CCNA 200-301 Official Cert Guide, Volume 1, Second Edition

Companion Website and Pearson Test Prep Access Code

Access interactive study tools on this book's companion website, including practice test software, review exercises, Key Term flash card application, a study planner, and more!

To access the companion website, simply follow these steps:

1. Go to www.ciscopress.com/register.

2. Enter the **print book ISBN**: 9780138229634.

3. Answer the security question to validate your purchase.

4. Go to your account page.

5. Click on the **Registered Products** tab.

6. Under the book listing, click on the **Access Bonus Content** link.

When you register your book, your Pearson Test Prep practice test access code will automatically be populated with the book listing under the Registered Products tab. You will need this code to access the practice test that comes with this book. You can redeem the code at **PearsonTestPrep.com**. Simply choose Pearson IT Certification as your product group and log into the site with the same credentials you used to register your book. Click the **Activate New Product** button and enter the access code. More detailed instructions on how to redeem your access code for both the online and desktop versions can be found on the companion website.

If you have any issues accessing the companion website or obtaining your Pearson Test Prep practice test access code, you can contact our support team by going to **ciscopress.com/support**.

T0293440

CCNA
200-301

Official Cert Guide
Volume 1

Second Edition

WENDELL ODOM, CCIE No. 1624

Cisco Press

CCNA 200-301 Official Cert Guide, Volume 1, Second Edition

Wendell Odom

Copyright© 2024 Pearson Education, Inc.

Published by:
Cisco Press
Hoboken, New Jersey

1 2024

Library of Congress Control Number: 2024934291

ISBN-13: 978-0-13-822963-4

ISBN-10: 0-13-822963-5

Warning and Disclaimer

This book is designed to provide information about the Cisco CCNA 200-301 exam. Every effort has been made to make this book as complete and as accurate as possible, but no warranty or fitness is implied.

The information is provided on an "as is" basis. The author, Cisco Press, and Cisco Systems, Inc. shall have neither liability nor responsibility to any person or entity with respect to any loss or damages arising from the information contained in this book or from the use of the discs or programs that may accompany it.

The opinions expressed in this book belong to the author and are not necessarily those of Cisco Systems, Inc.

Trademark Acknowledgments

All terms mentioned in this book that are known to be trademarks or service marks have been appropriately capitalized. Cisco Press or Cisco Systems, Inc., cannot attest to the accuracy of this information. Use of a term in this book should not be regarded as affecting the validity of any trademark or service mark.

Figure Credits

Figure 2.7 a: Anton Samsonov/123RF

Figure 2.7 b: indigolotos/123RF

Figure 19.10: Microsoft Corporation

Figures 19.11, 28.12: Apple Inc

Figure 19.12: Linux Foundation

Special Sales

For information about buying this title in bulk quantities, or for special sales opportunities (which may include electronic versions; custom cover designs; and content particular to your business, training goals, marketing focus, or branding interests), please contact our corporate sales department at corpsales@pearsoned.com or (800) 382-3419.

For government sales inquiries, please contact governmentsales@pearsoned.com.

For questions about sales outside the U.S., please contact intlcs@pearson.com.

Feedback Information

At Cisco Press, our goal is to create in-depth technical books of the highest quality and value. Each book is crafted with care and precision, undergoing rigorous development that involves the unique expertise of members from the professional technical community.

Readers' feedback is a natural continuation of this process. If you have any comments regarding how we could improve the quality of this book, or otherwise alter it to better suit your needs, you can contact us through email at feedback@ciscopress.com. Please make sure to include the book title and ISBN in your message.

We greatly appreciate your assistance.

Please contact us with concerns about any potential bias at https://www.pearson.com/report-bias.html.

GM K12, Early Career and Professional Learning: Soo Kang

Alliances Manager, Cisco Press: Caroline Antonio

Director, ITP Product Management: Brett Bartow

Managing Editor: Sandra Schroeder

Development Editor: Christopher Cleveland

Senior Project Editor: Tonya Simpson

Copy Editor: Chuck Hutchinson

Technical Editor: Denise Donohue

Editorial Assistant: Cindy Teeters

Cover Designer: Chuti Prasertsith

Composition: codeMantra

Indexer: Ken Johnson

Proofreader: Donna E. Mulder

Americas Headquarters
Cisco Systems, Inc.
San Jose, CA

Asia Pacific Headquarters
Cisco Systems (USA) Pte. Ltd.
Singapore

Europe Headquarters
Cisco Systems International BV
Amsterdam, The Netherlands

Cisco has more than 200 offices worldwide. Addresses, phone numbers, and fax numbers are listed on the Cisco Website at **www.cisco.com/go/offices.**

CCDE, CCENT, Cisco Eos, Cisco HealthPresence, the Cisco logo, Cisco Lumin, Cisco Nexus, Cisco StadiumVision, Cisco TelePresence, Cisco WebEx, DCE, and Welcome to the Human Network are trademarks; Changing the Way We Work, Live, Play, and Learn and Cisco Store are service marks; and Access Registrar, Aironet, AsyncOS, Bringing the Meeting To You, Catalyst, CCDA, CCDP, CCIE, CCIP, CCNA, CCNP, CCSP, CCVP, Cisco, the Cisco Certified Internetwork Expert logo, Cisco IOS, Cisco Press, Cisco Systems, Cisco Systems Capital, the Cisco Systems logo, Cisco Unity, Collaboration Without Limitation, EtherFast, EtherSwitch, Event Center, Fast Step, Follow Me Browsing, FormShare, GigaDrive, HomeLink, Internet Quotient, IOS, iPhone, iQuick Study, IronPort, the IronPort logo, LightStream, Linksys, MediaTone, MeetingPlace, MeetingPlace Chime Sound, MGX, Networkers, Networking Academy, Network Registrar, PCNow, PIX, PowerPanels, ProConnect, ScriptShare, SenderBase, SMARTnet, Spectrum Expert, StackWise, The Fastest Way to Increase Your Internet Quotient, TransPath, WebEx, and the WebEx logo are registered trademarks of Cisco Systems, Inc. and/or its affiliates in the United States and certain other countries.

All other trademarks mentioned in this document or website are the property of their respective owners. The use of the word partner does not imply a partnership relationship between Cisco and any other company. (0812R)

About the Author

Wendell Odom, CCIE Enterprise No. 1624, was the first Cisco Press author for
Cisco certification guides. He wrote all prior editions of this book, along with books
on topics ranging from introductory networking to CCENT, CCNA R&S, CCNA DC,
CCNP ROUTE, CCNP QoS, and CCIE R&S. In his four decades as a networker, he has
worked as a network engineer, consultant, systems engineer, instructor, and course
developer. He now spends his time focused on updating the CCNA books, his blog
(www.certskills.com), building his new CCNA YouTube channel (www.youtube.com/
@NetworkUpskill), and teaching online (www.certskills.com/courses). You can find him at
www.LinkedIn.com/in/WendellOdom, Twitter (@WendellOdom), and at his blog, which
provides a variety of free CCNA learning resources.

About the Technical Reviewer

Denise Donohue, CCIE No. 9566 (Routing and Switching), has worked with information
systems since the mid-1990s and network architecture since 2004. During that time, she
has worked with a wide range of networks, private and public, of all sizes, across most
industries. Her focus is on aligning business and technology. Denise has authored several
Cisco Press books and frequently shares her knowledge in webinars and seminars, and at
conferences.

Dedications

For Fay York Odom (1938–2022), the best mom ever.

Acknowledgments

Brett Bartow and I have been a team for a few decades. He has had more to do with the successes of the Cisco Press product line than anyone else. More than ever, his insights and wisdom have been a key to navigating Cisco's big changes to certifications back in 2020. Now with Cisco's 2023 pivot to a lean development model for certifications, with the possibility of new exam content annually, Brett's leadership matters more than ever. (See "Your Study Plan" for more about what that new lean development cycle means.) He's always a great partner in working through big-picture direction as well as features to make the books the best they can be for our readers. It is always appreciated, but not voiced every time—so thanks, Brett, for your consistent leadership and wisdom!

Chris Cleveland did the development editing for the very first Cisco Press exam certification guide way back in 1998, and he still can't seem to get away from us! Seriously, when Brett and I first discuss any new book, my first priority is to ask whether Chris has time to develop the book—and lobby if there are any barriers! It's always a pleasure working with you, Chris.

The technical editors also have a meaningful positive impact on the books. And we got Denise Donohue to do it! Denise and I teamed up to write the *CCIE R&S Official Cert Guide* for two editions, and she has written extensively herself—which is why I wondered if we could get her help. Her deep technical skills, along with her unique insights into the book authoring process, have been a great help to both weed out the mistakes and get good advice on how to improve the chapters.

Cisco's move to an annual exam update cadence (they at least consider updating each exam once per year) has more impact on the production side of our publishing process than it does on the authoring side. Knowing early that both Sandra and Tonya are back at it, finding ways to continue the high quality while being creative with the new publication cycle sets me more at ease. When writing, I could rest knowing that the second half of the process, which happens after I've finished 99 percent of my work, will be done well!

Thanks to all the production team for making the magic happen. I usually do not interact with you directly, beyond Sandra and Tonya, but I see your work, and the books truly improve through the process! From fixing all my grammar and passive-voice sentences to pulling the design and layout together, they do it all; thanks for putting it all together and making it look easy.

A special thank you to you readers who write in with suggestions and possible errors, and especially those of you who post online at the Cisco Learning Network and at my blog (www.certskills.com). More so than any edition I can remember, reader comments have had more to do with changes I made to improve existing content in these editions. The comments I received directly and those I overheard by participating at CLN made this edition a better book. (See the heading "Feedback Information" just a page or so back to see how to get in touch with us!)

My wonderful wife, Kris, and I reached our 25th anniversary while working on this edition. She makes this challenging work lifestyle a breeze, even happily scheduling our 25th-anniversary vacation around the book schedule! Thanks to my daughter Hannah for the perspectives on how 20 somethings think about learning and studying. And thanks to Jesus Christ, Lord of everything in my life.

Contents at a Glance

Online Appendixes

Reader Services

To access additional content for this book, simply register your product. To start the registration process, go to www.ciscopress.com/register and log in or create an account.* Enter the product ISBN 9780138229634 and click **Submit**. After the process is complete, you will find any available bonus content under Registered Products.

*Be sure to check the box that you would like to hear from us to receive exclusive discounts on future editions of this product.

Contents

Online Appendixes

Icons Used in This Book

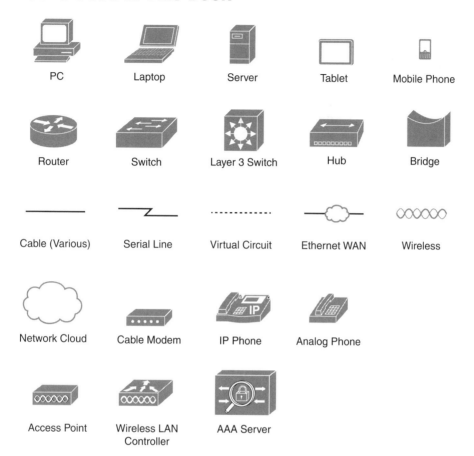

Command Syntax Conventions

The conventions used to present command syntax in this book are the same conventions used in the IOS Command Reference. The Command Reference describes these conventions as follows:

- **Boldface** indicates commands and keywords that are entered literally as shown. In actual configuration examples and output (not general command syntax), boldface indicates commands that are manually input by the user (such as a **show** command).

- *Italic* indicates arguments for which you supply actual values.

- Vertical bars (|) separate alternative, mutually exclusive elements.

- Square brackets ([ ]) indicate an optional element.

- Braces ({ }) indicate a required choice.

- Braces within brackets ([{ }]) indicate a required choice within an optional element.

Introduction

Do not skip the intro!

You are setting out on a journey to achieve your CCNA certification. For many, that step happens at the beginning of a new career path. For others, CCNA validates their knowledge and skills already learned on the job.

Regardless of your path, the journey takes some time and effort. I encourage you to spend some time in the Introduction to learn more about CCNA and the books so you can have the best experience preparing for CCNA! To that end, this introduction discusses these main points:

Cisco Certifications and the CCNA

Book Features

Book Elements (Reference)

About Getting Hands-on Skills

About IP Subnetting

Cisco Certifications and the CCNA

Congratulations! If you're reading far enough to look at this book's Introduction, you've probably already decided to go for your Cisco certification. Cisco has been the dominant vendor in networking for decades. If you want to be taken seriously as a network engineer, building your Cisco skills using Cisco certifications makes perfect sense. Where to start? CCNA.

Cisco Certifications as of 2024

The changes Cisco made in 2020 consolidated the certification tracks from about ten tracks down to the five tracks shown in Figure I-1. Cisco next made changes to various exams in 2023 and 2024; those changes updated the exams but maintained the same five tracks. The CCNA, CCNP, and CCIE certification levels progress through higher challenge levels, with CCNA as the foundation for all.

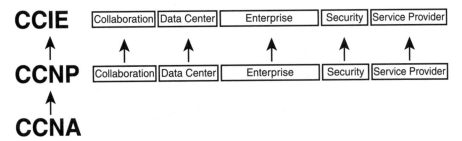

Figure I-1 *Cisco CCNA, CCNP, and CCIE Certifications*

The following list gives a few details of the history of these certification tracks: They are

CCNA – Cisco Certified Network Associate: Cisco began CCNA with a single CCNA certification back in 1998. They later expanded CCNA to include ten different CCNA certifications about different technology areas. Cisco retired all the varieties of CCNA back in 2020, leaving us again with a single CCNA certification, now referred to as simply "CCNA."

CCNP – Cisco Certified Network Professional: Cisco followed the same progression with different CCNP certifications over time, starting with one in 1998. The big changes in 2020 consolidated the lineup to five CCNP certifications, all of which benefit from having knowledge of CCNA before moving on to CCNP.

CCIE – Cisco Certified Internetwork Expert: First introduced in 1993, these expert-level certifications require both a written exam plus a one-day practical exam with extensive hands-on lab challenges.

Beyond the CCNA, CCNP, and CCIE certifications, Cisco offers two other certification tracks, one for network automation and another for cybersecurity. The CCNA certification can be helpful as a foundation for those tracks as well. They are

DevNet Certifications: The DevNet Associate, DevNet Professional, and DevNet Expert certifications mirror the progression of CCNA/CCNP/CCIE, just without using those specific acronyms. The DevNet certifications focus on software development and APIs that matter to managing networks.

CyberOps Certifications: The CyberOps Associate and CyberOps Professional certifications mirror the progression of CCNA/CCNP. These security exams focus on security concepts, security monitoring, host-based analysis, network intrusion analysis, and security policies and procedures.

How to Get Your CCNA Certification

As you saw in Figure I-1, all career certification paths now begin with CCNA. So how do you get the CCNA certification? Today, you have one and only one option to achieve CCNA certification:

Take and pass one exam: The Cisco 200-301 CCNA exam.

To take the 200-301 exam, or any Cisco exam, you will use the services of Pearson VUE. The process works something like this:

1. Establish a login at https://vue.com/cisco (or use your existing login).

2. Register for, schedule a time and place, and pay for the Cisco 200-301 exam, all from the VUE website.

3. Take the exam at the VUE testing center or from home with a video proctor watching to prevent cheating.

4. You will receive a notice of your score, and whether you passed, before you leave the testing center.

Content in the CCNA 200-301 Exam

We've all thought it, wondered, for almost every important test we ever took, and maybe even asked the teacher: "What's on the test?" For the CCNA exam, and for all Cisco certification exams, Cisco tells us.

Cisco publishes an exam blueprint for every Cisco exam, with the blueprint listing the exam topics for the exam. To find them, browse www.cisco.com/go/certifications, look for the CCNA page, and navigate until you see the exam topics. And if you haven't already done so, create a bookmark folder for CCNA content in your web browser and bookmark a link to this page.

The exam blueprint organizes the exam topics into groups called domains. The document also tells us the percentage of points on the exam that come from each domain. For instance, every CCNA exam should score 25 percent of your points from the exam topics in the IP Connectivity domain. The exam does not tell you the domain associated with each question, but the percentages give us a better idea of the importance of the domains for the exam. Figure I-2 shows the domains of the CCNA 200-301 Version 1.1 blueprint, the percentages, and the number of primary exam topics in each.

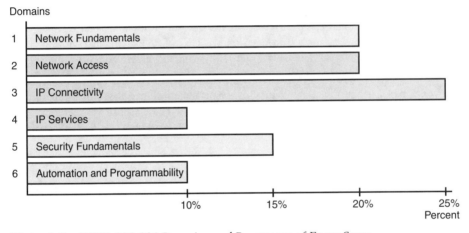

Figure I-2   *CCNA 200-301 Domains and Percentage of Exam Score*

Within each domain, the exam topic document lists exam topics that follow two different styles of wording. The main exam topics use a verb in the phrase that tells you the level of mastery required; I call those primary exam topics. The exam topics document shows subtopics that I refer to as secondary exam topics. Those do not have a verb, but list more technology details (nouns), and assume the verb from the primary exam topic. For instance, the following excerpt from the exam topics document lists one primary exam topic with the *describe* verb, with more detail added by two secondary exam topics.

    1.13 Describe switching concepts

       1.13.a MAC learning and aging

       1.13.b Frame switching

Exam Topic Verbs (Depth) and Nouns (Breadth)

Understanding an exam topic requires that you think about each exam topic wording, focusing on the verbs and nouns. The nouns identify the technical topics, such as LAN switching, IP routing, protocols like OSPF, and so on. The verbs in each primary exam topic inform us about the type and depth of knowledge and skill tested per the exam topics.

For example, consider the following primary exam topic:

Describe IPsec remote access and site-to-site VPNs

I'm sure you know what the word *describe* means in the normal use of the term. But for people who build exams, the verb has special meaning as to what the exam questions should and should not require of the test taker. For instance, you should be ready to describe whatever "IPsec remote access and site-to-site VPNs" are. But the exam should not ask you to perform higher performance verbs, like *analyze* or *configure*.

Figure I-3 shows a pyramid with verbs found in Cisco exam blueprints. It shows the lower-skill verbs at the bottom and higher skills at the top. An exam topic with a lower verb should not be tested with questions from higher knowledge and skill levels. For instance, with the exam topic "describe...first hop redundancy protocols," you should not expect to need to configure, verify, or troubleshoot the feature.

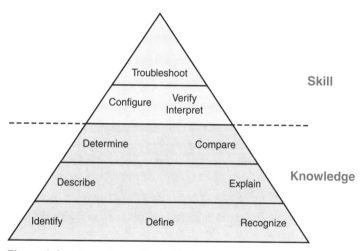

Figure I-3 *Cisco Exam Topic Verbs*

Knowing that, how should you study? Well, instead of a many-layer pyramid, think of it as two layers: Knowledge and Skill. When learning content whose exam topics use verbs from the lower three rows of the pyramid, study the same way no matter which of those verbs the exam topic uses. Learn the topic well. Be ready to describe it, explain it, and interpret the meaning. For content with exam topics with the verbs *configure* and *verify*, think of those as including the first level of knowledge, plus also requiring configuration and verification skills. Also, think about the common configuration mistakes so you can troubleshoot those mistakes.

Comparing the Exam and Exam Topics

Cisco tells us that the exam can include more technical topics than those listed as nouns in the exam topics. Cisco also tells us that the exam topics give us general guidance. Once you get into the content, you will understand what they mean: any noun listed in the exam topics has many related protocols, standards, features, concepts, or device commands that Cisco did not list in the exam topics. Let's explore that concept to give you some perspective.

First, to see what Cisco tells us about the exam versus the exam topics, return to cs.co/go/certifications or cisco.com/go/ccna. Find the CCNA exam topics and open the PDF version (the text we need to consider is currently only in the PDF version). Open the PDF and spend 10–15 seconds scanning it.

Did you read the first two paragraphs, the ones before the list of exam topics? Or did you skip those and move straight to the long list of exam topics? Many people skip those paragraphs. One of those tells us much about the exam versus the exam topics, so I've copied it here, with emphasis added:

> The following topics are *general guidelines* for the content likely to be included on the exam. However, *other related topics may also appear on any specific delivery of the exam*. To better reflect the contents of the exam and for clarity purposes, the *guidelines below may change at any time without notice.*

Together, the first two emphasized phrases tell us that the exam may go beyond the literal words in the exam topics. Let me give you a couple of examples. First, prerequisite knowledge must be inferred from the literal exam topics. For instance, consider this exam topic:

Configure and verify IPv4 addressing and subnetting

The skills to configure IPv4 addresses take only a few minutes to learn. Understanding what the numbers mean takes much longer. In fact, I'd say 95 percent of your work will be to understand the prerequisite knowledge—but the exam topics do not list those prerequisites, like understanding subnetting concepts, applying the subnet mask to an address, calculating the range of addresses in a subnet, and so on.

I develop the scope of the books with the preceding in mind. You will certainly read about all topics that appear in the exam topics. Consider that view a narrow interpretation of the exam topics. But you will also learn about terms, concepts, and product features not specifically mentioned in the exam topics, from my broad and deep interpretation of the exam topics, based on Cisco's approach to their exams. We try to predict what Cisco will include, starting from the exam topics. Figure I-4 shows the idea.

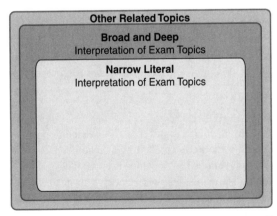

Figure I-4 *Scope Concept: Exam Versus Exam Topics*

Although we can build a book around the exam topics, we cannot predict every concept and command included in the actual CCNA exam. The general nature of the exam topics, the allowance of "other related topics," plus other factors, make predicting all exam content impossible. But we do promise to discuss 100 percent of the exam topic details and to diligently seek the right balance of a broad interpretation of those topics to make you well prepared for the exam.

How to Prepare for the Generalized Exam Topics

Given the possibility of topic areas not listed in the exam topics, how should you go about preparing for the CCNA exam? Let me give you a few suggestions.

1. Follow the suggestions in the upcoming section "Your Study Plan" just before Chapter 1.

2. Practice hands-on Command Line Interface (CLI) skills. The later section of the Introduction titled "About Building Hands-On Skills" discusses some ways to practice.

3. Pay close attention to troubleshooting topics in the book.

4. Practice all math-related skills, over time, until you master them.

5. Ensure you know all exam topic content as listed in the exam topics. Read the exam topics, consider your own literal interpretation, and when uncertain or confused, dig in and study further.

6. Trust that the book uses its broad interpretation of the exam topics to help you learn as much as possible that might be on the exam.

Types of Questions on the CCNA 200-301 Exam

You can expect the following kinds of questions on the exam; just be aware that the style of questions may change over time.

- Multiple-choice, single-answer
- Multiple-choice, multiple-answer
- Drag-and-drop
- Lab

For the multichoice questions, the exam software gives us a few important advantages:

- There is no penalty for guessing.
- Multichoice questions with a single correct answer require you to answer and allow only one answer.
- Multichoice questions with multiple correct answers tell you the number of correct answers and warn you if you have not selected that many answers.

For instance, if a question tells you there are two correct answers, and you select only one and then try to move to the next question, the app reminds you that you should choose another answer before moving on.

As for drag-and-drop, some questions use simple text blocks that you move from one list to another. However, you might see questions where you move items in a network diagram or some other creative use of drag-and-drop.

Finally, Cisco introduced lab questions (formally called performance-based questions) in 2022. Lab questions present you with a lab scenario with a lab pod of virtual routers and switches running in the background; you get console access to a few devices. Your job: find the missing or broken configuration and reconfigure the devices so that the lab scenario works. The best way to practice for these questions is to practice in the lab; more on that in the section titled "About Building Hands-On Skills."

As an aside, prior Cisco exams had Sim questions instead of lab questions. Sim questions required the same from us: read the scenario and fix the configuration. However, Sim questions used simulated Cisco devices with limited command support, which frustrated some test takers. The lab questions use real Cisco operating systems running in a virtual environment, so they provide a much more realistic experience compared to old Sim questions.

Book Features

This book includes many study features beyond the core explanations and examples in each chapter. This section acts as a reference to the various features in the book.

The CCNA Books: Volume 1 and Volume 2

The CCNA exam covers a large amount of content, and it does not fit in a single volume. As a result, Cisco Press has long published books for the CCNA exam as a two-book set. Volume 1 covers about half of the content, and Volume 2 covers the rest, as shown in Figure I-5. To best use both books, start in Volume 1 and work through the book in order, and then do the same with Volume 2.

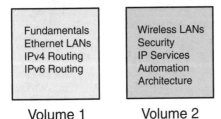

Volume 1

Volume 2

Figure I-5 *Two Books for CCNA 200-301*

When you start each new chapter, review the list of exam topics that begins the chapter. The book does not follow the same order of exam topics in the blueprint, but instead follows a more effective order for learning the topics. For reference, look to Appendix B, "Exam Topics Cross-Reference," in the back of the book. The appendix includes:

- A list of exam topics and the chapter(s) covering each topic

- A list of chapters and the exam topics covered in each chapter

Exam Blueprint Versions and Book Editions

Cisco made minor changes to the CCNA exam blueprint in 2024, the first change to the CCNA 200-301 exam since the year 2020. The much more important change (announced in 2023) had to do with the entire Cisco certification program about how Cisco announces and releases new exams and exam blueprints. Before 2023, when Cisco changed any CCNA or CCNP exam, they also changed the exam number, and the announcement was sudden. Those days are gone.

You should read and understand Cisco's long-term strategy for being more forthright about exam plans as detailed at www.cisco.com/go/certroadmap. Summarizing some key points, when Cisco changes an exam in the future, Cisco will keep the same exam number. To identify the changes, they will use a major.minor version numbering plan for every exam blueprint. More importantly, Cisco tells us when they will consider changing CCNA each year, but we know when Cisco will announce changes and when the new exam will be released, within a few months' timing.

The exam blueprint version changes based on two determinations: 1) whether Cisco will change the exam that year at all, and 2) if so, whether Cisco considers the changes to be major or minor. For instance, Cisco considered making a change to CCNA during February–April 2023 but chose not to change it, announcing that fact in the May–July 2023 timeframe. In 2024, Cisco chose to make minor changes to the CCNA blueprint. As a result, the former CCNA blueprint version 1.0 (major version 1, minor version 0) changed to version 1.1, increasing the minor version by 1.

Looking forward, if the next three future CCNA blueprint changes are also minor, they would be blueprint versions 1.2, 1.3, and 1.4. However, if any of them are major, that version would move to the next major version (2.0), with subsequent minor version changes as 2.1, 2.2, and so on.

Cisco also tells us that each year, internally, Cisco considers what to do with CCNA in the February–April timeframe. They will announce their plans to us all between May–July, and they will release the new exam (if changes are being made) sometime in the six months or so following the announcement.

As for the publishing plans to support that new update cycle, you should read and monitor the publisher's web page at www.ciscopress.com/newcerts. Also, opt in for communications on that page so the publisher will email you about future plans and updates.

Summarizing a few key points about the publisher's plans, this book, the second edition, was written for version 1.1 of the CCNA 200-301 blueprint, but it should be the book used for CCNA for subsequent blueprint versions as well. During the life of this second edition book, Cisco may update the CCNA 200-301 exam blueprint a few times, while this book (plus the Volume 2 second edition book) may remain unchanged. New exam content may be made available as electronic downloads. At some point, a new edition will be appropriate. (Figure I-6 shows one example of what might happen over time, with downloadable PDFs between editions.)

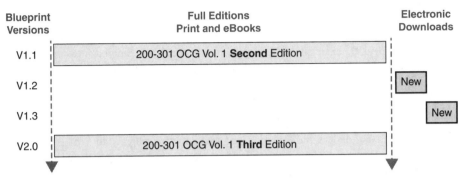

Figure I-6   *Possible Progression of Book Editions, New Content Release, Versus Exams*

NOTE   I cannot stress enough: monitor both the Cisco Press and Cisco pages linked in the preceding paragraphs, and opt in for communications at those pages, to stay aware of any exam and publishing plans. Also, consider watching my blog (www.certskills.com), where I expect to post about changes.

When you finish the technology chapters in this book (Chapters 1–29), make sure to also read Chapter 30, "Exam Updates." We post updated versions of that chapter online. We use that chapter to deliver small content updates to you as well as to inform you about future content updates. Make sure to read through that chapter and learn how to download the latest version of the chapter, discovering if new content has been posted after this book was published.

Also, just to reduce confusion about the book titles, note that the prior edition of this book is nearly identical to this book's title. Comparing the titles:

- *CCNA 200-301 Official Cert Guide, Volume 1* (the prior edition, published in 2019, for 200-301 exam blueprint version 1.0)

- *CCNA 200-301 Official Cert Guide, Volume 1*, Second Edition (this edition, published in 2024, for 200-301 exam blueprint version 1.1 and beyond)

Comparing This Edition to the Previous

This book replaces a similar book that applied to the former CCNA 200-301 exam blueprint 1.0. Some of you may buy this book but have already begun studying with the prior edition. The following list of major changes to this book versus the previous one may help you avoid rereading identical or similar content in this book.

Chapter 4: Added a short topic comparing Cisco switch operating systems. Also introduced the WebUI interface for Cisco routers and switches per an exam topic change.

Chapter 6: Explored the differences in the **transport input** configuration command based on device models and operating systems. Also showed how to configure the WebUI on a switch per an exam topic change.

Chapter 7: Revised and expanded sections about Ethernet autonegotiation concepts and auto-MDIX.

Chapter 8: Added a large closing section about troubleshooting VLANs and VLAN trunks.

Chapter 9: Removed EtherChannel load distribution concept details, and added concept details about BPDU Guard, BPDU filter, loop guard, and root guard.

Chapter 10: Expanded/revised the second half of the chapter (Layer 2 EtherChannels), and added a new middle section about verifying BPDU Guard, BPDU filter, loop guard, and root guard.

Chapter 12: Added a few pages comparing public IP networks and public CIDR blocks.

Chapter 15: Added an entire new chapter about subnetting design issues. The chapter was in the prior edition but as a PDF-only appendix.

Chapter 16: (Formerly Chapter 15) Expanded the discussion of router interface autonegotiation and differences between IOS and IOS XE.

Chapter 17: (Formerly Chapter 16) Added a small section discussing possible mistakes with the **ip address** interface subcommand.

Chapter 18: (Formerly Chapter 17) Added two topics: SVI interface auto-state and the configuration of Ethernet switch ports in a router.

Chapter 19: (Formerly Volume 2, Chapter 7) Moved the chapter to Volume 1 from Volume 2 and expanded the discussion of host commands.

Chapters 21–24: (Formerly Chapters 19–21) Chapters 21–24 reorganize and expand the OSPF topics. Chapter 24 closes with a revised section about route selection.

Chapter 28: This new chapter contains the final topic of former Chapter 25 (IPv6 NDP), unchanged. The second half of the chapter has new content about host IPv6 commands and IPv6 address attributes.

If you find the preceding information useful, consider looking in two other places that allow us to provide ongoing updates and to answer questions. First, I expect to post blog posts about the new CCNA exam changes, as always, at my blog (www.certskills.com). Look there for posts in the News section (click the General menu item and then News), for posts made around the time the new exams release.

Second, look to the companion website for this book for details about future exam revisions and publishing plans. The companion website gives the publisher a place to list details about changes moving forward. See this Introduction's later section titled "The Companion Website for Online Content" for the instructions for finding the site.

Chapter Features

Beginning to study CCNA can be overwhelming at first due to the volume. The best way to overcome that reaction requires a change in mindset: *treat each chapter as a separate study task*. Breaking your study into manageable tasks helps a lot.

Each chapter of this book is a self-contained short course about one small topic area, organized for reading and study. I create chapters so they average about 20 pages to cover the technology so that no one chapter takes too long to complete. Each chapter breaks down as follows:

"Do I Know This Already?" quizzes: Each chapter begins with a pre-chapter quiz so you can self-assess how much you know coming into the chapter.

Foundation Topics: This is the heading for the core content section of the chapter, with average length of 20 pages.

Chapter Review: This section includes a list of study tasks useful to help you remember concepts, connect ideas, and practice skills-based content in the chapter.

Do not read the "Foundation Topics" section of chapter after chapter without pausing to review and study. Each "Chapter Review" section uses a variety of other book features to help you study and internalize that chapter's content, including the following:

- **Review Key Topics:** All the content in the books matters, but some matters more. Cisco Press certification guides use a Key Topic icon next to those items in the "Foundation Topics" section. The "Chapter Review" section lists the key topics in a table. You can scan the chapter to review them or review the Key Topics more conveniently using the companion website.

- **Complete Tables from Memory:** We convert some tables in the book to interactive study tables called memory tables. You access memory tables from the companion website. Memory tables repeat the table, but with parts of the table removed. You can then fill in the table to exercise your memory and click to check your work.

- **Key Terms You Should Know:** The "Chapter Review" section lists the key terminology from the chapter. For a manual process with the book, think about each term and use the Glossary to cross-check your own mental definitions. Alternately, review the key terms with the "Key Terms Flashcards" app on the companion website.

- **Labs:** You should practice hands-on skills for any exam topics with the *configure* and *verify* verbs. The upcoming section titled "About Building Hands-On Skills" discusses your lab options. Also, the Chapter and Part Reviews refer you to lab exercises specific to the chapter or part.

- **Command References:** Some book chapters discuss the configure and verify exam topics, so they list various router and switch commands. The "Chapter Review" section of those chapters includes command reference tables, useful both for reference and for study. Just cover one column of the table and see how much you can remember and complete mentally.

- **Review DIKTA Questions:** Even if you used the DIKTA questions to begin the chapter, re-answering those questions can prove a useful way to review facts. By design, I do not mention the DIKTA questions in the "Chapter Review" sections but do suggest using them again for all chapters in a part during Part Review. Use the Pearson Test Prep (PTP) web app to easily use those questions any time you have a few minutes, a device, and Internet access.

- **Subnetting Exercises:** Several chapters ask you to perform some math processes related to either IPv4 or IPv6 addressing. The "Chapter Review" section asks you to do additional practice problems, where applicable. The problems can be found in Appendices D through I, in PDF form, on the companion website, along with those same exercises as interactive web apps.

Part Features

Your second mindset change: Use the book parts as major milestones in your study journey. Each part groups a small number of related chapters together. Take the time at the end of each part to review all topics in the part, effectively rewarding yourself with a chance to deepen your knowledge and internalize more of the content before moving to the next part. Figure I-7 shows the concept.

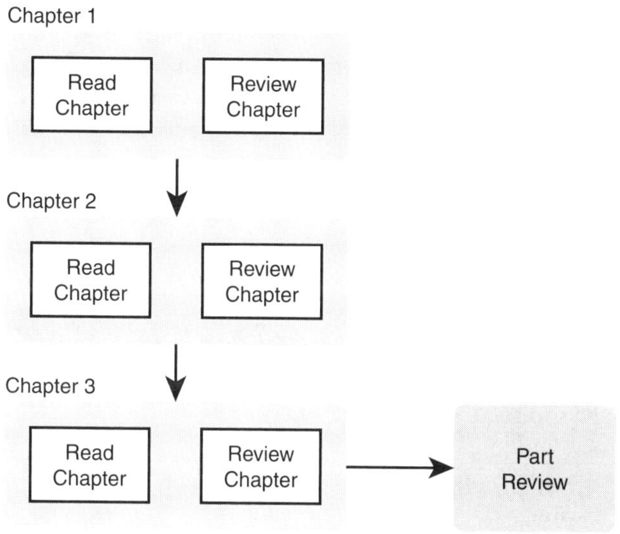

Figure I-7   *Part Review: The Second Review of Most Content*

The Part Review element at the end of each part suggests review and study activities. Spaced reviews—that is, reviewing content several times over the course of your study—help improve retention. Using the Chapter and Part Review process, the Part Review serves as your second review of the content in each chapter. The Part Review repeats some Chapter Review activities and offers some new ones, including a reminder to use practice questions set aside specifically for Part Review.

The Companion Website for Online Content

Some Chapter and Part Review tasks can be done from the book. However, several of them work better as an interactive online tool. For instance, you can take a "Do I Know This Already?" quiz by reading the pages of the book, but you can also use the PTP testing software. As another example, when you want to review the key terms from a chapter, you can find all those in electronic flashcards.

This book's companion website hosts all the electronic components of the book. The companion website gives you a big advantage: you can do most of your Chapter and

Part Review work from anywhere using the interactive tools on the site. The advantages include

- **Easier to use:** Instead of having to print out copies of the appendices and do the work on paper, you can use these new apps, which provide you with an easy-to-use, interactive experience that you can easily run over and over.

- **Convenient:** When you have a spare 5–10 minutes, go to the book's website and review content from one of your recently finished chapters.

- **Good break from reading:** Sometimes looking at a static page after reading a chapter lets your mind wander. Breaking up your reading with some review from the keyboard can help keep you focused on the activity.

The interactive Chapter Review elements should improve your chances of passing as well. Our in-depth reader surveys over the years show that those who do the Chapter and Part Reviews learn more. Those who use the interactive review elements tend to do the review tasks more often. So, take advantage of the tools and maybe you will be more successful as well. Table I-1 summarizes these interactive applications and the traditional book features that cover the same content.

Table I-1   *Book Features with Both Traditional and App Options*

Feature	Traditional	App
Key Topic	The "Chapter Review" section lists the key topics. To review, flip pages in the chapter.	Key Topics Table app with links to view each key topic
Config Checklist	This list of steps, in text, describes how to configure a feature.	Config Checklist app, where you complete the checklist by adding commands
Key Terms	Terms are listed in each "Chapter Review" section; review using the end-of-book Glossary.	Key Terms Flash Cards app
Appendices Subnetting Practice	Appendices D–I provide static text practice problems and answers in the PDF appendices.	A variety of apps, one per problem type, in the "Memory Tables and Practice Exercises" section
In-chapter Subnetting practice	Look at the problems in the chapter and refer to the answer tables at the end of the chapter.	App that offers a fill-in-the-blank answer space and grades your answer

The companion website also includes links to download, navigate, or stream for these types of content:

- Pearson Sim Lite Desktop App

- Pearson Test Prep (PTP) Desktop App

- Pearson Test Prep (PTP) Web App

- Videos

How to Access the Companion Website

To access the companion website, which gives you access to the electronic content with this book, start by establishing a login at www.ciscopress.com and register your book. To do so, simply go to www.ciscopress.com/register and enter the ISBN of the print book: 9780138229634. After you have registered your book, go to your account page and click the **Registered Products** tab. From there, click the **Access Bonus Content** link to get access to the book's companion website.

Note that if you buy the *Premium Edition eBook and Practice Test* version of this book from Cisco Press, your book will automatically be registered on your account page. Simply go to your account page, click the **Registered Products** tab, and select **Access Bonus Content** to access the book's companion website.

How to Access the Pearson Test Prep (PTP) App

You have two options for installing and using the Pearson Test Prep application: a web app and a desktop app. To use the Pearson Test Prep application, start by finding the registration code that comes with the book. You can find the code in these ways:

- You can get your access code by registering the print ISBN 9780138229634 on ciscopress.com/register. Make sure to use the print book ISBN, regardless of whether you purchased an eBook or the print book. After you register the book, your access code will be populated on your account page under the Registered Products tab. Instructions for how to redeem the code are available on the book's companion website by clicking the Access Bonus Content link.

- If you purchase the Premium Edition eBook and Practice Test directly from the Cisco Press website, the code will be populated on your account page after purchase. Just log in at ciscopress.com, click Account to see details of your account, and click the digital purchases tab.

NOTE   After you register your book, your code can always be found in your account under the Registered Products tab.

Once you have the access code, to find instructions about both the PTP web app and the desktop app, follow these steps:

Step 1.   Open this book's companion website as shown earlier in this Introduction under the heading, "How to Access the Companion Website."

Step 2.   Click the **Practice Exams** button.

Step 3.   Follow the instructions listed there for both installing the desktop app and using the web app.

Note that if you want to use the web app only at this point, just navigate to pearsontestprep.com, log in using the same credentials used to register your book or purchase the Premium Edition, and register this book's practice tests using the registration code you just found. The process should take only a couple of minutes.

Feature Reference

The following list provides an easy reference to get the basic idea behind each book feature:

- **Practice exam:** The book gives you the rights to the Pearson Test Prep (PTP) testing software, available as a web app and a desktop app. Use the access code on a piece of cardboard in the sleeve in the back of the book, and use the companion website to download the desktop app or navigate to the web app (or just go to www.pearsontestprep.com).

- **eBook:** Pearson offers an eBook version of this book that includes extra practice tests as compared to the print book. The product includes two versions of the eBook: PDF (for reading on your computer) and EPUB (for reading on your tablet, mobile device, or Kindle, Nook, or other e-reader). It also includes additional practice test questions and enhanced practice test features, including links from each question to the specific heading in the eBook file.

- **Mentoring videos:** The companion website also includes a number of videos about other topics as mentioned in individual chapters. Some of the videos explain common mistakes made with CCNA topics, whereas others provide sample CCNA questions with explanations.

- **Subnetting videos:** The companion website contains a series of videos that show you how to calculate various facts about IP addressing and subnetting (in particular, using the shortcuts described in this book).

- **Subnetting practice appendices/web apps:** The companion website contains appendices with a set of subnetting practice problems and answers. This is a great resource to practice building subnetting skills. You can use these same practice problems with applications from the "Memory Tables and Practice Exercises" section of the companion website.

- **CCNA 200-301 Network Simulator Lite:** This lite version of the best-selling CCNA Network Simulator from Pearson provides you with a means, right now, to experience the Cisco command-line interface (CLI). No need to go buy real gear or buy a full simulator to start learning the CLI. Just install it from the companion website.

- **CCNA Simulator:** If you are looking for more hands-on practice, you might want to consider purchasing the CCNA Network Simulator. You can purchase a copy of this software from Pearson at http://pearsonitcertification.com/networksimulator or other retail outlets. To help you with your studies, Pearson has created a mapping guide that maps each of the labs in the simulator to the specific sections in each volume of the CCNA Cert Guide. You can get this mapping guide free on the Extras tab on the book product page: www.ciscopress.com/title/9780138229634.

- **Author's websites:** The author maintains a blog site that has a large number of free lab exercises about CCNA content, additional sample questions, and other exercises. Additionally, the site indexes all content so you can study based on the book chapters and parts. To find it, navigate to www.certskills.com. Additionally, look for CCNA activities and lectures at his YouTube channel (www.youtube.com/@networkupskill).

Book Organization, Chapters, and Appendices

This book contains 29 chapters about CCNA topics organized into seven parts. The core chapters cover the following topics:

- Part I: Introduction to Networking

  - Chapter 1, "Introduction to TCP/IP Networking," introduces the central ideas and terms used by TCP/IP and explains the TCP/IP networking model.

  - Chapter 2, "Fundamentals of Ethernet LANs," introduces the concepts and terms used when building Ethernet LANs.

  - Chapter 3, "Fundamentals of WANs and IP Routing," covers the basics of the data-link layer for WANs in the context of IP routing but emphasizes the main network layer protocol for TCP/IP. This chapter introduces the basics of IPv4, including IPv4 addressing and routing.

- Part II: Implementing Ethernet LANs

  - Chapter 4, "Using the Command-Line Interface," explains how to access the text-based user interface of Cisco Catalyst LAN switches.

  - Chapter 5, "Analyzing Ethernet LAN Switching," shows how to use the Cisco CLI to verify the current status of an Ethernet LAN and how it switches Ethernet frames.

  - Chapter 6, "Configuring Basic Switch Management," explains how to configure Cisco switches for basic management features, such as remote access using Telnet and SSH.

  - Chapter 7, "Configuring and Verifying Switch Interfaces," shows how to configure a variety of switch features that apply to interfaces, including duplex/speed.

- Part III: Implementing VLANs and STP

  - Chapter 8, "Implementing Ethernet Virtual LANs," explains the concepts and configuration surrounding virtual LANs, including VLAN trunking.

  - Chapter 9, "Spanning Tree Protocol Concepts," discusses the concepts behind IEEE Spanning Tree Protocol (STP), including Rapid STP (RSTP) and how they make some switch interfaces block frames to prevent frames from looping continuously around a redundant switched LAN.

  - Chapter 10, "RSTP and EtherChannel Configuration," shows how to configure and verify RSTP and Layer 2 EtherChannels on Cisco switches.

- Part IV: IPv4 Addressing

  - Chapter 11, "Perspectives on IPv4 Subnetting," walks you through the entire concept of subnetting, from starting with a Class A, B, or C network to a completed subnetting design as implemented in an enterprise IPv4 network.

  - Chapter 12, "Analyzing Classful IPv4 Networks," explains how IPv4 addresses originally fell into several classes, with unicast IP addresses being in Class A, B, and C. This chapter explores all things related to address classes and the IP network concept created by those classes.

- Chapter 13, "Analyzing Subnet Masks," shows how an engineer can analyze the key facts about a subnetting design based on the subnet mask. This chapter shows how to look at the mask and IP network to determine the size of each subnet and the number of subnets.

- Chapter 14, "Analyzing Existing Subnets," describes how most troubleshooting of IP connectivity problems starts with an IP address and mask. This chapter shows how to take those two facts and find key facts about the IP subnet in which that host resides.

- Chapter 15, "Subnet Design," discusses IPv4 subnetting from the perspective of creating a list of useful subnets, based on a subnet mask, from one Class A, B, or C network.

- Part V: IPv4 Routing

  - Chapter 16, "Operating Cisco Routers," is like Chapter 8, focusing on basic device management, but it focuses on routers instead of switches.

  - Chapter 17, "Configuring IPv4 Addresses and Static Routes," discusses how to add IPv4 address configuration to router interfaces and how to configure static IPv4 routes.

  - Chapter 18, "IP Routing in the LAN," shows to a configuration and trouble-shooting depth different methods to route between VLANs, including Router-on-a-Stick (ROAS), Layer 3 switching with SVIs, Layer 3 switching with routed ports, and using Layer 3 EtherChannels.

  - Chapter 19, "IP Addressing on Hosts," discusses how IP hosts receive their IPv4 settings from either static configuration or using DHCP.

  - Chapter 20, "Troubleshooting IPv4 Routing," focuses on how to use two key troubleshooting tools to find routing problems: the **ping** and **traceroute** commands.

- Part VI: OSPF

  - Chapter 21, "Understanding OSPF Concepts," introduces the fundamental operation of the Open Shortest Path First (OSPF) protocol, focusing on link state fundamentals, neighbor relationships, flooding link state data, and calculating routes based on the lowest cost metric.

  - Chapter 22, "Implementing Basic OSPF Features," shows the most basic OSPF configuration using two methods: OSPF router subcommands and interface subcommands.

  - Chapter 23, "Implementing Optional OSPF Features," discusses a wide variety of OSPF configuration options.

  - Chapter 24, "OSPF Neighbors and Route Selection," examines the conditions that must be true before two routers will succeed in becoming OSPF neighbors. It also takes a closer look at the choices a router makes when choosing between competing routes and how the router uses those routes.

- Part VII: IP Version 6

  - Chapter 25, "Fundamentals of IP Version 6," discusses the most basic concepts of IP version 6, focusing on the rules for writing and interpreting IPv6 addresses.

  - Chapter 26, "IPv6 Addressing and Subnetting," works through the two branches of unicast IPv6 addresses—global unicast addresses and unique local addresses—that act somewhat like IPv4 public and private addresses, respectively.

  - Chapter 27, "Implementing IPv6 Addressing on Routers," shows how to configure IPv6 routing and addresses on routers, while discussing a variety of special IPv6 addresses.

  - Chapter 28, "Implementing IPv6 Addressing on Hosts," discusses how IPv6 hosts receive their IPv6 settings from either static configuration, DHCP, or SLAAC. It also discusses the NDP protocol suite.

  - Chapter 29, "Implementing IPv6 Routing," shows how to add static routes to an IPv6 router's routing table.

- Part VIII: Exam Updates

  - Chapter 30, "*CCNA 200-301 Official Cert Guide, Volume 1*, Second Edition, Exam Updates," has two purposes. First, the author will update this appendix with new content mid-edition as needed. The appendix details the download instructions. Additionally, it discusses Cisco's open approach to exam revision and release, called the Cisco Certification Roadmap.

- Part IX: Appendixes

  - Appendix A, "Numeric Reference Tables," lists several tables of numeric information, including a binary-to-decimal conversion table and a list of powers of 2.

  - Appendix B, "Exam Topics Cross-Reference," provides some tables to help you find where each exam objective is covered in the book.

  - Appendix C, "Answers to the 'Do I Know This Already?' Quizzes," includes the explanations to all the "Do I Know This Already" quizzes.

  - The **Glossary** contains definitions for all the terms listed in the "Key Terms You Should Know" sections at the conclusion of the chapters.

- Online Appendixes

- Practice Appendices

The following appendixes are available in digital format from the companion website. These appendixes provide additional practice for several networking processes that use some math.

  - Appendix D, "Practice for Chapter 12: Analyzing Classful IPv4 Networks"

  - Appendix E, "Practice for Chapter 13: Analyzing Subnet Masks"

  - Appendix F, "Practice for Chapter 14: Analyzing Existing Subnets"

  - Appendix G, "Practice for Chapter 15: Subnet Design"

- Appendix H, "Practice for Chapter 25: Fundamentals of IP Version 6"

- Appendix I, "Practice for Chapter 27: Implementing IPv6 Addressing on Routers"

- Miscellaneous Appendices

  - Appendix J, "Study Planner," is a spreadsheet with major study milestones, where you can track your progress through your study.

- Content from Previous Editions

  From edition to edition, some readers have asked that we keep some select chapters with the book. Keeping content that Cisco removed from the exam, but that may still be useful, can help the average reader as well as instructors who use the materials to teach courses with this book. The following appendices hold this edition's content from previous editions:

  - Appendix K, "Topics from Previous Editions," is a collection of small topics from prior editions. None of the topics justify a complete appendix by themselves, so we collect the small topics into this single appendix.

  - Appendix L, "LAN Troubleshooting," examines the most common LAN switching issues and how to discover those issues when troubleshooting a network.

  - Appendix M, "Variable-Length Subnet Masks," moves away from the assumption of one subnet mask per network to multiple subnet masks per network, which makes subnetting math and processes much more challenging. This appendix explains those challenges.

About Building Hands-On Skills

To do well on the CCNA exam, you need skills in using Cisco routers and switches, specifically the Cisco command-line interface (CLI). The Cisco CLI is a text-based command-and-response user interface; you type a command, and the device (a router or switch) displays messages in response.

For the exam, CLI skills help you in a couple of ways. First, lab questions require CLI skills. Each lab question can take 7–8 minutes if you know the topic, so poor CLI skills can cost several minutes per lab question. Additionally, any question type can ask about CLI commands, so the more comfortable you are remembering commands, parameters, and what they do, the more points you will pick up on the exam.

This next section walks through the options of what is included in the book, with a brief description of lab options outside the book.

Config Lab Exercises

I created some lab exercises called Config Labs and put them on my blog. Each Config Lab details a straightforward lab exercise. It begins with a scenario, a topology, and existing configuration. You choose the configuration to add to each device to meet the goals of the scenario.

To make the labs accessible to all, the blog has no login requirements and no cost. You can do each lab just by viewing the page, reading, and writing your answer on paper or typing it in an editor. Optionally, you can attempt most labs in the Cisco Packet Tracer Simulator. In either case, the Config Lab page lists the intended answer, so you can check your work.

To find the Config Labs, first go to www.certskills.com. Navigate from the top menus for "Labs." Alternatively, use the advanced search link, from which you can combine search parameters to choose a book chapter or part, and to search for Config Lab posts.

Note that the blog organizes these Config Lab posts by book chapter, so you can easily use them at both Chapter Review and Part Review. See the "Your Study Plan" element that follows the Introduction for more details about those review sections.

A Quick Start with Pearson Network Simulator Lite

The decision of how to get hands-on skills can be a little scary at first. The good news: You have a free and simple first step to experience the CLI: install a desktop simulator app called Pearson Network Simulator Lite (or NetSim Lite) that comes with this book.

Pearson builds a CCNA Simulator app designed to help you learn most of the CCNA configure and verify exam topics. They also make a free lite version of the Simulator, included with this book. The lite version gives you the means to experience the Cisco CLI just after a 5–10-minute installation process. No need to go buy real gear or buy a full simulator to start learning the CLI. Just install the Sim Lite from the companion website.

This latest version of NetSim Lite includes labs associated with Part II of this book, plus a few more from Part III. (Part II is the first book part that includes any CLI commands.) So, make sure to use the NetSim Lite to learn the basics of the CLI to get a good start.

Of course, one reason that you get access to the NetSim Lite is that the publisher hopes you will buy the full product. However, even if you do not use the full product, you can still learn from the labs that come with NetSim Lite while deciding about what options to pursue.

The Pearson Network Simulator

The Config Labs and the Pearson Network Simulator Lite both fill specific needs, and they both come with the book. However, you need more than those two tools.

The single best option for lab work to do along with this book is the paid version of the Pearson Network Simulator. This simulator product simulates Cisco routers and switches so that you can learn for CCNA certification. But more importantly, it focuses on learning for the exam by providing a large number of useful lab exercises. Reader surveys tell us that those people who use the Simulator along with the book love the learning process and rave about how the book and Simulator work well together.

Of course, you need to make a decision for yourself and consider all the options. Thankfully, you can get a great idea of how the full Simulator product works by using the Pearson Network Simulator Lite product included with the book. Both have the same base code, same user interface, and same types of labs. Try the Lite version to decide if you want to buy the full product.

On a practical note, when you want to do labs when reading a chapter or doing Part Review, the Simulator organizes the labs to match the book. Just look for the Sort by Chapter tab in the Simulator's user interface.

At the time this book was published, Pearson had no plan to update its CCNA Simulator product to a new version, as the current edition covers the latest exam topics. A software update will be issued that maps the labs to the organization of the new Cert Guide chapter structure by the summer of 2024.

More Lab Options

Many other lab options exist. For instance, you can use real Cisco routers and switches. You can buy them, new or used, or borrow them at work. For example, you can buy routers and switches that are useful for CCNA learning but are two or three product generations old. You can also find sites from which you can rent time on real devices or virtual devices.

Cisco also makes a free simulator that works very well as a learning tool: Cisco Packet Tracer. Unlike the Pearson Network Simulator, it does not include lab exercises that direct you as to how to go about learning each topic. However, you can usually find lab exercises that rely on Packet Tracer, like the Config Labs at my blog. If interested in more information about Packet Tracer, check out www.certskills.com/ptinstall.

Cisco offers a virtualization product that lets you run router and switch operating system (OS) images in a virtual environment on your PC. This tool, the Cisco Modeling Labs–Personal Edition (CML PE), lets you create a lab topology, start the operating system for each device, and connect to the CLI of real router and switch OS images. There is a fee, and you may need a PC hardware upgrade to use it effectively. Check out www.cisco.com/go/cml for more information, and inquire for more information at the Cisco Learning Network's CML community (learningnetwork.cisco.com).

The next two options work somewhat like CML PE, but with free software but no Cisco Operating Systems supplied. GNS3 (gns3.com) and EVE-NG (eve-ng.net) support creating topologies of virtual routers and switches that run real Cisco operating systems. Both have free options. However, both require that you provide the OS images. Also, as with CML PE, you may need to buy a small server or at least upgrade your personal computer to run more than a few routers and switches in a lab topology.

This book does not tell you what option to use, but you should plan on getting some hands-on practice somehow. For people starting with CCNA, many use some simulator like Pearson Sim Lite and the free Cisco Packet Tracer simulator. If you go far in your Cisco certification journey, you will likely try at least one of the virtualization options and also use real gear. The important thing to know is that most people need to practice using the Cisco CLI to be ready to pass these exams.

About IP Subnetting

IP addressing and subnetting skills remain as one of the top five most important topics for real networking jobs and for the CCNA exam. This book devotes Part IV to the topic, with several practice problem appendices to match. You can learn all you need for CCNA from those in-book chapters, and you can practice with the appendices. You can even use the interactive versions of the appendices on the companion website.

Because IP subnetting is so important, I created a video course called "IP Subnetting from Beginning to Mastery LiveLessons." You can buy the course outright from Cisco Press or access the course at O'Reilly Learning (learning.oreilly.com). This video course teaches IPv4 subnetting from start to finish. The course includes instruction on all aspects of IPv4 subnetting, many examples, and close to 100 video practice exercises.

However, to be clear, you do not need to buy the subnetting course; the book has all you need to learn subnetting well. But if you prefer to use the IP Subnetting video course, you do not have to use the course and read the chapters in this book's Part IV. Instead, use one of these plans if you get the video course:

- Learn from the first 19 lessons in the course, which cover the same content as Part IV of this book—and again ignore the chapters in Part IV.

- Study primarily from the book chapters and supplement your reading with the video course. Because the course teaches the topics in a different order, use the information in Table I-2 to decide what video course lessons to use.

Table I-2 *Using the IP Subnetting Video Course Instead of Volume 1, Part IV*

Volume 1 Chapter	Video Course Lessons
11	1–3, 10
12	11, 12
13	8, 9
14	4–7
15	13–19

For More Information

If you have any comments about the book, submit them via www.ciscopress.com. Just go to the website, select **Contact Us**, and type your message.

Cisco might make changes that affect the CCNA certification from time to time. You should always check www.cisco.com/go/ccna for the latest details.

CCNA 200-301 Official Cert Guide, *Volume 1*, Second Edition, helps you attain CCNA certification. This is the CCNA certification book from the only Cisco-authorized publisher. We at Cisco Press believe that this book certainly can help you achieve CCNA certification, but the real work is up to you! I trust that your time will be well spent.

Your Study Plan

You just got this book. You have probably already read (or quickly skimmed) the Introduction. You are probably now wondering whether to start reading here or skip ahead to Chapter 1, "Introduction to TCP/IP Networking."

Stop to read this section about how to create your own study plan for the CCNA 200-301 exam. Your study will go much better if you take time (maybe 15 minutes) to think about a few key points about studying before starting this journey. That is what this section will help you do.

A Brief Perspective on Cisco Certification Exams

Cisco sets the bar pretty high for passing the CCNA 200-301 exam. Most anyone can study and pass the exam, but it takes more than just a quick read through the book and the cash to pay for the exam.

The challenge of the exam comes from many angles. First, the exam covers many concepts and commands specific to Cisco devices. Beyond knowledge, all these Cisco exams also require deep skills. You must be able to analyze and predict what really happens in a network, configure Cisco devices to work correctly in those networks, and troubleshoot problems when the network does not work correctly.

The more challenging questions on these exams work a lot like a jigsaw puzzle, but with four out of every five puzzle pieces not even in the room. To solve the puzzle, you have to mentally re-create the missing pieces. To do that, you must know each networking concept and remember how the concepts work together.

For instance, you might encounter a question that asks you why two routers cannot exchange routing information using the OSPF routing protocol. The question would supply some of the information, like some jigsaw puzzle pieces, as represented with the white pieces in Figure 1. You have to apply your knowledge of IPv4 routing, IPv4 addressing, and the OSPF protocol to the scenario in the question to come up with some of the other pieces of the puzzle. For a given question, some pieces of the puzzle might remain a mystery, but with enough of the puzzle filled in, you should be able to answer the question. And some pieces will just remain unknown for a given question.

These skills require that you prepare by doing more than just reading and memorizing. Of course, you need to read many pages in this book to learn many individual facts and how these facts relate to each other. But a big part of this book lists exercises that require more than just simply reading, exercises that help you build the skills to solve these networking puzzles.

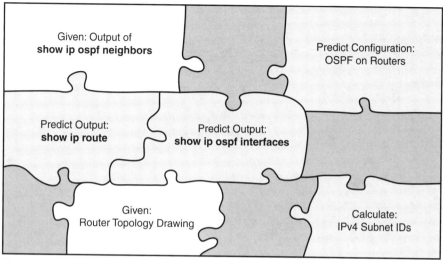

Figure 1 *Filling In Puzzle Pieces with Your Analysis Skills*

Five Study Plan Steps

What do you need to do to be ready to pass, beyond reading and remembering all the facts? You need to develop skills. You need to mentally link each idea with other related ideas. Doing that requires additional work. To help you along the way, the next few pages give you five key planning steps to take so that you can more effectively build those skills and make those connections, before you dive into this exciting but challenging world of learning networking on Cisco gear.

Step 1: Think in Terms of Parts and Chapters

The first step in your study plan is to get the right mindset about the size and nature of the task you have set out to accomplish. This is a large book, and to be ready for the CCNA 200-301 exam, you need to complete it and then the *CCNA 200-301 Official Cert Guide, Volume 2*, Second Edition. You cannot think about these two books as one huge task, or you might get discouraged. So, break the task down into smaller tasks.

The good news here is that the book is designed with obvious breakpoints and built-in extensive review activities. In short, the book is more of a study system than a book.

The first step in your study plan is to visualize this book not as one large book but as components. First, visualize the book as seven smaller parts. Then, within each part, visualize each part as three-to-five chapters. Your study plan has you working through the chapters and then reviewing the material in that part before moving on, as shown in Figure 2.

Now your plan has the following:

    1 large task: Read and master all content in the book.

    7 medium tasks/book: Read and master a part.

    4 small tasks/part: Read and master a chapter.

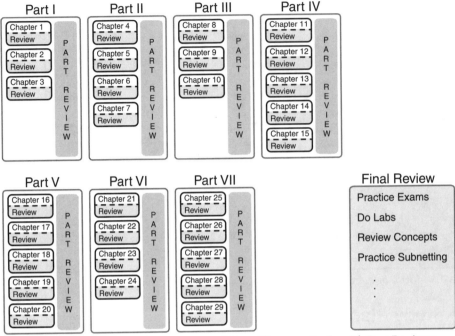

Figure 2   *Seven Parts, with an Average of Four Chapters Each, with Part Reviews*

Step 2: Build Your Study Habits Around the Chapter

For your second step, possibly the most important step, approach each chapter with the same process as shown in Figure 3. The chapter pre-quiz (called a DIKTA quiz, or "Do I Know This Already?" quiz) helps you decide how much time to spend reading versus skimming the core of the chapter, called the "Foundation Topics." The "Chapter Review" section then gives instructions on studying and reviewing what you just read.

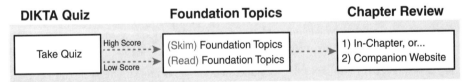

Figure 3   *Suggested Approach to Each Chapter*

The book has no long chapters, on purpose. They average about 20 pages for the Foundation Topics (which is the part of the chapter with new content). Because we keep the size reasonable, you can complete all of a chapter in one or two short study sessions. For instance, when you begin a new chapter, if you have an hour or an hour and a half, you should be able to complete a first reading of the chapter and at least make a great start on it. And even if you do not have enough time to read the entire chapter, look for the major headings inside the chapter; each chapter has two to three major headings, and those make a great place to stop reading when you need to wait to complete the reading in the next study sessions.

The Chapter Review tasks are very important to your exam-day success. Doing these tasks after you've read the chapter really does help you get ready. Do not ignore Chapter Review! The chapter-ending review tasks help you with the first phase of deepening your knowledge and skills of the key topics, remembering terms, and linking the concepts together in your brain so that you can remember how it all fits together. The following list describes most of the activities you will find in the "Chapter Review" sections:

- Review key topics
- Review key terms
- Answer the DIKTA questions
- Re-create config checklists
- Review command tables
- Review memory tables
- Do lab exercises
- Watch video
- Do subnetting exercises

Step 3: Use Book Parts for Major Milestones

Studies show that to master a concept and/or skill, you should plan to go through multiple study sessions to review the concept and to practice the skill. The "Chapter Review" section at the end of each chapter is the first such review, while the Part Review acts as that second review at the end of each part.

Plan time to do the Part Review task at the end of each part, using the Part Review elements found at the end of each part. You should expect to spend about as much time on one Part Review as you would on one entire chapter. So, in terms of planning your time, think of the Part Review itself as another chapter.

Figure 4 lists the names of the parts in this book. Note that Parts II and III are related (Ethernet), and Parts IV through VI discuss IP version 4 (IPv4). Part VII then moves on to IP Version 6 (IPv6). Each part ends with a Part Review section of two to four pages, with notes about what tools and activities to use.

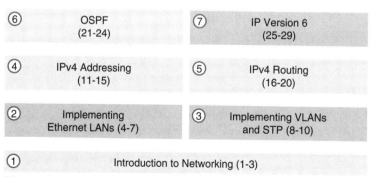

Figure 4 *Parts as Major Milestones*

Also, consider setting a goal date for finishing each part of the book (and a reward, as well). Plan a break, some family time, some time out exercising, eating some good food, whatever helps you get refreshed and motivated for the next part.

Step 4: Use Volume 2's Final Review Chapter

Your fourth step has one overall task: perform the details outlined in the "Final Exam Review" chapter at the end of the *CCNA 200-301 Official Cert Guide, Volume 2*, Second Edition. Note that you have no exam to take at the end of this Volume 1 book, so keep working with Volume 2 when you complete this book. Once you're finished with both books, Volume 2's "Final Exam Review" will direct you.

Step 5: Set Goals and Track Your Progress

Your fifth study plan step spans the entire timeline of your study effort. Before you start reading the book and doing the rest of these study tasks, take the time to make a plan, set some goals, and be ready to track your progress.

While making lists of tasks may or may not appeal to you, depending on your personality, goal setting can help everyone studying for these exams. And to do the goal setting, you need to know what tasks you plan to do.

As for the list of tasks to do when studying, you do not have to use a detailed task list. (You could list every single task in every chapter-ending "Chapter Review" section, every task in the Part Reviews, and every task in the "Final Review" chapter.) However, listing the major tasks can be enough.

You should track at least two tasks for each typical chapter: reading the "Foundation Topics" section and doing the Chapter Review at the end of the chapter. And, of course, do not forget to list tasks for Part Reviews and Final Review. Table 1 shows a sample for Part I of this book.

Table 1   Sample Excerpt from a Planning Table

Element	Task	Goal Date	First Date Completed	Second Date Completed (Optional)
Chapter 1	Read Foundation Topics			
Chapter 1	Do Chapter Review tasks			
Chapter 2	Read Foundation Topics			
Chapter 2	Do Chapter Review tasks			
Chapter 3	Read Foundation Topics			
Chapter 3	Do Chapter Review tasks			
Part I Review	Do Part Review activities			

NOTE   Appendix J, "Study Planner," on the companion website, contains a complete planning checklist like Table 1 for the tasks in this book. This spreadsheet allows you to update and save the file to note your goal dates and the tasks you have completed.

Use your goal dates to manage your study, and not as a way to get discouraged if you miss a date. Pick reasonable dates that you can meet. When setting your goals, think about how fast you read and the length of each chapter's "Foundation Topics" section, as listed in the table of contents. Then, when you finish a task sooner than planned, move up the next few goal dates.

If you miss a few dates, do *not* start skipping the tasks listed at the ends of the chapters! Instead, think about what is impacting your schedule—real life, commitment, and so on—and either adjust your goals or work a little harder on your study.

Things to Do Before Starting the First Chapter

Now that you understand the big ideas behind a good study plan for the book, take a few more minutes for a few overhead actions that will help. Before leaving this section, look at some other tasks you should do either now or around the time you read the first few chapters to help make a good start in the book.

Bookmark the Companion Website

The companion website contains links to all the tools you need for chapter and part review. In fact, it includes a chapter-by-chapter and part-by-part breakdown of all the review activities. Before you finish the first chapter, make sure and follow the instructions in the Introduction's section titled "The Companion Website for Online Content," get access, and bookmark the page.

Also, if you did not yet read about the companion website in the Introduction or explore the site, take a few minutes to look at the resources available on the site.

Bookmark/Install Pearson Test Prep

Like many other Cisco Press books, this book includes the rights to use the Pearson Test Prep (PTP) software and the rights to use some exam questions related to this book. PTP has many useful study features:

- Both a web and desktop version for your convenience and choice

- History tracking of your simulated exam attempts, synchronized between web and desktop

- Study mode, which lets you see the correct answers with each question and the related explanations

- Practice exam mode, which simulates exam conditions, hiding answers/explanations and timing the exam event

- Filters to let you choose questions based on chapter(s) and/or part(s)

You should take a few minutes to set up your PTP installation. Refer to the Introduction's section titled "How to Access the Pearson Test Prep (PTP) App" for details.

Understand This Book's PTP Databases and Modes

When you activate a product in PTP, you gain the rights to that product's exams. Understanding those exams helps you choose when to use them and when to delay using different exams to save those questions for later. The publisher includes different exams with different products, so this section works through the various options with you.

Exams in the Retail (Print) Editions

The retail edition—that is, the printed book—of Volume 1 comes with four exams, as shown on the left side of Figure 5. Volume 2 comes with four similar exams, plus four exams described as CCNA exams. If you buy the retail edition of the CCNA Library, you receive all the exams shown in the figure.

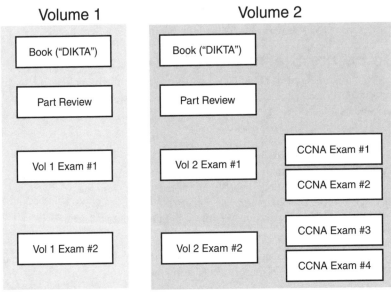

Figure 5   *PTP Exams/Exam Databases with the Retail (Print) Editions*

First, note that the exams found in both volumes contain only questions about that volume and not the other volume. For instance, the Part Review exam in Volume 1 has questions only about Volume 1, while the Part Review exam in Volume 2 has questions only about Volume 2. The CCNA exams have questions across the breadth of both books.

Use the book exams during chapter review for each chapter. Each chapter begins with a short pre-chapter quiz called a "Do I Know This Already?" or DIKTA quiz. You will likely read the DIKTA quizzes inside each chapter without using the PTP app; however, when reviewing the chapter after reading it, answer that chapter's DIKTA questions again using the PTP app. (The app refers to the exam with all that volume's DIKTA questions as the book exam.)

Use the Part Review exam during part review. Unlike the book exams, these questions exist only inside a PTP exam. In fact, we created them specifically as a review exercise at the end of each book part.

Use Volume 1 Exams 1 and 2 whenever you like. Those exams (and the similarly named exams for Volume 2) contain more unique questions, usually a little more than 90 per exam. Each question has an assigned objective, which matches the most relevant chapter. From the PTP app, you can use PTP questions for any combination of chapters, with any combination of these exams, for an impromptu study session. For example, after finishing the first 10 chapters of Volume 1, you could select both these exams, Chapters 1–10, and answer those questions.

Use the exams called CCNA exams for timed practice exams. Volume 2 (but not Volume 1) includes four CCNA exams. Only the CCNA exams contain questions from Volumes 1 and 2, built to provide individual exams useful for a practice exam event. When ready, pick any CCNA exam (a little more than 90 questions), use them as a practice exam, and give yourself 120 minutes. You build your test-taking skills with time pressure, and later, you can return to the results, identify missed questions, and dig in to learn those topics.

Be aware that the exams labeled Volume X Exam Y contain the same questions used to create the CCNA exams. The questions in the CCNA exams come from the Volume 1 and 2 exams, as shown in Figure 6.

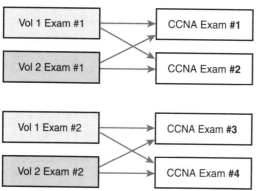

Figure 6 *Source of Questions for the CCNA Exams*

Some readers do not care about the overlaps shown in Figure 6, but others do. Those who do care want to protect their timed practice exam events so that they do not see those questions before taking a timed practice exam event. If that sounds like you, choose now which exams to use and which to avoid using.

- If you do not plan on using timed practice exam events, use Volume 1 exams 1 and 2 plus Volume 2 exams 1 and 2, at any time, and ignore the CCNA exams.

- If you plan to use all four CCNA exams for timed practice exams, avoid using Volume 1 exams 1 and 2 plus Volume 2 exams 1 and 2, to avoid seeing the questions before the timed events.

- Split the difference. Use Volume 1 exam 1 and Volume 2 Exam 1 at any time. Later, use CCNA exams 3 and 4.

I recommend using study mode in all cases except for the timed practice exam, as follows:

Study mode: Study mode works best when you are still working on understanding and learning the content. In study mode, you can see the answers immediately, so you can study the topics more easily. Study mode also shows an "answer" button that reveals an explanation to each question, so you can get immediate insights into questions you miss.

Practice mode: This mode lets you practice an exam event somewhat like the actual exam. It gives you a preset number of questions from all chapters with a timed event. Practice exam mode also gives you a score for that timed event.

Exams with Individual Premium Edition eBooks

The publisher sells these related Premium Edition eBook and Practice Test products:

■ *CCNA 200-301 Official Cert Guide, Volume 1 Premium Edition and Practice Test,* Second Edition

■ *CCNA 200-301 Official Cert Guide, Volume 2 Premium Edition and Practice Test,* Second Edition

■ *CCNA 200-301 Official Cert Guide Library Premium Edition eBook and Practice Test,* Second Edition

With the retail editions, purchasing the two volumes individually gives you the same PTP exams as purchasing the retail CCNA Library, which is a box with both volumes. With the Premium Edition eBooks, you see different exams depending on whether you buy each volume separately or as a two-book library. This section examines what you receive when you buy both individual volumes, with the following section detailing the exams that come with the Premium Edition Library.

Exams with Two Individual Premium Edition eBooks

If you purchase the Premium Edition eBook products for both Volumes 1 and 2, you get each in various formats (PDF, ePub). Also, owning the eBooks enables PTP to link all questions' explanations to a book page that gives more detail about the topics—a great study feature. So, if you are confused by an answer, just click that link in that question's explanation to open the PDF and read more.

As for the PTP exams, you receive all the exams shown earlier in Figure 5, plus additional exams. The phrase "…and Practice Test" at the end of the long formal name of the products refers to the additional practice questions. Figure 7 shows the additional exams you receive if you buy both the Volume 1 and Volume 2 Premium Edition products, adding more than 350 additional unique questions.

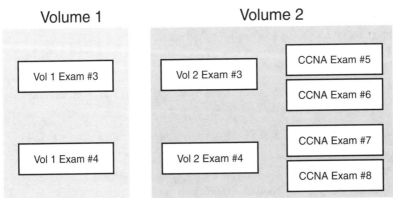

Figure 7   *Exams Added: Volume 1 and Volume 2 Premium Edition vs. Print Edition*

As with the other CCNA exams listed in Figure 6, the questions in CCNA exams 5–8 come from the Volume X Exam Y exams in Figure 7. Volume 1 and 2 exams 3 feed into CCNA exams 5 and 6, with Volume 1 and 2 exams 4 feeding into CCNA exams 7 and 8. So, you have the same choices to make about avoiding using some exams—just with many more questions to use.

Exams with CCNA Premium Edition Library

If you do not yet own any Premium Edition eBooks but want to choose, the CCNA Premium Edition Library version makes more sense for most people. It is cheaper than buying both Volume 1 and Volume 2 Premium Editions. It also includes the same questions as when purchasing the two individual products, but organizes the questions differently.

The CCNA Premium Edition Library has the book and part review exams for both volumes—the same exams as the other options. Plus, it has the same eight CCNA exams as seen in the other options, with content spread across the breadth of CCNA exam topics, which you can use at any time, in study mode or practice exam mode, as shown in Figure 8.

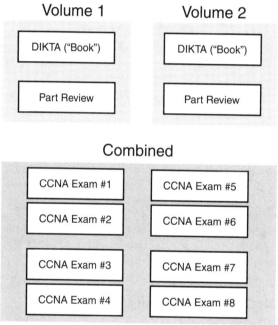

Figure 8   *PTP Exams/Exam Databases with CCNA Library Premium Edition*

The CCNA Premium Edition Library includes all the same questions you would get if you bought the individual Volume 1 and Volume 2 Premium Edition products—it just doesn't have the exams labeled Vol 1 Exam N and Vol 2 Exam N. You do not lose any function, but be more thoughtful about using the exams. For example, you can use some CCNA exams in study mode for review any time. For example, you could take this approach:

- Use CCNA exams 1–5 in study mode throughout the study experience for extra practice during chapter review, part review, or any time.

- Reserve CCNA exams 6–8 for timed practice exam events at the end of your study.

If you have this product, take the time right now to choose an approach. How many timed practice CCNA exams do you expect to take? Choose which CCNA exams to reserve for that purpose and use the other CCNA exams in study mode. Then, experiment with the PTP app to get comfortable choosing the exams, the objectives, and the mode (study or practice exam).

If you like practice questions when studying, you should have enough. The retail product exams, per Figure 5, have around 900 unique questions. Adding the CCNA Premium Edition Library bumps that to over 1200 unique questions.

Practice Viewing Per-Chapter Book (DIKTA) Questions

Take a few minutes to experiment with and understand how to use PTP to answer questions from a single chapter's book quiz, as follows:

Step 1.   Start the PTP web or desktop app.

Step 2.   From the main (home) menu, select the item for this product, with a name like *CCNA 200-301 Official Cert Guide, Volume 1*, Second Edition, and click **Open Exam**.

Step 3.   The top of the next window that appears should list some exams. Check the **Book Questions** box, and uncheck the other boxes. This selects the "book" questions (that is, the DIKTA questions from the beginning of each chapter).

Step 4.   On this same window, click at the bottom of the screen to deselect all objectives (chapters). Then select the box beside each chapter in the part of the book you are reviewing.

Step 5.   Select any other options on the right side of the window.

Step 6.   Click **Start** to start reviewing the questions.

Practice by Using Per-Part Review Questions

Your PTP access also includes a Part Review exam created solely for study during the Part Review process. To view these questions, follow the same process as you did with DIKTA/book questions, but select the Part Review database rather than the book database. PTP has a clear name for this database: Part Review Questions.

Join the Cisco Learning Network CCNA Community

Register (for free) at learningnetwork.cisco.com (the Cisco Learning Network, or CLN) and join the CCNA community. This group allows you to both lurk and participate in discussions about topics related to the CCNA exam. Register (for free), join the group, and set up an email filter to redirect the messages to a separate folder. Even if you do not spend time reading all the posts yet, later, when you have time to read, you can browse through the posts to find interesting topics (or just search the posts).

Also, the CLN CCNA community, along with my blog and YouTube channel, are the best places to find me online.

Getting Started: Now

Now dive in to your first of many short, manageable tasks: reading the relatively short Chapter 1. Enjoy!

This first part of the book introduces the fundamentals of the most important topics in TCP/IP networking. Chapter 1 provides a broad look at TCP/IP, introducing the common terms, big concepts, and major protocols for TCP/IP. Chapter 2 then examines local-area networks (LANs), which are networks that connect devices that are located near to each other, for instance, in the same building. Chapter 3 then shows how to connect those LANs across long distances with wide-area networks (WANs) with a focus on how routers connect LANs and WANs to forward data between any two devices in the network.

Part I

Introduction to Networking

CHAPTER 1

Introduction to TCP/IP Networking

This chapter covers the following exam topics:

1.0 Network Fundamentals

    1.3 Compare physical interface and cabling types

        1.3.a Single-mode fiber, multimode fiber, copper

        1.3.b Connections (Ethernet shared media and point-to-point)

Welcome to the first chapter in your study for CCNA! This chapter begins Part I, which focuses on the basics of networking.

Networks work correctly because the various devices and software follow the rules. Those rules come in the form of standards and protocols, which are agreements of a particular part of how a network should work. However, the sheer number of standards and protocols available can make it difficult for the average network engineer to think about and work with networks—so the world of networking has used several networking models over time. Networking models define a structure and different categories (layers) of standards and protocols. As new standards and protocols emerge over time, networkers can think of those new details in the context of a working model.

You can think of a networking model as you think of a set of architectural plans for building a house. A lot of different people work on building your house, such as framers, electricians, bricklayers, painters, and so on. The blueprint helps ensure that all the different pieces of the house work together as a whole. Similarly, the people who make networking products, and the people who use those products to build their own computer networks, follow a particular networking model. That networking model defines rules about how each part of the network should work, as well as how the parts should work together so that the entire network functions correctly.

Today, TCP/IP rules as the most pervasive networking model in use. You can find support for TCP/IP on practically every computer operating system (OS) in existence today, from mobile phones to mainframe computers. Every network built using Cisco products today supports TCP/IP. And not surprisingly, the CCNA exam focuses heavily on TCP/IP. This chapter uses TCP/IP for one of its main purposes: to present various concepts about networking using the context of the different roles and functions in the TCP/IP model.

Note that most chapters cover topics about some specific CCNA exam topic. However, this chapter does not. Instead, it describes background information about the TCP/IP model and ideas you need to know about so you can better understand the detail included in CCNA.

"Do I Know This Already?" Quiz

Take the quiz (either here or use the PTP software) if you want to use the score to help you decide how much time to spend on this chapter. The letter answers are listed at the bottom of the page following the quiz. Appendix C, found both at the end of the book as well as on the companion website, includes both the answers and explanations. You can also find both answers and explanations in the PTP testing software.

Table 1-1 "Do I Know This Already?" Foundation Topics Section-to-Question Mapping

Foundation Topics Section	Questions
Perspectives on Networking	None
TCP/IP Networking Model	1–4
Data Encapsulation Terminology	5–6

1. Which of the following protocols are examples of TCP/IP transport layer protocols? (Choose two answers.)
   a. Ethernet
   b. HTTP
   c. IP
   d. UDP
   e. SMTP
   f. TCP

2. Which of the following protocols are examples of TCP/IP data-link layer protocols? (Choose two answers.)
   a. Ethernet
   b. HTTP
   c. IP
   d. UDP
   e. SMTP
   f. TCP
   g. 802.11

3. The process of HTTP asking TCP to send some data and making sure that it is received correctly is an example of what?
   a. Same-layer interaction
   b. Adjacent-layer interaction
   c. TCP/IP model
   d. All of these answers are correct.

4. The process of TCP on one computer marking a TCP segment as segment 1 and the receiving computer then acknowledging the receipt of TCP segment 1 is an example of what?
   a. Data encapsulation
   b. Same-layer interaction

    c. Adjacent-layer interaction

    d. TCP/IP model

    e. All of these answers are correct.

5. The process of a web server adding a TCP header to the contents of a web page, followed by adding an IP header and then adding a data-link header and trailer, is an example of what?

    a. Data encapsulation

    b. Same-layer interaction

    c. TCP/IP model

    d. All of these answers are correct.

6. Which of the following terms is used specifically to identify the entity created when encapsulating data inside data-link layer headers and trailers?

    a. Data

    b. Chunk

    c. Segment

    d. Frame

    e. Packet

Foundation Topics

Perspectives on Networking

So, you are new to networking. If you're like many people, your perspective about networks might be that of a user of the network, as opposed to the network engineer who builds networks. For some, your view of networking might be based on how you use the Internet, from home, using a high-speed Internet connection like fiber Ethernet or cable TV, as shown in Figure 1-1.

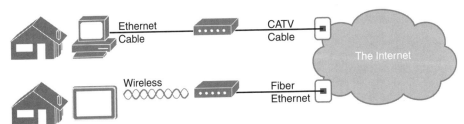

Figure 1-1 *End-User Perspective on High-Speed Internet Connections*

The top part of the figure shows a typical high-speed cable Internet user. The PC connects to a cable modem using an Ethernet cable. The cable modem then connects to a cable TV (CATV) outlet in the wall using a round coaxial cable—the same kind of cable used to connect your TV to the CATV wall outlet. Because cable Internet services provide service continuously, the user can just sit down at the PC and start sending email, browsing websites, making Internet phone calls, and using other tools and applications.

The lower part of the figure uses Ethernet between the home and service provider. First, the tablet computer uses wireless technology that goes by the name *wireless local-area network (wireless LAN).* In this example, the router uses a different technology, Ethernet, using a fiber-optic cable, to communicate with the Internet.

Both home-based networks and networks built for use by a company make use of similar networking technologies. The Information Technology (IT) world refers to a network created by one corporation, or enterprise, for the purpose of allowing its employees to communicate, as an *enterprise network*. The smaller networks at home, when used for business purposes, often go by the name small office/home office (SOHO) networks.

Users of enterprise networks have some idea about the enterprise network at their company or school. People realize that they use a network for many tasks. PC users might realize that their PC connects through an Ethernet cable to a matching wall outlet, as shown at the top of Figure 1-2. Those same users might use wireless LANs with their laptop when going to a meeting in the conference room as well. Figure 1-2 shows these two end-user perspectives on an enterprise network.

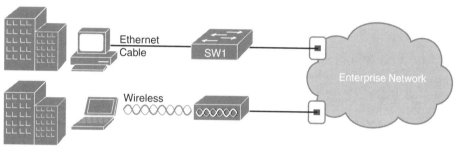

Figure 1-2 *Example Representation of an Enterprise Network*

NOTE   In networking diagrams, a cloud represents a part of a network whose details are not important to the purpose of the diagram. In this case, Figure 1-2 ignores the details of how to create an enterprise network.

Some users might not even have a concept of the network at all. Instead, these users just enjoy the functions of the network—the ability to post messages to social media sites, make phone calls, search for information on the Internet, listen to music, and download countless apps to their phones—without caring about how it works or how their favorite device connects to the network.

Regardless of how much you already know about how networks work, this book and the related certification help you learn how networks do their job. That job is simply this: moving data from one device to another. The rest of this chapter—and the rest of this first part of the book—reveals the basics of how to build enterprise networks so that they can deliver data between two devices.

TCP/IP Networking Model

A **networking model**, sometimes also called either a *networking architecture* or *networking blueprint*, refers to a comprehensive set of documents. Individually, each document describes one small function required for a network; collectively, these documents define everything that should happen for a computer network to work. Some documents define a *protocol*, which is a set of logical rules that devices must follow to communicate. Other documents define some physical requirements for networking. For example, a document could define the voltage and current levels used on a particular cable when transmitting data.

You can think of a networking model as you think of an architectural blueprint for building a house. Sure, you can build a house without the blueprint. However, the blueprint can ensure that the house has the right foundation and structure so that it will not fall down, and it has the correct hidden spaces to accommodate the plumbing, electrical, gas, and so on. Also, the many different people who build the house using the blueprint—such as framers, electricians, bricklayers, painters, and so on—know that if they follow the blueprint, their part of the work should not cause problems for the other workers.

Similarly, you could build your own network—write your own software, build your own networking cards, and so on—to create a network. However, it is much easier to simply buy and use products that already conform to some well-known networking model or blueprint. Because the networking product vendors build their products with some networking model in mind, their products should work well together.

History Leading to TCP/IP

Today, the world of computer networking uses one networking model: TCP/IP. However, the world has not always been so simple. Once upon a time, networking protocols didn't exist, including TCP/IP. Vendors created the first networking protocols; these protocols supported only that vendor's computers.

For example, IBM, the computer company with the largest market share in many markets back in the 1970s and 1980s, published its Systems Network Architecture (SNA) networking model in 1974. Other vendors also created their own proprietary networking models. As a result, if your company bought computers from three vendors, network engineers often had to create three different networks based on the networking models created by each company, and then somehow connect those networks, making the combined networks much more complex. The left side of Figure 1-3 shows the general idea of what a company's enterprise network might have looked like back in the 1980s, before TCP/IP became common in enterprise internetworks.

Although vendor-defined proprietary networking models often worked well, having an open, vendor-neutral networking model would aid competition and reduce complexity. The International Organization for Standardization (ISO) took on the task to create such a model, starting as early as the late 1970s, beginning work on what would become known as the Open Systems Interconnection (OSI) networking model. ISO had a noble goal for the OSI model: to standardize data networking protocols to allow communication among all computers across the entire planet. ISO worked toward this ambitious and noble goal, with participants from most of the technologically developed nations on Earth participating in the process.

Answers to the "Do I Know This Already?" quiz:

1 D and F **2** A and G **3** B **4** B **5** A **6** D

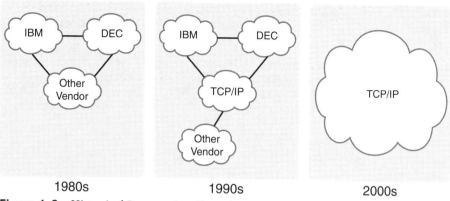

Figure 1-3 *Historical Progression: Proprietary Models to the Open TCP/IP Model*

A second, less-formal effort to create an open, vendor-neutral, public networking model sprouted forth from a U.S. Department of Defense (DoD) contract. Researchers at various universities volunteered to help further develop the protocols surrounding the original DoD work. These efforts resulted in a competing open networking model called TCP/IP.

During the 1990s, companies began adding OSI, TCP/IP, or both to their enterprise networks. However, by the end of the 1990s, TCP/IP had become the common choice, and OSI fell away. The center part of Figure 1-3 shows the general idea behind enterprise networks in that decade—still with networks built upon multiple networking models but including TCP/IP.

Here in the twenty-first century, TCP/IP dominates. Some proprietary networking models still exist, but they have mostly been discarded in favor of TCP/IP. The OSI model, whose development suffered in part due to a standard-first-code-second approach, never succeeded in the marketplace. And TCP/IP, the networking model originally created almost entirely by a bunch of volunteers, with a code-first-standardize-second approach, has become the most prolific networking model ever, as shown on the right side of Figure 1-3.

In this chapter, you will read about some of the basics of TCP/IP. Although you will learn some interesting facts about TCP/IP, the true goal of this chapter is to help you understand what a networking model or networking architecture really is and how it works.

Also in this chapter, you will learn about some of the jargon used with OSI. Will any of you ever work on a computer that is using the full OSI protocols instead of TCP/IP? Probably not. However, you will often use terms relating to OSI.

Overview of the TCP/IP Networking Model

The TCP/IP model both defines and references a large collection of protocols that allow computers to communicate. To define a protocol, TCP/IP uses documents called *Requests For Comments (RFC)*. (You can find these RFCs using any online search engine.) Each layer broadly defines a set of functions that helps create a working communication system, and each RFC gives the specifics about an option to implement one or more of the functions at some layer of the model.

The TCP/IP model also avoids repeating work already done by some other standards body or vendor consortium by simply referring to standards or protocols created by those groups.

For example, the Institute of Electrical and Electronics Engineers (IEEE) defines Ethernet LANs; the TCP/IP model does not define Ethernet in RFCs, but refers to IEEE Ethernet as an option.

To help people understand a networking model, each model breaks the functions into a small number of categories called *layers*. Each layer includes protocols and standards that relate to that category of functions, as shown in Figure 1-4.

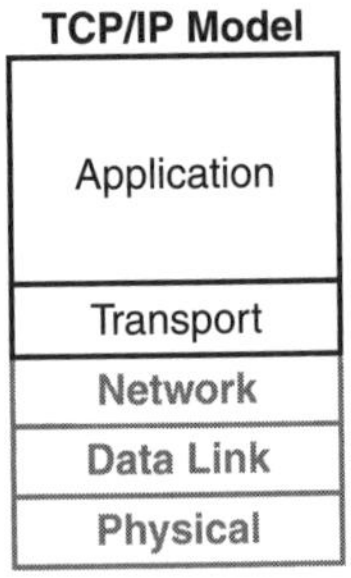

TCP/IP Model

Application
Transport
Network
Data Link
Physical

Figure 1-4 *The TCP/IP Networking Model*

> **NOTE** The network layer, shown as the middle layer of the TCP/IP model in Figure 1-4, may also be called the *Internet* layer in reference to its primary protocol, the Internet Protocol (IP).

On a single computer, different components implement different protocols and standards from different layers. Imagine buying a new computer and connecting it to either your home network or network at work using a cable or wireless. You would expect that you can open a web browser and connect to a website without much more effort. To make all that work, the network hardware in your computer—an integrated network interface card (NIC)—implements some physical layer standards to support physical communications. That NIC also supports the related data-link standards. The OS on the computer implements protocols from the network and transport layers. Finally, that web browser implements some application layer protocols (for instance, HTTP or HTTPS.)

More generally, the TCP/IP model in Figure 1-4 shows the more common terms and layers used when people talk about TCP/IP today. The physical layer focuses on how to transmit bits over each link. The data-link layer focuses on the rules that control the use of the physical link, analogous to how we need standards for roads, cars, and traffic signals. The network layer focuses on delivering data over the entire path from the original sending computer to the final destination computer, analogous to how a national postal service arranges for unique postal addresses and a system to deliver mail to all those addresses. The top two layers focus more on the applications that need to send and receive data—for instance, how to identify data, how to ask for the data to be sent, and how to recover the data if lost in transmission.

Many of you will have already heard of several TCP/IP protocols, like the examples listed in Table 1-2. Most of the protocols and standards in this table will be explained in more detail as you work through this book. Following the table, this section takes a closer look at the layers of the TCP/IP model.

Table 1-2   TCP/IP Architectural Model and Example Protocols

TCP/IP Architecture Layer	Example Protocols
Application	HTTPS, POP3, SMTP
Transport	TCP, UDP
Network	IP, ICMP
Data Link & Physical	Ethernet, 802.11 (Wi-Fi)

TCP/IP Application Layer

TCP/IP application layer protocols provide services to the application software running on a computer. The application layer does not define the application itself, but it defines services that applications need. For example, application protocol HTTP defines how web browsers can pull the contents of a web page from a web server. In short, the application layer provides an interface between software running on a computer and the network itself.

Arguably, the most popular TCP/IP application today is the web browser. Many major software vendors either have already changed or are changing their application software to support access from a web browser. And thankfully, using a web browser is easy: You start a web browser on your computer and select a website by typing the name of the website, and the web page appears.

HTTP Overview

What really happens to allow that web page to appear on your web browser?

Imagine that Bob opens his browser. His browser has been configured to automatically ask for web server Larry's default web page, or *home page*. The general logic looks like Figure 1-5.

Web Server - Larry   Web Browser - Bob

Figure 1-5   *Basic Application Logic to Get a Web Page*

So, what really happened? Bob's initial request actually asks Larry to send his home page back to Bob. Larry's web server software has been configured to know that the default web page is contained in a file called home.htm. Bob receives the file from Larry and displays the contents of the file in Bob's web browser window.

HTTP Protocol Mechanisms

Taking a closer look, this example shows how applications on each endpoint computer—specifically, the web browser application and web server application—use a TCP/IP application layer protocol. To make the request for a web page and return the contents of the web page, the applications use the Hypertext Transfer Protocol (HTTP).

HTTP did not exist until Tim Berners-Lee created the first web browser and web server in the early 1990s. Berners-Lee gave HTTP functionality to ask for the contents of web pages, specifically by giving the web browser the ability to request files from the server and giving the server a way to return the content of those files. The overall logic matches what was shown in Figure 1-5; Figure 1-6 shows the same idea, but with details specific to HTTP.

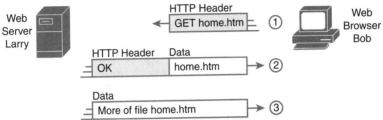

Figure 1-6   *HTTP GET Request, HTTP Reply, and One Data-Only Message*

NOTE   The full version of most web addresses—also called Uniform Resource Locators (URL) or Universal Resource Identifiers (URI)—begins with the letters *http*, which means that HTTP is used to transfer the web pages.

To get the web page from Larry, at Step 1, Bob sends a message with an HTTP header. Generally, protocols use headers as a place to put information used by that protocol. This HTTP header includes the request to "get" a file. The request typically contains the name of the file (home.htm, in this case), or if no filename is mentioned, the web server assumes that Bob wants the default web page.

Step 2 in Figure 1-6 shows the response from web server Larry. The message begins with an HTTP header, with a return code (200), which means something as simple as "OK" returned in the header. HTTP also defines other return codes so that the server can tell the browser whether the request worked. (Here is another example: If you ever looked for a web page that was not found, and then received an HTTP 404 "not found" error, you received an HTTP return code of 404.) The second message also includes the first part of the requested file.

Step 3 in Figure 1-6 shows another message from web server Larry to web browser Bob, but this time without an HTTP header. HTTP transfers the data by sending multiple messages, each with a part of the file. Rather than wasting space by sending repeated HTTP headers that list the same information, these additional messages simply omit the header.

Chapter 5 in *CCNA 200-301 Official Cert Guide, Volume 2*, revisits both HTTP going into more depth about HTTP, secure HTTP, and the various versions of HTTP.

TCP/IP Transport Layer

Although many TCP/IP application layer protocols exist, the TCP/IP transport layer includes a smaller number of protocols. The two most commonly used transport layer protocols are the Transmission Control Protocol (TCP) and the User Datagram Protocol (UDP).

Transport layer protocols provide services to the application layer protocols that reside one layer higher in the TCP/IP model. How does a transport layer protocol provide a service to a higher-layer protocol? This section introduces that general concept by focusing on a single service provided by TCP: error recovery. The *CCNA 200-301 Official Cert Guide, Volume 2*, Second Edition includes a chapter, "Introduction to TCP/IP Transport and Applications," which examines the transport layer in more detail.

TCP Error Recovery Basics

To appreciate what the transport layer protocols do, you must think about the layer above the transport layer, the application layer. Why? Well, each layer provides a service to the layer above it, like the error-recovery service provided to application layer protocols by TCP.

For example, in Figure 1-5, Bob and Larry used HTTP to transfer the home page from web server Larry to Bob's web browser. But what would have happened if Bob's HTTP GET request had been lost in transit through the TCP/IP network? Or, what would have happened if Larry's response, which included the contents of the home page, had been lost? Well, as you might expect, in either case, the page would not have shown up in Bob's browser.

TCP/IP needs a mechanism to guarantee delivery of data across a network. Because many application layer protocols probably want a way to guarantee delivery of data across a network, the creators of TCP included an error-recovery feature. To recover from errors, TCP uses the concept of acknowledgments. Figure 1-7 outlines the basic idea behind how TCP notices lost data and asks the sender to try again.

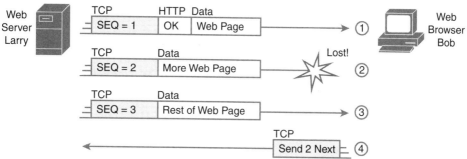

Figure 1-7   *TCP Error-Recovery Services as Provided to HTTP*

Figure 1-7 shows web server Larry sending a web page to web browser Bob, using three separate messages. Note that this figure shows the same HTTP headers as Figure 1-6, but it also shows a TCP header. The TCP header shows a sequence number (SEQ) with each message. In this example, the network has a problem, and the network fails to deliver the TCP message (called a **segment**) with sequence number 2. When Bob receives messages with sequence numbers 1 and 3, but does not receive a message with sequence number 2, Bob realizes that message 2 was lost. That realization by Bob's TCP logic causes Bob to send a TCP segment back to Larry, asking Larry to send message 2 again.

Same-Layer and Adjacent-Layer Interactions

Figure 1-7 also demonstrates a function called **adjacent-layer interaction**, which refers to the concepts of how adjacent layers in a networking model, on the same computer, work together. In this example, the higher-layer protocol (HTTP) wants error recovery, so it uses the next lower-layer protocol (TCP) to perform the service of error recovery; the lower layer provides a service to the layer above it.

Figure 1-7 also shows an example of a similar function called **same-layer interaction**. When a particular layer on one computer wants to communicate with the same layer on another computer, the two computers use headers to hold the information that they want to communicate. For example, in Figure 1-7, Larry set the sequence numbers to 1, 2, and 3 so that Bob could notice when some of the data did not arrive. Larry's TCP process created that TCP header with the sequence number; Bob's TCP process received and reacted to the TCP segments.

Table 1-3 summarizes the key points about how adjacent layers work together on a single computer and how one layer on one computer works with the same networking layer on another computer.

Table 1-3   Summary: Same-Layer and Adjacent-Layer Interactions

Concept	Description
Same-layer interaction on different computers	The two computers use a protocol to communicate with the same layer on another computer. The protocol defines a header that communicates what each computer wants to do.
Adjacent-layer interaction on the same computer	On a single computer, one lower layer provides a service to the layer just above. The software or hardware that implements the higher layer requests that the next lower layer perform the needed function.

TCP/IP Network Layer

The application layer includes many protocols. The transport layer includes fewer protocols, most notably, TCP and UDP. The TCP/IP network layer includes a small number of protocols, but only one major protocol: the Internet Protocol (IP). In fact, the name TCP/IP is simply the names of the two most common protocols (TCP and IP) separated by a /.

IP provides several features, most importantly, addressing and routing. This section begins by comparing IP's addressing and routing with another commonly known system that uses addressing and routing: the postal service. Following that, this section introduces IP addressing and routing. (More details follow in Chapter 3, "Fundamentals of WANs and IP Routing.")

Internet Protocol and the Postal Service

Imagine that you just wrote two letters: one to a friend on the other side of the country and one to a friend on the other side of town. You addressed the envelopes and put on the stamps, so both are ready to give to the postal service. Is there much difference in how you treat each letter? Not really. Typically, you would just put them in the same mailbox and expect the postal service to deliver both letters.

The postal service, however, must think about each letter separately, and then make a decision of where to send each letter so that it is delivered. For the letter sent across town, the people in the local post office probably just need to put the letter on another truck.

For the letter that needs to go across the country, the postal service sends the letter to another post office, then another, and so on, until the letter gets delivered across the country. At each post office, the postal service must process the letter and choose where to send it next.

To make it all work, the postal service has regular routes for small trucks, large trucks, planes, boats, and so on, to move letters between postal service sites. The service must be able to receive and forward the letters, and it must make good decisions about where to send each letter next, as shown in Figure 1-8.

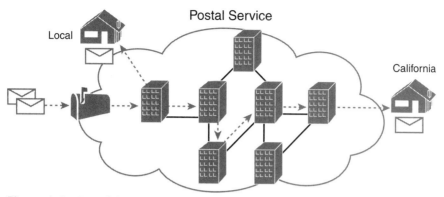

Figure 1-8 *Postal Service Forwarding (Routing) Letters*

Still thinking about the postal service, consider the difference between the person sending the letter and the work that the postal service does. The person sending the letters expects that the postal service will deliver the letter most of the time. However, the person sending the letter does not need to know the details of exactly what path the letters take. In contrast, the postal service does not create the letter, but it accepts the letter from the customer. Then, the postal service must know the details about addresses and postal codes that group addresses into larger groups, and it must have the ability to deliver the letters.

The TCP/IP application and transport layers act like the person sending letters through the postal service. These upper layers work the same way regardless of whether the endpoint host computers are on the same LAN or are separated by the entire Internet. To send a message, these upper layers ask the layer below them, the network layer, to deliver the message.

The lower layers of the TCP/IP model act more like the postal service to deliver those messages to the correct destinations. To do so, these lower layers must understand the underlying physical network because they must choose how to best deliver the data from one host to another.

So, what does this all matter to networking? Well, the network layer of the TCP/IP networking model, primarily defined by the Internet Protocol (IP), works much like the postal service. IP defines that each host computer should have a different IP address, just as the postal service defines addressing that allows unique addresses for each house, apartment, and business. Similarly, IP defines the process of routing so that devices called routers can work like the post office, forwarding **packets** of data so that they are delivered to the correct destinations. Just as the postal service created the necessary infrastructure to deliver letters—post offices, sorting machines, trucks, planes, and personnel—the network layer defines the details of how a network infrastructure should be created so that the network can deliver data to all computers in the network.

Internet Protocol Addressing Basics

IP defines addresses for several important reasons. First, each device that uses TCP/IP—each TCP/IP *host*—needs a unique address so that it can be identified in the network. IP also defines how to group addresses together, just like the postal system groups addresses based on postal codes (like ZIP codes in the United States).

To understand the basics, examine Figure 1-9, which shows the familiar web server Larry and web browser Bob; but now, instead of ignoring the network between these two computers, part of the network infrastructure is included.

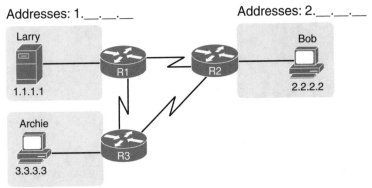

Addresses: 3.__.__.__

Figure 1-9 *Simple TCP/IP Network: Three Routers with IP Addresses Grouped*

First, note that Figure 1-9 shows some sample IP addresses. Each IP address has four numbers, separated by periods. In this case, Larry uses IP address 1.1.1.1, and Bob uses 2.2.2.2. This style of number is called a dotted-decimal notation (DDN).

Figure 1-9 also shows three groups of addresses. In this example, all IP addresses that begin with 1 must be on the upper left, as shown in shorthand in the figure as 1.__.__.__. All addresses that begin with 2 must be on the right, as shown in shorthand as 2.__.__.__. Finally, all IP addresses that begin with 3 must be at the bottom of the figure.

In addition, Figure 1-9 introduces icons that represent IP routers. Routers are networking devices that connect the parts of the TCP/IP network together for the purpose of routing (forwarding) IP packets to the correct destination. Routers do the equivalent of the work done by each post office site: They receive IP packets on various physical interfaces, make decisions based on the IP address included with the packet, and then physically forward the packet out some other network interface.

IP Routing Basics

The TCP/IP network layer, using the IP protocol, provides a service of forwarding IP packets from one device to another. Any device with an IP address can connect to the TCP/IP network and send packets. This section shows a basic IP routing example for perspective.

> **NOTE** The term *IP host* refers to any device, regardless of size or power, that has an IP address and connects to any TCP/IP network.

Figure 1-10 repeats the familiar case in which web server Larry wants to send part of a web page to Bob, but now with details related to IP. On the lower left, note that server Larry has the familiar application data, HTTP header, and TCP header ready to send. In addition, the message now contains an IP header. The IP header includes a source IP address of Larry's IP address (1.1.1.1) and a destination IP address of Bob's IP address (2.2.2.2).

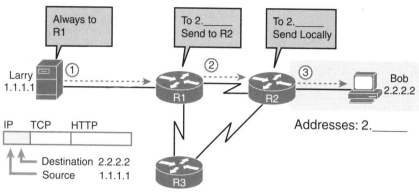

Figure 1-10   *Basic Routing Example*

Step 1, on the left of Figure 1-10, begins with Larry being ready to send an IP packet. Larry's IP process chooses to send the packet to some router—a nearby router on the same LAN—with the expectation that the router will know how to forward the packet. (This logic is much like you or me sending all our letters by putting them in a nearby mailbox.) Larry doesn't need to know anything more about the topology or the other routers.

At Step 2, Router R1 receives the IP packet, and R1's IP process makes a decision. R1 looks at the destination address (2.2.2.2), compares that address to its known IP routes, and chooses to forward the packet to Router R2. This process of forwarding the IP packet is called *IP routing* (or simply *routing*).

At Step 3, Router R2 repeats the same kind of logic used by Router R1. R2's IP process will compare the packet's destination IP address (2.2.2.2) to R2's known IP routes and make a choice to forward the packet to the right, on to Bob.

You will learn IP to more depth than any other protocol while preparing for CCNA. More than half the chapters in this book discuss some feature that relates to addressing, IP routing, and how routers perform routing.

TCP/IP Data-Link and Physical Layers

The TCP/IP model's data-link and physical layers define the protocols and hardware required to deliver data across some physical network. The two work together quite closely; in fact, some standards define both the data-link and physical layer functions. The physical layer defines the cabling and energy (for example, electrical signals) that flow over the cables. Some rules and conventions exist when sending data over the cable, however; those rules exist in the data-link layer of the TCP/IP model.

Focusing on the data-link layer for a moment, just like every layer in any networking model, the TCP/IP data-link layer provides services to the layer above it in the model (the network layer). When a host's or router's IP process chooses to send an IP packet to another router or host, that host or router then uses link-layer details to send that packet to the next host/router.

Because each layer provides a service to the layer above it, take a moment to think about the IP logic related to Figure 1-10. In that example, host Larry's IP logic chooses to send the IP packet to a nearby router (R1). However, while Figure 1-10 shows a simple line between Larry and router R1, that drawing means that some Ethernet LAN sits between the two. Figure 1-11 shows four steps of what occurs at the link layer to allow Larry to send the IP packet to R1.

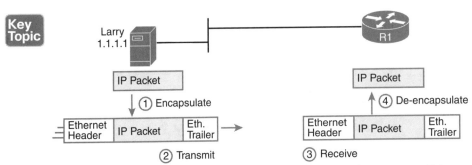

Figure 1-11   *Larry Using Ethernet to Forward an IP Packet to Router R1*

> **NOTE**   Figure 1-11 depicts the Ethernet as a series of lines. Networking diagrams often use this convention when drawing Ethernet LANs, in cases where the actual LAN cabling and LAN devices are not important to some discussion, as is the case here. The LAN would have cables and devices, like LAN switches, which are not shown in this figure.

Figure 1-11 shows four steps. The first two occur on Larry, and the last two occur on Router R1, as follows:

Step 1.   Larry encapsulates the IP packet between an Ethernet header and Ethernet trailer, creating an Ethernet **frame.**

Step 2.   Larry physically transmits the bits of this Ethernet frame, using electricity flowing over the Ethernet cabling.

Step 3.   Router R1 physically receives the electrical signal over a cable and re-creates the same bits by interpreting the meaning of the electrical signals.

Step 4.   Router R1 **de-encapsulates** the IP packet from the Ethernet frame by removing and discarding the Ethernet header and trailer.

By the end of this process, Larry and R1 have worked together to deliver the packet from Larry to Router R1.

> **NOTE**   Protocols define both headers and trailers for the same general reason, but headers exist at the beginning of the message and trailers exist at the end.

The data-link and physical layers include a large number of protocols and standards. For example, the link layer includes all the variations of Ethernet protocols and wireless LAN protocols discussed throughout this book.

In short, the TCP/IP physical and data-link layers include two distinct functions, respectively: functions related to the physical transmission of the data, plus the protocols and rules that control the use of the physical media.

Data Encapsulation Terminology

As you can see from the explanations of how HTTP, TCP, IP, and Ethernet do their jobs, when sending data, each layer adds its own header (and for data-link protocols, also a trailer) to the data supplied by the higher layer. The term **encapsulation** refers to the process of putting headers (and sometimes trailers) around some data.

Many of the examples in this chapter show the encapsulation process. For example, web server Larry encapsulated the contents of the home page inside an HTTP header in Figure 1-6. The TCP layer encapsulated the HTTP headers and data inside a TCP header in Figure 1-7. IP encapsulated the TCP headers and the data inside an IP header in Figure 1-10. Finally, the Ethernet link layer encapsulated the IP packets inside both a header and a trailer in Figure 1-11.

The process by which a TCP/IP host sends data can be viewed as a five-step process. The first four steps relate to the encapsulation performed by the four TCP/IP layers, and the last step is the actual physical transmission of the data by the host. In fact, if you use the five-layer TCP/IP model, one step corresponds to the role of each layer. The steps are summarized in the following list:

Step 1.   Create and encapsulate the application data with any required application layer headers. For example, the HTTP OK message can be returned in an HTTP header, followed by part of the contents of a web page.

Step 2.   Encapsulate the data supplied by the application layer inside a transport layer header. For end-user applications, a TCP or UDP header is typically used.

Step 3.   Encapsulate the data supplied by the transport layer inside a network layer (IP) header. IP defines the IP addresses that uniquely identify each computer.

Step 4.   Encapsulate the data supplied by the network layer inside a data-link layer header and trailer. This layer uses both a header and a trailer.

Step 5.   Transmit the bits. The physical layer encodes a signal onto the medium to transmit the frame.

The numbers in Figure 1-12 correspond to the five steps in this list, graphically showing the same concepts. Note that because the application layer often does not need to add a header, the figure does not show a specific application layer header, but the application layer will also at times add a header as well.

Names of TCP/IP Messages

One reason this chapter takes the time to show the encapsulation steps in detail has to do with terminology. When talking and writing about networking, people use *segment*, *packet*, and *frame* to refer to the messages shown in Figure 1-13 and the related list. Each term has a specific meaning, referring to the headers (and possibly trailers) defined by a particular layer and the data encapsulated following that header. Each term, however, refers to a different layer: segment for the transport layer, packet for the network layer, and frame for the link layer. Figure 1-13 shows each layer along with the associated term.

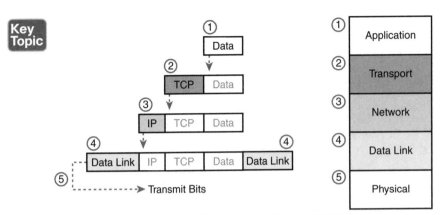

Figure 1-12   *Five Steps of Data Encapsulation: TCP/IP*

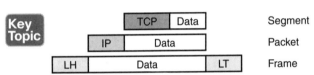

Figure 1-13   *Perspectives on Encapsulation and "Data"**

* The letters *LH* and *LT* stand for link header and link trailer, respectively, and refer to the data-link layer header and trailer.

Figure 1-13 also shows the encapsulated data as simply "data." When you are focusing on the work done by a particular layer, the encapsulated data typically is unimportant. For example, an IP packet can indeed have a TCP header after the IP header, an HTTP header after the TCP header, and data for a web page after the HTTP header. However, when discussing IP, you probably just care about the IP header, so everything after the IP header is just called data. So, when you are drawing IP packets, everything after the IP header is typically shown simply as data.

> **NOTE**   You will also see the generic term *protocol data unit*, or *PDU*, used to refer to any message defined by a protocol. A TCP segment, IP packet, and Ethernet frame are all PDUs, for instance.

OSI Networking Model and Terminology

At one point in the history of the OSI model, many people thought that OSI would win the battle of the networking models discussed earlier. If that had occurred, instead of running TCP/IP on every computer in the world, those computers would be running with OSI.

However, OSI did not win. In fact, OSI no longer exists as a networking model that could be used instead of TCP/IP, although some of the original protocols referenced by the OSI model still exist.

So, why is OSI even in this book? Terminology. During those years in which many people thought the OSI model would become commonplace in the world of networking (mostly in the late 1980s and early 1990s), many vendors and protocol documents started using terminology from the OSI model. That terminology remains today. So, while you will never need to work with a computer that uses OSI, to understand modern networking terminology, you need to understand something about OSI.

Comparing OSI and TCP/IP Layer Names and Numbers

The OSI model has many similarities to the TCP/IP model from a basic conceptual perspective. It has layers, and each layer defines a set of typical networking functions. As with TCP/IP, the OSI layers each refer to multiple protocols and standards that implement the functions specified by each layer. Just as for TCP/IP, the OSI committees did not create new protocols or standards in some cases, instead referencing other protocols that were already defined. For example, the IEEE defines Ethernet standards, so the OSI committees did not waste time specifying a new type of Ethernet; it simply referred to the IEEE Ethernet standards.

Today, the OSI model can be used as a standard of comparison to other networking models. Figure 1-14 compares the seven-layer OSI model with the commonly used five-layer TCP/IP model and the old original four-layer TCP/IP model.

	OSI		TCP/IP (Common)		TCP/IP (RFC 1122)
7	Application	5 - 7	Application	5 - 7	Application
6	Presentation				
5	Session				
4	Transport	4	Transport	4	Transport
3	Network	3	Network	3	Internet
2	Data Link	2	Data Link	1-2	Link
1	Physical	1	Physical		

Figure 1-14 *OSI Model Compared to the Two TCP/IP Models*

NOTE The CCNA exam topics no longer mention the OSI or TCP/IP models; however, you should know both and the related terminology for everyday network engineering discussions. While today you will see the five-layer model used throughout the industry, and in this book, the figure includes the original RFC 1122 four-layer model for perspective.

Note that the TCP/IP model in use today, in the middle of the figure, uses the exact same layer names as OSI at the lower layers. The functions generally match as well, so for the purpose of discussing networking, and reading networking documentation, think of the bottom four layers as equivalent, in name, in number, and in meaning.

Even though the world uses TCP/IP today rather than OSI, we tend to use the numbering from the OSI layer. For instance, when referring to an application layer protocol in a TCP/IP network, the world still refers to the protocol as a "Layer 7 protocol." Also, while TCP/IP includes more functions at its application layer, OSI breaks those into session, presentation, and application layers. Most of the time, no one cares much about the distinction, so you will see references like "Layer 5–7 protocol," again using OSI numbering.

For the purposes of this book, know the mapping between the five-layer TCP/IP model and the seven-layer OSI model shown in Figure 1-14, and know that layer number references to Layer 7 really do match the application layer of TCP/IP as well.

Chapter Review

The "Your Study Plan" element, just before Chapter 1, discusses how you should study and practice the content and skills for each chapter before moving on to the next chapter. That element introduces the tools used here at the end of each chapter. If you haven't already done so, take a few minutes to read that section. Then come back here and do the useful work of reviewing the chapter to help lock into memory what you just read.

Review this chapter's material using either the tools in the book or the interactive tools for the same material found on the book's companion website. Table 1-4 outlines the key review elements and where you can find them. To better track your study progress, record when you completed these activities in the second column.

Table 1-4   Chapter Review Tracking

Review Element	Review Date(s)	Resource Used
Review key topics		Book, website
Review key terms		Book, website
Answer DIKTA questions		Book, PTP Online

Review All the Key Topics

Table 1-5   Key Topics for Chapter 1

Key Topic Elements	Description	Page Number
Figure 1-10	Shows the general concept of IP routing	29
Figure 1-11	Depicts the data-link services provided to IP for the purpose of delivering IP packets from host to host	30
Figure 1-12	Identifies the five steps to encapsulate data on the sending host	32
Figure 1-13	Shows the meaning of the terms *segment*, *packet*, and *frame*	32
Figure 1-14	Compares the OSI and TCP/IP networking models	33

Key Terms You Should Know

adjacent-layer interaction, de-encapsulation, encapsulation, frame, networking model, packet, same-layer interaction, segment

CHAPTER 2

Fundamentals of Ethernet LANs

This chapter covers the following exam topics:

1.0 Network Fundamentals

> **1.1 Explain the role and function of network components**
>
>> **1.1.b Layer 2 and Layer 3 switches**
>
> **1.2 Describe characteristics of network topology architectures**
>
>> **1.2.e Small office/home office (SOHO)**
>
> **1.3 Compare physical interface and cabling types**
>
>> **1.3.a Single-mode fiber, multimode fiber, copper**
>
>> **1.3.b Connections (Ethernet shared media and point-to-point)**

Most enterprise computer networks can be separated into two general types of technology: local-area networks (LANs) and wide-area networks (WANs). LANs typically connect nearby devices: devices in the same room, in the same building, or in a campus of buildings. In contrast, WANs connect devices that are typically relatively far apart. Together, LANs and WANs create a complete enterprise computer network, working together to do the job of a computer network: delivering data from one device to another.

Many types of LANs have existed over the years, but today's networks use two general types of LANs: Ethernet LANs and wireless LANs. Ethernet LANs happen to use cables for the links between nodes, and because many types of cables use copper wires, Ethernet LANs are often called **wired LANs**. Ethernet LANs also make use of fiber-optic cabling, which includes a fiberglass core that devices use to send data using light. In comparison to Ethernet, **wireless LANs** do not use wires or cables, instead using radio waves for the links between nodes; Part I of the *CCNA 200-301 Official Cert Guide, Volume 2*, Second Edition, discusses wireless LANs at length.

This chapter introduces Ethernet LANs, with more detailed coverage in Parts II and III of this book.

"Do I Know This Already?" Quiz

Take the quiz (either here or use the PTP software) if you want to use the score to help you decide how much time to spend on this chapter. The letter answers are listed at the bottom of the page following the quiz. Appendix C, found both at the end of the book as well as on the companion website, includes both the answers and explanations. You can also find both answers and explanations in the PTP testing software.

Table 2-1 "Do I Know This Already?" Foundation Topics Section-to-Question Mapping

Foundation Topics Section	Questions
An Overview of LANs	1–2
Building Physical Ethernet LANs with UTP	3–4
Building Physical Ethernet LANs with Fiber	5
Sending Data in Ethernet Networks	6–9

1. Some end-user devices connect to a LAN using a cable while others use wireless. Which answer best characterizes which devices use Ethernet to connect to the LAN?

   a. Only the end-user devices that use cables are using Ethernet.

   b. Only the end-user devices that use wireless are using Ethernet.

   c. Both the end-user devices using cables and those using wireless are using Ethernet.

   d. Neither the end-user devices using cables nor those using wireless are using Ethernet.

2. Which of the following Ethernet standards defines Gigabit Ethernet over UTP cabling?

   a. 10GBASE-T

   b. 100BASE-T

   c. 1000BASE-T

   d. None of the other answers are correct.

3. Which of the following is true about Ethernet crossover cables for Fast Ethernet?

   a. Pins 1 and 2 are reversed on the other end of the cable.

   b. Pins 1 and 2 on one end of the cable connect to pins 3 and 6 on the other end of the cable.

   c. Pins 1 and 2 on one end of the cable connect to pins 3 and 4 on the other end of the cable.

   d. The cable can be up to 1000 meters long to cross over between buildings.

   e. None of the other answers are correct.

4. Each answer lists two types of devices used in a 100BASE-T network. If these devices were connected with UTP Ethernet cables, which pairs of devices would require a straight-through cable? (Choose three answers.)

   a. PC and router

   b. PC and switch

   c. Hub and switch

   d. Router and hub

   e. Wireless access point (Ethernet port) and switch

5. Which of the following are advantages of using multimode fiber for an Ethernet link instead of UTP or single-mode fiber? (Choose two answers.)

   a. To achieve the longest distance possible for that single link.

   b. To extend the link beyond 100 meters while keeping initial costs as low as possible.

   c. To make use of an existing stock of laser-based SFP/SFP+ modules.

   d. To make use of an existing stock of LED-based SFP/SFP+ modules.

6. Which of the following is true about the CSMA/CD algorithm?

   a. The algorithm never allows collisions to occur.

   b. Collisions can happen, but the algorithm defines how the computers should notice a collision and how to recover.

   c. The algorithm works with only two devices on the same Ethernet.

   d. None of the other answers are correct.

7. Which of the following is true about the Ethernet FCS field?

   a. Ethernet uses FCS for error recovery.

   b. It is 2 bytes long.

   c. It resides in the Ethernet trailer, not the Ethernet header.

   d. It is used for encryption.

8. Which of the following are true about the format of Ethernet addresses? (Choose three answers.)

   a. Each manufacturer puts a unique OUI code into the first 2 bytes of the address.

   b. Each manufacturer puts a unique OUI code into the first 3 bytes of the address.

   c. Each manufacturer puts a unique OUI code into the first half of the address.

   d. The part of the address that holds the manufacturer's code is called the MAC.

   e. The part of the address that holds the manufacturer's code is called the OUI.

   f. The part of the address that holds the manufacturer's code has no specific name.

9. Which of the following terms describe Ethernet addresses that can be used to send one frame that is delivered to multiple devices on the LAN? (Choose two answers.)

   a. Burned-in address

   b. Unicast address

   c. Broadcast address

   d. Multicast address

Foundation Topics

An Overview of LANs

The term **Ethernet** refers to a family of LAN standards that together define the physical and data-link layers of the world's most popular wired LAN technology. The standards, defined by the Institute of Electrical and Electronics Engineers (**IEEE**), define the cabling, the connectors on the ends of the cables, the protocol rules, and everything else required to create an Ethernet LAN.

Typical SOHO LANs

To begin, first think about a small office/home office (SOHO) LAN today, specifically a LAN that uses only Ethernet LAN technology. First, the LAN needs a device called an Ethernet *LAN switch*, which provides many physical ports into which cables can be connected. An Ethernet uses *Ethernet cables*, which is a general reference to any cable that conforms to any of several Ethernet standards. The LAN uses Ethernet cables to connect different Ethernet devices or nodes to one of the switch's Ethernet ports.

Figure 2-1 shows a drawing of a SOHO Ethernet LAN. The figure shows a single LAN switch, five cables, and five other Ethernet nodes: three PCs, a printer, and one network device called a *router*. (The router connects the LAN to the WAN, in this case to the Internet.)

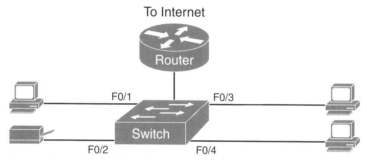

Figure 2-1   *Typical Small Ethernet-Only SOHO LAN*

Although Figure 2-1 shows the switch and router as separate devices, many SOHO Ethernet LANs today combine the router and switch into a single device. Vendors sell consumer-grade integrated networking devices that work as a router and Ethernet switch, as well as doing other functions. These devices typically have "router" on the packaging, but many models also have four-port or eight-port Ethernet LAN switch ports built into the device.

Typical SOHO LANs today also support wireless LAN connections. You can build a single SOHO LAN that includes both Ethernet LAN technology as well as wireless LAN technology, which is also defined by the IEEE. Wireless LANs, defined by the IEEE using standards that begin with 802.11, use radio waves to send the bits from one node to the next.

Most wireless LANs rely on yet another networking device: a wireless LAN access point (AP). The AP acts somewhat like an Ethernet switch, in that all the wireless LAN nodes communicate with the wireless AP. If the network uses an AP that is a separate physical device, the AP then needs a single Ethernet link to connect the AP to the Ethernet LAN, as shown in Figure 2-2.

Note that Figure 2-2 shows the router, Ethernet switch, and wireless LAN access point as three separate devices so that you can better understand the different roles. However, most SOHO networks today would use a single device, often labeled as a "wireless router," that does all these functions.

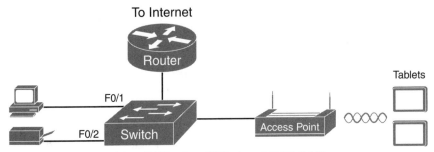

Figure 2-2 *Typical Small Wired and Wireless SOHO LAN*

Typical Enterprise LANs

Enterprise networks have similar needs compared to a SOHO network, but on a much larger scale. For example, enterprise Ethernet LANs begin with LAN switches installed in a wiring closet behind a locked door on each floor of a building. The electricians install the Ethernet cabling from that wiring closet to cubicles and conference rooms where devices might need to connect to the LAN. At the same time, most enterprises also support wireless LANs in the same space, to allow people to roam around and still work and to support a growing number of devices that do not have an Ethernet LAN interface.

Figure 2-3 shows a conceptual view of a typical enterprise LAN in a three-story building. Each floor has an Ethernet LAN switch and a wireless LAN AP. To allow communication between floors, each per-floor switch connects to one centralized distribution switch. For example, PC3 can send data to PC2, but it would first flow through switch SW3 to the first floor to the distribution switch (SWD) and then back up through switch SW2 on the second floor.

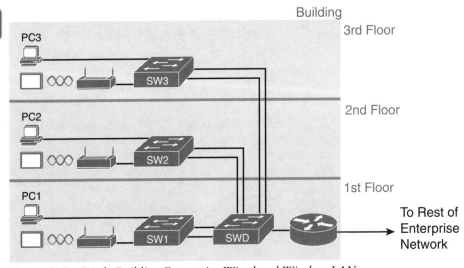

Figure 2-3 *Single-Building Enterprise Wired and Wireless LAN*

Answers to the "Do I Know This Already?" quiz:

1 A **2** C **3** B **4** B, D, and E **5** B and D **6** B **7** C **8** B, C, and E **9** C and D

The figure also shows the typical way to connect a LAN to a WAN using a router. LAN switches and wireless access points work to create the LAN itself. Routers connect to both the LAN and the WAN. To connect to the LAN, the router simply uses an Ethernet LAN interface and an Ethernet cable, as shown on the lower right of Figure 2-3.

The rest of this chapter focuses on Ethernet in particular.

The Variety of Ethernet Physical Layer Standards

The term *Ethernet* refers to an entire family of standards. Some standards define the specifics of how to send data over a particular type of cabling, and at a particular speed. Other standards define protocols, or rules, that the Ethernet nodes must follow to be a part of an Ethernet LAN. All these Ethernet standards come from the IEEE and include the number 802.3 as the beginning part of the standard name.

Ethernet supports a large variety of options for physical Ethernet links given its long history over the last 40 or so years. Today, Ethernet includes many standards for different kinds of optical and copper cabling, and for speeds from 10 megabits per second (Mbps) up to 400 gigabits per second (Gbps). The standards also differ as far as the types and length of the cables.

The most fundamental cabling choice has to do with the materials used inside the cable for the physical transmission of bits: either copper wires or glass fibers. Devices using unshielded twisted-pair (UTP) cabling transmit data over electrical circuits via the copper wires inside the cable. Fiber-optic cabling, the more expensive alternative, allows Ethernet nodes to send light over glass fibers in the center of the cable. Although more expensive, optical cables typically allow longer cabling distances between nodes.

To be ready to choose the products to purchase for a new Ethernet LAN, a network engineer must know the names and features of the different Ethernet standards supported in Ethernet products. The IEEE defines Ethernet physical layer standards using a couple of naming conventions. The formal name begins with 802.3 followed by some suffix letters. The IEEE also uses more meaningful shortcut names that identify the speed, as well as a clue about whether the cabling is UTP (with a suffix that includes *T*) or fiber (with a suffix that includes *X*). Table 2-2 lists a few Ethernet physical layer standards. First, the table lists enough names so that you get a sense of the IEEE naming conventions.

Table 2-2   Examples of Types of Ethernet

Speed	Common Name	Informal IEEE Standard Name	Formal IEEE Standard Name	Cable Type, Maximum Length
10 Mbps	Ethernet	10BASE-T	802.3	Copper, 100 m
100 Mbps	Fast Ethernet	100BASE-T	802.3u	Copper, 100 m
1000 Mbps	Gigabit Ethernet	1000BASE-LX	802.3z	Fiber, 5000 m
1000 Mbps	Gigabit Ethernet	1000BASE-T	802.3ab	Copper, 100 m
10 Gbps	10 Gig Ethernet	10GBASE-T	802.3an	Copper, 100 m

NOTE   Fiber-optic cabling contains long thin strands of fiberglass. The attached Ethernet nodes send light over the glass fiber in the cable, encoding the bits as changes in the light.

NOTE You might expect that a standard that began at the IEEE over 40 years ago would be stable and unchanging, but the opposite is true. The IEEE, along with active industry partners, continue to develop new Ethernet standards with longer distances, different cabling options, and faster speeds. Check out the Ethernet Alliance web page (www.EthernetAlliance.org) and look for the roadmap for some great graphics and tables about the latest happenings with Ethernet.

Consistent Behavior over All Links Using the Ethernet Data-Link Layer

Although Ethernet includes many physical layer standards, Ethernet acts like a single LAN technology because it uses the same data-link layer standard over all types of Ethernet physical links. That standard defines a common Ethernet header and trailer. (As a reminder, the header and trailer are bytes of overhead data that Ethernet uses to do its job of sending data over a LAN.) No matter whether the data flows over a UTP cable or any kind of fiber cable, and no matter the speed, the data-link header and trailer use the same format.

While the physical layer standards focus on sending bits over a cable, the Ethernet data-link protocols focus on sending an **Ethernet frame** from source to destination Ethernet node. From a data-link perspective, nodes build and forward frames. As first defined in Chapter 1, "Introduction to TCP/IP Networking," the term *frame* specifically refers to the header and trailer of a data-link protocol, plus the data encapsulated inside that header and trailer. The various Ethernet nodes simply forward the frame, over all the required links, to deliver the frame to the correct destination.

Figure 2-4 shows an example of the process. In this case, PC1 sends an Ethernet frame to PC3. The frame travels over a UTP link to Ethernet switch SW1, then over fiber links to Ethernet switches SW2 and SW3, and finally over another UTP link to PC3. Note that the bits actually travel at four different speeds in this example: 10 Mbps, 1 Gbps, 10 Gbps, and 100 Mbps, respectively.

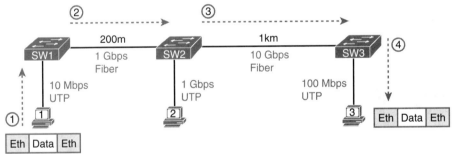

Figure 2-4 *Ethernet LAN Forwards a Data-Link Frame over Many Types of Links*

So, what is an Ethernet LAN? It is a combination of user devices, LAN switches, and different kinds of cabling. Each link can use different types of cables, at different speeds. However, they all work together to deliver Ethernet frames from the one device on the LAN to some other device.

The rest of this chapter takes these concepts a little deeper. The next section examines how to build a physical Ethernet network using UTP cabling, followed by a similar look at using fiber cabling to build Ethernet LANs. The chapter ends with some discussion of the rules for forwarding frames through an Ethernet LAN.

Building Physical Ethernet LANs with UTP

The next section of this chapter focuses on the individual physical links between any two Ethernet nodes, specifically those that use unshielded twisted-pair (UTP) cabling. Before the Ethernet network as a whole can send Ethernet frames between user devices, each node must be ready and able to send data over an individual physical link.

This section focuses on the three most commonly used Ethernet standards: **10BASE-T** (Ethernet), **100BASE-T** (**Fast Ethernet**, or FE), and **1000BASE-T** (**Gigabit Ethernet**, or GE). Specifically, this section looks at the details of sending data in both directions over a UTP cable. It then examines the specific wiring of the UTP cables used for 10-Mbps, 100-Mbps, and 1000-Mbps Ethernet.

Transmitting Data Using Twisted Pairs

While it is true that Ethernet sends data over UTP cables, the physical means to send the data uses electricity that flows over the wires inside the UTP cable. To better understand how Ethernet sends data using electricity, break the idea down into two parts: how to create an electrical circuit and then how to make that electrical signal communicate 1s and 0s.

First, to create one electrical circuit, Ethernet defines how to use the two wires inside a single twisted pair of wires, as shown in Figure 2-5. The figure does not show a UTP cable between two nodes, but instead shows two individual wires that are inside the UTP cable. An electrical circuit requires a complete loop, so the two nodes, using circuitry on their Ethernet ports, connect the wires in one pair to complete a loop, allowing electricity to flow.

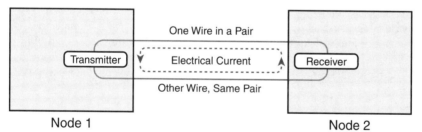

Figure 2-5   *Creating One Electrical Circuit over One Pair to Send in One Direction*

To send data, the two devices follow some rules called an *encoding scheme*. The idea works a lot like when two people talk using the same language: The speaker says some words in a particular language, and the listener, because she speaks the same language, can understand the spoken words. With an encoding scheme, the transmitting node changes the electrical signal over time, while the other node, the receiver, using the same rules, interprets those changes as either 0s or 1s. (For example, 10BASE-T uses an encoding scheme that encodes a binary 0 as a transition from higher voltage to lower voltage during the middle of a 1/10,000,000th-of-a-second interval.)

Note that in an actual UTP cable, the wires will be twisted together, instead of being parallel, as shown in Figure 2-5. The twisting helps solve some important physical transmission issues. When electrical current passes over any wire, it creates **electromagnetic interference (EMI)** that interferes with the electrical signals in nearby wires, including the wires in the same cable. (EMI between wire pairs in the same cable is called *crosstalk*.) Twisting the wire pairs together helps cancel out most of the EMI, so most networking physical links that use copper wires use twisted pairs.

Breaking Down a UTP Ethernet Link

The term **Ethernet link** refers to any physical cable between two Ethernet nodes. To learn about how a UTP Ethernet link works, it helps to break down the physical link into those basic pieces, as shown in Figure 2-6: the cable itself, the connectors on the ends of the cable, and the matching ports on the devices into which the connectors will be inserted.

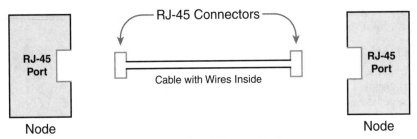

Figure 2-6 *Basic Components of an Ethernet Link*

First, think about the UTP cable itself. The cable holds some copper wires, grouped as twisted pairs. The 10BASE-T and 100BASE-T standards require two pairs of wires, while the 1000BASE-T standard requires four pairs. Each wire has a color-coded plastic coating, with the wires in a pair having a color scheme. For example, for the blue wire pair, one wire's coating is all blue, while the other wire's coating is blue-and-white striped.

Many Ethernet UTP cables use an RJ-45 connector on both ends. The **RJ-45** connector has eight physical locations into which the eight wires in the cable can be inserted, called *pin positions*, or simply *pins*. These pins create a place where the ends of the copper wires can touch the electronics inside the nodes at the end of the physical link so that electricity can flow.

> **NOTE**   If available, find a nearby Ethernet UTP cable and examine the connectors closely. Look for the pin positions and the colors of the wires in the connector.

To complete the physical link, the nodes each need an RJ-45 **Ethernet port** that matches the RJ-45 connectors on the cable so that the connectors on the ends of the cable can connect to each node. PCs often include this RJ-45 Ethernet port as part of a **network interface card (NIC)**, which can be an expansion card on the PC or can be built into the system itself. Switches typically have many RJ-45 ports because switches give user devices a place to connect to the Ethernet LAN. Figure 2-7 shows photos of the cables, connectors, and ports.

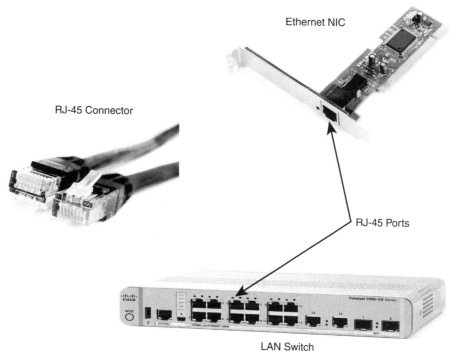

Figure 2-7 *RJ-45 Connectors and Ports*

The figure shows a connector on the left and ports on the right. The left shows the eight pin positions in the end of the RJ-45 connector. The upper right shows an Ethernet NIC that is not yet installed in a computer. The lower-right part of the figure shows the side of a Cisco switch, with multiple RJ-45 ports, allowing multiple devices to easily connect to the Ethernet network.

Finally, while RJ-45 connectors with UTP cabling can be common, Cisco LAN switches often support other types of connectors as well. When you buy one of the many models of Cisco switches, you need to think about the mix and numbers of each type of physical ports you want on the switch.

To give its customers flexibility as to the type of Ethernet links, even after the customer has bought the switch, Cisco switches include some physical ports whose port hardware (the **transceiver**) can be changed later, after you purchase the switch.

For example, Figure 2-8 shows a photo of a Cisco switch with one of the swappable transceivers. In this case, the figure shows an enhanced small form-factor pluggable plus (SFP+) transceiver, which runs at 10 Gbps, just outside two SFP+ slots on a Cisco 3560CX switch. The SFP+ itself is the silver-colored part below the switch, with a black cable connected to it.

Figure 2-8   *10-Gbps SFP+ with Cable Sitting Just Outside a Catalyst 3560CX Switch*

Gigabit Ethernet Interface Converter (GBIC): The original form factor for a removable transceiver for Gigabit interfaces; larger than SFPs.

Small Form-Factor Pluggable (SFP): The replacement for GBICs, used on Gigabit interfaces, with a smaller size, taking less space on the side of the networking card or switch.

Small Form-Factor Pluggable Plus (SFP+): Same size as the SFP, but used on 10-Gbps interfaces. (The Plus refers to the increase in speed compared to SFPs.)

UTP Cabling Pinouts for 10BASE-T and 100BASE-T

So far in this section, you have learned about the equivalent of how to drive a truck on a 1000-acre ranch: You could drive the truck all over the ranch, any place you wanted to go, and the police would not mind. However, as soon as you get on the public roads, the police want you to behave and follow the rules. Similarly, so far this chapter has discussed the general principles of how to send data, but it has not yet detailed some important rules for Ethernet cabling: the rules of the road so that all the devices send data using the right wires inside the cable.

This next topic discusses some of those rules, specifically for the 10-Mbps 10BASE-T and the 100-Mbps 100BASE-T. Both use UTP cabling in similar ways (including the use of only two wire pairs). A short comparison of the wiring for 1000BASE-T (Gigabit Ethernet), which uses four pairs, follows.

Straight-Through Cable Pinout

10BASE-T and 100BASE-T use two pairs of wires in a UTP cable, one for each direction, as shown in Figure 2-9. The figure shows four wires, all of which sit inside a single UTP cable that connects a PC and a LAN switch. In this example, the PC on the left transmits using the top pair, and the switch on the right transmits using the bottom pair.

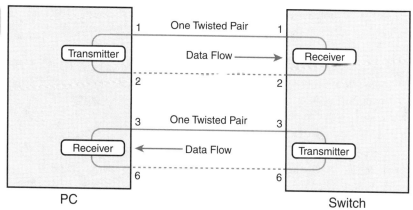

Figure 2-9 *Using One Pair for Each Transmission Direction with 10- and 100-Mbps Ethernet*

For correct transmission over the link, the wires in the UTP cable must be connected to the correct pin positions in the RJ-45 connectors. For example, in Figure 2-9, the transmitter on the PC on the left must know the pin positions of the two wires it should use to transmit. Those two wires must be connected to the correct pins in the RJ-45 connector on the switch so that the switch's receiver logic can use the correct wires.

To understand the wiring of the cable—which wires need to be in which pin positions on both ends of the cable—you need to first understand how the NICs and switches work. As a rule, Ethernet NIC transmitters use the pair connected to pins 1 and 2; the NIC receivers use a pair of wires at pin positions 3 and 6. LAN switches, knowing those facts about what Ethernet NICs do, do the opposite: Their receivers use the wire pair at pins 1 and 2, and their transmitters use the wire pair at pins 3 and 6. The switch effectively reverses the transmit and receive logic of the endpoint device.

To make the preceding logic work, the UTP cable must use a **straight-through cable** *pinout* convention. The term *pinout* refers to the wiring of which color wire is placed in each of the eight numbered pin positions in the RJ-45 connector. An Ethernet straight-through cable connects the wire at pin 1 on one end of the cable to pin 1 at the other end of the cable; the wire at pin 2 needs to connect to pin 2 on the other end of the cable; pin 3 on one end connects to pin 3 on the other, and so on. Figure 2-10 shows the concept of straight-through pinout with two pairs—one pair at pins 1,2 and another at pins 3,6, as used by 10BASE-T and 100BASE-T.

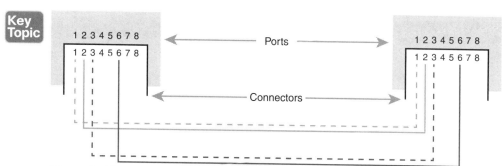

Figure 2-10 *10BASE-T and 100BASE-T Straight-Through Cable Pinout*

They effectively reverse or cross over the transmit and receive functions, so that for links between a switch and an endpoint device, the cable can use the straight-through pinout shown in Figure 2-9.

A straight-through cable works correctly when the nodes use opposite pairs for transmitting data, as seen in Figure 2-9. However, when connecting two devices that transmit on the same pins, you then need another type of cabling pinout called a **crossover cable** pinout. The crossover cable pinout crosses the pair at the transmit pins on each device to the receive pins on the opposite device.

While that previous sentence is true, this concept is much clearer with a figure such as Figure 2-11. The figure shows what happens on a link between two switches. The two switches both transmit on the pair at pins 3 and 6, and they both receive on the pair at pins 1 and 2. So, the cable must connect a pair at pins 3 and 6 on each side to pins 1 and 2 on the other side, connecting to the other node's receiver logic.

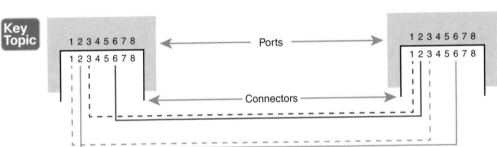

Figure 2-11   *Crossover Ethernet Cable Pinouts*

Choosing the Right Cable Pinouts

For the exam, you should be well prepared to choose which type of cable (straight-through or crossover) is needed in each part of the network. The key is to know whether a device acts like a PC NIC, transmitting at pins 1 and 2, or like a switch, transmitting at pins 3 and 6. Then, just apply the following logic:

Crossover cable: If the endpoints transmit on the same pin pair

Straight-through cable: If the endpoints transmit on different pin pairs

Table 2-3 lists the devices and the pin pairs they use, assuming that they use 10BASE-T and 100BASE-T.

Table 2-3   10BASE-T and 100BASE-T Pin Pairs Used

Transmits on Pins 1,2	Transmits on Pins 3,6
PC NICs	Hubs
Routers	Switches
Wireless access point (Ethernet interface)	—

For example, Figure 2-12 shows a campus LAN in a single building. In this case, several straight-through cables are used to connect PCs to switches. In addition, the cables connecting the switches require *crossover cables*.

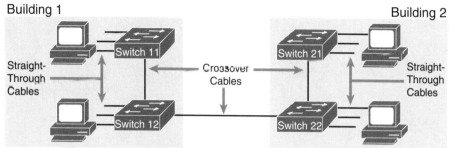

Figure 2-12 *Typical Uses for Straight-Through and Crossover Ethernet Cables*

Automatic Rewiring with Auto-MDIX

Using the wrong cabling pinout with a UTP cable happens to be one of the more common implementation mistakes. Back in 1998, with the introduction of Gigabit Ethernet, the IEEE added a new feature to Ethernet that defines how any device can use electrical pulses to sense if the cable has the wrong cable pinout. For instance, if the link needs a crossover cable, but the installer connected a straight-through cable, this feature can sense the incorrect pinout, and then redirect the electrical signals to the correct pairs to compensate so that the link works. The Ethernet standard calls this feature *automatic medium-dependent interface crossover* (**auto-MDIX**).

Auto-MDIX allows sites to use straight-through pinouts on all cables. For instance, the entire cable plant could use a straight-through pinout. On the links that need a crossover pinout, the auto-MDIX on the switch port will sense the use of the straight-through pinout and then internally swap the pairs used by the transceiver to make the link work. (Additionally, most installations use four-pair UTP cables that support Gigabit Ethernet so that all links support 10-, 100-, or 1000-Mbps Ethernet.)

UTP Cabling Pinouts for 1000BASE-T

1000BASE-T (*Gigabit Ethernet*) differs from 10BASE-T and 100BASE-T as far as the cabling and pinouts. First, 1000BASE-T requires four wire pairs. Second, it uses more advanced electronics that allow both ends to transmit and receive simultaneously on each wire pair. However, the wiring pinouts for 1000BASE-T work almost identically to the earlier standards, adding details for the additional two pairs.

The straight-through cable for 1000BASE-T uses the four wire pairs to create four circuits, but the pins need to match. It uses the same pinouts for two pairs as do the 10BASE-T and 100BASE-T standards, and it adds a pair at pins 4 and 5 and another pair at pins 7 and 8, as shown in Figure 2-13.

Just as with 10BASE-T and 100BASE-T, 1000BASE-T (Gigabit Ethernet) uses straight-through cable pinout for some links but crossover cables in other cases. The Gigabit Ethernet crossover cable crosses pairs A and B in the figure (the pairs at pins 1,2 and 3,6) and also pairs C and D (the pair at pins 4,5 with the pair at pins 7,8). You need a crossover cable pinout in the same cases listed earlier in Table 2-3—for instance, between two switches.

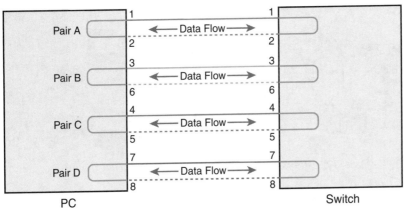

Figure 2-13 *Four-Pair Straight-Through Cable to 1000BASE-T*

Building Physical Ethernet LANs with Fiber

The capability of many UTP-based Ethernet standards to use a cable length up to 100 meters means that the majority of Ethernet cabling in an enterprise uses UTP cables. The distance from an Ethernet switch to every endpoint on the floor of a building will likely be less than 100m. In some cases, however, an engineer might prefer to use fiber cabling for some links in an Ethernet LAN, first to reach greater distances, but for other reasons as well. This next section examines a few of the tradeoffs after discussing the basics of how to transmit data over fiber cabling.

Fiber Cabling Transmission Concepts

Fiber-optic cabling uses glass as the medium through which light passes, varying that light over time to encode 0s and 1s. It might seem strange at first to use glass given that most of us think of glass in windows. Window glass is hard, unbending, and if you hit or bend it enough, the glass will probably shatter—all bad characteristics for a cabling material.

Instead, fiber-optic cables use fiberglass, which allows a manufacturer to spin a long thin string (fiber) of flexible glass. A **fiber-optic cable** holds the fiber in the middle of the cable, allowing the light to pass through the glass—which is a very important attribute for the purposes of sending data.

Although sending data through a glass fiber works well, the glass fiber by itself needs some help. The glass could break, so the glass fiber needs some protection and strengthening. Figure 2-14 shows a cutout with the components of a fiber cable for perspective.

The three outer layers of the cable protect the interior of the cable and make the cables easier to install and manage, while the inner **cladding** and **core** work together to create the environment to allow transmission of light over the cable. A light source, called the *optical transmitter*, shines a light into the core. Light can pass through the core; however, light reflects off the cladding back into the core. Figure 2-15 shows an example with a light-emitting diode (LED) transmitter. You can see how the cladding reflects the light back into the core as it travels through the core.

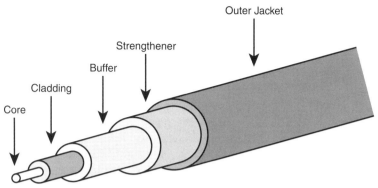

Figure 2-14   *Components of a Fiber-Optic Cable*

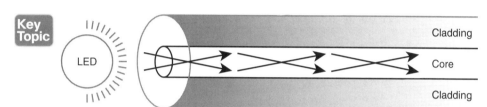

Figure 2-15   *Transmission on Multimode Fiber with Internal Reflection*

The figure shows the normal operation of a **multimode fiber**, characterized by the fact that the cable allows for multiple angles (modes) of light waves entering the core.

In contrast, **single-mode fiber** uses a smaller-diameter core, around one-fifth the diameter of common multimode cables (see Figure 2-16). To transmit light into a much smaller core, a laser-based transmitter sends light at a single angle (hence the name *single-mode*).

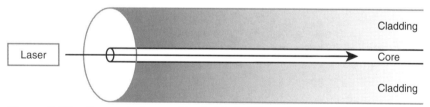

Figure 2-16   *Transmission on Single-Mode Fiber with Laser Transmitter*

Both multimode and single-mode cabling have important roles in Ethernet and meet different needs. Multimode improves the maximum distances over UTP, and it uses less expensive transmitters as compared with single-mode. Standards do vary; for instance, the standards for 10 Gigabit Ethernet over Fiber allow for distances up to 400m, which would often allow for connection of devices in different buildings in the same office park. Single-mode allows distances into the tens of kilometers, but with slightly more expensive SFP/SFP+ hardware.

To transmit between two devices, you need two cables, one for each direction, as shown in Figure 2-17. The concept works much like having two electrical circuits with the original UTP Ethernet standards. Note that the transmit port on one device connects to a cable that connects to a receive port on the other device, and vice versa with the other cable.

Figure 2-17   *Two Fiber Cables with Tx Connected to Rx on Each Cable*

Using Fiber with Ethernet

To use fiber with Ethernet switches, you need to use a switch with either built-in ports that support a particular optical Ethernet standard, or a switch with modular ports that allow you to change the Ethernet standard used on the port. Refer back to Figure 2-8, which shows a photo of a switch with two SFP+ ports, into which you could insert any of the supported SFP+ modules. Those SFP+ ports support a variety of 10-Gbps standards like those listed in Table 2-4.

Table 2-4   A Sampling of IEEE 802.3 10-Gbps Fiber Standards

Standard	Cable Type	Max Distance*
10GBASE-S	MM	400m
10GBASE-LX4	MM	300m
10GBASE-LR	SM	10km
10GBASE-E	SM	30km

* The maximum distances are based on the IEEE standards with no repeaters.

For instance, to build an Ethernet LAN in an office park, you might need to use some multi-mode and single-mode fiber links. In fact, many office parks might already have fiber cabling installed for the expected future use by the tenants in the buildings. If each building was within a few hundred meters of at least one other building, you could use multimode fiber between the buildings and connect switches to create your LAN.

NOTE   Outside of the need to study for CCNA, if you need to look more deeply at fiber Ethernet and SFP/SFP+, check out tmgmatrix.cisco.com as a place to search for and learn about compatible SFP/SFP+ hardware from Cisco.

Although distance might be the first criterion to consider when thinking about whether to use UTP or fiber cabling, a few other tradeoffs exist as well. UTP wins again on cost, because the cost goes up as you move from UTP, to multimode, and then to single-mode, due to the extra cost for the transmitters like the SFP and SFP+ modules. UTP has some negatives, however. First, UTP might work poorly in some electrically noisy environments such as factories, because UTP can be affected by electromagnetic interference (EMI). Also, UTP cables emit a faint signal outside the cable, so highly secure networks may choose to use fiber, which does not create similar emissions, to make the network more secure. Table 2-5 summarizes these tradeoffs.

Table 2-5 Comparisons Between UTP, MM, and SM Ethernet Cabling

Criteria	UTP	Multimode	Single-Mode
Relative Cost of Cabling	Low	Medium	Medium
Relative Cost of a Switch Port	Low	Medium	High
Approximate Max Distance	100m	500m	40km
Relative Susceptibility to Interference	Some	None	None
Relative Risk of Copying from Cable Emissions	Some	None	None

Sending Data in Ethernet Networks

Although physical layer standards vary quite a bit, other parts of the Ethernet standards work the same regardless of the type of physical Ethernet link. Next, this final major section of this chapter looks at several protocols and rules that Ethernet uses regardless of the type of link. In particular, this section examines the details of the Ethernet data-link layer protocol, plus how Ethernet nodes, switches, and hubs forward Ethernet frames through an Ethernet LAN.

Ethernet Data-Link Protocols

One of the most significant strengths of the Ethernet family of protocols is that these protocols use the same data-link standard. In fact, the core parts of the data-link standard date back to the original Ethernet standards.

The Ethernet data-link protocol defines the Ethernet frame: an Ethernet header at the front, the encapsulated data in the middle, and an Ethernet trailer at the end. Ethernet actually defines a few alternate formats for the header, with the frame format shown in Figure 2-18 being commonly used today.

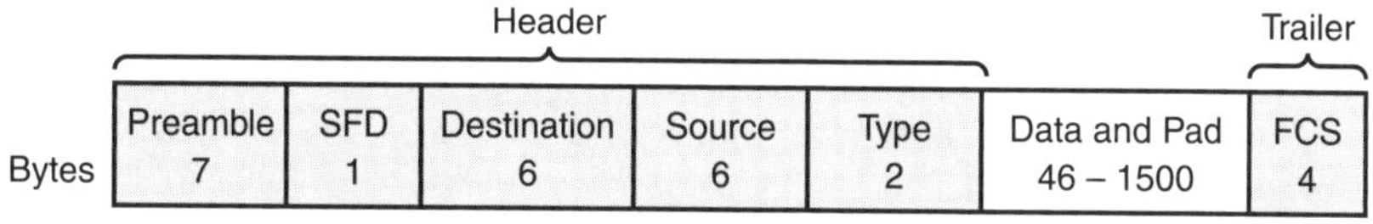

	Preamble	SFD	Destination	Source	Type	Data and Pad	FCS
Bytes	7	1	6	6	2	46 – 1500	4

Header spans Preamble through Type. Trailer is FCS.

Figure 2-18 *Commonly Used Ethernet Frame Format*

While all the fields in the frame matter, some matter more to the topics discussed in this book. Table 2-6 lists the fields in the header and trailer and a brief description for reference, with the upcoming pages including more detail about a few of these fields.

Table 2-6 IEEE 802.3 Ethernet Header and Trailer Fields

Field	Bytes	Description
Preamble	7	Synchronization.
Start Frame Delimiter (SFD)	1	Signifies that the next byte begins the Destination MAC Address field.
Destination MAC Address	6	Identifies the intended recipient of this frame.
Source MAC Address	6	Identifies the sender of this frame.

Field	Bytes	Description
Type	2	Defines the type of protocol listed inside the frame; today, most likely identifies IP version 4 (IPv4) or IP version 6 (IPv6).
Data and Pad*	46–1500	Holds data from a higher layer, typically an L3PDU (usually an IPv4 or IPv6 packet). The sender adds padding to meet the minimum length requirement for this field (46 bytes).
Frame Check Sequence (FCS)	4	Provides a method for the receiving NIC to determine whether the frame experienced transmission errors.

* The IEEE 802.3 specification limits the data portion of the 802.3 frame to a minimum of 46 and a maximum of 1500 bytes. The term *maximum transmission unit* (MTU) defines the maximum Layer 3 packet that can be sent over a medium. Because the Layer 3 packet rests inside the data portion of an Ethernet frame, 1500 bytes is the largest IP MTU allowed over an Ethernet.

Ethernet Addressing

The source and destination Ethernet address fields play a huge role in how Ethernet LANs work. The general idea for each is relatively simple: The sending node puts its own address in the source address field and the intended Ethernet destination device's address in the destination address field. The sender transmits the frame, expecting that the Ethernet LAN, as a whole, will deliver the frame to that correct destination.

Ethernet addresses, also called *Media Access Control (MAC) addresses*, are 6-byte-long (48-bit-long) binary numbers. For convenience, most computers list MAC addresses as 12-digit hexadecimal numbers. Cisco devices typically add some periods to the number for easier readability as well; for example, a Cisco switch might list a MAC address as 0000.0C12.3456.

Most MAC addresses represent a single NIC or other Ethernet port, so these addresses are often called a *unicast* Ethernet address. The term *unicast* is simply a formal way to refer to the fact that the address represents one interface to the Ethernet LAN. (This term also contrasts with two other types of Ethernet addresses, *broadcast* and *multicast*, which will be defined later in this section.)

The entire idea of sending data to a destination unicast MAC address works well, but it works only if all the unicast MAC addresses are unique. If two NICs tried to use the same MAC address, there could be confusion. (The problem would be like the confusion caused to the postal service if you and I both tried to use the same mailing address. Would the postal service deliver mail to your house or mine?) If two PCs on the same Ethernet tried to use the same MAC address, to which PC should frames sent to that MAC address be delivered?

Ethernet solves this problem using an administrative process so that, at the time of manufacture, all Ethernet devices are assigned a universally unique MAC address. Before a manufacturer can build Ethernet products, it must ask the IEEE to assign the manufacturer a universally unique 3-byte code, called the organizationally unique identifier (OUI). The manufacturer agrees to give all NICs (and other Ethernet products) a MAC address that begins with its assigned 3-byte OUI. The manufacturer also assigns a unique value for the last 3 bytes, a number that manufacturer has never used with that OUI. As a result, the MAC address of every device in the universe is unique.

> **NOTE** The IEEE also calls these universal MAC addresses *global MAC addresses*.

Figure 2-19 shows the structure of the unicast MAC address, with the OUI.

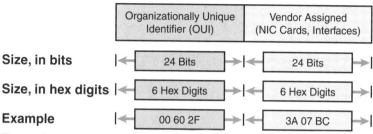

Figure 2-19 *Structure of Unicast Ethernet Addresses*

Ethernet addresses go by many names: LAN address, Ethernet address, hardware address, burned-in address, physical address, universal address, or MAC address. For example, the term burned-in address (BIA) refers to the idea that a permanent MAC address has been encoded (burned into) the ROM chip on the NIC. As another example, the IEEE uses the term *universal address* to emphasize the fact that the address assigned to a NIC by a manufacturer should be unique among all MAC addresses in the universe.

In addition to unicast addresses, Ethernet also uses group addresses. *Group addresses* identify more than one LAN interface card. A frame sent to a group address might be delivered to a small set of devices on the LAN, or even to all devices on the LAN. In fact, the IEEE defines two general categories of group addresses for Ethernet:

Broadcast address: Frames sent to this address should be delivered to all devices on the Ethernet LAN. It has a value of FFFF.FFFF.FFFF.

Multicast addresses: Frames sent to a multicast Ethernet address will be copied and forwarded to a subset of the devices on the LAN that volunteers to receive frames sent to a specific multicast address.

Table 2-7 summarizes most of the details about MAC addresses.

Table 2-7 LAN MAC Address Terminology and Features

LAN Addressing Term or Feature	Description
MAC address	Media Access Control. 802.3 (Ethernet) defines the MAC sublayer of IEEE Ethernet.
Ethernet address, NIC address, LAN address	Other names often used instead of MAC address. These terms describe the 6-byte address of the LAN interface card.
Burned-in address	The 6-byte address assigned by the vendor making the card.
Unicast address	A term for a MAC address that represents a single LAN interface.
Broadcast address	An address that means "all devices that reside on this LAN right now."
Multicast address	On Ethernet, a multicast address implies some subset of all devices currently on the Ethernet LAN.

Identifying Network Layer Protocols with the Ethernet Type Field

While the Ethernet header's address fields play an important and more obvious role in Ethernet LANs, the Ethernet Type field plays a much less obvious role. The Ethernet Type field, or EtherType, sits in the Ethernet data-link layer header, but its purpose is to directly help the network processing on routers and hosts. Basically, the Type field identifies the type of network layer (Layer 3) packet that sits inside the Ethernet frame.

First, think about what sits inside the data part of the Ethernet frame shown earlier in Figure 2-19. Typically, it holds the network layer packet created by the network layer protocol on some device in the network. Over the years, those protocols have included IBM Systems Network Architecture (SNA), Novell NetWare, Digital Equipment Corporation's DECnet, and Apple Computer's AppleTalk. Today, the most common network layer protocols are both from TCP/IP: IP version 4 (IPv4) and IP version 6 (IPv6).

The original host has a place to insert a value (a hexadecimal number) to identify the type of packet encapsulated inside the Ethernet frame. However, what number should the sender put in the header to identify an IPv4 packet as the type? Or an IPv6 packet? As it turns out, the IEEE manages a list of EtherType values, so that every network layer protocol that needs a unique EtherType value can have a number. The sender just has to know the list. (Anyone can view the list; just go to www.ieee.org and search for *EtherType*.)

For example, a host can send one Ethernet frame with an IPv4 packet and the next Ethernet frame with an IPv6 packet. Each frame would have a different Ethernet Type field value, using the values reserved by the IEEE, as shown in Figure 2-20.

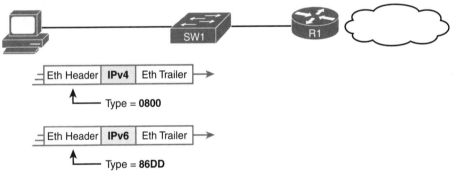

Figure 2-20 *Use of Ethernet Type Field*

Error Detection with FCS

Ethernet also defines a way for nodes to find out whether a frame's bits changed while crossing over an Ethernet link. (Usually, the bits could change because of some kind of electrical interference, or a bad NIC.) Ethernet, like most data-link protocols, uses a field in the data-link trailer for the purpose of error detection.

The Ethernet **Frame Check Sequence** *(FCS)* field in the Ethernet trailer—the only field in the Ethernet trailer—gives the receiving node a way to compare results with the sender, to discover whether errors occurred in the frame. The sender applies a complex math formula to the frame before sending it, storing the result of the formula in the FCS field. The receiver applies the same math formula to the received frame. The receiver then compares its own results with the sender's results. If the results are the same, the frame did not change; otherwise, an error occurred and the receiver discards the frame.

Note that *error detection* does not also mean *error recovery*. Ethernet defines that the errored frame should be discarded, but Ethernet does not attempt to recover the lost frame. Other protocols, notably TCP, recover the lost data by noticing that it is lost and sending the data again.

Sending Ethernet Frames with Switches and Hubs

Ethernet LANs behave slightly differently depending on whether the LAN has mostly modern devices, in particular, LAN switches instead of some older LAN devices called LAN hubs. Basically, the use of more modern switches allows the use of full-duplex logic, which is much faster and simpler than half-duplex logic, which is required when using hubs. The final topic in this chapter looks at these basic differences.

Sending in Modern Ethernet LANs Using Full Duplex

Modern Ethernet LANs use a variety of Ethernet physical standards, but with standard Ethernet frames that can flow over any of these types of physical links. Each individual link can run at a different speed, but each link allows the attached nodes to send the bits in the frame to the next node. They must work together to deliver the data from the sending Ethernet node to the destination node.

The process is relatively simple, on purpose; the simplicity lets each device send a large number of frames per second. Figure 2-21 shows an example in which PC1 sends an Ethernet frame to PC2.

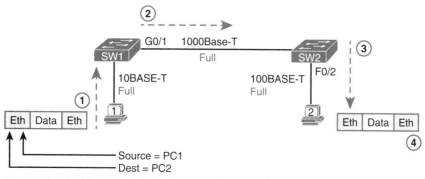

Figure 2-21 *Example of Sending Data in a Modern Ethernet LAN*

Following the steps in the figure:

1. PC1 builds and sends the original Ethernet frame, using its own MAC address as the source address and PC2's MAC address as the destination address.

2. Switch SW1 receives and forwards the Ethernet frame out its G0/1 interface (short for Gigabit interface 0/1) to SW2.

3. Switch SW2 receives and forwards the Ethernet frame out its F0/2 interface (short for Fast Ethernet interface 0/2) to PC2.

4. PC2 receives the frame, recognizes the destination MAC address as its own, and processes the frame.

The Ethernet network in Figure 2-21 uses full duplex on each link, but the concept might be difficult to see.

Full duplex means that the NIC or switch port has no half-duplex restrictions. So, to understand full duplex, you need to understand half duplex, as follows:

Half duplex: The device must wait to send if it is currently receiving a frame; in other words, it cannot send and receive at the same time.

Full duplex: The device does not have to wait before sending; it can send and receive at the same time.

So, with all PCs and LAN switches, and no LAN hubs, all the nodes can use full duplex. All nodes can send and receive on their port at the same instant in time. For example, in Figure 2-21, PC1 and PC2 could send frames to each other simultaneously, in both directions, without any half-duplex restrictions.

Using Half Duplex with LAN Hubs

To understand the need for half-duplex logic in some cases, you have to understand a little about an older type of networking device called a LAN hub. When the IEEE first introduced 10BASE-T in 1990, Ethernet switches did not exist yet; instead, networks used a device called a LAN hub. Like a switch, a LAN hub provided a number of RJ-45 ports as a place to connect links to PCs; however, hubs used different rules for forwarding data.

LAN hubs forward data using physical layer standards rather than data-link standards and are therefore considered to be Layer 1 devices. When an electrical signal comes in one hub port, the hub repeats that electrical signal out all other ports (except the incoming port). By doing so, the data reaches all the rest of the nodes connected to the hub, so the data hopefully reaches the correct destination. The hub has no concept of Ethernet frames, of addresses, making decisions based on those addresses, and so on.

The downside of using LAN hubs is that if two or more devices transmitted a signal at the same instant, the electrical signals collide and become garbled. The hub repeats all received electrical signals, even if it receives multiple signals at the same time. For example, Figure 2-22 shows the idea, with PCs Archie and Bob sending an electrical signal at the same instant of time (at Steps 1A and 1B) and the hub repeating both electrical signals out toward Larry on the left (Step 2).

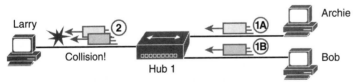

Figure 2-22 *Collision Occurring Because of LAN Hub Behavior*

NOTE For completeness, note that the hub floods each frame out all other ports (except the incoming port). So, Archie's frame goes to both Larry and Bob; Bob's frame goes to Larry and Archie.

If you replace the hub in Figure 2-22 with a LAN switch, the switch prevents the collision on the left. The switch operates as a Layer 2 device, meaning that it looks at the data-link header and trailer. A switch would look at the MAC addresses, and even if the switch needed to forward both frames to Larry on the left, the switch would send one frame and queue the other frame until the first frame was finished.

Now back to the issue created by the hub's logic: collisions. To prevent these collisions, the Ethernet nodes must use half-duplex logic instead of full-duplex logic. A problem occurs only when two or more devices send at the same time; half-duplex logic tells the nodes that if someone else is sending, wait before sending.

For example, back in Figure 2-22, imagine that Archie began sending his frame early enough so that Bob received the first bits of that frame before Bob tried to send his own frame. Bob, at Step 1B, would notice that he was receiving a frame from someone else, and using half-duplex logic, would simply wait to send the frame listed at Step 1B.

Nodes that use half-duplex logic actually use a relatively well-known algorithm called carrier sense multiple access with collision detection (CSMA/CD). The algorithm takes care of the obvious cases but also the cases caused by unfortunate timing. For example, two nodes could check for an incoming frame at the exact same instant, both realize that no other node is sending, and both send their frames at the exact same instant, causing a collision. CSMA/CD covers these cases as well, as follows:

Step 1.   A device with a frame to send listens until the Ethernet is not busy.

Step 2.   When the Ethernet is not busy, the sender begins sending the frame.

Step 3.   The sender listens while sending to discover whether a collision occurs; collisions might be caused by many reasons, including unfortunate timing. If a collision occurs, all currently sending nodes do the following:

    a.   They send a jamming signal that tells all nodes that a collision happened.

    b.   They independently choose a random time to wait before trying again, to avoid unfortunate timing.

    c.   The next attempt starts again at Step 1.

Although most modern LANs do not often use hubs and therefore do not need to use half duplex, enough old hubs still exist in enterprise networks so that you need to be ready to understand duplex issues. Each NIC and switch port has a duplex setting. For all links between PCs and switches, or between switches, use full duplex. However, for any link connected to a LAN hub, the connected LAN switch and NIC port should use half duplex. Note that the hub itself does not use half-duplex logic, instead just repeating incoming signals out every other port.

Figure 2-23 shows an example, with full-duplex links on the left and a single LAN hub on the right. The hub then requires SW2's F0/2 interface to use half-duplex logic, along with the PCs connected to the hub.

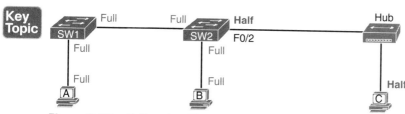

Figure 2-23   *Full and Half Duplex in an Ethernet LAN*

Before I close the chapter, note that the discussion of full and half duplex connects to two specific terms from CCNA exam topic 1.3.b, but those connections may not be obvious. First, the term *Ethernet shared media* (from the exam topic) refers to designs that use hubs, require CSMA/CD, and therefore share the bandwidth. The idea behind the term comes from the fact that the devices connected to the hub share the network because they must use CSMA/CD, and CSMA/CD enforces rules that allow only one device to successfully send a frame at any point in time.

By contrast, the term *Ethernet point-to-point* in that same exam topic emphasizes the fact that in a network built with switches, each (point-to-point) link works independently of the others. Because of the full-duplex logic discussed in this section, a frame can be sent on every point-to-point link in an Ethernet at the same time.

Chapter Review

One key to doing well on the exams is to perform repetitive spaced review sessions. Review this chapter's material using either the tools in the book or interactive tools for the same material found on the book's companion website. Refer to the "Your Study Plan" element for more details. Table 2-8 outlines the key review elements and where you can find them. To better track your study progress, record when you completed these activities in the second column.

Table 2-8   Chapter Review Tracking

Review Element	Review Date(s)	Resource Used
Review key topics		Book, website
Review key terms		Book, website
Answer DIKTA questions		Book, PTP
Review memory tables		Book, website

Review All the Key Topics

Table 2-9   Key Topics for Chapter 2

Key Topic Element	Description	Page Number
Figure 2-3	Drawing of a typical wired and wireless enterprise LAN	40
Table 2-2	Several types of Ethernet LANs and some details about each	41
Figure 2-9	Conceptual drawing of transmitting in one direction each over two different electrical circuits between two Ethernet nodes	47
Figure 2-10	10- and 100-Mbps Ethernet straight-through cable pinouts	47
Figure 2-11	10- and 100-Mbps Ethernet crossover cable pinouts	48
Table 2-3	List of devices that transmit on wire pair 1,2 and pair 3,6	48
Figure 2-12	Typical uses for straight-through and crossover Ethernet cables	49
Figure 2-15	Physical transmission concepts in a multimode cable	51
Table 2-5	Comparison between UTP, MM, and SM Ethernet cabling	53
Figure 2-19	Format of Ethernet MAC addresses	55

Key Topic Element	Description	Page Number
List	Definitions of half duplex and full duplex	58
Figure 2-23	Examples of which interfaces use full duplex and which interfaces use half duplex	59

2

Key Terms You Should Know

10BASE-T, 100BASE-T, 1000BASE-T, auto-MDIX, broadcast address, cladding, core, crossover cable, electromagnetic interference (EMI), Ethernet, Ethernet address, Ethernet frame, Ethernet link, Ethernet port, Fast Ethernet, fiber-optic cable, Frame Check Sequence, Gigabit Ethernet, IEEE, MAC address, multimode fiber, network interface card (NIC), RJ-45, single-mode fiber, straight-through cable, transceiver, unicast address, wired LAN, wireless LAN

CHAPTER 3

Fundamentals of WANs and IP Routing

This chapter covers the following exam topics:

1.0 Network Fundamentals

    1.1 Explain the role and function of network components

        1.1.a Routers

    1.2 Describe characteristics of network topology architectures

        1.2.d WAN

This chapter introduces WANs and the various features of the TCP/IP network layer.

First, for WANs, note that the current CCNA blueprint does not examine WANs in detail as an end to themselves. However, to understand IP routing, you need to understand the basics of the two types of WAN links introduced in the first major section of this chapter: serial links and Ethernet WAN links. In their most basic form, these WAN links connect routers that sit at sites that can be miles to hundreds of miles apart, allowing communications between remote sites.

The rest of the chapter then turns to the TCP/IP Network layer, with IP as the center of the discussion. The second section of the chapter discusses the major features of IP: routing, addressing, and routing protocols. The final section of the chapter examines a few protocols other than IP that also help the TCP/IP Network layer create a network that allows end-to-end communication between endpoints.

"Do I Know This Already?" Quiz

Take the quiz (either here or use the PTP software) if you want to use the score to help you decide how much time to spend on this chapter. The letter answers are listed at the bottom of the page following the quiz. Appendix C, found both at the end of the book as well as on the companion website, includes both the answers and explanations. You can also find both answers and explanations in the PTP testing software.

Table 3-1 "Do I Know This Already?" Foundation Topics Section-to-Question Mapping

Foundation Topics Section	Questions
Wide-Area Networks	1, 2
IP Routing	3–6
Other Network Layer Features	7

1. Which of the following terms is not commonly used to describe a serial link?

   a. Private line

   b. Point-to-point link

   c. Leased circuit

   d. E-line

2. Two routers, R1 and R2, connect using an Ethernet WAN service. The service provides point-to-point service between these two routers only, as a Layer 2 Ethernet service. Which of the following are the most likely to be true about this WAN? (Choose two answers.)

   a. R1 will connect to a physical Ethernet link, with the other end of the cable connected to R2.

   b. R1 will connect to a physical Ethernet link, with the other end of the cable connected to a device at the WAN service provider point of presence.

   c. R1 will forward data-link frames to R2 using an HDLC header/trailer.

   d. R1 will forward data-link frames to R2 using an Ethernet header/trailer.

3. Imagine a network in which PC1 connects to the same Ethernet LAN as Router1, PC2 connects to the same LAN as Router2, and the two routers connect to each other with a PPP serial link. When PC1 sends data to PC2, and Router1 removes the Ethernet header and trailer, which of the following is true?

   a. Router1 does not use the removed Ethernet header/trailer again.

   b. Router1 re-encapsulates the packet in a PPP frame that uses the Ethernet addresses from the removed header.

   c. Router1 also removes the IP header before forwarding the data to Router2.

   d. Router1 re-encapsulates the packet in a new Ethernet frame before forwarding the packet to Router2.

4. Which of the following does a router normally use when making a decision about routing TCP/IP packets?

   a. Destination MAC address

   b. Source MAC address

   c. Destination IP address

   d. Source IP address

   e. Destination MAC and IP addresses

5. Which of the following are true about a LAN-connected TCP/IP host and its IP routing (forwarding) choices?

   a. The host always sends packets to its default gateway.

   b. The host never sends packets to its default gateway.

   c. The host sends packets to its default gateway if the destination IP address is in a different subnet than the host.

   d. The host sends packets to its default gateway if the destination IP address is in the same subnet as the host.

6. Which of the following are functions of a routing protocol? (Choose two answers.)

   a. Advertising known routes to neighboring routers

   b. Learning routes to directly connected subnets

   c. Learning routes as advertised to the router by neighboring routers

   d. Forwarding IP packets based on a packet's destination IP address

7. A company implements a TCP/IP network, with PC1 sitting on an Ethernet LAN. Which of the following protocols and features requires PC1 to learn information from some other server device?

   a. ARP

   b. ping

   c. DNS

   d. None of these answers are correct.

Foundation Topics

Wide-Area Networks

Imagine a typical day at the branch office at some enterprise. The user sits at some endpoint device: a PC, tablet, phone, and so on. It connects to a LAN, either via an Ethernet cable or using a wireless LAN. However, the user happens to be checking information on a website, and that web server sits at the home office of the company. To make that work, the data travels over one or more **wide-area network (WAN)** links.

WAN technologies define the physical (Layer 1) standards and data-link (Layer 2) protocols used to communicate over long distances. This first section examines two WAN technologies: leased-line WANs and Ethernet WANs. Leased-line WANs have been an option since the 1960s, but are seldom used today. However, because leased-line WANs have been around many years, and have been a part of CCNA for its entire history, you need to know the basics of leased-line WANs for the current CCNA.

Conversely, companies use *Ethernet WAN* links much more often today as compared to leased lines. Those links use the same Ethernet data-link protocols as discussed in the previous chapter, but they use physical layer Ethernet standards that work over the much longer distances required for WANs. The next few pages examine leased-line WANs first, followed by Ethernet WANs.

Leased-Line WANs

To connect LANs using a WAN, the internetwork uses a router connected to each LAN, with a WAN link between the routers. For the WAN link, the enterprise's network engineer must do some planning and then order some kind of WAN link from a WAN service provider. That provider installs the WAN link between the two routers, as shown in Figure 3-1. Note that drawings of leased-line WAN links represent the link with a crooked line (a lightning bolt) to imply the WAN link is a leased line.

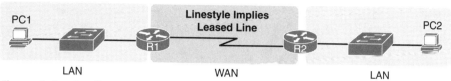

Figure 3-1   *Small Enterprise Network with One Leased Line*

This section begins by examining the physical details of leased lines, followed by a discussion of the two common data-link protocols for leased lines, HDLC and PPP.

Physical Details of Leased Lines

The **leased line** service, a physical layer service, delivers bits in both directions, at a predetermined speed, using full-duplex logic. In fact, conceptually it acts as if you had a full-duplex crossover Ethernet link between two routers, as shown in Figure 3-2. The leased line uses two pairs of wires, one pair for each direction of sending data, which allows full-duplex operation.

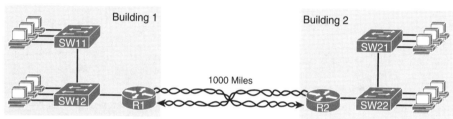

Figure 3-2   *Conceptual View of the Leased-Line Service*

To create a leased line, some physical path must exist between the two routers on the ends of the link. The physical cabling must leave the customer buildings where each router sits; however, the **telco** does not simply install one cable between the two buildings. Instead, it uses what is typically a large and complex network that creates the appearance of a cable between the two routers.

Figure 3-3 shows a conceptual view of a small part of the telco network. Telcos put their equipment in buildings called central offices (COs). The telco installs cables from the CO to most every other building in the city, expecting to sell services to the people in those buildings one day. The telco would then configure its switches to use some of the capacity on each cable to send data in both directions, creating the equivalent of a crossover cable between the two routers.

Given the long history of leased lines, the industry uses a variety of terms to refer to the same kind of WAN link. For instance, the term *leased line* emphasizes the fact that the telco leases the use of the leased line to a customer, but the customer does not permanently own the line. Table 3-2 lists some of the many names for leased lines, mainly so that in a networking job, you have a chance to translate from the terms each person uses with a basic description as to the meaning of the name.

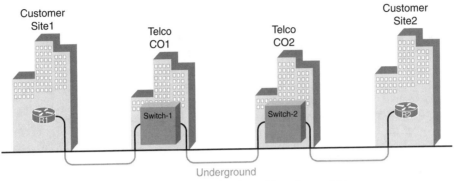

Figure 3-3   *Possible Cabling Inside a Telco for a Short Leased Line*

Table 3-2   Different Names for a Leased Line

Name	Meaning or Reference
Leased circuit, Circuit	The words *line* and *circuit* are often used as synonyms in telco terminology; *circuit* makes reference to the electrical circuit between the two endpoints.
Serial link, Serial line	The words *link* and *line* are also often used as synonyms. *Serial* in this case refers to the fact that the bits flow serially and that routers use **serial interfaces.**
Point-to-point link, Point-to-point line	These terms refer to the fact that the topology stretches between two points, and two points only. (Some older leased lines allowed more than two devices.)
T1	This specific type of leased line transmits data at 1.544 megabits per second (1.544 Mbps).
WAN link, Link	Both of these terms are very general, with no reference to any specific technology.
Private line	This term refers to the fact that the data sent over the line cannot be copied by other telco customers, so the data is private.

Data-Link Details of Leased Lines

A leased line provides a Layer 1 service. In other words, it promises to deliver bits between the devices connected to the leased line. However, the leased line itself does not define a data-link layer protocol to be used on the leased line. So, to make use of the leased line, the routers on the ends of the line use one of two data-link protocols: High-Level Data Link Control (**HDLC**) or Point-to-Point Protocol (PPP).

All data-link protocols perform a similar role: to control the correct delivery of data over a physical link of a particular type. For example, the Ethernet data-link protocol uses a destination address field to identify the correct device that should receive the data and an FCS field that allows the receiving device to determine whether the data arrived correctly. The WAN data-link protocols HDLC and PPP provide similar functions.

Answers to the "Do I Know This Already?" quiz:

1 D **2** B, D **3** A **4** C **5** C **6** A, C **7** C

HDLC and PPP have even less work to do than Ethernet because of the simple point-to-point topology of a leased line. Using HDLC as an example, when one router sends an HDLC frame over a leased line, the frame can go to only one destination device: to the router on the other end of the link. So, while HDLC has an address field, the destination is implied, and the actual address value is unimportant. The idea is sort of like when I have lunch with my friend Gary, and only Gary. I do not need to start every sentence with "Hey, Gary." He knows I am talking to him.

Figure 3-4 shows the HDLC frame format as an example, with Table 3-3 that follows describing the fields. However, note that HDLC and PPP have a similar frame format, although the newer PPP (defined in the 1990s) has more features and functions (plus additional optional headers) than the older HDLC (defined in the 1970s.)

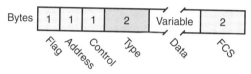

Figure 3-4   *HDLC Framing*

Table 3-3   Comparing HDLC and PPP Header Fields to Ethernet

HDLC & PPP Field	Ethernet Equivalent	Description
Flag	Preamble, SFD	Lists a recognizable bit pattern so that the receiving nodes realize that a new frame is arriving.
Address	Destination Address	Identifies the destination device, but not interesting for leased line point-to-point topologies.
Control	N/A	No longer of use today for links between routers.
Type	Type	Identifies the type of Layer 3 packet encapsulated inside the data portion of the frame.
FCS	FCS	Identifies a field used by the error detection process. (It is the only trailer field in this table.)

How Routers Use a WAN Data Link

Leased lines connect to routers, and routers focus on delivering packets to a destination host. However, routers physically connect to both LANs and WANs, with those LANs and WANs requiring that data be sent inside data-link frames. So, now that you know a little about HDLC and PPP, it helps to think about how routers use these data-link protocols when sending data.

First, the TCP/IP network layer focuses on forwarding **IP packets** from the sending host to the destination host. The underlying LANs and WANs just act as a way to move the packets to the next router or end-user device. Figure 3-5 shows that network layer perspective.

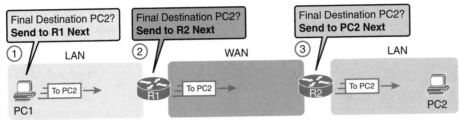

Figure 3-5 *IP Routing Logic over LANs and WANs*

Following the steps in the figure, for a packet sent by PC1 to PC2's IP address:

1. PC1's network layer (IP) logic tells it to send the packet to a nearby router (R1).

2. Router R1's network layer logic tells it to forward (route) the packet out the leased line to Router R2 next.

3. Router R2's network layer logic tells it to forward (route) the packet out the LAN link to PC2 next.

While Figure 3-5 shows the network layer logic, the PCs and routers must rely on the LANs and WANs in the figure to actually move the bits in the packet. Figure 3-6 shows the same figure, with the same packet, but this time showing some of the data-link layer logic used by the hosts and routers. Basically, three separate data-link layer steps encapsulate the packet, inside a data-link frame, over three hops through the internetwork: from PC1 to R1, from R1 to R2, and from R2 to PC2.

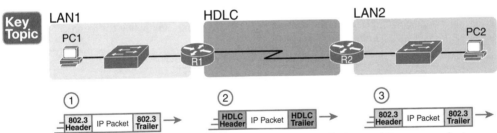

Figure 3-6 *General Concept of Routers De-encapsulating and Re-encapsulating IP Packets*

Following the steps in the figure, again for a packet sent by PC1 to PC2's IP address:

1. To send the IP packet to Router R1 next, PC1 encapsulates the IP packet in an Ethernet frame that has the destination MAC address of R1.

2. Router R1 de-encapsulates (removes) the IP packet from the Ethernet frame, encapsulates (inserts) the packet into an HDLC frame using an HDLC header and trailer, and forwards the HDLC frame to Router R2 next.

3. Router R2 de-encapsulates (removes) the IP packet from the HDLC frame, encapsulates (inserts) the packet into an Ethernet frame that has the destination MAC address of PC2, and forwards the Ethernet frame to PC2.

In summary, a leased line with HDLC creates a WAN link between two routers so that they can forward packets for the devices on the attached LANs. The leased line itself provides the physical means to transmit the bits, in both directions. The HDLC frames provide the means to encapsulate the network layer packet correctly so that it crosses the link between routers. Similarly, if the routers use PPP instead of HDLC, then the routers encapsulate the packets in PPP frames rather than HDLC frames.

Leased lines have many benefits that have led to their relatively long life in the WAN market-place. These lines are simple for the customer, are widely available, are of high quality, and are private. However, they do have some negatives as well compared to newer WAN technologies, including a higher cost and typically longer lead times to get the service installed. Additionally, by today's standards, leased-line WAN links are slow, with the fastest leased line speeds in the tens of megabits per second (Mbps). Newer and faster WAN technology has moved the WAN market away from leased lines, with Ethernet WANs being common here in the 2020s.

Ethernet as a WAN Technology

For the first several decades of the existence of Ethernet, Ethernet was only appropriate for LANs. The restrictions on cable lengths and devices might allow a LAN that stretched a kilometer or two, to support a campus LAN, but that was the limit.

As time passed, the IEEE improved Ethernet standards in ways that made Ethernet a reasonable WAN technology. For example, the 1000BASE-LX standard uses single-mode fiber cabling, with support for a 5-km cable length; the 1000BASE-ZX standard supports an even longer 70-km cable length. As time went by, and as the IEEE improved cabling distances for fiber Ethernet links, Ethernet became a reasonable WAN technology.

Today, many WAN service providers (SP) offer WAN services that take advantage of Ethernet. SPs offer a wide variety of these Ethernet WAN services, with many different names. But all of them use a similar model, with Ethernet used between the customer site and the SP's network, as shown in Figure 3-7.

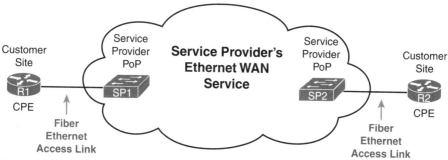

Figure 3-7 *Fiber Ethernet Link to Connect a CPE Router to a Service Provider's WAN*

The model shown in Figure 3-7 has many of the same ideas of how a telco creates a leased line, as shown earlier in Figure 3-3, but now with Ethernet links and devices. The customer connects to an Ethernet link using a router interface. The (fiber) Ethernet link leaves the customer building and connects to some nearby SP location called a point of presence (PoP). Instead of a telco switch as shown in Figure 3-3, the SP uses an Ethernet switch. Inside the SP's network, the SP uses any technology that it wants to create the specific Ethernet WAN services.

Ethernet WANs That Create a Layer 2 Service

Ethernet WAN services include a variety of specific services that vary in ways that change how routers use those services. However, for the purposes of CCNA, you just need to understand the most basic Ethernet WAN service, one that works much like an Ethernet crossover cable—just over a WAN. In other words:

- Logically, behaves like a point-to-point connection between two routers

- Physically, behaves as if a physical fiber Ethernet link existed between the two routers

This book refers to this particular Ethernet WAN service with a couple of the common names:

Ethernet WAN: A generic name to differentiate it from an Ethernet LAN.

Ethernet point-to-point link: A term that emphasizes the topology of a typical Ethernet WAN link that has exactly two endpoints: the routers on the two ends of the link.

Ethernet Line Service (E-Line): A term from the Metro Ethernet Forum (MEF) for the kind of point-to-point Ethernet WAN service shown throughout this book.

Ethernet over MPLS (EoMPLS): A term that refers to Multiprotocol Label Switching (MPLS), a technology that can be used to create the Ethernet service for the customer.

So, if you can imagine two routers, with a single Ethernet link between the two routers, you understand what this particular Ethernet WAN service does, as shown in Figure 3-8. In this case, the two routers, R1 and R2, connect with an Ethernet WAN service instead of a serial link. The routers use Ethernet interfaces, and they can send data in both directions at the same time. Physically, each router actually connects to some SP PoP, as shown earlier in Figure 3-7, but logically, the two routers can send Ethernet frames to each other over the link.

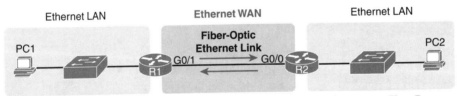

Figure 3-8   *Ethernet WAN Acting Like a Simple Ethernet Link Between Two Routers*

How Routers Route IP Packets Using Ethernet WAN Links

WANs, by their very nature, give IP routers a way to forward IP packets from a LAN at one site, over the WAN, and to another LAN at another site. The routing logic works the same whether the WAN link happens to be a serial link or an Ethernet WAN link, with the encapsulation details being slightly different. With an Ethernet WAN link, the link uses Ethernet for both Layer 1 and Layer 2 functions, so the routers encapsulate using the familiar Ethernet header and trailer, as shown in the middle of Figure 3-9. Also, note that the figure shows a small cloud over the Ethernet link as a way to tell us that the link is an Ethernet WAN link, rather than an Ethernet LAN link.

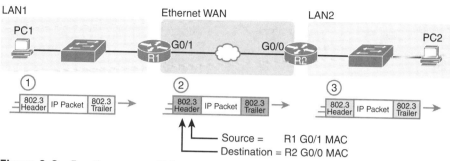

Figure 3-9 *Routing over an Ethernet WAN Link*

NOTE The 802.3 headers/trailers in the figure are different at each stage! Make sure to notice the reasons in the step-by-step explanations that follow.

The figure shows the same three routing steps as shown with the serial link in the earlier Figure 3-6. In this case, all three routing steps use the same Ethernet (802.3) protocol. However, note that each frame's data-link header and trailer are different. Each router discards the old data-link header/trailer and adds a new set, as described in these steps. Focus mainly on Step 2, because compared to the similar example shown in Figure 3-6, Steps 1 and 3 are unchanged:

1. To send the IP packet to Router R1 next, PC1 encapsulates (inserts) the IP packet in an Ethernet frame that has the destination MAC address of R1.

2. Router R1 de-encapsulates (removes) the IP packet from the Ethernet frame and encapsulates (inserts) the packet into a new Ethernet frame, with a new Ethernet header and trailer. The destination MAC address is R2's G0/0 MAC address, and the source MAC address is R1's G0/1 MAC address. R1 forwards this frame over the Ethernet WAN service to R2 next.

3. Router R2 de-encapsulates (removes) the IP packet from the Ethernet frame, encapsulates (inserts) the packet into an Ethernet frame that has the destination MAC address of PC2, and forwards the Ethernet frame to PC2.

Throughout this book, the WAN links (serial and Ethernet) will connect routers as shown here, with the focus being on the LANs and IP routing. The rest of the chapter turns our attention to a closer look at IP routing.

IP Routing

Many protocol models have existed over the years, but today the TCP/IP model dominates. And at the network layer of TCP/IP, two options exist for the main protocol around which all other network layer functions revolve: IP version 4 (IPv4) and IP version 6 (IPv6). Both IPv4 and IPv6 define the same kinds of network layer functions, but with different details. This chapter introduces these network layer functions for IPv4, leaving the IPv6 details for Part VII of this book.

NOTE All references to IP in this chapter refer to the older and more established IPv4, and all use of the term **IP address** refers to an IPv4 address.

Internet Protocol (IP) focuses on the job of routing data, in the form of IP packets, from the source host to the destination host. IP does not concern itself with the physical transmission of data, instead relying on the lower TCP/IP layers for those functions. Instead, IP concerns itself with the logical details, rather than physical details, of delivering data. In particular, the network layer specifies how packets travel end to end over a TCP/IP network, even when the packet crosses many different types of LAN and WAN links.

This next major section of the chapter examines IP routing in more depth. First, IP defines what it means to route an IP packet from sending host to destination host, while using successive data-link protocols. This section then examines how IP addressing rules help to make IP routing much more efficient by grouping addresses into subnets. This section closes by looking at the role of IP **routing protocols**, which give routers a means by which to learn routes to all the IP subnets in an internetwork.

Network Layer Routing (Forwarding) Logic

Routers and end-user computers (called *hosts* in a TCP/IP network) work together to perform IP routing. The host operating system (OS) has TCP/IP software, including the software that implements the network layer. Hosts use that software to choose where to send IP packets, often to a nearby router. Those routers make choices of where to send the IP packet next. Together, the hosts and routers deliver the IP packet to the correct destination, as shown in the example in Figure 3-10.

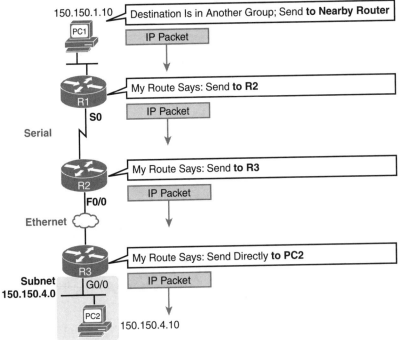

Figure 3-10 *Routing Logic: PC1 Sending an IP Packet to PC2*

The IP packet, created by PC1, goes from the top of the figure all the way to PC2 at the bottom of the figure. The next few pages discuss the network layer routing logic used by each device along the path.

NOTE   The term *path selection* is sometimes used to refer to the routing process shown in Figure 3-10. At other times, it refers to routing protocols, specifically how routing protocols select the best route among the competing routes to the same destination.

Host Forwarding Logic: Send the Packet to the Default Router

In this example, PC1 does some basic analysis and then chooses to send the IP packet to the router so that the router will forward the packet. PC1 analyzes the destination address and realizes that PC2's address (150.150.4.10) is not on the same LAN as PC1. So PC1's logic tells it to send the packet to a device whose job it is to know where to route data: a nearby router, on the same LAN, called PC1's **default router**.

To send the IP packet to the default router, the sender sends a data-link frame across the medium to the nearby router; this frame includes the packet in the data portion of the frame. That frame uses data-link layer (Layer 2) addressing in the data-link header to ensure that the nearby router receives the frame.

NOTE   The *default router* is also referred to as the *default gateway*.

R1 and R2's Logic: Routing Data Across the Network

All routers use the same general process to route the packet. Each router keeps an *IP* **routing table**. This table lists IP address *groupings*, called **IP networks** and **IP subnets**. When a router receives a packet, it compares the packet's destination IP address to the entries in the routing table and makes a match. This matching entry also lists directions that tell the router where to forward the packet next.

In Figure 3-10, R1 would have matched the destination address (150.150.4.10) to a routing table entry, which in turn told R1 to send the packet to R2 next. Similarly, R2 would have matched a routing table entry that told R2 to send the packet, over an Ethernet WAN link, to R3 next.

The routing concept works a little like driving down the freeway when approaching a big interchange. You look up and see signs for nearby towns, telling you which exits to take to go to each town. Similarly, the router looks at the IP routing table (the equivalent of the road signs) and directs each packet over the correct next LAN or WAN link (the equivalent of a road).

R3's Logic: Delivering Data to the End Destination

The final router in the path, R3, uses almost the same logic as R1 and R2, but with one minor difference. R3 needs to forward the packet directly to PC2, not to some other router. On the surface, that difference seems insignificant. In the next section, when you read about how the network layer uses LANs and WANs, the significance of the difference will become obvious.

How Network Layer Routing Uses LANs and WANs

While the network layer routing logic ignores the physical transmission details, the bits still have to be transmitted. To do that work, the network layer logic in a host or router must hand off the packet to the data-link layer protocols, which, in turn, ask the physical layer to actually send the data. The data-link layer adds the appropriate header and trailer to the packet, creating a frame, before sending the frames over each physical network.

The routing process forwards the network layer packet from end to end through the network, while each data-link frame only takes a smaller part of the trip. Each successive data-link layer frame moves the packet to the next device that thinks about network layer logic. In short, the network layer thinks about the bigger view of the goal, like "Send this packet to the specified next router or host...," while the data-link layer thinks about the specifics, like "Encapsulate the packet in a data-link frame and transmit it." The following list summarizes the major steps in a router's internal network layer routing for each packet beginning with the frame arriving in a router interface:

Step 1. Use the data-link Frame Check Sequence (FCS) field to ensure that the frame had no errors; if errors occurred, discard the frame.

Step 2. Assuming that the frame was not discarded at Step 1, discard the old data-link header and trailer, leaving the IP packet.

Step 3. Compare the IP packet's destination IP address to the routing table, and find the route that best matches the destination address. This route identifies the outgoing interface of the router and possibly the next-hop router IP address.

Step 4. Encapsulate the IP packet inside a new data-link header and trailer, appropriate for the outgoing interface, and forward the frame.

Figure 3-11 works through a repeat example of a packet sent by PC1 to PC2, followed by a detailed analysis of each device's routing logic. Each explanation includes the details about how PC1 and each of the three routers builds the appropriate new data-link headers.

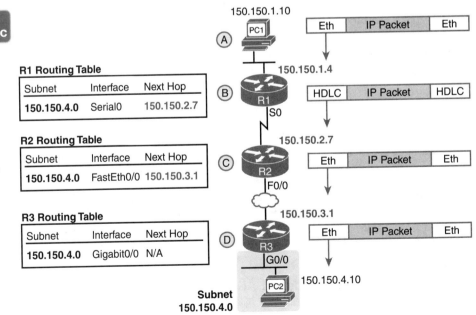

Figure 3-11 *Network Layer and Data-Link Layer Encapsulation*

The following list explains the forwarding logic at each router, focusing on how the routing integrates with the data link.

Step A. **PC1 sends the packet to its default router.** PC1's network layer logic builds the IP packet, with a destination address of PC2's IP address (150.150.4.10). The network layer also performs the analysis to decide that 150.150.4.10 is not in the local IP subnet, so PC1 needs to send the packet to R1 (PC1's default router). PC1 places the IP packet into an Ethernet data-link frame, with a destination Ethernet address of R1's Ethernet address. PC1 sends the frame on to the Ethernet.

Step B. **R1 processes the incoming frame and forwards the packet to R2.** Because the incoming Ethernet frame has a destination MAC of R1's Ethernet MAC, R1 decides to process the frame. R1 checks the frame's FCS for errors, and if none, R1 discards the Ethernet header and trailer. Next, R1 compares the packet's destination address (150.150.4.10) to its routing table and finds the entry for subnet 150.150.4.0. Because the destination address of 150.150.4.10 is in that subnet, R1 forwards the packet out the interface listed in that matching route (Serial0) to next-hop Router R2 (150.150.2.7). R1 must first encapsulate the IP packet into an HDLC frame.

Step C. **R2 processes the incoming frame and forwards the packet to R3.** R2 repeats the same general process as R1 when R2 receives the HDLC frame. R2 checks the FCS field and finds that no errors occurred and then discards the HDLC header and trailer. Next, R2 compares the packet's destination address (150.150.4.10) to its routing table and finds the entry for subnet 150.150.4.0, a route that directs R2 to send the packet out interface Fast Ethernet 0/0 to next-hop router 150.150.3.1 (R3). But first, R2 must encapsulate the packet in an Ethernet header. That header uses R2's MAC address and R3's MAC address on the Ethernet WAN link as the source and destination MAC address, respectively.

Step D. **R3 processes the incoming frame and forwards the packet to PC2.** Like R1 and R2, R3 checks the FCS, discards the old data-link header and trailer, and matches its own route for subnet 150.150.4.0. R3's routing table entry for 150.150.4.0 shows that the outgoing interface is R3's Ethernet interface, but there is no next-hop router because R3 is connected directly to subnet 150.150.4.0. All R3 has to do is encapsulate the packet inside a new Ethernet header and trailer, but with a destination Ethernet address of PC2's MAC address.

Because the routers build new data-link headers and trailers, and because the new headers contain data-link addresses, the PCs and routers must have some way to decide what data-link addresses to use. An example of how the router determines which data-link address to use is the IP Address Resolution Protocol (ARP). *ARP dynamically learns the data-link address of an IP host connected to a LAN.* For example, at the last step, at the bottom of Figure 3-11, Router R3 would use ARP once to learn PC2's MAC address before sending any packets to PC2.

How IP Addressing Helps IP Routing

IP defines network layer addresses that identify any host or router interface that connects to a TCP/IP network. The idea basically works like a postal address: Any interface that expects to receive IP packets needs an IP address, just like you need a postal address before receiving mail from the postal service. This next short topic introduces the idea of IP networks and subnets, which are the groups of addresses defined by IP.

> **NOTE**   IP defines the word *network* to mean a very specific concept. To avoid confusion when writing about IP addressing, this book (and others) often avoids using the term *network* for other uses. In particular, this book uses the term *internetwork* to refer more generally to a network made up of routers, switches, cables, and other equipment.

Rules for Groups of IP Addresses (Networks and Subnets)

TCP/IP groups IP addresses together so that IP addresses used on the same physical network are part of the same group. IP calls these address groups an *IP network* or an *IP subnet*. Using that same postal service analogy, each IP network and IP subnet works like a postal code (or in the United States, a ZIP code). All nearby postal addresses are in the same postal code (ZIP code), while all nearby IP addresses must be in the same IP network or IP subnet.

IP defines specific rules about which IP address should be in the same IP network or IP subnet. Numerically, the addresses in the same group have the same value in the first part of the addresses. For example, Figures 3-10 and 3-11 could have used the following conventions:

- Hosts on the top Ethernet: Addresses start with 150.150.1

- Hosts on the R1–R2 serial link: Addresses start with 150.150.2

- Hosts on the R2–R3 Ethernet WAN link: Addresses start with 150.150.3

- Hosts on the bottom Ethernet: Addresses start with 150.150.4

From the perspective of IP routing, the grouping of IP addresses means that the routing table can be much smaller. A router can list one routing table entry for each IP network or subnet, representing a group of addresses, instead of one entry for every single IP address.

While the list shows just one example of how IP addresses may be grouped, the rules for how to group addresses using subnets will require some work to master the concepts and math. Part IV of this book details IP addressing and subnetting, along with other subnetting videos and practice questions. However, the brief version of two of the foundational rules of **subnetting** can be summarized as follows:

- Two IP addresses, not separated from each other by a router, must be in the same group (subnet).

- Two IP addresses, separated from each other by at least one router, must be in different groups (subnets).

It's similar to the USPS ZIP code system and how it requires local governments to assign addresses to new buildings. It would be ridiculous to have two houses next door to each other with different postal/ZIP codes. Similarly, it would be silly to have people who live on opposite sides of the country to have addresses with the same postal/ZIP code.

The IP Header

The routing process also makes use of the IPv4 header, as shown in Figure 3-12. The header lists a 32-bit source IP address, as well as a 32-bit destination IP address. The header, of course, has other fields, a few of which matter for other discussions in this book. The book will refer to this figure as needed, but otherwise, be aware of the 20-byte IP header and the existence of the source and destination IP address fields. Note that in the examples so far in this chapter, while routers remove and add data-link headers each time they route a packet, the IP header remains, with the IP addresses unchanged by the IP routing process.

4 Bytes			
Version	Length	DS Field	Packet Length
Identification		Flags	Fragment Offset
Time to Live		Protocol	Header Checksum
Source IP Address			
Destination IP Address			

Figure 3-12 *IPv4 Header, Organized as 4 Bytes Wide for a Total of 20 Bytes*

How IP Routing Protocols Help IP Routing

For routing logic to work on both hosts and routers, each host and router needs to know something about the TCP/IP internetwork. Hosts need to know the IP address of their default router so that hosts can send packets to remote destinations. Routers, however, need to know routes so they forward packets to each and every reachable IP network and IP subnet.

The best method for routers to know all the useful routes is to configure the routers to use the same IP routing protocol. If you enable the same routing protocol on all the routers in a TCP/IP internetwork, with the correct settings, the routers will send routing protocol messages to each other. As a result, all the routers will learn routes for all the IP networks and subnets in the TCP/IP internetwork.

IP supports a small number of different IP routing protocols. All use some similar ideas and processes to learn IP routes, but different routing protocols do have some internal differences. All the routing protocols use the same general steps for learning routes:

Step 1.   Each router, independent of the routing protocol, adds a route to its routing table for each subnet directly connected to the router.

Step 2.   Each router's routing protocol tells its neighbors about the routes in its routing table, including the directly connected routes and routes learned from other routers.

Step 3.   Each router's routing protocol listens to messages from neighboring routers and learns routes, with the next-hop router of that route typically being the neighbor from which the route was learned.

Also, note that at the final step, routers may have to choose between multiple routes to reach a single subnet. When that happens, routers place the best currently available route to reach a subnet (based on a measurement called a metric) into the routing table.

Figure 3-13 shows an example of how a routing protocol works, using the same diagram as in Figures 3-10 and 3-11. In this case, IP subnet 150.150.4.0, which consists of all addresses that begin with 150.150.4.0, sits on the Ethernet at the bottom of the figure. The figure shows the advertisement of routes for subnet 150.150.4.0 from bottom to top, as described in detail following the figure.

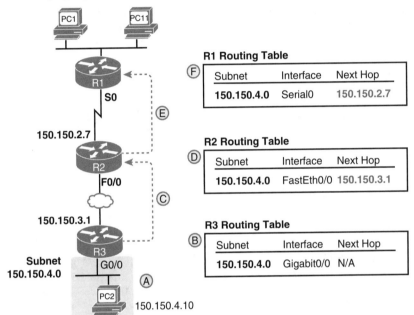

Figure 3-13   *Example of How Routing Protocols Advertise About Networks and Subnets*

Follow items A through F shown in the figure to see how each router learns its route to 150.150.4.0.

Step A.   Subnet 150.150.4.0 exists as a subnet at the bottom of the figure, connected to Router R3.

Step B.   R3 adds a connected route for 150.150.4.0 to its IP routing table; this happens without help from the routing protocol.

Step C.   R3 sends a routing protocol message, called a *routing update*, to R2, causing R2 to learn about subnet 150.150.4.0.

Step D.   R2 adds a route for subnet 150.150.4.0 to its routing table.

Step E.   R2 sends a similar routing update to R1, causing R1 to learn about subnet 150.150.4.0.

Step F.   R1 adds a route for subnet 150.150.4.0 to its routing table. The route lists R1's own Serial0 as the outgoing interface and R2 as the next-hop router IP address (150.150.2.7).

Other Network Layer Features

The TCP/IP network layer defines many functions beyond IP. Sure, IP plays a huge role in networking today, defining IP addressing and IP routing. However, other protocols and standards, defined in other Requests For Comments (RFC), play an important role for network layer functions as well. For example, routing protocols like Open Shortest Path First (OSPF) exist as separate protocols, defined in separate RFCs.

This last short section of the chapter introduces three other network layer features that should be helpful to you when reading through the rest of this book. These last three topics just help fill in a few holes, helping to give you some perspective and helping you make sense of later discussions as well. The three topics are

- Domain Name System (DNS)

- Address Resolution Protocol (ARP)

- Ping

Using Names and the Domain Name System

Can you imagine a world in which every time you used an application, you had to refer to it by IP address? Instead of using easy names like google.com or cisco.com, you would have to remember and type IP addresses, like 64.233.177.100. (At press time, 64.233.177.100 was an address used by Google, and you could reach Google's website by typing that address in a browser.) Certainly, asking users to remember IP addresses would not be user friendly and could drive some people away from using computers at all.

Thankfully, TCP/IP defines a way to use **hostnames** to identify other computers. The user either never thinks about the other computer or refers to the other computer by name. Then, protocols dynamically discover all the necessary information to allow communications based on that name.

For example, when you open a web browser and type in the hostname **www.google.com**, your computer does not send an IP packet with destination IP address www.google.com; it sends an IP packet to an IP address used by the web server for Google. TCP/IP needs a way to let a computer find the IP address used by the listed hostname, and that method uses the Domain Name System (**DNS**).

Enterprises use the DNS process to resolve names into the matching IP address, as shown in the example in Figure 3-14. In this case, PC11, on the left, needs to connect to a server named Server1. At some point, the user either types in the name Server1 or some application on PC11 refers to that server by name. At Step 1, PC11 sends a DNS message—a DNS query—to the DNS server. At Step 2, the DNS server sends back a DNS reply that lists Server1's IP address. At Step 3, PC11 can now send an IP packet to destination address 10.1.2.3, the address used by Server1.

Note that the example in Figure 3-14 shows a cloud for the TCP/IP network because the details of the network, including routers, do not matter to the name resolution process. Routers treat the DNS messages just like any other IP packet, routing them based on the destination IP address. For example, at Step 1 in the figure, the DNS query will list the DNS server's IP address as the destination address, which any routers will use to forward the packet.

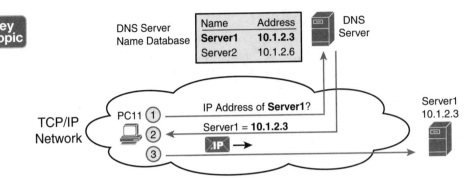

Figure 3-14   *Basic DNS Name Resolution Request*

Finally, DNS defines much more than just a few messages. DNS defines protocols, as well as standards for the text names used throughout the world, and a worldwide set of distributed DNS servers. The domain names that people use every day when web browsing, which look like www.example.com, follow the DNS naming standards. Also, no single DNS server knows all the names and matching IP addresses, but the information is distributed across many DNS servers. So, the DNS servers of the world work together, forwarding queries to each other, until the server that knows the answer supplies the desired IP address information.

The Address Resolution Protocol

As discussed in depth throughout this chapter, IP routing logic requires that hosts and routers encapsulate IP packets inside data-link layer frames. For Ethernet interfaces, how does a router know what MAC address to use for the destination? It uses **ARP**.

On Ethernet LANs, whenever a host or router needs to encapsulate an IP packet in a new Ethernet frame, the host or router knows all the important facts to build that header—except for the destination MAC address. The host knows the IP address of the next device, either another host IP address or the default router IP address. A router knows the IP route used for forwarding the IP packet, which lists the next router's IP address. However, the hosts and routers do not know those neighboring devices' MAC addresses beforehand.

TCP/IP defines the Address Resolution Protocol (ARP) as the method by which any host or router on a LAN can dynamically learn the MAC address of another IP host or router on the same LAN. ARP defines a protocol that includes the *ARP Request*, which is a message that makes the simple request "if this is your IP address, please reply with your MAC address." ARP also defines the *ARP Reply* message, which indeed lists both the original IP address and the matching MAC address.

Figure 3-15 shows an example that uses the same router and host from the bottom part of the earlier Figure 3-13. The figure shows the ARP Request sent by router R3, on the left of the figure, as a LAN broadcast. All devices on the LAN will then process the received frame. On the right, at Step 2, host PC2 sends back an ARP Reply, identifying PC2's MAC address. The text beside each message shows the contents inside the ARP message itself, which lets PC2 learn R3's IP address and matching MAC address, and R3 learn PC2's IP address and matching MAC address.

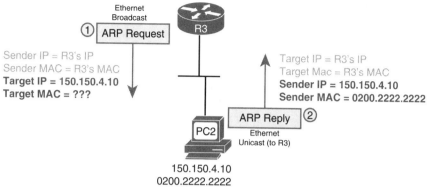

Figure 3-15   *Sample ARP Process*

Note that hosts and routers remember the ARP results, keeping the information in their *ARP cache* or *ARP table*. A host or router only needs to use ARP occasionally, to build the ARP cache the first time. Each time a host or router needs to send a packet encapsulated in an Ethernet frame, it first checks its ARP cache for the correct IP address and matching MAC address. Hosts and routers will let ARP cache entries time out to clean up the table, so occasional ARP Requests can be seen.

NOTE   You can see the contents of the ARP cache on most PC operating systems by using the **arp -a** command from a command prompt.

ICMP Echo and the ping Command

After you have implemented a TCP/IP internetwork, you need a way to test basic IP connectivity without relying on any applications to be working. The primary tool for testing basic network connectivity is the **ping** command.

Ping uses the Internet Control Message Protocol (ICMP), sending a message called an *ICMP echo request* to another IP address. The computer with that IP address should reply with an *ICMP echo reply*. If that works, you successfully have tested the IP network. In other words, you know that the network can deliver a packet from one host to the other and back. ICMP does not rely on any application, so it really just tests basic IP connectivity— Layers 1, 2, and 3 of the OSI model. Figure 3-16 outlines the basic process.

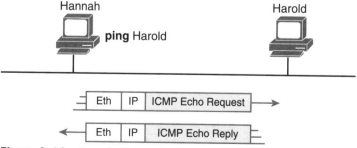

Figure 3-16   *Sample Network, ping Command*

Note that while the **ping** command uses ICMP, ICMP does much more. ICMP defines many messages that devices can use to help manage and control the IP network.

Chapter Review

The "Your Study Plan" element, just before Chapter 1, discusses how you should study and practice the content and skills for each chapter before moving on to the next chapter. That element introduces the tools used here at the end of each chapter. If you haven't already done so, take a few minutes to read that section. Then come back here and do the useful work of reviewing the chapter to help lock into memory what you just read.

Review this chapter's material using either the tools in the book or interactive tools for the same material found on the book's companion website. Table 3-4 outlines the key review elements and where you can find them. To better track your study progress, record when you completed these activities in the second column.

Table 3-4   Chapter Review Tracking

Review Element	Review Date(s)	Resource Used
Review key topics		Book, website
Review key terms		Book, website
Answer DIKTA questions		Book, PTP
Review memory tables		Book, website

Review All the Key Topics

Table 3-5   Key Topics for Chapter 3

Key Topic Element	Description	Page Number
Figure 3-6	Router de-encapsulation and re-encapsulation	68
Figure 3-7	Ethernet WAN—physical connections	69
List	Common terms to describe an Ethernet WAN link	70
List	Four-step process of how routers route (forward) packets	74
Figure 3-11	IP Routing and Encapsulation	74
List	Two statements about how IP expects IP addresses to be grouped into networks or subnets	76
List	Three-step process of how routing protocols learn routes	77
Figure 3-13	IP Routing Protocol Basic Process	78
Figure 3-14	Example that shows the purpose and process of DNS name resolution	80
Figure 3-15	Example of the purpose and process of ARP	81

Key Terms You Should Know

ARP, default router (default gateway), DNS, Ethernet Line Service (E-Line), Ethernet WAN, HDLC, hostname, IP address, IP network, IP packet, IP subnet, leased line, ping, routing protocol, routing table, serial interface, subnetting, telco, wide-area network (WAN)

Part I Review

Keep track of your part review progress with the checklist shown in Table P1-1. Details on each task follow the table.

Table P1-1 Part I Review Checklist

Activity	1st Date Completed	2nd Date Completed
Repeat All DIKTA Questions		
Answer Part Review Questions		
Review Key Topics		
Chapter Review Interactive Elements		

Repeat All DIKTA Questions

For this task, answer the "Do I Know This Already?" questions again for the chapters in this part of the book, using the PTP software. Refer to the Introduction to this book, the section titled "How to View Only DIKTA Questions by Chapter or Part," for help with how to make the PTP software show you DIKTA questions for this part only.

Answer Part Review Questions

For this task, answer the Part Review questions for this part of the book, using the PTP software. Refer to the Introduction to this book, the section titled "How to View Part Review Questions," for help with how to make the PTP software show you Part Review questions for this part only. (Note that if you use the questions but then want even more, get the Premium Edition of the book, as detailed in the Introduction, in the section "Other Features," under the item labeled "eBook.")

Review Key Topics

Browse back through the chapters and look for the Key Topic icons. If you do not remember some details, take the time to reread those topics, or use the Key Topics application(s) found on the companion website.

Take the time to find the companion website for this book and bookmark that page as detailed in the Introduction section titled "Bookmark the Companion Website," in the Your Study Plan section just before Chapter 1.

Use Per-Chapter Interactive Review Elements

Using the companion website, browse through the interactive review elements, like memory tables and key term flashcards, to review the content from each chapter.

Part I provided a broad look at the fundamentals of all parts of networking, focusing on Ethernet LANs, WANs, and IP routing. Parts II and III now drill into depth about the details of Ethernet, which was introduced in Chapter 2, "Fundamentals of Ethernet LANs."

Part II begins that journey by discussing the basics of building a small Ethernet LAN with Cisco Catalyst switches. The journey begins by showing how to access the user interface of a Cisco switch so that you can see evidence of what the switch is doing and to configure the switch to act in the ways you want it to act. At this point, you should start using whatever lab practice option you chose in the "Your Study Plan" section that preceded Chapter 1, "Introduction to TCP/IP Networking." (And if you have not yet finalized your plan for how to practice your hands-on skills, now is the time.)

After you complete Chapter 4 and see how to get into the command-line interface (CLI) of a switch, the next three chapters step through some important foundations of how to implement LANs—foundations used by every company that builds LANs with Cisco gear. Chapter 5 takes a close look at Ethernet switching—that is, the logic used by a switch—and how to know what a particular switch is doing. Chapter 6 shows the ways to configure a switch for remote access with Telnet and Secure Shell (SSH), along with a variety of other useful commands that will help you when you work with any real lab gear, simulator, or any other practice tools. Chapter 7, the final chapter in Part II, shows how to configure and verify the operation of switch interfaces for several important features, including speed, duplex, and autonegotiation.

Part II

Implementing Ethernet LANs

CHAPTER 4

Using the Command-Line Interface

This chapter covers the following exam topics:

2.0 Network Access

2.8 Describe network device management access (Telnet, SSH, HTTP, HTTPS, console, TACACS+/RADIUS, and cloud managed)

The CCNA exam focuses on skills like understanding how LANs work, configuring different switch features, verifying that those features work correctly, and finding the root cause of the problem when a feature is not working correctly. Before doing the more important work, you must first learn how to access and use the user interface of the switch, called the **command-line interface (CLI)**.

This chapter begins that process by showing the basics of how to access the switch's CLI. These skills include how to access the CLI and how to issue verification commands to check on the status of the LAN. This chapter also includes the processes of how to configure the switch and how to save that configuration.

Note that this chapter focuses on processes that provide a foundation for the exam topics which include the verbs *identify*, *configure*, or *verify*. Most of the rest of the chapters in Parts II and III of this book then go on to include details of the particular commands you can use to verify and configure different switch features.

"Do I Know This Already?" Quiz

Take the quiz (either here or use the PTP software) if you want to use the score to help you decide how much time to spend on this chapter. The letter answers are listed at the bottom of the page following the quiz. Appendix C, found both at the end of the book as well as on the companion website, includes both the answers and explanations. You can also find both answers and explanations in the PTP testing software.

Table 4-1 "Do I Know This Already?" Foundation Topics Section-to-Question Mapping

Foundation Topics Section	Questions
Accessing the Cisco Catalyst Switch CLI	1–3
Configuring Cisco IOS Software	4–6

1. In what modes can you type the command **show mac address-table** and expect to get a response with MAC table entries? (Choose two answers.)

   a. User mode

   b. Enable mode

   c. Global configuration mode

   d. Interface configuration mode

2. In which of the following modes of the CLI could you type the command **reload** and expect the switch to reboot?

   a. User mode

   b. Enable mode

   c. Global configuration mode

   d. Interface configuration mode

3. Which of the following is a difference between Telnet and SSH as supported by a Cisco switch?

   a. SSH encrypts the passwords used at login, but not other traffic; Telnet encrypts nothing.

   b. SSH encrypts all data exchange, including login passwords; Telnet encrypts nothing.

   c. Telnet is used from Microsoft operating systems, and SSH is used from UNIX and Linux operating systems.

   d. Telnet encrypts only password exchanges; SSH encrypts all data exchanges.

4. What type of switch memory is used to store the configuration used by the switch when it is up and working?

   a. RAM

   b. ROM

   c. Flash

   d. NVRAM

   e. Bubble

5. What command copies the configuration from RAM into NVRAM?

   a. copy running-config tftp

   b. copy tftp running-config

   c. copy running-config start-up-config

   d. copy start-up-config running-config

   e. copy startup-config running-config

   f. copy running-config startup-config

6. A switch user is currently in console line configuration mode. Which of the following would place the user in enable mode? (Choose two answers.)

   a. Using the **exit** command once

   b. Using the **end** command once

   c. Pressing the Ctrl+Z key sequence once

   d. Using the **quit** command

Foundation Topics

Accessing the Cisco Catalyst Switch CLI

Cisco uses the concept of a command-line interface (CLI) with its router and LAN switch products. The CLI is a text-based interface in which the user, typically a network engineer, enters a text command and presses Enter. Pressing Enter sends the command to the switch, which tells the device to do something. The switch does what the command says, and in some cases, the switch replies with some messages stating the results of the command.

Cisco Catalyst switches also support other methods to both monitor and configure a switch. For example, a switch can provide a web interface so that an engineer can open a web browser to connect to a web server running in the switch. Switches also can be controlled and operated using network management software.

This book discusses only Cisco Catalyst enterprise-class switches, and in particular, how to use the Cisco CLI to monitor and control these switches. This first major section of the chapter first examines these Catalyst switches in more detail and then explains how a network engineer can get access to the CLI to issue commands.

Cisco Catalyst Switches

When I was updating this chapter for expected publication in the year 2023, Cisco LAN switches fell into three product families:

- **Cisco Catalyst switches,** which serve as typical enterprise switches for use throughout an enterprise.

- **Cisco Nexus switches,** which Cisco designs for use in data centers. In comparison to Catalyst switches, Nexus switches support faster ports and more high-speed ports on a single switch, plus other features optimized for data centers.

- **Cisco Meraki switches,** built for enterprises, meet a need for LAN switches (and other network devices) that use a simple, cloud-based management portal that provides easy onboarding of new devices.

Throughout its history, when the CCNA exam mentions *switches*, it refers to Cisco Catalyst switches, and not to Nexus or Meraki switches.

Within the Cisco Catalyst brand of LAN switches, Cisco produces a wide variety of switch series or families. Each switch series includes several specific models of switches that have similar features, similar price-versus-performance tradeoffs, and similar internal components.

For example, when I was writing the latest version of this chapter, Cisco offered the Cisco Catalyst 9000 switch family as its primary Enterprise switch family. That family includes series that go by numbers like 9200, 9300, 9400, and so on, with specific models within each series. For instance, Cisco positions the 9200 and 9300 series of switches as full-featured access layer switches for enterprises.

Answers to the "Do I Know This Already?" quiz:

1 A, B **2** B **3** B **4** A **5** F **6** B, C

Figure 4-1 shows two models of 9200 switches. The lower switch in the figure has 48 fixed RJ-45 unshielded twisted-pair (UTP) 10/100/1000 ports, meaning that these ports can auto-negotiate the use of 10BASE-T (10 Mbps), 100BASE-T (100 Mbps), or 1000BASE-T (1 Gbps) Ethernet. The upper switch has 24 such ports.

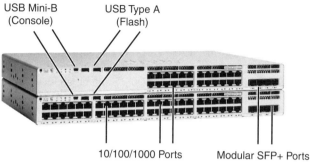

USB Mini-B (Console)
USB Type A (Flash)
10/100/1000 Ports
Modular SFP+ Ports

Figure 4-1 *Cisco Catalyst 9200L Switch Models, Front View*

Cisco refers to a switch's physical connectors as either *interfaces* or *ports*, with an interface type and interface number. Switches use interface types such as Ethernet, FastEthernet, GigabitEthernet, TenGigabit, and so on for faster speeds. For Ethernet interfaces that support running at multiple speeds, the switch uses the interface type of the fastest supported speed. For example, the switch refers to a 10/100/1000 interface (that is, an interface that runs at 10 Mbps, 100 Mbps, or 1000 Mbps) as a GigabitEthernet port, no matter the current speed used on the interface.

LAN switches also use a numeric interface identifier (interface ID) to identify the specific port. Interface IDs can use one, two, or three digits, with the digits separated by a slash, as chosen by Cisco when they designed the switch. For instance, Cisco Catalyst 9000 switches typically use three-digit identifiers like GigabitEthernet 1/0/1 and GigabitEthernet 1/0/2. Table 4-2 lists a few examples of interface identifiers and abbreviations for those identifiers based on the speeds supported by an interface.

Table 4-2   LAN Switch Interface ID Examples with Abbreviations

Speeds Supported	Common Name	Example Switch Interface ID	Valid Abbreviations
10 Mbps	Ethernet	Ethernet0/0	E0/0, Et0/0, Eth0/0
10/100 Mbps	10/100	FastEthernet 0/1	F0/1, Fa0/1
10/100/1000 Mbps	10/100/1000	GigabitEthernet 1/0/1	G1/0/1, Gi1/0/1
1G/2.5G/5G/10G	Multigig	TenGigabit 1/0/2	T1/0/2, Te1/0/2

Accessing the Cisco IOS XE CLI

The operating system (OS) in Catalyst switches creates a human-focused interface in which you can type commands and see lines of text in response. The next topic introduces that interface, called the command-line interface (CLI), but first the text gives a few background details about the operating system itself.

The Operating System in Cisco Catalyst Switches

Initially in its history, Cisco switches used an OS called CatOS, short for Catalyst OS. Cisco did not develop its first switch family, instead purchasing a company (Crescendo Communications) in 1993—a company that had named its switch family "Catalyst," with the OS called CatOS.

When Cisco first got into the LAN switch business, Cisco routers used an OS written by Cisco, called Internetwork Operating System (**IOS**)—not IOS XE, simply IOS. Unsurprisingly, the router IOS CLI in Cisco routers worked differently than the switch CatOS CLI produced by the vendor that Cisco bought. Over time, Cisco created a switch OS based on IOS, so, mostly in the 1990s and 2000s, when Cisco released a new switch product family, it used IOS for Catalyst switches instead of CatOS. By moving its switches to use IOS, eventually all Cisco enterprise-class routers and switches used the same IOS CLI, making them easier to manage for networkers. Figure 4-2 depicts the migration timeline in general terms.

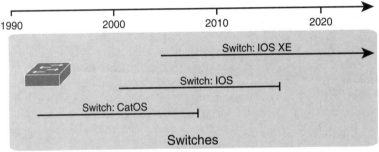

Figure 4-2 *Cisco Catalyst Operating System Long-Term Migration*

Cisco made yet another migration to a different OS for Catalyst switches, this time to use **IOS XE**. To create IOS XE, Cisco took IOS and modernized the internal software architecture. IOS XE, often referred to simply as XE, has features to improve uptime and the ability to maintain devices without requiring rebooting (reloading) the device. But it keeps the same familiar CLI; in fact, if you learned the CLI using a device running IOS, you might not even notice when later using a device running IOS XE.

For the purposes of CCNA, almost everything you see with commands and the CLI applies to older IOS-based switches as well as newer switches that use IOS XE. However, when a difference exists, the text will point out the difference.

> **NOTE** The book refers to IOS and IOS XE with the common term *IOS*, unless the need exists to differentiate between the two.

Accessing the IOS XE CLI

Cisco IOS Software for Catalyst switches implements and controls logic and functions performed by a Cisco switch. Besides controlling the switch's performance and behavior, Cisco IOS also defines an interface for humans called the CLI. The Cisco IOS CLI allows the user to use a terminal emulation program, which accepts text entered by the user. When the user presses Enter, the terminal emulator sends that text to the switch. The switch processes the text as if it is a command, does what the command says, and sends text back to the terminal emulator.

The switch CLI can be accessed through three popular methods: the console, **Telnet**, and **Secure Shell (SSH)**. Two of these methods (Telnet and SSH) use the IP network in which the switch resides to reach the switch. The console is a physical port built specifically to allow access to the CLI. Figure 4-3 depicts the options.

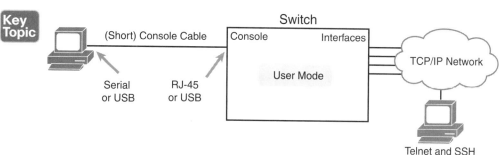

Figure 4-3 *CLI Access Options*

Console access requires both a physical connection between a PC (or other user device) and the switch's console port, as well as some software on the PC. Telnet and SSH require software on the user's device, but they rely on the existing TCP/IP network to transmit data. The next few pages detail how to connect the console and set up the software for each method to access the CLI.

Cabling the Console Connection

The physical console connection, both old and new, uses three main components: the physical console port on the switch, a physical serial port on the PC, and a cable that works with the console and serial ports. However, the physical cabling details have changed slowly over time, mainly because of advances and changes with serial interfaces on PC hardware. For this next topic, the text looks at three cases: newer connectors on both the PC and the switch, older connectors on both, and a third case with the newer (USB) connector on the PC but with an older connector on the switch.

Most PCs today use a familiar standard USB connector for the console connection. Cisco has been including USB console ports in new router and switch models for well over a decade. All you have to do is look at the switch to make sure you have the correct style of USB connector to match the USB console port (often a USB mini-B connector.) In the simplest form, you can use any USB port on the PC, with a USB cable, connected to the USB console port on the switch or router, as shown on the far-right side of Figure 4-4.

The case on the far left in the figure shows an older console connection, typical of how you would have connected to a switch over ten years ago. Before PCs used USB ports, they used serial ports for serial communications. The PC serial port had a D-shell connector (roughly rectangular) with nine pins (often called a DB-9). The console port looks like any Ethernet RJ-45 port (but is typically colored in blue and with the word *console* beside it on the switch). The older-style cabling used a standard RJ-45 to DB-9 converter plug and a UTP **rollover cable** with RJ-45 connectors on each end. The rollover pinout uses eight wires, rolling the wire at pin 1 to pin 8, pin 2 to pin 7, pin 3 to pin 6, and so on.

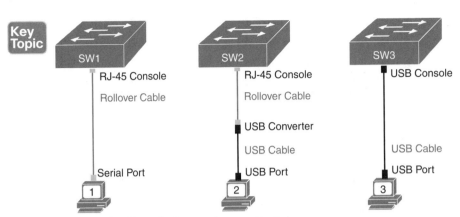

Figure 4-4   *Console Connection to a Switch*

The center case in the figure shows a variation that you might use on occasion that combines the cabling concepts from the left and right cases in the figure. You use the USB port on your PC but the RJ-45 console port on the switch. In fact, for some very old switch models, the switch has only an RJ-45 console port but no USB console port, requiring this kind of console cabling. In this case, you need a USB converter plug that converts from the older rollover console cable (with RJ-45 connectors) to a USB connector, as shown in the middle of Figure 4-4.

NOTE   When using the USB options, you typically also need to install a software driver so that your PC's OS knows that the device on the other end of the USB connection is the console of a Cisco device. Also, you can easily find photos of these cables and components online, with searches like "cisco console cable," "cisco usb console cable," or "console cable converter."

Figure 4-5 shows a Cisco 9200L switch, rear view, which shows the RJ-45 console connector. The 9200L locates the USB console port (a mini-B USB port) on the front panel, as seen earlier in Figure 4-1.

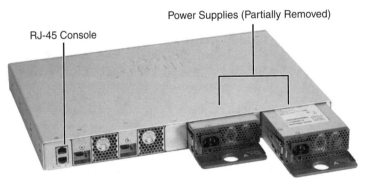

Figure 4-5   *Cisco Catalyst 9200L Switch, Rear View*

Configuring a Terminal Emulator

After the PC is physically connected to the console port, a terminal emulator software package must be installed and configured on the PC. The terminal emulator software treats all data as text. It accepts the text typed by the user and sends it over the console connection to the switch. Similarly, any bits coming into the PC over the console connection are displayed as text for the user to read.

The emulator must be configured to use the PC's serial port to match the settings on the switch's console port settings. The default console port settings on a switch are as follows. Note that the last three parameters are referred to collectively as 8N1:

- 9600 bits/second

- No hardware flow control

- 8-bit ASCII

- No parity bits

- 1 stop bit

Figure 4-6 shows one such terminal emulator. The image shows the window created by the emulator software in the background, with some output of a **show** command. The foreground, in the upper right, shows a settings window that lists the default console settings as listed just before this paragraph.

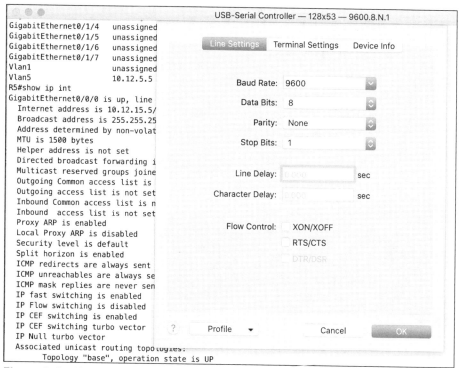

Figure 4-6   *Terminal Settings for Console Access*

Accessing the CLI with Telnet and SSH

For many years, terminal emulator applications have supported far more than the ability to communicate over a USB (or serial) port to a local device (like a switch's console). Terminal emulators support a variety of TCP/IP applications as well, including Telnet and SSH. Telnet and SSH both allow the user to connect to another device's CLI, but instead of connecting through a console cable to the console port, the traffic flows over the same IP network that the networking devices are helping to create.

Telnet uses the concept of a Telnet client (the terminal application) and a Telnet server (the switch in this case). A *Telnet client*, the device that sits in front of the user, accepts keyboard input and sends those commands to the *Telnet server*. The Telnet server accepts the text, interprets the text as a command, and replies back.

Cisco Catalyst switches enable a Telnet server by default, but switches need a few more configuration settings before you can successfully use Telnet to connect to a switch. Chapter 6, "Configuring Basic Switch Management," covers switch configuration to support Telnet and SSH in detail.

Using Telnet in a lab today makes sense, but Telnet poses a significant security risk in production networks. Telnet sends all data (including any username and password for login to the switch) as clear-text data. SSH gives us a much better option.

Think of SSH as the much more secure Telnet cousin. Outwardly, you still open a terminal emulator, connect to the switch's IP address, and see the switch CLI, no matter whether you use Telnet or SSH. The differences exist behind the scenes: SSH encrypts the contents of all messages, including the passwords, avoiding the possibility of someone capturing packets in the network and stealing the password to network devices.

User and Enable (Privileged) Modes

All three CLI access methods covered so far (console, Telnet, and SSH) place the user in an area of the CLI called *user EXEC mode*. User EXEC mode, sometimes also called **user mode**, allows the user to look around but not break anything. The "EXEC mode" part of the name refers to the fact that in this mode, when you enter a command, the switch executes the command and then displays messages that describe the command's results.

> **NOTE**   If you have not used the CLI before, you might want to experiment with the CLI from the Sim Lite product. You can find this resource on the companion website as mentioned in the Introduction.

Cisco IOS supports a more powerful EXEC mode called *privileged* mode (also known as **enable mode**). The formal name, *privileged mode*, refers to the fact that IOS allows powerful (or privileged) commands from that mode. Informally, engineers refer to the mode as *enable mode* because of the **enable** EXEC command, which moves the user from user mode to enable mode, as shown in Figure 4-7. For example, you can use the **reload** command, which tells the switch to reinitialize or reboot Cisco IOS, only from privileged mode.

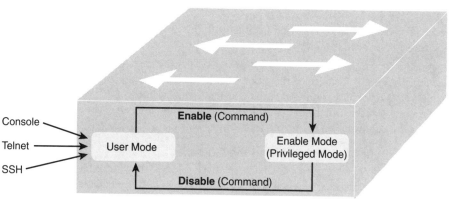

Figure 4-7 *User and Privileged Modes*

NOTE   If the command prompt ends with a >, the user is in user mode; if it ends with a #, the user is in enable mode.

Example 4-1 demonstrates the differences between user and enable modes. The example shows the output that you could see in a terminal emulator window, for instance, when connecting from the console. In this case, the user sits at the user mode prompt ("Certskills1>") and tries the **reload** command. The **reload** command tells the switch to reinitialize or reboot Cisco IOS, so IOS allows this powerful command to be used only from enable mode. IOS rejects the **reload** command from user mode. Then the user moves to privileged (enable) mode using the **enable** EXEC command. At that point, IOS accepts the **reload** command now that the user is in enable mode.

Example 4-1   *Example of Privileged Mode Commands Being Rejected in User Mode*

```
Press RETURN to get started.


User Access Verification


Password:
Certskills1>
Certskills1> reload
Translating "reload"
% Unknown command or computer name, or unable to find computer address
Certskills1> enable
Password:
Certskills1#
Certskills1# reload

Proceed with reload? [confirm] y
00:08:42: %SYS-5-RELOAD: Reload requested by console. Reload Reason: Reload Command.
```

NOTE   The commands that can be used in either user (EXEC) mode or enable (EXEC) mode are called EXEC commands.

This example is the first instance of this book showing you the output from the CLI, so it is worth noting a few conventions. The bold text represents what the user typed, and the nonbold text is what the switch sent back to the terminal emulator. Also, the typed passwords do not show up on the screen for security purposes.

Password Security for CLI Access from the Console

A Cisco switch, with default settings, remains relatively secure when locked inside a wiring closet, because by default, a switch allows console access only. By default, the console requires no password at all, and no password to reach enable mode for users that happened to connect from the console. The reason is that if you have access to the physical console port of the switch, you already have pretty much complete control over the switch. You could literally get out your screwdriver, remove the switch from the rack, and walk off with it, or you could unplug the power, or follow well-published procedures to go through password recovery to break into the CLI and then configure anything you want to configure.

However, many people use simple password protection for console users. Simple passwords can be configured at two points in the login process from the console: when the user connects from the console, and when any user moves to enable mode (using the **enable** EXEC command). You may have noticed that back in Example 4-1, the user saw a password prompt at both points.

Example 4-2 shows the additional configuration commands that were configured prior to collecting the output in Example 4-1. The output holds an excerpt from the EXEC command **show running-config**, which lists the current configuration in the switch.

Example 4-2   *Nondefault Basic Configuration*

```
Certskills1# show running-config
! Output has been formatted to show only the parts relevant to this discussion
hostname Certskills1
!
enable secret love
!
line console 0
 login

password faith
! The rest of the output has been omitted
Certskills1#
```

Working from top to bottom, note that the first configuration command listed by the **show running-config** command sets the switch's hostname to Certskills1. The switch uses the hostname to begin the command prompt.

Next, note that the lines with a ! in them are comment lines, both in the text of this book and in the real switch CLI.

The **enable secret love** configuration command defines the password that all users must use to reach enable mode. So, no matter whether users connect from the console, Telnet, or SSH, they would use the password love when prompted for a password after typing the **enable** EXEC command.

Finally, the last three lines configure the console password. The first line (**line console 0**) is the command that identifies the console, basically meaning "these next commands apply to the console only." The **login** command tells IOS to perform simple password checking (at the console). Remember, by default, the switch does not ask for a password for console users. Finally, the **password faith** command defines the password the console user must type when prompted.

This example just scratches the surface of the kinds of security configuration you might choose to configure on a switch, but it does give you enough detail to configure switches in your lab and get started (which is the reason I put these details in this first chapter of Part II). Note that Chapter 6 shows the configuration steps to add support for Telnet and SSH (including password security), and Chapter 9 of the *CCNA 200-301 Official Cert Guide, Volume 2*, Second Edition, "Securing Network Devices," shows additional security configuration as well.

Accessing the CLI with the WebUI

Engineers use SSH to access the network device CLI as a routine part of their daily work. Cisco also provides a graphical interface to manage individual Cisco switches and routers, referred to as the device's HTTP server or, in later years, as the WebUI (Web User Interface). Once configured, an engineer can use any web browser to connect to the IP address of the switch or router, supply the correct login information, and see web pages that allow management of that single device. That web interface also includes a method to access the CLI.

First, Figures 4-8 and 4-9 show a couple of example pages of the graphical interface. Figure 4-8 shows a screenshot of the web server dashboard's Switch View. This page shows an image representing the side of the switch, with all switch ports shown and colored lights representing the same status colors you would see on the physical switch.

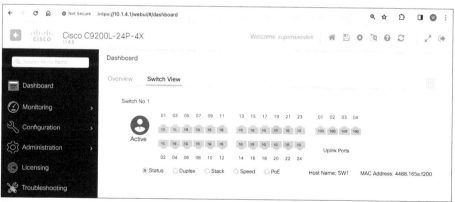

Figure 4-8   *Cisco Switch Web Interface Dashboard: Switch View*

NOTE   The examples in this section come from a Cisco Catalyst 9200L switch running IOS XE Version 17.6.3, visible in the upper left of the screenshot in Figure 4-8. However, the specifics of the user interface and available options in the left-side menus vary across device types, models, and IOS versions. So, use the figures in this section only to get a general idea of the functions of this tool.

The WebUI supports direct configuration and verification options that do not require knowledge of the CLI. For example, Figure 4-9 shows a screenshot with the user's mouse hovering over the word "Configuration" in the left menu, causing the page to reveal various configuration options. Earlier, the user had chosen the STP option, so the background in the screenshot shows a partial view of the Spanning Tree Protocol (STP) configuration screen. So, you could point and click through the user interface to configure some of the options covered for CCNA.

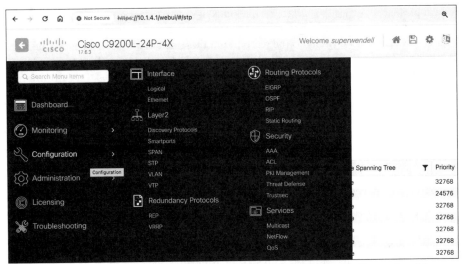

Figure 4-9 *Configuration Options in the Switch Web Server Configuration Menu*

If you have a Cisco switch or router available, you should take the time to use the WebUI and look around at some of the configuration and verification options. Again, be aware that your device might show different layouts and options versus the screenshots shown here.

The more recent versions of the WebUI provide access to the CLI without your device needing to have an SSH or Telnet client installed, as seen in Figure 4-10. Once you navigate to the correct page (**Administration > Command Line Interface**), you type the CLI command into the upper box, click a button to send it to the device, and the response messages appear in the lower box. The figure shows the output of the **show interfaces status** command.

The WebUI can be pretty useful when you do not have any of your devices with you. If your devices with SSH clients installed are back at your desk and you need to log in to a few network devices, borrow any device with a web browser, and connect to routers and switches. Although the WebUI is useful, most engineers prefer using an SSH client when working in the CLI because the clients are much more usable. For instance, in Figure 4-10, note the poor column alignment of the command output. An SSH client would typically not have those kinds of alignment issues, which can make reading the output more difficult.

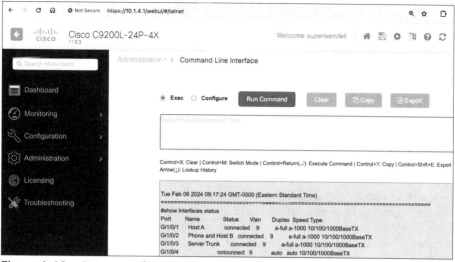

Figure 4-10   *CLI Access from the Switch Web Server Interface*

> **NOTE**   On a related note, vendors like Cisco also sell sophisticated stand-alone network management applications. These typically have graphical interfaces and comprehensive management for all available features and support all devices using one user interface. In comparison, the WebUI provides basic features on a per-device basis. You will learn more about one such application, Cisco Catalyst Center, in Chapter 22, "Cisco Software-Defined Access (Cisco SD-Access)," in the book *CCNA 200-301 Official Cert Guide, Volume 2, Second Edition.*

CLI Help Features

If you printed the Cisco IOS Command Reference documents, you would end up with a stack of paper several feet tall. No one should expect to memorize all the commands—and no one does. You can use several easy, convenient tools to help remember commands and save time typing. As you progress through your Cisco certifications, the exams will cover progressively more commands. However, you should know the methods of getting command help.

Table 4-3 summarizes command-recall help options available at the CLI. Note that, in the first column, *command* represents any command. Likewise, *parm* represents a command's parameter. For example, the third row lists *command* **?**, which means that commands such as **show ?** and **copy ?** would list help for the **show** and **copy** commands, respectively.

Table 4-3   Cisco IOS Software Command Help

What You Enter	What Help You Get
?	This option provides help for all commands available in this mode.
command ?	With a space between the command and the ?, the switch lists text to describe all the first parameter options for the command.
com?	This option lists commands that start with **com**.
command parm?	This option lists all parameters beginning with the **parameter typed so far**. (Notice that there is no space between *parm* and the ?.)

What You Enter	What Help You Get
command *parm<Tab>*	Pressing the Tab key causes IOS to spell out the rest of the word, assuming that you have typed enough of the word so there is only one option that begins with that string of characters.
command parm1 ?	If a space is inserted before the question mark, the CLI lists all the next parameters and gives a brief explanation of each.

When you enter the ?, the Cisco IOS CLI reacts immediately; that is, you don't need to press the Enter key or any other keys. The device running Cisco IOS also redisplays what you entered before the ? to save you some keystrokes. If you press Enter immediately after the ?, Cisco IOS tries to execute the command with only the parameters you have entered so far.

The information supplied by using help depends on the CLI mode. For example, when ? is entered in user mode, the commands allowed in user mode are displayed, but commands available only in enable mode (not in user mode) are not displayed. Also, help is available in **configuration mode**, which is the mode used to configure the switch. In fact, configuration mode has many different subconfiguration modes, as explained in the section "Configuration Submodes and Contexts," later in this chapter. So, you can get help for the commands available in each configuration submode as well. (Note that this might be a good time to use the free Sim Lite product on the companion website: to do so, open any lab, use the question mark, and try some commands.)

Cisco IOS stores the commands that you enter in a history buffer, storing ten commands by default. The CLI allows you to move backward and forward in the historical list of commands and then edit the command before reissuing it. These key sequences can help you use the CLI more quickly on the exams. Table 4-4 lists the commands used to manipulate previously entered commands.

Table 4-4   Key Sequences for Command Edit and Recall

Keyboard Command	What Happens
Up arrow or Ctrl+P	This keyboard command displays the most recently used command. If you press it again, the next most recent command appears, until the history buffer is exhausted. (The *P* stands for previous.)
Down arrow or Ctrl+N	If you have gone too far back into the history buffer, these keys take you forward to the more recently entered commands. (The *N* stands for next.)
Left arrow or Ctrl+B	This keyboard command moves the cursor backward in the currently displayed command without deleting characters. (The *B* stands for back.)
Right arrow or Ctrl+F	This keyboard command moves the cursor forward in the currently displayed command without deleting characters. (The *F* stands for forward.)
Backspace	This keyboard command moves the cursor backward in the currently displayed command, deleting characters.

The debug and show Commands

By far, the single most popular Cisco IOS command is the **show** command. The **show** command has a large variety of options, and with those options, you can find the status of almost every feature of Cisco IOS. Essentially, the **show** command lists the currently known facts about the switch's operational status.

For example, consider the output from the **show mac address-table dynamic** command listed in Example 4-3. This **show** command, issued from user mode, lists the table the switch uses to make forwarding decisions. A switch's MAC address table basically lists the data that a switch uses to do its primary job.

Example 4-3 *Example MAC Address Table*

```
Certskills1> show mac address-table dynamic
 Mac Address Table
-------------------------------------------


Vlan    Mac Address       Type        Ports
----    -----------       --------    -----
  31    0200.1111.1111    DYNAMIC     Gi0/1
  31    0200.3333.3333    DYNAMIC     Fa0/3
  31    1833.9d7b.0e9a    DYNAMIC     Gi0/1
  10    1833.9d7b.0e9a    DYNAMIC     Gi0/1
  10    30f7.0d29.8561    DYNAMIC     Gi0/1
   1    1833.9d7b.0e9a    DYNAMIC     Gi0/1
  12    1833.9d7b.0e9a    DYNAMIC     Gi0/1
Total Mac Addresses for this criterion: 7
Certskills1>
```

The **debug** command also tells the user details about the operation of the switch. However, while the **show** command lists status information at one instant of time—more like a photograph—the **debug** command acts more like a live video camera feed. Once you issue a **debug** command, IOS remembers, issuing messages over time as events continue to occur. Any switch user can choose to receive those messages, with the switch sending the messages to the console by default. Most of the commands used throughout this book to verify operation of switches and routers are **show** commands.

Configuring Cisco IOS Software

You will want to configure every switch in an Enterprise network, even though the switches will forward traffic even with default configuration. This section covers the basic configuration processes, including the concept of a configuration file and the locations in which the configuration files can be stored. Although this section focuses on the configuration process, and not on the configuration commands themselves, you should know all the commands covered in this chapter for the exams, in addition to the configuration processes.

Configuration mode accepts *configuration commands*—commands that tell the switch the details of what to do and how to do it. User and privileged modes accept EXEC commands, which return output, or possibly take an action like reloading the switch, but commands in these modes do not change any configuration settings. Figure 4-11 illustrates the navigation among configuration mode, user EXEC mode, and privileged EXEC mode.

Commands entered in configuration mode update the active configuration file. *These changes to the configuration occur immediately each time you press the Enter key at the end of a command.* Be careful when you enter a configuration command!

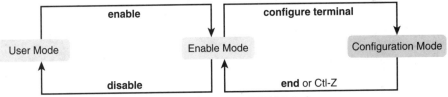

Figure 4-11   *CLI Configuration Mode Versus EXEC Modes*

Configuration Submodes and Contexts

Configuration mode supports a multitude of commands. To help organize the configuration, IOS groups some kinds of configuration commands together. To do that, when using configuration mode, you move from the initial mode—global configuration mode—into subcommand modes. *Context-setting commands* move you from one configuration subcommand mode, or context, to another. These context-setting commands tell the switch the topic about which you will enter the next few configuration commands. More importantly, the context tells the switch the topic you care about right now, so when you use the ? to get help, the switch gives you help about that topic only.

NOTE   *Context-setting* is not a Cisco term. It is just a description used here to help make sense of configuration mode.

The best way to learn about configuration submodes is to use them, but first, take a look at these upcoming examples. For instance, the **interface** command is one of the most commonly used context-setting configuration commands. For example, the CLI user could enter interface configuration mode by entering the **interface FastEthernet 0/1** configuration command. Asking for help in interface configuration mode displays only commands that are useful when configuring Ethernet interfaces. Commands used in this context are called *subcommands*—or, in this specific case, *interface subcommands*. When you begin practicing with the CLI using real equipment, the navigation between modes can become natural. For now, consider Example 4-4, which shows the following:

- Movement from enable mode to global configuration mode by using the **configure terminal** EXEC command.

- Use of a **hostname Fred** global configuration command to configure the switch's name. Using a global command from global configuration mode leaves you in global configuration mode.

- Movement from global configuration mode to console line configuration mode (using the **line console 0** command). The **line** command is another of the small set of context-setting commands that move you to another submode.

- Setting the console's simple password to **hope** (using the **password hope** line subcommand). Using a subcommand while in that submode leaves the command prompt in that submode.

- Movement from console configuration mode to interface configuration mode (using the **interface** *type number* command). The **interface** command is another of the small set of context-setting commands that move you to another submode.

- Setting the speed to 100 Mbps for interface Fa0/1 (using the **speed 100** interface subcommand).

- Movement from interface configuration mode back to global configuration mode (using the **exit** command).

Example 4-4 *Navigating Between Different Configuration Modes*

```
Switch# configure terminal
Switch(config)# hostname Fred
Fred(config)# line console 0
Fred(config-line)# password hope
Fred(config-line)# interface FastEthernet 0/1
Fred(config-if)# speed 100
Fred(config-if)# exit
Fred(config)#
```

The text inside parentheses in the command prompt identifies the configuration mode. For example, the first command prompt after you enter configuration mode lists (config), meaning global configuration mode. After the **line console 0** command, the text expands to (config-line), meaning line configuration mode. Each time the command prompt changes within config mode, you have moved to another configuration mode.

Table 4-5 shows the most common command prompts in configuration mode, the names of those modes, and the context-setting commands used to reach those modes.

Table 4-5 Common Switch Configuration Modes

Prompt	Name of Mode	Context-Setting Command(s) to Reach This Mode
hostname(config)#	Global	None—first mode after **configure terminal**
hostname(config-line)#	Line	**line console 0** **line vty 0 15**
hostname(config-if)#	Interface	**interface** *type number*
hostname(config-vlan)#	VLAN	**vlan** *number*

You should practice until you become comfortable moving between the different configuration modes, back to enable mode, and then back into the configuration modes. However, you can learn these skills just doing labs about the topics in later chapters of the book. For now, Figure 4-12 shows most of the navigation between global configuration mode and the four configuration submodes listed in Table 4-5.

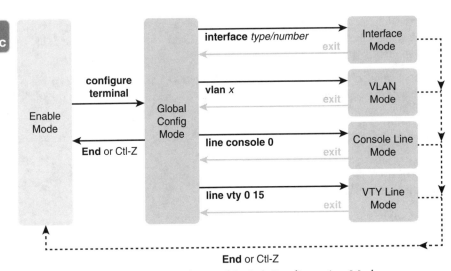

Figure 4-12 *Navigation In and Out of Switch Configuration Modes*

You really should stop and try navigating around these configuration modes. If you have not yet decided on a lab strategy, install the Pearson Sim Lite software from the companion website. It includes the simulator and a couple of lab exercises. Start any lab, ignore the instructions, and just get into configuration mode and move around between the configuration modes shown in Figure 4-12.

No set rules exist for what commands happen to be global commands or subcommands. Instead, you learn new commands, see whether they are global commands, or if subcommands, you also learn the required mode. But generally, Cisco uses global commands for settings that apply to the entire switch and subcommands that apply to one component or feature. For example:

The global command **hostname** sets the one hostname for the entire switch.

The interface subcommand **speed** configures a setting for a specific interface, so it works only in interface configuration submode.

Storing Switch Configuration Files

When you configure a switch, it needs to use the configuration. It also needs to be able to retain the configuration in case the switch loses power. Cisco switches contain random-access memory (RAM) to store data while Cisco IOS is using it, but RAM loses its contents when the switch loses power or is reloaded. To store information that must be retained when the switch loses power or is reloaded, Cisco switches use several types of more permanent memory, none of which has any moving parts. By avoiding components with moving parts (such as traditional disk drives), switches can maintain better uptime and availability.

The following list details the four main types of memory found in Cisco switches, as well as the most common use of each type:

■ **RAM:** Sometimes called DRAM, for dynamic random-access memory, RAM is used by the switch just as it is used by any other computer: for working storage. The running (active) configuration file is stored here.

■ **Flash memory:** Either a chip inside the switch or a removable memory card, flash memory stores fully functional Cisco IOS images and is the default location where the switch gets its Cisco IOS at boot time. Flash memory also can be used to store any other files, including backup copies of configuration files.

■ **ROM:** Read-only memory (ROM) stores a bootstrap (or boothelper) program that is loaded when the switch first powers on. This bootstrap program then finds the full Cisco IOS image and manages the process of loading Cisco IOS into RAM, at which point Cisco IOS takes over operation of the switch.

■ **NVRAM:** Nonvolatile RAM (NVRAM) stores the initial or startup configuration file that is used when the switch is first powered on and when the switch is reloaded.

Figure 4-13 summarizes this same information in a briefer and more convenient form for memorization and study.

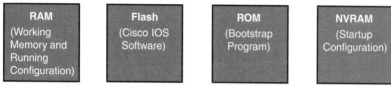

Figure 4-13 *Cisco Switch Memory Types*

Cisco IOS stores the collection of configuration commands in a *configuration file*. In fact, switches use multiple configuration files—one file for the initial configuration used when powering on, and another configuration file for the active, currently used running configuration as stored in RAM. Table 4-6 lists the names of these two files, their purpose, and their storage location.

Table 4-6   Names and Purposes of the Two Main Cisco IOS Configuration Files

Configuration Filename	Purpose	Where It Is Stored
startup-config	Stores the initial configuration used anytime the switch reloads Cisco IOS.	NVRAM
running-config	Stores the currently used configuration commands. This file changes dynamically when someone enters commands in configuration mode.	RAM

Essentially, when you use configuration mode, you change only the **running-config file**. This means that the configuration example earlier in this chapter (Example 4-4) updates only the running-config file. However, if the switch lost power right after that example, all that configuration would be lost. If you want to keep that configuration, you have to copy the running-config file into NVRAM, overwriting the old **startup-config file**.

Example 4-5 demonstrates that commands used in configuration mode change only the running configuration in RAM. The example shows the following concepts and steps:

Step 1. The example begins with both the running and startup-config having the same hostname, per the **hostname hannah** command.

Step 2. The hostname is changed in configuration mode using the **hostname harold** command.

Step 3. The **show running-config** and **show startup-config** commands show the fact that the hostnames are now different, with the **hostname harold** command found only in the running-config.

Example 4-5 *How Configuration Mode Commands Change the Running-Config File, Not the Startup-Config File*

```
! Step 1 next (two commands)
!
hannah# show running-config
! (lines omitted)
hostname hannah
! (rest of lines omitted)


hannah# show startup-config
! (lines omitted)
hostname hannah
! (rest of lines omitted)
! Step 2 next. Notice that the command prompt changes immediately after
! the hostname command.


hannah# configure terminal
hannah(config)# hostname harold
harold(config)# exit
! Step 3 next (two commands)
!
harold# show running-config
! (lines omitted) - just showing the part with the hostname command
hostname harold
!
harold# show startup-config
! (lines omitted) - just showing the part with the hostname command
hostname hannah
```

Copying and Erasing Configuration Files

The configuration process updates the running-config file, which is lost if the router loses power or is reloaded. Clearly, IOS needs to provide us a way to copy the running configuration so that it will not be lost, so it will be used the next time the switch reloads or powers on. For instance, Example 4-5 ended with a different running configuration (with the **hostname harold** command) versus the startup configuration.

In short, the EXEC command **copy running-config startup-config** backs up the running-config to the startup-config file. This command overwrites the current startup-config file with what is currently in the running-config file.

In addition, in the lab, you may want to just get rid of all existing configuration and start over with a clean configuration. To do that, you can erase the startup-config file using three different commands:

```
write erase
erase startup-config
erase nvram:
```

Once the startup-config file is erased, you can reload or power off/on the switch, and it will boot with the now-empty startup configuration.

Note that Cisco IOS does not have a command that erases the contents of the running-config file. To clear out the running-config file, simply erase the startup-config file, and then **reload** the switch, and the running-config will be empty at the end of the process.

NOTE   Cisco uses the term *reload* to refer to what most PC operating systems call rebooting or restarting. In each case, it is a re-initialization of the software. The **reload** EXEC command causes a switch to reload.

Chapter Review

One key to doing well on the exams is to perform repetitive spaced review sessions. Review this chapter's material using either the tools in the book or on the book's companion website. Refer to the "Your Study Plan" element section titled "Step 2: Build Your Study Habits Around the Chapter" for more details. Table 4-7 outlines the key review elements and where you can find them. To better track your study progress, record when you completed these activities in the second column.

Table 4-7   Chapter Review Tracking

Review Element	Review Date(s)	Resource Used
Review key topics		Book, website
Review key terms		Book, website
Answer DIKTA questions		Book, PTP
Review memory tables		Book, website
Review command tables		Book

Review All the Key Topics

Table 4-8   Key Topics for Chapter 4

Key Topic Element	Description	Page Number
Figure 4-3	Three methods to access a switch CLI	93
Figure 4-4	Cabling options for a console connection	94
List	A Cisco switch's default console port settings	95
Figure 4-11	Navigation between user, enable, and global config modes	104
Table 4-5	A list of configuration mode prompts, the name of the configuration mode, and the command used to reach each mode	105
Figure 4-12	Configuration mode context-setting commands	106
Table 4-6	The names and purposes of the two configuration files in a switch or router	107

Key Terms You Should Know

command-line interface (CLI), configuration mode, enable mode, IOS, IOS XE, rollover cable, running-config file, Secure Shell (SSH), startup-config file, Telnet, user mode

Command References

Tables 4-9 and 4-10 list configuration and verification commands used in this chapter, respectively. As an easy review exercise, cover the left column in a table, read the right column, and try to recall the command without looking. Then repeat the exercise, covering the right column, and try to recall what the command does.

Table 4-9   Chapter 4 Configuration Commands

Command	Mode and Purpose
line console 0	Global command that changes the context to console configuration mode.
login	Line (console and vty) configuration mode. Tells IOS to prompt for a password (no username).
password *pass-value*	Line (console and vty) configuration mode. Sets the password required on that line for login if the **login** command (with no other parameters) is also configured.
interface *type port-number*	Global command that changes the context to interface mode—for example, **interface FastEthernet 0/1**.
speed *value*	Interface subcommand that sets the Ethernet interface speed on interfaces that support multiple speeds.
hostname *name*	Global command that sets this switch's hostname, which is also used as the first part of the switch's command prompt.
exit	Command that moves back to the next higher mode in configuration mode.

Command	Mode and Purpose
end	Command that exits configuration mode and goes back to enable mode from any of the configuration submodes.
Ctrl+Z	This is not a command, but rather a two-key combination (pressing the Ctrl key and the letter Z) that together do the same thing as the **end** command.

Table 4-10   Chapter 4 EXEC Command Reference

Command	Purpose
no debug all undebug all	Privileged mode EXEC command to disable all currently enabled debugs.
reload	Privileged mode EXEC command that reboots the switch or router.
copy running-config startup-config	Privileged mode EXEC command that saves the active config, replacing the startup-config file used when the switch initializes.
copy startup-config running-config	Privileged mode EXEC command that merges the startup-config file with the currently active config file in RAM.
show running-config	Privileged mode EXEC command that lists the contents of the running-config file.
write erase erase startup-config erase nvram:	Privileged mode EXEC command that erases the startup-config file.
quit	EXEC command that disconnects the user from the CLI session.
show startup-config	Privileged mode EXEC command that lists the contents of the startup-config (initial config) file.
enable	User mode EXEC command that moves the user from user mode to enable (privileged) mode and prompts for a password if one is configured.
disable	Privileged mode EXEC command that moves the user from privileged mode to user mode.
configure terminal	Privileged mode EXEC command that moves the user into configuration mode.
show mac address-table	EXEC command that lists the contents of a switch forwarding (MAC) table.

CHAPTER 5

Analyzing Ethernet LAN Switching

This chapter covers the following exam topics:

1.0 Network Fundamentals

    1.1 Explain the role and function of network components

        1.1.b Layer 2 and Layer 3 switches

    1.13 Describe switching concepts

        1.13.a MAC learning and aging

        1.13.b Frame switching

        1.13.c Frame flooding

        1.13.d MAC address table

2.0 Network Access

    2.5 Interpret basic operations of Spanning Tree Protocols

When you buy a Cisco Catalyst Ethernet switch, the switch is ready to work. All you have to do is take it out of the box, power on the switch by connecting the power cable to the switch and a power outlet, and connect hosts to the switch using the correct unshielded twisted-pair (UTP) cables. You do not have to configure anything else, or connect to the console and login, or do anything: the switch just starts forwarding Ethernet frames.

In Part II of this book, you will learn how to build, configure, and verify the operation of Ethernet LANs. In Chapter 4, "Using the Command-Line Interface," you learned how to move around in the CLI, issue commands, and configure the switch. This chapter takes a short but important step in that journey by explaining the logic a switch uses when forwarding Ethernet frames.

This chapter breaks the content into two major sections. The first reviews and then further develops the concepts behind LAN switching, which were first introduced back in Chapter 2, "Fundamentals of Ethernet LANs." The second section then uses IOS **show** commands to verify that Cisco switches actually learned the MAC addresses, built its MAC address table, and forwarded frames.

"Do I Know This Already?" Quiz

Take the quiz (either here or use the PTP software) if you want to use the score to help you decide how much time to spend on this chapter. The letter answers are listed at the bottom of the page following the quiz. Appendix C, found both at the end of the book as well as on the companion website, includes both the answers and explanations. You can also find both answers and explanations in the PTP testing software.

Table 5-1 "Do I Know This Already?" Foundation Topics Section-to-Question Mapping

Foundation Topics Section	Questions
LAN Switching Concepts	1–4
Verifying and Analyzing Ethernet Switching	5–6

1. Which of the following statements describes part of the process of how a switch decides to forward a frame destined for a known unicast MAC address?

   a. It compares the unicast destination address to the bridging, or MAC address, table.

   b. It compares the unicast source address to the bridging, or MAC address, table.

   c. It forwards the frame out all interfaces in the same VLAN except for the incoming interface.

   d. It compares the destination IP address to the destination MAC address.

   e. It compares the frame's incoming interface to the source MAC entry in the MAC address table.

2. Which of the following statements best describes the forwarding logic that a LAN switch, with all interfaces assigned to VLAN 1 as per default settings, uses for an incoming frame with a destination MAC address of FFFF.FFFF.FFFF?

   a. It forwards the frame out all switch ports.

   b. It forwards the frame out all switch ports except the arrival port.

   c. It forwards the frame out all ports that had earlier registered to ask to receive broadcasts.

   d. It discards the frame.

3. Which of the following statements best describes what a switch does with a frame destined for an unknown unicast address?

   a. It forwards out all interfaces in the same VLAN except for the incoming interface.

   b. It forwards the frame out the one interface identified by the matching entry in the MAC address table.

   c. It compares the destination IP address to the destination MAC address.

   d. It compares the frame's incoming interface to the source MAC entry in the MAC address table.

4. Which of the following comparisons does a switch make when deciding whether a new MAC address should be added to its MAC address table?

   a. It compares the unicast destination address to the bridging, or MAC address, table.

   b. It compares the unicast source address to the bridging, or MAC address, table.

   c. It compares the VLAN ID to the bridging, or MAC address, table.

   d. It compares the destination IP address's ARP cache entry to the bridging, or MAC address, table.

5. A Cisco Catalyst switch has 24 10/100 ports, numbered 0/1 through 0/24. Ten PCs connect to the ten lowest numbered ports, with those PCs working and sending data over the network. The other ports are not connected to any device. Which of the following answers lists facts displayed by the **show interfaces status** command?

a. Port Ethernet 0/1 is in a connected state.

b. Port Fast Ethernet 0/11 is in a connected state.

c. Port Fast Ethernet 0/5 is in a connected state.

d. Port Ethernet 0/15 is in a notconnected state.

6. Consider the following output from a Cisco Catalyst switch:

```
SW1# show mac address-table dynamic

           Mac Address Table
-------------------------------------------


Vlan    Mac Address       Type       Ports
----    -----------       --------   -----
   1    02AA.AAAA.AAAA    DYNAMIC    Gi0/1

   1    02BB.BBBB.BBBB    DYNAMIC    Gi0/2

   1    02CC.CCCC.CCCC    DYNAMIC    Gi0/3
Total Mac Addresses for this criterion: 3
```

Which of the following answers is true about this switch?

a. The output proves that port Gi0/2 connects directly to a device that uses address 02BB.BBBB.BBBB.

b. The switch has learned three MAC addresses since the switch powered on.

c. The three listed MAC addresses were learned based on the destination MAC address of frames forwarded by the switch.

d. Address 02CC.CCCC.CCCC was learned from the source MAC address of a frame that entered port Gi0/3.

Foundation Topics

LAN Switching Concepts

A modern Ethernet LAN connects user devices as well as servers into some switches, with the switches then connecting to each other, sometimes in a design like Figure 5-1. Part of the LAN, called a campus LAN, supports the end-user population as shown on the left of the figure. End-user devices connect to LAN switches, which in turn connect to other switches so that a path exists to the rest of the network. The campus LAN switches sit in wiring closets close to the end users. On the right, the servers used to provide information to the users also connect to the LAN. Those servers and switches often sit in a closed room called a *data center*, with connections to the campus LAN to support traffic to/from the users.

To forward traffic from a user device to a server and back, each switch performs the same kind of logic, independently from each other. The first half of this chapter examines the logic—how a switch chooses to forward an Ethernet frame, when the switch chooses to not forward the frame, and so on.

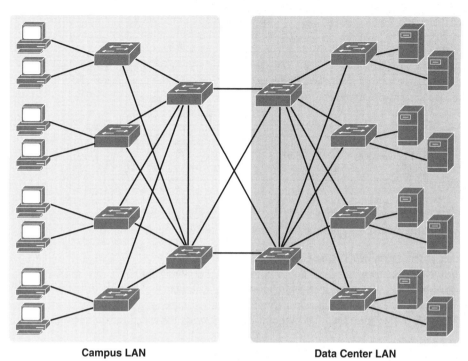

Campus LAN   **Data Center LAN**

Figure 5-1   *Campus LAN and Data Center LAN, Conceptual Drawing*

Overview of Switching Logic

Ultimately, the role of a LAN switch is to forward Ethernet frames. LANs exist as a set of user devices, servers, and other devices that connect to switches, with the switches connected to each other. The LAN switch has one primary job: to forward frames to the correct destination (MAC) address. And to achieve that goal, switches use logic—logic based on the source and destination MAC address in each frame's Ethernet header.

LAN switches receive Ethernet frames and then make a switching decision: either forward the frame out some other ports or ignore the frame. To accomplish this primary mission, switches perform three actions:

1. Deciding when to forward a frame or when to filter (not forward) a frame, based on the destination MAC address

2. Preparing to forward future frames by learning the source MAC address of each frame received by the switch

3. Cooperating with all switches to prevent the endless looping of frames by using Spanning Tree Protocol (STP)

The first action is the switch's primary job, whereas the other two items are overhead functions.

> **NOTE**   Throughout this book's discussion of LAN switches, the terms *switch port* and *switch interface* are synonymous.

Most of the upcoming discussions and figures about Ethernet switching focus on the use of the ever-present destination and source MAC address fields in the header. Both are 6 bytes long (represented as 12 hex digits in the book) and are a key part of the switching logic discussed in this section. Refer back to Chapter 2's section titled "Ethernet Data-Link Protocols" for a discussion of the header in detail for more info on the rest of the Ethernet frame. Figure 5-2 repeats the frame format here for reference.

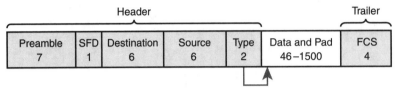

Figure 5-2 *IEEE 802.3 Ethernet Frame (One Variation)*

Now on to the details of how Ethernet switching works!

Forwarding Known Unicast Frames

To decide whether to forward a frame, a switch uses a dynamically built table that lists MAC addresses and outgoing interfaces. Switches compare the frame's destination MAC address to this table to decide whether the switch should forward a frame or simply ignore it. For example, consider the simple network shown in Figure 5-3, with Fred sending a frame to Barney.

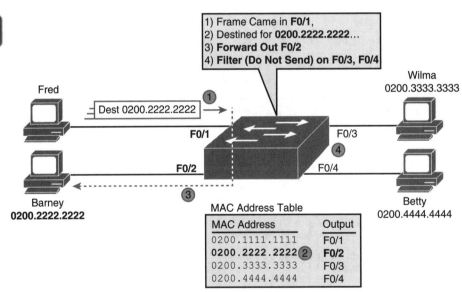

Figure 5-3 *Sample Switch Forwarding and Filtering Decision*

Answers to the "Do I Know This Already?" quiz:

1 A **2** B **3** A **4** B **5** C **6** D

In this figure, Fred sends a frame with destination address 0200.2222.2222 (Barney's MAC address). The switch compares the destination MAC address (0200.2222.2222) to the MAC address table, matching the bold table entry. That matched table entry tells the switch to forward the frame out port F0/2, and only port F0/2.

NOTE   A switch's **MAC address table** is also called the *switching table*, or *bridging table*, or even the *content-addressable memory (CAM) table*, in reference to the type of physical memory used to store the table.

A switch's MAC address table lists the location of each MAC relative to that one switch. In LANs with multiple switches, each switch makes an independent forwarding decision based on its own MAC address table. Together, they forward the frame so that it eventually arrives at the destination.

For example, Figure 5-4 shows the first switching decision in a case in which Fred sends a frame to Wilma, with destination MAC 0200.3333.3333. The topology has changed versus the previous figure, this time with two switches, and Fred and Wilma connected to two different switches. Figure 5-4 shows the first switch's logic, in reaction to Fred sending the original frame. Basically, the switch receives the frame in port F0/1, finds the destination MAC (0200.3333.3333) in the MAC address table, sees the outgoing port of G0/1, so SW1 forwards the frame out its G0/1 port.

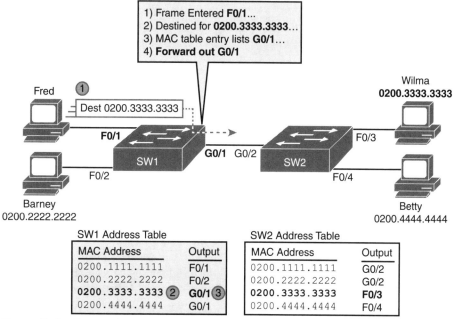

Figure 5-4   *Forwarding Decision with Two Switches: First Switch*

That same frame, after being forwarded by switch SW1, arrives at switch SW2, entering SW2's G0/2 interface. As shown in Figure 5-5, SW2 uses the same logic steps, but using SW2's table. The MAC table lists the forwarding instructions for that switch only. In this case, switch SW2 forwards the frame out its F0/3 port, based on SW2's MAC address table.

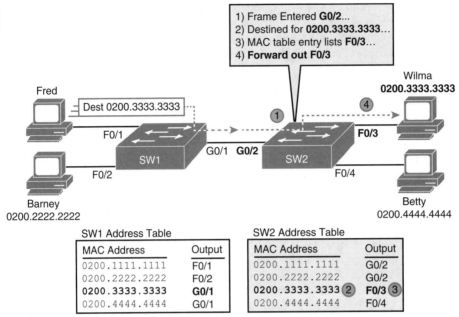

Figure 5-5 *Forwarding Decision with Two Switches: Second Switch*

> **NOTE** The term *forward-versus-filter decision* emphasizes the switch's choice to forward the frame out some ports but not forward (filter) the frame from being sent out other ports.

The examples so far use switches that happen to have a MAC table with all the MAC addresses listed. As a result, the destination MAC address in the frame is known to the switch. The frames are called **known unicast frames**, or simply known unicasts, because the destination address is a unicast address, and the destination is known. As shown in these examples, switches forward known unicast frames out one port: the port as listed in the MAC table entry for that MAC address.

Learning MAC Addresses

Thankfully, the networking staff does not have to type in all those MAC table entries. Instead, the switches do their second main function: to learn the MAC addresses and interfaces to put into its address table. With a complete MAC address table, the switch can make accurate forwarding and filtering decisions as just discussed.

Switches build the address table by listening to incoming frames and examining the *source MAC address* in the frame. If a frame enters the switch and the source MAC address is not in the MAC address table, the switch creates an entry in the table. That table entry lists the interface from which the frame arrived. Switch learning logic is that simple.

Figure 5-6 depicts the same single-switch topology network as Figure 5-3, but before the switch has built any address table entries. The figure shows the first two frames sent in this network: first a frame from Fred addressed to Barney, and then Barney's response, addressed to Fred.

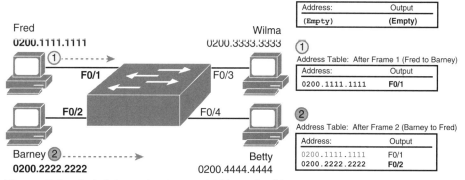

Figure 5-6 *Switch Learning: Empty Table and Adding Two Entries*

The figure does not show lines for where the frames flow, focusing instead on the arrival of the frames into the switch.

Focus on the learning process and how the MAC table grows at each step as shown on the right side of the figure. The switch begins with an empty MAC table, as shown in the upper-right part of the figure. Then Fred sends his first frame (labeled "1") to Barney, so the switch adds an entry for 0200.1111.1111, Fred's MAC address, associated with interface F0/1. Why F0/1? The frame sent by Fred entered the switch's F0/1 port. SW1's logic runs something like this: "The source is MAC 0200.1111.1111, the frame entered F0/1, so from my perspective, 0200.1111.1111 must be reachable out my port F0/1."

Continuing the example, when Barney replies in Step 2, the switch adds a second entry, this one for 0200.2222.2222, Barney's MAC address, along with interface F0/2. Why F0/2? The frame Barney sent entered the switch's F0/2 interface. Learning always occurs by looking at the source MAC address in the frame and adds the incoming interface as the associated port.

Flooding Unknown Unicast and Broadcast Frames

Now again turn your attention to the forwarding process, using the topology in Figure 5-5. What do you suppose the switch does with Fred's first frame, the one that occurred when there were no entries in the MAC address table? As it turns out, when there is no matching entry in the table, switches **forward** the frame out all interfaces (except the incoming interface) using a process called *flooding*. And the frame whose destination address is unknown to the switch is called an **unknown unicast frame**, or simply an *unknown unicast*.

Switches **flood** unknown unicast frames. Flooding means that the switch forwards copies of the frame out all ports, except the port on which the frame was received. The idea is simple: if you do not know where to send it, send it everywhere, to deliver the frame. And, by the way, that device will likely then send a reply—and then the switch can learn that device's MAC address and forward future frames out one port as a known unicast frame.

Switches also flood LAN **broadcast frames** (frames destined to the Ethernet broadcast address of FFFF.FFFF.FFFF) because this process helps deliver a copy of the frame to all devices in the LAN.

Figure 5-7 shows the same scenario as in Figure 5-6, with the first frame sent by Fred, when the switch's MAC table is empty—but focusing on switch forwarding. At Step 1, Fred sends the frame. At Step 2, the switch floods a copy of the frame out all three of the other interfaces.

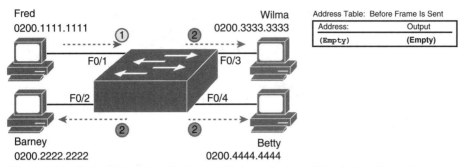

Figure 5-7 *Switch Flooding: Unknown Unicast Arrives, Floods Out Other Ports*

Avoiding Loops Using Spanning Tree Protocol

The third primary feature of LAN switches is loop prevention, as implemented by the **Spanning Tree Protocol (STP)**. Without STP, any flooded frames would loop for an indefinite period of time in Ethernet networks with physically redundant links. To prevent looping frames, STP blocks some ports from forwarding frames so that only one active path exists between any pair of LAN segments.

A simple example makes the need for STP more obvious. Remember, switches flood unknown unicast frames and broadcast frames. Figure 5-8 shows an unknown unicast frame, sent by Larry to Bob, which loops forever because the network has redundancy but no STP. Note that the figure shows one direction of the looping frame only, just to reduce clutter, but a copy of the frame would also loop the other direction.

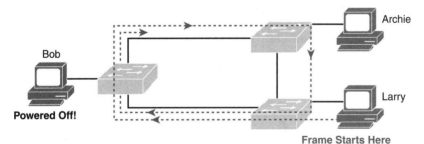

Figure 5-8 *Network with Redundant Links but Without STP: The Frame Loops Forever*

The flooding of this frame would cause the frame to rotate around the three switches; because none of the switches list Bob's MAC address in their address tables, each switch floods the frame. And while the flooding process is a good mechanism for forwarding unknown unicasts and broadcasts, the continual flooding of traffic frames as in the figure can completely congest the LAN to the point of making it unusable.

A topology like Figure 5-8, with redundant links, is good, but we need to prevent the bad effect of those looping frames. To avoid Layer 2 loops, all switches need to use STP. STP causes each interface on a switch to settle into either a blocking state or a forwarding state. *Blocking* means that the interface cannot forward or receive data frames, while *forwarding* means that the interface can send and receive data frames. If a correct subset of the interfaces is blocked, only a single currently active logical path exists between each pair of LANs.

Chapter 9 of this book, "Spanning Tree Protocol Concepts," examines STP in depth, including how STP prevents loops.

LAN Switching Summary

Switches use Layer 2 logic, examining the Ethernet data-link header to choose how to process frames. In particular, switches make decisions to forward and filter frames, learn MAC addresses, and use STP to avoid loops, as follows:

Step 1. Switches forward frames based on the destination MAC address:

    a. If the destination MAC address is a broadcast, multicast, or unknown destination unicast (a unicast not listed in the MAC table), the switch floods the frame.

    b. If the destination MAC address is a known unicast address (a unicast address found in the MAC table):

        i. If the outgoing interface listed in the MAC address table is different from the interface in which the frame was received, the switch forwards the frame out the outgoing interface.

        ii. If the outgoing interface is the same as the interface in which the frame was received, the switch filters the frame, meaning that the switch simply ignores the frame and does not forward it.

Step 2. Switches learn MAC address table entries based on the source MAC address:

    a. For each received frame, note the source MAC address and incoming interface ID.

    b. If not yet in the MAC address table, add an entry listing the MAC address and incoming interface.

Step 3. Switches use STP to prevent loops by causing some interfaces to block, meaning that they do not send or receive frames.

Verifying and Analyzing Ethernet Switching

A Cisco Catalyst switch comes from the factory ready to switch frames. All you have to do is connect the power cable, plug in the Ethernet cables, and the switch starts switching incoming frames. Connect multiple switches together, and they are ready to forward frames between the switches as well. And the big reason behind this default behavior has to do with the default settings on the switches.

Cisco Catalyst switches come ready to get busy switching frames because of settings like these:

- The interfaces are enabled by default, ready to start working once a cable is connected.

- All interfaces are assigned to VLAN 1.

- 10/100 and 10/100/1000 interfaces use autonegotiation by default.

■ The MAC learning, forwarding, flooding logic all works by default.

■ STP is enabled by default.

This second section of the chapter examines how switches will work with these default settings, showing how to verify the Ethernet learning and forwarding process.

Demonstrating MAC Learning

To see a switch's MAC address table, use the **show mac address-table** command. With no additional parameters, this command lists all known MAC addresses in the MAC table, including some overhead static MAC addresses that you can ignore. To see all the dynamically learned MAC addresses only, instead use the **show mac address-table dynamic** command, as seen in Example 5-1.

Example 5-1   show mac address-table dynamic *for Figure 5-9*

```
SW1# show mac address-table dynamic
          Mac Address Table
-------------------------------------------


Vlan    Mac Address       Type       Ports
----    -----------       --------   -----
   1    0200.1111.1111    DYNAMIC    Fa0/1
   1    0200.2222.2222    DYNAMIC    Fa0/2
   1    0200.3333.3333    DYNAMIC    Fa0/3
   1    0200.4444.4444    DYNAMIC    Fa0/4
Total Mac Addresses for this criterion: 4
SW1#
```

First, focus on two columns of the table: the MAC Address and Ports columns of the table. The values should look familiar: they match the earlier single-switch example, as repeated here as Figure 5-9. Note the four MAC addresses listed, along with their matching ports, as shown in the figure.

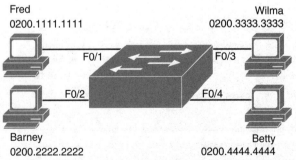

Figure 5-9 *Single Switch Topology Used in Verification Section*

Next, look at the Type field in the heading of the output table. The column tells us how the switch learned the MAC address as described earlier in this chapter; in this case, the switch learned all MAC addresses dynamically. You can also statically predefine MAC table entries using a couple of different features, including port security, and those would appear as Static in the Type column.

Finally, the VLAN column of the output gives us a chance to briefly discuss how virtual LANs (VLANs) impact switching logic. LAN switches forward Ethernet frames inside a VLAN. What that means is if a frame enters via a port in VLAN 1, then the switch will forward or flood that frame out other ports in VLAN 1 only, and not out any ports that happen to be assigned to another VLAN. Chapter 8, "Implementing Ethernet Virtual LANs," looks at all the details of how switches forward frames when using VLANs.

Switch Interfaces

The first example assumes that you installed the switch and cabling correctly, and that the switch interfaces work. You can easily check the status of those interfaces with the **show interfaces status** command, as shown in Example 5-2.

Example 5-2   **show interfaces status** *on Switch SW1*

```
SW1# show interfaces status

Port      Name          Status       Vlan     Duplex  Speed  Type
Fa0/1                   connected    1         a-full  a-100  10/100BaseTX
Fa0/2                   connected    1         a-full  a-100  10/100BaseTX
Fa0/3                   connected    1         a-full  a-100  10/100BaseTX
Fa0/4                   connected    1         a-full  a-100  10/100BaseTX
Fa0/5                   notconnect   1         auto    auto   10/100BaseTX
Fa0/6                   notconnect   1         auto    auto   10/100BaseTX
Fa0/7                   notconnect   1         auto    auto   10/100BaseTX
Fa0/8                   notconnect   1         auto    auto   10/100BaseTX
Fa0/9                   notconnect   1         auto    auto   10/100BaseTX
Fa0/10                  notconnect   1         auto    auto   10/100BaseTX
Fa0/11                  notconnect   1         auto    auto   10/100BaseTX
Fa0/12                  notconnect   1         auto    auto   10/100BaseTX
Fa0/13                  notconnect   1         auto    auto   10/100BaseTX
Fa0/14                  notconnect   1         auto    auto   10/100BaseTX
Fa0/15                  notconnect   1         auto    auto   10/100BaseTX
Fa0/16                  notconnect   1         auto    auto   10/100BaseTX
Fa0/17                  notconnect   1         auto    auto   10/100BaseTX
Fa0/18                  notconnect   1         auto    auto   10/100BaseTX
Fa0/19                  notconnect   1         auto    auto   10/100BaseTX
Fa0/20                  notconnect   1         auto    auto   10/100BaseTX
Fa0/21                  notconnect   1         auto    auto   10/100BaseTX
Fa0/22                  notconnect   1         auto    auto   10/100BaseTX
Fa0/23                  notconnect   1         auto    auto   10/100BaseTX
Fa0/24                  notconnect   1         auto    auto   10/100BaseTX
Gi0/1                   notconnect   1         auto    auto   10/100/1000BaseTX
Gi0/2                   notconnect   1         auto    auto   10/100/1000BaseTX
```

Focus on the Port column for a moment. As a reminder, Cisco Catalyst switches name their ports based on the fastest specification supported, so in this case, the switch has 24 interfaces named FastEthernet and two named GigabitEthernet. Many commands abbreviate those terms, this time as Fa for FastEthernet and Gi for GigabitEthernet. (The example happens to come from a Cisco Catalyst switch that has 24 10/100 ports and two 10/100/1000 ports.)

The Status column, of course, tells us the status or state of the port. In this case, the lab switch had cables and devices connected to ports F0/1–F0/4 only, with no other cables connected. As a result, those first four ports have a state of connected, meaning that the ports have a cable and are functional. The notconnect state means that the port is not yet functioning. It may mean that there is no cable installed, but other problems may exist as well. (The section "Analyzing Switch Interface Status and Statistics," in Chapter 7, "Configuring and Verifying Switch Interfaces," works through the details of what causes a switch interface to fail.)

> **NOTE** You can see the status for a single interface in a couple of ways. For instance, for F0/1, the command **show interfaces f0/1 status** lists the status in a single line of output as in Example 5-2. The **show interfaces f0/1** command (without the **status** keyword) displays a detailed set of messages about the interface.

The **show interfaces** command has a large number of options. One particular option, the **counters** option, lists statistics about incoming and outgoing frames on the interfaces. In particular, it lists the number of unicast, multicast, and broadcast frames (both the in and out directions), and a total byte count for those frames. Example 5-3 shows an example, again for interface F0/1.

Example 5-3   show interfaces f0/1 counters *on Switch SW1*

```
SW1# show interfaces f0/1 counters

Port            InOctets      InUcastPkts      InMcastPkts      InBcastPkts
Fa0/1           1223303          10264              107               18


Port            OutOctets     OutUcastPkts     OutMcastPkts     OutBcastPkts
Fa0/1           3235055         13886             22940              437
```

Finding Entries in the MAC Address Table

With a single switch and only four hosts connected to them, you can just read the details of the MAC address table and find the information you want to see. However, in real networks, with lots of interconnected hosts and switches, just reading the output to find one MAC address can be hard to do. You might have hundreds of entries—page after page of output—with each MAC address looking like a random string of hex characters. (The book uses easy-to-recognize MAC addresses to make it easier to learn.)

Thankfully, Cisco IOS supplies several more options on the **show mac address-table** command to make it easier to find individual entries. First, if you know the MAC address, you can search for it—just type in the MAC address at the end of the command, as shown in Example 5-4. All you have to do is include the **address** keyword, followed by the actual MAC address. If the address exists, the output lists the address. Note that the output lists the exact same information in the exact same format, but it lists only the line for the matching MAC address.

Example 5-4   show mac address-table dynamic *with the* address *Keyword*

```
SW1# show mac address-table dynamic address 0200.1111.1111
          Mac Address Table
-------------------------------------------

Vlan     Mac Address      Type          Ports
----     -----------      --------      -----
   1     0200.1111.1111   DYNAMIC       Fa0/1
Total Mac Addresses for this criterion: 1
```

While this information is useful, often the engineer troubleshooting a problem does not know the MAC addresses of the devices connected to the network. Instead, you might be troubleshooting while looking at a network topology diagram and want to look at all the MAC addresses learned off a particular port. IOS supplies that option with the **show mac address-table dynamic interface** command. Example 5-5 shows one example, for switch SW1's F0/1 interface.

Example 5-5   show mac address-table dynamic *with the* interface *Keyword*

```
SW1# show mac address-table dynamic interface fastEthernet 0/1
          Mac Address Table
-------------------------------------------

Vlan     Mac Address      Type          Ports
----     -----------      --------      -----
   1     0200.1111.1111   DYNAMIC       Fa0/1
Total    Mac Addresses for this criterion: 1
```

Finally, you may also want to find the MAC address table entries for one VLAN. You guessed it—you can add the **vlan** parameter, followed by the VLAN number. Example 5-6 shows two such examples from the same switch SW1 from Figure 5-9—one for VLAN 1, where all four devices reside, and one for a nonexistent VLAN 2.

Example 5-6   *The* show mac address-table vlan *command*

```
SW1# show mac address-table dynamic vlan 1
          Mac Address Table
-------------------------------------------

Vlan     Mac Address      Type          Ports
----     -----------      --------      -----
   1     0200.1111.1111   DYNAMIC       Fa0/1
```

5

```
  1    0200.2222.2222    DYNAMIC    Fa0/2
  1    0200.3333.3333    DYNAMIC    Fa0/3
  1    0200.4444.4444    DYNAMIC    Fa0/4
Total Mac Addresses for this criterion: 4
SW1#
SW1# show mac address-table dynamic vlan 2
         Mac Address Table
-------------------------------------------


Vlan    Mac Address     Type       Ports
----    -----------     --------   -----
SW1#
```

Managing the MAC Address Table (Aging, Clearing)

This chapter closes with a few comments about how switches manage their MAC address tables. MAC addresses do not remain in the table indefinitely. The switch will remove the entries due to age, due to the table filling, and you can remove entries using a command.

First, for aging out MAC table entries, switches remove entries that have not been used for a defined number of seconds (default of 300 seconds). To do that, switches keep a timer for each MAC table entry that increases over time. However, the switch resets the timer to 0 when it receives another frame with that same source MAC address. Timers that have not been reset continue to grow, and once a timer reaches the aging setting, the switch removes the MAC table entry.

Example 5-7 shows the aging timer setting for the entire switch. The aging time can be configured to a different time, globally and per-VLAN using the **mac address-table aging-time** *time-in-seconds* [**vlan** *vlan-number*] global configuration command. The example shows a case with all defaults, with the global setting of 300 seconds, and no per-VLAN overrides.

Example 5-7 *The MAC Address Default Aging Timer Displayed*

```
SW1# show mac address-table aging-time
Global Aging Time:  300
Vlan    Aging Time
----    ----------
SW1#


SW1# show mac address-table count


Mac Entries for Vlan 1:
-------------------------
Dynamic Address Count  : 4
Static  Address Count  : 0
Total Mac Addresses    : 4


Total Mac Address Space Available: 7299
```

Each switch also removes the oldest table entries, even if they are younger than the aging time setting, if the table fills. The MAC address table uses content-addressable memory (CAM), a physical memory that has great table lookup capabilities. However, the size of the table depends on the size of the CAM in a particular model of switch and based on some configurable settings in the switch. When a switch tries to add a new MAC table entry and finds the table full, the switch removes the oldest table entry to make space. For perspective, the end of Example 5-7 lists the size of a Cisco Catalyst switch's MAC table at about 8000 entries—the same four existing entries from the earlier examples, with space for 7299 more.

Finally, you can remove the dynamic entries from the MAC address table with the **clear mac address-table dynamic** command. Note that the **show** commands in this chapter can be executed from user and enable mode, but the **clear** command happens to be an enable mode command. The command also allows parameters to limit the types of entries cleared, as follows:

- By VLAN: **clear mac address-table dynamic vlan** *vlan-number*

- By Interface: **clear mac address-table dynamic interface** *interface-id*

- By MAC address: **clear mac address-table dynamic address** *mac-address*

MAC Address Tables with Multiple Switches

Finally, to complete the discussion, it helps to think about an example with multiple switches, just to emphasize how MAC learning, forwarding, and flooding happen independently on each LAN switch.

Consider the topology in Figure 5-10, and pay close attention to the port numbers. The ports were purposefully chosen so that neither switch used any of the same ports for this example. That is, switch SW2 does have a port F0/1 and F0/2, but I did not plug any devices into those ports when making this example. Also note that all ports are in VLAN 1, and as with the other examples in this chapter, all default configuration is used other than the host-name on the switches.

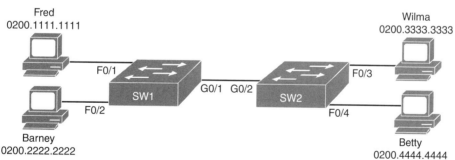

Figure 5-10 *Two-Switch Topology Example*

Think about a case in which both switches learn all four MAC addresses. For instance, that would happen if the hosts on the left communicate with the hosts on the right. SW1's MAC address table would list SW1's own port numbers (F0/1, F0/2, and G0/1) because SW1 uses that information to decide where SW1 should forward frames. Similarly, SW2's MAC table lists SW2's port numbers (F0/3, F0/4, G0/2 in this example). Example 5-8 shows the MAC address tables on both switches for that scenario.

Example 5-8   *The MAC Address Table on Two Switches*

```
SW1# show mac address-table dynamic
          Mac Address Table
-------------------------------------------


Vlan    Mac Address      Type        Ports
----    -----------      --------    -----
   1    0200.1111.1111   DYNAMIC     Fa0/1
   1    0200.2222.2222   DYNAMIC     Fa0/2
   1    0200.3333.3333   DYNAMIC     Gi0/1
   1    0200.4444.4444   DYNAMIC     Gi0/1
Total Mac Addresses for this criterion: 4

! The next output is from switch SW2
SW2# show mac address-table dynamic
   1    0200.1111.1111   DYNAMIC     Gi0/2
   1    0200.2222.2222   DYNAMIC     Gi0/2
   1    0200.3333.3333   DYNAMIC     Fa0/3
   1    0200.4444.4444   DYNAMIC     Fa0/4
Total Mac Addresses for this criterion: 4
```

Chapter Review

Review this chapter's material using either the tools in the book or interactive tools for the same material found on the book's companion website. Table 5-2 outlines the key review elements and where you can find them. To better track your study progress, record when you completed these activities in the second column.

Table 5-2   Chapter Review Tracking

Review Element	Review Date(s)	Resource Used
Review key topics		Book, website
Review key terms		Book, website
Answer DIKTA questions		Book, PTP
Do labs		Book, Sim Lite, blog
Review command tables		Book
Watch video		Website

Review All the Key Topics

Table 5-3   Key Topics for Chapter 5

Key Topic Element	Description	Page Number
List	Three main functions of a LAN switch	115
Figure 5-3	Process to forward a known unicast frame	116
Figure 5-5	Process to forward a known unicast, second switch	118
Figure 5-6	Process to learn MAC addresses	119
List	Summary of switch forwarding logic	121
Example 5-1	The **show mac address-table dynamic** command	122

Do Labs

The Sim Lite software is a version of Pearson's full simulator learning product with a subset of the labs, included free with this book. The subset of labs mostly relates to this part of the book, so take the time to try some of the labs.

As always, also check the author's blog site pages for configuration exercises (Config Labs) at http://www.certskills.com.

Key Terms You Should Know

broadcast frame, flood, forward, known unicast frame, MAC address table, Spanning Tree Protocol (STP), unknown unicast frame

Command References

Table 5-4 lists the verification commands used in this chapter. As an easy review exercise, cover the left column, read the right, and try to recall the command without looking. Then repeat the exercise, covering the right column, and try to recall what the command does.

Table 5-4   Chapter 5 EXEC Command Reference

Command	Mode/Purpose/Description
show mac address-table	Shows all MAC table entries of all types
show mac address-table dynamic	Shows all dynamically learned MAC table entries
show mac address-table dynamic vlan *vlan-id*	Shows all dynamically learned MAC table entries in that VLAN
show mac address-table dynamic address *mac-address*	Shows the dynamically learned MAC table entries with that MAC address
show mac address-table dynamic interface *interface-id*	Shows all dynamically learned MAC table entries associated with that interface
show mac address-table count	Shows the number of entries in the MAC table and the total number of remaining empty slots in the MAC table

Command	Mode/Purpose/Description
show mac address-table aging-time	Shows the global and per-VLAN aging timeout for inactive MAC table entries
show interfaces *id* counters	Lists packet counters for the listed interface ID
show interfaces status	Lists one line per interface on the switch, with basic status and operating/ information for each
clear mac address-table dynamic [vlan *vlan-number*] [interface *interface-id*] [address *mac-address*]	Clears (removes) dynamic MAC table entries: either all (with no parameters), or a subset based on VLAN ID, interface ID, or a specific MAC address

Note that this chapter also includes reference to one configuration command, so it does not call for the use of a separate table. For review, the command is

mac address-table aging-time *time-in-seconds* [**vlan** *vlan-number*]

CHAPTER 6

Configuring Basic Switch Management

This chapter covers the following exam topics:

  1.0 Network Fundamentals

   1.6 Configure and verify IPv4 addressing and subnetting

  2.0 Network Access

   2.8 Describe network device management access (Telnet, SSH, HTTP, HTTPS, console, RADIUS/TACACS+)

  4.0 IP Services

   4.6 Configure and verify DHCP client and relay

   4.8 Configure network devices for remote access using SSH

  5.0 Security Fundamentals

   5.3 Configure device access control using local passwords

The tasks of a switch fall into a small set of categories called planes. The data plane includes the process of forwarding frames received by the switch. The control plane refers to the processes that control and change the switch's data plane. The control plane includes configuration to enable or disable an interface, to control the speed used by each interface, and the dynamic processes of Spanning Tree to block some ports to prevent loops, and so on. The third plane, the management plane, refers to device management features. Those include Telnet and SSH, used to connect to the CLI, and other management features.

This chapter discusses the most basic management plane features in a Cisco switch. The first section of the chapter discusses configuring different kinds of login security for console, Telnet, and SSH users. The second section shows how to enable remote switch management by configuring switch IPv4 settings. The last section then explains a few practical matters that can make your life in the lab a little easier.

"Do I Know This Already?" Quiz

Take the quiz (either here or use the PTP software) if you want to use the score to help you decide how much time to spend on this chapter. The letter answers are listed at the bottom of the page following the quiz. Appendix C, found both at the end of the book as well as on the companion website, includes both the answers and explanations. You can also find both answers and explanations in the PTP testing software.

Table 6-1 "Do I Know This Already?" Foundation Topics Section-to-Question Mapping

Foundation Topics Section	Questions
Securing the Switch CLI	1–3
Enabling IPv4 for Remote Access	4–5
Miscellaneous Settings Useful in the Lab	6

1. Imagine that you have configured the **enable secret** command, followed by the **enable password** command, from the console. You log out of the switch and log back in at the console. Which command defines the password that you had to enter to access privileged mode?

   a. enable password

   b. enable secret

   c. Neither

   d. The **password** command, if it is configured

2. An engineer wants to set up simple password protection with no usernames for some switches in a lab, for the purpose of keeping curious coworkers from logging in to the lab switches from their desktop PCs. Which of the following commands would be a useful part of that configuration?

   a. A **login** vty mode subcommand

   b. A **password** *password* console subcommand

   c. A **login local** vty subcommand

   d. A **transport input ssh** vty subcommand

3. An engineer had formerly configured a Cisco 2960 switch to allow Telnet access so that the switch expected a password of **mypassword** from the Telnet user. The engineer then changed the configuration to support Secure Shell. Which of the following commands could have been part of the new configuration? (Choose two answers.)

   a. A **username** *name* **secret** *password* vty mode subcommand

   b. A **username** *name* **secret** *password* global configuration command

   c. A **login local** vty mode subcommand

   d. A **transport input ssh** global configuration command

4. An engineer's desktop PC connects to a switch at the main site. A router at the main site connects to each branch office through a serial link, with one small router and switch at each branch. Which of the following commands must be configured on the branch office switches, in the listed configuration mode, to allow the engineer to telnet to the branch office switches and supply only a password to log in? (Choose three answers.)

   a. The **ip address** command in interface configuration mode

   b. The **ip address** command in global configuration mode

   c. The **ip default-gateway** command in VLAN configuration mode

   d. The **ip default-gateway** command in global configuration mode

   e. The **password** command in console line configuration mode

   f. The **password** command in vty line configuration mode

5. A Layer 2 switch configuration places all its physical ports into VLAN 2. An attached router uses address/mask 172.16.2.254/24. The IP address plan calls for the switch to use address/mask 172.16.2.250/24 and to use the router as its default gateway. The switch needs to support SSH connections into the switch from any subnet in the network. Which of the following commands are part of the required configuration in this case? (Choose two answers.)

   a. The ip address 172.16.2.250 255.255.255.0 command in interface vlan 1 configuration mode.

   b. The ip address 172.16.2.250 255.255.255.0 command in interface vlan 2 configuration mode.

   c. The ip default-gateway 172.16.2.254 command in global configuration mode.

   d. The switch cannot support SSH because all its ports connect to VLAN 2, and the IP address must be configured on interface VLAN 1.

6. Which of the following line subcommands tells a switch to wait until a show command's output has completed before displaying log messages on the screen?

   a. logging synchronous

   b. no ip domain-lookup

   c. exec-timeout 0 0

   d. history size 15

Foundation Topics

Securing the Switch CLI

By default, a user can connect to the console and reach **enable mode** with no security checks and no passwords required. In contrast, the default settings disallow all **Telnet** and **Secure Shell (SSH)** users from even seeing a login prompt. Those defaults make sense, given that if you can get to the console port of the switch, you already have control over the switch physically. But clearly, protecting the console makes sense, as does opening up SSH and Telnet access to appropriate users.

This first topic in the chapter examines how to configure login security for a Cisco Catalyst switch. Securing the CLI includes protecting access to enable mode, because from enable mode, an attacker could reload the switch or change the configuration. Protecting user mode is also important, because attackers can see the status of the switch, learn about the network, and find new ways to attack the network.

In particular, this section covers the following login security topics:

- Securing user mode and privileged mode with simple passwords

- Securing user mode access with local usernames

- Securing user mode access with external authentication servers

- Securing remote access with Secure Shell (SSH)

Note that all remote management protocols, like Telnet and SSH, require IP configuration on the switch, which is not discussed until the second major section of this chapter, "Enabling IPv4 for Remote Access."

Securing User Mode and Privileged Mode with Simple Passwords

The defaults work great for a brand new switch, but in production, you will want to secure access through the console as well as enable remote login via Telnet and/or SSH so you can sit at your desk and log in to all the switches in the LAN. Keep in mind, however, that you should not open the switch for just anyone to log in and change the configuration, so some type of secure login should be used.

Most people use a simple shared password for access to lab gear. This method uses a password only—with no username—with one password for console users and a different password for Telnet users. Console users must supply the *console password*, as configured in console line configuration mode. Telnet users must supply the *Telnet password*, also called the vty password, so called because the configuration sits in vty line configuration mode. Figure 6-1 summarizes these options for using shared passwords from the perspective of the user logging in to the switch.

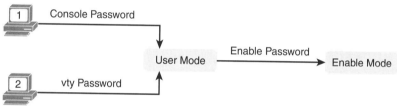

Figure 6-1 *Simple Password Security Concepts*

> **NOTE**   This section refers to several passwords as *shared* passwords. Users share these passwords in that all users must know and use that same password. In other words, each user does not have a unique username/password to use, but rather, all the appropriate staff knows and uses the same password.

In addition, Cisco switches protect enable mode (also called privileged mode) with yet another shared password called the *enable password*. From the perspective of the network engineer connecting to the CLI of the switch, once in user mode, the user types the **enable** EXEC command. This command prompts the user for this enable password; if the user types the correct password, IOS moves the user to enable mode.

Example 6-1 shows an example of the user experience of logging in to a switch from the console when the shared console password and the shared enable password have both been set. Note that before this example began, the user started the terminal emulator, physically connected a laptop to the console cable, and then pressed the Enter key to make the switch respond as shown at the top of the example.

Example 6-1 *Console Login and Movement to Enable Mode*

```
(User now presses enter to start the process. This line of text does not appear.)


User Access Verification


Password: faith
Switch> enable
Password: love
Switch#
```

Note that the example shows the password text as if typed (faith and love), along with the **enable** command that moves the user from user mode to enable mode. In reality, the switch hides the passwords when typed, to prevent someone from reading over your shoulder to see the passwords.

To configure the shared passwords for the console, Telnet, and for enable mode, you need to configure several commands. However, the parameters of the commands can be pretty intuitive. Figure 6-2 shows the configuration of all three of these passwords.

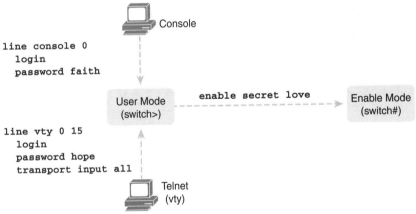

Figure 6-2 *Simple Password Security Configuration*

The configuration for these three passwords does not require a lot of work. First, the console and vty password configuration sets the password based on the context: console mode for the console (**line con 0**), and vty line configuration mode for the Telnet password (**line vty 0 15**). Then inside console mode and vty mode, respectively, the two commands in each mode are as follows:

> **password** *password-value*: Defines the actual password used on the console or vty
>
> **login:** Tells IOS to enable the use of a simple shared password (with no username) on this line (console or vty), so that the switch asks the user for a password

---

Answers to the "Do I Know This Already?" quiz:

1 B **2** A **3** B, C **4** A, D, F **5** B, C **6** A

The configured enable password, shown on the right side of the figure, applies to all users, no matter whether they connect to user mode via the console, Telnet, or otherwise. The command to configure the enable password is a global configuration command: **enable secret** *password-value*.

NOTE   Older IOS versions used the command **enable password** *password-value* to set the enable password, and that command still exists in IOS. However, the **enable secret** command is much more secure. In real networks, use **enable secret**. Chapter 10, "Securing Network Devices," in the *CCNA 200-301 Official Cert Guide, Volume 2*, Second Edition, explains more about the security levels of various password mechanisms, including a comparison of the **enable secret** and **enable password** commands.

To help you follow the process, and for easier study later, use the configuration checklist before the example. The configuration checklist collects the required and optional steps to configure a feature as described in this book. The configuration checklist for shared passwords for the console, Telnet, and enable passwords is

Config Checklist

Step 1.   Configure the enable password with the **enable secret** *password-value* command.

Step 2.   Configure the console password:

    a.   Use the **line con 0** command to enter console configuration mode.

    b.   Use the **password** *password-value* subcommand to set the value of the console password.

    c.   Use the **login** subcommand to enable console password security using a simple password.

Step 3.   Configure the Telnet (vty) password:

    a.   Use the **line vty 0 15** command to enter vty configuration mode for all 16 vty lines (numbered 0 through 15).

    b.   Use the **password** *password-value* subcommand to set the value of the vty password.

    c.   Use the **login** subcommand to enable console password security using a simple password.

    d.   Use the **transport input all** subcommand (or similar) to enable Telnet as an input protocol for the vty lines.

NOTE   The section "Securing Remote Access with Secure Shell," later in this chapter, provides more detail about the **transport input** subcommand.

Example 6-2 shows the configuration process as noted in the configuration checklist, along with setting the enable secret password. Note that the lines which begin with a ! are comment lines; they are there to guide you through the configuration.

Example 6-3 shows the resulting configuration in the switch per the **show running-config** command. The gray lines highlight the new configuration. Note that many unrelated lines of output have been deleted from the output to keep focused on the password configuration.

Example 6-2 *Configuring Basic Passwords*

```
! Enter global configuration mode and set the enable password.
!
Switch# configure terminal
Switch(config)# enable secret love
!
! At Step 2 in the checklist, enter console configuration mode, set the
! password value to "faith" and enable simple passwords for the console.
! The exit command moves the user back to global config mode.
!
Switch#(config)# line console 0
Switch#(config-line)# password faith
Switch#(config-line)# login
Switch#(config-line)# exit
!
! The next few lines do basically the same configuration, except it is
! for the vty lines. Telnet users will use "hope" to login.
!
Switch#(config)# line vty 0 15
Switch#(config-line)# password hope
Switch#(config-line)# login
Switch#(config-line)# transport input all
Switch#(config-line)# end
Switch#
```

Example 6-3 *Resulting Running-Config File (Subset) per Example 6-2 Configuration*

```
Switch# show running-config
!
Building configuration...

Current configuration: 1333 bytes
!
version 12.2
!
enable secret 5 $1$OwtI$A58c2XgqWyDNeDnv51mNR.
!
interface FastEthernet0/1
!
interface FastEthernet0/2
!
! Several lines have been omitted here - in particular, lines for
! FastEthernet interfaces 0/3 through 0/23.
!
interface FastEthernet0/24
```

```
!
interface GigabitEthernet0/1
!
interface GigabitEthernet0/2
!
line con 0
 password faith
login
!
line vty 0 4
 password hope
 login
 transport input all
!
line vty 5 15
 password hope
 login
 transport input all
```

NOTE   For historical reasons, the output of the **show running-config** command, in the last six lines of Example 6-3, separates the first five vty lines (0 through 4) from the rest (5 through 15).

Securing User Mode Access with Local Usernames and Passwords

Cisco switches support two other login security methods that both use per-user username/password pairs instead of a shared password with no username. One method, referred to as **local usernames** and passwords, configures the username/password pairs locally—that is, in the switch's configuration. Switches support this local username/password option for the console, for Telnet, and even for SSH, but do not replace the enable password used to reach enable mode.

The configuration to migrate from using the simple shared passwords to instead using local usernames/passwords requires only some small configuration changes, as shown in Figure 6-3.

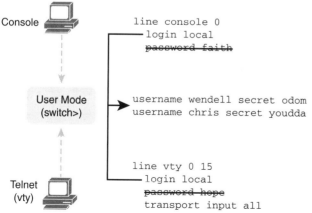

Figure 6-3   *Configuring Switches to Use Local Username Login Authentication*

Working through the configuration in the figure, first, the switch of course needs to know the list of username/password pairs. To create these, repeatedly use the **username** *name* **secret** *password* global configuration command. Then, to enable this different type of console or Telnet security, simply enable this login security method with the **login local** line. Basically, this command means "use the local list of usernames for login." You can also use the **no password** command (without even typing in the password) to clean up any remaining password subcommands from console or vty mode because these commands are not needed when using local usernames and passwords.

The following checklist details the commands to configure local username login, mainly as a method for easier study and review:

Step 1. Use the **username** *name* **secret** *password* global configuration command to add one or more username/password pairs on the local switch.

Step 2. Configure the console to use locally configured username/password pairs:

  a. Use the **line con 0** command to enter console configuration mode.

  b. Use the **login local** subcommand to enable the console to prompt for both username and password, checked versus the list of local usernames/passwords.

  c. (Optional) Use the **no password** subcommand to remove any existing simple shared passwords, just for good housekeeping of the configuration file.

Step 3. Configure Telnet (vty) to use locally configured username/password pairs.

  a. Use the **line vty 0 15** command to enter vty configuration mode for all 16 vty lines (numbered 0 through 15).

  b. Use the **login local** subcommand to enable the switch to prompt for both username and password for all inbound Telnet users, checked versus the list of local usernames/passwords.

  c. (Optional) Use the **no password** subcommand to remove any existing simple shared passwords, just for good housekeeping of the configuration file.

  d. Use the **transport input all** subcommand (or similar) to enable Telnet as an input protocol for the vty lines.

When a Telnet user connects to the switch configured as shown in Figure 6-3, the user will be prompted first for a username and then for a password, as shown in Example 6-4. The username/password pair must be from the list of local usernames; otherwise, the login is rejected.

Example 6-4   *Telnet Login Process After Applying Configuration in Figure 6-3*

```
SW2# telnet 10.9.9.19
Trying 10.9.9.19 ... Open


User Access Verification
```

```
Username: wendell
Password:
SW1> enable
Password:
SW1# configure terminal
Enter configuration commands, one per line. End with CNTL/Z.
SW1(config)#^Z
SW1#
*Mar 1 02:00:56.229: %SYS-5-CONFIG_I: Configured from console by wendell on vty0
(10.9.9.19)
```

NOTE   Example 6-4 does not show the password value as having been typed because Cisco switches do not display the typed password for security reasons.

Securing User Mode Access with External Authentication Servers

The end of Example 6-4 points out one of the many security improvements when requiring each user to log in with their own username. The end of the example shows the user entering configuration mode (**configure terminal**) and then immediately leaving (**end**). Note that when a user exits configuration mode, the switch generates a **log message**. If the user logged in with a username, the log message identifies that username; note the "wendell" in the log message.

However, using a username/password configured directly on the switch causes some administrative headaches. For instance, every switch and router needs the configuration for all users who might need to log in to the devices. Then, when any changes need to happen, like an occasional change to the passwords for good security practices, the configuration of all devices must be changed.

A better option would be to use tools like those used for many other IT login functions. Those tools allow for a central place to securely store all username/password pairs, with tools to make users change their passwords regularly, tools to revoke users when they leave their current jobs, and so on.

Cisco switches allow exactly that option using an external server called an authentication, authorization, and accounting (**AAA**) server. These servers hold the usernames/passwords. Typically, these servers allow users to do self-service and forced maintenance to their passwords. Many production networks use AAA servers for their switches and routers today.

The underlying login process requires some additional work on the part of the switch for each user login, but once set up, the username/password administration is much less. When an **AAA server** is used for authentication, the switch (or router) simply sends a message to the AAA server asking whether the username and password are allowed, and the AAA server replies. Figure 6-4 shows an example, with the user first supplying a username/password, the switch asking the AAA server, and the server replying to the switch stating that the username/password is valid.

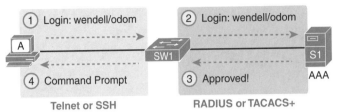

Figure 6-4 *Basic Authentication Process with an External AAA Server*

While the figure shows the general idea, note that the information flows with a couple of different protocols. On the left, the connection between the user and the switch or router uses Telnet or SSH. On the right, the switch and AAA server typically use either the RADIUS or TACACS+ protocol, both of which encrypt the passwords as they traverse the network.

Securing Remote Access with Secure Shell

So far, this chapter has focused on the console and on Telnet, mostly ignoring SSH. Telnet has one serious disadvantage: all data in the Telnet session flows as clear text, including the password exchanges. So, anyone who can capture the messages between the user and the switch (in what is called a man-in-the-middle attack) can see the passwords. SSH encrypts all data transmitted between the SSH client and server, protecting the data and passwords.

SSH can use the same local login authentication method as Telnet, with the locally configured username and password. (SSH cannot rely on authentication methods that do not include a username, like shared passwords.) So, the configuration to support local usernames for Telnet, as shown previously in Figure 6-3, also enables local username authentication for incoming SSH connections.

Figure 6-5 shows one example configuration of what is required to support SSH. The figure repeats the local username configuration as shown earlier in Figure 6-3, as used for Telnet. Figure 6-5 shows three additional commands required to complete the configuration of SSH on the switch.

SSH-Specific Configuration

```
hostname sw1
ip domain-name example.com
! Next Command Uses FQDN "sw1.example.com"
crypto key generate rsa
```

Local Username Configuration (Like Telnet)

```
username wendell secret odom
username chris secret youdda
!
line vty 0 15
  login local
  transport input all
```

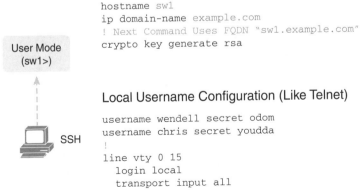

Figure 6-5 *Adding SSH Configuration to Local Username Configuration*

IOS uses the three SSH-specific configuration commands in the figure to create the SSH encryption keys. The SSH server uses the fully qualified domain name (FQDN) of the switch as input to create that key. The switch creates the FQDN from the hostname and domain name of the switch. Figure 6-5 begins by setting both values (just in case they are not already configured). Then the third command, the **crypto key generate rsa** command, generates the SSH encryption keys.

Seeing the configuration happen in configuration mode, step by step, can be particularly helpful with SSH configuration. Note in particular that in this example, the **crypto key** command prompts the user for the key modulus; you could also add the parameters **modulus** *modulus-value* to the end of the **crypto key** command to add this setting on the command. Example 6-5 shows the commands in Figure 6-5 being configured, with the encryption key as the final step.

Example 6-5 *SSH Configuration Process to Match Figure 6-5*

```
SW1# configure terminal
Enter configuration commands, one per line. End with CNTL/Z.
!
! Step 1 next. The hostname is already set, but it is repeated just
! to be obvious about the steps.
!
SW1(config)# hostname SW1
SW1(config)# ip domain name example.com
SW1(config)# crypto key generate rsa
The name for the keys will be: SW1.example.com

Choose the size of the key modulus in the range of 512 to 2048 for your
  General Purpose Keys. Choosing a key modulus greater than 512 may take
  a few minutes.

How many bits in the modulus [1024]: 1024
% Generating 1024 bit RSA keys, keys will be non-exportable...
[OK] (elapsed time was 4 seconds)
SW1(config)#
!
! Optionally, set the SSH version to version 2 (only) - preferred
!
SW1(config)# ip ssh version 2
!
! Next, configure the vty lines for local username support, just like
! with Telnet
!
SW1(config)# line vty 0 15
SW1(config-line)# login local
SW1(config-line)# transport input all
SW1(config-line)# exit
!
```

6

```
! Define the local usernames, just like with Telnet
!
SW1(config)# username wendell secret odom
SW1(config)# username chris secret youdaman
SW1(config)# ^Z
SW1#
```

NOTE Older IOS versions used the syntax **ip domain-name** *domain-name* rather than the newer **ip domain name** *domain-name* (with a space instead of a dash.)

Both the Telnet and SSH examples throughout this chapter so far list the **transport input all** subcommand in vty configuration mode. The **transport input** command identifies the protocols allowed in the vty ports, with the **all** keyword including SSH and Telnet. Using **transport input all** lets you support everything when getting started learning, but for production devices you might want to instead choose some different options, like not supporting Telnet at all due to its poor security. Some common options include

transport input all or **transport input telnet ssh**: Support both Telnet and SSH

transport input none: Support neither

transport input telnet: Support only Telnet

transport input ssh: Support only SSH

Over the years, the default settings for this command have varied a bit based on device type, OS, and OS version. As a result, for production devices, it makes sense to pick the setting you want and configure it, rather than relying on your memory of a default setting for a particular device and software version. For instance, many companies prefer to disable any possibility of Telnet access, but allow SSH, using **transport input ssh**.

For the exams, be ready to look for the **transport input** setting to ensure it supports SSH, or Telnet, or both, depending on the scenario. As a strategy for the exam, look for the command to confirm its settings when looking at any Telnet or SSH configuration. Also, be aware of the traditional defaults: Many older switches defaulted to **transport input all**, while older routers defaulted to **transport input none**, with more recent Cisco switches and routers now defaulting to the more-secure **transport input ssh**.

To complete this section about SSH, the following configuration checklist details the steps for one method to configure a Cisco switch to support SSH using local usernames. (SSH support in IOS can be configured in several ways; this checklist shows one simple way to configure it.) The process shown here ends with a comment to configure local username support on vty lines, as was discussed earlier in the section titled "Securing User Mode Access with Local Usernames and Passwords."

Step 1.   Configure the switch to generate a matched public and private key pair to use for encryption:

   a. If not already configured, use the **hostname** *name* in global configuration mode to configure a hostname for this switch.

> **b.** If not already configured, use the **ip domain name** *name* in global configuration mode to configure a domain name for the switch, completing the switch's FQDN.
>
> **c.** Use the **crypto key generate rsa** command in global configuration mode (or the **crypto key generate rsa modulus** *modulus-value* command to avoid being prompted for the key modulus) to generate the keys. (Use at least a 768-bit key to support SSH version 2.)

Step 2. (Optional) Use the **ip ssh version 2** command in global configuration mode to override the default of supporting both versions 1 and 2, so that only SSHv2 connections are allowed.

Step 3. (Optional) If not already configured with the setting you want, configure the vty lines to accept SSH and whether to also allow Telnet:

> **a.** Use the **transport input ssh** command in vty line configuration mode to allow SSH only.
>
> **b.** Use the **transport input all** command or **transport input telnet ssh** command in vty line configuration mode to allow both SSH and Telnet.

Step 4. Use various commands in vty line configuration mode to configure local username login authentication as discussed earlier in this chapter.

Two key commands give some information about the status of SSH on the switch. First, the **show ip ssh** command lists status information about the SSH server itself. The **show ssh** command then lists information about each SSH client currently connected to the switch. Example 6-6 shows samples of each, with user wendell currently connected to the switch.

Example 6-6 *Displaying SSH Status*

```
SW1# show ip ssh
SSH Enabled - version 2.0
Authentication timeout: 120 secs; Authentication retries: 3

SW1# show ssh
Connection Version Mode  Encryption   Hmac          State             Username
0           2.0     IN    aes126-cbc   hmac-sha1     Session started   wendell
0           2.0     OUT   aes126-cbc   hmac-sha1     Session started   wendell
%No SSHv1 server connections running.
```

Enabling and Securing the WebUI

The section "Accessing the CLI with the WebUI" in Chapter 4 shows examples of the WebUI user interface but does not discuss any configurations. Next, you will discover how to configure the most common settings to support this feature and to secure it using a **username** command—but with a new twist.

The HTTP server, the WebUI, has a long history as an integrated IOS feature in switches and routers. Over time, Cisco changed the user interface and some configuration commands. So, rather than focus on the trivial matters, focus on these steps that would be a common-sense configuration in a switch (or router) today:

■ Use the **no ip http server** global command to disable the HTTP server (port 80) (traditionally enabled by default).

■ Use the **ip http secure-server** global command to enable the HTTPS server (port 443, uses TLS) (traditionally enabled by default).

■ Use the **ip http authentication local** global command to define the authentication method to use locally defined usernames (traditionally defaults to use the enable password).

■ Use the **username** *name* **priority 15 password** *pass-value* global command to define one or more usernames with privilege level 15.

Talking through the items in the list, IOS has long used defaults that enable both the HTTP and HTTPS servers. With both enabled, users can connect from browsers by typing URLs that begin http:// (therefore not encrypting the traffic) or https:// (therefore encrypting the traffic). For better security, Cisco recommends disabling the HTTP server.

The HTTP server has long allowed three options to log in to a device from a web browser:

■ Using the enable password

■ Using a local username/password

■ Using the AAA settings on the device

More recent IOS versions move away from the **enable** option. Also, using both a username and a password makes more sense from a security perspective.

To access all the features of the HTTP server (the WebUI), when using local usernames for authentication, you must configure a privilege level of 15 for the user. IOS internally defines user privilege levels, by default creating two levels, 0 and 15. IOS assigns user mode to level 0 and privileged mode (enable mode) to level 15. When CLI users move from user mode to enable mode, they improve their priority level from 0 to 15.

For the WebUI, if you log in using a username with the **privilege 15** option, you receive access to all WebUI features, including the ability to use the CLI configuration mode, install new software, erase the configuration, and reload the router. So, the **username** *name* **priority 15 password** *pass-value* global command creates a way to enter privileged mode immediately. (If you omit the **priority 15** option and log in to the WebUI with that username you can log in, but you cannot do advanced features, including using the CLI to configure or verify a feature.)

Enabling IPv4 for Remote Access

To allow Telnet, SSH, or WebUI access to the switch, and to allow other IP-based management protocols (for example, Simple Network Management Protocol, or SNMP) to function as intended, the switch needs an IP address, as well as a few other related settings. The IP address has nothing to do with how switches forward Ethernet frames; it simply exists to support overhead management traffic (control plane traffic).

This next topic begins by explaining the IPv4 settings needed on a switch, followed by the configuration. Note that although switches can be configured with IPv6 addresses with commands similar to those shown in this chapter, this chapter focuses solely on IPv4. All references to IP in this chapter imply IPv4.

Host and Switch IP Settings

A switch needs the same kind of IP settings as a PC with a single Ethernet interface. For perspective, a PC has a CPU, with the operating system running on the CPU. It has an Ethernet network interface card (NIC). The OS configuration includes an IP address associated with the NIC, either configured or learned dynamically with Dynamic Host Configuration Protocol (DHCP).

A switch uses the same ideas, except that the switch needs to use a virtual NIC inside the switch. Like a PC, a switch has a real CPU, running an OS (called IOS). The switch obviously has lots of Ethernet ports, but instead of assigning its management IP address to any of those ports, the switch then uses a NIC-like concept called a switch virtual interface (SVI), or more commonly, a **VLAN interface**, that acts like the switch's own NIC. Then the settings on the switch look something like a host, with the switch configuration assigning IP settings, like an IP address, to this VLAN interface, as shown in Figure 6-6.

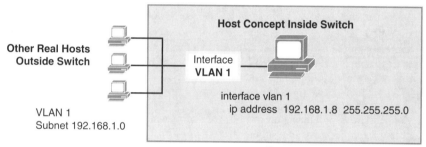

Figure 6-6 *Switch Virtual Interface (SVI) Concept Inside a Switch*

By using interface VLAN 1 for the IP configuration, the switch can then send and receive frames on any of the ports in VLAN 1. In a Cisco switch, by default, all ports are assigned to VLAN 1.

In most networks, switches configure many VLANs, so the network engineer has a choice of where to configure the IP address. That is, the management IP address does not have to be configured on the VLAN 1 interface (as configured with the **interface vlan 1** command seen in Figure 6-6).

A Layer 2 Cisco LAN switch needs only one IP address for management purposes. However, you can choose to use any VLAN to which the switch connects. The configuration then includes a VLAN interface for that VLAN number, with an appropriate IP address.

For example, Figure 6-7 shows a Layer 2 switch with some physical ports in two different VLANs (VLANs 1 and 2). The figure also shows the subnets used on those VLANs. The network engineer could choose to use either

- Interface VLAN 1, with an IP address in subnet 192.168.1.0

- Interface VLAN 2, with an IP address in subnet 192.168.2.0

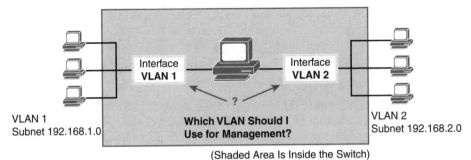

(Shaded Area Is Inside the Switch)

Figure 6-7 *Choosing One VLAN on Which to Configure a Switch IP Address*

Note that you should not try to use a VLAN interface for which there are no physical ports assigned to the same VLAN. If you do, the VLAN interface will not reach an up/up state, and the switch will not have the physical ability to communicate outside the switch.

> **NOTE** Some Cisco switches can be configured to act as either a Layer 2 switch or a Layer 3 switch. When acting as a Layer 2 switch, a switch forwards Ethernet frames as discussed in depth in Chapter 5, "Analyzing Ethernet LAN Switching." Alternatively, a switch can also act as a *multilayer switch* or *Layer 3 switch*, which means the switch can do both Layer 2 switching and Layer 3 IP routing of IP packets, using the Layer 3 logic normally used by routers. This chapter assumes all switches are Layer 2 switches. Chapter 18, "IP Routing in the LAN," discusses Layer 3 switching in depth along with using multiple VLAN interfaces at the same time.

Configuring the IP address (and mask) on one VLAN interface allows the switch to send and receive IP packets with other hosts in a subnet that exists on that VLAN; however, the switch cannot communicate outside the local subnet without another configuration setting called the **default gateway**. The reason a switch needs a default gateway setting is the same reason that hosts need the same setting—because of how hosts think when sending IP packets. Specifically:

- To send IP packets to hosts in the same subnet, send them directly

- To send IP packets to hosts in a different subnet, send them to the local router; that is, the default gateway

Figure 6-8 shows the ideas. In this case, the switch (on the right) will use IP address 192.168.1.200 as configured on interface VLAN 1. However, to communicate with host A, on the far left of the figure, the switch must use Router R1 (the default gateway) to forward IP packets to host A. To make that work, the switch needs to configure a default gateway setting, pointing to Router R1's IP address (192.168.1.1 in this case). Note that the switch and router both use the same mask, 255.255.255.0, which puts the addresses in the same subnet.

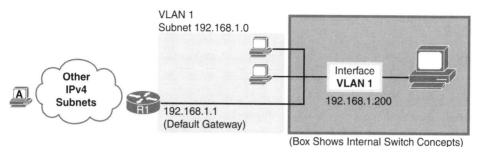

Figure 6-8 *The Need for a Default Gateway*

Configuring IPv4 on a Switch

A switch configures its IPv4 address and mask on this special NIC-like *VLAN interface*. The following steps list the commands used to configure IPv4 on a switch, assuming that the IP address is configured to be in VLAN 1, with Example 6-7 that follows showing an example configuration.

Step 1.   Use the **interface vlan 1** command in global configuration mode to enter interface VLAN 1 configuration mode.

Step 2.   Use the **ip address** *ip-address mask* command in interface configuration mode to assign an IP address and mask.

Step 3.   Use the **no shutdown** command in interface configuration mode to enable the VLAN 1 interface if it is not already enabled.

Step 4.   Add the **ip default-gateway** *ip-address* command in global configuration mode to configure the default gateway.

Step 5.   (Optional) Add the **ip name-server** *ip-address1 ip-address2 ...* command in global configuration mode to configure the switch to use the Domain Name System (**DNS**) to resolve names into their matching IP address.

Example 6-7 *Switch Static IP Address Configuration*

```
Emma# configure terminal
Emma(config)# interface vlan 1
Emma(config-if)# ip address 192.168.1.200 255.255.255.0
Emma(config-if)# no shutdown
00:25:07: %LINK-3-UPDOWN: Interface Vlan1, changed state to up
00:25:08: %LINEPROTO-5-UPDOWN: Line protocol on Interface Vlan1, changed
 state to up
Emma(config if)# exit
Emma(config)# ip default-gateway 192.168.1.1
```

On a side note, this example shows a particularly important and common command: the [no] **shutdown** command. To administratively enable an interface on a switch, use the **no shutdown** interface subcommand; to disable an interface, use the **shutdown** interface subcommand.

This command can be used on the physical Ethernet interfaces that the switch uses to switch Ethernet messages in addition to the VLAN interface shown here in this example.

Also, pause long enough to look at the messages that appear just below the **no shutdown** command in Example 6-7. Those messages are syslog messages generated by the switch stating that the switch did indeed enable the interface. Switches (and routers) generate syslog messages in response to a variety of events, and by default, those messages appear at the console. Chapter 13, "Device Management Protocols," in the *CCNA 200-301 Official Cert Guide, Volume 2*, Second Edition, discusses syslog messages in more detail.

Configuring a Switch to Learn Its IP Address with DHCP

The switch can also use Dynamic Host Configuration Protocol (DHCP) to dynamically learn its IPv4 settings. (Typically, engineers do not do so, instead statically configuring switch IP addresses, but this section covers the concept to be complete as compared to the exam topics.) Basically, all you have to do is tell the switch to use DHCP on the interface and enable the interface. Assuming that DHCP works in this network, the switch will learn all its settings. The following list details the steps, again assuming the use of interface VLAN 1, with Example 6-8 that follows showing an example:

Step 1.   Enter VLAN 1 configuration mode using the **interface vlan 1** global configuration command, and enable the interface using the **no shutdown** command as necessary.

Step 2.   Assign an IP address and mask using the **ip address dhcp** interface subcommand.

Example 6-8   *Switch Dynamic IP Address Configuration with DHCP*

```
Emma# configure terminal
Enter configuration commands, one per line. End with CNTL/Z.
Emma(config)# interface vlan 1
Emma(config-if)# ip address dhcp
Emma(config-if)# no shutdown
Emma(config-if)# ^Z
Emma#
00:38:20: %LINK-3-UPDOWN: Interface Vlan1, changed state to up
00:38:21: %LINEPROTO-5-UPDOWN: Line protocol on Interface Vlan1, changed state to up
```

Verifying IPv4 on a Switch

The switch IPv4 configuration can be checked in several places. First, you can always look at the current configuration using the **show running-config** command. Second, you can look at the IP address and mask information using the **show interfaces vlan** *x* command, which shows detailed status information about the VLAN interface in VLAN *x*. Finally, if using DHCP, use the **show dhcp lease** command to see the (temporarily) leased IP address and other parameters. (Note that the switch does not store the DHCP-learned IP configuration in the running-config file.) Example 6-9 shows sample output from these commands to match the configuration in Example 6-8.

Example 6-9   *Verifying DHCP-Learned Information on a Switch*

```
Emma# show dhcp lease
Temp IP addr: 192.168.1.101   for peer on Interface: Vlan1
Temp sub net mask: 255.255.255.0
   DHCP Lease server: 192.168.1.1, state: 3 Bound
   DHCP transaction id: 1966
   Lease: 86400 secs,  Renewal: 43200 secs,  Rebind: 75600 secs
Temp default-gateway addr: 192.168.1.1
   Next timer fires after: 11:59:45
   Retry count: 0   Client-ID: cisco-0019.e86a.6fc0-Vl1
   Hostname: Emma
Emma# show interfaces vlan 1
Vlan1 is up, line protocol is up
  Hardware is EtherSVI, address is 0019.e86a.6fc0 (bia 0019.e86a.6fc0)
  Internet address is 192.168.1.101/24
  MTU 1500 bytes, BW 1000000 Kbit, DLY 10 usec,
     reliability 255/255, txload 1/255, rxload 1/255
! lines omitted for brevity
Emma# show ip default-gateway
192.168.1.1
```

The output of the **show interfaces vlan 1** command lists two important details related to switch IP addressing. First, this **show** command lists the interface status of the VLAN 1 interface—in this case, "up and up." If the VLAN 1 interface is not up, the switch cannot use its IP address to send and receive management traffic. Notably, if you forget to issue the **no shutdown** command, the VLAN 1 interface remains in its default shutdown state and is listed as "administratively down" in the **show** command output.

Second, note that the output lists the interface's IP address on the third line. If you statically configure the IP address, as in Example 6-7, the IP address will always be listed; however, if you use DHCP and DHCP fails, the **show interfaces vlan** *x* command will not list an IP address here. When DHCP works, you can see the IP address with the **show interfaces vlan 1** command, but that output does not remind you whether the address is either statically configured or DHCP leased. So it does take a little extra effort to make sure you know whether the address is statically configured or DHCP-learned on the VLAN interface.

Miscellaneous Settings Useful in the Lab

This last short section of the chapter touches on a couple of commands that can help you be a little more productive when practicing in a lab.

History Buffer Commands

When you enter commands from the CLI, the switch saves the last several commands in the **history buffer**. Then, as mentioned in Chapter 4, "Using the Command-Line Interface," you can use the up-arrow key or press Ctrl+P to move back in the history buffer to retrieve a command you entered a few commands ago. This feature makes it easy and fast to use a set of commands repeatedly. Table 6-2 lists some of the key commands related to the history buffer.

Table 6-2   Commands Related to the History Buffer

Command	Description
show history	An EXEC command that lists the commands currently held in the history buffer.
terminal history size *x*	From EXEC mode, this command allows a single user to set, just for this one login session, the size of his or her history buffer.
history size *x*	A configuration command that, from console or vty line configuration mode, sets the default number of commands saved in the history buffer for the users of the console or vty lines, respectively.

The logging synchronous, exec-timeout, and no ip domain-lookup Commands

These next three configuration commands have little in common, other than the fact that they can be useful settings to reduce your frustration when using the console of a switch or router.

The console automatically receives copies of all unsolicited syslog messages on a switch. The idea is that if the switch needs to tell the network administrator some important and possibly urgent information, the administrator might be at the console and might notice the message.

Unfortunately, IOS (by default) displays these syslog messages on the console's screen at any time—including right in the middle of a command you are entering, or in the middle of the output of a **show** command. Having a bunch of text show up unexpectedly can be a bit annoying.

You could simply disable the feature that sends these messages to the console and then re-enable the feature later using the **no logging console** and **logging console** global configuration commands. For example, when working from the console, if you want to temporarily not be bothered by log messages, you can disable the display of these messages with the **no logging console** global configuration command, and then when finished, enable them again.

However, IOS supplies a reasonable compromise, telling the switch to display syslog messages only at more convenient times, such as at the end of output from a **show** command. To do so, just configure the **logging synchronous** console line subcommand, which basically tells IOS to synchronize the syslog message display with the messages requested using **show** commands.

Another way to improve the user experience at the console is to control timeouts of the login session from the console or when using Telnet or SSH. By default, the switch automatically disconnects console and vty (Telnet and SSH) users after 5 minutes of inactivity. The **exec-timeout** *minutes seconds* line subcommand enables you to set the length of that inactivity timer. In the lab (but not in production), you might want to use the special value of 0 minutes and 0 seconds, meaning "never time out."

Finally, IOS has an interesting combination of features that can make you wait for a minute or so when you mistype a command. First, IOS tries to use DNS **name resolution** on IP hostnames—a generally useful feature. If you mistype a command, however, IOS thinks you want to telnet to a host by that name. With all default settings in the switch, the switch tries to resolve the hostname, cannot find a DNS server, and takes about a minute to time out and give you control of the CLI again.

To avoid this problem, configure the **no ip domain-lookup** global configuration command, which disables IOS's attempt to resolve the hostname into an IP address.

Example 6-10 collects all these commands into a single example, as a template for some good settings to add in a lab switch to make you more productive.

Example 6-10 *Commands Often Used in the Lab to Increase Productivity*

```
no ip domain-lookup
!
line console 0
 exec-timeout 0 0
 logging synchronous
 history size 20
!
line vty 0 15
 exec-timeout 0 0
 logging synchronous
 history size 20
```

Chapter Review

One key to doing well on the exams is to perform repetitive spaced review sessions. Review this chapter's material using either the tools in the book or interactive tools for the same material found on the book's companion website. Refer to the "Your Study Plan" element section titled "Step 2: Build Your Study Habits Around the Chapter" for more details. Table 6-3 outlines the key review elements and where you can find them. To better track your study progress, record when you completed these activities in the second column.

Table 6-3 Chapter Review Tracking

Review Element	Review Date(s)	Resource Used
Review key topics		Book, website
Review key terms		Book, website
Answer DIKTA questions		Book, PTP
Review config checklists		Book, website
Do labs		Sim Lite, blog
Review command tables		Book
Watch video		Website

Review All the Key Topics

Table 6-4   Key Topics for Chapter 6

Key Topic Element	Description	Page Number
Example 6-2	Example of configuring password login security (no usernames)	138
Figure 6-5	SSH configuration commands with related username login security	142

Key Terms You Should Know

AAA, AAA server, default gateway, DNS, enable mode, history buffer, local username, log message, name resolution, Secure Shell (SSH), Telnet, VLAN interface

Do Labs

The Sim Lite software is a version of Pearson's full simulator learning product with a subset of the labs, included with this book for free. The subset of labs mostly relates to this chapter. Take the time to try some of the labs. As always, also check the author's blog site pages for configuration exercises (Config Labs) at https://www.certskills.com.

Command References

Tables 6-5, 6-6, 6-7, and 6-8 list configuration and verification commands used in this chapter. As an easy review exercise, cover the left column in a table, read the right column, and try to recall the command without looking. Then repeat the exercise, covering the right column, and try to recall what the command does.

Table 6-5   Login Security Commands

Command	Mode/Purpose/Description
line console 0	Changes the context to console configuration mode.
line vty *1st-vty last-vty*	Changes the context to vty configuration mode for the range of vty lines listed in the command.
login	Console and vty configuration mode. Tells IOS to prompt for a password.
password *pass-value*	Console and vty configuration mode. Lists the password required if the **login** command (with no other parameters) is configured.
login local	Console and vty configuration mode. Tells IOS to prompt for a username and password, to be checked against locally configured **username** global configuration commands on this switch or router.
username *name* **secret** *pass-value*	Global command. Defines one of possibly multiple usernames and associated passwords, used for user authentication. Used when the **login local** line configuration command has been used.

Command	Mode/Purpose/Description
crypto key generate rsa [modulus *512..2048*]	Global command. Creates and stores (in a hidden location in flash memory) the keys required by SSH.
transport input {**telnet** | **ssh** | **all** | **none**}	vty line configuration mode. Defines whether Telnet/SSH access is allowed into this switch. Both values can be configured on one command to allow both Telnet and SSH access (the default).
ip domain name *fqdn*	Global command. Defines the fully-qualified domain name (*fqdn*) for the DNS domain in which the switch or router resides.
hostname *name*	Global command. Sets the *name* that the device uses for itself, which is also used at the initial text in the command prompt.
ip ssh version 2	Global command. Sets the SSH server to use only version 2, rather than the default of supporting both versions 1 and 2.

Table 6-6   Switch IPv4 Configuration

Command	Mode/Purpose/Description
interface vlan *number*	Changes the context to VLAN interface mode. For VLAN 1, allows the configuration of the switch's IP address.
ip address *ip-address subnet-mask*	VLAN interface mode. Statically configures the switch's IP address and mask.
ip address dhcp	VLAN interface mode. Configures the switch as a DHCP client to discover its IPv4 address, mask, and default gateway.
ip default-gateway *address*	Global command. Configures the switch's default gateway IPv4 address. Not required if the switch uses DHCP.
ip name-server *server-ip-1 server-ip-2 ...*	Global command. Configures the IPv4 addresses of DNS servers, so any commands when logged in to the switch will use the DNS for name resolution.

Table 6-7   Other Switch Configuration

Command	Mode/Purpose/Description
hostname *name*	Global command. Sets this switch's hostname, which is also used as the first part of the switch's command prompt.
enable secret *pass-value*	Global command. Sets this switch's password that is required for any user to reach enable mode.
history size *length*	Line config mode. Defines the number of commands held in the history buffer, for later recall, for users of those lines.
logging synchronous	Console or vty mode. Tells IOS to send log messages to the user at natural break points between commands rather than in the middle of a line of output.
[no] logging console	Global command. Disables or enables the display of log messages to the console.

6

Command	Mode/Purpose/Description
exec-timeout *minutes* [*seconds*]	Console or vty mode. Sets the inactivity timeout so that after the defined period of no action, IOS closes the current user login session.
no ip domain-lookup	Global command. Disables the use of the DNS client on the switch.

Table 6-8   Chapter 6 EXEC Command Reference

Command	Purpose
show running-config	Lists the currently used configuration.
show running-config | begin line vty	Pipes (sends) the command output to the **begin** command, which only lists output beginning with the first line that contains the text "line vty."
show dhcp lease	Lists any information the switch acquires as a DHCP client. This includes IP address, subnet mask, and default gateway information.
show crypto key mypubkey rsa	Lists the public and shared key created for use with SSH using the **crypto key generate rsa** global configuration command.
show ip ssh	Lists status information for the SSH server, including the SSH version.
show ssh	Lists status information for current SSH connections into and out of the local switch.
show interfaces vlan *number*	Lists the interface status, the switch's IPv4 address and mask, and much more.
show ip default-gateway	Lists the switch's setting for its IPv4 default gateway.
terminal history size *x*	Changes the length of the history buffer for the current user only, only for the current login to the switch.
show history	Lists the commands in the current history buffer.

CHAPTER 7

Configuring and Verifying Switch Interfaces

This chapter covers the following exam topics:

1.0 Network Fundamentals

    1.1 Explain the role and function of network components

        1.1.b Layer 2 and Layer 3 switches

    1.3 Compare physical interface and cabling types

        1.3.b Connections (Ethernet shared media and point-to-point)

    1.4 Identify interface and cable issues (collisions, errors, mismatch duplex, and/or speed)

The chapters in Part II of this book move back and forth between switch administration and core switch functions. In Chapter 4, "Using the Command-Line Interface," you read about the fundamentals of the command-line interface (CLI) and how to use commands that configure and verify switch features. In Chapter 5, "Analyzing Ethernet LAN Switching," you learned about the primary purpose of a switch—forwarding Ethernet frames—and how to see that process in action by looking at the switch MAC address table. Chapter 6, "Configuring Basic Switch Management," then moved back to more administrative tasks, where you learned a few management plane features, like how to configure the switch to support Telnet and Secure Shell (SSH) by configuring IP address and login security.

This chapter focuses on more core switch features, specifically how to configure switch interfaces so that they work. The first section shows how to configure switch interfaces to use the correct speed and duplex, primarily by using IEEE autonegotiation. The second section examines some administrative settings on switches, including how to disable and re-enable an interface. The final section then focuses on how to use **show** commands on a switch to verify switch interface status and interpret the output to find some of the more common issues with switch interfaces.

"Do I Know This Already?" Quiz

Take the quiz (either here or use the PTP software) if you want to use the score to help you decide how much time to spend on this chapter. The letter answers are listed at the bottom of the page following the quiz. Appendix C, found both at the end of the book and on the companion website, includes answers and explanations. You can also find both answers and explanations in the PTP testing software.

Table 7-1 "Do I Know This Already?" Foundation Topics Section-to-Question Mapping

Foundation Topics Section	Questions
Configuring Switch Interface Speed and Duplex	1–3
Managing Switch Interface Configuration	4–5
Analyzing Switch Interface Status and Statistics	6–8

1. Switch SW1 connects its G1/0/1 port to PC1. Both devices use IEEE autonegotiation and have 10/100/1000 ports. Which answer describes how the switch chooses its G1/0/1 speed and duplex settings? (Choose two answers.)

    a. Speed by comparing capabilities per received autonegotiation messages

    b. Speed by analyzing the electrical signal of incoming Ethernet frames from PC1

    c. Duplex by comparing capabilities per received autonegotiation messages

    d. Duplex by analyzing the electrical signal of incoming Ethernet frames from PC1

    e. Duplex by choosing a default based on the chosen speed

2. In which of the following modes of the CLI could you configure the duplex setting for interface Fast Ethernet 0/5?

    a. User mode

    b. Enable mode

    c. Global configuration mode

    d. VLAN mode

    e. Interface configuration mode

3. Switch SW1 connects its G1/0/1 port to PC1. Both devices are 10/100/1000 ports. While the switch port uses IEEE autonegotiation, PC1 has disabled it. Which answer describes how the switch chooses its G1/0/1 speed and duplex settings?

    a. Speed by comparing capabilities per received autonegotiation messages

    b. Speed by analyzing the electrical signal of incoming Ethernet frames from PC1

    c. Duplex by comparing capabilities per received autonegotiation messages

    d. Duplex by analyzing the electrical signal of incoming Ethernet frames from PC1

    e. Duplex by choosing a default based on the chosen speed

4. Switch interface G1/0/5 has been cabled correctly in anticipation of some weekend work. However, the engineer needs to prevent the interface from being used until she enables it remotely during a change window this weekend. Which action helps achieve that goal?

    a. Unplug the cable.

    b. Issue the **shutdown g1/0/5** global configuration command.

    c. Issue the **shutdown** interface subcommand under interface **g1/0/5**.

    d. Issue the **disable g1/0/5** global configuration command.

    e. Issue the **enable** interface subcommand under interface **g1/0/5**.

5. An engineer configures Cisco switch SW1 with the commands **interface range G1/0/10-20** and then **description connected to endpoint device**. The engineer exits configuration mode and issues a **show running-config** command. Which answers best describe the related output? (Choose two answers.)

   a. The output includes the **interface range** command.

   b. The output does not include the **interface range** command.

   c. The output lists one **description connected to endpoint device** interface subcommand.

   d. The output lists 11 **description connected to endpoint device** interface subcommands.

6. The output from the switch command **show interfaces status** shows interface Fa0/1 in a "disabled" state. Which of the following is true about interface Fa0/1? (Choose three answers.)

   a. The interface is configured with the **shutdown** command.

   b. The **show interfaces fa0/1** command will list the interface with two status codes of administratively down and line protocol down.

   c. The **show interfaces fa0/1** command will list the interface with two status codes up and down.

   d. The interface cannot currently be used to forward frames.

   e. The interface can currently be used to forward frames.

7. Switch SW1 Gigabit 1/0/1 connects to switch SW2's Gigabit 1/0/2 interface, both 10/100/1000 ports. The switch SW2 configuration includes the **speed** and **duplex** commands, the combination of which happens to disable autonegotiation on that port. Which combination of settings in SW2's **speed** and **duplex** commands results in a duplex mismatch between SW1 and SW2? (Choose two answers.)

   a. **speed 100** and **duplex full**

   b. **speed 100** and **duplex half**

   c. **speed 10** and **duplex full**

   d. **speed 10** and **duplex half**

8. Switch SW1 connects via a cable to switch SW2's G1/0/1 port. Which of the following conditions is the most likely to cause SW1's late collision counter to continue to increment?

   a. SW2's G1/0/1 has been configured with a **shutdown** interface subcommand.

   b. The two switches have been configured with different values on the **speed** interface subcommand.

   c. A duplex mismatch exists with SW1 set to full duplex.

   d. A duplex mismatch exists with SW1 set to half duplex.

Foundation Topics

Configuring Switch Interface Speed and Duplex

When physically creating an Ethernet LAN, you must consider the cabling and connectors that match the dozens of physical layer Ethernet standards that help you meet the physical requirements for the LAN. Once chosen and installed, any interfaces connected to fiber cabling require no additional configuration; however, UTP cabling can have different pinouts, and UTP supports different speeds and duplex settings. So once installed, interfaces that use UTP cabling may need additional configuration.

This first major section of the chapter examines interface speed and duplex settings, along with the IEEE autonegotiation process. It also discusses auto-MDIX, a feature that deals with pinout issues. Finally, this entire chapter continues the goal of helping you learn more about CLI navigation and conventions.

IEEE Autonegotiation Concepts

Ethernet NICs and switch ports often support multiple standards and therefore support multiple speeds. For instance, you will see designations like these:

10/100: A port that supports 10- and 100-Mbps Ethernet

10/100/1000: A port that supports 10-, 100-, and 1000-Mbps Ethernet

Using hardware that supports multiple standards and speeds allows for much easier growth and migration over time—mainly because the devices can automatically sense the fastest speed using the IEEE autonegotiation feature. For instance, many switches today have many 10/100/1000 ports. Many newer end-user devices also have a 10/100/1000 Ethernet NIC, so the PC and switch can autonegotiate to 1000 Mbps (1 Gbps). Older devices, and some specialized devices that might not need faster speeds, might support only 10 Mbps or 100 Mbps. **Autonegotiation** gives the devices on each link the means to agree to use the best speed without manually configuring the speed on each switch port.

IEEE autonegotiation defines a process by which both devices on each link tell the neighboring device their capabilities. Once both endpoints learn about the other, they use the standard with the fastest speed. Autonegotiation also defines **full duplex** as the preferred option over **half duplex**, assuming both devices support that option.

Autonegotiation Under Working Conditions

With IEEE autonegotiation, a device declares its capabilities by sending a series of Fast Link Pulses (FLPs). The data in the FLP messages include bits that identify the Ethernet standards supported by the device and the duplex ability supported, in effect declaring the speeds and duplex settings supported by the device.

The FLPs work even before the endpoints choose a physical layer standard. FLPs use out-of-band electrical signaling, independent of the various physical layer standards for Ethernet frame transmission. Any device that supports autonegotiation supports using these out-of-band FLP messages. The FLPs solve the problem of how the devices can send information to each other even before the link is up and working for normal data transmission.

7

Figure 7-1 shows three examples of autonegotiation working as intended. First, the company installs cabling that supports 10BASE-T, 100BASE-T, and 1000BASE-T, that is, cabling with four wire pairs of appropriate quality. In the three examples, the PC and switch both use autonegotiation. The cables work with correct straight-through pinouts. The switch, in this case, has all 10/100/1000 ports, while the PC NICs support different options (10 only, 10/100, and 10/100/1000), as per the figure.

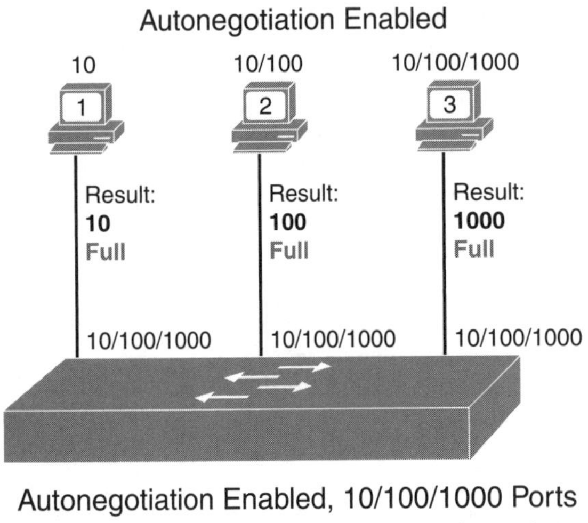

Autonegotiation Enabled

Figure 7-1   *IEEE Autonegotiation Results with Both Nodes Working Correctly*

The following list breaks down the logic, one PC at a time:

- **PC1:** PC1 sends autonegotiation FLPs that declare support for 10 Mbps only (not 100 or 1000 Mbps) and support for both full and half duplex. The switch announces support for 10, 100, and 1000 Mbps and both duplex settings. As a result, both the PC and the switch choose the fastest speed (10 Mbps) and the best duplex (full) that both support.

- **PC2:** PC2 declares support for 10 and 100 Mbps and both full and half duplex. The switch again claims support for 10, 100, and 1000 Mbps and both full and half duplex. Both devices use the best common speed and duplex (100 Mbps and full duplex).

- **PC3:** PC3 uses a 10/100/1000 NIC, supporting all three speeds, so both the NIC and switch port choose 1000 Mbps and full duplex.

Summarizing, the following list details autonegotiation rules when both endpoints use it:

- Both endpoints send messages, out-of-band compared to any specific data transmission standard, using Fast Link Pulses (FLPs).

Answers to the "Do I Know This Already?" quiz:

1 A, C **2** E **3** B, E **4** C **5** B, D **6** A, B, D **7** A, C **8** D

- The messages declare all supported speed and duplex combinations.

- After hearing from the link partner, each device chooses the fastest speed supported by both devices and the best duplex (full being better than half duplex).

Autonegotiation Results When Only One Node Uses Autonegotiation

With both devices using autonegotiation, the result is obvious. Both devices use the fastest speed and best duplex supported by both devices.

Cisco repeatedly recommends using autonegotiation on both ends of all Ethernet links that support it—but if you must disable it, make sure to configure both speed and duplex on both ends of the link. For instance, some installations prefer to predefine the speed and duplex on links between two switches. To do so, use commands such as **speed 1000** (meaning 1000 Mbps, or 1 Gbps) and **duplex full.** If configured with these same values on both ends of the link, the link will work due to matching settings of 1000BASE-T with full duplex.

However, many devices have the capability to disable autonegotiation, which means an engineer can make the poor choice to disable autonegotiation on one end of the link but not the other. In real networks, do not do that, because it can cause problems like a *duplex mismatch* and *late collisions*.

To understand what happens, first consider the device with autonegotiation disabled. It must use some physical layer standard (typically due to a static configuration setting), so it begins sending Ethernet frames that conform to that standard—but it does not send FLPs. The other device (the one that uses autonegotiation) sends FLPs, but receives none. Once the device that is attempting autonegotiation realizes it is not receiving FLPs, it can examine the incoming electrical signal of those Ethernet frames and notice the differences between the signals used for 10BASE-T, 100BASE-T, and so on in the incoming signals. Knowing that, it uses the same standard, solving the question of what speed to use.

The choice of duplex requires using a default. If the speed is 10 or 100 Mbps, the device attempting autonegotiation uses half duplex. Otherwise, it chooses full duplex.

The IEEE refers to the logic used by autonegotiation when the other device has disabled autonegotiation as **parallel detection**, summarized as follows:

- **Speed:** Detect the neighboring device's physical layer standard by analyzing the neighbor's incoming frames. Use that speed.

- **Duplex:** Make a default choice based on speed—half duplex if the speed is 10 or 100 Mbps, and full duplex if faster.

> **NOTE** Ethernet interfaces using speeds more than 1 Gbps always use full duplex.

Figure 7-2 shows three examples of autonegotiation parallel detection logic. In each case, the PC configuration has disabled autonegotiation while the switch (with all 10/100/1000 ports) continues to use autonegotiation. The top of the figure shows the configured settings on each PC NIC, with the choices made by the switch listed next to each switch port.

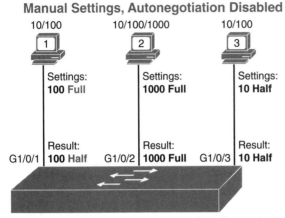

Figure 7-2 *IEEE Autonegotiation Results Using Parallel Detection Logic*

Reviewing each link, left to right:

- **PC1:** The PC uses 100 Mbps and full duplex settings. The switch receives no autonegotiation FLP messages on port G1/0/1, instead sensing that PC1 is sending frames at 100 Mbps. Then the switch chooses to use half duplex per the defaults (half duplex if the speed is 10 or 100 Mbps).

- **PC2:** The switch uses the same steps and logic as for the link to PC1. Switch port G1/0/2 senses the use of 1000BASE-T signaling, with a speed of 1 Gbps, and chooses a full duplex per the speed-based defaults.

- **PC3:** The PC uses the worst settings possible, with the slower speed (10 Mbps) and the worse duplex setting (half). The switch port receives no FLP messages, so it senses the use of 10BASE-T per the incoming frames, uses 10 Mbps, and chooses half duplex per the speed-based defaults.

Take a closer look at the PC1 example: It shows a poor result called a **duplex mismatch**. The two nodes (PC1 and SW1's port G1/0/1) both use the same 100 Mbps so that they can send data. However, PC1, using full duplex, does not attempt to use carrier sense multiple access with collision detection (CSMA/CD) logic and sends frames at any time. Switch port G1/0/1, using half duplex, does use CSMA/CD. As a result, switch port G1/0/1 will believe collisions occur on the link if, when sending a frame, PC1 also sends a frame. When that happens, the switch port will stop transmitting, back off, resend frames, and so on. As a result, the link is up, but it performs poorly. The upcoming section titled "The Duplex Mismatch Issue" will explore this problem with a focus on how to recognize the symptoms of a duplex mismatch.

NOTE To emphasize, in real networks, use autonegotiation. If you have specific reasons not to use it, ensure you configure the devices on both ends of the link and use the same settings.

Autonegotiation and LAN Hubs

LAN hubs also impact how autonegotiation works. Hubs do not participate in autonegotiation, they do not generate FLP messages, and they do not forward the autonegotiation FLP messages sent by connected devices. As a result, devices connected to a hub receive no FLP messages and use only IEEE autonegotiation parallel detection rules. That can work, but it often results in the devices using 10 Mbps and half duplex.

Figure 7-3 shows an example of a small Ethernet LAN that uses an old 10BASE-T hub. The devices on the right (PC3 and PC4) sense the speed as 10 Mbps per the incoming signal, and then they choose to use the default duplex when using 10 Mbps of half duplex. Using 10 Mbps and half duplex works well in this case: The PCs on the right need to use half duplex because the hub requires any attached devices to use half duplex to avoid collisions.

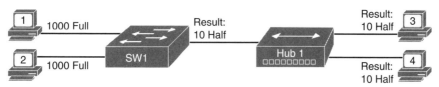

Figure 7-3   *IEEE Autonegotiation with a LAN Hub*

Configuring Autonegotiation, Speed, and Duplex

For an Ethernet link to work correctly, the link needs a working cable, and the endpoints need to use the same physical layer standard and duplex setting. With Cisco switches, the default switch setting to use autonegotiation should make the switch use the right speed and duplex so that the link works. The following pages show how to verify the autonegotiation process to see what a switch has chosen to use on an interface, along with how to manually set the speed and duplex with some other related commands.

Using Autonegotiation on Cisco Switches

Figure 7-4 shows a small network used in the next few examples. The figure shows a working link with an installed cable, a powered-on device (PC1), and both devices using IEEE autonegotiation. The other two links do not work because, in one case, no cable has been connected, and in the other, the cable is installed, but the device is powered off.

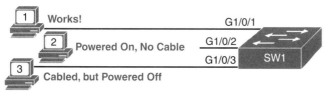

Figure 7-4   *Network Topology to Match Examples 7-1 Through 7-4*

The switch (SW1) uses the default autonegotiation settings in the first few examples. To configure those settings overtly, you would configure the interface subcommands **speed auto** and **duplex auto**. However, because the **show running-config** and **show startup-config** commands generally do not show default configuration commands, the absence of the **speed** and **duplex** commands in Example 7-1 confirms the interfaces use autonegotiation.

Example 7-1 *Confirming All Default Settings on the Switch Interfaces in Figure 7-1*

```
SW1# show running-config
! Lines omitted for brevity
interface GigabitEthernet1/0/1
!
interface GigabitEthernet1/0/2
!
interface GigabitEthernet1/0/3
!
! Lines omitted for brevity
SW1#
```

Example 7-2 shows how you can overcome your doubts about whether the absence of the **speed auto** and **duplex auto** interface subcommands confirms those settings. The example shows the commands configured on an interface. Even after configuring the commands, the **show running-config** command does not display them, confirming them as the default settings. (You can use that process for any configuration command, by the way.)

Example 7-2 *Confirming Autonegotiation Is the Default Setting*

```
SW1# configure terminal
SW1(config)# interface gigabitEthernet 1/0/1
SW1(config-if)# speed auto
SW1(config-if)# duplex auto
SW1(config-if)# ^Z
SW1# show running-config interface gigabitEthernet 1/0/1
Building configuration...

Current configuration : 38 bytes
!
interface GigabitEthernet1/0/1
end
SW1#
```

Also, as a quick way to check interface configuration, note the **show running-config interface GigabitEthernet1/0/1** command at the end of the example. It is a supported command that shows only the configuration for the listed interface.

The better way to confirm the operation of autonegotiation on a switch interface relies on the **show interfaces status** command. Example 7-3 shows the output based on the state from Figure 7-4. In particular, note the Duplex and Speed columns of the output, with the following list identifying the meaning:

   a-full: Full duplex, with the a- meaning the switch learned the value using autonegotiation.

   a-1000: 1000 Mbps (1 Gbps), with the a- meaning the switch learned the setting using autonegotiation.

   auto: The interface will use autonegotiation when the link physically works.

Example 7-3 *Interpreting Autonegotiation Clues Before/After Completion*

```
SW1# show interfaces status
Port        Name            Status         Vlan       Duplex  Speed Type
Gi1/0/1                     connected      1          a-full a-1000 10/100/1000BaseTX
Gi1/0/2                     notconnect     1          auto     auto 10/100/1000BaseTX
Gi1/0/3                     notconnect     1          auto     auto 10/100/1000BaseTX
Gi1/0/4                     notconnect     1          auto     auto 10/100/1000BaseTX
Gi1/0/5                     notconnect     1          auto     auto 10/100/1000BaseTX
Gi1/0/6                     notconnect     1          auto     auto 10/100/1000BaseTX
Gi1/0/7                     notconnect     1          auto     auto 10/100/1000BaseTX
Gi1/0/8                     notconnect     1          auto     auto 10/100/1000BaseTX
Gi1/0/9                     notconnect     1          auto     auto 10/100/1000BaseTX
Gi1/0/10                    notconnect     1          auto     auto 10/100/1000BaseTX
Gi1/0/11                    notconnect     1          auto     auto 10/100/1000BaseTX
Gi1/0/12                    notconnect     1          auto     auto 10/100/1000BaseTX
Gi1/0/13                    notconnect     1          auto     auto 10/100/1000BaseTX
Gi1/0/14                    notconnect     1          auto     auto 10/100/1000BaseTX
Gi1/0/15                    notconnect     1          auto     auto 10/100/1000BaseTX
Gi1/0/16                    notconnect     1          auto     auto 10/100/1000BaseTX
Gi1/0/17                    notconnect     1          auto     auto 10/100/1000BaseTX
Gi1/0/18                    notconnect     1          auto     auto 10/100/1000BaseTX
Gi1/0/19                    notconnect     1          auto     auto 10/100/1000BaseTX
Gi1/0/20                    notconnect     1          auto     auto 10/100/1000BaseTX
Gi1/0/21                    notconnect     1          auto     auto 10/100/1000BaseTX
Gi1/0/22                    notconnect     1          auto     auto 10/100/1000BaseTX
Gi1/0/23                    notconnect     1          auto     auto 10/100/1000BaseTX
Gi1/0/24                    notconnect     1          auto     auto 10/100/1000BaseTX
Te1/1/1                     connected      1          full      10G SFP-10GBase-SR
Te1/1/2                     notconnect     1          auto     auto unknown
Te1/1/3                     notconnect     1          auto     auto unknown
Te1/1/4                     notconnect     1          auto     auto unknown
```

The first few output lines in Example 7-3 confirm that port G1/0/1 works with autonegotiation. Given the highlighted values in the duplex and speed columns, you can see that port G1/0/1 uses 1000BASE-T and full duplex, as learned by autonegotiation (per the a- prefix).

The output lines for ports G1/0/2 and G1/0/3 show the normal state for a nonworking port. The notconnect state per the Status column means that the link is not functional—in PC2's case because no cable exists and in PC3's case because PC3 is powered off. Autonegotiation can work only if the physical link works.

Beyond the **show interfaces status**, the **show interfaces** command also gives some autonegotiation data. Example 7-4 shows the output for working interface G1/0/1 from Figure 7-4. Note the highlighted text about seven lines into the example, which shows the speed and duplex used on the link; however, note that this command on working interface G1/0/1 lists no information on whether it used autonegotiation.

7

Example 7-4 show interfaces *Command Autonegotiation Clues*

```
SW1# show interfaces gigabitEthernet 1/0/1
GigabitEthernet1/0/1 is up, line protocol is up (connected)
  Hardware is Gigabit Ethernet, address is 4488.165a.f201 (bia 4488.165a.f201)
  MTU 1500 bytes, BW 1000000 Kbit/sec, DLY 10 usec,
     reliability 255/255, txload 1/255, rxload 1/255
  Encapsulation ARPA, loopback not set
  Keepalive set (10 sec)
  Full-duplex, 1000Mb/s, media type is 10/100/1000BaseTX
  input flow-control is on, output flow-control is unsupported
  ARP type: ARPA, ARP Timeout 04:00:00
  Last input 00:00:01, output 00:00:00, output hang never
  Last clearing of "show interface" counters never
  Input queue: 0/2000/0/0 (size/max/drops/flushes); Total output drops: 0
  Queueing strategy: fifo
  Output queue: 0/40 (size/max)
  5 minute input rate 0 bits/sec, 0 packets/sec
  5 minute output rate 0 bits/sec, 0 packets/sec
     14228 packets input, 1870879 bytes, 0 no buffer
     Received 14223 broadcasts (14222 multicasts)
     0 runts, 0 giants, 0 throttles
     0 input errors, 0 CRC, 0 frame, 0 overrun, 0 ignored
     0 watchdog, 14222 multicast, 0 pause input
     0 input packets with dribble condition detected
     56865 packets output, 7901974 bytes, 0 underruns
     Output 17109 broadcasts (0 multicasts)
     0 output errors, 0 collisions, 2 interface resets
     0 unknown protocol drops
     0 babbles, 0 late collision, 0 deferred
     0 lost carrier, 0 no carrier, 0 pause output
     0 output buffer failures, 0 output buffers swapped out

SW1# show interfaces g1/0/2
GigabitEthernet1/0/2 is down, line protocol is down (notconnect)
  Hardware is Gigabit Ethernet, address is 4488.165a.f202 (bia 4488.165a.f202)
  MTU 1500 bytes, BW 1000000 Kbit/sec, DLY 10 usec,
     reliability 255/255, txload 1/255, rxload 1/255
  Encapsulation ARPA, loopback not set
  Keepalive set (10 sec)
  Auto-duplex, Auto-speed, media type is 10/100/1000BaseTX
! Lines omitted for brevity
```

However, the **show interfaces** command does give some insight into autonegotiation for a nonworking interface such as G1/0/2, as seen at the end of Example 7-4. On an interface with default settings **speed auto** and **duplex auto**, the command output implies those settings with the auto-duplex and auto-speed text. However, the output shows those specific settings if configured to a specific speed or duplex.

Setting Speed and Duplex Manually

The switch **speed** and **duplex** interface subcommands can set an interface's specific speed and duplex. Risking being repetitive: In production networks, use and trust autonegotiation. However, for exam preparation, to cover all the combinations, if you want to configure the settings instead, Cisco recommends that you configure both devices on the ends of the link (to the same values, of course).

Figure 7-5 and Example 7-5 show an example of manually configuring the speed and duplex on a link between two switches. As per the recommendation, the engineer configures both devices with the same settings, and the link works.

Figure 7-5   *Configuring Speed and Duplex on a Switch-to-Switch Link*

Example 7-5   *Configuring Speed and Duplex on Both Ends of a Link*

```
SW1# show running-config interface g1/0/19
Building configuration...

Current configuration : 63 bytes
!
interface GigabitEthernet1/0/19
 speed 1000
 duplex full
end
```

```
! Now, on switch SW2
SW2# show running-config interface g1/0/20
Building configuration...

Current configuration : 64 bytes
!
interface GigabitEthernet1/0/20
 speed 1000
 duplex full
end
SW1#
```

In the scenario shown in Example 7-5, the two switches set both the speed and duplex, so they do not need to use autonegotiation. In this case, they just begin using the 1000BASE-T standard with full duplex, and the link works.

Example 7-6 shows a hidden gem in the output of the **show interfaces status** command that tells you the switch did not use autonegotiation in this case. First, note that switch SW1's

G1/0/19 interface reaches a connected state, so the link works. The Duplex and Speed columns list full and 1000 without the "a-" prefix. The absence of the "a-" means that the interface did not use autonegotiation to choose the setting, instead using the configuration. (See Example 7-3 for the earlier example showing values of a-full and a-1000.)

Example 7-6   show interfaces status *Without Using Autonegotiation*

```
SW1# show interfaces g1/0/20 status


Port          Name           Status      Vlan       Duplex  Speed Type
Gi1/0/19                     connected   1           full    1000
10/100/1000BaseTX


SW1# show interfaces g1/0/19
GigabitEthernet1/0/19 is up, line protocol is up (connected)
  Hardware is Gigabit Ethernet, address is 4488.165a.f213 (bia 4488.165a.f213)
  MTU 1500 bytes, BW 1000000 Kbit/sec, DLY 10 usec,
     reliability 255/255, txload 1/255, rxload 1/255
  Encapsulation ARPA, loopback not set
  Keepalive set (10 sec)
  Full-duplex, 1000Mb/s, media type is 10/100/1000BaseTX
! Lines omitted for brevity
```

NOTE   On some Cisco Catalyst switch ports, configuring both speed and duplex disables autonegotiation on that port. On others, it does not. In real networks, should you ever need to configure both the speed and duplex to specific values, take extra care to confirm that the speed and duplex match on both ends of the link.

Using Auto-MDIX on Cisco Switches

For switch interfaces to work, meaning they reach a connected state, the engineer should install a correct cable between the switch port and some other connected device. For UTP cabling, the cables often terminate with RJ-45 connectors. The cables must also conform to a straight-through or crossover cable pinout, as discussed in the section, "Building Physical Ethernet LANs with UTP," in Chapter 2, "Fundamentals of Ethernet LANs."

Chapter 2 also introduced a related concept called **auto-MDIX**, or automatic medium-dependent interface crossover. Auto-MDIX, when enabled, gives an Ethernet interface the ability to sense when the attached cable uses the wrong cable pinout and to overcome the problem. For instance, a link between two switches should use a crossover cable pinout. If the cable has a straight-through pinout, the auto-MDIX feature can sense the issue and swap pairs in the interface electronics, achieving the same effect as a crossover cable.

Figure 7-6 and Examples 7-7 and 7-8 demonstrate auto-MDIX. The figure shows a case with two switches connected with a straight-through cable. Cisco Catalyst switches use auto-MDIX by default, with a default interface subcommand of **mdix auto**. As with the **speed** and **duplex** commands earlier in this chapter, the default interface subcommand **mdix auto** command does not appear in the configuration. Example 7-7 confirms the absence of the **mdix auto** subcommand but confirms that the link reaches a connected state.

Figure 7-6   *Switch-Switch Link That Needs Crossover but Uses Straight-Through Cable*

Example 7-7   *Switch-Switch Link Works with All Default Settings*

```
SW1# running-config interface GigabitEthernet 1/0/19
Building configuration...

Current configuration : 39 bytes
!
interface GigabitEthernet1/0/19
end

SW1# show interfaces 1/0/19 status

Port         Name         Status       Vlan     Duplex  Speed Type
Gi1/0/19                  connected    1        a-full a-1000 10/100/1000BaseTX
```

Auto-MDIX works if either one or both endpoints on the link enable auto-MDIX. In Example 7-7, both switches default to auto-MDIX, but only one needs to swap the wire pairs. If you disable auto-MDIX on just one side, the other side swaps the pairs. To prevent auto-MDIX from doing its valuable work, disable it on both ends of the link using the **no mdix auto** interface subcommand.

Example 7-8 shows just that example. Before the example, the engineer configured switch SW2 with the **no mdix auto** interface subcommand. The example shows the process to disable it on switch SW1. As a result, neither switch uses auto-MDIX, and the interface fails to a notconnect state.

Example 7-8   *Switch-Switch Link Fails with Auto-MDIX Disabled on Both Ends*

```
SW1# running-config interface GigabitEthernet 1/0/19
SW1# config t
Enter configuration commands, one per line.  End with CNTL/Z.
SW1(config)# int g1/0/19
SW1(config-if)# no mdix auto
SW1(config-if)#
*Oct  5 12:50:22.177: %LINEPROTO-5-UPDOWN: Line protocol on Interface
GigabitEthernet1/0/19, changed state to down
*Oct  5 12:50:23.175: %LINK-3-UPDOWN: Interface GigabitEthernet1/0/19, changed state
to down
SW1(config-if)# ^Z
SW1#
SW1# show interfaces g1/0/19 status

Port         Name         Status       Vlan     Duplex  Speed Type
Gi1/0/19                  notconnect   1        auto    auto 10/100/1000BaseTX
```

On a side note, IOS supports many valid abbreviations for the **interface GigabitEthernet 1/0/19** global configuration command, including the **int g1/0/19** command shown in the example.

Managing Switch Interface Configuration

This next section of the chapter examines a small number of additional interface subcommands, specifically the **description** and **shutdown** commands. The first gives you the ability to document facts about each interface, while the second gives you the means to disable and enable the interface administratively.

This section also explains more about the mechanisms of the IOS CLI for interfaces, with some discussion and examples of removing configuration from an interface using the **no** command.

The Description and Interface Range Commands

The **description** *text* interface subcommand lets you add a text description to the interface. For the text, you can use keyboard characters, including spaces, with Cisco switches typically supporting around 200 characters of description text. For instance, if you want to store some information in the switch about the interface and the device connected to it, you could document the details with the **description** interface subcommand.

Example 7-9 demonstrates the mechanics of the process with a simple description added to interface G1/0/1 from Figure 7-4. The example shows the configuration plus the output from some **show** commands that repeat the detail. Note that the **show interfaces status** command does not leave enough space for the entire **description** command's text, but the **show interface** command does.

Example 7-9   *Configuring and Verifying the* **description** *Command on Switch SW1*

```
SW1# configure terminal
Enter configuration commands, one per line. End with CNTL/Z.
SW1(config)# interface GigabitEthernet 1/0/1
SW1(config-if)# description Link to PC1, using autonegotiation
SW1(config-if)# ^Z
SW1# show interfaces g1/0/1 status


Port            Name            Status      Vlan    Duplex  Speed Type
Gi1/0/1         Link to PC1, using connected 1            a-full a-1000
10/100/1000BaseTX
SW1# show interfaces g1/0/1
GigabitEthernet1/0/1 is up, line protocol is up (connected)
  Hardware is Gigabit Ethernet, address is 4488.165a.f201 (bia 4488.165a.f201)
  Description: Link to PC1, using autonegotiation
! Lines omitted for brevity
SW1#
```

Example 7-10 demonstrates how to configure the same interface subcommand on multiple interfaces simultaneously, saving effort. The example uses the **description** command again but after the **interface range GigabitEthernet 1/0/2 - 10** command. The **interface range** command tells IOS to apply subsequent subcommands to multiple interfaces, in this case, Gi1/0/2 through Gi1/0/10.

Example 7-10 *Configuring Multiple Interfaces Using the* **interface range** *Command*

```
SW1# configure terminal
SW1(config)# interface range g1/0/2 - 10
SW1(config-if-range)# description Interface not in use
SW1(config-if-range)# ^Z
SW1#
```

IOS does not put the **interface range** command into the configuration. Instead, it acts as if you had typed the subcommands under every single interface in the specified range. Example 7-11 shows an excerpt from the **show running-config** command, listing the configuration of interfaces G1/0/2 –3 from the configuration in Example 7-10. The example shows the same **description** command on both interfaces; to save space, the example does not bother to show all interfaces G1/0/2 through G1/0/10.

Example 7-11 *How IOS Expands the Subcommands Typed After* **interface range**

```
SW1# show running-config
! Lines omitted for brevity
interface GigabitEthernet1/0/2
 description Interface not in use
!
interface GigabitEthernet1/0/3
 description Interface not in use
! Lines omitted for brevity
SW1# show interfaces description
Interface              Status          Protocol Description
Vl1                    up              up
Gi0/0                  admin down      down
Gi1/0/1                up              up       Link to PC1, using
autonegotiation
Gi1/0/2                down            down     Interface not in use
Gi1/0/3                down            down     Interface not in use
! Lines omitted for brevity
```

Administratively Controlling Interface State with shutdown

As you might imagine, network engineers need a way to enable and disable an interface using a command. In an odd turn of phrase, Cisco switches use the **shutdown** command to disable an interface and the **no shutdown** command to enable an interface. While the **no shutdown** command might seem like an odd command to enable an interface at first, you will use this command a lot in the lab, and it will become second nature. (Most people use the abbreviations **shut** and **no shut**.)

Example 7-12 shows an example of disabling an interface using the **shutdown** subcommand. In this case, switch SW1 has a working interface G1/0/1. The user connects to the switch console and disables the interface. IOS generates a log message each time an interface fails or recovers, and log messages appear at the console, as shown in the example.

Example 7-12 *Administratively Disabling an Interface with* **shutdown**

```
SW1# configure terminal
Enter configuration commands, one per line. End with CNTL/Z.
SW1(config)# interface GigabitEthernet 1/0/1
SW1(config-if)# shutdown
*Oct  6 16:33:14.911: %LINK-5-CHANGED: Interface GigabitEthernet1/0/1, changed state
to administratively down
*Oct  6 16:33:15.911: %LINEPROTO-5-UPDOWN: Line protocol on Interface
GigabitEthernet1/0/1, changed state to down
SW1(config-if)#
```

To bring the interface back up again, you must follow the same process but use the **no shutdown** command instead.

Before leaving the simple but oddly named **shutdown/no shutdown** commands, examine the new status codes in the output in Example 7-13. The **show interfaces status** command lists one line of output per interface and, when shut down, lists the interface status as "disabled." That makes logical sense to most people. The **show interfaces** command (without the **status** keyword) lists many lines of output per interface, giving a much more detailed picture of interface status and statistics. With that command, the interface status comes in two parts, with one part using the phrase "administratively down," matching the highlighted log message in Example 7-12.

Example 7-13 *Interface Status When Configured with the* **shutdown** *Command*

```
SW1# show interfaces g1/0/1 status

Port           Name                    Status      Vlan     Duplex  Speed Type
Gi1/0/1        Link to PC1, using      disabled    1                auto   auto
10/100/1000BaseTX

SW1# show interfaces g1/0/1
GigabitEthernet1/0/1 is administratively down, line protocol is down (disabled)
  Hardware is Gigabit Ethernet, address is 4488.165a.f201 (bia 4488.165a.f201)
  Description: Link to PC1, using autonegotiation
! Lines omitted for brevity
```

Removing Configuration with the no Command

The chapters in Part II of this book have two broad goals: to help you learn some specific topics about LAN switches and to also learn about how to use the switch CLI. Some examples have more to do with learning about the CLI, which is the case for the examples that follow.

For any IOS configuration command that you might configure, you also need to consider this question: How can you remove that configuration? With some IOS configuration commands (but not all), you can revert to the default setting by issuing a **no** version of the command. What does that mean? Let me give you a few examples:

- If you configured **speed 1000** on an interface, the **no speed** command on that same interface reverts to the default speed setting (which happens to be **speed auto**).

- Similarly, if you configured an earlier **duplex half** or **duplex full** command, the **no duplex** command in interface mode for the same interface reverts the configuration to the default **duplex auto**.

- If you configured a **description** command with some text, to go back to the default state of having no **description** command for that interface, you can use the **no description** command when in interface configuration mode for that same interface.

Example 7-14 shows a sample interface configuration with four interface subcommands configured. Example 7-15 demonstrates the configuration's removal using various **no** commands.

Example 7-14 *Existing Configuration on Switch SW1 Interface G1/0/21*

```
SW1# show running-config interface g1/0/21
Building configuration...

Current configuration : 96 bytes
!
interface GigabitEthernet1/0/21
 description link to switch SW2
 speed 1000
 duplex full
 shutdown
end
```

Example 7-15 *Removing Various Configuration Settings Using the* no *Command*

```
SW1# configure terminal
Enter configuration commands, one per line. End with CNTL/Z.
SW1(config)# interface gigabitethernet 1/0/21
SW1(config-if)# no speed
SW1(config-if)# no duplex
SW1(config-if)# no description
SW1(config-if)# no shutdown
SW1(config-if)# ^Z
SW1#
SW1# show running-config interface g1/0/21
Building configuration...

Current configuration : 39 bytes
!
interface GigabitEthernet1/0/21
end
SW1#
```

In particular, interface g1/0/21 has no interface subcommands at the bottom of Example 7-15.

NOTE The **show running-config** and **show startup-config** commands typically do not display default configuration settings. Hence, the absence of interface subcommands under an interface means that all possible subcommands use default values. You can see the configured and default settings using the **show running-config all** command. (Be warned, the **show running-config all** command lists many commands, about ten times the output of the **show running-config** command.)

Alternatively, if the goal is to revert all interface subcommands to their default settings, later IOS versions provide a single command: the **default interface** *interface-id* global configuration command. For instance, if switch SW1 had the configuration shown in Example 7-14 again, the global configuration command **default interface g1/0/21** would accomplish the same result as the list of **no** commands seen in Example 7-15, resulting in all default configuration on the interface.

Analyzing Switch Interface Status and Statistics

This final major section of the chapter examines how to verify the interfaces work correctly. This section also looks at those more unusual cases in which the interface is working but not working well, as revealed by different interface status codes and statistics.

Interface Status Codes

Cisco switches use two different sets of interface status codes. The switch **show interfaces** and **show interfaces description** commands list a two-code status named the *line status* and *protocol status*. Together, these two status values identify the state of the interface. Generally, the line status refers to whether the Layer 1 standard works, while the protocol status refers to whether Layer 2 works.

> **NOTE** This book refers to these two status codes in shorthand by just listing the two codes with a slash between them, such as *up/up* or *down/down*.

Other commands, like the **show interfaces status** command, use a single-code interface status. The single-word status words correlate to different combinations of the two-code interface status codes, as seen in Table 7-2. For example, the **show interfaces status** command lists the *connected* state for working interfaces, while the **show interfaces** and **show interfaces description** commands list an *up/up* state.

Table 7-2 LAN Switch Interface Status Codes

Line Status	Protocol Status	Interface Status	Typical Root Cause
administratively down	down	disabled	The **shutdown** command is configured on the interface.
down	down	notconnect	No cable; bad cable; wrong cable pinouts with MDIX disabled; speed mismatch; the neighboring device is (a) powered off, (b) **shutdown**, or (c) error disabled.
up	down	notconnect	Not expected on LAN switch physical interfaces.
down	down (err-disabled)	err-disabled	Port security (or other feature) has disabled the local interface.
up	up	connected	The interface is working.

Examining the notconnect state for a moment, note that this state has many causes. For example, this state includes the more obvious cases, like a missing or broken cable. Some examples of the root causes of cabling problems that result in a notconnect state include the following:

- The installation of any equipment that uses electricity, even non-IT equipment, can interfere with the transmission on the cabling and link fail.

- The cable could be damaged, for example, if it lies under the carpet. The electrical signal can eventually degrade if the user's chair squashes the cable.

- Although optical cables do not suffer from electromagnetic interference (EMI), someone can try to be helpful and move a fiber-optic cable out of the way—by bending it too much. A bend into too tight a shape can prevent the cable from transmitting bits (called *macrobending*).

The Duplex Mismatch Issue

You might think the up/up (connected) state means everything works. Indeed, you want your switch interfaces in that state; however, a variety of problems can occur on a working interface in that state, one being a *duplex mismatch*, as discussed next.

If the devices on the ends of a link use the same physical layer standard with a working cable, the interfaces reach the up/up (connected) state. However, the endpoints can also have opposite duplex settings (a duplex mismatch), with full on one side and half on the other. The interfaces remain up/up and data flows; however, the device that uses half duplex experiences unnecessary errors and retransmissions.

You should remember the recommendation by now: Avoid problems like duplex mismatches by using autonegotiation on both devices on each link. However, because the CCNA exam topics have mentioned the duplex mismatch problem for most of its history, take a closer look at how a duplex mismatch can occur.

Figure 7-7 shows a classic case that results in a duplex mismatch with some Cisco switch ports. Some Cisco switch ports disable autonegotiation on interfaces configured with both a specific speed and duplex setting. The device that uses autonegotiation uses parallel detection rules to discover the speed and then uses a default duplex based on that speed, but that default duplex setting may not match the device on the other end.

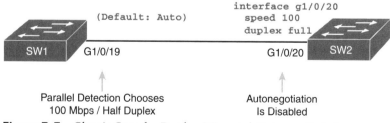

Figure 7-7 *Classic Case for Duplex Mismatch Between Switches*

Figure 7-7 shows that scenario, with switch SW2's G1/0/20 interface configured with **speed 100** and **duplex full**, disabling autonegotiation. The logic runs like this:

1. Switch SW2 sets speed 100 and duplex full.

2. SW2 disables autonegotiation FLP messages.

3. Because it receives no FLP messages, switch SW1 moves on to use autonegotiation parallel detection logic:

   a. SW1 senses that SW2 uses 100 Mbps speed.

   b. SW1 chooses to use half duplex based on the default table (half duplex if the speed is 10 or 100 Mbps; otherwise, full duplex).

Finding a duplex mismatch can be much more difficult than finding a speed mismatch because speed mismatches result in a failed link, but a duplex mismatch does not. In the duplex mismatch case as shown in Figure 7-7, *if the duplex settings do not match on the ends of an Ethernet segment, the switch interface will still be in a connected state.*

To identify duplex mismatch problems, you have to check the duplex setting on each end of the link to see if the values mismatch. You can also watch for incrementing collision and late collision counters, as explained in the next section.

NOTE Some Cisco switch ports do not disable autonegotiation when configured with both **speed** and **duplex** as shown in Figure 7-7. It appears that switch ports that support Power over Ethernet (PoE) do not disable autonegotiation, while ports that do not support PoE do disable autonegotiation, as shown in the figure. However, I found these facts only from experimentation, and not from any Cisco documentation, so be cautious and test if you decide to configure both speed and duplex. Also, the fact that some ports disable autonegotiation when configured with both speed and duplex, but some do not, provides yet another reason to simply use autonegotiation on both ends of the link.

On switch ports that continue using autonegotiation, even after you configure the speed and duplex commands, a duplex mismatch should not occur, because autonegotiation works. Working through the Figure 7-7 example again, but assuming a port that does not disable autonegotiation, consider this sequence:

1. Switch SW2 sets speed 100 and duplex full.

2. SW2 continues to send autonegotiation FLP messages, declaring it can support only 100 Mbps and full duplex.

3. SW1, using autonegotiation, receives SW2's FLPs, and agrees to use 100 Mbps and full duplex—avoiding the duplex mismatch.

Common Layer 1 Problems on Working Interfaces

When the interface reaches the connected (up/up) state, the switch considers the interface to be working. The switch, of course, tries to use the interface, and at the same time, the switch keeps various interface counters. These interface counters can help identify problems that can occur even though the interface reaches a connected state, like issues related to the just-completed duplex mismatch problem. This section explains some of the related concepts and a few of the most common problems.

The receiving device might receive a frame whose bits have changed values whenever the physical transmission has problems. These frames do not pass the error detection logic as implemented in the FCS field in the Ethernet trailer, as covered in Chapter 2. The receiving device discards the frame and counts it as an *input error*. Cisco switches list this error as a CRC error, as highlighted in Example 7-16. (Cyclic redundancy check [CRC] is a term related to how the frame check sequence [FCS] math detects an error.)

Example 7-16 *Interface Counters for Layer 1 Problems*

```
SW1# show interfaces gi1/0/1
! lines omitted for brevity
     Received 3943 broadcasts (3941 multicasts)
     0 runts, 0 giants, 0 throttles
     0 input errors, 0 CRC, 0 frame, 0 overrun, 0 ignored
     0 watchdog, 3941 multicast, 0 pause input
     0 input packets with dribble condition detected
     18843 packets output, 1726956 bytes, 0 underruns
     Output 10 broadcasts (16378 multicasts)
     0 output errors, 0 collisions, 3 interface resets
     0 unknown protocol drops
     0 babbles, 0 late collision, 0 deferred
     0 lost carrier, 0 no carrier, 0 pause output
     0 output buffer failures, 0 output buffers swapped out
```

The numbers of input and CRC errors are just a few of the counters in the output of the **show interfaces** command. The challenge is to decide which counters you need to think about, which ones show that a problem is happening, and which ones are normal and of no concern.

The example highlights several counters as examples so that you can start to understand which ones point to problems and which ones are just counting everyday events that are not problems. The following list shows a short description of each highlighted counter in the order shown in the example:

Runts: Frames that did not meet the minimum frame size requirement (64 bytes, including the 18-byte destination MAC, source MAC, type, and FCS). Collisions can cause it.

Giants: Frames that exceed the maximum frame size requirement (default 1518 bytes, including the 18-byte destination MAC, source MAC, type, and FCS).

Input Errors: A total of many counters, including runts, giants, no buffer, CRC, frame, overrun, and ignored counts.

CRC: Received frames that did not pass the FCS math; can be caused by collisions.

Frame: Received frames that have an illegal format, for example, ending with a partial byte, can be caused by collisions.

Packets Output: Total number of packets (frames) forwarded out the interface.

Output Errors: Total number of packets (frames) that the switch port tried to transmit but for which some problem occurred.

Collisions: Counter of all collisions that occur when the interface is transmitting a frame.

Late Collisions: The subset of all collisions that happen after the 64th byte of the frame has been transmitted. (In a properly working Ethernet LAN, collisions should occur within the first 64 bytes; **late collisions** today often point to a duplex mismatch.)

7

Note that many of these counters increment on a properly working interface that uses the CSMA/CD process to implement half duplex. So, a switch interface with an increasing collision counter might not have a problem. However, one problem, called late collisions, points to the classic duplex mismatch problem.

If a LAN design follows cabling guidelines, all collisions should occur by the end of the 64th byte of any frame. When a half-duplex switch interface has already sent 64 bytes of a frame and receives a frame on that same interface, the switch senses a collision. In this case, the collision is a late collision, and the switch increments the late collision counter in addition to the usual CSMA/CD actions to send a jam signal, wait a random time, and try again.

With a duplex mismatch, like the mismatch between SW1 and SW2 in Figure 7-7, the half-duplex interface will likely see the late collisions counter increment. Why? The half-duplex interface sends a frame (SW1), but the full-duplex neighbor (SW2) sends at any time, even after the 64th byte of the frame sent by the half-duplex switch. So, just keep repeating the **show interfaces** command, and if you see the late collisions counter incrementing on a half-duplex interface, you might have a duplex mismatch problem.

A working interface (in an up/up state) can also suffer from issues related to the physical cabling. The cabling problems might not be bad enough to cause a complete failure, but the transmission failures result in some frames failing to pass successfully over the cable. For example, excessive interference on the cable can cause the various input error counters to keep growing, especially the CRC counter. In particular, if the CRC errors grow, but the collision counters do not, the problem might simply be interference on the cable.

Chapter Review

One key to doing well on the exams is to perform repetitive spaced review sessions. Review this chapter's material using either the tools in the book or interactive tools for the same material found on the book's companion website. Refer to the "Your Study Plan" element section titled "Step 2: Build Your Study Habits Around the Chapter" for more details. Table 7-3 outlines the key review elements and where you can find them. To better track your study progress, record when you completed these activities in the second column.

Table 7-3   Chapter Review Tracking

Review Element	Review Date(s)	Resource Used
Review key topics		Book, website
Review key terms		Book, website
Answer DIKTA questions		Book, PTP
Review command tables		Book
Review memory tables		Book, website
Do labs		Sim Lite, blog

Review All the Key Topics

Table 7-4 Key Topics for Chapter 7

Key Topic Element	Description	Page Number
List	IEEE autonegotiation rules when both link partners participate	162
List	IEEE autonegotiation rules when only one link partner participates (parallel detection)	163
Example 7-1	Confirming All Default Settings on the Switch Interfaces	166
Example 7-3	Interpreting Autonegotiation Clues Before/After Completion	167
Example 7-4	**show interfaces** Command Autonegotiation Clues	168
Example 7-5	Configuring Speed and Duplex on Both Ends of a Link	169
Example 7-6	**show interfaces status** Without Using Autonegotiation	170
Example 7-9	Configuring and Verifying the **description** Command on Switch SW1	172
Example 7-12	Administratively Disabling an Interface with **shutdown**	174
Example 7-13	Interface Status When Configured with the **shutdown** Command	174
Table 7-2	Two types of interface state terms and their meanings	176
List	Explanations of different error statistics on switch interfaces	179

Key Terms You Should Know

10/100, 10/100/1000, auto-MDIX, autonegotiation, duplex mismatch, full duplex, half duplex, late collisions, parallel detection

Do Labs

The Sim Lite software is a version of Pearson's full simulator learning product with a subset of the labs, included free with this book. The subset of labs mostly relates to this part. Take the time to try some of the labs. As always, also check the author's blog site pages for configuration exercises (Config Labs) at https://www.certskills.com.

Command References

Tables 7-5 and 7-6 list configuration and verification commands used in this chapter. As an easy review exercise, cover the left column in a table, read the right column, and try to recall the command without looking. Then repeat the exercise, covering the right column, and try to recall what the command does.

Table 7-5   Switch Interface Configuration

Command	Mode/Purpose/Description
interface *type port-number*	Changes context to interface mode. The type is typically Fast Ethernet or Gigabit Ethernet. The possible port numbers vary depending on the model of switch—for example, Fa0/1, Fa0/2, and so on.
interface range *type port-number - end-port-number*	Changes the context to interface mode for a range of consecutively numbered interfaces. The subcommands that follow then apply to all interfaces in the range.
shutdown | no shutdown	Interface mode. Disables or enables the interface, respectively.
speed {10 | 100 | 1000 | auto}	Interface mode. Manually sets the speed to the listed speed or, with the auto setting, automatically negotiates the speed.
duplex {auto | full | half}	Interface mode. Manually sets the duplex to half or full, or to autonegotiate the duplex setting.
description *text*	Interface mode. Lists any information text the engineer wants to track for the interface, such as the expected device on the other end of the cable.
no duplex no speed no description	Reverts to the default setting for each interface subcommand of **speed auto**, **duplex auto**, and the absence of a **description** command.
default interface *interface-id*	Reverts to the default setting for all interface subcommands on an interface.
[no] mdix auto	Interface subcommand. Enables (**auto mdix**) or disables (**no auto mdix**) the auto-MDIX feature.

Table 7-6   Chapter 7 EXEC Command Reference

Command	Purpose
show running-config	Lists the currently used configuration while omitting most default settings
show running-config interface *type number*	Displays the running-configuration excerpt of the listed interface and its subcommands only
show running-config all	Displays the running-configuration while including all default settings
show interfaces [*type number*] status	Lists one output line per interface (or for only the listed interface if included), noting the description, operating state, and settings for duplex and speed on each interface
show interfaces [*type number*]	Lists detailed status and statistical information about all interfaces (or the listed interface only)
show interfaces description	Displays one line of information per interface, with a two-item status (similar to the **show interfaces** command status), and includes any description configured on the interfaces

Part II Review

Keep track of your part review progress with the checklist shown in Table P2-1. Details on each task follow the table.

Table P2-1   Part II Part Review Checklist

Activity	1st Date Completed	2nd Date Completed
Repeat All DIKTA Questions		
Answer Part Review Questions		
Review Key Topics		
Do Labs		
Review Appendix L on the Companion Website		
Watch video		
Use Per-Chapter Interactive Review		

Repeat All DIKTA Questions

For this task, answer the "Do I Know This Already?" questions again for the chapters in this part of the book, using the PTP software.

Answer Part Review Questions

For this task, answer the Part Review questions for this part of the book, using the PTP software.

Review Key Topics

Review all key topics in all chapters in this part, either by browsing the chapters or by using the Key Topics application on the companion website.

Labs

Depending on your chosen lab tool, here are some suggestions for what to do in lab:

Pearson Network Simulator: If you use the full Pearson ICND1 or CCNA simulator, focus more on the configuration scenario and troubleshooting scenario labs associated with the topics in this part of the book. These types of labs include a larger set of topics and work well as Part Review activities. (See the Introduction for some details about how to find which labs are about topics in this part of the book.)

Blog: Config Labs: The author's blog includes a series of configuration-focused labs that you can do on paper or with Cisco Packet Tracer in about 15 minutes. To find them, open https://www.certskills.com and look under the Labs menu item.

Other: If using other lab tools, as a few suggestions: make sure to experiment heavily with VLAN configuration and VLAN trunking configuration. Also, spend some time changing interface settings like **speed** and **duplex** on a link between two switches, to make sure that you understand which cases would result in a duplex mismatch.

Review Appendix L on the Companion Website

Appendix L on the companion website contains a chapter from the previous edition of the book that focused on troubleshooting. That appendix, named "LAN Troubleshooting," can be useful as a tool to review the topics in this part of the book. (Note that if you use this extra appendix, you can ignore the mentions of Port Security until you have reached that topic in the *CCNA 200-301 Official Cert Guide, Volume 2*, Second Edition.)

Watch Videos

The companion website includes a variety of common mistake and Q&A videos organized by part and chapter. Use these videos to challenge your thinking, dig deeper, review topics, and better prepare for the exam. Make sure to bookmark a link to the companion website and use the videos for review whenever you have a few extra minutes.

Use Per-Chapter Interactive Review

Using the companion website, browse through the interactive review elements, like memory tables and key term flashcards, to review the content from each chapter.

Part II of this book introduces the basics of Ethernet LANs, both in concept and in how to implement the features. However, the two primary features discussed in Part III of this book—Virtual LANs (VLANs) and Spanning Tree Protocol (STP)—impact almost everything you have learned about Ethernet so far.

VLANs allow a network engineer to create separate Ethernet LANs through simple configuration choices. The ability to separate some switch ports into one VLAN and other switch ports into another VLAN gives network designers a powerful tool for creating networks. Once created, VLANs also have a huge impact on how a switch works, which then impacts how you verify and troubleshoot the operation of a campus LAN.

The two VLAN-related exam topics (2.1 and 2.2) use the verbs *configure* and *verify*. To support that depth, Chapter 8 opens this part with details about the concepts related to VLANs, VLAN trunks, and EtherChannels. It then shows a variety of configuration options, sprinkled with some troubleshooting topics.

STP acts to prevent frames from looping repeatedly around a LAN that has redundant links. Without STP, switches would forward broadcasts and some other frames around and around the LAN, eventually clogging the LAN so much as to make it unusable.

The CCNA 200-301 version 1.1 exam blueprint refers to STP using only topic 2.5. That topic uses the plural phrase *Spanning Tree Protocols*, in reference to the original Spanning Tree Protocol (STP) and its replacement Rapid STP (RSTP). That exam topic uses the verb *identify*, which places more importance on interpreting STP operations using **show** commands rather than every configuration option.

As for this part of the book, Chapter 9 focuses on STP concepts, with Chapter 10 focusing on configuration and verification—but with emphasis on interpreting STP behavior. It also discusses Layer 2 EtherChannel configuration.

Part III

Implementing VLANs and STP

CHAPTER 8

Implementing Ethernet Virtual LANs

This chapter covers the following exam topics:

1.0 Network Fundamentals

    1.13 Describe switching concepts

        1.13.a MAC learning and aging

        1.13.b Frame switching

        1.13.c Frame flooding

        1.13.d MAC address table

2.0 Network Access

    2.1 Configure and verify VLANs (normal range) spanning multiple switches

        2.1.a Access ports (data and voice)

        2.1.b Default VLAN

        2.1.c InterVLAN connectivity

    2.2 Configure and verify interswitch connectivity

        2.2.a Trunk ports

        2.2.b 802.1Q

        2.2.c Native VLAN

So far in this book, you have learned that Ethernet switches receive Ethernet frames, make decisions, and then forward (switch) those Ethernet frames. That core logic revolves around MAC addresses, the interface in which the frame arrives, and the interfaces out which the switch forwards the frame.

While true, that logic omits any consideration of virtual LANs (VLANs). VLANs impact the switching logic for each frame because each VLAN acts as a subset of the switch ports in an Ethernet LAN. Switches believe each Ethernet frame to be received in an identifiable VLAN, forwarded based on MAC table entries for that VLAN, and forwarded out ports in that VLAN. This chapter explores those concepts and others related to VLANs.

As for the organization of the chapter, the first major section of the chapter explains the core concepts. These concepts include how VLANs work on a single switch, how to use VLAN trunking to create VLANs that span across multiple switches, and how to forward traffic between VLANs using a router. The second major section shows how to configure VLANs and VLAN trunks: how to statically assign interfaces to a VLAN. The final major section discusses some issues that can arise when using VLANs and trunks and how to avoid those issues.

Also, this chapter goes beyond the normal chapter page length. If you want to break up your study into two reading sections, stop the first session when you reach the heading "Implementing Interfaces Connected to Phones."

"Do I Know This Already?" Quiz

Take the quiz (either here or use the PTP software) if you want to use the score to help you decide how much time to spend on this chapter. The letter answers are listed at the bottom of the page following the quiz. Appendix C, found both at the end of the book as well as on the companion website, includes both the answers and explanations. You can also find both answers and explanations in the PTP testing software.

Table 8-1 "Do I Know This Already?" Foundation Topics Section-to-Question Mapping

Foundation Topics Section	Questions
Virtual LAN Concepts	1–3
VLAN and VLAN Trunking Configuration and Verification	4–6
Troubleshooting VLANs and VLAN Trunks	7–8

1. In a LAN, which of the following terms best equates to the term *VLAN*?

   a. Collision domain

   b. Broadcast domain

   c. Subnet

   d. Single switch

   e. Trunk

2. Imagine a small lab network with one LAN switch, with the ports configured to be in three different VLANs. How many IP subnets do you need for the hosts connected to the switch ports, assuming that all hosts in all VLANs want to use TCP/IP?

   a. 0

   b. 1

   c. 2

   d. 3

   e. You cannot tell from the information provided.

3. Switch SW1 sends a frame to switch SW2 using 802.1Q trunking. Which of the answers describes how SW1 changes or adds to the Ethernet frame before forwarding the frame to SW2?

   a. Inserts a 4-byte header and does change the MAC addresses.

   b. Inserts a 4-byte header and does not change the MAC addresses.

   c. Encapsulates the original frame behind an entirely new Ethernet header.

   d. None of the other answers are correct.

4. You are told that switch 1 is configured with the **switchport mode dynamic auto** command on its Fa0/5 interface, which is connected to switch 2. Which of the following settings on the **switchport mode** command on switch 2 would allow trunking to work? (Choose two answers.)

   a. trunk

   b. dynamic auto

   c. dynamic desirable

   d. access

   e. None of the other answers are correct.

5. A switch has just arrived from Cisco. The switch has never been configured with any VLANs, but VTP has been disabled. An engineer configures the **vlan 22** and **name Hannahs-VLAN** commands and then exits configuration mode. Which of the following are true? (Choose two answers.)

   a. VLAN 22 is listed in the output of the **show vlan brief** command.

   b. VLAN 22 is listed in the output of the **show running-config** command.

   c. VLAN 22 is not created by this process.

   d. VLAN 22 does not exist in that switch until at least one interface is assigned to that VLAN.

6. Which of the following commands identify switch interfaces as being trunking interfaces—interfaces that currently operate as VLAN trunks? (Choose two answers.)

   a. show interfaces

   b. show interfaces switchport

   c. show interfaces trunk

   d. show trunks

7. In a switch that disables VTP, an engineer configures the commands **vlan 30** and **shutdown vlan 30**. Which answers should be true about this switch? (Choose two answers.)

   a. The **show vlan brief** command should list VLAN 30.

   b. The **show running-config** command should list VLAN 30.

   c. The switch should forward frames that arrive in access ports in VLAN 30.

   d. The switch should forward frames that arrive in trunk ports tagged with VLAN 30.

8. The **show interfaces g0/1 trunk** command provides three lists of VLAN IDs. Which items would limit the VLANs that appear in the first of the three lists of VLANs?

   a. A **shutdown vlan 30** global command

   b. A **switchport trunk allowed vlan** interface subcommand

   c. An STP choice to block on G0/1

   d. A **no vlan 30** global command

Foundation Topics

Virtual LAN Concepts

Before understanding **VLANs**, you must first have a specific understanding of the definition of a LAN. For example, from one perspective, a LAN includes all the user devices, servers, switches, routers, cables, and wireless access points in one location. However, an alternative narrower definition of a LAN can help in understanding the concept of a virtual LAN:

A LAN includes all devices in the same broadcast domain.

A broadcast domain includes the set of all LAN-connected devices, so that when any of the devices sends a broadcast frame, all the other devices get a copy of the frame. So, from one perspective, you can think of a LAN and a broadcast domain as being basically the same thing.

Using only default settings, a switch considers all its interfaces to be in the same broadcast domain. That is, for one switch, when a broadcast frame entered one switch port, the switch forwarded that broadcast frame out all other ports. With that logic, to create two different LAN broadcast domains, you had to buy two different Ethernet LAN switches, as shown in Figure 8-1.

Figure 8-1 *Creating Two Broadcast Domains with Two Physical Switches and No VLANs*

By using two VLANs, a single switch can accomplish the same goals of the design in Figure 8-1—to create two broadcast domains—with a single switch. With VLANs, a switch can configure some interfaces into one broadcast domain and some into another, creating multiple broadcast domains. These individual broadcast domains created by the switch are called *virtual LANs (VLANs)*.

For example, in Figure 8-2, the single switch creates two VLANs, treating the ports in each VLAN as being completely separate. The switch would never forward a frame sent by Dino (in VLAN 1) over to either Wilma or Betty (in VLAN 2).

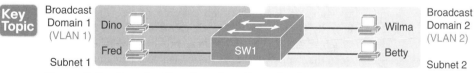

Figure 8-2 *Creating Two Broadcast Domains Using One Switch and VLANs*

Designing campus LANs to use more VLANs, each with a smaller number of devices, often helps improve the LAN in many ways. For example, a broadcast sent by one host in a VLAN will be received and processed by all the other hosts in the VLAN—but not by hosts in a different VLAN. Limiting the number of hosts that receive a single broadcast frame reduces the number of hosts that waste effort processing unneeded broadcasts. It also reduces security risks because fewer hosts see frames sent by any one host. These are just a few reasons for separating hosts into different VLANs. The following list summarizes the most common reasons for choosing to create smaller broadcast domains (VLANs):

- To reduce CPU overhead on each device, improving host performance, by reducing the number of devices that receive each broadcast frame

- To reduce security risks by reducing the number of hosts that receive copies of frames that the switches flood (broadcasts, multicasts, and unknown unicasts)

- To improve security for hosts through the application of different security policies per VLAN

- To create more flexible designs that group users by department, or by groups that work together, instead of by physical location

- To solve problems more quickly, because the failure domain for many problems is the same set of devices as those in the same broadcast domain

- To reduce the workload for the Spanning Tree Protocol (STP) by limiting a VLAN to a single access switch

The rest of this chapter looks closely at the mechanics of how VLANs work across multiple Cisco switches, including the required configuration. To that end, the next section examines VLAN trunking, a feature required when installing a VLAN that exists on more than one LAN switch.

Creating Multiswitch VLANs Using Trunking

Configuring VLANs on a single switch requires only a little effort: you simply configure each port to tell it the VLAN number to which the port belongs. With multiple switches, you have to consider additional concepts about how to forward traffic between the switches.

When you are using VLANs in networks that have multiple interconnected switches, the switches need to use *VLAN trunking* on the links between the switches. VLAN trunking causes the switches to use a process called *VLAN tagging*, by which the sending switch adds another header to the frame before sending it over the **trunk**. This extra trunking header includes a *VLAN identifier* (VLAN ID) field so that the sending switch can associate the frame with a particular VLAN ID, and the receiving switch can then know in what VLAN each frame belongs.

Figure 8-3 shows an example that demonstrates VLANs that exist on multiple switches, but it does not use trunking. First, the design uses two VLANs: VLAN 10 and VLAN 20. Each switch has two ports assigned to each VLAN, so each VLAN exists in both switches. To forward traffic in VLAN 10 between the two switches, the design includes a link between switches, with that link fully inside VLAN 10. Likewise, to support VLAN 20 traffic between switches, the design uses a second link between switches, with that link inside VLAN 20.

Answers to the "Do I Know This Already?" quiz:

1 B **2** D **3** B **4** A, C **5** A, B **6** B, C **7** A, B **8** B

The design in Figure 8-3 functions perfectly. For example, PC11 (in VLAN 10) can send a frame to PC14. The frame flows into SW1, over the top link (the one that is in VLAN 10) and over to SW2.

VLAN 10

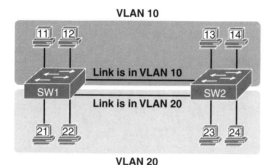

VLAN 20

Figure 8-3 *Multiswitch VLAN Without VLAN Trunking*

The design shown in Figure 8-3 works, but it simply does not scale very well. It requires one physical link between switches to support every VLAN. If a design needed 10 or 20 VLANs, you would need 10 or 20 links between switches, and you would use 10 or 20 switch ports (on each switch) for those links.

VLAN Tagging Concepts

VLAN trunking creates one link between switches that supports as many VLANs as you need. As a VLAN trunk, the switches treat the link as if it were a part of all the VLANs. At the same time, the trunk keeps the VLAN traffic separate, so frames in VLAN 10 would not go to devices in VLAN 20, and vice versa, because each frame is identified by VLAN number as it crosses the trunk. Figure 8-4 shows the idea, with a single physical link between the two switches.

VLAN 10

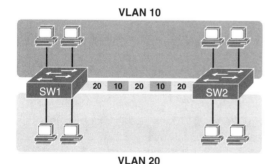

VLAN 20

Figure 8-4 *Multiswitch VLAN with Trunking*

The use of trunking allows switches to forward frames from multiple VLANs over a single physical connection by adding a small header to the Ethernet frame. For example, Figure 8-5 shows PC11 sending a broadcast frame on interface Fa0/1 at Step 1. To flood the frame, switch SW1 needs to forward the broadcast frame to switch SW2. However, SW1 needs to let SW2 know that the frame is part of VLAN 10, so that after the frame is received, SW2 will flood the frame only into VLAN 10, and not into VLAN 20. So, as shown at Step 2, before sending the frame, SW1 adds a VLAN header to the original Ethernet frame, with the VLAN header listing a VLAN ID of 10 in this case.

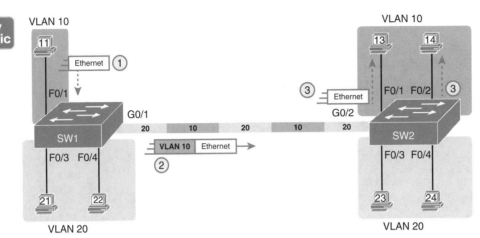

Figure 8-5   *VLAN Trunking Between Two Switches*

When SW2 receives the frame, it understands that the frame is in VLAN 10. SW2 then removes the VLAN header, forwarding the original frame out its interfaces in VLAN 10 (Step 3).

For another example, consider the case when PC21 (in VLAN 20) sends a broadcast. SW1 sends the broadcast out port Fa0/4 (because that port is in VLAN 20) and out Gi0/1 (because it is a trunk, meaning that it supports multiple different VLANs). SW1 adds a trunking header to the frame, listing a VLAN ID of 20. SW2 strips off the trunking header after determining that the frame is part of VLAN 20, so SW2 knows to forward the frame out only ports Fa0/3 and Fa0/4, because they are in VLAN 20, and not out ports Fa0/1 and Fa0/2, because they are in VLAN 10.

The 802.1Q and ISL VLAN Trunking Protocols

Cisco has supported two different trunking protocols over the years: Inter-Switch Link (ISL) and IEEE **802.1Q**. Cisco created the ISL years before 802.1Q, in part because the IEEE had not yet defined a VLAN trunking standard. Today, 802.1Q has become the more popular trunking protocol, with Cisco not even bothering to support ISL in many of its switch models today.

While both ISL and 802.1Q tag each frame with the VLAN ID, the details differ. 802.1Q inserts an extra 4-byte 802.1Q VLAN header into the original frame's Ethernet header, as shown at the top of Figure 8-6. As for the fields in the 802.1Q header, only the 12-bit VLAN ID field inside the 802.1Q header matters for topics discussed in this book. This 12-bit field supports a theoretical maximum of 212 (4096) VLANs, but in practice it supports a maximum of 4094. (Both 802.1Q and ISL use 12 bits to tag the VLAN ID, with two reserved values [0 and 4095].)

Cisco switches break the range of VLAN IDs (1–4094) into two ranges: the normal range and the extended range. All switches can use normal-range VLANs with values from 1 to 1005. Only some switches can use extended-range VLANs with VLAN IDs from 1006 to 4094. The rules for which switches can use extended-range VLANs depend on the configuration of the VLAN Trunking Protocol (**VTP**), which is discussed briefly in the section "VLAN Trunking Configuration," later in this chapter.

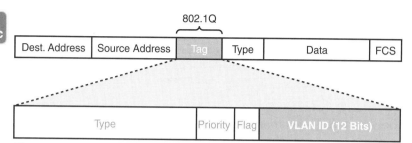

Figure 8-6 *802.1Q Trunking*

802.1Q also defines one special VLAN ID on each trunk as the **native VLAN** (defaulting to use VLAN 1). In a normally working 802.1Q trunk, both endpoints use trunking, and both use the same native VLAN. Neither end, when sending a frame assigned to this native VLAN, adds the 802.1Q header. Both switches, knowing that untagged frames mean that the frame is part of the native VLAN, treat untagged frames as being part of the native VLAN.

The IEEE included the native VLAN concept for cases in which one device operates as a trunk while the other side does not. The nontrunking endpoint may do so temporarily or permanently (typically because of misconfiguration or a lack of 802.1Q support). In such cases, the nontrunking device will be confused and discard any received frames that contain a trunking header. However, when the trunking side sends frames as part of the native VLAN—untagged—the nontrunking side will understand the frame and consider it to be part of the access VLAN assigned to the interface. So, the native VLAN gives engineers a tool to allow for cases of making one VLAN work over the link, even when some trunking issue might exist.

Forwarding Data Between VLANs

If you create a campus LAN that contains many VLANs, you typically still need all devices to be able to send data to all other devices. This next topic discusses some concepts about how to route data between those VLANs.

The Need for Routing Between VLANs

LAN switches that forward data based on Layer 2 logic, as discussed so far in this book, often go by the name *Layer 2 switch*. For example, Chapter 5, "Analyzing Ethernet LAN Switching," discussed how LAN switches receive Ethernet frames (a Layer 2 concept), look at the destination Ethernet MAC address (a Layer 2 address), and forward the Ethernet frame out some other interface. All those concepts are defined by Layer 2 protocols, hence the name Layer 2 switch.

Layer 2 switches perform their logic per VLAN. For example, in Figure 8-7, the two PCs on the left sit in VLAN 10, in subnet 10. The two PCs on the right sit in a different VLAN (20), with a different subnet (20). Note that the figure repeats earlier Figure 8-2, but with the switch broken into halves, to emphasize the point that Layer 2 switches will not forward data between two VLANs.

Figure 8-7 *Layer 2 Switch Does Not Route Between the VLANs*

As shown in the figure, when configured with some ports in VLAN 10 and others in VLAN 20, the switch acts like two separate switches in which it will forward traffic. In fact, one goal of VLANs is to separate traffic in one VLAN from another, preventing frames in one VLAN from leaking over to other VLANs. For example, when Dino (in VLAN 10) sends any Ethernet frame, if SW1 is a Layer 2 switch, that switch will not forward the frame to the PCs on the right in VLAN 20.

Routing Packets Between VLANs with a Router

When VLANs are included in a campus LAN design, the devices in a VLAN need to be in the same subnet. Following the same design logic, devices in different VLANs need to be in different subnets.

To forward packets between VLANs, the network must use a device that acts as a router. You can use an actual router or use a switch that can perform some functions like a router. These switches that also perform Layer 3 routing functions go by the name *multilayer switch* or **Layer 3 switch**. This section first discusses how to forward data between VLANs when using Layer 2 switches and ends with a brief discussion of how to use Layer 3 switches.

For example, Figure 8-8 shows a router that can route packets between subnets 10 and 20. The figure shows the same Layer 2 switch as shown in Figure 8-7, with the same perspective of the switch being split into parts with two different VLANs, and with the same PCs in the same VLANs and subnets. Now Router R1 has one LAN physical interface connected to the switch and assigned to VLAN 10, and a second physical interface connected to the switch and assigned to VLAN 20. With an interface connected to each subnet, the Layer 2 switch can keep doing its job—forwarding frames inside a VLAN, while the router can do its job—routing IP packets between the subnets.

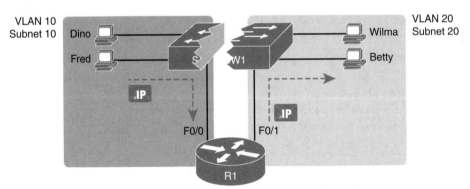

Figure 8-8   *Routing Between Two VLANs on Two Physical Interfaces*

The figure shows an IP packet being routed from Fred, which sits in one VLAN/subnet, to Betty, which sits in the other. The Layer 2 switch forwards two different Layer 2 Ethernet frames: one in VLAN 10, from Fred to R1's F0/0 interface, and the other in VLAN 20, from R1's F0/1 interface to Betty. From a Layer 3 perspective, Fred sends the IP packet to its default router (R1), and R1 routes the packet out another interface (F0/1) into another subnet where Betty resides.

The design in Figure 8-8 works, but there are several different solutions for routing packets between VLANs. This chapter shows the option of using a separate physical router, with a separate link per VLAN, because it can be the easiest of the options to understand and visualize. Chapter 18, "IP Routing in the LAN," works through those other features for routing packets between VLANs.

VLAN and VLAN Trunking Configuration and Verification

Cisco switches do not require any configuration to work. You can purchase Cisco switches, install devices with the correct cabling, turn on the switches, and they work. You would never need to configure the switch, and it would work fine, even if you interconnected switches, until you needed more than one VLAN. But if you want to use VLANs—and most enterprise networks do—you need to add some configuration.

This chapter separates the VLAN configuration details into two major sections. The first section looks at how to configure *static access interfaces*—switch interfaces configured to be in one VLAN only, therefore not using VLAN trunking. The second part shows how to configure interfaces that do use VLAN trunking.

Creating VLANs and Assigning Access VLANs to an Interface

This section shows how to create a VLAN, give the VLAN a name, and assign interfaces to a VLAN. To focus on these basic details, this section shows examples using a single switch, so VLAN trunking is not needed.

For a Cisco switch to forward frames in a particular VLAN, the switch must be configured to believe that the VLAN exists. In addition, the switch must have nontrunking interfaces (called **access interfaces** or **static access interfaces**) assigned to the VLAN and/or trunks that support the VLAN. The configuration steps for access interfaces are as follows:

Step 1.   To configure a new VLAN, follow these steps:

    a. From configuration mode, use the **vlan** *vlan-id* command in global configuration mode to create the VLAN and to move the user into VLAN configuration mode.

    b. (Optional) Use the **name** *name* command in VLAN configuration mode to list a name for the VLAN. If not configured, the VLAN name is VLANZZZZ, where *ZZZZ* is the four-digit decimal VLAN ID.

Step 2.   For each access interface, follow these steps:

    a. Use the **interface** *type number* command in global configuration mode to move into interface configuration mode for each desired interface.

    b. Use the **switchport access vlan** *id-number* command in interface configuration mode to specify the VLAN number associated with that interface.

    c. (Optional) Use the **switchport mode access** command in interface configuration mode to make this port always operate in access mode (that is, to not trunk).

While the list might look a little daunting, the process on a single switch is actually pretty simple. For example, if you want to put the switch's ports in three VLANs—11, 12, and 13—you first add three **vlan** commands: **vlan 11**, **vlan 12**, and **vlan 13**. Then, for each interface, add a **switchport access vlan 11** (or **12** or **13**) command to assign that interface to the proper VLAN.

8

NOTE The term **default VLAN** (as shown in the exam topics) refers to the default setting on the **switchport access vlan** *vlan-id* command, and that default is VLAN ID 1. In other words, by default, each port is assigned to access VLAN 1.

VLAN Configuration Example 1: Full VLAN Configuration

Examples 8-1, 8-2, and 8-3 work through one scenario with VLAN configuration and verification. To begin, Example 8-1 begins by showing the VLANs in switch SW1 in Figure 8-9, with all default settings related to VLANs.

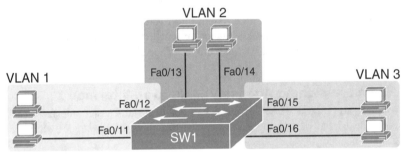

Figure 8-9 *Network with One Switch and Three VLANs*

Example 8-1 *Configuring VLANs and Assigning VLANs to Interfaces*

```
SW1# show vlan brief
VLAN Name                             Status    Ports
---- -------------------------------- --------- ------------------------------
1    default                          active    Fa0/1, Fa0/2, Fa0/3, Fa0/4
                                                Fa0/5, Fa0/6, Fa0/7, Fa0/8
                                                Fa0/9, Fa0/10, Fa0/11, Fa0/12
                                                Fa0/13, Fa0/14, Fa0/15, Fa0/16
                                                Fa0/17, Fa0/18, Fa0/19, Fa0/20
                                                Fa0/21, Fa0/22, Fa0/23, Fa0/24
                                                Gi0/1, Gi0/2
1002 fddi-default                     act/unsup
1003 token-ring-default               act/unsup
1004 fddinet-default                  act/unsup
1005 trnet-default                    act/unsup
```

The example begins with the **show vlan brief** command, confirming the default settings of five nondeletable VLANs, with all interfaces assigned to VLAN 1. VLAN 1 cannot be deleted but can be used. VLANs 1002–1005 cannot be deleted and cannot be used as access VLANs today. In particular, note that this switch has 24 Fast Ethernet ports (Fa0/1–Fa0/24) and two Gigabit Ethernet ports (Gi0/1 and Gi0/2), all of which are listed as being in VLAN 1 per that first command's output, confirming that by default, Cisco switches assign all ports to VLAN 1.

Next, Example 8-2 shows steps that mirror the VLAN configuration checklist, namely the configuration of VLAN 2, plus the assignment of VLAN 2 as the access VLAN on two ports: Fa0/13 and Fa0/14.

Example 8-2 *Configuring VLANs and Assigning VLANs to Interfaces*

```
SW1# configure terminal
Enter configuration commands, one per line. End with CNTL/Z.
SW1(config)# vlan 2
SW1(config-vlan)# name Freds-vlan
SW1(config-vlan)# exit
SW1(config)# interface range fastethernet 0/13 - 14
SW1(config-if)# switchport access vlan 2
SW1(config-if)# switchport mode access
SW1(config-if)# end

SW1# show vlan brief

VLAN Name                             Status    Ports
---- -------------------------------- --------- -------------------------------
1    default                          active    Fa0/1, Fa0/2, Fa0/3, Fa0/4
                                                Fa0/5, Fa0/6, Fa0/7, Fa0/8
                                                Fa0/9, Fa0/10, Fa0/11, Fa0/12
                                                Fa0/15, Fa0/16, Fa0/17, Fa0/18
                                                Fa0/19, Fa0/20, Fa0/21, Fa0/22
                                                Fa0/23, Fa0/24, Gi0/1, Gi0/2
2    Freds-vlan                       active    Fa0/13, Fa0/14
1002 fddi-default                     act/unsup
1003 token-ring-default               act/unsup
1004 fddinet-default                  act/unsup
1005 trnet-default                    act/unsup
```

Take a moment to compare the output of the **show vlan brief** commands in Example 8-2 (after adding the configuration) versus Example 8-1. Example 8-2 shows new information about VLAN 2, with ports Fa0/13 and Fa0/14 no longer being listed with VLAN 1, but now listed as assigned to VLAN 2.

To complete this scenario, Example 8-3 shows a little more detail about the VLAN itself. First, the **show running-config** command lists both the **vlan 2** and **switchport access vlan 2** commands as configured in Example 8-2. Also, note that earlier Example 8-2 uses the **interface range** command, with one instance of the **switchport access vlan 2** interface sub-command. However, Example 8-3 shows how the switch actually applied that command to both Fa0/13 and Fa0/14. Example 8-3 ends with the **show vlan id 2** command, which confirms the operational status that ports Fa0/13 and Fa0/14 are assigned to VLAN 2.

8

Example 8-3 *Configuring VLANs and Assigning VLANs to Interfaces*

```
SW1# show running-config
! Many lines omitted for brevity
! Early in the output:
vlan 2
 name Freds-vlan
!
! more lines omitted for brevity
interface FastEthernet0/13
 switchport access vlan 2
 switchport mode access
!
interface FastEthernet0/14
 switchport access vlan 2
 switchport mode access
!

SW1# show vlan id 2
VLAN Name                             Status    Ports
---- -------------------------------- --------- -------------------------------
2    Freds-vlan                       active    Fa0/13, Fa0/14

VLAN Type  SAID       MTU   Parent RingNo BridgeNo Stp  BrdgMode Trans1 Trans2
---- ----- ---------- ----- ------ ------ -------- ---- -------- ------ ------
2    enet  100010     1500  -      -      -        -    -        0      0

Remote SPAN VLAN
----------------
Disabled

Primary Secondary Type              Ports
------- --------- ----------------- -------------------------------------------
```

The example surrounding Figure 8-9 uses six switch ports, all of which need to operate as access ports. That is, each port should not use trunking but instead should be assigned to a single VLAN, as assigned by the **switchport access vlan** *vlan-id* command. For ports that should always act as access ports, add the optional interface subcommand **switchport mode access**. This command tells the switch to always be an access interface and disables the protocol that negotiates trunking (Dynamic Trunking Protocol [DTP]) with the device on the other end of the link. (The upcoming section "VLAN Trunking Configuration" discusses more details about the commands that allow a port to negotiate whether it should use trunking.)

NOTE The companion website for this book includes a video that works through a different VLAN configuration example.

VLAN Configuration Example 2: Shorter VLAN Configuration

Example 8-2 shows how to configure a VLAN and add two ports to the VLAN as access ports. Example 8-4 does the same, this time with VLAN 3, and this time with a much briefer alternative configuration. The configuration completes the configuration of the design shown in Figure 8-9, by adding two ports to VLAN 3.

Example 8-4 *Shorter VLAN Configuration Example (VLAN 3)*

```
SW1# configure terminal
Enter configuration commands, one per line. End with CNTL/Z.
SW1(config)# interface range Fastethernet 0/15 - 16
SW1(config-if-range)# switchport access vlan 3
% Access VLAN does not exist. Creating vlan 3
SW1(config-if-range)# ^Z

SW1# show vlan brief

VLAN Name                             Status    Ports
---- -------------------------------- --------- -------------------------------
1 default                             active     Fa0/1, Fa0/2, Fa0/3, Fa0/4
                                                 Fa0/5, Fa0/6, Fa0/7, Fa0/8
                                                 Fa0/9, Fa0/10, Fa0/11, Fa0/12
                                                 Fa0/17, Fa0/18, Fa0/19, Fa0/20
                                                 Fa0/21, Fa0/22, Fa0/23, Fa0/24
                                                 Gi0/1, Gi0/2
2 Freds-vlan                          active    Fa0/13, Fa0/14
3 VLAN0003                            active    Fa0/15, Fa0/16
1002 fddi-default                     act/unsup
1003 token-ring-default               act/unsup
1004 fddinet-default                  act/unsup
1005 trnet-default                    act/unsup
```

Example 8-4 shows how a switch can dynamically create a VLAN—the equivalent of the **vlan** *vlan-id* global config command—when the **switchport access vlan** interface subcommand refers to a currently unconfigured VLAN. This example begins with SW1 not knowing about VLAN 3. With the addition of the **switchport access vlan 3** interface subcommand, the switch realized that VLAN 3 did not exist, and as noted in the shaded message in the example, the switch created VLAN 3, using a default name (VLAN0003). The engineer did not need to type the **vlan 3** global command to create VLAN 3; the switch did that automatically. No other steps are required to create the VLAN. At the end of the process, VLAN 3 exists in the switch, and interfaces Fa0/15 and Fa0/16 are in VLAN 3, as noted in the shaded part of the **show vlan brief** command output.

VLAN Trunking Protocol

Before showing more configuration examples, you also need to know something about a Cisco protocol and tool called the VLAN Trunking Protocol (VTP). VTP is a Cisco proprietary tool on Cisco switches that advertises each VLAN configured in one switch (with the **vlan** *number* command) so that all the other switches in the campus learn about that VLAN.

This book does not discuss VTP as an end to itself for a few different reasons. First, the current CCNA 200-301 exam blueprint ignores VTP, as do the CCNP Enterprise Core and CCNP Enterprise Advanced Routing blueprints. Additionally, many enterprises choose to disable VTP.

Also, you can easily disable VTP so that it has no impact on your switches in the lab, which is exactly what I did when building all the examples in this book.

However, VTP has some small impact on how every Cisco Catalyst switch works, even if you avoid using VTP. This brief section introduces enough details of VTP so that you can understand the impact of VTP in a Cisco Catalyst switch.

First, all examples in this book (and in Volume 2) use switches that disable VTP in some way. Interestingly, for much of VTP's decades of existence, most switches did support an option to completely disable VTP. Instead, to effectively disable VTP, the engineer would set the switch to use **VTP transparent mode** (with the **vtp mode transparent** global command). Many newer switches now have an option to disable VTP completely with the **vtp mode off** global command. For the purposes of this book, configuring a switch with either transparent mode or off mode disables VTP.

Note that both transparent and off modes prevent VTP from learning and advertising about VLAN configuration. Those modes allow a switch to configure all VLANs, including standard- and extended-range VLANs. Additionally, switches using transparent or off modes list the **vlan** configuration commands in the running-config file.

In contrast, switches in VTP server or client mode behave differently. Just in case you do lab exercises with real switches or with simulators, and you see unusual results with VLANs, check the VTP status with the **show vtp status** command. If your switch uses VTP server or client mode, you will find

- The server switches can configure VLANs in the standard range only (1–1005).

- The client switches cannot configure VLANs.

- Both servers and clients may be learning new VLANs from other switches and seeing their VLANs deleted by other switches because of VTP.

- The **show running-config** command does not list any **vlan** commands; you must use other **show** commands to find out about the configured VLANs.

If possible in the lab, disable VTP for your switch configuration practice until you decide to learn more about VTP for other purposes.

NOTE   Do not change VTP settings on any switch that also connects to the production network until you know how VTP works and you talk with experienced colleagues. Doing so can cause real harm to your LAN. For example, if the switch you configure connects to other switches, which in turn connect to switches used in the production LAN, you could accidentally change the VLAN configuration in other switches with serious impact to the operation of the network. You could delete VLANs and cause outages. Be careful and never experiment with VTP settings on a switch unless it and the other switches connected to it have absolutely no physical links connected to the production LAN.

VLAN Trunking Configuration

Trunking configuration between two Cisco switches can be simple if you just statically configure trunking. You could literally add one interface subcommand for the switch interface on each side of the link (**switchport mode trunk**), and you would create a VLAN trunk that supported all the VLANs known to each switch.

However, trunking configuration on Cisco switches includes many more options, including several options for dynamically negotiating various trunking settings. The configuration can either predefine different settings or tell the switch to negotiate the settings, as follows:

- **The type of trunking:** IEEE 802.1Q, ISL, or negotiate which one to use, on switches that support both types of trunking.

- **The administrative mode:** Whether to always trunk, always not trunk, or negotiate whether to trunk or not.

First, consider the type of trunking. For many years, Cisco has not bothered to include ISL support in new switch product families, preferring IEEE 802.1Q. On older switches that support both, use the **switchport trunk encapsulation {dot1q | isl | negotiate}** interface subcommand to either configure the type to use or to allow Dynamic Trunking Protocol (DTP) to negotiate the type (which prefers ISL if both support it).

DTP can also negotiate whether the two devices on the link agree to trunk at all, as guided by the local switch port's administrative mode. The **administrative mode** refers to the configuration setting for whether trunking should be used. Cisco switches use the **switchport mode** interface subcommand to define the administrative trunking mode, as listed in Table 8-2. The switch interface's **operational mode** shows whether the interface operates as a trunk or an access port, which depends on the configuration on both switches plus other factors.

Table 8-2   Trunking Administrative Mode Options with the **switchport mode** Command

Command Option	Description
access	Always act as an access (nontrunk) port
trunk	Always act as a trunk port
dynamic desirable	Initiates negotiation messages and responds to negotiation messages to dynamically choose whether to start using trunking
dynamic auto	Passively waits to receive trunk negotiation messages, at which point the switch will respond and negotiate whether to use trunking

For example, consider the two switches shown in Figure 8-10. This figure expands the design shown earlier in Figure 8-9, with a trunk to a new switch (SW2) and with parts of VLANs 1 and 3 on ports attached to SW2. The two switches use a Gigabit Ethernet link for the trunk. In this case, the trunk does not dynamically form by default because both switches default to an administrative mode of *dynamic auto*, meaning that neither switch initiates the trunk negotiation process. When one switch is changed to use *dynamic desirable* mode, which does initiate the negotiation, the switches negotiate to use trunking, specifically 802.1Q because the switches support only 802.1Q.

Example 8-5 begins with SW1 configured as shown in Examples 8-2 and 8-4; that is, SW1 has two ports each assigned to VLANs 1, 2, and 3. However, both SW1 and SW2 currently

8

have all default settings on the interfaces that connect the two switches. With the default setting of **switchport mode dynamic auto**, the two switches do not trunk.

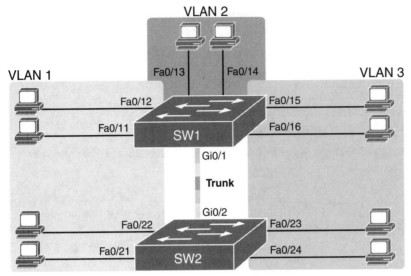

Figure 8-10   *Network with Two Switches and Three VLANs*

Example 8-5   *Initial (Default) State: Not Trunking Between SW1 and SW2*

```
SW1# show interfaces gigabit 0/1 switchport
Name: Gi0/1
Switchport: Enabled
Administrative Mode: dynamic auto
Operational Mode: static access
Administrative Trunking Encapsulation: dot1q
Operational Trunking Encapsulation: native
Negotiation of Trunking: On
Access Mode VLAN: 1 (default)
Trunking Native Mode VLAN: 1 (default)
Administrative Native VLAN tagging: enabled
Voice VLAN: none
Access Mode VLAN: 1 (default)
Trunking Native Mode VLAN: 1 (default)
Administrative Native VLAN tagging: enabled
Voice VLAN: none
Administrative private-vlan host-association: none
Administrative private-vlan mapping: none
Administrative private-vlan trunk native VLAN: none
Administrative private-vlan trunk Native VLAN tagging: enabled
Administrative private-vlan trunk encapsulation: dot1q
Administrative private-vlan trunk normal VLANs: none
Administrative private-vlan trunk private VLANs: none
Operational private-vlan: none
```

```
Trunking VLANs Enabled: ALL
Pruning VLANs Enabled: 2-1001
Capture Mode Disabled
Capture VLANs Allowed: ALL


Protected: false
Unknown unicast blocked: disabled
Unknown multicast blocked: disabled
Appliance trust: none


! Note that the next command results in a single empty line of output.
SW1# show interfaces trunk
SW1#
```

First, focus on the highlighted items from the output of the **show interfaces switchport** command at the beginning of Example 8-5. The output lists the default administrative mode setting of dynamic auto. Because SW2 also defaults to dynamic auto, the command lists SW1's operational status as "access," meaning that it is not trunking. ("Dynamic auto" tells both switches to sit there and wait on the other switch to start the negotiations.) The third shaded line points out the only supported type of trunking (802.1Q). (On a switch that supports both ISL and 802.1Q, this value would by default list "negotiate," to mean that the type of encapsulation is negotiated.) Finally, the operational trunking type is listed as "native," which is a reference to the 802.1Q native VLAN.

The end of the example shows the output of the **show interfaces trunk** command, but with no output. This command lists information about all interfaces that currently operationally trunk; that is, it lists interfaces that currently use VLAN trunking. With no interfaces listed, this command also confirms that the link between switches is not trunking.

Next, consider Example 8-6, which shows the new configuration that enables trunking. In this case, SW1 is configured with the **switchport mode dynamic desirable** command, which asks the switch to both negotiate as well as to begin the negotiation process, rather than waiting on the other device. The example shows that as soon as the command is issued, log messages appear showing that the interface goes down and then back up again, which happens when the interface transitions from access mode to trunk mode.

Example 8-6 *SW1 Changes from Dynamic Auto to Dynamic Desirable*

```
SW1# configure terminal
Enter configuration commands, one per line. End with CNTL/Z.
SW1(config)# interface gigabit 0/1
SW1(config-if)# switchport mode dynamic desirable
SW1(config-if)# ^Z
SW1#
%LINEPROTO-5-UPDOWN: Line protocol on Interface GigabitEthernet0/1, changed state to
down
%LINEPROTO-5-UPDOWN: Line protocol on Interface GigabitEthernet0/1, changed state to
up
SW1# show interfaces gigabit 0/1 switchport
```

```
Name: Gi0/1
Switchport: Enabled
Administrative Mode: dynamic desirable
Operational Mode: trunk
Administrative Trunking Encapsulation: dot1q
Operational Trunking Encapsulation: dot1q
Negotiation of Trunking: On
Access Mode VLAN: 1 (default)
Trunking Native Mode VLAN: 1 (default)
! lines omitted for brevity
```

Example 8-6 repeats the **show interfaces gi0/1 switchport** command seen in Example 8-5, but after configuring VLAN trunking, so this time the output shows that SW1's G0/1 interface now operates as a trunk. Note that the command still lists the administrative settings, which denote the configured values along with the operational settings, which list what the switch is currently doing. SW1 now claims to be in an operational mode of *trunk*, with an operational trunking encapsulation of dot1Q.

Example 8-7 now repeats the same **show interfaces trunk** command that showed no output at all back in Example 8-5. Now that SW1 trunks on its G0/1 port, the output in Example 8-7 lists G0/1, confirming that G0/1 is now operationally trunking. The next section discusses the meaning of the output of this command. Also, note that the end of the example repeats the **show vlan id 2** command; of note, it includes the trunk port G0/1 in the output because the trunk port can forward traffic in VLAN 2.

Example 8-7   *A Closer Look at SW1's G0/1 Trunk Port*

```
SW1# show interfaces trunk

Port        Mode            Encapsulation  Status       Native vlan
Gi0/1       desirable       802.1q         trunking     1

Port        Vlans allowed on trunk
Gi0/1       1-4094

Port        Vlans allowed and active in management domain
Gi0/1       1-3

Port        Vlans in spanning tree forwarding state and not pruned
Gi0/1       1-3

SW1# show vlan id 2
VLAN Name                             Status    Ports
---- -------------------------------- --------- -------------------------------
2    Freds-vlan                       active    Fa0/13, Fa0/14, G0/1
```

```
VLAN Type  SAID        MTU    Parent RingNo BridgeNo Stp  BrdgMode Trans1 Trans2
---- ----- ----------  -----  ------ ------ -------- ---- -------- ------ ------
2    enet  100010      1500   -      -      -        -    -        0      0


Remote SPAN VLAN
----------------


Disabled
Primary Secondary Type               Ports
------- --------- ----------------   -------------------------------------------
```

For the exams, you should be ready to interpret the output of the **show interfaces switchport** command, realize the administrative mode implied by the output, and know whether the link should operationally trunk based on those settings. Table 8-3 lists the combinations of the trunking administrative modes and the expected operational mode (trunk or access) resulting from the configured settings. The table lists the administrative mode used on one end of the link on the left and the administrative mode on the switch on the other end of the link across the top of the table.

Key Topic

Table 8-3 Expected Trunking Operational Mode Based on the Configured Administrative Modes

Administrative Mode	Access	Dynamic Auto	Trunk	Dynamic Desirable
access	Access	Access	Do Not Use*	Access
dynamic auto	Access	Access	Trunk	Trunk
trunk	Do Not Use*	Trunk	Trunk	Trunk
dynamic desirable	Access	Trunk	Trunk	Trunk

* When two switches configure a mode of "access" on one end and "trunk" on the other, problems occur. Avoid this combination.

Finally, before we leave the discussion of configuring trunks, Cisco recommends disabling trunk negotiation on most ports for better security. The majority of switch ports on most switches will be used to connect to users and configured with the command **switchport mode access**, which also disables DTP. For ports without the **switchport mode access** command—for instance, ports statically configured to trunk with the **switchport mode trunk** command—DTP still operates, but you can disable DTP negotiations altogether using the **switchport nonegotiate** interface subcommand.

Implementing Interfaces Connected to Phones

This next topic is strange, at least in the context of access links and trunk links. In the world of IP telephony, telephones use Ethernet ports to connect to an Ethernet network so they can use IP to send and receive voice traffic sent via IP packets. To make that work, the switch's Ethernet port acts like an access port, but at the same time, the port acts like a trunk in some ways. This last topic of the chapter works through those main concepts.

8

Data and Voice VLAN Concepts

Before IP telephony, a PC could sit on the same desk as a phone. The phone happened to use UTP cabling, with that phone connected to some voice device (often called a *voice switch* or a *private branch exchange [PBX]*). The PC, of course, connected using a unshielded twisted-pair (UTP) cable to the usual LAN switch that sat in the wiring closet—sometimes in the same wiring closet as the voice switch. Figure 8-11 shows the idea.

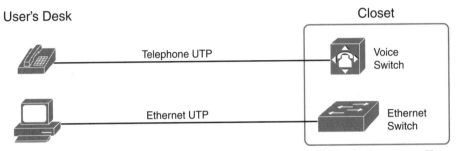

Figure 8-11 *Before IP Telephony: PC and Phone, One Cable Each, Connect to Two Different Devices*

The term *IP telephony* refers to the branch of networking in which the telephones use IP packets to send and receive voice as represented by the bits in the data portion of the IP packet. The phones connect to the network like most other end-user devices, using either Ethernet or Wi-Fi. These new IP phones did not connect via cable directly to a voice switch, instead connecting to the IP network using an Ethernet cable and an Ethernet port built in to the phone. The phones then communicated over the IP network with software that replaced the call setup and other functions of the PBX. (The current products from Cisco that perform this IP telephony control function are called *Cisco Unified Communication Manager*.)

The migration from using the already-installed telephone cabling to these new IP phones that needed UTP cables that supported Ethernet caused some problems in some offices. In particular:

- The older non-IP phones used a category of UTP cabling that often did not support 100-Mbps or 1000-Mbps Ethernet.

- Most offices had a single UTP cable running from the wiring closet to each desk, but now two devices (the PC and the new IP phone) both needed a cable from the desktop to the wiring closet.

- Installing a new cable to every desk would be expensive; plus you would need more switch ports.

To solve this problem, Cisco embedded small three-port switches into each phone.

IP telephones have included a small LAN switch, on the underside of the phone, since the earliest IP telephone products. Figure 8-12 shows the basic cabling, with the wiring closet cable connecting to one physical port on the embedded switch, the PC connecting with a short patch cable to the other physical port, and the phone's internal CPU connecting to an internal switch port.

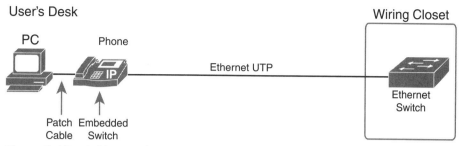

Figure 8-12 *Cabling with an IP Phone, a Single Cable, and an Integrated Switch*

Sites that use IP telephony, which includes most every company today, now have two devices off each access port. In addition, Cisco best practices for IP telephony design tell us to put the phones in one VLAN and the PCs in a different VLAN. To make that happen, the switch port acts a little like an access link (for the PC's traffic) and a little like a trunk (for the phone's traffic). The configuration defines two VLANs on that port, as follows:

Data VLAN: Same idea and configuration as the access VLAN on an access port but defined as the VLAN on that link for forwarding the traffic for the device connected to the phone on the desk (typically the user's PC).

Voice VLAN: The VLAN defined on the link for forwarding the phone's traffic. Traffic in this VLAN is typically tagged with an 802.1Q header.

Figure 8-13 illustrates this design with two VLANs on access ports that support IP telephones.

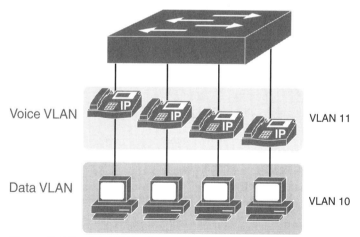

Figure 8-13 *A LAN Design, with Data in VLAN 10 and Phones in VLAN 11*

Data and Voice VLAN Configuration and Verification

Configuring a switch port to support IP phones, once you know the planned voice and data VLAN IDs, requires just a few easy commands. Making sense of the **show** commands once it is configured, however, can be a challenge. The port acts like an access port in many ways. However, with most configuration options, the voice frames flow with an 802.1Q header so that the link supports frames in both VLANs on the link. But that makes for some different **show** command output.

Example 8-8 shows an example configuration. In this case, all four switch ports F0/1–F0/4 begin with a default configuration. The configuration adds the new data and **voice VLANs**. The example then configures all four ports as access ports and defines the access VLAN, which is also called the **data VLAN** when discussing IP telephony. Finally, the configuration includes the **switchport voice vlan 11** command, which defines the voice VLAN used on the port. The example matches Figure 8-13, using ports F0/1–F0/4.

Example 8-8 *Configuring the Voice and Data VLAN on Ports Connected to Phones*

```
SW1# configure terminal
Enter configuration commands, one per line. End with CNTL/Z.
SW1(config)# vlan 10
SW1(config-vlan)# vlan 11
SW1(config-vlan)# interface range FastEthernet0/1 - 4
SW1(config-if)# switchport mode access
SW1(config-if)# switchport access vlan 10
SW1(config-if)# switchport voice vlan 11
SW1(config-if)#^Z
SW1#
```

NOTE Cisco phones exchange configuration data with the switch using the Cisco Discovery Protocol (CDP) or Link-Layer Discovery Protocol (LLDP). Switches enable CDP by default, so the configuration shows no specific configuration commands for it. *CCNA 200-301 Official Cert Guide, Volume 2*, Second Edition, Chapter 13, "Device Management Protocols," discusses CDP concepts and configuration.

The following list details the configuration steps for easier review and study:

Step 1.   Use the **vlan** *vlan-id* command in global configuration mode to create the data and voice VLANs if they do not already exist on the switch.

Step 2.   Configure the data VLAN like an access VLAN, as usual:

   a. Use the **interface** *type number* command in global configuration mode to move into interface configuration mode.

   b. Use the **switchport access vlan** *id-number* command in interface configuration mode to define the data VLAN.

   c. Use the **switchport mode access** command in interface configuration mode to make this port always operate in access mode (that is, to not trunk).

Step 3.   Use the **switchport voice vlan** *id-number* command in interface configuration mode to set the voice VLAN ID.

Verifying the status of a switch port configured like Example 8-8 shows some different output compared to the pure access port and pure trunk port configurations seen earlier in this chapter. For example, the **show interfaces switchport** command shows details about the operation of an interface, including many details about access ports. Example 8-9 shows those details for port F0/4 after the configuration in Example 8-8 was added.

Example 8-9   *Verifying the Data VLAN (Access VLAN) and Voice VLAN*

```
SW1# show interfaces FastEthernet 0/4 switchport
Name: Fa0/4
Switchport: Enabled
Administrative Mode: static access
Operational Mode: static access
Administrative Trunking Encapsulation: dot1q
Operational Trunking Encapsulation: native
Negotiation of Trunking: Off
Access Mode VLAN: 10 (VLAN0010)
Trunking Native Mode VLAN: 1 (default)
Administrative Native VLAN tagging: enabled
Voice VLAN: 11 (VLAN0011)
! The rest of the output is omitted for brevity
```

Working through the first three highlighted lines in the output, all those details should look familiar for any access port. The **switchport mode access** configuration command statically configures the administrative mode to be an access port, so the port of course operates as an access port. Also, as shown in the third highlighted line, the **switchport access vlan 10** configuration command defined the access mode VLAN as highlighted here.

The fourth highlighted line shows the one small new piece of information: the voice VLAN ID, as set with the **switchport voice vlan 11** command in this case. This small line of output is the only piece of information in the output that differs from the earlier access port examples in this chapter.

These ports act more like access ports than trunk ports. In fact, the **show interfaces** *type number* **switchport** command boldly proclaims, "Operational Mode: static access." However, one other **show** command reveals just a little more about the underlying operation with 802.1Q tagging for the voice frames.

As mentioned earlier, the **show interfaces trunk** command—that is, the command that does not include a specific interface in the middle of the command—lists the operational trunks on a switch. With IP telephony ports, the ports do not show up in the list of trunks either—providing evidence that these links are *not* treated as trunks. Example 8-10 shows just such an example.

However, the **show interfaces trunk** command with the interface listed in the middle of the command, as is also shown in Example 8-10, does list some additional information. Note that in this case, the **show interfaces F0/4 trunk** command lists the status as not-trunking, but with VLANs 10 and 11 allowed on the trunk. (Normally, on an access port, only the access VLAN is listed in the "VLANs allowed on the trunk" list in the output of this command.)

8

Example 8-10 *Allowed VLAN List and the List of Active VLANs*

```
SW1# show interfaces trunk
SW1# show interfaces F0/4 trunk


Port          Mode              Encapsulation  Status        Native vlan
Fa0/4         off               802.1q         not-trunking  1


Port          Vlans allowed on trunk
Fa0/4         10-11


Port          Vlans allowed and active in management domain
Fa0/4         10-11


Port          Vlans in spanning tree forwarding state and not pruned
Fa0/4         10-11
```

Summary: IP Telephony Ports on Switches

It might seem as though this short topic about IP telephony and switch configuration includes a lot of small twists and turns and trivia, and it does. The most important items to remember are as follows:

- Configure these ports like a normal access port to begin: Configure it as a static access port and assign it an access VLAN.

- Add one more command to define the voice VLAN (**switchport voice vlan** *vlan-id*).

- Look for the mention of the voice VLAN ID, but no other new facts, in the output of the **show interfaces** *type number* **switchport** command.

- Look for both the voice and data (access) VLAN IDs in the output of the **show interfaces** *type number* **trunk** command.

- Do not expect to see the port listed in the list of operational trunks as listed by the **show interfaces trunk** command.

Troubleshooting VLANs and VLAN Trunks

A switch's data plane forwarding processes depend in part on VLANs and VLAN trunking. This final section of the chapter focuses on issues related to VLANs and VLAN trunks that could prevent LAN switching from working properly, focusing on a few items not yet discussed in the chapter. In particular, this section examines these steps an engineer can take to avoid issues:

Step 1. Confirm that the correct access VLANs have been assigned.

Step 2. Confirm that all VLANs are both defined and active.

Step 3. Check the allowed VLAN lists on both ends of each trunk to ensure that all VLANs intended to be used are included.

Step 4.   Check for incorrect trunk configuration settings that result in one switch operating as a trunk, with the neighboring switch not operating as a trunk.

Step 5.   Check the native VLAN settings on both ends of the trunk to ensure the settings match.

Confirm the Correct Access VLAN Is Assigned

To ensure that each access interface has been assigned to the correct VLAN, engineers need to confirm an interface operates as an access interface (as opposed to a **trunk interface**), determine the access VLAN assigned to the access interface, and compare the information to the documentation. The **show** commands listed in Table 8-4 can be particularly helpful in this process.

Table 8-4   Commands That Can Find Access Ports and VLANs

EXEC Command	Description
show vlan brief show vlan	Lists each VLAN and all interfaces assigned to that VLAN (but does not include operational trunks)
show vlan id *num*	Lists both access and trunk ports in the VLAN
show interfaces status	On ports operating as access ports, it lists the access VLAN, and on ports operating as trunk ports, it lists the word *trunk*.
show interfaces *type number* switchport	Identifies the interface's access VLAN and voice VLAN, plus the configured and operational mode (access or trunk)
show mac address-table	Lists MAC table entries, including the associated VLAN

If possible, start this step with the **show vlan** and **show vlan brief** commands. Both commands list all known VLANs and all access interfaces assigned to each VLAN, whether the interface is in a working or nonworking state. Be aware, however, that these two commands do not list operational trunks, so if you want to also see the trunk ports that support a VLAN, use the **show vlan id** *number* command.

After you determine the access interfaces and associated VLANs, if the interface is assigned to the wrong VLAN, use the **switchport access vlan** *vlan-id* interface subcommand to assign the correct VLAN ID.

Access VLANs Undefined or Disabled

Switches do not forward frames for VLANs that are (a) not known because the VLAN is not configured or has not been learned with VTP or (b) the VLAN is known but is disabled (shut down). This next topic summarizes the best ways to confirm that a switch knows that a particular VLAN exists, and if it exists, determines the shutdown state of the VLAN.

First, on the issue of whether a VLAN exists on a switch, a VLAN can be defined to a switch in two ways: using the **vlan** *number* global configuration command, or it can be learned from another switch using VTP. As mentioned earlier in this chapter, the examples in this book assume that you are not using VTP. If you discover that a VLAN does not exist on a switch, simply configure the VLAN as discussed earlier in the section, "Creating VLANs and Assigning Access VLANs to an Interface."

In addition to checking the configuration, you can check for the status of the VLAN (as well as whether it is known to the switch) using the **show vlan** command. No matter the VTP

8

mode, this command will list all VLANs known to the switch, plus one of two VLAN state values, depending on the current state: either *active* or *act/lshut*. The second of these states means that the VLAN is shut down. Shutting down a VLAN disables the VLAN on that switch only, so *the switch will not forward frames in that VLAN.*

Switch IOS gives you two similar configuration methods with which to disable (**shutdown**) and enable (**no shutdown**) a VLAN. Example 8-11 shows how, first by using the global command [**no**] **shutdown vlan** *number* and then using the VLAN mode subcommand [**no**] **shutdown**. The example shows the global commands enabling and disabling VLANs 10 and 20, respectively, and using VLAN subcommands to enable and disable VLANs 30 and 40, respectively. The **show vlan brief** command at the end of the example confirms the shutdown (act/lshut) state of VLANs 10 and 30.

Example 8-11 *Enabling and Disabling VLANs on a Switch*

```
SW1# configure terminal
Enter configuration commands, one per line. End with CNTL/Z.
SW1(config)# no shutdown vlan 10
SW1(config)# shutdown vlan 20
SW1(config)# vlan 30
SW1(config-vlan)# no shutdown
SW1(config-vlan)# vlan 40
SW1(config-vlan)# shutdown
SW2(config-vlan)# end

SW1# show vlan brief

VLAN Name                             Status    Ports
---- -------------------------------- --------- ------------------------------
1    default                          active    Gi1/0/1, Gi1/0/2, Gi1/0/3
                                                Gi1/0/4, Gi1/0/5, Gi1/0/6
                                                Gi1/0/7, Gi1/0/8, Gi1/0/9
                                                Gi1/0/10, Gi1/0/11, Gi1/0/12
                                                Gi1/0/13, Gi1/0/14, Gi1/0/15
                                                Gi1/0/16, Gi1/0/17, Gi1/0/18
                                                Gi1/0/19, Gi1/0/20, Gi1/0/21
                                                Gi1/0/22, Gi1/0/23, Gi1/0/24
                                                Te1/1/1, Te1/1/2, Te1/1/3
                                                Te1/1/4
10   VLAN0010                         act/lshut
20   VLAN0020                         active
30   VLAN0030                         act/lshut
40   VLAN0040                         active
1002 fddi-default                     act/unsup
1003 token-ring-default               act/unsup
1004 fddinet-default                  act/unsup
1005 trnet-default                    act/unsup
```

NOTE The output of the **show vlan brief** command also lists a state of "act/unsup" for the reserved VLAN IDs 1002–1005, with "unsup" meaning "unsupported."

Example 8-12 shows another way to find the access VLANs on different ports by using the **show interfaces status** command. The switch has been configured before gathering the output in Example 8-12. First, the switch configures the first three ports as access ports in VLAN 10 and the next three as access ports in VLAN 20. The switch also configures two TenGigabitEthernet interfaces as trunks; note the word *trunk* under the VLAN heading for those interfaces.

Example 8-12 *Displaying Access Port VLANs with* **show interfaces status**

```
SW1# show interfaces status

Port       Name              Status       Vlan      Duplex  Speed  Type
Gi1/0/1                      connected    10        a-full  a-1000 10/100/1000BaseTX
Gi1/0/2                      connected    10        a-full  a-1000 10/100/1000BaseTX
Gi1/0/3                      connected    10        a-full  a-1000 10/100/1000BaseTX
Gi1/0/4                      connected    20        a-full  a-1000 10/100/1000BaseTX
Gi1/0/5                      connected    20        a-full  a-1000 10/100/1000BaseTX
Gi1/0/6                      connected    20        a-full  a-1000 10/100/1000BaseTX
! Lines For G1/0/7 - G1/0/24 omitted for brevity
Te1/1/1                      connected    trunk       full    10G  SFP-10Gbase-SR
Te1/1/2                      connected    trunk       full    10G  SFP-10Gbase-SR
Te1/1/3                      notconnect   1           auto    auto unknown
Te1/1/4                      notconnect   1           auto    auto unknown
```

Mismatched Trunking Operational States

Trunking can be configured correctly so that both switches use trunking. However, trunks can also be misconfigured, with a couple of different results: either both switches do not trunk, or one switch trunks and the other does not. Both results cause problems.

The most common incorrect configuration—which results in both switches not trunking—is a configuration that uses the **switchport mode dynamic auto** command on both switches on the link. The word *auto* just makes us all want to think that the link would trunk automatically, but this command is both automatic and passive. As a result, both switches passively wait on the other device on the link to begin negotiations. Example 8-13 highlights those parts of the output from the **show interfaces switchport** command that confirm both the configured and operational states. Note that the output lists the operational mode as "static access" rather than "trunking."

8

Example 8-13 *Operational Trunking State*

```
SW1# show interfaces TenGigabitEthernet1/1/1 switchport
Name: Te1/1/1
Switchport: Enabled
Administrative Mode: dynamic auto
Operational Mode: static access
Administrative Trunking Encapsulation: dot1q
Operational Trunking Encapsulation: native
! lines omitted for brevity
```

A different incorrect trunking configuration has an even worse result: one switch trunks, sending tagged frames, but the neighboring switch does not trunk, so the neighboring switch discards any frames it receives that have a VLAN tag in the header. When this combination of events happens, the interface works in that the status on each end will be up/up or connected. Traffic in the native VLAN will actually cross the link successfully because those frames have no VLAN tags (headers). However, traffic in all the rest of the VLANs will not cross the link.

Figure 8-14 shows the incorrect configuration along with which side trunks and which does not. The side that trunks (SW1 in this case) enables trunking using the command **switchport mode trunk** but also disables Dynamic Trunking Protocol (DTP) negotiations using the **switchport nonegotiate** command. SW2's configuration also helps create the problem, by using one of the two trunking options that rely on DTP. Because SW1 has disabled DTP, SW2's DTP negotiations fail, and SW2 chooses to not trunk.

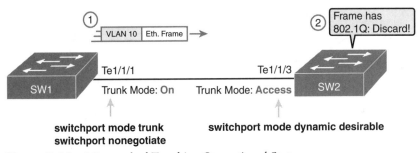

Figure 8-14 *Mismatched Trunking Operational States*

The figure shows what happens when using this incorrect configuration. At Step 1, SW1 could (for example) forward a frame in VLAN 10. However, SW2 would view any frame that arrives with an 802.1Q header as illegal because the frame has an 802.1Q header, and SW2 treats its G0/2 port as an access port. So, SW2 discards any 802.1Q frames received on that port.

The trunking issues shown here can be easily avoided by checking the configuration and by checking the trunk's operational state (mode) on both sides of the trunk. The best commands to check trunking-related facts are **show interfaces trunk** and **show interfaces switchport**. Just be aware that the switches do not prevent you from making these configuration mistakes.

The Supported VLAN List on Trunks

A Cisco switch can forward traffic for all defined and active VLANs. However, a particular VLAN trunk may not forward traffic for a defined and active VLAN for a variety of other reasons. You should learn how to identify which VLANs a particular trunk port currently supports and the reasons why the switch might not be forwarding frames for a VLAN on that trunk port.

The first category in this step can be easily done using the **show interfaces** *interface-id* **trunk** command, which lists information only about currently operational trunks. The best place to begin with this command is the last section of output, which lists the VLANs whose traffic will be forwarded over the trunk. Any VLANs that make it to this final list of VLANs in the command output meet the following criteria:

- The VLAN has not been removed from the *allowed VLAN list* on the trunk (as configured with the **switchport trunk allowed vlan** interface subcommand).

- The VLAN exists and is active on the local switch (as seen in the **show vlan** command).

- The VLAN has not been VTP-pruned from the trunk because the switch has disabled VTP. The trunk is in an STP forwarding state in that VLAN (as also seen in the **show spanning-tree vlan** *vlan-id* command).

The **switchport trunk allowed vlan** interface subcommand gives the network engineer a method to administratively limit the VLANs whose traffic uses a trunk. If the engineer wants all defined VLANs to be supported on a trunk, the engineer simply does not configure this command. If the engineer would like to limit the trunk to support a subset of the VLANs known to the switch, however, the engineer can add one or more **switchport trunk allowed vlan** interface subcommands.

For instance, in a switch that has configured VLANs 1 through 100, but no others, by default the switch would allow traffic in all 100 VLANs. However, the trunk interface command **switchport trunk allowed vlan 1-60** would limit the trunk to forward traffic for VLANs 1 through 60, but not the rest of the VLANs. Example 8-14 shows a sample of the command output from the **show interfaces trunk** command, which confirms the first list of VLAN IDs now lists VLANs 1–60. Without the **switchport trunk allowed vlan** command, the first list would have included VLANs 1–4094.

Example 8-14 *Allowed VLAN List and List of Active VLANs*

```
SW1# show interfaces trunk

Port          Mode          Encapsulation   Status        Native vlan
Te1/1/1       desirable     802.1q          trunking      1

Port          Vlans allowed on trunk
Te1/1/1       1-60

Port          Vlans allowed and active in management domain
Te1/1/1       1-59

Port          Vlans in spanning tree forwarding state and not pruned
Te1/1/1       1-58
```

The output of the **show interfaces trunk** command creates three separate lists of VLANs, each under a separate heading. These three lists show a progression of reasons why a VLAN is not forwarded over a trunk. Table 8-5 summarizes the headings that precede each list and the reasons why a switch chooses to include or not include a VLAN in each list. For instance, in Example 8-14, VLAN 60 has been shut down, and VLAN 59 happens to be in an STP blocking state. (Chapter 9, "Spanning Tree Protocol Concepts," has more information about STP.)

Table 8-5   VLAN Lists in the **show interfaces trunk** Command

List Position	Heading	Reasons
First	VLANs allowed	VLANs 1–4094, minus those removed by the **switchport trunk allowed** command
Second	VLANs allowed and active...	The first list, minus VLANs not defined to the local switch (that is, there is not a **vlan** global configuration command or the switch has not learned of the VLAN with VTP), and also minus those VLANs in shutdown mode
Third	VLANs in spanning tree...	The second list, minus VLANs in an STP blocking state for that interface, and minus VLANs VTP pruned from that trunk

Mismatched Native VLAN on a Trunk

Unfortunately, it *is* possible to set the native VLAN ID to different VLANs on either end of the trunk, using the **switchport trunk native vlan** *vlan-id* command. If the native VLANs differ according to the two neighboring switches, the switches will cause frames sent in the native VLAN to jump from one VLAN to the other.

For example, if switch SW1 sends a frame using native VLAN 1 on an 802.1Q trunk, SW1 does not add a VLAN header, as is normal for the native VLAN. When switch SW2 receives the frame, noticing that no 802.1Q header exists, SW2 assumes that the frame is part of SW2's configured native VLAN. If SW2 has been configured to think VLAN 2 is the native VLAN on that trunk, SW2 will try to forward the received frame into VLAN 2. (This effect of a frame being sent in one VLAN but then being believed to be in a different VLAN is called *VLAN hopping*.)

Chapter Review

Review this chapter's material using either the tools in the book or the interactive tools for the same material found on the book's companion website. Table 8-6 outlines the key review elements and where you can find them. To better track your study progress, record when you completed these activities in the second column.

Table 8-6   Chapter Review Tracking

Review Element	Review Date(s)	Resource Used
Review key topics		Book, website
Review key terms		Book, website
Answer DIKTA questions		Book, PTP

Review Element	Review Date(s)	Resource Used
Review config checklists		Book, website
Review command tables		Book
Review memory tables		Website
Do labs		Sim Lite, blog
Watch Video		Website

Review All the Key Topics

Table 8-7   Key Topics for Chapter 8

Key Topic Element	Description	Page Number
Figure 8-2	Basic VLAN concept	191
List	Reasons for using VLANs	192
Figure 8-5	Diagram of VLAN trunking	194
Figure 8-6	802.1Q header	195
Table 8-2	Options of the **switchport mode** command	203
Table 8-3	Expected trunking results based on the configuration of the **switchport mode** command	207
List	Definitions of data VLAN and voice VLAN	209
List	Summary of data and voice VLAN concepts, configuration, and verification	212
Table 8-4	Commands to find access ports and assigned VLANs	213
Table 8-5	Analysis of the three VLAN lists in the output from the **show interfaces** *interface-id* **trunk** command	218

Key Terms You Should Know

802.1Q, access interface, data VLAN, default VLAN, Layer 3 switch, native VLAN, static access interface, trunk, trunk interface, trunking administrative mode, trunking operational mode, VLAN, voice VLAN, VTP, VTP transparent mode

Do Labs

The Sim Lite software is a version of Pearson's full simulator learning product with a subset of the labs, included free with this book. The Sim Lite with this book includes a couple of labs about VLANs. Also, check the author's blog site pages for configuration exercises (Config Labs) at https://www.certskills.com.

Command References

Tables 8-8 and 8-9 list configuration and verification commands used in this chapter, respectively. As an easy review exercise, cover the left column in a table, read the right column, and try to recall the command without looking. Then repeat the exercise, covering the right column, and try to recall what the command does.

8

Table 8-8   Chapter 8 Configuration Command Reference

Command	Description
vlan *vlan-id*	Global config command that both creates the VLAN and puts the CLI into VLAN configuration mode.
name *vlan-name*	VLAN subcommand that names the VLAN.
[no] shutdown	VLAN mode subcommand that enables (**no shutdown**) or disables (**shutdown**) the VLAN.
[no] shutdown vlan *vlan-id*	Global config command that has the same effect as the [no] **shutdown** VLAN mode subcommands.
vtp mode {server | client | transparent | off}	Global config command that defines the VTP mode.
switchport mode {access | dynamic {auto | desirable} | trunk}	Interface subcommand that configures the trunking administrative mode on the interface.
switchport access vlan *vlan-id*	Interface subcommand that statically configures the interface into that one VLAN.
switchport trunk encapsulation {dot1q | isl | negotiate}	Interface subcommand that defines which type of trunking to use, assuming that trunking is configured or negotiated.
switchport trunk native vlan *vlan-id*	Interface subcommand that defines the native VLAN for a trunk port.
switchport nonegotiate	Interface subcommand that disables the negotiation of VLAN trunking.
switchport voice vlan *vlan-id*	Interface subcommand that defines the voice VLAN on a port, meaning that the switch uses 802.1Q tagging for frames in this VLAN.
switchport trunk allowed vlan *vlan-list*	Interface subcommand that defines the list of allowed VLANs. Ignores the existing list of allowed VLANs.
switchport trunk allowed vlan {add | remove} *vlan-list*	Interface subcommand that adds to or removes from the current set of allowed VLANs on a trunk, adjusting from the existing list of allowed VLANs.
switchport trunk allowed vlan {all | none | except *vlan-list*}	Interface subcommand that defines the allowed VLAN list as either all VLANs, no VLANs, or all except those in the configured list. Ignores the existing list of allowed VLANs.

Table 8-9   Chapter 8 EXEC Command Reference

Command	Description
show interfaces status	On ports operating as access ports, it lists the access VLAN, and on ports operating as trunk ports, it lists the word *trunk*.
show interfaces *interface-id* switchport	Lists information about any interface regarding administrative settings and operational state.

Command	Description
show interfaces trunk	Lists information about all operational trunks (but no other interfaces), including the list of VLANs that can be forwarded over the trunk.
show interfaces *interface-id* **trunk**	Lists trunking status about the listed interface, regardless of whether the interface currently operates as a trunk.
show vlan [brief]	Lists each VLAN and all interfaces assigned to that VLAN (but does not include operational trunks).
show vlan {id *vlan-id* **| name** *vlan-name***}**	Lists information about a specific VLAN by ID or name, and interfaces, including trunks.
show vtp status	Lists VTP configuration and status information.

8

CHAPTER 9

Spanning Tree Protocol Concepts

This chapter covers the following exam topics:

2.0 Network Access

  2.4 Configure and verify (Layer 2/Layer 3) EtherChannel (LACP)

  2.5 Interpret basic operations of Rapid PVST+ Spanning Tree Protocol

    2.5.a Root port, root bridge (primary/secondary), and other port names

    2.5.b Port states and roles

    2.5.c PortFast

    2.5.d Root Guard, loop guard, BPDU filter, and BPDU guard

Spanning Tree Protocol (STP) allows Ethernet LANs to have redundant links in a LAN while overcoming the known problems that occur when adding those extra links. Using redundant links in a LAN design allows the LAN to keep working even when some links fail or even when some entire switches fail. Proper LAN design should add enough redundancy so that no single point of failure crashes the LAN; STP allows the design to use redundancy without causing other problems.

Historically, the IEEE first standardized STP as part of the IEEE 802.1D standard back in 1990, with pre-standard versions working even before that time. Over time, the industry and IEEE improved STP, with the eventual replacement of STP with an improved protocol: Rapid Spanning Tree Protocol (RSTP). The IEEE first released RSTP as amendment 802.1w and, in 2004, integrated RSTP into the 802.1D standard.

Today, most networks use RSTP rather than STP; however, STP and RSTP share many of the same mechanisms, and RSTP's improvements can be best understood in comparison to STP. For that reason, this chapter presents some details that apply only to STP, as a learning tool to help you understand RSTP.

This chapter organizes the material into four sections. The first section presents some core concepts about how both STP and RSTP discover a tree made of nodes (switches) and links so that no loops exist in a network. The second section then takes a brief look at the area in which STP differs the most from RSTP: in how STP reacts to changes in the network. The third section then shows how RSTP works much better than STP when reacting to changes. The final section touches on a variety of small optional STP and RSTP features.

Finally, be warned that this chapter, as well as Chapter 10, are a little longer than expected. If you like to think of each chapter as one study session, you might need to think about splitting this chapter into two study sessions. For the first study session, you should stop at the section, "Rapid STP Concepts." The second study session would consist of the "Rapid STP Concepts" and "Optional STP Features" sections.

"Do I Know This Already?" Quiz

Take the quiz (either here or use the PTP software) if you want to use the score to help you decide how much time to spend on this chapter. The letter answers are listed at the bottom of the page following the quiz. Appendix C, found both at the end of the book as well as on the companion website, includes both the answers and explanations. You can also find both answers and explanations in the PTP testing software.

Table 9-1 "Do I Know This Already?" Foundation Topics Section-to-Question Mapping

Foundation Topics Section	Questions
STP and RSTP Basics	1–2
Details Specific to STP (and Not RSTP)	3–4
Rapid STP Concepts	5–6
Optional STP Features	7–8

1. Which of the following port states are stable states used when STP has completed convergence? (Choose two answers.)

   a. Blocking

   b. Forwarding

   c. Listening

   d. Learning

   e. Discarding

2. Which of the following bridge IDs wins election as root, assuming that the switches with these bridge IDs are in the same network?

   a. 32769:0200.1111.1111

   b. 32769:0200.2222.2222

   c. 4097:0200.1111.1111

   d. 4097:0200.2222.2222

   e. 40961:0200.1111.1111

3. Which of the following are transitory port states used only during the process of STP convergence? (Choose two answers.)

   a. Blocking

   b. Forwarding

   c. Listening

   d. Learning

   e. Discarding

4. Which of the following facts determines how often a nonroot bridge or switch sends an STP Hello BPDU message?

   a. The Hello timer as configured on that switch.

   b. The Hello timer as configured on the root switch.

   c.   It is always every 2 seconds.

   d.   The switch reacts to BPDUs received from the root switch by sending another BPDU 2 seconds after receiving the root BPDU.

5.   Which of the following RSTP port states have the same name and purpose as a port state in traditional STP? (Choose two answers.)

   a.   Blocking

   b.   Forwarding

   c.   Listening

   d.   Learning

   e.   Discarding

6.   RSTP adds features beyond STP that enable ports to be used for a role if another port on the same switch fails. Which of the following statements correctly describe a port role that is waiting to take over for another port role? (Choose two answers.)

   a.   An alternate port waits to become a root port.

   b.   A backup port waits to become a root port.

   c.   An alternate port waits to become a designated port.

   d.   A backup port waits to become a designated port.

7.   What STP/RSTP feature causes an interface to be placed in the forwarding state as soon as the interface is physically active?

   a.   STP

   b.   EtherChannel

   c.   Root Guard

   d.   PortFast

8.   Which optional STP feature reacts to a subset of incoming STP BPDUs to disable the port, but allows and processes some other STP BPDUs?

   a.   Loop Guard

   b.   BPDU Guard

   c.   Root Guard

   d.   PortFast

Foundation Topics

STP and RSTP Basics

Without some mechanism like **Spanning Tree Protocol (STP)** or **Rapid STP (RSTP)**, a LAN with redundant links would cause Ethernet frames to loop for an indefinite period of time. With STP or RSTP enabled, some switches block ports so that these ports do not forward frames. STP and RSTP intelligently choose which ports block, with two goals in mind:

   ■   All devices in a VLAN can send frames to all other devices. In other words, STP or RSTP does not block too many ports, cutting off some parts of the LAN from other parts.

   ■   Frames have a short life and do not loop around the network indefinitely.

STP and RSTP strike a balance, allowing frames to be delivered to each device, without causing the problems that occur when frames loop through the network over and over again.

> **NOTE**   This first major section of the chapter explains details of both STP and RSTP, so this section uses the term *STP/RSTP* to refer to these protocols together. Note that this term is just a convenient shorthand. Later in the chapter, the text will point out differences between STP and RSTP and begin using the terms *STP* and *RSTP* separately, referring to only the specific protocol.

STP/RSTP prevents looping frames by adding an additional check on each interface before a switch uses it to send or receive user traffic. That check: If the port is in STP/RSTP **forwarding state** in that VLAN, use it as normal; if it is in STP/RSTP **blocking state**, however, block all user traffic and do not send or receive user traffic on that interface in that VLAN.

Note that these STP/RSTP states do not change the other information you already know about switch interfaces. The interface's state of connected/notconnect does not change. The interface's operational state as either an access or trunk port does not change. STP/RSTP adds this additional state, with the blocking state basically disabling the interface.

In many ways, the preceding two paragraphs sum up what STP/RSTP does. However, the details of how STP/RSTP does its work can take a fair amount of study and practice. This first major section of the chapter begins by explaining the need for STP/RSTP and the basic ideas of what STP/RSTP does to solve the problem of looping frames. The majority of this section then looks at how STP/RSTP goes about choosing which switch ports to block to accomplish its goals.

The Need for Spanning Tree

STP/RSTP prevents three common problems in Ethernet LANs. All three problems occur as a side effect of one fact: without STP/RSTP, some Ethernet frames would loop around the network for a long time (hours, days, literally forever if the LAN devices and links never failed).

Just one looping frame causes what is called a *broadcast storm*. Broadcast storms happen when any kind of Ethernet frames—broadcast frames, multicast frames, or unknown-destination unicast frames—loop around a LAN indefinitely. Broadcast storms can saturate all the links with copies of that one single frame, crowding out good frames, as well as significantly impacting end-user device performance by making the PCs process too many broadcast frames.

To help you understand how this occurs, Figure 9-1 shows a sample network in which Bob sends a broadcast frame. The dashed lines show how the switches forward the frame when STP/RSTP does not exist.

Remember that LAN switch? That logic tells switches to flood broadcasts out all interfaces in the same VLAN except the interface in which the frame arrived. In Figure 9-1, that means SW3 forwards Bob's frame to SW2, SW2 forwards the frame to SW1, SW1 forwards the frame back to SW3, and SW3 forwards it back to SW2 again.

9

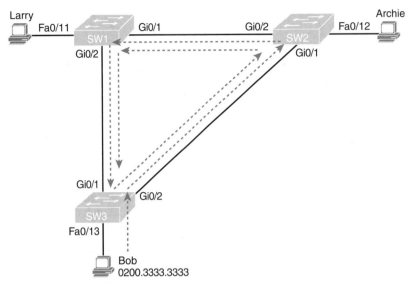

Figure 9-1 *Broadcast Storm*

When broadcast storms happen, frames like the one in Figure 9-1 keep looping until some-thing changes—someone shuts down an interface, reloads a switch, or does something else to break the loop. Also note that the same event happens in the opposite direction. When Bob sends the original frame, SW3 also forwards a copy to SW1, SW1 forwards it to SW2, and so on.

The storm also causes a much more subtle problem called *MAC table instability*. MAC table instability means that the switches' MAC address tables keep changing because frames with the same source MAC arrive on different ports. To see why, follow this example, in which SW3 begins Figure 9-1 with a MAC table entry for Bob, at the bottom of the figure, associated with port Fa0/13:

    0200.3333.3333   Fa0/13   VLAN 1

However, now think about the switch-learning process that occurs when the looping frame goes to SW2, then SW1, and then back into SW3's Gi0/1 interface. SW3 thinks, "Hmm...the source MAC address is 0200.3333.3333, and it came in my Gi0/1 interface. Update my MAC table!" This results in the following entry on SW3, with interface Gi0/1 instead of Fa0/13:

    0200.3333.3333   Gi0/1   VLAN 1

At this point, SW3 itself cannot correctly deliver frames to Bob's MAC address. At that instant, if a frame arrives at SW3 destined for Bob—a different frame than the looping frame that causes the problems—SW3 incorrectly forwards the frame out Gi0/1 to SW1, creating even more congestion.

The looping frames in a broadcast storm also cause a third problem: multiple copies of the frame arrive at the destination. Consider a case in which Bob sends a frame to Larry but

Answers to the "Do I Know This Already?" quiz:

1 A, B **2** C **3** C, D **4** B **5** B, D **6** A, D **7** D, **8** C

none of the switches know Larry's MAC address. Switches flood frames sent to unknown destination unicast MAC addresses. When Bob sends the frame destined for Larry's MAC address, SW3 sends a copy to both SW1 and SW2. SW1 and SW2 also flood the frame, causing copies of the frame to loop. SW1 also sends a copy of each frame out Fa0/11 to Larry. As a result, Larry gets multiple copies of the frame, which may result in an application failure, if not more pervasive networking problems.

Table 9-2 summarizes the main three classes of problems that occur when STP/RSTP is not used in a LAN that has redundancy.

Table 9-2   Three Classes of Problems Caused by Not Using STP in Redundant LANs

Problem	Description
Broadcast storms	The forwarding of a frame repeatedly on the same links, consuming significant parts of the links' capacities
MAC table instability	The continual updating of a switch's MAC address table with incorrect entries, in reaction to looping frames, resulting in frames being sent to the wrong locations
Multiple frame transmission	A side effect of looping frames in which multiple copies of one frame are delivered to the intended host, confusing the host

What Spanning Tree Does

STP/RSTP prevents loops by placing each switch port in either a forwarding state or a blocking state. Interfaces in the forwarding state act as normal, forwarding and receiving frames. However, interfaces in a blocking state do not process any frames except STP/RSTP messages (and some other overhead messages). Interfaces that block do not forward user frames, do not learn MAC addresses of received frames, and do not process received user frames.

Figure 9-2 shows a simple STP/RSTP tree that solves the problem shown in Figure 9-1 by placing one port on SW3 in the blocking state.

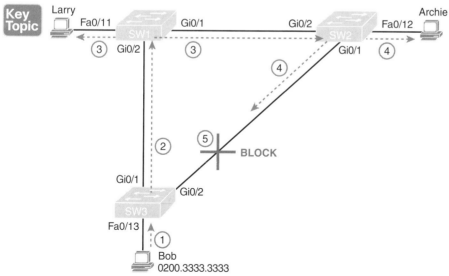

Figure 9-2   *What STP/RSTP Does: Blocks a Port to Break the Loop*

Now when Bob sends a broadcast frame, the frame does not loop. As shown in the steps in the figure:

Step 1.   Bob sends the frame to SW3.

Step 2.   SW3 forwards the frame only to SW1, but not out Gi0/2 to SW2, because SW3's Gi0/2 interface is in a blocking state.

Step 3.   SW1 floods the frame out both Fa0/11 and Gi0/1.

Step 4.   SW2 floods the frame out Fa0/12 and Gi0/1.

Step 5.   SW3 physically receives the frame, but it ignores the frame received from SW2 because SW3's Gi0/2 interface is in a blocking state.

With the STP/RSTP topology in Figure 9-2, the switches simply do not use the link between SW2 and SW3 for traffic in this VLAN, which is the minor negative side effect of STP. However, if either of the other two links fails, STP/RSTP converges so that SW3 forwards instead of blocks on its Gi0/2 interface.

> **NOTE**   The term *STP convergence* refers to the process by which the switches collectively realize that something has changed in the LAN topology and determine whether they need to change which ports block and which ports forward.

That completes the description of what STP/RSTP does, placing each port into either a forwarding or blocking state. The more interesting question, and the one that takes a lot more work to understand, is how and why STP/RSTP makes its choices. How does STP/RSTP manage to make switches block or forward on each interface? And how does it converge to change state from blocking to forwarding to take advantage of redundant links in response to network outages? The following pages answer these questions.

How Spanning Tree Works

The STP/RSTP algorithm creates a spanning tree of interfaces that forward frames. The tree structure of forwarding interfaces creates a single path to and from each Ethernet link, just like you can trace a single path in a living, growing tree from the base of the tree to each leaf.

> **NOTE**   STP existed before LAN switches, with the STP processes performed by devices called bridges. Some terms and command output still use the older term *bridge*, so when working with STP/RSTP, consider the terms *bridge* and *switch* synonymous.

The process used by STP, sometimes called the *spanning-tree algorithm* (STA), chooses the interfaces that should be placed into a forwarding state. For any interfaces not chosen to be in a forwarding state, STP/RSTP places the interfaces in a blocking state. In other words, STP/RSTP simply picks which interfaces should forward, and any interfaces left over go to a blocking state.

STP/RSTP uses three criteria to choose whether to put an interface in a forwarding state:

- STP/RSTP elects a **root switch**. STP puts all working interfaces on the root switch in a forwarding state.

- Each nonroot switch calculates the least-cost path between itself and the root switch based on STP/RSTP interface costs. The switch port that begins that least-cost path is its *root port* (RP), and the cost is the switch's **root cost**.

- In a modern Ethernet that uses switches, each physical link connects two devices only. With two switches on a link, the switch with the lowest root cost becomes the *designated switch,* and its port connected to that link is the **designated port** (DP) on the link.

NOTE   A root switch places all interfaces into a forwarding state because each port on the root switch always wins its designated port (DP) election. However, it is easier to just remember that all the root switches' working interfaces will forward frames.

All other interfaces are placed in a blocking state. Table 9-3 summarizes the reasons STP/RSTP places a port in a forwarding or blocking state.

Table 9-3   STP/RSTP: Reasons for Forwarding or Blocking

Characterization of Port	STP State	Description
All the root switch's ports	Forwarding	The root switch is always the designated switch on all connected segments.
Each nonroot switch's root port	Forwarding	The port through which the switch has the least cost to reach the root switch (lowest root cost).
Each LAN's designated port	Forwarding	The switch forwarding the Hello on to the segment, with the lowest root cost, is the designated switch for that segment.
All other working ports	Blocking	The port is not used for forwarding user frames, nor are any frames received on these interfaces considered for forwarding.

NOTE   STP/RSTP should not use nonworking interfaces in the working STP/RSTP topology. To remove all nonworking interfaces from consideration—that is, all that are not in a connected (up/up) interface state—STP/RSTP assigns nonworking ports with the *disabled port role*. STP/RSTP does not consider these ports as potential RP or DP ports. STP also places these ports into a **disabled state** (much like blocking).

The STP Bridge ID and Hello BPDU

The STA begins with an election of one switch to be the root switch. To better understand this election process, you need to understand the STP/RSTP messages sent between switches as well as the concept and format of the identifier used to uniquely identify each switch.

The STP/RSTP **bridge ID** (BID) is an 8-byte value unique to each switch. The bridge ID consists of a 2-byte priority field and a 6-byte system ID, with the system ID being based on a universal (burned-in) MAC address in each switch. Using a burned-in MAC address ensures that each switch's bridge ID will be unique.

STP/RSTP defines messages called **bridge protocol data units (BPDU)**, also called configuration BPDUs, which switches use to exchange information with each other. The most common BPDU, called a **Hello BPDU**, lists many details, including the sending switch's BID. By listing its own unique BID, switches can tell which switch sent which Hello BPDU. Table 9-4 lists some of the key information in the Hello BPDU.

Table 9-4   Fields in the STP Hello BPDU

Field	Description
Root bridge ID	The bridge ID of the switch that the sender of this Hello currently believes to be the root switch
Sender's bridge ID	The bridge ID of the switch sending this Hello BPDU
Sender's root cost	The STP/RSTP cost between this switch and the current root
Timer values on the root switch	Includes the Hello timer, MaxAge timer, and **forward delay** timer

For the time being, just keep the first three items from Table 9-4 in mind as the following sections work through the three steps in how STP/RSTP chooses the interfaces to place into a forwarding state. Next, the text examines the three main steps in the STP/RSTP process.

Electing the Root Switch

Switches elect a root switch based on the BIDs in the BPDUs. The root switch is the switch with the lowest numeric value for the BID. Because the two-part BID starts with the priority value, essentially the switch with the lowest priority becomes the root. For example, if one switch has priority 4096, and another switch has priority 8192, the switch with priority 4096 wins, regardless of what MAC address was used to create the BID for each switch.

If a tie occurs based on the priority portion of the BID, the switch with the lowest MAC address portion of the BID is the root. No other tiebreaker should be needed because switches use one of their own universal (burned-in) MAC addresses as the second part of their BIDs. So, if the priorities tie, and one switch uses a MAC address of 0200.0000.0000 as part of the BID and the other uses 0811.1111.1111, the first switch (MAC 0200.0000.0000) becomes the root switch.

STP/RSTP elects a root switch in a manner not unlike a political election. The process begins with all switches claiming to be the root by sending Hello BPDUs listing their own BID as the root BID. If a switch hears a Hello that lists a better (lower) BID, that switch stops advertising itself as root and starts forwarding the superior Hello. The Hello sent by the better switch lists the better switch's BID as the root. It works like a political race in which a less-popular candidate gives up and leaves the race, throwing his support behind the more popular candidate. Eventually, everyone agrees which switch has the best (lowest) BID, and everyone supports the elected switch—which is where the political race analogy falls apart.

> **NOTE** A better Hello, meaning that the listed root's BID is better (numerically lower), is called a *superior Hello*; a worse Hello, meaning that the listed root's BID is not as good (numerically higher), is called an *inferior Hello*.

Figure 9-3 shows the beginning of the root election process. In this case, SW1 has advertised itself as root, as have SW2 and SW3. However, SW2 now believes that SW1 is a better root, so SW2 is now forwarding the Hello originating at SW1. So, at this point, the figure shows SW1 is saying Hello, claiming to be root; SW2 agrees and is forwarding SW1's Hello that lists SW1 as root; but SW3 is still claiming to be best, sending its own Hello BPDUs, listing SW3's BID as the root.

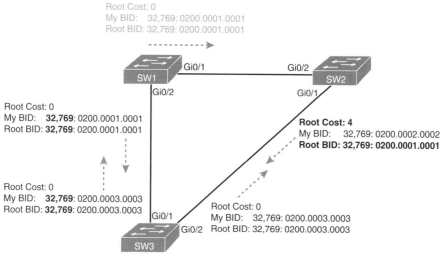

Figure 9-3 *Beginnings of the Root Election Process*

Two candidates still exist in Figure 9-3: SW1 and SW3. So, who wins? Well, from the BID, the lower-priority switch wins; if a tie occurs, the lower MAC address wins. As shown in the figure on the left, the switch priority values (32,769) tie, but SW1 has a lower BID (32,769:0200.0001.0001) than SW3 (32,769:0200.0003.0003) due to its lower MAC address. SW1 wins, and SW3 now also believes that SW1 is the better switch. Figure 9-4 shows the resulting Hello messages sent by the switches.

Summarizing, the root election happens through each switch claiming to be root, with the best switch being elected based on the numerically lowest BID. Breaking down the BID into its components, the comparisons can be made as:

- The lowest priority

- If that ties, the lowest switch MAC address

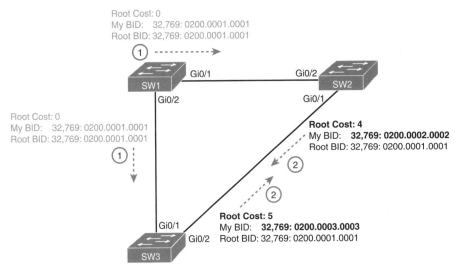

Figure 9-4 *SW1 Wins the Election*

Choosing Each Switch's Root Port

The second part of the STP/RSTP process occurs when each nonroot switch chooses its one and only *root port* (RP). A switch's RP is its interface through which it has the least STP/RSTP cost to reach the root switch (least root cost).

You can easily see the idea behind a switch's cost to reach the root. Just look at a network diagram that shows the root switch, lists the STP/RSTP cost associated with each switch port, and identifies the nonroot switch in question. Switches use a different process than you can see by looking at a network diagram, of course, but using a diagram can make it easier to learn the idea.

Figure 9-5 shows just such a figure, with the same three switches shown in the last several figures. SW1 has already won the election as root, and the figure considers the cost from SW3's perspective. (Note that the figure uses some nondefault cost settings.)

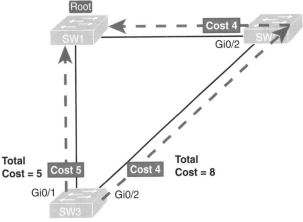

Figure 9-5 *How a Human Might Calculate STP/RSTP Cost from SW3 to the Root (SW1)*

SW3 has two possible physical paths to send frames to the root switch: the direct path to the left and the indirect path to the right through switch SW2. The cost is the sum of the costs of all the *switch ports the frame would exit* if it flowed over that path. (The calculation ignores the inbound ports.) As you can see, the cost over the direct path out SW3's G0/1 port has a total cost of 5, and the other path has a total cost of 8. SW3 picks its G0/1 port as root port because it is the port that is part of the least-cost path to send frames to the root switch.

Switches come to the same conclusion but using a different process. Instead, they add their local interface STP/RSTP cost to the root cost listed in each received Hello BPDU. The STP/RSTP port cost is simply an integer value assigned to each interface, per VLAN, for the purpose of providing an objective measurement that allows STP/RSTP to choose which interfaces to add to the STP/RSTP topology. The switches also look at their neighbor's root cost, as announced in Hello BPDUs received from each neighbor.

Figure 9-6 shows an example of how switches calculate their best root cost and then choose their root port, using the same topology and STP/RSTP costs as shown in Figure 9-5. STP/RSTP on SW3 calculates its cost to reach the root over the two possible paths by adding the advertised cost (in Hello messages) to the interface costs listed in the figure.

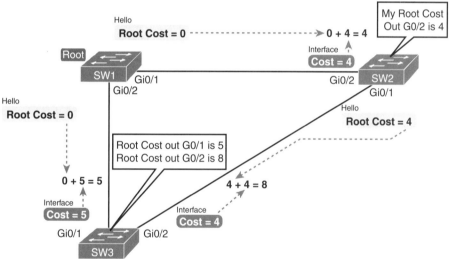

Figure 9-6 *How STP/RSTP Actually Calculates the Cost from SW3 to the Root*

Focus on the process for a moment. The root switch sends Hellos, with a listed root cost of 0. The idea is that the root's cost to reach itself is 0.

Next, look on the left of the figure. SW3 takes the received cost (0) from the Hello sent by SW1 and adds the interface cost (5) of the interface on which that Hello was received. SW3 calculates that the cost to reach the root switch, out that port (G0/1), is 5.

On the right side, SW2 has realized its best cost to reach the root is cost 4. So, when SW2 forwards the Hello toward SW3, SW2 lists a root cost 4. SW3's STP/RSTP port cost on port G0/2 is 4, so SW3 determines a total cost to reach root out its G0/2 port of 8.

As a result of the process depicted in Figure 9-6, SW3 chooses Gi0/1 as its RP because the cost to reach the root switch through that port (5) is lower than the other alternative (Gi0/2, cost 8). Similarly, SW2 chooses Gi0/2 as its RP, with a cost of 4 (SW1's advertised cost of 0 plus SW2's Gi0/2 interface cost of 4). Each switch places its root port into a forwarding state.

Switches need a tiebreaker to use in case the best root cost ties for two or more paths. If a tie occurs, the switch applies these three tiebreakers to the paths that tie, in order, as follows:

1. Choose based on the lowest neighbor bridge ID.

2. Choose based on the lowest neighbor port priority.

3. Choose based on the lowest neighbor internal port number.

Choosing the Designated Port on Each LAN Segment

The final STP/RSTP step determines the designated port on each LAN segment. The switch with the lowest root cost wins the competition. With two switches on the ends of a link, the switch with the lower cost to reach the root becomes the designated switch, with its port on that link becoming the DP on that segment. On a link with a switch and a second device that does not use STP/RSTP (for instance, a router or PC), the switch becomes the DP.

The process to choose the DP begins with the switch(es) forwarding Hellos onto the link. The Hello messages include a field to list the root cost of the switch that forwarded the Hello. Determining which switch has the lowest root cost requires a simple comparison. Once a switch port becomes the DP, it continues to forward Hellos onto the link.

For example, earlier Figure 9-4 shows in bold text the parts of the Hello messages from both SW2 and SW3 that determine the choice of DP on that segment. Note that both SW2 and SW3 list their respective root cost (cost 4 on SW2 and cost 5 on SW3). SW2 lists the lower cost, so SW2's Gi0/1 port is the designated port on that LAN segment.

All DPs are placed into a forwarding state; in this case, SW2's Gi0/1 interface will be in a forwarding state.

If the advertised costs tie, the switches break the tie by choosing the switch with the lower BID. In this case, SW2 would also have won, with a BID of 32769:0200.0002.0002 versus SW3's 32769:0200.0003.0003.

> **NOTE** Two additional tiebreakers are needed in some cases, although these would be unlikely today. A single switch can connect two or more interfaces to the same collision domain by connecting to a hub. In that case, the one switch hears its own BPDUs. So, if a switch ties with itself, two additional tiebreakers are used: the lowest interface STP/RSTP priority and, if that ties, the lowest internal interface number.

The only interface that does not have a reason to be in a forwarding state on the three switches in the examples shown in Figures 9-3 through 9-6 is SW3's Gi0/2 port. So, the STP/RSTP process is now complete. Table 9-5 outlines the state of each port and shows why it is in that state.

Table 9-5 State of Each Interface

Switch Interface	State	Reason Why the Interface Is in Forwarding State
SW1, Gi0/1	Forwarding	The interface is on the root switch, so it becomes the DP on that link.
SW1, Gi0/2	Forwarding	The interface is on the root switch, so it becomes the DP on that link.
SW2, Gi0/2	Forwarding	The root port of SW2.
SW2, Gi0/1	Forwarding	The designated port on the LAN segment to SW3.
SW3, Gi0/1	Forwarding	The root port of SW3.
SW3, Gi0/2	Blocking	Not the root port and not the designated port.

Note that the examples in this section focus on the links between the switches, but switch ports connected to endpoint devices should become DPs and settle into a forwarding state. Working through the logic, each switch will forward BPDUs on each port as part of the process to determine the DP on that LAN. Endpoints should ignore those messages because they do not run STP/RSTP, so the switch will win and become the DP on every access port.

Configuring to Influence the STP Topology

STP/RSTP works by default on Cisco switches, so all the settings needed by a switch have a useful default. Switches have a default BID, based on a default priority value and adding a universal MAC address that comes with the switch hardware. Additionally, switch interfaces have default STP/RSTP costs based on the current operating speed of the switch interfaces.

Network engineers often want to change the STP/RSTP settings to then change the choices STP/RSTP makes in a given LAN. Two main tools available to the engineer are to configure the bridge ID and to change STP/RSTP port costs.

First, to change the BID, the engineer can set the priority used by the switch, while continuing to use the universal MAC address as the final 48 bits of the BID. For instance, giving a switch the lowest priority value among all switches will cause that switch to win the root election.

Port costs also have default values, per port, per VLAN. You can configure these port costs, which will in turn impact many switch's calculations of the root cost. For instance, to favor one link, give the ports on that link a lower cost, or to avoid a link, give the ports a higher cost.

Table 9-6 lists the default port costs suggested by IEEE. IOS on Cisco switches has long used the default settings as defined as far back as the 1998 version of the STP standard. The latest IEEE standards suggest values that are more useful when using links faster than 10 Gbps. You can configure a switch to use the old (short) or new (long) defaults using the global command (**spanning-tree pathcost method {short | long}**)—but it makes sense to use the same setting on all switches in the same campus.

9

Table 9-6 Default Port Costs According to IEEE

Ethernet Speed	IEEE Cost: 1998 (and Before)	IEEE Cost: 2004 (and After)
10 Mbps	100	2,000,000
100 Mbps	19	200,000
1 Gbps	4	20,000
10 Gbps	2	2000
100 Gbps	N/A	200
1 Tbps	N/A	20

Also, be aware that Cisco switches choose the default cost based on the operating speed of the link, not the maximum speed. That is, if a 10/100/1000 port runs at 10 Mbps for some reason, its default STP cost on a Cisco switch is 100.

Details Specific to STP (and Not RSTP)

As promised in the introduction to this chapter, the first section showed features that apply to both STP and RSTP. This next heading acts as the turning point, with the next several pages being about STP only. The upcoming section titled "Rapid STP Concepts" then shows details specific to RSTP, in contrast to STP.

Once the engineer has finished all STP configuration, the STP topology should settle into a stable state and not change, at least until the network topology changes. This section examines the ongoing operation of STP while the network is stable, and then it covers how STP converges to a new topology when something changes.

Note that almost all the differences between STP and RSTP revolve around the activities of waiting for and reacting to changes in the topology. STP performed well for the era and circumstances in which it was created. The "rapid" in RSTP refers to the improvements to how fast RSTP could react when changes occur—so understanding how STP reacts will be useful to understand why RSTP reacts faster. These next few pages show the specifics of STP (and not RSTP) and how STP reacts to and manages convergence when changes happen in an Ethernet LAN.

STP Activity When the Network Remains Stable

When the network remains stable, the root switch generates a new Hello BPDU, with the nonroot switches forwarding copies of the Hello so that the Hellos traverse the spanning tree. The root generates a new Hello every Hello time (default 2 seconds), with each nonroot switch forwarding the Hello out any interfaces in a forwarding state after updating the Hello. The following steps summarize the steady-state operation when nothing is currently changing in the STP topology:

Step 1.   The root creates and sends a Hello BPDU, with a root cost of 0, out all its working interfaces (those in a forwarding state).

Step 2.   The nonroot switches receive the Hello on their root ports. After changing the Hello to list their own BID as the sender's BID and listing that switch's root cost, the switch forwards the Hello out all designated ports.

Step 3.   Steps 1 and 2 repeat every Hello time until something changes.

When a switch fails to receive a Hello in its root port, it knows a problem might be occurring in the network. Each switch relies on these periodically received Hellos from the root as a way to know that its path to the root is still working. When a switch ceases to receive the Hellos, or receives a Hello that lists different details, something has failed, so the switch reacts and starts the process of changing the spanning-tree topology.

STP Timers That Manage STP Convergence

For various reasons, the STP convergence process requires the use of three timers, listed in Table 9-7. Note that all switches use the timers as dictated by the root switch, which the root lists in its periodic Hello BPDU messages.

Table 9-7   STP Timers

Timer	Default Value	Description
Hello	2 seconds	The time period between Hellos created by the root.
MaxAge	10 times Hello	How long any switch should wait, after ceasing to hear Hellos, before trying to change the STP topology.
Forward delay	15 seconds	Delay that affects the process that occurs when an interface changes from a blocking state to a forwarding state. A port stays in an interim **listening state**, and then an interim **learning state**, for the number of seconds defined by the forward delay timer.

If a switch does not get one expected Hello BPDU within the Hello time, the switch continues as normal. However, if the Hellos do not show up again within MaxAge time, the switch reacts by taking steps to change the STP topology. With default settings, MaxAge is 20 seconds (ten times the default Hello timer of 2 seconds). So, a switch would go 20 seconds without hearing a Hello before reacting.

After MaxAge expires, the switch essentially makes all its STP choices again, based on any Hellos it receives from other switches. It reevaluates which switch should be the root switch. If the local switch is not the root, it chooses its RP. And it determines whether it is the DP on each of its other links.

The best way to describe STP convergence is to show an example using the same familiar topology. Figure 9-7 shows the same familiar figure, with SW3's Gi0/2 in a blocking state, but SW1's Gi0/2 interface has just failed.

In the scenario shown in the figure, SW3 reacts to the change because SW3 fails to receive its expected Hellos on its Gi0/1 interface. However, SW2 does not need to react because SW2 continues to receive its periodic Hellos in its Gi0/2 interface. In this case, SW3 reacts either when **MaxAge** time passes without hearing the Hellos, or as soon as SW3 notices that interface Gi0/1 has failed. (If the interface fails, the switch can assume that the Hellos will not be arriving in that interface anymore.)

Now that SW3 can act, it begins by reevaluating the choice of root switch. SW3 still receives the Hellos from SW2, as forwarded from the root (SW1). SW1 still has a lower BID than SW3; otherwise, SW1 would not have already been the root. So, SW3 decides that SW1 wins the root election and that SW3 is not the root.

9

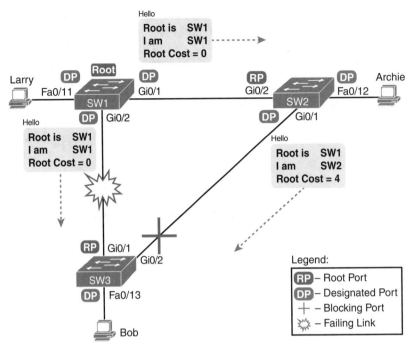

Figure 9-7   *Initial STP State Before SW1-SW3 Link Fails*

Next, SW3 reevaluates its choice of RP. At this point, SW3 is receiving Hellos on only one interface: Gi0/2. Whatever the calculated root cost, Gi0/2 becomes SW3's new RP. (The cost would be 8, assuming the same STP costs in earlier Figures 9-5 and 9-6.)

SW3 then reevaluates its role as DP on any other interfaces. In this example, no real work needs to be done. SW3 was already the DP on interface Fa0/13, and it continues to be the DP because no other switches connect to that port.

Changing Interface States with STP

STP uses the idea of roles and states. *Roles*, like root port role and designated port role, relate to how STP analyzes the LAN topology. *States*, like forwarding and blocking, tell a switch whether to send or receive frames. When STP converges, a switch chooses new port roles, and the port roles determine the state (forwarding or blocking).

Switches using STP can simply move immediately from a forwarding to a blocking state, but they must take extra time to transition from a blocking state to a forwarding state. For instance, when switch SW3 in Figure 9-7 formerly used port G0/1 as its RP (a role), that port was in a forwarding state. After convergence, G0/1 might be neither an RP nor a DP; the switch can immediately move that port to a blocking state.

However, when a port that formerly blocked needs to transition to forwarding, the switch first puts the port through two intermediate interface states. These temporary STP states help prevent temporary loops:

- **Listening:** Like the blocking state, the interface does not forward frames. The switch removes old stale (unused) MAC table entries for which no frames are received from each MAC address during this period. These stale MAC table entries could be the cause of the temporary loops.

- **Learning:** Interfaces in this state still do not forward frames, but the switch begins to learn the MAC addresses of frames received on the interface.

STP moves an interface from blocking to listening, then to learning, and then to a forwarding state. STP leaves the interface in each interim state for a time equal to the forward delay timer, which defaults to 15 seconds. As a result, a convergence event that causes an interface to change from blocking to forwarding requires 30 seconds to transition from blocking to forwarding. In addition, a switch might have to wait MaxAge seconds (default 20 seconds) before even choosing to move an interface from a blocking to a forwarding state.

For example, follow what happens with an initial STP topology as shown in Figures 9-3 through 9-6, with the SW1-to-SW3 link failing as shown in Figure 9-7. If SW1 simply quit sending Hello messages to SW3, but the link between the two did not fail, SW3 would wait MaxAge seconds before reacting (20 seconds is the default). SW3 would actually quickly choose its ports' STP roles, but then wait 15 seconds each in listening and learning states on interface Gi0/2, resulting in a 50-second convergence delay.

Table 9-8 summarizes spanning tree's various interface states for easier review.

Table 9-8 IEEE STP (not RSTP) States

State	Forwards Data Frames?	Learns MACs Based on Received Frames?	Transitory or Stable State?
Blocking	No	No	Stable
Listening	No	No	Transitory
Learning	No	Yes	Transitory
Forwarding	Yes	Yes	Stable
Disabled	No	No	Stable

Rapid STP Concepts

The original STP worked well given the assumptions about networks and networking devices in that era. However, as with any computing or networking standard, as time passes, hardware and software capabilities improve, so new protocols emerge to take advantage of those new capabilities. For STP, one of the most significant improvements over time has been the introduction of Rapid Spanning Tree Protocol (RSTP), introduced as standard IEEE 802.1w.

NOTE Just to make sure you are clear about the terminology: Throughout the rest of the chapter, *STP* refers to the original STP standard only, and use of the term *RSTP* does not include STP.

Before getting into the details of RSTP, it helps to make sense of the standards numbers a bit: 802.1w was actually an amendment to the 802.1D standard. The IEEE first published 802.1D in 1990, and anew in 1998. After the 1998 version of 802.1D, the IEEE published the 802.1w amendment to 802.1D in 2001, which first standardized RSTP.

Over the years, other meaningful changes happened in the standards as well, although those changes probably do not impact most networkers' thinking when it comes to working with STP or RSTP. But to be complete, the IEEE replaced STP with RSTP in the revised 802.1D standard in 2004. In another move, in 2011 the IEEE moved all the RSTP details into a revised 802.1Q standard. As it stands today, RSTP actually sits in the 802.1Q standards document.

As a result, when reading about RSTP, you will see documents, books, videos, and the like that refer to RSTP and include various references to 802.1w, 802.1D, and 802.1Q—and they might all be correct based on timing and context. At the same time, many people refer to RSTP as 802.1w because that was the first IEEE document to define it. However, for the purposes of this book, focus instead on the RSTP acronym rather than the IEEE standards numbers used with RSTP over its history.

> **NOTE** The IEEE sells its standards, but through the "Get IEEE 802" program, you can get free PDFs of the current 802 standards. To read about RSTP today, you will need to download the 802.1Q standard and then look for the sections about RSTP.

Now on to the details about RSTP in this chapter. As discussed throughout this chapter, RSTP and STP have many similarities, so this section next compares and contrasts the two. Following that, the rest of this section discusses the concepts unique to RSTP that are not found in STP—alternate root ports, different port states, backup ports, and the port roles used by RSTP.

Comparing STP and RSTP

RSTP works just like STP in several ways, as discussed in the first major section of the chapter. To review:

- RSTP and STP elect the root switch using the same rules and tiebreakers.

- RSTP and STP switches select their root ports with the same rules.

- RSTP and STP elect designated ports on each LAN segment with the same rules and tiebreakers.

- RSTP and STP place each port in either forwarding or blocking state, although RSTP calls the blocking state the **discarding state**.

In fact, RSTP works so much like STP that they can both be used in the same network. RSTP and STP switches can be deployed in the same network, with RSTP features working in switches that support it and traditional STP features working in the switches that support only STP.

With all these similarities, you might be wondering why the IEEE bothered to create RSTP in the first place. The overriding reason is convergence. STP takes a relatively long time to converge (50 seconds with the default settings when all the wait times must be followed). RSTP improves network convergence when topology changes occur, usually converging within a few seconds (or in slow conditions, in about 10 seconds).

RSTP changes and adds to STP in ways that avoid waiting on STP timers, resulting in quick transitions from forwarding to discarding (blocking) state and vice versa. Specifically, RSTP, compared to STP, defines more cases in which the switch can avoid waiting for a timer to expire, such as the following:

- RSTP adds a mechanism by which a switch can replace its root port, without any waiting to reach a forwarding state (in some conditions).

- RSTP adds a new mechanism to replace a designated port, without any waiting to reach a forwarding state (in some conditions).

- RSTP lowers waiting times for cases in which RSTP must wait for a timer.

For instance, imagine a failure case in which a link remains up, but for some reason, a non-root switch stops hearing the Hello BPDUs it had been hearing in the past. STP requires a switch to wait for MaxAge seconds, which STP defines based on ten times the Hello timer, or 20 seconds, by default. RSTP shortens this timer, defining MaxAge as three times the Hello timer. Additionally, RSTP can send messages to the neighboring switch to inquire whether a problem has occurred rather than wait for timers.

The best way to get a sense for these mechanisms is to see how the RSTP alternate port role and the backup port role both work. RSTP uses the term *alternate port* to refer to a switch's other ports that could be used as the root port if the root port ever fails. The *backup port* concept provides a backup port on the local switch for a designated port. (Note that backup ports apply only to designs that use hubs, so they are unlikely to be useful today.) However, both are instructive about how RSTP works. Table 9-9 lists these RSTP port roles.

Table 9-9 Port Roles in RSTP

Function	Port Role
Nonroot switch's best path to the root	**Root port**
Port that will be used to replace the root port when the root port fails	**Alternate port**
Switch port designated to forward onto a collision domain	**Designated port**
Port that will be used to replace a designated port when a designated port fails	**Backup port**
Port in a nonworking interface state—that is, anything other than connected (up/up)	**Disabled port**

RSTP differs from STP in a few other ways as well. For instance, with STP, the root switch creates a Hello, with all other switches updating and forwarding the Hello. With RSTP, each switch independently generates its own Hellos. Additionally, RSTP allows for queries between neighbors, rather than waiting on timers to expire, as a means to avoid waiting to learn information. These types of protocol changes help RSTP-based switches isolate what has changed in a network and react quickly to choose a net RSTP topology.

The next few pages work through some of those overt RSTP features that differ from STP.

RSTP and the Alternate (Root) Port Role

With STP, each nonroot switch places one port in the STP root port (RP) role. RSTP follows that same convention, with the same exact rules for choosing the RP. RSTP then takes another step beyond STP, naming other possible RPs, identifying them as *alternate ports*.

9

To be an alternate port, both the RP and the alternate port must receive Hellos that identify the same root switch. For instance, in Figure 9-8, SW1 is the root. SW3 will receive Hello BPDUs on two ports: G0/1 and G0/2. Both Hellos list SW1's bridge ID (BID) as the root switch, so whichever port is not the root port meets the criteria to be an alternate port. SW3 picks G0/1 as its root port in this case and then makes G0/2 an alternate port.

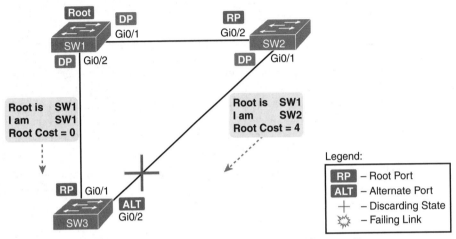

Figure 9-8   *Example of SW3 Making G0/2 Become an Alternate Port*

An alternate port basically works like the second-best option for the root port. The alternate port can take over for the former root port, often very rapidly, without requiring a wait in other interim RSTP states. For instance, when the root port fails, the switch changes the former root port's role and state: (a) the role from root port to a *disabled port* (because the interface failed), and (b) the state from forwarding to discarding (RSTP uses the discarding state for ports in the disabled port role). Then, without waiting on any timers, the switch changes the alternate port to be the root port and immediately changes its port state from discarding to forwarding.

Notably, the new root port also does not need to spend time in other states, such as the learning state, instead moving immediately to the forwarding state.

Figure 9-9 shows an example of RSTP convergence. SW3's root port before the failure shown in this figure is SW3's G0/1, the link connected directly to SW1 (the root switch). Then SW3's link to SW1 fails as shown in Step 1 of the figure.

Following the steps in Figure 9-9:

Step 1.   The link between SW1 and SW3 fails, so SW3's current root port (Gi0/1) fails.

Step 2.   SW3 and SW2 exchange RSTP messages to confirm that SW3 will now transition its former alternate port (Gi0/2) to be the root port. This action causes SW2 to flush the required MAC table entries.

Step 3.   SW3 transitions G0/1 to the disabled port role and G0/2 to the root port role.

Step 4.   SW3 transitions G0/2 to a forwarding state immediately, without using the learning state, because this is one case in which RSTP knows the transition will not create a loop.

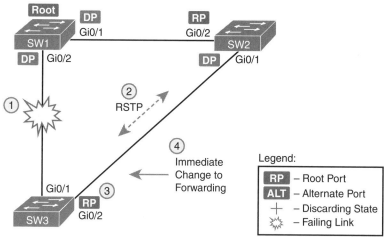

Figure 9-9 *Convergence Events with SW3 G0/1 Failure*

As soon as SW3 realizes its G0/1 interface has failed, the process shown in the figure takes very little time. None of the processes rely on timers, so as soon as the work can be done, the convergence completes. (This particular convergence example takes about 1 second in a lab.)

RSTP States and Processes

The depth of the previous example does not point out all the details of RSTP, of course; however, the example does show enough details to discuss RSTP states and internal processes.

Both STP and RSTP use *port states*; however, RSTP differs from STP in a few of the details. Both use the forwarding state for the same purpose. For the two interim states used by STP during convergence (listening and learning), RSTP does not use the listening state, considering it unnecessary, but it uses the learning state for the same purpose as STP. Finally, RSTP uses the *discarding* state instead of the STP *blocking* state.

To be complete, note that both RSTP and STP have port roles and states related to ports that are not currently working. Those rules are

- Both STP and RSTP define and use a disabled port role for any port in a nonworking interface state. (For instance, interfaces with no cable installed or interfaces configured with the **shutdown** command configured.)

- STP uses the disabled state for such ports. RSTP does not have a separate disabled state but instead uses the discarding state.

Honestly, the intricacies of the disabled role and states probably do not matter much; it seems obvious that nonworking interfaces cannot be a useful part of a working spanning tree. Regardless, Table 9-10 shows the list of STP and RSTP states for comparison and easier study.

9

Table 9-10 Port States Compared: STP and RSTP

Function	STP State	RSTP State
Port is not in a working (connected) state, either due to failure or due to shutdown	Disabled	Discarding
Stable state that ignores incoming data frames and is not used to forward data frames	Blocking	Discarding
Interim state without MAC learning and without forwarding	Listening	Not used
Interim state with MAC learning and without forwarding	Learning	Learning
Stable state that allows MAC learning and forwarding of data frames	Forwarding	Forwarding

RSTP uses different internal processes compared to STP in an effort to speed convergence. As an example, consider what happens when STP changes a port's role, resulting in the need to move from a blocking to a forwarding state:

1. The switch changes the timer it uses to timeout MAC table entries to be equal to the STP forward delay timer (default 15 seconds).

2. The switch transitions the interface to the listening state, remaining there for the forward delay time (default 15 seconds).

3. After the forward delay time passes:

   a. All MAC table entries affected by this topology change will have been timed out of the table, removing the possibility of loops.

   b. The switch can now transition the port to the learning state, remaining there for the forward delay time.

4. After spending the forward delay time in the learning state, the switch transitions the port to the forwarding state.

To converge more quickly, RSTP avoids relying on timers. RSTP switches tell each other (using messages) that the topology has changed. Those messages also direct neighboring switches to flush the contents of their MAC tables in a way that removes all the potentially loop-causing entries, without a wait. As a result, RSTP creates more scenarios in which a formerly discarding port can immediately transition to a forwarding state, without waiting, and without using the learning state, as shown in the example in Figure 9-9.

RSTP and the Backup (Designated) Port Role

The RSTP backup port role also improves convergence. It provides fast failover for the designated port role, but only in designs like Figure 9-10, when one switch connects with multiple ports to the same hub. Because moderns LANs do not use hubs, you will be unlikely to see this RSTP feature in practice, but to be ready for all RSTP features, consider this example.

Figure 9-10 shows a design in which switch SW3 connects with one port and SW4 connects with two ports to the same hub. SW4's port F0/1 happens to win the election as designated port (DP). In this topology, switch SW4's port F0/2 can act as a backup port.

With a backup port, if the current designated port fails, SW4 can start using the backup port as the new designated port with rapid convergence. For instance, if SW4's F0/1 interface were to fail, SW4 could transition F0/2 to the designated port role, without any delay in moving from the discarding state to a forwarding state.

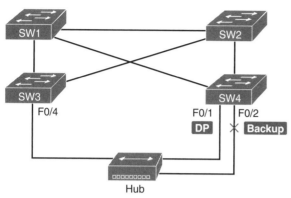

Figure 9-10   *RSTP Backup Port Example*

RSTP Port Types

The final RSTP concept included here relates to some terms RSTP uses to refer to different types of ports and the links that connect to those ports.

To begin, consider the basic image in Figure 9-11. It shows several links between two switches. RSTP considers these links to be point-to-point links and the ports connected to them to be point-to-point ports because the link connects exactly two devices (points).

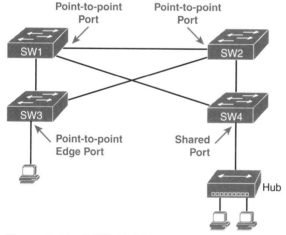

Figure 9-11   *RSTP Link Types*

RSTP further classifies point-to-point ports into two categories. Point-to-point ports that connect two switches are not at the edge of the network and are simply called *point-to-point ports*. Ports that instead connect to a single endpoint device at the edge of the network, like a PC or server, are called *point-to-point edge ports*, or simply *edge ports*. In Figure 9-11, SW3's switch port connected to a PC is an edge port.

Finally, RSTP defines the term *shared* to describe ports connected to a hub. The term *shared* comes from the fact that hubs create a shared Ethernet; hubs also force the attached switch port to use half-duplex logic. RSTP assumes that all half-duplex ports may be connected to hubs, treating ports that use half duplex as shared ports. RSTP converges more slowly on shared ports as compared to all point-to-point ports.

Optional STP Features

To close out the chapter, the last major section describes optional features that make STP work even better or be more secure: EtherChannel, PortFast, BPDU Guard, Root Guard, and Loop Guard.

EtherChannel

One of the best ways to lower STP's convergence time is to avoid convergence altogether. **EtherChannel** provides a way to prevent STP convergence from being needed when only a single port or cable failure occurs.

EtherChannel combines multiple parallel segments of equal speed (up to eight) between the same pair of switches, bundled into an EtherChannel. The switches treat the EtherChannel as a single interface with regard to STP. As a result, if one of the links fails, but at least one of the links is up, STP convergence does not have to occur. For example, Figure 9-12 shows the familiar three-switch network, but now with two Gigabit Ethernet connections between each pair of switches.

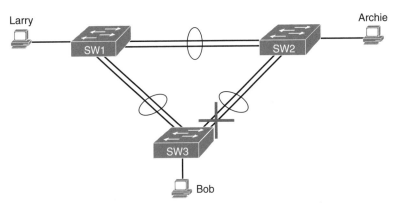

Figure 9-12 *Two-Segment EtherChannels Between Switches*

With each pair of Ethernet links configured as an EtherChannel, STP treats each EtherChannel as a single link. In other words, both links to the same switch must fail for a switch to need to cause STP convergence. Without EtherChannel, if you have multiple parallel links between two switches, STP blocks all the links except one. With EtherChannel, all the parallel links can be up and working simultaneously while reducing the number of times STP must converge, making the network more available.

The current CCNA exam blueprint includes a topic for configuring both Layer 2 EtherChannels (as described here) and Layer 3 EtherChannels. Chapter 10, "RSTP and EtherChannel Configuration," shows how to configure Layer 2 EtherChannels, while Chapter 18, "IP Routing in the LAN," shows how to configure Layer 3 EtherChannels. Note that Layer 2 EtherChannels combine links that switches use as switch ports, with the switches using Layer 2 switching logic to forward and receive Ethernet frames over the EtherChannels. Layer 3 EtherChannels also combine links, but the switches use Layer 3 routing logic to forward packets over the EtherChannels.

PortFast

Switch ports that connect directly to endpoints rather than to other switches eventually use the designated port (DP) role and a forwarding state. However, with default port settings, they go through some interim steps:

1. After the interface reaches the connected (up/up) state, the switch STP logic initially places the port in the STP discarding (blocking) state.

2. The switch begins sending BPDUs out of the port and listens for incoming BPDUs, to decide whether the switch port should take on a root port (RP) or a DP role.

3. Because the connected device is not a switch, the local switch receives no incoming BPDUs. As a result, the switch port wins the DP election and becomes a DP.

4. The switch takes interim steps to transition to a forwarding state:

    a. STP moves the port first to the listening state, then to the learning state, and then to the forwarding state. The interim states require 15 seconds each by default (per the default Forward Delay timer).

    b. RSTP follows the same process, except it has no listening state. It moves from discarding to learning to forwarding.

PortFast bypasses the process. After the interface reaches a connected state, STP PortFast immediately moves the port to the DP role and the forwarding state without delay. As long as the interface remains up, the STP role remains as DP with a forwarding state.

PortFast exists to support access links connected to endpoints, as shown in Figure 9-13. You know the switch always wins the DP election on those links because the endpoints do not use STP. Those endpoints can include single computers, phones with connected computers, or a trunk connected to a server.

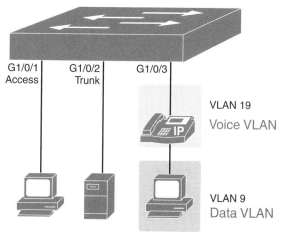

Figure 9-13 *Access Ports Appropriate for the PortFast Feature*

As you might guess from the fact that PortFast speeds convergence, STP did not include the PortFast feature, but RSTP included it as one of its rapid convergence optimizations. You might recall the mention of RSTP port types, particularly point-to-point edge port types, around Figure 9-11. RSTP, by design of the protocol, converges quickly on these ports of type point-to-point edge by bypassing the learning state. Note that Cisco introduced this idea with its PortFast years before the IEEE finalized RSTP, which is why we still call the feature PortFast many decades later. In practice, Cisco switches enable RSTP point-to-point edge ports by enabling PortFast on the port.

While very useful and popular, PortFast also introduces the risk of creating loops. PortFast ports should never connect to bridges or switches. With PortFast enabled, the port ignores incoming BPDUs, always acts as a designated port, and always forwards. As a result, an unexpected or rogue switch connected to a PortFast-enabled port can create a forwarding loop.

BPDU Guard

PortFast creates an exposure: the possibility of a forwarding loop if an unexpected switch connects to a PortFast port. The Cisco **BPDU Guard** feature helps defeat these kinds of problems by disabling a port if it receives any BPDUs in the port. So, this feature is handy on ports that should be used only as an access port and never connected to another switch.

Figure 9-14 shows the basic idea. The device on the right should be an endpoint device such as a PC. Instead, a new switch named Rogue-1 connects to the legitimate switch SW3—a switch that uses BPDU Guard to protect against this scenario. At Step 2, as soon as switch Rogue-1 sends a BPDU into SW3, SW3's BPDU Guard logic reacts, disabling the port.

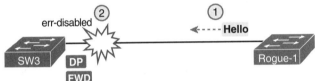

Figure 9-14 *Basic Logic of BPDU Guard*

Most switch access port configurations combine PortFast and BPDU Guard, although both can be used independently. Using PortFast without protection against the scenario in Figure 9-14 risks a loop. Using BPDU Guard on these same ports makes sense because if another switch connects to such a port, the local switch can disable the port to prevent a loop.

BPDU Filter

The **BPDU Filter** feature defines two different functions under one named feature. Both fall under the name BPDU filter because, behind the scenes, they filter (discard) STP BPDUs.

First, the BPDU Filter feature can be used as an alternative to BPDU Guard when used along with PortFast. Both BPDU Guard and BPDU Filter prevent loops when unexpected BPDUs arrive in a PortFast-enabled port. However, BPDU Filter reacts to those incoming BPDUs by disabling PortFast logic (which creates the possibility of a forwarding loop) and restoring normal STP logic on the port (which prevents the possibility of a forwarding loop).

The other BPDU Filter feature disables STP on an interface. When enabled, BPDU Filter discards all sent and received BPDUs on an interface.

The following pages take a closer look at each logic branch.

BPDU Filter to Prevent Loops on PortFast Ports

Most campus LANs make widespread use of PortFast, both on access ports and on server ports that use trunking. However, with PortFast alone but with no other features, you risk someone unplugging those devices and replacing them with switches to create a forwarding loop. Figure 9-15 shows such a case, where switch SW1's two ports use PortFast but the endpoints were replaced with two rogue switches.

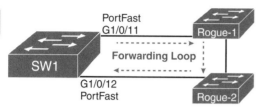

Figure 9-15 *Possible Loop on PortFast Ports with Rogue Switches*

To protect against such a case, you can use either BPDU Guard or BPDU Filter. Ports that use PortFast should not receive BPDUs under normal circumstances, but nothing prevents people from replacing devices as shown in Figure 9-15. If that happens, BPDU Filter reacts by disabling PortFast on the port. The port then reverts to normal STP rules. STP will then determine a new port role and status as needed, use STP rules, and prevent any forwarding loop. The port may block or forward, depending on the results of that normal STP logic.

The previous paragraph gets at the reason why an engineer might choose this BPDU Filter feature; however, the following list details the specific steps, which includes some BPDU filtering.

1. To enable this branch of BPDU Filter logic, use the related global command **spanning-tree portfast bpdufilter default**.

2. IOS finds all ports that currently use PortFast and enables conditional BPDU Filter on those ports.

3. When any such port comes up:

    a. BPDU Filter allows STP to send BPDUs as normal for 10 × Hello Time (2 × 10 seconds, or 20 seconds total by default).

    b. If the port receives zero BPDUs in that time, BPDU Filter begins filtering (discarding) sent BPDUs.

4. BPDU Filter monitors to notice any incoming BPDUs. If they begin to arrive:

    a. It disables PortFast on the port.

    b. It reverts the port to use STP with normal STP rules.

BPDU Filter to Disable STP on a Port

The BPDU Filter feature can be configured to enable a completely different style of logic. As you will see in Chapter 10's section titled "BPDU Filter," the configuration does not make it obvious which style the configuration enables. However, when enabled with an interface subcommand, BPDU Filter does just what the name says: It filters (discards) all BPDUs on the ports, both outgoing and incoming.

Using BPDU Filter in this way effectively disables STP on the port. Using this feature is dangerous: Do not use it in production until you fully test and understand it.

9

As an example of why you might want to use BPDU Filter to disable STP on a port, consider the scenario in Figure 9-16. Two IT groups build networks inside the same company. They want to connect their LANs together, but the two groups (Left and Right) do not want the other group's STP to influence theirs—for example, which switch would be allowed to win the root election, a left or a right switch? The two groups meet and decide to keep their STP topologies separate. To do so, they filter all BPDUs sent between the two using BPDU Filter, disabling STP on the one link that connects the two LANs.

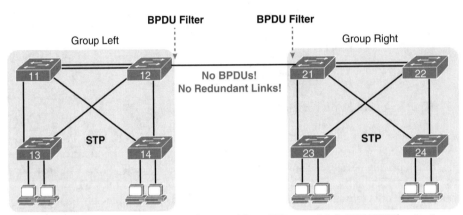

Figure 9-16   *A Scenario to Consider Disabling STP on a Link (BPDU Filtering)*

Root Guard

The **Root Guard** feature monitors incoming BPDUs on a port and reacts if the received BPDU would change the root switch in the VLAN. To understand why that might be useful, consider the topology with six switches in Figure 9-17. The notation by each switch defines how good the priority is on each switch. If you configure the switches with different priorities, you know and control which switches will become the root switch, with switches SW5 and SW6 being the least likely.

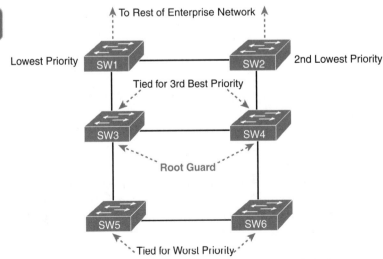

Figure 9-17   *Larger LAN Showing Most and Least Likely Root Switches*

Now imagine that your organization planned the design in the figure, but you directly control switches SW1 through SW4 while another organization controls switches SW5 and SW6. Both groups agree that SW1 should be the root switch, with SW2 taking over if SW2 fails; however, that agreement does not prevent a configuration mistake on switch SW5 or SW6.

For example, someone in the other group could configure switch SW5 with a priority lower than SW1's priority, and SW5 would become the root switch, creating a suboptimal STP topology. Switch SW5 would send a superior BPDU into the network if such an unplanned configuration occurred. With this topology, SW3 would receive the superior BPDU. Similarly, SW4 might receive a superior BPDU from SW6 if someone lowered switch SW6's priority.

Root Guard, enabled per port, enables the port to operate normally with STP except in this one special case: when it receives a **superior BPDU** in the port. So, you enable Root Guard on ports connected to other switches, usually trunks, and STP works normally; however, Root Guard on a port also prevents the election of a different root switch that is reachable through that port. Root Guard achieves that by listening for incoming Hellos on the port, and if it is a superior Hello, the switch disables the port by using a special STP port state (the **broken state**). Root Guard recovers the port automatically when the superior Hellos no longer occur.

The choice to use Root Guard begins with a close analysis of the topology. You must agree which switches should never become root and which ports should never receive superior BPDUs.

Loop Guard

The final optional tool mentioned here, Loop Guard, protects against a specific case in an STP topology. This feature helps protect the worst priority switch (highest BID) in a typical STP design, such as switch SW3 in Figure 9-18. The mechanisms apply to regular operation in a typical STP design, forcing some review of topics from earlier in the chapter.

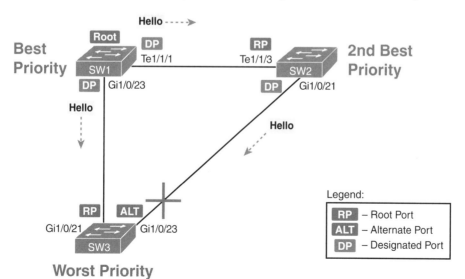

Figure 9-18 *Typical STP Design*

A typical STP design uses one switch as the known root under normal circumstances. To achieve that, you assign that switch the lowest priority. Another switch has the role of being the best backup, so you assign it the second-best priority value. Switches SW1 and SW2 play those roles in Figure 9-18. All the other switches have a lower priority than SW1 and SW2, such as switch SW3.

Next, consider an observation about this design, about the worst switch (SW3). SW3's ports on its switch-to-switch links seldom become designated ports. Why? STP determines the DP based on lowest root cost of the switches on the link, and breaks ties based on the better (lower) BID. SW3 loses the DP election tiebreaker in this scenario.

However, SW3's ports have other roles, just not the DP role, as follows:

- One link will be its root port (G1/0/21 in Figure 9-18) and settle into a forwarding state.

- The other will be an alternate port (G1/0/23 in Figure 9-18) and settle into a discarding state.

The second meaningful observation is that the worst switch (SW3) receives repeated Hellos in both switch-to-switch links. The figure shows the Hellos. The rule is that switches forward Hellos out designated ports every Hello time (the default is 2 seconds).

The third fact that helps you understand Loop Guard involves unidirectional links. Figure 9-19 shows the idea. The interfaces on the ends of a fiber link will be up and in a connected state, but one of the two fibers has a problem. The problem could prevent frames from arriving at the other end of the fiber. Figure 9-19 shows such a case, with only the right-to-left direction working.

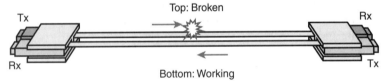

Figure 9-19   *Unidirectional Fiber Link*

To summarize, Loop Guard relies on these underlying facts:

- A switch with the worst (highest) priority in a design has switch-to-switch ports in the root port (RP) and alternate port (ALT) roles but seldom the designated port (DP) role.

- Those same ports normally receive Hellos every Hello time because each link's neighboring switch is the DP.

- A **unidirectional link** can occur, in which the interface state remains up (connected) on both ends but frames cannot flow in one direction.

The **Loop Guard** feature takes advantage of the above observations to protect against a class of failures that, without Loop Guard, results in one of switch SW3's switch-switch links becoming a DP. Figure 9-20 shows an adjustment to Figure 9-18 for one scenario, with the SW2-SW3 link becoming unidirectional:

1. The SW2-SW3 link's fiber for transmitting from SW2 to SW3 fails.

2. Because SW2's G1/0/21 and SW3's G1/0/23 ports remain in a connected state, there is no interface failure to influence STP.

3. SW3 ceases to receive incoming Hello messages on its G1/0/23 port.

4. After the appropriate timeouts, SW3 believes it is the only switch on the link connected to its G1/0/23 interface, so it changes the port to a DP and moves toward a forwarding state.

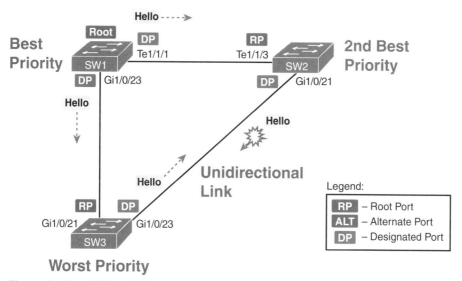

Figure 9-20 *SW3's ALT Port Becomes DP, Forwards; All Links Forward, Create Loop*

Take a moment and look at the ends of the switch-to-switch links. All ports are either an RP or DP, both of which use a forwarding state. As a result, a forwarding loop exists. Note that with the unidirectional link between switches SW2 and SW3, broken in the direction from SW2 to SW3, the forwarding loop exists only in the opposite (counter-clockwise) direction.

Finally, you can now appreciate the Loop Guard feature. You enable it on an interface and it takes the following actions:

If the port is a root or alternate port, prevent it from becoming a designated port by moving it to the special broken STP state.

As with Root Guard, you must work through the underlying concepts to decide the ports on which to enable Loop Guard. Generally, you need it only on fiber-optic links connected to other switches. You should also only choose ports on switches with a poor (high) STP priority, so they normally have switch-to-switch ports in the RP or ALT roles but not the DP role.

9

Chapter Review

One key to doing well on the exams is to perform repetitive spaced review sessions. Review this chapter's material using either the tools in the book or interactive tools for the same material found on the book's companion website. Refer to the "Your Study Plan" element for more details. Table 9-11 outlines the key review elements and where you can find them. To better track your study progress, record when you completed these activities in the second column.

Table 9-11   Chapter Review Tracking

Review Element	Review Date(s)	Resource Used
Review key topics		Book, website
Review key terms		Book, website
Answer DIKTA questions		Book, PTP
Review memory tables		Website

Review All the Key Topics

Table 9-12   Key Topics for Chapter 9

Key Topic Element	Description	Page Number
Table 9-2	Lists the three main problems that occur when not using STP in a LAN with redundant links	227
Figure 9-2	How STP blocks to break a loop	227
Table 9-3	Lists the reasons why a switch chooses to place an interface into forwarding or blocking state	229
Table 9-4	Lists the most important fields in Hello BPDU messages	230
List	Logic for the root switch election	231
Figure 9-6	Shows how switches calculate their root cost	233
Table 9-6	Lists the original and current default STP port costs for various interface speeds	236
Step list	A summary description of steady-state STP operations	236
Table 9-7	STP timers	237
List	Definitions of what occurs in the listening and learning states	239
Table 9-8	Summary of STP and RSTP states	239
List	Key similarities between 802.1D STP and 802.1w RSTP	240
List	RSTP mechanisms for faster convergence compared to STP	241
Table 9-9	List of 802.1w port roles	241
Table 9-10	Comparisons of port states with 802.1D and 802.1w	244
Figure 9-14	Basic logic for BPDU Guard	248
Figure 9-15	An example forwarding loop risk with PortFast	249
List	Conditional BPDU Filter logic applied to PortFast ports	249
Figure 9-17	Locations to apply Root Guard	250
Paragraph	Loop Guard rules	253

Key Terms You Should Know

alternate port (role), backup port (role), blocking state, BPDU Filter, BPDU Guard, bridge ID, bridge protocol data unit (BPDU), broken state, designated port, designated port (role), disabled port (role), disabled state, discarding state, EtherChannel, forward delay, forwarding state, Hello BPDU, learning state, listening state, Loop Guard, MaxAge, PortFast, Rapid STP (RSTP), root cost, Root Guard, root port (role), root switch, Spanning Tree Protocol (STP), superior BPDU, unidirectional link

9

CHAPTER 10

RSTP and EtherChannel Configuration

This chapter covers the following exam topics:

2.0 Network Access

    2.4 Configure and verify (Layer 2/Layer 3) EtherChannel (LACP)

    2.5 Interpret basic operations of Rapid PVST+ Spanning Tree Protocol

        2.5.a Root port, root bridge (primary/secondary), and other port names

        2.5.b Port states and roles

        2.5.c PortFast

        2.5.d Root guard, loop guard, BPDU filter, and BPDU guard

This chapter shows how to configure Rapid Spanning Tree Protocol (RSTP) and Layer 2 EtherChannels.

The first two sections take a little different approach than many other CLI-focused parts of the book, based on exam topic 2.5. That exam topic begins with the phrase "interpret basic operations," which emphasizes the concepts behind what happens in the CLI. The first major section examines STP concepts using some configuration, with much focus on interpreting **show** command output. The second major section, about exam topics 2.5.c and 2.5.d, takes the same approach.

The EtherChannel content, in the final major section of the chapter, follows a typical flow for most configuration/verification topics in a certification guide: it reviews concepts, shows configurations, followed by **show** commands that point out the configuration settings and operational state. The details include how to manually configure a channel, how to cause a switch to dynamically create a channel, and how EtherChannel load distribution works.

I encourage you to practice and experiment with STP from the CLI. If you're looking for lab exercises, check out the Config Labs at my blog site related to this chapter, as detailed in the introduction to this book. (Or, just go to certskills.com/config-labs for more info.)

Finally, like Chapter 9, this chapter is longer than I prefer. If you like to think of each chapter as one study session, you might need to think about splitting this chapter into two study sessions. Stop the first study session just as you reach the third major section, titled "Configuring Layer 2 EtherChannel." The second study session would consist of the "Configuring Layer 2 EtherChannel" section.

"Do I Know This Already?" Quiz

Take the quiz (either here or use the PTP software) if you want to use the score to help you decide how much time to spend on this chapter. The letter answers are listed at the bottom of the page following the quiz. Appendix C, found both at the end of the book as well as on the companion website, includes both the answers and explanations. You can also find both answers and explanations in the PTP testing software.

Table 10-1 "Do I Know This Already?" Foundation Topics Section-to-Question Mapping

Foundation Topics Section	Questions
Understanding RSTP Through Configuration	1–3
Identifying Optional STP Features	4–5
Configuring Layer 2 EtherChannel	6–8

1. Which type value on the **spanning-tree mode** *type* global command enables the use of RSTP?

   a. rapid-pvst

   b. pvst

   c. rstp

   d. rpvst

2. Examine the following output from the **show spanning-tree vlan 5** command, which describes a root switch in a LAN. Which answers accurately describe facts related to the root's bridge ID? (Choose two answers.)

   ```
   SW1# show spanning-tree vlan 5


   VLAN0005
       Spanning tree enabled protocol rstp
       Root ID Priority 32773
               Address     1833.9d7b.0e80
               Cost        15
               Port        25 (GigabitEthernet0/1)
               Hello Time 2 sec Max Age 20 sec Forward Delay 15 sec
   ```

   a. The system ID extension value, in decimal, is 5.

   b. The root's configured priority value is 32773.

   c. The root's configured priority value is 32768.

   d. The system ID extension value, in hexadecimal, is 1833.9d7b.0e80.

3. With Cisco's RPVST+, which of the following actions does a switch take to identify which VLAN is described by a BPDU? (Choose three answers.)

   a. Adds a VLAN tag when forwarding a BPDU on trunks

   b. Adds the VLAN ID in an extra TLV in the BPDU

   c. Lists the VLAN ID as the middle 12 bits of the System ID field of the BPDU

   d. Lists the VLAN ID in the System ID Extension field of the BPDU

4. A switch port in access mode connects to a single laptop. An attacker replaces the laptop with a LAN switch that uses STP. Which combination of features, enabled on the access port, results in the switch changing the port's interface state to err-disabled? (Choose two answers.)

   a. PortFast enabled but BPDU Guard not enabled

   b. PortFast and BPDU Guard enabled

   c. PortFast disabled but BPDU Guard enabled

   d. PortFast and BPDU Guard disabled

5. Root Guard has acted to disable port G1/0/1. An engineer uses the **show interfaces status** and **show spanning-tree vlan 1** commands to investigate the current status. Which answers list facts expected due to Root Guard's actions? (Choose two answers.)

   a. The STP port state per **show spanning-tree vlan 1** shows BKN (broken).

   b. The interface state per **show interfaces status** shows err-disabled.

   c. The STP port state per **show spanning-tree vlan 1** shows FWD (forwarding).

   d. The STP port state per **show spanning-tree vlan 1** shows BLK (blocking).

   e. The interface state per **show interfaces status** shows connected.

6. An engineer configures a switch to put interfaces G0/1 and G0/2 into the same Layer 2 EtherChannel. Which of the following terms is used in the configuration commands?

   a. EtherChannel

   b. PortChannel

   c. Ethernet-Channel

   d. Channel-group

7. Which combinations of keywords on the **channel-group** interface subcommand on two neighboring switches will cause the switches to use LACP and attempt to add the link to the EtherChannel? (Choose two answers.)

   a. **desirable** and **active**

   b. **passive** and **active**

   c. **active** and **auto**

   d. **active** and **active**

8. A Cisco Catalyst switch needs to send frames over a Layer 2 EtherChannel. Which answer best describes how the switch balances the traffic over the four active links in the channel?

   a. Breaks each frame into fragments of approximately one-fourth of the original frame, sending one fragment over each link

   b. Sends the entire frame over one link, alternating links in sequence for each successive frame

   c. Sends the entire frame over one link, choosing the link by applying some math to fields in each frame's headers

   d. Sends the entire frame over one link, using the link with the lowest percent utilization as the next link to use

Foundation Topics

Understanding RSTP Through Configuration

Cisco IOS switches today typically default to using RSTP rather than STP, with default settings so that RSTP works with no configuration. You can buy some Cisco switches and connect them with Ethernet cables in a redundant topology, and RSTP will ensure that frames do not loop. And even if some switches use RSTP and some use STP, the switches can interoperate and still build a working spanning tree—and you never even have to think about changing any settings!

Although RSTP works without any configuration, most medium-size to large-size campus LANs benefit from some RSTP configuration. For instance, Figure 10-1 shows a typical LAN design model, with two distribution layer switches (D1 and D2). The design may have dozens of access layer switches that connect to end users; the figure shows just three access switches (A1, A2, and A3). For a variety of reasons, most network engineers make the distribution layer switches be the root.

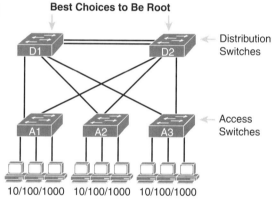

Figure 10-1   *Typical Configuration Choice: Making Distribution Switch Be Root*

> **NOTE**   Cisco uses the term *access switch* to refer to switches used to connect to endpoint devices. The term *distribution switch* refers to switches that do not connect to endpoints but rather connect to each access switch, providing a means to distribute frames throughout the LAN. The term *uplink* refers to the switch-to-switch links, usually trunks, between access and distribution switches. If you want to read more about LAN design concepts and terms, refer to the *CCNA 200-301 Official Cert Guide, Volume 2*, Second Edition, Chapter 17, "LAN Architecture."

As discussed in the introduction to this chapter, this first section of the chapter examines a variety of STP/RSTP configuration topics, but with a goal of revealing a few more details about how STP/RSTP operate. Following this opening section about STP/RSTP configuration, the next section examines how to configure Layer 2 EtherChannels and how that impacts STP/RSTP.

The Need for Multiple Spanning Trees

The IEEE first standardized STP as the IEEE 802.1D standard, first published back in 1990. To put some perspective on that date, Cisco did not have a LAN switch product line at the time, and virtual LANs did not exist yet. Instead of multiple VLANs in a physical Ethernet LAN, the physical Ethernet LAN existed as one single broadcast domain, with one instance of STP.

By the mid-1990s, VLANs had appeared on the scene, along with LAN switches. The emergence of VLANs posed a challenge for STP—the only type of STP available at the time—because STP defined a single common spanning tree (CST) topology for the entire LAN. The IEEE needed an option to create multiple spanning trees so that traffic could be balanced across the available links, as shown in Figure 10-2. With two different STP instances, SW3 could block on a different interface in each VLAN, as shown in the figure.

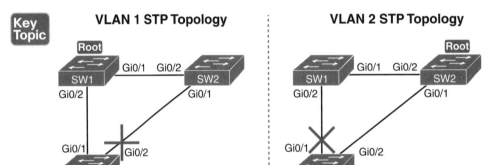

Figure 10-2 *Load Balancing with One Tree for VLAN 1 and Another for VLAN 2*

STP Modes and Standards

Because of the sequence of events over the history of the various STP family of protocols, vendors like Cisco needed to create their own proprietary features to create the per-VLAN spanning tree concept shown in Figure 10-2. That sequence resulted in the following:

- When STP was the only STP standard back in the 1990s with 802.1D, Cisco created the STP-based Per VLAN Spanning Tree Plus (**PVST+**) protocol, which creates one spanning tree instance per VLAN.

- When the IEEE introduced RSTP (in 802.1D amendment 802.1w, in 2001), they again defined it as a means to create a single spanning tree.

- When Cisco added support for RSTP to its switches, it created the **Rapid PVST+** (RPVST+) protocol. RPVST+ provided more features than standardized RSTP, including one tree per VLAN.

- To create multiple spanning trees, the IEEE did not adopt Cisco's PVST+ or RPVST+. Instead, the IEEE created a different method: Multiple Spanning Tree Protocol (MSTP), originally defined in 802.1Q amendment 802.1s.

Answers to the "Do I Know This Already?" quiz:

1 A **2** A, C **3** A, B, D **4** B, C **5** A, E **6** D **7** B, D **8** C

Figure 10-3 shows the features as a timeline for perspective.

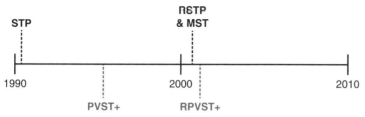

Figure 10-3   *Timeline of Per-VLAN and Multiple STP Features*

Today, Cisco Catalyst switches give us three options to configure on the **spanning-tree mode** command, which tells the switch which type of STP to use. Note that the switches do not support STP or RSTP with the single tree (CST). They can use either the Cisco-proprietary and STP-based PVST+, Cisco-proprietary and RSTP-based RPVST+, or the IEEE standard MSTP. Table 10-2 summarizes some of the facts about these standards and options, along with the keywords used on the **spanning-tree mode** global configuration command. Example 10-1, which follows, shows the command options in global configuration mode.

Table 10-2   STP Standards and Configuration Options

Name	Based on STP or RSTP?	# Trees	Original IEEE Standard	Config Parameter
STP	STP	1 (CST)	802.1D	N/A
PVST+	STP	1/VLAN	802.1D	**pvst**
RSTP	RSTP	1 (CST)	802.1w	N/A
Rapid PVST+	RSTP	1/VLAN	802.1w	**rapid-pvst**
MSTP	RSTP	1 or more*	802.1s	**mst**

* MSTP allows the definition of as many instances (multiple spanning tree instances, or MSTIs) as chosen by the network designer but does not require one per VLAN.

Example 10-1   *Cisco Switch Spanning Tree modes*

```
SW1(config)# spanning-tree mode ?
  mst         Multiple spanning tree mode
  pvst        Per-Vlan spanning tree mode
  rapid-pvst  Per-Vlan rapid spanning tree mode
SW1(config)#
```

The Bridge ID and System ID Extension

To support the idea of multiple spanning trees, whether one per VLAN or simply multiple as created with MSTP, the protocols must consider the VLANs and VLAN trunking. (That's one reason why RSTP and MSTP now exist as part of the 802.1Q standard, which defines VLANs and VLAN trunking.) To help make that work, the IEEE redefined the format of the original BID value to help make per-VLAN instances of STP/RSTP become a reality.

Originally, a switch's BID was formed by combining the switch's 2-byte priority and its 6-byte MAC address. The IEEE later revised the 2-byte priority field as shown in

Figure 10-4 as a 4-bit priority field and a 12-bit subfield called the **system ID extension** (which represents the VLAN ID).

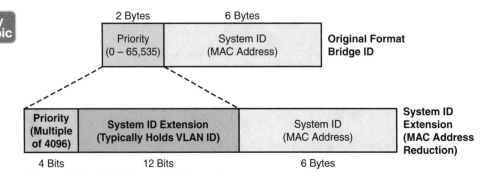

Figure 10-4 *STP System ID Extension*

Cisco switches enable you to configure only the priority part of the BID. The switch fills in its universal (burned-in) MAC address as the system ID. It also plugs in the VLAN ID of a VLAN in the 12-bit system ID extension field; you cannot change that behavior either.

However, configuring the priority field may be one of the strangest things to configure on a Cisco router or switch. Focusing on the top of Figure 10-4, the priority field was originally a 16-bit number, which represented a decimal number from 0 to 65,535. Because of that history, the configuration command (**spanning-tree vlan** *vlan-id* **priority** *x*) requires a decimal number between 0 and 65,535. However, because the modern use of this field reserves the final 12 bits for the VLAN ID, IOS restricts the command to multiples of 4096. Table 10-3 shows the reason: The allowed decimal values, when viewed as 16-bit binary values, have all zeros in the final 12 bits.

Table 10-3 STP/RSTP Configurable Priority Values

Decimal Value	16-bit Binary Equivalent	Decimal Value	16-bit Binary Equivalent
0	0000 0000 0000 0000	32768	1000 0000 0000 0000
4096	0001 0000 0000 0000	36864	1001 0000 0000 0000
8192	0010 0000 0000 0000	40960	1010 0000 0000 0000
12288	0011 0000 0000 0000	45056	1011 0000 0000 0000
16384	0100 0000 0000 0000	49152	1100 0000 0000 0000
20480	0101 0000 0000 0000	53248	1101 0000 0000 0000
24576	0110 0000 0000 0000	57344	1110 0000 0000 0000
28672	0111 0000 0000 0000	61440	1111 0000 0000 0000

Example 10-2 shows how to configure the priority setting for each VLAN. Note that switches default to a base priority of 32,768.

Example 10-2 *Help Shows Requirements for Using Increments of 4096 for Priority*

```
SW1(config)# spanning-tree vlan 1 priority ?
  <0-61440>  bridge priority in increments of 4096
SW1(config)#
```

Identifying Switch Priority and the Root Switch

Cisco Catalyst switches configure the priority value using a number that represents a 16-bit value; however, the system ID extension exists as the low-order 12 bits of that same number. This next topic works through connecting those ideas.

When the switch builds its BID to use for RSTP in a VLAN, it must combine the configured priority with the VLAN ID of that VLAN. Interestingly, the configured priority results in a 16-bit priority that always ends with 12 binary 0s. That fact makes the process of combining values to create the BID a little simpler for the switch and possibly a little simpler for network engineers once you understand it all.

First, consider the process shown in Figure 10-5. The top shows the configured priority value (decimal 32768), in 16-bit binary form, with a System ID Extension of 12 zeros. Moving down the figure, you see the binary version of a VLAN ID (decimal 9). At the last step, the switch replaces those last 12 bits of the System ID Extension with the value that matches the VLAN ID and uses that value as the first 16 bits of the BID.

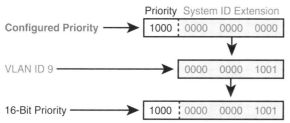

Figure 10-5 *Configured Priority (16-Bit) and System ID Extension (12-Bit) Added*

Switch Priority and Identifying the Root Switch

In most STP designs, you favor two switches to become the root switch. Often, the design calls for one switch to be the root switch, with a second switch ready to take over as root if the first switch fails. Figure 10-6 shows the idea, with switch SW1 as the primary and switch SW2 as the secondary. Additionally, note that the figure uses the interface type abbreviation of Te for Ten-GigabitEthernet. Also, the switch shows only links between switches to simplify the discussion.

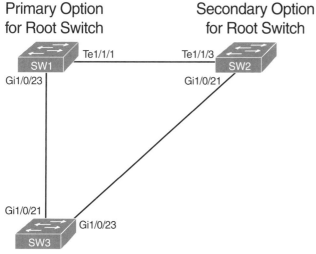

Figure 10-6 *Sample Network for Root Switch Election Configuration*

Cisco switches default to use a default base priority of 32,768. To achieve the STP goals in the figure, the engineer needs to lower switch SW2's priority to lower than the default value and the value on switch SW1 to even lower. For example, to do just that for the STP instance for VLAN 9, the engineer could do the following:

■ **On SW1:** Configure the **spanning-tree vlan 9 priority 24576** global command.

■ **On SW2:** Configure the **spanning-tree vlan 9 priority 28672** global command.

■ **On SW3:** Rely on the default base priority of 32,768.

The **show spanning-tree vlan 9** command, featured in Example 10-3, shows many facts about STP operation. Of particular importance, it lists about five lines of output about the root switch, starting with the line that begins with "Root ID." Following that, it lists several lines about the local switch: the switch on which this command was run. In this case, the output comes from nonroot switch SW3, so the section about the root switch refers to another switch (SW1).

Example 10-3 *Examining the 16-bit Priority from Nonroot Switch SW3*

```
SW3# show spanning-tree vlan 9
VLAN0009
  Spanning tree enabled protocol rstp
  Root ID    Priority    24585
             Address     4488.165a.f200
             Cost        4
             Port        21 (GigabitEthernet1/0/21)
             Hello Time   2 sec  Max Age 20 sec  Forward Delay 15 sec

  Bridge ID  Priority    32777  (priority 32768 sys-id-ext 9)
             Address     5cfc.6608.2880
             Hello Time   2 sec  Max Age 20 sec  Forward Delay 15 sec
             Aging Time  300 sec


Interface           Role Sts Cost      Prio.Nbr Type
------------------- ---- --- --------- -------- --------------------------------
Gi1/0/1             Desg FWD 4          128.1    P2p
Gi1/0/2             Desg FWD 4          128.2    P2p
Gi1/0/3             Desg FWD 4          128.3    P2p
Gi1/0/21            Root FWD 4          128.21   P2p
Gi1/0/23            Altn BLK 4          128.23   P2p
```

Look closely at those early message groups that begin with Root ID (about the root switch) and bridge ID (about the local switch). Both sections identify a bridge ID in two parts: the priority and MAC address. The output for the local switch breaks the priority down into the base priority and the VLAN ID. You can also confirm that the local switch is not the root switch based on two different facts:

■ The bridge ID values (priority plus MAC address) in the two message sections differ, with the one in the root ID section identifying the root switch.

- The "Root ID" section lists a line with a port number (G1/0/21). That line identifies the local switch's root port. Only nonroot switches have a root port, confirming the local switch is not the root switch.

The output also notes the priority of the root switch and the local switch. The highlighted line for the local switch shows a priority of 32,777, broken down in the same line as a base priority of the (default) value of 32,768 and the system ID extension, or VLAN, of 9 in this case. Earlier, the section about the root switch lists a priority of 24,585. Knowing the output is about VLAN 9, subtract 9 to get the base priority of 24,576.

Consider the output in Example 10-4 from root switch SW1 for comparison. Of note:

- The sections about the root switch and the local switch both list the same priority and MAC address, confirming the local switch is the root switch.

- The section about the root switch does not list a root port; root switches do not have root ports.

- The section about the root switch states, "This bridge is the root."

Example 10-4 *Examining the 16-bit Priority from Root Switch SW1*

```
SW1# show spanning-tree vlan 9
VLAN0009
  Spanning tree enabled protocol rstp
  Root ID    Priority    24585
             Address     4488.165a.f200
             This bridge is the root
             Hello Time   2 sec  Max Age 20 sec  Forward Delay 15 sec

  Bridge ID  Priority    24585   (priority 24576 sys-id-ext 9)
             Address     4488.165a.f200
             Hello Time   2 sec  Max Age 20 sec  Forward Delay 15 sec
             Aging Time   300 sec


Interface           Role Sts Cost      Prio.Nbr Type
------------------- ---- --- --------- -------- -------------------------------
Gi1/0/23            Desg FWD 4         128.23   P2p
Te1/1/1             Desg FWD 2         128.25   P2p
```

Finally, for one more fact of many in the detailed output from this command, note that the first highlighted line in Examples 10-3 and 10-4 both show the phrase "protocol rstp." That phrase occurs when using PVST+, per the **spanning-tree mode rapid-pvst** global command.

Switch Priority Using Root Primary and Secondary

Examples 10-3 and 10-4 relied on the direct configuration of the best priority in switch SW1 (24,576) and second best in switch SW2 (28,672). However, knowing that most STP designs identify the best and second-best switches to use as the root switch, Cisco provides two

10

related commands that mirror that idea. To configure two switches to be the two most likely switches to be the root switch, simply configure

> **spanning-tree vlan** *x* **root primary** (on the switch that should be primary)

> **spanning-tree vlan** *x* **root secondary** (on the switch that should be secondary)

Both of these commands use some different IOS logic compared to most configuration commands. Both commands cause IOS to choose a priority value when the command is added to the configuration. Then, IOS does not store the above commands; instead, it stores the priority setting in the **spanning-tree vlan** *x* **priority** *value* command. The command with **root primary** or **root secondary** does not appear in the configuration.

When configuring **root primary**, the switch looks at the priority of the current root switch and chooses either (a) 24,576 or (b) 4096 less than the current root's priority (if the current root's priority is 24,576 or less). The **root secondary** option always results in that switch using a priority of 28,672; the value will be less (better) than other switches that use the default of 32,768 and higher (worse) than any switch configured as **root primary**.

RSTP (One Tree) and RPVST+ (One Tree Per VLAN)

To complete some of the conceptual discussion about the bridge ID, focus on the standard RSTP and its Cisco-proprietary cousin RPVST+. Both use the RSTP mechanisms as discussed in Chapter 9, "Spanning Tree Protocol Concepts," but RPVST+ uses the mechanisms for every VLAN, while standard RSTP does not. So how do their methods differ?

- RSTP creates one tree—the common spanning tree (CST)—while RPVST+ creates one tree for each and every VLAN.

- RSTP sends one set of RSTP messages (BPDUs) in the network, while RPVST+ sends one set of messages per VLAN.

- RSTP sends messages to multicast address 0180.C200.0000 (per the IEEE standard), while RPVST+ uses multicast address 0100.0CCC.CCCD (an address chosen by Cisco).

- On VLAN trunks, RSTP sends all BPDUs in the native VLAN without a VLAN header/tag. RPVST+ sends BPDUs for each VLAN, respectively. For instance, BPDUs about VLAN 9 have an 802.1Q header that lists VLAN 9.

- RSTP sets the BID's VLAN field (extended system ID) value to 0000.0000.0000, meaning "no VLAN," while RPVST+ uses the VLAN ID.

In other words, standard RSTP behaves as if VLANs do not exist, while Cisco's RPVST+ integrates VLAN information into the entire process.

> **NOTE** Some documents refer to the feature of sending BPDUs over trunks with VLAN tags matching the same VLAN as *BPDU tunneling*.

Identifying Port Cost, Role, and State

Only the bridge ID values impact the root switch choice, and that choice has a direct impact on the STP topology. However, changes to STP interface costs change each nonroot switch's calculation of its root cost. The root cost then impacts the choice of root port and designated ports, which can impact the STP topology.

To explore those concepts, configure Figure 10-7. It repeats the topology of Figure 10-6, assuming that switch SW1 is the root switch and all port costs in VLAN 9 use default values. The figure focuses the discussion on switch SW3, which calculates possible root costs over two paths. The lower root cost, which uses SW3's port G1/0/21, becomes SW3's root port. SW3's G1/0/23 loses the designated port election due to SW3's root cost of 4 versus SW2's root cost of 2.

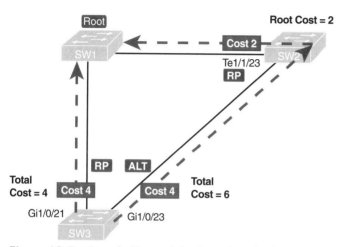

Figure 10-7 *Sample Network for Root Switch Election Configuration*

The **show spanning-tree vlan 9** command identifies those same facts. Example 10-5 shows an excerpt, with only the two interfaces that connect to other switches listed. The Role column lists the STP roles of Root and Altn (Alternate), while the abbreviated Sts heading refers to the State or Status. (Note that even though the switch uses RSTP, the output still uses the term BLK for blocking rather than the correct RSTP term of discarding.) Finally, the output lists the STP interface cost.

Example 10-5 *Switch SW3 Port Costs, Roles, and States with Default Costs*

```
SW1# show spanning-tree vlan 9 | begin Interface
Interface          Role Sts Cost      Prio.Nbr Type
------------------ ---- --- --------- -------- --------------------------------
Gi1/0/21           Root FWD 4         128.21   P2p
Gi1/0/23           Altn BLK 4         128.23   P2p
```

As for the root cost, look back to Example 10-3, which also shows output from switch SW3. Find the initial section about the root switch and the line that shows "Cost 4"—that line identifies switch SW3's root cost rather than an interface's cost.

The STP topology shown in Figure 10-7 works well and you would likely not want to change it. But just to show how to do so, consider Example 10-6. It changes SW3's post cost on its root port (G1/0/21) from 4 to 10. As a result, the path out SW3's G1/0/23 port toward switch SW2 has a lower root cost. The example begins with a **debug** command, so you can see interesting facts about the actions IOS takes with this straightforward configuration.

10

Example 10-6 *Changing SW3 Port Cost Setting Triggers New Root and Alternate Port Choices*

```
SW3# debug spanning-tree events
Spanning Tree event debugging is on

SW3# conf t
Enter configuration commands, one per line.  End with CNTL/Z.
SW3(config)# int g1/0/21
SW3(config-if)# spanning-tree vlan 9 cost 10
SW3(config-if)#
Oct 19 11:34:38.983: RSTP(9): updt roles, received superior bpdu on Gi1/0/23
Oct 19 11:34:38.983: RSTP(9): Gi1/0/23 is now root port
Oct 19 11:34:38.987: RSTP(9): Gi1/0/21 blocked by re-root
Oct 19 11:34:38.987: RSTP(9): Gi1/0/21 is now alternate
Oct 19 11:34:38.987: STP[9]: Generating TC trap for port GigabitEthernet1/0/23
SW3(config-if)# end
SW3# show spanning-tree vlan 9
VLAN0009
  Spanning tree enabled protocol rstp
  Root ID    Priority    24585
             Address     4488.165a.f200
             Cost        6
             Port        23 (GigabitEthernet1/0/23)
             Hello Time   2 sec  Max Age 20 sec  Forward Delay 15 sec

  Bridge ID  Priority    32777  (priority 32768 sys-id-ext 9)
             Address     5cfc.6608.2880
             Hello Time   2 sec  Max Age 20 sec  Forward Delay 15 sec
             Aging Time  300 sec


Interface          Role Sts Cost      Prio.Nbr Type
------------------ ---- --- --------- -------- --------------------------------
Gi1/0/21           Altn BLK 10        128.21   P2p
Gi1/0/23           Root FWD 4         128.23   P2p
```

Comparing the output from Example 10-6 to Example 10-5, you can see that switch SW3's ports swapped roles. G1/0/21 now blocks, with G1/0/23 now in a FWD or forwarding state. Also, in the highlighted lines toward the top of the **show spanning-tree vlan 9** output, you see the updated root cost of 6 and another reference to the root port, G1/0/23.

Author's Note Alternately, you can configure the STP port cost on an interface, for all VLANs, with the **spanning-tree cost** *value* interface subcommand. Doing so sets that value as the cost on that interface for any VLANs for which the interface does not also have a VLAN-specific version of the command (as shown in Example 10-6).

Identifying Optional STP Features

Chapter 9's section titled "Optional STP Features" introduced the concepts behind four STP features: PortFast, BPDU Guard, Root Guard, and Loop Guard. This next major section, with a similar title, focuses on identifying the presence of each feature and the results of using it. Along the way, you will also learn the basics of how to configure each.

PortFast and BPDU Guard

As discussed back in Chapter 9, PortFast provides both a useful feature but also a notable risk. Once the interface reaches a connected state, PortFast logic moves a port immediately to the STP designated port (DP) role and to a forwarding state. However, that behavior can cause a forwarding loop if the port becomes connected to a switch (with other connections to the rest of the network) instead of to an endpoint device. By combining PortFast with BPDU Guard, you prevent loops by disabling the port if any BPDUs arrive in the port. So, it makes sense to examine both features together.

PortFast and BPDU Guard on an Access Port with One Endpoint

First, consider the classic case to use both features: a switch port (G1/0/1) connected to a PC. Example 10-7 shows the configuration for both features on that port. Take time to read the long warning messages IOS generates in response to the **spanning-tree portfast** interface subcommand, basically suggesting the use of BPDU Guard.

Example 10-7   *Enabling PortFast and BPDU Guard on Access Port G1/0/1*

```
SW1# configure terminal
Enter configuration commands, one per line.  End with CNTL/Z.
SW1(config)#
SW1(config)# interface g1/0/1
SW1(config-if)# switchport mode access
SW1(config-if)# switchport access vlan 9
SW1(config-if)# spanning-tree portfast
%Warning: portfast should only be enabled on ports connected to a single
 host. Connecting hubs, concentrators, switches, bridges, etc... to this
 interface  when portfast is enabled, can cause temporary bridging loops.
 Use with CAUTION

%Portfast has been configured on GigabitEthernet1/0/1 but will only
have effect when the interface is in a non-trunking mode.
SW1(config-if)# spanning-tree bpduguard ?
  disable  Disable BPDU guard for this interface
  enable   Enable BPDU guard for this interface

SW1(config-if)# spanning-tree bpduguard enable
SW1(config-if)#
```

First, the **spanning-tree portfast** subcommand (with no additional keywords) tells IOS to enable PortFast logic only on an access port. If the port operates as a trunk, IOS does not apply PortFast logic. In fact, the highlighted portion of the long message that IOS generates when you configure the command reminds you of that fact.

10

As for BPDU Guard, the **spanning-tree bpduguard enable** interface subcommand applies BPDU Guard logic to the port regardless of whether operating as an access or trunk port and regardless of whether PortFast is used. Once enabled, BPDU Guard uses the following trigger, action, and recovery steps:

- **Trigger:** Any BPDU arrives in a port that has BPDU Guard enabled.

- **Actions:**

  - IOS places the interface into an error disabled (err-disabled) interface state.

  - STP removes the interface from the STP instance because the interface fails—that it, it is no longer up (connected).

- **Recovery:**

  - By default, the interface must be configured first with a **shutdown** command and then with a **no shutdown** command.

  - Alternately, and not discussed here, you can configure error disable recovery parameters to automatically recover the port after some time.

Example 10-8 shows a before-and-after example. It begins with switch SW1 port G1/0/1 as configured in Example 10-7, with both PortFast and BPDU Guard enabled. Example 10-8 begins with port G1/0/1 in an STP port role of Desg (designated) and a port state of FWD (forwarding), as consistent with a port in PortFast mode. It also reveals an interface state of connected. Also, in that first command's output, the highlighted port type of "P2p Edge" has great importance: the word "Edge" appears only if PortFast is both configured and enabled, so it confirms that the port uses PortFast.

Example 10-8   *Example of BPDU Guard Disabling a Port*

```
SW1# show spanning-tree interface g1/0/1

Vlan                    Role Sts Cost       Prio.Nbr Type
------------------- ---- --- --------- -------- -------------------------------
VLAN0009                Desg FWD 4          128.1    P2p Edge


SW1# show interfaces g1/0/1 status


Port          Name          Status        Vlan        Duplex  Speed Type
Gi1/0/1       Host A        connected     9           a-full a-1000
10/100/1000BaseTX
SW1#
SW1# ! The cable was removed from the PC and connected to a LAN switch.
SW1#
*Jan 30 17:08:19.024: %LINEPROTO-5-UPDOWN: Line protocol on Interface GigabitEther-
net1/0/1, changed state to down
*Jan 30 17:08:20.024: %LINK-3-UPDOWN: Interface GigabitEthernet1/0/1, changed state
to down
*Jan 30 17:08:30.364: %SPANTREE-2-BLOCK_BPDUGUARD: Received BPDU on port Gi1/0/1
with BPDU Guard enabled. Disabling port.
```

```
*Jan 30 17:08:30.364: %PM-4-ERR_DISABLE: bpduguard error detected on Gi1/0/1, put-
ting Gi1/0/1 in err-disable state
SW1#
SW1# show spanning-tree interface g1/0/1
no spanning tree info available for GigabitEthernet1/0/1

SW1# show interfaces g1/0/1 status

Port          Name           Status        Vlan     Duplex  Speed Type
Gi1/0/1       Host A         err-disabled 9          auto    auto
10/100/1000BaseTX
```

In the middle of the example we replaced the attached PC with a switch. The log messages reveal SW1's port G1/0/1 failing and recovering. As soon as the port came up again, BPDU Guard noticed the incoming BPDUs from the neighboring switch—and disabled the port, as seen in the highlighted log messages.

The bottom of the example repeats the same two **show** commands as the top of the example, revealing the actions taken. The interface state of err-disabled (error disabled) confirms BPDU Guard disabled the interface due to errors. The response from the **show spanning tree interface g1/0/1** command no longer lists information about this port, implying that the interface is no longer part of that spanning tree.

PortFast on VLAN Trunks and Voice Pseudo-Trunks

Cisco IOS also supports PortFast on trunk ports. You should not use PortFast on trunk ports connected to other switches, but you can use it on trunk ports connected to endpoints, as seen in the center of Figure 10-8. You can also use it on the pseudo-trunk created for voice ports connected to IP phones, as seen in port G1/0/3 in the figure. (For a review of voice VLAN configuration, refer to Chapter 8's section titled "Data and Voice VLAN Configuration and Verification.")

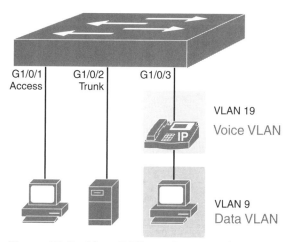

Figure 10-8   *Three Different Scenarios for Portfast and BPDU Guard*

The PortFast configuration for the voice port looks identical to the access ports. The only small difference happens with IOS automatically adding the **spanning-tree portfast** interface subcommand when you first configure the voice VLAN using the **switchport voice vlan** *vlan-id* interface subcommand.

Note that the **spanning-tree portfast** interface subcommand requires IOS to decide whether to apply PortFast logic or not, based on whether the command does or does not include the **trunk** keyword. The logic is:

> **spanning-tree portfast:** Use PortFast if the port operates as an access port.

> **spanning-tree portfast trunk:** Use PortFast if the port operates as a trunk.

Example 10-9 shows the configuration for switch SW1 port G1/0/2, attached via a trunk to a server. Note the different warning message in Example 10-9 versus Example 10-7's sample configuration.

Example 10-9 *Configuring Portfast and BPDU Guard on a Trunk*

```
SW1# configure terminal
Enter configuration commands, one per line.  End with CNTL/Z.
SW1(config)# interface g1/0/2
SW1(config-if)# switchport mode trunk
SW1(config-if)# spanning-tree portfast trunk
%Warning: portfast should only be enabled on ports connected to a single
 host. Connecting hubs, concentrators, switches, bridges, etc... to this
 interface  when portfast is enabled, can cause temporary bridging loops.
 Use with CAUTION
SW1(config-if)# spanning-tree bpduguard enable
SW1(config-if)#
```

You must be ready to discover whether IOS decided to apply PortFast logic to a port. To do so, use the **show spanning-tree** command (without the **interface** keyword) as seen in Example 10-10. The lower part of the command output lists one line per interface for all interfaces active in that spanning tree, including both access and trunk links. The value under the Type heading in the **show spanning-tree** command output reveals whether PortFast is being used:

- **P2p Edge:** Port operates with PortFast logic

- **P2p (without "Edge"):** Port does not use PortFast logic

Example 10-10 *Confirming Portfast with Port Type Edge*

```
SW1# show spanning-tree vlan 9 | begin Interface
Interface           Role Sts Cost      Prio.Nbr Type
------------------- ---- --- --------- -------- ---------------------------
Gi1/0/1             Desg FWD 4         128.1    P2p Edge
Gi1/0/2             Desg FWD 4         128.2    P2p Edge
Gi1/0/3             Desg FWD 4         128.3    P2p Edge
Gi1/0/23            Desg FWD 4         128.23   P2p
Te1/1/1             Desg FWD 2         128.25   P2p
```

Global Configuration of PortFast and BPDU Guard

The configuration examples so far use interface subcommands that override any global settings. IOS defaults to global settings whose values disable both features per port; however, you can enable each feature globally. For interfaces with no related subcommands, IOS enables the feature on the interface. Then, you should identify the interfaces for which the feature should be disabled and use another interface subcommand to disable the feature per interface, as needed.

For example, consider an access layer switch with 48 access ports connected to endpoints, plus two trunk ports connected to other switches. You probably want to enable both PortFast and BPDU Guard on all 48 access ports. Rather than requiring the interface subcommands on all 48 of those ports, enable both the features globally, and then disable them on the uplink ports.

First, consider PortFast. Configuring the **spanning-tree portfast default** global command tells IOS to apply PortFast to some ports, based on the following conditions:

- Enable PortFast on ports operating as access ports only.

- Ignore ports configured to disable PortFast with the **spanning-tree portfast disable** interface subcommand.

To see that logic in action, work through the examples in Figure 10-9. The switch uses the global command **spanning-tree portfast default**. Port G1/0/11 has no **spanning-tree portfast** subcommands and is configured to be an access port, so IOS applies PortFast to that port. However, port G1/0/12 has a **spanning-tree portfast disable** subcommand, so IOS does not apply PortFast. Port G1/0/13 fails to meet the required conditions because it uses trunking.

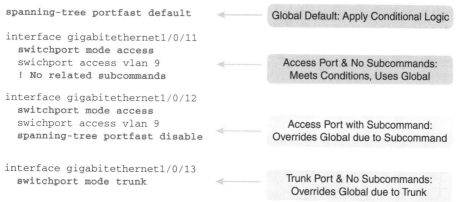

Figure 10-9 *Conditional PortFast Global Configuration Logic*

IOS also supports a similar configuration process for BPDU Guard, but with this configuration, BPDU Guard is tied to PortFast. You configure the **spanning-tree portfast bpduguard default** global command. Doing so asks IOS to enable BPDU Guard under these conditions:

- Enable BPDU Guard on ports that currently use PortFast.

- Ignore ports configured to disable BPDU Guard with the **spanning-tree bpduguard disable** interface subcommand.

For the exam, interpreting **show** command output might be more important than the intricacies of the configuration. For example, exam topic 2.5, the only one that mentions STP features, uses the verb *interpret* rather than *configure* or *verify*. So, be ready to interpret **show** command output and even predict the related configuration.

As an example of determining the configuration from the **show** commands, consider interfaces G1/0/7 and G1/0/8 on switch SW1. The configuration (not shown) uses this convention:

- **G1/0/7:** Uses interface subcommands **spanning-tree portfast** and **spanning-tree bpduguard enable**, not relying on the global configuration commands.

- **G1/0/8:** Uses no relevant interface subcommands, instead relying on the global configuration commands **spanning-tree portfast default** and **spanning-tree portfast bpduguard default**.

Example 10-11 shows truncated output from the **show spanning-tree interface** command for both interfaces. Compare the highlighted lines about PortFast and BPDU Guard to see the different information. On port G1/0/8, the phrase "by default" confirms that G1/0/8 uses the default setting per the global command. The absence of "by default" in the output for port G1/0/7 means those settings come from interface subcommands.

Example 10-11   *Interpreting the Source of PortFast and BPDU Guard Configuration*

```
SW1# show spanning-tree interface g1/0/7 detail | begin portfast
  The port is in the portfast mode
  Link type is point-to-point by default
  Bpdu guard is enabled
  BPDU: sent 387, received 0

SW1# show spanning-tree interface g1/0/8 detail | begin portfast
  The port is in the portfast mode by default
  Link type is point-to-point by default
  Bpdu guard is enabled by default
  BPDU: sent 774, received 0
```

BPDU Filter

In Chapter 9's section about this same topic, also titled "BPDU Filter," you learned about the two different logic branches of this feature. To review:

1.   Using a global configuration command, enable BPDU Filter, after which IOS applies BPDU Filter on PortFast ports only. While applied, it monitors for incoming BPDUs. When incoming BPDUs occur, BPDU Filter disables PortFast logic, so that the port then uses normal STP logic on the port.

2.   Using an interface subcommand, enable BPDU filter on the port. BPDU Filter discards all outgoing and incoming BPDUs on the port, effectively disabling STP on the port.

This section examines both logic branches in order.

Conditional BPDU Filtering with Global Configuration

To enable the conditional logic of BPDU Filter, you must toggle from the default global set-ting of **no spanning-tree portfast bpdufilter enable** to the same command without the **no** option: the **spanning-tree portfast bpdufilter enable** global command.

Similar to the effect of the **spanning-tree portfast bpduguard enable** global command, the **spanning-tree portfast bpdufilter enable** global command asks IOS to enable BPDU Filter under these conditions:

■ Enable BPDU Filter on ports that currently use PortFast.

■ Ignore ports configured to disable BPDU Filter with the **spanning-tree bpdufilter disable** interface subcommand.

Example 10-12 shows a straightforward scenario on switch SW1 port G1/0/23. It shows a classic access port, in VLAN 9, with PortFast enabled with an interface subcommand—along with conditional BPDU Filter enabled globally.

Example 10-12   *BPDU Filter as Global Default, Applied to Port G1/0/23*

```
spanning-tree portfast bpdufilter enable
!
interface GigabitEthernet1/0/23
  switchport mode access
  switchport access vlan 9
  spanning-tree portfast
  ! No BPDU Filter subcommands present
```

You should be ready to think about the configuration and understand the rules IOS applies—and to also see the evidence of the choices in IOS command output. First, to review how IOS interprets and applies the configuration:

■ The combination of port G1/0/23 as an access port (from the **switchport mode access** subcommand), with the command to enable PortFast on access ports (the **spanning-tree portfast** subcommand without the **trunk** keyword), enables PortFast.

■ The one global command tells IOS to find current PortFast ports (no matter whether access or trunk port) and enable BPDU Filter conditional logic.

Example 10-13 shows evidence of these listed results, while an endpoint connects to the port rather than a rogue switch. Look for the following:

1. The first command, **show spanning-tree**, lists interfaces in the tree for that VLAN. It lists the port type for G1/0/23 as P2p Edge—the word Edge confirms that the port currently uses Portfast.

2. The final command, in the final line, lists a counter of 11 sent BPDUs and 0 received. That confirms the switch sent 11 Hellos before BPDU Filter stopped sending them after 20 seconds. If nothing changes, the received BPDU counter remains at 0 because the attached endpoint device does not send BPDUs to the switch.

10

3. The phrase at the end of the example "Bpdu filter is enabled by default," at the end of the **show spanning-tree interface** command, reveals that the BPDU Filter configuration uses a global command. This command's output includes the phrase "by default" when the global configuration setting is the reason the feature is enabled.

4. Conversely, that same **show spanning-tree interface** command output reveals that the PortFast configuration uses an interface subcommand. The phrase "by default" does not occur at the end of the line about PortFast, implying the configuration comes from an interface subcommand.

Example 10-13 *Key Status Values When an Endpoint Connects to Port G1/0/23*

```
SW1# show spanning-tree vlan 9 | begin Interface
Interface         Role Sts Cost      Prio.Nbr Type
----------------- ---- --- --------- -------- --------------------------------
Gi1/0/1           Desg FWD 4         128.1    P2p Edge
Gi1/0/2           Desg FWD 4         128.2    P2p Edge
Gi1/0/3           Desg FWD 4         128.3    P2p Edge
Gi1/0/23          Desg FWD 4         128.23   P2p Edge
Te1/1/1           Desg FWD 2         128.25   P2p


SW1# show spanning-tree interface g1/0/23

Vlan              Role Sts Cost      Prio.Nbr Type
----------------- ---- --- --------- -------- --------------------------------
VLAN0009          Desg FWD 4         128.23   P2p Edge


SW1# show spanning-tree interface g1/0/23 detail | begin portfast
   The port is in the portfast mode
   Link type is point-to-point by default
   Bpdu filter is enabled by default
   BPDU: sent 11, received 0
```

As configured using the global command, IOS applies conditional BPDU Filter logic. To see that in action, Example 10-14 begins with the replacement of the attached PC with a rogue switch. The example does not show the related log messages, but know that the interface fails and recovers. The example repeats the same **show** commands as in the previous example, but with these differences:

1. The first command, **show spanning-tree**, lists the port type for G1/0/23 as P2p but without the word Edge. That output change is what confirms IOS no longer applies PortFast logic to this port.

2. The final command, in the final line, lists BPDU counters. In this case, the neighboring switch becomes root and continues to send BPDUs into port G1/0/23. The received BPDU counter will continue to increment over time.

3. The **show spanning-tree interface** command no longer includes the line that mentions the BPDU Filter feature.

Example 10-14   *SW1 Port G1/0/23 Connects to a Rogue Switch*

```
! Someone disconnects the endpoint off SW1's G1/0/23 and attaches a switch:
! G1/0/23 fails and recovers…

SW1# show spanning-tree vlan 9 | begin Interface
Interface           Role Sts Cost      Prio.Nbr Type
------------------- ---- --- --------- -------- --------------------------------
Gi1/0/23            Root FWD 4         128.23   P2p

SW1# show spanning-tree interface g1/0/23 detail | begin portfast
   The port is in the portfast mode
   Link type is point-to-point by default
   BPDU: sent 6, received 138
! Line "bpdu filter is enabled by default" does not appear above.
```

Disabling STP with BPDU Filter Interface Configuration

The other type of BPDU Filter logic always filters all outgoing and incoming BPDUs on a port, in effect disabling STP on the interface. To configure it, simply configure the **spanning-tree bpdufilter enable** interface subcommand.

> **NOTE**   That previous statement ought to scare you—one simple command can disable STP on one link. With redundant links in the LAN, that one command, on one port, can create a forwarding loop that makes the entire LAN unusable. That is not an exaggeration. Be very careful before using this command!

Example 10-15 shows a typical configuration. This feature makes sense on links between switches, so it would likely be a trunk port.

Example 10-15   *Disabling STP on a Port Between STP Domains*

```
interface TenGigabitEthernet 1/1/1
  switchport mode trunk
  spanning-tree bpdufilter enable
```

Example 10-16 shows just a few lines of output that are the keys to confirming the feature works. The end of the **show spanning-tree interface** command has a line that confirms the BPDU Filter feature is enabled; however, that line does not end with "by default" as seen near the end of Example 10-14. That tiny difference in the text signals a huge difference in logic! The absence of "by default" means IOS enables BPDU Filter in this case due to an interface subcommand, which means IOS applies the absolute filtering logic of BPDU Filter—disabling STP on the interface.

Example 10-16   *Typical Evidence of BPDU Filter to Disable STP*

```
SW1# show spanning-tree vlan 9 interface te1/1/1 detail | begin Bpdu
   Bpdu filter is enabled
   BPDU: sent 0, received 0
```

10

To support the claim that IOS applies absolute filtering of all outgoing and incoming BPDUs on the port, note that the counters in the final output line show 0s. Over time, it will continue to show 0s, because BPDU Filter discards all BPDUs on the port.

Root Guard

The most challenging part of working with Root Guard involves analyzing the STP design to decide which ports might benefit from using it. Chapter 9's section with this same title, "Root Guard," discusses the logic, but to summarize, you consider only ports connected to other switches. Then you look for special cases of switch ports that should never receive a superior Hello from a new root switch based on the intended STP design. Root Guard then monitors for incoming superior Hellos, disabling the port when that occurs. Root Guard may not apply to any ports for some networks, but the choice of ports begins by thinking about the STP design, as discussed in Chapter 9.

If ports need to use Root Guard, the implementation and verification take a few short steps. The configuration uses a single option: the **spanning-tree guard root** interface subcommand. There is no global command to change the default, with the default being not to use Root Guard on an interface.

As for the actions taken by Root Guard, Chapter 9 described the big concepts, but the following list provides more detail that you will see in the upcoming CLI examples.

- **Trigger:** Root Guard acts after receiving a superior BPDU in the port.
- **Actions:** Once triggered, Root Guard takes these actions:
  - The actions occur per VLAN, based on the VLAN of the superior Hello.
  - STP places the port in a broken (BRK) state for that VLAN, which discards all traffic (like the discarding and blocking states).
  - STP describes the port as being in a root inconsistent state in the port type information in show commands.
- **Recovery:** When the incoming superior BPDUs cease for a time, STP reverts to its prior STP state without any operator intervention.

Examples 10-17 and 10-18 combine to show an example of Root Guard in action. First, Example 10-17 shows the simple configuration, with the log message that confirms IOS enabled the feature.

Example 10-17 *Configuring Root Guard on Switch SW3 Port G1/0/11*

```
SW3# configure terminal
Enter configuration commands, one per line.  End with CNTL/Z.
SW3(config)# interface g1/0/11
SW3(config-if)# spanning-tree guard root
SW3(config-if)#
Oct 21 11:02:31.145: %SPANTREE-2-ROOTGUARD_CONFIG_CHANGE: Root guard enabled on port
GigabitEthernet1/0/11.
SW3#
```

To see Root Guard in action, look for log messages, the BRK (broken) port state, and the root inconsistent state. Example 10-18 does just that, as follows:

1. The first two commands confirm port G1/0/11's interface state (connected), STP role (Desg, or designated), STP forwarding state (FWD), and port type (P2P).

2. A log message reveals that Root Guard blocked the port. (Just before that, but not shown, I lowered the priority of the neighboring switch.)

3. The last two commands at the bottom of the example reveal:

    a. No change in in port G1/0/11's interface state (connected) or STP role (designated).

    b. A change to the STP forwarding state BKN, meaning broken, and port type P2p ROOT Inc, meaning Root Inconsistent.

Example 10-18 *Identifying Root Guard Root Inconsistent State*

```
SW3# show interfaces g1/0/11 status


Port        Name                Status      Vlan      Duplex  Speed Type
Gi1/0/11                        connected   trunk     a-full a-1000 10/100/1000BaseTX


SW3# show spanning-tree vlan 9 int g1/0/11


Vlan                  Role Sts Cost      Prio.Nbr Type
------------------    ---- --- --------- -------- --------------------------------
VLAN0009              Desg FWD 4         128.11   P2p


SW3#! Neighboring switch priority was lowered so it sends a superior BPDU.


Oct 21 11:03:14.472: %SPANTREE-2-ROOTGUARD_BLOCK: Root guard blocking port
GigabitEthernet1/0/11 on VLAN0009.


SW3# show interfaces g1/0/11 status
Port        Name                Status      Vlan      Duplex  Speed Type
Gi1/0/11                        connected   trunk     a-full a-1000 10/100/1000BaseTX


SW3# show spanning-tree vlan 9 int g1/0/11


Vlan                  Role Sts Cost      Prio.Nbr Type
------------------    ---- --- --------- -------- --------------------------------
VLAN0009              Desg BKN*4         128.11   P2p *ROOT_Inc
```

Loop Guard

Chapter 9's section with this same title, "Loop Guard," discusses the compound factors that lead to the specific scenario where you can apply Loop Guard. Understanding those conditions and choosing ports that can effectively use Loop Guard takes some effort. However, the configuration takes only a little effort once chosen, as seen in the following list. You can either enable it directly on the interface or change the global default to enable it on all switch interfaces—but then disable it on selected interfaces as needed. Use these steps.

Step 1.   Use the **spanning-tree guard loop** interface subcommand to enable Loop
            Guard on the interfaces selected to use the feature.

Step 2.   To use the global default:

    a.   Use the **spanning-tree loopguard default** global command to change the
            Loop Guard default from disabled to enabled on all point-to-point switch
            interfaces.

    b.   Use the **no spanning-tree guard loop** interface subcommand to disable
            Loop Guard on the interfaces selected not to use the feature.

Example 10-19 shows the simple configuration on a single port. The **show spanning-tree
interface** command then confirms that Loop Guard is enabled, with the absence of the "by
default" phrase implying it was configured using an interface subcommand.

Example 10-19 *Configuring Loop Guard on a Port*

```
SW3# configure terminal
Enter configuration commands, one per line.  End with CNTL/Z.
SW3(config)# interface g1/0/21
SW3(config-if)# spanning-tree guard loop
SW3(config-if)#

SW3# show spanning-tree vlan 9 int g1/0/21 detail
 Port 21 (GigabitEthernet1/0/21) of VLAN0009 is root forwarding
   Port path cost 4, Port priority 128, Port Identifier 128.21.
   Designated root has priority 24585, address 4488.165a.f200
   Designated bridge has priority 24585, address 4488.165a.f200
   Designated port id is 128.23, designated path cost 0
   Timers: message age 16, forward delay 0, hold 0
   Number of transitions to forwarding state: 7
   Link type is point-to-point by default
   Loop guard is enabled on the port
   BPDU: sent 139, received 165425

! Link becomes unidirectional; switch SW3 G1/0/21 ceases to receive BPDUs
*Feb 23 17:11:19.087: %SPANTREE-2-LOOPGUARD_BLOCK: Loop guard blocking port
GigabitEthernet1/0/23 on VLAN0009.
SW3# show spanning-tree vlan 9 int g1/0/21 detail | include 1/0/21
 Port 21 (GigabitEthernet1/0/21) of VLAN0009 is broken  (Loop Inconsistent)
```

The example ends by showing what happens when a unidirectional link occurs on this port.
The end of the example shows a comment to show when the failure occurs and the log message noting the Loop Guard acted for VLAN 9. The final output shows how Loop Guard
moved the port to a broken state (Loop Inconsistent) in that VLAN, similar to the Root
Inconsistent state used by Root Guard. Loop Guard also recovers automatically when Hellos
begin to arrive in the port again.

Configuring Layer 2 EtherChannel

As introduced in Chapter 9, "Spanning Tree Protocol Concepts," two neighboring switches can treat multiple parallel links between each other as a single logical link called an *EtherChannel*. Without EtherChannel, a switch treats each physical port as an independent port, applying MAC learning, forwarding, and STP logic per physical port. With EtherChannel, the switch applies all those same processes to a group of physical ports as one entity: the EtherChannel. Without EtherChannel, with parallel links between two switches, STP/RSTP would block all links except one, but with EtherChannel, the switch can use all the links, load balancing the traffic over the links.

> **NOTE**   All references to EtherChannel in this chapter refer to Layer 2 EtherChannels, not to Layer 3 EtherChannels (as discussed in Chapter 18, "IP Routing in the LAN"). CCNA 200-301 exam topics include both Layer 2 and Layer 3 EtherChannels.

EtherChannel might be one of the most challenging switch features to make work. First, the configuration has several options, so you have to remember the details of which options work together. Second, the switches also require a variety of other interface settings to match among all the links in the channel, so you have to know those settings as well.

This section shows how to configure a Layer 2 EtherChannel, first through manual (static) configuration and then by allowing dynamic protocols to create the channel. Cisco recommends using the dynamic method, but the static method can be a little easier to learn initially, so we begin with the static or manual option. This section closes with some information about some common configuration issues that occur with Layer 2 EtherChannels.

Configuring a Manual Layer 2 EtherChannel

To configure a Layer 2 EtherChannel so that all the ports always attempt to be part of the channel, simply add the correct **channel-group** configuration command to each physical interface, on each switch, all with the **on** keyword, and all with the same number. The **on** keyword tells the switches to place a physical interface into an EtherChannel, and the number identifies the PortChannel interface number that the interface should be a part of.

Before getting into the configuration and verification, however, you need to start using three terms as synonyms: **EtherChannel**, **PortChannel**, and **Channel-group**. Oddly, IOS uses the **channel-group** configuration command, but then to display its status, IOS uses the **show etherchannel** command. Then the output of this **show** command refers to neither an "EtherChannel" nor a "Channel-group," instead using "PortChannel." So, pay close attention to these three terms in the example.

To configure an EtherChannel manually, follow these steps:

Step 1.   Add the **channel-group** *number* **mode on** command in interface configuration mode under each physical interface that should be in the channel to add it to the channel.

Step 2.   Use the same number for all commands on the same switch, but the channel-group number on the neighboring switch can differ.

10

Example 10-20 shows a simple example, with two links between switches SW1 and SW2, as shown in Figure 10-10. The example begins with all default interface configuration on the interfaces used for the EtherChannel. The configuration first shows the ports being configured as VLAN trunks and then manually configured to be in channel-group 1 (SW1) and channel-group 2 (SW2).

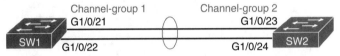

Figure 10-10 *Sample LAN Used in EtherChannel Example*

Example 10-20 *Configuring EtherChannel—Both SW1 and SW2*

```
! First, on switch SW1
SW1# configure terminal
Enter configuration commands, one per line. End with CNTL/Z.
SW1(config)# interface range g1/0/21-22
SW1(config-if-range)# switchport mode trunk
SW1(config-if-range)# channel-group 1 mode on

! Next, on switch SW2
SW2# configure terminal
Enter configuration commands, one per line. End with CNTL/Z.
SW2(config)# interface range g1/0/23-24
SW2(config-if-range)# switchport mode trunk
SW2(config-if-range)# channel-group 2 mode on
```

Interestingly, IOS reacts to the **channel-group** interface subcommands to create a matching port-channel interface on the switch. Example 10-21 shows an excerpt from the **show running-config** command on switch SW1, listing the new port-channel 1 interface in the configuration, along with the two physical interfaces.

Example 10-21 *Configuration Results from Example 10-20*

```
SW1# show running-config
! Lines omitted for brevity
!
interface Port-channel1
 switchport mode trunk
!
! Lines omitted for brevity
interface GigabitEthernet1/0/21
 switchport mode trunk
 channel-group 1 mode on
!
```

```
interface GigabitEthernet1/0/22
 switchport mode trunk
 channel-group 1 mode on

SW1# show interfaces portchannel 1
Port-channel1 is up, line protocol is up (connected)
  Hardware is EtherChannel, address is 4488.165a.f215 (bia 4488.165a.f215)
  MTU 1500 bytes, BW 2000000 Kbit/sec, DLY 10 usec,
     reliability 255/255, txload 1/255, rxload 1/255
  Encapsulation ARPA, loopback not set
  Keepalive set (10 sec)
  Full-duplex, 1000Mb/s, link type is auto, media type is N/A
  input flow-control is on, output flow-control is unsupported
  Members in this channel: Gi1/0/21 Gi1/0/22
  ARP type: ARPA, ARP Timeout 04:00:00
  Last input 02:12:51, output 00:00:00, output hang never
  Last clearing of "show interface" counters never
! Interface statistics output removed for brevity
```

The end of Example 10-21 gives more insight into the portchannel interface in the output of the **show interfaces portchannel 1** command. Like all output from the **show interfaces** command, the output lists both an interface and protocol state ("up" and "up" in this case), and the interface bandwidth, noted with the text "BW." However, the output shows the bandwidth as 2,000,000 Kbps, or 2 Gbps, because the portchannel has two active 1-Gbps links. Also, in the final highlighted line, the output lists the currently active interfaces in the portchannel.

The **show etherchannel** command, shown at the top of Example 10-22, lists basic configuration information about the channel per earlier Example 10-20. In this case, it identifies the configured portchannel number (1), with two ports configured to be in the channel. It lists the protocol as a dash (–), meaning that it does not use LACP or PAgP, implying the use of the **channel-group mode on** command. Note that this command does not list status information, only configuration information.

Example 10-22 *Exploring SW1 PortChannel Configuration and Status*

```
SW1# show etherchannel
                Channel-group listing:
                ----------------------

Group: 1
----------
Group state = L2
Ports: 2   Maxports = 8
Port-channels: 1 Max Port-channels = 1
Protocol:     -
Minimum Links: 0
```

10

```
SW1# show etherchannel summary
Flags:  D - down       P - bundled in port-channel
        I - stand-alone s - suspended
        H - Hot-standby (LACP only)
        R - Layer3      S - Layer2
        U - in use      f - failed to allocate aggregator

        M - not in use, minimum links not met
        u - unsuitable for bundling
        w - waiting to be aggregated
        d - default port

        A - formed by Auto LAG

Number of channel-groups in use: 1
Number of aggregators:           1

Group  Port-channel  Protocol    Ports
------+-------------+-----------+-----------------------------------------------
1      Po1(SU)          -        Gi1/0/21(P)    Gi1/0/22(P)
```

The **show etherchannel summary** command at the end of Example 10-22 provides status information. The output begins with an extensive status code legend. The lines at the bottom list each PortChannel along with the ports and their status. In the lowest line of output with highlights, note the code P, which means that both of those ports are bundled (working) in the channel. A status of (SU), per the legend, means the channel is in use and acts as a Layer 2 EtherChannel (rather than a Layer 3 EtherChannel).

Configuring Dynamic EtherChannels

Cisco switches also support two different configuration options that use a dynamic protocol to negotiate whether a particular link becomes part of an EtherChannel or not. Basically, the configuration enables a protocol for a particular channel-group number. At that point, the switch can use the protocol to send messages to/from the neighboring switch and discover whether their configuration settings pass all checks. If a given physical link passes, the link is added to the EtherChannel and used; if not, it is placed in a down state, and not used, until the configuration inconsistency can be resolved.

Most Cisco Catalyst switches support the Cisco-proprietary Port Aggregation Protocol (**PAgP**) and the IEEE standard Link Aggregation Control Protocol (**LACP**). Although differences exist between the two, to the depth discussed here, they both accomplish the same task: negotiate so that only links that pass the configuration checks are actually used in an EtherChannel. (Note that the IEEE originally defined LACP in amendment 802.3ad but now defines it in IEEE standard 802.1AX.)

One difference of note is that LACP does support more links in a channel—16—as compared to PaGP's maximum of 8. With LACP, only 8 can be active at one time, with the others waiting to be used should any of the other links fail.

To configure either protocol, a switch uses the **channel-group** configuration commands on each switch, but with a keyword that either means "use this protocol and begin negotiations" or "use this protocol and wait for the other switch to begin negotiations." As shown in Figure 10-11, the **desirable** and **auto** keywords enable PAgP, and the **active** and **passive** keywords enable LACP. With these options, at least one side has to begin the negotiations. In other words, with PAgP, at least one of the two sides must use **desirable**, and with LACP, at least one of the two sides must use **active**.

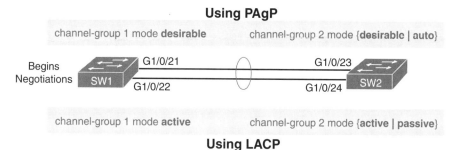

Figure 10-11 *Correct EtherChannel Configuration Combinations*

NOTE   Do not use the **on** parameter on one end, and either **auto** or **desirable** (or for LACP, **active** or **passive**) on the neighboring switch. The **on** option uses neither PAgP nor LACP, so a configuration that uses **on**, with PAgP or LACP options on the other end, would prevent the EtherChannel from working.

As an example, consider the topology in Figure 10-11, which uses the same switches and ports as Figure 10-10 and the last several examples. However, the next example starts fresh, with the manual EtherChannel no longer configured and no interface commands on any of the interfaces in use. Example 10-23 shows a dynamic configuration with LACP on both switches, with the **channel-group 1 mode active** interface subcommand on SW1 and **channel-group 2 mode passive** on SW2.

Example 10-23 *Configuring an LACP Dynamic EtherChannel—Both SW1 and SW2*

```
! First, on switch SW1
SW1# configure terminal
Enter configuration commands, one per line. End with CNTL/Z.
SW1(config)# interface range g1/0/21-22
SW1(config-if-range)# switchport mode trunk
SW1(config-if-range)# channel-group 1 mode active
```

```
! Next, on switch SW2
SW2# configure terminal
Enter configuration commands, one per line. End with CNTL/Z.
SW2(config)# interface range g1/0/23-24
SW2(config-if-range)# switchport mode trunk
SW2(config-if-range)# channel-group 2 mode passive
```

10

As with the manual configuration and verification in Examples 10-20 and 10-21, the switch creates a portchannel interface in reaction to the configuration shown in Example 10-23. Example 10-24 confirms the related settings, with group or portchannel 1, two ports in the channel, specifically SW1's G1/0/21 and G1/0/22. Also, note that the output lists the protocol as LACP, because the configuration commands in Example 10-23 use keywords **active** and **passive**, both of which enable LACP.

Example 10-24 *EtherChannel Verification: SW1 with LACP Active Mode*

```
SW1# show etherchannel port-channel
                Channel-group listing:
                ----------------------


Group: 1
----------
                Port-channels in the group:
                ---------------------------


Port-channel: Po1    (Primary Aggregator)


------------


Age of the Port-channel   = 0d:00h:11m:35s
Logical slot/port    = 31/1         Number of ports = 2
HotStandBy port = null
Port state           = Port-channel Ag-Inuse
Protocol             =    LACP
Port security        = Disabled
Fast-switchover      = disabled
Fast-switchover Dampening = disabled


Ports in the Port-channel:


Index   Load    Port        EC state         No of bits
------+------+------+------------------+-----------
   0    00    Gi1/0/21       Active            0
   0    00    Gi1/0/22       Active            0


Time since last port bundled:    0d:00h:02m:17s    Gi1/0/22
Time since last port Un-bundled: 0d:00h:02m:25s    Gi1/0/22
```

Before leaving the core EtherChannel configuration and verification topics, think about EtherChannels and Spanning Tree together. STP/RSTP prefers the better links based on STP/RSTP link costs. An EtherChannel may have more than one working link, and the number of active links changes as links fail and recover. So, by default, IOS calculates the default STP cost for EtherChannel based on the number of active links.

For example, the STP/RSTP default costs prefer 10 Gbps over EtherChannels with 1 Gbps links, and EtherChannels of multiple 1 Gbps links over a single 1 Gbps link, with the following default port costs:

- **Default Cost 4:** EtherChannels with one active 1 Gbps link and any single 1 Gbps link (without an EtherChannel)

- **Default Cost 3:** EtherChannels with 2 to 8 active 1 Gbps links

- **Default Cost 2:** A single 10 Gbps link

Example 10-25 shows the default STP cost on a couple of 1 Gbps interfaces along with interface PortChannel 1, whose configuration resides earlier in Example 10-23.

Example 10-25 *EtherChannel Verification: SW1 with LACP Active Mode*

```
SW1# show spanning-tree vlan 1 | begin Interface
Interface          Role Sts Cost      Prio.Nbr Type
------------------ ---- --- --------- -------- -------------------------------
Gi1/0/23           Desg FWD 4         128.23   P2p
Gi1/0/24           Desg FWD 4         128.24   P2p
Po1                Desg FWD 3         128.456  P2p
```

Interface Configuration Consistency with EtherChannels

Even when the **channel-group** commands have all been configured correctly, other configuration settings can prevent a switch from using a physical port in an EtherChannel—even physical ports manually configured to be part of the channel. The next topic examines those reasons.

First, before using a physical port in a dynamic EtherChannel, the switch compares the new physical port's configuration to the existing ports in the channel. That new physical interface's settings must be the same as the existing ports' settings; otherwise, the switch does not add the new link to the list of approved and working interfaces in the channel. That is, the physical interface remains configured as part of the PortChannel, but it is not used as part of the channel, often being placed into some nonworking state.

The list of items the switch checks includes the following:

- Speed

- Duplex

- Operational access or trunking state (all must be access, or all must be trunks)

- If an access port, the access VLAN

- If a trunk port, the allowed VLAN list (per the **switchport trunk allowed** command)

- If a trunk port, the native VLAN

Example 10-26 shows a failure of one link in the EtherChannel due to a purposeful misconfiguration of the native VLAN on SW1's G1/0/21 port. Example 10-26 begins with the configuration of VLAN 21 as the native VLAN on port G1/0/21; port G1/0/22 defaults to

10

native VLAN 1. The log messages following that configuration show the interface failing, with the **show interfaces g1/0/21** command listing a "down (suspended)" protocol state for that interface. The usual **show etherchannel port-channel** command lists only one port as bundled in the channel.

Example 10-26   *Native VLAN Mismatch Removes SW1 G1/0/21 from EtherChannel*

```
SW1# configure terminal
Enter configuration commands, one per line.  End with CNTL/Z.
SW1(config)# interface g1/0/21
SW1(config-if)# switchport trunk native vlan 21
SW1(config-if)# ^Z
SW1#
Jun 17 16:11:34.217: %EC-5-CANNOT_BUNDLE2: Gi1/0/21 is not compatible with Gi1/0/22
and will be suspended (native vlan of Gi1/0/21 is 21, Gi1/0/22 id 1)
Jun 17 16:11:35.220: %LINEPROTO-5-UPDOWN: Line protocol on Interface
GigabitEthernet1/0/21, changed state to down

SW1# show interfaces gigabitethernet 1/0/21
GigabitEthernet1/0/21 is up, line protocol is down (suspended)
  Hardware is Gigabit Ethernet, address is 4488.165a.f215 (bia 4488.165a.f215)
! lines omitted for brevity

SW1# show etherchannel port-channel
                Channel-group listing:
                ----------------------


Group: 1
----------
                Port-channels in the group:
                --------------------------


Port-channel: Po1    (Primary Aggregator)


------------

Age of the Port-channel   = 0d:05h:26m:48s
Logical slot/port    = 31/1          Number of ports = 1
HotStandBy port = null
Port state          = Port-channel Ag-Inuse
Protocol            =    LACP
Port security       = Disabled
Fast-switchover     = disabled
Fast-switchover Dampening = disabled


Ports in the Port-channel:
```

```
Index   Load    Port         EC state         No of bits

------+------+------+-------------------+-----------
   0     00    Gi1/0/22        Active              0


Time since last port bundled:     0d:00h:05m:44s     Gi1/0/22
Time since last port Un-bundled: 0d:00h:01m:09s     Gi1/0/21
```

The output in Example 10-26 closes with two useful messages at the end of the **show etherchannel port-channel** command output: the interface ID and the timing of the most recent ports bundled and unbundled with the EtherChannel. In this case, it shows the most recent addition of the still-working G1/0/22 interface and the just-suspended G1/0/21 interface.

EtherChannel Load Distribution

When using Layer 2 EtherChannels, a switch's MAC learning process associates MAC addresses with the PortChannel interfaces and not the underlying physical ports. Later, when a switch makes a forwarding decision to send a frame out a PortChannel interface, the switch must do more work: to decide which specific physical port to use to forward the frame. IOS documentation refers to those rules as **EtherChannel load distribution** or *load balancing*. Figure 10-12 shows the main idea.

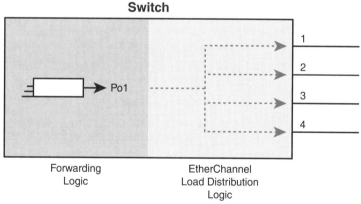

Figure 10-12   *Forwarding Concepts from Outgoing PortChannel to Physical Interfaces*

EtherChannel load distribution makes the choice for each frame based on various numeric values found in the Layer 2, 3, and 4 headers. The process uses one configurable setting as input: the load distribution method as defined with the **port-channel load-balance** *method* global command. The process then performs some match against the fields identified by the configured method.

Table 10-4 lists the most common methods. However, note that some switches may support only MAC-based methods, or only MAC- and IP-based methods, depending on the model and software version.

10

Table 10-4   EtherChannel Load Distribution Methods

Configuration Keyword	Math Uses...	Layer
src-mac	Source MAC address	2
dst-mac	Destination MAC address	2
src-dst-mac	Both source and destination MAC	2
src-ip	Source IP address	3
dst-ip	Destination IP address	3
src-dst-ip	Both source and destination IP	3
src-port	Source TCP or UDP port	4
dst-port	Destination TCP or UDP port	4
src-dst-port	Both source and destination TCP or UDP port	4

To appreciate why you might want to use different methods, you need to consider the results of how switches make their choice. (The discussion here focuses on the result, and not the logic, because the logic remains internal to the switch, and Cisco does not document how each switch model or IOS version works internally.) However, the various load distribution algorithms do share some common goals:

- To cause all messages in a single application flow to use the same link in the channel, rather than being sent over different links. Doing so means that the switch will not inadvertently reorder the messages sent in that application flow by sending one message over a busy link that has a queue of waiting messages, while immediately sending the next message out an unused link.

- To integrate the load distribution algorithm work into the hardware forwarding ASIC so that load distribution works just as quickly as the work to forward any other frame.

- To use all the active links in the EtherChannel, adjusting to the addition and removal of active links over time.

- Within the constraints of the other goals, balance the traffic across those active links.

In short, the algorithms first intend to avoid message reordering, make use of the switch forwarding ASICs, and use all the active links. However, the algorithm does not attempt to send the exact same number of bits over each link over time. The algorithm does try to balance the traffic, but always within the constraints of the other goals.

Whatever load distribution method you choose, the method identifies fields in the message headers. Any messages in the same application flow will then have the same values in the fields used by the load distribution algorithm and will always be forwarded over the same link. For example, when a user connects to a website, that web server may return thousands of packets to the client. Those thousands of packets should flow over the same link in the EtherChannel.

For instance, with the load distribution method of **src-mac** (meaning source MAC address), all frames with the same MAC address flow over one link. Figure 10-13 shows the idea with pseudo (generic) MAC addresses, with the load distribution sending frames with source MAC 1 over link 1, source MAC 2 over link 2, and source MAC 3 over link 3.

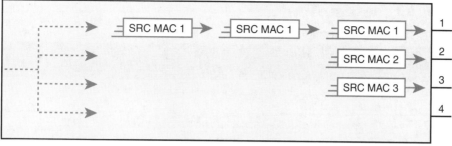

EtherChannel Load Distribution

Figure 10-13 *Distributing All Frames with the Same MAC Out the Same Interface*

Cisco provides a variety of load distribution options so that the engineer can examine the flows in the network with the idea of finding which fields have the most variety in their values: source and destination MAC, or IP address, or transport layer port numbers. The more variety in the values in the fields, the better the balancing effects, and the lower the chance of sending disproportionate amounts of traffic over one link.

NOTE The algorithm focuses on the low-order bits in the fields in the headers because the low-order bits typically differ the most in real networks, while the high-order bits do not differ much. By focusing on the lower-order bits, the algorithm achieves better balancing of traffic over the links.

Chapter Review

One key to doing well on the exams is to perform repetitive spaced review sessions. Review this chapter's material using either the tools in the book or interactive tools for the same material found on the book's companion website. Refer to the "Your Study Plan" element for more details. Table 10-5 outlines the key review elements and where you can find them. To better track your study progress, record when you completed these activities in the second column.

Table 10-5 Chapter Review Tracking

Review Element	Review Date(s)	Resource Used
Review key topics		Book, website
Review key terms		Book, website
Answer DIKTA questions		Book, PTP
Review config checklists		Book, website
Review command tables		Book
Review memory tables		Website
Do labs		Blog
Watch video		Website

10

Review All the Key Topics

Table 10-6   Key Topics for Chapter 10

Key Topic Element	Description	Page Number
Figure 10-1	Typical design choice for which switches should be made to be root	259
Figure 10-2	Conceptual view of load-balancing benefits of PVST+	260
Table 10-2	STP Standards and Configuration Options	261
Figure 10-4	Shows the format of the system ID extension of the STP priority field	262
List	Facts about RPVST+'s methods versus RSTP	266
List	Trigger, actions, and recovery for BPDU Guard	270
List	Trigger, actions, and recovery for Root Guard	278
List	Configuration options with Loop Guard	280
List	Steps to manually configure an EtherChannel	281
List	Items a switch compares in a new physical port's configuration to the existing ports in the channel	287

Key Terms You Should Know

Channel-group, EtherChannel, EtherChannel load distribution, LACP, PAgP, PortChannel, PVST+, Rapid PVST+, system ID extension

Command References

Tables 10-7 and 10-8 list configuration and verification commands used in this chapter. As an easy review exercise, cover the left column in a table, read the right column, and try to recall the command without looking. Then repeat the exercise, covering the right column, and try to recall what the command does.

Table 10-7   Chapter 10 Configuration Command Reference

Command	Description
**spanning-tree mode {pvst	rapid-pvst	mst}**	Global configuration command to set the STP mode.
spanning-tree [vlan *vlan-number*] **root primary**	Global configuration command that changes this switch to the root switch. The switch's priority is changed to the lower of either 24,576 or 4096 less than the priority of the current root bridge when the command was issued.
spanning-tree [vlan *vlan-number*] **root secondary**	Global configuration command that sets this switch's STP base priority to 28,672.
spanning-tree vlan *vlan-id* **priority** *priority*	Global configuration command that changes the bridge priority of this switch for the specified VLAN.
spanning-tree [vlan *vlan-number*] **cost** *cost*	Interface subcommand that changes the STP cost to the configured value.

Command	Description
spanning-tree [vlan *vlan-number*] port-priority *priority*	Interface subcommand that changes the STP port priority in that VLAN (0 to 240, in increments of 16).
spanning-tree portfast	Interface subcommand that enables PortFast if the port is also an access port.
spanning-tree portfast trunk	Interface subcommand that enables PortFast if the port is also a trunk port.
spanning-tree bpduguard enable	Interface subcommand that enables BPDU Guard on the interface under all conditions.
spanning-tree portfast disable	Interface subcommand that reverses the **spanning-tree portfast** command.
spanning-tree bpduguard disable	Interface subcommand that reverses the **spanning-tree bpduguard enable** command.
spanning-tree portfast enable	Global command that changes the default interface setting to the same logic as if the **spanning-tree portfast** interface subcommand were configured.
spanning-tree portfast bpduguard default	Global command that changes the default interface setting to enable BPDU Guard if the port is also actively using PortFast.
spanning-tree bpdufilter enable	Interface subcommand that enables BPDU Filter on the interface under all conditions, disabling STP on the interface.
spanning-tree portfast bpdufilter default	Global command that directs IOS to enable BPDU Filter conditional logic, which toggles away from using PortFast as needed if the port is also actively using PortFast.
[no] spanning-tree guard root	Interface subcommand to enable or disable (with the **no** option) Root Guard.
[no] spanning-tree guard loop	Interface subcommand to enable or disable (with the **no** option) Loop Guard.
spanning-tree loopguard default	Global command to change the default setting on interfaces to enable Loop Guard.
channel-group *channel-group-number* mode {auto	desirable	active	passive	on}	Interface subcommand that enables EtherChannel on the interface.

Table 10-8   Chapter 10 EXEC Command Reference

Command	Description
show spanning-tree	Lists details about the state of STP on the switch, including the state of each port.
show spanning-tree vlan *vlan-id*	Lists STP information for the specified VLAN.
show spanning-tree vlan *vlan-id* interface *interface-id* [detail]	Lists STP information for the specified VLAN about the specific interface.

10

Command	Description
show etherchannel [*channel-group-number*] {brief | detail | port | port-channel | summary}	Lists information about the state of EtherChannels on this switch.
show interfaces portchannel *number*	Lists information typical of the **show interfaces** command and also lists the interfaces included in the EtherChannel.
show etherchannel	Displays configuration settings for each EtherChannel.
show etherchannel [*number*] {summary | portchannel | detail}	Displays status information about all EtherChannels, or the one specific EtherChannel. The final parameter suggests the briefest option (**summary**) to the most detailed (**detail**).

Part III Review

Keep track of your part review progress with the checklist shown in Table P3-1. Details on each task follow the table.

Table P3-1 Part III Part Review Checklist

Activity	1st Date Completed	2nd Date Completed
Repeat All DIKTA Questions		
Answer Part Review Questions		
Review Key Topics		
Do Labs		
Review Appendices		
Watch Video		
Use Per-Chapter Interactive Review		

Repeat All DIKTA Questions

For this task, answer the "Do I Know This Already?" questions again for the chapters in this part of the book, using the PTP software.

Answer Part Review Questions

For this task, answer the Part Review questions for this part of the book, using the PTP software.

Review Key Topics

Review all key topics in all chapters in this part, either by browsing the chapters or by using the Key Topics application on the companion website.

Do Labs

Depending on your chosen lab tool, here are some suggestions for what to do in the labs:

Pearson Network Simulator: If you use the full Pearson CCNA simulator, focus more on the configuration scenario and troubleshooting scenario labs associated with the topics in this part of the book. These types of labs include a larger set of topics and work well as Part Review activities. (See the Introduction for some details about how to find which labs are about topics in this part of the book.) Note that the Sim Lite that comes with this book also has a couple of labs about VLANs.

Blog: Config Labs: The author's blog includes a series of configuration-focused labs that you can do on paper or with Cisco Packet Tracer in about 15 minutes. To find them, open https://www.certskills.com and look under the Labs menu item.

Other: If using other lab tools, as a few suggestions: make sure to experiment heavily with VLAN configuration and VLAN trunking configuration.

Dig Deeper with Appendices on the Companion Website

The chapters in Part III of the book recommended the following appendices for extra reading. If you care to read further, consider

- **Appendix L, "LAN Troubleshooting":** An appendix from the previous edition of the book. It includes topics about VLANs, trunks, and STP and how to troubleshoot each.

Watch Video

The companion website includes a variety of common mistake and Q&A videos organized by part and chapter. Use these videos to challenge your thinking, dig deeper, review topics, and better prepare for the exam. Make sure to bookmark a link to the companion website and use the videos for review whenever you have a few extra minutes.

Use Per-Chapter Interactive Review

Using the companion website, browse through the interactive review elements, like memory tables and key term flashcards, to review the content from each chapter.

The book makes a big transition at this point. Part I gave you a broad introduction to networking, and Parts II and III went into some detail about the dominant LAN technology today: Ethernet. Part IV transitions from Ethernet to the network layer details that sit above Ethernet and WAN technology, specifically IP version 4 (IPv4).

Thinking about the network layer requires engineers to shift how they think about addressing. Ethernet allows the luxury of using universal MAC addresses, assigned by the manufacturers, with no need to plan or configure addresses. Although the network engineer needs to understand MAC addresses, MAC already exists on each Ethernet NIC, and switches learn the Ethernet MAC addresses dynamically without even needing to be configured to do so. As a result, most people operating the network can ignore the specific MAC address values for most tasks.

Conversely, IP addressing gives you flexibility and allows choice; however, those features require planning, along with a much deeper understanding of the internal structure of the addresses. People operating the network must be more aware of the network layer addresses when doing many tasks. To better prepare you for these Layer 3 addressing details, this part breaks down the addressing details into five chapters, with an opportunity to learn more in preparation for the CCNP Enterprise certification.

Part IV examines most of the basic details of IPv4 addressing and subnetting, mostly from the perspective of operating an IP network. Chapter 11 takes a grand tour of IPv4 addressing as implemented inside a typical enterprise network. Chapters 12 through 15 look at some of the specific questions people must ask themselves when operating an IPv4 network.

This section includes all the details you need to learn for the CCNA 200-301 V1.1 blueprint's IPv4 addressing and subnetting exam topics. Many people have learned subnetting from these chapters over the years; however, some people have asked for video and more practice with subnetting—and understandably so. If that's you, consider these additional products as well, both of which can be found at ciscopress.com:

> IP Subnetting: From Beginning to Mastery (Video Course)
>
> IP Subnetting Practice Question Kit (Practice Questions Product)

We mention these here before you begin Part IV because, if you decide to use them, you might want to use them alongside the chapters in this part.

Part IV

IPv4 Addressing

CHAPTER 11

Perspectives on IPv4 Subnetting

This chapter covers the following exam topics:

1.0 Network Fundamentals

    1.6 Configure and verify IPv4 addressing and subnetting

    1.7 Describe private IPv4 addressing

Most entry-level networking jobs require you to operate and troubleshoot a network using a preexisting IP addressing and subnetting plan. The CCNA exam assesses your readiness to use preexisting IP addressing and subnetting information to perform typical operations tasks, such as monitoring the network, reacting to possible problems, configuring addresses for new parts of the network, and troubleshooting those problems.

However, you also need to understand how networks are designed and why. Anyone monitoring a network must ask the question, "Is the network working *as designed*?" If a problem exists, you must consider questions such as "What happens when the network works normally, and what is different right now?" Both questions require you to understand the intended design of the network, including details of the IP addressing and subnetting design.

This chapter provides some perspectives and answers for the bigger issues in IPv4 addressing. What addresses can be used so that they work properly? What addresses should be used? When told to use certain numbers, what does that tell you about the choices made by some other network engineer? How do these choices impact the practical job of configuring switches, routers, hosts, and operating the network on a daily basis? This chapter helps to answer these questions while revealing details of how IPv4 addresses work.

"Do I Know This Already?" Quiz

Take the quiz (either here or use the PTP software) if you want to use the score to help you decide how much time to spend on this chapter. The letter answers are listed at the bottom of the page following the quiz. Appendix C, found both at the end of the book as well as on the companion website, includes both the answers and explanations. You can also find both answers and explanations in the PTP testing software.

Table 11-1 "Do I Know This Already?" Foundation Topics Section-to-Question Mapping

Foundation Topics Section	Questions
Analyze Subnetting and Addressing Needs	1–3
Make Design Choices	4–7

1. Host A is a PC, connected to switch SW1 and assigned to VLAN 1. Which of the following are typically assigned an IP address in the same subnet as host A? (Choose two answers.)

   a. The local router's WAN interface

   b. The local router's LAN interface

   c. All other hosts attached to the same switch

   d. Other hosts attached to the same switch and also in VLAN 1

2. Why does the formula for the number of hosts per subnet (2^H 2) require the subtraction of two hosts?

   a. To reserve two addresses for redundant default gateways (routers)

   b. To reserve the two addresses required for DHCP operation

   c. To reserve addresses for the subnet ID and default gateway (router)

   d. To reserve addresses for the subnet broadcast address and subnet ID

3. A Class B network needs to be subnetted such that it supports 100 subnets and 100 hosts/subnet. Which of the following answers list a workable combination for the number of network, subnet, and host bits? (Choose two answers.)

   a. Network = 16, subnet = 7, host = 7

   b. Network = 16, subnet = 8, host = 8

   c. Network = 16, subnet = 9, host = 7

   d. Network = 8, subnet = 7, host = 17

4. Which of the following are private IP networks? (Choose two answers.)

   a. 172.31.0.0

   b. 172.32.0.0

   c. 192.168.255.0

   d. 192.1.168.0

   e. 11.0.0.0

5. Which of the following are public IP networks? (Choose three answers.)

   a. 9.0.0.0

   b. 172.30.0.0

   c. 192.168.255.0

   d. 192.1.168.0

   e. 1.0.0.0

6. Before Class B network 172.16.0.0 is subnetted by a network engineer, what parts of the structure of the IP addresses in this network already exist, with a specific size? (Choose two answers.)

   a. Network

   b. Subnet

   c. Host

   d. Broadcast

7. Consider the size of the network, subnet, and host parts of the address structure for Class B network 172.16.0.0 without any subnetting. Compare that to an updated plan that subnets the network using one mask for all subnets. Which answer describes what changed in the network, subnet, or host fields for the new plan that uses subnetting in comparison to the earlier plan that does not?

a. The subnet part got smaller.

b. The host part got smaller.

c. The network part got smaller.

d. The host part was removed.

e. The network part was removed.

Foundation Topics

Introduction to Subnetting

Say you just happened to be at the sandwich shop when it was selling the world's longest sandwich. You're pretty hungry, so you go for it. Now you have one sandwich, but because it's over 2 kilometers long, you realize it's a bit more than you need for lunch all by yourself. To make the sandwich more useful (and more portable), you chop the sandwich into meal-size pieces and give the pieces to other folks around you who are also ready for lunch.

Huh? Well, subnetting, at least the main concept, is similar to this sandwich story. You start with one network, but it is just one large network. As a single large entity, it might not be useful, and it is probably far too large. To make it useful, you chop it into smaller pieces, called **subnets**, and assign those subnets to be used in different parts of the enterprise internetwork.

This short first section of the chapter introduces IP subnetting. First, it shows the general ideas behind a completed subnet design that indeed chops (or subnets) one **network** into subnets. The rest of this section describes the many design steps that you would take to create just such a subnet design. By the end of this section, you should have the right context to then read through the subnetting design steps introduced throughout the rest of this chapter.

NOTE All the chapters from this chapter up until Chapter 25, "Fundamentals of IP Version 6," focus on IPv4 rather than IPv6. All references to *IP* refer to IPv4 unless otherwise stated.

Subnetting Defined Through a Simple Example

An IP network—in other words, a Class A, B, or C network—is simply a set of consecutively numbered IP addresses that follow some preset rules. These Class A, B, and C rules define that for a given network, all the addresses in the network have the same value in some of the octets of the addresses. For example, Class B network 172.16.0.0 consists of all IP addresses that begin with 172.16: 172.16.0.0, 172.16.0.1, 172.16.0.2, and so on, through 172.16.255.255. Another example: Class A network 10.0.0.0 includes all addresses that begin with 10.

An IP subnet is simply a subset of a Class A, B, or C network. If fact, the word *subnet* is a shortened version of the phrase *subdivided network*. For example, one subnet of Class B network 172.16.0.0 could be the set of all IP addresses that begin with 172.16.1, and would include 172.16.1.0, 172.16.1.1, 172.16.1.2, and so on, up through 172.16.1.255. Another subnet of that same Class B network could be all addresses that begin with 172.16.2.

To give you a general idea, Figure 11-1 shows some basic documentation from a completed subnet design that could be used when an engineer subnets Class B network 172.16.0.0.

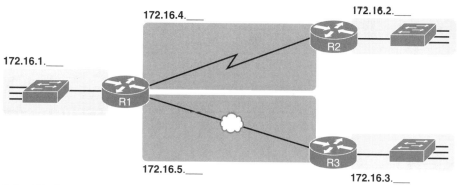

Subnet Design:

> **Class B 172.16.0.0**
> **First 3 Octets are Equal**

Figure 11-1   *Subnet Plan Document*

The design shows five subnets—one for each of the three LANs and one each for the two WAN links. The small text note shows the rationale used by the engineer for the subnets: each subnet includes addresses that have the same value in the first three octets. For example, for the LAN on the left, the number shows 172.16.1.__, meaning "all addresses that begin with 172.16.1." Also, note that the design, as shown, does not use all the addresses in Class B network 172.16.0.0, so the engineer has left plenty of room for growth.

Operational View Versus Design View of Subnetting

Most IT jobs require you to work with subnetting from an operational view. That is, someone else, before you got the job, designed how IP addressing and subnetting would work for that particular enterprise network. You need to interpret what someone else has already chosen.

To fully understand IP addressing and subnetting, you need to think about subnetting from both a design and operational perspective. For example, Figure 11-1 simply states that in all these subnets, the first three octets must be equal. Why was that convention chosen? What alternatives exist? Would those alternatives be better for your internetwork today? All these questions relate more to subnetting design rather than to operation.

To help you see both perspectives, this chapter focuses more on design issues by moving through the entire design process for the purpose of introducing the bigger picture of IP subnetting. The next three chapters each examine one topic from this chapter from an operational perspective, with the final chapter in this part returning to subnet design for a closer look.

The remaining three main sections of this chapter examine each of the steps listed in Figure 11-2, in sequence.

11

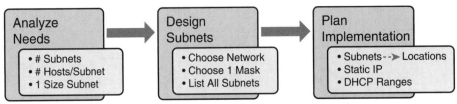

Figure 11-2 *Subnet Planning, Design, and Implementation Tasks*

Analyze Subnetting and Addressing Needs

This section discusses the meaning of four basic questions that can be used to analyze the addressing and subnetting needs for any new or changing enterprise network:

1. Which hosts should be grouped together into a subnet?

2. How many subnets does this internetwork require?

3. How many host IP addresses does each subnet require?

4. Will we use a single subnet size for simplicity, or not?

Rules About Which Hosts Are in Which Subnet

Every device that connects to an IP internetwork needs to have an IP address. These devices include computers used by end users, servers, mobile phones, laptops, IP phones, tablets, and networking devices like routers, switches, and firewalls. In short, any device that uses IP to send and receive packets needs an IP address.

> **NOTE** In a discussion of IP addressing, the term *network* has specific meaning: a Class A, B, or C IP network. To avoid confusion with that use of the term *network*, this book uses the terms *internetwork* and *enterprise network* when referring to a collection of hosts, routers, switches, and so on.

The IP addresses must be assigned according to some basic rules—and for good reasons. To make routing work efficiently, IP addressing rules group addresses into groups called subnets. The rules are as follows:

■ Addresses in the same subnet are not separated by a router.

■ Addresses in different subnets are separated by at least one router.

Figure 11-3 shows the general concept, with hosts A and B in one subnet and host C in another. In particular, note that hosts A and B are not separated from each other by any routers. However, host C, separated from A and B by at least one router, must be in a different subnet.

The idea that hosts on the same link must be in the same subnet is much like the postal code concept. All mailing addresses in the same town use the same postal code (ZIP codes in the United States). Addresses in another town, whether relatively nearby or on the other side of the country, have a different postal code. The postal code gives the postal service a better ability to automatically sort the mail to deliver it to the right location. For the same general reasons, hosts on the same LAN are in the same subnet, and hosts in different LANs are in different subnets.

Answers to the "Do I Know This Already?" quiz:

1 B, D **2** D **3** B, C **4** A, C **5** A, D, E **6** A, C **7** B

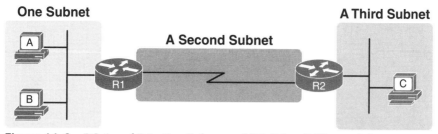

Figure 11-3   *PC A and B in One Subnet and PC C in a Different Subnet*

Note that the point-to-point WAN link in the figure also needs a subnet. Figure 11-3 shows Router R1 connected to the LAN subnet on the left and to a WAN subnet on the right. Router R2 connects to that same WAN subnet. To do so, both R1 and R2 will have IP addresses on their WAN interfaces, and the addresses will be in the same subnet. (An Ethernet WAN link has the same IP addressing needs, with each of the two routers having an IP address in the same subnet.)

The Ethernet LANs in Figure 11-3 also show a slightly different style of drawing, using simple lines with no Ethernet switch. Drawings of Ethernet LANs when the details of the LAN switches do not matter simply show each device connected to the same line, as shown in Figure 11-3. (This kind of drawing mimics the original Ethernet cabling before switches and hubs existed.)

Finally, because the routers' main job is to forward packets from one subnet to another, routers typically connect to multiple subnets. For example, in this case, Router R1 connects to one LAN subnet on the left and one WAN subnet on the right. To do so, R1 will be configured with two different IP addresses, one per interface. These addresses will be in different subnets because the interfaces connect the router to different subnets.

Determining the Number of Subnets

To determine the number of subnets required, the engineer must think about the internetwork as documented and count the locations that need a subnet. To do so, the engineer requires access to network diagrams, VLAN configuration details, and details about WAN links. For the types of links discussed in this book, you should plan for one subnet for every one of the following:

- VLAN

- Point-to-point serial link

- Ethernet WAN (Ethernet Line Service)

NOTE   Other WAN technologies outside the scope of the CCNA exam topics allow subnetting options other than one subnet per pair of routers on the WAN (as shown here). However, this book only uses point-to-point WAN technologies—serial links and Ethernet WAN links—that have one subnet for each point-to-point WAN connection between two routers.

11

For example, imagine that the network planner has only Figure 11-4 on which to base the subnet design.

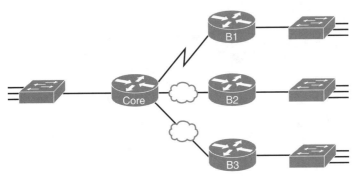

Figure 11-4 *Four-Site Internetwork with Small Central Site*

The number of subnets required cannot be fully predicted with only this figure. Certainly, three subnets will be needed for the WAN links, one per link. However, each LAN switch can be configured with a single VLAN or with multiple VLANs. You can be certain that you need at least one subnet for the LAN at each site, but you might need more.

Next, consider the more detailed version of the same figure as shown in Figure 11-5. In this case, the figure shows VLAN counts in addition to the same Layer 3 topology (the routers and the links connected to the routers). It also shows that the central site has many more switches, but the key fact on the left, regardless of how many switches exist, is that the central site has a total of 12 VLANs. Similarly, the figure lists each branch as having two VLANs. Along with the same three WAN subnets, this internetwork requires 21 subnets.

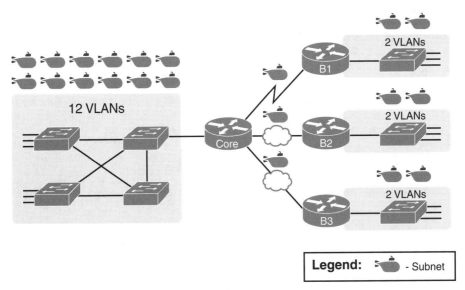

Figure 11-5 *Four-Site Internetwork with Larger Central Site*

Finally, in a real job, you would consider the needs today as well as how much growth you expect in the internetwork over time. Any subnetting plan should include a reasonable estimate of the number of subnets you need to meet future needs.

Determining the Number of Hosts per Subnet

Determining the number of hosts per subnet requires knowing a few simple concepts and then doing a lot of research and questioning. Every device that connects to a subnet needs an IP address. For a totally new network, you can look at business plans—numbers of people at the site, devices on order, and so on—to get some idea of the possible devices. When expanding an existing network to add new sites, you can use existing sites as a point of comparison and then find out which sites will get bigger or smaller. And don't forget to count the router interface IP address in each subnet and the switch IP address used to remotely manage the switch.

Instead of gathering data for each and every site, planners often just use a few typical sites for planning purposes. For example, maybe you have some large sales offices and some small sales offices. You might dig in and learn a lot about only one large sales office and only one small sales office. Add that analysis to the fact that point-to-point links need a subnet with just two addresses, plus any analysis of more one-of-a-kind subnets, and you have enough information to plan the addressing and subnetting design.

For example, in Figure 11-6, the engineer has built a diagram that shows the number of hosts per LAN subnet in the largest branch, B1. For the two other branches, the engineer did not bother to dig to find out the number of required hosts. As long as the number of required IP addresses at sites B2 and B3 stays below the estimate of 50, based on larger site B1, the engineer can plan for 50 hosts in each branch LAN subnet and have plenty of addresses per subnet.

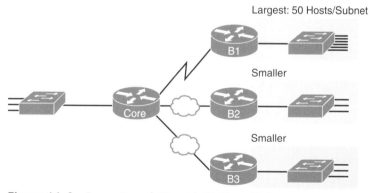

Figure 11-6 *Large Branch B1 with 50 Hosts/Subnet*

One Size Subnet Fits All—Or Not

The final choice in the initial planning step is to decide whether you will use a simpler design by using a one-size-subnet-fits-all philosophy. A subnet's size, or length, is simply the number of usable IP addresses in the subnet. A subnetting design can either use one size subnet or varied sizes of subnets, with pros and cons for each choice.

11

Defining the Size of a Subnet

Before you finish this book, you will learn all the details of how to determine the size of the subnet. For now, you just need to know a few specific facts about the size of subnets. Chapter 12, "Analyzing Classful IPv4 Networks," and Chapter 13, "Analyzing Subnet Masks," give you a progressively deeper knowledge of the details.

The engineer assigns each subnet a **subnet mask**, and that mask, among other things, defines the size of that subnet. The mask sets aside a number of *host bits* whose purpose is to number different host IP addresses in that subnet. Because you can number 2^x things with x bits, if the mask defines H host bits, the subnet contains 2^H unique numeric values.

However, the subnet's size is not 2^H. It's $2^H - 2$ because two numbers in each subnet are reserved for other purposes. Each subnet reserves the numerically lowest value for the *subnet number* and the numerically highest value as the *subnet broadcast address*. As a result, the number of usable IP addresses per subnet is $2^H - 2$.

> **NOTE**   The terms *subnet number*, *subnet ID*, and *subnet address* all refer to the number that represents or identifies a subnet.

Figure 11-7 shows the general concept behind the three-part structure of an IP address (as defined by the subnet mask), focusing on the host part and the resulting subnet size.

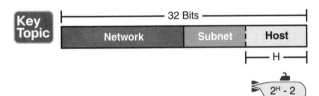

Figure 11-7 *Subnet Size Concepts*

One Size Subnet Fits All

To choose to use a single-size subnet in an enterprise network, you must use the same mask for all subnets because the mask defines the size of the subnet. But which mask?

One requirement to consider when choosing that one mask is this: that one mask must provide enough host IP addresses to support the largest subnet. To do so, the number of host bits (H) defined by the mask must be large enough so that $2^H - 2$ is larger than (or equal to) the number of host IP addresses required in the largest subnet.

For example, consider Figure 11-8. It shows the required number of hosts per LAN subnet. (The figure ignores the subnets on the WAN links, which require only two IP addresses each.) The branch LAN subnets require only 50 host addresses, but the main site LAN subnet requires 200 host addresses. To accommodate the largest subnet, you need at least 8 host bits. Seven host bits would not be enough because $2^7 - 2 = 126$. Eight host bits would be enough because $2^8 - 2 = 254$, which is more than enough to support 200 hosts in a subnet.

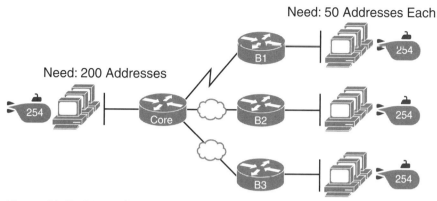

Figure 11-8 *Network Using One Subnet Size*

What's the big advantage when using a single-size subnet? Operational simplicity. In other words, keeping it simple. Everyone on the IT staff who has to work with networking can get used to working with one mask—and one mask only. Staff members will be able to answer all subnetting questions more easily because everyone gets used to doing subnetting math with that one mask.

The big disadvantage for using a single-size subnet is that it wastes IP addresses. For example, in Figure 11-8, all the branch LAN subnets support 254 addresses, while the largest branch subnet needs only 50 addresses. The WAN subnets need only two IP addresses, but each supports 254 addresses, again wasting more IP addresses.

The wasted IP addresses do not actually cause a problem in most cases, however. Most organizations use private IP networks in their enterprise internetworks, and a single Class A or Class B private network can supply plenty of IP addresses, even with the waste.

Multiple Subnet Sizes (Variable-Length Subnet Masks)

To create multiple sizes of subnets in one Class A, B, or C network, the engineer must create some subnets using one mask, some with another, and so on. Different masks mean different numbers of host bits, and a different number of hosts in some subnets based on the $2^H - 2$ formula.

For example, consider the requirements listed earlier in Figure 11-8. It showed one LAN subnet on the left that needs 200 host addresses, three branch subnets that need 50 addresses, and three WAN links that need two addresses. To meet those needs, but waste fewer IP addresses, three subnet masks could be used, creating subnets of three different sizes, as shown in Figure 11-9.

The smaller subnets now waste fewer IP addresses compared to the design shown earlier in Figure 11-8. The subnets on the right that need 50 IP addresses have subnets with 6 host bits, for $2^6 - 2 = 62$ available addresses per subnet. The WAN links use masks with 2 host bits, for $2^2 - 2 = 2$ available addresses per subnet.

11

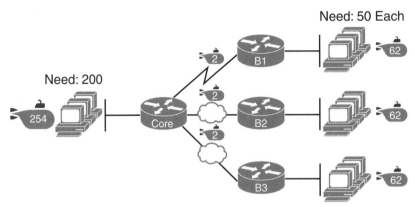

Figure 11-9   *Three Masks, Three Subnet Sizes*

However, some are still wasted because you cannot set the size of the subnet as some arbitrary size. All subnets will be a size based on the $2^H - 2$ formula, with H being the number of host bits defined by the mask for each subnet.

One Mask for All Subnets, or More Than One

For the most part, this book explains subnetting using designs that use a single mask, creating a single subnet size for all subnets. Why? First, it makes the process of learning subnetting easier. Second, some types of analysis that you can do about a network—specifically, calculating the number of subnets in the classful network—make sense only when a single mask is used.

However, you still need to be ready to work with designs that use more than one mask in different subnets of the same Class A, B, or C network. In fact, a design that does just that is said to be using **variable-length subnet masks (VLSM)**. For example, the internetwork in Figure 11-10 shows 11 subnets: two with a mask of /30 and nine with a mask of /24. By using more than one mask among all the subnets of one Class A network (10.0.0.0), the design uses VLSM.

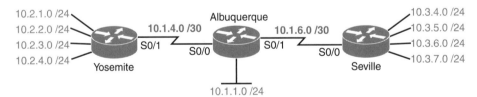

Figure 11-10   *Internetwork with VLSM: Network 10.0.0.0, >1 Mask*

Although VLSM causes problems when using some older IP routing protocols, the CCNA 200-301 V1.1 blueprint includes only the OSPF routing protocol, and VLSM causes no problems with OSPF. Just be aware of the term and what it means and that it should not impact the features included in the current CCNA exam.

> **NOTE** VLSM has been featured in the CCNA exam topics in the past. If you want to read a little more about VLSM, check out Appendix M, "Variable-Length Subnet Masks," on the companion website for this book.

Make Design Choices

Now that you know how to analyze the IP addressing and subnetting needs, the next major step examines how to apply the rules of IP addressing and subnetting to those needs and make some choices. In other words, now that you know how many subnets you need and how many host addresses you need in the largest subnet, how do you create a useful subnetting design that meets those requirements? The short answer is that you need to do the three tasks shown on the right side of Figure 11-11.

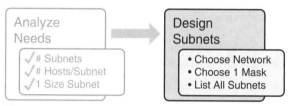

Figure 11-11 *Input to the Design Phase, and Design Questions to Answer*

Choose a Classful Network

In the original design for what we know of today as the Internet, companies used registered *public* **classful IP networks** when implementing TCP/IP inside the company. By the mid-1990s, an alternative became more popular: **private IP networks**. This section discusses the background behind these two choices because it impacts the choice of what IP network a company will then subnet and implement in its enterprise internetwork.

Public IP Networks

The original design of the Internet required that any company that connected to the Internet had to use a *registered* **public IP network**. To do so, the company would complete some paperwork, describing the enterprise's internetwork and the number of hosts existing, plus plans for growth. After submitting the paperwork, the company would receive an assignment of either a Class A, B, or C network.

Public IP networks—and the administrative processes surrounding them—ensure that all the companies that connect to the Internet use unique IP addresses. In particular, after a public IP network is assigned to a company, only that company should use the addresses in that network. That guarantee of uniqueness means that Internet routing can work well because there are no duplicate public IP addresses.

For example, consider the example shown in Figure 11-12. Company 1 has been assigned public Class A network 1.0.0.0, and company 2 has been assigned public Class A network 2.0.0.0. Per the original intent for public addressing in the Internet, after these public network assignments have been made, no other companies can use addresses in Class A networks 1.0.0.0 or 2.0.0.0.

11

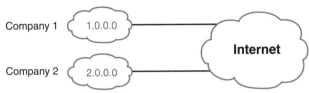

Figure 11-12   *Two Companies with Unique Public IP Networks*

This original address assignment process ensured unique IP addresses across the entire planet. The idea is much like the fact that your telephone number should be unique in the universe, your postal mailing address should also be unique, and your email address should also be unique. If someone calls you, your phone rings, but no one else's phone rings. Similarly, if company 1 is assigned Class A network 1.0.0.0, and the engineers at Company 1 assign address 1.1.1.1 to a particular PC, that address should be unique in the universe. A packet sent through the Internet to destination 1.1.1.1 should arrive only at this one PC inside company 1, instead of being delivered to some other host.

Growth Exhausts the Public IP Address Space

By the early 1990s, the world was running out of public IP networks that could be assigned. During most of the 1990s, the number of hosts newly connected to the Internet was growing at a double-digit pace *per month*. Companies kept following the rules, asking for public IP networks, and it was clear that the current address-assignment scheme could not continue without some changes. Simply put, the number of Class A, B, and C networks supported by the 32-bit address in IP version 4 (IPv4) was not enough to support one public classful network per organization, while also providing enough IP addresses in each company.

> **NOTE**   The universe has run out of public IPv4 addresses in a couple of significant ways. IANA, which assigns public IPv4 address blocks to the five Regional Internet Registries (RIR) around the globe, assigned the last of the IPv4 address spaces in early 2011. By 2015, ARIN, the RIR for North America, exhausted its supply of IPv4 addresses, so companies must return unused public IPv4 addresses to ARIN before they have more to assign to new companies. Try an online search for "ARIN depletion" to see pages about the current status of available IPv4 address space for just one RIR example.

The Internet community worked hard during the 1990s to solve this problem, coming up with several solutions, including the following:

- A new version of IP (IPv6), with much larger addresses (128 bit)

- Assigning a subset of a public IP network to each company, instead of an entire public IP network, to reduce waste, using a feature called classless interdomain routing (CIDR)

- Network Address Translation (NAT), which allows the use of private IP networks

These three solutions matter to real networks today. However, to stay focused on the topic of subnet design, this chapter focuses on the third option, and in particular, the private IP networks that can be used by an enterprise when also using NAT. (Be aware that Chapter 14, "Network Address Translation," in the *CCNA 200-301 Official Cert Guide, Volume 2,*

Second Edition, gives more detail about the last two bullets in the list, while Part VII of this book discusses the first bullet item (IPv6) in more depth.

Focusing on the third item in the bullet list, NAT allows multiple companies to use the exact same *private IP network*, using the same IP addresses as other companies while still connecting to the Internet. For example, Figure 11-13 shows the same two companies connecting to the Internet as in Figure 11-12, but now with both using the same private Class A network 10.0.0.0.

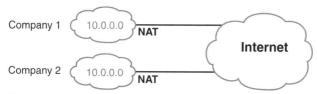

Figure 11-13 *Reusing the Same Private Network 10.0.0.0 with NAT*

Both companies use the same classful IP network (10.0.0.0). Both companies can implement their subnet design internal to their respective enterprise internetworks, without discussing their plans. The two companies can even use the exact same IP addresses inside network 10.0.0.0. And amazingly, at the same time, both companies can even communicate with each other through the Internet.

The technology called Network Address Translation makes it possible for companies to reuse the same IP networks, as shown in Figure 11-13. NAT does this by translating the IP addresses inside the packets as they go from the enterprise to the Internet, using a small number of public IP addresses to support tens of thousands of private IP addresses. That one bit of information is not enough to understand how NAT works; however, to keep the focus on subnetting, the book defers the discussion of how NAT works until *CCNA 200-301 Official Cert Guide, Volume 2*, Second Edition. For now, accept that most companies use NAT, and therefore, they can use private IP networks for their internetworks.

Private IP Networks

When using NAT—and almost every organization that connects to the Internet uses NAT—the company can simply pick one or more of the private IP networks from the list of reserved private IP network numbers. RFC 1918 defines the list of available private IP networks, which is summarized in Table 11-2.

Table 11-2 RFC 1918 Private Address Space

Class of Networks	Private IP Networks	Number of Networks
A	10.0.0.0	1
B	172.16.0.0 through 172.31.0.0	16
C	192.168.0.0 through 192.168.255.0	256

NOTE In each class I teach online, I survey students about who uses network 10.0.0.0 in their company, with an average response of 60–70 percent using private class A network 10.0.0.0.

11

From the perspective of making IPv4 work for the entire world, private IP networks have helped preserve and extend IPv4 and its use in every enterprise and throughout the Internet. In particular, private networks have improved IPv4's implementation worldwide by

- **Avoiding using another organization's public address range for private networks:** Some organizations have a part of their networks that need zero Internet access. The hosts in that part of their network need IP addresses. RFC 1918 suggests that truly private networks—that is, networks with no need for Internet connectivity—use addresses from the RFC 1918 list of private networks.

- **Delaying IPv4 address exhaustion:** To delay the day in which all public IPv4 addresses were assigned to organizations as public addresses, RFC 1918 calls for the use of NAT along with private networks for the addresses internal to an organization.

- **Reducing Internet routers' routing table size:** Using private networks also helps reduce the size of the IP routing tables in Internet routers. For instance, routers in the Internet do not need routes for the private IP networks used inside organizations (in fact, ISPs filter those routes).

Choosing an IP Network During the Design Phase

Today, most organizations use private IP networks along with NAT, which requires a small CIDR block of public addresses. Some companies use a public address block, like a public Class A, B, or C network, per the original plan that would allow each company to have its own unique public network. Some smaller number of companies might use a public CIDR block for all addresses—in effect a subset of a Class A, B, or C network—and subnet that block.

For the purposes of this book, most examples use private IP network numbers. For the design step to choose a network number, just choose a private Class A, B, or C network from the list of RFC 1918 private networks. Regardless, the subnetting math works the same whether you begin with a public or private IP network.

After the choice to use a private IP network has been made, just pick one that has enough IP addresses. You can have a small internetwork and still choose to use private Class A network 10.0.0.0. It might seem wasteful to choose a Class A network that has over 16 million IP addresses, especially if you need only a few hundred. However, there's no penalty or problem with using a private network that is too large for your current or future needs.

Choose the Mask

If design engineers followed the topics in this chapter so far, in order, they would know the following:

- The number of subnets required

- The number of hosts/subnet required

- That a choice was made to use only one mask for all subnets so that all subnets are the same size (same number of hosts/subnet)

- The classful IP network number that will be subnetted

This section completes the design process, at least the parts described in this chapter, by discussing how to choose that one mask to use for all subnets. First, this section examines default masks, used when a network is not subnetted, as a point of comparison. Next, the concept of borrowing host bits to create subnet bits is explored. Finally, this section ends with an example of how to create a subnet mask based on the analysis of the requirements.

Classful IP Networks Before Subnetting

Before an engineer subnets a classful network, the network is a single group of addresses. In other words, the engineer has not yet subdivided the network into many smaller subsets called *subnets*.

When thinking about an unsubnetted classful network, the addresses in a network have only two parts: the **network part** and **host part**. Comparing any two addresses in the classful network:

- The addresses have the same value in the network part.
- The addresses have different values in the host part.

The actual sizes of the network and host parts of the addresses in a network can be easily predicted, as shown in Figure 11-14.

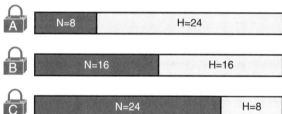

Figure 11-14 *Format of Unsubnetted Class A, B, and C Networks*

In Figure 11-14, N and H represent the number of network and host bits, respectively. Class rules define the number of network octets (1, 2, or 3) for Classes A, B, and C, respectively; the figure shows these values as a number of bits. The number of host octets is 3, 2, or 1, respectively.

Continuing the analysis of a classful network before subnetting, the number of addresses in one classful IP network can be calculated with the same $2^H - 2$ formula previously discussed. In particular, the size of an unsubnetted Class A, B, or C network is as follows:

- Class A: $2^{24} - 2 = 16,777,214$
- Class B: $2^{16} - 2 = 65,534$
- Class C: $2^8 - 2 = 254$

Borrowing Host Bits to Create Subnet Bits

To subnet a network, the designer thinks about the network and host parts, as shown in Figure 11-15, and then the engineer adds a third part in the middle: the **subnet part**. However, the designer cannot change the size of the network part or the size of the entire address (32 bits). To create a subnet part of the address structure, the engineer borrows bits from the host part. Figure 11-15 shows the general idea.

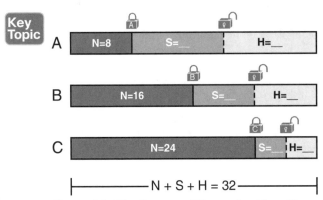

Figure 11-15   *Concept of Borrowing Host Bits*

Figure 11-15 shows a rectangle that represents the subnet mask. N, representing the number of network bits, remains locked at 8, 16, or 24, depending on the class. Conceptually, the designer moves a (dashed) dividing line into the host field, with subnet bits (S) between the network and host parts, and the remaining host bits (H) on the right. The three parts must add up to 32 because IPv4 addresses consist of 32 bits.

Choosing Enough Subnet and Host Bits

The design process requires a choice of where to place the dashed line shown in Figure 11-15. But what is the right choice? How many subnet and host bits should the designer choose? The answers hinge on the requirements gathered in the early stages of the planning process:

- Number of subnets required

- Number of hosts/subnet

The bits in the subnet part create a way to uniquely number the different subnets that the design engineer wants to create. With 1 subnet bit, you can number 2^1 or 2 subnets. With 2 bits, 2^2 or 4 subnets; with 3 bits, 2^3 or 8 subnets; and so on. The number of subnet bits must be large enough to uniquely number all the subnets, as determined during the planning process.

At the same time, the remaining number of host bits must also be large enough to number the host IP addresses in the largest subnet. Remember, in this chapter, we assume the use of a single mask for all subnets. This single mask must support both the required number of subnets and the required number of hosts in the largest subnet. Figure 11-16 shows the concept.

Figure 11-16 shows the idea of the designer choosing a number of subnet (S) and host (H) bits and then checking the math. 2^S must be more than the number of required subnets, or the mask will not supply enough subnets in this IP network. Also, $2^H - 2$ must be more than the required number of hosts/subnet.

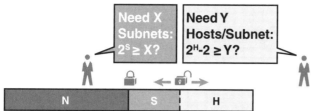

Figure 11-16   *Borrowing Enough Subnet and Host Bits*

NOTE   The idea of calculating the number of subnets as 2^S applies only in cases where a single mask is used for all subnets of a single classful network, as is being assumed in this chapter.

To effectively design masks, or to interpret masks that were chosen by someone else, you need a good working memory of the powers of 2. Appendix A, "Numeric Reference Tables," lists a table with powers of 2 up through 2^{32} for your reference.

Example Design: 172.16.0.0, 200 Subnets, 200 Hosts

To help make sense of the theoretical discussion so far, consider an example that focuses on the design choice for the subnet mask. In this case, the planning and design choices so far tell us the following:

- Use a single mask for all subnets.

- Plan for 200 subnets.

- Plan for 200 host IP addresses per subnet.

- Use private Class B network 172.16.0.0.

To choose the mask, the designer asks this question:

   How many subnet (S) bits do I need to number 200 subnets?

You can see that S = 7 is not large enough ($2^7 = 128$), but S = 8 is enough ($2^8 = 256$). So, you need *at least* 8 subnet bits.

Next, the designer asks a similar question, based on the number of hosts per subnet:

   How many host (H) bits do I need to number 200 hosts per subnet?

The math is basically the same, but the formula subtracts 2 when counting the number of hosts/subnet. You can see that H = 7 is not large enough ($2^7 - 2 = 126$), but H = 8 is enough ($2^8 - 2 = 254$).

Only one possible mask meets all the requirements in this case. First, the number of network bits (N) must be 16 because the design uses a Class B network. The requirements tell us that the mask needs at least 8 subnet bits and at least 8 host bits. The mask has only 32 bits in it; Figure 11-17 shows the resulting mask.

11

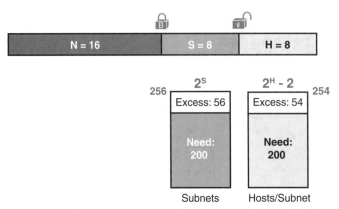

Figure 11-17   *Example Mask Choice, N = 16, S = 8, H = 8*

Masks and Mask Formats

Although engineers think about IP addresses in three parts when making design choices (network, subnet, and host), the subnet mask gives the engineer a way to communicate those design choices to all the devices in the subnet.

The subnet mask is a 32-bit binary number with a number of binary 1s on the left and with binary 0s on the right. By definition, the number of binary 0s equals the number of host bits; in fact, that is exactly how the mask communicates the idea of the size of the host part of the addresses in a subnet. The beginning bits in the mask equal binary 1, with those bit positions representing the combined network and subnet parts of the addresses in the subnet.

Because the network part always comes first, then the subnet part, and then the host part, the subnet mask, in binary form, cannot have interleaved 1s and 0s. Each subnet mask has one unbroken string of binary 1s on the left, with the rest of the bits as binary 0s.

After the engineer chooses the classful network and the number of subnet and host bits in a subnet, creating the binary subnet mask is easy. Just write down N 1s, S 1s, and then H 0s (assuming that N, S, and H represent the number of network, subnet, and host bits). Figure 11-18 shows the mask based on the previous example, which subnets a Class B network by creating 8 subnet bits, leaving 8 host bits.

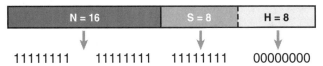

11111111   11111111   11111111   00000000

Figure 11-18   *Creating the Subnet Mask—Binary—Class B Network*

In addition to the binary mask shown in Figure 11-18, masks can also be written in two other formats: the familiar **dotted-decimal notation** (DDN) seen in IP addresses and an even briefer *prefix* notation. Chapter 13 discusses these formats and how to convert between the different formats.

Build a List of All Subnets

Building a list of all subnets, the final task of the subnet design step, determines the actual subnets that can be used, based on all the earlier choices. The earlier design work determined the Class A, B, or C network to use, and the (one) subnet mask to use that supplies enough subnets and enough host IP addresses per subnet. But what are those subnets? How do you identify or describe a subnet? This section answers these questions.

A subnet consists of a group of consecutive numbers. Most of these numbers can be used as IP addresses by hosts. However, each subnet reserves the first and last numbers in the group, and these two numbers cannot be used as IP addresses. In particular, each subnet contains the following:

- **Subnet number:** Also called the *subnet ID* or *subnet address*, this number identifies the subnet. It is the numerically smallest number in the subnet. It cannot be used as an IP address by a host.

- **Subnet broadcast:** Also called the *subnet broadcast address* or *directed broadcast address*, this is the last (numerically highest) number in the subnet. It also cannot be used as an IP address by a host.

- **IP addresses:** All the numbers between the subnet ID and the subnet broadcast address can be used as a host IP address.

For example, consider the earlier case in which the design results were as follows:

Network	172.16.0.0 (Class B)
Mask	255.255.255.0 (for all subnets)

With some math, the facts about each subnet that exists in this Class B network can be calculated. In this case, Table 11-3 shows the first ten such subnets. It then skips many subnets and shows the last two (numerically largest) subnets.

Table 11-3   First Ten Subnets, Plus the Last Few, from 172.16.0.0, 255.255.255.0

Subnet Number	IP Addresses	Broadcast Address
172.16.0.0	172.16.0.1 – 172.16.0.254	172.16.0.255
172.16.1.0	172.16.1.1 – 172.16.1.254	172.16.1.255
172.16.2.0	172.16.2.1 – 172.16.2.254	172.16.2.255
172.16.3.0	172.16.3.1 – 172.16.3.254	172.16.3.255
172.16.4.0	172.16.4.1 – 172.16.4.254	172.16.4.255
172.16.5.0	172.16.5.1 – 172.16.5.254	172.16.5.255
172.16.6.0	172.16.6.1 – 172.16.6.254	172.16.6.255
172.16.7.0	172.16.7.1 – 172.16.7.254	172.16.7.255
172.16.8.0	172.16.8.1 – 172.16.8.254	172.16.8.255
172.16.9.0	172.16.9.1 – 172.16.9.254	172.16.9.255
Skipping many…		
172.16.254.0	172.16.254.1 – 172.16.254.254	172.16.254.255
172.16.255.0	172.16.255.1 – 172.16.255.254	172.16.255.255

11

After you have the network number and the mask, calculating the subnet IDs and other details for all subnets requires some math. In real life, most people use subnet calculators or subnet-planning tools. For the CCNA exam, you need to be ready to find this kind of information, as discussed in Chapter 15, "Subnet Design."

Plan the Implementation

The next step, planning the implementation, is the last step before actually configuring the devices to create a subnet. The engineer first needs to choose where to use each subnet. For example, at a branch office in a particular city, which subnet from the subnet planning chart (Table 11-3) should be used for each VLAN at that site? Also, for any interfaces that require static IP addresses, which addresses should be used in each case? Finally, what range of IP addresses from inside each subnet should be configured in the DHCP server, to be dynamically leased to hosts for use as their IP address? Figure 11-19 summarizes the list of implementation planning tasks.

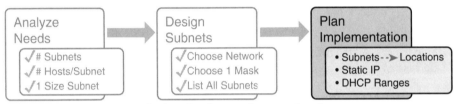

Figure 11-19 *Facts Supplied to the Plan Implementation Step*

Assigning Subnets to Different Locations

The job is simple: Look at your network diagram, identify each location that needs a subnet, and pick one from the table you made of all the possible subnets. Then, track it so that you know which ones you use where, using a spreadsheet or some other purpose-built subnet-planning tool. That's it! Figure 11-20 shows a sample of a completed design using Table 11-3, which happens to match the initial design sample shown way back in Figure 11-1.

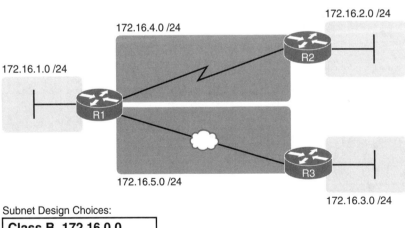

Figure 11-20 *Example of Subnets Assigned to Different Locations*

Although this design could have used any five subnets from Table 11-3, in real networks, engineers usually give more thought to some strategy for assigning subnets. For example, you might assign all LAN subnets lower numbers and WAN subnets higher numbers. Or you might slice off large ranges of subnets for different divisions of the company. Or you might follow that same strategy but ignore organizational divisions in the company, paying more attention to geographies.

For example, for a U.S.-based company with a smaller presence in both Europe and Asia, you might plan to reserve ranges of subnets based on continent. This kind of choice is particularly useful when later trying to use a feature called route summarization. Figure 11-21 shows the general benefit of placing addressing in the network for easier route summarization, using the same subnets from Table 11-3 again.

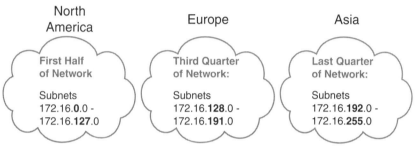

Figure 11-21 *Reserving 50 Percent of Subnets for North America and 25 Percent Each for Europe and Asia*

Choose Static and Dynamic Ranges per Subnet

Devices receive their IP address and mask assignment in one of two ways: dynamically by using Dynamic Host Configuration Protocol (DHCP) or statically through configuration. For DHCP to work, the network engineer must tell the DHCP server the subnets for which it must assign IP addresses. In addition, that configuration limits the DHCP server to only a subset of the addresses in the subnet. For static addresses, you simply configure the device to tell it what IP address and mask to use.

To keep things as simple as possible, most shops use a strategy to separate the static IP addresses on one end of each subnet, and the DHCP-assigned dynamic addresses on the other. It does not really matter whether the static addresses sit on the low end of the range of addresses or the high end.

For example, imagine that the engineer decides that, for the LAN subnets in Figure 11-20, the DHCP pool comes from the high end of the range, namely, addresses that end in .101 through .254. (The address that ends in .255 is, of course, reserved.) The engineer also assigns static addresses from the lower end, with addresses ending in .1 through .100. Figure 11-22 shows the idea.

11

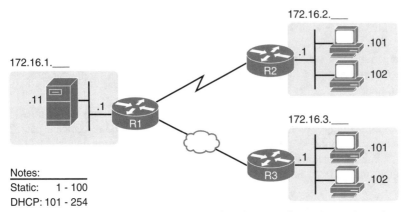

172.16.1.___

172.16.2.___

.101

.102

172.16.3.___

.101

.102

Notes:
Static: 1 - 100
DHCP: 101 - 254

Figure 11-22   *Static from the Low End and DHCP from the High End*

Figure 11-22 shows all three routers with statically assigned IP addresses that end in .1. The only other static IP address in the figure is assigned to the server on the left, with address 172.16.1.11 (abbreviated simply as .11 in the figure).

On the right, each LAN has two PCs that use DHCP to dynamically lease their IP addresses. DHCP servers often begin by leasing the addresses at the bottom of the range of addresses, so in each LAN, the hosts have leased addresses that end in .101 and .102, which are at the low end of the range chosen by design.

Chapter Review

One key to doing well on the exams is to perform repetitive spaced review sessions. Review this chapter's material using either the tools in the book or interactive tools for the same material found on the book's companion website. Refer to the "Your Study Plan" element for more details. Table 11-4 outlines the key review elements and where you can find them. To better track your study progress, record when you completed these activities in the second column.

Table 11-4   Chapter Review Tracking

Review Element	Review Date(s)	Resource Used
Review key topics		Book, website
Review key terms		Book, website
Answer DIKTA questions		Book, PTP
Review memory tables		Website

Review All the Key Topics

Table 11-5   Key Topics for Chapter 11

Key Topic Element	Description	Page Number
List	Key facts about subnets	304
List	Rules about what places in a network topology need a subnet	305
Figure 11-7	Locations of the network, subnet, and host parts of an IPv4 address	308
List	Features that extended the life of IPv4	312
List	Motivations for using private IP networks	314
Figure 11-14	Formats of Class A, B, and C addresses when not subnetted	315
Figure 11-15	Formats of Class A, B, and C addresses when subnetted	316
Figure 11-16	General logic when choosing the size of the subnet and host parts of addresses in a subnet	317
List	Items that together define a subnet	319

Key Terms You Should Know

classful IP network, dotted-decimal notation, host part, network, network part, private IP network, public IP network, subnet, subnet mask, subnet part, variable-length subnet masks (VLSM)

11

CHAPTER 12

Analyzing Classful IPv4 Networks

This chapter covers the following exam topics:

1.0 Network Fundamentals

    1.6 Configure and verify IPv4 addressing and subnetting

    1.7 Describe private IPv4 addressing

When operating a network, you often start investigating a problem based on an IP address and mask. Based on the IP address alone, you should be able to determine several facts about the Class A, B, or C network in which the IP address resides.

This chapter lists the key facts about classful IP networks and explains how to discover these facts. Following that, this chapter lists some practice problems. Before moving to the next chapter, you should practice until you can consistently determine all these facts, quickly and confidently, based on an IP address.

"Do I Know This Already?" Quiz

Take the quiz (either here or use the PTP software) if you want to use the score to help you decide how much time to spend on this chapter. The letter answers are listed at the bottom of the page following the quiz. Appendix C, found both at the end of the book as well as on the companion website, includes both the answers and explanations. You can also find both answers and explanations in the PTP testing software.

Table 12-1 "Do I Know This Already?" Foundation Topics Section-to-Question Mapping

Foundation Topics Section	Questions
Classful Network Concepts	1–5

1. Which of the following are not valid Class A network IDs? (Choose two answers.)

    a. 1.0.0.0

    b. 130.0.0.0

    c. 127.0.0.0

    d. 9.0.0.0

2. Which of the following are not valid Class B network IDs?

    a. 130.0.0.0

    b. 191.255.0.0

    c. 128.0.0.0

    d. 150.255.0.0

    e. All are valid Class B network IDs.

3. Which of the following are true about IP address 172.16.99.45's IP network? (Choose two answers.)

   a. The network ID is 172.0.0.0.

   b. The network is a Class B network.

   c. The default mask for the network is 255.255.255.0.

   d. The number of host bits in the unsubnetted network is 16.

4. Which of the following are true about IP address 192.168.6.7's IP network? (Choose two answers.)

   a. The network ID is 192.168.6.0.

   b. The network is a Class B network.

   c. The default mask for the network is 255.255.255.0.

   d. The number of host bits in the unsubnetted network is 16.

5. Which of the following is a network broadcast address?

   a. 10.1.255.255

   b. 192.168.255.1

   c. 224.1.1.255

   d. 172.30.255.255

Foundation Topics

Classful Network Concepts

Imagine that you have a job interview for your first IT job. As part of the interview, you're given an IPv4 address and mask: 10.4.5.99, 255.255.255.0. What can you tell the interviewer about the classful **network** (in this case, the Class A network) in which the IP address resides?

This section, the first of two major sections in this chapter, reviews the concepts of **classful IP networks** (in other words, Class A, B, and C networks). In particular, this chapter examines how to begin with a single IP address and then determine the following facts:

- Class (A, B, or C)

- Default mask

- Number of network octets/bits

- Number of host octets/bits

- Number of host addresses in the network

- Network ID

- Network broadcast address

- First and last usable address in the network

Before getting into this chapter's processes, the text first discusses the context. Analyzing Class A, B, and C networks has a valuable purpose, and it remains an important skill—but it might not be as useful in some networks. This section begins by setting that context regarding public networks, large public CIDR blocks, and small public CIDR blocks. Then the rest of the section dives into finding all the facts about the classful IP network an address would reside in if the assignment process still assigned the entire Class A, B, or C network.

Setting the Context of Public Networks and CIDR Blocks

As discussed in Chapter 11, "Perspectives on IPv4 Subnetting," the original plan called for every organization to register for and use a public IP network of one of three classes: A, B, or C. That approach existed in the 1980s up through the 2010s when the Regional Internet Registries (RIRs) assigned their final IP **network numbers**. Even with the RIRs exhausting their supply of IPv4 addresses, companies that received assignments for a public Class A, B, or C network continue to use them. Figure 12-1 shows a conceptual diagram with some Class A networks that could still be used today.

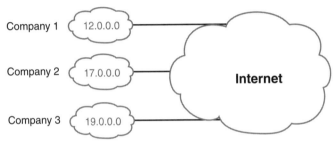

Figure 12-1   *Concept: Companies Using Separate Public Class A Networks*

One of the address conservation options that emerged in the 1990s called for using more than the three set sizes of Class A, B, and C networks, instead allowing for any block size that is a power of 2. Starting in that decade, the Internet Assigned Numbers Authority (IANA), the global owner of the address space, along with the five RIRs, began assigning public *classless interdomain routing (CIDR) blocks*. Doing so allowed companies to receive assignments that did not waste as many addresses.

For instance, instead of assigning public network 1.0.0.0 to one company, an RIR could subdivide that network into smaller blocks that followed some simple rules. For instance, each block has to include a power of 2 number of addresses. Figure 12-2 shows the concept, with three other companies receiving assignments of public CIDR blocks that look like subsets of former Class A network 1.0.0.0.

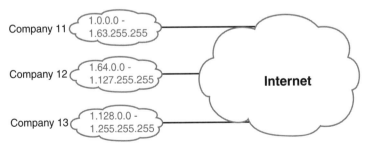

Figure 12-2   *Concept: Companies Using Public CIDR Blocks*

Answers to the "Do I Know This Already?" quiz:

1 B, C **2** E **3** B, D **4** A, C **5** D

A company using a large public **CIDR block** implements it like a public Class A, B, or C network. Whether starting with a public Class A, B, or C network, or a public CIDR block, the company has one large block of public addresses. The company can then create a subnetting plan to subdivide the large block further, picking which subnets to use in each location. All the hosts in the network use an address from the large public address block.

Over time, a third option emerged that used even fewer public addresses—and it became the most popular option. A company uses a private IP network to address all the hosts within the company. The company also needs a small public CIDR block, while using NAT to translate addresses for packets that flow to and from the Internet. Often, a block of 4, 8, or 16 addresses gives even a large company plenty of public IP address capacity to use with NAT. All companies can use any private IP network for hosts inside the company, as shown in Figure 12-3.

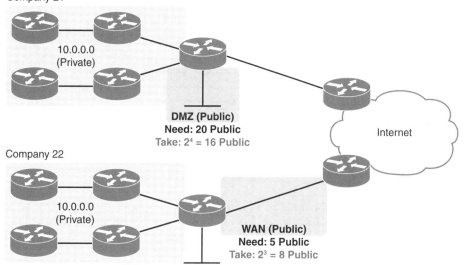

Figure 12-3   *Concept: Small CIDR Block with Private IP Network*

Now back to the main point of this chapter, which focuses on processes to find key facts about Class A, B, and C networks, when starting with a **unicast IP address**. Regardless of whether the address happens to be from a public classful network, a public CIDR block, or a private classful network, learning the processes in this chapter will help you in your journey to understand networks and subnetting math. Most of you will use these foundational skills at your company or your clients' companies, and it helps prepare you for the exam.

To complete the discussion of the context, be aware that if you start with one public IP address, you cannot tell from that address whether it comes from a public classful network or a public CIDR block. However, this chapter focuses on determining the facts about a Class A, B, or C network, assuming it comes from a public IP network rather than a public CIDR block. Now on to the math and processes!

NOTE   You can discover if a public unicast address is part of a public classful network assignment, or a public CIDR block, with a search of WHOIS records. As for the process, go to ARIN's WHOIS search page (https://search.arin.net/rdap/), with a search for any public IP address. For example, on that page, a search for 17.1.1.1 reveals an address block of 17.0.0.0/8. As you will learn in this chapter and the next, the 17.0.0.0/8 notation represents Class A network 17.0.0.0, meaning that the 17.1.1.1 address comes from a public Class A assignment.

IPv4 Network Classes and Related Facts

IP version 4 (IPv4) defines five address classes. Three of the classes, Classes A, B, and C, consist of unicast IP addresses. Unicast addresses identify a single host or interface so that the address uniquely identifies the device. Class D addresses serve as multicast addresses, so that one packet sent to a Class D multicast IPv4 address can actually be delivered to multiple hosts. Finally, Class E addresses were originally intended for experimentation but were changed to simply be reserved for future use. The class can be identified based on the value of the first octet of the address, as shown in Table 12-2.

Table 12-2   IPv4 Address Classes Based on First Octet Values

Class	First Octet Values	Purpose
A	1–126	Unicast (large networks)
B	128–191	Unicast (medium-sized networks)
C	192–223	Unicast (small networks)
D	224–239	Multicast
E	240–255	Reserved (formerly experimental)

After you identify the class of a unicast address as either A, B, or C, many other related facts can be derived just through memorization. Table 12-3 lists that information for reference and later study; each of these concepts is described in this chapter.

Table 12-3   Key Facts for Classes A, B, and C

	Class A	Class B	Class C
First octet range	1–126	128–191	192–223
Valid network numbers	1.0.0.0–126.0.0.0	128.0.0.0–191.255.0.0	192.0.0.0–223.255.255.0
Total networks	$2^7 - 2 = 126$	$2^{14} = 16,384$	$2^{21} = 2,097,152$
Hosts per network	$2^{24} - 2$	$2^{16} - 2$	$2^8 - 2$
Octets (bits) in network part	1 (8)	2 (16)	3 (24)
Octets (bits) in host part	3 (24)	2 (16)	1 (8)
Default mask	255.0.0.0	255.255.0.0	255.255.255.0

Note that the address ranges of all addresses that begin with 0 and all addresses that begin with 127 are reserved. Had they not been reserved since the creation of Class A networks, as listed in RFC 791 (published in 1981), then they might have been known as Class A networks

0.0.0.0 and 127.0.0.0. Because they are reserved, however, the address space has 126 Class A networks, and not 128. Also, note that there are no similar reserved ranges to begin/end the Class B and C ranges.

In addition to the reservation of what would be Class A networks 0.0.0.0 and 127.0.0.0 for other purposes, other newer RFCs have also reserved small pieces of the Class A, B, and C address space. So, tables like Table 12-3, with the count of the numbers of Class A, B, and C networks, are a good place to get a sense of the size of the number; however, the number of reserved networks does change slightly over time (albeit slowly) based on these other reserved address ranges.

NOTE   If you are interested in seeing all the reserved IPv4 address ranges, just do an Internet search on "IANA IPv4 special-purpose address registry."

The Number and Size of the Class A, B, and C Networks

Table 12-3 lists the range of Class A, B, and C network numbers; however, some key points can be lost just referencing a table of information. This section examines the Class A, B, and C network numbers, focusing on the more important points and the exceptions and unusual cases.

First, the number of networks from each class significantly differs. Only 126 Class A networks exist: network 1.0.0.0, 2.0.0.0, 3.0.0.0, and so on, up through network 126.0.0.0. However, 16,384 Class B networks exist, with more than 2 million Class C networks.

Next, note that the size of networks from each class also significantly differs. Each Class A network is relatively large—over 16 million host IP addresses per network—so they were originally intended to be used by the largest companies and organizations. Class B networks are smaller, with over 65,000 hosts per network. Finally, Class C networks, intended for small organizations, have 254 hosts in each network. Figure 12-4 summarizes those facts.

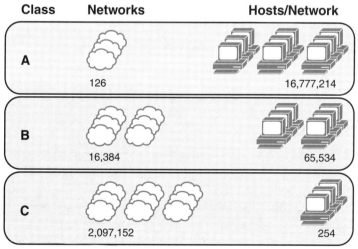

Figure 12-4   *Numbers and Sizes of Class A, B, and C Networks*

Address Formats

In some cases, an engineer might need to think about a Class A, B, or C network as if the network has not been subdivided through the subnetting process. In such a case, the addresses in the classful network have a structure with two parts: the **network part** (sometimes called the *prefix*) and the **host part**. Then, comparing any two IP addresses in one network, the following observations can be made:

The addresses in the same network have the same values in the network part.

The addresses in the same network have different values in the host part.

For example, in Class A network 10.0.0.0, by definition, the network part consists of the first octet. As a result, all addresses have an equal value in the network part, namely a 10 in the first octet. If you then compare any two addresses in the network, the addresses have a different value in the last three octets (the host octets). For example, IP addresses 10.1.1.1 and 10.1.1.2 have the same value (10) in the network part, but different values in the host part.

Figure 12-5 shows the format and sizes (in number of bits) of the network and host parts of IP addresses in Class A, B, and C networks, before any subnetting has been applied.

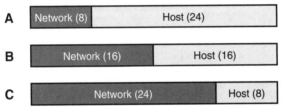

Figure 12-5 *Sizes (Bits) of the Network and Host Parts of Unsubnetted Classful Networks*

Default Masks

Although we humans can easily understand the concepts behind Figure 12-5, computers prefer numbers. To communicate those same ideas to computers, each network class has an associated **default mask** that defines the size of the network and host parts of an unsubnetted Class A, B, and C network. To do so, the mask lists binary 1s for the bits considered to be in the network part and binary 0s for the bits considered to be in the host part.

For example, Class A network 10.0.0.0 has a network part of the first single octet (8 bits) and a host part of the last three octets (24 bits). As a result, the Class A default mask is 255.0.0.0, which in binary is

11111111 00000000 00000000 00000000

Figure 12-6 shows default masks for each network class, both in binary and dotted-decimal format.

NOTE Decimal 255 converts to the binary value 11111111. Decimal 0, converted to 8-bit binary, is 00000000. See Appendix A, "Numeric Reference Tables," for a conversion table.

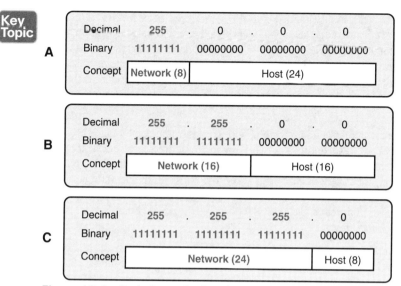

Figure 12-6 *Default Masks for Classes A, B, and C*

Number of Hosts per Network

Calculating the number of hosts per network requires some basic binary math. First, consider a case where you have a single binary digit. How many unique values are there? There are, of course, two values: 0 and 1. With 2 bits, you can make four combinations: 00, 01, 10, and 11. As it turns out, the total combination of unique values you can make with N bits is 2^N.

Host addresses—the IP addresses assigned to hosts—must be unique. The host bits exist for the purpose of giving each host a unique IP address by virtue of having a different value in the host part of the addresses. So, with H host bits, 2^H unique combinations exist.

However, the number of hosts in a network is not 2^H; instead, it is $2^H - 2$. Each network reserves two numbers that would have otherwise been useful as host addresses but have instead been reserved for special use: one for the **network ID** and one for the **network broadcast address**. As a result, the formula to calculate the number of host addresses per Class A, B, or C network is

$$2^H - 2$$

where *H* is the number of host bits.

Deriving the Network ID and Related Numbers

Each classful network has four key numbers that describe the network. You can derive these four numbers if you start with just one IP address in the network. The numbers are as follows:

- Network number
- First (numerically lowest) usable address
- Last (numerically highest) usable address
- Network broadcast address

First, consider both the network number and first usable IP address. The *network number*, also called the *network ID* or **network address**, identifies the network. By definition, the network number is the numerically lowest number in the network. However, to prevent any ambiguity, the people who made up IP addressing added the restriction that the network number cannot be assigned as an IP address. So, the lowest number in the network is the network ID. Then, the first (numerically lowest) host IP address is *one larger than* the network number.

Next, consider the network broadcast address along with the last (numerically highest) usable IP address. The TCP/IP RFCs define a network broadcast address as a special address in each network. This broadcast address could be used as the destination address in a packet, and the routers would forward a copy of that one packet to all hosts in that classful network. Numerically, a network broadcast address is always the highest (last) number in the network. As a result, the highest (last) number usable as an IP address is the address that is *one less than* the network broadcast address.

Simply put, if you can find the network number and network broadcast address, finding the first and last usable IP addresses in the network is easy. For the exam, you should be able to find all four values with ease; the process is as follows:

Step 1.   Determine the class (A, B, or C) based on the first octet.

Step 2.   Mentally divide the network and host octets based on the class.

Step 3.   To find the network number, change the IP address's host octets to 0.

Step 4.   To find the first address, add 1 to the fourth octet of the network ID.

Step 5.   To find the broadcast address, change the network ID's host octets to 255.

Step 6.   To find the last address, subtract 1 from the fourth octet of the network broadcast address.

The written process actually looks harder than it is. Figure 12-7 shows an example of the process, using Class A IP address 10.17.18.21, with the circled numbers matching the process.

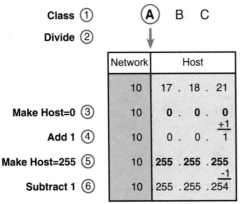

Figure 12-7   *Example of Deriving the Network ID and Other Values from 10.17.18.21*

Figure 12-7 shows the identification of the class as Class A (Step 1) and the number of network/host octets as 1 and 3, respectively. So, to find the network ID at Step 3, the figure copies only the first octet, setting the last three (host) octets to 0. At Step 4, just copy the network ID and add 1 to the fourth octet. Similarly, to find the broadcast address at Step 5, copy the network octets but set the host octets to 255. Then, at Step 6, subtract 1 from the fourth octet to find the last (numerically highest) usable IP address.

Just to show an alternative example, consider IP address 172.16.8.9. Figure 12-8 shows the process applied to this IP address.

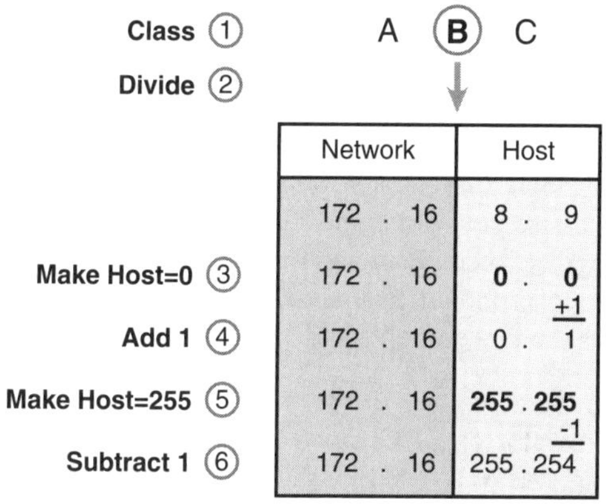

Figure 12-8 *Example Deriving the Network ID and Other Values from 172.16.8.9*

Figure 12-8 shows the identification of the class as Class B (Step 1) and the number of network/host octets as 2 and 2, respectively. So, to find the network ID at Step 3, the figure copies only the first two octets, setting the last two (host) octets to 0. Similarly, Step 5 shows the same action, but with the last two (host) octets being set to 255.

Unusual Network IDs and Network Broadcast Addresses

Some of the more unusual numbers in and around the range of Class A, B, and C network numbers can cause some confusion. This section lists some examples of numbers that make many people make the wrong assumptions about the meaning of the number.

For Class A, the first odd fact is that the range of values in the first octet omits the numbers 0 and 127. As it turns out, what would be Class A network 0.0.0.0 was originally reserved for some broadcasting requirements, so all addresses that begin with 0 in the first octet are reserved. What would be Class A network 127.0.0.0 is still reserved because of a special address used in software testing, called the loopback address (127.0.0.1).

For Class B (and C), some of the network numbers can look odd, particularly if you fall into a habit of thinking that 0s at the end mean the number is a network ID, and 255s at the end mean it's a network broadcast address. First, Class B network numbers range from 128.0.0.0 to 191.255.0.0, for a total of 2^{14} networks. However, even the first (lowest number) Class B network number (128.0.0.0) looks a little like a Class A network number because it ends with three 0s. However, the first octet is 128, making it a Class B network with a two-octet network part (128.0).

For another Class B example, the high end of the Class B range also might look strange at first glance (191.255.0.0), but this is indeed the numerically highest of the valid Class B network numbers. This network's broadcast address, 191.255.255.255, might look a little like a Class A broadcast address because of the three 255s at the end, but it is indeed the broadcast address of a Class B network.

Similarly to Class B networks, some of the valid Class C network numbers do look strange. For example, Class C network 192.0.0.0 looks a little like a Class A network because of the last three octets being 0, but because it is a Class C network, it consists of all addresses that begin with three octets equal to 192.0.0. Similarly, 223.255.255.0, another valid Class C network, consists of all addresses that begin with 223.255.255.

Practice with Classful Networks

As with all areas of IP addressing and subnetting, you need to practice to be ready for the CCNA exam. You should practice some while reading this chapter to make sure that you understand the processes. At that point, you can use your notes and this book as a reference, with a goal of understanding the process. After that, keep practicing this and all the other subnetting processes. Before you take the exam, you should be able to always get the right answer, and with speed. Table 12-4 summarizes the key concepts and suggestions for this two-phase approach.

Table 12-4 Keep-Reading and Take-Exam Goals for This Chapter's Topics

Time Frame	After Reading This Chapter	Before Taking the Exam
Focus on...	Learning how	Being correct and fast
Tools Allowed	All	Your brain and a notepad
Goal: Accuracy	90% correct	100% correct
Goal: Speed	Any speed	10 seconds

Practice Deriving Key Facts Based on an IP Address

Practice finding the various facts that can be derived from an IP address, as discussed throughout this chapter. To do so, complete Table 12-5.

Table 12-5 Practice Problems: Find the Network ID and Network Broadcast

	IP Address	Class	Network Octets	Host Octets	Network ID	Network Broadcast Address
1	1.1.1.1					
2	128.1.6.5					
3	200.1.2.3					
4	192.192.1.1					
5	126.5.4.3					
6	200.1.9.8					
7	192.0.0.1					
8	191.255.1.47					
9	223.223.0.1					

The answers are listed in the section "Answers to Earlier Practice Problems," later in this chapter.

Practice Remembering the Details of Address Classes

Tables 12-2 and 12-3, shown earlier in this chapter, summarized some key information about IPv4 address classes. Tables 12-6 and 12-7 show sparse versions of these same tables. To practice recalling those key facts, particularly the range of values in the first octet that identifies the address class, complete these tables. Then, refer to Tables 12-2 and 12-3 to check your answers. Repeat this process until you can recall all the information in the tables.

Table 12-6   Sparse Study Table Version of Table 12-2

Class	First Octet Values	Purpose
A		
B		
C		
D		
E		

Table 12-7   Sparse Study Table Version of Table 12-3

	Class A	Class B	Class C
First octet range			
Valid network numbers			
Total networks			
Hosts per network			
Octets (bits) in network part			
Octets (bits) in host part			
Default mask			

Chapter Review

One key to doing well on the exams is to perform repetitive spaced review sessions. Review this chapter's material using either the tools in the book or interactive tools for the same material found on the book's companion website. Refer to the "Your Study Plan" element for more details. Table 12-8 outlines the key review elements and where you can find them. To better track your study progress, record when you completed these activities in the second column.

Table 12-8   Chapter Review Tracking

Review Element	Review Date(s)	Resource Used
Review key topics		Book, website
Review key terms		Book, website
Answer DIKTA questions		Book, PTP
Review memory tables		Website

Review Element	Review Date(s)	Resource Used
Practice analyzing classful IPv4 networks		Website, Appendix D
Watch video		Website

Review All the Key Topics

Table 12-9   Key Topics for Chapter 12

Key Topic Elements	Description	Page Number
Table 12-2	Address classes	328
Table 12-3	Key facts about Class A, B, and C networks	328
List	Comparisons of network and host parts of addresses in the same classful network	330
Figure 12-6	Default masks	331
Paragraph	Function to calculate the number of hosts per network	331
List	Steps to find information about a classful network	332

Key Terms You Should Know

CIDR block, classful IP network, default mask, host part, network, network address, network broadcast address, network ID, network number, network part, unicast IP address

Additional Practice for This Chapter's Processes

For additional practice with analyzing classful networks, you may do a set of practice problems using your choice of tools:

Application: From the companion website, in the section titled "Memory Tables and Practice Exercises," use the "Practice Exercise: Analyzing Classful IPv4 Networks."

PDF: Practice the same problems using companion website Appendix D, "Practice for Chapter 12: Analyzing Classful IPv4 Networks."

Answers to Earlier Practice Problems

Table 12-5, shown earlier, listed several practice problems. Table 12-10 lists the answers.

Table 12-10   Practice Problems: Find the Network ID and Network Broadcast

	IP Address	Class	Network Octets	Host Octets	Network ID	Network Broadcast
1	1.1.1.1	A	1	3	1.0.0.0	1.255.255.255
2	128.1.6.5	B	2	2	128.1.0.0	128.1.255.255
3	200.1.2.3	C	3	1	200.1.2.0	200.1.2.255
4	192.192.1.1	C	3	1	192.192.1.0	192.192.1.255
5	126.5.4.3	A	1	3	126.0.0.0	126.255.255.255

	IP Address	Class	Network Octets	Host Octets	Network ID	Network Broadcast
6	200.1.9.8	C	3	1	200.1.9.0	200.1.9.255
7	192.0.0.1	C	3	1	192.0.0.0	192.0.0.255
8	191.255.1.47	B	2	2	191.255.0.0	191.255.255.255
9	223.223.0.1	C	3	1	223.223.0.0	223.223.0.255

The class, number of network octets, and number of host octets all require you to look at the first octet of the IP address to determine the class. If a value is between 1 and 126, inclusive, the address is a Class A address, with one network and three host octets. If a value is between 128 and 191 inclusive, the address is a Class B address, with two network and two host octets. If a value is between 192 and 223, inclusive, it is a Class C address, with three network octets and one host octet.

The last two columns can be found based on Table 12-3, specifically the number of network and host octets along with the IP address. To find the network ID, copy the IP address, but change the host octets to 0. Similarly, to find the network broadcast address, copy the IP address, but change the host octets to 255.

The last three problems can be confusing and were included on purpose so that you could see an example of these unusual cases, as follows.

Answers to Practice Problem 7 (from Table 12-5)

Consider IP address 192.0.0.1. First, 192 is on the lower edge of the first octet range for Class C; as such, this address has three network octets and one host octet. To find the network ID, copy the address, but change the single host octet (the fourth octet) to 0, for a network ID of 192.0.0.0. It looks strange, but it is indeed the network ID.

The network broadcast address choice for problem 7 can also look strange. To find the broadcast address, copy the IP address (192.0.0.1), but change the last octet (the only host octet) to 255, for a broadcast address of 192.0.0.255. In particular, if you decide that the broadcast should be 192.255.255.255, you might have fallen into the trap of logic, like "Change all 0s in the network ID to 255s," which is not the correct logic. Instead, change all host octets in the IP address (or network ID) to 255s.

Answers to Practice Problem 8 (from Table 12-5)

The first octet of problem 8 (191.255.1.47) sits on the upper edge of the Class B range for the first octet (128–191). As such, to find the network ID, change the last two octets (host octets) to 0, for a network ID of 191.255.0.0. This value sometimes gives people problems because they are used to thinking that 255 somehow means the number is a broadcast address.

The broadcast address, found by changing the two host octets to 255, means that the broadcast address is 191.255.255.255. It looks more like a broadcast address for a Class A network, but it is actually the broadcast address for Class B network 191.255.0.0.

Answers to Practice Problem 9 (from Table 12-5)

Problem 9, with IP address 223.223.0.1, is near the high end of the Class C range. As a result, only the last (host) octet is changed to 0 to form the network ID 223.223.0.0. It looks a little like a Class B network number at first glance because it ends in two octets of 0. However, it is indeed a Class C network ID (based on the value in the first octet).

CHAPTER 13

Analyzing Subnet Masks

This chapter covers the following exam topics:

1.0 Network Fundamentals

    1.6 Configure and verify IPv4 addressing and subnetting

The subnet mask used in one or many subnets in an IP internetwork says a lot about the intent of the subnet design. First, the mask divides addresses into two parts: *prefix* and *host*, with the host part defining the size of the subnet (that is, the number of hosts in the subnet). Then, the class (A, B, or C) further divides the structure of addresses in a subnet, breaking the prefix part into the *network* and *subnet* parts. The subnet part defines the number of subnets that could exist inside one classful IP network, assuming that one mask is used throughout the classful network.

The subnet mask holds the key to understanding several important subnetting design points. However, to analyze a subnet mask, you first need some basic math skills with masks. The math converts masks between the three different formats used to represent a mask:

- Binary

- Dotted-decimal notation (DDN)

- Prefix (also called classless interdomain routing [CIDR])

This chapter has two major sections. The first focuses on the mask formats and the math used to convert between the three formats. The second section explains how to take an IP address and its subnet mask and analyze those values. In particular, it shows how to determine the three-part format of the IPv4 address and describes the facts about the subnetting design that are implied by the mask.

> **NOTE** The majority of the chapter assumes subnetting of a Class A, B, or C network. The end of the chapter provides some discussion of the similar case of subnetting a public CIDR block.

"Do I Know This Already?" Quiz

Take the quiz (either here or use the PTP software) if you want to use the score to help you decide how much time to spend on this chapter. The letter answers are listed at the bottom of the page following the quiz. Appendix C, found both at the end of the book as well as on the companion website, includes both the answers and explanations. You can also find both answers and explanations in the PTP testing software.

Table 13-1 "Do I Know This Already?" Foundation Topics Section-to-Question Mapping

Foundation Topics Section	Questions
Subnet Mask Conversion	1–3
Identifying Subnet Design Choices Using Masks	4–7

1. Which of the following answers lists the prefix (CIDR) format equivalent of 255.255.254.0?

   a. /19

   b. /20

   c. /23

   d. /24

   e. /25

2. Which of the following answers lists the prefix (CIDR) format equivalent of 255.255.255.240?

   a. /26

   b. /28

   c. /27

   d. /30

   e. /29

3. Which of the following answers lists the dotted-decimal notation (DDN) equivalent of /30?

   a. 255.255.255.192

   b. 255.255.255.252

   c. 255.255.255.240

   d. 255.255.254.0

   e. 255.255.255.0

4. Working at the help desk, you receive a call and learn a user's PC IP address and mask (10.55.66.77, mask 255.255.255.0). When thinking about this using classful logic, you determine the number of network (N), subnet (S), and host (H) bits. Which of the following is true in this case?

   a. N=12

   b. S=12

   c. H=8

   d. S=8

   e. N=24

5. Working at the help desk, you receive a call and learn a user's PC IP address and mask (192.168.9.1/27). When thinking about this using classful logic, you determine the number of network (N), subnet (S), and host (H) bits. Which of the following is true in this case?

   a. N=24

   b. S=24

     c. H=8

     d. H=7

  6. Which of the following statements is true about classless IP addressing concepts?

     a. Uses a 128-bit IP address

     b. Applies only for Class A and B networks

     c. Separates IP addresses into network, subnet, and host parts

     d. Ignores Class A, B, and C network rules

  7. Which of the following masks, when used as the only mask within a Class B network, would supply enough subnet bits to support 100 subnets? (Choose two answers.)

     a. /24

     b. 255.255.255.252

     c. /20

     d. 255.255.252.0

Foundation Topics

Subnet Mask Conversion

This section describes how to convert between different formats for the subnet mask. You can then use these processes when you practice. If you already know how to convert from one format to the other, go ahead and move to the section "Practice Converting Subnet Masks," later in this chapter.

Three Mask Formats

Subnet masks can be written as 32-bit binary numbers, but not just any binary number. In particular, the binary subnet mask must follow these rules:

- The value must not interleave 1s and 0s.

- If 1s exist, they are on the left.

- If 0s exist, they are on the right.

For example, the following values would be illegal. The first is illegal because the value interleaves 0s and 1s, and the second is illegal because it lists 0s on the left and 1s on the right:

```
10101010 01010101 11110000 00001111
00000000 00000000 00000000 11111111
```

The following two binary values meet the requirements, in that they have all 1s on the left, followed by all 0s, with no interleaving of 1s and 0s:

```
11111111 00000000 00000000 00000000
11111111 11111111 11111111 00000000
```

Two alternative subnet mask formats exist so that we humans do not have to work with 32-bit binary numbers. One format, **dotted-decimal notation (DDN)**, converts each set of 8 bits into the decimal equivalent. For example, the two previous binary masks would convert to the following DDN subnet masks because binary 11111111 converts to decimal 255, and binary 00000000 converts to decimal 0:

255.0.0.0

255.255.255.0

Although the DDN format has been around since the beginning of IPv4 addressing, the third mask format was added later, in the early 1990s: the *prefix* format. This format takes advantage of the rule that the subnet mask starts with some number of 1s, and then the rest of the digits are 0s. Prefix format lists a slash (/) followed by the number of binary 1s in the **binary mask**. Using the same two examples as earlier in this section, the prefix format equivalent masks are as follows:

/8

/24

Note that although the terms *prefix* or **prefix mask** can be used, the terms **CIDR mask** or *slash mask* can also be used. This newer prefix style mask was created around the same time as the classless interdomain routing (CIDR) specification back in the early 1990s, and the acronym CIDR grew to be used for anything related to CIDR, including prefix-style masks. In addition, the term *slash mask* is sometimes used because the value includes a slash mark (/).

You need to get comfortable working with masks in different formats. The rest of this section examines how to convert between the three formats.

Converting Between Binary and Prefix Masks

Converting between binary and prefix masks should be relatively intuitive after you know that the prefix value is simply the number of binary 1s in the binary mask. For the sake of completeness, the processes to convert in each direction are

Binary to prefix: Count the number of binary 1s in the binary mask, and write the total, in decimal, after a /.

Prefix to binary: Write P binary 1s, where P is the prefix value, followed by as many binary 0s as required to create a 32-bit number.

Tables 13-2 and 13-3 show some examples.

Table 13-2   Example Conversions: Binary to Prefix

Binary Mask	Logic	Prefix Mask
11111111 11111111 11000000 00000000	Count 8 + 8 + 2 = 18 binary 1s	/18
11111111 11111111 11111111 11110000	Count 8 + 8 + 8 + 4 = 28 binary 1s	/28
11111111 11111000 00000000 00000000	Count 8 + 5 = 13 binary 1s	/13

Table 13-3   Example Conversions: Prefix to Binary

Prefix Mask	Logic	Binary Mask
/18	Write 18 1s, then 14 0s, total 32	11111111 11111111 11000000 00000000
/28	Write 28 1s, then 4 0s, total 32	11111111 11111111 11111111 11110000
/13	Write 13 1s, then 19 0s, total 32	11111111 11111000 00000000 00000000

Converting Between Binary and DDN Masks

By definition, a dotted-decimal number (DDN) used with IPv4 addressing contains four decimal numbers, separated by dots. Each decimal number represents 8 bits. So, a single DDN shows four decimal numbers that together represent some 32-bit binary number.

Conversion from a DDN mask to the binary equivalent is relatively simple to describe but can be laborious to perform. First, to do the conversion, the process is as follows:

> For each octet, perform a decimal-to-binary conversion.

However, depending on your comfort level with doing decimal-to-binary conversions, that process can be difficult or time-consuming. If you want to think about masks in binary for the exam, consider picking one of the following methods to do the conversion and practicing until you can do it quickly and accurately:

- Do the decimal-binary conversions, but practice your decimal-binary conversions to get fast. If you choose this path, consider the Cisco Binary Game, which you can find by searching its name at the Cisco Learning Network (CLN), or try this link: https://learningnetwork.cisco.com/s/binary-game.

- Use the decimal-binary conversion chart in Appendix A, "Numeric Reference Tables." This lets you find the answer more quickly now, but you cannot use the chart on exam day.

- Memorize the nine possible decimal values that can be in a **decimal mask**, and practice using a reference table with those values.

The third method, which is the method recommended in this book, takes advantage of the fact that any and every DDN mask octet must be one of only nine values. Why? Well, remember how a binary mask cannot interleave 1s and 0s, and the 0s must be on the right? It turns out that only nine different 8-bit binary numbers conform to these rules. Table 13-4 lists the values, along with other relevant information.

Table 13-4   Nine Possible Values in One Octet of a Subnet Mask

Binary Mask Octet	Decimal Equivalent	Number of Binary 1s
00000000	0	0
10000000	128	1
11000000	192	2
11100000	224	3

Binary Mask Octet	Decimal Equivalent	Number of Binary 1s
11110000	240	4
11111000	248	5
11111100	252	6
11111110	254	7
11111111	255	8

Many subnetting processes can be done with or without binary math. Some of those processes—mask conversion included—use the information in Table 13-4. You should plan to memorize the information in the table. I recommend making a copy of the table to keep handy while you practice. (You will likely memorize the contents of this table simply by practicing the conversion process enough to get both good and fast at the conversion.)

Using the table, the conversion processes in each direction with binary and decimal masks are as follows:

Binary to decimal: Organize the bits into four sets of eight. For each octet, find the binary value in the table and write down the corresponding decimal value.

Decimal to binary: For each octet, find the decimal value in the table and write down the corresponding 8-bit binary value.

Tables 13-5 and 13-6 show some examples.

Table 13-5   Conversion Example: Binary to Decimal

Binary Mask	Logic	Decimal Mask
11111111 11111111 11000000 00000000	11111111 maps to 255 11000000 maps to 192 00000000 maps to 0	255.255.192.0
11111111 11111111 11111111 11110000	11111111 maps to 255 11110000 maps to 240	255.255.255.240
11111111 11111000 00000000 00000000	11111111 maps to 255 11111000 maps to 248 00000000 maps to 0	255.248.0.0

Table 13-6   Conversion Examples: Decimal to Binary

Decimal Mask	Logic	Binary Mask
255.255.192.0	255 maps to 11111111 192 maps to 11000000 0 maps to 00000000	11111111 11111111 11000000 00000000
255.255.255.240	255 maps to 11111111 240 maps to 11110000	11111111 11111111 11111111 11110000

Decimal Mask	Logic	Binary Mask
255.248.0.0	255 maps to 11111111	11111111 11111000 00000000 00000000
	248 maps to 11111000	
	0 maps to 00000000	

Converting Between Prefix and DDN Masks

When you are learning, the best way to convert between the prefix and decimal formats is to first convert to binary. For example, to move from decimal to prefix, first convert decimal to binary and then from binary to prefix.

For the exams, set a goal to master these conversions doing the math in your head. While learning, you will likely want to use paper. To train yourself to do all this without writing it down, instead of writing each octet of binary, just write the number of binary 1s in that octet.

Figure 13-1 shows an example with a prefix-to-decimal conversion. The left side shows the conversion to binary as an interim step. For comparison, the right side shows the binary interim step in shorthand that just lists the number of binary 1s in each octet of the binary mask.

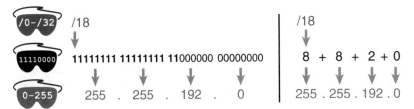

Figure 13-1 *Conversion from Prefix to Decimal: Full Binary Versus Shorthand*

Similarly, when converting from decimal to prefix, mentally convert to binary along the way, and as you improve, just think of the binary as the number of 1s in each octet. Figure 13-2 shows an example of such a conversion.

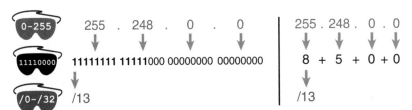

Figure 13-2 *Conversion from Decimal to Prefix: Full Binary Versus Shorthand*

Note that Appendix A has a table that lists all 33 legal subnet masks, with all three formats shown.

Practice Converting Subnet Masks

Before moving to the second half of this chapter, and thinking about what these subnet masks mean, first do some practice. Practice the processes discussed in this chapter until you get the right answer most of the time. Later, before taking the exam, practice more until you master the topics in this chapter and can move pretty fast, as outlined in the right column of Table 13-7.

Table 13-7 Keep-Reading and Take-Exam Goals for This Chapter's Topics

Time Frame	Before Moving to the Next Section	Before Taking the Exam
Focus On...	Learning how	Being correct and fast
Tools Allowed	All	Your brain and a notepad
Goal: Accuracy	90% correct	100% correct
Goal: Speed	Any speed	10 seconds

Table 13-8 lists eight practice problems. The table has three columns, one for each mask format. Each row lists one mask, in one format. Your job is to find the mask's value in the other two formats for each row. Table 13-12, located in the section "Answers to Earlier Practice Problems," later in this chapter, lists the answers.

Table 13-8 Practice Problems: Find the Mask Values in the Other Two Formats

Prefix	Binary Mask	Decimal
	11111111 11111111 11000000 00000000	
		255.255.255.252
/25		
/16		
		255.0.0.0
	11111111 11111111 11111100 00000000	
		255.254.0.0
/27		

Identifying Subnet Design Choices Using Masks

Subnet masks have many purposes. In fact, if ten experienced network engineers were independently asked, "What is the purpose of a subnet mask?" the engineers would likely give a variety of true answers. The subnet mask plays several roles.

This chapter focuses on one particular use of a subnet mask: defining the prefix part of the IP addresses in a subnet. The prefix part must be the same value for all addresses in a subnet. In fact, a single subnet can be defined as all IPv4 addresses that have the same value in the prefix part of their IPv4 addresses.

While the previous paragraph might sound a bit formal, the idea is relatively basic, as shown in Figure 13-3. The right side of the figure shows a subnet of all addresses that begin with 172.16.2 and another subnet made of all addresses that begin with 172.16.3. In this example, the prefix—the part that has the same value in all the addresses in the subnet—is the first three octets.

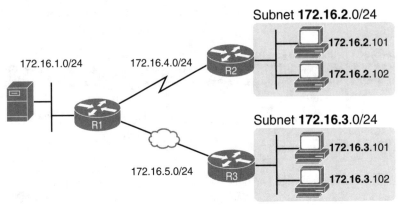

Figure 13-3 *Simple Subnet Design, with Mask /24*

While people can sit around a conference table and talk about how a prefix is three octets long, computers communicate that same concept using a subnet mask. In this case, the subnets use a subnet mask of /24, which means that the prefix part of the addresses is 24 bits (3 octets) long.

This section explains more about how to use a subnet mask to understand this concept of a prefix part of an IPv4 address, along with these other uses for a subnet mask. Note that this section discusses the first five items in the list.

- Defines the size of the prefix (combined network and subnet) part of the addresses in a subnet

- Defines the size of the host part of the addresses in the subnet

- Can be used to calculate the number of hosts in the subnet

- Provides a means for the network designer to communicate the design details—the number of subnet and host bits—to the devices in the network

- Under certain assumptions, can be used to calculate the number of subnets in the entire classful network

- Can be used in binary calculations of both the subnet ID and the subnet broadcast address

Masks Divide the Subnet's Addresses into Two Parts

The subnet mask subdivides the IP addresses in a subnet into two parts: the *prefix*, or *subnet part*, and the *host part*.

The prefix part identifies the addresses that reside in the same subnet because all IP addresses in the same subnet have the same value in the prefix part of their addresses. The idea is much like the postal code (ZIP codes in the United States) in mailing addresses. All mailing addresses in the same town have the same postal code. Likewise, all IP addresses in the same subnet have identical values in the prefix part of their addresses.

The host part of an address identifies the host uniquely inside the subnet. If you compare any two IP addresses in the same subnet, their host parts will differ, even though the prefix parts of their addresses have the same value. To summarize these key comparisons:

Prefix (subnet) part: Equal in all addresses in the same subnet

Host part: Different in all addresses in the same subnet

For example, imagine a subnet that, in concept, includes all addresses whose first three octets are 10.1.1. So, the following list shows several addresses in this subnet:

10.1.1.**1**

10.1.1.**2**

10.1.1.**3**

In this list, the prefix or subnet parts (the first three octets of 10.1.1) are equal. The host part (the last octet [in bold]) is different. So, the prefix or subnet part of the address identifies the group, and the host part identifies the specific member of the group.

The subnet mask defines the dividing line between the prefix and the host part. To do so, the mask creates a conceptual line between the binary 1s in the binary mask and the binary 0s in the mask. In short, if a mask has P binary 1s, the prefix part is P bits long and the rest of the bits are host bits. Figure 13-4 shows the concept.

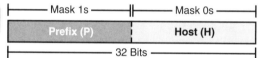

Figure 13-4 *Prefix (Subnet) and Host Parts Defined by Mask 1s and 0s*

Figure 13-5, shows a specific example using mask 255.255.255.0. Mask 255.255.255.0 (/24) has 24 binary 1s, for a prefix length of 24 bits.

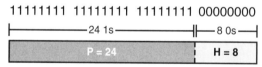

Figure 13-5 *Mask 255.255.255.0: P=24, H=8*

Masks and Class Divide Addresses into Three Parts

In addition to the two-part view of IPv4 addresses, you can also think about IPv4 addresses as having three parts. When subnetting a class A, B, or C network, just apply Class A, B, and C rules to the address format to define the network part at the beginning of the address. This added logic divides the prefix into two parts: the *network* part and the *subnet* part. The class defines the length of the network part, with the subnet part simply being the rest of the prefix. Figure 13-6 shows the idea.

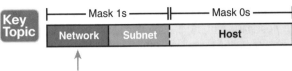

Size: 8, 16, 24 (A, B, C)

Figure 13-6 *Class Concepts Applied to Create Three Parts*

The combined network and subnet parts act like the prefix because all addresses in the same subnet must have identical values in the network and subnet parts. The size of the host part remains unchanged, whether viewing the addresses as having two parts or three parts.

To be complete, Figure 13-7 shows the same example as in the previous section, with the subnet of "all addresses that begin with 10.1.1." In that example, the subnet uses mask 255.255.255.0, and the addresses are all in Class A network 10.0.0.0. The class defines 8 network bits, and the mask defines 24 prefix bits, meaning that 24 – 8 = 16 subnet bits exist. The host part remains as 8 bits per the mask.

11111111 11111111 11111111 00000000

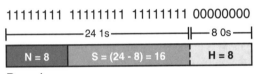

Based on
Class

Figure 13-7 *Subnet 10.1.1.0, Mask 255.255.255.0: N=8, S=16, H=8*

Classless and Classful Addressing

The terms **classless addressing** and **classful addressing** refer to the two different ways to think about IPv4 addresses as described so far in this chapter. Classful addressing means that you think about Class A, B, and C rules, so the prefix is separated into the network and subnet parts, as shown in Figures 13-6 and 13-7. Classless addressing means that you ignore the Class A, B, and C rules and treat the prefix part as one part, as shown in Figures 13-4 and 13-5. The following more formal definitions are listed for reference and study:

Classless addressing: The concept that an IPv4 address has two parts—the prefix part plus the host part—as defined by the mask, with *no consideration of the class* (A, B, or C).

Classful addressing: The concept that an IPv4 address has three parts—network, subnet, and host—as defined by the mask *and Class A, B, and C rules.*

NOTE Unfortunately, the networking world uses the terms *classless* and *classful* in a couple of different ways. In addition to the classless and classful addressing described here, each routing protocol can be categorized as either a *classless routing protocol* or a *classful routing protocol*. In another use, the terms *classless routing* and *classful routing* refer to some details of how Cisco routers forward (route) packets using the default route in some cases. As a result, these terms can be easily confused and misused. So, when you see the words *classless* and *classful*, be careful to note the context: addressing, routing, or routing protocols.

Calculations Based on the IPv4 Address Format

After you know how to break an address down using both classless and classful addressing rules, you can easily calculate a couple of important facts using some basic math formulas.

First, for any subnet, after you know the number of host bits, you can calculate the number of host IP addresses in the subnet. Next, if you know the number of subnet bits (using classful addressing concepts) and you know that only one subnet mask is used throughout the network, you can also calculate the number of subnets in the network. The formulas just require that you know the powers of 2:

Hosts in the subnet: $2^H - 2$, where H is the number of host bits.

Subnets in the network: 2^S, where S is the number of subnet bits. Only use this formula if only one mask is used throughout the network.

NOTE The section "Choose the Mask" in Chapter 11, "Perspectives on IPv4 Subnetting," details many concepts related to masks, including comments about this assumption of one mask throughout a single Class A, B, or C network.

The sizes of the parts of IPv4 addresses can also be calculated. The math is basic, but the concepts are important. Keeping in mind that IPv4 addresses are 32 bits long, the two parts with classless addressing must add up to 32 (P + H = 32), and with classful addressing, the three parts must add up to 32 (N + S + H = 32). Figure 13-8 shows the relationships.

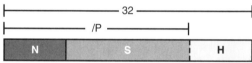

Class:
 A: N = 8
 B: N = 16
 C: N = 24

Figure 13-8 *Relationship Between /P, N, S, and H*

You often begin with an IP address and mask, both when answering questions on the CCNA exam and when examining problems that occur in real networks. Based on the information in this chapter and earlier chapters, you should be able to find all the information in Figure 13-8 and then calculate the number of hosts/subnet and the number of subnets in the network. For reference, the following process spells out the steps:

Step 1. Convert the mask to prefix format (/P) as needed. (See the earlier section "Practice Converting Subnet Masks" for review.)

Step 2. Determine N based on the class. (See Chapter 12, "Analyzing Classful IPv4 Networks," for review.)

Step 3. Calculate S = P – N.

Step 4. Calculate H = 32 – P.

Step 5. Calculate hosts/subnet: $2^H - 2$.

Step 6. Calculate number of subnets: 2^S.

For example, consider the case of IP address 8.1.4.5 with mask 255.255.0.0 by following this process:

Step 1.   255.255.0.0 = /16, so P=16.

Step 2.   8.1.4.5 is in the range 1–126 in the first octet, so it is Class A; so N=8.

Step 3.   S = P – N = 16 – 8 = 8.

Step 4.   H = 32 – P = 32 – 16 = 16.

Step 5. 2^{16} – 2 = 65,534 hosts/subnet.

Step 6. 2^{8} = 256 subnets.

Figure 13-9 shows a visual analysis of the same problem.

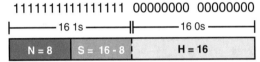

Figure 13-9   *Visual Representation of Problem: 8.1.4.5, 255.255.0.0*

For another example, consider address 200.1.1.1, mask 255.255.255.252 by following this process:

Step 1.   255.255.255.252 = /30, so P=30.

Step 2.   200.1.1.1 is in the range 192–223 in the first octet, so it is Class C; so N=24.

Step 3.   S = P – N = 30 – 24 = 6.

Step 4.   H = 32 – P = 32 – 30 = 2.

Step 5. 2^{2} – 2 = 2 hosts/subnet.

Step 6. 2^{6} = 64 subnets.

This example uses a popular mask for serial links because serial links require only two host addresses, and the mask supports only two host addresses.

Practice Analyzing Subnet Masks

As with the other subnetting math in this book, using a two-phase approach may help. Take time now to practice until you feel as though you understand the process. Then, before the exam, make sure you master the math. Table 13-9 summarizes the key concepts and suggestions for this two-phase approach.

Table 13-9   Keep-Reading and Take-Exam Goals for This Chapter's Topics

Time Frame	Before Moving to the Next Chapter	Before Taking the Exam
Focus On...	Learning how	Being correct and fast
Tools Allowed	All	Your brain and a notepad
Goal: Accuracy	90% correct	100% correct
Goal: Speed	Any speed	15 seconds

On a piece of scratch paper, answer the following questions. In each case:

- Determine the structure of the addresses in each subnet based on the class and mask, using classful IP addressing concepts. In other words, find the size of the network, subnet, and host parts of the addresses.

- Calculate the number of hosts in the subnet.

- Calculate the number of subnets in the network, assuming that the same mask is used throughout.

13

1. 8.1.4.5, 255.255.254.0
2. 130.4.102.1, 255.255.255.0
3. 199.1.1.100, 255.255.255.0
4. 130.4.102.1, 255.255.252.0
5. 199.1.1.100, 255.255.255.224

The answers are listed in the section "Answers to Earlier Practice Problems," later in this chapter.

Masks and CIDR Blocks

As described in the Introduction, most of this chapter, particularly the second major section, expects the more typical case of subnetting a Class A, B, or C network. However, in some cases, a company will use a large public *CIDR block* instead of a classful public IP network or a classful private IP network. While more common today for enterprises to use private Class A, B, and C IP networks for the addresses for most of their hosts, it still helps to understand how you would subnet if using a large public CIDR block instead.

First, the classless addressing view of the mask need not change. However, the classful view of the mask, which interprets the address structure with a network field length based on Class A, B, and C rules, needs to be adjusted. Thankfully, the concepts are straightforward and do not require new processes or math. In short:

Formerly, you defined a network field based on Class A, B, and C rules. With a CIDR block, instead, use the prefix length specified by the CIDR block.

To explain a little more, note that a CIDR block assignment lists a prefix ID and length. The prefix ID represents the group, like a network ID or subnet ID, and is the numerically lowest number in the CIDR block. The CIDR block's prefix length acts like the block's default mask. For example, the numbers 1.1.0.0/16 imply "all addresses that begin with 1.1." The /16 mask means that all addresses in the CIDR block have the same value in their first 16 bits.

To summarize using Figure 13-10, instead of using Class A, B, or C rules to create an 8-, 16-, or 24-bit network field, begin with a CIDR field based on the prefix length of the CIDR field (16 bits in the previous example).

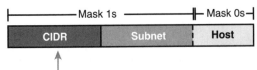

Size: Per CIDR Block Prefix Length

Figure 13-10 *CIDR and Subnet Masks Divide Addresses into Three Parts*

Just as with the classful view of the address structure, when subnetting the CIDR block, the width of the CIDR field remains the same. When you choose a mask, the more binary 1s, the more subnet bits and subnets in the design. The more host bits in the mask, the more hosts/subnet.

Chapter Review

One key to doing well on the exams is to perform repetitive spaced review sessions. Review this chapter's material using either the tools in the book or interactive tools for the same material found on the book's companion website. Refer to the "Your Study Plan" element for more details. Table 13-10 outlines the key review elements and where you can find them. To better track your study progress, record when you completed these activities in the second column.

Table 13-10 Chapter Review Tracking

Review Element	Review Date(s)	Resource Used
Review key topics		Book, website
Review key terms		Book, website
Answer DIKTA questions		Book, PTP
Review memory tables		Website
Practice analyzing subnet masks		Website, Appendix E
Watch video		Website

Review All the Key Topics

Table 13-11 Key Topics for Chapter 13

Key Topic Element	Description	Page Number
List	Rules for binary subnet mask values	340
List	Rules to convert between binary and prefix masks	341
Table 13-4	Nine possible values in a decimal subnet mask	342
List	Rules to convert between binary and DDN masks	343
List	Some functions of a subnet mask	346
List	Comparisons of IP addresses in the same subnet	347
Figure 13-4	Two-part classless view of an IP address	347
Figure 13-6	Three-part classful view of an IP address	348
List	Definitions of classful addressing and classless addressing	348
List	Formal steps to analyze masks and calculate values	349

Key Terms You Should Know

binary mask, CIDR mask, classful addressing, classless addressing, decimal mask, dotted-decimal notation (DDN), prefix mask

Additional Practice for This Chapter's Processes

You can do more practice with the processes in this chapter with a pair of practice sets. One focuses on interpreting existing masks, while the other gives you practice with converting between mask formats. You may do each practice set using the following tools:

Application: From the companion website, in the section titled "Memory Tables and Practice Exercises," use the "Analyzing Subnet Masks" and "Converting Masks" applications, listed under the Chapter Review for this chapter.

PDF: Practice the same problems found in both these apps using companion website Appendix E, "Practice for Chapter 13: Analyzing Subnet Masks."

Answers to Earlier Practice Problems

Table 13-8, shown earlier, listed several practice problems for converting subnet masks; Table 13-12 lists the answers.

Table 13-12   Answers to Problems in Table 13-8

Prefix	Binary Mask	Decimal
/18	11111111 11111111 11000000 00000000	255.255.192.0
/30	11111111 11111111 11111111 11111100	255.255.255.252
/25	11111111 11111111 11111111 10000000	255.255.255.128
/16	11111111 11111111 00000000 00000000	255.255.0.0
/8	11111111 00000000 00000000 00000000	255.0.0.0
/22	11111111 11111111 11111100 00000000	255.255.252.0
/15	11111111 11111110 00000000 00000000	255.254.0.0
/27	11111111 11111111 11111111 11100000	255.255.255.224

Table 13-13 lists the answers to the practice problems from the earlier section "Practice Analyzing Subnet Masks."

Table 13-13   Answers to Problems from Earlier in the Chapter

	Problem	/P	Class	N	S	H	2^S	$2^H - 2$
1	8.1.4.5 255.255.254.0	23	A	8	15	9	32,768	510
2	130.4.102.1 255.255.255.0	24	B	16	8	8	256	254
3	199.1.1.100 255.255.255.0	24	C	24	0	8	N/A	254
4	130.4.102.1 255.255.252.0	22	B	16	6	10	64	1022
5	199.1.1.100 255.255.255.224	27	C	24	3	5	8	30

The following list reviews the problems:

1. For 8.1.4.5, the first octet (8) is in the 1–126 range, so it is a Class A address, with 8 network bits. Mask 255.255.254.0 converts to /23, so P – N = 15, for 15 subnet bits. H can be found by subtracting /P (23) from 32, for 9 host bits.

2. The address 130.4.102.1 is in the 128–191 range in the first octet, making it a Class B address, with N = 16 bits. The 255.255.255.0 converts to /24, so the number of subnet bits is 24 – 16 = 8. With 24 prefix bits, the number of host bits is 32 – 24 = 8.

3. The third problem purposely shows a case where the mask does not create a subnet part of the address. The address, 199.1.1.100, has a first octet between 192 and 223, making it a Class C address with 24 network bits. The prefix version of the mask is /24, so the number of subnet bits is 24 – 24 = 0. The number of host bits is 32 minus the prefix length (24), for a total of 8 host bits. So in this case, the mask shows that the network engineer is using the default mask, which creates no subnet bits and no subnets.

4. With the same address as the second problem, 130.4.102.1 is a Class B address with N = 16 bits. This problem uses a different mask, 255.255.252.0, which converts to /22. This makes the number of subnet bits 22 – 16 = 6. With 22 prefix bits, the number of host bits is 32 – 22 = 10.

5. With the same address as the third problem, 199.1.1.100 is a Class C address with N = 24 bits. This problem uses a different mask, 255.255.255.224, which converts to /27. This makes the number of subnet bits 27 – 24 = 3. With 27 prefix bits, the number of host bits is 32 – 27 = 5.

CHAPTER 14

Analyzing Existing Subnets

This chapter covers the following exam topics:

> **1.0 Network Fundamentals**
>
> > **1.6 Configure and verify IPv4 addressing and subnetting**

Often, a networking task begins with the discovery of the IP address and mask used by some host. Then, to understand how the internetwork routes packets to that host, you must find key pieces of information about the subnet, specifically the following:

- Subnet ID

- Subnet broadcast address

- Subnet's range of usable unicast IP addresses

This chapter discusses the concepts and math to take a known IP address and mask, and then fully describe a subnet by finding the values in this list. These specific tasks might well be the most important IP skills in the entire IP addressing and subnetting topics in this book because they might be the most commonly used tasks when operating and troubleshooting real networks. Also note that as with the other chapters, this chapter shows examples that subnet a Class A, B, or C network, rather than a CIDR block.

"Do I Know This Already?" Quiz

Take the quiz (either here or use the PTP software) if you want to use the score to help you decide how much time to spend on this chapter. The letter answers are listed at the bottom of the page following the quiz. Appendix C, found both at the end of the book as well as on the companion website, includes both the answers and explanations. You can also find both answers and explanations in the PTP testing software.

Table 14-1 "Do I Know This Already?" Foundation Topics Section-to-Question Mapping

Foundation Topics Section	Questions
Defining a Subnet	1
Analyzing Existing Subnets: Binary	2
Analyzing Existing Subnets: Decimal	3–6

1. When you think about an IP address using classful addressing rules, an address can have three parts: network, subnet, and host. If you examined all the addresses in one subnet, in binary, which of the following answers correctly states which of the three parts of the addresses will be equal among all addresses? (Choose the best answer.)

   a. Network part only

   b. Subnet part only

   c. Host part only

   d. Network and subnet parts

   e. Subnet and host parts

2. Which of the following statements are true regarding the binary subnet ID, subnet broadcast address, and host IP address values in any single subnet? (Choose two answers.)

   a. The host part of the broadcast address is all binary 0s.

   b. The host part of the subnet ID is all binary 0s.

   c. The host part of a usable IP address can have all binary 1s.

   d. The host part of any usable IP address must not be all binary 0s.

3. Which of the following is the resident subnet ID for IP address 10.7.99.133/24?

   a. 10.0.0.0

   b. 10.7.0.0

   c. 10.7.99.0

   d. 10.7.99.128

4. Which of the following is the resident subnet for IP address 192.168.44.97/30?

   a. 192.168.44.0

   b. 192.168.44.64

   c. 192.168.44.96

   d. 192.168.44.128

5. Which of the following is the subnet broadcast address for the subnet in which IP address 172.31.77.201/27 resides?

   a. 172.31.201.255

   b. 172.31.255.255

   c. 172.31.77.223

   d. 172.31.77.207

6. A fellow engineer tells you to configure the DHCP server to lease the last 100 usable IP addresses in subnet 10.1.4.0/23. Which of the following IP addresses could be leased as a result of your new configuration?

   a. 10.1.4.156

   b. 10.1.4.254

   c. 10.1.5.200

   d. 10.1.7.200

   e. 10.1.255.200

Foundation Topics

Defining a Subnet

An IP subnet is a subset of a classful network, created by choice of some network engineer. However, that engineer cannot pick just any arbitrary subset of addresses; instead, the engineer must follow certain rules, such as the following:

- The subnet contains a set of consecutive numbers.

- The subnet holds 2^H numbers, where H is the number of host bits defined by the subnet mask.

- Two special numbers in the range cannot be used as IP addresses:

    - The first (lowest) number acts as an identifier for the subnet (subnet ID).

    - The last (highest) number acts as a *subnet broadcast address*.

- The remaining addresses, whose values sit between the subnet ID and subnet broadcast address, are used as *unicast IP addresses*.

This section reviews and expands the basic concepts of the subnet ID, subnet broadcast address, and range of addresses in a subnet.

An Example with Network 172.16.0.0 and Four Subnets

Imagine that you work at the customer support center, where you receive all initial calls from users who have problems with their computer. You coach the user through finding her IP address and mask: 172.16.150.41, mask 255.255.192.0. One of the first and most common tasks you will do based on that information is to find the subnet ID of the subnet in which that address resides. (In fact, this subnet ID is sometimes called the **resident subnet** because the IP address exists in or resides in that subnet.)

Before getting into the math, examine the mask (255.255.192.0) and classful network (172.16.0.0) for a moment. From the mask, based on what you learned in Chapter 13, "Analyzing Subnet Masks," you can find the structure of the addresses in the subnet, including the number of host and subnet bits. That analysis tells you that two subnet bits exist, meaning that there should be four (2^2) subnets. Figure 14-1 shows the idea.

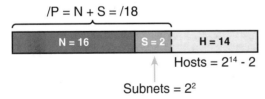

Figure 14-1   *Address Structure: Class B Network, /18 Mask*

> **NOTE**   This chapter, like the others in this part of the book, assumes that one mask is used throughout an entire classful network.

Because each subnet uses a single mask, all subnets of this single IP network must be the same size, because all subnets have the same structure. In this example, all four subnets will have the structure shown in the figure, so all four subnets will have $2^{14} - 2$ host addresses.

Next, consider the big picture of what happens with this example subnet design: the one Class B network now has four subnets of equal size. Conceptually, if you represent the entire Class B network as a number line, each subnet consumes one-fourth of the number line, as shown in Figure 14-2. Each subnet has a subnet ID—the numerically lowest number in the subnet—so it sits on the left of the subnet. And each subnet has a **subnet broadcast address**—the numerically highest number in the subnet—so it sits on the right side of the subnet.

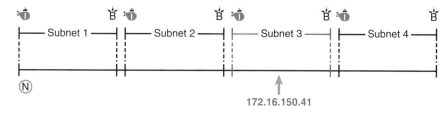

Legend:

- Ⓝ Network ID
- ⬆ Subnet ID
- B̌ Subnet Broadcast Address

Figure 14-2   *Network 172.16.0.0, Divided into Four Equal Subnets*

The rest of this chapter focuses on how to take one IP address and mask and discover the details about that one subnet in which the address resides. In other words, you see how to find the resident subnet of an IP address. Again, using IP address 172.16.150.41 and mask 255.255.192.0 as an example, Figure 14-3 shows the resident subnet, along with the subnet ID and subnet broadcast address that bracket the subnet.

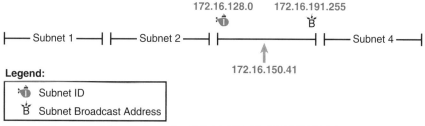

Legend:

- ⬆ Subnet ID
- B̌ Subnet Broadcast Address

Figure 14-3   *Resident Subnet for 172.16.150.41, 255.255.192.0*

Subnet ID Concepts

A subnet ID is simply a number used to succinctly represent a subnet. When listed along with its matching subnet mask, the subnet ID identifies the subnet and can be used to derive the subnet broadcast address and range of addresses in the subnet. Rather than having to write down all these details about a subnet, you simply need to write down the subnet ID and mask, and you have enough information to fully describe the subnet.

The subnet ID appears in many places, but it is seen most often in IP routing tables. For example, when an engineer configures a router with its IP address and mask, the router calculates the subnet ID and puts a route into its routing table for that subnet. The router typically then advertises the subnet ID/mask combination to neighboring routers with some IP routing protocol. Eventually, all the routers in an enterprise learn about the subnet—again using the subnet ID and subnet mask combination—and display it in their routing tables. (You can display the contents of a router's IP routing table using the **show ip route** command.)

Unfortunately, the terminology related to subnets can sometimes cause problems. First, the terms **subnet ID**, **subnet number**, and **subnet address** are synonyms. In addition, people sometimes simply say *subnet* when referring to both the idea of a subnet and the number that is used as the subnet ID. When talking about routing, people sometimes use the term *prefix* instead of *subnet*. The term *prefix* refers to the same idea as *subnet*; it just uses terminology from the classless addressing way to describe IP addresses, as discussed in Chapter 13's section "Classless and Classful Addressing."

The biggest terminology confusion arises between the terms *network* and *subnet*. In the real world, people often use these terms synonymously, and that is perfectly reasonable in some cases. In other cases, the specific meaning of these terms, and their differences, matter to what is being discussed.

For example, people often might say, "What is the network ID?" when they really want to know the subnet ID. In another case, they might want to know the Class A, B, or C network ID. So, when one engineer asks something like, "What's the net ID for 172.16.150.41 slash 18?" use the context to figure out whether he wants the literal classful network ID (172.16.0.0, in this case) or the literal subnet ID (172.16.128.0, in this case).

For the exams, be ready to notice when the terms *subnet* and *network* are used, and then use the context to figure out the specific meaning of the term in that case.

Table 14-2 summarizes the key facts about the subnet ID, along with the possible synonyms, for easier review and study.

Table 14-2   Summary of Subnet ID Key Facts

Definition	Number that represents the subnet
Numeric Value	First (smallest) number in the subnet
Literal Synonyms	Subnet number, subnet address, prefix, resident subnet
Common-Use Synonyms	Network, network ID, network number, network address
Typically Seen In...	Routing tables, documentation

Subnet Broadcast Address

The subnet broadcast address has two main roles: to be used as a destination IP address for the purpose of sending packets to all hosts in the subnet, and as a means to find the high end of the range of addresses in a subnet.

The original purpose for the subnet broadcast address was to give hosts a way to send one packet to all hosts in a subnet and to do so efficiently. For example, a host in subnet A could send a packet with a destination address of subnet B's subnet broadcast address. The routers would forward this one packet just like a unicast IP packet sent to a host in subnet B. After the packet arrives at the router connected to subnet B, that last router would then forward the packet to all hosts in subnet B, typically by encapsulating the packet in a data-link layer broadcast frame. As a result, all hosts in host B's subnet would receive a copy of the packet.

The subnet broadcast address also helps you find the range of addresses in a subnet because the subnet broadcast address is the last (highest) number in a subnet's range of addresses. To find the low end of the range, calculate the subnet ID; to find the high end of the range, calculate the subnet broadcast address.

Table 14-3 summarizes the key facts about the subnet broadcast address, along with the possible synonyms, for easier review and study.

Table 14-3   Summary of Subnet Broadcast Address Key Facts

Definition	A reserved number in each subnet that, when used as the destination address of a packet, causes the device to forward the packet to all hosts in that subnet
Numeric Value	Last (highest) number in the subnet
Literal Synonyms	Directed broadcast address
Broader-Use Synonyms	Network broadcast
Typically Seen In...	Calculations of the range of addresses in a subnet

Range of Usable Addresses

The engineers implementing an IP internetwork need to know the range of unicast IP addresses in each subnet. Before you can plan which addresses to use as statically assigned IP addresses, which to configure to be leased by the DHCP server, and which to reserve for later use, you need to know the range of usable addresses.

To find the range of usable IP addresses in a subnet, first find the subnet ID and the subnet broadcast address. Then, just add 1 to the fourth octet of the subnet ID to get the first (lowest) usable address, and subtract 1 from the fourth octet of the subnet broadcast address to get the last (highest) usable address in the subnet.

For example, Figure 14-3 showed subnet ID 172.16.128.0, mask /18. The first usable address is simply one more than the subnet ID (in this case, 172.16.128.1). That same figure showed a subnet broadcast address of 172.16.191.255, so the last usable address is one less, or 172.16.191.254.

Now that this section has described the concepts behind the numbers that collectively define a subnet, the rest of this chapter focuses on the math used to find these values.

Analyzing Existing Subnets: Binary

What does it mean to "analyze a subnet"? For this book, it means that you should be able to start with an IP address and mask and then define key facts about the subnet in which that address resides. Specifically, that means discovering the subnet ID, subnet broadcast address, and range of addresses. The analysis can also include the calculation of the number of addresses in the subnet as discussed in Chapter 13, but this chapter does not review those concepts.

Many methods exist to calculate the details about a subnet based on the address/mask. This section begins by discussing some calculations that use binary math, with the next section showing alternatives that use only decimal math. Although many people prefer the decimal method for going fast on the exams, the binary calculations ultimately give you a better understanding of IPv4 addressing. In particular, if you plan to move on to attain Cisco certifications beyond CCNA, you should take the time to understand the binary methods discussed in this section, even if you use the decimal methods for the exams.

Finding the Subnet ID: Binary

The two following statements summarize the logic behind the binary value of any subnet ID:

All numbers in the subnet (subnet ID, subnet broadcast address, and all usable IP addresses) have the same value in the prefix part of the numbers.

The subnet ID is the lowest numeric value in the subnet, so its host part, in binary, is all 0s.

To find the subnet ID in binary, you take the IP address in binary and change all host bits to binary 0. To do so, you need to convert the IP address to binary. You also need to identify the prefix and host bits, which can be easily done by converting the mask (as needed) to prefix format. Figure 14-4 shows the idea, using the same address/mask as in the earlier examples in this chapter: 172.16.150.41, mask /18.

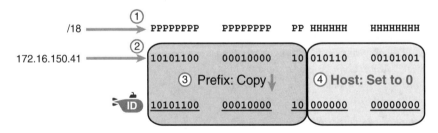

Figure 14-4   *Binary Concept: Convert the IP Address to the Subnet ID*

Starting at the top of Figure 14-4, the format of the IP address is represented with 18 prefix (P) and 14 host (H) bits in the mask (Step 1). The second row (Step 2) shows the binary version of the IP address, converted from the dotted-decimal notation (DDN) value 172.16.150.41.

The next two steps show the action to copy the IP address's prefix bits (Step 3) and give the host bits a value of binary 0 (Step 4). This resulting number is the subnet ID (in binary).

The last step, not shown in Figure 14-4, is to convert the subnet ID from binary to decimal. This book shows that conversion as a separate step, in Figure 14-5, mainly because many people make a mistake at this step in the process. When converting a 32-bit number (like an IP address or IP subnet ID) back to an IPv4 DDN, you must follow this rule:

Convert 8 bits at a time from binary to decimal, regardless of the line between the prefix and host parts of the number.

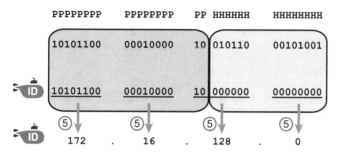

Figure 14-5 *Converting the Subnet ID from Binary to DDN*

Figure 14-5 shows this final step. Note that the third octet (the third set of 8 bits) has 2 bits in the prefix and 6 bits in the host part of the number, but the conversion occurs for all 8 bits.

NOTE You can do the numeric conversions in Figures 14-4 and 14-5 by relying on the conversion table in Appendix A, "Numeric Reference Tables." To convert from DDN to binary, for each octet, find the decimal value in the table and then write down the 8-bit binary equivalent. To convert from binary back to DDN, for each octet of 8 bits, find the matching binary entry in the table and write down the corresponding decimal value. For example, 172 converts to binary 10101100, and 00010000 converts to decimal 16.

Finding the Subnet Broadcast Address: Binary

Finding the subnet broadcast address uses a similar process. To find the subnet broadcast address, use the same binary process used to find the subnet ID, but instead of setting all the host bits to the lowest value (all binary 0s), set the host part to the highest value (all binary 1s). Figure 14-6 shows the concept.

The process in Figure 14-6 demonstrates the same first three steps shown in Figure 14-4. Specifically, it shows the identification of the prefix and host bits (Step 1), the results of converting the IP address 172.16.150.41 to binary (Step 2), and the copying of the prefix bits (first 18 bits, in this case) at Step 3. The difference occurs in the host bits on the right at Step 4, changing all host bits (the last 14, in this case) to the largest possible value (all binary 1s). Step 5 then converts the 32-bit subnet broadcast address to DDN format. Also, remember that with any conversion from DDN to binary or vice versa, the process always converts using 8 bits at a time. In particular, in this case, the entire third octet of binary 10111111 is converted to decimal 191.

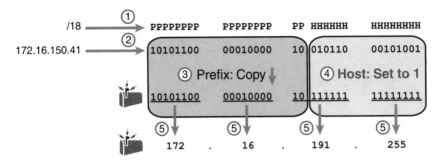

Figure 14-6 *Finding a Subnet Broadcast Address: Binary*

Binary Practice Problems

Figures 14-4 and 14-5 demonstrate a process to find the subnet ID using binary math. The following process summarizes those steps in written form for easier reference and practice:

Step 1. Convert the mask to prefix format to find the length of the prefix (/P) and the length of the host part (32 − P).

Step 2. Convert the IP address to its 32-bit binary equivalent.

Step 3. Copy the prefix bits of the IP address.

Step 4. Write down 0s for the host bits.

Step 5. Convert the resulting 32-bit number, 8 bits at a time, back to decimal.

The process to find the subnet broadcast address is exactly the same, except in Step 4, you set the bits to 1s, as shown in Figure 14-6.

Take a few moments and run through the following five practice problems on scratch paper. In each case, find both the subnet ID and subnet broadcast address. Also, record the prefix style mask:

1. 8.1.4.5, 255.255.0.0
2. 130.4.102.1, 255.255.255.0
3. 199.1.1.100, 255.255.255.0
4. 130.4.102.1, 255.255.252.0
5. 199.1.1.100, 255.255.255.224

Tables 14-4 through 14-8 show the results for the five different examples. The tables show the host bits in bold, and they include the binary version of the address and mask and the binary version of the subnet ID and subnet broadcast address.

Table 14-4   Subnet Analysis for Subnet with Address 8.1.4.5, Mask 255.255.0.0

Prefix Length	/16	11111111 11111111 **00000000 00000000**
Address	8.1.4.5	00001000 00000001 **00000100 00000101**
Subnet ID	8.1.0.0	00001000 00000001 **00000000 00000000**
Broadcast Address	8.1.255.255	00001000 00000001 **11111111 11111111**

Table 14-5   Subnet Analysis for Subnet with Address 130.4.102.1, Mask 255.255.255.0

Prefix Length	/24	11111111 11111111 11111111 **00000000**
Address	130.4.102.1	10000010 00000100 01100110 **00000001**
Subnet ID	130.4.102.0	10000010 00000100 01100110 **00000000**
Broadcast Address	130.4.102.255	10000010 00000100 01100110 **11111111**

Table 14-6   Subnet Analysis for Subnet with Address 199.1.1.100, Mask 255.255.255.0

Prefix Length	/24	11111111 11111111 11111111 **00000000**
Address	199.1.1.100	11000111 00000001 00000001 **01100100**
Subnet ID	199.1.1.0	11000111 00000001 00000001 **00000000**
Broadcast Address	199.1.1.255	11000111 00000001 00000001 **11111111**

Table 14-7   Subnet Analysis for Subnet with Address 130.4.102.1, Mask 255.255.252.0

Prefix Length	/22	11111111 11111111 **111111**00 **00000000**
Address	130.4.102.1	10000010 00000100 011001**10 00000001**
Subnet ID	130.4.100.0	10000010 00000100 011001**00 00000000**
Broadcast Address	130.4.103.255	10000010 00000100 011001**11 11111111**

Table 14-8   Subnet Analysis for Subnet with Address 199.1.1.100, Mask 255.255.255.224

Prefix Length	/27	11111111 11111111 11111111 **111**00000
Address	199.1.1.100	11000111 00000001 00000001 01**100100**
Subnet ID	199.1.1.96	11000111 00000001 00000001 01**100000**
Broadcast Address	199.1.1.127	11000111 00000001 00000001 01**111111**

Shortcut for the Binary Process

The binary process described in this section so far requires that all four octets be converted to binary and then back to decimal. However, you can easily predict the results in at least three of the four octets, based on the DDN mask. You can then avoid the binary math in all but one octet and reduce the number of binary conversions you need to do.

First, consider an octet, and that octet only, whose DDN mask value is 255. The mask value of 255 converts to binary 11111111, which means that all 8 bits are prefix bits. Thinking through the steps in the process, at Step 2, you convert the address to some number. At Step 3, you copy the number. At Step 4, you convert the same 8-bit number back to decimal. All you did in those three steps, in this one octet, is convert from decimal to binary and convert the same number back to the same decimal value!

In short, for any mask octet of value 255, the subnet ID and subnet broadcast address octet equal the IP address's value in that same octet.

For example, the resident subnet ID for 172.16.150.41, mask 255.255.192.0 is 172.16.128.0. The first two mask octets are 255. Rather than think about the binary math, you could just start by copying the address's value in those two octets: 172.16.

Another shortcut exists for octets whose DDN mask value is decimal 0, or binary 00000000. With a decimal mask value of 0, the math always results in a decimal 0 for the subnet ID, no matter the beginning value in the IP address. Specifically, just look at Steps 4 and 5 in this case: At Step 4, you would write down 8 binary 0s, and at Step 5, you would convert 00000000 back to decimal 0.

The following revised process steps take these two shortcuts into account. However, when the mask is neither 0 nor 255, the process requires the same conversions. At most, you have to do only one octet of the conversions. To find the subnet ID, apply the logic in these steps for each of the four octets:

Step 1.   If the mask = 255, copy the decimal IP address for that octet.

Step 2.   If the mask = 0, write down a decimal 0 for that octet.

Step 3.   If the mask is neither 0 nor 255 in this octet, use the same binary logic as shown in the section "Finding the Subnet ID: Binary," earlier in this chapter.

Figure 14-7 shows an example of this process, again using 172.16.150.41, 255.255.192.0.

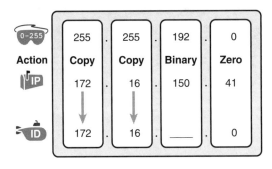

Figure 14-7   *Binary Shortcut Example*

To find the subnet broadcast address, you can use a decimal shortcut similar to the one used to find the subnet ID: for DDN mask octets equal to decimal 0, set the decimal subnet broadcast address value to 255 instead of 0, as noted in the following list:

Step 1.   If the mask = 255, copy the decimal IP address for that octet.

Step 2.   If the mask = 0, write down a decimal 255 for that octet.

Step 3.   If the mask is neither 0 nor 255 in this octet, use the same binary logic as shown in the section "Finding the Subnet Broadcast Address: Binary," earlier in this chapter.

A Brief Note About Boolean Math

So far, this chapter has described how humans can use binary math to find the subnet ID and subnet broadcast address. However, computers typically use an entirely different binary process to find the same values, using a branch of mathematics called *Boolean algebra*. Computers already store the IP address and mask in binary form, so they do not have to do any conversions to and from decimal. Then, certain Boolean operations allow the computers to calculate the subnet ID and subnet broadcast address with just a few CPU instructions.

You do not need to know Boolean math to have a good understanding of IP subnetting. However, in case you are interested, computers use the following Boolean logic to find the subnet ID and subnet broadcast address, respectively:

Perform a *Boolean AND* of the IP address and mask. This process converts all host bits to binary 0s.

Invert the mask and then perform a *Boolean OR* of the IP address and inverted subnet mask. This process converts all host bits to binary 1s.

Finding the Range of Addresses

Finding the range of usable addresses in a subnet, after you know the subnet ID and subnet broadcast address, requires only simple addition and subtraction. To find the first (lowest) usable IP address in the subnet, simply add 1 to the fourth octet of the subnet ID. To find the last (highest) usable IP address, simply subtract 1 from the fourth octet of the subnet broadcast address.

Analyzing Existing Subnets: Decimal

Analyzing existing subnets using the binary process works well. However, some of the math takes time for most people, particularly the decimal-binary conversions. And you need to do the math quickly for the Cisco CCNA exam. For the exam, you really should be able to take an IP address and mask, and calculate the subnet ID and range of usable addresses within about 15 seconds. When using binary methods, most people require a lot of practice to be able to find these answers, even when using the abbreviated binary process.

This section discusses how to find the subnet ID and subnet broadcast address using only decimal math. Most people can find the answers more quickly using this process, at least after a little practice, as compared with the binary process. However, the decimal process does not tell you anything about the meaning behind the math. So, if you have not read the earlier section "Analyzing Existing Subnets: Binary," it is worthwhile to read it for the sake of understanding subnetting. This section focuses on getting the right answer using a method that, after you have practiced, should be faster.

Analysis with Easy Masks

With three easy subnet masks in particular, finding the subnet ID and subnet broadcast address requires only easy logic and literally no math. Three easy masks exist:

255.0.0.0

255.255.0.0

255.255.255.0

These easy masks have only 255 and 0 in decimal. In comparison, difficult masks have one octet that has neither a 255 nor a 0 in the mask, which makes the logic more challenging.

NOTE   The terms *easy mask* and *difficult mask* are created for use in this book to describe the masks and the level of difficulty when working with each.

When the problem uses an easy mask, you can quickly find the subnet ID based on the IP address and mask in DDN format. Just use the following process for each of the four octets to find the subnet ID:

Step 1.   If the mask octet = 255, copy the decimal IP address.

Step 2.   If the mask octet = 0, write a decimal 0.

A similar simple process exists to find the subnet broadcast address, as follows:

Step 1.   If the mask octet = 255, copy the decimal IP address.

Step 2.   If the mask octet = 0, write a decimal 255.

Before moving to the next section, take some time to fill in the blanks in Table 14-9. Check your answers against Table 14-15 in the section "Answers to Earlier Practice Problems," later in this chapter. Complete the table by listing the subnet ID and subnet broadcast address.

Table 14-9   Practice Problems: Find Subnet ID and Broadcast, Easy Masks

	IP Address	Mask	Subnet ID	Broadcast Address
1	10.77.55.3	255.255.255.0		
2	172.30.99.4	255.255.255.0		
3	192.168.6.54	255.255.255.0		
4	10.77.3.14	255.255.0.0		
5	172.22.55.77	255.255.0.0		
6	1.99.53.76	255.0.0.0		

Predictability in the Interesting Octet

Although three masks are easier to work with (255.0.0.0, 255.255.0.0, and 255.255.255.0), all other subnet masks make the decimal math a little more difficult, so we call these masks *difficult masks*. With difficult masks, one octet has a value of neither a 0 nor a 255. To bring attention to the one octet with the most difficult value, this book refers to that octet as the *interesting octet*.

If you take some time to think about different problems and focus on the interesting octet, you will begin to see a pattern. This section takes you through that examination so that you can learn how to predict the pattern, in decimal, and find the subnet ID.

First, the subnet ID value has a predictable decimal value because of the assumption that a single subnet mask is used for all subnets of a single classful network. The chapters in this part of the book assume that, for a given classful network, the design engineer chooses to use a single subnet mask for all subnets. (See the section "One Size Subnet Fits All—Or Not" in Chapter 11, "Perspectives on IPv4 Subnetting," for more details.)

To see that predictability, consider some planning information written down by a network engineer, as shown in Figure 14-8. The figure shows four different masks the engineer is considering using in an IPv4 network, along with Class B network 172.16.0.0. The figure shows the third-octet values for the subnet IDs that would be created when using masks 255.255.128.0, 255.255.192.0, 255.255.224.0, and 255.255.240.0, from top to bottom in the figure.

Subnets of 172.16.0.0:   172.16.____.0

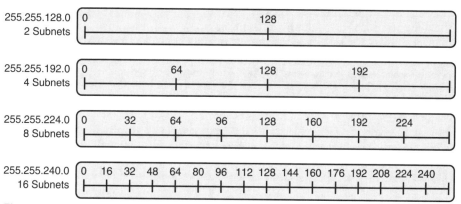

Figure 14-8 *Numeric Patterns in the Interesting Octet*

First, to explain the figure further, look at the top row of the figure. If the engineer uses 255.255.128.0 as the mask, the mask creates two subnets, with subnet IDs 172.16.0.0 and 172.16.128.0. If the engineer uses mask 255.255.192.0, the mask creates four subnets, with subnet IDs 172.16.0.0, 172.16.64.0, 172.16.128.0, and 172.16.192.0.

If you take the time to look at the figure, the patterns become obvious. In this case:

Mask: 255.255.128.0   Pattern: Multiples of 128

Mask: 255.255.192.0   Pattern: Multiples of 64

Mask: 255.255.224.0   Pattern: Multiples of 32

Mask: 255.255.240.0   Pattern: Multiples of 16

To find the subnet ID, you just need a way to figure out what the pattern is. If you start with an IP address and mask, just find the subnet ID closest to the IP address, without going over, as discussed in the next section.

Finding the Subnet ID: Difficult Masks

The following written process lists all the steps to find the subnet ID, using only decimal math. This process adds to the earlier process used with easy masks. For each octet:

Step 1.   If the mask octet = 255, copy the decimal IP address.

Step 2.   If the mask octet = 0, write a decimal 0.

Step 3.   If the mask is neither, refer to this octet as the *interesting octet*:

  a.   Calculate the *magic number* as 256 − mask.

  b.   Set the subnet ID's value to the multiple of the magic number that is closest to the IP address without going over.

The process uses two new terms created for this book: *magic number* and *interesting octet*. The term *interesting octet* refers to the octet identified at Step 3 in the process; in other words, it is the octet with the mask that is neither 255 nor 0. Step 3A then uses the term *magic number*, which is derived from the DDN mask. Conceptually, the magic number is the number you add to one subnet ID to get the next subnet ID in order, as shown in Figure 14-8. Numerically, it can be found by subtracting the DDN mask's value, in the interesting octet, from 256, as mentioned in Step 3A.

The best way to learn this process is to see it happen. In fact, if you can, stop reading now, use the companion website for this book, and watch the videos about finding the subnet ID with a difficult mask. These videos demonstrate this process. You can also use the examples on the next few pages that show the process being used on paper. Then follow the practice opportunities outlined in the section "Practice Analyzing Existing Subnets," later in this chapter.

Resident Subnet Example 1

For example, consider the requirement to find the resident subnet for IP address 130.4.102.1, mask 255.255.240.0. The process does not require you to think about prefix bits versus host bits, convert the mask, think about the mask in binary, or convert the IP address to and from binary. Instead, for each of the four octets, choose an action based on the value in the mask. Figure 14-9 shows the results; the circled numbers in the figure refer to the step numbers in the written process to find the subnet ID, as listed in the previous few pages.

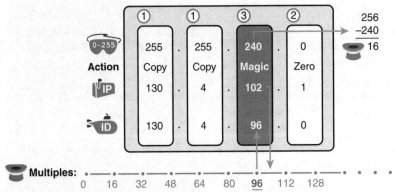

Figure 14-9   *Find the Subnet ID: 130.4.102.1, 255.255.240.0*

First, examine the three uninteresting octets (1, 2, and 4, in this example). The process keys on the mask, and the first two octets have a mask value of 255, so simply copy the IP address to the place where you intend to write down the subnet ID. The fourth octet has a mask value of 0, so write down a 0 for the fourth octet of the subnet ID.

The most challenging logic occurs in the interesting octet, which is the third octet in this example, because of the mask value 240 in that octet. For this octet, Step 3A asks you to calculate the magic number as 256 – mask. That means you take the mask's value in the interesting octet (240, in this case) and subtract it from 256: 256 – 240 = 16. The subnet ID's value in this octet must be a multiple of decimal 16, in this case.

Step 3B then asks you to find the multiples of the magic number (16, in this case) and choose the one closest to the IP address without going over. Specifically, that means that you should mentally calculate the multiples of the magic number, starting at 0. (Do not forget to start at 0!) Count, starting at 0: 0, 16, 32, 48, 64, 80, 96, 112, and so on. Then, find the multiple closest to the IP address value in this octet (102, in this case), without going over 102. So, as shown in Figure 14-9, you make the third octet's value 96 to complete the subnet ID of 130.4.96.0.

Resident Subnet Example 2

Consider another example: 192.168.5.77, mask 255.255.255.224. Figure 14-10 shows the results.

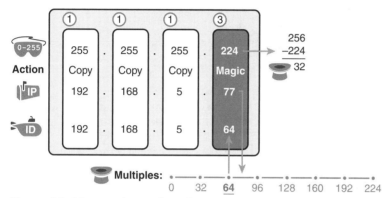

Figure 14-10   *Resident Subnet for 192.168.5.77, 255.255.255.224*

The three uninteresting octets (1, 2, and 3, in this case) require only a little thought. For each octet, each with a mask value of 255, just copy the IP address.

For the interesting octet, at Step 3A, the magic number is 256 − 224 = 32. The multiples of the magic number are 0, 32, 64, 96, and so on. Because the IP address value in the fourth octet is 77, in this case, the multiple must be the number closest to 77 without going over; therefore, the subnet ID ends with 64, for a value of 192.168.5.64.

Resident Subnet Practice Problems

Before moving to the next section, take some time to fill in the blanks in Table 14-10. Check your answers against Table 14-16 in the section "Answers to Earlier Practice Problems," later in this chapter. Complete the table by listing the subnet ID in each case. The text following Table 14-16 also lists explanations for each problem.

Table 14-10   Practice Problems: Find Subnet ID, Difficult Masks

Problem	IP Address	Mask	Subnet ID
1	10.77.55.3	255.248.0.0	
2	172.30.99.4	255.255.192.0	
3	192.168.6.54	255.255.255.252	
4	10.77.3.14	255.255.128.0	
5	172.22.55.77	255.255.254.0	
6	1.99.53.76	255.255.255.248	

Finding the Subnet Broadcast Address: Difficult Masks

To find a subnet's broadcast address, you can use a similar process. For simplicity, this process begins with the subnet ID, rather than the IP address. If you happen to start with an IP address instead, use the processes in this chapter to first find the subnet ID, and then use the following process to find the subnet broadcast address for that same subnet. For each octet:

Step 1.   If the mask octet = 255, copy the subnet ID.

Step 2.   If the mask octet = 0, write 255.

Step 3.   If the mask is neither, identify this octet as the *interesting octet*:

  a.   Calculate the *magic number* as 256 – mask.

  b.   Take the subnet ID's value, add the magic number, and subtract 1 (ID + magic – 1).

Subnet Broadcast Example 1

The first example continues the first example from the section "Finding the Subnet ID: Difficult Masks," earlier in this chapter, as demonstrated in Figure 14-9. That example started with the IP address/mask of 130.4.102.1, 255.255.240.0, and showed how to find subnet ID 130.4.96.0. Figure 14-11 now begins with that subnet ID and the same mask.

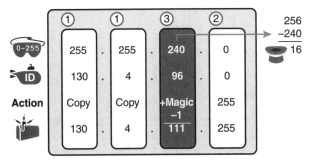

Figure 14-11   *Find the Subnet Broadcast: 130.4.96.0, 255.255.240.0*

First, examine the three uninteresting octets (1, 2, and 4). The process keys on the mask, and the first two octets have a mask value of 255, so simply copy the subnet ID to the place where you intend to write down the subnet broadcast address. The fourth octet has a mask value of 0, so write down a 255 for the fourth octet.

The logic related to the interesting octet occurs in the third octet in this example because of the mask value 240. First, Step 3A asks you to calculate the magic number, as 256 – mask. (If you had already calculated the subnet ID using the decimal process in this book, you should already know the magic number.) At Step 3B, you take the subnet ID's value (96), add the magic number (16), and subtract 1, for a total of 111. That makes the subnet broadcast address 130.4.111.255.

Subnet Broadcast Example 2

Again, this example continues an earlier example, from the section "Resident Subnet Example 2," as demonstrated in Figure 14-10. That example started with the IP address/mask of 192.168.5.77, mask 255.255.255.224 and showed how to find subnet ID 192.168.5.64. Figure 14-12 now begins with that subnet ID and the same mask.

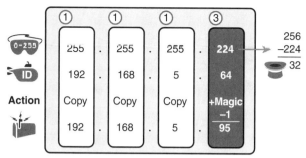

Figure 14-12   *Find the Subnet Broadcast: 192.168.5.64, 255.255.255.224*

First, examine the three uninteresting octets (1, 2, and 3). The process keys on the mask, and the first three octets have a mask value of 255, so simply copy the subnet ID to the place where you intend to write down the subnet broadcast address.

The interesting logic occurs in the interesting octet, the fourth octet in this example, because of the mask value 224. First, Step 3A asks you to calculate the magic number, as 256 – mask. (If you had already calculated the subnet ID, it is the same magic number because the same mask is used.) At Step 3B, you take the subnet ID's value (64), add magic (32), and subtract 1, for a total of 95. That makes the subnet broadcast address 192.168.5.95.

Subnet Broadcast Address Practice Problems

Before moving to the next section, take some time to do several practice problems on a scratch piece of paper. Go back to Table 14-10, which lists IP addresses and masks, and practice by finding the subnet broadcast address for all the problems in that table. Then check your answers against Table 14-17 in the section "Answers to Earlier Practice Problems," later in this chapter.

Practice Analyzing Existing Subnets

As with the other subnetting math in this book, using a two-phase approach may help. Take time now to practice until you feel like you understand the process. Then, before the exam, make sure you master the math. Table 14-11 summarizes the key concepts and suggestions for this two-phase approach.

Table 14-11   Keep-Reading and Take-Exam Goals for This Chapter's Topics

Time Frame	Before Moving to the Next Chapter	Before Taking the Exam
Focus On…	Learning how	Being correct and fast
Tools Allowed	All	Your brain and a notepad
Goal: Accuracy	90% correct	100% correct
Goal: Speed	Any speed	20–30 seconds

A Choice: Memorize or Calculate

As described in this chapter, the decimal processes to find the subnet ID and subnet broadcast address do require some calculation, including the calculation of the magic number (256 – mask). The processes also use a DDN mask, so if an exam question gives you a prefix-style mask, you need to convert to DDN format before using the process in this book.

Over the years, some people have told me they prefer to memorize a table to find the magic number. These tables could list the magic number for different DDN masks and prefix masks, so you avoid converting from the prefix mask to DDN. Table 14-12 shows an example of such a table. Feel free to ignore this table, use it, or make your own.

Table 14-12 Reference Table: DDN Mask Values, Binary Equivalent, Magic Numbers, and Prefixes

Prefix, interesting octet 2	/9	/10	/11	/12	/13	/14	/15	/16
Prefix, interesting octet 3	/17	/18	/19	/20	/21	/22	/23	/24
Prefix, interesting octet 4	/25	/26	/27	/28	/29	/30		
Magic number	128	64	32	16	8	4	2	1
DDN mask in the interesting octet	128	192	224	240	248	252	254	255

Chapter Review

One key to doing well on the exams is to perform repetitive spaced review sessions. Review this chapter's material using either the tools in the book or interactive tools for the same material found on the book's companion website. Refer to the "Your Study Plan" element for more details. Table 14-13 outlines the key review elements and where you can find them. To better track your study progress, record when you completed these activities in the second column.

Table 14-13 Chapter Review Tracking

Review Element	Review Date(s)	Resource Used
Review key topics		Book, website
Review key terms		Book, website
Answer DIKTA questions		Book, PTP
Review memory tables		Website
Practice mask analysis		Website, Appendix F
Practice analyzing existing subnets		Website, Appendix F
Watch video		Website

Review All the Key Topics

Table 14-14 Key Topics for Chapter 14

Key Topic Element	Description	Page Number
List	Definition of a subnet's key numbers	358
Table 14-2	Key facts about the subnet ID	360
Table 14-3	Key facts about the subnet broadcast address	361
List	Steps to use binary math to find the subnet ID	364
List	General steps to use binary and decimal math to find the subnet ID	366

Key Topic Element	Description	Page Number
List	Steps to use decimal and binary math to find the subnet broadcast address	366
List	Steps to use only decimal math to find the subnet ID	369
List	Steps to use only decimal math to find the subnet broadcast address	372

Key Terms You Should Know

resident subnet, subnet address, subnet broadcast address, subnet ID, subnet number

Additional Practice for This Chapter's Processes

You can do more practice with the processes in this chapter with a pair of practice sets. Both give you practice at analyzing existing subnets. You may do each practice set using the following tools:

Application: From the companion website, in the section titled "Memory Tables and Practice Exercises," use the "Analyzing Existing Subnets" exercises 1 and 2, listed under the Chapter Review for this chapter.

PDF: Practice the same problems found in these apps using companion website Appendix F, "Practice for Chapter 14: Analyzing Existing Subnets."

Answers to Earlier Practice Problems

This chapter includes practice problems spread around different locations in the chapter. The answers are located in Tables 14-15, 14-16, and 14-17.

Table 14-15   Answers to Problems in Table 14-9

	IP Address	Mask	Subnet ID	Broadcast Address
1	10.77.55.3	255.255.255.0	10.77.55.0	10.77.55.255
2	172.30.99.4	255.255.255.0	172.30.99.0	172.30.99.255
3	192.168.6.54	255.255.255.0	192.168.6.0	192.168.6.255
4	10.77.3.14	255.255.0.0	10.77.0.0	10.77.255.255
5	172.22.55.77	255.255.0.0	172.22.0.0	172.22.255.255
6	1.99.53.76	255.0.0.0	1.0.0.0	1.255.255.255

Table 14-16   Answers to Problems in Table 14-10

	IP Address	Mask	Subnet ID
1	10.77.55.3	255.248.0.0	10.72.0.0
2	172.30.99.4	255.255.192.0	172.30.64.0
3	192.168.6.54	255.255.255.252	192.168.6.52
4	10.77.3.14	255.255.128.0	10.77.0.0
5	172.22.55.77	255.255.254.0	172.22.54.0
6	1.99.53.76	255.255.255.248	1.99.53.72

The following list explains the answers for Table 14-16:

1. The second octet is the interesting octet, with magic number 256 – 248 = 8. The multiples of 8 include 0, 8, 16, 24, ..., 64, 72, and 80. Here, 72 is closest to the IP address value in that same octet (77) without going over, making the subnet ID 10.72.0.0.

2. The third octet is the interesting octet, with magic number 256 – 192 = 64. The multiples of 64 include 0, 64, 128, and 192. Here, 64 is closest to the IP address value in that same octet (99) without going over, making the subnet ID 172.30.64.0.

3. The fourth octet is the interesting octet, with magic number 256 – 252 = 4. The multiples of 4 include 0, 4, 8, 12, 16, ..., 48, 52, and 56. Here, 52 is the closest to the IP address value in that same octet (54) without going over, making the subnet ID 192.168.6.52.

4. The third octet is the interesting octet, with magic number 256 – 128 = 128. Only two multiples exist that matter: 0 and 128. Here, 0 is the closest to the IP address value in that same octet (3) without going over, making the subnet ID 10.77.0.0.

5. The third octet is the interesting octet, with magic number 256 – 254 = 2. The multiples of 2 include 0, 2, 4, 6, 8, and so on—essentially all even numbers. Here, 54 is closest to the IP address value in that same octet (55) without going over, making the subnet ID 172.22.54.0.

6. The fourth octet is the interesting octet, with magic number 256 – 248 = 8. The multiples of 8 include 0, 8, 16, 24, ..., 64, 72, and 80. Here, 72 is closest to the IP address value in that same octet (76) without going over, making the subnet ID 1.99.53.72.

Table 14-17   Answers to Problems in the Section "Subnet Broadcast Address Practice Problems"

	Subnet ID	Mask	Broadcast Address
1	10.72.0.0	255.248.0.0	10.79.255.255
2	172.30.64.0	255.255.192.0	172.30.127.255
3	192.168.6.52	255.255.255.252	192.168.6.55
4	10.77.0.0	255.255.128.0	10.77.127.255
5	172.22.54.0	255.255.254.0	172.22.55.255
6	1.99.53.72	255.255.255.248	1.99.53.79

The following list explains the answers for Table 14-17:

1. The second octet is the interesting octet. Completing the three easy octets means that the broadcast address in the interesting octet will be 10.___.255.255. With magic number 256 – 248 = 8, the second octet will be 72 (from the subnet ID), plus 8, minus 1, or 79.

2. The third octet is the interesting octet. Completing the three easy octets means that the broadcast address in the interesting octet will be 172.30.___.255. With magic number 256 – 192 = 64, the interesting octet will be 64 (from the subnet ID), plus 64 (the magic number), minus 1, for 127.

3. The fourth octet is the interesting octet. Completing the three easy octets means that the broadcast address in the interesting octet will be 192.168.6.___. With magic number 256 − 252 = 4, the interesting octet will be 52 (the subnet ID value), plus 4 (the magic number), minus 1, or 55.

4. The third octet is the interesting octet. Completing the three easy octets means that the broadcast address will be 10.77.___.255. With magic number 256 − 128 = 128, the interesting octet will be 0 (the subnet ID value), plus 128 (the magic number), minus 1, or 127.

5. The third octet is the interesting octet. Completing the three easy octets means that the broadcast address will be 172.22.___.255. With magic number 256 − 254 = 2, the broadcast address in the interesting octet will be 54 (the subnet ID value), plus 2 (the magic number), minus 1, or 55.

6. The fourth octet is the interesting octet. Completing the three easy octets means that the broadcast address will be 1.99.53.___. With magic number 256 − 248 = 8, the broadcast address in the interesting octet will be 72 (the subnet ID value), plus 8 (the magic number), minus 1, or 79.

14

CHAPTER 15

Subnet Design

This chapter covers the following exam topics:

1.0 Network Fundamentals

    1.6 Configure and verify IPv4 addressing and subnetting

So far in this book, most of the discussion about IPv4 used examples with the addresses and masks already given. This book has shown many examples already, but the examples so far do not ask you to pick the IP address or pick the mask. Instead, as discussed back in Chapter 11, "Perspectives on IPv4 Subnetting," this book so far has assumed that someone else designed the IP addressing and subnetting plan, and this book shows how to implement it.

This chapter turns that model around. It goes back to the progression of building and implementing IPv4, as discussed in Chapter 11, as shown in Figure 15-1. This chapter picks up the story right after some network engineer has chosen a Class A, B, or C network to use for the enterprise's IPv4 network. And then this chapter discusses the design choices related to picking one subnet mask to use for all subnets (the first major section) and what subnet IDs that choice creates (the second major section).

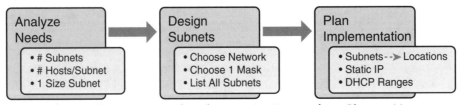

Figure 15-1 *Subnet Design and Implementation Process from Chapter 11*

"Do I Know This Already?" Quiz

Take the quiz (either here or use the PTP software) if you want to use the score to help you decide how much time to spend on this chapter. The letter answers are listed at the bottom of the page following the quiz. Appendix C, found both at the end of the book as well as on the companion website, includes both the answers and explanations. You can also find both answers and explanations in the PTP testing software.

Table 15-1 "Do I Know This Already?" Foundation Topics Section-to-Question Mapping

Foundation Topics Section	Questions
Choosing the Mask(s) to Meet Requirements	1–3
Finding All Subnet IDs	4–6

1. An IP subnetting design effort is under way at a company. So far, the senior engineer has decided to use private Class B network 172.23.0.0. The design calls for 100 subnets, with the largest subnet needing 500 hosts. Management requires that the design accommodate 50 percent growth in the number of subnets and the size of the largest subnet. The requirements also state that a single mask must be used throughout the Class B network. How many masks meet the requirements?

   a. 0
   b. 1
   c. 2
   d. 3+

2. An IP subnetting design requires 200 subnets and 120 hosts/subnet for the largest subnets, and requires that a single mask be used throughout the one private IP network that will be used. The design also requires planning for 20 percent growth in the number of subnets and number of hosts/subnet in the largest subnet. Which of the following answers lists a private IP network and mask that, if chosen, would meet the requirements?

   a. 10.0.0.0/25
   b. 10.0.0.0/22
   c. 172.16.0.0/23
   d. 192.168.7.0/24

3. An engineer has planned to use private Class B network 172.19.0.0 and a single subnet mask throughout the network. The answers list the masks considered by the engineer. Choose the mask that, among the answers, supplies the largest number of hosts per subnet, while also supplying enough subnet bits to support 1000 subnets.

   a. 255.255.255.0
   b. /26
   c. 255.255.252.0
   d. /28

4. An engineer has calculated the list of subnet IDs, in consecutive order, for network 172.30.0.0, assuming that the /22 mask is used throughout the network. Which of the following are true? (Choose two answers.)

   a. Any two consecutive subnet IDs differ by a value of 22 in the third octet.
   b. Any two consecutive subnet IDs differ by a value of 16 in the fourth octet.
   c. The list contains 64 subnet IDs.
   d. The last subnet ID is 172.30.252.0.

5. Which of the following are valid subnet IDs for private network 192.168.9.0, using mask /29, assuming that mask /29 is used throughout the network?

   a. 192.168.9.144
   b. 192.168.9.58
   c. 192.168.9.242
   d. 192.168.9.9

6. Which of the following is not a valid subnet ID for private network 172.19.0.0, using mask /24, assuming that mask /24 is used throughout the network?

    a. 172.19.0.0

    b. 172.19.1.0

    c. 172.19.255.0

    d. 172.19.0.16

Foundation Topics

Choosing the Mask(s) to Meet Requirements

This first major section examines how to find all the masks that meet the stated requirements for the number of subnets and the number of hosts per subnet. To that end, the text assumes that the designer has already determined these requirements and has chosen the network private number to be subnetted. The designer has also made the choice to use a single subnet mask value throughout the classful network.

Armed with the information in this chapter, you can answer questions such as the following, a question that matters both for real engineering jobs and the Cisco exams:

You are using Class B network 172.16.0.0. You need 200 subnets and 200 hosts/subnet. Which of the following subnet mask(s) meet the requirements? (This question is then followed by several answers that list different subnet masks.)

To begin, this section reviews the concepts in Chapter 11's section "Choose the Mask." That section introduced the main concepts about how an engineer, when designing subnet conventions, must choose the mask based on the requirements.

After reviewing the related concepts from Chapter 11, this section examines this topic in more depth. In particular, this chapter looks at three general cases:

■ No masks meet the requirements.

■ One and only one mask meets the requirements.

■ Multiple masks meet the requirements.

For this last case, the text discusses how to determine all masks that meet the requirements and the tradeoffs related to choosing which one mask to use.

Review: Choosing the Minimum Number of Subnet and Host Bits

The network designer must examine the requirements for the number of subnets and number of hosts/subnet, and then choose a mask. As discussed in detail in Chapter 13, "Analyzing Subnet Masks," a classful view of IP addresses defines the three-part structure of an IP address: network, subnet, and host. The network designer must choose the mask so that the number of subnet and host bits (S and H, respectively, in Figure 15-2) meet the requirements.

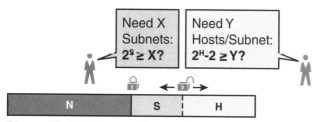

Figure 15-2   *Choosing the Number of Subnet and Host Bits*

Basically, the designer must choose S subnet bits so that the number of subnets that can be uniquely numbered with S bits (2^S) is at least as large as the required number of subnets. The designer applies similar logic to the number of host bits H, while noting that the formula is $2^H - 2$, because of the two reserved numbers in each subnet. So, keeping the powers of 2 handy, as shown in Table 15-2, will be useful when working through these problems.

Table 15-2   Powers of 2 Reference for Designing Masks

Number of Bits	2^X	Number of Bits	2^X	Number of Bits	2^X	Number of Bits	2^X
1	2	5	32	9	512	13	8192
2	4	6	64	10	1024	14	16,384
3	8	7	128	11	2048	15	32,768
4	16	8	256	12	4096	16	65,536

More formally, the process must determine the minimum values for both S and H that meet the requirements. The following list summarizes the initial steps to choose the mask:

Step 1.   Determine the number of network bits (N) based on the class.

Step 2.   Determine the smallest value of S, so that 2^S => X, where X represents the required number of subnets.

Step 3.   Determine the smallest value of H, so that $2^H - 2$ => Y, where Y represents the required number of hosts/subnet.

The next three sections examine how to use these initial steps to choose a subnet mask.

No Masks Meet Requirements

After you determine the required number of subnet and host bits, those bits might not fit into a 32-bit IPv4 subnet mask. Remember, the mask always has a total of 32 bits, with binary 1s in the network and subnet parts and binary 0s in the host part. For the exam, a question might provide a set of requirements that simply cannot be met with 32 total bits.

For example, consider the following sample exam question:

A network engineer is planning a subnet design. The engineer plans to use Class B network 172.16.0.0. The network has a need for 300 subnets and 280 hosts per subnet. Which of the following masks could the engineer choose?

The three-step process shown in the previous section shows that these requirements mean that a total of 34 bits will be needed, so no mask meets the requirements. First, as a Class B network, 16 network bits exist, with 16 host bits from which to create the subnet part and to leave enough host bits to number the hosts in each subnet. For the number of subnet bits, S=8 does not work, because $2^8 = 256 < 300$. However, S=9 works, because $2^9 = 512 => 300$. Similarly, because $2^8 - 2 = 254$, which is less than 300, 8 host bits are not enough but 9 host bits ($2^9 - 2 = 510$) are just enough.

These requirements do not leave enough space to number all the hosts and subnet, because the network, subnet, and host parts add up to more than 32:

N=16, because as a Class B network, 16 network bits exist.

The minimum S=9, because S=8 provides too few subnets ($2^8 = 256 < 300$) but S=9 provides $2^9 = 512$ subnets.

The minimum H=9, because H=8 provides too few hosts ($2^8 - 2 = 254 < 280$) but H=9 provides $2^9 - 2 = 510$ hosts/subnet.

Figure 15-3 shows the resulting format for the IP addresses in this subnet, after the engineer has allocated 9 subnet bits on paper. Only 7 host bits remain, but the engineer needs 9 host bits.

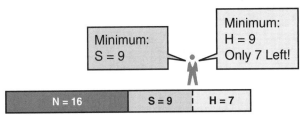

Figure 15-3 *Too Few Bits for the Host Part, Given the Requirements*

One Mask Meets Requirements

The process discussed in this chapter in part focuses on finding the smallest number of subnet bits and the smallest number of host bits to meet the requirements. If the engineer tries to use these minimum values, and the combined network, subnet, and host parts add up to exactly 32 bits, exactly one mask meets the requirements.

For example, consider a revised version of the example in the previous section, with smaller numbers of subnets and hosts, as follows:

A network engineer is planning a subnet design. The engineer plans to use Class B network 172.16.0.0. The network has a need for 200 subnets and 180 hosts per subnet. Which of the following masks could the engineer choose?

The three-step process to determine the numbers of network, minimum subnet, and minimum host bits results in a need for 16, 8, and 8 bits, respectively. As before, with a Class B network, 16 network bits exist. With a need for only 200 subnets, S=8 does work, because $2^8 = 256 => 200$; 7 subnet bits would not supply enough subnets ($2^7 = 128$). Similarly, because $2^8 - 2 = 254 => 180$, 8 host bits meet the requirements; 7 host bits (for 126 total hosts/subnet) would not be enough.

Figure 15-4 shows the resulting format for the IP addresses in this subnet.

Answers to the "Do I Know This Already?" quiz:

1 A **2** B **3** B **4** C, D **5** A **6** D

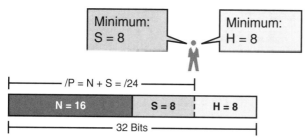

Figure 15-4 *One Mask That Meets the Requirements*

Figure 15-4 shows the mask conceptually. To find the actual mask value, simply record the mask in prefix format (/P), where P = N + S or, in this case, /24.

Multiple Masks Meet Requirements

Depending on the requirements and choice of network, several masks might meet the requirements for the numbers of subnets and hosts/subnet. In these cases, you need to find all the masks that could be used. Then, you have a choice, but what should you consider when choosing one mask among all those that meet your requirements? This section shows how to find all the masks, as well as the facts to consider when choosing one mask from the list.

Finding All the Masks: Concepts

To help you better understand how to find all the subnet masks in binary, this section uses two major steps. In the first major step, you build the 32-bit binary subnet mask on paper. You write down binary 1s for the network bits, binary 1s for the subnet bits, and binary 0s for the host bits, just as always. However, you will use the minimum values for S and H. And when you write down these bits, you will not have 32 bits yet!

For example, consider the following problem, similar to the earlier examples in this chapter but with some changes in the requirements:

A network engineer is planning a subnet design. The engineer plans to use Class B network 172.16.0.0. The network has a need for 50 subnets and 180 hosts per subnet. Which of the following masks could the engineer choose?

This example is similar to an earlier example, except that only 50 subnets are needed in this case. Again, the engineer is using private IP network 172.16.0.0, meaning 16 network bits. The design requires only 6 subnet bits in this case, because $2^6 = 64 => 50$, and with only 5 subnet bits, $2^5 = 32 < 50$. The design then requires a minimum of 8 host bits.

One way to discuss the concepts and find all the masks that meet these requirements is to write down the bits in the subnet mask: binary 1s for the network and subnet parts and binary 0s for the host part. However, think of the 32-bit mask as 32-bit positions, and when writing the binary 0s, *write them on the far right*. Figure 15-5 shows the general idea.

Figure 15-5 shows 30 bits of the mask, but the mask must have 32 bits. The 2 remaining bits might become subnet bits, being set to binary 1. Alternatively, these 2 bits could be made host bits, being set to binary 0. The engineer simply needs to choose based on whether he would like more subnet bits, to number more subnets, or more host bits, to number more hosts/subnet.

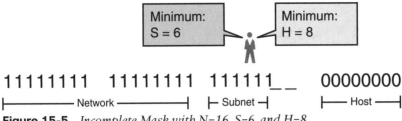

Figure 15-5 *Incomplete Mask with N=16, S=6, and H=8*

Regardless of the requirements, when choosing any IPv4 subnet mask, you must always follow this rule:

A subnet mask begins with all binary 1s, followed by all binary 0s, with no interleaving of 1s and 0s.

With the example shown in Figure 15-5, with 2 open bits, one value (binary 01) breaks this rule. However, the other three combinations of 2 bits (00, 10, and 11) do not break the rule. As a result, three masks meet the requirements in this example, as shown in Figure 15-6.

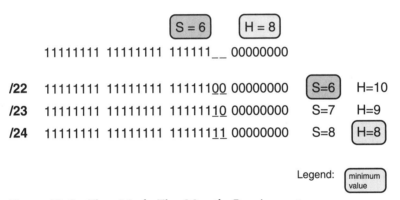

Figure 15-6 *Three Masks That Meet the Requirements*

In the three masks, the first has the least number of subnet bits among the three masks, but therefore has the most number of host bits. So, the first mask maximizes the number of hosts/subnet. The last mask uses the minimum value for the number of host bits, therefore using the most number of subnet bits allowed while still meeting the requirements. As a result, the last mask maximizes the number of subnets allowed.

Finding All the Masks: Math

Although the concepts related to the example shown in Figures 15-5 and 15-6 are important, you can find the range of masks that meets the requirements more easily just using some simple math. The process to find the masks requires only a few steps, after you know N and the minimum values of S and H. The process finds the value of /P when using the least number of subnet bits, and when using the least number of host bits, as follows:

Step 1. Calculate the shortest prefix mask (/P) based on the *minimum value of S*, where P = N + S.

Step 2. Calculate the longest prefix mask (/P) based on the *minimum value of H*, where P = 32 − H.

Step 3. The range of valid masks includes all /P values between the two values calculated in the previous steps.

For example, in the example shown in Figure 15-6, N=16, the minimum S=6, and the minimum H=8. The first step identifies the shortest prefix mask (the /P with the smallest value of P) of /22 by adding N and S (16 + 6). The second step identifies the longest prefix mask that meets the requirements by subtracting the smallest possible value for H (8, in this case) from 32, for a mask of /24. The third step reminds us that the range is from /22 to /24, meaning that /23 is also an option.

Choosing the Best Mask

When multiple possible masks meet the stated requirements, the engineer has a choice of masks. That, of course, begs some questions: Which mask should you choose? Why would one mask be better than the other? The reasons can be summarized into three main options:

To maximize the number of hosts/subnet: To make this choice, use the shortest prefix mask (that is, the mask with the smallest /P value), because this mask has the largest host part.

To maximize the number of subnets: To make this choice, use the longest prefix mask (that is, the mask with the largest /P value), because this mask has the largest subnet part.

To increase both the numbers of supported subnets and hosts: To make this choice, choose a mask in the middle of the range, which gives you both more subnet bits and more host bits.

For example, in Figure 15-6, the range of masks that meet the requirements is /22 – /24. The shortest mask, /22, has the least subnet bits but the largest number of host bits (10) of the three answers, maximizing the number of hosts/subnet. The longest mask, /24, maximizes the number of subnet bits (8), maximizing the number of subnets, at least among the options that meet the original requirements. The mask in the middle, /23, provides some growth in both subnets and hosts/subnet.

The Formal Process

Although this chapter has explained various steps in finding a subnet mask to meet the design requirements, it has not yet collected these concepts into a list for the entire process. The following list collects all these steps into one place for reference. Note that this list does not introduce any new concepts compared to the rest of this chapter; it just puts all the ideas in one place.

Step 1. Find the number of network bits (N) per class rules.

Step 2. Calculate the minimum number of subnet bits (S) so that 2^S => the number of required subnets.

Step 3. Calculate the minimum number of host bits (H) so that $2^H - 2$ => the number of required hosts/subnet.

Step 4. If N + S + H > 32, no mask meets the need.

Step 5. If N + S + H = 32, one mask meets the need. Calculate the mask as /P, where P = N + S.

Step 6.   If N + S + H < 32, multiple masks meet the need:

   a. Calculate mask /P based on the minimum value of S, where P = N + S. This mask maximizes the number of hosts/subnet.

   b. Calculate mask /P based on the minimum value of H, where P = 32 – H. This mask maximizes the number of possible subnets.

   c. Note that the complete range of masks includes all prefix lengths between the two values calculated in Steps 6A and 6B.

Practice Choosing Subnet Masks

Take the usual two-phase approach to learning new subnetting math and processes. Take the time now to practice to make sure you understand the fundamentals, using the book and notes as needed. Then, sometime before taking the exam, practice until you can reach the goals in the right column of Table 15-3.

Table 15-3   Keep-Reading and Take-Exam Goals for Choosing a Subnet Mask

Time Frame	Before Moving to the Next Chapter	Before Taking the Exam
Focus On...	Learning how	Being correct and fast
Tools Allowed	All	Your brain and a notepad
Goal: Accuracy	90% correct	100% correct
Goal: Speed	Any speed	15 seconds

Practice Problems for Choosing a Subnet Mask

The following list shows three separate problems, each with a classful network number and a required number of subnets and hosts/subnet. For each problem, determine the minimum number of subnet and host bits that meet the requirements. If more than one mask exists, note which mask maximizes the number of hosts/subnet and which maximizes the number of subnets. If only one mask meets the requirements, simply list that mask. List the masks in prefix format:

   1. Network 10.0.0.0, need 1500 subnets, need 300 hosts/subnet

   2. Network 172.25.0.0, need 130 subnets, need 127 hosts/subnet

   3. Network 192.168.83.0, need 8 subnets, need 8 hosts/subnet

Table 15-8, found in the later section "Answers to Earlier Practice Problems," lists the answers.

Finding All Subnet IDs

After the person designing the IP subnetting plan has chosen the one mask to use throughout the Class A, B, or C network, that person will soon need to start assigning specific subnet IDs for use in specific VLANs, WAN links, and other places in the internetwork that need a subnet. But what are those subnet IDs? As it turns out, after the network ID and one subnet mask for all subnets have been chosen, finding all the subnet IDs just requires doing a little math. This second major section of this chapter focuses on that math, which focuses on a single question:

Given a single Class A, B, or C network, and the single subnet mask to use for all subnets, what are all the subnet IDs?

When learning how to answer this question, you can think about the problem in either binary or decimal. This chapter approaches the problem using decimal. Although the process itself requires only simple math, the process requires practice before most people can confidently answer this question.

The decimal process begins by identifying the first, or numerically lowest, subnet ID. After that, the process identifies a pattern in all subnet IDs for a given subnet mask so that you can find each successive subnet ID through simple addition. This section examines the key ideas behind this process first; then you are given a formal definition of the process.

> **NOTE**   Some videos included on the companion website describe the same fundamental processes to find all subnet IDs. You can view those videos before or after reading this section, or even instead of reading this section, as long as you learn how to find all subnet IDs. The process step numbering in the videos might not match the steps shown in this edition of the book.

15

First Subnet ID: The Zero Subnet

The first step in finding all subnet IDs of one network is incredibly simple: Copy the network ID. That is, take the Class A, B, or C network ID—in other words, the classful network ID—and write it down as the first subnet ID. No matter what Class A, B, or C network you use, and no matter what subnet mask you use, the first (numerically lowest) subnet ID is equal to the network ID.

For example, if you begin with classful network 172.20.0.0, no matter what the mask is, the first subnet ID is 172.20.0.0.

This first subnet ID in each network goes by two special names: either **subnet zero** or **zero subnet**. The origin of these names is related to the fact that a network's zero subnet, when viewed in binary, has a subnet part of all binary 0s. In decimal, the zero subnet can be easily identified, because the zero subnet always has the exact same numeric value as the network ID itself.

In the past, engineers avoided using zero subnets because of the ambiguity with one number that could represent the entire classful network, or it could represent one subnet inside the classful network. To help control that, IOS has a global command that can be set one of two ways:

> **ip subnet-zero**, which allows the configuration of addresses in the zero subnet.

> **no ip subnet-zero**, which prevents the configuration of addresses in the zero subnet.

Although most sites use the default setting to allow zero subnets, you can use the **no ip subnet-zero** command to prevent configuring addresses that are part of a zero subnet. Example 15-1 shows how a router rejects an **ip address** command after changing to use **no ip subnet-zero**. Note that the error message does not mention the zero subnet, instead simply stating "bad mask."

Example 15-1 *Effects of* [no] ip subnet-zero *on a Local Router*

```
R1# configure terminal
Enter configuration commands, one per line. End with CNTL/Z.
R1(config)# no ip subnet-zero
R1(config)# interface g0/1
R1(config-if)# ip address 10.0.0.1 255.255.255.0
Bad mask /24 for address 10.0.0.1
```

Note that the **no ip subnet-zero** command affects the local router's **ip address** commands, as well as the local router's **ip route** commands (which define static routes). However, it does not affect the local router's routes as learned with a routing protocol.

Finding the Pattern Using the Magic Number

Subnet IDs follow a predictable pattern, at least when using our assumption of a single subnet mask for all subnets of a network. The pattern uses the *magic number*, as discussed in Chapter 14, "Analyzing Existing Subnets." To review, the magic number is 256, minus the mask's decimal value, in a particular octet that this book refers to as the *interesting octet*.

Figure 15-7 shows four examples of these patterns with four different masks. For example, just look at the top of the figure to start. It lists mask 255.255.128.0 on the left. The third octet is the interesting octet, with a mask value other than 0 or 255 in that octet. The left side shows a magic number calculated as 256 – 128 = 128. So, the pattern of subnet IDs is shown in the highlighted number line; that is, the subnet IDs when using this mask will have either a 0 or 128 in the third octet. For example, if using network 172.16.0.0, the subnet IDs would be 172.16.0.0 and 172.16.128.0.

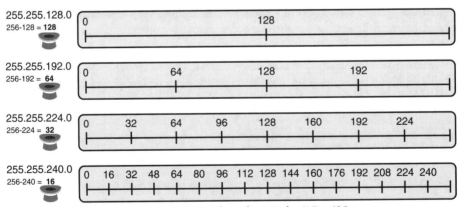

Figure 15-7 *Patterns with Magic Numbers for Masks /17 – /20*

Now focus on the second row, with another example, with mask 255.255.192.0. This row shows a magic number of 64 (256 – 192 = 64), so the subnet IDs will use a value of 0, 64, 128, or 192 (multiples of 64) in the third octet. For example, if used with network 172.16.0.0, the subnet IDs would be 172.16.0.0, 172.16.64.0, 172.16.128.0, and 172.16.192.0.

Looking at the third row/example, the mask is 255.255.224.0, with a magic number of 256 – 224 = 32. So, as shown in the center of the figure, the subnet ID values will be multiples of 32. For example, if used with network 172.16.0.0 again, this mask would tell us that the subnet IDs are 172.16.0.0, 172.16.32.0, 172.16.64.0, 172.16.96.0, and so on.

Finally, for the bottom example, mask 255.255.240.0 makes the magic number, in the third octet, be 16. So, all the subnet IDs will be a multiple of 16 in the third octet, with those values shown in the middle of the figure.

A Formal Process with Fewer Than 8 Subnet Bits

Although it can be easy to see the patterns in Figure 15-7, it might not be as obvious exactly how to apply those concepts to find all the subnet IDs in every case. This section outlines a specific process to find all the subnet IDs.

To simplify the explanations, this section assumes that fewer than 8 subnet bits exist. Later, the section "Finding All Subnets with More Than 8 Subnet Bits," describes the full process that can be used in all cases.

First, to organize your thoughts, you might want to organize the data into a chart like Table 15-4. This book refers to this chart as the list-all-subnets chart.

Table 15-4   Generic List-All-Subnets Chart

Octet	1	2	3	4
Mask				
Magic Number				
Network Number/Zero Subnet				
Next Subnet				
Next Subnet				
Next Subnet				
Broadcast Subnet				
Out of Range— Used by Process				

A formal process to find all subnet IDs, given a network and a single subnet mask, is as follows:

Step 1.   Write down the subnet mask, in decimal, in the first empty row of the table.

Step 2.   Identify the interesting octet, which is the one octet of the mask with a value other than 255 or 0. Draw a rectangle around the column of the interesting octet.

Step 3.   Calculate and write down the magic number by subtracting the *subnet mask's interesting octet* from 256.

Step 4.   Write down the classful network number, which is the same number as the zero subnet, in the next empty row of the list-all-subnets chart.

Step 5.   To find each successive subnet number:

   a. For the three uninteresting octets, copy the previous subnet number's values.

   b. For the interesting octet, add the magic number to the previous subnet number's interesting octet.

Step 6.   When the sum calculated in Step 5B reaches 256, stop the process. The number with the 256 in it is out of range, and the previous subnet number is the broadcast subnet.

Although the written process is long, with practice, most people can find the answers much more quickly with this decimal-based process than by using binary math. As usual, most people learn this process best by seeing it in action, exercising it, and then practicing it. To that end, review the two following examples, and watch the related videos on the companion website for additional examples.

Example 1: Network 172.16.0.0, Mask 255.255.240.0

To begin this example, focus on the first four of the six steps, when subnetting network 172.16.0.0 using mask 255.255.240.0. Figure 15-8 shows the results of these first four steps:

Step 1.   Record mask 255.255.240.0, which was given as part of the problem statement. (Figure 15-8 also shows the network ID, 172.16.0.0, for easy reference.)

Step 2.   The mask's third octet is neither 0 nor 255, which makes the third octet interesting.

Step 3.   Because the mask's value in the third octet is 240, the magic number = 256 − 240 = 16.

Step 4.   Because the network ID is 172.16.0.0, the first subnet ID, the zero subnet, is also 172.16.0.0.

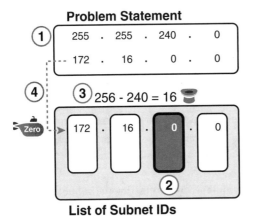

Figure 15-8   *Results of First Four Steps: 172.16.0.0, 255.255.240.0*

These first four steps discover the first subnet (the zero subnet) and get you ready to do the remaining steps by identifying the interesting octet and the magic number. Step 5 in the process tells you to copy the three boring octets and add the magic number (16, in this case) in the interesting octet (octet 3, in this case). Keep repeating this step until the interesting octet value equals 256 (per Step 6). When the total is 256, you have listed all the subnet IDs, and the line with 256 on it is not a correct subnet ID. Figure 15-9 shows the results of the Step 5 actions.

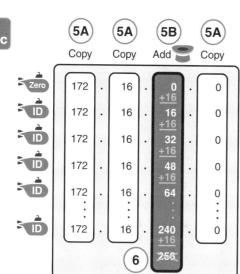

Figure 15-9   *List of Subnet IDs: 172.16.0.0, 255.255.240.0*

NOTE   In any list of all the subnet IDs of a network, the numerically highest subnet ID is called the **broadcast subnet**. Decades ago, engineers avoided using the broadcast subnet. However, using the broadcast subnet causes no problems. The term *broadcast subnet* has its origins in the fact that if you determine the subnet broadcast address inside the broadcast subnet, it has the same numeric value as the network-wide broadcast address.

NOTE   People sometimes confuse the terms *broadcast subnet* and *subnet broadcast address*. The *broadcast subnet* is one subnet, namely the numerically highest subnet; only one such subnet exists per network. The term *subnet broadcast address* refers to the one number in each and every subnet that is the numerically highest number in that subnet.

Example 2: Network 192.168.1.0, Mask 255.255.255.224

With a Class C network and a mask of 255.255.255.224, this example makes the fourth octet the interesting octet. However, the process works the same, with the same logic, just with the interesting logic applied in a different octet. As with the previous example, the following list outlines the first four steps, with Figure 15-10 showing the results of the first four steps:

Step 1.   Record mask 255.255.255.224, which was given as part of the problem statement, and optionally record the network number (192.168.1.0).

Step 2.   The mask's fourth octet is neither 0 nor 255, which makes the fourth octet interesting.

Step 3.   Because the mask's value in the fourth octet is 224, the magic number = 256 − 224 = 32.

Step 4.   Because the network ID is 192.168.1.0, the first subnet ID, the zero subnet, is also 192.168.1.0.

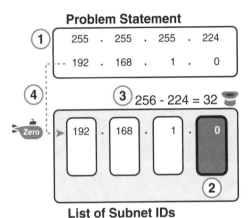

Figure 15-10   *Results of First Four Steps: 192.168.1.0, 255.255.255.224*

From this point, Step 5 in the process tells you to copy the values in the first three octets and then add the magic number (32, in this case) in the interesting octet (octet 4, in this case). Keep doing so until the interesting octet value equals 256 (per Step 6). When the total is 256, you have listed all the subnet IDs, and the line with 256 on it is not a correct subnet ID. Figure 15-11 shows the results of these steps.

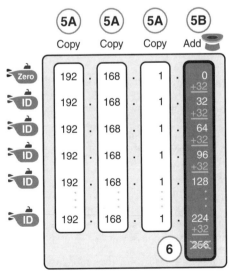

Figure 15-11   *List of Subnet IDs: 192.168.1.0, 255.255.255.224*

Finding All Subnets with Exactly 8 Subnet Bits

The formal process in the earlier section "A Formal Process with Fewer Than 8 Subnet Bits" identified the interesting octet as the octet whose mask value is neither a 255 nor a 0. If the mask defines exactly 8 subnet bits, you must use a different logic to identify the interesting octet; otherwise, the same process can be used. In fact, the actual subnet IDs can be a little more intuitive.

Only two cases exist with exactly 8 subnet bits:

A Class A network with mask 255.255.0.0; the entire second octet contains subnet bits.

A Class B network with mask 255.255.255.0; the entire third octet contains subnet bits.

In each case, use the same process as with less than 8 subnet bits, but identify the interesting octet as the one octet that contains subnet bits. Also, because the mask's value is 255, the magic number will be 256 − 255 = 1, so the subnet IDs are each 1 larger than the previous subnet ID.

For example, for 172.16.0.0, mask 255.255.255.0, the third octet is the interesting octet and the magic number is 256 − 255 = 1. You start with the zero subnet, equal in value to network number 172.16.0.0, and then add 1 in the third octet. For example, the first four subnets are as follows:

172.16.0.0 (zero subnet)

172.16.1.0

172.16.2.0

172.16.3.0

Finding All Subnets with More Than 8 Subnet Bits

Earlier, the section "A Formal Process with Fewer Than 8 Subnet Bits" assumed fewer than 8 subnet bits for the purpose of simplifying the discussions while you learn. In real life, you need to be able to find all subnet IDs with any valid mask, so you cannot assume fewer than 8 subnet bits.

The examples that have at least 9 subnet bits have a minimum of 512 subnet IDs, so writing down such a list would take a lot of time. To conserve space, the examples will use shorthand rather than list hundreds or thousands of subnet IDs.

The process with fewer than 8 subnet bits told you to count in increments of the magic number in one octet. With more than 8 subnet bits, the new expanded process must tell you how to count in multiple octets. So, this section breaks down two general cases: (a) when 9–16 subnet bits exist, which means that the subnet field exists in only two octets, and (b) cases with 17 or more subnet bits, which means that the subnet field exists in three octets.

Process with 9–16 Subnet Bits

To understand the process, you need to know a few terms that the process will use. Figure 15-12 shows the details, with an example that uses Class B network 130.4.0.0 and mask 255.255.255.192. The lower part of the figure details the structure of the addresses per the mask: a network part of two octets because it is a Class B address, a 10-bit subnet part per the mask (/26), and 6 host bits.

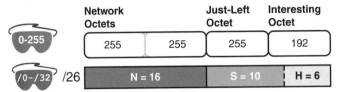

Figure 15-12   *Fundamental Concepts and Terms for the >8 Subnet Bit Process*

In this case, subnet bits exist in two octets: octets 3 and 4. For the purposes of the process, the rightmost of these octets is the interesting octet, and the octet just to the left is the cleverly named *just-left* octet.

The updated process, which makes adjustments for cases in which the subnet field is longer than 1 octet, tells you to count in increments of the magic number in the interesting octet, but count by 1s in the just-left octet. Formally:

Step 1.   Calculate subnet IDs using the 8-subnet-bits-or-less process. However, when the total adds up to 256, move to the next step; consider the subnet IDs listed so far as a *subnet block*.

Step 2.   Copy the previous subnet block, but add 1 to the just-left octet in all subnet IDs in the new block.

Step 3.   Repeat Step 2 until you create the block with a just-left octet of 255, but go no further.

To be honest, the formal concept can cause you problems until you work through some examples, so even if the process remains a bit unclear in your mind, you should work through the following examples instead of rereading the formal process.

First, consider an example based on Figure 15-12, with network 130.4.0.0 and mask 255.255.255.192. Figure 15-12 already showed the structure, and Figure 15-13 shows the subnet ID block created at Step 1.

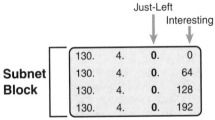

Figure 15-13   *Step 1: Listing the First Subnet ID Block*

The logic at Step 1, to create this subnet ID block of four subnet IDs, follows the same magic number process seen before. The first subnet ID, 130.4.0.0, is the zero subnet. The next three subnet IDs are each 64 bigger, because the magic number, in this case, is 256 − 192 = 64.

Steps 2 and 3 from the formal process tell you how to create 256 subnet blocks, and by doing so, you will list all 1024 subnet IDs. To do so, create 256 total subnet blocks: one with a 0 in the just-left octet, one with a 1 in the just-left octet, and another with a 2 in the just-left octet, up through 255. The process continues through the step at which you create the subnet block with 255 in the just-left octet (third octet, in this case). Figure 15-14 shows the idea, with the addition of the first few subnet blocks.

Just-Left				Just-Left				Just-Left		
130.	4.	**0.**	0	130.	4.	**1.**	0	130.	4.	**2.**	0
130.	4.	**0.**	64	130.	4.	**1.**	64	130.	4.	**2.**	64
130.	4.	**0.**128		130.	4.	**1.**128		130.	4.	**2.**128	
130.	4.	**0.**192		130.	4.	**1.**192		130.	4.	**2.**192	

Figure 15-14 *Step 2: Replicating the Subnet Block with +1 in the Just-Left Octet*

This example, with 10 total subnet bits, creates 256 blocks of four subnets each, for a total of 1024 subnets. This math matches the usual method of counting subnets, because $2^{10} = 1024$.

Process with 17 or More Subnet Bits

To create a subnet design that allows 17 or more subnet bits to exist, the design must use a Class A network. In addition, the subnet part will consist of the entire second and third octets, plus part of the fourth octet. That means a lot of subnet IDs: at least 2^{17} (or 131,072) subnets. Figure 15-15 shows an example of just such a structure, with a Class A network and a /26 mask.

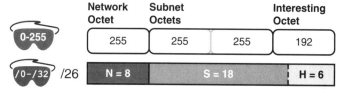

Figure 15-15 *Address Structure with 18 Subnet Bits*

To find all the subnet IDs in this example, you use the same general process as with 9–16 subnet bits, but with many more subnet blocks to create. In effect, you have to create a subnet block for all combinations of values (0–255, inclusive) in both the second and third octets. Figure 15-16 shows the general idea. Note that with only 2 subnet bits in the fourth octet in this example, the subnet blocks will have four subnets each.

10.	**0.**	**0.**	0	10.	**0.**	**1.**	0	10.	**0.255.**	0
10.	**0.**	**0.**	64	10.	**0.**	**1.**	64	10.	**0.255.**	64
10.	**0.**	**0.**128		10.	**0.**	**1.**128		10.	**0.255.**128	
10.	**0.**	**0.**192		10.	**0.**	**1.**192		10.	**0.255.**192	

10.	**1.**	**0.**	0	10.	**1.**	**1.**	0	10.	**1.255.**	0
10.	**1.**	**0.**	64	10.	**1.**	**1.**	64	10.	**1.255.**	64
10.	**1.**	**0.**128		10.	**1.**	**1.**128		10.	**1.255.**128	
10.	**1.**	**0.**192		10.	**1.**	**1.**192		10.	**1.255.**192	

10.**255.**	**0.**	0	10.**255.**	**1.**	0	10.**255.255.**	0
10.**255.**	**0.**	64	10.**255.**	**1.**	64	10.**255.255.**	64
10.**255.**	**0.**128		10.**255.**	**1.**128		10.**255.255.**128	
10.**255.**	**0.**192		10.**255.**	**1.**192		10.**255.255.**192	

Figure 15-16 *256 Times 256 Subnet Blocks of Four Subnets*

Practice Finding All Subnet IDs

Before moving to the next chapter, practice until you get the right answer most of the time—but use any tools you want and take all the time you need. Then, you can move on with your reading. *Before taking the exam*, practice until you reach the goals in the right column of Table 15-5, which summarizes the key concepts and suggestions for this two-phase approach.

Table 15-5   Keep-Reading and Take-Exam Goals for This Chapter's Topics

Time Frame	Before Moving to the Next Chapter	Before Taking the Exam
Focus On…	Learning how	Being correct and fast
Tools Allowed	All	Your brain and a notepad
Goal: Accuracy	90% correct	100% correct
Goal: Speed	Any speed	45 seconds

Practice Problems for Finding All Subnet IDs

The following list shows three separate problems, each with a classful network number and prefix-style mask. Find all subnet IDs for each problem:

1. 192.168.9.0/27

2. 172.30.0.0/20

3. 10.0.0.0/17

The section "Answers to Earlier Practice Problems," later in this chapter, lists the answers.

Chapter Review

One key to doing well on the exams is to perform repetitive spaced review sessions. Review this chapter's material using either the tools in the book or interactive tools for the same material found on the book's companion website. Refer to the "Your Study Plan" element for more details. Table 15-6 outlines the key review elements and where you can find them. To better track your study progress, record when you completed these activities in the second column.

Table 15-6   Chapter Review Tracking

Review Element	Review Date(s)	Resource Used
Review key topics		Book, website
Review key terms		Book, website
Answer DIKTA questions		Book, PTP
Practice subnet design		Website, Appendix G
Watch video		Website

Review All the Key Topics

Table 15-7 Key Topics for Chapter 15

Key Topic Element	Description	Page Number
Definition	Facts about binary values in subnet masks	384
List	The shorter three-step process to find all prefix masks that meet certain requirements	384
List	Reasons to choose one subnet mask versus another	385
Step list	The complete process for finding and choosing masks to meet certain requirements	385
Step list	Formal steps to find all subnet IDs when fewer than 8 subnet bits exist	389
Figure 15-9	An example of adding the magic number in the interesting octet to find all subnet IDs	391
Step list	Formal steps to find all subnet IDs when more than 8 subnet bits exist	394

15

Key Terms You Should Know

broadcast subnet, subnet zero, zero subnet

Additional Practice for This Chapter's Processes

For additional practice with subnet mask design and finding all subnet IDs, you may do the same set of practice problems using your choice of tools:

> **PDF:** Practice using online Appendix G, "Practice for Chapter 15: Subnet Design."

Answers to Earlier Practice Problems

Answers to Practice Choosing Subnet Masks

The earlier section "Practice Choosing Subnet Masks" listed three practice problems. The answers are listed here so that the answers are nearby but not visible from the list of problems. Table 15-8 lists the answers, with notes related to each problem following the table.

Table 15-8 Practice Problems: Find the Masks That Meet Requirements

Problem	Class	Minimum Subnet Bits	Minimum Host Bits	Prefix Range	Prefix to Maximize Subnets	Prefix to Maximize Hosts
1	A	11	9	/19 – /23	/23	/19
2	B	8	8	/24	—	—
3	C	3	4	/27 – /28	/28	/27

1. N=8, because the problem lists Class A network 10.0.0.0. With a need for 1500 subnets, 10 subnet bits supply only 1024 subnets (per Table 15-2), but 11 subnet bits (S) would provide 2048 subnets—more than the required 1500. Similarly, the smallest number of host bits would be 9, because $2^8 - 2 = 254$, and the design requires 300 hosts/subnet. The shortest prefix mask would then be /19, found by adding N (8) and the smallest usable number of subnet bits S (11). Similarly, with a minimum H value of 9, the longest prefix mask, maximizing the number of subnets, is $32 - H = /23$.

2. N=16, because the problem lists Class B network 172.25.0.0. With a need for 130 subnets, 7 subnet bits supply only 128 subnets (per Table 15-2), but 8 subnet bits (S) would provide 256 subnets—more than the required 130. Similarly, the smallest number of host bits would be 8, because $2^7 - 2 = 126$—close to the required 127, but not quite enough, making H=8 the smallest number of host bits that meets requirements. Note that the network, minimum subnet bits, and minimum host bits add up to 32, so only one mask meets the requirements, namely /24, found by adding the number of network bits (16) to the minimum number of subnet bits (8).

3. N=24, because the problem lists Class C network 192.168.83.0. With a need for 8 subnets, 3 subnet bits supply enough, but just barely. The smallest number of host bits would be 4, because $2^3 - 2 = 6$, and the design requires 8 hosts/subnet. The shortest prefix mask would then be /27, found by adding N (24) and the smallest usable number of subnet bits S (3). Similarly, with a minimum H value of 4, the longest prefix mask, maximizing the number of subnets, is $32 - H = /28$.

Answers to Practice Finding All Subnet IDs

The earlier section "Practice Finding All Subnet IDs" listed three practice problems. The answers are listed here so that they are not visible from the same page as the list of problems.

Answer, Practice Problem 1

Problem 1 lists network 192.168.9.0, mask /27. The mask converts to DDN mask 255.255.255.224. When used with a Class C network, which has 24 network bits, only 3 subnet bits exist, and they all sit in the fourth octet. So, this problem is a case of fewer than 8 subnet bits, with the fourth octet as the interesting octet.

To get started listing subnets, first write down the zero subnet and then start adding the magic number in the interesting octet. The zero subnet equals the network ID (192.168.9.0, in this case). The magic number, calculated as $256 - 224 = 32$, should be added to the previous subnet ID's interesting octet. Table 15-9 lists the results.

Table 15-9   List-All-Subnets Chart: 192.168.9.0/27

Octet	1	2	3	4
Mask	255	255	255	224
Magic Number	—	—	—	32
Classful Network/Subnet Zero	192	168	9	0
First Nonzero Subnet	192	168	9	32
Next Subnet	192	168	9	64

Octet	1	2	3	4
Next Subnet	192	168	9	96
Next Subnet	192	168	9	128
Next Subnet	192	168	9	160
Next Subnet	192	168	9	192
Broadcast Subnet	192	168	9	224
Invalid—Used by Process	192	168	9	256

Answer, Practice Problem 2

Problem 2 lists network 172.30.0.0, mask /20. The mask converts to DDN mask 255.255.240.0. When used with a Class B network, which has 16 network bits, only 4 subnet bits exist, and they all sit in the third octet. So, this problem is a case of fewer than 8 subnet bits, with the third octet as the interesting octet.

To get started listing subnets, first write down the zero subnet and then start adding the magic number in the interesting octet. The zero subnet equals the network ID (or 172.30.0.0, in this case). The magic number, calculated as 256 − 240 = 16, should be added to the previous subnet ID's interesting octet. Table 15-10 lists the results.

Table 15-10   List-All-Subnets Chart: 172.30.0.0/20

Octet	1	2	3	4
Mask	255	255	240	0
Magic Number	—	—	16	—
Classful Network/Subnet Zero	172	30	0	0
First Nonzero Subnet	172	30	16	0
Next Subnet	172	30	32	0
Next Subnet	172	30	Skipping...	0
Next Subnet	172	30	224	0
Broadcast Subnet	172	30	240	0
Invalid—Used by Process	172	30	256	0

Answer, Practice Problem 3

Problem 3 lists network 10.0.0.0, mask /17. The mask converts to DDN mask 255.255.128.0. When used with a Class A network, which has 8 network bits, 9 subnet bits exist. Using the terms unique to this chapter, octet 3 is the interesting octet, with only 1 subnet bit in that octet, and octet 2 is the just-left octet, with 8 subnet bits.

In this case, begin by finding the first subnet block. The magic number is 256 − 128 = 128. The first subnet (zero subnet) equals the network ID. So, the first subnet ID block includes the following:

10.0.0.0

10.0.128.0

Then, you create a subnet block for all 256 possible values in the just-left octet, or octet 2 in this case. The following list shows the first three subnet ID blocks, plus the last subnet ID block, rather than listing page upon page of subnet IDs:

10.0.0.0 (zero subnet)

10.0.128.0

10.1.0.0

10.1.128.0

10.2.0.0

10.2.128.0

...

10.255.0.0

10.255.128.0 (broadcast subnet)

Part IV Review

Keep track of your part review progress with the checklist in Table P4-1. Details on each task follow the table.

Table P4-1   Part IV Part Review Checklist

Activity	1st Date Completed	2nd Date Completed
Repeat All DIKTA Questions		
Answer Part Review Questions		
Review Key Topics		
Subnetting Exercises in PDF Appendices on Companion Website		
Interactive Subnetting Exercises on Companion Website		
Watch Video		

Repeat All DIKTA Questions

For this task, use the PTP software to answer the "Do I Know This Already?" questions again for the chapters in this part of the book.

Answer Part Review Questions

For this task, use PTP to answer the Part Review questions for this part of the book.

Review Key Topics

Review all key topics in all chapters in this part, either by browsing the chapters or by using the Key Topics application on the companion website.

Watch Video

The companion website includes a variety of subnetting videos. Some have the familiar common mistake and Q&A format as the other chapters, whereas others simply work through various subnetting processes. Use these videos to challenge your thinking, dig deeper, review topics, and better prepare for the exam. Make sure to bookmark a link to the companion website and use the videos for review whenever you have a few extra minutes.

Subnetting Exercises

Chapters 12 through 15 list some subnetting exercises, along with time and accuracy goals. Now is a good time to work on those goals. Some options include the following:

Practice from this book's appendices or web applications: This book includes four appendices of subnetting practice exercises, all available from the companion website. From that website, to use the static PDFs, look to the section titled "Study Resources." To find the interactive versions of the exercises in those same appendices, look to the section titled "Memory Tables and Practice Exercises." Look for these topics/appendices:

Appendix D, "Practice for Chapter 12: Analyzing Classful IPv4 Networks"

Appendix E, "Practice for Chapter 13: Analyzing Subnet Masks"

Appendix F, "Practice for Chapter 14: Analyzing Existing Subnets"

Appendix G, "Practice for Chapter 15: Subnet Design"

IP Subnetting Practice Question Kit: As mentioned in the Introduction to the book, if you want large amounts of subnetting practice, with explanations that match the processes in the book, consider purchasing the IP Subnetting Practice Question Kit, available at ciscopress.com.

Author's blog: I've written a few dozen subnetting exercises on the blog over the years. Just look at the Questions menu item at the top of the page, and you will see a variety of IPv4 addressing and subnetting question types. Start at https://www.certskills.com.

Parts V and VI work together to reveal the details of how to implement IPv4 routing in Cisco routers. To that end, Part V focuses on the most common features for Cisco routers, including IP address configuration, connected routes, and static routes. Part VI then goes into some detail about the one IP routing protocol discussed in this book: OSPF Version 2 (OSPFv2).

Part V follows a progression of topics. First, Chapter 16 examines the fundamentals of routers—the physical components, how to access the router command-line interface (CLI), and the configuration process. Chapter 16 makes a close comparison of the switch CLI and its basic administrative commands so that you need to learn only new commands that apply to routers but not to switches.

Chapter 17 then moves on to discuss how to configure routers to route IPv4 packets in the most basic designs. Those designs require a simple IP address/mask configuration on each interface, with the addition of a static route command—a command that directly configures a route into the IP routing table—for each destination subnet.

Chapter 18 continues the progression into more challenging but more realistic configurations related to routing between subnets in a LAN environment. Most LANs use many VLANs, with one subnet per VLAN. Cisco routers and switches can be configured to route packets between those subnets, with more than a few twists in the configuration.

Chapter 19 moves the focus from routers to hosts. Hosts rely on a working internetwork of routers, but the hosts need IP settings as well, with an IP address, mask, default gateway, and DNS server list. This chapter examines how hosts can dynamically learn these IP settings using Dynamic Host Configuration Protocol (DHCP), and the role the routers play in that process. The chapter also shows how to display and understand IP settings on hosts.

Finally, Part V closes with a chapter about troubleshooting IPv4 routing. Chapter 20 features the **ping** and **traceroute** commands, two commands that can help you discover not only whether a routing problem exists but also where the problem exists. The other chapters show how to confirm whether a route has been added to one router's routing table, while the commands discussed in Chapter 20 teach you how to test the end-to-end routes from sending host to receiving host.

Part V

IPv4 Routing

CHAPTER 16

Operating Cisco Routers

This chapter covers the following exam topics:

1.0 Network Fundamentals

    1.1 Explain the role and function of network components

        1.1.a Routers

    1.2 Describe characteristics of network topology architectures

        1.2.e Small office/home office (SOHO)

    1.6 Configure and verify IPv4 addressing and subnetting

This chapter begins a series of chapters that focus on specific Cisco router features. It begins by discussing Cisco routers: hardware, operating system, interfaces, and other components that comprise a router. This first section helps give you concrete examples of interfaces and devices before getting into the many concept and topology drawings to come.

The second section of the chapter then discusses the command-line interface (CLI) on a Cisco router, which has the same look and feel as the Cisco switch CLI. However, unlike switches, routers require some minimal configuration before they will do their primary job: to forward IP packets. The second section of this chapter discusses the concepts and commands to configure a router so it begins forwarding IP packets on its interfaces.

"Do I Know This Already?" Quiz

Take the quiz (either here or use the PTP software) if you want to use the score to help you decide how much time to spend on this chapter. The letter answers are listed at the bottom of the page following the quiz. Appendix C, found both at the end of the book as well as on the companion website, includes both the answers and explanations. You can also find both answers and explanations in the PTP testing software.

Table 16-1 "Do I Know This Already?" Foundation Topics Section-to-Question Mapping

Foundation Topics Section	Questions
Installing Cisco Routers	1
Enabling IPv4 Support on Cisco Router Interfaces	2–6

    1. Which operating systems run on Cisco enterprise routers and use a CLI that works much like the CLI on Cisco LAN switches? (Choose two answers.)

        a. CatOS

        b. IOS

        c. Windows

        d. IOS XE

2. Which action would you expect to be true of a router CLI interaction that is not true when configuring a LAN switch that performs only Layer 2 switching functions?

   a. Moving from global to physical interface configuration mode

   b. Configuring an IP address in physical interface configuration mode

   c. Configuring a 10/100/1000 port's settings related to speed and autonegotiation

   d. Configuring a console password

3. Which answers list a task that could be helpful in making a router interface G0/0 ready to route packets? (Choose two answers.)

   a. Configuring the **ip address** *address mask* command in G0/0 configuration mode

   b. Configuring the **ip address** *address* and **ip mask** *mask* commands in G0/0 configuration mode

   c. Configuring the **no shutdown** command in G0/0 configuration mode

   d. Setting the interface **description** in G0/0 configuration mode

4. The output of the **show ip interface brief** command on R1 lists interface status codes of "down" and "down" for interface GigabitEthernet 0/0. The interface connects to a LAN switch with a UTP straight-through cable. Which of the following could be true?

   a. The **shutdown** command is currently configured for router interface G0/0.

   b. The **shutdown** command is currently configured for the switch interface on the other end of the cable.

   c. The router was never configured with an **ip address** command on the interface.

   d. The router was configured with the **no ip address** command.

5. Which of the following commands list the IP address but not the subnet mask of an interface?

   a. show running-config

   b. show protocols *type number*

   c. show ip interface brief

   d. show interfaces

6. Which of the following is different on the Cisco switch CLI for a Layer 2 switch as compared with the Cisco router CLI?

   a. The commands used to configure simple password checking for the console

   b. The number of IP addresses configured

   c. The configuration of the device's hostname

   d. The configuration of an interface description

Foundation Topics

Installing Cisco Routers

Routers collectively provide the main feature of the network layer—the capability to forward packets end to end through a network. As introduced in Chapter 3, "Fundamentals of WANs and IP Routing," routers forward packets by connecting to various physical network links, like Ethernet LAN, Ethernet WAN, and serial WAN links, then using Layer 3 routing logic to choose where to forward each packet. As a reminder, Chapter 2, "Fundamentals of Ethernet LANs," covered the details of making those physical connections to Ethernet networks, while Chapter 3 covered the basics of cabling with WAN links.

This section examines some of the details of router installation and cabling, first from the enterprise perspective and then from the perspective of connecting a typical small office/ home office (SOHO) to an ISP using high-speed Internet.

Installing Enterprise Routers

A typical enterprise network has a few centralized sites as well as lots of smaller remote sites. To support devices at each site (the computers, IP phones, printers, and other devices), the network includes at least one LAN switch at each site. In addition, each site has a router, which connects to the LAN switch and to some WAN link. The WAN link provides connectivity from each remote site, back to the central site, and to other sites through the connection to the central site.

Figures 16-1 and 16-2 show a couple of different kinds of network diagrams that might be used to represent an enterprise network. The style of Figure 16-1 supports discussions about Layer 3 topics, showing the subnet IDs, masks, and interface IP addresses in shorthand. The figure also keeps the physical and data-link details to a minimum with these conventions:

Ethernet LAN: Simple straight lines with one or more LAN switches implied but not shown.

Ethernet WAN: Shown as a straight line, often with a cloud over it, with some kind of Ethernet interface identifier shown by the router (in this case, G0/1/0 and G0/0/0, which refers to GigabitEthernet interfaces).

Serial WAN: A line with a crooked part in the middle (a "lightning bolt") represents a typical point-to-point serial link as introduced in Chapter 3.

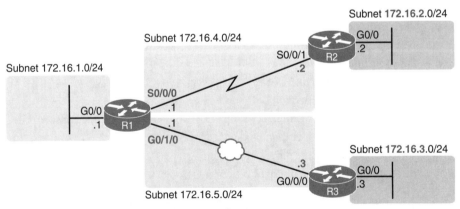

Figure 16-1   *Generic Enterprise Network Diagram*

In comparison, Figure 16-2 shows the same network, with more detail about the physical cabling but with IP details removed. Focusing on the LANs, all the lines connected to the LAN switches could be the standard UTP cabling with RJ-45 connectors,

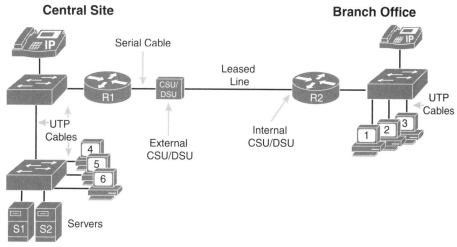

Central Site   **Branch Office**

Serial Cable

Leased
Line

UTP
Cables

UTP
Cables

External
CSU/DSU

Internal
CSU/DSU

Servers

Figure 16-2   *More Detailed Cabling Diagram for the Same Enterprise Network*

Next, consider the hardware on the ends of the serial link between the two routers. In a real serial link that runs through a service provider, the link terminates at a channel service unit/ data service unit (CSU/DSU). The CSU/DSU can either sit outside the router as a separate device (as shown on the left at Router R1) or integrated into the router's serial interface hardware (as shown on the right).

As for cabling, the service provider will run the cable into the enterprise's wiring closet and often put an RJ-48 connector (same size as an RJ-45 connector) on the end of the cable. That cable should connect to the CSU/DSU. With an internal CSU/DSU (as with Router R2 in Figure 16-2), the router serial port has an RJ-48 port to which the serial cable should connect. With an external CSU/DSU, the CSU/DSU must be connected to the router's serial card via a short serial cable.

The Cisco Router Operating Systems

All routers have the usual components found in a computer: a CPU, RAM, permanent memory (usually flash memory), and other electronics. They also run an operating system (OS), which goes by the name **IOS**. The original Cisco routers used IOS; even today, some current router products use IOS. However, Cisco has created other enterprise-class router product families that use a different variation of IOS named **IOS XE**.

Cisco created IOS XE in the 2000s to improve the IOS software architecture. Those improvements may not be evident to the casual observer, but to name a few, IOS XE reduces unplanned and planned downtime, better protects against cyberattacks, and aids network automation. For instance, IOS XE devices can support upgrading the OS while continuing to forward frames and packets, while IOS cannot.

Thankfully, IOS XE uses the same familiar CLI as IOS. Both use the same commands, for the most part, the same command syntax, navigation and modes, and so on. If you learned the CLI using an IOS router, you might not even notice when using a router that runs IOS XE later.

Because the differences between IOS and IOS XE do not matter in most cases in this book, the book uses the term *IOS* almost exclusively to refer to the router OS. When differences in IOS versus IOS XE matter, the text will note the differences.

Cisco Integrated Services Routers

Product vendors, including Cisco, typically provide several different types of router hardware. Today, routers often do much more work than simply routing packets; in fact, they serve as a device or platform from which to provide many network services.

As an example, consider the networking functions needed at a typical branch office. A typical enterprise branch office needs a router for WAN/LAN connectivity, and a LAN switch to provide a high-performance local network and connectivity into the router and WAN. Many branches also need voice-over-IP (VoIP) services to support IP phones, and several security services as well. Plus, it is hard to imagine a site with users that does not have Wi-Fi access today. So, rather than require multiple separate devices at one site, as shown in Figure 16-2, Cisco offers single devices that act as both router and switch and provide other functions as well.

For the sake of learning and understanding the different functions, this book focuses on using a separate switch and separate router, which provides a much cleaner path for learning the basics. However, most Cisco products and product families support a variety of functions in one device.

The Cisco **Integrated Services Router (ISR)** product families include routers that perform much more than routing. Cisco introduced the first ISRs in the mid-2000s, with some ISR families still in existence in the early 2020s when this chapter was most recently updated. The name itself emphasizes the role of being a router, while also integrating other functions (services).

Figure 16-3 shows a Cisco 4321 ISR, with some of the more important features highlighted. The top part of the figure shows a full view of the back of the router. This model comes with two built-in Gigabit Ethernet interfaces and two modular slots that allow you to add small cards called Network Interface Modules (NIMs). The bottom of the figure shows one sample NIM (a NIM that provides two serial interfaces). The router has other items as well, including both an RJ-45 and USB console port.

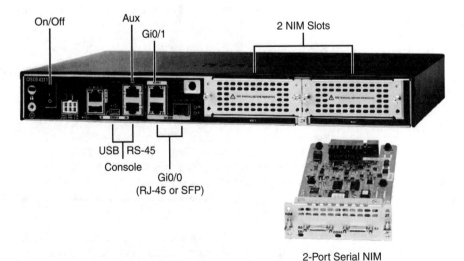

2-Port Serial NIM

Figure 16-3 *Photos of a Model 4321 Cisco Integrated Services Router (ISR)*

The figure shows an important feature for using routers to connect to both Ethernet LANs and Ethernet WAN services. Look closely at Figure 16-3's Gigabit interfaces. G0/1 refers to interface GigabitEthernet0/1 and is an RJ-45 port that supports UTP cabling only. However, interface G0/0 (short for GigabitEthernet0/0) has some interesting features:

- The router has two ports for one interface (G0/0).

- You can use one or the other at any point in time, but not both.

- One physical port is an RJ-45 port that supports copper cabling (implying that it is used to connect to a LAN).

- The other G0/0 physical port is a small form pluggable (SFP) port that would support various fiber Ethernet standards, allowing the port to be used for Ethernet WAN purposes.

Cisco commonly makes one or more of the Ethernet ports on its Enterprise class routers support SFPs so that the engineer can choose an SFP that supports the type of Ethernet cabling provided by the Ethernet WAN service provider.

16

NOTE   When building a lab network to study for CCNA or CCNP, because your devices will be in the same place, you can create Ethernet WAN links by using the RJ-45 ports and a UTP cable without the need to purchase an SFP for each router.

The Cisco Catalyst Edge Platform

In 2020, Cisco announced a new router family with the **Cisco Catalyst Edge Platform** branding, a departure from the previous ISR branding. The new family includes models in the 8000 series, such as the 8200, 8300, and 8500. These new models replaced some existing Cisco ISR families in the Cisco product lineup, but not all.

If the ISR brand emphasized the multifunction nature of modern routers, the *Catalyst Edge Platform* emphasizes that point even more. First, the name does not even use the word *router*, even though the devices use IOS XE and act primarily as routers. The word *platform* emphasizes that the device serves as a platform to run various network services.

Also, note that the new branding uses the term *Catalyst*, a term historically used only for switches. Before the Catalyst 8000 series, the term *Catalyst* always referred to switches, but now Cisco uses the term more broadly. Just be aware in your travels outside of your CCNA studies that when you come across the Catalyst 8000 series devices, think of them as routers.

As for exam preparation, this chapter provides information about ISRs and Catalyst 8000s to provide some context. However, the exam topics do not mention specific Cisco product families. But knowing something about router models and families can help you connect the more generalized topics in CCNA to the devices in your network at work.

Physical Installation

Armed with the cabling details in images like Figure 16-2 and the router hardware details in photos like Figure 16-3, you can physically install a router. To install a router, follow these steps:

Step 1. For any Ethernet LAN interface, connect the RJ-45 connector of an appropriate copper Ethernet cable between the RJ-45 Ethernet port on the router and one of the LAN switch ports.

Step 2. For any serial WAN ports:

  Step A. If using an external CSU/DSU, connect the router's serial interface to the CSU/DSU and the CSU/DSU to the line from the telco.

  Step B. If using an internal CSU/DSU, connect the router's serial interface to the line from the telco.

Step 3. For any Ethernet WAN ports:

  Step A. When ordering the Ethernet WAN service, confirm the required Ethernet standard and SFP type required to connect to the link, and order the SFPs.

  Step B. Install the SFPs into the routers, and connect the Ethernet cable for the Ethernet WAN link to the SFP on each end of the link.

Step 4. Connect the router's console port to a PC (as discussed in Chapter 4, "Using the Command-Line Interface"), as needed, to configure the router.

Step 5. Connect a power cable from a power outlet to the power port on the router.

Step 6. Power on the router using the on/off switch.

Note that Cisco enterprise routers typically have an on/off switch, while switches do not.

Installing SOHO Routers

The terms **enterprise router** and *small office/home office (SOHO) router* act as a pair of contrasting categories for routers, both in terms of how vendors like Cisco provide to the market, and how enterprises use and configure those devices. The term *enterprise router* typically refers to a router that a company would use in a permanent business location, while a **SOHO router** would reside at an employee's home or at a small permanent site with just a few people. However, as you might guess, the line between a router acting as an enterprise router and a SOHO router is blurry, so use these terms as general categories.

Even with that general comparison, SOHO routers typically have two features that an enterprise router would be less likely to have:

- SOHO routers almost always use the Internet and virtual private network (VPN) technology for its WAN connection to send data back and forth to the rest of the enterprise.

- SOHO routers almost always use a multifunction device that does routing, LAN switching, VPN, wireless, and maybe other features.

For instance, at an enterprise business location, the building may contain enterprise routers, separate Ethernet switches, and separate wireless access points (APs), all connected together.

At a permanent business site with four employees and 10 total devices in the network, one SOHO router could provide all those same features in one device.

For instance, Figure 16-4 shows a typical SOHO site. The three icons that represent a router, switch, and access point all exist inside one box; the figure shows them separately to emphasize the fact that the one SOHO router provides several functions. On the left, the SOHO router provides wired and wireless LAN servers, and on the right, it provides WAN access through a cable Internet connection.

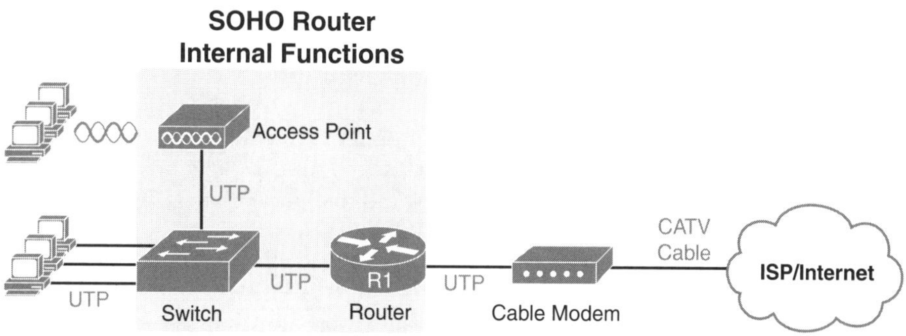

Figure 16-4 *Devices in a SOHO Network with High-Speed CATV Internet*

Figure 16-4 does not reflect the physical reality of a SOHO router, so Figure 16-5 shows one cabling example. The figure shows user devices on the left, connecting to the router via wireless or via Ethernet UTP cabling. On the right in this case, the router uses an external cable modem to connect to the coaxial cable provided by the ISP. Then the router must use a normal UTP Ethernet port to connect a short Ethernet cable between the SOHO router and the cable modem.

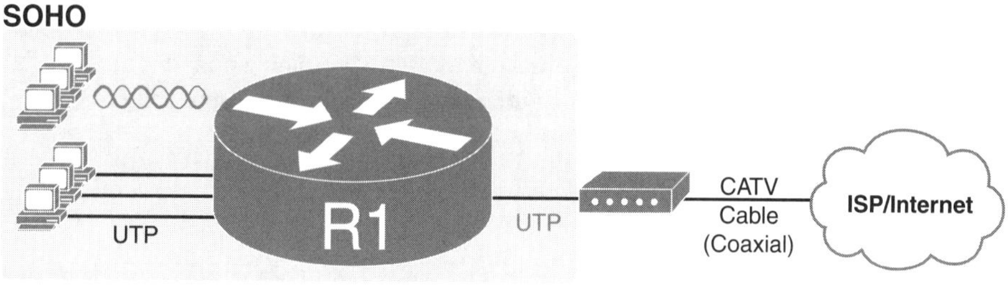

Figure 16-5 *SOHO Network, Using Cable Internet and an Integrated Device*

Enabling IPv4 Support on Cisco Router Interfaces

Routers support a relatively large number of features, with a large number of configuration and EXEC commands to support those features. You will learn about many of these features throughout the rest of this book.

NOTE For perspective, the Cisco router documentation includes a command reference, with an index to every single router command. A quick informal count listed over 5000 CLI commands.

This second section of the chapter focuses on commands related to router interfaces. To make routers work—that is, to route IPv4 packets—the interfaces must be configured. This section introduces the most common commands that configure interfaces, make them work, and give the interfaces IP addresses and masks.

Accessing the Router CLI

The router command-line interface (CLI) works much like a switch. In fact, rather than repeat the detail in Chapter 4, just assume the CLI details from that chapter also apply to routers. If the details from Chapter 4 are not fresh in your memory, it might be worthwhile to spend a few minutes briefly reviewing that chapter as well as Chapter 7, "Configuring and Verifying Switch Interfaces," before reading further. The following list reviews some of the basic CLI features in common between switches and routers:

- User and Privileged (enable) mode

- Entering and exiting configuration mode, using the **configure terminal**, **end**, and **exit** commands and the Ctrl+Z key sequence

- Configuration of console, Telnet (vty), and enable secret passwords

- Configuration of Secure Shell (SSH) encryption keys and username/password login credentials

- Configuration of the hostname and interface description

- Configuration of an interface to be administratively disabled (**shutdown**) and administratively enabled (**no shutdown**)

- Navigation through different configuration mode contexts using commands like **line console 0** and **interface** *type number*

- CLI help, command editing, and command recall features

- The meaning and use of the startup-config (in NVRAM), running-config (in RAM), and external servers (like TFTP), along with how to use the **copy** command to copy the configuration files and IOS images

The most significant differences in the CLI between Cisco routers and switches come from the primary functions of each device: Layer 2 LAN switching by switches and Layer 3 IP routing by routers. LAN switches consider physical interfaces *Layer 2 interfaces*, or *switched interfaces*, meaning the switch should receive Ethernet frames on the interface and pass those into the LAN switching logic. Routers consider their physical interfaces to be *Layer 3 interfaces* or *routed interfaces*. Layer 3 interfaces expect to receive frames, then de-encapsulate the packet found inside the frame, and pass the packet off to the internal routing processes of the router.

The best way to become comfortable with the differences between switches and routers is to learn more and more commands on each. The chapters from here to the end of this book, and several in *CCNA 200-301 Official Cert Guide, Volume 2*, Second Edition, reveal more detail about router features and the related commands. Here are a few of the router CLI topics you will learn about for routers, with one sample command each:

- Configuring interface IP addresses (**ip address** *address mask*)

- Configuring IP routing protocols (e.g., OSPF) (**router ospf** *process-id*)

- Verifying the IP routing table (**show ip route**)

- Configuring static IP routes (**ip route** *subnet mask next-hop-address*)

> **NOTE** Modern routers and switches often support both routing and switching features. Network engineers can then decide whether they need a switch in a particular location in a network design (usually when stronger switching features are required) or a router (when stronger routing features are needed). When studying for CCNA, be aware that routers and switches often support commands for both routing and switching, commands that you might otherwise expect to see only in one or the other.

Cisco routers require the same commands to secure Telnet and SSH, so take some time to review the "Securing the Switch CLI" section in Chapter 6, "Configuring Basic Switch Management." Additionally, take extra care with one command related to Telnet and SSH configuration: the **transport input** line subcommand. The command has different defaults on switches and routers, and the default has migrated to a new setting as well. For instance, older enterprise-class routers using IOS (not IOS XE) often default to use **transport input none**, meaning the router supported neither Telnet nor SSH. Enterprise-class routers running IOS XE often default to **transport input ssh**, supporting SSH but not Telnet.

Router Interfaces

One minor difference between Cisco switches and routers is that routers support a much wider variety of interfaces. Today, LAN switches support only Ethernet interfaces of various speeds. Routers support a variety of other types of interfaces, including serial interfaces, cable TV, 4G/5G wireless, and others not mentioned in this book.

Most Cisco routers have at least one Ethernet interface of some type. Many of those Ethernet interfaces support multiple speeds and use autonegotiation, so for consistency, the router IOS refers to these interfaces based on the fastest speed. For example, a 10-Mbps-only Ethernet interface would be configured with the **interface ethernet** *number* configuration command, a 10/100 interface with the **interface fastethernet** *number* command, and a 10/100/1000 interface with the **interface gigabitethernet** *number* command. However, when discussing these interfaces all together, engineers would simply call them *ethernet interfaces*, regardless of the maximum speed.

Some Cisco routers have serial interfaces. As you might recall from Chapter 3, Cisco routers use serial interfaces to connect to a serial link. Each point-to-point serial link can then use High-Level Data Link Control (HDLC, the default) or Point-to-Point Protocol (PPP).

Router commands refer to interfaces first by the type of interface (Ethernet, Fast Ethernet, Gigabit Ethernet, Serial, and so on) and then with a unique interface identifier (a number) on that router. Depending on the router model, the interface identifiers might be a single number, two numbers separated by a slash, or three numbers separated by slashes. For example, all of the following configuration commands are correct on at least one model of Cisco router:

```
interface ethernet 0
interface fastethernet 0/1
interface gigabitethernet 0/0
interface gigabitethernet 0/1/0
interface serial 1/0/1
interface cellular 0/0/1
```

Two of the most common commands to display the interfaces, and their status, are the **show ip interface brief** and **show interfaces** commands. The first of these commands displays a list with one line per interface, with some basic information, including the interface IP address and interface status. The second command lists the interfaces, but with a large amount of information per interface. Example 16-1 shows a sample of each command. The output comes from an ISR router that has both a GigabitEthernet0/0 interface and a GigabitEthernet0/1/0 interface, showing a case with both two-digit and three-digit interface identifiers.

Example 16-1 *Listing the Interfaces in a Router*

```
R1# show ip interface brief
Interface                    IP-Address     OK? Method Status                Protocol
Embedded-Service-Engine0/0   unassigned     YES NVRAM  administratively down down
GigabitEthernet0/0           172.16.1.1     YES NVRAM  down                  down
GigabitEthernet0/1           unassigned     YES NVRAM  administratively down down
Serial0/0/0                  172.16.4.1     YES manual up                    up
Serial0/0/1                  unassigned     YES unset  administratively down down
GigabitEthernet0/1/0         172.16.5.1     YES NVRAM  up                    up


R1# show interfaces gigabitEthernet 0/1/0
GigabitEthernet0/1/0 is up, line protocol is up
  Hardware is EHWIC-1GE-SFP-CU, address is 0201.a010.0001 (bia 30f7.0d29.8570)
  Description: Link in lab to R3's G0/0/0
  Internet address is 172.16.5.1/24
  MTU 1500 bytes, BW 1000000 Kbit/sec, DLY 10 usec,
     reliability 255/255, txload 1/255, rxload 1/255
  Encapsulation ARPA, loopback not set
  Keepalive set (10 sec)
  Full Duplex, 1Gbps, media type is RJ45
  output flow-control is XON, input flow-control is XON
  ARP type: ARPA, ARP Timeout 04:00:00
  Last input 00:00:29, output 00:00:08, output hang never
  Last clearing of "show interface" counters never
  Input queue: 0/75/0/0 (size/max/drops/flushes); Total output drops: 0
  Queueing strategy: fifo
  Output queue: 0/40 (size/max)
  5 minute input rate 0 bits/sec, 0 packets/sec
  5 minute output rate 0 bits/sec, 0 packets/sec
     12 packets input, 4251 bytes, 0 no buffer
     Received 12 broadcasts (0 IP multicasts)
     0 runts, 0 giants, 0 throttles
     0 input errors, 0 CRC, 0 frame, 0 overrun, 0 ignored
     0 watchdog, 0 multicast, 0 pause input
     55 packets output, 8098 bytes, 0 underruns
     0 output errors, 0 collisions, 0 interface resets
```

```
0 unknown protocol drops
0 babbles, 0 late collision, 0 deferred
0 lost carrier, 0 no carrier, 0 pause output
0 output buffer failures, 0 output buffers swapped out
```

NOTE Commands that refer to router interfaces can be significantly shortened by truncating the words. For example, **sh int gi0/0** or **sh int g0/0** can be used instead of **show interfaces gigabitethernet0/0**. In fact, many network engineers, when looking over someone's shoulder, would say something like "just do a show int G-I-oh-oh command" in this case, rather than speaking the long version of the command.

Also, note that the **show interfaces** command lists a text interface description on about the third line, if configured. In this case, interface G0/1/0 had been previously configured with the **description Link in lab to R3's G0/0/0** command in interface configuration mode for interface G0/1/0. The **description** interface subcommand provides an easy way to keep small notes about what router interfaces connect to which neighboring devices, with the **show interfaces** command listing that information.

Interface Status Codes

Each interface has two *interface status codes*. To be usable, the two interface status codes must be in an "up" state. The first status code refers to whether Layer 1 is working, and the second status code generally (but not always) refers to whether the data-link layer protocol is working. Table 16-2 summarizes these two status codes.

Table 16-2   Interface Status Codes and Their Meanings

Name	Location	General Meaning
Line status	First status code	Refers to the Layer 1 status. (For example, is the cable installed, is it the right/wrong cable, is the device on the other end powered on?)
Protocol status	Second status code	Refers generally to the Layer 2 status. It is always down if the line status is down. If the line status is up, a protocol status of down is usually caused by a mismatched data-link layer configuration.

Several combinations of interface status codes exist, as summarized in Table 16-3. The table lists the status codes in order, from being disabled on purpose by the configuration to a fully working state.

Table 16-3   Typical Combinations of Interface Status Codes

Line Status	Protocol Status	Typical Reasons
Administratively down	Down	The interface has a **shutdown** command configured on it.
Down	Down	The interface is not **shutdown**, but the physical layer has a problem. For example, no cable has been attached to the interface, or with Ethernet, the switch interface on the other end of the cable is shut down, or the switch is powered off, or the devices on the ends of the cable use a different transmission speed.

16

Line Status	Protocol Status	Typical Reasons
Up	Down	Almost always refers to data-link layer problems, most often configuration problems. For example, serial links have this combination when one router was configured to use PPP and the other defaults to use HDLC.
Up	Up	Both Layer 1 and Layer 2 of this interface are functioning.

For some examples, look back at Example 16-1's **show ip interface brief** command, to the three interfaces in the following list. The interfaces in this list each have a different combination of interface status codes; the list details the specific reasons for this status code in the lab used to create this example for the book.

G0/0: The interface is down/down, in this case because no cable was connected to the interface.

G0/1: The interface is administratively down/down, because the configuration includes the **shutdown** command under the G0/1 interface.

S0/0/0: The interface is up/up because a serial cable is installed, is connected to another router in a lab, and is working.

Router Interface IP Addresses

Cisco enterprise routers require at least some configuration beyond the default configuration before they will do their primary job: routing IP packets. First, default router behavior may place an interface in a disabled (shutdown) state. Second, routers use a default interface command of **no ip address**, meaning the interface has no IP address or mask configured. For a router interface to function for routing packets, the interface must be up and configured with an IP address and mask.

To configure the address and mask, simply use the **ip address** *address mask* interface subcommand and ensure that the interface is enabled by using the **no shutdown** command. Figure 16-6 shows a simple IPv4 network with IPv4 addresses on Router R1, with Example 16-2 showing the matching configuration.

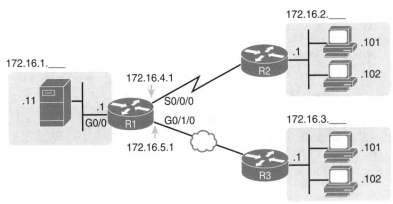

Figure 16-6 *IPv4 Addresses Used in Example 16-2*

Example 16-2 *Configuring IP Addresses on Cisco Routers*

```
R1# configure terminal
Enter configuration commands, one per line. End with CNTL/Z.
R1config)# interface G0/0
R1(config-if)# ip address 172.16.1.1 255.255.255.0
R1(config-if)# no shutdown
R1(config-if)# interface S0/0/0
R1(config-if)# ip address 172.16.4.1 255.255.255.0
R1(config-if)# no shutdown
R1(config-if)# interface G0/1/0
R1(config-if)# ip address 172.16.5.1 255.255.255.0
R1(config-if)# no shutdown
R1(config-if)# ^Z
R1#
```

The **show protocols** command in Example 16-3 confirms the state of each of the three R1 interfaces in Figure 16-6 and the IP address and mask configured on those same interfaces.

Example 16-3 *Verifying IP Addresses on Cisco Routers*

```
R1# show protocols
Global values:
    Internet Protocol routing is enabled
Embedded-Service-Engine0/0 is administratively down, line protocol is down
GigabitEthernet0/0 is up, line protocol is up
    Internet address is 172.16.1.1/24
GigabitEthernet0/1 is administratively down, line protocol is down
Serial0/0/0 is up, line protocol is up
    Internet address is 172.16.4.1/24
Serial0/0/1 is administratively down, line protocol is down
GigabitEthernet0/1/0 is up, line protocol is up
    Internet address is 172.16.5.1/24
```

One of the first actions to take when verifying whether a router is working is to find the interfaces, check the interface status, and check to see whether the correct IP addresses and masks are used. Examples 16-1 and 16-3 showed samples of the key **show** commands, while Table 16-4 summarizes those commands and the types of information they display.

Table 16-4 Key Commands to List Router Interface Status

Command	Lines of Output per Interface	IP Configuration Listed	Interface Status Listed?
show ip interface brief	1	Address	Yes
show protocols [*type number*]	1 or 2	Address/mask	Yes
show interfaces [*type number*]	Many	Address/mask	Yes

Ethernet Interface Autonegotiation

The first step to make a router Ethernet interface reach an up/up state requires the installation of the correct cable. For instance, for Ethernet WAN links, the physical standard may need to support distances of several kilometers, so the interface hardware typically requires fiber-optic cabling. Router LAN interfaces often use UTP cabling that connects to nearby LAN switches, with the expected straight-through cable pinout.

For Ethernet interfaces that allow multiple standards and speeds, you also need to ensure the interfaces use autonegotiation or use correct static settings. IOS routers use the same concepts and commands as Cisco switches, as discussed in the section, "Configuring Autonegotiation, Speed, and Duplex," in Chapter 7. IOS XE routers use the same autonegotiation processes but with different commands, so read the next few pages to work through those differences.

First, for the familiar, the top part of Figure 16-7 shows an example with an IOS Router R1 connected to a Cisco switch. The figure shows all the default settings on both the router and the switch, which cause both devices to perform IEEE autonegotiation.

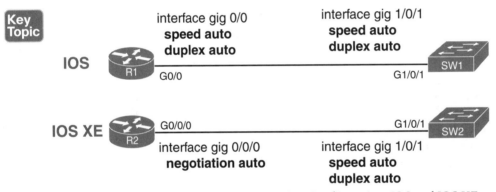

Figure 16-7 *Default Ethernet Autonegotiation Configuration: IOS and IOS XE*

The bottom half of the figure focuses on the different configuration in IOS XE Router R2. The IOS XE default interface subcommand, **negotiation auto**, does just what it appears to do—it enables IEEE autonegotiation. As a result, both devices use autonegotiation to choose the link speed and duplex.

The **show interfaces** EXEC command reveals the chosen duplex and speed. For an IOS (not IOS XE) example, refer to Example 16-1, about nine lines into the **show interfaces** command output, to see the speed (1Gbps) and duplex (full) listed. However, none of the IOS **show** commands specifically note that the router used autonegotiation.

For the IOS XE case, several commands reveal the use of IEEE autonegotiation, as seen in Example 16-4's output from IOS XE Router R2 from Figure 16-7. The **show interfaces** command (in the highlighted line) confirms the speed and duplex. The highlighted line also lists "link type is auto," meaning it autonegotiated the values.

Example 16-4   *Verifying IOS XE Autonegotiation Results (Default)*

```
! Output below is from IOS XE router R2
R2# show interfaces g0/0/0
GigabitEthernet0/0/0 is up, line protocol is up
  Hardware is C1111-2x1GE, address is 0200.1111.1111 (bia 2436.dadf.5680)
  Internet address is 10.1.1.1/24
  MTU 1500 bytes, BW 1000000 Kbit/sec, DLY 10 usec,
     reliability 255/255, txload 1/255, rxload 1/255
  Encapsulation ARPA, loopback not set
  Keepalive not supported
  Full Duplex, 1000Mbps, link type is auto, media type is RJ45
! Lines omitted for brevity
R2# show interfaces g0/0/0 controller | include Autoneg
Admin State Up MTU 1500 Speed 1000mbps Duplex full Autoneg On Stats Interval 5
```

The IOS XE **show interfaces g0/0/0 controller** command at the end of the example filters the output to show only the subset of lines that include the text "Autoneg." That line also confirms the use of autonegotiation.

Whether you are using IOS or IOS XE, the recommendations for using autonegotiation on router Ethernet interfaces mirror the recommendations for switch interfaces, summarized here as follows:

- Use autonegotiation on both ends of an Ethernet link.

- If you must set the speed or duplex, ensure you configure the devices on both ends of the link to use the same speed and duplex.

- Avoid configuring speed and duplex on one end while relying on autonegotiation on the other.

If you must manually configure the settings, IOS and IOS XE differ slightly in how to configure speed and duplex manually. IOS routers use the same conventions as switches: just configure both the **speed** and **duplex** interface subcommands to specific settings, as shown in the left of Figure 16-8. With IOS routers, configuring both speed and duplex also disables autonegotiation.

Figure 16-8   *Router Ethernet Speed, Duplex, and Autonegotiation Configuration*

IOS XE requires the commands shown by Router R2 in the figure, with Example 16-5 demonstrating those same configuration steps. The example begins by showing how IOS XE does not allow the configuration of the **speed** or **duplex** commands until you disable autonegotiation with the **no negotiation auto** interface subcommand. After disabling autonegotiation, IOS XE allows setting the specific **speed** and **duplex** values. The example then shows log messages informing you that the interface failed and then recovered, which is common when using new speed and duplex settings, with approximately ten seconds to work through the process.

Example 16-5   *IOS XE Router: Setting Speed and Duplex*

```
R2# configure terminal
Enter configuration commands, one per line.  End with CNTL/Z.
R2(config)# interface g0/0/0
R2(config-if)# speed 1000
Auto-negotiation is enabled. Speed cannot be set

R2(config-if)# no negotiation auto
R2(config-if) # speed 1000
R2(config-if) # duplex full
*Oct 14 12:24:16.014: %LINEPROTO-5-UPDOWN: Line protocol on Interface
GigabitEthernet0/0/0, changed state to down
*Oct 14 12:24:24.207: %LINEPROTO-5-UPDOWN: Line protocol on Interface
GigabitEthernet0/0/0, changed state to up
R2(config-if)# ^Z
*Oct 14 12:19:10.210: %LINK-3-UPDOWN: Interface GigabitEthernet0/0/0, changed state
to up
R2#
R2# show interfaces g0/0/0 controller
GigabitEthernet0/0/0 is up, line protocol is up
  Hardware is C1111-2x1GE, address is 0200.1111.1111 (bia 2436.dadf.5680)
  Internet address is 10.1.1.1/24
  MTU 1500 bytes, BW 1000000 Kbit/sec, DLY 10 usec,
     reliability 255/255, txload 1/255, rxload 1/255
  Encapsulation ARPA, loopback not set
  Keepalive not supported
  Full Duplex, 1000Mbps, link type is force-up, media type is RJ45
  output flow-control is on, input flow-control is on
! Lines omitted for brevity
Driver Configuration Block:
Admin State Up MTU 1500 Speed 1000mbps Duplex full Autoneg Off Stats Interval 5
! More lines omitted for brevity
```

The highlighted text near the end of Example 16-5 confirms the resulting speed and duplex. It also identifies that autonegotiation was not used, with the phrase "link type is force-up," in contrast to the "link type is auto" text in the autonegotiation in Example 16-4. Later in the output, one line explicitly lists the fact that autonegotiation is off.

> **NOTE** On IOS XE routers, the **[no] negotiation auto** command controls autonegotiation. In IOS routers, configuring **speed** and **duplex** to specific values disables autonegotiation.

Bandwidth and Clock Rate on Serial Interfaces

Cisco included serial WAN topics in the CCNA exam topic from its inception in 1998 until the CCNA 200-301 Version 1.0 blueprint in early 2020. Even though Cisco no longer mentions serial links in the exam topics, the exam might show them with the expectation that you at least understand the basics, such as the fact that two routers can send data over a serial link if the router interfaces on both ends are up/up and the routers have IP addresses in the same subnet.

However, some of you will want to make serial links work in a lab because you have some serial interface cards in your lab. If so, take the time to look at a few pages in the section titled "Bandwidth and Clock Rate on Serial Interfaces," in Appendix K, "Topics from Previous Editions," which shows how to cable and configure a WAN serial link in the lab.

Router Auxiliary Port

Both routers and switches have a console port to allow administrative access, but most Cisco routers have an extra physical port called an auxiliary (Aux) port. The Aux port typically serves as a means to make a phone call to connect into the router to issue commands from the CLI.

The Aux port works like the console port, except that the Aux port is typically connected through a cable to an external analog modem, which in turn connects to a phone line. Then, the engineer uses a PC, terminal emulator, and modem to call the remote router. After being connected, the engineer can use the terminal emulator to access the router CLI, starting in user mode as usual.

Aux ports can be configured beginning with the **line aux 0** command to reach aux line configuration mode. From there, all the commands for the console line, covered mostly in Chapter 6, can be used. For example, the **login** and **password** *password* subcommands on the aux line could be used to set up simple password checking when a user dials in.

Chapter Review

One key to doing well on the exams is to perform repetitive spaced review sessions. Review this chapter's material using either the tools in the book or interactive tools for the same material found on the book's companion website. Refer to the "Your Study Plan" element for more details. Table 16-5 outlines the key review elements and where you can find them. To better track your study progress, record when you completed these activities in the second column.

Table 16-5 Chapter Review Tracking

Review Element	Review Date(s)	Resource Used
Review key topics		Book, website
Review key terms		Book, website
Answer DIKTA questions		Book, PTP

Review Element	Review Date(s)	Resource Used
Review command tables		Book
Review memory tables		Website
Do labs		Blog
Watch video		Website

Review All the Key Topics

Table 16-6   Key Topics for Chapter 16

Key Topic	Description	Page Number
List	Steps required to install a router	412
List	Similarities between a router CLI and a switch CLI	414
List	IOS features typical of routers (and all devices that perform routing)	414
Table 16-2	Router interface status codes and their meanings	417
Table 16-3	Combinations of the two interface status codes and the likely reasons for each combination	417
Table 16-4	Commands useful to display interface IPv4 addresses, masks, and interface status	419
Figure 16-7	Comparison of default autonegotiation configuration, routers with IOS and IOS XE	420
Figure 16-8	Comparison of configuration to disable autonegotiation and use a set speed/duplex, routers with IOS and IOS XE	421

Key Terms You Should Know

Cisco Catalyst Edge Platform, enterprise router, Integrated Services Router (ISR), IOS, IOS XE, SOHO router

Command References

Tables 16-7 and 16-8 list configuration and verification commands used in this chapter. As an easy review exercise, cover the left column in a table, read the right column, and try to recall the command without looking. Then repeat the exercise, covering the right column, and try to recall what the command does.

Table 16-7   Chapter 16 Configuration Command Reference

Command	Description
interface *type number*	Global command that moves the user into configuration mode of the named interface.
ip address *address mask*	Interface subcommand that sets the router's IPv4 address and mask.
[no] shutdown	Interface subcommand that enables (no shutdown) or disables (shutdown) the interface.

Command	Description
duplex {full | half | auto}	IOS (not XE) interface command that sets the duplex, or sets the use of IEEE autonegotiation, for router LAN interfaces that support multiple speeds.
speed {10 | 100 | 1000 | auto}	IOS (not XE) interface command for router Gigabit (10/100/1000) interfaces that sets the speed at which the router interface sends and receives data, or sets the use of IEEE autonegotiation.
description *text*	An interface subcommand with which you can type a string of text to document information about that particular interface.
[no] negotiation auto	IOS XE (not IOS) interface command that enables or disables (**y**) the use of IEEE autonegotiation on the interface. There is no equivalent for routers that use IOS.
duplex {full | half }	IOS XE (not IOS) interface command that sets the duplex, allowed only if the interface is already configured with the **no negotiation auto** subcommand.
speed {10 | 100 | 1000}	IOS XE (not IOS) interface command that sets the speed, allowed only if the interface is already configured with the **no negotiation auto** subcommand.

Table 16-8   Chapter 16 EXEC Command Reference

Command	Purpose
show interfaces [*type number*]	Lists a large set of informational messages about each interface, or about the one specifically listed interface.
show ip interface brief	Lists a single line of information about each interface, including the IP address, line and protocol status, and the method with which the address was configured (manual or Dynamic Host Configuration Protocol [DHCP]).
show protocols [*type number*]	Lists information about the listed interface (or all interfaces if the interface is omitted), including the IP address, mask, and line/protocol status.
show interfaces [*type number*] controller	IOS XE (not IOS) command that lists detail about interface hardware and driver behavior, including detail about Ethernet autonegotiation processes and results.

16

CHAPTER 17

Configuring IPv4 Addresses and Static Routes

This chapter covers the following exam topics:

1.0 Network Fundamentals

    1.6 Configure and verify IPv4 addressing and subnetting

3.0 IP Connectivity

    3.1 Interpret the components of routing table

        3.1.a Routing protocol code

        3.1.b Prefix

        3.1.c Network mask

        3.1.d Next hop

        3.1.e Administrative distance

        3.1.f Metric

        3.1.g Gateway of last resort

    3.2 Determine how a router makes a forwarding decision by default

        3.2.a Longest prefix match

        3.2.b Administrative distance

    3.3 Configure and verify IPv4 and IPv6 static routing

        3.3.a Default route

        3.3.b Network route

        3.3.c Host route

        3.3.d Floating static

Routers route IPv4 packets. That simple statement actually carries a lot of hidden meaning. For routers to route packets, routers follow a routing process, and that routing process relies on information called IP routes. Each IP route lists a destination—an IP network, IP subnet, or some other group of IP addresses. Each route also lists instructions that tell the router where to forward packets sent to addresses in that IP network or subnet. For routers to do a good job of routing packets, routers need to have a detailed, accurate list of IP routes.

Routers use three methods to add IPv4 routes to their IPv4 routing tables. Routers first learn **connected routes**, which are routes for subnets attached to a router interface. Routers can also use **static routes**, which are routes created through a configuration command (**ip route**) that tells the router what route to put in the IPv4 **routing table**. And routers can use a routing protocol, in which routers tell each other about all their known routes, so that all routers can learn and build dynamic routes to all networks and subnets.

This chapter examines IP routing in depth with the most straightforward routes that can be added to a router's routing table. The router starts with a detailed look at the IP packet routing (forwarding process)—a process that relies on each router having useful IP routes in their routing tables. The second section then examines connected routes, which are routes to subnets that exist on the interfaces connected to the local router. The third section then examines static routes, which are routes the network engineer configures directly.

"Do I Know This Already?" Quiz

Take the quiz (either here or use the PTP software) if you want to use the score to help you decide how much time to spend on this chapter. The letter answers are listed at the bottom of the page following the quiz. Appendix C, found both at the end of the book as well as on the companion website, includes both the answers and explanations. You can also find both answers and explanations in the PTP testing software.

Table 17-1 "Do I Know This Already?" Foundation Topics Section-to-Question Mapping

Foundation Topics Section	Questions
IP Routing	1, 2
Configuring IP Addresses and Connected Routes	3
Configuring Static Routes	4–6

1. Router R1 lists a route in its routing table. Which of the following answers list a fact from a route that the router uses when matching the packet's destination address? (Choose two answers.)

   a. Mask

   b. Next-hop router

   c. Subnet ID

   d. Outgoing interface

2. PC1 sends an IP packet to PC2. To do so, PC1 sends the packet to Router R1, which routes it to Router R2, which routes it to Router R3, which routes it to the final destination (PC2). All links use Ethernet. How many routers de-encapsulate the IP packet from an Ethernet frame during its journey from PC1 to PC2?

   a. 0

   b. 1

   c. 2

   d. 3

3. After configuring a working router interface with IP address/mask 10.1.1.100/26, which of the following routes would you expect to see in the output of the **show ip route** command? (Choose two answers.)

   a. A connected route for subnet 10.1.1.64 255.255.255.192

   b. A connected route for subnet 10.1.1.0 255.255.255.0

    c.   A local route for host 10.1.1.100 255.255.255.192

    d.   A local route for host 10.1.1.100 255.255.255.255

    e.   A local route for host 10.1.1.64 255.255.255.255

4. Which of the following pieces of information could be listed in a correct **ip route** command on a local router? (Choose two answers.)

    a.   The local router's IP address on the link between the two routers

    b.   The next-hop router's IP address on the link between the two routers

    c.   The next-hop router's interface ID on the link between the two routers

    d.   The local router's interface ID on the link between the two routers

5. Which of the following commands correctly configures a static route?

    a.   **ip route 10.1.3.0 255.255.255.0 10.1.130.253**

    b.   **ip route 10.1.3.0 serial 0**

    c.   **ip route 10.1.3.0 /24 10.1.130.253**

    d.   **ip route 10.1.3.0 /24 serial 0**

6. A network engineer configures the **ip route 10.1.1.0 255.255.255.0 s0/0/0** command on a router and then issues a **show ip route** command from enable mode. No routes for subnet 10.1.1.0/24 appear in the output. Which of the following could be true?

    a.   The **ip route** command has incorrect syntax and was rejected in config mode.

    b.   Interface s0/0/0 is down.

    c.   The router has no up/up interfaces in Class A network 10.0.0.0.

    d.   The **ip route** command is missing a next-hop router IP address.

Foundation Topics

IP Routing

IP routing—the process of forwarding IP packets—delivers packets across entire TCP/IP networks, from the device that originally builds the IP packet to the device that is supposed to receive the packet. In other words, IP routing delivers IP packets from the sending host to the destination host.

The complete end-to-end routing process relies on network layer logic on hosts and on routers. The sending host uses Layer 3 concepts to create an IP packet, forwarding the IP packet to the host's default gateway (default router). The process requires Layer 3 logic on the routers as well, by which the routers compare the destination address in the packet to their routing tables, to decide where to forward the IP packet next.

The routing process also relies on data-link and physical details at each link. IP routing relies on serial WAN links, Ethernet WAN links, Ethernet LANs, wireless LANs, and many other networks that implement data-link and physical layer standards. These lower-layer devices and protocols move the IP packets around the TCP/IP network by encapsulating and trans-mitting the packets inside data-link layer frames.

The previous two paragraphs summarize the key concepts about IP routing as introduced back in Chapter 3, "Fundamentals of WANs and IP Routing." Next, this section reviews IP routing, while taking the discussion another step or two deeper, taking advantage of the additional depth of knowledge discussed in all the earlier chapters in this book.

IPv4 Routing Process Reference

Because you already saw the basics back in Chapter 3, this section collects the routing process into steps for reference. The steps use many specific Ethernet LAN terms discussed in Parts II and III of this book and some IP addressing terms discussed in Part IV. The upcoming descriptions and example then discuss these summaries of routing logic to make sure that each step is clear.

The routing process starts with the host that creates the IP packet. First, the host asks the question: Is the destination IP address of this new packet in my local subnet? The host uses its own IP address/mask to determine the range of addresses in the local subnet. Based on its own opinion of the range of addresses in the local subnet, a LAN-based host acts as follows:

Step 1. If the destination is local, send directly:

    a. Find the destination host's MAC address. Use the already-known Address Resolution Protocol (ARP) table entry, or use ARP messages to learn the information.

    b. Encapsulate the IP packet in a data-link frame, with the destination data-link address of the destination host.

Step 2. If the destination is not local, send to the default gateway:

    a. Find the default gateway's MAC address. Use the already-known Address Resolution Protocol (ARP) table entry, or use ARP messages to learn the information.

    b. Encapsulate the IP packet in a data-link frame, with the destination data-link address of the default gateway.

Figure 17-1 summarizes these same concepts. In the figure, host A sends a local packet directly to host D. However, for packets to host B, on the other side of a router and therefore in a different subnet, host A sends the packet to its default router (R1). (As a reminder, the terms *default gateway* and *default router* are synonyms.)

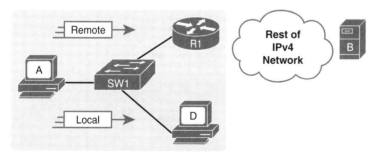

Figure 17-1 *Host Routing Logic Summary*

Routers have a little more routing work to do as compared with hosts. While the host logic began with an IP packet sitting in memory, a router has some work to do before getting to that point. With the following five-step summary of a router's routing logic, the router takes the first two steps just to receive the frame and extract the IP packet, before thinking about the packet's destination address at Step 3. The steps are as follows:

1. For each received data-link frame, choose whether or not to process the frame. Process it if

    a.   The frame has no errors (per the data-link trailer Frame Check Sequence [FCS] field).

    b.   The frame's destination data-link address is the router's address (or an appropriate multicast or broadcast address).

2. If choosing to process the frame at Step 1, de-encapsulate the packet from inside the data-link frame.

3. Make a routing decision. To do so, compare the packet's destination IP address to the routing table and find the route that matches the destination address. This route identifies the **outgoing interface** of the router and possibly the **next-hop router**.

4. Encapsulate the packet into a data-link frame appropriate for the outgoing interface. When forwarding out LAN interfaces, use ARP as needed to find the next device's MAC address.

5. Transmit the frame out the outgoing interface, as listed in the matched IP route.

This routing process summary lists many details, but sometimes you can think about the routing process in simpler terms. For example, leaving out some details, this paraphrase of the step list details the same big concepts:

> The router receives a frame, removes the packet from inside the frame, decides where to forward the packet, puts the packet into another frame, and sends the frame.

To give you a little more perspective on these steps, Figure 17-2 breaks down the same five-step routing process as a diagram. The figure shows a packet arriving from the left, entering a router Ethernet interface, with an IP destination of host C. The figure shows the packet arriving, encapsulated inside an Ethernet frame (both header and trailer).

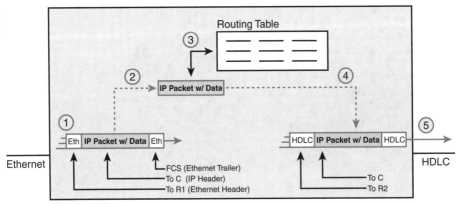

Figure 17-2 *Router Routing Logic Summary*

Answers to the "Do I Know This Already?" quiz:

1 A, C **2** D **3** A, D **4** B, C **5** A **6** B

Router R1 processes the frame and packet as shown with the numbers in the figure, matching the same five-step process described just before the figure, as follows:

1. Router R1 notes that the received Ethernet frame passes the FCS check and that the destination Ethernet MAC address is R1's MAC address, so R1 processes the frame.

2. R1 de-encapsulates the IP packet from inside the Ethernet frame's header and trailer.

3. R1 compares the IP packet's destination IP address to R1's IP routing table.

4. R1 encapsulates the IP packet inside a new data-link frame, in this case, inside a High-Level Data Link Control (HDLC) header and trailer.

5. R1 transmits the IP packet, inside the new HDLC frame, out the serial link on the right.

NOTE   This chapter uses several figures that show an IP packet encapsulated inside a data-link layer frame. These figures often show both the data-link header as well as the data-link trailer, with the IP packet in the middle. The IP packets all include the IP header, plus any encapsulated data.

An Example of IP Routing

The next several pages walk you through an example that discusses each routing step, in order, through multiple devices. The example uses a case in which host A (172.16.1.9) sends a packet to host B (172.16.2.9), with host routing logic and the five steps showing how R1 forwards the packet.

Figure 17-3 shows a typical IP addressing diagram for an IPv4 network with typical address abbreviations. The diagram can get a little too messy if it lists the full IP address for every router interface. When possible, these diagrams usually list the subnet and then the last octet or two of the individual IP addresses—just enough so that you know the IP address but with less clutter. For example, host A uses IP address 172.16.1.9, taking from subnet 172.16.1.0/24 (in which all addresses begin 172.16.1) and the .9 beside the host A icon. As another example, R1 uses address 172.16.1.1 on its LAN interface, 172.16.4.1 on one serial interface, and 172.16.5.1 on an Ethernet WAN interface.

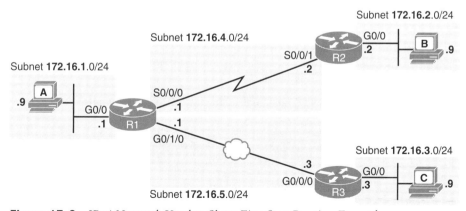

Figure 17-3   *IPv4 Network Used to Show Five-Step Routing Example*

Now on to the example, with host A (172.16.1.9) sending a packet to host B (172.16.2.9).

Host Forwards the IP Packet to the Default Router (Gateway)

In this example, host A uses some application that sends data to host B (172.16.2.9). After host A has the IP packet sitting in memory, host A's logic reduces to the following:

- My IP address/mask is 172.16.1.9/24, so my local subnet contains numbers 172.16.1.0–172.16.1.255 (including the subnet ID and subnet broadcast address).

- The destination address is 172.16.2.9, which is clearly not in my local subnet.

- Send the packet to my default gateway, which is set to 172.16.1.1.

- To send the packet, encapsulate it in an Ethernet frame. Make the destination MAC address be R1's G0/0 MAC address (host A's default gateway).

Figure 17-4 pulls these concepts together, showing the destination IP address and destination MAC address in the frame and packet sent by host A in this case. Note that the figure uses a common drawing convention in networking, showing an Ethernet as a few lines, hiding all the detail of the Layer 2 switches.

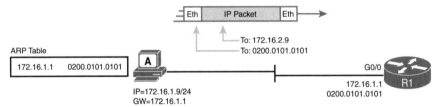

Figure 17-4 *Host A Sends Packet Through Router R1 to Host B*

Routing Step 1: Decide Whether to Process the Incoming Frame

Routers receive many frames in an interface, particularly LAN interfaces. However, a router can and should ignore some of those frames. So, the first step in the routing process begins with a decision of whether a router should process the frame or silently discard (ignore) the frame.

First, the router does a simple but important check (Step 1A in the process summary) so that the router ignores all frames that had bit errors during transmission. The router uses the data-link trailer's FCS field to check the frame, and if errors occurred in transmission, the router discards the frame. (The router makes no attempt at error recovery; that is, the router does not ask the sender to retransmit the data.)

The router also checks the destination data-link address (Step 1B in the summary) to decide whether the frame is intended for the router. For example, frames sent to the router's unicast MAC address for that interface are clearly sent to that router. However, a router can actually receive a frame sent to some other unicast MAC address, and routers should ignore these frames.

For example, think back to how LAN switches forward unknown unicast frames—frames for which the switch does not list the destination MAC address in the MAC address table. The LAN switch floods those frames. The result? Routers sometimes receive frames destined for some other device, with some other device's MAC address listed as the destination MAC address. Routers should ignore those frames.

Figure 17-5 shows a working example in which host A sends a frame destined for R1's MAC address. After receiving the frame, R1 confirms with the FCS that no errors occurred, and R1 confirms that the frame is destined for R1's MAC address (0200.0101.0101 in this case). All checks have been passed, so R1 will process the frame. (Note that the large rectangle in the figure represents the internals of Router R1.)

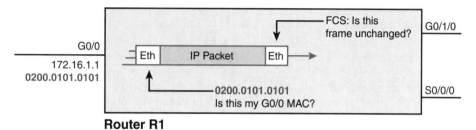

Router R1

Figure 17-5   *Routing Step 1, on Router R1: Checking FCS and Destination MAC*

Routing Step 2: De-encapsulation of the IP Packet

After the router knows that it ought to process the received frame (per Step 1), the next step is relatively simple: de-encapsulating the packet. In router memory, the router no longer needs the original frame's data-link header and trailer, so the router removes and discards them, leaving the IP packet, as shown in Figure 17-6. Note that the destination IP address remains unchanged (172.16.2.9).

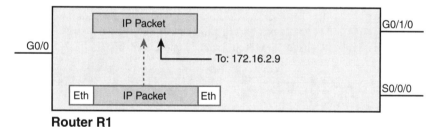

Router R1

Figure 17-6   *Routing Step 2 on Router R1: De-encapsulating the Packet*

Routing Step 3: Choosing Where to Forward the Packet

While routing Step 2 required little thought, Step 3 requires the most thought of all the steps. At this point, the router needs to make a choice about where to forward the packet next. That process uses the router's IP routing table, with some matching logic to compare the packet's destination address with the table.

First, an IP routing table lists multiple routes. Each individual route contains several facts, which in turn can be grouped as shown in Figure 17-7. Part of each route is used to match the destination address of the packet, while the rest of the route lists forwarding instructions: where to send the packet next.

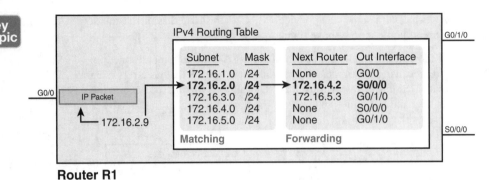

Router R1

Figure 17-7   *Routing Step 3 on Router R1: Matching the Routing Table*

Focus on the entire routing table for a moment, and notice the fact that it lists five routes. Earlier, Figure 17-3 showed the entire example network, with five subnets, so R1 has a route for each of the five subnets.

Next, look at the part of the five routes that Router R1 will use to match packets. To fully define each subnet, each route lists both the subnet ID and the subnet mask. When matching the IP packet's destination with the routing table, the router looks at the packet's destination IP address (172.16.2.9) and compares it to the range of addresses defined by each subnet. Specifically, the router looks at the subnet and mask information; with a little math, the router can figure out in which of these subnets 172.16.2.9 resides (the route for subnet 172.16.2.0/24).

Finally, look to the right side of the figure, to the forwarding instructions for these five routes. After the router matches a specific route, the router uses the forwarding information in the route to tell the router where to send the packet next. In this case, the router matched the route for subnet 172.16.2.0/24, so R1 will forward the packet out its own interface S0/0/0, to Router R2 next, listed with its next-hop router IP address of 172.16.4.2.

NOTE   Routes for remote subnets typically list both an outgoing interface and next-hop router IP address. Routes for subnets that connect directly to the router list only the outgoing interface because packets to these destinations do not need to be sent to another router.

Routing Step 4: Encapsulating the Packet in a New Frame

At this point, the router knows how it will forward the packet. However, routers cannot forward a packet without first wrapping a data-link header and trailer around it (encapsulation).

Encapsulating packets for serial links does not require a lot of thought, but the current CCNA exam does not require a lot from us. Point-to-point serial WAN links use either HDLC (the default) or PPP as the data-link protocol. However, we can ignore any data-link logic, even ignoring data-link addressing, because serial links have only two devices on the link: the sender and the then-obvious receiver; the data-link addressing does not matter. In this example, R1 forwards the packet out S0/0/0, after encapsulating the packet inside an HDLC frame, as shown in Figure 17-8.

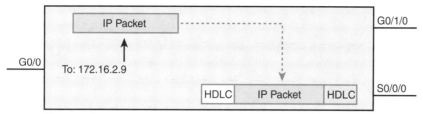

Router R1

Figure 17-8   *Routing Step 4 on Router R1: Encapsulating the Packet*

Note that with some other types of data links, the router has a little more work to do at this routing step. For example, sometimes a router forwards packets out an Ethernet interface. To encapsulate the IP packet, the router would need to build an Ethernet header, and that Ethernet header's destination MAC address would need to list the correct value.

For example, consider a packet sent by that same PC A (172.16.1.9) in Figure 17-3 but with a destination of PC C (172.16.3.9). When R1 processes the packet, R1 matches a route that tells R1 to forward the packet out R1's G0/1/0 Ethernet interface to 172.16.5.3 (R3) next. R1 needs to put R3's MAC address in the header, and to do that, R1 uses its IP ARP table information, as shown in Figure 17-9. If R1 did not have an ARP table entry for 172.16.5.3, R1 would first have to use ARP to learn the matching MAC address.

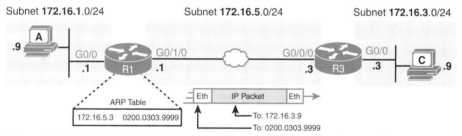

Figure 17-9   *Routing Step 4 on Router R1 with a LAN Outgoing Interface*

Routing Step 5: Transmitting the Frame

After the frame has been prepared, the router simply needs to transmit the frame. The router might have to wait, particularly if other frames are already waiting their turn to exit the interface.

Configuring IP Addresses and Connected Routes

Cisco routers enable IPv4 routing globally, by default. Then, to make the router be ready to route packets on a particular interface, the interface must be configured with an IP address and the interface must be configured such that it comes up, reaching a "line status up, line protocol up" state. Only at that point can routers route IP packets in and out a particular interface.

After a router can route IP packets out one or more interfaces, the router needs some routes. Routers can add routes to their routing tables through three methods:

Connected routes: Added because of the configuration of the **ip address** interface subcommand on the local router

Static routes: Added because of the configuration of the **ip route** global command on the local router

Routing protocols: Added as a function by configuration on all routers, resulting in a process by which routers dynamically tell each other about the network so that they all learn routes

This second of three sections discusses several variations on how to configure connected routes, while the next major section discusses static routes.

Connected Routes and the ip address Command

A Cisco router automatically adds a route to its routing table for the subnet connected to each interface, assuming that the following two facts are true:

- The interface is in a working state. In other words, the interface status in the **show interfaces** command lists a line status of up and a protocol status of up.

- The interface has an IP address assigned through the **ip address** interface subcommand.

The concept of connected routes is relatively basic. The router, of course, needs to know the subnet number connected to each of its interfaces, so the router can route packets to that subnet. The router does the math, taking the interface IP address and mask and calculating the subnet ID. However, the router only needs that route when the interface is up and working, so the router includes a connected route in the routing table only when the interface is working.

Example 17-1 shows the connected routes on Router R1 in Figure 17-10. The first part of the example shows the configuration of IP addresses on all three of R1's interfaces. The end of the example lists the output from the **show ip route** command, which lists these routes with a C as the route code, meaning *connected*.

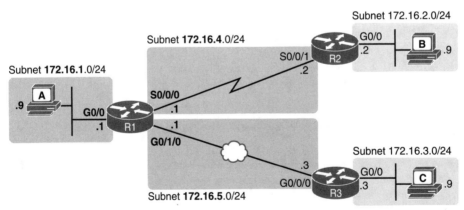

Figure 17-10 *Sample Network to Show Connected Routes*

Example 17-1 *Connected and Local Routes on Router R1*

```
! Excerpt from show running-config follows...
!
interface GigabitEthernet0/0
 ip address 172.16.1.1 255.255.255.0
!
interface Serial0/0/0
 ip address 172.16.4.1 255.255.255.0
!
interface GigabitEthernet0/1/0
 ip address 172.16.5.1 255.255.255.0

R1# show ip route
Codes: L - local, C - connected, S - static, R - RIP, M - mobile, B - BGP
       D - EIGRP, EX - EIGRP external, O - OSPF, IA - OSPF inter area
       N1 - OSPF NSSA external type 1, N2 - OSPF NSSA external type 2
       E1 - OSPF external type 1, E2 - OSPF external type 2
       i - IS-IS, su - IS-IS summary, L1 - IS-IS level-1, L2 - IS-IS level-2
       ia - IS-IS inter area, * - candidate default, U - per-user static route
       o - ODR, P - periodic downloaded static route, H - NHRP, l - LISP
       a - application route
       + - replicated route, % - next hop override, p - overrides from PfR

Gateway of last resort is not set

      172.16.0.0/16 is variably subnetted, 6 subnets, 2 masks
C        172.16.1.0/24 is directly connected, GigabitEthernet0/0
L        172.16.1.1/32 is directly connected, GigabitEthernet0/0
C        172.16.4.0/24 is directly connected, Serial0/0/0
L        172.16.4.1/32 is directly connected, Serial0/0/0
C        172.16.5.0/24 is directly connected, GigabitEthernet0/1/0
L        172.16.5.1/32 is directly connected, GigabitEthernet0/1/0
```

Each time you do a lab or see an example with output from the **show ip route** command, look closely at the heading line for each classful network and the indented lines that follow. The indented lines list routes to specific subnets. In Example 17-1, the heading line shows Class B network 172.16.0.0 as "172.16.0.0/16", with /16 representing the default mask for a Class B network. Why? IOS groups the output by Class A, B, or C network. In this case, the output shows a heading line that tells us that the following indented lines have to do with network 172.16.0.0/16.

Take a moment to look closely at each of the three highlighted routes below the heading line that references Class B network 172.16.0.0. Each lists a C in the first column, and each has text that says "directly connected"; both identify the route as connected to the router. The early part of each route lists the matching parameters (subnet ID and mask), as shown in the earlier example in Figure 17-7. The end of each of these routes lists the outgoing interface.

Note that the router also automatically produces a different kind of route, called a *local route*. The local routes define a route for the one specific IP address configured on the router interface. Each local route has a /32 prefix length, defining a *host route*, which defines a route just for that one IP address. For example, the last local route, for 172.16.5.1/32, defines a route that matches only the IP address of 172.16.5.1. Routers use these local routes that list their own local IP addresses to more efficiently forward packets sent to the router itself.

The **show ip route** command in the example reveals a few of the specific subitems within exam topic 3.1 (per CCNA 200-301 V1.1), with later examples in this chapter revealing even more details. This section shows details related to the following terms from the exam topics:

- **Routing Protocol Code:** The legend at the top of the **show ip route** output (about nine lines) lists all the routing protocol codes (exam topic 3.1.a). This book references the codes for connected routes (C), local (L), static (S), and OSPF (O).

- **Prefix:** The word *prefix* (exam topic 3.1.b) is just another name for subnet ID.

- **Mask:** Each route lists a prefix (subnet ID) and network mask (exam topic 3.1.c) in prefix format, for example, /24.

Common Mistakes with the ip address Subcommand

If you follow a correct IP address plan, the **ip address** commands on your routers should be accepted. They should also work correctly to support endpoint hosts in LANs in their roles as the default gateway. However, several mistakes are possible with this command, mistakes that might not be obvious at first glance.

This next topic examines a few of those mistakes, using Figure 17-11 as a backdrop. The figure shows a more detailed view of the LAN connected to Router R1 in Figure 17-10, now with two PCs in it.

Subnet 172.16.1.0/24

Subnet ID:	172.16.1.0
Lowest IP:	172.16.1.1
Highest IP:	172.16.1.254
Broadcast:	172.16.1.255

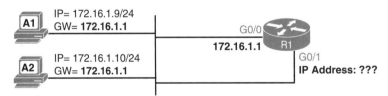

Figure 17-11 *More Detailed and Expanded View of Router R1 LAN*

First, IOS rejects the **ip address** command in configuration mode if it uses a reserved number in the subnet, such as the subnet ID or the subnet broadcast address. Example 17-2 shows three rejected **ip address** commands. The first attempts to configure the subnet ID as the address, while the second attempts to configure the subnet broadcast address. The final example shows the command with an invalid subnet mask (which is also rejected). Note that the error message does not reveal the specific reason, instead giving a cryptic reference to the idea that the values have a problem when using that mask.

Example 17-2   *IOS Rejects* ip address *Commands with Reserved Addresses*

```
R1# configure terminal
Enter configuration commands, one per line.  End with CNTL/Z.
R1(config)# interface gigabitEthernet 0/0
R1(config-if)# ip address 172.16.1.0 255.255.255.0
Bad mask /24 for address 172.16.1.0
R1(config-if)# ip address 172.16.1.255 255.255.255.0
Bad mask /24 for address 172.16.1.255
R1(config-if)# ip address 172.16.1.1 255.0.255.0
Bad mask 0xFF00FF00 for address 172.16.1.1
R1(config-if)#
```

You can also configure the **ip address** command with values that IOS accepts but that are incorrect per your address plan—resulting in problems in the network. For example, looking at Figure 17-11, the default gateway setting on the two PCs implies that router R1's address should be 172.16.1.1. Router R1 would accept the **ip address 172.16.1.2 255.255.255.0** command on its G0/0 interface, setting the wrong address value—but the router has no mechanism to know that its address does not match the PC's default gateway settings. Instead, the PCs cannot communicate outside the subnet. The solution: Configure the correct address on Router R1.

As a third issue, one router may connect only one interface to a subnet. In Figure 17-11, Router R1 has two interfaces (G0/0 and G0/1) connected to the same LAN. If you attempted to assign both interfaces an IP address in that same 172.16.1.0/24 subnet, and both interfaces were in an up/up state, IOS would reject the second **ip address** command. Example 17-3 shows that sequence, with R1's G0/0 configured first and R1's G0/1 configured second (with the rejection).

Example 17-3   *IOS Rejects* ip address *Command for Second Interface in the Same Subnet*

```
R1# configure terminal
Enter configuration commands, one per line.  End with CNTL/Z.
R1(config)# interface gigabitEthernet 0/0
R1(config-if)# ip address 172.16.1.1 255.255.255.0
R1(config)# interface gigabitEthernet 0/1
R1(config-if)# ip address 172.16.1.2 255.255.255.0
% 172.16.1.0 overlaps with GigabitEthernet0/0
R1(config-if)#
```

The ARP Table on a Cisco Router

After a router has added these connected routes, the router can route IPv4 packets between those subnets. To do so, the router makes use of its IP ARP table.

The IPv4 **ARP table** lists the IPv4 address and matching MAC address of hosts connected to the same subnet as the router. When forwarding a packet to a host on the same subnet, the router encapsulates the packet, with a destination MAC address as found in the ARP table. If the router wants to forward a packet to an IP address on the same subnet as the router but does not find an ARP table entry for that IP address, the router will use ARP messages to learn that device's MAC address.

Example 17-4 shows R1's ARP table based on the previous example. The output lists R1's own IP address of 172.16.1.1, with an age of -, meaning that this entry does not time out. Dynamically learned ARP table entries have an upward counter, like the 35-minute value for the ARP table entry for IP address 172.16.1.9. By default, IOS will time out (remove) an ARP table entry after 240 minutes in which the entry is not used. (IOS resets the timer to 0 when an ARP table entry is used.) Note that to experiment in the lab, you might want to empty all dynamic entries (or a single entry for one IP address) using the **clear ip arp** [*ip-address*] EXEC command.

Example 17-4 *Displaying a Router's IP ARP Table*

```
R1# show ip arp
Protocol  Address        Age (min)  Hardware Addr   Type   Interface
Internet  172.16.1.1            -   0200.0101.0101  ARPA   GigabitEthernet0/0
Internet  172.16.1.9           35   0200.aaaa.aaaa  ARPA   GigabitEthernet0/0
```

Thinking about how Router R1 forwards a packet to host A (172.16.1.9), over that final subnet, R1 does the following:

1. R1 looks in the ARP table for an entry for 172.16.1.9.

2. R1 encapsulates the IP packet in an Ethernet frame, adding destination 0200.aaaa.aaaa to the Ethernet header (as taken from the ARP table).

3. R1 transmits the frame out interface G0/0.

Configuring Static Routes

In real networks, you will find connected routes on every router, which the routers create for subnets connected to their interfaces. You will use dynamic routing protocols like OSPF and EIGRP to learn routes for the rest of the subnets in the enterprise, routes for subnets remote from the local router.

Enterprises use static routes—that is, routes added to a routing table through direct configuration of the **ip route** command—much less often than connected routes and routes learned with dynamic routing protocols. However, static routes can be useful at times. Studying static routes also happens to be a wonderful learning tool as well. And, of course, the exam topics list several variations of static routes, so you need to learn the topic for the exam.

NOTE The CCNA 200-301 exam V1.1, exam topic 3.3, subdivides IPv4 (and IPv6) static routes into four subtopics: network routes, default routes, host routes, and floating static routes. This section explains all four types for IPv4 as noted in the upcoming headings.

Static Network Routes

IOS allows the definition of individual static routes using the **ip route** global configuration command. Every **ip route** command defines a destination subnet with a subnet ID and mask. The command also lists the forwarding instructions, listing the outgoing interface or the next-hop router's IP address (or both). IOS then takes that information and adds that route to the IP routing table.

A static **network route** defines either a subnet or an entire Class A, B, or C network in the **ip route** command. In contrast, a **default route** defines the set of all destination IP addresses, while a **host route** defines a single IP address (that is, an address of one host).

Figure 17-12 shows a new network diagram to be used in the upcoming examples. Note that the design uses the same subnets as some previous figures in this chapter, but it uses two GigabitEthernet WAN links and no serial links.

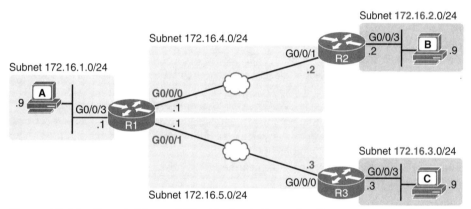

Figure 17-12   *Sample Network Used in Static Route Configuration Examples*

Figure 17-13 shows the concepts behind the potential network routes on Router R1 for the subnet to the right of Router R2 (subnet 172.16.2.0/24). To create that static network route on R1, R1 will configure the subnet ID and mask. For the forwarding instructions, R1 will configure either R1's outgoing interface (G0/0/0) or R2's IP address as the next-hop router IP address (172.16.4.2).

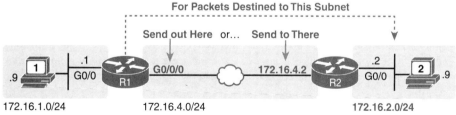

Figure 17-13   *Static Route Configuration Concept*

Example 17-5 shows the configuration of a couple of sample static routes, using the three-router topology in Figure 17-12. The example shows static routes on R1, one route for each of the two subnets on the right side of the figure. The first command defines a route for subnet 172.16.2.0 255.255.255.0, the subnet off Router R2. The forwarding instruction parameters list only R1's outgoing interface, G0/0/0. This route basically states: To send packets to the subnet off Router R2, send them out my local G0/0/0 interface.

Example 17-5 *Static Routes Added to R1*

```
ip route 172.16.2.0 255.255.255.0 G0/0/0
ip route 172.16.3.0 255.255.255.0 172.16.5.3
```

The second route has the same kind of logic, except listing the neighboring router's IP address on the WAN link as the next-hop router. This route basically says this: To send packets to the subnet off Router R3 (172.16.3.0 255.255.255.0), send the packets to R3's WAN IP address next (172.16.5.3).

Verifying Static Network Routes

Static routes, when seen in the IP routing table, list the same parameters included in the configuration command. To see how, closely compare the output in Example 17-6's **show ip route static** command. This command lists only static routes, in this case listing the two static routes configured in Example 17-5. First, the two lines listing the static routes begin with legend code S, meaning static. Both list the subnet and mask defined in the respective routes, although the output uses prefix-style masks. But note the key difference: for the route configured with only the outgoing interface, the route lists only the outgoing interface, and for the route configured with only the next-hop IP address, the output lists only the next-hop address.

Example 17-6 *Static Routes Added to R1*

```
R1# show ip route static
Codes: L - local, C - connected, S - static, R - RIP, M - mobile, B - BGP
! Legend lines omitted for brevity

      172.16.0.0/16 is variably subnetted, 8 subnets, 2 masks
S        172.16.2.0/24 is directly connected, GigabitEthernet0/0/0S
S        172.16.3.0/24 [1/0] via 172.16.5.3
```

Although statically configured, IOS adds and removes static routes from the routing table over time based on whether the outgoing interface is working or not. For example, in this case, if R1's G0/0/0 interface fails, R1 removes the static route to 172.16.2.0/24 from the IPv4 routing table. Later, when the interface comes up again, IOS adds the route back to the routing table.

Examples 17-3 and 17-4 show how to configure static network routes to support left-to-right packet flow in Figure 17-12, but routers need routes for all subnets to support packet flow in all directions. Even in a small lab used for CCNA learning, if you use only static routes, you need static routes for all subnets for both directions of packet flow. For instance, in Figure 17-13, to support packet flow from PC A to PC B, you need:

A route on Router R1 for PC B's subnet 172.16.2.0/24

A route on Router R2 for PC A's subnet 172.16.1.0/24

Ethernet Outgoing Interfaces and Proxy ARP

While both styles of static routes in Example 17-5 work—with either next-hop IP address or outgoing interface—using the next-hop address is better. Both work, but using a next-hop address causes much less confusion when the staff begin to wonder about how those static routes work behind the scenes. In short, using the next-hop address does not force the use of proxy ARP on the neighboring router, but using an outgoing interface on an Ethernet link does require proxy ARP.

This section attempts to explain how proxy ARP works and how static routes make use of it. To begin, consider this general definition of proxy ARP:

1. A router receives in interface X an ARP request, whose target is not in the subnet connected to interface X.

2. The router has a route to forward packets to that target address, and that route should not forward the packet back out onto the same interface causing a loop. In other words, the router has a useful route to forward packets to the target.

3. The router is therefore willing and useful to act as a proxy for the target host. To do so, the router supplies its own MAC address in the ARP Reply.

While true, it helps to work through an example. Consider Example 17-5 again with the **ip route 172.16.2.0 255.255.255.0 G0/0/0** command. Imagine PC A sends a packet to PC B at address 172.16.2.9. The packet arrives at Router R1, R1 matches the packet to the static route for subnet 172.16.2.0/24, and now Router R1 must decide from the forwarding instructions how to forward the packet. Router R1 uses logic as follows:

1. The route's forwarding instructions show the destination subnet as connected to interface G0/0/0. That causes R1 to send an ARP Request looking for 172.16.2.9 as the target address. In effect, R1's route makes R1 behave as if the destination subnet 172.16.2.0/24 is connected to port G0/0/0. Of course, PC B will not receive the ARP Request, as it resides on the other side of a router.

2. R2 receives R1's ARP for target 172.16.2.9. The ARP meets the requirements of proxy ARP (an address not in the local subnet, but R2 has a useful route matching address 172.16.2.9). R2 sends an ARP reply listing R2's interface G0/0/1 MAC—a proxy ARP Reply.

3. R1 receives the ARP Reply, so R1 can now forward packets meant for 172.16.2.9. R1 forwards these packets encapsulated in an Ethernet frame, with R2's G0/0/1 MAC as the destination MAC address.

4. R2 receives the frame and routes the encapsulated packet to PC B, as with normal routing processes.

As you can understand from the previous page or so, the underlying logic behind using an outgoing Ethernet interface on a route requires quite a lot of analysis. For real-world applications, use static routes with a next-hop address instead.

Static Default Routes

When a router tries to route a packet, the router might not match the packet's destination IP address with any route. When that happens, the router normally just discards the packet.

Routers can use a *default route* to match all packets, so that if a packet does not match any other more specific route in the routing table, the router will forward the packet based on the default route. Routers can learn default routes with a routing protocol, or you can configure a default static route.

Figure 17-14 shows one classic example in which a company has many branch office routers, like R2 and R3 in the figure, each of which has a single WAN connection. No matter how many routes a router might learn for specific subnets in those isolated branch offices, all the forwarding details in those routes would be the same for each route. For instance, all routes on Router R2, for remote subnets, would use outgoing interface G0/0/1 and next-hop address 172.16.4.1. Router R2 could instead use a default route, which matches all destinations, with the same forwarding instructions.

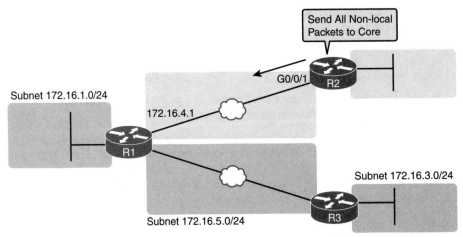

Figure 17-14 *Example Use of Static Default Routes*

IOS allows the configuration of a static default route by using special values for the subnet and mask fields in the **ip route** command: 0.0.0.0 and 0.0.0.0. For example, the command **ip route 0.0.0.0 0.0.0.0 172.16.4.1** creates the static route depicted in Figure 17-14 on Router R2—a route that matches all IP packets—and sends those packets to R1 (172.16.4.1). Example 17-7 shows that static default route, but take care to notice the unexpected location of the route for 0.0.0.0/0.

Example 17-7 *Adding a Static Default Route on R2 (Figure 17-14)*

```
R2# configure terminal
Enter configuration commands, one per line. End with CNTL/Z.
R2(config)# ip route 0.0.0.0 0.0.0.0 172.16.4.1
R2(config)# ^Z
R2# show ip route
Codes: L - local, C - connected, S - static, R - RIP, M - mobile, B - BGP
       D - EIGRP, EX - EIGRP external, O - OSPF, IA - OSPF inter area
       N1 - OSPF NSSA external type 1, N2 - OSPF NSSA external type 2
       E1 - OSPF external type 1, E2 - OSPF external type 2
       i - IS-IS, su - IS-IS summary, L1 - IS-IS level-1, L2 - IS-IS level-2
       ia - IS-IS inter area, * - candidate default, U - per-user static route
```

```
          o - ODR, P - periodic downloaded static route, H - NHRP, l - LISP
          + - replicated route, % - next hop override

Gateway of last resort is 172.16.4.1 to network 0.0.0.0S*

S*      0.0.0.0/0 [1/0] via 172.16.4.1
        172.16.0.0/16 is variably subnetted, 4 subnets, 2 masks
C          172.16.2.0/24 is directly connected, GigabitEthernet0/0/0
L          172.16.2.2/32 is directly connected, GigabitEthernet0/0/0
C          172.16.4.0/24 is directly connected, GigabitEthernet0/0/1
L          172.16.4.2/32 is directly connected, GigabitEthernet0/0/1
```

The output of the **show ip route** command lists a few new and interesting facts. First, it lists the route as 0.0.0.0/0, another notation for a subnet and mask of 0.0.0.0 and 0.0.0.0. The output lists a code of S, meaning static, but also with a *, meaning it is a *candidate default route*. (A router can learn about more than one default route, and the router then has to choose which one to use; the * means that it is at least a candidate to become the default route.) Just above the list of routes, the "Gateway of Last Resort" line refers to the chosen default route; in this case, R2 has only one candidate, so the output shows the just-configured static default route with next-hop address 172.16.4.1.

NOTE   If you attempt to re-create some of the examples from the book as part of your lab practice, note that if you configure the network as shown in Figures 17-13 and 17-14, with the configuration in Examples 17-5 and 17-7, PCs A and B should be able to ping each other. As an exercise, you can think about what network or default static routes to add to R3 so that PC C can ping the other two PCs as well.

Static Host Routes

The term *network route* refers to a route that matches addresses in an entire IP network or subnet, while a default route refers to a route that matches all destinations. In contrast, the term *host route* defines a route to a single host address. To configure such a static route, the **ip route** command uses an IP address plus a mask of 255.255.255.255 so that the matching logic matches just that one address.

Why use a static host route? Honestly, it is the least likely style of static route to use because network engineers seldom need to solve some routing problem for which a static host route will help. However, just to get the gist of what it can do, consider the topology in Figure 17-15, which expands the topology shown in the previous few figures.

First, imagine you run a dynamic routing protocol like OSPF, and Router R1 learns a route for subnet 172.16.10.0/26. Depending on the conditions of the network, R1's route for 172.16.10.0/26 may send packets to R2 next or R3 next. Most enterprises would be content in either case. The figure shows that route running through the lower router, R3.

Now imagine there was some unusual business reason such that all packets meant for host D must flow through Router R2 if it is working. The figure also shows that route, for host D only (172.16.10.4).

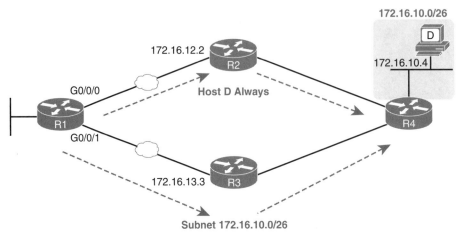

Figure 17-15 *An Example Possible Use for a Static Host Route*

The preceding scenario creates a need for a static host route. For instance, all the routers use OSPF to dynamically learn network routes for all subnets in the design. However, the engineer also configures the one host route on R1 as discussed in the last few paragraphs, as seen at the top of Example 17-8.

Example 17-8 *Host Route Configuration Versus an Overlapping Static Network Route*

```
R1# configure terminal
! The static host route for one IP address within that same subnet
R1(config)# ip route 172.16.10.4 255.255.255.255 172.16.4.2
R1(config)# ^Z
R1# show ip route
! Irrelevant portions omitted for brevity


     172.16.0.0/16 is variably subnetted, 12 subnets, 4 masks
O IA    172.16.10.0/26 [110/3] via 172.16.5.3, 01:52:58, GigabitEthernet0/0/1
S       172.16.10.4/32 [1/0] via 172.16.4.2
```

Note that it is normal for a host route to overlap with some other network route as seen here. A router always attempts to place the best route for each prefix (subnet) into the IP routing table. However, the host route uses a mask of 255.255.255.255 (/32), and the dynamic route for the subnet that address resides in uses a different mask. Router R1 does not view those routes as routes for the same subnet, but as different routes, and places both into its routing table.

Once in the routing table, when a packet arrives for that one special host address (172.16.10.4), R1 uses the host route. Why? Routers use the most specific route (that is, the route with the longest prefix length) when the packet's destination address matches multiple routes in the routing table. So, a packet sent to 172.16.10.4 would match the host route because a /32 mask is longer and more specific than the route with a /26 mask. Router R1 will forward that packet to next-hop router 172.16.4.2 per the host route. Packets sent to other destinations in subnet 172.16.10.0/26 would be sent to next-hop router 172.16.5.3, because those match only one route.

Note that the section "IP Forwarding with the Longest Prefix Match" near the end of Chapter 25, "Fundamentals of IP Version 6," gets into more detail about how a router chooses a route when multiple routes match a packet destination.

Floating Static Routes

Floating static routes exist in the configuration of a router, but the router floats the route into the routing table and out of the routing table based on certain conditions. Why? As part of a broader configuration that lets the router create a temporary WAN link when the primary WAN link fails.

To see how that works, consider the example illustrated in Figure 17-16, which shows routers R1 and R2 from the previous few figures. The Ethernet WAN link serves as the only working WAN link most of the time, but now both routers have a cellular interface. The routers can connect to each other using a 4G/LTE/5G network when the primary link goes down.

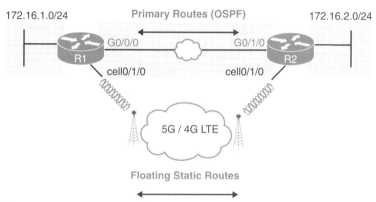

Figure 17-16 *Using a Floating Static Route to Key Subnet 172.16.2.0/24*

Interestingly, the configuration to use the cellular network to back up the Ethernet WAN link hinges on the routes. Routers use a routing protocol like OSPF on the permanent links, so in this case, R1 learns an OSPF route to subnet 172.16.2.0/24 that uses the Ethernet WAN link. R1 also defines a floating static route for that same subnet that directs packets over the cellular interface to Router R2. Although configured, Router R1 then chooses to add that floating static route to the routing table *only when the OSPF route is not available*. If the Ethernet link is up, R1 routes packets over that link. If not, it routes packets over the cellular network.

To create a floating static route, you configure a route but assign it a higher (worse) administrative distance than the competing dynamically learned route. When a router learns of more than one route to the same subnet/mask combination, the router must first decide which routing source has the better **administrative distance**, with lower being better, and then use the route learned from the better source. Default settings make routers treat static routes as better than any routes learned by a dynamic routing protocol. A floating static route reverses that logic.

To implement a floating static route, you need to use a parameter on the **ip route** command that sets the administrative distance for just that route, making the value larger than the default administrative distance of the routing protocol. For example, the **ip route 172.16.2.0 255.255.255.0 cell0/1/0 130** command on R1 (in Figure 17-15) would do exactly that—setting the static route's administrative distance to 130. As long as the primary link stays up, and OSPF on R1 learns a route for 172.16.2.0/24, with a default OSPF administrative distance of 110, R1 ignores the floating static route. When the Ethernet WAN link fails, R1 loses its OSPF-learned route for that subnet, so R1 places the floating static route into the routing table. (The rest of the configuration, not shown here, tells the router how to make the call to create the backup link over the cellular network.)

Finally, note that while the **show ip route** command lists the administrative distance of most routes, as the first of two numbers inside two brackets, the **show ip route** *subnet* command plainly lists the administrative distance. Example 17-9 shows a sample, matching this most recent example.

Example 17-9 *Displaying the Administrative Distance of the Static Route*

```
R1# show ip route static
! Legend omitted for brevity
        172.16.0.0/16 is variably subnetted, 6 subnets, 2 masks
S          172.16.2.0/24 is directly connected, Cellular0/1/0


R1# show ip route 172.16.2.0
Routing entry for 172.16.2.0/24
  Known via "static", distance 130, metric 0 (connected)
  Routing Descriptor Blocks:
  * directly connected, via Cellular0/1/0
      Route metric is 0, traffic share count is 1
```

Troubleshooting Static Routes

These final few pages about IPv4 static routes examine some issues that can occur with static routes, both reviewing some reasons mentioned over the last few pages, while adding more detail. This topic breaks static route troubleshooting into three perspectives:

- The route is in the routing table but is incorrect.

- The route is not in the routing table.

- The route is in the routing table and is correct, but the packets do not arrive at the destination host.

Incorrect Static Routes That Appear in the IP Routing Table

This first troubleshooting item can be obvious, but it is worth pausing to think about. A static route is only as good as the input typed into the **ip route** command. IOS checks the syntax, and as mentioned earlier, makes a few other checks that this section reviews in the next heading. But once those checks are passed, IOS puts the route into the IP routing table, even if the route had poorly chosen parameters.

For instance, if you wanted to configure a static route for subnet 172.16.2.0/24, but configured the route for subnet 172.16.222.0/24, the router will accept the command—but it is for the wrong subnet. Or, when choosing the next-hop router address, you looked at a network diagram, and used the next-hop address of a router to the left—but the destination subnet was on the right side of the figure. Or you could look at documentation and choose the next-hop address for the command, and it is in the correct destination subnet—but it is not the address of the next-hop router. In all these cases, the router would accept the command and even add the route to the routing table, but the route would not be useful.

As another example, IOS will reject the **ip route** command if the first two parameters reveal the configuration of an IP address within the subnet rather than the subnet ID. For instance, back in Example 17-5, the commands used mask 255.255.255.0, with subnet IDs 172.16.2.0 and 172.16.3.0. Example 17-10 shows a repeat of those same commands, but now with addresses from within those subnets: 172.16.2.1 and 172.16.3.1. In both cases, IOS shows an error message and does not add the command to the configuration.

Example 17-10 *IOS Rejects* **ip route** *Commands That Use an Address in the Subnet*

```
R1# configure terminal
Enter configuration commands, one per line.  End with CNTL/Z.
R1-8200(config)# ip route 172.16.2.1 255.255.255.0 G0/0/0
%Inconsistent address and mask
R1-8200(config)# ip route 172.16.3.1 255.255.255.0 172.16.5.3
%Inconsistent address and mask
R1-8200(config)#
```

When you see an exam question that has static routes, and you see them in the output of **show ip route**, remember to check on these items:

■ Are the subnet ID and mask correct?

■ Is the next-hop IP address correct and referencing an IP address on a neighboring router?

■ Does the next-hop IP address identify the correct router?

■ Is the outgoing interface correct and referencing an interface on the local router (that is, the same router where the static route is configured)?

The Static Route Does Not Appear in the IP Routing Table

After configuring an **ip route** command, IOS might or might not add the route to the IP routing table. IOS also considers the following before adding the route to its routing table:

■ For **ip route** commands that list an outgoing interface, that interface must be in an up/up state.

■ For **ip route** commands that list a next-hop IP address, the local router must have a route to reach that next-hop address.

For example, earlier in Example 17-5, R1's command **ip route 172.16.3.0 255.255.255.0 172.16.5.3** defines a static route. Before adding the route to the IP routing table, R1 looks for an existing IP route to reach 172.16.5.3. In that case, R1 will find a connected route for subnet 172.16.5.0/24 as long as its Ethernet WAN link is up. As a result, R1 adds the static route to subnet 172.16.3.0/24. Later, if R1's G0/0/1 were to fail, R1 would remove its connected route to 172.16.5.0/24 from the IP routing table—an action that would also then cause R1 to remove its static route to 172.16.3.0/24.

17

You can configure a static route so that IOS ignores these basic checks, always putting the IP route in the routing table. To do so, just use the **permanent** keyword on the **ip route** command. For example, if you add the **permanent** keyword to the end of the two commands as demonstrated in Example 17-11, R1 would now add these routes, regardless of whether the two WAN links were up.

Example 17-11 *Permanently Adding Static Routes to the IP Routing Table (Router R1)*

```
ip route 172.16.2.0 255.255.255.0 G0/0/0 permanent
ip route 172.16.3.0 255.255.255.0 172.16.5.3 permanent
```

Note that although the **permanent** keyword lets the router keep the route in the routing table without checking the outgoing interface or route to the next-hop address, it does not magically fix a broken route. For example, if the outgoing interface fails, the route will remain in the routing table, but the router cannot forward packets because the outgoing interface is down.

The Correct Static Route Appears but Works Poorly

This last section is a place to make two points—one mainstream and one point to review a bit of trivia.

First, on the mainstream point, the static route can be perfect, but the packets might not arrive because of other problems. An incorrect static route is just one of many items to check when you're troubleshooting problems like "host A cannot connect to server B." The root cause may be the static route, or it may be something else. Chapter 20, "Troubleshooting IPv4 Routing," goes into some depth about troubleshooting these types of problems.

On the more specific point, be wary of any **ip route** command with the **permanent** keyword. IOS puts these routes in the routing table with no checks for accuracy. You should check whether the outgoing interface is down and/or whether the router has a route to reach the next-hop address.

Chapter Review

One key to doing well on the exams is to perform repetitive spaced review sessions. Review this chapter's material using either the tools in the book or interactive tools for the same material found on the book's companion website. Refer to the "Your Study Plan" element for more details. Table 17-2 outlines the key review elements and where you can find them. To better track your study progress, record when you completed these activities in the second column.

Table 17-2 Chapter Review Tracking

Review Element	Review Date(s)	Resource Used
Review key topics		Book, website
Review key terms		Book, website
Answer DIKTA questions		Book, PTP
Review command tables		Book
Do labs		Blog
Watch video		Website

Review All the Key Topics

Table 17-3   Key Topics for Chapter 17

Key Topic Element	Description	Page Number
List	Steps taken by a host when forwarding IP packets	429
List	Steps taken by a router when forwarding IP packets	430
Figure 17-2	Diagram of five routing steps taken by a router	430
Figure 17-7	Breakdown of IP routing table with matching and forwarding details	434
List	Three common sources from which routers build IP routes	435
List	Rules regarding when a router creates a connected route	436
Figure 17-13	Static route configuration concept	441
List	Troubleshooting checklist for routes that do appear in the IP routing table	449
List	Troubleshooting checklist for static routes that do not appear in the IP routing table	449

Key Terms You Should Know

administrative distance, ARP table, connected route, default route, floating static route, host route, network route, next-hop router, outgoing interface, routing table, static route

Command References

Tables 17-4 and 17-5 list configuration and verification commands used in this chapter. As an easy review exercise, cover the left column in a table, read the right column, and try to recall the command without looking. Then repeat the exercise, covering the right column, and try to recall what the command does.

Table 17-4   Chapter 17 Configuration Command Reference

Command	Description
ip address *ip-address mask*	Interface subcommand that assigns the interface's IP address
interface *type number.subint*	Global command to create a subinterface and to enter configuration mode for that subinterface
[**no**] **ip routing**	Global command that enables (**ip routing**) or disables (**no ip routing**) the routing of IPv4 packets on a router or Layer 3 switch
ip route *prefix mask* {*ip-address* | *interface-type interface-number*} [*distance*] [**permanent**]	Global configuration command that creates a static route

17

Table 17-5   Chapter 17 EXEC Command Reference

Command	Description
show ip route	Lists the router's entire routing table
show ip route [connected | static | ospf]	Lists a subset of the IP routing table
show ip route *ip-address*	Lists detailed information about the route that a router matches for the listed IP address
show arp, show ip arp	Lists the router's IPv4 ARP table
clear ip arp [ip-address]	Removes all dynamically learned ARP table entries, or if the command lists an IP address, removes the entry for that IP address only

CHAPTER 18

IP Routing in the LAN

This chapter covers the following exam topics:

1.0 Network Fundamentals

   1.1 Explain the role and function of network components

      1.1.a Routers

      1.1.b Layer 2 and Layer 3 switches

   1.6 Configure and verify IPv4 addressing and subnetting

2.0 Network Access

   2.1 Configure and verify VLANs (normal range) spanning multiple switches

      2.1.c InterVLAN connectivity

   2.4 Configure and verify (Layer 2/Layer 3) EtherChannel (LACP)

The preceding two chapters showed how to configure an IP address and mask on a router interface, making the router ready to route packets to/from the subnet implied by that address/mask combination. While true and useful, all the examples so far ignored the LAN switches and the possibility of VLANs. In fact, the examples so far show the simplest possible cases: the attached switches as Layer 2 switches, using only one VLAN, with the router configured with one **ip address** command on its physical interface. This chapter takes a detailed look at how to configure routers so that they route packets to/from the subnets that exist on each and every VLAN.

Because Layer 2 switches do not forward Layer 2 frames between VLANs, a network must use a device that performs IP routing to route IP packets between subnets. That device can be a router, or it can be a switch that also includes routing features.

To review, Ethernet defines the concept of a VLAN, while IP defines the concept of an IP subnet, so a VLAN is not equivalent to a subnet. However, the devices in one VLAN typically use IP addresses in one subnet. By the same reasoning, devices in two different VLANs are normally in two different subnets. For two devices in different VLANs to communicate with each other, routers must connect to the subnets that exist on each VLAN, and then the routers forward IP packets between the devices in those subnets.

This chapter discusses multiple methods of routing between VLANs, all of which can be useful in different scenarios:

- **VLAN Routing with Router 802.1Q Trunks:** The first section discusses configuring a router to use VLAN trunking on a link connected to a Layer 2 switch. The router does the routing, with the switch creating the VLANs. The link between the router and switch uses VLAN trunking so that the router has an interface connected to each

VLAN/subnet. This feature is known as routing over a VLAN trunk and also known as **router-on-a-stick (ROAS)**.

■ **VLAN Routing with Layer 3 Switch SVIs:** The second section discusses using a LAN switch that supports both Layer 2 switching and Layer 3 routing (called a **Layer 3 switch** or **multilayer switch**). To route, the Layer 3 switch configuration uses interfaces called switched virtual interfaces (SVIs), which are also called VLAN interfaces.

■ **VLAN Routing with Layer 3 Switch Routed Ports:** The third major section of the chapter discusses an alternative to SVIs called **routed ports**, in which the physical switch ports are made to act like interfaces on a router. This third section also introduces the concept of an EtherChannel as used as a routed port in a feature called **Layer 3 EtherChannel (L3 EtherChannel)**.

■ **VLAN Routing on a Router's LAN Switch Ports:** The final major section discusses Cisco routers that include integrated LAN switch ports. For instance, rather than installing a small router plus a separate small switch at a branch office, you could install a router that has a small set of integrated switch ports. This section shows how to configure the router's switch ports and the internal logic, so the router routes packets for the subnets on those switch ports.

"Do I Know This Already?" Quiz

Take the quiz (either here or use the PTP software) if you want to use the score to help you decide how much time to spend on this chapter. The letter answers are listed at the bottom of the page following the quiz. Appendix C, found both at the end of the book as well as on the companion website, includes both the answers and explanations. You can also find both answers and explanations in the PTP testing software.

Table 18-1 "Do I Know This Already?" Foundation Topics Section-to-Question Mapping

Foundation Topics Section	Questions
VLAN Routing with Router 802.1Q Trunks	1, 2
VLAN Routing with Layer 3 Switch SVIs	3, 4
VLAN Routing with Layer 3 Switch Routed Ports	5, 6
VLAN Routing on a Router's LAN Switch Ports	7

1. Router 1 has a Fast Ethernet interface 0/0 with IP address 10.1.1.1. The interface is connected to a switch. This connection is then migrated to use 802.1Q trunking. Which of the following commands could be part of a valid configuration for Router 1's Fa0/0 interface, assuming the trunk uses VLAN 4 as one of the supported VLANs? (Choose two answers.)

   a. interface fastethernet 0/0.4
   b. dot1q enable
   c. dot1q enable 4
   d. trunking enable
   e. trunking enable 4
   f. encapsulation dot1q 4

2. Router R1 has a router-on-a-stick (ROAS) configuration with two subinterfaces of interface G0/1: G0/1.1 and G0/1.2. Physical interface G0/1 is currently in a down/down state. The network engineer then configures a **shutdown** command when in interface configuration mode for G0/1.1 and a **no shutdown** command when in interface configuration mode for G0/1.2. Which answers are correct about the interface state for the subinterfaces? (Choose two answers.)

   a. G0/1.1 will be in a down/down state.

   b. G0/1.2 will be in a down/down state.

   c. G0/1.1 will be in an administratively down state.

   d. G0/1.2 will be in an up/up state.

3. A Layer 3 switch has been configured to route IP packets between VLANs 1, 2, and 3 using SVIs, which connect to subnets 172.20.1.0/25, 172.20.2.0/25, and 172.20.3.0/25, respectively. The engineer issues a **show ip route connected** command on the Layer 3 switch, listing the connected routes. Which of the following answers lists a piece of information that should be in at least one of the routes?

   a. Interface Gigabit Ethernet 0/0.3

   b. Next-hop router 172.20.2.1

   c. Interface VLAN 2

   d. Mask 255.255.255.0

4. An engineer has successfully configured a Layer 3 switch with SVIs for VLANs 2 and 3 with autostate enabled by default. Hosts in the subnets using VLANs 2 and 3 can ping each other with the Layer 3 switch routing the packets. The next week, the network engineer receives a call that those same users can no longer ping each other. If the problem is with the Layer 3 switching function, which of the following could have caused the problem? (Choose two answers.)

   a. Six (or more) out of ten working VLAN 2 access ports failing due to physical problems

   b. A **shutdown** command issued from interface VLAN 4 configuration mode

   c. A **no vlan 2** command issued from global configuration mode

   d. A **shutdown** command issued from VLAN 2 configuration mode

5. A LAN design uses a Layer 3 EtherChannel between two switches SW1 and SW2, with port-channel interface 1 used on both switches. SW1 uses ports G0/1, G0/2, G0/3, and G0/4 in the channel. Which of the following is true about SW1's configuration to enable the channel to route IPv4 packets correctly? (Choose two answers.)

   a. The **ip address** command must be on the port-channel 1 interface.

   b. The **ip address** command must be on interface G0/1 (lowest numbered port).

   c. The port-channel 1 interface must be configured with the **no switchport** command.

   d. Interface G0/1 must be configured with the **routedport** command.

6. A LAN design uses a Layer 3 EtherChannel between two switches: SW1 and SW2. An engineer adds SW1 port G0/1 to the channel successfully but later fails when adding SW1 port G0/2 to the channel. Which answers list a configuration setting on port G0/2 that would cause this issue? (Choose two answers.)

  a. A different STP cost (**spanning-tree cost** *value*)

  b. A different speed (**speed** *value*)

  c. A default setting for switchport (**switchport**)

  d. A different access VLAN (**switchport access vlan** *vlan-id*)

7. A router has some routed and some switched physical ports. Which interface subcommands would you expect to be supported only on the switched ports?

  a. The **switchport access vlan** *vlan-id* subcommand

  b. The **ip address** *address mask* subcommand

  c. The **description** *text* subcommand

  d. The **hostname** *name* subcommand

Foundation Topics

VLAN Routing with Router 802.1Q Trunks

Almost all enterprise networks use VLANs. To route IP packets in and out of those VLANs, some devices (either routers or Layer 3 switches) need to have an IP address in each subnet and have a connected route to each of those subnets. Then the IP addresses on those routers or Layer 3 switches can serve as the default gateways in those subnets.

This chapter breaks down the LAN routing options into five categories:

- Use a router, with one router LAN interface and cable connected to the switch for each and every VLAN (typically not used)

- Use a router, with a VLAN trunk connecting to a LAN switch (known as router-on-a-stick, or ROAS)

- Use a Layer 3 switch with switched virtual interfaces (SVIs)

- Use a Layer 3 switch with routed interfaces (which may or may not be Layer 3 EtherChannels)

- Use a router with integrated switch ports, configuring it much like a Layer 3 switch with SVIs

Of the items in the list, the first option works, but to be practical, it requires far too many interfaces. It is mentioned here only to make the list complete.

As for the other options, this chapter discusses each in turn. Real networks use these features, with the choice to use one or the other driven by the design and needs for a particular part of the network. Figure 18-1 shows cases in which these options could be used.

18

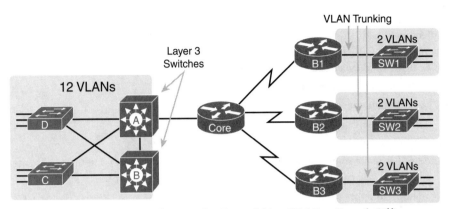

Figure 18-1   *Layer 3 Switching at the Central Site, ROAS at Branch Offices*

Figure 18-1 shows two switches, labeled A and B, which could act as Layer 3 switches—both with SVIs and routed interfaces. The figure shows a central site campus LAN on the left, with 12 VLANs. At the central site, two of the switches act as Layer 3 switches, combining the functions of a router and a switch, routing between all 12 subnets/VLANs. Those Layer 3 switches could use SVIs, routed interfaces, or both.

Figure 18-1 also shows a classic case for using a router with a VLAN trunk. Sites like the remote sites on the right side of the figure may have a WAN-connected router and a LAN switch. These sites might use ROAS to take advantage of the router's ability to route over an 802.1Q trunk.

Note that Figure 18-1 just shows an example. The engineer could use Layer 3 switching at each site or routers with VLAN trunking at each site.

Configuring ROAS

This next topic discusses how routers route packets to subnets associated with VLANs connected to a router 802.1Q trunk. That long description can be a bit of a chore to repeat each time someone wants to discuss this feature, so over time, the networking world has instead settled on a shorter and more interesting name for this feature: router-on-a-stick (ROAS).

ROAS uses router VLAN trunking configuration to give the router a logical interface connected to each VLAN. Because the router then has an interface connected to each VLAN, the router can also be configured with an IP address in the subnet that exists on each VLAN.

The router needs to have an IP address/mask associated with each VLAN on the trunk. However, the router has only one physical interface for the link connected to the trunk. Cisco solves this problem by creating multiple virtual router interfaces, one for each supported VLAN on that trunk. Cisco calls these virtual interfaces **subinterfaces**, and the router configuration includes an **ip address** command for each subinterface.

Figure 18-2 shows the concept with Router B1, one of the branch routers from Figure 18-1. Because this router needs to route between only two VLANs, the figure also shows two

---

Answers to the "Do I Know This Already?" quiz:

1 A, F **2** B, C **3** C **4** C, D **5** A, C **6** B, C **7** A

subinterfaces, named G0/0/0.10 and G0/0/0.20, which create a new place in the configuration where the per-VLAN configuration settings can be made. The router treats frames tagged with VLAN 10 as if they came in or out of G0/0/0.10 and frames tagged with VLAN 20 as if they came in or out G0/0/0.20.

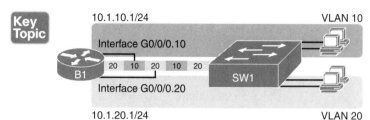

Figure 18-2 *Subinterfaces on Router B1*

In addition, note that most Cisco routers do not attempt to negotiate trunking, so both the router and switch need to manually configure trunking. This chapter discusses the router side of that trunking configuration; the matching switch interface would need to be configured with the **switchport mode trunk** command.

Example 18-1 shows a full example of the 802.1Q trunking configuration required on Router B1 in Figure 18-2. More generally, these steps detail how to configure 802.1Q trunking on a router:

Step 1.   Use the **interface** *type number.subint* command in global configuration mode to create a unique subinterface for each VLAN that needs to be routed.

Step 2.   Use the **encapsulation dot1q** *vlan_id* command in subinterface configuration mode to enable 802.1Q and associate one specific VLAN with the subinterface.

Step 3.   Use the **ip address** *address mask* command in subinterface configuration mode to configure IP settings (address and mask).

Example 18-1 *Router 802.1Q Configuration per Figure 18-2*

```
B1# show running-config
! Only pertinent lines shown
interface gigabitethernet 0/0/0
! No IP address or encapsulation up here!
!
interface gigabitethernet 0/0/0.10
 encapsulation dot1q 10
 ip address 10.1.10.1 255.255.255.0
!
interface gigabitethernet 0/0/0.20
 encapsulation dot1q 20
 ip address 10.1.20.1 255.255.255.0
```

First, look at the subinterface numbers. The subinterface number begins with the period, like .10 and .20 in this case. These numbers can be any number from 1 up through a very large number (over 4 billion). The number just needs to be unique among all subinterfaces associated with this one physical interface. In fact, the subinterface number does not even have to match the associated VLAN ID. (The **encapsulation** command, and not the subinterface number, defines the VLAN ID associated with the subinterface.)

> **NOTE** Although not required, most sites do choose to make the subinterface number match the VLAN ID, as shown in Example 18-1, just to avoid confusion.

Each subinterface configuration lists two subcommands. One command (**encapsulation**) enables trunking and defines the VLAN the router associates with the frames entering and exiting the subinterface. The **ip address** command works the same way it does on any other router interface.

Now that the router has a working interface, with IPv4 addresses configured, the router can route IPv4 packets on these subinterfaces. That is, the router treats these subinterfaces like any physical interface in terms of adding connected routes, matching those routes, and forwarding packets to/from those connected subnets.

Example 18-1 uses two VLANs, 10 and 20, neither of which is the native VLAN on the trunk. ROAS can make use of the native VLAN, with two variations in the configuration, so it requires a little extra thought. The native VLAN can be configured on a subinterface, or on the physical interface, or ignored as in Example 18-1. Each 802.1Q trunk has one native VLAN, and if the router needs to route packets for a subnet that exists in the native VLAN, then the router needs some configuration to support that subnet. The two options to define a router interface for the native VLAN are

- Configure the **ip address** command on the physical interface, but without an **encapsulation** command; the router considers this physical interface to be using the native VLAN.

- Configure the **ip address** command on a subinterface and use the **encapsulation dot1q** *vlan-id* **native** subcommand to tell the router both the VLAN ID and the fact that it is the native VLAN.

Example 18-2 shows both native VLAN configuration options with a small change to the same configuration in Example 18-1. In this case, VLAN 10 becomes the native VLAN. The top part of the example shows the option to configure the router physical interface to use native VLAN 10. The second half of the example shows how to configure that same native VLAN on a subinterface. In both cases, the switch configuration also needs to be changed to make VLAN 10 the native VLAN.

Example 18-2 *Two Configuration Options for Native VLAN 10 on Router B1*

```
! First option: put the native VLAN IP address on the physical interface
interface gigabitethernet 0/0/0
 ip address 10.1.10.1 255.255.255.0
!
interface gigabitethernet 0/0/0.20
 encapsulation dot1q 20
 ip address 10.1.20.1 255.255.255.0
```

```
! Second option: like Example 18-1, but add the native keyword
interface gigabitethernet 0/0/0.10
 encapsulation dot1q 10 native
 ip address 10.1.10.1 255.255.255.0
!
interface gigabitethernet 0/0/0.20
 encapsulation dot1q 20
 ip address 10.1.20.1 255.255.255.0
```

Verifying ROAS

Beyond using the **show running-config** command, ROAS configuration on a router can be best verified with two commands: **show ip route [connected]** and **show vlans**. As with any router interface, as long as the interface is in an up/up state and has an IPv4 address configured, IOS will put a connected (and local) route in the IPv4 routing table. So, a first and obvious check would be to see if all the expected connected routes exist. Example 18-3 lists the connected routes per the configuration shown in Example 18-1.

Example 18-3 *Connected Routes Based on Example 18-1 Configuration*

```
B1# show ip route connected
Codes: L - local, C - connected, S - static, R - RIP, M - mobile, B - BGP
! Legend omitted for brevity

      10.0.0.0/8 is variably subnetted, 4 subnets, 2 masks
C        10.1.10.0/24 is directly connected, GigabitEthernet0/0/0.10
L        10.1.10.1/32 is directly connected, GigabitEthernet0/0/0.10
C        10.1.20.0/24 is directly connected, GigabitEthernet0/0/0.20
L        10.1.20.1/32 is directly connected, GigabitEthernet0/0/0.20
```

As for interface and subinterface state, note that the ROAS subinterface state does depend to some degree on the physical interface state. In particular, the subinterface state cannot be better than the state of the matching physical interface. For instance, so far, the physical interface and related subinterfaces on Router B1 rested in an up/up state. If you unplugged the cable from that physical port, the physical and subinterfaces all fail to a down/down state. Or, if you shut down the physical interface, the physical and subinterfaces move to an administratively down state, as seen in Example 18-4.

Example 18-4 *Subinterface State Tied to Physical Interface State*

```
B1# configure terminal
Enter configuration commands, one per line. End with CNTL/Z.
B1(config)# interface g0/0/0
B1(config-if)# shutdown
B1(config-if)# ^Z
B1# show ip interface brief | include 0/0/0
GigabitEthernet0/0/0       unassigned     YES manual administratively down down
GigabitEthernet0/0/0.10    10.1.10.1      YES manual administratively down down
GigabitEthernet0/0/0.20    10.1.20.1      YES manual administratively down down
```

Additionally, the subinterface state can also be enabled and disabled independently from the physical interface, using the **no shutdown** and **shutdown** commands in subinterface configuration mode. For instance, the physical interface and subinterface .10 can remain up/up, while subinterface .20 can be independently shut down.

Another useful ROAS verification command, **show vlans**, spells out which router trunk interfaces use which VLANs, which VLAN is the native VLAN, plus some packet statistics. The fact that the packet counters are increasing can be useful when verifying whether traffic is happening or not. Example 18-5 shows a sample, based on the Router B1 configuration in Example 18-2 (bottom half), in which native VLAN 10 is configured on subinterface G0/0/0.10. Note that the output identifies VLAN 1 associated with the physical interface, VLAN 10 as the native VLAN associated with G0/0/0.10, and VLAN 20 associated with G0/0/0.20. It also lists the IP addresses assigned to each interface/subinterface.

Example 18-5 *Router* show vlans *Command Reveals Router ROAS Configuration*

```
B1# show vlans
VLAN ID: 1 (IEEE 802.1Q Encapsulation)


   Protocols Configured:        Received:        Transmitted:


VLAN trunk interfaces for VLAN ID 1:
GigabitEthernet0/0/0


GigabitEthernet0/0/0 (1)
      Total 5 packets, 330 bytes input
      Total 20 packets, 3134 bytes output


VLAN ID: 10 (IEEE 802.1Q Encapsulation)

  This is configured as native Vlan for the following interface(s) :
GigabitEthernet0/0/0    Native-vlan Tx-type: Untagged

   Protocols Configured:        Received:        Transmitted:
                   IP               0                   0


VLAN trunk interfaces for VLAN ID 10:
GigabitEthernet0/0/0.10


GigabitEthernet0/0/0.10 (10)
                   IP: 10.1.10.1
      Total 38 packets, 5696 bytes input
      Total 2 packets, 128 bytes output


VLAN ID: 20 (IEEE 802.1Q Encapsulation)
```

```
   Protocols Configured:         Received:        Transmitted:
                      IP              0                 0

VLAN trunk interfaces for VLAN ID 20:
GigabitEthernet0/0/0.20


GigabitEthernet0/0/0.20 (20)
                    IP: 10.1.20.1
      Total 0 packets, 0 bytes input
      Total 2 packets, 128 bytes output
```

Troubleshooting ROAS

The biggest challenge when troubleshooting ROAS has to do with the fact that if you mis-configure only the router or misconfigure only the switch, the other device on the trunk has no way to know that the other side is misconfigured. That is, the router configuration might be correct, but routing might still fail because of problems on the attached switch. So, troubleshooting ROAS often begins with checking the configuration on both the router and switch because there is no status output on either device that tells you where the problem might be.

First, to check ROAS on the router, you need to start with the intended configuration and ask questions about the configuration:

1. Is each non-native VLAN configured on the router with an **encapsulation dot1q** *vlan-id* command on a subinterface?

2. Do those same VLANs exist on the trunk on the neighboring switch (**show interfaces trunk**), and are they in the allowed list, not VTP pruned, and not STP blocked?

3. Does each router ROAS subinterface have an IP address/mask configured per the planned configuration?

4. If using the native VLAN, is it configured correctly on the router either on a subinter-face (with an **encapsulation dot1q** *vlan-id* **native** command) or implied on the physical interface?

5. Is the same native VLAN configured on the neighboring switch's trunk in comparison to the native VLAN configured on the router?

6. Are the router physical or ROAS subinterfaces configured with a **shutdown** command?

For some of these steps, you need to be ready to investigate possible VLAN trunking issues on the LAN switch. Many Cisco router interfaces do not negotiate trunking. As a result, ROAS relies on static trunk configuration on both the router and switch. If the switch has any problems with VLANs or the VLAN trunking configuration on its side of the trunk, the router has no way to realize that the problem exists.

For example, imagine you configured ROAS on a router just like in Example 18-1 or Example 18-2. However, the switch on the other end of the link had no matching configu-ration. For instance, maybe the switch did not even define VLANs 10 and 20. Maybe the switch did not configure trunking on the port connected to the router. Even with blatant misconfiguration or missing configuration on the switch, the router still shows up/up ROAS interfaces and subinterfaces, IP routes in the output of **show ip route**, and meaningful configuration information in the output of the **show vlans** command. The router will forward packets (encapsulated inside frames) to the switch, but the switch's configuration does not give it enough information to forward the frame correctly.

VLAN Routing with Layer 3 Switch SVIs

Using a router with ROAS to route packets makes sense in some cases, particularly at small remote sites. In sites with a larger LAN, network designers choose to use Layer 3 switches for most inter-VLAN routing.

A Layer 3 switch (also called a multilayer switch) is one device, but it executes logic at two layers: Layer 2 LAN switching and Layer 3 IP routing. The Layer 2 switch function forwards frames inside each VLAN, but it will not forward frames between VLANs. The Layer 3 forwarding (routing) logic forwards IP packets between VLANs by applying IP routing logic to IP packets sent by the devices in those VLANs.

Layer 3 switches typically support two configuration options to enable IPv4 routing inside the switch, specifically to enable IPv4 on switch interfaces. This section explains one option, an option that uses switched virtual interfaces (SVI). The following major section of the chapter deals with the other option for configuring IPv4 addresses on Layer 3 switches: routed interfaces.

Configuring Routing Using Switch SVIs

The configuration of a Layer 3 switch mostly looks like the Layer 2 switching configuration shown back in Parts II and III of this book, with a small bit of configuration added for the Layer 3 functions. The Layer 3 switching function needs a virtual interface connected to each VLAN internal to the switch. These **VLAN interfaces** act like router interfaces, with an IP address and mask. The Layer 3 switch has an IP routing table, with connected routes off each of these VLAN interfaces. Cisco refers to these virtual interfaces as **switched virtual interfaces (SVIs)**.

To show the concept of Layer 3 switching with SVIs, the following example uses the same branch office with two VLANs shown in the earlier examples, but now the design will use Layer 3 switching in the LAN switch. Figure 18-3 details the physical connections, subnets, and VLAN IDs. Figure 18-4 then shows the internal routing logic and SVIs.

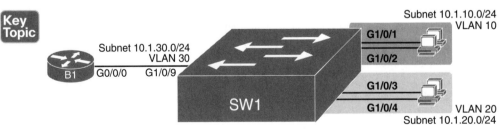

Figure 18-3 *Physical Interfaces and Subnets for Layer 3 Switching Example*

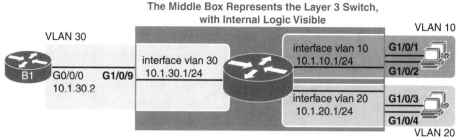

Figure 18-4   *Internal VLAN Interfaces for Layer 3 Switching Example*

Note that Figure 18-4 represents the internals of the Layer 3 switch within the box in the middle of the figure. The branch still has two user VLANs (10 and 20), so the Layer 3 switch needs one VLAN interface (SVI) for each VLAN. The figure shows a router icon inside the gray box to represent the Layer 3 switching (routing) function, with two VLAN interfaces on the right side of that icon. In addition, the traffic still needs to get to Router B1 (a physical router) to access the WAN, so the switch uses a third VLAN (VLAN 30 in this case) for the link to Router B1. The switch treats the link between the Layer 3 switch and Router B1 as an access link; the router would be unaware of any VLANs and would not need VLAN trunking configuration.

The following steps show how to configure Layer 3 switching using SVIs.

Step 1.   Enable IP routing on the switch, as needed:

     a.   (As needed) Use a model-specific command to change the switch forwarding ASIC settings to make space for IPv4 routes and reload the switch to make those settings take effect.

     c.   Use the **ip routing** command in global configuration mode to enable the IPv4 routing function in IOS software and to enable key commands like **show ip route**.

Step 2.   Configure each SVI interface, one per VLAN for which routing should be done by this Layer 3 switch:

     a.   Use the **interface vlan** *vlan_id* command in global configuration mode to create a VLAN interface and to give the switch's routing logic a Layer 3 interface connected into the VLAN of the same number.

     b.   Use the **ip address** *address mask* command in VLAN interface configuration mode to configure an IP address and mask on the VLAN interface, enabling IPv4 routing on that VLAN interface.

     c.   (As needed) Use the **no shutdown** command in interface configuration mode to enable the VLAN interface (if it is currently in a shutdown state).

NOTE   Regarding Step 1A, some older switch models do not support IP routing until you reprogram the switch's forwarding ASIC. For instance, the 2960 and 2960-XR switches popularly sold by Cisco in the 2010s required the **sdm prefer** global command followed by a reload of the switch. Newer Cisco switch models default to support IP routing and do not require similar steps.

18

Example 18-6 shows the configuration to match Figure 18-4. In this case, the switch defaulted to support IP routing in the forwarding ASIC without any special commands. The example shows the related configuration on all three VLAN interfaces.

Example 18-6 *VLAN Interface Configuration for Layer 3 Switching*

```
ip routing
!
interface vlan 10
 ip address 10.1.10.1 255.255.255.0
!
interface vlan 20
 ip address 10.1.20.1 255.255.255.0
!
interface vlan 30
 ip address 10.1.30.1 255.255.255.0
```

Verifying Routing with SVIs

With the VLAN configuration shown in the previous section, the switch is ready to route packets between the VLANs as shown in Figure 18-4. To support the routing of packets, the switch adds connected IP routes as shown in Example 18-7; note that each route is listed as being connected to a different VLAN interface.

Example 18-7 *Connected Routes on a Layer 3 Switch*

```
SW1# show ip route connected
! legend omitted for brevity


      10.0.0.0/8 is variably subnetted, 6 subnets, 2 masks
C        10.1.10.0/24 is directly connected, Vlan10
L        10.1.10.1/32 is directly connected, Vlan10
C        10.1.20.0/24 is directly connected, Vlan20
L        10.1.20.1/32 is directly connected, Vlan20
C        10.1.30.0/24 is directly connected, Vlan30
L        10.1.30.1/32 is directly connected, Vlan30
```

The switch would also need additional routes to the rest of the network (not shown in the figures in this chapter). The Layer 3 switch could use static routes or a routing protocol, depending on the capabilities of the switch. For instance, if you then enabled OSPF on the Layer 3 switch, the configuration and verification would work the same as it does on a router, as discussed in Part VI, "OSPF." The routes that IOS adds to the Layer 3 switch's IP routing table list the VLAN interfaces as outgoing interfaces.

NOTE Some models of Cisco enterprise switches, based on the specific model, IOS version, and IOS feature set, support different capabilities for IP routing and routing protocols. For use in real networks, check the capabilities of the switch model by using the Cisco Feature Navigator (CFN) tool at www.cisco.com/go/cfn.

Troubleshooting Routing with SVIs

On a physical router, when using physical interfaces, the router can assign a state to the interface based on physical factors, like whether the cable is installed or if the router receives any electricity or light over the cable. However, SVIs act as a virtual interface for the routing function in a Layer 3 switch. The switch must use some other logic to decide whether to place the SVI into a working (up/up) state.

Layer 3 switches use one of two interface configuration settings to dictate the logic to determine interface state: either **autostate** or **no autostate**. The default setting on a VLAN interface, **autostate**, checks several factors about the underlying VLAN to determine the state of the VLAN interface. By configuring the **no autostate** VLAN interface subcommand, the switch instead uses much simpler logic with fewer checks. The following few pages explain both.

SVI Interface State with Autostate Enabled

The VLAN interface acts as the interface between the switch's routing function and the VLAN. For that VLAN interface to work properly, the VLAN must work properly. In particular, for a VLAN interface to be in an up/up state when using the autostate setting:

Step 1. The VLAN must be defined on the local switch (either explicitly or learned with VTP).

Step 2. The switch must have at least one up/up interface using the VLAN, including:

    a. An up/up access interface assigned to that VLAN

    b. A trunk interface for which the VLAN is in the allowed list, is STP forwarding, and is not VTP pruned

Step 3. The VLAN must be administratively enabled (that is, not **shutdown**).

Step 4. The VLAN interface must be administratively enabled (that is, not **shutdown**).

18

Do not miss this point: VLAN and the VLAN interface are related but separate ideas, each configured separately in the CLI. A VLAN interface, configured with the **interface vlan** *vlan-id* global command, creates a switch's Layer 3 interface connected to the VLAN. A VLAN, created with the **vlan** *vlan-id* global command, creates the VLAN. If you want to route packets for the subnets on VLANs 11, 12, and 13, using SVIs, you must configure the VLAN interfaces with those same VLAN IDs 11, 12, and 13. The VLANs with those same VLAN IDs must also exist.

IOS supports the function to disable and enable both a VLAN and a VLAN interface with the **shutdown** and **no shutdown** commands (as mentioned in Steps 3 and 4 in the preceding list). As part of the configuration checklist tasks, check the status to ensure that all the configuration enables all the related VLANs and VLAN interfaces.

Example 18-8 shows three scenarios, each of which leads to one of the VLAN interfaces in the previous configuration example (Figure 18-4, Example 18-6) to fail. At the beginning of the example, all three VLAN interfaces are up/up. To begin the example, VLANs 10, 20, and 30 each have at least one access interface up and working. The example works through three scenarios:

- **Scenario 1:** The last access interface in VLAN 10 is shut down (G1/0/1), so IOS shuts down the VLAN 10 interface.

- **Scenario 2:** VLAN 20 (not VLAN interface 20, but VLAN 20) is deleted, which results in IOS then bringing down (not shutting down) the VLAN 20 interface.

- **Scenario 3:** VLAN 30 (not VLAN interface 30, but VLAN 30) is shut down, which results in IOS then bringing down (not shutting down) the VLAN 30 interface.

Example 18-8   *Three Examples That Cause VLAN Interfaces to Fail*

```
SW1# show interfaces status
! Only ports related to the example are shown
Port       Name             Status      Vlan    Duplex  Speed Type
Gi1/0/1                     connected   10      a-full  a-100 10/100/1000BaseTX
Gi1/0/2                     notconnect  10       auto    auto 10/100/1000BaseTX
Gi1/0/3                     connected   20      a-full  a-100 10/100/1000BaseTX
Gi1/0/4                     connected   20      a-full  a-100 10/100/1000BaseTX
Gi1/0/9                     connected   30      a-full a-1000 10/100/1000BaseTX


SW1# configure terminal
Enter configuration commands, one per line. End with CNTL/Z.

! Case 1: Interface G1/0/1, the last up/up access interface in VLAN 10, is shutdown
SW1(config)# interface GigabitEthernet 1/0/1
SW1(config-if)# shutdown
SW1(config-if)#
*Apr 2 19:54:08.784: %LINEPROTO-5-UPDOWN: Line protocol on Interface Vlan10, changed
state to down
*Apr 2 19:54:10.772: %LINK-5-CHANGED: Interface GigabitEthernet1/0/1, changed state
to administratively down
*Apr 2 19:54:11.779: %LINEPROTO-5-UPDOWN: Line protocol on Interface GigabitEther-
net1/0/1, changed state to down

! Case 2: VLAN 20 is deleted
SW1(config)# no vlan 20
SW1(config)#
*Apr 2 19:54:39.688: %LINEPROTO-5-UPDOWN: Line protocol on Interface Vlan20, changed
state to down

! Case 3: VLAN 30, the VLAN from the switch to the router, is shutdown
SW1(config)# vlan 30
SW1(config-vlan)# shutdown
SW1(config-vlan)# exit
SW1(config)#
*Apr 2 19:55:25.204: %LINEPROTO-5-UPDOWN: Line protocol on Interface Vlan30, changed
state to down
```

```
! Final status of all three VLAN interfaces is below
SW1# show ip interface brief | include Vlan
Vlan1                 unassigned      YES manual administratively down down
Vlan10                10.1.10.1       YES manual up                    down
Vlan20                10.1.20.1       YES manual up                    down
Vlan30                10.1.30.1       YES manual up                    down
```

Note that the example ends with the three VLAN interfaces in an up/down state per the **show ip interface brief** command.

SVI Interface State with Autostate Disabled

With autostate disabled, the switch checks only whether the VLAN is defined on the switch, either explicitly or learned by VTP. It ignores all the other checks performed when using autostate. If no matching VLAN exists, the switch places the VLAN interface in an up/down state.

Example 18-9 shows how to determine whether autostate is enabled from the **show interfaces vlan** command output. In the example, the engineer already configured the **no autostate** command under interface VLAN 10, with interface VLAN 20 using the default setting of **autostate**.

Example 18-9 *Recognizing the Autostate Setting on VLAN Interfaces*

```
SW1# show interfaces vlan 10
Vlan10 is up, line protocol is up , Autostate Disabled
! Lines omitted for brevity
SW1# show interfaces vlan 20
Vlan10 is up, line protocol is up , Autostate Enabled
! Lines omitted for brevity
```

VLAN Routing with Layer 3 Switch Routed Ports

When Layer 3 switches use SVIs, the physical interfaces on the switches act like they always have: as Layer 2 interfaces. That is, the physical interfaces receive Ethernet frames, the switch learns the source MAC address of the frame, and the switch forwards the frame based on the destination MAC address. That logic occurs independently from any configured routing logic.

When using a Layer 3 switch, the switch acts as the default router for endpoint hosts. As usual, to send a packet to a default router, a host uses ARP to learn the default router's MAC address and then encapsulates the packet in a frame destined to the default router's MAC address. As a result, when using a Layer 3 switch with SVIs, hosts send their frames to the SVI's MAC address. Those frames arrive in a physical switch port, which forwards the frame based on the destination MAC address, but to the internal destination of the VLAN interface. That process triggers internal routing actions like stripping data-link headers, making a routing decision, and so on.

Alternately, the Layer 3 switch configuration can make a physical port act like a router interface instead of a switch interface. To do so, the switch configuration makes that port a routed port. On a *routed port*, the switch does not perform Layer 2 switching logic on that frame. Instead, frames arriving in a routed port trigger the Layer 3 routing logic, including

1. Stripping off the incoming frame's Ethernet data-link header/trailer

2. Making a Layer 3 forwarding decision by comparing the destination IP address to the IP routing table

3. Adding a new Ethernet data-link header/trailer to the packet

4. Forwarding the packet, encapsulated in a new frame

This third major section of the chapter examines routed interfaces as configured on Cisco Layer 3 switches, but with a particular goal in mind: to also discuss Layer 3 EtherChannels. L3 EtherChannels use routed ports, so before learning about L3 EtherChannels you must first understand routed ports.

Implementing Routed Interfaces on Switches

When a Layer 3 switch needs a Layer 3 interface connected to a subnet, and only one physical interface connects to that subnet, the design can use a routed port instead of an SVI. Stated differently, when routing over a point-to-point link connected to one other device only, using a routed port makes sense. Conversely, when the Layer 3 switch needs a Layer 3 interface connected to a subnet, and many physical interfaces on the switch connect to that subnet, the design must use an SVI.

To see why, consider the design in Figure 18-5, which repeats the same design from Figure 18-4, which was used in the SVI examples. In that design, the gray rectangle on the right represents the switch and its internals. On the right of the switch, at least two access ports sit in both VLAN 10 and VLAN 20. The Layer 3 switch must use SVIs as an interface into those VLANs because two or more ports connect to the VLAN.

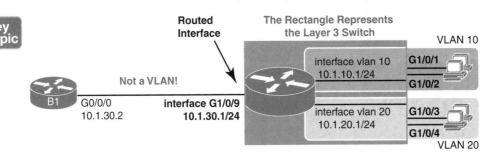

Figure 18-5   *Routing on a Routed Interface on a Switch*

The link on the left of the figure connects from the switch to Router B1. The design needs routing between Router B1 and the switch. While earlier Example 18-6 and Example 18-7 show how to accomplish that routing with an access port and an SVI on the switch, using a routed port works as well, given that the design creates a point-to-point topology between the two devices.

Enabling a switch interface to be a routed interface instead of a switched interface is simple: just use the **no switchport** subcommand on the physical interface. Cisco switches capable of being a Layer 3 switch use a default of the **switchport** command to each switch physical interface. Think about the word *switchport* for a moment. With that term, Cisco tells the switch to treat the port like it is a port on a switch—that is, a Layer 2 port on a switch. To make the port stop acting like a switch port and instead act like a router port, use the **no switchport** command on the interface.

Once the port is acting as a routed port, think of it like a router interface. That is, configure the IP address on the physical port, as implied in Figure 18-5. Example 18-10 shows a completed configuration for the interfaces configured on the switch in Figure 18-5. Note that the design uses the exact same IP subnets as the example that showed SVI configuration in Example 18-6, but now, the port connected to subnet 10.1.30.0 has been converted to a routed port. All you have to do is add the **no switchport** command to the physical interface and configure the IP address on the physical interface.

Example 18-10   *Configuring Interface G0/1 on Switch SW1 as a Routed Port*

```
ip routing
!
interface vlan 10
 ip address 10.1.10.1 255.255.255.0
!
interface vlan 20
 ip address 10.1.20.1 255.255.255.0
!
interface gigabitethernet 1/0/9
 no switchport
 ip address 10.1.30.1 255.255.255.0
```

Once configured, the routed interface will show up differently in command output in the switch. In particular, for an interface configured as a routed port with an IP address, like interface GigabitEthernet1/0/9 in the previous example:

show interfaces: Similar to the same command on a router, the output will display the IP address of the interface. (Conversely, for switch ports, this command does not list an IP address.)

show interfaces status: Under the "VLAN" heading, instead of listing the access VLAN or the word *trunk*, the output lists the word *routed*, meaning that it is a routed port.

show ip route: Lists the routed port as an outgoing interface in routes.

show interfaces *type number* **switchport:** If a routed port, the output is short and confirms that the port is not a switch port. (If the port is a Layer 2 port, this command lists many configuration and status details.)

Example 18-11 shows samples of all four of these commands as taken from the switch as configured in Example 18-10.

18

Example 18-11 *Verification Commands for Routed Ports on Switches*

```
SW1# show interfaces g1/0/9
GigabitEthernet1/0/9 is up, line protocol is up (connected)
  Hardware is Gigabit Ethernet, address is 4488.165a.f277 (bia 4488.165a.f277)
  Internet address is 10.1.30.1/24
! lines omitted for brevity

SW1# show interfaces status
! Only ports related to the example are shown; the command lists physical only
Port       Name            Status      Vlan      Duplex  Speed Type
Gi1/0/1                    connected   10        a-full a-1000 10/100/1000BaseTX
Gi1/0/2                    connected   10        a-full a-1000 10/100/1000BaseTX
Gi1/0/3                    connected   20        a-full a-1000 10/100/1000BaseTX
Gi1/0/4                    connected   20        a-full a-1000 10/100/1000BaseTX
Gi1/0/9                    connected   routed    a-full a-1000 10/100/1000BaseTX

SW1# show ip route
! legend omitted for brevity

      10.0.0.0/8 is variably subnetted, 6 subnets, 2 masks
C        10.1.10.0/24 is directly connected, Vlan10
L        10.1.10.1/32 is directly connected, Vlan10
C        10.1.20.0/24 is directly connected, Vlan20
L        10.1.20.1/32 is directly connected, Vlan20
C        10.1.30.0/24 is directly connected, GigabitEthernet1/0/9
L        10.1.30.1/32 is directly connected, GigabitEthernet1/0/9

SW1# show interfaces g0/1 switchport
Name: Gi1/0/9
Switchport: Disabled
```

So, with two options—SVI and routed ports—where should you use each?

For any topologies with a point-to-point link between two devices that do routing, a routed interface works better. For any other topology, you must use SVIs.

Figure 18-6 shows an example of where to use SVIs and where to use routed ports in a typical core/distribution/access design. In this design, the core (Core1, Core2) and distribution (D11, D12, D21, D22) switches perform Layer 3 switching. The access switches (labeled A11, A12, and so on) perform only Layer 2 switching. All the ports that are links directly between the Layer 3 switches can be routed interfaces. For VLANs for which many interfaces (access and trunk) connect to the VLAN, SVIs make sense because the SVIs can send and receive traffic out multiple ports in the same VLAN on the same switch. In this design, all the ports on Core1 and Core2 will be routed ports, while the four distribution switches will use some routed ports and some SVIs.

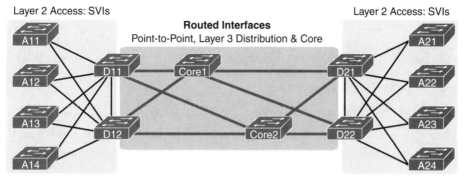

Figure 18-6 *Using Routed Interfaces for Core and Distribution Layer 3 Links*

Implementing Layer 3 EtherChannels

So far, this section has stated that routed interfaces can be used with a single point-to-point link between pairs of Layer 3 switches, or between a Layer 3 switch and a router. However, in most designs, the network engineers use at least two links between each pair of distribution and core switches, as shown in Figure 18-7.

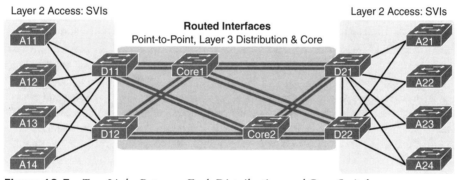

Figure 18-7 *Two Links Between Each Distribution and Core Switch*

While each individual port in the distribution and core could be treated as a separate routed port, it is better to combine each pair of parallel links into a Layer 3 EtherChannel. Without using EtherChannel, you can still make each port on each switch in the center of the figure be a routed port. It works. However, once you enable a routing protocol but don't use EtherChannels, each Layer 3 switch will now learn two IP routes with the same neighboring switch as the next hop—one route over one link, another route over the other link.

Using a Layer 3 EtherChannel makes more sense with multiple parallel links between two switches. By doing so, each pair of links acts as one Layer 3 link. So, each pair of switches has one routing protocol neighbor relationship with the neighbor, and not two. Each switch learns one route per destination per pair of links, and not two. IOS then balances the traffic, often with better balancing than the balancing that occurs with the use of multiple IP routes to the same subnet. Overall, the Layer 3 EtherChannel approach works much better than leaving each link as a separate routed port and using Layer 3 balancing.

18

Compared to what you have already learned, configuring a Layer 3 EtherChannel takes only a little more work. Chapter 10, "RSTP and EtherChannel Configuration," already showed you how to configure an EtherChannel. This chapter has already shown how to make a port a Layer 3 routed port. Next, you have to combine the two ideas by combining both the Ether-Channel and routed port configuration. The following checklist shows the steps, assuming a static definition for the EtherChannel.

Step 1. Configure the physical interfaces as follows, in interface configuration mode:

    a. Add the **no switchport** command to make each physical port a routed port.

    b. Add the **channel-group** *number* **mode on** command to add it to the channel. Use the same number for all physical interfaces on the same switch, but the number used (the channel-group number) can differ on the two neighboring switches.

Step 2. Configure the PortChannel interface:

    a. Use the **interface port-channel** *number* command to move to port-channel configuration mode for the same channel number configured on the physical interfaces.

    b. Add the **no switchport** command to make sure that the port-channel inter-face acts as a routed port. (IOS may have already added this command.)

    c. Use the **ip address** *address mask* command to configure the address and mask.

> **NOTE** Cisco uses the term *EtherChannel* in concepts discussed in this section and then uses the term *PortChannel*, with command keyword **port-channel**, when verifying and con-figuring EtherChannels. For the purposes of understanding the technology, you may treat these terms as synonyms. However, it helps to pay close attention to the use of the terms *PortChannel* and *EtherChannel* as you work through the examples in this section because IOS uses both.

Example 18-12 shows an example of the configuration for a Layer 3 EtherChannel for switch SW1 in Figure 18-8. The EtherChannel defines port-channel interface 12 and uses subnet 10.1.12.0/24. The design makes use of TenGigabit interfaces between the two switches.

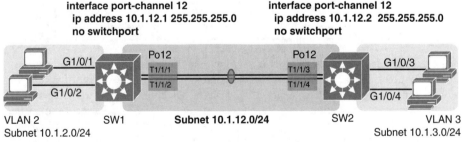

Figure 18-8 *Design Used in EtherChannel Configuration Examples*

Example 18-12 *Layer 3 EtherChannel Configuration on Switch SW1*

```
interface TenGigabit1/1/1
 no switchport
 no ip address
 channel-group 12 mode on
!
interface TenGigabit1/1/2
 no switchport
 no ip address
 channel-group 12 mode on
!
interface Port-channel12
 no switchport
 ip address 10.1.12.1 255.255.255.0
```

Of particular importance, note that although the physical interfaces and PortChannel interface are all routed ports, the IP address should be placed on the PortChannel interface only. In fact, when the **no switchport** command is configured on an interface, IOS adds the **no ip address** command to the interface. Then configure the IP address on the PortChannel interface only.

Once configured, the PortChannel interface appears in several commands, as shown in Example 18-13. The commands that list IP addresses and routes refer to the PortChannel interface. Also, note that the **show interfaces status** command lists the fact that the physical ports and the port-channel 12 interface are all routed ports.

Example 18-13 *Verification Commands Listing Interface Port-Channel12 from Switch SW1*

```
SW1# show interfaces port-channel 12
Port-channel12 is up, line protocol is up (connected)
  Hardware is EtherChannel, address is 4488.165a.f26c (bia 4488.165a.f26c)
  Internet address is 10.1.12.1/24
! lines omitted for brevity


SW1# show interfaces status
! Only ports related to the example are shown.
Port          Name             Status       Vlan      Duplex  Speed Type
Te1/1/1                        connected    routed      full   10G SFP-10GBase-SR
Te1/1/2                        connected    routed      full   10G SFP-10GBase-SR
Po12                           connected    routed    a-full   a-10G N/A


SW1# show ip route
! legend omitted for brevity
      10.0.0.0/8 is variably subnetted, 4 subnets, 2 masks
C        10.1.2.0/24 is directly connected, Vlan2
L        10.1.2.1/32 is directly connected, Vlan2
C        10.1.12.0/24 is directly connected, Port-channel12
L        10.1.12.1/32 is directly connected, Port-channel12
```

18

For a final bit of verification, you can examine the EtherChannel directly with the **show etherchannel summary** command as listed in Example 18-14. Note in particular that it lists a flag legend for characters that identify key operational states, such as whether a port is bundled (included) in the PortChannel (P) and whether it is acting as a routed (R) or switched (S) port.

Example 18-14   *Verifying the EtherChannel*

```
SW1# show etherchannel 12 summary
Flags:  D - down         P - bundled in port-channel
        I - stand-alone  s - suspended
        H - Hot-standby (LACP only)
        R - Layer3       S - Layer2
        U - in use       f - failed to allocate aggregator

        M - not in use, minimum links not met
        u - unsuitable for bundling
        w - waiting to be aggregated
        d - default port

        A - formed by Auto LAG

Number of channel-groups in use: 1
Number of aggregators:           1

Group  Port-channel  Protocol    Ports
------+-------------+-----------+-----------------------------------------------
12     Po12(RU)         -        Te1/1/1(P)    Te1/1/2(P)
```

Troubleshooting Layer 3 EtherChannels

When you are troubleshooting a Layer 3 EtherChannel, there are two main areas to consider. First, you need to look at the configuration of the **channel-group** command, which enables an interface for an EtherChannel. Second, you should check a list of settings that must match on the interfaces for a Layer 3 EtherChannel to work correctly.

As for the **channel-group** interface subcommand, this command can enable EtherChannel statically or dynamically. If dynamic, this command's keywords imply either Port Aggregation Protocol (PAgP) or Link Aggregation Control Protocol (LACP) as the protocol to negotiate between the neighboring switches whether they put the link into the EtherChannel.

If all this sounds vaguely familiar, it is the exact same configuration covered way back in the Chapter 10 section "Configuring Dynamic EtherChannels." The configuration of the **channel-group** subcommand is exactly the same, with the same requirements, whether configuring Layer 2 or Layer 3 EtherChannels. So, it might be a good time to review those

EtherChannel configuration details from Chapter 10. Regardless of when you review and master those commands, note that the configuration of the EtherChannel (with the **channel-group** subcommand) is the same, whether Layer 2 or Layer 3.

Additionally, you must do more than just configure the **channel-group** command correctly for all the physical ports to be bundled into the EtherChannel. Layer 2 EtherChannels have a longer list of requirements, but Layer 3 EtherChannels also require a few consistency checks between the ports before they can be added to the EtherChannel. The following is the list of requirements for Layer 3 EtherChannels:

no switchport: The PortChannel interface must be configured with the **no switchport** command, and so must the physical interfaces. If a physical interface is not also configured with the **no switchport** command, it will not become operational in the EtherChannel.

Speed: The physical ports in the channel must use the same speed.

duplex: The physical ports in the channel must use the same duplex.

VLAN Routing on a Router's LAN Switch Ports

The earlier major sections of this chapter all show designs with hosts connected to a switch. The switch might do the routing, or a router connected to the switch might do the routing, but the hosts are connected via a cable to the switch.

This last major section discusses a design with only a router, specifically one whose hardware includes a set of LAN switch ports. In effect, the router hardware embeds a LAN switch into the hardware. As a result, the router needs to implement both routing and switching.

Designs that include small branch offices can make good use of a router with embedded switch ports. Those sites need a router that can route over the WAN and may need only a few LAN ports. Many vendors (Cisco included) offer router products that include a small set of LAN switch ports for such cases. Many consumer-grade routers, like the one you have at home for Internet access, also embed a small number of switch ports.

As an example of the hardware, Figure 18-9 shows photos of an ISR1K router and a Catalyst 8200L edge router. Some ISR1Ks, positioned by Cisco as enterprise-class routers for smaller sites, include a few routed ports plus a set of **switched ports**. The routed ports act like ports on routers, as discussed so far in this book, receiving and forwarding IP packets while requiring the configuration of an IP address and mask. The switch ports work like ports on a LAN switch, forwarding and receiving Ethernet frames, with the router's switching logic learning entries for a MAC address table.

The bottom of the figure shows a photo of three Catalyst 8200 edge platforms (routers). The models in the figure each support four fixed routed Ethernet ports (two RJ-45 and two modular SFP slots). The Network Interface Module (NIM) slot allows for expansion with modular NIMs, including NIMs with four and eight LAN switch ports.

18

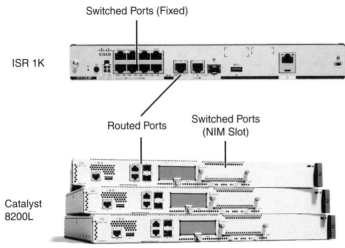

Figure 18-9 *Cisco ISR 1000 and Catalyst 8200L Routers*

Configuring Routing for Embedded Switch Ports

Routers that have switch ports implement both routing and switching. To make that work, configure LAN switching commands on the switch ports and routing commands for the routed interfaces. To stitch the logic together, use a concept familiar from multilayer switch configuration: SVI interfaces.

Figures 18-10 and Figure 18-11 give the context for an example. Figure 18-10 shows Router B1, at a branch office, with four switch ports connected to some PCs. The design calls for two VLANs with the same VLAN IDs and subnets, as in several earlier examples in this chapter. The router (the same model of ISR1K shown in Figure 18-9) uses routed port G0/0/1 to connect to the WAN.

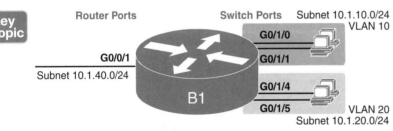

Figure 18-10 *Physical Representation of Router with Routed and Switched Ports*

Figure 18-11 shows the internal logic using SVIs that give the routing process inside Router B1 interfaces that connect directly to the subnets that reside on VLANs 10 and 20. The concepts should look familiar; the internal concepts work like a Layer 3 switch.

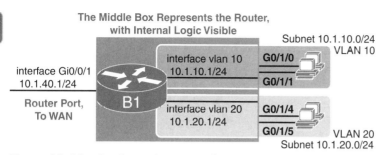

Figure 18-11   *Configuration View of a Router with Routed and Switched Ports*

The configuration steps include familiar tasks for the LAN switch, other familiar tasks for IP routing and the routed ports, and the additional task of configuring the SVIs. To review, the following configuration checklist lists a minimal set of tasks, beginning with a default configuration, to enable IP on the three interfaces so that the router has connected routes to all three subnets and can route packets between those connected subnets.

Step 1.   Configure VLANs and assign access VLANs to the switch ports.

   a.   Use the **vlan** *vlan-number* command in global configuration mode to create each VLAN.

   b.   Use the **switchport access vlan** *vlan-id* command in interface configuration mode on the switched interfaces to assign the correct access VLAN.

   c.   (As needed) Use the **no shutdown** command in interface configuration mode to enable the interface.

Step 2.   Configure an SVI interface for each VLAN used by the switch ports.

   a.   Use the **interface vlan** *vlan_id* command in global configuration mode to create a VLAN interface. Use the same number as the VLAN ID.

   b.   Use the **ip address** *address mask* command in VLAN interface configuration mode to assign an IP address and mask to the interface, enabling IPv4 processing on the interface.

   c.   (As needed) Use the **no shutdown** command in interface configuration mode to enable the VLAN interface.

Step 3.   Configure any routed interfaces with IP addresses.

   a.   Use the **ip address** *address mask* command in interface configuration mode to assign an IP address and mask to the interface, enabling IPv4 processing.

   b.   Configure any routing protocols as needed.

Example 18-15 shows a sample configuration to match Figure 18-11. The top of the configuration adds VLANs 10 and 20, assigning them as access VLANs to the ports per the figure. The **interface vlan** commands create the SVIs, with IP address configuration added to each. The final interface, G0/0/1, a routed port, shows traditional router interface configuration with an **ip address** command but without a **switchport access** subcommand.

Example 18-15 *VLAN Interface Configuration for Routing to/from Switch Port VLANs*

```
vlan 10
vlan 20
!
interface GigabitEthernet0/1/0
 switchport access vlan 10
!
interface GigabitEthernet0/1/1
 switchport access vlan 10
!
interface GigabitEthernet0/1/4
 switchport access vlan 20
!
interface GigabitEthernet0/1/5
 switchport access vlan 20
!
interface vlan 10
 ip address 10.1.10.1 255.255.255.0
!
interface vlan 20
 ip address 10.1.20.1 255.255.255.0
!
interface gigabitEthernet0/0/1
 description physical, routed interface

ip address 10.1.40.1 255.255.255.0
```

Verifying Routing for Embedded Switch Ports

With the VLAN configuration shown in the previous section, the router is ready to route packets between the subnets as shown in Figure 18-11. The output in Example 18-16 lists two routes as connected to different VLAN interfaces, with one route connected to the one routed interface (G0/0/1). Beyond those routes, the router also needs routes to remote subnets. The router could use static routes or a routing protocol.

Example 18-16 *Connected Routes on Router B1 from Example 18-15*

```
B1# show ip route connected
Codes: L - local, C - connected, S - static, R - RIP, M - mobile, B - BGP
       D - EIGRP, EX - EIGRP external, O - OSPF, IA - OSPF inter area
! Remaining legend omitted for brevity


      10.0.0.0/8 is variably subnetted, 13 subnets, 2 masks
C        10.1.10.0/24 is directly connected, Vlan10
L        10.1.10.1/32 is directly connected, Vlan10
C        10.1.20.0/24 is directly connected, Vlan20
L        10.1.20.1/32 is directly connected, Vlan20
C        10.1.30.0/24 is directly connected, GigabitEthernet0/0/1
L        10.1.30.1/32 is directly connected, GigabitEthernet0/0/1
```

The router adds the connected routes when the related interface reaches an up/up state. For SVIs, the state varies based on rules related to the state of the underlying VLAN and the ports in that VLAN. Those rules work just as described in this chapter's earlier section titled "Troubleshooting Routing with SVIs."

The router performs LAN switching with the same conventions you learned about LAN switches in Parts II and III of this book. For instance, the router supports the exact commands you expect to find on LAN switches to support the LAN switch ports. Example 18-17 shows the MAC addresses learned on the four switch ports shown in the most recent figures. It confirms that addresses learned on ports G0/1/0 and G0/1/1 exist in VLAN 10 while those learned on ports G0/1/4 and G0/1/5 exist in VLAN 20.

Example 18-17   *MAC Address Table on the Router*

```
B1# show mac address-table dynamic
          Mac Address Table
-------------------------------------------


Vlan    Mac Address      Type       Ports
----    -----------      --------   -----
  10    0200.aaaa.aaaa   DYNAMIC    Gi0/1/0
  10    0200.bbbb.bbbb   DYNAMIC    Gi0/1/1
  20    0200.cccc.cccc   DYNAMIC    Gi0/1/4
  20    0200.dddd.dddd   DYNAMIC    Gi0/1/5
Total Mac Addresses for this criterion: 4
```

NOTE   Switches use the **show vlan [brief]** command to display VLAN configuration. Routers with embedded switch ports have a command that mimics the switch command: **show vlan-switch [brief]** (IOS) and **show vlan [brief]** (IOS XE). As a reminder, the similar **show vlans** command on routers does not list VLANs but rather ROAS configuration.

18

Identifying Switched Ports in Routers

When you look at a router or use the CLI of a router, how do you know which Ethernet ports happen to be routed ports and which are switch ports? Finding the answer can be difficult. This last short section tells you how.

First, you do not configure a router port's role as a routed or switch port. Instead, Cisco creates router interfaces that act as one or the other. You can research the router model and family at www.cisco.com and learn about the fixed ports that come with each model. That documentation also identifies modular options for cards like NIMs.

You can also discover the router's switched ports from the CLI, but the conventions are not obvious. Most **show** commands do not help, but a few do. Of note:

show running-config, show startup-config: These commands do not identify routed versus switched ports.

show interfaces, show interfaces description, show ip interface brief, show protocols: All these commands list all interfaces, routed and switched, with no notation of which is which.

show interfaces status: This command lists only switched ports.

Using **show interfaces status** to identify the switch ports makes the most sense.

Additionally, you can confirm which ports act as routed versus switched ports by trying to configure commands supported only on one or the other. For instance, routed ports accept the **ip address** *address mask* subcommand but reject the **switchport access vlan** *vlan-id* subcommand. Switched ports accept the opposite.

Example 18-18 shows a few cases of identifying routed and switched ports using Router B1 from the previous examples. It first shows only the switched ports G0/1/0–G0/1/7 in the **show interfaces status** command output. Note the output follows the format from LAN switches, identifying the access VLAN assigned to each interface. Following that, the output shows a switched port rejecting the **ip address** interface subcommand.

Example 18-18 *Displaying Switched Interfaces but Omitting Routed Interfaces*

```
B1# show interfaces status

Port         Name          Status       Vlan      Duplex  Speed Type
Gi0/1/0                    connected    10        a-full a-1000 10/100/1000BaseTX
Gi0/1/1                    connected    10        a-full a-1000 10/100/1000BaseTX
Gi0/1/2                    notconnect   1          auto   auto 10/100/1000BaseTX
Gi0/1/3                    notconnect   1          auto   auto 10/100/1000BaseTX
Gi0/1/4                    connected    20        a-full a-1000 10/100/1000BaseTX
Gi0/1/5                    connected    20        a-full a-1000 10/100/1000BaseTX
Gi0/1/6                    notconnect   1          auto   auto 10/100/1000BaseTX
Gi0/1/7                    notconnect   1          auto   auto 10/100/1000BaseTX
B1# configure terminal
Enter configuration commands, one per line.  End with CNTL/Z.
B1(config)# interface g0/1/7
B1(config-if)# ip address 10.1.90.1 255.255.255.0
                ^
% Invalid input detected at '^' marker.
B1(config-if)#
```

Chapter Review

One key to doing well on the exams is to perform repetitive spaced review sessions. Review this chapter's material using either the tools in the book or interactive tools for the same material found on the book's companion website. Refer to the "Your Study Plan" element for more details. Table 18-2 outlines the key review elements and where you can find them. To better track your study progress, record when you completed these activities in the second column.

Table 18-2 Chapter Review Tracking

Review Element	Review Date(s)	Resource Used
Review key topics		Book, website
Review key terms		Book, website
Answer DIKTA questions		Book, PTP
Review config checklists		Book, website
Review command tables		Book
Do labs		Blog
Watch video		Website

Review All the Key Topics

Table 18-3 Key Topics for Chapter 18

Key Topic Element	Description	Page Number
Figure 18-2	Concept of VLAN subinterfaces on a router	459
List	Two alternative methods to configure the native VLAN in a ROAS configuration	460
List	Troubleshooting suggestions for ROAS configuration	463
Figure 18-3	Layer 3 switching with SVIs concept and configuration	464
Figure 18-4	Layer 3 switching with routed ports concept and configuration	465
List	Troubleshooting suggestions for correct operation of a Layer 3 switch that uses SVIs	467
Figure 18-5	A figure showing the concepts behind IP routing on a routed interface on a switch	470
List	**show** commands that list Layer 3 routed ports in their output	471
Figure 18-8	Layer 3 EtherChannel concept and configuration	474
List	List of configuration settings that must be consistent before IOS will bundle a link with an existing Layer 3 EtherChannel	477
Figure 18-10	A concept diagram showing a router with routed and switched ports	478
Figure 18-11	Conceptual view of the configuration for a router with integrated LAN switch ports	479
List	Router commands and whether they list routed ports, switched ports, or both	481

Key Terms You Should Know

Layer 3 EtherChannel (L3 EtherChannel), Layer 3 switch, multilayer switch, routed port, router-on-a-stick (ROAS), subinterfaces, switched port, switched virtual interface (SVI), VLAN interface

18

Command References

Tables 18-4 and 18-5 list configuration and verification commands used in this chapter. As an easy review exercise, cover the left column in a table, read the right column, and try to recall the command without looking. Then repeat the exercise, covering the right column, and try to recall what the command does.

Table 18-4   Chapter 18 Configuration Command Reference

Command	Description
interface *type number.subint*	Router global command to create a subinterface and to enter configuration mode for that subinterface
encapsulation dot1q *vlan-id* [native]	Router subinterface subcommand that tells the router to use 802.1Q trunking, for a particular VLAN, and with the **native** keyword, to not encapsulate in a trunking header
[no] ip routing	Global command that enables (**ip routing**) or disables (**no ip routing**) the routing of IPv4 packets on a router or Layer 3 switch
interface vlan *vlan-id*	Global command to create a VLAN interface and to enter VLAN interface configuration mode; valid on Layer 3 switches and on routers that have embedded LAN switch ports
[no] switchport	Layer 3 switch subcommand that makes the port act as a Layer 2 port (**switchport**) or Layer 3 routed port (**no switchport**)
interface port-channel *channel-number*	A switch command to enter PortChannel configuration mode and also to create the PortChannel if not already created
channel-group *channel-number* mode {auto | desirable | active | passive | on}	Interface subcommand that enables EtherChannel on the interface
[no] autostate	Interface subcommand on VLAN interfaces that enables (**autostate**) or disables (**no autostate**) the autostate feature.
vlan *vlan-id*	Global config command that both creates the VLAN and puts the CLI into VLAN configuration mode
name *vlan-name*	VLAN subcommand that names the VLAN
[no] shutdown	VLAN mode subcommand that enables (**no shutdown**) or disables (**shutdown**) the VLAN

Table 18-5   Chapter 18 EXEC Command Reference

Command	Description
show ip route	Lists the router's entire routing table
show ip route [connected]	Lists a subset of the IP routing table
show vlans	Lists VLAN configuration and statistics for VLAN trunks configured on routers

Command	Description
show interfaces [interface *type number*]	Lists detailed status and statistical information, including IP address and mask, about all interfaces (or the listed interface only)
show interfaces [interface *type number*] **status**	Among other facts, for switch ports, lists the access VLAN or the fact that the interface is a trunk; or, for routed ports, lists "routed"
show interfaces *interface-id* **switchport**	For switch ports, lists information about any interface regarding administrative settings and operational state; for routed ports, the output simply confirms the port is a routed (not switched) port
show interfaces vlan *number*	Lists the interface status, the switch's IPv4 address and mask, and much more
show etherchannel [*channel-group-number*] **summary**	Lists information about the state of EtherChannels on this switch, including whether the channel is a Layer 2 or Layer 3 EtherChannel
show mac address-table dynamic	Shows all dynamically learned MAC table entries on LAN switches and on routers that have embedded switch ports
show vlan-switch [brief]	(IOS only) On a router with embedded LAN switch ports, lists the VLAN configuration
show vlan [brief]	(IOS XE only) On a router with embedded LAN switch ports, lists the VLAN configuration

18

CHAPTER 19

IP Addressing on Hosts

This chapter covers the following exam topics:

1.0 Network Fundamentals

    1.10 Verify IP parameters for Client OS (Windows, Mac OS, Linux)

4.0 IP Services

    4.3 Explain the role of DHCP and DNS within the network

    4.6 Configure and verify DHCP client and relay

In the world of TCP/IP, the word *host* refers to any device with an IP address: your phone, your tablet, a PC, a server, a router, a switch—any device that uses IP to provide a service or just needs an IP address to be managed. The term *host* includes some less-obvious devices as well: the electronic advertising video screen at the mall, your electrical power meter that uses the same technology as mobile phones to submit your electrical usage information for billing, your new car.

No matter the type of host, any host that uses IPv4 needs four IPv4 settings to work properly:

- IP address
- Subnet mask
- Default routers
- DNS server IP addresses

This chapter discusses these basic IP settings on hosts. The chapter begins by discussing how a host can dynamically learn these four settings using the Dynamic Host Configuration Protocol (DHCP). The second half of this chapter then shows how to find the settings on hosts and the key facts to look for when displaying the settings.

"Do I Know This Already?" Quiz

Take the quiz (either here or use the PTP software) if you want to use the score to help you decide how much time to spend on this chapter. The letter answers are listed at the bottom of the page following the quiz. Appendix C, found both at the end of the book as well as on the companion website, includes both the answers and explanations. You can also find both answers and explanations in the PTP testing software.

Table 19-1 "Do I Know This Already?" Foundation Topics Section-to-Question Mapping

Foundation Topics Section	Questions
Dynamic Host Configuration Protocol	1–4
Identifying Host IPv4 Settings	5, 6

1. A PC connects to a LAN and uses DHCP to lease an IP address for the first time. Of the usual four DHCP messages that flow between the PC and the DHCP server, which ones does the client send? (Choose two answers.)

   a. Acknowledgment

   b. Discover

   c. Offer

   d. Request

2. Which of the following kinds of information are part of a DHCP server configuration? (Choose two answers.)

   a. Ranges of IP addresses in subnets that the server should lease

   b. Ranges of IP addresses to not lease per subnet

   c. DNS server hostnames

   d. The default router IP and MAC address in each subnet

3. Which answers list a criterion for choosing which router interfaces need to be configured as a DHCP relay agent? (Choose two answers.)

   a. If the subnet off the interface does not include a DHCP server

   b. If the subnet off the interface does include a DHCP server

   c. If the subnet off the interface contains DHCP clients

   d. If the router interface already has an **ip address dhcp** command

4. A router connects to an Internet service provider (ISP) using its G0/0/0 interface, with the **ip address dhcp** command configured. What does the router do with the DHCP-learned default gateway information?

   a. The router ignores the default gateway value learned from the DHCP server.

   b. The router uses the default gateway just like a host, ignoring its routing table.

   c. The router forwards received packets based on its routing table but uses its default gateway setting to forward packets it generates itself.

   d. The router adds a default route based on the default gateway to its IP routing table.

5. In the following excerpt from a command on a Mac, which of the following parts of the output represent information learned from a DHCP server? (Choose two answers.)

   ```
   Macprompt$ ifconfig en0

   En1: flags=8863<UP,BROADCAST,SMART,RUNNING,SIMPLEX,MULTICAST> mtu 1500
           options=10b<RXCSUM,TXCSUM,VLAN_HWTAGGING,AV>
           ether 00:6d:e7:b1:9a:11
           inet 172.16.4.2 netmask 0xffffff00 broadcast 172.16.4.255
   ```

    a.   00:6d:e7:b1:9a:11

    b.   172.16.4.2

    c.   0xffffff00

    d.   172.16.4.255

6. Which of the following commands on a Windows OS should list both the host's IP address and DNS servers' IP addresses as learned with DHCP?

    a.   ifconfig

    b.   ipconfig

    c.   ifconfig /all

    d.   ipconfig /all

Foundation Topics

Dynamic Host Configuration Protocol

Dynamic Host Configuration Protocol (DHCP) provides one of the most commonly used services in a TCP/IP network. The vast majority of hosts in a TCP/IP network are user devices, and the vast majority of user devices learn their IPv4 settings using DHCP.

Using DHCP has several advantages over the other option of manually configuring IPv4 settings. The configuration of host IP settings sits in a DHCP server, with each client learning these settings using DHCP messages. As a result, the host IP configuration is controlled by the IT staff, rather than on local configuration on each host, resulting in fewer user errors. DHCP allows the permanent assignment of host addresses, but more commonly, a temporary lease of IP addresses. With these leases, the **DHCP server** can reclaim IP addresses when a device is removed from the network, making better use of the available addresses.

DHCP also enables mobility. For example, every time a user moves to a new location with a tablet computer—to a coffee shop, a client location, or back at the office—the user's device can connect to another wireless LAN, use DHCP to lease a new IP address in that LAN, and begin working on the new network. Without DHCP, the user would have to ask for information about the local network and configure settings manually, with more than a few users making mistakes.

Although DHCP works automatically for user hosts, it does require some preparation from the network, with some configuration on routers. In some enterprise networks, that router configuration can be a single command on many of the router's LAN interfaces (**ip helper-address** *server-ip*), which identifies the DHCP server by its IP address. In other cases, the router acts as the DHCP server. Regardless, the routers have some role to play.

This first major section of the chapter takes a tour of DHCP, including concepts and the router configuration to enable the routers to work well with a separate DHCP server.

DHCP Concepts

Sit back for a moment and think about the role of DHCP for a host computer. The host acts as a **DHCP client**. As a DHCP client, the host begins with no IPv4 settings—no IPv4 address, no mask, no default router, and no **DNS server** IP addresses. But a DHCP client does have knowledge of the DHCP protocol, so the client can use that protocol to (a) discover a DHCP server and (b) request to lease an IPv4 address.

DHCP uses the following four messages between the client and server. (Also, to help remember the messages, note that the first letters spell DORA):

Discover: Sent by the DHCP client to find a willing DHCP server

Offer: Sent by a DHCP server to offer to lease to that client a specific IP address (and inform the client of its other parameters)

Request: Sent by the DHCP client to ask the server to lease the IPv4 address listed in the Offer message

Acknowledgment: Sent by the DHCP server to assign the address and to list the mask, default router, and DNS server IP addresses

DHCP clients, however, have a somewhat unique problem: they do not have an IP address yet, but they need to send these DHCP messages inside IP packets. To make that work, DHCP messages make use of two special IPv4 addresses that allow a host that has no IP address to still be able to send and receive messages on the local subnet:

Key Topic

0.0.0.0: An address reserved for use as a source IPv4 address for hosts that do not yet have an IP address.

255.255.255.255: The local broadcast IP address. Packets sent to this destination address are broadcast on the local data link, but routers do not forward them.

To see how these addresses work, Figure 19-1 shows an example of the IP addresses used between a host (A) and a DHCP server on the same LAN. Host A, a client, sends a Discover message, with source IP address of 0.0.0.0 because Host A does not have an IP address to use yet. Host A sends the packet to destination 255.255.255.255, which is sent in a LAN broadcast frame, reaching all hosts in the subnet. The client hopes that there is a DHCP server on the local subnet. Why? Packets sent to 255.255.255.255 only go to hosts in the local subnet; Router R1 will not forward this packet.

NOTE   Figure 19-1 shows one example of the addresses that can be used in a DHCP request. This example shows details assuming the DHCP client chooses to use a DHCP option called the *broadcast flag*; all examples in this book assume the broadcast flag is used.

19

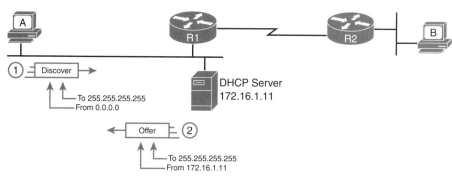

Figure 19-1   *DHCP Discover and Offer*

Now look at the Offer message sent back by the DHCP server. The server sets the destination IP address to 255.255.255.255 again. Why? Host A still does not have an IP address, so the server cannot send a packet directly to host A. So, the server sends the packet to "all local hosts in the subnet" address (255.255.255.255). (The packet is also encapsulated in an Ethernet broadcast frame.)

Note that all hosts in the subnet receive the Offer message. However, the original Discover message lists a number called the client ID, which includes the host's MAC address, that identifies the original host (Host A in this case). As a result, Host A knows that the Offer message is meant for host A. The rest of the hosts will receive the Offer message, but notice that the message lists another device's DHCP client ID, so the rest of the hosts ignore the Offer message.

APIPA IP Addresses (169.254.x.x)

If the DHCP process fails for a DHCP client, hosts have a default means to self-assign an IP address using a feature called Automatic Private IP Addressing (**APIPA**). When the DHCP process fails, the DHCP client self-assigns an APIPA IP address from within a subset of the 169.254.0.0 Class B network, along with default mask 255.255.0.0.

Using an APIPA address does not help devices work like a normal host. For instance, hosts do not know of a default router or learn a list of DNS servers. The host can send packets only to other APIPA hosts on the same LAN.

The APIPA process works like this:

1. The client chooses any IP address from network 169.254.0.0 (actual address range: 169.54.1.0 – 169.254.254.255).

2. The DHCP client discovers if any other host on the same link already uses the APIPA address it chose by using ARP to perform Duplicate Address Detection (DAD). If another host already uses the same address, the client stops using the address and chooses another.

3. The client can send/receive packets on the local network only.

Supporting DHCP for Remote Subnets with DHCP Relay

Network engineers have a major design choice to make with DHCP: Do they put a DHCP server in every LAN subnet or locate a DHCP server in a central site? The question is legitimate. Cisco routers can act as the DHCP server, so a distributed design could use the router at each site as the DHCP server. With a DHCP server in every subnet, as shown in Figure 19-1, the protocol flows stay local to each LAN.

However, a centralized DHCP server approach has advantages as well. In fact, some Cisco design documents suggest a centralized design as a best practice, in part because it allows for centralized control and configuration of all the IPv4 addresses assigned throughout the enterprise.

Answers to the "Do I Know This Already?" quiz:

1 B, D **2** A, B **3** A, C **4** D **5** B, C **6** D

With a centralized DHCP server, those DHCP messages that flowed only on the local subnet in Figure 19-1 somehow need to flow over the IP network to the centralized DHCP server and back. To make that work, the routers connected to the remote LAN subnets need an interface subcommand: the **ip helper-address** *server-ip* command.

The **ip helper-address** *server-ip* subcommand tells the router to do the following for the messages coming in an interface, from a DHCP client:

1. Watch for incoming DHCP messages, with destination IP address 255.255.255.255.
2. Change that packet's source IP address to the router's incoming interface IP address.
3. Change that packet's destination IP address to the address of the DHCP server (as configured in the **ip helper-address** command).
4. Route the packet to the DHCP server.

This command gets around the "do not route local subnet broadcast packets sent to address 255.255.255.255" rule by changing the destination IP address. Once the destination has been set to match the DHCP server's IP address, the network can route the packet to the server.

> **NOTE** This feature, by which a router relays DHCP messages by changing the IP addresses in the packet header, is called *DHCP relay*.

Figure 19-2 shows an example of the process. Host A sits on the left, as a DHCP client. The DHCP server (172.16.2.11) sits on the right. R1 has an **ip helper-address 172.16.2.11** command configured, under its G0/0 interface. At Step 1, Router R1 notices the incoming DHCP packet destined for 255.255.255.255. Step 2 shows the results of changing both the source and destination IP address, with R1 routing the packet.

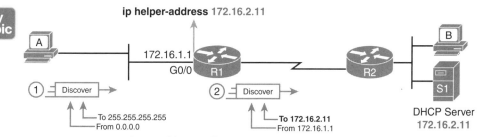

Figure 19-2 *IP Helper Address Effect*

The router uses a similar process for the return DHCP messages from the server. First, for the return packet from the DHCP server, the server simply reverses the source and destination IP address of the packet received from the router (relay agent). For example, in Figure 19-2, the Discover message lists source IP address 172.16.1.1, so the server sends the Offer message back to destination IP address 172.16.1.1.

When a router receives a DHCP message addressed to one of the router's own IP addresses, the router realizes the packet might be part of the DHCP relay feature. When that happens, the **DHCP relay agent** (Router R1) needs to change the destination IP address so that the real DHCP client (host A), which does not have an IP address yet, can receive and process the packet.

Figure 19-3 shows one example of how these addresses work, when R1 receives the DHCP Offer message sent to R1's own 172.16.1.1 address. R1 changes the packet's destination to 255.255.255.255 and forwards it out G0/0, because the packet was destined to G0/0's 172.16.1.1 IP address. As a result, all hosts in that LAN (including the DHCP client A) will receive the message.

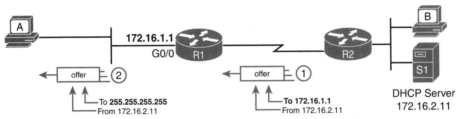

Figure 19-3 *IP Helper Address for the Offer Message Returned from the DHCP Server*

Many enterprise networks use a centralized DHCP server, so the normal router configuration includes an **ip helper-address** command on every LAN interface/subinterface. With that standard configuration, user hosts off any router LAN interface can always reach the DHCP server and lease an IP address.

Information Stored at the DHCP Server

A DHCP server might sound like some large piece of hardware, sitting in a big locked room with lots of air conditioning to keep the hardware cool. However, like most servers, the server is actually software, running on some server OS. The DHCP server could be a piece of software downloaded for free and installed on an old PC. However, because the server needs to be available all the time, to support new DHCP clients, most companies install the software on a very stable and highly available data center, with high availability features. The DHCP service is still created by software, however.

To be ready to answer DHCP clients and to supply them with an IPv4 address and other information, the DHCP server (software) needs configuration. DHCP servers organize these IPv4 settings per subnet, listing an address pool and a default router setting—settings that differ from subnet to subnet. The following list shows the types of settings the DHCP server needs to know to support DHCP clients:

Subnet ID and mask: The DHCP server can use this information to know all addresses in the subnet. (The DHCP server knows to not lease the subnet ID or subnet broadcast address.)

Reserved (excluded) addresses: The server needs to know which addresses in the subnet to *not* lease. This list allows the engineer to reserve addresses to be used as static IP addresses. For example, most router and switch IP addresses, server addresses, and addresses of most anything other than user devices use a statically assigned IP address. Most of the time, engineers use the same convention for all subnets, either reserving the lowest IP addresses in all subnets or reserving the highest IP addresses in all subnets.

Default router(s): This is the IP address of the router on that subnet.

DNS IP address(es): This is a list of DNS server IP addresses.

Figure 19-4 shows the concept behind the preconfiguration on a DHCP server for two LAN-based subnets: 172.16.1.0/24 and 172.16.2.0/24. The DHCP server sits on the right. For each subnet, the server defines all the items in the list. In this case, the configuration reserves the lowest IP addresses in the subnet to be used as static addresses.

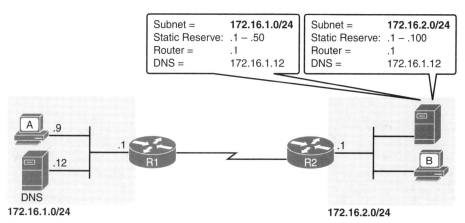

Figure 19-4   *Preconfiguration on a DHCP Server*

The configuration can list other parameters as well. For example, it can set the time limit for leasing an IP address. The server leases an address for a time (usually a number of days), and then the client can ask to renew the lease. If the client does not renew, the server can reclaim the IP address and put it back in the pool of available IP addresses. The server configuration sets the maximum time for the lease.

DHCP uses three allocation modes, based on small differences in the configuration at the DHCP server. *Dynamic allocation* refers to the DHCP mechanisms and configuration described throughout this chapter. Another method, *automatic allocation*, sets the DHCP lease time to infinite. As a result, once the server chooses an address from the pool and assigns the IP address to a client, the IP address remains with that same client indefinitely. A third mode, *static allocation*, preconfigures the specific IP address for a client based on the client's MAC address. That specific client is the only client that then uses the IP address. (Note that this chapter shows examples and configuration for dynamic allocation only.)

Additionally, the DHCP server can be configured to supply some other useful configuration settings. For instance, a server can supply the IP address of a Trivial File Transfer Protocol (TFTP) server. TFTP servers provide a basic means of storing files that can then be transferred to a client host. For instance, Cisco IP phones rely on TFTP to retrieve several configuration files when the phone initializes. DHCP plays a key role by supplying the IP address of the TFTP server that the phones should use.

Configuring DHCP Features on Routers and Switches

Cisco routers and switches support a variety of features. Routers can be configured to act as a DHCP server with just a few straightforward commands—a feature useful in the lab and

19

in some limited cases. More commonly, the enterprise uses a centralized DHCP server (that does not run on a router) but with the DHCP relay feature on most every router interface. Finally, Cisco routers and switches can also act as DHCP clients, learning their IP addresses from a DHCP server.

This section discusses the DHCP configuration topics mentioned for the CCNA 200-301 V1.1 exam blueprint. Those include the router DHCP relay feature and the configuration to enable DHCP client services on both switches and routers.

> **NOTE**   The CCNA 200-301 V1.1 exam blueprint does not mention the DHCP server function, but many people like to use the IOS DHCP server in the lab for testing with DHCP. If interested in how to configure a DHCP server on a router, refer to Appendix K, "Topics from Previous Editions."

Configuring DHCP Relay

Configuring DHCP relay requires a simple decision and a single straightforward configuration command. First, you must identify the interfaces that need the feature. The DHCP relay feature must be configured for any router interface that connects to a subnet where

- DHCP clients exist in the subnet

- DHCP servers do not exist in the subnet

Once such interfaces have been identified, the configuration requires the **ip helper-address** interface subcommand on each of those interfaces. For instance, in the topology of the previous three figures, R1's G0/0 interface needs to be configured with the **ip helper-address 172.16.2.11** interface subcommand. Once enabled on an interface, the IOS DHCP relay agent makes changes in the incoming DHCP messages' addresses as described earlier in the chapter. Without the DHCP relay agent, the DHCP request never arrives at the server.

To verify the relay agent, you can use the **show running-config** command and look for the single configuration command or use the **show ip interface g0/0** command as shown in Example 19-1. The highlighted line confirms the configured setting. Note that if there were no **ip helper-address** commands configured on the interface, the highlighted line would instead read "Helper address is not set."

Example 19-1   *Listing the Current Helper Address Setting with* **show ip interface**

```
R1# show ip interface g0/0
GigabitEthernet0/0 is up, line protocol is up
 Internet address is 172.16.1.1/24
 Broadcast address is 255.255.255.255
 Address determined by non-volatile memory
 MTU is 1500 bytes
 Helper address is 172.16.2.11
! Lines omitted for brevity
```

Configuring a Switch as DHCP Client

A switch can act as a DHCP client to lease its management IP address. In most cases, you will want to instead use a static IP address so that the staff can more easily identify the switch's address for remote management. However, as an example of how a DHCP client can work, this next topic shows how to configure and verify DHCP client operations on a switch.

> **NOTE** Chapter 6, "Configuring Basic Switch Management," also shows this same example of how to configure a switch to be a DHCP client. This chapter repeats the example here so you can see all the related DHCP configuration details in a single place in this volume.

To configure a switch to use DHCP to lease an address, configure a switch's IP address as normal, but with the **ip address dhcp** interface subcommand. Example 19-2 shows a sample.

Example 19-2 *Switch Dynamic IP Address Configuration with DHCP*

```
Emma# configure terminal
Enter configuration commands, one per line. End with CNTL/Z.
Emma(config)# interface vlan 1
Emma(config-if)# ip address dhcp
Emma(config-if)# no shutdown
Emma(config-if)# ^Z
Emma#
00:38:20: %LINK-3-UPDOWN: Interface Vlan1, changed state to up
00:38:21: %LINEPROTO-5-UPDOWN: Line protocol on Interface Vlan1, changed state to up
```

To verify that DHCP worked, start with the traditional way to check IP addresses on switch VLAN interfaces: the **show interfaces vlan** *x* command as demonstrated in Example 19-3. First, check the interface state, because the switch does not attempt DHCP until the VLAN interface reaches an up/up state. Notably, if you forget to issue the **no shutdown** command, the VLAN 1 interface will remain in a shutdown state and be listed as "administratively down" in the **show** command output. Then, if DHCP has not yet worked, you will see the highlighted line shown in the upper part of the example. Once the switch leases an IP address, you will see the different text shown in the bottom half of the example.

Example 19-3 *Verifying DHCP-Learned IP Address on a Switch*

```
! First, output when the switch has not yet leased an IP address
Emma# show interfaces vlan 1
Vlan1 is up, line protocol is up, Autostate Enabled
 Hardware is Ethernet SVI, address is 4488.165a.f247 (bia 4488.165a.f247)
  Internet address will be negotiated using DHCP
! lines omitted for brevity
! Next, the output after DHCP works
Emma# show interfaces vlan 1
Vlan1 is up, line protocol is up, Autostate Enabled
 Hardware is Ethernet SVI, address is 4488.165a.f247 (bia 4488.165a.f247)
  Internet address is 192.168.1.101/24
! lines omitted for brevity
```

19

Interestingly, output line three, which lists the address, appears the same whether you configure the address explicitly or whether the switch leases the address. For instance, the latter half of Example 19-3 lists 192.168.1.101 as the address, but with no information to identify whether the IP address is a static or DHCP-learned IP address.

To see more details specific to DHCP, instead use the **show dhcp lease** command to see the (temporarily) leased IP address and other parameters. (Note that the switch does not store the DHCP-learned IP configuration in the running-config file.) Example 19-4 shows sample output. Note also that the switch learns its default-gateway setting using DHCP as well.

Example 19-4 *Verifying DHCP-Learned Information on a Switch*

```
Emma# show dhcp lease
Temp IP addr: 192.168.1.101 for peer on Interface: Vlan1
Temp sub net mask: 255.255.255.0
 DHCP Lease server: 192.168.1.1, state: 3 Bound
 DHCP transaction id: 1966
 Lease: 86400 secs, Renewal: 43200 secs, Rebind: 75600 secs
Temp default-gateway addr: 192.168.1.1
 Next timer fires after: 11:59:45
 Retry count: 0 Client-ID: cisco-0019.e86a.6fc0-Vl1
 Hostname: Emma


Emma# show ip default-gateway
192.168.1.1
```

Configuring a Router as DHCP Client

Just as with switches, you can configure router interfaces to lease an IP address using DHCP rather than using a static IP address, although those cases will be rare. In most every case it makes more sense to statically configure router interface IP addresses with the address listed in the **ip address** *address mask* interface subcommand. However, configuring a router to lease an address using DHCP makes sense in some cases with a router connected to the Internet; in fact, most every home-based router does just that.

A router with a link to the Internet can learn its IP address and mask with DHCP and also learn the neighboring ISP router's address as the **default gateway**. Figure 19-5 shows an example, with three routers on the left at one enterprise site. Router R1 uses DHCP to learn its IP address (192.0.2.2) from the ISP router over a connection to the Internet.

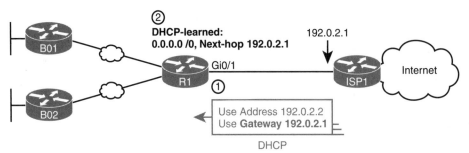

Figure 19-5 *Enterprise Router Building and Advertising Default Routes with DHCP Client*

The DHCP process supplies a default gateway IP address to Router R1, but routers do not normally use a default gateway setting; only hosts use a default gateway setting. However, the router takes advantage of that information by turning that default gateway IP address into the basis for a default route. For instance, in Figure 19-5, Router R1 dynamically adds a default route to its routing table with the default gateway IP address from the DHCP message—which is the ISP router's IP address—as the next-hop address. At that point, R1 has a good route to use to forward packets into the Internet.

Additionally, Router R1 can distribute that default route to the rest of the routers using an interior routing protocol like OSPF. See the section "OSPF Default Routes" in Chapter 23, "Implementing Optional OSPF Features," for more information.

Example 19-5 shows the configuration on Router R1 to match Figure 19-5. Note that it begins with R1 configuring its G0/1 interface to use DHCP to learn the IP address to use on the interface, using the **ip address dhcp** command.

Example 19-5 *Learning an Address and Default Static Route with DHCP*

```
R1# configure terminal
R1(config)# interface gigabitethernet0/1
R1(config-if)# ip address dhcp
R1(config-if)# end
R1#
R1# show ip route static
! Legend omitted
Gateway of last resort is 192.0.2.1 to network 0.0.0.0

S* 0.0.0.0/0 [254/0] via 192.0.2.1
```

The end of the example shows the resulting default route. Oddly, IOS displays this route as a static route (destination 0.0.0.0/0), although the route is learned dynamically based on the DHCP-learned default gateway. To recognize this route as a DHCP-learned default route, look to the administrative distance value of 254. IOS uses a default administrative distance of 1 for static routes configured with the **ip route** configuration command but a default of 254 for default routes added because of DHCP.

Identifying Host IPv4 Settings

Whether learned using DHCP or not, every host that uses IP version 4 needs to have some settings to work correctly. This second major section of the chapter examines those settings and shows examples of those settings on Windows, Linux, and macOS.

Host Settings for IPv4

To work correctly, an IPv4 host needs to know these values:

- DNS server IP addresses

- Default gateway (router) IP address

- Device's own IP address

- Device's own subnet mask

19

To review the basics, the host must know the IP address of one or more DNS servers to send the servers' name resolution requests. For enterprises, the servers may reside in the enterprise, as shown in Figure 19-6. The host on the left (sometimes called an endpoint) typically knows the addresses of at least two DNS servers for redundancy. If the first DNS fails to respond, the endpoint can then attempt name resolution with the next DNS server.

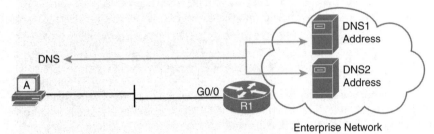

Figure 19-6 *Host A Needs to Know the IP Address of the DNS Servers*

Each endpoint needs to know the IP address of a router that resides in the same subnet. The endpoint uses that router as its default router or default gateway, as shown in Figure 19-7. From a host logic perspective, the host can then forward packets destined for addresses outside the subnet to the default router, with that router then forwarding the packet based on its routing table.

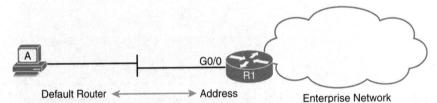

Figure 19-7 *Host Default Router Setting Should Equal Router Interface Address*

Of course, each device needs its own IP address and subnet mask. Equally as important, note that the host and the default router must agree on the addresses inside the subnet. The host will use the address and mask to do the math to determine which addresses are in the same subnet and which are in other subnets. For routing to work correctly, the default router's interface address and mask should result in the same definition of the subnet with the same addresses, as shown in Figure 19-8.

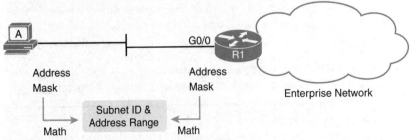

Figure 19-8 *The Need for Subnet Agreement Between Host and Default Router*

The rest of this section shows examples of these settings in the graphical user interface (GUI) and command-line interface (CLI) of three different host operating systems.

The examples for the remainder of the chapter use hosts in subnet 10.1.1.0/24, as shown on the left side of Figure 19-9.

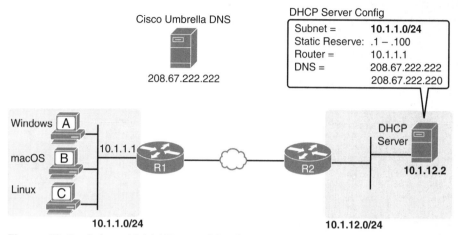

Figure 19-9   *Subnet 10.1.1.0/24 Used for the Upcoming Host Examples*

Host IP Settings on Windows

Almost every OS in the world—certainly the more common OSs people work with every day—have a fairly easy-to-reach settings window that lists most if not all the IPv4 settings in one place.

For example, Figure 19-10 shows the Network configuration screen from a Windows host from the network area of the Windows Control Panel. This image shows the four significant settings: address, mask, router, and DNS. Note that this host, Windows Host A in Figure 19-9, uses DHCP to learn its settings from the DHCP server in that figure.

Figure 19-10   *Windows DHCP Client IP Address, Mask, and Default Router Settings*

However, beyond the GUI, most OSs have a variety of networking commands available from a command line. For many decades and Windows versions, the **ipconfig** and **ipconfig /all** commands supply the most direct help, as shown in Example 19-6. As you can see, both list the address, mask, and default gateway. The **ipconfig /all** command lists much more detail, including the **DNS server list**, confirmation that the host used DHCP, along with the IP address of the DHCP server.

Key Topic

Example 19-6   ipconfig *and* ipconfig /all *(Windows)*

```
Windows_A> ipconfig
! Lines omitted for brevity
Ethernet adapter Ethernet 5:

   Connection-specific DNS Suffix . :
   Link-local IPv6 Address . . . . . : fe80::6878:1f3d:6223:f4db%6
   IPv4 Address. . . . . . . . . . . : 10.1.1.103
   Subnet Mask . . . . . . . . . . . : 255.255.255.0
   Default Gateway . . . . . . . . . : 10.1.1.1


Windows_A> ipconfig /all
! Lines omitted for brevity
Ethernet adapter Ethernet 5:

   Connection-specific DNS Suffix . . :
   Description . . . . . . . . . . . : Realtek USB GbE Family Controller
   Physical Address. . . . . . . . . : 00-E0-4C-69-08-47
   DHCP Enabled. . . . . . . . . . . : Yes
   Autoconfiguration Enabled . . . . : Yes
   Link-local IPv6 Address . . . . . : fe80::6878:1f3d:6223:f4db%6(Preferred)
   IPv4 Address. . . . . . . . . . . : 10.1.1.103(Preferred)
   Subnet Mask . . . . . . . . . . . : 255.255.255.0
   Lease Obtained. . . . . . . . . . : Tuesday, October 25, 2022 8:25:19 AM
   Lease Expires . . . . . . . . . . : Wednesday, October 26, 2022 8:25:19 AM
   Default Gateway . . . . . . . . . : 10.1.1.1
   DHCP Server . . . . . . . . . . . : 10.1.12.2
   DHCPv6 IAID . . . . . . . . . . . : 100720716
   DHCPv6 Client DUID. . . . . . . . : 00-01-00-01-19-A0-DC-F0-24-FD-52-CB-50-C9
   DNS Servers . . . . . . . . . . . : 208.67.222.222
                                       208.67.222.220
   NetBIOS over Tcpip. . . . . . . . : Enabled
```

While Example 19-6 shows the traditional **ipconfig** Windows command, Example 19-7 shows a similar command as part of the Windows network shell. The network shell commands replace some of the older Windows command-line commands like **ipconfig**.

Example 19-7   *Windows Network Shell* show config *Command*

```
Windows_A> netsh interface ip show config


Configuration for interface "Ethernet 5"
    DHCP enabled:                      Yes
    IP Address:                        10.1.1.103
    Subnet Prefix:                     10.1.1.0/24  (mask 255.255.255.0)
    Default Gateway:                   10.1.1.1
    Gateway Metric:                    0
    InterfaceMetric:                   25
    DNS servers configured through DHCP: 208.67.222.222
                                       208.67.222.220
    Register with which suffix:        Primary only
    WINS servers configured through DHCP: None


! Next, use the network shell to allow repeated commands.
Windows_A> netsh
netsh> interface ip
netsh interface ip> show config


Configuration for interface "Ethernet 5"
    DHCP enabled:                      Yes
    IP Address:                        10.1.1.103
    Subnet Prefix:                     10.1.1.0/24  (mask 255.255.255.0)
! Remaining lines omitted; same output as at the top of the example.

netsh interface ip> show dnsservers


Configuration for interface "Ethernet 5"
    DNS servers configured through DHCP: 208.67.222.222
                                       208.67.222.220
    Register with which suffix:        Primary only
```

Interestingly, you can issue network shell commands as a single command (as seen at the top of Example 19-7) or by navigating within the network shell interface. The example shows the use of the **netsh** command and then **interface ip** so that you reach a mode where you can use short versions of many IP-related commands, like the **show config** and **show dnsservers** commands. (Note that all output has been edited to show only the entries related to the Ethernet interface used in the example.)

19

You should also look at the host's IP routing table, focusing on two routes that direct most routing in the host. When using DHCP, the host creates these routes based on information learned from the DHCP server:

- A default route, with the default gateway as the next-hop address, with the destination subnet and mask listed as 0.0.0.0 and 0.0.0.0.

- A route to the subnet connected to the working interface, subnet 10.1.1.0/24 in this case, calculated from the interface IP address and mask.

Example 19-8 displays Windows host A's routing table with two commands: the older **netstat -rn** command and the newer **netsh interface ip show route** command. The example has been edited to list only routes related to subnet 10.1.1.0/24 and the Ethernet LAN interface used in the example. Note that a gateway of "on-link" means that the PC thinks the destination is on the local subnet (link).

Example 19-8 *Windows Host IPv4 Routes*

```
Windows_A> netstat -rn
IPv4 Route Table
===========================================================================
Active Routes:
Network Destination        Netmask      Gateway     Interface  Metric
          0.0.0.0          0.0.0.0      10.1.1.1    10.1.1.103    25
         10.1.1.0    255.255.255.0     On-link     10.1.1.103   281
       10.1.1.103  255.255.255.255    On-link     10.1.1.103   281
       10.1.1.255  255.255.255.255    On-link     10.1.1.103   281
! Lines omitted for brevity
Windows_A> netsh interface ip show route
Publish Type      Met Prefix                     Idx Gateway/Interface Name
------- -------- --- ----------------------- --- ------------------------
No      Manual     0  0.0.0.0/0                   6 10.1.1.1
No      System   256 10.1.1.0/24                 6 Ethernet 5
No      System   256 10.1.1.103/32               6 Ethernet 5
No      System   256 10.1.1.255/32               6 Ethernet 5
!       Lines     omitted for brevity
```

Host IP Settings on macOS

Although the details vary as compared to Windows, macOS has a graphical interface to see network settings and a variety of network commands. This section shows examples of each, beginning with Figure 19-11. It shows the network settings in macOS for an Ethernet interface, with the address, mask, default router, and DNS server addresses. Also note the setting states that the interface is using DHCP.

Both macOS and Linux support the **ifconfig** command to list information similar to the Windows **ipconfig /all** command. However, the **ifconfig** command lacks an option like **/all**, listing no information about the default gateway or DNS servers. Example 19-9 gives an example of the **ifconfig** command from Mac Host B in Figure 19-11, along with another command that lists the default router.

Figure 19-11 *macOS DHCP Client IP Address, Mask, and Default Router Settings*

Example 19-9 ifconfig *and* networksetup -getinfo *(macOS)*

```
Mac_B$ ifconfig en8
 en8: flags=8863<UP,BROADCAST,SMART,RUNNING,SIMPLEX,MULTICAST> mtu 1500
        options=6467<RXCSUM,TXCSUM,VLAN_MTU,TSO4,TSO6,CHANNEL_IO,PARTIAL_CSUM,
        ZEROINVERT_CSUM>
            ether 00:e0:4c:68:1f:26
            inet6 fe80::184c:56f9:fd3b:d6e7%en8 prefixlen 64 secured scopeid 0x14
            inet 10.1.1.104 netmask 0xffffff00 broadcast 10.1.1.255
            nd6 options=201<PERFORMNUD,DAD>
            media: autoselect (1000baseT <full-duplex>)
            status: active

Mac_B$ networksetup -getinfo "USB 10/100/1000 LAN"
DHCP Configuration
IP address: 10.1.1.104
Subnet mask: 255.255.255.0
Router: 10.1.1.1
Client ID:
```

```
IPv6: Automatic
IPv6 IP address: none
IPv6 Router: none
Ethernet Address: 00:e0:4c:68:1f:26
```

Focusing on the **ifconfig** command, it lists the subnet mask in hex, listing 0xffffff00 in the example. To convert the mask to dotted decimal, convert each pair of hex digits to binary and then from binary to the decimal equivalent, giving you four octets for the dotted-decimal mask. In this case, the 0xffffff00 begins with three pairs of ff, which convert to binary 11111111. Each binary 11111111 converts to decimal 255: the last hex pair, 00, converts to binary 00000000, which converts to decimal 0. The final decimal mask is the familiar value 255.255.255.0.

The **networksetup** command in Example 19-9 lists more detail than the older **ifconfig** command. It lists the usual IP settings, other than the DNS server list. Note that the **networksetup** macOS command has a large variety of options.

Like Windows, macOS adds a default route to its host routing table based on the default gateway and a route to the local subnet calculated based on the IP address and mask. And like Windows, macOS uses the **netstat -rn** command to list those routes—but with several differences in the output. Of note, in the macOS sample shown in Example 19-10, the output represents the default route using the word *default* rather than the destination subnet and mask of 0.0.0.0 and 0.0.0.0. The example highlights the default route and the route to the connected subnet. As usual, the example aids readability by limiting the output to those routes related to network 10.0.0.0.

Example 19-10   netstat -rn *Command (macOS)*

```
Mac_B> netstat -rn
Routing tables

Internet:
Destination       Gateway            Flags      Netif Expire
default           10.1.1.1           UGScg      en8
10.1.1/24         link#20            UCS        en8        !
10.1.1.1/32       link#20            UCS        en8        !
10.1.1.1          2:0:11:11:11:11    UHLWIir    en8        385
10.1.1.104/32     link#20            UCS        en8        !
! lines omitted for brevity
```

Host IP Settings on Linux

As with the other desktop OSs, Linux shows networking settings from the GUI as well as with commands. However, be aware that the Linux world includes many different Linux distributions. Additionally, the Linux architecture separates the OS from the desktop (the graphical interface). So, other Linux users may use different GUI administration tools and commands to see network settings.

Figure 19-12 shows an example from the Ubuntu Linux distribution using the Mate desktop (www.ubuntu-mate.org). The host, Host C in Figure 19-9, uses DHCP and learns an address in subnet 10.1.1.0/24. Figure 19-12 shows IP details about an Ethernet adapter and includes the IPv4 address, mask, default router, and DNS IP addresses.

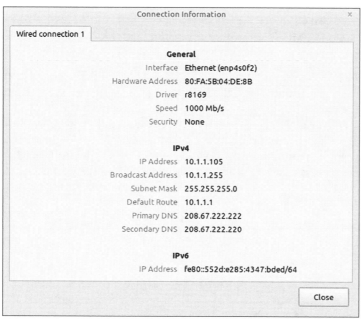

Figure 19-12 *Linux DHCP Client IP Address, Mask, and Default Router Settings*

Linux hosts often support a large set of commands from the command line. However, an older set of commands, referenced together as *net-tools*, has been deprecated in Linux to the point that some Linux distributions do not include net-tools. (You can easily add net-tools to most Linux distributions.) The net-tools library has popular commands like **ifconfig** and **netstat -rn**. To replace those tools, Linux uses the *iproute* library, which includes a set of replacement commands and functions, many performed with the **ip** command and some parameters.

Example 19-11 shows a sample of the Linux **ifconfig** command and the replacement command **ip address** for the same interface detailed in Figure 19-12. Both commands list the Ethernet MAC and IPv4 addresses, along with the subnet mask.

Example 19-11   ifconfig *and* ip address *Commands (Linux)*

```
Linux_C$ ifconfig
enp4s0f2: flags=4163<UP,BROADCAST,RUNNING,MULTICAST> mtu 1500
        inet 10.1.1.105 netmask 255.255.255.0 broadcast 10.1.1.255
        inet6 fe80::552d:e285:4347:bded prefixlen 64 scopeid 0x20<link>
        ether 80:fa:5b:04:de:8b txqueuelen 1000 (Ethernet)
        RX packets 4958 bytes 384498 (384.4 KB)
        RX errors 0 dropped 0 overruns 0 frame 0
        TX packets 16270 bytes 1320108 (1.3 MB)
        TX errors 0 dropped 0 overruns 0 carrier 0 collisions 0
```

```
Linux_C$ ip address
2: enp4s0f2: <BROADCAST,MULTICAST,UP,LOWER_UP> mtu 1500 qdisc fq_codel state UP
group default qlen 1000
    link/ether 80:fa:5b:04:de:8b brd ff:ff:ff:ff:ff:ff
    inet 10.1.1.105/24 brd 10.1.1.255 scope global dynamic noprefixroute enp4s0f2
      valid_lft 81056sec preferred_lft 81056sec
    inet6 fe80::552d:e285:4347:bded/64 scope link noprefixroute
      valid_lft forever preferred_lft forever
```

Example 19-12 shows another pair of older and newer Linux commands: the **netstat -rn** and **ip route** commands. The **netstat -rn** command lists the default route with a style that shows the destination and mask both as 0.0.0.0. As usual, the default route uses the learned default gateway IP address (10.1.1.1) as the next-hop IP address. The **netstat -rn** output also lists a route to the local subnet (10.1.1.0/24). The **ip route** command lists those same routes but with much different formatting and phrasing.

Example 19-12   netstat -rn *and* ip route *Commands (Linux)*

```
Linux_C$ netstat -rn
Kernel IP routing table
Destination     Gateway         Genmask         Flags   MSS Window irtt Iface
0.0.0.0         10.1.1.1        0.0.0.0         UG        0 0           0 enp4s0f2
10.1.1.0        0.0.0.0         255.255.255.0   U         0 0           0 enp4s0f2
! Lines omitted for brevity


Linux_C$ ip route
default via 10.1.1.1 dev enp4s0f2 proto dhcp metric 20100
10.1.1.0/24 dev enp4s0f2 proto kernel  scope link  src 10.1.1.105 metric 100
! Lines omitted for brevity
```

Troubleshooting Host IP Settings

The examples for Windows, macOS, and Linux shown over the last few pages show the successful results for DHCP clients A, B, and C per Figure 19-9. To round out your perspective, the final few examples in this section show a few different scenarios with the resulting output from the popular Windows **ipconfig /all** command. The scenarios, all from Windows Host A in the figure, are as follows:

1. Host A with static IP configuration, using correct settings.
2. Host A as a DHCP client, but with a network issue that prevents the DHCP client and server from communicating.
3. Host A as a DHCP client with a working network so that DHCP works, but with the DHCP server supplying some incorrect information (wrong default gateway address).

A Working Windows Host with Static IP Configuration

Example 19-13 shows the first scenario. Someone has disabled DHCP on Windows Host A and configured all IP settings manually. They chose well, using correct values per

Figure 19-9. In particular, the figure shows addresses .1 – .100 reserved for static addresses, so the person who manually configured Host A assigned 10.1.1.99.

Example 19-13   *Working Windows Host with Static IP Setting (No DHCP)*

```
Windows_A> ipconfig /all
! Showing only the Ethernet adapter connected to subnet 10.1.1.0/24
Ethernet adapter Ethernet 5:

   Connection-specific DNS Suffix .  :
   Description . . . . . . . . . . . : Realtek USB GbE Family Controller
   Physical Address. . . . . . . . . : 00-E0-4C-69-08-47
   DHCP Enabled. . . . . . . . . . . : No
   Autoconfiguration Enabled . . . . : Yes
   Link-local IPv6 Address . . . . . : fe80::6878:1f3d:6223:f4db%6(Preferred)
   IPv4 Address. . . . . . . . . . . : 10.1.1.99(Preferred)
   Subnet Mask . . . . . . . . . . . : 255.255.255.0
   Default Gateway . . . . . . . . . : 10.1.1.1
   DHCPv6 IAID . . . . . . . . . . . : 100720716
   DHCPv6 Client DUID. . . . . . . . : 00-01-00-01-19-A0-DC-F0-24-FD-52-CB-50-C9
   DNS Servers . . . . . . . . . . . : 208.67.222.222
                                       208.67.222.220
   NetBIOS over Tcpip. . . . . . . . : Enabled
```

The **ipconfig /all** command output in Example 19-13 implies that the host uses static settings by noting that DHCP is disabled (per the first highlighted line). Take a moment to compare that line to the same line back in Example 19-7, in which Host A acts as a DHCP client.

The output here in Example 19-13 also signals that the host uses a static setting rather than DHCP, but it tells us that by the absence of several lines of output usually shown for DHCP clients, omitting the lines for

- DHCP Enabled
- Lease Obtained
- Lease Expires

Knowing those facts, you should be able to distinguish between cases in which the Windows host does and does not use DHCP.

A Failed Windows DHCP Client Due to IP Connectivity Issues

The following example, again taken from Windows Host A, shows a case in which the host similarly acts as a DHCP client to follow the design from Figure 19-9. However, any problem that prevents the DHCP DORA messages from flowing between the client and DHCP server results in a failure of the DHCP process. The client does not lease an address or learn the other IP details from the DHCP server, but it self-assigns an APIPA address and uses the APIPA default mask of 255.255.0.0. (For a review of APIPA, see the section titled "APIPA IP Addresses (169.254.x.x)" earlier in this chapter.)

19

Example 19-14 shows the resulting **ipconfig /all** command. The output confirms the client enables DHCP. However, the following facts identify that the process failed:

- It omits the output line that would list the DHCP server's IP address.

- It omits the two output lines that list DHCP lease details.

- It shows an APIPA IP address that begins 169.254.

- It lists no IPv4 default gateway address.

- It lists no IPv4 DNS servers.

Example 19-14 *Windows DHCP Client Fails Due to IP Connectivity Failure*

```
Windows_A> ipconfig /all
! Showing only the Ethernet adapter connected to subnet 10.1.1.0/24
Ethernet adapter Ethernet 5:

   Connection-specific DNS Suffix  .  :
   Description . . . . . . . . . . . : Realtek USB GbE Family Controller
   Physical Address. . . . . . . . . : 00-E0-4C-69-08-47
   DHCP Enabled. . . . . . . . . . . : Yes
   Autoconfiguration Enabled . . . . : Yes
   Link-local IPv6 Address . . . . . : fe80::6878:1f3d:6223:f4db%6(Preferred)
   Autoconfiguration IPv4 Address. . : 169.254.244.219(Preferred)
   Subnet Mask . . . . . . . . . . . : 255.255.0.0
   Default Gateway . . . . . . . . . :
   DHCPv6 IAID . . . . . . . . . . . : 100720716
   DHCPv6 Client DUID. . . . . . . . : 00-01-00-01-19-A0-DC-F0-24-FD-52-CB-50-C9
   DNS Servers . . . . . . . . . . . : fec0:0:0:ffff::1%1
                                       fec0:0:0:ffff::2%1
                                       fec0:0:0:ffff::3%1
   NetBIOS over Tcpip. . . . . . . . : Enabled
```

A Working Windows DHCP Client with Incorrect Settings

For one final scenario, imagine a case in which the DHCP process works but the server configuration is incorrect. As a result, the DHCP client can learn incorrect information and not be able to communicate in some cases. For instance, the DHCP process could complete with the client learning these inaccurate or incomplete settings:

- Wrong subnet mask

- Wrong or missing default gateway

- Wrong or missing DNS server list

Example 19-15 shows a case with the incorrect default gateway (10.1.1.254) configured in the DHCP server's settings for subnet 10.1.1.0/24. The correct default gateway per the design is Router R1 (10.1.1.1). The **ipconfig /all** output in Example 19-15 shows the usual indications that DHCP worked, showing it as enabled, with a lease start and end time. It also shows the host's IP address, mask, default gateway, and DNS servers. But compared to the intended design, the output shows that the host learned a default gateway setting for a nonexistent router.

Example 19-15   *Windows DHCP Client Learns Incorrect Default Gateway*

```
Windows_A> ipconfig /all


Ethernet adapter Ethernet 5:

   Connection-specific DNS Suffix  . :
   Description . . . . . . . . . . . : Realtek USB GbE Family Controller
   Physical Address. . . . . . . . . : 00-E0-4C-69-08-47
   DHCP Enabled. . . . . . . . . . . : Yes
   Autoconfiguration Enabled . . . . : Yes
   Link-local IPv6 Address . . . . . : fe80::6878:1f3d:6223:f4db%6(Preferred)
   IPv4 Address. . . . . . . . . . . : 10.1.1.103(Preferred)
   Subnet Mask . . . . . . . . . . . : 255.255.255.0
   Lease Obtained. . . . . . . . . . : Tuesday, October 25, 2022 7:54:17 AM
   Lease Expires . . . . . . . . . . : Wednesday, October 26, 2022 7:54:16 AM
   Default Gateway . . . . . . . . . : 10.1.1.254
   DHCP Server . . . . . . . . . . . : 10.1.12.2
   DHCPv6 IAID . . . . . . . . . . . : 100720716
   DHCPv6 Client DUID. . . . . . . . : 00-01-00-01-19-A0-DC-F0-24-FD-52-CB-50-C9
   DNS Servers . . . . . . . . . . . : 208.67.222.222
                                       208.67.222.220
   NetBIOS over Tcpip. . . . . . . . : Enabled

Windows_A> netstat -rn


IPv4 Route Table
===========================================================================
Active Routes:
Network Destination        Netmask          Gateway    Interface  Metric
          0.0.0.0          0.0.0.0       10.1.1.254     10.1.1.103     25
         10.1.1.0    255.255.255.0        On-link      10.1.1.103    281
! Lines omitted for brevity
```

The underlying solution to this problem is to fix the configuration mistake in the DHCP server. For the exam, the more likely scenario would be for you to think about the design and notice a difference between what the DHCP client learned and the correct settings. Also, note that the next chapter, "Troubleshooting IPv4 Routing," gives some insights into how to explore different symptoms for problems in an IP network.

Chapter Review

One key to doing well on the exams is to perform repetitive spaced review sessions. Review this chapter's material using either the tools in the book or interactive tools for the same material found on the book's companion website. Refer to the "Your Study Plan" element for more details. Table 19-2 outlines the key review elements and where you can find them. To better track your study progress, record when you completed these activities in the second column.

Table 19-2 Chapter Review Tracking

Review Element	Review Date(s)	Resource Used
Review key topics		Book, website
Review key terms		Book, website
Answer DIKTA questions		Book, PTP
Review command tables		Book
Watch video		Website

Review All the Key Topics

Table 19-3 Key Topics for Chapter 19

Key Topic Element	Description	Page Number
List	Definitions of special IPv4 addresses 0.0.0.0 and 255.255.255.255	489
List	Four logic steps created by the **ip helper-address** command	491
Figure 19-2	What the **ip helper-address** command changes in a DHCP Discover message	491
List	The two facts that must be true about a subnet for a router to need to be a DHCP relay agent for that subnet	494
Example 19-4	Switch commands that confirm the details of DHCP client operations based on the **ip address dhcp** interface subcommand	496
List	The IPv4 settings expected on an end-user host	497
Example 19-6	Output from a Windows **ipconfig /all** command when the host successfully uses DHCP	500
Example 19-8	IP routes on a Windows host	502
Example 19-9	Output from a macOS **ifconfig** command plus two **networksetup** commands	503
Example 19-13	Output from a Windows **ipconfig /all** command when the host uses static IP configuration	507

Key Terms You Should Know

APIPA, default gateway, DHCP client, DHCP relay agent, DHCP server, DNS server, DNS server list

Command References

Tables 19-4, 19-5, and 19-6 list configuration and verification commands used in this chapter. As an easy review exercise, cover the left column in a table, read the right column, and try to recall the command without looking. Then repeat the exercise, covering the right column, and try to recall what the command does.

Table 19-4   Chapter 19 Configuration Command Reference

Command	Description
ip helper-address *IP-address*	An interface subcommand that tells the router to notice local subnet broadcasts (to 255.255.255.255) that use UDP, and change the source and destination IP address, enabling DHCP servers to sit on a remote subnet
ip address dhcp	An interface subcommand that tells the router or switch to use DHCP to attempt to lease a DHCP address from a DHCP server

Table 19-5   Chapter 19 EXEC Command Reference

Command	Description
show arp, show ip arp	Command that lists the router's IPv4 ARP table
show dhcp lease	Switch command that lists information about addresses leased because of the configuration of the **ip address dhcp** command
show ip default-gateway	Switch command that lists the switch's default gateway setting, no matter whether learned by DHCP or statically configured

Table 19-6   Chapter 19 Generic Host Networking Command Reference

Command	Description
ipconfig /all	(Windows) Lists IP address, mask, gateway, and DNS servers
ifconfig	(Mac, Linux) Lists IP address and mask for an interface
networksetup -getinfo *interface*	(Mac) Lists IP settings including default router
netstat -rn	(Windows, Mac, Linux) Lists the host's routing table, including a default route that uses the DHCP-learned default gateway
arp -a	(Windows, Mac, Linux) Lists the host's ARP table
ip address	(Linux) Lists IP address and mask information for interfaces; the Linux replacement for **ifconfig**
ip route	(Linux) Lists routes, including the default route and a route to the local subnet; the Linux replacement for **netstat -rn**
netsh interface ip show addresses	(Windows) Windows network shell command to list interface IP address configuration settings; a replacement for the **ipconfig /all** command
netsh interface ip show route	(Windows) Windows network shell command to list IPv4 routes; a replacement for the **netstat -rn** command

19

CHAPTER 20

Troubleshooting IPv4 Routing

This chapter covers the following exam topics:

2.0 Network Access

2.8 Describe network device management access (Telnet, SSH, HTTP, HTTPS, console, TACACS+/RADIUS, and cloud managed)

3.0 IP Connectivity

3.3 Configure and verify IPv4 and IPv6 static routing

3.3.a Default route

3.3.b Network route

3.3.c Host route

3.3.d Floating static

This chapter turns our attention to routing from end-to-end across an entire enterprise network. How do you troubleshoot an IPv4 network? How do you verify correct operation, identify root causes, and fix those for various IP routing features? How do you do that in the presence of an IP addressing and subnetting plan, requiring you to apply all that subnetting math from Part IV of this book and the basic address/mask and static route configuration from the other chapters here in Part V? This chapter answers some of those questions.

In particular, this chapter focuses on two tools and how to use them: *ping* and *traceroute*. Both tools test the IPv4 data plane; that is, the ability of each networking device to route or forward IPv4 packets. This chapter devotes a major section each to **ping** and **traceroute**. The chapter then ends with a short discussion of two other router tools that can also be useful for troubleshooting: Telnet and Secure Shell (SSH).

"Do I Know This Already?" Quiz

I put DIKTA quizzes in most of the chapters as a tool to help you decide how to approach reading a chapter. However, this chapter does not have a DIKTA quiz because I think you should read it regardless of your prior knowledge. As with all chapters in this book, this chapter introduces new concepts, but it also acts as a tool to review and deepen your understanding of IP routing. Hope you enjoy the perspectives on using **ping** and **traceroute** in this chapter.

Foundation Topics

Problem Isolation Using the ping Command

Someone sends you an email or text, or a phone message, asking you to look into a user's network problem. You Secure Shell (SSH) to a router and issue a **ping** command that works. What does that result rule out as a possible reason for the problem? What does it rule in as still being a possible root cause?

Then you issue another **ping** to another address, and this time the ping fails. Again, what does the failure of that **ping** command tell you? What parts of IPv4 routing may still be a problem, and what parts do you now know are not a problem?

The **ping** command gives us one of the most common network troubleshooting tools. When the **ping** command succeeds, it confirms many individual parts of how IP routing works, ruling out some possible causes of the current problem. When a **ping** command fails, it often helps narrow down where in the internetwork the root cause of the problem may be happening, further isolating the problem.

This section begins with a brief explanation of how ping works. It then moves on to some suggestions and analysis of how to use the **ping** command to isolate problems by removing some items from consideration.

Ping Command Basics

The **ping** command tests connectivity by sending packets to an IP address, expecting the device at that address to send packets back. The command sends packets that mean "if you receive this packet, and it is addressed to you, send a reply back." Each time the **ping** command sends one of these packets and receives the message sent back by the other host, the **ping** command knows a packet made it from the source host to the destination and back.

More formally, the **ping** command uses the Internet Control Message Protocol (ICMP), specifically the **ICMP echo request** and **ICMP echo reply** messages. ICMP defines many other messages as well, but these two messages were made specifically for connectivity testing by commands like **ping**. As a protocol, ICMP does not rely on TCP or UDP, and it does not use any application layer protocol. It functions as part of Layer 3, as a control protocol to assist IP by helping manage the IP network functions.

Figure 20-1 shows the ICMP messages, with IP headers, in an example. In this case, the user at host A opens a command prompt and issues the **ping 172.16.2.101** command, testing connectivity to host B. The command sends one echo request and waits (Step 1); host B receives the messages and sends back an echo reply (Step 2).

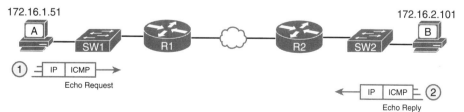

Figure 20-1 *Concept Behind* **ping 172.16.2.101** *on Host A*

The **ping** command is supported on many different devices and many common operating systems. The command has many options: the name or IP address of the destination, how many times the command should send an echo request, how long the command should wait (timeout) for an echo reply, how big to make the packets, and many other options. Example 20-1 shows a sample from host A, with the same command that matches the concept in Figure 20-1: a **ping 172.16.2.101** command on host A.

Example 20-1   *Sample Output from Host A's* **ping 172.16.2.101** *Command*

```
Mac_A$ ping 172.16.2.101
PING 172.16.2.101 (172.16.2.101): 56 data bytes
64 bytes from 172.16.2.101: icmp_seq=0 ttl=64 time=1.112 ms
64 bytes from 172.16.2.101: icmp_seq=1 ttl=64 time=0.673 ms
64 bytes from 172.16.2.101: icmp_seq=2 ttl=64 time=0.631 ms
64 bytes from 172.16.2.101: icmp_seq=3 ttl=64 time=0.674 ms
64 bytes from 172.16.2.101: icmp_seq=4 ttl=64 time=0.642 ms
64 bytes from 172.16.2.101: icmp_seq=5 ttl=64 time=0.656 ms
^C
--- 172.16.2.101 ping statistics ---
6 packets transmitted, 6 packets received, 0.0% packet loss
round-trip min/avg/max/stddev = 0.631/0.731/1.112/0.171 ms
```

Strategies and Results When Testing with the ping Command

Often, the person handling initial calls from users about problems (often called a customer support rep, or CSR) cannot issue **ping** commands from the user's device. In some cases, talking users through typing the right commands and making the right clicks on their machines can be a problem. Or the user just might not be available. As an alternative, using different **ping** commands from different routers can help isolate the problem.

The problem with using **ping** commands from routers, instead of from the host that has the problem, is that no single router **ping** command can exactly replicate a **ping** command done from the user's device. However, each different **ping** command can help isolate a problem further. The rest of this section of **ping** commands discusses troubleshooting IPv4 routing by using various **ping** commands from the command-line interface (CLI) of a router.

Testing Longer Routes from Near the Source of the Problem

Most problems begin with some idea like "host X cannot communicate with host Y." A great first troubleshooting step is to issue a **ping** command from X for host Y's IP address. However, assuming the engineer does not have access to host X, the engineer can instead issue the **ping** from the router nearest X, typically the router acting as host X's default gateway.

For instance, in Figure 20-1, imagine that the user of host A had called IT support with a problem related to sending packets to host B. A **ping 172.16.2.101** command on host A would be a great first troubleshooting step, but the CSR cannot access host A or get in touch with the user of host A. So, the CSR telnets to Router R1 and pings host B from there, as shown in Example 20-2.

Example 20-2 *Router R2 Pings Host B (Two Commands)*

```
R1# ping 172.16.2.101
Type escape sequence to abort.
Sending 5, 100-byte ICMP Echos to 172.16.2.101, timeout is 2 seconds:
.!!!!
Success rate is 80 percent (4/5), round-trip min/avg/max = 1/2/4 ms
R1# ping 172.16.2.101
Type escape sequence to abort.
Sending 5, 100-byte ICMP Echos to 172.16.2.101, timeout is 2 seconds:
!!!!!
Success rate is 100 percent (5/5), round-trip min/avg/max = 1/2/4 ms
```

First, take a moment to review the output of the first IOS **ping** command. By default, the Cisco IOS **ping** command sends five echo messages, with a timeout of 2 seconds. If the command does not receive an echo reply within 2 seconds, the command considers that message to be a failure, and the command lists a period. If a successful reply is received within 2 seconds, the command displays an exclamation point. So, in this first command, the first echo reply timed out, whereas the other four received a matching echo reply within 2 seconds.

As a quick aside, the example shows a common and normal behavior with **ping** commands: the first **ping** command shows one failure to start, but then the rest of the messages work. This usually happens because some device in the end-to-end route is missing an ARP table entry.

Now think about troubleshooting and what a working **ping** command tells us about the current behavior of this internetwork. First, focus on the big picture for a moment:

- R1 can send ICMP echo request messages to host B (172.16.2.101).

- R1 sends these messages from its outgoing interface's IP address (by default), 172.16.4.1 in this case.

- Host B can send ICMP echo reply messages to R1's 172.16.4.1 IP address (hosts send echo reply messages to the IP address from which the echo request was received).

Figure 20-2 shows the packet flow.

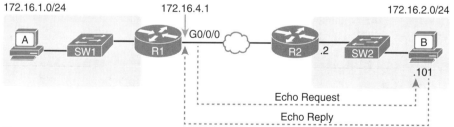

Figure 20-2 *Standard* ping 172.6.2.101 *Command Using the Source Interface IP Address*

Next, think about IPv4 routing. In the forward direction, R1 must have a route that matches host B's address (172.16.2.101); this route will be either a static route or one learned with a routing protocol. R2 also needs a route for host B's address, in this case a connected route to B's subnet (172.16.2.0/24), as shown in the top arrow lines in Figure 20-3.

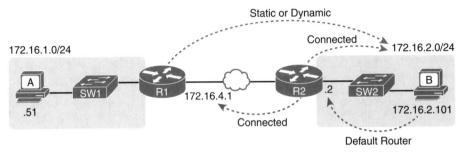

Figure 20-3   *Layer 3 Routes Needed for R1's* **ping 172.16.2.101** *to Work*

The arrow lines on the bottom of Figure 20-3 show the routes needed to forward the ICMP echo reply message back to Router R1's 172.16.4.1 interface. First, host B must have a valid default router setting because 172.16.4.1 sits in a different subnet than host B. R2 must also have a route that matches destination 172.16.4.1 (in this case, likely to be a connected route).

The working **ping** commands in Example 20-2 also require the data-link and physical layer details to be working. The WAN link must be working: The router interfaces must be up/up, which typically indicates that the link can pass data. On the LAN, R2's LAN interface must be in an up/up state. In addition, everything discussed about Ethernet LANs must be working because the **ping** confirmed that the packets went all the way from R1 to host B and back. In particular

■ The switch interfaces in use are in a connected (up/up) state.

■ Port security (discussed in the *CCNA 200-301 Official Cert Guide, Volume 2, Second Edition*) does not filter frames sent by R2 or host B.

■ STP has placed the right ports into a forwarding state.

The **ping 172.16.2.101** command in Example 20-2 also confirms that IP access control lists (ACLs) did not filter the ICMP messages. One ACL contains a set of matching rules and actions: some matched packets are filtered (discarded), while others can continue on their path as normal. ACLs can examine packets as they enter or exit a router interface, so Figure 20-4 shows the various locations on routers R1 and R2 where an ACL could have filtered (discarded) the ICMP messages. (Note that an outbound ACL on Router R1 would not filter packets created on R1, so there is no rightward-facing arrow over R1.)

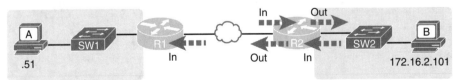

Figure 20-4   *Locations Where IP ACLs Could Have Filtered the Ping Messages*

Finally, the working **ping 172.16.2.101** command on R1 can also be used to reasonably predict that ARP worked and that switch SW2 learned MAC addresses for its MAC address table. R2 and host B need to know each other's MAC addresses so that they can encapsulate the IP packet inside an Ethernet frame, which means both must have a matching ARP table entry. The switch learns the MAC address used by R2 and by host B when it sends the ARP messages or when it sends the frames that hold the IP packets. Figure 20-5 shows the type of information expected in those tables.

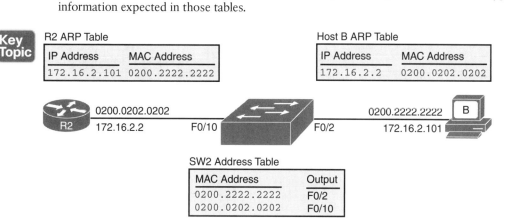

Figure 20-5 *Router and Host ARP Tables, with the Switch MAC Address Table*

As you can see from the last few pages, a strategy of using a **ping** command from near the source of the problem can rule out a lot of possible root causes of any problems between two hosts—assuming the **ping** command succeeds. However, this **ping** command does not act exactly like the same **ping** command on the actual host. To overcome some of what is missing in the **ping** command from a nearby router, the next several examples show some strategies for testing other parts of the path between the two hosts that might have a current problem.

Using Extended Ping to Test the Reverse Route

Pinging from the default router, as discussed in the past few pages, misses an opportunity to test IP routes more fully. Such tests check the **forward route**, that is, the route toward the destination. However, a ping from the default route does not test the **reverse route** back toward the original host.

For instance, referring to the internetwork in Figure 20-2 again, note that the reverse routes do not point to an address in host A's subnet. When R1 processes the **ping 172.16.2.101** command, R1 has to pick a source IP address to use for the echo request, and routers choose the *IP address of the outgoing interface*. The echo request from R1 to host B flows with source IP address 172.16.4.1 (R1's G0/0/0 IP address). The echo reply flows back to that same address (172.16.4.1).

A standard ping often does not test the reverse route that you need to test. In this case, the standard **ping 172.16.2.101** command on R1 does not test whether the routers can route back to subnet 172.16.1.0/24, instead testing their routes for subnet 172.16.4.0. A better ping test would test the route back to host A's subnet; an *extended ping* from R1 can cause that test to happen. An extended ping allows R1's **ping** command to use R1's LAN IP address from within subnet 172.16.1.0/24. Then, the echo reply messages would flow to host A's subnet, as shown in Figure 20-6.

20

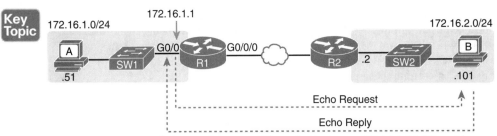

Figure 20-6 *Extended Ping Command Tests the Route to 172.16.1.51 (Host A)*

The extended **ping** command does allow the user to type all the parameters on a potentially long command, but it also allows users to simply issue the **ping** command, press Enter, with IOS then asking the user to answer questions to complete the command, as shown in Example 20-3. The example shows the **ping** command on R1 that matches the logic in Figure 20-6. This same command could have been issued from the command line as **ping 172.16.2.101 source 172.16.1.1**.

Example 20-3 *Testing the Reverse Route Using the Extended Ping*

```
R1# ping
Protocol [ip]:
Target IP address: 172.16.2.101
Repeat count [5]:
Datagram size [100]:
Timeout in seconds [2]:
Extended commands [n]: y
Source address or interface: 172.16.1.1
Type of service [0]:
Set DF bit in IP header? [no]:
Validate reply data? [no]:
Data pattern [0xABCD]:
Loose, Strict, Record, Timestamp, Verbose[none]:
Sweep range of sizes [n]:
Type escape sequence to abort.
Sending 5, 100-byte ICMP Echos to 172.16.2.101, timeout is 2 seconds:
Packet sent with a source address of 172.16.1.1
!!!!!
Success rate is 100 percent (5/5), round-trip min/avg/max = 1/2/4 ms
```

This particular extended **ping** command tests the same routes for the echo request going to the right, but it forces a better test of routes pointing back to the left for the ICMP echo reply. For that direction, R2 needs a route that matches address 172.16.1.1, which is likely to be a route for subnet 172.16.1.0/24—the same subnet in which host A resides.

From a troubleshooting perspective, using both standard and extended **ping** commands can be useful. However, neither can exactly mimic a **ping** command created on the host itself because the routers cannot send packets with the host's IP address. For instance, the extended **ping** in Example 20-3 uses source IP address 172.16.1.1, which is not host A's IP address. As a result, neither the standard nor extended **ping** commands in these two examples so far in this chapter can test for some kinds of problems, such as the following:

- IP ACLs that discard packets based on host A's IP address but allow packets that match the router's IP address

- LAN switch port security that filters A's frames (based on A's MAC address)

- IP routes on routers that happen to match host A's 172.16.1.51 address, with different routes that match R1's 172.16.1.1 address

- Problems with host A's default router setting

> **NOTE**   IP ACLs and LAN switch port security are covered in the *CCNA 200-301 Official Cert Guide, Volume 2*, Second Edition. For now, know that IP ACLs can filter packets on routers, focusing on the Layer 3 and 4 headers. Port security can be enabled on Layer 2 switches to filter based on source MAC addresses.

Testing LAN Neighbors with Standard Ping

Testing using a **ping** of another device on the LAN can quickly confirm whether the LAN can pass packets and frames. Specifically, a working **ping** rules out many possible root causes of a problem. For instance, Figure 20-7 shows the ICMP messages that occur if R1 issues the command **ping 172.16.1.51**, pinging host A, which sits on the same VLAN as R1.

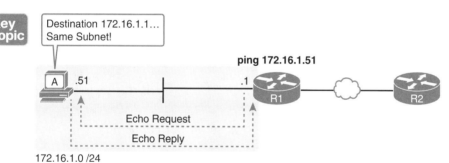

Figure 20-7   *Standard* ping *Command Confirms That the LAN Works*

If the ping works, it confirms the following, which rules out some potential issues:

- The host with address 172.16.1.51 replied.

- The LAN can pass unicast frames from R1 to host 172.16.1.51 and vice versa.

- You can reasonably assume that the switches learned the MAC addresses of the router and the host, adding those to the MAC address tables.

- Host A and Router R1 completed the ARP process and list each other in their respective Address Resolution Protocol (ARP) tables.

The failure of a ping, even with two devices on the same subnet, can point to a variety of problems, like those mentioned in this list. For instance, if the **ping 172.16.1.51** on R1 fails (refer to Figure 20-7), that result points to this list of potential root causes:

- **IP addressing problem:** Host A or the router could be configured with the wrong IP address.

- **IP mask problem:** Using an incorrect subnet mask on either the host or the router would change their calculation view of the range of addresses in the attached subnet, which would affect their forwarding logic. For example, the host, with address 172.16.1.51 but incorrect mask 255.255.255.240, would think that the router's address of 172.16.1.1 is in a different subnet.

- **DHCP problems:** If you are using Dynamic Host Configuration Protocol (DHCP), many problems could exist. Chapter 19, "IP Addressing on Hosts," discusses those possibilities in some depth.

- **VLAN trunking problems:** The router could be configured for 802.1Q trunking, when the switch is not (or vice versa).

- **LAN problems:** A wide variety of issues could exist with the Layer 2 switches, preventing any frames from flowing between host A and the router.

So, whether the ping works or fails, simply pinging a LAN host from a router can help further isolate the problem.

Testing LAN Neighbors with Extended Ping

A standard ping of a LAN host from a router does not test that host's default router setting. However, an extended ping can test the host's default router setting. Both tests can be useful, especially for problem isolation, because

- If a standard ping of a local LAN host works...

- But an extended ping of the same LAN host fails...

- The problem likely relates somehow to the host's default router setting.

First, to understand why the standard and extended ping results have different effects, consider first the standard **ping 172.16.1.51** command on R1, as shown previously in Figure 20-7. As a standard **ping** command, R1 used its LAN interface IP address (172.16.1.1) as the source of the ICMP Echo. So, when the host (A) sent back its ICMP echo reply, host A considered the destination of 172.16.1.1 as being on the same subnet. Host A's ICMP echo reply message, sent back to 172.16.1.1, would work even if host A did not have a default router setting at all!

In comparison, Figure 20-8 shows the difference when using an extended ping on Router R1. An extended ping from local Router R1, using R1's WAN IP address of 172.16.4.1 as the source of the ICMP echo request, means that host A's ICMP echo reply will flow to an address in another subnet, which makes host A use its default router setting.

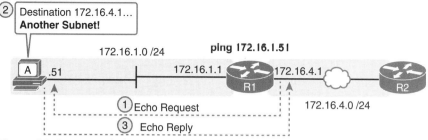

Figure 20-8 *Extended* **ping** *Command Does Test Host A's Default Router Setting*

The comparison between the previous two figures shows one of the most classic mistakes when troubleshooting networks. Sometimes, the temptation is to connect to a router and ping the host on the attached LAN, and it works. So, the engineer moves on, thinking that the network layer issues between the router and host work fine, when the problem still exists with the host's default router setting.

Testing WAN Neighbors with Standard Ping

As with a standard ping test across a LAN, a standard ping test between routers over a serial or Ethernet WAN link tests whether the link can pass IPv4 packets. With a properly designed IPv4 addressing plan, two routers on the same serial or Ethernet WAN link should have IP addresses in the same subnet. A ping from one router to the IP address of the other router confirms that an IP packet can be sent over the link and back, as shown in the **ping 172.16.4.2** command on R1 in Figure 20-9.

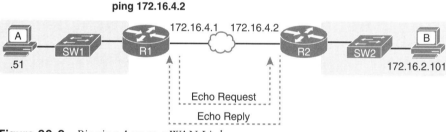

Figure 20-9 *Pinging Across a WAN Link*

A successful ping of the IP address on the other end of an Ethernet WAN link that sits between two routers confirms several specific facts, such as the following:

■ Both routers' WAN interfaces are in an up/up state.

■ The Layer 1 and 2 features of the link work.

■ The routers believe that the neighboring router's IP address is in the same subnet.

■ Inbound ACLs on both routers do not filter the incoming packets, respectively.

■ The remote router is configured with the expected IP address (172.16.4.2 in this case).

Pinging the other neighboring router does not test many other features. However, although the test is limited in scope, it does let you rule out WAN links as having a Layer 1 or 2 problem, and it rules out some basic Layer 3 addressing problems.

Using Ping with Names and with IP Addresses

All the ping examples so far in this chapter show a ping of an IP address. However, the **ping** command can use **hostnames**, and pinging a hostname allows the network engineer to further test whether the Domain Name System (**DNS**) process works.

First, most every TCP/IP application uses hostnames rather than IP addresses to identify the other device. No one opens a web browser and types in 72.163.4.185. Instead, they type in a web address, like https://www.cisco.com, which includes the hostname www.cisco.com. Then, before a host can send data to a specific IP address, the host must first ask a DNS server to resolve that hostname into the matching IP address.

For example, in the small internetwork used for several examples in this chapter, a **ping B** command on host A tests A's DNS settings, as shown in Figure 20-10. When host A sees the use of a hostname (B), it first looks in its local DNS name cache to find out whether it has already resolved the name B. If not, host A first asks the DNS to supply (resolve) the name into its matching IP address (Step 1 in the figure). Only then does host A send a packet to 172.16.2.101, host B's IP address (Step 2).

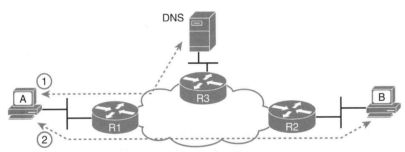

Figure 20-10 *DNS Name Resolution by Host A*

When troubleshooting, testing from the host by pinging using a hostname can be very helpful. The command, of course, tests the host's own DNS client settings. For instance, a classic comparison is to first ping the destination host using the hostname, which requires a DNS request. Then, repeat the same test, but use the destination host's IP address instead of its name, which does not require the DNS request. If the ping of the hostname fails but the ping of the IP address works, the problem usually has something to do with DNS.

Routers and switches can also use name resolution for commands that refer to hosts, such as the **ping** and **traceroute** commands. The networking device can use DNS, locally defined hostnames, or both. Example 20-4 shows an example DNS configuration on Router R1 from the most recent examples. In particular:

- The **ip domain lookup** command tells the router to attempt to use a DNS server.

- The **ip name-server** {*address* [*address address*]} command defines the list of DNS server IP addresses.

- The **ip domain name** *domain-name* command defines the domain used by the device.

In the example, note that once configured to use DNS, the **ping hostB** command works. The command output shows the IP address the DNS resolution process found for name hostB, 172.16.2.101.

Example 20-4 *Configuring to Use DNS (Router R1), DNS Has hostB Name*

```
R1# configure terminal
Enter configuration commands, one per line.  End with CNTL/Z.
R1(config)# ip domain lookup
R1(config)# ip domain name example.com
R1(config)# ip name-server 8.8.8.8 8.8.8.4
R1(config)# ^Z
R1#
R1# ping hostB
Type escape sequence to abort.
Sending 5, 100-byte ICMP Echos to 172.16.2.101, timeout is 2 seconds:
!!!!!
Success rate is 100 percent (5/5), round-trip min/avg/max = 1/1/4 ms
```

NOTE Older IOS versions used a syntax of **ip domain-name** *domain-name* rather than the newer **ip domain name** *domain-name* (with a space instead of a dash).

NOTE When practicing, you might want to disable DNS resolution, particularly in lab devices, using the **no ip domain lookup** command. Cisco routers and switches enable DNS resolution by default with a setting of **ip domain lookup**, but with no name servers identified with the **ip name-server** command. The result of these two default settings causes the router or switch to perform name resolution on a name by broadcasting for a DNS server on each connected subnet. Additionally, if you mistype the first word of a command, IOS thinks you mean that word to be a hostname, and it attempts to perform name resolution on the mistyped command. The result: for any typo of the first word in a command, the default name resolution settings cause a few minutes wait until you get control of the CLI again.

In a lab environment, when not expecting to use DNS, disable DNS resolution with the **no ip domain lookup** command.

You can also configure the router or switch to use locally configured hostnames (or to use both locally configured names and DNS). Use a configuration like that in Example 20-5, adding the **ip host** *name address* global configuration command for each hostname. The router or switch will look for local hostnames whether you use DNS or have the **ip domain lookup** command configured.

Example 20-5 *Configuring to Use Local Hostnames, R1 Config Has hostB Name*

```
R1# configure terminal
Enter configuration commands, one per line.  End with CNTL/Z.
R1(config)# ip host hostB 172.16.2.101
R1(config)# ^Z
R1#
```

20

```
R1# show hosts
Default domain is example.com
Name servers are 8.8.8.8, 8.8.8.4
NAME  TTL  CLASS   TYPE      DATA/ADDRESS
-----------------------------------------
101.2.16.172.in-addr.arpa    10      IN      PTR     hostB
hostB                        10      IN      A       172.16.2.101
```

Problem Isolation Using the traceroute Command

Like **ping**, the **traceroute** command helps network engineers isolate problems. Here is a comparison of the two:

- Both send messages in the network to test connectivity.

- Both rely on other devices to send back a reply.

- Both have wide support on many different operating systems.

- Both can use a hostname or an IP address to identify the destination.

- On routers, both have a standard and extended version, allowing better testing of the reverse route.

The biggest differences relate to the more detailed results in the output of the **traceroute** command and the extra time and effort it takes **traceroute** to build that output. This next major section examines how traceroute works; plus it provides some suggestions on how to use this more detailed information to more quickly isolate IP routing problems.

traceroute Basics

Imagine some network engineer or CSR starts to troubleshoot some problem. The engineer pings from the user's host, pings from a nearby router, and after a few commands, convinces herself that the host can indeed send and receive IP packets. The problem might not be solved yet, but the problem does not appear to be a network problem.

Now imagine the next problem comes along, and this time the **ping** command fails. It appears that some problem does exist in the IP network. Where is the problem? Where should the engineer look more closely? Although the **ping** command can prove helpful in isolating the source of the problem, the **traceroute** command may be a better option. The **traceroute** command systematically helps pinpoint routing problems by showing how far a packet goes through an IP network before being discarded.

The **traceroute** command identifies the routers in the forward route from source host to destination host. Specifically, it lists the next-hop IP address of each router that would be in each of the individual routes. For instance, a **traceroute 172.16.2.101** command on host A in Figure 20-11 would identify an IP address on Router R1, another on Router R2, and then host B, as shown in the figure. Example 20-6, which follows, lists the output of the command, taken from host A.

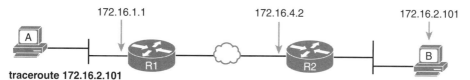

172.16.1.1   172.16.4.2   172.16.2.101

traceroute 172.16.2.101

Figure 20-11 *IP Addresses Identified by a Successful* **traceroute** *172.16.2.101 Command*

Example 20-6 *Output from* **traceroute** *172.16.2.101 on Host A*

```
Mac_A$ traceroute 172.16.2.101
traceroute to 172.16.2.101, 64 hops max, 52 byte packets
  1 172.16.1.1 (172.16.1.1) 0.870 ms 0.520 ms 0.496 ms
  2 172.16.4.2 (172.16.4.2) 8.263 ms 7.518 ms 9.319 ms
  3 172.16.2.101 (172.16.2.101) 16.770 ms 9.819 ms 9.830 ms
```

How the traceroute Command Works

The **traceroute** command gathers information by generating packets that trigger error messages from routers; these messages identify the routers, letting the **traceroute** command list the routers' IP addresses in the output of the command. That error message is the ICMP Time-to-Live Exceeded (TTL Exceeded) message, originally meant to notify hosts when a packet had been looping around a network.

Ignoring traceroute for a moment and instead focusing on IP routing, IPv4 routers defeat routing loops in part by discarding looping IP packets. To do so, the IPv4 header holds a field called Time To Live (TTL). The original host that creates the packet sets an initial TTL value. Then each router that forwards the packet decrements the TTL value by 1. When a router decrements the TTL to 0, the router perceives the packet is looping, and the router discards the packet. The router also notifies the host that sent the discarded packet by sending an ICMP TTL Exceeded message.

Now back to traceroute. Traceroute sends messages with low TTL values to make the routers send back a TTL Exceeded message. Specifically, a **traceroute** command begins by sending several packets (usually three), each with the header TTL field equal to 1. When that packet arrives at the next router—host A's default Router R1 in the example of Figure 20-12—the router decrements TTL to 0 and discards the packet. The router then sends host A the TTL Exceeded message, which identifies the router's IP address to the **traceroute** command.

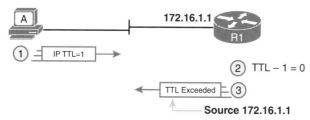

A   172.16.1.1   R1

① IP TTL=1
② TTL – 1 = 0
TTL Exceeded ③
Source 172.16.1.1

Figure 20-12 *How* **traceroute** *Identifies the First Router in the Route*

20

The **traceroute** command sends several TTL=1 packets, checking them to see whether the TTL Exceeded messages flow from the same router, based on the source IP address of the TTL Exceeded message. Assuming the messages come from the same router, the **traceroute** command lists that IP address as the next line of output on the command.

To find all the routers in the path, and finally confirm that packets flow all the way to the destination host, the **traceroute** command sends a small set of packets with TTL=1, then a small set with TTL=2, then 3, 4, and so on, until the destination host replies. Figure 20-13 shows the packet from the second set with TTL=2. In this case, one router (R1) actually forwards the packet, while another router (R2) happens to decrement the TTL to 0, causing a TTL Exceeded message to be sent back to host A.

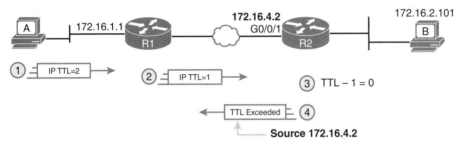

Figure 20-13 *TTL=2 Message Sent by* traceroute

The figure shows these four steps:

1. The **traceroute** command sends a packet from the second set with TTL=2.
2. Router R1 processes the packet and decrements TTL to 1. R1 forwards the packet.
3. Router R2 processes the packet and decrements TTL to 0. R2 discards the packet.
4. R2 notifies the sending host of the discarded packet by sending a TTL Exceeded ICMP message. The source IP address of that message is 172.16.4.2.

Finally, the choice of source IP address to use on the time-exceeded message returned by routers has a big impact on the output of the **traceroute** command. Most routers use simpler logic that also makes command output like **traceroute** more consistent and meaningful. That logic: choose the TTL Exceeded message's source IP address based on the interface in which the discarded original message arrived. In the example in Figure 20-13, the original message at Step 2 arrived on R2's G0/0/1 interface, so at Step 3, R2 uses G0/0/1's IP address as the source IP address of the TTL Exceeded message, and as the interface out which to send the message.

Standard and Extended traceroute

The standard and extended options for the **traceroute** command give you many of the same options as the **ping** command. For instance, Example 20-7 lists the output of a standard **traceroute** command on Router R1. Like the standard **ping** command, a standard **traceroute** command chooses an IP address based on the outgoing interface for the packet sent by the command. So, in this example, the packets sent by R1 come from source IP address 172.16.4.1, R1's G0/0/0 IP address.

Example 20-7 *Standard* traceroute *Command on R1*

```
R1# traceroute 172.16.2.101
Type escape sequence to abort.
Tracing the route to 172.16.2.101
VRF info: (vrf in name/id, vrf out name/id)
   1 172.16.4.2 0 msec 0 msec 0 msec
   2 172.16.2.101 0 msec 0 msec *
```

The extended **traceroute** command, as shown in Example 20-8, follows the same basic command structure as the extended **ping** command. The user can type all the parameters on one command line, but it is much easier to just type **traceroute**, press Enter, and let IOS prompt for all the parameters, including the source IP address of the packets (172.16.1.1 in this example).

Example 20-8 *Extended* traceroute *Command on R1*

```
R1# traceroute
Protocol [ip]:
Target IP address: 172.16.2.101
Source address: 172.16.1.1
Numeric display [n]:
Timeout in seconds [3]:
Probe count [3]:
Minimum Time to Live [1]:
Maximum Time to Live [30]:
Port Number [33434]:
Loose, Strict, Record, Timestamp, Verbose[none]:
Type escape sequence to abort.
Tracing the route to 172.16.2.101
VRF info: (vrf in name/id, vrf out name/id)
   1 172.16.4.2 0 msec 0 msec 0 msec
   2 172.16.2.101 0 msec 0 msec *
```

Both the **ping** and **traceroute** commands exist on most operating systems, including Cisco IOS. However, some operating systems use a slightly different syntax for **traceroute**. For example, most Windows operating systems support **tracert** and **pathping**, and not **traceroute**. Linux and OS X support the **traceroute** command.

20

> **NOTE** Host OS **traceroute** commands usually create ICMP echo requests. The Cisco IOS **traceroute** command instead creates IP packets with a UDP header. This bit of information may seem trivial at this point. However, note that an ACL may actually filter the traffic from a host's **traceroute** messages but not the router **traceroute** command, or vice versa.

Telnet and SSH

The **ping** and **traceroute** commands do give networkers two great tools to begin isolating the cause of an IP routing problem. However, these two commands tell us nothing about the operation state inside the various network devices. Once you begin to get an idea of the kinds of problems and the possible locations of the problems using **ping** and **traceroute**, the next step is to look at the status of various router and switch features. One way to do that is to use Telnet or Secure Shell (SSH) to log in to the devices.

Common Reasons to Use the IOS Telnet and SSH Client

Normally, a network engineer would log in to the remote device using a Telnet or SSH client on a PC, tablet, or any other user device. In fact, often, the same software package does both Telnet and SSH. However, in some cases, you might want to take advantage of the Telnet and SSH client built in to IOS on the routers and switches to Telnet/SSH from one Cisco device to the next.

To understand why, consider the example shown in Figure 20-14. The figure shows arrowed lines to three separate IP addresses on three separate Cisco routers. PC1 has attempted to Telnet to each address from a different tab in PC1's Telnet/SSH client. However, R2 happens to have an error in its routing protocol configuration, so R1, R2, and R3 fail to learn any routes from each other. As a result, PC1's Telnet attempt to both 10.1.2.2 (R2) and 10.1.3.3 (R3) fails.

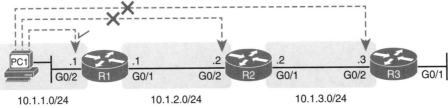

Figure 20-14 *Telnet Works from PC1 to R1 but Not to R2 or R3*

In some cases, like this one, a Telnet or SSH login from the network engineer's device can fail, while you could still find a way to log in using the **telnet** and **ssh** commands to use the Telnet and SSH clients on the routers or switches. With this particular scenario, all the individual data links work; the problem is with the routing protocol exchanging routes. PC1 can ping R1's 10.1.1.1 IP address, R1 can ping R2's 10.1.2.2 address, and R2 can ping R3's 10.1.3.3 address. Because each link works, and each router can send and receive packets with its neighbor on the shared data link, you could Telnet/SSH to each successive device.

Figure 20-15 shows the idea. PC1 begins with a Telnet/SSH connection into Router R1, as shown on the left. Then the user issues the **telnet 10.1.2.2** command from R1 to Telnet to R2. Once logged in to R2, the user can issue commands on R2. Then from R2, the user could issue the **telnet 10.1.3.3** command to Telnet to R3, from which the user could issue commands on R3.

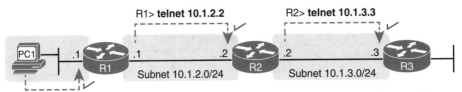

Figure 20-15 *Successive Telnet Connections: PC1 to R1, R1 to R2, and R2 to R3*

The Telnet connections shown in Figure 20-15 work because each Telnet in this case uses source and destination addresses in the same subnet. For example, R1's **telnet 10.1.2.2** command uses 10.1.2.2 as the destination, of course. R1 uses the outgoing interface IP address used to send packets to 10.1.2.2, 10.1.2.1 in this case. Because each of these **telnet** commands connects to an IP address in a connected subnet, the routing protocol could be completely misconfigured, and you could still Telnet/SSH to each successive device to troubleshoot and fix the problem.

Network engineers also use the IOS Telnet and SSH client just for preference. For instance, if you need to log in to several Cisco devices, you could open several windows and tabs on your PC, and log in from your PC (assuming the network was not having problems). Or you could log in from your PC to some nearby Cisco router or switch, and from there Telnet or SSH to other Cisco devices.

IOS Telnet and SSH Examples

Using the IOS Telnet client via the **telnet** *host* command is pretty simple. Just use the IP address or hostname to identify the host to which you want to connect, and press Enter. Example 20-9 shows an example based on Figure 20-15, with R1 using Telnet to connect to 10.1.2.2 (R2).

Example 20-9 *Telnet from R1 to R2 to View Interface Status on R2*

```
R1# telnet 10.1.2.2
Trying 10.1.2.2 ... Open

User Access Verification

Username: wendell
Password:
R2>
R2> show ip interface brief
Interface               IP-Address      OK? Method Status                Protocol
GigabitEthernet0/0      unassigned      YES unset  administratively down  down
GigabitEthernet0/1      10.1.3.2        YES manual up                     up
GigabitEthernet0/2      10.1.2.2        YES manual up                     up
GigabitEthernet0/3      unassigned      YES unset  administratively down  down
```

Take the time to pay close attention to the command prompts. The example begins with the user logged in to Router R1, with the R1# command prompt. After the user issues the **telnet 10.1.2.2** command, R2 asks the user for both a username and password because Router R2 uses local username authentication, which requires those credentials. The **show ip interfaces brief** command at the end of the output shows Router R2's interfaces and IP addresses again per Example 20-9 and Figure 20-15.

The **ssh -l** *username host* command in Example 20-10 follows the same basic ideas as the **telnet** *host* command, but with an SSH client. The -l flag means that the next parameter is the login username. In this case, the user begins logged in to Router R1 and then uses the **ssh -l wendell 10.1.2.2** command to SSH to Router R2. R2 expects a username/password of wendell/odom, with wendell supplied in the command and odom supplied when R2 prompts the user.

20

Example 20-10   *SSH Client from R1 to R2 to View Interface Status on R2*

```
R1# ssh -l wendell 10.1.2.2

Password:

R2>
Interface                IP-Address       OK? Method Status                 Protocol
GigabitEthernet0/0       unassigned       YES unset  administratively down  down
GigabitEthernet0/1       10.1.3.2         YES manual up                     up
GigabitEthernet0/2       10.1.2.2         YES manual up                     up
GigabitEthernet0/3       unassigned       YES unset  administratively down  down
```

When you have finished using the other router, you can log out from your Telnet or SSH connection using the **exit** or **quit** command.

Finally, note that IOS supports a mechanism to use hotkeys to move between multiple Telnet or SSH sessions from the CLI. Basically, starting at one router, you could telnet or SSH to a router, do some commands, and instead of using the **exit** command to end your connection, you could keep the connection open while still moving back to the command prompt of the original router. For instance, if starting at Router R1, you could telnet to R2, R3, and R4, suspending but not exiting those Telnet connections. Then you could easily move between the sessions to issue new commands with a few keystrokes.

Chapter Review

One key to doing well on the exams is to perform repetitive spaced review sessions. Review this chapter's material using either the tools in the book or interactive tools for the same material found on the book's companion website. Refer to the "Your Study Plan" element for more details. Table 20-1 outlines the key review elements and where you can find them. To better track your study progress, record when you completed these activities in the second column.

Table 20-1   Chapter Review Tracking

Review Element	Review Date(s)	Resource Used
Review key topics		Book, website
Review key terms		Book, website

Review All the Key Topics

Table 20-2   Key Topics for Chapter 20

Key Topic Element	Description	Page Number
Figure 20-5	ARP tables on Layer 3 hosts, with MAC address tables on Layer 2 switch	517
Figure 20-6	How extended ping in IOS performs a better test of the reverse route	518

Key Topic Element	Description	Page Number
Figure 20-7	Why a standard ping over a LAN does not exercise a host's default router logic	519
List	Network layer problems that could cause a ping to fail between a router and host on the same LAN subnet	520
List	Testing a host's default router setting using extended ping	520
List	DNS configuration commands	522
List	Comparisons between the **ping** and **traceroute** commands	524

Key Terms You Should Know

DNS, extended ping, forward route, hostname, ICMP echo reply, ICMP echo request, ping, reverse route, traceroute

Command References

Tables 20-3 and 20-4 list configuration and verification commands used in this chapter. As an easy review exercise, cover the left column in a table, read the right column, and try to recall the command without looking. Then repeat the exercise, covering the right column, and try to recall what the command does.

Table 20-3   Chapter 20 Configuration Command Reference

Command	Description
[no] ip domain lookup	Router/switch global command to enable or disable (**no**) the device from using DNS resolution when commands use a hostname
ip domain name *name*	Router/switch global command to define the DNS domain used by this device
ip name-server *address* [*address...*]	Global command to define one or more DNS server IP addresses
ip host *name address*	Global command that defines a hostname available on the local device

Table 20-4   Chapter 20 EXEC Command Reference

Command	Description
ping {*hostname* | *address*}	EXEC command that sends ICMP Echo Request packets to the address, expecting the distant host to send ICMP Echo Reply messages in return
traceroute {*hostname* | *address*}	EXEC command that messages to a distance host, expecting to force intermediate routes to send ICMP destination unreachable messages, to identify the routers in the path to the distant host
show host	Command to list the device's known hostnames and corresponding IP addresses

20

Command	Description
show ip interface brief	A router command that lists its interfaces and IP addresses, plus a few more facts, with one line per interface
telnet {*hostname* | *address*}	Command to initiate a Telnet connection to a remote host
ssh -l *username* {*hostname* | *address*}	Command to initiate an SSH connection, for the listed username, to a remote host

Part V Review

Keep track of your part review progress with the checklist in Table P5-1. Details on each task follow the table.

Table P5-1 Part V Part Review Checklist

Activity	1st Date Completed	2nd Date Completed
Repeat All DIKTA Questions		
Answer Part Review Questions		
Review Key Topics		
Do Labs		
Watch Video		
Use Per-Chapter Interactive Review		

Repeat All DIKTA Questions

For this task, answer the "Do I Know This Already?" questions again for the chapters in this part of the book, using the PTP software.

Answer Part Review Questions

For this task, use PTP to answer the Part Review questions for this part of the book.

Review Key Topics

Review all key topics in all chapters in this part, either by browsing the chapters or by using the Key Topics application on the companion website.

Do Labs

Depending on your chosen lab tool, here are some suggestions for what to do in lab:

Pearson Network Simulator: If you use the full Pearson CCNA simulator, focus more on the configuration scenario and troubleshooting scenario labs associated with the topics in this part of the book. These types of labs include a larger set of topics and work well as Part Review activities. (See the Introduction for some details about how to find which labs are about topics in this part of the book.)

Blog Config Labs: The author's blog includes a series of configuration-focused labs that you can do on paper or with Cisco Packet Tracer in about 15 minutes. To find them, open https://www.certskills.com and look under the Labs menu item.

Other: If using other lab tools, here are a few suggestions: Make sure to experiment heavily with IPv4 addressing, static routing, and Layer 3 switching. In each case, test all your routes using **ping** and **traceroute**.

Watch Video

The companion website includes a variety of common mistake and Q&A videos organized by part and chapter. Use these videos to challenge your thinking, dig deeper, review topics, and better prepare for the exam. Make sure to bookmark a link to the companion website and use the videos for review whenever you have a few extra minutes.

Part IV began the story in this book about IP Version 4 (IPv4) addressing. Part V continued that story with how to implement addressing in Cisco routers, along with a variety of methods to route packets between local interfaces. But those topics delayed the discussion of one of the most important topics in TCP/IP, namely IP routing protocols, as discussed in Part VI.

Routers use IP routing protocols to learn about the subnets in an internetwork, choose the current-best routes to reach each subnet, and add those routes to each router's IP routing table. Cisco chose to include one and only one IP routing protocol in the CCNA 200-301 Version 1.1 blueprint: the Open Shortest Path First (OSPF) routing protocol. This entire part focuses on OSPF as an end to itself and to show the principles of routing protocols.

Part VI

OSPF

CHAPTER 21

Understanding OSPF Concepts

This chapter covers the following exam topics:

3.0 IP Connectivity

 3.2 Determine how a router makes a forwarding decision by default

  3.2.b Administrative distance

  3.2.c Routing protocol metric

 3.4 Configure and verify single area OSPFv2

  3.4.a Neighbor adjacencies

  3.4.b Point-to-point

  3.4.c Broadcast (DR/BR selection)

  3.4.d Router ID

Every enterprise uses some dynamic routing protocol inside their network so that the routers cooperatively learn routes to all subnets. But in the decades that led to TCP/IP becoming the common networking model used on all computers, several routing protocols emerged as candidates to be used by those enterprises. As a result, even today, enterprises choose from a small set of alternative routing protocols. Of those, Cisco includes Open Shortest Path First (OSPF) in the CCNA 200-301 V1.1 blueprint.

To establish come context, this chapter begins by examining the different routing protocols, their similar goals, and their differences in implementation. With that context in mind, the rest of the chapter then examines the basic concepts of how OSPF operates. The second major section of the chapter gets into the foundations of OSPF: running OSPF on each router, becoming neighbors, exchanging data about routes, and calculating IP routes to be used by the IP routing table. The final major section then looks more closely at how OSPF internally represents network topologies as a database of network links and their states—the OSPF link-state database (LSDB).

"Do I Know This Already?" Quiz

Take the quiz (either here or use the PTP software) if you want to use the score to help you decide how much time to spend on this chapter. The letter answers are listed at the bottom of the page following the quiz. Appendix C, found both at the end of the book as well as on the companion website, includes both the answers and explanations. You can also find both answers and explanations in the PTP testing software.

Table 21-1 "Do I Know This Already?" Foundation Topics Section-to-Question Mapping

Foundation Topics Section	Questions
Comparing Dynamic Routing Protocol Features	1–3
OSPF Concepts and Operation	4, 5
OSPF Areas and LSAs	6

1. Which of the following routing protocols uses link-state logic?

    a. RIPv1

    b. RIPv2

    c. EIGRP

    d. OSPF

2. Which of the following routing protocols use a metric that is, by default, at least partially affected by link bandwidth? (Choose two answers.)

    a. RIPv1

    b. RIPv2

    c. EIGRP

    d. OSPF

3. Which of the following interior routing protocols support VLSM? (Choose three answers.)

    a. RIPv1

    b. RIPv2

    c. EIGRP

    d. OSPF

4. Two routers using OSPFv2 have become neighbors and exchanged all LSAs. As a result, Router R1 now lists some OSPF-learned routes in its routing table. Which of the following best describes how R1 uses those recently learned LSAs to choose which IP routes to add to its IP routing table?

    a. R1 copies a route from every LSA into its routing table.

    b. R1 copies a route from certain types of LSAs into its routing table.

    c. R1 runs SPF against the LSAs to calculate the routes.

    d. R1 does not use the LSAs when choosing what routes to add.

5. Which of the following OSPF neighbor states is expected when the exchange of topology information is complete between two OSPF neighbors?

    a. 2-way

    b. Full

    c. Up/up

    d. Final

6. A company has a small/medium-sized network with 15 routers and 40 subnets and uses OSPFv2. Which of the following is considered an advantage of using a single-area design as opposed to a multiarea design?

   a. It reduces the CPU processing overhead on most routers.

   b. It reduces the frequency of running the SPF algorithm due to interface status changes.

   c. It allows for simpler planning and operations.

   d. It reduces memory consumption.

Foundation Topics

Comparing Dynamic Routing Protocol Features

Routers add IP routes to their routing tables using three methods: connected routes, static routes, and routes learned by using dynamic routing protocols. Before we get too far into the discussion, however, it is important to define a few related terms and clear up any misconceptions about the terms *routing protocol*, *routed protocol*, and *routable protocol*. These terms are generally defined as follows:

- **Routing protocol:** A set of messages, rules, and algorithms used by routers for the overall purpose of learning routes. This process includes the exchange and analysis of routing information. Each router chooses the best route to each subnet (path selection) and finally places those best routes in its IP routing table. Examples include RIP, EIGRP, OSPF, and BGP.

- **Routed protocol and routable protocol:** Synonyms, both terms refer to a protocol that defines packets that can be routed (forwarded) by a router. Routers forward packets defined by routed protocols. Examples include IP Version 4 (IPv4) and IP Version 6 (IPv6).

NOTE The term *path selection* sometimes refers to part of the job of a routing protocol, in which the routing protocol chooses the best route.

Even though routing protocols (such as OSPF) are different from routed protocols (such as IP), they do work together very closely. The routing process forwards IP packets, but if a router does not have any routes in its IP routing table that match a packet's destination address, the router discards the packet. Routers need routing protocols so that the routers can learn all the possible routes and add them to the routing table so that the routing process can forward (route) routable protocols such as IP.

Routing Protocol Functions

Cisco IOS software supports several IP routing protocols, performing the same general functions:

1. Learn routing information about IP subnets from neighboring routers.
2. Advertise routing information about IP subnets to neighboring routers.
3. If more than one possible route exists to reach one subnet, pick the best route based on a **metric**.
4. If the network topology changes—for example, a link fails—react by advertising that some routes have failed and pick a new currently best route. (This process is called **convergence**.)

NOTE A neighboring router connects to the same link as another router, such as the same WAN link or the same Ethernet LAN.

Figure 21-1 shows an example of three of the four functions in the list. Router R1, in the lower left of the figure, must choose the best route to reach the subnet connected off Router R2, on the bottom right of the figure. Following the steps in the figure:

Step 1. R2 advertises a route to the lower right subnet—172.16.3.0/24—to both Router R1 and R3.

Step 2. After R3 learns about the route to 172.16.3.0/24 from R2, R3 advertises that route to R1.

Step 3. R1 must choose between the two routes it learned about for reaching subnet 172.16.3.0/24—one with metric 1 from R2 and one with metric 2 from R3. R1 chooses the lower metric route through R2 (function 3).

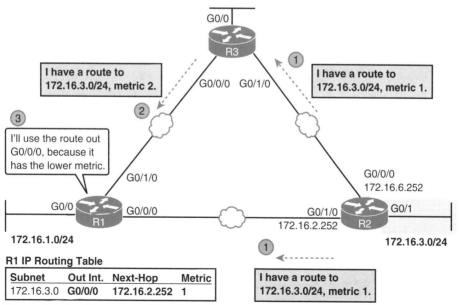

Figure 21-1 *Three of the Four Basic Functions of Routing Protocols*

The other routing protocol function, *convergence*, occurs when the topology changes—that is, when either a router or link fails or comes back up again. When something changes, the best routes available in the network can change. Convergence simply refers to the process by which all the routers collectively realize something has changed, advertise the information about the changes to all the other routers, and all the routers then choose the currently best routes for each subnet. The ability to converge quickly, without causing loops, is one of the most important considerations when choosing which IP routing protocol to use.

In Figure 21-1, convergence might occur if the link between R1 and R2 failed. In that case, R1 should stop using its old route for subnet 172.16.3.0/24 (directly through R2) and begin sending packets to R3.

Interior and Exterior Routing Protocols

IP routing protocols fall into one of two major categories: **interior gateway protocols (IGP)** or *exterior gateway protocols* (EGP). The definitions of each are as follows:

- **IGP:** A routing protocol that was designed and intended for use inside a single autonomous system (AS)

- **EGP:** A routing protocol that was designed and intended for use between different autonomous systems

NOTE   The terms *IGP* and *EGP* include the word *gateway* because routers used to be called gateways.

These definitions use another new term: *autonomous system* (AS). An AS is a network under the administrative control of a single organization. For example, a network created and paid for by a single company is probably a single AS, and a network created by a single school system is probably a single AS. Other examples include large divisions of a state or national government, where different government agencies might be able to build their own networks. Each ISP is also typically a single different AS.

Some routing protocols work best inside a single AS by design, so these routing protocols are called IGPs. Conversely, routing protocols designed to exchange routes between routers in different autonomous systems are called EGPs. Today, Border Gateway Protocol (BGP) is the only EGP.

Each AS can be assigned a number called (unsurprisingly) an *AS number* (ASN). Like public IP addresses, the Internet Assigned Numbers Authority (IANA, www.iana.org) controls the worldwide rights to assigning ASNs. It delegates that authority to other organizations around the world, typically to the same organizations that assign public IP addresses. For example, in North America, the American Registry for Internet Numbers (ARIN, www.arin.net) assigns public IP address ranges and ASNs.

Figure 21-2 shows a small view of the worldwide Internet. The figure shows two enterprises and three ISPs using IGPs (OSPF and EIGRP) inside their own networks and with BGP being used between the ASNs.

Answers to the "Do I Know This Already?" quiz:

1 D **2** C, D **3** B, C, D **4** C **5** B **6** C

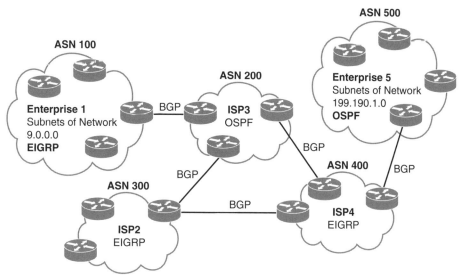

Figure 21-2 *Comparing Locations for Using IGPs and EGPs*

Comparing IGPs

Before getting into the details of OSPF, it helps to consider some comparisons between OSPF and the other IGP options. This section takes a brief look at all three routing protocols.

IGP Routing Protocol Algorithms

A routing protocol's underlying algorithm determines how the routing protocol does its job. The term *routing protocol algorithm* simply refers to the logic and processes used by different routing protocols to solve the problem of learning all routes, choosing the best route to each subnet, and converging in reaction to changes in the internetwork. Three main branches of routing protocol algorithms exist for IGP routing protocols:

- **Distance vector** (sometimes called Bellman-Ford after its creators)

- Advanced distance vector (sometimes called balanced hybrid)

- **Link-state**

Historically speaking, distance vector protocols were invented first, mainly in the early 1980s. Routing Information Protocol (RIP) was the first popularly used IP distance vector protocol, with the Cisco-proprietary Interior Gateway Routing Protocol (IGRP) being introduced a little later.

By the early 1990s, distance vector protocols' somewhat slow convergence and potential for routing loops drove the development of new alternative routing protocols that used new algorithms. Link-state protocols—in particular, Open Shortest Path First (OSPF) and Integrated Intermediate System to Intermediate System (IS-IS)—solved the main issues. They also came with a price: they required extra CPU and memory on routers, with more planning required from the network engineers.

21

NOTE All references to OSPF in this chapter refer to OSPF Version 2 (OSPFv2) unless otherwise stated.

Around the same time as the introduction of OSPF, Cisco created a proprietary routing protocol called Enhanced Interior Gateway Routing Protocol (EIGRP), which used some features of the earlier IGRP protocol. EIGRP solved the same problems as did link-state routing protocols, but EIGRP required less planning and less CPU/RAM overhead. As time went on, EIGRP was classified as a unique type of routing protocol. However, it used more distance vector features than link-state, so the industry refers to its algorithm as either an advanced distance vector protocol or as a balanced hybrid protocol.

Metrics

Routing protocols choose the best route to reach a subnet by choosing the route with the lowest metric. For example, RIP uses a counter of the number of routers (hops) between a router and the destination subnet, as shown in the example of Figure 21-1. OSPF totals the cost associated with each interface in the end-to-end route, with the cost based on link bandwidth. Table 21-2 lists the most common IP routing protocols and some details about the metric in each case.

Table 21-2   IP IGP Metrics

IGP	Metric	Description
RIPv2	Hop count	The number of routers (hops) between a router and the destination subnet
OSPF	Cost	The sum of all interface cost settings for all links in a route, with the cost default based on interface bandwidth
EIGRP	Calculation based on bandwidth and delay	Calculated based on the route's slowest link and the cumulative delay associated with each interface in the route

A brief comparison of the metric used by the older RIP versus the metric used by OSPF shows some insight into why OSPF and EIGRP surpassed RIP. Figure 21-3 shows an example in which Router B has two possible routes to subnet 10.1.1.0 on the left side of the network: a shorter route over a very slow serial link at 1544 Kbps, or a longer route over two Gigabit Ethernet WAN links.

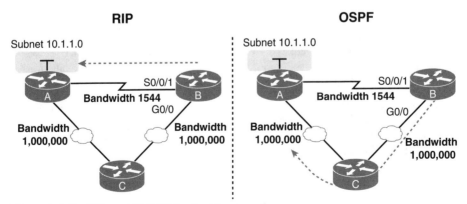

Figure 21-3 *RIP and OSPF Metrics Compared*

The left side of the figure shows the results of RIP in this network. Using hop count, Router B learns of a one-hop route directly to Router A through B's S0/0/1 interface. B also learns of a two-hop route through Router C, through B's G0/0 interface. Router B chooses the lower hop count route, which happens to go over the slow-speed serial link.

The right side of the figure shows the better choice made by OSPF based on its better metric. To cause OSPF to make the right choice, the engineer could use default settings based on the correct interface bandwidth to match the actual link speeds, thereby allowing OSPF to choose the faster route. (The **bandwidth** interface subcommand does not change the actual physical speed of the interface. It just tells IOS what speed to assume the interface is using.)

Other IGP Comparisons

Routing protocols can be compared based on many features, some of which matter to the current CCNA exam, whereas some do not. Table 21-3 introduces a few more points and lists the comparison points mentioned in this book for easier study, with a few supporting comments following the table.

Table 21-3   Interior IP Routing Protocols Compared

Feature	RIPv2	EIGRP	OSPF
Classless/sends mask in updates/supports VLSM	Yes	Yes	Yes
Algorithm (DV, advanced DV, LS)	DV	Advanced DV	LS
Supports manual summarization	Yes	Yes	Yes
Cisco-proprietary	No	Yes*	No
Routing updates are sent to a multicast IP address	Yes	Yes	Yes
Convergence	Slow	Fast	Fast
Multicast addresses used	224.0.0.9	224.0.0.10	224.0.0.5, 224.0.0.6

* Although Cisco created EIGRP and has kept it as a proprietary protocol for many years, Cisco chose to publish EIGRP as an informational RFC in 2013. This allows other vendors to implement EIGRP, while Cisco retains the rights to the protocol.

Regarding the top row of the table, classless routing protocols support variable-length subnet masks (VLSM) as well as manual route summarization by sending routing protocol messages that include the subnet masks in the message. The older RIPv1 and IGRP routing protocols—both classful routing protocols—do not.

Also, note that the older routing protocols (RIPv1, IGRP) sent routing protocol messages to IP broadcast addresses, while the newer routing protocols in the table all use IP multicast destination addresses. The use of multicasts makes the protocol more efficient and causes less overhead and fewer issues with the devices in the subnet that are not running the routing protocol.

21

OSPF Concepts and Operation

Routing protocols basically exchange information so routers can learn routes. The routers learn information about subnets, routes to those subnets, and metric information about how good each route is compared to others. The routing protocol can then choose the currently best route to each subnet, building the IP routing table.

Link-state protocols like OSPF take a little different approach to the particulars of what information they exchange and what the routers do with that information once learned. This next (second) major section narrows the focus to only link-state protocols, specifically OSPFv2.

This section begins with an overview of what OSPF does by exchanging data about the network in data structures called **link-state advertisements (LSAs)**. Then the discussion backs up a bit to provide more details about each of three fundamental parts of how OSPF operates: how OSPF routers use *neighbor* relationships, how routers exchange LSAs with neighbors, and then how routers calculate the best routes once they learn all the LSAs.

OSPF Overview

Link-state protocols build IP routes with a couple of major steps. First, the routers together build a lot of information about the network: routers, links, IP addresses, status information, and so on. Then the routers flood the information, so all routers know the same information. At that point, each router can calculate routes to all subnets, but from each router's own perspective.

Topology Information and LSAs

Routers using link-state routing protocols need to collectively advertise practically every detail about the internetwork to all the other routers. At the end of the process of *flooding* the information to all routers, every router in the internetwork has the exact same information about the internetwork. Flooding a lot of detailed information to every router sounds like a lot of work, and relative to distance vector routing protocols, it is.

Open Shortest Path First (OSPF), the most popular link-state IP routing protocol, organizes topology information using LSAs and the **link-state database (LSDB)**. Figure 21-4 represents the ideas. Each LSA is a data structure with some specific information about the network topology; the LSDB is simply the collection of all the LSAs known to a router.

Link-State Database (LSDB)

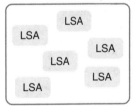

Figure 21-4 *LSA and LSDB Relationship*

Figure 21-5 shows the general idea of the flooding process, with R8 creating and flooding its *router LSA*. The router LSA for Router R8 describes the router itself, including the existence of subnet 172.16.3.0/24, as seen on the right side of the figure. (Note that Figure 21-5 shows only a subset of the information in R8's router LSA.)

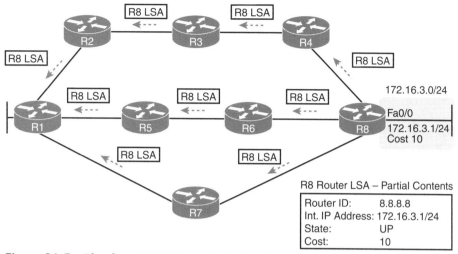

Figure 21-5 *Flooding LSAs Using a Link-State Routing Protocol*

Figure 21-5 shows the rather basic flooding process, with R8 sending the original LSA for itself, and the other routers flooding the LSA by forwarding it until every router has a copy. The flooding process causes every router to learn the contents of the LSA while preventing the LSA from being flooded around in circles. Basically, before sending an LSA to yet another neighbor, routers communicate, asking "Do you already have this LSA?" and then sending the LSA to the next neighbor only if the neighbor has not yet learned about the LSA.

Once flooded, routers do occasionally reflood each LSA. Routers reflood an LSA when some information changes (for example, when a link goes up or comes down). They also reflood each LSA based on each LSA's separate aging timer (default 30 minutes).

Applying Dijkstra SPF Math to Find the Best Routes

The link-state flooding process results in every router having an identical copy of the LSDB in memory, but the flooding process alone does not cause a router to learn what routes to add to the IP routing table. Although incredibly detailed and useful, the information in the LSDB does not explicitly state each router's best route to reach a destination.

To build routes, link-state routers have to do some math. Thankfully, you and I do not have to know the math! However, all link-state protocols use a type of math algorithm, called the Dijkstra **Shortest Path First (SPF) algorithm**, to process the LSDB. That algorithm analyzes (with math) the LSDB and builds the routes that the local router should add to the IP routing table—routes that list a subnet number and mask, an outgoing interface, and a next-hop router IP address.

Now that you have the big ideas down, the next several topics walk through the three main phases of how OSPF routers accomplish the work of exchanging LSAs and calculating routes. Those three phases are

21

Becoming neighbors: A relationship between two routers that connect to the same data link, created so that the neighboring routers have a means to exchange their LSDBs.

Exchanging databases: The process of sending LSAs to neighbors so that all routers learn the same LSAs.

Adding the best routes: The process of each router independently running SPF, on their local copy of the LSDB, calculating the best routes, and adding those to the IPv4 routing table.

Becoming OSPF Neighbors

Of everything you learn about OSPF in this chapter, OSPF neighbor concepts have the most to do with how you will configure and troubleshoot OSPF in Cisco routers. You configure OSPF to cause routers to run OSPF and become neighbors with other routers. Once that happens, OSPF does the rest of the work to exchange LSAs and calculate routers in the background, with no additional configuration required. This section discusses the fundamental concepts of OSPF neighbors.

The Basics of OSPF Neighbors

Two routers must meet some compatibility requirements to become neighbors. First, they must both use OSPF and both connect to the same data link. Two routers can become OSPF neighbors if connected to the same VLAN, or same serial link, or same Ethernet WAN link.

Additionally, the two routers must send OSPF messages that declare some OSPF settings, and those settings must be compatible. To do so, the routers send OSPF Hello messages, introducing themselves to the potential neighbor. Assuming the two potential neighbors have compatible OSPF parameters, the two form an OSPF neighbor relationship, and would be displayed in the output of the **show ip ospf neighbor** command.

The OSPF neighbor relationship also lets OSPF know when a neighbor might not be a good option for routing packets right now. Imagine R1 and R2 form a neighbor relationship, learn LSAs, and calculate routes that send packets through the other router. Months later, R1 notices that the neighbor relationship with R2 fails. That failed neighbor connection to R2 makes R1 react: R1 refloods LSAs impacted by the failed link, and R1 runs SPF to recalculate its own routes.

Finally, the OSPF neighbor model allows new routers to be dynamically discovered. That means new routers can be added to a network without requiring every router to be reconfigured. Instead, OSPF routers listen for OSPF Hello messages from new routers and react to those messages, attempting to become neighbors and exchange LSDBs.

Meeting Neighbors and Learning Their Router ID

The OSPF neighbor relationship begins by exchanging OSPF *Hello* messages, which list each router's **router ID (RID)**. OSPF RIDs are 32-bit numbers, so most command output lists these as dotted-decimal numbers (DDN). By default, IOS chooses one of the router interface's IPv4 addresses to use as its OSPF RID. However, the OSPF RID can be directly configured, as covered in the section "Configuring the OSPF Router ID" in Chapter 22, "Implementing Basic OSPF Features."

As soon as a router has chosen its OSPF RID and some interfaces come up, the router is ready to meet its OSPF neighbors. OSPF routers can become neighbors if they are connected to the same subnet. To discover other OSPF-speaking routers, a router sends multicast OSPF Hello packets to each interface and hopes to receive OSPF Hello packets from other routers connected to those interfaces. Figure 21-6 outlines the basic concept.

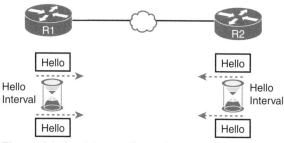

Figure 21-6 *OSPF Hello Packets*

Routers R1 and R2 both send Hello messages onto the link. They continue to send Hellos at a regular interval based on their Hello timer settings. The Hello messages themselves have the following features:

- The Hello message follows the IP packet header, with IP protocol type 89.

- Hello packets are sent to multicast IP address 224.0.0.5, a multicast IP address intended for all OSPF-speaking routers.

- OSPF routers listen for packets sent to IP multicast address 224.0.0.5, in part hoping to receive Hello packets and learn about new neighbors.

Taking a closer look, Figure 21-7 shows several of the neighbor states used by the early formation of an OSPF neighbor relationship. The figure shows the Hello messages in the center and the resulting neighbor states on the left and right edges of the figure. Each router keeps an OSPF state variable for how it views the neighbor.

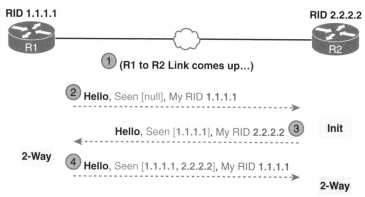

Figure 21-7 *Early Neighbor States*

Following the steps in the figure, the scenario begins with the link down, so the routers have no knowledge of each other as OSPF neighbors. As a result, they have no state (status) information about each other as neighbors, and they would not list each other in the output of the **show ip ospf neighbor** command. At Step 2, R1 sends the first Hello, so R2 learns of the existence of R1 as an OSPF router. At that point, R2 lists R1 as a neighbor, with an interim beginning state of init.

The process continues at Step 3, with R2 sending back a Hello. This message tells R1 that R2 exists, and it allows R1 to move through the init state and quickly to a 2-way state. At Step 4, R2 receives the next Hello from R1, and R2 can also move to a 2-way state.

The **2-way state** is a particularly important OSPF state. At that point, the following major facts are true:

- The router received a Hello from the neighbor, with that router's own RID listed as being seen by the neighbor.

- The router has performed all checks of settings in the Hello and considers the potential neighbor to have passed all checks so they can become neighbors.

- If both routers reach a 2-way state with each other, they are neighbors and ready to exchange their LSDB with each other.

Exchanging the LSDB Between Neighbors

One purpose of forming OSPF neighbor relationships is to allow the two neighbors to exchange their databases. This next topic works through some of the details of OSPF database exchange.

Fully Exchanging LSAs with Neighbors

Once two routers on a link reach the 2-way state, they can immediately move on to the process of database exchange. The database exchange process can be quite involved, with several OSPF messages and several interim neighbor states. This chapter is more concerned with a few of the messages and the final state when database exchange has completed: the **full state**.

After two routers decide to exchange databases, they do not simply send the contents of the entire database. First, they tell each other a list of LSAs in their respective databases—not all the details of the LSAs, just a list. (Think of these lists as checklists.) Next, each router can check which LSAs it already has and then ask the other router for only the LSAs that are not known yet.

For instance, R1 might send R2 a checklist that lists ten LSAs (using an OSPF Database Description, or DD, packet). R2 then checks its LSDB and finds six of those ten LSAs. So, R2 asks R1 (using a Link-State Request packet) to send the four additional LSAs.

Thankfully, most OSPFv2 work does not require detailed knowledge of these specific protocol steps. However, a few of the terms are used quite a bit and should be remembered. In particular, the OSPF messages that actually send the LSAs between neighbors are called **link-state update** (LSU) packets. That is, the LSU packet holds data structures called *link-state advertisements (LSAs)*. The LSAs are not packets, but rather data structures that sit inside the LSDB and describe the topology.

Figure 21-8 pulls some of these terms and processes together, with a general example. The story picks up the example shown in Figure 21-7, with Figure 21-8 showing an example of the database exchange process between Routers R1 and R2. The center shows the protocol messages, and the outer items show the neighbor states at different points in the process. Focus on two items in particular:

- The routers exchange the LSAs inside LSU packets.

- When finished, the routers reach a full state, meaning they have fully exchanged the contents of their LSDBs.

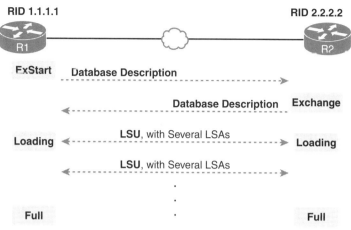

RID 1.1.1.1   **RID 2.2.2.2**

FxStart   **Database Description**

                                                  Database Description   **Exchange**

Loading   **LSU**, with Several LSAs   **Loading**

                          LSU, with Several LSAs

Full   **Full**

Figure 21-8   *Database Exchange Example, Ending in a Full State*

Maintaining Neighbors and the LSDB

Once two neighbors reach a full state, they have done all the initial work to exchange OSPF information between them. However, neighbors still have to do some small ongoing tasks to maintain the neighbor relationship.

First, routers monitor each neighbor relationship using Hello messages and two related timers: the **Hello interval** and the **Dead interval**. Routers send Hellos every Hello interval to each neighbor. Each router expects to receive a Hello from each neighbor based on the Hello interval, so if a neighbor is silent for the length of the Dead interval (by default, four times as long as the Hello interval), the loss of Hellos means that the neighbor has failed.

Next, routers must react when the topology changes as well, and neighbors play a key role in that process. When something changes, one or more routers change one or more LSAs. Then the routers must flood the changed LSAs to each neighbor so that the neighbor can change its LSDB.

For example, imagine a LAN switch loses power, so a router's G0/0 interface fails from up/up to down/down. That router updates an LSA that shows the router's G0/0 as being down. That router then sends the LSA to its neighbors, and that neighbor in turn sends it to its neighbors, until all routers again have an identical copy of the LSDB. Each router's LSDB now reflects the fact that the original router's G0/0 interface failed, so each router will then use SPF to recalculate any routes affected by the failed interface.

A third maintenance task done by neighbors is to reflood each LSA occasionally, even when the network is completely stable. By default, each router that creates an LSA also has the responsibility to reflood the LSA every 30 minutes (the default), even if no changes occur. (Note that each LSA has a separate timer, based on when the LSA was created, so there is no single big event where the network is overloaded with flooding LSAs.)

The following list summarizes these three maintenance tasks for easier review:

- Maintain neighbor state by sending Hello messages based on the Hello interval and listening for Hellos before the Dead interval expires

21

■ Flood any changed LSAs to each neighbor

■ Reflood unchanged LSAs as their lifetime expires (default 30 minutes)

Using Designated Routers on Ethernet Links

OSPF behaves differently on some types of interfaces based on a per-interface setting called the OSPF *network type*. On Ethernet links, OSPF defaults to use a network type of *broadcast*, which causes OSPF to elect one of the routers on the same subnet to act as the **designated router (DR)**. The DR plays a key role in how the database exchange process works, with different rules than with point-to-point links.

To see how, consider the example that begins with Figure 21-9. The figure shows five OSPFv2 routers on the same Ethernet VLAN. These five OSPF routers elect one router to act as the DR and one router to be a **backup designated router (BDR)**. The figure shows A and B as DR and BDR, for no other reason than the subnet with OSPF network type broadcast will have one of each.

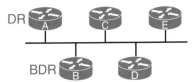

Figure 21-9   *Routers A and B Elected as DR and BDR*

The database exchange process on an Ethernet link does not happen between every pair of routers on the same VLAN/subnet. Instead, it happens between the DR and each of the other routers, with the DR making sure that all the other routers get a copy of each LSA. In other words, the database exchange happens over the flows shown in Figure 21-10.

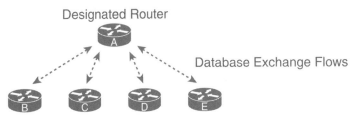

Figure 21-10   *Database Exchange to and from the DR on an Ethernet*

OSPF defines the backup designated router (BDR) role so that some router can take over for the DR should it fail. When the DR fails, the BDR takes over as DR, and some other router is elected as the new BDR.

The use of a DR/BDR, along with the use of multicast IP addresses, makes the exchange of OSPF LSDBs more efficient on networks that allow more than two routers on the same link. The DR can send a packet to all OSPF routers in the subnet by using multicast IP address 224.0.0.5. IANA reserves this address as the "All SPF Routers" multicast address just for this purpose. For instance, in Figure 21-10, the DR can send one set of messages to all the OSPF routers rather than sending one message to each router.

Similarly, any OSPF router needing to send a message to the DR and also to the BDR (so it remains ready to take over for the DR) can send those messages to the "All SPF DRs" multicast address 224.0.0.6. So, instead of having to send one set of messages to the DR and another set to the BDR, an OSPF router can send one set of messages, making the exchange more efficient.

You will see quite a bit of the DR and BDR theory in **show** commands on a router. Because the DR and BDR both do full database exchange with all the other OSPF routers in the LAN, they reach a full state with all neighbors. However, routers that are neither a DR nor a BDR—called *DROthers* by OSPF—never reach a full state because they do not exchange LSDBs directly with each other. As a result, the **show ip ospf neighbor** command on these DROther routers lists some neighbors in a 2-way state, remaining in that state under normal operation.

For instance, with OSPF working normally on the Ethernet LAN in Figure 21-10, a **show ip ospf neighbor** command on Router C (which is a DROther router) would show the following:

- Two neighbors (A and B, the DR and BDR, respectively) with a full state (called *fully adjacent neighbors*)

- Two neighbors (D and E, which are DROthers) with a 2-way state (called **neighbors**)

OSPF requires some terms to describe all neighbors versus the subset of all neighbors that reach the full state. First, all OSPF routers on the same link that reach the 2-way state—that is, they send Hello messages and the parameters match—are called *neighbors*. The subset of neighbors for which the neighbor relationship reaches the full state are called *adjacent neighbors*. Additionally, OSPFv2 RFC 2328 emphasizes this point by defining two synonyms to the term *adjacent neighbor*: **fully adjacent** and *fully adjacent neighbor*. Finally, while the terms so far refer to the neighbor, two other terms refer to the relationship: *neighbor relationship* refers to any OSPF neighbor relationship, while the term *adjacency* refers to neighbor relationships that reach a full state. Table 21-4 details the terms.

Table 21-4 Stable OSPF Neighbor States and Their Meanings

Neighbor State	Term for Neighbor	Term for Relationship
2-way	Neighbor	Neighbor Relationship
Full	Adjacent Neighbor Fully Adjacent Neighbor	Adjacency

Calculating the Best Routes with SPF

OSPF LSAs contain useful information, but they do not contain the specific information that a router needs to add to its IPv4 routing table. In other words, a router cannot just copy information from the LSDB into a route in the IPv4 routing table. The LSAs individually are more like pieces of a jigsaw puzzle, with the picture shown by the completed puzzle showing a topology map of the entire network. So, to know what routes to add to the routing table, each router must do some SPF math to choose the best routes from that router's perspective. The router then adds each route to its routing table: a route with a subnet number and mask, an outgoing interface, and a next-hop router IP address.

Although engineers do not need to know the details of how SPF does the math, they do need to know how to predict which routes SPF will choose as the best route. The SPF algorithm calculates all the routes for a subnet—that is, all possible routes from the router to the destination subnet. If more than one route exists, the router compares the metrics, picking the best (lowest) metric route to add to the routing table. Although the SPF math can be complex, engineers with a network diagram, router status information, and simple addition can calculate the metric for each route, predicting what SPF will choose.

Once SPF has identified a route, OSPF calculates the metric for a route as follows:

The sum of the OSPF interface costs for all outgoing interfaces in the route.

Figure 21-11 shows an example with three possible routes from R1 to Subnet X (172.16.3.0/24) at the bottom of the figure.

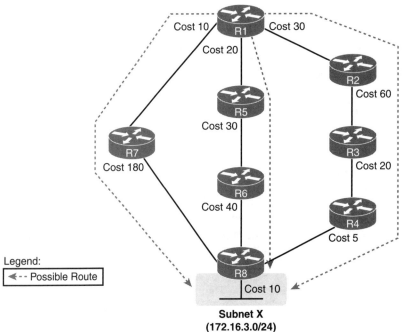

Figure 21-11 *SPF Tree to Find R1's Route to 172.16.3.0/24*

> **NOTE** OSPF considers the costs of the outgoing interfaces (only) in each route. It does not add the cost for incoming interfaces in the route.

Table 21-5 lists the three routes shown in Figure 21-11, with their cumulative costs, showing that R1's best route to 172.16.3.0/24 starts by going through R5.

Table 21-5 Comparing R1's Three Alternatives for the Route to 172.16.3.0/24

Route	Location in Figure 21-11	Cumulative Cost
R1–R7–R8	Left	10 + 180 + 10 = 200
R1–R5–R6–R8	Middle	20 + 30 + 40 + 10 = 100
R1–R2–R3–R4–R8	Right	30 + 60 + 20 + 5 + 10 = 125

As a result of the SPF algorithm's analysis of the LSDB, R1 adds a route to subnet 172.16.3.0/24 to its routing table, with the next-hop router of R5.

In real OSPF networks, an engineer can do the same process by knowing the OSPF cost for each interface. Armed with a network diagram, the engineer can examine all routes, add the costs, and predict the metric for each route.

OSPF Areas and LSAs

OSPF can be used in some networks with very little thought about design issues. You just turn on OSPF in all the routers, put all interfaces into the same area (usually area 0), and it works! Figure 21-12 shows one such network example, with 11 routers and all interfaces in area 0.

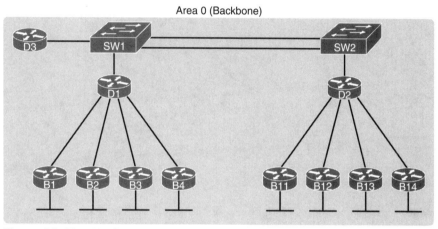

Figure 21-12 *Single-Area OSPF*

Using a single-area design works well in small- to medium-sized networks. In fact, the CCNA 200-301 V1.1 blueprint specifically mentions **single-area OSPF**, omitting **multiarea OSPF**. However, it helps to think through the concept of areas even for CCNA preparation. The next few pages look at how OSPF area design works, with more reasons as to why areas help make larger OSPF networks work better.

OSPF Areas

OSPF area design follows a couple of basic rules. To apply the rules, start with a clean drawing of the internetwork, with routers, and all interfaces. Then choose the area for each router interface, as follows:

- Put all interfaces connected to the same subnet inside the same area.

- An area should be contiguous.

- Some routers may be internal to an area, with all interfaces assigned to that single area.

- Some routers may be Area Border Routers (ABRs) because some interfaces connect to the backbone area, and some connect to nonbackbone areas.

- All nonbackbone areas must have a path to reach the backbone area (area 0) by having at least one ABR connected to both the backbone area and the nonbackbone area.

Figure 21-13 shows one example. An engineer started with a network diagram that showed all 11 routers and their links. On the left, the engineer put four WAN links and the LANs connected to branch routers B1 through B4 into area 1. Similarly, he placed the links to branches B11 through B14 and their LANs in area 2. Both areas need a connection to the backbone area, area 0, so he put the LAN interfaces of D1 and D2 into area 0, along with D3, creating the backbone area.

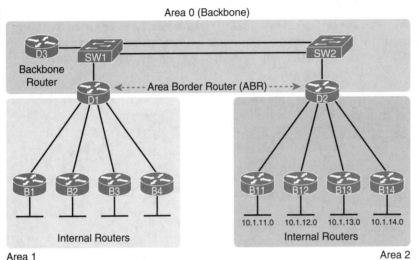

Figure 21-13   *Three-Area OSPF with D1 and D2 as ABRs*

The figure also shows a few important OSPF area design terms. Table 21-6 summarizes the meaning of these terms, plus some other related terms, but pay closest attention to the terms from the figure.

Table 21-6   OSPF Design Terminology

Term	Description
Area Border Router (ABR)	An OSPF router with interfaces connected to the backbone area and to at least one other area
Backbone router	A router connected to the backbone area (includes ABRs)
Internal router	A router in one area (not the backbone area)
Area	A set of routers and links that shares the same detailed LSDB information, but not with routers in other areas, for better efficiency
Backbone area	A special OSPF area to which all other areas must connect—area 0
Intra-area route	A route to a subnet inside the same area as the router
Interarea route	A route to a subnet in an area of which the router is not a part

How Areas Reduce SPF Calculation Time

Figure 21-13 shows a sample area design and some terminology related to areas, but it does not show the power and benefit of the areas. To understand how areas reduce the work SPF has to do, you need to understand what changes about the LSDB inside an area, as a result of the area design.

SPF spends most of its processing time working through all the topology details, namely routers and the links that connect routers. Areas reduce SPF's workload because, for a given area, the LSDB lists only routers and links inside that area, as shown on the left side of Figure 21-14.

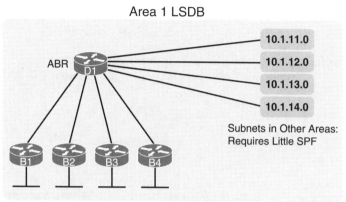

Detailed Topology Data (Routers and Links):
Requires Heavy SPF

Figure 21-14   *Smaller Area 1 LSDB Concept*

While the LSDB has less topology information, it still needs information about all subnets in all areas so that each router can create IPv4 routes for all subnets. So, with an area design, OSPFv2 uses brief summary information about the subnets in other areas. These summary LSAs do not include topology information about the other areas; however, each summary LSA *does* list a subnet ID and mask of a subnet in some other area. Summary LSAs do not require SPF processing at all. Instead, these subnets all appear like subnets connected to the ABR (in Figure 21-14, ABR D1).

Using multiple areas improves OSPF operations in many ways for larger networks. The following list summarizes some of the key points arguing for the use of multiple areas in larger OSPF networks:

- Routers require fewer CPU cycles to process the smaller per-area LSDB with the SPF algorithm, reducing CPU overhead and improving convergence time.

- The smaller per-area LSDB requires less memory.

- Changes in the network (for example, links failing and recovering) require SPF calculations only on routers in the area where the link changed state, reducing the number of routers that must rerun SPF.

- Less information must be advertised between areas, reducing the bandwidth required to send LSAs.

(OSPFv2) Link-State Advertisements

Many people tend to get a little intimidated by OSPF LSAs when first learning about them. Commands like **show ip ospf database** in its many variations list a lot of information about the LSDB. Those details appear to be in some kind of code, using lots of numbers. It can seem like a bit of a mess.

However, if you examine LSAs while thinking about OSPF areas and area design, some of the most common LSA types will make a lot more sense. For instance, think about the LSDB in one area. The topology in one area includes routers and the links between the routers. As it turns out, OSPF defines the first two types of LSAs to define those exact details, as follows:

■ One *router LSA* for each router in the area

■ One *network LSA* for each network that has a DR plus one neighbor of the DR

Next, think about the subnets in the other areas. The ABR creates summary information about each subnet in one area to advertise into other areas—basically just the subnet IDs and masks—as a third type of LSA:

■ One *summary LSA* for each subnet ID that exists in a different area

The next few pages discuss these three LSA types in a little more detail; Table 21-7 lists some information about all three for easier reference and study.

Table 21-7   The Three OSPFv2 LSA Types Seen with a Multiarea OSPF Design

LSA Name	LSA Type	Primary Purpose	Contents of LSA
Router	1	Describe a router	RID, interfaces, IP address/mask, current interface state (status)
Network	2	Describe a network that has a DR and BDR	DR and BDR IP addresses, subnet ID, mask
Summary	3	Describe a subnet in another area	Subnet ID, mask, RID of ABR that advertises the LSA

Router LSAs Build Most of the Intra-Area Topology

OSPF needs very detailed topology information inside each area. The routers inside area X need to know all the details about the topology inside area X. And the mechanism to give routers all these details is for the routers to create and flood router (Type 1) and network (Type 2) LSAs about the routers and links in the area.

Router LSAs, also known as Type 1 LSAs, describe the router in detail. Each lists a router's RID, its interfaces, its IPv4 addresses and masks, its interface state, and notes about what neighbors the router knows about via each of its interfaces.

To see a specific instance, first review Figure 21-15. It lists internetwork topology, with subnets listed. Because it's a small internetwork, the engineer chose a single-area design, with all interfaces in backbone area 0.

With the single-area design planned for this small internetwork, the LSDB will contain four router LSAs. Each router creates a router LSA for itself, with its own RID as the LSA identifier. The LSA lists that router's own interfaces, IP address/mask, with pointers to neighbors.

Once all four routers have copies of all four router LSAs, SPF can mathematically analyze the LSAs to create a model. The model looks a lot like the concept drawing in Figure 21-16. Note that the drawing shows each router with an obvious RID value. Each router has pointers that represent each of its interfaces, and because the LSAs identify neighbors, SPF can figure out which interfaces connect to which other routers.

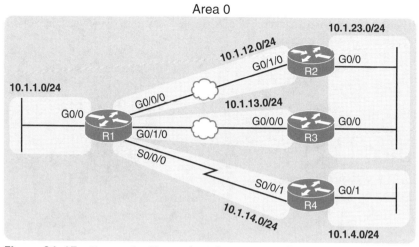

Figure 21-15 *Enterprise Network with Six IPv4 Subnets*

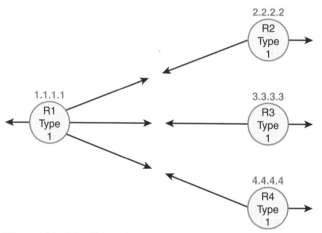

Figure 21-16 *Type 1 LSAs, Assuming a Single-Area Design*

Network LSAs Complete the Intra-Area Topology

Whereas router LSAs define most of the intra-area topology, network LSAs define the rest. As it turns out, when OSPF elects a DR on some subnet *and* that DR has at least one neighbor, OSPF treats that subnet as another node in its mathematical model of the network. To represent that network, the DR creates and floods a network (Type 2) LSA for that network (subnet).

For instance, back in Figure 21-15, one Ethernet LAN and two Ethernet WANs exist. The Ethernet LAN between R2 and R3 will elect a DR, and the two routers will become neighbors; so, whichever router is the DR will create a network LSA. Similarly, R1 and R2 connect with an Ethernet WAN, so the DR on that link will create a network LSA. Likewise, the DR on the Ethernet WAN link between R1 and R3 will also create a network LSA.

21

Figure 21-17 shows the completed version of the intra-area LSAs in area 0 with this design. Note that the router LSAs reference the network LSAs when they exist, which lets the SPF processes connect the pieces together.

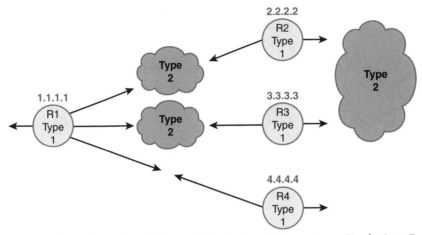

Figure 21-17   *Type 1 and Type 2 LSAs in Area 0, Assuming a Single-Area Design*

Finally, note that in this single-area design example, no summary (Type 3) LSAs exist at all. These LSAs represent subnets in other areas, and there are no other areas. Given that the CCNA 200-301 V1.1 exam blueprint refers specifically to single-area OSPF designs, this section stops at showing the details of the intra-area LSAs (Types 1 and 2).

Chapter Review

One key to doing well on the exams is to perform repetitive spaced review sessions. Review this chapter's material using either the tools in the book or interactive tools for the same material found on the book's companion website. Refer to the "Your Study Plan" element for more details. Table 21-8 outlines the key review elements and where you can find them. To better track your study progress, record when you completed these activities in the second column.

Table 21-8   Chapter Review Tracking

Review Element	Review Date(s)	Resource Used:
Review key topics		Book, website
Review key terms		Book, website
Answer DIKTA questions		Book, PTP
Review memory tables		Website

Review All the Key Topics

Table 21-9   Key Topics for Chapter 21

Key Topic Element	Description	Page Number
List	Functions of IP routing protocols	541
List	Definitions of IGP and EGP	542
List	Types of IGP routing protocols	543
Table 21-2	IGP metrics	544
List	Key facts about the OSPF 2-way state	550
Table 21-4	Key OSPF neighbor states	553
Item	Definition of how OSPF calculates the cost for a route	554
Figure 21-11	Example of calculating the cost for multiple competing routes	554
List	OSPF area design rules	555
Figure 21-13	Sample OSPF multiarea design with terminology	556
Table 21-6	OSPF design terms and definitions	556

Key Terms You Should Know

2-way state, Area Border Router (ABR), backbone area, backup designated router (BDR), convergence, Dead interval, designated router (DR), distance vector, full state, fully adjacent, Hello interval, interior gateway protocol (IGP), internal router, link-state, link-state advertisement (LSA), link-state database (LSDB), link-state update, metric, multiarea OSPF, neighbor, router ID (RID), Shortest Path First (SPF) algorithm, single-area OSPF

21

CHAPTER 22

Implementing Basic OSPF Features

This chapter covers the following exam topics:

3.0 IP Connectivity

    3.2 Determine how a router makes a forwarding decision by default

        3.2.b Administrative distance

        3.2.c Routing protocol metric

    3.4 Configure and verify single area OSPFv2

        3.4.a Neighbor adjacencies

        3.4.b Point-to-point

        3.4.c Broadcast (DR/BR selection)

        3.4.d Router ID

OSPFv2 requires only a few configuration commands if you rely on default settings. To use OSPF, all you need to do is enable OSPF on each interface you intend to use in the network, and OSPF uses messages to discover neighbors and learn routes through those neighbors. OSPF performs many background tasks, and you can discover details about that work using a large number of OSPF **show** commands. However, configuring OSPF, using mostly default settings for all the optional features, requires only a few commands. This chapter sets about to help you learn those minimal settings.

The first major section of this chapter focuses on traditional OSPFv2 configuration using the **network** command, along with the large variety of associated **show** commands. This section teaches you how to make OSPFv2 operate with default settings and convince yourself that it really is working through use of those **show** commands.

The second major section shows an alternative configuration option called OSPF interface mode, in contrast with the traditional OSPF configuration shown in the first section of the chapter. This mode uses the **ip ospf** *process-id* **area** *area-number* configuration command instead of the **network** command.

Along the way, the first major section includes the detail of how to set the OSPF router ID (RID). While optional, configuring a predictable and stable OSPF RID allows easier operation and troubleshooting of OSPF and may be the most important of the optional OSPF settings.

"Do I Know This Already?" Quiz

Take the quiz (either here or use the PTP software) if you want to use the score to help you decide how much time to spend on this chapter. The letter answers are listed at the bottom of the page following the quiz. Appendix C, found both at the end of the book as well as on the companion website, includes both the answers and explanations. You can also find both answers and explanations in the PTP testing software.

Table 22-1 "Do I Know This Already?" Foundation Topics Section-to-Question Mapping

Foundation Topics Section	Questions
Implementing OSPFv2 Using network Commands	1–4
Implementing OSPFv2 Using Interface Subcommands	5, 6

1. Which of the following **network** commands, following the command **router ospf 1**, enables OSPF on interfaces whose IP addresses are 10.1.1.1, 10.1.100.1, and 10.1.120.1?

   a. network 10.0.0.0 0.0.0.0 area 0

   b. network 10.0.0.0 0.255.255.255 area 0

   c. network 10.0.0.0 0.0.0.255 area 0

   d. network 10.0.0.0 0.0.255.255 area 0

2. Which of the following **network** commands, following the command **router ospf 1**, tells this router to start using OSPF on interfaces whose IP addresses are 10.1.1.1, 10.1.100.1, and 10.1.120.1?

   a. network 10.1.0.0 0.0.255.255 area 0

   b. network 10.0.0.0 0.255.255.0 area 0

   c. network 10.1.1.0 0.x.1x.0 area 0

   d. network 10.1.1.0 255.0.0.0 area 0

3. Which of the following commands list the OSPF neighbors off interface serial 0/0? (Choose two answers.)

   a. show ip ospf neighbor

   b. show ip ospf interface brief

   c. show ip neighbor

   d. show ip interface

   e. show ip ospf neighbor serial 0/0

4. When reloading and choosing a new OSPF router ID (RID), a router had working interfaces loopback 1 with IP address 10.8.8.8, loopback 2 with address 10.7.7.7, and GigabitEthernet0/0/0 with 10.9.9.9. The router did not have a **router-id** command in the OSPF process configuration. What RID did the router choose?

   a. 10.7.7.7

   b. 10.8.8.8

   c. 10.9.9.9

   d. The router would fail to choose an RID.

5. An engineer migrates from a more traditional OSPFv2 configuration that uses **network** commands in OSPF configuration mode to instead use OSPFv2 interface configuration. Which of the following commands configures the area number assigned to an interface in this new configuration?

  a. The **area** command in interface configuration mode

  b. The **ip ospf** command in interface configuration mode

  c. The **router ospf** command in interface configuration mode

  d. The **network** command in interface configuration mode

6. An enterprise avoids using the OSPF **network** command, instead preferring to enable OSPF per-interface with the **ip ospf** *process-id* **area** *area-id* interface subcommand. Which **show** command identifies whether an interface has been configured with the **ip ospf** *process-id* **area** *area-id* interface subcommand? (Choose two answers.)

  a. The **show ip ospf interface** command

  b. The **show ip ospf interface brief** command

  c. The **show ip ospf neighbor** command

  d. The **show ip protocols** command

Foundation Topics

Implementing OSPFv2 Using network Commands

After an OSPF design has been chosen—a task that can be complex in larger IP internetworks—the configuration can be as simple as enabling OSPF on each router interface and placing that interface in the correct OSPF area. This first major section of the chapter focuses on the required configuration using the traditional OSPFv2 **network** command along with one optional configuration setting: how to set the **OSPF router-id**. Additionally, this section works through how to show the various lists and tables that confirm how OSPF is working.

For reference and study, the following list outlines the configuration steps covered in this first major section of the chapter:

Step 1. Use the **router ospf** *process-id* global command to enter OSPF configuration mode for a particular OSPF process.

Step 2. (Optional) Configure the OSPF router ID by doing the following:

  a. Use the **router-id** *id-value* router subcommand to define the router ID, or

  b. Use the **interface loopback** *number* global command, along with an **ip address** *address mask* command, to configure an IP address on a loopback interface (chooses the highest IP address of all working loopbacks), or

  c. Rely on an interface IP address (chooses the highest IP address of all working nonloopbacks).

Step 3. Use one or more **network** *ip-address wildcard-mask* **area** *area-id* router subcommands to enable OSPFv2 on any interfaces matched by the configured address and mask, enabling OSPF on the interface for the listed area.

Figure 22-1 shows the relationship between the OSPF configuration commands, with the idea that the configuration creates a routing process in one part of the configuration, and then indirectly enables OSPF on each interface. The configuration does not name the interfaces on which OSPF is enabled, instead requiring IOS to apply some logic by comparing the OSPF **network** command to the interface **ip address** commands. The upcoming example discusses more about this logic.

Configuration

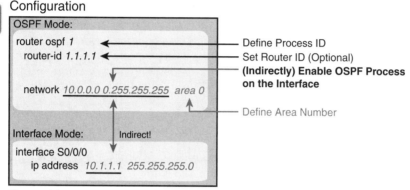

Figure 22-1   *Organization of OSPFv2 Configuration with the* network *Command*

OSPF Single-Area Configuration

Figure 22-2 shows a sample network that will be used for most examples throughout this chapter. All links reside in area 0, making the area design a single-area design, with four routers. You can think of Router R1 as a router at a central site, with WAN links to each remote site. Routers R2 and R3 might be at one large remote site that needs two WAN links and two routers for WAN redundancy, with both routers connected to the LAN at that remote site. Router R4 might be a typical smaller remote site with a single router needed for that site.

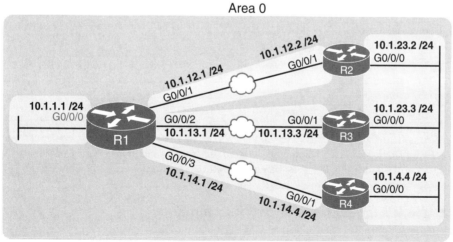

Figure 22-2   *Sample Network for OSPF Single-Area Configuration*

22

Example 22-1 shows the IPv4 addressing configuration on Router R1, before getting into the OSPF detail.

Example 22-1   *IPv4 Address Configuration on R1*

```
interface GigabitEthernet0/0/0
 ip address 10.1.1.1 255.255.255.0
!
interface GigabitEthernet0/0/1
 ip address 10.1.12.1 255.255.255.0
!
interface GigabitEthernet0/0/2
 ip address 10.1.13.1 255.255.255.0
!
interface GigabitEthernet0/0/3
 ip address 10.1.14.1 255.255.255.0
```

The OSPF configuration begins with the **router ospf** *process-id* global command, which puts the user in OSPF configuration mode, and sets the OSPF *process-id* value. The *process-id* number just needs to be unique on the local router, matching between various commands in a router. The *process-id* does not need to match between neighboring routers or other routers in the same area. The value can be any integer between 1 and 65,535.

Second, the configuration needs one or more **network** commands in OSPF mode. These commands tell the router to find its local interfaces that match the first two parameters on the **network** command. Then, for each matched interface, the router enables OSPF on those interfaces, discovers neighbors, creates neighbor relationships, and assigns the interface to the area listed in the **network** command. (Note that the area can be configured as either an integer or a dotted-decimal number, but this book makes a habit of configuring the area number as an integer. The integer area numbers range from 0 through 4,294,967,295.)

Example 22-2 shows an example configuration on Router R1 from Figure 22-2. The **router ospf 1** command enables OSPF process 1, and the single **network** command enables OSPF on all interfaces shown in the figure.

Example 22-2   *OSPF Single-Area Configuration on R1 Using One* **network** *Command*

```
router ospf 1
 network 10.0.0.0 0.255.255.255 area 0
```

For the specific **network** command in Example 22-2, any matched interfaces are assigned to area 0. However, the first two parameters—the *ip_address* and *wildcard_mask* parameter values of 10.0.0.0 and 0.255.255.255—need some explaining. In this case, the command matches all interfaces shown for Router R1; the next topic explains why.

Wildcard Matching with the network Command

The key to understanding the traditional OSPFv2 configuration shown in this first example is to understand the OSPF **network** command. The OSPF **network** command compares the

---

Answers to the "Do I Know This Already?" quiz:

1 B **2** A **3** A, E **4** B **5** B **6** A, D

first parameter in the command to each interface IP address on the local router, trying to find a match. However, rather than comparing the entire number in the **network** command to the entire IPv4 address on the interface, the router can compare a subset of the octets, based on the wildcard mask, as follows:

Wildcard 0.0.0.0: Compare all four octets. In other words, the numbers must exactly match.

Wildcard 0.0.0.255: Compare the first three octets only. Ignore the last octet when comparing the numbers.

Wildcard 0.0.255.255: Compare the first two octets only. Ignore the last two octets when comparing the numbers.

Wildcard 0.255.255.255: Compare the first octet only. Ignore the last three octets when comparing the numbers.

Wildcard 255.255.255.255: Compare nothing; this wildcard mask means that all addresses will match the **network** command.

Basically, a wildcard mask value of decimal 0 in an octet tells IOS to compare to see if the numbers match, and a value of 255 tells IOS to ignore that octet when comparing the numbers.

The **network** command provides many flexible options because of the wildcard mask. For example, in Router R1, many **network** commands could be used, with some matching all interfaces, and some matching a subset of interfaces. Table 22-2 shows a sampling of options, with notes.

Table 22-2   Example OSPF **network** Commands on R1, with Expected Results

Command	Logic in Command	Matched Interfaces
network 10.1.0.0 0.0.255.255	Match addresses that begin with 10.1	G0/0/0
		G0/0/1
		G0/0/1
		G0/0/2
network 10.0.0.0 0.255.255.255	Match addresses that begin with 10	G0/0/0
		G0/0/1
		G0/0/1
		G0/0/2
network 0.0.0.0 255.255.255.255	Match all addresses	G0/0/0
		G0/0/1
		G0/0/1
		G0/0/2
network 10.1.13.0 0.0.0.255	Match addresses that begin with 10.1.13	G0/0/2
network 10.1.13.1 0.0.0.0	Match one address: 10.1.13.1	G0/0/2

The wildcard mask gives the local router its rules for matching its own interfaces. To show examples of the different options, Example 22-3 shows the configuration on routers R2, R3, and R4, each using different wildcard masks. Note that all three routers (R2, R3, and R4) enable OSPF on all the interfaces shown in Figure 22-2.

22

Example 22-3 *OSPF Configuration on Routers R2, R3, and R4*

```
! R2 configuration next - one network command enables OSPF on both interfaces
interface GigabitEthernet0/0/0
 ip address 10.1.23.2 255.255.255.0
!
interface GigabitEthernet0/0/1
 ip address 10.1.12.2 255.255.255.0
!
router ospf 1
 network 10.0.0.0 0.255.255.255 area 0
```
```
! R3 configuration next - One network command per interface
interface GigabitEthernet0/0/0
 ip address 10.1.23.3 255.255.255.0
!
interface GigabitEthernet0/0/1
 ip address 10.1.13.3 255.255.255.0
!
router ospf 1
 network 10.1.13.3 0.0.0.0 area 0
 network 10.1.23.3 0.0.0.0 area 0
```
```
! R4 configuration next - One network command per interface with wildcard 0.0.0.255
interface GigabitEthernet0/0/0
 ip address 10.1.4.4 255.255.255.0
!
interface GigabitEthernet0/0/1
 ip address 10.1.14.4 255.255.255.0
!
router ospf 1
 network 10.1.14.0 0.0.0.255 area 0
 network 10.1.4.0 0.0.0.255 area 0
```

Finally, note that OSPF uses the same wildcard mask logic as defined by Cisco IOS access control lists. The section titled "Finding the Right Wildcard Mask to Match a Subnet" section in Chapter 6 of the *CCNA 200-301 Official Cert Guide, Volume 2*, Second Edition, provides more detail about wildcard masks.

NOTE If the wildcard mask octet in a **network** command is 255, the matching address octet should be configured as a 0. Interestingly, IOS will accept a **network** command that breaks this rule, but if you configure a wildcard mask octet as 255, then IOS changes the corresponding address octet to a 0 before putting it into the running configuration file. For example, IOS will change a typed command that begins with **network 1.2.3.4 0.0.255.255** to **network 1.2.0.0 0.0.255.255**.

Verifying OSPF Operation

As mentioned in Chapter 21, "Understanding OSPF Concepts," OSPF routers use a three-step process to eventually add OSPF-learned routes to the IP routing table. First, they create neighbor relationships. Then they build and flood LSAs between those neighbors so each router in the same area has a copy of the same LSDB. Finally, each router independently computes its own IP routes using the SPF algorithm and adds them to its routing table. This next topic works through how to display the results of each of those steps, which lets you confirm whether OSPF has worked correctly or not.

The **show ip ospf neighbor, show ip ospf database**, and **show ip route** commands display information to match each of these three steps, respectively. Figure 22-3 summarizes the commands you can use (and others) when verifying OSPF.

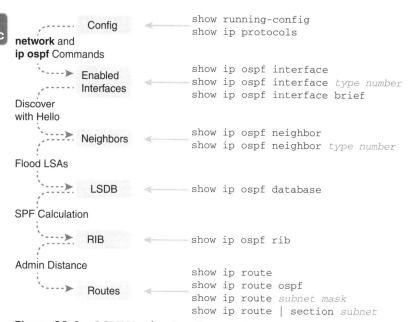

Figure 22-3   *OSPF Verification Commands*

Many engineers begin OSPF verification by looking at the output of the **show ip ospf neighbor** command. For instance, Example 22-4 shows a sample from Router R1, which should have one neighbor relationship each with routers R2, R3, and R4. Example 22-4 shows all three.

Example 22-4   *OSPF Neighbors on Router R1 from Figure 22-2*

```
R1# show ip ospf neighbor
Neighbor ID     Pri   State         Dead Time   Address       Interface
2.2.2.2           1   FULL/DR       00:00:37    10.1.12.2     GigabitEthernet0/0/1
3.3.3.3           1   FULL/DR       00:00:37    10.1.13.3     GigabitEthernet0/0/2
4.4.4.4           1   FULL/BDR      00:00:34    10.1.14.4     GigabitEthernet0/0/3
```

22

The detail in the output mentions several important facts, and for most people, working right to left works best in this case. For example, look at the headings:

Interface: This is the local router's interface connected to the neighbor. For example, the first neighbor in the list is reachable through R1's G0/0/1 interface.

Address: This is the neighbor's IP address on that link. Again, this first neighbor, the neighbor, which is R2, uses IP address 10.1.12.2.

State: While many possible states exist, for the details discussed in this chapter, FULL is the correct and fully working state in this case.

Neighbor ID: This is the router ID of the neighbor.

> **NOTE**   Examples 22-4 through 22-8 use configuration not shown here that sets the RID values to easily identify the routers, using 2.2.2.2 for Router R2, 3.3.3.3 for Router R3, and so on. The upcoming section "Configuring the OSPF Router ID" shows how to set the RID.

Once OSPF convergence has completed, a router should list each neighbor. On links that use a designated router (DR), the state will also list the role of the neighboring router after the / (DR, BDR, or DROther). As a result, the normal working states will be:

FULL/ -: The neighbor state is full, with the "-" instead of letters meaning that the link does not use a DR/BDR.

FULL/DR: The neighbor state is full, and the neighbor is the DR.

FULL/BDR: The neighbor state is full, and the neighbor is the backup DR (BDR).

FULL/DROTHER: The neighbor state is full, and the neighbor is neither the DR nor BDR. (It also implies that the local router is a DR or BDR because the state is FULL.)

2WAY/DROTHER: The neighbor state is 2-way, and the neighbor is neither the DR nor BDR—that is, a DROther router. (It also implies that the local router is also a DROther router because otherwise the state would reach a full state.)

Once a router's OSPF process forms a working neighbor relationship, the routers exchange the contents of their LSDBs, either directly or through the DR on the subnet. Example 22-5 shows the contents of the LSDB on Router R1. Interestingly, with a single-area design, all the routers will have the same LSDB contents once all neighbors are up and all LSAs have been exchanged. So, the **show ip ospf database** command in Example 22-5 should list the same exact information, no matter on which of the four routers it is issued.

Example 22-5   *OSPF Database on Router R1 from Figure 22-2*

```
R1# show ip ospf database

            OSPF Router with ID (1.1.1.1) (Process ID 1)



            Router Link States (Area 0)
```

```
Link ID            ADV Router        Age        Seq#           Checksum Link count
1.1.1.1            1.1.1.1           431        0x8000008F 0x00DCCA 5
2.2.2.2            2.2.2.2           1167       0x8000007F 0x009DA1 2
3.3.3.3            3.3.3.3           441        0x80000005 0x002FB1 1
4.4.4.4            4.4.4.4           530        0x80000004 0x007F39 2



                   Net Link States (Area 0)


Link ID            ADV Router        Age        Seq#           Checksum
10.1.12.2          2.2.2.2           1167       0x8000007C 0x00BBD5
10.1.13.3          3.3.3.3           453        0x80000001 0x00A161
10.1.14.1          4.4.4.4           745        0x8000007B 0x004449
10.1.23.3          3.3.3.3           8          0x80000001 0x00658F
```

For the purposes of this book, do not be concerned about the specifics in the output of this command. However, for perspective, note that the LSDB should list one "Router Link State" (Type 1 Router LSA) for each of the routers in the same area, so with the design based on Figure 22-2, the output lists four Type 1 LSAs. Also, with all default settings in this design, the routers will create a total of four Type 2 Network LSAs as shown, one each for the subnets that have a DR and contain at least two routers in that subnet (the three WAN links plus the LAN to which both R2 and R3 connect).

Next, Example 22-6 shows R4's IPv4 routing table with the **show ip route** command. As configured, with all links working, R4 has connected routes to two of those subnets and should learn OSPF routes to the other subnets.

Example 22-6 *IPv4 Routes Added by OSPF on Router R4 from Figure 22-2*

```
R4# show ip route
Codes: L - local, C - connected, S - static, R - RIP, M - mobile, B - BGP
       D - EIGRP, EX - EIGRP external, O - OSPF, IA - OSPF inter area
       N1 - OSPF NSSA external type 1, N2 - OSPF NSSA external type 2
       E1 - OSPF external type 1, E2 - OSPF external type 2
! Additional legend lines omitted for brevity


Gateway of last resort is not set


      10.0.0.0/8 is variably subnetted, 9 subnets, 2 masks
O        10.1.1.0/24 [110/2] via 10.1.14.1, 00:27:24, GigabitEthernet0/0/1
C        10.1.4.0/24 is directly connected, GigabitEthernet0/0/0
L        10.1.4.4/32 is directly connected, GigabitEthernet0/0/0
O        10.1.12.0/24 [110/2] via 10.1.14.1, 00:27:24, GigabitEthernet0/0/1
O        10.1.13.0/24 [110/2] via 10.1.14.1, 00:25:15, GigabitEthernet0/0/1
C        10.1.14.0/24 is directly connected, GigabitEthernet0/0/1
L        10.1.14.4/32 is directly connected, GigabitEthernet0/0/1
O        10.1.23.0/24 [110/3] via 10.1.14.1, 00:27:24, GigabitEthernet0/0/1
```

22

Any time you want to check OSPF on a router in a small design like the ones in the book, you can count all the subnets, then count the subnets connected to the local router, and know that OSPF should learn routes to the rest of the subnets. Then just use the **show ip route** command and add up how many connected and OSPF routes exist as a quick check of whether all the routes have been learned or not.

In this case, Router R4 has two connected subnets, but six subnets exist per the figure, so Router R4 should learn four OSPF routes. Next look for the code of "O" on the left, which identifies a route as being learned by OSPF. The output lists four such IP routes: one for the LAN subnet off Router R1, one for the LAN subnet connected to both R2 and R3, and one each for the WAN subnets from R1 to R2 and R1 to R3.

Next, examine the first route (to subnet 10.1.1.0/24). It lists the subnet ID and mask, identifying the subnet. It also lists two numbers in brackets. The first, 110, is the administrative distance of the route. All the OSPF routes in this example use the default of 110 (see Table 24-4 in Chapter 24, "OSPF Neighbors and Route Selection," for the list of administrative distance values). The second number, 2, is the OSPF metric for this route. The route also lists the forwarding instructions: the next-hop IP address (10.1.14.1) and R4's outgoing interface (G0/0/1).

> **NOTE** The section "Floating Static Routes" in Chapter 17, "Configuring IPv4 Addresses and Static Routes," introduced the concept of administrative distance; however, the section "Multiple Routes Learned from Competing Sources," in Chapter 24 discusses the topic in more depth.

Verifying OSPF Configuration

Once you can configure OSPF with confidence, you will likely verify OSPF focusing on **OSPF neighbors** and the IP routing table as just discussed. However, if OSPF does not work immediately, you may need to circle back and check the configuration. To do so, you can use these steps:

- If you have enable mode access, use the **show running-config** command to examine the configuration.

- If you have only user mode access, use the **show ip protocols** command to re-create the OSPF configuration.

- Use the **show ip ospf interface [brief]** command to determine whether the router enabled OSPF on the correct interfaces or not based on the configuration.

The best way to verify the configuration begins with the **show running-config** command, of course. However, the **show ip protocols** command repeats the details of the OSPFv2 configuration and does not require enable mode access. Example 22-7 does just that for Router R3.

Example 22-7   *Router R3 Configuration and the* **show ip protocols** *Command*

```
R3# show running-config | section router ospf 1
router ospf 1
  network 10.1.13.3 0.0.0.0 area 0
  network 10.1.23.3 0.0.0.0 area 0
  router-id 3.3.3.3

R3# show ip protocols
*** IP Routing is NSF aware ***

Routing Protocol is "ospf 1"
  Outgoing update filter list for all interfaces is not set
  Incoming update filter list for all interfaces is not set
  Router ID 3.3.3.3
  Number of areas in this router is 1. 1 normal 0 stub 0 nssa
  Maximum path: 4
  Routing for Networks:
    10.1.13.3 0.0.0.0 area 0
    10.1.23.3 0.0.0.0 area 0
  Routing Information Sources:
    Gateway          Distance       Last Update
    1.1.1.1                110        02:05:26
    4.4.4.4                110        02:05:26
    2.2.2.2                110        01:51:16
  Distance: (default is 110)
```

The highlighted output emphasizes some of the configuration. The first highlighted line repeats the parameters on the **router ospf 1** global configuration command. (The second highlighted item points out the router's router ID, which will be discussed in the next section.) The third set of highlighted lines begins with a heading of "Routing for Networks:" followed by two lines that closely resemble the parameters on the configured **network** commands. In fact, closely compare those last two highlighted lines with the **network** configuration commands at the top of the example, and you will see that they mirror each other, but the **show** command just leaves out the word *network*. For instance:

Configuration: **network 10.1.13.3 0.0.0.0 area 0**

show Command: **10.1.13.3 0.0.0.0 area 0**

IOS interprets the **network** commands to choose interfaces on which to run OSPF, so it could be that IOS chooses a different set of interfaces than you predicted. To check the list of interfaces chosen by IOS, use the **show ip ospf interface brief** command, which lists all interfaces that have been enabled for OSPF processing. Verifying the interfaces can be a useful step if you have issues with OSPF neighbors because OSPF must first be enabled on an interface before a router will attempt to discover neighbors on that interface. Example 22-8 shows a sample from Router R1.

22

Example 22-8 *Router R1* show ip ospf interface brief *Command*

```
R1# show ip ospf interface brief
Interface    PID   Area            IP Address/Mask    Cost   State   Nbrs F/C
Gi0/0/0      1     0               10.1.1.1/24        1      DR      0/0
Gi0/0/1      1     0               10.1.12.1/24       1      BDR     1/1
Gi0/0/2      1     0               10.1.13.1/24       1      BDR     1/1
Gi0/0/3      1     0               10.1.14.1/24       1      DR      1/1
```

The **show ip ospf interface brief** command lists one line per interface, showing all the interfaces on which OSPF has been enabled. Each line identifies the OSPF process ID (per the **router ospf** *process-id* command), the area, the interface IP address, and the number of neighbors found via each interface.

You may use the command in Example 22-8 quite often, but the **show ip ospf interface** command (without the **brief** keyword) gives much more detail about OSPF per-interface settings. Example 23-4 in Chapter 23, "Implementing Optional OSPF Features," shows an example of the entire output of that command.

Configuring the OSPF Router ID

While OSPF has many other optional features, most enterprise networks that use OSPF choose to configure each router's OSPF router ID. OSPF-speaking routers must have a router ID (RID) for proper operation. By default, routers will choose an interface IP address to use as the RID. However, many network engineers prefer to choose each router's router ID, so command output from commands like **show ip ospf neighbor** lists more recognizable router IDs.

To choose its RID, a Cisco router uses the following process when the router reloads and brings up the OSPF process. Note that the router stops looking for a router ID to use once one of the steps identifies a value to use.

1. If the **router-id** *rid* OSPF subcommand is configured, this value is used as the RID.

2. If any loopback interfaces have an IP address configured, and the interface has an interface status of up, the router picks the highest numeric IP address among these loopback interfaces.

3. The router picks the highest numeric IP address from all other interfaces whose interface status code (first status code) is up. (In other words, an interface in up/down state will be included by OSPF when choosing its router ID.)

The first and third criteria should make some sense right away: the RID is either configured or is taken from a working interface's IP address. However, this book has not yet explained the concept of a *loopback interface*, as mentioned in Step 2.

A loopback interface is a virtual interface that can be configured with the **interface loopback** *interface-number* command, where *interface-number* is an integer. Loopback interfaces are always in an "up and up" state unless administratively placed in a shutdown state. For example, a simple configuration of the command **interface loopback 0**, followed by **ip address 2.2.2.2 255.255.255.0**, would create a loopback interface and assign it an IP address. Because loopback interfaces do not rely on any hardware, these interfaces can be up/up whenever IOS is running, making them good interfaces on which to base an OSPF RID.

Example 22-9 shows the configuration that existed in Routers R1 and R2 before the creation of the **show** command output earlier in this chapter. R1 set its router ID using the direct method, while R2 used a loopback IP address. Example 22-10 that follows shows the output of the **show ip ospf** command on R1, which identifies the OSPF RID used by R1.

Example 22-9 *OSPF Router ID Configuration Examples*

```
! R1 Configuration first
router ospf 1
 router-id 1.1.1.1
 network 10.1.0.0 0.0.255.255 area 0

! R2 Configuration next
!
interface Loopback2
 ip address 2.2.2.2 255.255.255.255
```

Example 22-10 *Confirming the Current OSPF Router ID*

```
R1# show ip ospf
 Routing Process "ospf 1" with ID 1.1.1.1
! lines omitted for brevity
```

Routers need a stable OSPF RID because any change to the OSPF RID causes a router to close existing neighbor relationships and remove all routes learned through those neighbors. To keep the RID stable, a router chooses its RID when the router first initializes (at power-on or per the **reload** command). So the RID might change at the next reload when the router re-evaluates the RID choice rules based on the current conditions.

However, routers do support one scenario to update their RID without a **reload**, which can be useful for testing in lab. To do so, configure the OSPF **router-id** OSPF subcommand followed by the **clear ip ospf process** EXEC command.

Implementing Multiarea OSPF

Even though the current CCNA 200-301 V1.1 exam blueprint mentions single area but not multiarea OSPF, you only need to learn one more idea to know how to configure multiarea OSPF. So, this chapter takes a brief page to show how.

For example, consider a multiarea OSPF design as shown in Figure 22-4. It uses the same routers and IP addresses as shown earlier in Figure 22-2, on which all the examples in this chapter have been based so far. However, the design shows three areas instead of the single-area design shown in Figure 22-2.

Configuring the routers in a multiarea design is almost just like configuring OSPFv2 for a single area. To configure multiarea OSPF, all you need is a valid OSPF area design (for instance, like Figure 22-4) and a configuration that places each router interface into the correct area per that design. For example, both of R4's interfaces connect to links in area 4, making R4 an internal router, so any **network** commands on Router R4 will list area 4.

22

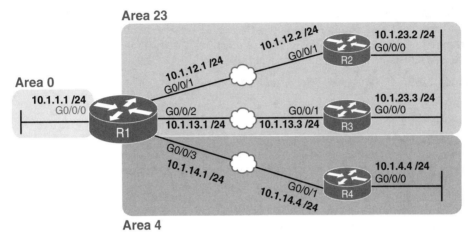

Figure 22-4   *Area Design for an Example Multiarea OSPF Configuration*

Example 22-11 shows a sample configuration for Router R1. To make the configuration clear, it uses **network** commands with a wildcard mask of 0.0.0.0, meaning each **network** command matches a single interface. Each interface will be placed into either area 0, 23, or 4 to match the figure.

Example 22-11   *OSPF Configuration on R1, Placing Interfaces into Different Areas*

```
router ospf 1
 network 10.1.1.1 0.0.0.0 area 0
 network 10.1.12.1 0.0.0.0 area 23
 network 10.1.13.1 0.0.0.0 area 23
 network 10.1.14.1 0.0.0.0 area 4
```

Implementing OSPFv2 Using Interface Subcommands

From the earliest days of OSPFv2 support in Cisco routers, the configuration used the OSPF **network** command as discussed in this chapter. However, that configuration style can be confusing, and it does require some interpretation. As a result, Cisco added another option for OSPFv2 configuration called OSPF interface configuration.

The newer interface-style OSPF configuration still enables OSPF on interfaces, but it does so directly with the **ip ospf** interface subcommand. Instead of matching interfaces with indirect logic using **network** commands, you directly enable OSPFv2 on interfaces by configuring an interface subcommand on each interface.

OSPF Interface Configuration Example

To show how OSPF interface configuration works, this example basically repeats the example shown earlier in the chapter using the traditional OSPFv2 configuration with **network** commands. So, before looking at the OSPFv2 interface configuration, take a moment to look back to review traditional OSPFv2 configuration with Figure 22-2 and Examples 22-2 and 22-3.

After reviewing the traditional configuration, consider this checklist, which details how to convert from the old-style configuration in Example 22-2 and Example 22-3 to use interface configuration:

Step 1. Use the **no network** *network-id* **area** *area-id* subcommands in OSPF configuration mode to remove the **network** commands.

Step 2. Add one **ip ospf** *process-id* **area** *area-id* command in interface configuration mode under each interface on which OSPF should operate, with the correct OSPF process (*process-id*) and the correct OSPF area number.

Figure 22-5 repeats the design for both the original examples in this chapter and for this upcoming interface configuration example.

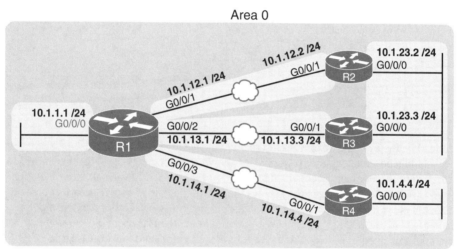

Figure 22-5   *Area Design Used in the Upcoming OSPF Interface Config Example*

Example 22-2 shows a single **network** command: **network 10.0.0.0 0.255.255.255 area 0**. Example 22-12 follows the steps in the migration checklist, beginning with the removal of the previous configuration using the **no network 10.0.0.0 0.255.255.255 area 0** command. The example then shows the addition of the **ip ospf 1 area 0** command on each of the interfaces on Router R1, enabling OSPF process 1 on the interface and placing each interface into area 0.

Example 22-12   *Migrating to Use OSPF Interface Subcommand Configuration*

```
R1# configure terminal
Enter configuration commands, one per line.  End with CNTL/Z.
R1(config)# router ospf 1
R1(config-router)# no network 10.0.0.0 0.255.255.255 area 0
R1(config-router)#
*Apr  8 19:35:24.994: %OSPF-5-ADJCHG: Process 1, Nbr 2.2.2.2 on GigabitEthernet0/0/1
from FULL to DOWN, Neighbor Down: Interface down or detached
*Apr  8 19:35:24.994: %OSPF-5-ADJCHG: Process 1, Nbr 3.3.3.3 on GigabitEthernet0/0/2
from FULL to DOWN, Neighbor Down: Interface down or detached
```

22

```
*Apr  8 19:35:24.994: %OSPF-5-ADJCHG: Process 1, Nbr 4.4.4.4 on GigabitEthernet0/0/3
from FULL to DOWN, Neighbor Down: Interface down or detached
R1(config-router)# interface g0/0/0
R1(config-if)# ip ospf 1 area 0
R1(config-if)# interface g0/0/1
R1(config-if)# ip ospf 1 area 0
R1(config-if)#
*Apr  8 19:35:52.970: %OSPF-5-ADJCHG: Process 1, Nbr 2.2.2.2 on GigabitEthernet0/0/1
from LOADING to FULL, Loading Done
R1(config-if)# interface g0/0/2
R1(config-if)# ip ospf 1 area 0
R1(config-if)#
*Apr  8 19:36:13.362: %OSPF-5-ADJCHG: Process 1, Nbr 3.3.3.3 on GigabitEthernet0/0/2
from LOADING to FULL, Loading Done
R1(config-if)# interface g0/0/3
R1(config-if)# ip ospf 1 area 0
R1(config-if)#
*Apr  8 19:37:05.398: %OSPF-5-ADJCHG: Process 1, Nbr 4.4.4.4 on GigabitEthernet0/0/3
from LOADING to FULL, Loading Done
R1(config-if)#
```

When reading the example, read from top to bottom, and also consider the details about the failed and recovered neighbor relationships shown in the log messages. Removing the network command disabled OSPF on all interfaces on Router R1, causing all three neighbor relationships to fail. The example then shows the addition of the **ip ospf 1 area 0** command on the LAN interface, which enables OSPF but does not cause a neighbor relationship to form, because no other OSPF routers exist in that subnet. Then the example shows the same command added to each of the WAN links in succession, and in each case, the OSPF neighbor available over that WAN link comes up (as noted in the log messages).

NOTE A router's configuration can include both a **network** router subcommand and an **ip ospf** interface subcommand that enable OSPF on the same interface. If those commands refer to different area numbers, IOS uses the area number from the **ip ospf** interface subcommand. Additionally, multiple **network** commands can match the same interface. In that case, IOS uses the order in which the commands appear in OSPF configuration mode.

Verifying OSPF Interface Configuration

OSPF operates the same way whether you use the new style or old style of configuration. The OSPF area design works the same, neighbor relationships form the same way, routers negotiate to become the DR and BDR the same way, and so on. However, you can see a few small differences in **show** command output when using the newer OSPFv2 configuration if you look closely.

The **show ip protocols** command relists most of the routing protocol configuration, so it does list some different details if you use interface configuration versus the **network** command. With the **ip ospf** interface subcommands, the output lists the phrase "Interfaces Configured Explicitly," as highlighted in Example 22-13. The example first shows the relevant parts of the

show ip protocols command when using interface configuration on Router R1, and then lists the same portions of the command from when R1 used **network** commands.

Example 22-13 *Differences in* show ip protocols *Output: Old- and New-Style OSPFv2 Configuration*

```
! First, with the new interface configuration
R1# show ip protocols
! … beginning lines omitted for brevity
  Routing for Networks:
  Routing on Interfaces Configured Explicitly (Area 0):
    GigabitEthernet0/0/0
    GigabitEthernet0/0/1
    GigabitEthernet0/0/2
    GigabitEthernet0/0/3
  Routing Information Sources:
    Gateway         Distance       Last Update
    4.4.4.4              110       00:09:30
    2.2.2.2              110       00:10:49
    3.3.3.3              110       05:20:07
  Distance: (default is 110)

! For comparison, the old results with the use of the OSPF network command
R1# show ip protocols
! … beginning lines omitted for brevity
  Routing for Networks:
    10.1.0.0 0.0.255.255 area 0
! … ending line omitted for brevity
```

Another small piece of different output exists in the **show ip ospf interface** [*interface*] command. The command lists details about OSPF settings for the interface(s) on which OSPF is enabled. The output also makes a subtle reference to whether that interface was enabled for OSPF with the old or new configuration style. Example 22-14 also begins with output based on interface configuration on Router R1, followed by the output that would exist if R1 still used the old-style **network** command.

Example 22-14 *Differences in* show ip ospf interface *Output with OSPFv2 Interface Configuration*

```
! First, with the new interface configuration
R1# show ip ospf interface g0/0/1
GigabitEthernet0/0/0 is up, line protocol is up
  Internet Address 10.1.12.1/24, Area 0, Attached via Interface Enable
! Lines omitted for brevity

! For comparison, the old results with the use of the OSPF network command
R1# show ip ospf interface g0/0/1
GigabitEthernet0/0/0 is up, line protocol is up
  Internet Address 10.1.12.1/24, Area 0, Attached via Network Statement
! … ending line omitted for brevity
```

22

Other than these small differences in a few **show** commands, the rest of the commands show nothing different depending on the style of configuration. For instance, the **show ip ospf interface brief** command does not change depending on the configuration style, nor do the **show ip ospf database**, **show ip ospf neighbor**, or **show ip route** commands.

Chapter Review

One key to doing well on the exams is to perform repetitive spaced review sessions. Review this chapter's material using either the tools in the book or interactive tools for the same material found on the book's companion website. Refer to the "Your Study Plan" element for more details. Table 22-3 outlines the key review elements and where you can find them. To better track your study progress, record when you completed these activities in the second column.

Table 22-3   Chapter Review Tracking

Review Element	Review Date(s)	Resource Used
Review key topics		Book, website
Review key terms		Book, website
Answer DIKTA questions		Book, PTP
Review Config Checklists		Book, website
Review command tables		Book
Do labs		Blog
Watch video		Website

Review All the Key Topics

Table 22-4   Key Topics for Chapter 22

Key Topic Element	Description	Page Number
Figure 22-1	Organization of OSPFv2 configuration with the **network** command	565
List	Example OSPF wildcard masks and their meaning	567
Figure 22-3	OSPF verification commands	569
Example 22-4	Example of the **show ip ospf neighbor** command	569
List	Neighbor states and their meanings	570
List	Rules for setting the router ID	574
Example 22-14	Differences in **show ip ospf interface** output with OSPF interface configuration	579

Key Terms You Should Know

OSPF neighbor, OSPF router-id

Command References

Tables 22-5 and 22-6 list configuration and verification commands used in this chapter. As an easy review exercise, cover the left column in a table, read the right column, and try to recall the command without looking. Then repeat the exercise, covering the right column, and try to recall what the command does.

Table 22-5   Chapter 22 Configuration Command Reference

Command	Description
router ospf *process-id*	Global command that enters OSPF configuration mode for the listed process
network *ip-address wildcard-mask* area *area-id*	Router subcommand that enables OSPF on interfaces matching the address/wildcard combination and sets the OSPF area
ip ospf *process-id* area *area-number*	Interface subcommand to enable OSPF on the interface and to assign the interface to a specific OSPF area
ip ospf cost *interface-cost*	Interface subcommand that sets the OSPF cost associated with the interface
bandwidth *bandwidth*	Interface subcommand that directly sets the interface bandwidth (Kbps)
auto-cost reference-bandwidth *number*	Router subcommand that tells OSPF the numerator in the Reference_bandwidth/Interface_bandwidth formula used to calculate the OSPF cost based on the interface bandwidth
router-id *id*	OSPF command that statically sets the router ID
interface loopback *number*	Global command to create a loopback interface and to navigate to interface configuration mode for that interface

Table 22-6   Chapter 22 EXEC Command Reference

Command	Description
show ip ospf	Lists information about the OSPF process running on the router, including the OSPF router ID, areas to which the router connects, and the number of interfaces in each area.
show ip ospf interface brief	Lists the interfaces on which the OSPF protocol is enabled (based on the **network** commands), including passive interfaces.
show ip ospf interface [*type number*]	Lists a long section of settings, status, and counters for OSPF operation on all interfaces, or on the listed interface, including the Hello and Dead Timers.
show ip protocols	Shows routing protocol parameters and current timer values.
show ip ospf neighbor [*type number*]	Lists brief output about neighbors, identified by neighbor router ID, including current state, with one line per neighbor; optionally, limits the output to neighbors on the listed interface.
show ip ospf neighbor *neighbor-ID*	Lists the same output as the **show ip ospf neighbor** detail command, but only for the listed neighbor (by neighbor RID).

22

Command	Description
show ip ospf database	Lists a summary of the LSAs in the database, with one line of output per LSA. It is organized by LSA type (first type 1, then type 2, and so on).
show ip route	Lists all IPv4 routes.
show ip route ospf	Lists routes in the routing table learned by OSPF.
clear ip ospf process	Resets the OSPF process, resetting all neighbor relationships and also causing the process to make a choice of OSPF RID.

CHAPTER 23

Implementing Optional OSPF Features

This chapter covers the following exam topics:

3.0 IP Connectivity

> **3.2 Determine how a router makes a forwarding decision by default**
>
> > **3.2.b Administrative distance**
> >
> > **3.2.c Routing protocol metric**
>
> **3.4 Configure and verify single area OSPFv2**
>
> > **3.4.a Neighbor adjacencies**
> >
> > **3.4.b Point-to-point**
> >
> > **3.4.c Broadcast (DR/BR selection)**
> >
> > **3.4.d Router ID**

The previous chapter showed how to configure the core OSPF settings to make OSPF work. This chapter examines a variety of optional OSPF settings, chosen for two reasons. First, the CCNA exam topics mention or imply coverage of many of the optional features mentioned in this chapter. Second, the optional features listed here happen to be relatively popular in production networks.

The chapter begins with a section about OSPF network types. As a setting on each interface, the OSPF network type dictates whether the router attempts to dynamically discover neighbors, and once discovered, whether routers on the link use a designated router (DR) or not. The section also discusses how to influence which router wins the DR election using OSPF priority and router IDs (RIDs).

The final section then moves on to discuss a variety of smaller optional OSPF configuration topics. The features include topics such as how to use passive interfaces, how to change OSPF costs (which influences the routes OSPF chooses), and how to create a default route advertised by OSPF.

"Do I Know This Already?" Quiz

Take the quiz (either here or use the PTP software) if you want to use the score to help you decide how much time to spend on this chapter. The letter answers are listed at the bottom of the page following the quiz. Appendix C, found both at the end of the book as well as on the companion website, includes both the answers and explanations. You can also find both answers and explanations in the PTP testing software.

Table 23-1 "Do I Know This Already?" Foundation Topics Section-to-Question Mapping

Foundation Topics Section	Questions
OSPF Network Types	1–4
Additional Optional OSPFv2 Features	5–6

1. Routers R1 and R2, with router IDs 1.1.1.1 and 2.2.2.2, connect over an Ethernet WAN link. If using all default OSPF settings, if the WAN link initializes for both routers at the same time, which of the following answers are true? (Choose two answers.)

   a. Router R1 will become the DR.

   b. Router R1 will dynamically discover the existence of Router R2.

   c. Router R2 will be neither the DR nor the BDR.

   d. Router R1's **show ip ospf neighbor** command will list R2 with a state of "FULL/DR."

2. Routers R1 and R2, with router IDs 1.1.1.1 and 2.2.2.2, connect over an Ethernet WAN link. The configuration uses all defaults, except giving R1 an interface priority of 11 and changing both routers to use OSPF network type point-to-point. If the WAN link initializes for both routers at the same time, which of the following answers are true? (Choose two answers.)

   a. Router R1 will become the DR.

   b. Router R1 will dynamically discover the existence of Router R2.

   c. Router R2 will be neither the DR nor the BDR.

   d. Router R2's **show ip ospf neighbor** command will list R1 with a state of "FULL/DR."

3. Per the command output, with how many routers is Router R9 fully adjacent over its Gi0/0 interface?

   ```
   R9# show ip ospf interface brief
   Interface    PID   Area      IP Address/Mask    Cost  State Nbrs F/C
   Gi0/0        1     0         10.1.1.1/24        1     DROTH 2/5
   ```

   a. 7

   b. 0

   c. 5

   d. 2

4. Routers R1 and R2, which use default priority settings, become neighbors, with R1 as the DR and R2 as the BDR. The engineer then configures R2's interface to use OSPF priority 100. Which answers correctly predict any changes in the OSPF neighbor relationship?

   a. Router R2 will immediately become the DR.

   b. Router R2 will become the DR after the neighbor relationship fails.

   c. Router R2 will immediately stop filling the BDR role.

   d. Router R2 will become the DR after four OSPF Hello intervals.

5. Which of the following configuration settings on a router does not influence which IPv4 route a router chooses to add to its IPv4 routing table when using OSPFv2?

   a. **auto-cost reference-bandwidth**

   b. **delay**

   c. **bandwidth**

   d. **ip ospf cost**

6. A network engineer configures the **ip ospf hello-interval 15** subcommand under the interfaces that connect OSPF neighbors R1 and R2 but with no use of the **ip ospf dead-interval** subcommand. Eventually, Router R1's OSPF process fails, but the link between R1 and R2 remains working. How long after Router R1's last Hello does R2 consider its neighbor relationship with R1 to fail?

   a. 10 seconds

   b. 15 seconds

   c. 40 seconds

   d. 60 seconds

Foundation Topics

OSPF Network Types

Two CCNA 200-301 V1.1 exam topics might be completely misunderstood without taking a closer look at some default OSPF settings. In particular, the following exam topics refer to a specific per-interface OSPF setting called the *network type*—even listing the keywords used to configure the setting in the exam topics:

   3.4.b: **point-to-point**

   3.4.c: **broadcast** (DR/BDR selection)

OSPF includes a small number of network types as a setting on each OSPF-enabled interface. The setting tells the router whether or not to dynamically discover OSPF neighbors (versus requiring the static configuration of the neighboring router's IP address) and whether or not the router should attempt to use a designated router (DR) and backup designated router (BDR) in the subnet. Of the two OSPF network types included in the CCNA exam topics, both cause routers to dynamically discover neighbors, but one calls for the use of a DR, whereas the other does not. Table 23-2 summarizes the features of the two OSPF network types mentioned in the exam topics.

Table 23-2 Two OSPF Network Types and Key Behaviors

Network Type Keyword	Dynamically Discovers Neighbors	Uses a DR/BDR
broadcast	Yes	Yes
point-to-point	Yes	No

The rest of this first major section of the chapter explores each type.

23

The OSPF Broadcast Network Type

OSPF defaults to use a **broadcast network type** on all types of Ethernet interfaces. Note that all the Ethernet interfaces in the examples in Chapter 22, "Implementing Basic OSPF Features," relied on that default setting.

To see all the details of how the OSPF broadcast network type works, this chapter begins with a different design than the examples in Chapter 22, instead using a single-area design that connects four routers to the same subnet, as shown in Figure 23-1. All links reside in area 0, making the design a single-area design.

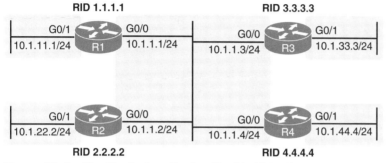

Figure 23-1 *The Single-Area Design Used in This Chapter*

To get a sense for how OSPF operates with the broadcast network type, imagine that all four routers use a straightforward OSPF interface configuration like the Router R1 configuration shown in Example 23-1. Both GigabitEthernet interfaces on all four routers default to use network type broadcast. Note that the configuration on routers R2, R3, and R4 mirrors R1's configuration except that they use router IDs 2.2.2.2, 3.3.3.3, and 4.4.4.4, respectively, and they use the IP addresses shown in the figure.

Example 23-1 *R1 OSPF Configuration to Match Figure 23-1*

```
router ospf 1
 router-id 1.1.1.1
!
interface gigabitEthernet0/0
 ip ospf 1 area 0
!
interface gigabitEthernet0/1
 ip ospf 1 area 0
```

This simple design gives us a great backdrop from which to observe the results of the broadcast network type on each router. Both interfaces (G0/0 and G0/1) on each router use the broadcast network type and perform the following actions:

- Attempt to discover neighbors by sending OSPF Hellos to the 224.0.0.5 multicast address (an address reserved for sending packets to all OSPF routers in the subnet)

- Attempt to elect a DR and BDR on each subnet

- On the interface with no other routers on the subnet (G0/1), become the DR

■ On the interface with three other routers on the subnet (G0/0), be either DR, BDR, or a DROther router

■ When sending OSPF messages to the DR or BDR, send the messages to the all-OSPF-DRs multicast address 224.0.0.6

Example 23-2 shows some of the results using the **show ip ospf neighbor** command. Note that R1 lists R2, R3, and R4 as neighbors (based on their 2.2.2.2, 3.3.3.3, and 4.4.4.4 router IDs), confirming that R1 dynamically discovered the other routers. Also, note that the output lists 4.4.4.4 as the DR and 3.3.3.3 as the BDR.

Example 23-2   *R1's List of Neighbors*

```
R1# show ip ospf neighbor

Neighbor ID     Pri   State          Dead Time   Address      Interface
2.2.2.2          1    2WAY/DROTHER   00:00:35    10.1.1.2     GigabitEthernet0/0
3.3.3.3          1    FULL/BDR       00:00:33    10.1.1.3     GigabitEthernet0/0
4.4.4.4          1    FULL/DR        00:00:35    10.1.1.4     GigabitEthernet0/0
```

Verifying Operations with Network Type Broadcast

As discussed in the section "Using Designated Routers on Ethernet Links" in Chapter 21, "Understanding OSPF Concepts," all discovered routers on the link should become neighbors and at least reach the *2-way* state. For all neighbor relationships that include the DR and/or BDR, the neighbor relationship should further reach the *full* state. That section defined the term *fully adjacent* as a special term that refers to neighbors that reach this full state.

The design in Figure 23-1, with four routers on the same LAN, provides just enough routers so that one neighbor relationship will remain in a 2-way state and not reach the full state, as a perfectly normal way for OSPF to operate. Figure 23-2 shows the current conditions when the **show** commands in this chapter were gathered, with R4 as the DR, R3 as the BDR, and with R1 and R2 as DROther routers.

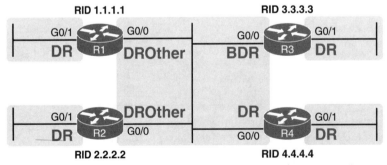

Figure 23-2   *OSPF DR, BDR, and DROther Roles in the Network*

Now consider Router R1's neighbors as listed in Example 23-2. R1 has three neighbors, all reachable out its G0/0 interface. However, R1's **show ip ospf neighbor** command refers to the state of R1's relationship with the neighbor: 2-way with router 2.2.2.2. Because both R1 and R2 currently serve as DROther routers—that is, they wait ready to become the BDR if either the DR or BDR fails—their neighbor relationship remains in a 2-way state.

Examining Example 23-2 one last time, R1, as a DROther router itself, has two neighbor relationships that reach a full state: R1's neighbor adjacency with DR R4 and R1's neighbor adjacency with BDR R3. But R1 has a total of three neighbors, all reachable off R1's G0/0 interface.

The next example emphasizes that R1 has three neighbors off its G0/0 interface, with only two as fully adjacent. The far right of the **show ip ospf interface brief** command output in Example 23-3 shows "2/3." meaning two fully adjacent neighbors and three total neighbors on that interface. Also, note that this command's "State" column differs from the **show ip ospf neighbor** commands, because it lists the local router's role on the interface, with R1's G0/1 acting as DR and R1's G0/0 acting as a DROther router.

Example 23-3 *Router R1 OSPF Interfaces: Local Role and Neighbor Counts*

```
R1# show ip ospf interface brief
Interface    PID    Area         IP Address/Mask    Cost   State  Nbrs F/C
Gi0/1        1      0            10.1.11.1/24       1      DR     0/0
Gi0/0        1      0            10.1.1.1/24        1      DROTH  2/3
```

So far, this topic has described the effect of the OSPF broadcast network type by taking advantage of the default setting on Ethernet interfaces. To see the setting, use the **show ip ospf interface** command, as shown in Example 23-4. The first highlighted item identifies the network type. However, this command's output restates many of the facts seen in both the **show ip ospf neighbor** and **show ip ospf interface brief** commands in Examples 23-2 and 23-3, so take the time to browse through all of Example 23-4 and focus on the additional highlights to see those familiar items.

Example 23-4 *Displaying OSPF Network Type Broadcast*

```
R1# show ip ospf interface g0/0
GigabitEthernet0/0 is up, line protocol is up
  Internet Address 10.1.1.1/24, Area 0, Attached via Interface Enable
  Process ID 1, Router ID 1.1.1.1, Network Type BROADCAST, Cost: 1
  Topology-MTID    Cost    Disabled    Shutdown      Topology Name
       0            1         no          no            Base
  Enabled by interface config, including secondary ip addresses
  Transmit Delay is 1 sec, State DROTHER, Priority 1
  Designated Router (ID) 4.4.4.4, Interface address 10.1.1.4
  Backup Designated router (ID) 3.3.3.3, Interface address 10.1.1.3
  Timer intervals configured, Hello 10, Dead 40, Wait 40, Retransmit 5
    oob-resync timeout 40
    Hello due in 00:00:00
  Supports Link-local Signaling (LLS)
```

```
Cisco NSF helper support enabled

IETF NSF helper support enabled

Index 1/1/1, flood queue length 0

Next 0x0(0)/0x0(0)/0x0(0)

Last flood scan length is 0, maximum is 1

Last flood scan time is 0 msec, maximum is 0 msec

Neighbor Count is 3, Adjacent neighbor count is 2

   Adjacent with neighbor 3.3.3.3   (Backup Designated Router)

   Adjacent with neighbor 4.4.4.4   (Designated Router)

Suppress hello for 0 neighbor(s)
```

Although you would not need to configure an Ethernet interface to use the broadcast network type, for reference, IOS defaults to that setting on Ethernet interfaces per default command **ip ospf network broadcast.**

Using Priority and RID to Influence the DR/BDR Election

In some cases, you might want to influence the OSPF DR election. However, before deciding that makes sense in every case, note that OSPF DR/BDR election rules will not result in a specific router always being the DR, and another always being the BDR, assuming that each is up and working. In short, here are the rules once a DR and BDR have been elected:

- If the DR fails, the BDR becomes the DR, and a new BDR is elected.

- When a better router enters the subnet, no preemption of the existing DR or BDR occurs.

As a result of these rules, while you can configure a router to be the best (highest priority) router to become the DR in an election, doing so only increases that router's statistical chances of being the DR at a given point in time. If the router with the highest priority fails, other routers will become DR and BDR, and the best router will not be DR again until the current DR and BDR fail, causing new elections.

However, in some cases, you may want to influence the DR/BDR election. To do so, use these settings, listed here in order of precedence:

- **The highest OSPF interface priority:** The highest value wins during an election, with values ranging from 0 to 255. (A value of 0 prevents the router from ever becoming the DR.)

- **The highest OSPF Router ID:** If the priority ties, the election chooses the router with the highest OSPF RID.

For example, imagine all four routers in the design shown in Figure 23-1 trying to elect the DR and BDR at the same time—for instance, after a power hit in which all four routers power off and back on again. No prior DR or BDR exists at this point. They all participate in the election. They all tie with default priority values of 1 (see Example 23-4 for R1's priority in the **show ip ospf interface** command output). In this case, R4 becomes the DR based on the numerically highest RID of 4.4.4.4, and R3 becomes the BDR based on the next highest RID of 3.3.3.3.

To influence the election, you could set the various RIDs with your preferred router with the highest RID value. However, many networks choose OSPF router IDs to help identify the router easily rather than choosing to make one value higher than its neighbor. Instead, using the **OSPF priority** setting makes better sense. For instance, if an engineer preferred that R1 be the DR, the engineer could add the configuration in Example 23-5 to set R1's interface priority to 99.

Example 23-5 *Influencing DR/BDR Election Using OSPF Priority*

```
R1# configure terminal
Configuring from terminal, memory, or network [terminal]?
Enter configuration commands, one per line.  End with CNTL/Z.
R1(config)# interface g0/0
R1(config-if)# ip ospf priority 99
R1(config-if)# ^Z
R1#
R1# show ip ospf interface g0/0 | include Priority
  Transmit Delay is 1 sec, State DROTHER, Priority 99


R1# show ip ospf neighbor
Neighbor ID     Pri   State          Dead Time   Address         Interface
2.2.2.2           1   2WAY/DROTHER   00:00:36    10.1.1.2        GigabitEthernet0/0
3.3.3.3           1   FULL/BDR       00:00:30    10.1.1.3        GigabitEthernet0/0
4.4.4.4           1   FULL/DR        00:00:37    10.1.1.4        GigabitEthernet0/0


R1# show ip ospf interface brief
Interface   PID   Area        IP Address/Mask    Cost  State Nbrs F/C
Gi0/1       1     0           10.1.11.1/24       1     DR    0/0
Gi0/0       1     0           10.1.1.1/24        1     DROTH 2/3
```

The top of the example shows R1's interface priority value now as 99, and the **show ip ospf interface G0/0** command that follows confirms the setting. However, the last two commands confirm that OSPF does not preempt the existing DR or BDR. Note that the **show ip ospf neighbor** command still lists R4's state as DR, meaning R4 still acts as the DR, so R1, with a higher priority, did not take over. The final command, **show ip ospf interface brief**, lists R1's State (role) as DROTH.

Just to complete the process and show R1 winning a DR election, Example 23-6 shows the results after forcing a free election by failing the LAN switch that sits between the four routers. As expected, R1 wins and becomes DR due to its higher priority, with the other three routers tying based on priority. R4 wins between R2, R3, and R4 due to its higher RID to become the BDR.

Example 23-6 *Results of a Completely New DR/BDR Election*

```
! Not shown: LAN fails, and then recovers, causing a new OSPF Election
R1# show ip ospf neighbor

Neighbor ID    Pri   State         Dead Time   Address       Interface
2.2.2.2          1   FULL/DROTHER   00:00:37   10.1.1.2      GigabitEthernet0/0
3.3.3.3          1   FULL/DROTHER   00:00:38   10.1.1.3      GigabitEthernet0/0
4.4.4.4          1   FULL/BDR       00:00:38   10.1.1.4      GigabitEthernet0/0


R1# show ip ospf interface brief
Interface   PID   Area           IP Address/Mask   Cost   State  Nbrs F/C
Gi0/1        1    0              10.1.11.1/24       1     DR     0/0
Gi0/0        1    0              10.1.1.1/24        1     DR     3/3
```

NOTE If you have begun to mentally compare OSPF DR elections to STP elections, keep some key differences in mind. First, STP uses lowest-is-best logic, whereas OSPF uses highest-is-best. STP elections allow preemption—for instance, if a new switch appears with a superior (lower) bridge ID (BID) than the current root, the new switch becomes the root switch. OSPF does not preempt, so a new router on a link, with the highest priority, does not take over as DR or BDR. Instead, it wins future elections, eventually becoming the DR.

The OSPF Point-to-Point Network Type

The other OSPF network type mentioned in the CCNA 200-301 V1.1 blueprint, point-to-point, works well for data links that by their nature have just two routers on the link. For example, consider the topology in Figure 23-3, which shows Router R1 with three WAN links—two Ethernet WAN links and one serial link.

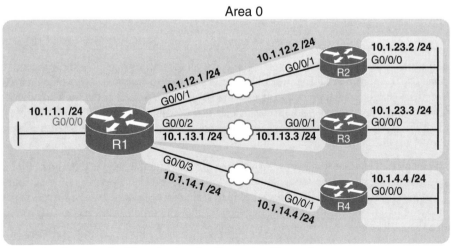

Figure 23-3 *Sample OSPF Design for Upcoming Examples*

First, consider the older-style serial links (not used in the figure). Serial links between routers do not support the capability to add a third router to the link. With only two devices on the link, using a DR/BDR provides no advantage; instead, it adds a little extra convergence time. Using a network type of point-to-point tells the router to not use a DR/BDR on the link, which makes sense on serial links. In fact, IOS defaults to a setting of **ip ospf network point-to-point** on serial interfaces.

While you might not see many serial links in networks today, some other point-to-point WAN topologies exist, including some Ethernet WAN links. All the Ethernet WAN links used in this book happen to use a point-to-point Ethernet WAN service called an Ethernet Private Wire Service or simply an Ethernet Line (E-Line). For that service, the service provider will send Ethernet frames between two devices (routers) connected to the service, but only those two devices. In other words, an E-Line is a point-to-point service in concept. So, like serial links, Ethernet WAN links with only two routers connected gain no advantage by using a DR/BDR. As a result, many engineers prefer to instead use an OSPF **point-to-point network type** on Ethernet WAN links that in effect act as a point-to-point link.

Example 23-7 shows the configuration of Router R1's G0/0/1 interface in Figure 23-3 to use OSPF network type point-to-point. R2, on the other end of the WAN link, would need the same configuration command on its matching interface.

Example 23-7 *OSPF Network Type Point-to-Point on an Ethernet WAN Interface on R1*

```
R1# configure terminal
Enter configuration commands, one per line.  End with CNTL/Z.
R1(config)# interface g0/0/1
R1(config-if)# ip ospf network point-to-point
R1(config-if)#

R1# show ip ospf interface g0/0/1
GigabitEthernet0/0/1 is up, line protocol is up
  Internet Address 10.1.12.1/24, Area 0, Attached via Interface Enable
  Process ID 1, Router ID 1.1.1.1, Network Type POINT_TO_POINT, Cost: 1
  Topology-MTID    Cost    Disabled    Shutdown      Topology Name
        0            4        no          no            Base
  Enabled by interface config, including secondary ip addresses
  Transmit Delay is 1 sec, State POINT_TO_POINT
  Timer intervals configured, Hello 10, Dead 40, Wait 40, Retransmit 5
    oob-resync timeout 40
    Hello due in 00:00:01
  Supports Link-local Signaling (LLS)
  Cisco NSF helper support enabled
  IETF NSF helper support enabled
  Index 1/3/3, flood queue length 0
  Next 0x0(0)/0x0(0)/0x0(0)
  Last flood scan length is 1, maximum is 3
  Last flood scan time is 0 msec, maximum is 0 msec
  Neighbor Count is 1, Adjacent neighbor count is 1
    Adjacent with neighbor 2.2.2.2
  Suppress hello for 0 neighbor(s)
```

Note the highlighted portions of the **show** command in Example 23-7. The first two high-lights note the network type. The final highlight with two lines notes that R1 has one neighbor on the interface, a neighbor with which it has become fully adjacent per the output.

Example 23-8 closes this section with a confirmation of some of those facts with two more commands. Note that the **show ip ospf neighbor** command on R1 lists Router R2 (RID 2.2.2.2) with a full state, but with no DR or BDR designation, instead listing a -. The - acts as a reminder that the link does not use a DR/BDR. The second command, **show ip ospf interface brief**, shows the state (the local router's role) as P2P, which is short for point-to-point, with a counter of 1 for the number of fully adjacent neighbors and total number of neighbors.

Example 23-8   *OSPF Network Type Point-to-Point on an Ethernet WAN Interface on R1*

```
R1# show ip ospf neighbor


Neighbor ID     Pri   State          Dead Time    Address      Interface
2.2.2.2           0   FULL/  -       00:00:39     10.1.12.2    GigabitEthernet0/0/1
! lines omitted for brevity


R1# show ip ospf interface brief
Interface     PID   Area           IP Address/Mask    Cost   State Nbrs F/C
Gi0/0/1        1     0             10.1.12.1/24        4     P2P   1/1
! lines omitted for brevity
```

When using Ethernet WAN links that behave as a point-to-point link, consider using OSPF network type point-to-point rather than using the default broadcast type.

Additional Optional OSPFv2 Features

This final major section of the chapter discusses some popular but optional OSPFv2 configuration features, as listed here in their order of appearance:

- Passive interfaces
- Default routes
- Metrics
- Hello and Dead intervals

OSPF Passive Interfaces

Once OSPF has been enabled on an interface, the router tries to discover neighboring OSPF routers and form a neighbor relationship. To do so, the router sends OSPF Hello messages on a regular time interval (called the Hello interval). The router also listens for incoming Hello messages from potential neighbors.

Sometimes, a router does not need to form neighbor relationships with neighbors on an interface. Often, no other routers exist on a particular link, so the router has no need to keep sending those repetitive OSPF Hello messages. In such cases, an engineer can make the interface passive, which means

■ OSPF continues to advertise about the subnet that is connected to the interface.

■ OSPF no longer sends OSPF Hellos on the interface.

■ OSPF no longer processes any received Hellos on the interface.

The result of enabling OSPF on an interface but then making it passive is that OSPF still advertises about the connected subnet, but OSPF also does not form neighbor relationships over the interface.

To configure an interface as passive, two options exist. First, you can add the following command to the configuration of the OSPF process, in router configuration mode:

passive-interface *type number*

Alternately, the configuration can change the default setting so that all interfaces are passive by default and then add a **no passive-interface** command for all interfaces that need to not be passive:

passive-interface default

no passive-interface *type number*

For example, in the sample internetwork in Figure 23-4, Router R1 connects to a LAN with its G0/0/0 interface. With no other OSPF routers on that LAN, R1 will never discover an OSPF neighbor on that interface. Example 23-9 shows two alternative configurations to make R1's G0/0/0 passive to OSPF.

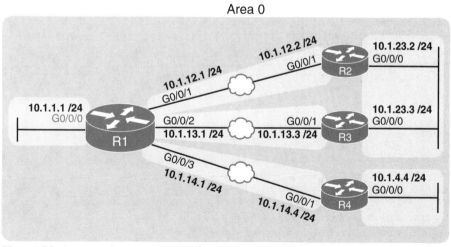

Figure 23-4   *Sample OSPF Design for Upcoming Examples*

Example 23-9 *Configuring Passive Interfaces on R1 from Figure 23-4*

```
! First, make each interface passive directly
router ospf 1
 passive-interface GigabitEthernet0/0/0

! Or, change the default to passive, and make the other interfaces not be passive
router ospf 1
 passive-interface default
 no passive-interface GigabitEthernet0/0/1
 no passive-interface GigabitEthernet0/0/2
 no passive-interface GigabitEthernet0/0/3
```

In real internetworks, use the configuration style that requires the least number of commands. For example, a router with 20 interfaces, 18 of which are passive to OSPF, has far fewer configuration commands when using the **passive-interface default** command to change the default to passive. If only two of those 20 interfaces need to be passive, use the default setting, in which all interfaces are not passive, to keep the configuration shorter.

Interestingly, OSPF makes it a bit of a challenge to use **show** commands to find out whether an interface is passive. The **show running-config** command lists the configuration directly, but if you cannot get into enable mode to use this command, note these two facts:

The **show ip ospf interface brief** command lists all interfaces on which OSPF is enabled, including **passive interfaces**.

The **show ip ospf interface** command lists several output lines per interface with a single line that mentions that the interface is passive.

Example 23-10 shows these commands on Router R1, based on the configuration shown in the top of Example 23-9. Note that passive interface G0/0/0 appears in the output of **show ip ospf interface brief**.

Example 23-10 *Displaying Passive Interfaces*

```
R1# show ip ospf interface brief
Interface     PID   Area        IP Address/Mask     Cost  State  Nbrs F/C
Gi0/0/0       1     0           10.1.1.1/24         1     DR     0/0
Gi0/0/1       1     0           10.1.12.1/24        1     BDR    1/1
Gi0/0/2       1     0           10.1.13.1/24        1     BDR    1/1
Gi0/0/3       1     0           10.1.14.1/24        1     DR     1/1

R1# show ip ospf interface g0/0/0
GigabitEthernet0/0/0 is up, line protocol is up
  Internet Address 10.1.1.1/24, Area 0, Attached via Network Statement
  Process ID 1, Router ID 1.1.1.1, Network Type BROADCAST, Cost: 1
  Topology-MTID    Cost    Disabled    Shutdown    Topology Name
        0           1        no          no          Base
```

```
   Transmit Delay is 1 sec, State DR, Priority 1
   Designated Router (ID) 1.1.1.1, Interface address 10.1.1.1
   No backup designated router on this network
   Timer intervals configured, Hello 10, Dead 40, Wait 40, Retransmit 5
     oob-resync timeout 40
     No Hellos (Passive interface)
! Lines omitted for brevity
```

OSPF Default Routes

Chapter 17, "Configuring IPv4 Addresses and Static Routes," showed some of the uses and benefits of default routes, with examples of static default routes. For those exact same reasons, networks can use OSPF to advertise default routes.

The most classic case for using a routing protocol to advertise a default route has to do with an enterprise's connection to the Internet. As a strategy, the enterprise engineer uses these design goals:

- All routers learn specific (nondefault) routes for subnets inside the company; a default route is not needed when forwarding packets to these destinations.

- One router connects to the Internet, and it has a default route that points toward the Internet.

- All routers should dynamically learn a default route, used for all traffic going to the Internet, so that all packets destined to locations in the Internet go to the one router connected to the Internet.

Figure 23-5 shows the idea of how OSPF advertises the default route, with the specific OSPF configuration. In this case, a company connects to an ISP with its Router R1. That router has a static default route (destination 0.0.0.0, mask 0.0.0.0) with a next-hop address of the ISP router. Then the use of the OSPF **default-information originate** command (Step 2) makes the router advertise a default route using OSPF to the remote routers (B1 and B2).

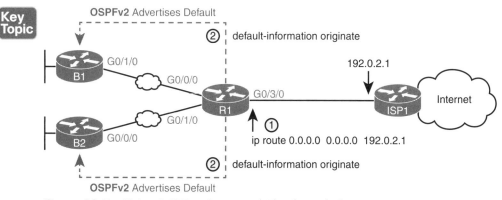

Figure 23-5 *Using OSPF to Create and Flood a Default Route*

Figure 23-6 shows the default routes that result from OSPF's advertisements in Figure 23-5. On the far left, the branch routers all have OSPF-learned default routes, pointing to R1. R1 itself also needs a default route, pointing to the ISP router, so that R1 can forward all Internet-bound traffic to the ISP.

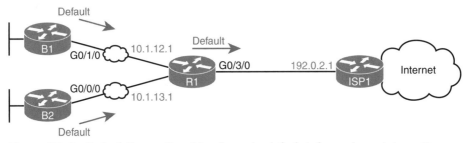

Figure 23-6 *Default Routes Resulting from the* **default-information originate** *Command*

Example 23-11 first highlights the two commands relevant to the default route on Router R1 in Figure 23-6. The router has a default static route referring to the ISP router as the next-hop router (192.0.2.1). It also has a **default-information originate** command configured under the OSPF process, telling the router to advertise a default route to other OSPF routers—but only if the router currently has a default route.

Example 23-11 *Relevant OSPF Configuration on Internet Edge Router R1*

```
! Excerpt from a show running-config command on router R1
ip route 0.0.0.0 0.0.0.0 192.0.2.1
!
router ospf 1
  network 10.0.0.0 0.255.255.255 area 0
  router-id 1.1.1.1
  default-information originate
```

Example 23-12 shows the status based on the configuration shown in Example 23-11. First, the top of the example confirms that R1 has a default route—that is, a route to 0.0.0.0/0. The "Gateway of last resort," which refers to the default route currently used by the router, points to next-hop IP address 192.0.2.1, which is the ISP router's IP address.

Example 23-12 *Default Routes on Routers R1 and B1*

```
! The next command is from Router R1. Note the static code for the default route
R1# show ip route static
Codes: L - local, C - connected, S - static, R - RIP, M - mobile, B - BGP
! Rest of the legend omitted for brevity

Gateway of last resort is 192.0.2.1 to network 0.0.0.0

S*    0.0.0.0/0 [254/0] via 192.0.2.1
```
```
! The next command is from router B1; notice the External route code for the default
```

```
B1# show ip route ospf
Codes: L - local, C - connected, S - static, R - RIP, M - mobile, B - BGP
       D - EIGRP, EX - EIGRP external, O - OSPF, IA - OSPF inter area
       N1 - OSPF NSSA external type 1, N2 - OSPF NSSA external type 2
       E1 - OSPF external type 1, E2 - OSPF external type 2
! Rest of the legend omitted for brevity


Gateway of last resort is 10.1.12.1 to network 0.0.0.0


O*E2   0.0.0.0/0 [110/1] via 10.1.12.1, 00:20:51, GigabitEthernet0/1/0
       10.0.0.0/8 is variably subnetted, 6 subnets, 2 masks
O          10.1.3.0/24 [110/3] via 10.1.12.1, 00:20:51, GigabitEthernet0/1/0
O          10.1.13.0/24 [110/2] via 10.1.12.1, 00:20:51, GigabitEthernet0/1/0
```

The bottom half of the example shows router B1's OSPF-learned default route. B1 lists a route for 0.0.0.0/0 as well. The next-hop router in this case is 10.1.12.1, which is Router R1's IP address on the WAN link. The code on the far left is O*E2, meaning an OSPF-learned route, which is a default route, and is specifically an external OSPF route. B1's gateway of last resort setting uses that one OSPF-learned default route, with next-hop router 10.1.12.1.

Finally, the OSPF subcommand **default-information originate** makes the logic conditional: only advertise a default route into OSPF if you already have some other default route. Adding the **always** keyword to the command (**default-information originate always**) tells OSPF to always advertise a default route into OSPF regardless of whether a default route currently exists.

OSPF Metrics (Cost)

The section "Calculating the Best Routes with SPF" in Chapter 21 discussed how SPF calculates the metric for each route, choosing the route with the best metric for each destination subnet. OSPF routers can influence that choice by changing the OSPF interface cost using three different configuration options:

- Directly, using the interface subcommand **ip ospf cost** x.

- Using the default calculation per interface, and changing the **interface bandwidth** setting, which changes the calculated value.

- Using the default calculation per interface, and changing the OSPF **reference bandwidth** setting, which changes the calculated value.

Setting the Cost Directly

Setting the cost directly requires a simple configuration command, as shown in Example 23-13. The example sets the cost of two interfaces on Router R1. This example uses the Figure 23-4 topology, with a single area, with OSPF enabled on all interfaces shown in the figure. The **show ip ospf interface brief** command that follows details the cost of each interface. Note that the **show** command confirms the cost settings.

Example 23-13 *Confirming OSPF Interface Costs*

```
R1# conf t
Enter configuration commands, one per line.  End with CNTL/Z.
R1(config)# interface g0/0/1
R1(config-if)# ip ospf cost 4
R1(config-if)# interface g0/0/2
R1(config-if)# ip ospf cost 5
R1(config-if)# ^Z
R1#
R1# show ip ospf interface brief
Interface    PID   Area           IP Address/Mask    Cost   State Nbrs F/C
Gi0/0/0      1     0              10.1.1.1/24        1      DR    0/0
Gi0/0/1      1     0              10.1.12.1/24       4      DR    1/1
Gi0/0/2      1     0              10.1.13.1/24       5      BDR   1/1
Gi0/0/3      1     0              10.1.14.1/24       1      DR    1/1
```

The output also shows a cost value of 1 for the other Gigabit interfaces, which is the default OSPF cost for any interface faster than 100 Mbps. The next topic discusses how IOS determines the default cost values.

Setting the Cost Based on Interface and Reference Bandwidth

Routers use a per-interface *bandwidth* setting to describe the speed of the interface. Note that the interface bandwidth setting does not influence the actual transmission speed. Instead, the interface bandwidth acts as a configurable setting to represent the speed of the interface, with the option to configure the bandwidth to match the actual transmission speed...or not. To support this logic, IOS sets a default interface bandwidth value that matches the physical transmission speed when possible, but also allows the configuration of the interface bandwidth using the **bandwidth** *speed* interface subcommand.

OSPF (as well as other IOS features) uses the interface bandwidth to make decisions, with OSPF using the interface bandwidth in its calculation of the default OSPF cost for each interface. IOS uses the following formula to choose an interface's OSPF cost for interfaces that do not have an **ip ospf cost** command configured. IOS puts the interface's bandwidth in the denominator and an OSPF setting called the *reference bandwidth* in the numerator:

Reference_bandwidth / Interface_bandwidth

Note that while you can change both the interface bandwidth and reference bandwidth via configuration, because several IOS features make use of the interface bandwidth setting, you should avoid changing the interface bandwidth to influence the default OSPF cost.

Today, most companies override the default IOS reference bandwidth setting. Cisco chose the default setting (100 Mbps) decades ago in an era with much slower links. As a result, when using that default, any interface bandwidth of 100 Mbps or faster results in a calculated OSPF cost of 1. So, when you re relying on the OSPF cost calculation, it helps to configure the reference bandwidth to a speed faster than the fastest speed link in the network.

To see the issue, consider Table 23-3, which lists several types of interfaces, the default interface bandwidth on those interfaces, and the OSPF cost calculated with the default OSPF reference bandwidth of 100 Mbps (that is, 100,000 Kbps). (OSPF rounds up for these calculations, resulting in a lowest possible OSPF interface cost of 1.)

Table 23-3   Faster Interfaces with Equal OSPF Costs

Interface	Interface Default Bandwidth (Kbps)	Formula (Kbps)	OSPF Cost
Serial	1544 Kbps	100,000 / 1544	64
Ethernet	10,000 Kbps	100,000 / 10,000	10
Fast Ethernet	100,000 Kbps	100,000/100,000	1
Gigabit Ethernet	1,000,000 Kbps	100,000/1,000,000	1
10 Gigabit Ethernet	10,000,000 Kbps	100,000/10,000,000	1
100 Gigabit Ethernet	100,000,000 Kbps	100,000/100,000,000	1

As you can see from the table, with a default reference bandwidth, all interfaces from Fast Ethernet's 100 Mbps and faster tie with their default OSPF cost. As a result, OSPF would treat a 100-Mbps link as having the same cost as a 10- or 100-Gbps link, which is probably not the right basis for choosing routes.

You can still use OSPF's default cost calculation (and many do) just by changing the reference bandwidth with the **auto-cost reference-bandwidth** *speed* OSPF mode subcommand. This command sets a value in a unit of megabits per second (Mbps). Set the reference bandwidth value to a value at least as much as the fastest link speed in the network, but preferably higher, in anticipation of adding even faster links in the future.

For instance, in an enterprise whose fastest links are 10 Gbps (10,000 Mbps), you could set all routers to use **auto-cost reference-bandwidth 10000**, meaning 10,000 Mbps or 10 Gbps. In that case, by default, a 10-Gbps link would have an OSPF cost of 1, while a 1-Gbps link would have a cost of 10, and a 100-MBps link a cost of 100.

Better still, in that same enterprise, use a reference bandwidth of a faster speed than the fastest interface in the network, to allow room for higher speeds. For instance, in that same enterprise, whose fastest link is 10 Gbps, set the reference bandwidth to 40 Gbps or even 100 Gbps to be ready for future upgrades to use 40-Gbps links, or even 100-Gbps links. (For example, use the **auto-cost reference-bandwidth 100000** command, meaning 100,000 Mbps or 100 Gbps.) That causes 100-Gbps links to have an OSPF cost of 1, 40-Gbps links to have a cost of 2, 10-Gbps links to have a cost of 10, and 1-Gbps links to have a cost of 100.

NOTE   Cisco recommends making the OSPF reference bandwidth setting the same on all OSPF routers in an enterprise network.

For convenient study, the following list summarizes the rules for how a router sets its OSPF interface costs:

1. Set the cost explicitly, using the **ip ospf cost** *x* interface subcommand, to a value between 1 and 65,535, inclusive.
2. Although it should be avoided, change the interface bandwidth with the **bandwidth** *speed* command, with *speed* being a number in kilobits per second (Kbps).
3. Change the reference bandwidth, using router OSPF subcommand **auto-cost reference-bandwidth** *ref-bw*, with a unit of megabits per second (Mbps).

OSPF Hello and Dead Intervals

OSPF does a lot of interesting work with the OSPF Hello message when initializing neighbors. As explained in the section, "Meeting Neighbors and Learning Their Router ID," in Chapter 21, an OSPF router uses Hello messages to announce the router's presence on the link, with those messages sent to the 224.0.0.5 all-OSPF-routers multicast address. The router also listens for incoming Hello messages from potential neighbors. Upon hearing Hellos from each other, two routers check the settings revealed in the Hello, and if compatible, the two routers can proceed to become neighbors.

This section looks at the other end of the story: what happens when the neighbor relationship fails.

First, while the neighbor relationship continues to work, routers send Hello messages regularly per a per-interface **Hello interval** (also called the *Hello timer*). Cisco IOS defaults to a 10-second Hello interval on all Ethernet interfaces. Why? When a router no longer receives the incoming Hello messages from a neighbor, the router believes the neighbor has failed, and takes the neighbor relationship down.

The process to decide when a neighbor fails uses the assumption on continual incoming Hello messages from the neighbor, combined with a second timer: the **Dead interval** (also called the *Dead timer*). The Dead timer tells the interface how long to wait. That is, how long since receiving a Hello message should a router wait before deciding that the neighbor failed.

Figure 23-7 shows an example of the interaction, focusing on what happens if Router R1 fails, and how Router R2 views the messages and timers. In this case, Router R1 loses power, but R2's Ethernet WAN link remains up because the link between R2 and the Ethernet WAN services does not have any problem. The sequence of events follows the circled step numbers as follows, using the default settings of a 10-second Hello timer and 40-second Dead timer:

1. Router R2 has a working neighbor relationship with R1 (full state).
2. R1 sends a Hello message, as usual; R2 resets its Dead timer to 40.
3. R1 sends another Hello message, 10 seconds later; R2 resets its Dead timer to 40.
4. R1 loses power; R2 receives no further Hellos from R1.
5. The Dead timer counts down to 0.
6. Router R2 changes the neighbor state for neighbor R1 to down and reconverges.

Under normal working conditions, with default settings, the Dead timer gets reset to 40, counts down to 30, and is reset to 40, over and over. However, the process also means that you might want to configure to use a lower Dead interval to improve the speed with which routers react to failures.

Example 23-14 shows the straightforward interface subcommands to set the Hello and Dead intervals. The example is based on the network in Figure 23-4, showing the configuration in Router R1, with the three WAN interfaces that connect to routers R2, R3, and R4. Although not shown, the neighboring routers must also be configured with the same Hello and Dead timer settings.

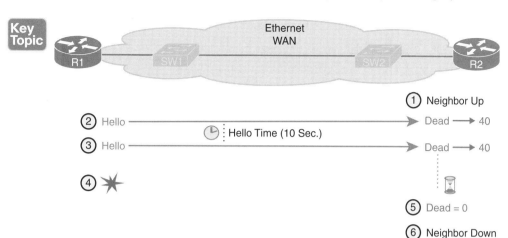

Figure 23-7   *An Example: R2's Use of the Hello and Dead Intervals*

Example 23-14   *Configuring OSPF Hello and Dead Intervals*

```
R1# conf t
Enter configuration commands, one per line.  End with CNTL/Z.
! Link connected to router R2
R1(config)# interface g0/0/1
R1(config-if)# ip ospf hello-interval 5
! Link connected to router R3
R1(config)# interface g0/0/2
R1(config-if)# ip ospf dead-interval 20
! Link connected to router R4
R1(config)# interface g0/0/3
R1(config-if)# ip ospf hello-interval 5
R1(config-if)# ip ospf dead-interval 15
R1(config-if)# Ctl-z
R1#
```

Example 23-15 confirms the settings configured in Example 23-14, but with a twist on interface G0/0/1. IOS uses a Hello interval default of 10 seconds on Ethernet interfaces, but a default of four times the Hello interval for the Dead interval. For interface G0/0/1, because only the Hello interval was configured, IOS uses a default dead interval based on 4 × Hello, or 20. However, the other two interfaces follow more predictable logic, summarized by this list, and then confirmed in the highlights in Example 23-15:

■ G0/0/1: Hello = 5 (configured) and Dead = 20 (calculated by IOS as 4X Hello)

■ G0/0/2: Hello = 10 (IOS default) and Dead = 20 (configured)

■ G0/0/3: Hello = 5 and Dead = 15 (both configured)

Example 23-15 *Confirming New OSPF Hello and Dead Intervals, Per Interface*

```
R1# show ip ospf interface g0/0/1 | include Hello
  Timer intervals configured, Hello 5, Dead 20, Wait 20, Retransmit 5
    Hello due in 00:00:02

R1# show ip ospf interface g0/0/2 | include Hello
  Timer intervals configured, Hello 10, Dead 20, Wait 20, Retransmit 5
    Hello due in 00:00:04

R1# show ip ospf interface g0/0/3 | include Hello
  Timer intervals configured, Hello 5, Dead 15, Wait 15, Retransmit 5
    Hello due in 00:00:03
```

IOS enables us to make poor configuration choices with these two settings. As a fair warning, consider these points:

- The default settings create a 4:1 ratio between the dead:hello timers. That ratio requires four consecutive lost Hellos before the Dead timer would expire. No matter the numbers, consider using the same 4:1 ratio, or at least a 3:1 ratio for your chosen numbers.

- Two neighboring routers must use the same Dead and Hello timer settings. However, IOS allows you to configure different settings on potential neighbors, preventing them from becoming neighbors, so take care to ensure the settings match.

- IOS enables you to make a poor choice to configure a Dead interval smaller than the Hello interval. In that case, the Dead interval expires before a router receives the next Hello. The neighbor relationship fails and recovers repeatedly once per Hello interval. Instead, always set the Dead interval higher than the Hello interval.

Chapter Review

One key to doing well on the exams is to perform repetitive spaced review sessions. Review this chapter's material using either the tools in the book or interactive tools for the same material found on the book's companion website. Refer to the "Your Study Plan" element for more details. Table 23-4 outlines the key review elements and where you can find them. To better track your study progress, record when you completed these activities in the second column.

Table 23-4 Chapter Review Tracking

Review Element	Review Date(s)	Resource Used
Review key topics		Book, website
Review key terms		Book, website
Answer DIKTA questions		Book, PTP
Review Config Checklists		Book, website
Review command tables		Book

Review Element	Review Date(s)	Resource Used
Do labs		Blog
Watch videos		Website

Review All the Key Topics

Table 23-5 Key Topics for Chapter 23

Key Topic Element	Description	Page Number
Table 23-2	Two OSPF network types and key behaviors	586
Example 23-3	OSPF interfaces, local roles, and neighbor counts	589
List	Rules for electing OSPF DR/BDR	590
Example 23-8	Evidence of OSPF network type point-to-point	594
List	Actions taken by OSPF when the interface is passive	595
Figure 23-5	Using OSPF to create and flood a default route	597
List	Rules for how OSPF sets its interface cost settings	601
Figure 23-7	Conceptual view of OSPF Hello and Dead timers	603

Key Terms You Should Know

broadcast network type, Dead interval, Hello interval, interface bandwidth, OSPF priority, passive interface, point-to-point network type, reference bandwidth

Command References

Tables 23-6 and 23-7 list configuration and verification commands used in this chapter. As an easy review exercise, cover the left column in a table, read the right column, and try to recall the command without looking. Then repeat the exercise, covering the right column, and try to recall what the command does.

Table 23-6 Chapter 23 Configuration Command Reference

Command	Description
ip ospf network {broadcast | point-to-point}	Interface subcommand used to set the OSPF network type on the interface
ip ospf priority *value*	Interface subcommand that sets the OSPF priority, used when electing a new DR or BDR
passive-interface *type number*	Router subcommand that makes the interface passive to OSPF, meaning that the OSPF process will not form neighbor relationships with neighbors reachable on that interface
passive-interface *default*	OSPF subcommand that changes the OSPF default for interfaces to be passive instead of active (not passive)
no passive-interface *type number*	OSPF subcommand that tells OSPF to be active (not passive) on that interface or subinterface

Command	Description
default-information originate [always]	OSPF subcommand to tell OSPF to create and advertise an OSPF default route, as long as the router has some default route (or to always advertise a default, if the **always** option is configured)
ip ospf cost *interface-cost*	Interface subcommand that sets the OSPF cost associated with the interface
bandwidth *bandwidth*	Interface subcommand that directly sets the interface bandwidth (Kbps)
auto-cost reference-bandwidth *number*	Router subcommand that tells OSPF the numerator in the Reference_bandwidth / Interface_bandwidth formula used to calculate the OSPF cost based on the interface bandwidth
ip ospf hello-interval *time*	Interface subcommand to set the OSPF Hello interval
ip ospf dead-interval *time*	Interface subcommand to set the OSPF Dead interval

Table 23-7   Chapter 23 EXEC Command Reference

Command	Description
show ip ospf interface brief	Lists the interfaces on which the OSPF protocol is enabled (based on the **network** commands), including passive interfaces
show ip ospf interface [*type number*]	Lists a long section of settings, status, and counters for OSPF operation on all interfaces, or on the listed interface, including the Hello and Dead timers
show ip ospf neighbor [*type number*]	Lists brief output about neighbors, identified by neighbor router ID, including current state, with one line per neighbor; optionally, limits the output to neighbors on the listed interface
show ip ospf neighbor *neighbor-ID*	Lists the same output as the **show ip ospf neighbor** detail command, but only for the listed neighbor (by neighbor RID)
show ip route	Lists all IPv4 routes
show ip route ospf	Lists routes in the routing table learned by OSPF

CHAPTER 24

OSPF Neighbors and Route Selection

This chapter covers the following exam topics:

3.0 IP Connectivity

    3.1 Interpret the components of routing table

        3.1.e Administrative distance

    3.2 Determine how a router makes a forwarding decision by default

        3.2.a Longest prefix match

        3.2.b Administrative distance

        3.2.c Routing protocol metric

    3.4 Configure and verify single area OSPFv2

        3.4.a Neighbor adjacencies

        3.4.b Point-to-point

        3.4.c Broadcast (DR/BDR selection)

        3.4.d Router ID

Chapter 21, "Understanding OSPF Concepts," and Chapter 22, "Implementing Basic OSPF Features," discuss the required and most common optional OSPF configuration settings, along with the many verification commands to show how OSPF works with those settings. This chapter continues with more OSPF implementation topics, both to round out the discussion of OSPF and to focus even more on the specific CCNA 200-301 exam topics.

The first major section focuses on neighbors and neighbor adjacencies, as mentioned in yet another of the OSPF exam topics. OSPF routers cannot exchange LSAs with another router unless they first become neighbors. This section discusses the various OSPF features that can prevent OSPF routers from becoming neighbors and how you can go about discovering if those bad conditions exist—even if you do not have access to the running configuration.

The chapter closes with a section called "Route Selection," which discusses OSPF logic plus IP routing logic. This section tackles the question of what route the router should choose, focusing on the cases in which multiple routes exist. The text discusses how OSPF chooses between competing routes and how routers match packet destination addresses to the routes that already exist in the IP routing table.

"Do I Know This Already?" Quiz

Take the quiz (either here or use the PTP software) if you want to use the score to help you decide how much time to spend on this chapter. The letter answers are listed at the bottom of the page following the quiz. Appendix C, found both at the end of the book as well as on the companion website, includes both the answers and explanations. You can also find both answers and explanations in the PTP testing software.

Table 24-1 "Do I Know This Already?" Foundation Topics Section-to-Question Mapping

Foundation Topics Section	Questions
OSPF Neighbor Relationships	1–3
Route Selection	4–7

1. An engineer connects Routers R11 and R12 to the same Ethernet LAN and configures them to use OSPFv2. Which answers describe a combination of settings that would prevent the two routers from becoming OSPF neighbors? (Choose two answers.)

   a. R11's interface uses area 11 while R12's interface uses area 12.

   b. R11's OSPF process uses process ID 11 while R12's uses process ID 12.

   c. R11's interface uses OSPF priority 11 while R12's uses OSPF priority 12.

   d. R11's interface uses an OSPF Hello timer value of 11 while R12's uses 12.

2. An engineer connects Routers R13 and R14 to the same Ethernet LAN and configures them to use OSPFv2. Which answers describe a combination of settings that would prevent the two routers from becoming OSPF neighbors?

   a. Both routers' interface IP addresses reside in the same subnet.

   b. Both routers' OSPF process uses process ID 13.

   c. Both routers' OSPF process uses router ID 13.13.13.13.

   d. Both routers' interfaces use an OSPF Dead interval of 40.

3. Router R15 has been a working part of a network that uses OSPFv2. An engineer then issues the **shutdown** command in OSPF configuration mode on R15. Which of the following occurs?

   a. R15 empties its IP routing table of all OSPF routes but keeps its LSDB intact.

   b. R15 empties its OSPF routes and LSDB but keeps OSPF neighbor relationships active.

   c. R15 keeps OSPF neighbors open but does not accept new OSPF neighbors.

   d. R15 keeps all OSPF configuration but ceases all OSPF activities (routes, LSDB, neighbors).

4. Using OSPF, Router R1 learns three routes to subnet 10.1.1.0/24. It first calculates a route through Router R2 with metric 15000, then a route through Router R3 with metric 15001, and then a route through Router R4 with metric 15000. Which routes does the router place into its routing table, assuming all default configuration settings for any features that would impact the answer?

   a. Only the route with R2 as the next-hop router

   b. Both routes with metric 15000

   c. All three routes to subnet 10.1.1.0/24

   d. Only the router with R3 as the next-hop router

5. Router R2 runs both EIGRP and OSPF. It learns two OSPF routes to subnet 172.16.1.0/24, one with metric 1000 and one with metric 2000. It learns two EIGRP routes with metrics 1,000,000 and 2,000,000. If using default settings for any settings that might impact the answer, which route(s) will the router place into the IP routing table?

    a. The metric 1000 OSPF route and the metric 1,0000,000 EIGRP route

    b. The metric 2000 OSPF route and the metric 2,0000,000 EIGRP route

    c. The metric 1000 OSPF route only

    d. The metric 1,0000,000 EIGRP route only

6. Router R3 receives a packet with destination IP address 172.20.89.100. How many of the address ranges defined in the routes per the **show ip route** command match the packet's destination address?

```
R3# show ip route
Gateway of last resort is 172.20.15.5 to network 0.0.0.0

O*E2  0.0.0.0/0 [110/1] via 172.20.15.5, 00:04:56, GigabitEthernet0/1
         172.20.0.0/16 is variably subnetted, 12 subnets, 4 masks
S        172.20.90.9/32 [1/0] via 172.20.11.1
O IA     172.20.88.0/23 [110/3] via 172.20.12.2, 00:03:44, GigabitEthernet0/0/2
O IA     172.20.80.0/20 [110/3] via 172.20.13.3, 00:04:55, GigabitEthernet0/0/3
O IA     172.20.0.0/16 [110/6] via 172.20.14.4, 00:02:14, GigabitEthernet0/0/4
```

    a. 1

    b. 2

    c. 3

    d. 4

    e. 5

7. Router R3 receives a packet with destination IP address 172.20.90.1. Which next-hop IP address does Router R3 use when forwarding the packet?

```
R3# show ip route
Gateway of last resort is 172.20.15.5 to network 0.0.0.0

O*E2  0.0.0.0/0 [110/1] via 172.20.15.5, 00:04:56, GigabitEthernet0/1
         172.20.0.0/16 is variably subnetted, 12 subnets, 4 masks
S        172.20.90.9/32 [1/0] via 172.20.11.1
O IA     172.20.88.0/23 [110/3] via 172.20.12.2, 00:03:44, GigabitEthernet0/0/2
O IA     172.20.80.0/20 [110/3] via 172.20.13.3, 00:04:55, GigabitEthernet0/0/3
O IA     172.20.0.0/16 [110/6] via 172.20.14.4, 00:02:14, GigabitEthernet0/0/4
```

    a. 172.20.11.1

    b. 172.20.12.2

    c. 172.20.13.3

    d. 172.20.14.4

    e. 172.20.15.5

Foundation Topics

OSPF Neighbor Relationships

A router's OSPF configuration enables OSPF on a set of interfaces. IOS then attempts to discover other neighbors on those interfaces by sending and listening for OSPF Hello messages. However, once discovered, two routers may not become neighbors. They must have compatible values for several settings as listed in the Hellos exchanged between the two routers. This second major section of the chapter examines those reasons.

OSPF Neighbor Requirements

After an OSPF router hears a Hello from a new neighbor, the routing protocol examines the information in the Hello and compares that information with the local router's own settings. If the settings match, great. If not, the routers do not become neighbors. Because there is no formal term for all these items that a routing protocol considers, this book just calls them *neighbor requirements*. Table 24-2 lists the neighbor requirements for OSPF, with some comments about the various issues following the table.

Table 24-2   Neighbor Requirements for OSPF

Requirement	Required for OSPF	Neighbor Missing If Incorrect
Interfaces must be in an up/up state.	Yes	Yes
Access control lists (ACL) must not filter routing protocol messages.	Yes	Yes
Interfaces must be in the same subnet.	Yes	Yes
Neighbors must pass routing protocol neighbor authentication (if configured).	Yes	Yes
Hello and dead timers must match.	Yes	Yes
Router IDs (RID) must be unique.	Yes	Yes
Neighbors must be in the same area.	Yes	Yes
OSPF process must not be shut down.	Yes	Yes
OSPF must not be shut down on the interface.	Yes	Yes
Neighboring interfaces must use same MTU setting.	Yes	No
Neighboring interfaces must use same OSPF network type.	Yes	No
Neighboring interfaces cannot both use priority 0.	Yes	No

First, consider the meaning of the two rightmost columns. The column labeled "Required for OSPF" means that the item must be working correctly for the neighbor relationship to work correctly. The last column heading notes whether the neighbor will be missing ("yes") in the list of OSPF neighbors in commands like the **show ip ospf neighbor** command.

The table breaks into three sections. The first section lists non-OSPF configuration while the second lists OSPF configuration—all of which prevents OSPF neighbor relationships from forming. The third section lists settings that allow OSPF neighbor relationships, but with other related problems that prevent the addition of correct OSPF routes to the IP routing table.

For reference, Table 24-3 relists some of the requirements from Table 24-2, along with the most useful commands to find the related settings.

Table 24-3   OSPF Neighbor Requirements and the Best **show/debug** Commands

Requirement	Best show Command
Hello and dead timers must match.	show ip ospf interface
Neighbors must be in the same area.	show ip ospf interface brief
RIDs must be unique.	show ip ospf
Neighbors must pass any neighbor authentication.	show ip ospf interface
OSPF process must not be shut down.	show ip ospf, show ip ospf interface

The rest of this section looks at some of the items from Table 24-3 in a little more detail.

> **NOTE**   One configuration choice that people sometimes think is an issue, but is not, is the process ID as defined by the **router ospf** *process-id* command. Neighboring routers can use the same process ID values, or different process ID values, with no impact on whether two routers become OSPF neighbors.

Issues That Prevent Neighbor Adjacencies

The next few pages look at three neighbor issues from Table 24-2, using Figure 24-1's topology in the examples. R1 begins with all correct configuration as listed in Example 24-1. However, later examples introduce configuration mistakes on Routers R2, R3, and R4 as follows:

- R2 has been reconfigured to place both LAN interfaces in area 1, whereas the other three routers' G0/0 interfaces remain in area 0.

- R3 has been reconfigured to use the same RID (1.1.1.1) as R1.

- R4 has been reconfigured with Hello/Dead timers of 5/20 on its G0/0 interface, instead of the default settings of 10/40 used by R1, R2, and R3.

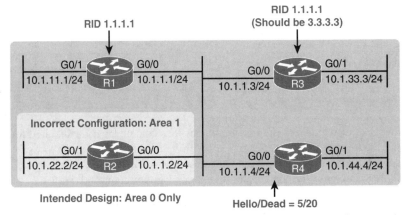

Figure 24-1   *Summary of Problems That Prevent OSPF Neighbors on the Central LAN*

Answers to the "Do I Know This Already?" quiz:

1 A, D **2** C **3** D **4** B **5** D **6** D **7** C

Example 24-1 *Router R1 Configuration with No Configuration Issues*

```
router ospf 1
 router-id 1.1.1.1
 !
 interface gigabitEthernet0/0
 ip address 10.1.1.1 255.255.255.0
 ip ospf 1 area 0
 !
interface gigabitEthernet0/1
 ip address 10.1.11.1 255.255.255.0
 ip ospf 1 area 0
```

Finding Area Mismatches

To create an area mismatch, the configuration on some router must place the interface into the wrong area per the design. Figure 24-1 shows the intent to make that mistake on Router R2, placing both its interfaces into area 1 instead of area 0. Example 24-2 shows the configuration, which uses the correct syntax (and is therefore accepted by the router) but sets the wrong area number.

Example 24-2 *Setting Area 1 on R2's Interfaces, When They Should Be in Area 0*

```
router ospf 1
 router-id 2.2.2.2
 !
interface gigabitEthernet0/0
 ip address 10.1.1.2 255.255.255.0
 ip ospf 1 area 1
 !
interface gigabitEthernet0/1
 ip address 10.1.22.2 255.255.255.0
 ip ospf 1 area 1
```

With an area mismatch error, the **show ip ospf neighbor** command will not list the neighbor. Because you see nothing in the OSPF neighbor table, to troubleshoot this problem, you need to find the area configuration on each interface on potentially neighboring routers. To do so:

- Check the output of **show running-config** to look for:
    - **ip ospf** *process-id* **area** *area-number* interface subcommands
    - **network** commands in OSPF configuration mode
- Use the **show ip ospf interface** [**brief**] command to list the area number

Finding Duplicate OSPF Router IDs

Next, Example 24-3 shows R1 and R3 both trying to use RID 1.1.1.1. Due to the duplicate RIDs, neither router will list the other in the output of the **show ip ospf neighbor** command. Interestingly, both routers automatically generate a log message for the duplicate OSPF RID problem between R1 and R3; the end of Example 24-3 shows one such message. For the exams, just use the **show ip ospf** commands on both R3 and R1 to easily list the RID on each router, noting that they both use the same value.

Example 24-3 *Comparing OSPF Router IDs on R1 and R3*

```
! Next, on R3: R3 lists the RID of 1.1.1.1
!
R3# show ip ospf
Routing Process "ospf 1" with ID 1.1.1.1
Start time: 00:00:37.136, Time elapsed: 02:20:37.200
! lines omitted for brevity


! Back to R1: R1 also uses RID 1.1.1.1
R1# show ip ospf
Routing Process "ospf 1" with ID 1.1.1.1
Start time: 00:01:51.864, Time elapsed: 12:13:50.904
! lines omitted for brevity


*May 29 00:01:25.679: %OSPF-4-DUP_RTRID_NBR: OSPF detected duplicate router-id
1.1.1.1 from 10.1.1.3 on interface GigabitEthernet0/0
```

First, focus on the problem: the duplicate RIDs. The first line of the **show ip ospf** command on the two routers quickly shows the duplicate use of 1.1.1.1. To solve the problem, assuming R1 should use 1.1.1.1 and R3 should use another RID (maybe 3.3.3.3), change the RID on R3 and restart the OSPF process. To do so, use the **router-id 3.3.3.3** OSPF subcommand and the EXEC mode command **clear ip ospf process**. (OSPF will not begin using a new RID value until the process restarts, either via command or reload.) At that point, the routers should become neighbors again and be displayed in the output of the **show ip ospf neighbor** command.

NOTE There are cases in which routers in different areas can use the same RID and cause no problems in OSPF. However, to be safe, use unique OSPF RIDs throughout the entire OSPF domain (that is, among all routers in your enterprise that use OSPF).

Finding OSPF Hello and Dead Timer Mismatches

First, as a reminder from chapters past:

- **Hello interval/timer:** The per-interface timer that tells a router how often to send OSPF Hello messages on an interface.

- **Dead interval/timer:** The per-interface timer that tells the router how long to wait without having received a Hello from a neighbor before believing that neighbor has failed. (Defaults to four times the Hello timer.)

Next, consider the problem created on R4, with the configuration of a different Hello timer and dead timer (5 and 20, respectively) as compared with the default settings on R1, R2, and R3 (10 and 40, respectively). A Hello or Dead interval mismatch prevents R4 from becoming neighbors with any of the other three OSPF routers. Routers list their Hello and Dead interval settings in their Hello messages and choose not to become neighbors if the values do not match. As a result, none of the routers become neighbors with Router R4 in this case.

Example 24-4 shows the easiest way to find the mismatch using the **show ip ospf interface** command on both R1 and R4. This command lists the Hello and Dead timers for each interface, as highlighted in the example. Note that R1 uses 10 and 40 (Hello and Dead), whereas R4 uses 5 and 20.

Example 24-4 *Finding Mismatched Hello/Dead Timers*

```
R1# show ip ospf interface G0/0
GigabitEthernet0/0 is up, line protocol is up
  Internet Address 10.1.1.1/24, Area 0, Attached via Network Statement
  Process ID 1, Router ID 1.1.1.1, Network Type BROADCAST, Cost: 1
  Topology-MTID  Cost  Disabled  Shutdown   Topology Name
       0          1      no        no          Base
  Transmit Delay is 1 sec, State DR, Priority 1
  Designated Router (ID) 1.1.1.1, Interface address 10.1.1.1
  No backup designated router on this network
  Timer intervals configured, Hello 10, Dead 40, Wait 40, Retransmit 5
! lines omitted for brevity

! Moving on to R4 next
!
R4# show ip ospf interface Gi0/0
GigabitEthernet0/0 is up, line protocol is up
   Internet Address 10.1.1.4/24, Area 0, Attached via Network Statement
   Process ID 4, Router ID 10.1.44.4, Network Type BROADCAST, Cost: 1
  Topology-MTID  Cost  Disabled  Shutdown   Topology Name
       0          1      no        no          Base
  Transmit Delay is 1 sec, State DR, Priority 1
  Transmit Delay is 1 sec, State DR, Priority 1
  Designated Router (ID) 10.1.44.4, Interface address 10.1.1.4
  No backup designated router on this network
  Timer intervals configured, Hello 5, Dead 20, Wait 20, Retransmit 5
! lines omitted for brevity
```

Shutting Down the OSPF Process

Like administratively disabling and enabling an interface, IOS also allows the OSPFv2 routing protocol process to be disabled and enabled with the **shutdown** and **no shutdown** router mode subcommands, respectively. When a routing protocol process is shut down, IOS does the following:

- Brings down all neighbor relationships and clears the OSPF neighbor table
- Clears the LSDB
- Clears the IP routing table of any OSPF-learned routes

At the same time, shutting down OSPF does retain some important details about OSPF, in particular:

- IOS retains all OSPF configuration.

- IOS still lists all OSPF-enabled interfaces in the OSPF interface list (**show ip ospf interface**) but in a DOWN state.

Shutting down the OSPF routing protocol process allows the network engineer to stop using the routing protocol on that router without having to remove all the configuration. Once the process is shut down, the **show ip ospf interface [brief]** command should still list some output, as will the **show ip ospf** command, but the rest of the commands will list nothing.

Example 24-5 shows an example on Router R5, as shown in Figure 24-2. R5 is a different router than the one used in earlier examples, but it begins the example with two OSPF neighbors, R2 and R3, with Router IDs 2.2.2.2 and 3.3.3.3. The example shows the OSPF process being shut down, the neighbors failing, and those two key OSPF **show** commands: **show ip ospf neighbor** and **show ip ospf interface brief**.

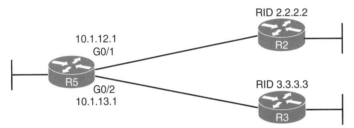

Figure 24-2 *Example Network to Demonstrate OSPF Process Shutdown*

Example 24-5 *Shutting Down an OSPF Process, and the Resulting Neighbor States*

```
R5# show ip ospf neighbor
Neighbor ID     Pri    State      Dead Time    Address       Interface
2.2.2.2          1     FULL/DR    00:00:35     10.1.12.2     GigabitEthernet0/1
3.3.3.3          1     FULL/DR    00:00:33     10.1.13.3     GigabitEthernet0/2
R5# configure terminal
Enter configuration commands, one per line. End with CNTL/Z.
R5(config)# router ospf 1
R5(config-router)# shutdown
R5(config-router)# ^Z
*Mar 23 12:43:30.634: %OSPF-5-ADJCHG: Process 1, Nbr 2.2.2.2 on GigabitEthernet0/1
from FULL to DOWN, Neighbor Down: Interface down or detached
*Mar 23 12:43:30.635: %OSPF-5-ADJCHG: Process 1, Nbr 3.3.3.3 on GigabitEthernet0/2
from FULL to DOWN, Neighbor Down: Interface down or detached
R5# show ip ospf interface brief
Interface    PID    Area     IP Address/Mask     Cost  State Nbrs F/C
Gi0/1         1      0       10.1.12.1/24         1    DOWN  0/0
Gi0/2         1      0       10.1.13.1/24         1    DOWN  0/0
```

```
R5# show ip ospf
 Routing Process "ospf 1" with ID 5.5.5.5
 Start time: 5d23h, Time elapsed: 1d04h
 Routing Process is shutdown
! lines omitted for brevity

R5# show ip ospf neighbor
R5#
R5# show ip ospf database
            OSPF Router with ID (3.3.3.3) (Process ID 1)
R5#
```

First, before the **shutdown**, the **show ip ospf neighbor** command lists two neighbors. After the **shutdown**, the same command lists no neighbors at all. Second, the **show ip ospf interface brief** command lists the interfaces on which OSPF is enabled, on the local router's interfaces. However, it lists a state of DOWN, which is a reference to the local router's state. Also, note that the **show ip ospf** command positively states that the OSPF process is in a shutdown state, while the **show ip ospf database** command output lists only a heading line, with no LSAs.

Shutting Down OSPF on an Interface

IOS also supports a feature to disable OSPF on an interface without having to remove any OSPF configuration to do so. The feature has the same motivations as the **shutdown** command in router configuration mode: to allow OSPF configuration to remain while stopping OSPF. However, shutting down OSPF on an interface ceases all OSPF operations on that interface rather than all OSPF operations on the router.

To shut down OSPF on an interface, use the **ip ospf shutdown** interface subcommand, and to enable it again, use the **no ip ospf shutdown** command. After you use the **ip ospf shutdown** command, the router changes as follows:

- The router stops sending Hellos on the interface, allowing existing OSPF neighbor relationships to time out.

- The neighbor failure(s) triggers OSPF reconvergence, resulting in the removal of any routes that use the interface as an outgoing interface.

- The router also stops advertising about the subnet on the link that is shut down.

If those ideas sound familiar, the feature works much like OSPF passive interfaces, except that when shut down, OSPF also stops advertising about the connected subnet.

Interestingly, using the **ip ospf shutdown** interface subcommand also does not change a few commands about interfaces. For instance, after you configure interface G0/0/0 with the **ip ospf shutdown** command, the **show ip ospf interface** and **show ip ospf interface brief** commands still show G0/0/0 in the list of interfaces.

Issues That Allow Neighbors but Prevent IP Routes

Some configuration mismatches prevent learning OSPF routes, but they do allow routers to become neighbors, as noted in the final section of Table 24-2. The issues are

- A mismatched MTU setting

- A mismatched OSPF network type

- Both neighbors using OSPF Priority 0

The next few pages explain the issues, with an example that shows all three misconfigurations along with the resulting **show** commands.

Mismatched MTU Settings

The maximum transmission unit (MTU) size defines a per-interface setting used by the router for its Layer 3 forwarding logic, defining the largest network layer packet that the router will forward out each interface. The IPv4 MTU size of an interface defines the maximum size IPv4 packet that the router can forward out an interface, and similarly, the IPv6 MTU size defines the largest IPv6 packet.

Routers often use a default IP MTU size of 1500 bytes, with the ability to set the value as well. The **ip mtu** *size* interface subcommand defines the IPv4 MTU setting, and the **ipv6 mtu** *size* command sets the equivalent for IPv6 packets.

Alternatively, you can set the MTU size for IPv4 and IPv6 using the **mtu** *size* interface subcommand. That command sets the MTU for IPv4 on the interface if the **ip mtu** *size* command does not appear and for IPv6 if the **ipv6 mtu** *size* command does not appear.

With different IPv4 MTU settings, two OSPFv2 routers become OSPF neighbors; however, they fail to complete regular OSPF database exchange, reaching other interim OSPF neighbor states and then failing to a down state. Over time, they repeat the process to become neighbors, try to exchange their LSDBs, fail, and fall back to a down state.

Mismatched OSPF Network Types

In the section, "OSPF Network Types," in Chapter 23, "Implementing Optional OSPF Features," you read about the OSPF broadcast network type, which uses a DR/BDR, and the OSPF point-to-point network type, which does not. Interestingly, if you misconfigure network type settings such that one router uses broadcast, and the other uses point-to-point, the two routers become neighbors and reach a full state. They remain stable in a full state, which means they exchanged their LSDBs; however, neither router can use routes based on LSAs learned from the neighbor.

The reason for not adding the routes has to do with the details of LSAs and how the use of a DR (or not) changes those LSAs. Basically, the two routers expect different details in the LSAs, and the SPF algorithm notices those differences and cannot resolve those differences when calculating routes.

Both Neighbors Using OSPF Priority 0

OSPF interface priority allows us to influence which router wins a DR or BDR election when using the broadcast network type. The highest priority router wins the election, with 1 as the default setting and allowed values ranging from 0 to 255 decimal.

Priority 0 acts as a special case meaning that the router will not serve as DR or BDR. For instance, in a topology with many routers sharing the same subnet, you could choose to make some routers use priority 0, effectively refusing to become DR or BDR so that you have more predictability when operating the network.

A problem occurs when you make the poor configuration choice to make all routers on a subnet use priority 0. If making that mistake, you have a subnet that must have a DR but for which all routers refuse the role. The routers proceed as normal to use Hellos to discover each other. They list each other as neighbors and reach a 2WAY state. However, because no router serves as the DR, the database exchange process stops at that point. The typical symptom is a stable neighbor in a 2WAY/DROTHER state.

Examples That Show OSPF Neighbors but No Routes

Figure 24-3 shows a router topology used in an upcoming example. In this case, R1 uses poor configuration choices that cause the problems discussed in the previous few pages. In particular:

R1 G0/0/1: Uses network type point-to-point; R2 uses default setting broadcast.

R1 G0/0/2: Uses an IPv4 MTU of 1600; R3 uses the default setting 1500.

R1 G0/0/3: Both R1 and R4 use an OSPF priority of 0.

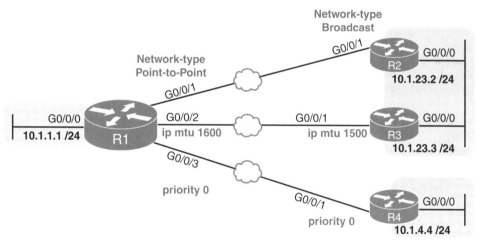

Figure 24-3 *OSPF Mistakes: Neighbors Formed, but Routes Not Learned*

To begin, Example 24-6 shows the Router R1 configuration to cause the problems shown in the figure. Routers R2, R3, and R4 use all default configuration related to these parameters other than R4, which also requires the **ip ospf priority 0** interface subcommand. The example shows only the relevant configuration.

Example 24-7 shows the results. First, note that Routers R2, R3, and R4 use OSPF RIDs 2.2.2.2, 3.3.3.3, and 4.4.4.4, respectively. The example begins with a **show ip ospf neighbor** command at a time when the neighbor relationships reach their best states.

Example 24-6   *OSPF Configuration Settings Matching Figure 24-3*

```
R1# show running-config interface g0/0/1
! Neighboring router R2 defaults to network type broadcast
interface GigabitEthernet0/0/1
 ip address 10.1.12.1 255.255.255.0
 ip ospf network point-to-point
 ip ospf 1 area 0

R1# show running-config interface g0/0/2
! Neighboring router R3 defaults to IP MTU 1500
interface GigabitEthernet0/0/2
 ip address 10.1.13.1 255.255.255.0
 ip mtu 1600
 ip ospf 1 area 0

R1# show running-config interface g0/0/3
! Neighboring router R4 is also configured for OSPF priority 0
interface GigabitEthernet0/0/3
 ip address 10.1.14.1 255.255.255.0
 ip ospf priority 0
 ip ospf 1 area 0
```

Example 24-7   *Resulting OSPF Neighbor Relationships on Router R1*

```
R1# show ip ospf neighbor

Neighbor ID    Pri    State            Dead Time    Address      Interface
4.4.4.4          0    2WAY/DROTHER     00:00:38     10.1.14.4    GigabitEthernet0/0/3
3.3.3.3          0    EXCHANGE/DROTHER 00:00:38     10.1.13.3    GigabitEthernet0/0/2
2.2.2.2          0    FULL/  -         00:00:39     10.1.12.2    GigabitEthernet0/0/1
R1#


*Nov  2 21:38:34.046: %OSPF-5-ADJCHG: Process 1, Nbr 3.3.3.3 on GigabitEthernet0/0/2
from EXCHANGE to DOWN, Neighbor Down: Too many retransmissions


R1# show ip ospf neighbor

Neighbor ID    Pri    State            Dead Time    Address      Interface
4.4.4.4          0    2WAY/DROTHER     00:00:31     10.1.14.4    GigabitEthernet0/0/3
3.3.3.3          0    DOWN/DROTHER     -            10.1.13.3    GigabitEthernet0/0/2
2.2.2.2          0    FULL/  -         00:00:34     10.1.12.2    GigabitEthernet0/0/1
```

In this case, R1's neighbor relationship with Router R3 (3.3.3.3) cycles through different states. The middle of the example shows messages about how this neighbor relationship fails. Then the end of the example shows neighbor 3.3.3.3 now in a DOWN state. Over time, the neighbor relationship cycles through repeated attempts.

Note that none of the three neighbor relationships result in any IP routes. In this case, the **show ip route ospf** command on R1 lists zero routes.

Route Selection

When OSPF calculates routes to a specific subnet, the competition between routes might be simple and obvious. A router might calculate a single route for a subnet and use that route. A router might calculate multiple routes to reach a subnet, so it finds the route with the lowest metric (cost), placing that route into the IP routing table.

However, other scenarios occur both inside and outside of OSPF, requiring more understanding of the logic used by a router. This final major section of the chapter discusses three topics that make us think about the following:

1. How one router chooses between multiple equal-cost OSPF routes for one subnet
2. How one router chooses between multiple routes for one subnet that were learned by different routing protocols
3. When forwarding packets, how routers match routes in the routing table, particularly when a packet's destination address matches more than one route

Equal-Cost Multipath OSPF Routes

Consider the routes that one OSPF router calculates for one destination subnet. When more than one route to that one subnet exists, one route may have the lowest metric, making OSPF's logic simple: Add that route to the IP routing table. However, when the metrics tie for multiple routes to the same subnet, the router applies different logic: It places multiple **equal-cost routes** in the routing table.

IOS limits the concurrent equal-cost OSPF routes for each destination subnet based on the **maximum-paths** *number* subcommand under **router ospf**. The default varies depending on the router platform, with a common default setting of four concurrent routes.

For example, consider the most recent Figure 24-3, but with all configuration errors fixed, all routers learn routes to all subnets. Router R1 has only one possible route to reach subnet 10.1.4.0/24, located off Router R4. However, R1 has two possible routes to reach subnet 10.1.23.0/24: one route through neighbor R2 and one through neighbor R3. If using OSPF costs 10 for all GigabitEthernet interfaces, both R1's routes to subnet 10.1.23.0/24 have a cost of 20. Example 24-8 shows that result with a list of OSPF-learned routes on Router R1.

Take an extra moment to look closely at the last two lines of output. Note that the output does not repeat the subnet ID and mask, listing it once, but leaving spaces in that position in the last line. That format should help you identify cases like this of multiple routes for the same subnet. Also, note the second number within brackets lists the metric, 20 for both routes, confirming they have an equal metric (cost).

Example 24-8 *OSPF Routes on Router R1 from Figure 24-3*

```
R1# show ip route ospf
! Legend omitted for brevity


Gateway of last resort is not set

      10.0.0.0/8 is variably subnetted, 14 subnets, 2 masks
O        10.1.4.0/24 [110/20] via 10.1.14.4, 00:00:17, GigabitEthernet0/0/3
O        10.1.23.0/24 [110/20] via 10.1.13.3, 00:00:20, GigabitEthernet0/0/2
                      [110/20] via 10.1.12.2, 00:00:23, GigabitEthernet0/0/1
```

Now, think about packet forwarding instead of thinking about the logic of placing routes into the routing table. Which of the two routes to subnet 10.1.23.0/24 should R1 use? How should it take advantage of the two equal-cost routes? A router could load balance the packets on a per-packet basis, but that is a poor choice for a few reasons. Instead, by default, routers balance based on the individual destination address. The router sends packets for one destination IP address using one route, another destination address using the other route, and so on. Using destination-based load balancing allows for much less router overhead and avoids some of the problems that occur with per-packet load balancing.

> **NOTE** The logic in this section often goes by the name **equal-cost multipath (ECMP)**.

Multiple Routes Learned from Competing Sources

A typical enterprise router first learns connected routes, based on interface IP addresses. Those routes happen to be the best routes to reach those subnets because those subnets connect directly to the router. Additionally, each enterprise router uses one routing protocol (for example, OSPF) to dynamically learn all other routes.

However, in several legitimate cases, one router learns routes using more than connected routes plus one routing protocol. For instance, some routers also have static routes, as discussed in Chapter 17, "Configuring IPv4 Addresses and Static Routes." A router configuration could define a static route to a subnet, while the IGP also learns a route to that same subnet. Which route is better? In other cases, one router might run both OSPF and BGP. Again, if both learn a route to the same subnet, which is better? Or a router might use multiple IGPs, like both OSPF and EIGRP. Again, both might learn a route to the same subnet, begging the same question.

> **NOTE** To consider routes to be to the same subnet, they must refer to the same subnet ID and subnet mask.

Routing protocol metrics do not help a router choose between competing routes in these cases. For instance, EIGRP commonly assigns metrics with values in the millions and billions, with OSPF using hundreds or thousands. Additionally, connected and static routes have no metrics. So metrics cannot help the router choose the best route in these cases, so IOS needs another method to choose between routes from different sources.

When IOS must choose between routes learned using different routing protocols, IOS uses a concept called **administrative distance**. Administrative distance (AD) is a number that denotes how believable an entire routing protocol is on a single router. The lower the number, the better, or more believable, the routing protocol. For example, RIP has a default administrative distance of 120, OSPF uses a default of 110, and EIGRP defaults to 90. When using OSPF and EIGRP, the router will believe the EIGRP route instead of the OSPF route (at least by default). The administrative distance values are configured on a single router and are not exchanged with other routers. Table 24-4 lists the various sources of routing information, along with the default administrative distances.

Table 24-4   Default Administrative Distances

Route Type	Administrative Distance
Connected	0
Static	1
BGP (external routes [eBGP])	20
EIGRP (internal routes)	90
OSPF	110
IS-IS	115
RIP	120
EIGRP (external routes)	170
BGP (internal routes [iBGP])	200
DHCP default route	254
Unusable	255

NOTE   The **show ip route** command lists each route's administrative distance as the first of the two numbers inside the brackets. The second number in brackets is the metric.

Figure 24-4 shows what might happen inside each routing process and the choice to prefer the EIGRP route instead of the OSPF route. The left side shows how OSPF learns three routes to subnet 10.1.1.0/24, while EIGRP learns two routes to the same subnet. Each routing protocol chooses the lowest metric route to offer as the best route. However, an additional logic step then considers the administrative distance (AD) of the route. With default settings, the router chooses the EIGRP (AD 90) route instead of the OSPF (AD 110) route for subnet 10.1.1.0/24.

You might wonder at the choice to use more than one routing protocol. One classic case occurs when two companies merge into one company, as shown in Figure 24-5. Company A on the left uses EIGRP with addresses from private network 10.0.0.0. Company B on the right uses OSPF with addresses from private network 172.16.0.0. As a first step to connect the networks, the network engineers install new WAN links between the A1 and B1 router plus the A2 and B2 router as shown in the figure.

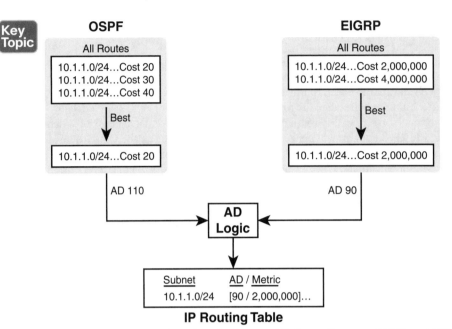

Figure 24-4   *Logic: Choosing the Lowest AD Route Between OSPF and EIGRP*

Next, the routers need to learn routes from both companies. The EIGRP routers on the left need to learn the company B routes known to OSPF on the right, and vice versa. To do that, the networking staff uses a feature called *route redistribution*, in which a *small set of routers run both routing protocols*. Internal to those routers, the router redistributes (takes routes from one protocol and advertises into the other), taking OSPF routes and advertising those subnets using EIGRP, and vice versa.

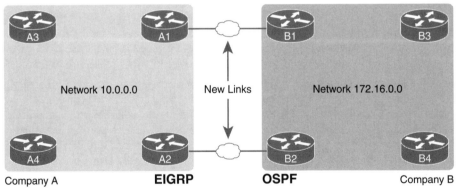

Figure 24-5   *First Step: Adding WAN Links Between Existing Company A and B Routers*

Figure 24-6 shows the updated scenario, with Routers A1 and A2 performing route redistribution. Most routers continue to run only OSPF or only EIGRP; in this case, Routers B1, B2, B3, and B4 continue to use only OSPF, whereas A3 and A4 use only EIGRP. However, the redistribution process on Routers A1 and A2 advertises routes so that all learn routes to all subnets in network 10.0.0.0 and network 172.16.0.0.

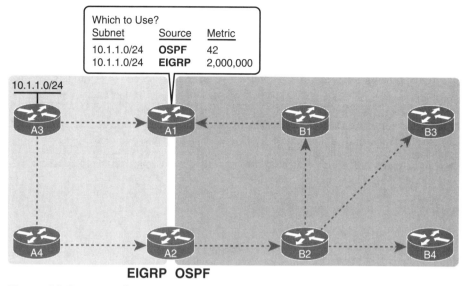

Figure 24-6 *Example: Router A1 Learns an EIGRP and OSPF Route to Subnet 10.1.1.0/24*

The figure uses dashed lines to show the propagation of routing information about subnet 10.1.1.0/24. First, focusing on the left, all four EIGRP routers in former Company A learn a route for subnet 10.1.1.0/24 using EIGRP. Next, follow the dashed lines along the bottom of the drawing, with Router A2 redistributing a route for 10.1.1.0/24 into OSPF. The OSPF routers all learn routes for 10.1.1.0/24 using OSPF. Now Router A1 has a route for subnet 10.1.1.0/24 learned with EIGRP and another learned with OSPF, creating a real-life scenario in which it must use administrative distance.

NOTE   The CCNP Enterprise certification discusses route redistribution, both concept and configuration. However, the CCNA V1.1 blueprint does not. It is mentioned here only to show a realistic case when a router needs to use administrative distance.

NOTE   The section "Floating Static Routes" in Chapter 17 discusses another example of how routers use the AD to choose routes. Take a moment to review that section if you do not recall the details.

Now that you understand the context, try memorizing the administrative distance values in Table 24-4.

IP Forwarding with the Longest Prefix Match

For the final few pages of this chapter, focus on how a router matches a packet's destination IP address to one of the routes already placed in the routing table. That process goes by a few terms, like *IP routing*, *forwarding*, or the *data plane*. Regardless, focus on the logic.

A router's IP routing process requires that the router compare the destination IP address of each packet with the existing contents of that router's IP routing table. Often, only one route matches a particular destination address. When only one route matches the packet's destination, the action is obvious: forward the packet based on the details listed in that route.

In some cases, multiple routes exist for the exact same subnet, that is, for the exact same subnet and mask. The earlier section, "Equal-Cost Multipath OSPF Routes," discussed how OSPF would choose to add these multiple routes to the routing table, and how a router will load balance packets that match those routes.

This section discusses a different case in which a set of routes lists different subnets whose address ranges overlap. In that case, some packets' destination addresses match multiple routes in the IP routing table. For instance, one route might list subnet 10.1.0.0/16, another 10.1.1.0/25, and another 10.1.1.1/32. The range of addresses in each of those subnets includes 10.1.1.1, so a packet sent to IP address 10.1.1.1 would match all those routes.

Many legitimate router features can cause these multiple overlapping routes to appear in a router's routing table, including

- Static routes (including host routes)

- Route autosummarization

- Manual route summarization

- Default routes

In this case, a router chooses the best route as follows:

When a particular destination IP address matches more than one route in a router's IPv4 routing table, and those routes list different rather than identical subnets (different subnet IDs and masks), the router uses **longest prefix match** logic to match the most specific route—the route with the longest prefix length mask.

Using Your Subnetting Math Skills to Predict the Choice of Best Route

One way to predict which route a router uses requires you to use your subnetting skills plus the output from the **show ip route** command. To see how it works, an upcoming example uses several overlapping routes learned by Router R1 in Figure 24-7. Example 24-9 focuses on routes that match PC D's IP address (172.16.10.4), matching four routes on Router R1.

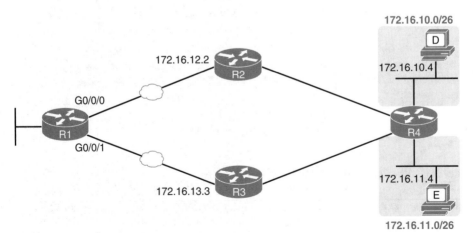

Figure 24-7 *Topology, Interfaces, and Next-Hop Addresses Used with Example 24-9*

Example 24-9   show ip route *Command with Overlapping Routes*

```
R1# show ip route
Codes: L - local, C - connected, S - static, R - RIP, M - mobile, B - BGP
       D - EIGRP, EX - EIGRP external, O - OSPF, IA - OSPF inter area
       N1 - OSPF NSSA external type 1, N2 - OSPF NSSA external type 2
       E1 - OSPF external type 1, E2 - OSPF external type 2
       i - IS-IS, su - IS-IS summary, L1 - IS-IS level-1, L2 - IS-IS level-2
       ia - IS-IS inter area, * - candidate default, U - per-user static route
       o - ODR, P - periodic downloaded static route, H - NHRP, l - LISP
       + - replicated route, % - next hop override

Gateway of last resort is 172.16.13.3 to network 0.0.0.0

O*E2  0.0.0.0/0 [110/1] via 172.16.13.3, 00:04:56, GigabitEthernet0/1
      172.16.0.0/16 is variably subnetted, 12 subnets, 4 masks
S        172.16.10.4/32 [1/0] via 172.16.12.2
O IA     172.16.10.0/26 [110/3] via 172.16.13.3, 00:04:56, GigabitEthernet0/0/1
O IA     172.16.10.0/23 [110/6] via 172.16.12.2, 00:04:56, GigabitEthernet0/0/0
O IA     172.16.11.0/26 [110/3] via 172.16.13.3, 00:04:56, GigabitEthernet0/0/1
! Non-overlapping routes omitted for brevity
```

On the exam, or in real life, you would look at each route's subnet ID and mask and do the math to list the range of addresses in each subnet. Table 24-5 shows the result to ensure the math does not get in the way of your understanding the concepts. All the subnets listed in the table match the destination address 172.16.10.4 (PC D).

Table 24-5   Analysis of Address Ranges for the Subnets in Example 24-9

Subnet/Prefix of a Route	Address Range	Next-Hop
172.16.10.4/32	172.16.10.4 (just this one address)	172.16.12.2 (R2)
172.16.10.0/26	172.16.10.0–172.16.10.63	172.16.13.3 (R3)
172.16.10.0/23	172.16.10.0–172.16.11.255	172.16.12.2 (R2)
0.0.0.0/0	0.0.0.0–255.255.255.255 (all addresses)	172.16.13.3 (R3)

NOTE   The route listed as 0.0.0.0/0 is the default route.

Working through the logic, note that packet destination 172.16.10.4 matches all routes highlighted in Example 24-9 (the routes also listed in Table 24-5). The various prefix lengths (masks) range from /0 to /32. The longest prefix (largest /P value, meaning the best and most specific route) is /32. So, a packet sent to 172.16.10.4 uses the route to 172.16.10.4/32, not the other routes.

It helps to think through a few more examples. The list identifies other destination addresses and explains why the router matches a specific route in Example 24-9.

172.16.10.4: PC D. Matches all four highlighted routes; the longest prefix is /32, the route to router 172.16.10.4/32.

172.16.10.1: A different host in PC D's subnet, this destination matches the default route (0 prefix length) and the routes with the /23 and /26 prefix lengths. R1 uses the /26 route for subnet 172.16.10.0/26.

172.16.10.100: Per Table 24-5, this address resides in the range of addresses for the /23 route, and it matches the default route as always. R1 uses the route with /23 prefix length for subnet 172.16.10.0/23.

172.16.12.1: Matches only the default route with /0 prefix length.

Using show ip route *address* to Find the Best Route

A second method to identify the route used by a router does not require you to use any subnetting math skills. Instead, use the **show ip route** *address* command, with the packet's destination IP address as the final parameter in the command. The router replies by listing its route when forwarding packets to that address.

For instance, Example 24-10 lists the output of the **show ip route 172.16.10.1** command on the same router used in Example 24-9. The first line of (highlighted) output lists the matched route: the route to 172.16.10.0/26. The rest of the output lists the details of that particular route, including the outgoing interface of GigabitEthernet0/0/1 and the next-hop router of 172.16.13.3.

Example 24-10   show ip route *Command with Overlapping Routes*

```
R1# show ip route 172.16.10.1
Routing entry for 172.16.10.0/26
  Known via "ospf 1", distance 110, metric 3, type inter area
  Last update from 172.16.13.3 on GigabitEthernet0/0/1, 00:44:09 ago
  Routing Descriptor Blocks:
  * 172.16.13.3, from 3.3.3.3, 00:44:09 ago, via GigabitEthernet0/0/1
      Route metric is 3, traffic share count is 1
```

Certainly, if answering a lab question on the exam, use this command because it tells you what the router will choose without you doing the subnetting math.

Interpreting the IP Routing Table

Here at the end of three consecutive book parts about IP and IP routing, before moving on to Part VII, "IP Version 6," this final topic reviews the most critical router command at the center of the discussion: the **show ip route** command. You have learned the various components of the command output through many examples. This final topic of the chapter pulls the concepts together in one place for easier reference and study.

Figure 24-8 shows the output of a sample **show ip route** command. The figure numbers various parts of the command output for easier reference, with Table 24-6 describing the output noted by each number.

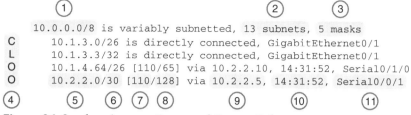

Figure 24-8   show ip route *Command Output Reference*

Table 24-6   Descriptions of the **show ip route** Command Output (refer to Figure 24-8)

Item	Idea	Value in the Figure	Description
1	Classful network	10.0.0.0/8	The routing table is organized by classful network. This line is the heading line for classful network 10.0.0.0; it lists the default mask for Class A networks (/8).
2	Number of subnets	13 subnets	The number of routes for subnets of the classful network known to this router, from all sources, including local routes—the /32 routes that match each router interface IP address.
3	Number of masks	5 masks	The number of different masks used in all routes known to this router inside this classful network.
4	Legend code	C, L, O	A short code that identifies the source of the routing information. *O* is for OSPF, *D* for EIGRP, *C* for Connected, *S* for static, and *L* for local. (See Example 24-11 for a sample of the legend.)
5	Prefix (Subnet ID)	10.2.2.0	The subnet number of this particular route.
6	Prefix length (Mask)	/30	The prefix mask used with this subnet.
7	Administrative distance	110	If a router learns routes for the listed subnet from more than one source of routing information, the router uses the source with the lowest administrative distance (AD).
8	Metric	128	The metric for this route.
9	Next-hop router	10.2.2.5	For packets matching this route, the IP address of the next router to which the packet should be forwarded.
10	Timer	14:31:52	For OSPF and EIGRP routes, this is the time since the route was first learned.
11	Outgoing interface	Serial0/0/1	For packets matching this route, the interface out which the packet should be forwarded.

You should also have a good mastery of the most common codes found in the legend at the beginning of the output from the **show ip route** command. Example 24-11 closes the chapter with one final example, showing the legend but without any routes. Make an effort to commit the highlighted codes to memory.

Example 24-11   show ip route—*Most Common Legend Codes*

```
R1# show ip route
Codes: L - local, C - connected, S - static, R - RIP, M - mobile, B - BGP
       D - EIGRP, EX - EIGRP external, O - OSPF, IA - OSPF inter area
       N1 - OSPF NSSA external type 1, N2 - OSPF NSSA external type 2
       E1 - OSPF external type 1, E2 - OSPF external type 2, m - OMP
       n - NAT, Ni - NAT inside, No - NAT outside, Nd - NAT DIA
       i - IS-IS, su - IS-IS summary, L1 - IS-IS level-1, L2 - IS-IS level-2
       ia - IS-IS inter area, * - candidate default, U - per-user static route
       H - NHRP, G - NHRP registered, g - NHRP registration summary
       o - ODR, P - periodic downloaded static route, l - LISP
       a - application route
       + - replicated route, % - next hop override, p - overrides from PfR
       & - replicated local route overrides by connected
! Lines omitted for brevity
```

Chapter Review

One key to doing well on the exams is to perform repetitive spaced review sessions. Review this chapter's material using either the tools in the book or interactive tools for the same material found on the book's companion website. Refer to the "Your Study Plan" element for more details. Table 24-7 outlines the key review elements and where you can find them. To better track your study progress, record when you completed these activities in the second column.

Table 24-7   Chapter Review Tracking

Review Element	Review Date(s)	Resource Used
Review key topics		Book, website
Review command tables		Book
Review memory tables		Website
Watch video		Website

Review All the Key Topics

Table 24-8   Key Topics for Chapter 24

Key Topic Element	Description	Page Number
Table 24-2	OSPF neighbor requirements	611
Table 24-3	**show** commands to display facts for OSPF neighbor requirements	612
List	Reasons why routers can become OSPF neighbors but fail to exchange routing information	618
Table 24-4	Default Cisco router administrative distance settings	623

Key Topic Element	Description	Page Number
Figure 24-4	Concept of how a router uses administrative distance to choose an EIGRP route over an OSPF route	624
Paragraph	Router logic when a packet's destination address matches multiple IP routes	626
Example 24-9	Example of an IP routing table with overlapping IP routes	627
Figure 24-8	The Cisco IP routing table field reference	629
Table 24-6	Explanations for Figure 24-8's IP routing table	629

24

Key Terms You Should Know

administrative distance, equal-cost multipath (ECMP), equal-cost route, longest prefix match

Command References

Tables 24-9 and 24-10 list configuration and verification commands used in this chapter. As an easy review exercise, cover the left column in a table, read the right column, and try to recall the command without looking. Then repeat the exercise, covering the right column, and try to recall what the command does.

Table 24-9 Chapter 24 Configuration Command Reference

Command	Description
router ospf *process-id*	Global command that enters OSPF configuration mode for the listed process
ip ospf *process-id* area *area-number*	Interface subcommand to enable OSPF on the interface and to assign the interface to a specific OSPF area
router-id *id*	OSPF command that statically sets the router ID
ip ospf hello-interval *seconds*	Interface subcommand that sets the interval for periodic Hellos
ip ospf dead-interval *number*	Interface subcommand that sets the OSPF dead timer
[no] shutdown	An OSPF configuration mode command to disable (**shutdown**) or enable (**no shutdown**) the OSPF process
[no] ip ospf shutdown	An interface subcommand to disable or enable OSPF functions on the selected interface
mtu *size*	An interface subcommand to set the largest packet size (MTU) for all Layer 3 protocols enabled on the interface
ip mtu *size*	An interface subcommand to set the largest packet size (MTU) for IPv4 packets on the interface, overriding the setting of the **mtu** *size* subcommand
ip ospf priority *value*	Interface subcommand that sets the OSPF priority, used when electing a new DR or BDR
ip ospf network {broadcast | point-to-point}	Interface subcommand used to set the OSPF network type on the interface
maximum-paths *number*	OSPF router subcommand that defines the maximum number of equal-cost multipath (ECMP) routes, learned by OSPF, to be added to the routing table at one time

Table 24-10 Chapter 24 **show** Command Reference

Command	Description
show ip protocols	Shows routing protocol parameters and current timer values, including an effective copy of the routing protocols' **network** commands and a list of passive interfaces
show ip ospf interface brief	Lists the interfaces on which the OSPF protocol is enabled (based on the **network** commands), including passive interfaces
show ip ospf interface [*type number*]	Lists detailed OSPF settings for all interfaces, or the listed interface, including Hello and Dead timers and OSPF area
show ip ospf neighbor	Lists neighbors and current status with neighbors, per interface
show ip ospf	Lists a group of messages about the OSPF process itself, listing the OSPF Router ID in the first line
show interfaces	Lists a long set of messages, per interface, that lists configuration, state, and counter information
show ip ospf database	Displays the contents of the router's OSPF LSDB
show ip route	Lists all IPv4 routes
show ip route ospf	Lists the OSPF-learned IPv4 routes in the routing table
show ip route *address*	Lists details about the one route this router would match for packets destined to the listed address
clear ip ospf process	Resets the OSPF process, resetting all neighbor relationships and also causing the process to make a choice of OSPF RID

Part VI Review

Keep track of your part review progress with the checklist in Table P6-1. Details about each task follow the table.

Table P6-1 Part VI Part Review Checklist

Activity	1st Date Completed	2nd Date Completed
Repeat All DIKTA Questions		
Answer Part Review Questions		
Review Key Topics		
Do Labs		
Watch Video		
Use Per-Chapter Interactive Review		

Repeat All DIKTA Questions

For this task, answer the "Do I Know This Already?" questions again for the chapters in this part of the book using the PTP software. See the section "How to View Only DIKTA Questions by Chapter or Part" in the Introduction to this book to learn how to make the PTP software show you DIKTA questions for this part only.

Answer Part Review Questions

For this task, answer the Part Review questions for this part of the book using the PTP software. See the section "How to View Part Review Questions" in the Introduction to this book to learn how to make the PTP software show you DIKTA questions for this part only.

Review Key Topics

Review all Key Topics in all chapters in this part, either by browsing the chapters or by using the Key Topics application on the companion website.

Do Labs

Depending on your chosen lab tool, here are some suggestions for what to do in lab:

Pearson Network Simulator: If you use the full Pearson CCNA simulator, focus more on the configuration scenario and troubleshooting scenario labs associated with the topics in this part of the book. These types of labs include a larger set of topics and work well as Part Review activities. (See the Introduction for some details about how to find which labs are about topics in this part of the book.)

Blog: Config Labs: The author's blog includes a series of configuration-focused labs that you can do on paper or with Cisco Packet Tracer in about 15 minutes. To find them, open https://www.certskills.com and look under the Labs menu item.

Other: If using other lab tools, here are a few suggestions: make sure to experiment heavily with OSPF configuration and all the optional settings that impact OSPF neighbor compatibility.

Watch Video

The companion website includes a variety of common mistake and Q&A videos organized by part and chapter. Use these videos to challenge your thinking, dig deeper, review topics, and better prepare for the exam. Make sure to bookmark a link to the companion website and use the videos for review whenever you have a few extra minutes.

So far, this book has mostly ignored IP version 6 (IPv6). This part reverses the trend, collecting all the specific IPv6 topics into five chapters.

The chapters in Part VII walk you through the same topics discussed throughout this book for IPv4, often using IPv4 as a point of comparison. Certainly, many details differ when comparing IPv4 and IPv6. However, many core concepts about IP addressing, subnetting, routing, and routing protocols remain the same. The chapters in this part build on those foundational concepts, adding the specific details about how IPv6 forwards IPv6 packets from one host to another.

Part VII

IP Version 6

CHAPTER 25

Fundamentals of IP Version 6

This chapter covers the following exam topics:

1.0 Network Fundamentals

    1.8 Configure and verify IPv6 addressing and prefix

    1.9 Describe IPv6 address types

IPv4 has been a solid and highly useful part of the growth of TCP/IP and the Internet. For most of the long history of the Internet, and for most corporate networks that use TCP/IP, IPv4 is the core protocol that defines addressing and routing. However, although IPv4 has many great qualities, it has some shortcomings, creating the need for a replacement protocol: IP version 6 (IPv6).

IPv6 defines the same general functions as IPv4, but with different methods of implementing those functions. For example, both IPv4 and IPv6 define addressing, the concepts of subnetting larger groups of addresses into smaller groups, headers used to create an IPv4 or IPv6 packet, and the rules for routing those packets. At the same time, IPv6 handles the details differently; for example, using a 128-bit IPv6 address rather than the 32-bit IPv4 address.

This chapter focuses on the core network layer functions of addressing and routing. The first section of this chapter looks at the big concepts, while the second section looks at the specifics of how to write and type IPv6 addresses.

"Do I Know This Already?" Quiz

Take the quiz (either here or use the PTP software) if you want to use the score to help you decide how much time to spend on this chapter. The letter answers are listed at the bottom of the page following the quiz. Appendix C, found both at the end of the book as well as on the companion website, includes both the answers and explanations. You can also find both answers and explanations in the PTP testing software.

Table 25-1 "Do I Know This Already?" Foundation Topics Section-to-Question Mapping

Foundation Topics Section	Questions
Introduction to IPv6	1–2
IPv6 Addressing Formats and Conventions	3–6

    1. Which of the following was a short-term solution to the IPv4 address exhaustion problem?

        a. IP version 6

        b. IP version 5

    c. NAT/PAT

    d. ARP

2. A router receives an Ethernet frame that holds an IPv6 packet. The router then decides to route the packet out an Ethernet WAN link. Which statement is true about how a router forwards an IPv6 packet?

    a. The router discards the received frame's Ethernet data-link header and trailer.

    b. The router makes the forwarding decision based on the packet's source IPv6 address.

    c. The router keeps the incoming frame's Ethernet header, encapsulating the entire frame inside a new IPv6 packet before sending it over the outgoing Ethernet WAN link.

    d. The router uses the IPv4 routing table when choosing where to forward the packet.

3. Which of the following is the shortest valid abbreviation for FE80:0000:0000:0000:0100:0000:0000:0123?

    a. FE80::100::123

    b. FE8::1::123

    c. FE80::100:0:0:0:123:4567

    d. FE80::100:0:0:123

4. Which of the following is the shortest valid abbreviation for 2000:0300:0040:0005:6000:0700:0080:0009?

    a. 2:3:4:5:6:7:8:9

    b. 2000:300:40:5:6000:700:80:9

    c. 2000:300:4:5:6000:700:8:9

    d. 2000:3:4:5:6:7:8:9

5. Which of the following is the unabbreviated version of IPv6 address 2001:DB8::200:28?

    a. 2001:0DB8:0000:0000:0000:0000:0200:0028

    b. 2001:0DB8::0200:0028

    c. 2001:0DB8:0:0:0:0:0200:0028

    d. 2001:0DB8:0000:0000:0000:0000:200:0028

6. Which of the following is the correct abbreviated subnet prefix for address 2000:0000:0000:0005:6000:0700:0080:0009, assuming a mask of /64?

    a. 2000::5::/64

    b. 2000::5:0:0:0:0/64

    c. 2000:0:0:5::/64

    d. 2000:0:0:5:0:0:0:0/64

Foundation Topics

Introduction to IPv6

IP version 6 (IPv6) serves as the replacement protocol for IP version 4 (IPv4). To do so, the network can perform a slow migration that uses both, with IPv6 overcoming some of the issues that drove the need for a protocol to replace IPv4.

Unfortunately, that introductory statement creates more questions than it answers. Why does IPv4 need to be replaced? If IPv4 needs to be replaced, when will that happen—and will it happen quickly? What exactly happens when a company or the Internet replaces IPv4 with IPv6? And the list goes on.

While this introductory chapter cannot get into every detail of why IPv4 needs to eventually be replaced by IPv6, the clearest and most obvious reason for migrating TCP/IP networks to use IPv6 is growth. IPv4 uses a 32-bit address, which totals to a few billion addresses. Interestingly, that seemingly large number of addresses is too small. IPv6 increases the address to 128 bits in length. For perspective, IPv6 supplies more than 10,000,000,000,000,000,000,000,000,000 times as many addresses as IPv4. IPv4 supplies just under 10^{10} addresses, while IPv6 supplies just under 10^{38} addresses.

The fact that IPv6 uses a different size address field, with some different addressing rules, means that many other protocols and functions change as well. For example, IPv4 routing—in other words, the packet-forwarding process—relies on an understanding of IPv4 addresses. To support IPv6 routing, routers must understand IPv6 addresses and routing. To dynamically learn routes for IPv6 subnets, routing protocols must support these different IPv6 addressing rules, including rules about how IPv6 creates subnets. As a result, the migration from IPv4 to IPv6 is much more than changing one protocol (IP), but it impacts many protocols.

This first section of the chapter discusses some of the reasons for the change from IPv4 to IPv6, along with the protocols that must change as a result.

The Historical Reasons for IPv6

In the last 50+ years, the Internet has gone from its infancy to being a huge influence in the world. It first grew through research at universities, from the ARPANET beginnings of the Internet in the late 1960s into the 1970s. The Internet kept growing fast in the 1980s, with the Internet's fast growth still primarily driven by research and the universities that joined in that research.

By the early 1990s, the Internet allowed commercial use, driving Internet growth even higher. Eventually, fixed Internet access from home became common, followed by the pervasive use of the Internet from mobile devices like smartphones. Now the Internet of Things (IoT) fuels Internet growth, adding all kinds of devices throughout industry that can communicate through an IP network. Figure 25-1 shows some of these major milestones with general dates.

Answers to the "Do I Know This Already?" quiz:

1 C **2** A **3** D **4** B **5** A **6** C

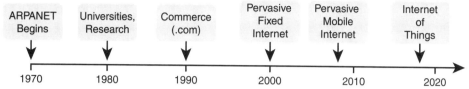

Figure 25-1 *Some Major Events in the Growth of the Internet*

The incredible growth of the Internet over a fairly long time created a big problem for public IPv4 addresses: the world was running out of addresses. As one example milestone, in 2011, the Internet Assigned Numbers Authority (IANA) allocated the final five /8 address blocks (the same size as a Class A network) to each of the five Regional Internet Registries (RIR). At that point, IANA had no more public IPv4 addresses to allocate to RIRs. The RIRs could no longer receive new allocations of public addresses from IANA but could continue to assign blocks from their remaining public address space.

In the 2010s, the five RIRs eventually assigned all of their public address space. For example, in late 2015, ARIN (North America) announced that it had exhausted its supply. All the RIRs have plans for how to deal with IPv4 address exhaustion, with all either being out of IPv4 address space or using a maintenance plan to reclaim unused IPv4 addresses for reassignment.

These events are significant in that the day has finally come in which new companies can attempt to connect to the Internet, but they can no longer simply use IPv4, ignoring IPv6. Their only option will be IPv6 because IPv4 has no public addresses left.

NOTE You can track ARIN's progress through this interesting transition in the history of the Internet at its IPv4 address depletion site: https://www.arin.net/resources/guide/ipv4/. You can also see a summary report at http://ipv4.potaroo.net.

Even though the media has rightfully made a big deal about running out of IPv4 addresses, those who care about the Internet knew about this potential problem since the late 1980s. The problem, generally called the **IPv4 address exhaustion** problem, could literally have caused the huge growth of the Internet in the 1990s to have come to a screeching halt! Something had to be done.

The IETF came up with several short-term solutions to make IPv4 addresses last longer, and one long-term solution: IPv6. However, several other tools like Network Address Translation (NAT) and classless interdomain routing (CIDR) helped extend IPv4's life another couple of decades. IPv6 creates a more permanent and long-lasting solution, replacing IPv4, with a new IPv6 header and new IPv6 addresses. The address size supports a huge number of addresses, solving the address shortage problem for generations (we hope). Figure 25-2 shows some of the major IPv4 address exhaustion timing events.

The rest of this first section examines IPv6, comparing it to IPv4, focusing on the common features of the two protocols. In particular, this section compares the protocols (including addresses), routing, routing protocols, and miscellaneous other related topics.

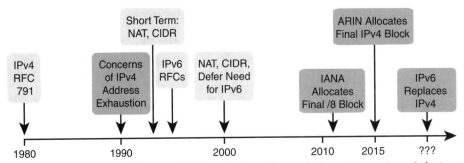

Figure 25-2   *Timeline for IPv4 Address Exhaustion and Short-/Long-Term Solutions*

> **NOTE**   You might wonder why the next version of IP is not called IP version 5. There was an earlier effort to create a new version of IP, and it was numbered version 5. IPv5 did not progress to the standards stage. However, to prevent any issues, because version 5 had been used in some documents, the next effort to update IP was numbered as version 6.

The IPv6 Protocols

The primary purpose of the core IPv6 protocol mirrors the same purpose of the IPv4 protocol. That core IPv6 protocol, as defined in RFC 8200, defines a packet concept, addresses for those packets, and the role of hosts and routers. These rules allow the devices to forward packets sourced by hosts, through multiple routers, so that they arrive at the correct destination host. (IPv4 defines those same concepts for IPv4 back in RFC 791.)

However, because IPv6 impacts so many other functions in a TCP/IP network, many more RFCs must define details of IPv6. Some other RFCs define how to migrate from IPv4 to IPv6. Others define new versions of familiar protocols or replace old protocols with new ones. For example:

Older OSPF Version 2 Upgraded to OSPF Version 3: The older Open Shortest Path First (OSPF) version 2 works for IPv4, but not for IPv6, so a newer version, **OSPF version 3 (OSPFv3),** was created to support IPv6. (Note: OSPFv3 was later upgraded to support advertising both IPv4 and IPv6 routes.)

ICMP Upgraded to ICMP Version 6: Internet Control Message Protocol (ICMP) worked well with IPv4 but needed to be changed to support IPv6. The new name is ICMPv6.

ARP Replaced by Neighbor Discovery Protocol: For IPv4, Address Resolution Protocol (ARP) discovers the MAC address used by neighbors. IPv6 replaces ARP with a more general Neighbor Discovery Protocol (NDP).

> **NOTE**   A huge number of Internet RFCs define IPv6. A recent search for "IPv6" at https://www.rfc-editor.org showed over 550 such RFCs.

Although the term *IPv6*, when used broadly, includes many protocols, the one specific protocol called IPv6 defines the new 128-bit IPv6 address. Of course, writing these addresses in binary would be a problem—they probably would not even fit on the width of a piece of paper! IPv6 defines a shorter hexadecimal format, requiring at most 32 hexadecimal digits (one hex digit per 4 bits), with methods to abbreviate the hexadecimal addresses as well.

For example, all of the following are IPv6 addresses, each with 32 or fewer hex digits.

```
2345:1111:2222:3333:4444:5555:6666:AAAA
2000:1:2:3:4:5:6:A
FE80::1
```

The upcoming section "IPv6 Addressing Formats and Conventions" discusses the specifics of how to represent IPv6 addresses, including how to legally abbreviate the hex address values.

Like IPv4, IPv6 defines a header, with places to hold both the source and destination address fields. Compared to IPv4, the IPv6 header does make some other changes besides simply making the address fields larger. However, even though the IPv6 header is larger than an IPv4 header, the IPv6 header is actually simpler (on purpose). Figure 25-3 shows the required 40-byte part of the IPv6 header.

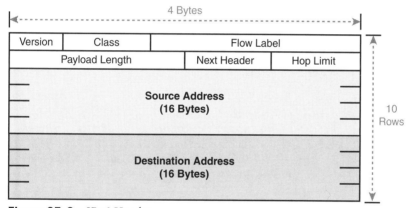

Figure 25-3   *IPv6 Header*

IPv6 Routing

As with many functions of IPv6, IPv6 routing looks just like IPv4 routing from a general perspective, with the differences being clear only once you look at the specifics. Keeping the discussion general for now, IPv6 uses these ideas the same way as IPv4:

- To be able to build and send IPv6 packets out an interface, end-user devices need an IPv6 address on that interface.

- End-user hosts need to know the IPv6 address of a default router, to which the host sends IPv6 packets if the destination host is in a different subnet.

- IPv6 routers de-encapsulate and re-encapsulate each IPv6 packet when routing the packet.

- IPv6 routers make routing decisions by comparing the IPv6 packet's destination address to the router's IPv6 routing table; the matched route lists directions of where to send the IPv6 packet next.

NOTE   You could take the preceding list and replace every instance of IPv6 with IPv4, and all the statements would be true of IPv4 as well.

The next few figures show the concepts with an example. First, Figure 25-4 shows a few settings on a host. The host (PC1) has an address of 2345::1. PC1 also knows its default gateway of 2345::2. (Both values are valid abbreviations for real IPv6 addresses.) To send an IPv6 packet to host PC2, on another IPv6 subnet, PC1 creates an IPv6 packet and sends it to R1, PC1's default gateway.

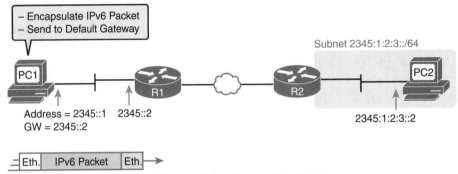

Figure 25-4   *IPv6 Host Building and Sending an IPv6 Packet*

The router (R1) has many small tasks to do when forwarding this IPv6 packet, but for now, focus on the work R1 does related to encapsulation. As seen in Step 1 of Figure 25-5, R1 receives the incoming data-link frame and extracts (de-encapsulates) the IPv6 packet from inside the frame, discarding the original data-link header and trailer. At Step 2, once R1 knows to forward the IPv6 packet to R2, R1 adds a correct outgoing data-link header and trailer to the IPv6 packet, encapsulating the IPv6 packet.

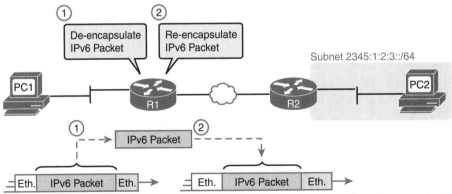

Figure 25-5   *IPv6 Router Performing Routine Encapsulation Tasks When Routing IPv6*

When a router like R1 de-encapsulates the packet from the data-link frame, it must also decide what type of packet sits inside the frame. To do so, the router must look at a protocol type field in the data-link header, which identifies the type of packet inside the data-link frame. Today, most data-link frames carry either an IPv4 packet or an IPv6 packet.

To route an IPv6 packet, a router must use its IPv6 routing table instead of the IPv4 routing table. The router must look at the packet's destination IPv6 address and compare that address to the router's current IPv6 routing table. The router uses the forwarding instructions in the matched IPv6 route to forward the IPv6 packet. Figure 25-6 shows the overall process.

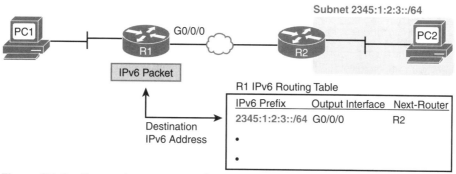

Figure 25-6   *Comparing an IPv6 Packet to R1's IPv6 Routing Table*

Note that again, the process works like IPv4, except that the IPv6 packet lists IPv6 addresses, and the IPv6 routing table lists routing information for IPv6 subnets (called subnet *prefixes*).

Finally, in most enterprise networks, the routers will route both IPv4 and IPv6 packets at the same time. That is, your company will not decide to adopt IPv6, and then late one weekend night turn off all IPv4 and enable IPv6 on every device. Instead, IPv6 allows for a slow migration, during which some or all routers forward both IPv4 and IPv6 packets. (The migration strategy of running both IPv4 and IPv6 is called *dual stack*.) All you have to do is configure the router to route IPv6 packets, in addition to the existing configuration for routing IPv4 packets.

IPv6 Routing Protocols

IPv6 routers need to learn routes for all the possible IPv6 subnet prefixes. Just like with IPv4, IPv6 routers use routing protocols, with familiar names, and generally speaking, with familiar functions.

None of the IPv4 routing protocols could be used to advertise IPv6 routes originally. They all required some kind of update to add messages, protocols, and rules to support IPv6. Over time, Routing Information Protocol (RIP), Open Shortest Path First (OSPF), Enhanced Interior Gateway Routing Protocol (EIGRP), and Border Gateway Protocol (BGP) were all updated to support IPv6. Table 25-2 lists the names of these routing protocols, with a few comments.

Table 25-2   IPv6 Routing Protocols

Routing Protocol	Defined By	Notes
RIPng (RIP next generation)	RFC	The "next generation" is a reference to a TV series, *Star Trek: The Next Generation.*
OSPFv3 (OSPF version 3)	RFC	The OSPF you have worked with for IPv4 is actually OSPF version 2, so the new version for IPv6 is OSPFv3.

Routing Protocol	Defined By	Notes
EIGRPv6 (EIGRP for IPv6)	Cisco	Cisco owns the rights to the EIGRP protocol, but Cisco also now publishes EIGRP as an informational RFC.
MP BGP-4 (Multiprotocol BGP version 4)	RFC	BGP version 4 was created to be highly extendable; IPv6 support was added to BGP version 4 through one such enhancement, MP BGP-4.

In addition, these routing protocols also follow the same interior gateway protocol (IGP) and exterior gateway protocol (EGP) conventions as their IPv4 cousins. RIPng, EIGRPv6, and OSPFv3 act as interior gateway protocols, advertising IPv6 routes inside an enterprise.

As you can see from this introduction, IPv6 uses many of the same big ideas as IPv4. Both define headers with a source and destination address. Both define the routing of packets, with the routing process discarding old data-link headers and trailers when forwarding the packets. And routers use the same general process to make a routing decision, comparing the packet's destination IP address to the routing table.

The big differences between IPv4 and IPv6 revolve around the bigger IPv6 addresses. The next topic begins looking at the specifics of these IPv6 addresses.

IPv6 Addressing Formats and Conventions

The CCNA exam requires some fundamental skills in working with IPv4 addresses. For example, you need to be able to interpret IPv4 addresses, like 172.21.73.14. You need to be able to work with prefix-style masks, like /25, and interpret what that means when used with a particular IPv4 address. And you need to be able to take an address and mask, like 172.21.73.14/25, and find the subnet ID.

This second major section of this chapter discusses these same ideas for IPv6 addresses. In particular, this section looks at

- How to write and interpret unabbreviated 32-digit IPv6 addresses

- How to abbreviate IPv6 addresses and how to interpret abbreviated addresses

- How to interpret the IPv6 prefix length (subnet mask)

- How to find the IPv6 subnet prefix ID based on an address and prefix length mask

The biggest challenge with these tasks lies in the sheer size of the numbers. Thankfully, the math to find the subnet ID—often a challenge for IPv4—is easier for IPv6, at least to the depth discussed in this book.

Representing Full (Unabbreviated) IPv6 Addresses

IPv6 uses a convenient hexadecimal (hex) format for addresses. To make it more readable, IPv6 uses a format with eight sets of four hex digits, with each set of four digits separated by a colon. For example:

```
2340:1111:AAAA:0001:1234:5678:9ABC:1234
```

> **NOTE** For convenience, this book uses the term **quartet** for one set of four hex digits, with eight quartets in each IPv6 address. Note that the IPv6 RFCs do not define an equivalent term.

IPv6 addresses also have a binary format, but thankfully, most of the time you do not need to look at the binary version of the addresses. However, in those cases, converting from hex to binary is relatively easy. Just change each hex digit to the equivalent 4-bit value listed in Table 25-3.

Table 25-3 Hexadecimal/Binary Conversion Chart

Hex	Binary	Hex	Binary
0	0000	8	1000
1	0001	9	1001
2	0010	A	1010
3	0011	B	1011
4	0100	C	1100
5	0101	D	1101
6	0110	E	1110
7	0111	F	1111

Abbreviating and Expanding IPv6 Addresses

IPv6 also defines ways to abbreviate or shorten how you write or type an IPv6 address. Why? Although using a 32-digit hex number works much better than working with a 128-bit binary number, 32 hex digits are still a lot of digits to remember, recognize in command output, and type on a command line. The IPv6 address abbreviation rules let you shorten these numbers.

Computers and routers use the shortest abbreviation, even if you type all 32 hex digits of the address. So even if you would prefer to use the longer unabbreviated version of the IPv6 address, you need to be ready to interpret the meaning of an abbreviated IPv6 address as listed by a router or host. This section first looks at abbreviating addresses and then at expanding addresses.

Abbreviating IPv6 Addresses

Two basic rules let you, or any computer, shorten or abbreviate an IPv6 address:

1. Inside each quartet of four hex digits, remove up to three leading 0s in the three positions on the left. (Note: At this step, a quartet of 0000 will leave a single 0.)
2. Replace the longest set of two or more consecutive 0000 quartets with a double colon. The abbreviation :: means "two or more quartets of all 0s." However, you can use this replacement only once inside a single address—for the longest set of consecutive 0000 quartets (or the first such set if a tie).

For example, consider the following IPv6 address. The bold digits represent digits in which the address could be abbreviated.

        2100:**0000**:**0000**:**000**1:**0000**:**0000**:**0000**:**00**56

Applying the first rule, you would look at all eight quartets independently. In each, remove all the leading 0s. Note that five of the quartets have four 0s, so for these, remove only three leading binary 0s, leaving the following value:

```
2100:0:0:1:0:0:0:56
```

While this abbreviation is valid, the address can be abbreviated further, using the second rule. In this case, two instances exist where more than one quartet in a row has only a 0. Pick the longest such sequence, and replace it with ::, giving you the shortest legal abbreviation:

```
2100:0:0:1::56
```

While 2100:0:0:1::56 is indeed the shortest abbreviation, this example happens to make it easier to see the two most common mistakes when abbreviating IPv6 addresses. First, never remove trailing 0s in a quartet (0s on the right side of the quartet). In this case, the first quartet of 2100 cannot be shortened at all because the two 0s trail. So, the following address, which begins now with only FE in the first quartet, is not a correct abbreviation of the original IPv6 address:

```
21:0:0:1::56
```

The second common mistake is to replace both sets of 0000 quartets with a double colon. For example, the following abbreviation would be incorrect for the original IPv6 address listed in this topic:

```
2100::1::56
```

The reason this abbreviation is incorrect is that now you do not know how many quartets of all 0s to substitute into each :: to find the original unabbreviated address.

Expanding Abbreviated IPv6 Addresses

To expand an IPv6 address back into its full unabbreviated 32-digit number, use two similar rules. The rules basically reverse the logic of the previous two rules:

1. In each quartet, add leading 0s as needed until the quartet has four hex digits.
2. If a double colon (::) exists, count the quartets currently shown; the total should be less than 8. Replace the :: with multiple quartets of 0000 so that eight total quartets exist.

The best way to get comfortable with these addresses and abbreviations is to do some yourself. Table 25-4 lists some practice problems, with the full 32-digit IPv6 address on the left and the best abbreviation on the right. The table gives you either the expanded or abbreviated address, and you need to supply the opposite value. The answers sit at the end of the chapter, in the section "Answers to Earlier Practice Problems."

Table 25-4 IPv6 Address Abbreviation and Expansion Practice

Full	Abbreviation
2340:0000:0010:0100:1000:ABCD:0101:1010	
	30A0:ABCD:EF12:3456:ABC:B0B0:9999:9009
2222:3333:4444:5555:0000:0000:6060:0707	
	3210::
210F:0000:0000:0000:CCCC:0000:0000:000D	

Full	Abbreviation
	`34BA:B:B::20`
`FE80:0000:0000:0000:DEAD:BEFF:FEEF:CAFE`	
	`FE80::FACE:BAFF:FEBE:CAFE`

Representing the Prefix Length of an Address

IPv6 uses a mask concept, called the **prefix length**, similar to IPv4 subnet masks. Similar to the IPv4 prefix-style mask, the IPv6 prefix length is written as a /, followed by a decimal number (there is no dotted-decimal equivalent mask for IPv6). The prefix length defines how many bits on the left side of an IPv6 address are the same value for all addresses within that subnet prefix. If you think of the ideas generically as prefix/length, all addresses in the subnet prefix begin with the same value in number of initial bits as defined by the length.

When writing an IPv6 address and prefix length in documentation, you can choose to leave a space before the /, or not, for readability. However, commands on Cisco devices typically do not allow spaces before or after the /.

```
2222:1111:0:1:A:B:C:D/64
2222:1111:0:1:A:B:C:D /64
```

Finally, note that the prefix length is a number of bits, so with IPv6, the legal value range is from 0 through 128, inclusive.

Calculating the IPv6 Subnet Prefix (Subnet ID)

With IPv4, you can take an IP address and the associated subnet mask, and calculate the subnet ID. With IPv6 subnetting, you can take an IPv6 address and the associated prefix length, and calculate the IPv6 equivalent of the subnet ID: an *IPv6* **subnet prefix**.

Like with different IPv4 subnet masks, some IPv6 prefix lengths make for an easy math problem to find the IPv6 subnet prefix, while some prefix lengths make the math more difficult. This section looks at the easier cases, mainly because the size of the IPv6 address space lets us all choose to use IPv6 prefix lengths that make the math much easier.

Finding the IPv6 Subnet Prefix

In IPv6, a subnet prefix represents a group of IPv6 addresses. For now, this section focuses on the math, and only the math, for finding the number that represents that subnet prefix. Chapter 26, "IPv6 Addressing and Subnetting," then starts putting more meaning behind the actual numbers.

Each IPv6 subnet prefix, or subnet if you prefer, has a number that represents the group. Many people just call it a subnet number or subnet ID, using the same terms as IPv4. As with IPv4, you can start with an IPv6 address and prefix length, and find the subnet prefix, with the same general rules that you use in IPv4. If the prefix length is /P, use these rules:

1. Copy the first P bits.

2. Change the rest of the bits to 0.

When using a prefix length that happens to be a multiple of 4, you do not have to think in terms of bits, but in terms of hex digits. A prefix length that is a multiple of 4 means that each hex digit is either copied or changed to hex 0. For example, a /44 prefix length implies 11 hex digits, a /48 prefix length implies 12 hex digits, and so on. Just for completeness, if the prefix length is indeed a multiple of 4, the process becomes

1. Identify the number of hex digits in the subnet prefix by dividing the prefix length (which is in bits) by 4.

2. Copy the hex digits determined to be in the subnet prefix per the first step.

3. Change the rest of the hex digits to 0.

Figure 25-7 shows an example, with a prefix length of 64. In this case, Step 1 looks at the /64 prefix length and calculates that the subnet prefix has 16 hex digits. Step 2 copies the first 16 digits of the IPv6 address, while Step 3 records hex 0s for the rest of the digits.

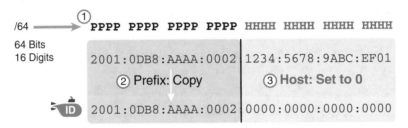

Legend:

 Subnet ID

Figure 25-7 *Creating the IPv6 Subnet Prefix from an Address/Length*

After you find the IPv6 subnet prefix, you should also be ready to abbreviate the IPv6 subnet prefix using the same rules you use to abbreviate IPv6 addresses. However, you should pay extra attention to the end of the subnet prefix because it often has several octets of all 0 values. As a result, the abbreviation typically ends with two colons (::).

For example, consider the following IPv6 address that is assigned to a host on a LAN:

    2000:1234:5678:9ABC:1234:5678:9ABC:1111/64

This example shows an IPv6 address that itself cannot be abbreviated. After you calculate the subnet prefix by zeroing out the last 64 bits (16 digits) of the address, you find the following subnet prefix value:

    2000:1234:5678:9ABC:**0000:0000:0000:0000**/64

This value can be abbreviated, with four quartets of all 0s at the end, as follows:

    2000:1234:5678:9ABC::/64

To get better at the math, take some time to work through finding the subnet prefix for several practice problems, as listed in Table 25-5. The answers sit at the end of the chapter, in the section "Answers to Earlier Practice Problems."

Table 25-5   Finding the IPv6 Subnet Prefix from an Address/Length Value

Address/Length	Subnet Prefix
2340:0:10:100:1000:ABCD:101:1010/64	
30A0:ABCD:EF12:3456:ABC:B0B0:9999:9009/64	
2222:3333:4444:5555::6060:707/64	
3210::ABCD:101:1010/64	
210F::CCCC:B0B0:9999:9009/64	
34BA:B:B:0:5555:0:6060:707/64	
3124::DEAD:CAFE:FF:FE00:1/64	
2BCD::FACE:BEFF:FEBE:CAFE/64	

25

Working with More-Difficult IPv6 Prefix Lengths

In Chapter 26, you will read more about IPv6 subnetting—a much simpler topic to learn as compared with IPv4 subnetting. One reason why IPv6 subnetting happens to be simple is that several RFCs, including RFC 4291, "IPv6 Addressing Architecture," recommends that all deployed subnets use a /64 prefix length.

You will also on occasion need to work with prefix lengths shorter than /64 when working through your enterprise's subnetting plan. To get ready for that, this last topic of the chapter provides some practice with other shorter prefix lengths, using the easier cases of prefix lengths that are multiples of 4.

For example, consider the following IPv6 address and prefix length:

    2000:1234:5678:9ABC:1234:5678:9ABC:1111/56

Because this example uses a /56 prefix length, the subnet prefix includes the first 56 bits, or first 14 complete hex digits, of the address. The rest of the hex digits will be 0, resulting in the following subnet prefix:

    2000:1234:5678:9A00:0000:0000:0000:0000/56

This value can be abbreviated, with four quartets of all 0s at the end, as follows:

    2000:1234:5678:9A00::/56

This example shows an easy place to make a mistake. Sometimes, people look at the /56 and think of that as the first 14 hex digits, which is correct. However, they then copy the first 14 hex digits and add a double colon, showing the following:

    2000:1234:5678:9A::/56

This abbreviation is not correct because it removes the trailing "00" at the end of the fourth quartet. If you later expanded this incorrect abbreviated value, it would begin with 2000:1234:5678:009A, not 2000:1234:5678:9A00. So, be careful when abbreviating when the boundary is not at the edge of a quartet.

Once again, some extra practice can help. Table 25-6 uses examples that have a prefix length that is a multiple of 4, but is not on a quartet boundary, just to get some extra practice. The answers sit at the end of the chapter, in the section "Answers to Earlier Practice Problems."

Table 25-6   Finding the IPv6 Subnet Prefix from an Address/Length Value

Address/Length	Subnet Prefix
34BA:B:B:0:5555:0:6060:707/48	
3124:1:20:DEAD:CAFE:FF:FE00:1/48	
2BCD::FACE:BEFF:FEBE:CAFE/48	
3FED:F:E0:D00:FACE:BAFF:FE00:0/48	
210F:A:B:C:CCCC:B0B0:9999:9009/40	
34BA:B:B:0:5555:0:6060:707/36	
3124::DEAD:CAFE:FF:FE00:1/60	
2BCD::FACE:1:BEFF:FEBE:CAFE/56	

Chapter Review

One key to doing well on the exams is to perform repetitive spaced review sessions. Review this chapter's material using either the tools in the book or interactive tools for the same material found on the book's companion website. Refer to the "Your Study Plan" element for more details. Table 25-7 outlines the key review elements and where you can find them. To better track your study progress, record when you completed these activities in the second column.

Table 25-7   Chapter Review Tracking

Review Element	Review Date(s)	Resource Used
Review key topics		Book, website
Review key terms		Book, website
Answer DIKTA questions		Book, PTP
Review command tables		Book
Review memory table		Book, website

Review All the Key Topics

Table 25-8   Key Topics for Chapter 25

Key Topic Element	Description	Page Number
List	Similarities between IPv4 and IPv6	643
List	Rules for abbreviating IPv6 addresses	647
List	Rules for expanding an abbreviated IPv6 address	648
List	Process steps to find an IPv6 prefix, based on the IPv6 address and prefix length	649

Key Terms You Should Know

EIGRP version 6 (EIGRPv6), IP version 6 (IPv6), IPv4 address exhaustion, OSPF version 3 (OSPFv3), prefix length, quartet, subnet prefix

Additional Practice for This Chapter's Processes

For additional practice with IPv6 abbreviations, you may do the same set of practice problems based on Appendix H, "Practice for Chapter 25: Fundamentals of IP Version 6." You have two options to use:

PDF: Navigate to the companion website and open the PDF for Appendix H.

Application: Navigate to the companion website and use these applications:

"Practice Exercise: Abbreviating and Expanding Addresses"

"Practice Exercise: Calculating the IPv6 Subnet Prefix"

"Practice Exercise: Calculating the IPv6 Subnet Prefix Round 2"

Answers to Earlier Practice Problems

This chapter includes practice problems spread around different locations in the chapter. The answers are located in Tables 25-9, 25-10, and 25-11.

Table 25-9 Answers to Questions in the Earlier Table 25-4

Full	Abbreviation
2340:0000:0010:0100:1000:ABCD:0101:1010	2340:0:10:100:1000:ABCD:101:1010
30A0:ABCD:EF12:3456:0ABC:B0B0:9999:9009	30A0:ABCD:EF12:3456:ABC:B0B0:9999:9009
2222:3333:4444:5555:0000:0000:6060:0707	2222:3333:4444:5555::6060:707
3210:0000:0000:0000:0000:0000:0000:0000	3210::
210F:0000:0000:0000:CCCC:0000:0000:000D	210F::CCCC:0:0:D
34BA:000B:000B:0000:0000:0000:0000:0020	34BA:B:B::20
FE80:0000:0000:0000:DEAD:BEFF:FEEF:CAFE	FE80::DEAD:BEFF:FEEF:CAFE
FE80:0000:0000:0000:FACE:BAFF:FEBE:CAFE	FE80::FACE:BAFF:FEBE:CAFE

Table 25-10 Answers to Questions in the Earlier Table 25-5

Address/Length	Subnet Prefix
2340:0:10:100:1000:ABCD:101:1010/64	2340:0:10:100::/64
30A0:ABCD:EF12:3456:ABC:B0B0:9999:9009/64	30A0:ABCD:EF12:3456::/64
2222:3333:4444:5555::6060:707/64	2222:3333:4444:5555::/64
3210::ABCD:101:1010/64	3210::/64
210F::CCCC:B0B0:9999:9009/64	210F::/64
34BA:B:B:0:5555:0:6060:707/64	34BA:B:B::/64
3124::DEAD:CAFE:FF:FE00:1/64	3124:0:0:DEAD::/64
2BCD::FACE:BEFF:FEBE:CAFE/64	2BCD::/64

Table 25-11 Answers to Questions in the Earlier Table 25-6

Address/Length	Subnet Prefix
34BA:B:B:0:5555:0:6060:707/48	34BA:B:B::/48
3124:1:20:DEAD:CAFE:FF:FE00:1/48	3124:1:20::/48
2BCD::FACE:BEFF:FEBE:CAFE/48	2BCD::/48
3FED:F:E0:D00:FACE:BAFF:FE00:0/48	3FED:F:E0::/48
210F:A:B:C:CCCC:B0B0:9999:9009/40	210F:A::/40
34BA:B:B:0:5555:0:6060:707/36	34BA:B::/36
3124::DEAD:CAFE:FF:FE00:1/60	3124:0:0:DEA0::/60
2BCD::FACE:1:BEFF:FEBE:CAFE/56	2BCD:0:0:FA00::/56

25

CHAPTER 26

IPv6 Addressing and Subnetting

This chapter covers the following exam topics:

1.0 Network Fundamentals

> **1.8 Configure and verify IPv6 addressing and prefix**
>
> **1.9 Describe IPv6 address types**
>
> > **1.9.a Unicast (global, unique local, and link local)**

The Internet Assigned Numbers Authority (IANA) assigns public IPv6 addresses using a process much like IPv4 with CIDR blocks. IANA first defines some IPv6 address space as unicast and other parts as multicast. The majority of the unicast address space serves as public addresses, with small parts of the address space reserved for particular purposes. IANA with the RIRs assign public address blocks as defined with a prefix length of any valid size, commonly in sizes that use /32 to /48 prefix lengths.

This chapter has two major sections. The first examines **global unicast addresses**, which serve as public IPv6 addresses. This section also discusses subnetting in IPv6, which happens to be much simpler than with IPv4. The second major section looks at **unique local addresses**, which serve as private IPv6 addresses.

"Do I Know This Already?" Quiz

Take the quiz (either here or use the PTP software) if you want to use the score to help you decide how much time to spend on this chapter. The letter answers are listed at the bottom of the page following the quiz. Appendix C, found both at the end of the book as well as on the companion website, includes both the answers and explanations. You can also find both answers and explanations in the PTP testing software.

Table 26-1 "Do I Know This Already?" Foundation Topics Section-to-Question Mapping

Foundation Topics Section	Questions
Global Unicast Addressing Concepts	1–4
Unique Local Unicast Addresses	5

1. Which of the following IPv6 addresses appears to be a unique local unicast address based on its first few hex digits?

    a. 3123:1:3:5::1

    b. FE80::1234:56FF:FE78:9ABC

    c. FDAD::1

    d. FF00::5

2. Which of the following IPv6 addresses appears to be a global unicast address, based on its first few hex digits?

    a. 3123:1:3:5::1

    b. FE80::1234:56FF:FE78:9ABC

    c. FDAD::1

    d. FF00::5

3. When subnetting an IPv6 address block, an engineer shows a drawing that breaks the address structure into three pieces. Comparing this concept to a three-part IPv4 address structure, which part of the IPv6 address structure is most like the IPv4 network part of the address?

    a. Subnet ID

    b. Interface ID

    c. Network ID

    d. Global routing prefix

    e. Subnet router anycast

4. When subnetting an IPv6 address block, an engineer shows a drawing that breaks the address structure into three pieces. Assuming that all subnets use the same /64 prefix length, which of the following answers lists the field's name on the far right side of the address?

    a. Subnet ID

    b. Interface ID

    c. Network ID

    d. Global routing prefix

    e. Subnet router anycast

5. For the IPv6 address FD00:1234:5678:9ABC:DEF1:2345:6789:ABCD, which part of the address is considered the global ID of the unique local address?

    a. None; this address has no global ID.

    b. 00:1234:5678:9ABC

    c. DEF1:2345:6789:ABCD

    d. 00:1234:5678

    e. FD00

Foundation Topics

Global Unicast Addressing Concepts

This first major section of the chapter focuses on one type of unicast IPv6 addresses: global unicast addresses. As it turns out, many of the general concepts and processes behind these global unicast IPv6 addresses follow the original intent for public IPv4 addresses. So, this section begins with a review of some IPv4 concepts, followed by the details of how a company can use global unicast addresses.

This first section also discusses IPv6 subnetting and the entire process of taking a block of global unicast addresses and creating subnets for one company. This process takes a globally unique global routing prefix, creates IPv6 subnets, and assigns IPv6 addresses from within each subnet, much like with IPv4.

Public and Private IPv6 Addresses

The original plan for worldwide IPv4 addresses called for each organization connected to the Internet to be assigned a unique public IPv4 network. Each organization could then subnet that network and assign addresses from within that network so that every host in every organization used an IPv4 address unique in the universe. Unfortunately, because the IPv4 address space had too few addresses for that plan to work once every company, organization, and home wanted to connect to the Internet, those responsible for the IPv4 addressing updated their plan.

As part of that revised plan, in the 1990s, companies started using addresses from the private IPv4 address range, as defined in RFC 1918, along with Network Address Translation (NAT). Using NAT and private IPv4 addresses allowed one organization to share a few public globally unique IPv4 addresses for all host connections into the Internet.

IPv6 allows two similar options of public and private unicast addressing, beginning with *global unicast* addresses as the public IPv6 address space. Similar to public IPv4 addresses, IPv6 global unicast addresses rely on an administrative process that assigns each company a unique IPv6 address block. Each company then subnets this IPv6 address block and only uses addresses from within that block. The result is that each company uses addresses that are unique across the globe as well.

The second IPv6 option uses *unique local* IPv6 addresses, which work like the IPv4 private addresses. Companies that do not plan to connect to the Internet and companies that plan to use IPv6 NAT can use unique local addresses. With IPv4, an organization simply picked numbers from the private networks in RFC 1918. With IPv6, you choose by referencing RFC 4193, which suggests a process to randomly choose a unique local prefix. And just as when using private networks with IPv4, when using IPv6 unique local addresses (ULAs), to connect to the Internet, the organization would need a small set of public IPv6 addresses and would need to use NAT.

The following lists summarizes the comparisons between global unicast addresses and unique local addresses:

Global Unicast Addresses (GUAs): These addresses work like public IPv4 addresses. The organization that needs IPv6 addresses asks for a registered IPv6 address block, which is assigned as a global routing prefix. After that, only that organization uses the addresses inside that block of addresses—that is, the addresses that begin with the assigned prefix.

Unique Local Addresses (ULAs): These addresses work somewhat like private IPv4 addresses, with the possibility that multiple organizations use the exact same addresses, and with no requirement for registering with any numbering authority.

Answers to the "Do I Know This Already?" quiz:

1 C **2** A **3** D **4** B **5** D

The rest of this first major section of the chapter examines global unicast addresses in more detail, while the second major section discusses unique local addresses.

The IPv6 Global Routing Prefix

IPv6 global unicast addresses (GUAs) allow IPv6 to work more like the original design of the IPv4 Internet. Each organization asks for a block of IPv6 addresses, which no one else can use. That organization further subdivides the address block into smaller chunks called *subnets*. Finally, the engineer chooses an address from the right subnet to assign for use by a host.

That reserved block of IPv6 addresses—a set of addresses only one company can use—is called a **global routing prefix**. Each organization that wants to connect to the Internet and use IPv6 GUAs should ask for and receive a global routing prefix. In comparison, you can think of the global routing prefix like an IPv4 Class A, B, or C network number from the range of public IPv4 addresses, or think of it like a public CIDR block.

The term *global routing prefix* might not make you think of a block of IPv6 addresses at first. The term refers to the idea that Internet routers can have one route that refers to all the addresses inside the address block, without a need to have routes for smaller parts of that block. For example, Figure 26-1 shows three companies with three different IPv6 global routing prefixes; the router on the right (R4) inside the Internet has one IPv6 route for each global routing prefix.

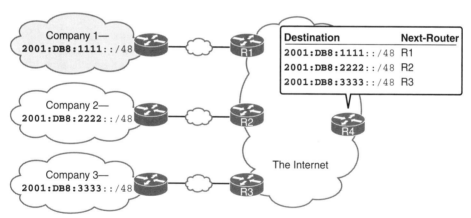

Figure 26-1   *Three Global Routing Prefixes, with One Route per Prefix*

The figure shows three global routing prefixes, each defining a range of GUAs reserved for use by the three companies in the figure. Consider prefix 2001:DB8:1111::/48. The prefix length, 48, happens to equal 12*4. So, the first phrase that follows gives a more literal and binary view of the meaning of "2001:DB8:1111::/48," while the second line shows the much easier hex view:

Addresses whose first 48 bits equal the first 48 bits of 2001:DB8:1111::

Addresses whose first 12 hex digits equal the first 12 hex digits of 2001:DB8:1111::

The address assignment process sets those IPv6 addresses apart for use by that one company, just like a public IPv4 network or a CIDR address block does in IPv4. All IPv6 addresses inside that company should begin with those first bits in the global routing prefix. No other companies should use IPv6 addresses with that same prefix. And thankfully, IPv6 has plenty of space to allow all companies to have a global routing prefix with plenty of addresses.

Both the IPv6 and IPv4 address assignment processes rely on the same organizations: IANA (along with ICANN), the Regional Internet Registries (RIR), and ISPs. For example, an imaginary company, Company1, received the assignment of a global routing prefix. The prefix means "All addresses whose first 12 hex digits are 2001:0DB8:1111," as represented by prefix 2001:0DB8:1111::/48. To receive that assignment, the process shown in Figure 26-2 happened.

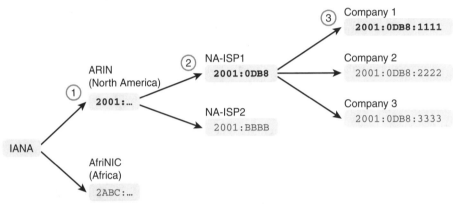

Figure 26-2   *Prefix Assignment with IANA, RIRs, and ISPs*

The event timeline in the figure uses a left-to-right flow; in other words, the event on the far left must happen first. Following the flow from left to right in the figure:

1.   **IANA allocates ARIN prefix 2001::/16:** ARIN (the RIR for North America) asks IANA to allocate a large block of addresses. In this imaginary example, IANA gives ARIN a prefix of "all addresses that begin 2001," or 2001::/16.

2.   **ARIN allocates NA-ISP1 prefix 2001:0DB8::/32:** NA-ISP1, an imaginary ISP based in North America, asks ARIN for a new IPv6 prefix. ARIN takes a subset of its 2001::/16 prefix, specifically all addresses that begin with the 32 bits (8 hex digits) 2001:0DB8, and allocates it to the ISP.

3.   **NA-ISP1 assigns Company 1 2001:0DB8:1111::/48:** Company 1 decides to start supporting IPv6, so it goes to its ISP, NA-ISP1, to ask for a block of GUAs. NA-ISP1 assigns Company 1 a "small" piece of NA-ISP1's address block, in this case, the addresses that begin with the 48 bits (12 hex digits) of 2001:0DB8:1111 (2001:0DB8:1111::/48).

NOTE   If you do not plan to connect to the Internet using IPv6 for a while and just want to experiment, you do not need to ask for an IPv6 global routing prefix to be assigned. Just make up IPv6 addresses and configure your devices, or use unique local addresses, as discussed toward the end of this chapter.

Address Ranges for Global Unicast Addresses

Global unicast addresses make up the majority of the IPv6 address space. However, unlike IPv4, the rules for which IPv6 addresses fall into which category are purposefully more flexible than they were with IPv4 and the rules for IPv4 Classes A, B, C, D, and E.

IANA allocates all IPv6 addresses that begin with hex 2 or 3 as global unicast addresses. The prefix 2000::/3 formally defines that range of numbers, meaning all addresses whose first three bits (per the /3 prefix length) match the first three bits of 2000::. To further explain:

- The first hex digit (2) is binary 0010.

- /3 means the number represents all addresses with the same first three bits as the listed prefix, or 001 binary in this case.

- The hex values whose first three bits are 001 are hex 2 and 3 but no others.

- Therefore, prefix 2000::/3 means all addresses that begin with hex 2 or 3.

IANA can expand the GUA address range beyond 2000::/3 over time if needed. RFC 4291, "IPv6 Addressing Architecture," which lays the foundation of IPv6 addressing, reserves all addresses not otherwise reserved for the GUA address space. However, by current policy, IANA allocates global unicasts only from the 2000::/3 range.

> **NOTE** For perspective, the 2000::/3 GUA address space, if allocated to organizations as only /48 prefixes, would provide more than 30 trillion /48 global routing prefixes. Each global routing prefix would allow for 65,536 subnets. IANA may never exhaust the 2000::/3 GUA address space.

Table 26-2 lists the address prefixes discussed in this book and their purpose.

Table 26-2 Some Types of IPv6 Addresses and Their First Hex Digit(s)

Address Type	First Hex Digits
Global unicast	2 or 3
Unique local	FD
Multicast	FF
Link local	FE80

IPv6 Subnetting Using Global Unicast Addresses

After an enterprise has a block of reserved GUAs—in other words, a global routing prefix—the company needs to subdivide that large address block into subnets.

Subnetting IPv6 addresses generally works like IPv4, but with mostly simpler math (hoorah!). Many IPv6 RFCs dictate that all subnets deployed in a network (that is, by configuration on endpoints and routers) use a /64 prefix length. Using /64 as the prefix length for all subnets makes the IPv6 subnetting math just as easy as using a /24 mask for all IPv4 subnets. In addition, the dynamic IPv6 address assignment process works better with a /64 prefix length as well; so in practice, and in this book, expect IPv6 designs to use a /64 prefix length for subnets.

This section progresses through the different parts of IPv6 subnetting while using examples that use a /64 prefix length. The discussion defines the rules about which addresses should be in the same subnet and which addresses need to be in different subnets. Plus, this section looks at how to analyze the global routing prefix and associated prefix length to find all the IPv6 subnet prefixes and the addresses in each subnet.

> **NOTE**   If the IPv4 subnetting concepts are a little vague, you might want to reread Chapter 11, "Perspectives on IPv4 Subnetting," which discusses the subnetting concepts for IPv4.

Deciding Where IPv6 Subnets Are Needed

First, IPv6 and IPv4 both use the same concepts about where a subnet is needed: one for each VLAN and one for each point-to-point WAN connection (serial and Ethernet). Figure 26-3 shows an example of the idea, using the small enterprise internetwork of Company 1. Company 1 has two LANs, with a point-to-point Ethernet WAN link connecting the sites. It also has an Ethernet WAN link connected to an ISP. Using the same logic you would use for IPv4, Company 1 needs four IPv6 subnets.

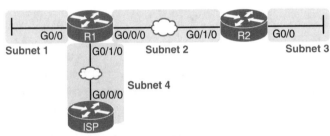

Figure 26-3 *Locations for IPv6 Subnets*

The Mechanics of Subnetting IPv6 Global Unicast Addresses

To understand how to subnet your one large block of IPv6 addresses, you need to understand some of the theories and mechanisms IPv6 uses. To learn those details, it can help to compare IPv6 with some similar concepts from IPv4.

With IPv4, without subnetting, an address has two parts: a network part and a host part. Class A, B, and C rules define the length of the network part, with the host part making up the rest of the 32-bit IPv4 address, as shown in Figure 26-4.

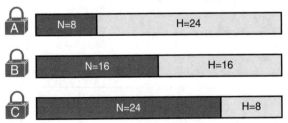

Figure 26-4 *Classful View of Unsubnetted IPv4 Networks*

To subnet an IPv4 Class A, B, or C network, the network engineer for the enterprise makes some choices. Conceptually, the engineer creates a three-part view of the addresses, adding a subnet field in the center while shortening the host field. (Many people call this "borrowing host bits.") The size of the network part stays locked per the Class A, B, and C rules, with the line between the subnet and host part being flexible, based on the choice of subnet mask. Figure 26-5 shows the field names and concepts idea for a subnetted Class B network.

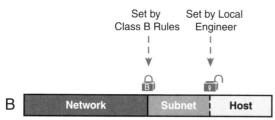

Figure 26-5 *Classful View of Subnetted IPv4 Networks with Field Names*

26

First, just think about the general idea with IPv6, comparing Figure 26-6 to Figure 26-5. The IPv6 global routing prefix (the prefix/length assigned by the RIR or ISP) acts like the IPv4 network part of the address structure. The IPv6 subnet ID acts like the IPv4 subnet field. And the right side of the IPv6 address, formally called the **interface ID** (short for interface identifier), or simply *IID*, acts like the IPv4 host field.

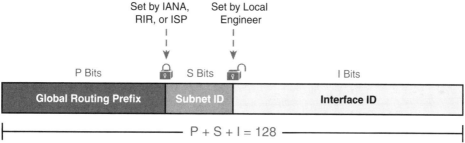

Figure 26-6 *Structure of Subnetted IPv6 Global Unicast Addresses*

Now focus on the IPv6 global routing prefix and its prefix length. Unlike IPv4, IPv6 has no concept of address classes, so no preset rules determine the prefix length of the global routing prefix. When a company applies to an ISP, RIR, or any other organization that can assign a global routing prefix, that assignment includes both the prefix and the prefix length. After a company receives a global routing prefix and that prefix length, the length of the prefix typically does not change over time and is locked. (Note that the prefix length of the global routing prefix is often between /32 and /48, or possibly as long as /56.)

Next, look to the right side of Figure 26-6 to the interface ID (IID) field. Several RFCs (including RFC 4291, "IPv6 Addressing Architecture") state that IIDs should be 64 bits long. A 64-bit IID works well with the IPv6 methods for dynamic IPv6 address assignment.

Finally, look to the subnet ID field in Figure 26-6. This field creates a place with which to number IPv6 subnets. The subnet ID field length depends on two facts: the global routing prefix's length and the interface ID's length. Assuming the typical 64-bit IID, the subnet ID field is typically 64–P bits, with P being the length of the global routing prefix.

As an example, consider the structure of a specific global unicast IPv6 address, 2001:0DB8:1111:0001:0000:0000:0000:0001, as seen in Figure 26-7. In this case:

- The company was assigned global routing prefix 2001:0DB8:1111/48.

- The company uses the usual 64-bit interface ID and /64 prefix length for the subnet.

- The company has a subnet field of 16 bits, allowing for 2^{16} IPv6 subnets.

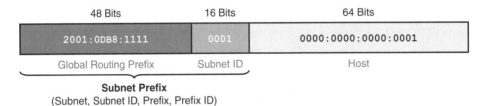

Figure 26-7 *Address Structure for Company 1 Example*

The example in Figure 26-7, along with a bit of math, shows one reason why so many companies embrace the recommendation of a 64-bit IID. With this structure, Company 1 can support 2^{16} possible subnets (65,536). Few companies need that many subnets. However, RIRs and ISPs can be generous in approving much larger blocks of public IPv6 addresses, so even if 65,536 subnets are enough, a company might apply for and receive a global routing prefix assignment with a shorter length, like /32, or /40. That would give them many more subnets (2^{32} and 2^{24}, respectively), opening up many possibilities for their subnet design and subnet numbering plans, beyond just having enough subnets.

Each subnet has far more than enough hosts per subnet with 64 bits in the interface ID. The motivation for the 64-bit IID comes from supporting various RFCs, particularly those related to dynamic IPv6 address assignment, including DHCP and SLAAC.

Listing the IPv6 Subnet Prefix (Subnet ID)

When working with IPv6 in Cisco routers, you often work with the numbers representing the subnet. For IPv6, you will use these terms:

Subnet prefix: The formal term for the number representing the subnet, including both the global routing prefix and subnet ID shown in Figure 26-7.

Subnet ID or **Prefix ID**: Informal terms used as synonyms for subnet prefix.

While the term *subnet prefix* comes from the RFCs, people tend to use the term *subnet ID*, given the history of that term in IPv4. However, note the potential miscommunication between the formal meaning of subnet ID (the middle portion of the address structure per Figure 26-7) or as a synonym for subnet prefix.

Chapter 25, "Fundamentals of IP Version 6," already discussed finding the subnet prefix, given an IPv6 address and prefix length. The math works the same whether working with global unicast addresses or with the unique local addresses discussed later in the chapter. Just to review an example, the subnet prefix for the address in Figure 26-7 would be

```
2001:DB8:1111:1::/64
```

List All IPv6 Subnets

With IPv4, if you choose to use a single subnet mask for all subnets, you can find all the subnets of a Class A, B, or C network using that one subnet mask. With IPv6, the same ideas apply, and the /64 prefix length means you can find all subnets with no binary math.

To find all the subnet IDs, you simply need to find all the unique values that will fit inside the subnet ID part of the three-part IPv6 address, as shown in Figure 26-6 and Figure 26-7, basically following these rules:

- All subnet IDs begin with the global routing prefix.

- Use a different value in the subnet field to identify each subnet.

- All subnet IDs have all 0s in the interface ID.

As an example, take the IPv6 design shown in Figure 26-7, and think about all the subnet IDs. First, all subnets will use the commonly used /64 prefix length. This company uses a global routing prefix of 2001:0DB8:1111::/48, which defines the first 12 hex digits of all the subnet IDs. The list of all possible IPv6 subnet prefixes provides all binary combinations in the subnet ID field, in this case, the fourth quartet. Also, represent the last four 0000 quartets with a :: symbol. Figure 26-8 shows the beginning of just such a list.

```
  2001:0DB8:1111:0000::      2001:0DB8:1111:0008::
✓ 2001:0DB8:1111:0001::      2001:0DB8:1111:0009::
✓ 2001:0DB8:1111:0002::      2001:0DB8:1111:000A::
✓ 2001:0DB8:1111:0003::      2001:0DB8:1111:000B::
✓ 2001:0DB8:1111:0004::      2001:0DB8:1111:000C::
  2001:0DB8:1111:0005::      2001:0DB8:1111:000D::
  2001:0DB8:1111:0006::      2001:0DB8:1111:000E::
  2001:0DB8:1111:0007::      2001:0DB8:1111:000F::
```
| Global Routing Prefix   Subnet   Global Routing Prefix   Subnet

Figure 26-8   *First 16 Possible Subnets with a 16-bit Subnet Field in This Example*

The example allows for 65,536 subnets, so clearly, the example will not list all the possible subnets. However, in that fourth quartet, all combinations of hex values would be allowed.

NOTE   Each IPv6 subnet ID, more formally called the **subnet router anycast address**, is reserved and should not be used as an IPv6 address for any host.

Assign Subnets to the Internetwork Topology

After an engineer lists all the possible subnet IDs (based on the subnet design), the next step is to choose which subnet ID to use for each link that needs an IPv6 subnet. As with IPv4, each VLAN, each serial link, each Ethernet WAN link, and many other data-link instances need an IPv6 subnet.

Figure 26-9 shows an example using Company 1 again. The figure uses the four subnets from Figure 26-8 that have check marks beside them. The check marks are just a reminder not to use those four subnets in other locations.

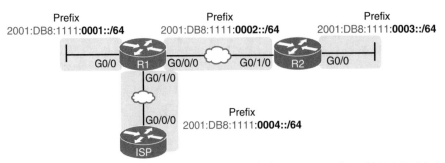

Figure 26-9   *Subnets in Company 1, with Global Routing Prefix of 2001:0DB8:1111::/48*

Assigning Addresses to Hosts in a Subnet

Now that the engineer has planned which IPv6 subnet to use in each location, the individual IPv6 addressing can be planned and implemented. Each address must be unique in that no other host interface uses the same IPv6 address. Also, the hosts cannot use the subnet ID itself.

The process of assigning IPv6 addresses to interfaces works similarly to IPv4. Addresses can be configured statically, along with the prefix length, default router, and Domain Name System (DNS) IPv6 addresses. Alternatively, hosts can learn these same settings dynamically, using either Dynamic Host Configuration Protocol (DHCP) or a built-in IPv6 mechanism called Stateless Address Autoconfiguration (SLAAC). Chapter 28, "Implementing IPv6 Addressing on Hosts," discusses IPv6 address assignment in more depth.

For example, Figure 26-10 shows some static IP addresses chosen for the router interfaces based on the subnet choices shown in Figure 26-9. In each case, the router interfaces use an interface ID that is a relatively low number and easily remembered.

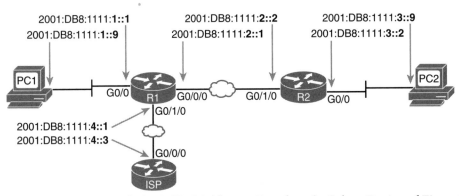

Figure 26-10   *Example Static IPv6 Addresses Based on the Subnet Design of Figure 26-9*

This chapter puts off the details of how to configure the IPv6 addresses until Chapter 27, "Implementing IPv6 Addressing on Routers."

Unique Local Unicast Addresses

Unique local addresses (ULAs) act as private IPv6 unicast addresses. These addresses have many similarities with global unicast addresses, particularly in how to subnet. The biggest difference lies in the literal number (ULAs begin with hex FD) and with the administrative process: the ULA prefixes are not registered with any numbering authority and can be used by multiple organizations.

Although the network engineer creates unique local addresses without any registration or assignment process, the addresses still need to follow some rules, as follows:

- Use FD as the first two hex digits.

- Choose a unique 40-bit global ID.

- Append the global ID to FD to create a 48-bit prefix, used as the prefix for all your addresses.

- Use the next 16 bits as a subnet field.

- Note that the structure leaves a convenient 64-bit interface ID field.

Figure 26-11 shows the format of these unique local unicast addresses.

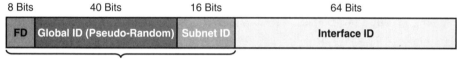

Figure 26-11   *IPv6 Unique Local Unicast Address Format*

> **NOTE**   Just to be entirely exact, IANA reserves prefix FC00::/7, and not FD00::/8, as the address range for ULAs. FC00::/7 includes all addresses that begin with hex FC and FD. However, the ULA RFC (4193) also requires setting the eighth bit to 1, which means that all ULAs begin with their first two hex digits as FD.

Subnetting with Unique Local IPv6 Addresses

Subnetting ULAs works like subnetting GUAs, assuming you begin with a 48-bit global routing prefix. The differences lie in that you must be assigned the GUA global routing prefix and prefix length. With ULAs, you create a prefix locally, with a prefix of /48.

To choose your 48-bit (12 hex digit) ULA prefix, you begin with hex FD and choose ten hex digits via a random number process. Per the ULA RFC, you should use a defined pseudo-random algorithm to determine your global ID. When practicing in lab, you can just make up a number. For example, imagine you chose a 10-hex-digit value of hex 00 0001 0001 and prepend a hex FD, making the entire prefix FD00:0001:0001::/48, or FD00:1:1::/48 when abbreviated.

To create subnets, just as you did in the earlier examples with a 48-bit global routing prefix, treat the entire fourth quartet as the subnet ID field, as shown in Figure 26-11.

Figure 26-12 shows an example subnetting plan using unique local addresses. The example repeats the same topology shown earlier in Figure 26-9; that figure showed subnetting with a global unicast prefix. This example uses the exact same numbers for the fourth quartet's subnet field, simply replacing the 48-bit global unicast prefix with this new local unique prefix of FD00:1:1.

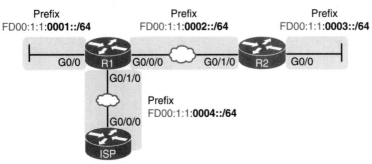

Figure 26-12 *Subnetting Using Unique Local Addresses*

The Need for Globally Unique Local Addresses

The example in Figure 26-12 shows an easy-to-remember prefix of FD00:1:1::/48. I made up the easy-to-remember global ID in this example. What global ID would you choose for your company? Would you pick a number that you could not abbreviate and make it shorter? If you had to pick the IPv6 prefix for your ULAs from the options in the following list, which would you pick for your company?

- `FDE9:81BE:A059::/48`
- `FDF0:E1D2:C3B4::/48`
- `FD00:1:1::/48`

Given the freedom to choose, most people would pick an easy-to-remember, short-to-type prefix, like FD00:1:1::/48. And in a lab or other small network used for testing, making up an easy-to-use number is reasonable. However, for use in real corporate networks, you should not just make up any global ID you like. Instead, follow the ULA rules to make your ULAs unique in the universe—even without registering a prefix with an ISP or RIR.

RFC 4193 stresses the importance of choosing your global ID to make it statistically unlikely to be used by other companies. What is the result of unique global IDs at every company? It makes all these **ULA global IDs** unique across the globe. So, if you plan on using ULAs in a real network, use the random number generator logic listed in RFC 4193 to create your prefix.

One of the big reasons to attempt to use a unique prefix, rather than everyone using the same easy-to-remember prefixes, is to be ready for the day your company merges with or buys another company. Today, with IPv4, a high percentage of companies use private IPv4 network 10.0.0.0. When they merge their networks, the fact that both use network 10.0.0.0 makes the network merger more painful than if the companies had used different private IPv4 networks. With IPv6 ULAs, if both companies did the right thing and randomly chose a prefix, they will most likely be using completely different prefixes, making the merger much simpler. However, companies that take the seemingly easy way out and choose an easy-to-remember prefix like FD00:1:1 significantly increase their risk of requiring extra effort when merging with another company that also chose to use that same prefix.

Chapter Review

One key to doing well on the exams is to perform repetitive spaced review sessions. Review this chapter's material using either the tools in the book or interactive tools for the same material found on the book's companion website. Refer to the "Your Study Plan" element for more details. Table 26-3 outlines the key review elements and where you can find them. To better track your study progress, record when you completed these activities in the second column.

Table 26-3   Chapter Review Tracking

Review Element	Review Date(s)	Resource Used
Review key topics		Book, website
Review key terms		Book, website
Answer DIKTA questions		Book, PTP
Review memory table		Website
Watch video		Website

26

Review All the Key Topics

Table 26-4   Key Topics for Chapter 26

Key Topic Element	Description	Page Number
List	Two types of IPv6 unicast addresses	656
Table 26-2	Values of the initial hex digits of IPv6 addresses, and the address type implied by each	659
Figure 26-6	Subnetting concepts for IPv6 global unicast addresses	661
List	Rules for how to find all IPv6 subnet IDs, given the global routing prefix, and prefix length used for all subnets	662
List	Rules for building unique local unicast addresses	665
Figure 26-11	Subnetting concepts for IPv6 unique local addresses	665

Key Terms You Should Know

global routing prefix, global unicast address, interface ID (IID), subnet ID (prefix ID), subnet prefix, subnet router anycast address, ULA global ID, unique local address

CHAPTER 27

Implementing IPv6 Addressing on Routers

This chapter covers the following exam topics:

1.0 Network Fundamentals

    1.8 Configure and verify IPv6 addressing and prefix

    1.9 Describe IPv6 address types

        1.9.a Unicast (global, unique local, and link local)

        1.9.b Anycast

        1.9.c Multicast

        1.9.d Modified EUI 64

With IPv4 addressing, some devices, like servers and routers, typically use static pre-defined IPv4 addresses. End-user devices do not mind if their address changes from time to time, and they typically learn an IPv4 address dynamically using DHCP. IPv6 uses the same approach, with servers, routers, and other devices in the control of the IT group often using predefined IPv6 addresses, and with end-user devices using dynamically learned IPv6 addresses.

This chapter focuses on IPv6 address configuration on routers, with the next chapter focusing on end-user devices. This chapter begins with the more obvious IPv6 addressing configuration, with features that mirror IPv4 features, showing how to configure interfaces with IPv6 addresses and view that configuration with **show** commands. The second half of the chapter introduces new IPv6 addressing concepts in comparison to IPv4, showing some other IPv6 addresses used by routers when doing different tasks.

"Do I Know This Already?" Quiz

Take the quiz (either here or use the PTP software) if you want to use the score to help you decide how much time to spend on this chapter. The letter answers are listed at the bottom of the page following the quiz. Appendix C, found both at the end of the book as well as on the companion website, includes both the answers and explanations. You can also find both answers and explanations in the PTP testing software.

Table 27-1 "Do I Know This Already?" Foundation Topics Section-to-Question Mapping

Foundation Topics Section	Questions
Implementing Unicast IPv6 Addresses on Routers	1–4
Special Addresses Used by Routers	5–8

1. Router R1 has an interface named Gigabit Ethernet 0/1, whose MAC address has been set to 0200.0001.000A. Which of the following commands, added in R1's Gigabit Ethernet 0/1 configuration mode, gives this interface a unicast IPv6 address of 2001:1:1:1:1:200:1:A with a /64 prefix length?

   a. ipv6 address 2001:1:1:1:1:200:1:A/64

   b. ipv6 address 2001:1:1:1:1:200:1:A/64 eui-64

   c. ipv6 address 2001:1:1:1:1:200:1:A /64 eui-64

   d. ipv6 address 2001:1:1:1:1:200:1:A /64

   e. None of the other answers are correct.

2. Router R1 has an interface named Gigabit Ethernet 0/1, whose MAC address has been set to 5055.4444.3333. This interface has been configured with the **ipv6 address 2000:1:1:1::/64 eui-64** subcommand. What unicast address will this interface use?

   a. 2000:1:1:1:52FF:FE55:4444:3333

   b. 2000:1:1:1:5255:44FF:FE44:3333

   c. 2000:1:1:1:5255:4444:33FF:FE33

   d. 2000:1:1:1:200:FF:FE00:0

3. Router R1 currently supports IPv4, routing packets in and out all its interfaces. R1's configuration must be migrated to support dual-stack operation, routing both IPv4 and IPv6. Which of the following tasks must be performed before the router can also support routing IPv6 packets? (Choose two answers.)

   a. Enable IPv6 on each interface using an **ipv6 address** interface subcommand.

   b. Enable support for both versions with the **ip versions 4 6** global command.

   c. Enable IPv6 routing using the **ipv6 unicast-routing** global command.

   d. Migrate to dual-stack routing using the **ip routing dual-stack** global command.

4. On a router configured with an **ipv6 address** interface subcommand on its G0/0/0 interface, which of the following commands reveals the IPv6 prefix that the router computed based on the address/prefix-length? (Choose two answers.)

   a. show ipv6 address

   b. show ipv6 route connected

   c. show ipv6 interface brief

   d. show ipv6 interface g0/0/0

5. Router R1 has an interface named Gigabit Ethernet 0/1, whose MAC address has been set to 0200.0001.000A. The interface is then configured with the **ipv6 address 2001:1:1:1:200:FF:FE01:B/64** interface subcommand; no other **ipv6 address** commands are configured on the interface. Which of the following answers lists the link-local address used on the interface?

   a. FE80::FF:FE01:A

   b. FE80::FF:FE01:B

   c. FE80::200:FF:FE01:A

   d. FE80::200:FF:FE01:B

   6. Which of the following multicast addresses is defined as the address for sending
   packets to only the IPv6 routers on the local link?

   a. FF02::1

   b. FF02::2

   c. FF02::5

   d. FF02::A

   7. Host C must forward a packet to its default gateway, 2001:db8:1:1::1234:5678. Host C
   does not yet have a neighbor table entry for that address. To which solicited-node multicast address will host C send its NDP neighbor solicitation (NS) request?

   a. FF02::1:ff34:5678

   b. FF02::1:ff12:3456

   c. FF02::1ff:1234:5678

   d. FF02::1ff:34:5678

   8. A router uses the **ipv6 enable** subcommand on interface G0/0/1, the **ipv6 address
   autoconfig** command on interface G0/0/2, and the **ipv6 address 2002:db8:1:1::1/64**
   command on interface G0/0/3. The commands succeed, dynamically or statically
   creating the expected addresses as typical for each command. Which answers are
   accurate about the link-local addresses (LLAs) on the various interfaces? (Choose two
   answers.)

   a. G0/0/1 has no LLA.

   b. G0/0/1 has an LLA.

   c. G0/0/2 has an LLA and global unicast address with identical interface IDs.

   d. G0/0/3 has a global unicast address but no LLA.

Foundation Topics

Implementing Unicast IPv6 Addresses on Routers

Every company bases its enterprise network on one or more protocol models or protocol
stacks. In the earlier days of networking, enterprise networks used one or more protocol
stacks from different vendors, as shown on the left of Figure 27-1. Over time, companies
added TCP/IP (based on IPv4) to the mix. Eventually, companies migrated fully to TCP/IP
as the only protocol stack in use.

IPv6 might fully replace IPv4 one day; however, for a long migration period, most enterprises will run IPv4 and IPv6 on hosts and routers simultaneously, effectively like in the
old days, with multiple protocol stacks. Over time, hosts will use IPv6 more and more
until one day, it might be possible to disable IPv4 and run with only IPv6, as shown in
Figure 27-2.

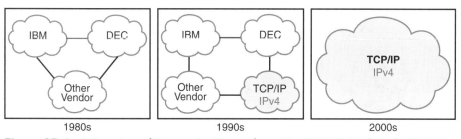

Figure 27-1 *Migration of Enterprise Networks to Use TCP/IP Stack Only, IPv4*

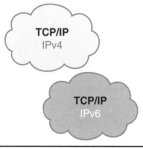

Figure 27-2 *Possible Path Through a Dual Stack (IPv4 and IPv6) over a Long Period*

Using **dual stacks**—that is, running both IPv4 and IPv6—makes great sense for today's enterprise networks. To do so, configure the routers to route IPv6 packets with IPv6 addresses on their interfaces, and advertise IPv6 routes with a routing protocol, while continuing to do the same with IPv4 addresses and routing protocols. On hosts and servers, implement IPv4 and IPv6 as well. The hosts have new methods to choose when to use IPv6 and when to use IPv4, giving preference to IPv6.

While using a dual-stack strategy works well, the configuration model for IPv6 works much as it does for IPv4. To that end, the first major section of this chapter shows how to configure and verify unicast IPv6 addresses on routers.

Static Unicast Address Configuration

Cisco routers give us two options for static configuration of IPv6 addresses. You configure the full 128-bit address and the standard /64 prefix length in one case. A second option allows you to configure a 64-bit prefix and let the router derive the second half of the address (the interface ID [IID]). The next few pages show both options.

Configuring the Full 128-Bit Address

To statically configure the full 128-bit unicast address—either global unicast address (GUA) or unique local address (ULA) —use the **ipv6 address** *address/prefix-length* interface subcommand. The command accepts abbreviated or expanded addresses, a slash, and then prefix length, with no spaces. Examples 27-1 and 27-2 show the configuration of the IPv6 GUAs on routers R1 and R2 from Figure 27-3, respectively.

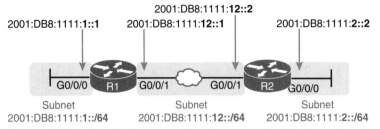

Figure 27-3 *Sample 128-bit IPv6 Addresses to Be Configured on Cisco Router Interfaces*

Example 27-1 *Configuring Static IPv6 Addresses on R1*

```
ipv6 unicast-routing
!
interface GigabitEthernet0/0/0
 ipv6 address 2001:DB8:1111:1::1/64
!
! Below, note the expanded address. IOS will abbreviate the address for you.
interface GigabitEthernet0/0/1
 ipv6 address 2001:0db8:1111:0012:0000:0000:0000:0001/64
```

Example 27-2 *Configuring Static IPv6 Addresses on R2*

```
ipv6 unicast-routing
!
interface GigabitEthernet0/0/0
 ipv6 address 2001:DB8:1111:2::2/64
!
interface GigabitEthernet0/0/1
 ipv6 address 2001:db8:1111:12::2/64
```

NOTE The configuration on R1 in Example 27-1 shows the commands as typed. One **ipv6 address** command uses an abbreviated address with uppercase hex digits, while the other uses an expanded address with lowercase hex digits. IOS accepts both commands but then changes them to their abbreviated form with uppercase hex digits.

Enabling IPv6 Routing

Interestingly, Cisco routers enable IPv4 routing by default but not IPv6 routing. The global command **ip routing** (the default setting) enables the routing of IPv4 packets. To route IPv6 packets, you must also configure the **ipv6 unicast-routing** global command.

If you forget to configure the **ipv6 unicast-routing** global command, the router will still accept your **ipv6 address** interface subcommands. In that case, the router acts as an IPv6 host, so it can send IPv6 packets it generates. However, the router will not route IPv6 packets (that is, forward IPv6 packets received in an interface) until you configure the **ipv6 unicast-routing** global command.

Verifying the IPv6 Address Configuration

IPv6 uses many **show** commands that mimic the syntax of IPv4 **show** commands. For example:

- The **show ipv6 interface brief** command gives you interface IPv6 address info but not prefix length info, similar to the IPv4 **show ip interface brief** command.

- The **show ipv6 interface** command gives the details of IPv6 interface settings, much like the **show ip interface** command does for IPv4.

The one notable difference in the most common commands is that the **show interfaces** command still lists the IPv4 address and mask but tells us nothing about IPv6. So, to see IPv6 interface addresses, use commands that begin with **show ipv6**. Example 27-3 lists a few samples from Router R1, with the explanations following.

Example 27-3   *Verifying Static IPv6 Addresses on Router R1*

```
! The first interface is in subnet 1
R1# show ipv6 interface GigabitEthernet 0/0/0
GigabitEthernet0/0/0 is up, line protocol is up
  IPv6 is enabled, link-local address is FE80::11FF:FE11:1111
  No Virtual link-local address(es):
  Global unicast address(es):
    2001:DB8:1111:1::1, subnet is 2001:DB8:1111:1::/64
  Joined group address(es):
    FF02::1
    FF02::2
    FF02::1:FF00:1
    FF02::1:FF11:1111
  MTU is 1500 bytes
  ICMP error messages limited to one every 100 milliseconds
  ICMP redirects are enabled
  ICMP unreachables are sent
  ND DAD is enabled, number of DAD attempts: 1
  ND reachable time is 30000 milliseconds (using 30000)
  ND advertised reachable time is 0 (unspecified)
  ND advertised retransmit interval is 0 (unspecified)
  ND router advertisements are sent every 200 seconds
  ND router advertisements live for 1800 seconds
  ND advertised default router preference is Medium
  Hosts use stateless autoconfig for addresses.

R1# show ipv6 interface brief
GigabitEthernet0/0/0      [up/up]
    FE80::11FF:FE11:1111
```

27

```
       2001:DB8:1111:1::1
GigabitEthernet0/0/1        [up/up]
       FE80::32F7:DFF:FE29:8568
       2001:DB8:1111:12::1
GigabitEthernet0/0/2        [administratively down/down]
     unassigned
GigabitEthernet0/0/3        [administratively down/down]
     unassigned
```

First, focus on the output of the **show ipv6 interface** command at the top of the example, which lists interface G0/0/0, showing output about that interface only. The output lists the configured IPv6 address and prefix length and the IPv6 subnet (2001:DB8:1111:1::/64), which the router calculated based on the IPv6 address.

To close the example, the **show ipv6 interface brief** command lists IPv6 addresses, not the prefix length or prefixes. Note that this command also lists all interfaces, whether configured with IPv6 addresses or not.

As with IPv4, the router adds IPv6 connected routes to the IPv6 routing table based on the IPv6 address configuration. Just as with IPv4, the router keeps these connected routes in the IPv6 routing table when the interface is working (up/up) and removes them when the interface is down. Example 27-4 shows the connected IPv6 on Router R1 from Figure 27-3.

Example 27-4 *Displaying Connected IPv6 Routes on Router R1*

```
R1# show ipv6 route connected
IPv6 Routing Table - default - 5 entries
Codes: C - Connected, L - Local, S - Static, U - Per-user Static route
       B - BGP, R - RIP, H - NHRP, I1 - ISIS L1
       I2 - ISIS L2, IA - ISIS interarea, IS - ISIS summary, D - EIGRP
       EX - EIGRP external, ND - ND Default, NDp - ND Prefix, DCE - Destination
       NDr - Redirect, O - OSPF Intra, OI - OSPF Inter, OE1 - OSPF ext 1
       OE2 - OSPF ext 2, ON1 - OSPF NSSA ext 1, ON2 - OSPF NSSA ext 2
       a - Application, m - OMP
C   2001:DB8:1111:1::/64 [0/0]
     via GigabitEthernet0/0/0, directly connected
C   2001:DB8:1111:12::/64 [0/0]
     via GigabitEthernet0/0/1, directly connected
```

Generating a Unique Interface ID Using Modified EUI-64

IOS supports two methods to configure a permanent, stable router IPv6 interface address. Examples 27-1 and 27-2 show the first method, in which you configure the entire 128-bit address. The second method uses the same **ipv6 address** command, but you configure only the 64-bit IPv6 prefix for the interface, letting the router automatically generate a unique IID.

To generate the second half of the address, this second method uses rules called *modified EUI-64* (extended unique identifier) or simply **EUI-64**. To use this method, add the **eui-64** keyword to the end of the command. The router then uses EUI-64 rules to create the IID part of the address, as follows:

1. Split the 6-byte (12-hex-digit) MAC address into two halves (6 hex digits each).

2. Insert FFFE between the two, making the interface ID 16 hex digits (64 bits).

3. Invert the seventh bit of the IID.

Figure 27-4 shows a visual representation of the modified EUI-64 process.

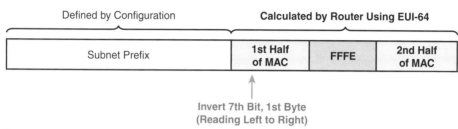

Figure 27-4 *IPv6 Address Format with Interface ID and EUI-64*

> **NOTE** You can find a video about the EUI-64 process on the companion website in the Chapter Review section for this chapter.

Although this process might seem a bit convoluted, it works. Also, with a little practice, you can look at an IPv6 address and quickly notice the FFFE in the middle of the IID and then easily find the two halves of the corresponding interface's MAC address. But you need to be ready to do the same math, in this case to predict the modified EUI-64 formatted IPv6 address on an interface.

Consider the two different examples in Figure 27-5, one on the left and another on the right. Both show all the work except the step to invert the 7th bit. Both start with the MAC address, breaking it into two halves (Step 2). The third step inserts FFFE in the middle, and the fourth step inserts a colon every four hex digits, keeping with IPv6 conventions.

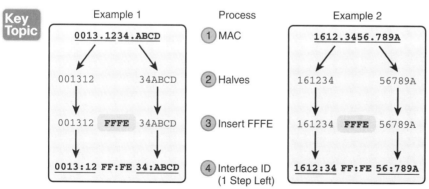

Figure 27-5 *Two Partial Examples of the EUI-64 Interface ID Process*

To complete the modified EUI-64 process, invert the 7th bit. Following the logic in Figure 27-6, convert the first byte (first two hex digits) from hex to binary. Then invert the seventh of the 8 bits: If it is a 0, make it a 1, or if it is a 1, make it a 0. Then convert the 8 bits back to two hex digits.

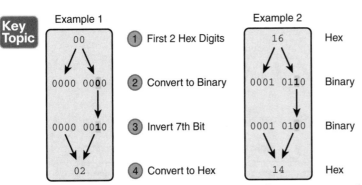

Figure 27-6 *Inverting the Seventh Bit of an EUI-64 Interface ID Field*

NOTE If you do not remember how to do hex-to-binary conversions, take a few moments to review the process. The conversion can be easy if you memorize the 16 hex values for digits 0 through F, with the corresponding binary values. If you do not have those handy in your memory, take a few moments to look at Table A-2 in Appendix A, "Numeric Reference Tables."

For those who prefer decimal shortcuts, you can do the bit-flip math without doing any hex-binary conversions with a little memorization. First, note that the process to invert the seventh bit, when working with a hexadecimal IPv6 address, flips the third of four bits one hex digit. With only 16 possible hex digits, you could memorize what each hex digit becomes if its third bit is inverted, and you can quickly memorize those values with Figure 27-7. To internalize the concepts, redraw the figure several times with these instructions. Just use any piece of scrap paper and use these steps:

Step 1. Write hex digits 0 through F, but arrange the digits as shown on the left of the figure, with spacing as shown. (You do not have to draw the arrow lines or the text "A Little Space"—those are instructions for you.)

Step 2. Draw lines to connect the nearby pairs of hex digits.

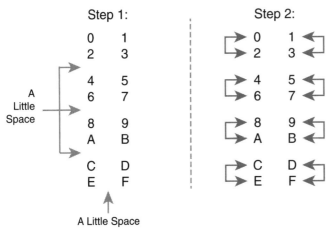

Figure 27-7 *A Mnemonic Device to Help Memorize Bit Inversion Shortcut*

When inverting the 7th bit, first remember that the 7th bit is in the 2nd hex digit. Then, refer to the right side of Figure 27-7 (or your version), and change the 2nd hex digit based on those pairs of digits. That is, 0 converts to 2; 2 converts to 0; 1 converts to 3; 3 converts to 1; 4 converts to 6; 6 converts to 4; and so on. So, on the exam, if you can arrange the hex digits in the pattern of Figure 27-7 on your notepad, you could avoid doing binary/hexadecimal conversion. Use whichever approach makes you more comfortable.

As usual, the best way to get comfortable forming these modified EUI-64 IIDs is to calculate some yourself. Table 27-2 lists some practice problems, with an IPv6 64-bit prefix in the first column and the MAC address in the second column. Your job is to calculate the full (unabbreviated) IPv6 address using modified EUI-64 rules. The answers are at the end of the chapter, in the section "Answers to Earlier Practice Problems."

Table 27-2   IPv6 EUI-64 Address Creation Practice

Prefix	MAC Address	Unabbreviated IPv6 Address
2001:DB8:1:1::/64	0013.ABAB.1001	
2001:DB8:1:1::/64	AA13.ABAB.1001	
2001:DB8:1:1::/64	000C.BEEF.CAFE	
2001:DB8:1:1::/64	B80C.BEEF.CAFE	
2001:DB8:FE:FE::/64	0C0C.ABAC.CABA	
2001:DB8:FE:FE::/64	0A0C.ABAC.CABA	

The **ipv6 address** *prefix/prefix-length* **eui-64** interface subcommand has two key differences with the earlier examples of the **ipv6 address** command. First, the **eui-64** keyword tells the router to build the IID using modified EUI-64 rules. Second, the command should not list an address but instead a prefix, because the router will calculate the IID.

Example 27-5 shows an example that converts Router R1 from earlier Example 27-1 to use EUI-64 for the interface IIDs. It uses the same subnet prefixes as per the earlier example (based on Figure 27-3).

Example 27-5   *Configuring R1's IPv6 Interfaces Using EUI-64*

```
ipv6 unicast-routing
!
! The ipv6 address command below lists a prefix, not the full address
interface GigabitEthernet0/0/0
 mac-address 0200.1111.1111
 ipv6 address 2001:DB8:1111:1::/64 eui-64
!
interface GigabitEthernet0/0/1
 ipv6 address 2001:DB8:1111:12::/64 eui-64

R1# show ipv6 interface brief
GigabitEthernet0/0/0   [up/up]
    FE80::11FF:FE11:1111
```

```
    2001:DB8:1111:1:0:11FF:FE11:1111
GigabitEthernet0/0/1   [up/up]
    FE80::32F7:DFF:FE29:8568
    2001:DB8:1111:12:32F7:DFF:FE29:8568
GigabitEthernet0/0/2   [administratively down/down]
    unassigned
GigabitEthernet0/0/3   [administratively down/down]
    unassigned
```

For this example, interface G0/0/1 uses its universal MAC address (its burned-in address), but interface G0/0/0 uses a configured MAC address. Following that math:

```
G0/0/0 - MAC 0200.1111.1111 - IID 0000.11FF.FE11.1111
G0/0/1 - MAC 30F7.0D29.8568 - IID 32F7.0DFF.FE29.8568
```

Also, be aware that for interfaces that do not have a MAC address, like serial interfaces, the router uses the MAC of the lowest-numbered router interface that does have a MAC.

NOTE   When you use modified EUI-64, the **ipv6 address** command should list a prefix rather than the full 128-bit IPv6 address. However, suppose you mistakenly type the complete address and still use the **eui-64** keyword. In that case, IOS accepts the command; however, it converts the address to the matching prefix before putting it into the running config file. For example, IOS converts **ipv6 address 2000:1:1:1::1/64 eui-64** to **ipv6 address 2000:1:1:1::/64 eui-64**.

IPv6 Address Attributes

IOS defines a set of attributes for some IPv6 addresses, displaying those with short all-caps codes in the output from commands like **show ipv6 interface** (but not listed in output from the **show ipv6 interface brief** command). The most common attributes include

EUI: The router generated the address using modified EUI-64.

TEN: Tentative. A temporary attribute that occurs while the router performs duplicate address detection (DAD).

CAL: Calendared. An address with a prescribed lifetime, including a valid and preferred lifetime. They are commonly listed when using DHCP and SLAAC.

PRE: Preferred. The preferred address to use on the interface that uses time-based (calendared) addresses. They are commonly listed when using DHCP and SLAAC.

Example 27-6 shows an example using R1's interface G0/0/0 in the previous example. The example shows two consecutive **show ipv6 interface g0/0/0** commands, the first issued immediately after the interface configuration in Example 27-5. At that time, the router had not completed DAD (which takes only a few seconds to complete), so the output lists the TEN attribute along with EUI. The subsequent repeat of the command no longer lists TEN, as DAD completed, but still lists EUI, confirming the router derived the address using EUI-64. (The section "Discovering Duplicate Addresses Using NDP NS and NA" in Chapter 28, "Implementing IPv6 Addressing on Hosts," explains DAD.)

Example 27-6 *An Example of IPv6 Address Attributes in* **show interfaces**

```
R1# show interfaces g0/0/0
GigabitEthernet0/0/0 is up, line protocol is up
  IPv6 is enabled, link-local address is FE80::11FF:FE11:1111
  No Virtual link-local address(es):
  Global unicast address(es):
    2001:DB8:1111:1:0:11FF:FE11:1111, subnet is 2001:DB8:1111:1::/64 [EUI/TEN]
! Lines omitted for brevity
! Next command gathered seconds later...
R1# show interfaces g0/0/0
GigabitEthernet0/0/0 is up, line protocol is up
  IPv6 is enabled, link-local address is FE80::11FF:FE11:1111
  No Virtual link-local address(es):
  Global unicast address(es):
    2001:DB8:1111:1:0:11FF:FE11:1111, subnet is 2001:DB8:1111:1::/64 [EUI]
! Lines omitted for brevity
```

Dynamic Unicast Address Configuration

In most cases, network engineers will statically configure the IPv6 addresses of router interfaces so that the addresses do not change until the engineer changes the router configuration. However, routers can dynamically learn IPv6 addresses. These can be useful for routers
connecting to the Internet through some types of Internet access technologies, like cable
modems or fiber Internet.

Cisco routers support two ways for the router interface to dynamically learn an IPv6 address
to use

- Stateful DHCP

- Stateless Address Autoconfiguration (SLAAC)

Both methods use the familiar **ipv6 address** command. Of course, neither option configures
the actual IPv6 address; instead, the commands configure a keyword that tells the router
which dynamic method to use to learn its IPv6 address. Example 27-7 shows the configuration, with one interface using stateful DHCP and one using SLAAC.

Example 27-7 *Router Configuration to Learn IPv6 Addresses with DHCP and SLAAC*

```
! This interface uses DHCP to learn its IPv6 address
interface GigabitEthernet0/0/0
 ipv6 address dhcp
!
! This interface uses SLAAC to learn its IPv6 address
interface GigabitEthernet0/0/1
 ipv6 address autoconfig
```

Endpoints often use one of the dynamic methods to learn their IPv6 address and related settings. Chapter 28, "Implementing IPv6 Addresses on Hosts," discusses the specifics of DHCP and SLAAC.

Special Addresses Used by Routers

IPv6 configuration on a router begins with the simple steps discussed in the first part of this chapter. After you configure the **ipv6 unicast-routing** global configuration command, to enable the function of IPv6 routing, the addition of a unicast IPv6 address on an interface causes the router to do the following:

- Gives the interface a unicast IPv6 address

- Enables the routing of IPv6 packets in/out that interface

- Defines the IPv6 prefix (subnet) that exists off that interface

- Tells the router to add a connected IPv6 route for that prefix, to the IPv6 routing table, when that interface is up/up

NOTE In fact, if you pause and look at the list again, the same ideas happen for IPv4 when you configure an IPv4 address on a router interface.

While all the IPv6 features in this list work much like similar features in IPv4, IPv6 also has a number of additional functions not seen in IPv4. Often, these additional functions use other IPv6 addresses, many of which are multicast addresses. This second major section of the chapter examines the additional IPv6 addresses seen on routers, with a brief description of how they are used.

Link-Local Addresses

IPv6 uses **link-local addresses (LLA)** as a special kind of unicast IPv6 address. Every interface that supports IPv6 must have an LLA. A small number of important IPv6 protocols then use LLAs to send and receive packets to help with overhead IPv6 functions, like neighbor and address discovery—sometimes even before the device has a GUA or ULA to use. This next topic first looks at how IPv6 uses LLAs and then how routers create them.

Link-Local Address Concepts

LLAs provide every device that supports IPv6 the capability to send and receive unicast packets on the local link, before dynamically learning or being configured with their routable IPv6 GUA or ULA. While hosts could send and receive application data using LLAs over a single subnet, LLAs do not exist to support normal application data. Instead, LLAs exist to support some overhead IPv6 protocols—protocols that need some working address to use.

The IPv6 designers wanted better options than IPv4 to support protocols that need to send packets before hosts have their normal unicast address assignment. For instance, before an IPv4 host leases an address with DHCP, it needs to send DHCP messages inside IP packets. To do that, IPv4 defines special addresses 0.0.0.0 and 255.255.255.255. The IPv6 designers looked for a better way, and LLAs provide a solution in some cases.

Hosts self-generate an LLA for themselves and can then use their LLA to send and receive IPv6 packets on the local link. All interfaces that use IPv6 must have an LLA, with the option for the device to dynamically create it without outside help. Once created, the host ensures no other hosts use the same LLA by using duplicate address detection (DAD). If unique, the host keeps using the LLA, but if DAD finds another host using the same LLA, the new host picks a different LLA. Some IPv6 protocols rely on using a host's LLA as the source of IPv6 protocol messages, including Neighbor Discovery Protocol (NDP, which replaces IPv4 ARP) and Dynamic Host Configuration Protocol (DHCP).

LLAs also appear in a surprising place: as the next-hop IPv6 addresses in IPv6 routes, as shown in Figure 27-8. For routes learned by a routing protocol, the **show ipv6 route** command lists the LLA of the neighboring router, rather than the GUA or ULA. For the default router setting on a host, the host refers to the router's LLA.

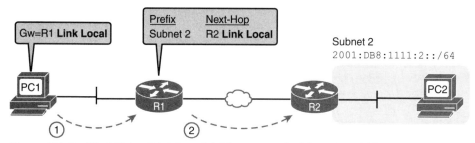

Figure 27-8 *IPv6 Using Link-Local Addresses as the Next-Hop Address*

The following list summarizes some key facts about link-local addresses:

Unicast (not multicast): LLAs represent a single host, and packets sent to a link-local address should be processed by only that one IPv6 host.

Forwarding scope is the local link only: Packets sent to a link-local address do not leave the local data link because routers do not forward packets with link-local destination addresses.

Automatically self-generated: Every IPv6 host interface (and router interface) can automatically create its own link-local address, solving some initialization problems for hosts before they learn a dynamically learned global unicast address.

Common uses: Link-local addresses are used for some overhead protocols that stay local to one subnet and as the next-hop address for IPv6 routes.

Creating Link-Local Addresses on Routers

By default, routers self-assign an LLA to each IPv6-enabled interface. To do so, the router sets the first half of the address to FE80:0000:0000:0000, as shown on the left side of Figure 27-9. Then the router creates the IID using modified EUI-64 rules (see the earlier section "Generating a Unique Interface ID Using Modified EUI-64" for a review of the process). As a result, a router's complete LLA should be unique because the MAC address that feeds into the EUI-64 process should be unique.

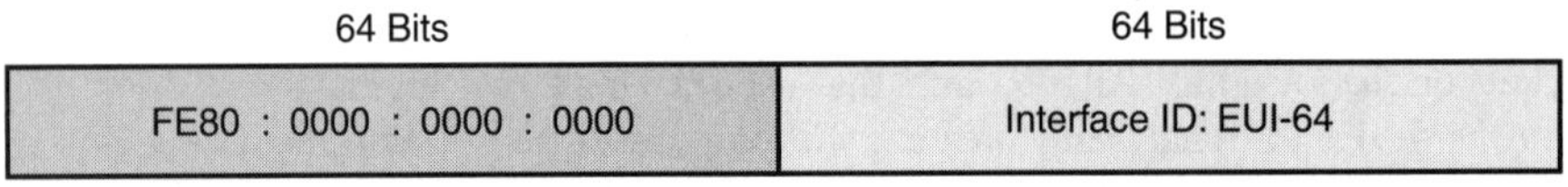

64 Bits	64 Bits
FE80 : 0000 : 0000 : 0000	Interface ID: EUI-64

Figure 27-9 *Link-Local Address Format*

In practice, LLAs begin with FE80, but formally, RFC 4291 reserves prefix FE80::/10, which includes addresses that begin FE8, FE9, FEA, or FEB. However, that same RFC also dictates that the first 64 bits should be FE80:0000:0000:0000. So in practice, LLAs begin with FE80:0000:0000:0000.

When a router automatically generates an interface's LLA, it does not create a matching configuration command. To see the LLA, instead of the **show running-config** command, just use the usual commands that also list the unicast IPv6 address: **show ipv6 interface** and **show ipv6 interface brief**. Example 27-8 shows an example from Router R1 just after it was configured as shown in Example 27-5 (with the **eui-64** keyword on the **ipv6 address** commands).

Example 27-8 *Comparing Link-Local Addresses with EUI-Generated Unicast Addresses*

```
R1# show ipv6 interface brief
GigabitEthernet0/0/0    [up/up]
    FE80::11FF:FE11:1111
    2001:DB8:1111:1:0:11FF:FE11:1111
GigabitEthernet0/0/1    [up/up]
    FE80::32F7:DFF:FE29:8568
    2001:DB8:1111:12:32F7:DFF:FE29:8568
GigabitEthernet0/0/2    [administratively down/down]
    unassigned
GigabitEthernet0/0/3    [administratively down/down]
    unassigned
```

First, examine the two pairs of highlighted entries in the example. For each of the two interfaces that have a global unicast address (G0/0/0 and G0/0/1), the output lists the GUAs, which happen to begin with 2001 in this case. At the same time, the output also lists the LLAs for each interface, beginning with FE80.

Next, focus on the two addresses listed under interface G0/0/0. If you look closely, you will see that both addresses have the same IID value. Because the GUA configuration used the **ipv6 address 2001:DB8:1111:1::/64 eui-64** command, the router used modified EUI-64 logic to form the IID portion of both the GUA and LLA. For both addresses, the router used the interface MAC address of 0200.1111.1111 and calculated the IID portion of both addresses as 0000:11FF:FE11:1111 (unabbreviated). After abbreviation, Router R1's LLA on interface G0/0/0 becomes FE80::11FF:FE11:1111.

NOTE While Cisco routers use the modified EUI-64 method to create the IID for LLAs, most end-user device OSs do not. Instead, to reduce security exposures, they randomly assign IPv6 address IIDs. Chapter 28, which focuses on host IPv6 address assignment, provides additional details and examples.

Cisco IOS also allows the direct configuration of the interface's LLA, with that configured LLA taking precedence, as follows:

- The **ipv6 address** *address* **link-local** interface subcommand configures the LLA; in this case, the router does not create an LLA using EUI-64 rules.

- If not configured, the IOS calculates the LLA using EUI-64 rules.

Routing IPv6 with Only Link-Local Addresses on an Interface

This chapter has shown four variations on the **ipv6 address** command to configure routable addresses (GUAs and ULAs) so far. To review:

ipv6 address *address/prefix-length*: Static configuration of the entire routable address and prefix length

ipv6 address *prefix/prefix-length* **eui-64**: Static configuration of the prefix and prefix length, with the router calculating the IID using EUI-64 rules

ipv6 address dhcp: Dynamic learning of the address and prefix length using DHCP

ipv6 address autoconfig: Dynamic learning of the prefix and prefix length, with the router calculating the IID using EUI-64 rules (SLAAC)

To complete the list, now consider the **ipv6 enable** interface subcommand. It enables IPv6 processing on the interface and causes the router to self-assign an LLA, but it leaves the interface with no routable (GUA or ULA) address.

The purpose of the **ipv6 enable** command will not make sense until you realize that some links, particularly WAN links, do not need a GUA or ULA. Using the backdrop of Figure 27-10, think about the destination of packets sent by hosts like PC1 and PC2. When PC1 sends PC2 an IPv6 packet, the packet holds PC1's and PC2's IPv6 addresses and never contains the WAN link's IPv6 addresses. The hosts do not need to know the routers' WAN interface addresses. (That same logic applies with IPv4 as well.)

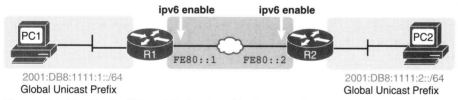

Figure 27-10 *Typical Use of the* **ipv6 enable** *Command*

Additionally, the routers do not need GUAs or ULAs on the WAN links for routing to work; they only need LLAs. For instance, IPv6 routing protocols use LLAs as the next-hop address when dynamically building IPv6 routes. Additionally, as discussed in Chapter 29, "Implementing IPv6 Routing," static routes can use LLAs for the next-hop address.

In short, IPv6 routing works on WAN links that use only LLAs, with no GUAs or ULAs. As a result, you would not even need to assign an IPv6 subnet prefix to each WAN link. Then to configure the WAN interfaces, use the **ipv6 enable** command, enabling IPv6 and giving each interface a generated link-local IPv6 address.

To use the command, just configure the **ipv6 enable** command on the interfaces on both ends of the WAN link.

IPv6 Multicast Addresses

IPv6 uses multicast IPv6 addresses for several purposes. Like IPv4, IPv6 includes a range of multicast addresses that can be used by multicast applications, with many of the same fundamental concepts as IPv4 multicasts. For instance, IANA defines the range FF30::/12 (all IPv6 addresses that begin with FF3) as the range of addresses used for multicast applications.

Additionally, different IPv6 RFCs reserve multicast addresses for specific purposes. For instance, OSPFv3 uses FF02::5 and FF02::6 as the all-OSPF-routers and all-DR-Routers multicast addresses, respectively, similar to how OSPFv2 uses IPv4 addresses 224.0.0.5 and 224.0.0.6. IANA and various RFCs use the term *well-known multicast address* to refer to these reserved predefined multicast addresses. IANA reserves address range FF00::/12 (all IPv6 addresses that begin FF0) for these addresses.

This next section focuses on the well-known permanent IPv6 multicast addresses. The first, **link-local multicast addresses**, have a scope that limits them to flow over a single link. The other type is a special overhead multicast address calculated for each host, called the **solicited-node multicast address**.

Well-Known Multicast Addresses

Stop for a moment and think about some of the control plane protocols discussed throughout this book so far. Some IPv4 control plane protocols use IPv4 broadcasts, meaning that the packet destination address was either 255.255.255.255 (the address for all hosts in the local subnet) or the subnet broadcast address (the address for all hosts in that specific subnet). The sender encapsulates the packet in an Ethernet broadcast frame, destined to the Ethernet broadcast address of FFFF.FFFF.FFFF.

While useful, the IPv4 approach of IPv4 broadcast and LAN broadcast requires every host in the VLAN to process the broadcast frame, even if only one other device needs to think about the message. LAN switches forward LAN broadcasts out every port in the same VLAN, so copies of each LAN broadcast arrive at each host in the subnet. As a result, each host has to process the frame, then the packet, read the type of message, and so on, before choosing to ignore the packet. For example, an IPv4 ARP Request—an IPv4 and LAN broadcast—requires a host to process the Ethernet and ARP details of the message before deciding whether to reply or not.

IPv6, instead of using Layer 3 and Layer 2 broadcasts, uses Layer 3 multicast addresses, which in turn causes Ethernet frames to use Ethernet multicast addresses. LAN switches can use a long-established multicast optimization feature that lets them forward multicast frames to only the hosts that care to receive a copy while not forwarding frames to disinterested hosts. As a result, the IPv6 protocols work more efficiently with fewer unnecessary interruptions to hosts.

For instance, OSPFv3 uses IPv6 multicast addresses FF02::5 and FF02::6. In a subnet, the OSPFv3 routers, when they initialize OSPF on an interface, send messages to register their interest in receiving packets sent to FF02::5 and FF02::6. However, hosts do not register an interest in receiving packets sent to those addresses. The LAN switches watch for those multicast registration messages and recall which ports connect to hosts interested in packets sent to each multicast address. When receiving frames sent to those multicast addresses, the switches forward them only to the OSPFv3 routers that preregistered to receive them, but no other hosts/routers.

All the IPv6 multicast addresses can benefit from the multicast optimizations. For reference, Table 27-3 lists the most common well-known IPv6 multicast addresses.

Table 27-3   Key IPv6 Local-Scope Multicast Addresses

Short Name	Multicast Address	Meaning	IPv4 Equivalent
All-nodes	FF02::1	All-nodes (all interfaces that use IPv6 that are on the link)	224.0.0.1
All-routers	FF02::2	All-routers (all IPv6 router interfaces on the link)	224.0.0.2
All-OSPF, All-OSPF-DR	FF02::5, FF02::6	All OSPF routers and all OSPF-designated routers, respectively	224.0.0.5, 224.0.0.6
RIPng Routers	FF02::9	All RIPng routers	224.0.0.9
EIGRPv6 Routers	FF02::A	All routers using EIGRP for IPv6 (EIGRPv6)	224.0.0.10
DHCP Relay Agent	FF02::1:2	All routers acting as a DHCPv6 relay agent	None

NOTE   An Internet search of "IPv6 Multicast Address Space Registry" will show the IANA page that lists all the reserved values and the RFC that defines the use of each address.

Example 27-9 repeats the output of the **show ipv6 interface** command to show the multicast addresses used by Router R1 on its G0/0/0 interface. In this case, the highlighted lines show the all-nodes address (FF02::1), all-routers (FF02::2), and two for OSPFv3 (FF02::5 and FF02::6). The highlighted section beginning with the heading "Joined group address(es)" lists the multicast addresses joined by the router on this interface.

Example 27-9   *Verifying Static IPv6 Addresses on Router R1*

```
R1# show ipv6 interface GigabitEthernet 0/0/0
GigabitEthernet0/0/0 is up, line protocol is up
  IPv6 is enabled, link-local address is FE80::11FF:FE11:1111
  No Virtual link-local address(es):
  Global unicast address(es):
    2001:DB8:1111:1::1, subnet is 2001:DB8:1111:1::/64
  Joined group address(es):
    FF02::1
    FF02::2
```

```
FF02::5
FF02::6
FF02::1:FF00:1
FF02::1:FF11:1111
! Lines omitted for brevity
```

Multicast Address Scopes

IPv6 RFC 4291 defines IPv6 unicast and multicast addressing details, including the ideas of **IPv6 address scope**. Each scope defines a different set of rules about whether routers should or should not forward a packet, and how far routers should forward packets, based on those scopes.

For instance, an LLA—a unicast IPv6 address—has a **link-local scope**. The scope definition called "link-local" dictates that packets sent to a link-local unicast address should remain on the link and not be forwarded by any router.

Most of the scope discussion in RFC 4291 applies to multicast addresses, using the term *multicast scope*. Per that RFC, the fourth digit of the multicast address identifies the scope, as noted in Table 27-4.

Table 27-4   IPv6 Multicast Scope Terms

Scope Name	Fourth Hex Digit	Scope Defined by...	Meaning
Interface-Local	1	Derived by Device	The packet remains within the device. Useful for internally sending packets to services running on that same host.
Link-Local	2	Derived by Device	The host that creates the packet can send it onto the link, but no routers forward it.
Site-Local	5	Configuration on Routers	Intended to be more than Link-Local, so routers forward, but must be less than Organization-Local; generally meant to limit packets so they do not cross WAN links.
Organization-Local	8	Configuration on Routers	Intended to be broad, probably for an entire company or organization. Must be broader than Site-Local.
Global	E	No Boundaries	No boundaries.

Breaking down the concepts a little further, packets sent to a multicast address with a link-local scope should stay on the local link, that is, the local subnet. Hosts know they can process a link-local packet if received, as do routers. However, routers know to not route the packet to other subnets because of the scope. Packets with an organization-local scope should be routed inside the organization but not out to the Internet or over a link to another company. (Note that routers can predict the boundaries of some scopes, like link-local, but they need configuration to know the boundaries of other scopes, for instance, organization-local.)

Comparing a few of the scopes in terms of where the packets can flow, the higher the value in the fourth hex digit, the further away from the sending host the scope allows the packet to be forwarded. Table 27-4 shows that progression top to bottom, while Figure 27-11 shows an example with three scopes: link-local, site-local, and organization-local. In the figure, site-local messages do not cross the WAN, and organization-local messages do not leave the organization over the link to the Internet.

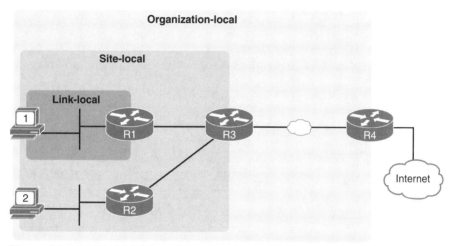

Figure 27-11 *IPv6 Multicast Scopes*

Finally, the term *link-local* has a couple of common uses in IPv6 and can be confusing. The following descriptions should clarify the different uses of the term:

Link-local address: A unicast IPv6 address that begins FE80 with a link-local scope. Devices create their own LLAs. A more complete term for comparison would be *link-local unicast address*.

Link-local multicast address: An IPv6 address that begins with FF02. These addresses serve as reserved multicast addresses to which devices apply a link-local scope.

Link-local scope: A reference to the scope itself, rather than an address. This scope defines that routers should not forward packets sent to an address in this scope.

Solicited-Node Multicast Addresses

IPv6 Neighbor Discovery Protocol (NDP) replaces IPv4 ARP, as discussed in Chapter 28. NDP improves the MAC-discovery process compared to IPv4 ARP by sending IPv6 multicast packets to communicate with a second host before the first host knows the second host's MAC address. The process uses the solicited-node multicast address associated with the unicast IPv6 address.

Figure 27-12 shows how to determine the solicited-node multicast address associated with a unicast address. Start with the predefined /104 prefix (26 hex digits) shown in

Figure 27-12. In other words, all the solicited-node multicast addresses begin with the abbreviated FF02::1:FF. In the last 24 bits (6 hex digits), copy the last 6 hex digits of the unicast address into the solicited-node address.

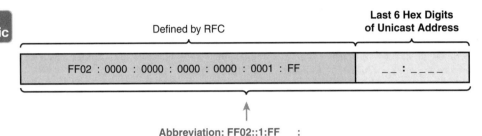

Figure 27-12 *Solicited-Node Multicast Address Format*

Note that a host or router calculates and uses a matching solicited-node multicast address for every unicast address (GUA, ULA, and LLA) on an interface. The device then registers to receive incoming multicast messages sent to that address. Example 27-10 shows an example in which the router interface has a GUA of 2001:DB8:1111:1::1/64 and an LLA of FE80::11FF:FE11:1111. (You saw these addresses earlier in Examples 27-1 and 27-3.) As a result, the interface has two solicited-node multicast addresses, shown at the end of the output.

Example 27-10 *Verifying Static IPv6 Addresses on Router R1*

```
R1# show ipv6 interface GigabitEthernet 0/0/0
GigabitEthernet0/0/0 is up, line protocol is up
  IPv6 is enabled, link-local address is FE80::11FF:FE11:1111
  No Virtual link-local address(es):
  Global unicast address(es):
    2001:DB8:1111:1::1, subnet is 2001:DB8:1111:1::/64
  Joined group address(es):
    FF02::1
    FF02::2
    FF02::5
    FF02::1:FF00:1
    FF02::1:FF11:1111
! Lines omitted for brevity
```

Note that in this case, R1's expanded GUA ends with its last six hex digits as 00:0001, resulting in an unabbreviated solicited-node multicast address of FF02:0000:0000:0000:0000:0001:FF00:0001. This value begins with the 26-hex-digit prefix shown in Figure 27-12, followed by 00:0001. The solicited-node multicast address corresponding to link-local address FE80::11FF:FE11:1111 ends in 11:1111, as shown in the last line of the example.

The Unspecified and Loopback Addresses

All IPv6 hosts can use two additional special addresses:

- The unspecified IPv6 address, ::, that is, all 0s

- The loopback IPv6 address, ::1, that is, 127 binary 0s with a single 1

Seldom used, a host can use the unspecified address when it has not yet learned a unicast address to use. The address can be used only as a source address, and only used before the host has an LLA or other unicast address to use.

The IPv6 loopback address gives each IPv6 host a way to test its protocol stack. Just like the IPv4 127.0.0.1 loopback address, packets sent to ::1 do not leave the host but are simply delivered down the stack to IPv6 and back up the stack to the application on the local host.

Anycast Addresses

Imagine that routers collectively need to implement some service. Rather than have one router supply that service, that service works best when implemented on several routers. But the hosts that use the service need to contact only the nearest such service, and the network wants to hide all these details from the hosts. Hosts can send just one packet to an IPv6 address, and the routers will forward the packet to the nearest router that supports that service by virtue of supporting that destination IPv6 address.

IPv6 **anycast addresses** provide that exact function. The *any* part of the name refers to the fact that any of the instances of the service can be used. Figure 27-13 shows this big concept, with two major steps:

Step 1.   Two routers configure the exact same IPv6 address, designated as an anycast address, to support some service.

Step 2.   In the future, when any router receives a packet for that anycast address, the other routers simply route the packet to the nearest of the routers that support the address.

Figure 27-13   *IPv6 Anycast Addresses*

To make this anycast process work, the routers implementing the anycast address must be configured and then advertise a route for the anycast address. The addresses do not come from a special reserved range of addresses; instead, they are from the unicast address range.

Often, the address is configured with a /128 prefix so that the routers advertise a host route for that one anycast address. At that point, the routing protocol advertises the route just like any other IPv6 route; the other routers cannot tell the difference.

Example 27-11 shows a sample configuration on a router. Note that the actual address (2001:1:1:2::99) looks like any other unicast address. However, note the different **anycast** keyword on the **ipv6 address** command, telling the local router that the address has a special purpose as an anycast address. Finally, note that the **show ipv6 interface** command does identify the address as an anycast address, but the **show ipv6 interface brief** command does not.

Example 27-11 *Configuring and Verifying IPv6 Anycast Addresses*

```
R1# configure terminal
Enter configuration commands, one per line. End with CNTL/Z.
R1(config)# interface gigabitEthernet 0/0/0
R1(config-if)# ipv6 address 2001:1:1:1::1/64
R1(config-if)# ipv6 address 2001:1:1:2::99/128 anycast
R1(config-if)# ^Z
R1#


R1# show ipv6 interface g0/0/0
GigabitEthernet0/0/0 is up, line protocol is up
    IPv6 is enabled, link-local address is FE80::11FF:FE11:1111
    No Virtual link-local address(es):
    Global unicast address(es):
        2001:1:1:1::1, subnet is 2001:1:1:1::/64
        2001:1:1:2::99, subnet is 2001:1:1:2::99/128 [ANY]
 ! Lines omitted for brevity
R1# show ipv6 interface brief g0/0/0
GigabitEthernet0/0/0 [up/up]
    FE80::11FF:FE11:1111
    2001:1:1:1::1
    2001:1:1:2::99
```

NOTE The term **subnet-router anycast address** represents a different concept than the anycast address just discussed. Instead, the *subnet-router anycast address* is one special anycast address in each subnet. It is reserved for routers to send a packet to any router on the subnet. The address's value in each subnet is the same number as the subnet ID; the address has the same prefix value as the other addresses and all binary 0s in the interface ID.

IPv6 Addressing Configuration Summary

This chapter completes the discussion of various IPv6 address types while showing how to enable IPv6 on interfaces. Many implementations will use the **ipv6 address** command on each router LAN interface, and either that same command or the **ipv6 enable** command on the WAN interfaces. For exam prep, Table 27-5 summarizes the various commands and the automatically generated IPv6 addresses in one place for review and study.

Table 27-5 Summary of IPv6 Address Types and the Commands That Create Them

Type	Prefix/Address Notes	Enabled with What Interface Subcommand
Global unicast	Many prefixes	**ipv6 address** *address/prefix-length*
		ipv6 address *prefix/prefix-length* **eui-64**
Unique local	FD00::/8	**ipv6 address** *address/prefix-length*
		ipv6 address *prefix/prefix-length* **eui-64**
Link local	FE80::/10	**ipv6 address** *address* **link-local**
		Autogenerated by all **ipv6 address** commands
		Autogenerated by the **ipv6 enable** command
All hosts multicast	FF02::1	Autogenerated by all **ipv6 address** commands
All routers multicast	FF02::2	Autogenerated by all **ipv6 address** commands
Routing protocol multicasts	Various	Added to the interface when the corresponding routing protocol is enabled on the interface
Solicited-node multicast	FF02::1:FF /104	Autogenerated by all **ipv6 address** commands

Chapter Review

One key to doing well on the exams is to perform repetitive spaced review sessions. Review this chapter's material using either the tools in the book or interactive tools for the same material found on the book's companion website. Refer to the "Your Study Plan" element for more details. Table 27-6 outlines the key review elements and where you can find them. To better track your study progress, record when you completed these activities in the second column.

Table 27-6 Chapter Review Tracking

Review Element	Review Date(s)	Resource Used
Review key topics		Book, website
Review key terms		Book, website
Answer DIKTA questions		Book, PTP
Review command tables		Book
Review memory tables		Website
Do labs		Blog
Watch video		Website

Review All the Key Topics

Table 27-7   Key Topics for Chapter 27

Key Topic Element	Description	Page Number
Figure 27-2	Conceptual drawing about the need for dual stacks for the foreseeable future	671
List	Rules for creating an IPv6 address using EUI-64 rules	675
Figure 27-4	IPv6 EUI-64 Address Format and Rules	675
Figure 27-5	Conceptual drawing of how to create an IPv6 address using EUI-64 rules	675
Figure 27-6	Example of performing the bit inversion when using EUI-64	676
List	Functions IOS enables when an IPv6 address is configured on a working interface	680
List	Key facts about IPv6 link-local addresses	681
Table 27-4	Link-local scope terms and meanings	686
List	Comparisons of the use of the term *link-local*	687
Figure 27-12	Conceptual drawing of how to make a solicited-node multicast address	688
List	Other special IPv6 addresses	689
Figure 27-13	Concept of IPv6 anycast addresses	689
Table 27-5	IPv6 address summary with the commands that enable each address type	691

Key Terms You Should Know

all-nodes multicast address, all-routers multicast address, anycast address, dual stack, EUI-64, interface-local scope, IPv6 address scope, link-local address (LLA), link-local multicast address, link-local scope, organization-local scope, site-local scope, solicited-node multicast address, subnet-router anycast address

Additional Practice for This Chapter's Processes

For additional practice with IPv6 abbreviations, you may do the same set of practice problems using your choice of tools:

For additional practice with calculating IPv6 addresses using EUI-64 rules and finding the solicited-node multicast address based on a unicast address, use the exercises in Appendix I, "Practice for Chapter 27: Implementing IPv6 Addressing on Routers." You have two options to use:

PDF: Navigate to the companion website and open the PDF for Appendix I.

Application: Navigate to the companion website and open the application "Practice Exercise: EUI-64 and Solicited-Node Multicast Problems."

Additionally, you can create your own problems using any real router or simulator: Get into the router CLI, into configuration mode, and configure the **mac-address** *address* and

ipv6 address *prefix*/**64 eui-64** command. Then predict the IPv6 unicast address, link-local address, and solicited-node multicast address; finally, check your predictions against the **show ipv6 interface** command.

Command References

Tables 27-8 and 27-9 list configuration and verification commands used in this chapter. As an easy review exercise, cover the left column in a table, read the right column, and try to recall the command without looking. Then repeat the exercise, covering the right column, and try to recall what the command does.

Table 27-8   Chapter 27 Configuration Command Reference

Command	Description
ipv6 unicast-routing	Global command that enables IPv6 routing on the router
ipv6 address *ipv6-address*/ *prefix-length*	Interface subcommand that manually configures the entire interface IP address and prefix length
ipv6 address *ipv6-prefix*/ *prefix-length* **eui-64**	Interface subcommand that manually configures an IPv6 prefix and prefix length, with the router building the EUI-64 format interface ID automatically
ipv6 address *ipv6-address*/ *prefix-length* [**anycast**]	Interface subcommand that manually configures an address to be used as an anycast address
ipv6 enable	Command that enables IPv6 on an interface and generates a link-local address
ipv6 address dhcp	Interface subcommand that enables IPv6 on an interface, causes the router to use DHCP client processes to try to lease an IPv6 address, and creates a link-local address for the interface
ipv6 address autoconfig	Interface subcommand that tells the router to use SLAAC to find/build its interface IPv6 address

Table 27-9   Chapter 27 EXEC Command Reference

Command	Description
show ipv6 route [**connected**] [**local**]	Lists all IPv6 routes, or the connected routes only, or the local routes only
show ipv6 interface [*type number*]	Lists IPv6 settings, including link-local and other unicast IP addresses, on all interfaces (or for the listed interface)
show ipv6 interface brief [*type number*]	Lists IPv6 interface status and unicast IPv6 addresses for all interfaces (or for only the listed interface if included)

Answers to Earlier Practice Problems

Table 27-2, earlier in this chapter, listed several practice problems in which you needed to calculate the IPv6 address based on EUI-64 rules. Table 27-10 lists the answers to those problems.

Table 27-10   Answers to IPv6 EUI-64 Address Creation Practice

Prefix	MAC Address	Unabbreviated IPv6 Address
2001:DB8:1:1::/64	0013.ABAB.1001	2001:0DB8:0001:0001:0213:ABFF:FEAB:1001
2001:DB8:1:1::/64	AA13.ABAB.1001	2001:0DB8:0001:0001:A813:ABFF:FEAB:1001
2001:DB8:1:1::/64	000C.BEEF.CAFE	2001:0DB8:0001:0001:020C:BEFF:FEEF:CAFE
2001:DB8:1:1::/64	B80C.BEEF.CAFE	2001:0DB8:0001:0001:BA0C:BEFF:FEEF:CAFE
2001:DB8:FE:FE::/64	0C0C.ABAC.CABA	2001:0DB8:00FE:00FE:0E0C:ABFF:FEAC:CABA
2001:DB8:FE:FE::/64	0A0C.ABAC.CABA	2001:0DB8:00FE:00FE:080C:ABFF:FEAC:CABA

CHAPTER 28

Implementing IPv6 Addressing on Hosts

This chapter covers the following exam topics:

1.0 Network Fundamentals

    1.8 Configure and verify IPv6 addressing and prefix

    1.9 Describe IPv6 address types

        1.9.a Unicast (global, unique local, and link local)

        1.9.d Modified EUI 64

IPv6 hosts act like IPv4 hosts in many ways, using similar ideas, similar protocols, and even similar or identical commands for the same purpose. At the same time, IPv6 sometimes takes a different approach than IPv4, using a different solution with a new protocol or command. For example:

- Like IPv4, IPv6 hosts use a unicast address, prefix length (mask), default router, and DNS server.

- Like IPv4, IPv6 uses a protocol to dynamically learn the MAC addresses of other hosts in the same LAN-based subnet.

- Unlike IPv4, IPv6 hosts use the Neighbor Discovery Protocol (NDP) for many functions, including those done by IPv4's ARP.

- Like IPv4, IPv6 hosts can use DHCP to learn their four primary IPv6 settings.

- Unlike IPv4, IPv6 supports a dynamic address assignment process other than DHCP, called Stateless Address Autoconfiguration (SLAAC).

This chapter focuses on the four primary IPv6 settings on hosts: the address, prefix length, default router address, and DNS server address. However, to understand how hosts dynamically learn those addresses, this chapter begins its first major section devoted to NDP, which plays a crucial role in several IPv6 processes. The middle section of the chapter then focuses on how hosts dynamically learn their IPv6 settings with DHCP and SLAAC. The final major section of this chapter looks at the tools to verify a host's IPv6 settings, many of which use the same commands used for IPv4.

"Do I Know This Already?" Quiz

Take the quiz (either here or use the PTP software) if you want to use the score to help you decide how much time to spend on this chapter. The letter answers are listed at the bottom of the page following the quiz. Appendix C, found both at the end of the book as well as on the companion website, includes both the answers and explanations. You can also find both answers and explanations in the PTP testing software.

Table 28-1 "Do I Know This Already?" Foundation Topics Section-to-Question Mapping

Foundation Topics Section	Questions
The Neighbor Discovery Protocol	1–4
Dynamic Configuration of Host IPv6 Settings	5–7
Troubleshooting Host IPv6 Addressing	8

1. PC1, PC2, and Router R1 all connect to the same VLAN and IPv6 subnet. PC1 wants to send its first IPv6 packet to PC2. What protocol message will PC1 use to begin the process of discovering PC2's MAC address?

   a. ARP Request

   b. NDP NS

   c. NDP RS

   d. SLAAC NS

2. Which of the following pieces of information does a router supply in an NDP Router Advertisement (RA) message? (Choose two answers.)

   a. Router IPv6 address

   b. Router hostname

   c. IPv6 prefix(es) on the link

   d. IPv6 address of DHCP server

3. Three routers (R1, R2, and R3) connect to the same VLAN and IPv6 subnet. All three routers have responded to various NDP RS messages with NDP RA messages. Which of the answers best describes the kind of NDP information held in the output of the **show ipv6 neighbors** command on R1?

   a. IPv6 neighbors (both routers and hosts) plus their MAC addresses, without noting which are routers

   b. IPv6 neighbors (both routers and hosts) plus their MAC addresses, also noting which are routers

   c. IPv6 routers, with no information about nonrouters, with no MAC address info

   d. IPv6 routers, with no information about nonrouters, but with MAC address info

4. PC1 and Router R1 connect to the same VLAN and IPv6 subnet. The user of PC1 pings the IPv6 address of a host that sits at a remote site so that the packets flow through R1, PC1's default router. PC1 learned all its IPv6 settings dynamically. Which of the following answers lists a protocol or message that PC1 could have used to learn what IPv6 address to use as its default router?

   a. EUI-64

   b. NDP NS

   c. DAD

   d. NDP RS

5. Host PC1 dynamically learns its IPv6 settings using Stateless Address Autoconfiguration (SLAAC). Which one of PC1's settings is most likely to be learned from the stateless DHCPv6 server?

    a. Host address

    b. Prefix length

    c. Default router address

    d. DNS server address(es)

6. Host PC1 dynamically learns its IPv6 settings using Stateless Address Autoconfiguration (SLAAC). Think about the host's unicast address as two parts: the subnet prefix and the interface ID. Which answers list a way that SLAAC learns or builds the value of the interface ID portion of the host's address? (Choose two answers.)

    a. Learned from a DHCPv6 server

    b. Built by the host using EUI-64 rules

    c. Learned from a router using NDP RS/RA messages

    d. Built by the host using a random value

7. An IPv6 host is configured to use DHCP to lease its IPv6 address. The DHCPv6 server is not on the same link but is located at another site. Which answer describes a mechanism the client and routers use to make the DHCPv6 messages flow between the client and server?

    a. The client sends the DHCPv6 Solicit message to multicast address FF02:1:2.

    b. The client sends the DHCPv6 Solicit message to broadcast address FFFF:FFFF: FFFF:FFFF:FFFF:FFFF:FFFF:FFFF.

    c. The client must learn the DHCPv6 server's unicast address from a local router using NDP messages.

    d. The routers use IPv6 multicast routing to forward the Solicit message, unchanged, to the DHCPv6 server.

8. All routers in the network have global unicast addresses (GUAs) configured on their interfaces. The user of PC1, on a LAN, issues a **traceroute** command for a distant host's address. The command succeeds, listing four lines with IPv6 addresses. Which answer best describes the addresses in the **traceroute** output and its use of link-local addresses (LLAs) and GUAs?

    a. All lines list LLAs with no GUAs.

    b. The first line lists an address that matches PC1's default route.

    c. All lines list GUAs with no LLAs.

    d. The last line lists the GUA of the final router in the route.

Foundation Topics

The Neighbor Discovery Protocol

IPv4 and IPv6 define a wide range of control and management functions as part of the Internet Control Message Protocol (ICMP). To support similar features in IPv6, the Internet community created ICMPv6, which defines protocols appropriate for IPv6. (For easier comparison, ICMP for IPv4 is often called ICMPv4.)

The **Neighbor Discovery Protocol (NDP)**, a part of ICMPv6 defined in RFC 4861, provides several vital functions in every IPv6 network. Notably, NDP defines the IPv6 equivalent of the IPv4 ARP function. Some of its functions are

Neighbor MAC Discovery: An IPv6 LAN-based host will need to learn the MAC address of other hosts in the same subnet. NDP replaces IPv4's ARP, providing messages that replace the ARP Request and Reply messages.

Router Discovery: Hosts learn the IPv6 addresses of the available IPv6 routers in the same subnet.

Prefix Discovery: Hosts learn the IPv6 subnet prefix and prefix length that the router(s) expect to exist on the link.

Duplicate Address Detection (DAD): Before using an IPv6 address, hosts use NDP to perform a Duplicate Address Detection process to ensure no other host uses the same IPv6 address before attempting to use it.

The next few pages explain the listed features.

Discovering Neighbor Link Addresses with NDP NS and NA

NDP replaces IPv4 ARP using the *Neighbor Solicitation (NS)* and *Neighbor Advertisement (NA)* messages. The NS acts like an IPv4 ARP Request, asking the host with a particular unicast IPv6 address to send back a reply. The NA message acts like an IPv4 ARP Reply, listing that host's MAC address. The following list summarizes the functions:

Neighbor Solicitation (NS): This message asks the host with a particular IPv6 address (the target address) to reply with an NA message that lists its MAC address.

Neighbor Advertisement (NA): This message lists the sender's IPv6 and MAC addresses. It can be sent in reply to an NS message; if so, the packet is sent to the IPv6 unicast address of the host that sent the original NS message. A host can also send an unsolicited NA, announcing its IPv6 and MAC addresses, in which case the message is sent to the all-IPv6-hosts local-scope multicast address FF02::1.

> **NOTE** With NDP, the word *neighbor* refers to hosts on the same data link—for example, the same VLAN.

Figure 28-1 shows an example of how a host (PC1) uses an NS message to learn the MAC address used by another host. The NS message lists a target IPv6 unicast address with the implied question: "What is your link address?" The NA message, in this example, sent back to the original host that asked the question, lists that link address.

At Step 1 of this particular example, PC1 sends the solicitation to find PC2's MAC address. PC1 first looks in its NDP neighbor table, the equivalent of the IPv4 ARP cache, and does not find the MAC address for IPv6 address 2001:DB8:1111:1::22. So, at Step 1, PC1 sends the NDP NS message to the target.

28

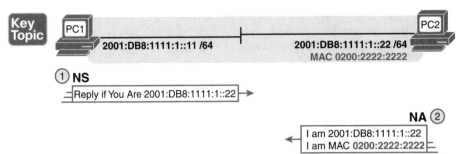

Figure 28-1 *Example NDP NS/NA Process to Find the Neighbor's Link Addresses*

As a brief aside, be aware that NDP NS messages use a destination IPv6 address of the target's solicited-node multicast address, in this case PC2's solicited-node multicast address FF02::1:FF00:22. PC1 would then encapsulate the IPv6 packet in a frame destined to a multicast Ethernet address. If the network engineers at this company also enabled the multicast optimization feature MLD Snooping, the switches would forward the multicast NS message only to hosts that had earlier registered to receive packets sent to that specific multicast address. The other hosts on the link will never see the NS message. If the LAN switches do not implement MLD, then the switches still flood the frame so that it reaches the intended destination.

At Step 2, PC2 reacts to the received NS message. PC2 sends back an NA message, listing PC2's MAC address. PC1 records PC2's MAC address in PC1's NDP neighbor table.

Example 28-1 shows an example of the **IPv6 neighbor table** on Router R1 based on Figure 28-2. In this case, R1 has learned the MAC addresses for Routers R2 and R3, associated with their respective LLAs. R1 has also learned PC A's LLA and GUA and the matching MAC address. (To connect the output to the figure, pay close attention to the interface column on the far right of the output.)

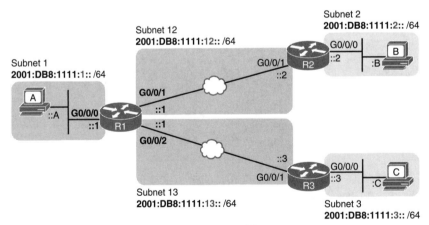

Figure 28-2 *Sample Network with IPv6 Addresses*

Answers to the "Do I Know This Already?" quiz:

1 B **2** A, C **3** A **4** D **5** D **6** B, D **7** A **8** C

Example 28-1 *IPv6 Neighbor Table on Router R1*

```
R1# show ipv6 neighbors
IPv6 Address                         Age Link-layer Addr State Interface
2001:DB8:1111:1::a                     0 0200.aaaa.aaaa  REACH Gi0/0/0
2001:DB8:1111:1:9EA:93AC:F7CE:D39F     0 3c8c.f8eb.710d  REACH Gi0/0/0
2001:DB8:1111:1:706A:5FDF:AA40:E576   16 3c8c.f8eb.710d  STALE Gi0/0/0
2001:DB8:1111:1:70D0:AE1F:4786:907D    0 80fa.5b04.de8b  STALE Gi0/0/0
2001:DB8:1111:1:7C6B:7B02:DB5C:873F   16 3c8c.f8eb.710d  STALE Gi0/0/0
2001:DB8:1111:1:90A1:C742:1B11:6F10    0 00e0.4c68.1f26  STALE Gi0/0/0
2001:DB8:1111:1:BD2C:9AA4:83E2:6D8F   16 3c8c.f8eb.710d  STALE Gi0/0/0
FE80::AAAA:AAAA                        0 0200.aaaa.aaaa  REACH Gi0/0/0
FE80::184C:56F9:FD3B:D6E7              0 00e0.4c68.1f26  REACH Gi0/0/0
FE80::552D:E285:4347:BDED              0 80fa.5b04.de8b  DELAY Gi0/0/0
FE80::706A:5FDF:AA40:E576              0 3c8c.f8eb.710d  REACH Gi0/0/0
FE80::FF:FE01:2                        0 2436.dadf.9281  REACH Gi0/0/1
FE80::72EA:1AFF:FE9A:D301              0 70ea.1a9a.d301  REACH Gi0/0/2
```

> **NOTE** To view a host's NDP neighbor table, use these commands: (Windows) **netsh interface ipv6 show neighbors**; (Linux) **ip -6 neighbor show**; (macOS) **ndp -an**.

Example 28-2 shows an excerpt from a Windows host neighbor table of a host in the same IPv6 subnet as PC A and Router R1 in Figure 28-2. The beginning output shows network shell command **netsh interface ipv6 show neighbors**, as issued in layers (which makes it much easier to issue additional **netsh** commands later). The highlighted entry lists R1's G0/0/0 link-local address (LLA) and MAC address. Also, the highlighted text at the far right of the line identifies this entry as representing a router. The output also lists several solicited-node multicast addresses.

Example 28-2 *Example Windows Neighbor Table with* **netsh interface ipv6 show neighbors** *Command*

```
C:\Users\Wendell> netsh
netsh> interface ipv6
netsh interface ipv6> show neighbors
Interface 7: En0

Internet Address                              Physical Address    Type
---------------------------------------------  -----------------  ----------
fe80::11ff:fe11:1111                          02-00-11-11-11-11   Reachable (Router)
ff02::1                                       33-33-00-00-00-01   Permanent
ff02::2                                       33-33-00-00-00-02   Permanent
ff02::1:ff11:1111                             33-33-ff-11-11-11   Permanent
! Lines omitted for brevity
```

28

```
! Next line shows a Powershell command


PS C:\Users\Wendell> get-NetNeighbor -AddressFamily IPv6
ifIndex IPAddress                    LinkLayerAddress        State        PolicyStore
------- ---------                    ----------------        -----        -----------
49      ff02::1:ff11:1111            33-33-FF-11-11-11       Permanent    ActiveStore
49      fe80::11ff:fe11:1111         02-00-11-11-11-11       Reachable    ActiveStore
49      ff02::2                      33-33-00-00-00-02       Permanent    ActiveStore
49      ff02::1                      33-33-00-00-00-01       Permanent    ActiveStore
! Lines omitted for brevity
```

The example ends with the PowerShell command equivalent to the **netsh interface ipv6
show neighbor** command: **get-NetNeighbor -AddressFamily IPv6**. The latter command lists
the same info. Be aware that Microsoft favors using PowerShell commands over older commands like those from netshell.

Discovering Routers with NDP RS and RA

IPv4 hosts use the concept of an IPv4 default gateway or default router. When the host
needs to send a packet to some IPv4 subnet other than the local subnet, the host sends the
IPv4 packet to the default router, expecting the router to be able to route the packet to the
destination. Note that IPv4 hosts either statically set the IP address of their default gateway
or learn it from a server called a Dynamic Host Configuration Protocol (DHCP) server.

IPv6 uses the same concept of a default gateway, but it improves the process using NDP.
With IPv6, IPv6 hosts use NDP to dynamically discover all IPv6 routers on the link, learning
what routers it can use as a default router. NDP defines two messages that allow any host to
discover all routers in the subnet:

Router Solicitation (RS): Hosts send this message to the "all-IPv6-routers" local-scope
multicast address of FF02::2 to ask all on-link routers to identify themselves.

Router Advertisement (RA): Routers send this message in response to an RS message,
listing many facts, including the link-local IPv6 address of the router. The message flows
to the unicast address of the host that sent the RS. Routers also send unsolicited RA messages, not in response to an RS, but periodically, announcing the same details to all hosts
on the link. Routers send unsolicited RA messages to the all-IPv6-hosts local-scope multicast address of FF02::1.

For example, Figure 28-3 shows how host PC A can learn R1's LLA. The process is simple,
with PC A first asking and R1 replying.

IPv6 does not use broadcasts, but it does use multicasts to improve efficiency compared to
IPv4. In this case, the RS message flows to the all-routers multicast address (FF02::2) so that
all routers will receive the message. It has the same good effect as a broadcast with IPv4,
without the negatives of a broadcast. In this case, only IPv6 routers will spend CPU cycles
processing the RS message, and IPv6 hosts will ignore the message.

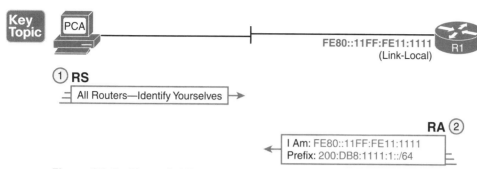

Figure 28-3 *Example NDP RS/RA Process to Find the Default Routers*

Routers list any neighboring routers they learn about in NDP RA messages with the **show ipv6 routers** command. As an example, consider the topology in earlier Figure 28-2. No routers exist on the LAN connected to R1's G0/0/0 (on the left of the figure), but R1 should learn of both R2 and R3 on its WAN links. Example 28-3 shows the output, highlighting the LLA of the router that sent the NDP RA message, the local R1 interface on which it was received, and the **on-link prefix** advertised by the neighboring router.

Example 28-3 *Listing All Routers with the* **show ipv6 routers** *Command*

```
R1# show ipv6 routers
Router FE80::FF:FE01:2 on GigabitEthernet0/0/1, last update 2 min
  Hops 64, Lifetime 1800 sec, AddrFlag=0, OtherFlag=0, MTU=1500
  HomeAgentFlag=0, Preference=Medium
  Reachable time 0 (unspecified), Retransmit time 0 (unspecified)
  Prefix 2001:DB8:1111:12::/64 onlink autoconfig
    Valid lifetime 2592000, preferred lifetime 604800
Router FE80::72EA:1AFF:FE9A:D301 on GigabitEthernet0/0/2, last update 0 min
  Hops 64, Lifetime 1800 sec, AddrFlag=0, OtherFlag=0, MTU=1500
  HomeAgentFlag=0, Preference=Medium
  Reachable time 0 (unspecified), Retransmit time 0 (unspecified)
  Prefix 2001:DB8:1111:13::/64 onlink autoconfig
    Valid lifetime 2592000, preferred lifetime 604800
```

28

NOTE To view the routers learned by a host, use these commands: (Windows) **netsh interface ipv6 show neighbors**; (Linux) **ip -6 neighbor**; (macOS) **ndp -rn**.

Discovering Prefixes with NDP RS and RA

Beyond identifying routers on a link, the NDP RA message also lists the IPv6 prefix and prefix length used on the link. As a result, hosts dynamically learn the subnet(s) that should exist on-link. For example, Figure 28-3 shows an RS/RA exchange example. The RA in the lower right of the figure not only shows the router identifying itself using its link-local address (LLA), but the message also lists one on-link prefix of 2001:db8:1111:1::/64.

IPv6 hosts use a routing table much like IPv4 hosts but build their routes differently. IPv4 hosts build a route for each on-link subnet, with that subnet calculated from the host's IPv4 address and mask. IPv6 hosts build a route for each on-link subnet, but hosts do no calculations. Instead, they rely on the prefixes advertised in the RA messages sent by routers. Routers can advertise multiple on-link prefixes, listing the subnet prefix and prefix length, with the hosts then considering destinations in those subnets as on-link. Also, hosts build a default route, using the information listed in the NDP RA message. To summarize, IPv6 hosts create two important routes based on the RA message, as follows:

- Create a route for each on-link prefix/length learned from a router in an NDP RA message. These on-link routes allow the host to forward packets directly to on-link destinations without using a router.

- Create a default route with a next-hop router address of the router LLA identified in the NDP RA message. The default route allows the host to forward packets destined off-link to the router that resides on-link.

Example 28-4 shows excerpts from two hosts on the same subnet as PC A in Figure 28-3—with the initial output from macOS and the latter output from a Windows PC. Both commands display the host's routing table entries for the default route and one on-link prefix. The example highlights each command's default route, the next-hop address ("gateway"), and on-link prefix 2001:db8:1111:1::/64.

Example 28-4 *Example macOS Host Routing Table with* **netstat -rn** *Command*

```
Mac% netstat -rnf inet6
default                      fe80::11ff:fe11:1111%en8      UGcg       en8
2001:db8:1111:1::/64         link#20                       UC         en8
fe80::11ff:fe11:1111%en8     2:0:11:11:11:11               UHLWIir    en8
! Lines omitted for brevity


Windows PC> netsh
netsh> interface ipv6
netsh interface ipv6> show route

Publish  Type      Met  Prefix                      Idx  Gateway/Interface Name
-------  --------  ---  ------------------------    ---  ------------------------
No       Manual    256  ::/0                        49   fe80::11ff:fe11:1111
No       Manual    256  2001:db8:1111:1::/64        49   Ethernet 6
! Lines omitted for brevity
```

You see some differences when looking closely at the output from macOS versus Windows. However, both hosts use information from RA messages from R1. Notably, macOS lists the default route with the word *default*, while Windows uses the numeric equivalent of ::/0, a number meant to represent all IPv6 addresses. Both list the router's LLA rather than its GUA as the next-hop address.

Discovering Duplicate Addresses Using NDP NS and NA

IPv6 hosts use the Duplicate Address Detection (DAD) process before they begin using a unicast address to ensure that no other node on that link is already using it. Hosts perform DAD when first using the address, and any time a host interface initializes. Hosts also use DAD, whether using static address configuration or any of the dynamic address configuration options. When performing DAD, if another host already uses that address, the first host simply does not use the address until the problem is resolved.

DAD refers to the function, but the function uses NDP NS and NA messages. A host sends an NS message for its own IPv6 address. No other host should be using that address, so no other host should send an NDP NA in reply. However, if another host already uses that address, that host will reply with an NA, identifying a duplicate use of the address.

Figure 28-4 shows an example of DAD. PC1 initializes and does a DAD check, but PC2 already uses the same address. The figure shows the following steps:

1. PC1, before using address 2001:DB8:1111:1::11, must use DAD.

2. PC1 sends an NS message, listing the address PC1 now wants to use (2001:DB8:1111:1::11) as the target.

3. PC2 receives the NS for the address PC2 currently uses, so PC2 sends back an NA.

4. PC1, on receiving the NA message for its IPv6 address, realizes a duplicate address exists.

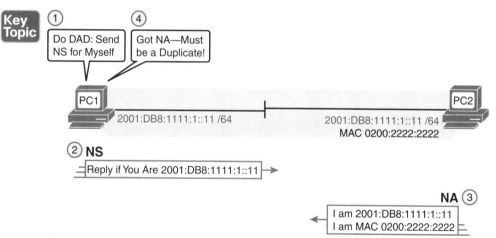

Figure 28-4 *Example Duplicate Address Detection (DAD) with NDP NS/NA*

NDP Summary

This chapter explains some of the many important functions performed by NDP. Use Table 28-2 as a study reference for the four NDP features discussed here.

Table 28-2   NDP Function Summary

Function	Protocol Messages	Who Discovers Info	Who Supplies Info	Info Supplied
Router discovery	RS and RA	Any IPv6 host	Any IPv6 router	Link-local IPv6 address of router
Prefix/length discovery	RS and RA	Any IPv6 host	Any IPv6 router	Prefix(es) and associated prefix lengths used on local link
Neighbor discovery	NS and NA	Any IPv6 host	Any IPv6 host	Link-layer address (for example, MAC address) used by a neighbor
Duplicate Address Detection	NS and NA	Any IPv6 host	Any IPv6 host	A simple confirmation of whether a unicast address is already in use

Dynamic Configuration of Host IPv6 Settings

Dynamic Host Configuration Protocol (DHCP) worked well for the dynamic assignment of IPv4 addresses. When the creators of IPv6 protocols looked for a solution for dynamic host address assignment, creating new DHCP protocols for IPv6 made perfect sense. Today, the DHCP Version 6 (DHCPv6) RFC 8415 defines one dynamic IPv6 address assignment method.

However, the creators of IPv6 also wanted another method to assign IPv6 addresses. DHCPv4 uses a server, requiring preconfiguration of the address pools used for each subnet. That model works well in some cases, but using the DHCPv4 model also requires the server to know all the address leases, keeping that information (called state information) about each host (client) and its address.

The creators of IPv6 made two methods for dynamic address assignment:

- **DHCPv6 (Stateful DHCPv6):** This method uses the same stateful model as DHCPv4 using a DHCP server.

- **Stateless Address Autoconfiguration (SLAAC):** The client self-assigns its IPv6 address. This method requires no preconfiguration of address pools and no need for servers to keep state information about the client.

This next major section of the chapter first looks at stateful DHCPv6, followed by SLAAC.

Using Stateful DHCP

DHCPv6 gives an IPv6 host a way to learn host IPv6 configuration settings using the same general concepts as DHCP for IPv4. The host exchanges messages with a DHCP server. The server supplies the host with configuration information, including a lease of an IPv6 address and DNS server address information.

More specifically, stateful DHCPv6 works like the more familiar DHCP for IPv4 in many other general ways, as follows:

- DHCP clients on a LAN send messages that flow only on the local LAN, hoping to find a DHCP server.

- If the DHCP server sits on the same LAN as the client, the client and server can exchange DHCP messages directly, without needing help from a router.

- If the DHCP server sits on another link as compared to the client, the client and server rely on a router to forward the DHCP messages.

- The router that forwards messages from one link to a server in a remote subnet must be configured as a DHCP relay agent, with knowledge of the DHCP server's IPv6 address.

- Servers have configuration that lists pools of addresses for each subnet from which the server allocates addresses.

- Servers offer a lease of an IP address to a client, from the pool of addresses for the client's subnet; the lease lasts a set time (usually days or weeks).

- The server tracks state information, specifically a client identifier (often based on the MAC address), along with the address currently leased to that client.

DHCPv6 defines two branches: **stateful DHCPv6** and **stateless DHCPv6**. Stateful DHCPv6 works more like the DHCPv4 model, especially related to that last item in the list. A stateful DHCPv6 server tracks information about which client has a lease for what IPv6 address; the fact that the server knows information about a specific client is called state information, making the DHCP server a stateful DHCP server.

Stateless DHCP servers do not lease an address to the client, so a stateless DHCP server does not track any per-client information. The upcoming section, "Using Stateless Address Autoconfiguration," discusses how stateless DHCPv6 servers have an important role when a company decides to use SLAAC.

Differences Between Stateful DHCPv6 and DHCPv4

While stateful DHCPv6 has many similarities to DHCPv4, many particulars differ as well. Figure 28-5 shows the differences: Stateful DHCPv6 supplies the address and the DNS server list. However, the host already relies on NDP RA messages to learn the default router address and the prefix length to use, with enough information to build default and on-link routes. So, with stateful DHCPv6, the server does not supply a default router address or prefix length.

DHCPv6 also updates the protocol messages to use IPv6 packets instead of IPv4 packets, with new messages and fields. For example, Figure 28-6 shows the names of the DHCPv6 messages, which replace the DHCPv4 Discover, Offer, Request, and Acknowledgment (DORA) messages. Instead, DHCPv6 uses the Solicit, Advertise, Request, and Reply (SARR) messages.

28

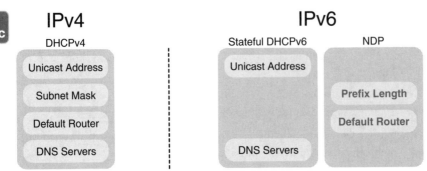

Figure 28-5 *Sources of Specific IPv6 Settings When Using Stateful DHCP*

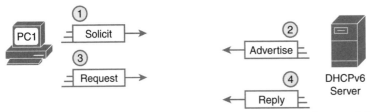

Figure 28-6 *Four Stateful DHCPv6 Messages Between Client and Server*

The four DHCPv6 messages work in two matched pairs with the same general flow as the similar DHCPv4 messages. The Solicit and Advertise messages complete the process of the client searching for the IPv6 address of a DHCPv6 server (the Solicit message) and the server advertising an address (and other configuration settings) for the client to possibly use (the Advertise message). The Request and Reply messages let the client ask to lease the address, with the server confirming the lease in the Reply message. (Note that stateful DHCPv6 supports a rapid commit option that completes the lease using only the Solicit and Reply messages.)

DHCPv6 Relay Agents

For enterprises that choose to use stateful DHCPv6, often the DHCP server sits at a central site, far away from many of the clients that use the DHCPv6 server. In those cases, the local router at each site must act as a DHCP relay agent.

The concepts of DHCPv6 relay work like DHCPv4 relay, as discussed in the section "Configuring DHCP Relay" in Chapter 19, "IP Addressing on Hosts." The client sends a message that normally has a link-local scope so that routers do not forward the packet. By enabling DHCPv6 relay, the router then changes the source and destination IP address, forwarding the packet to the DHCP server. When the server sends a reply, it flows to an address on the router (the relay agent). The router again changes the addresses in the packet for correct delivery to the client.

The differences for IPv6 become more apparent when you look at some of the IPv6 addresses used in DHCPv6 messages, like the Solicit message used to lead off a DHCPv6 flow. As shown in Figure 28-7, the client uses the following addresses in the solicit message:

Source of link-local: The client uses its link-local address as the packet's source address.

Destination address of "all-DHCP-agents" FF02::1:2: The client sends the Solicit message to the link-local scope multicast address FF02::1:2. Only DHCP servers and routers acting as DHCP relay agents listen for these packets.

With a link-local scope multicast destination address, the Solicit message sent by a host would flow only on the local LAN. Figure 28-7 shows how R1, acting as a DHCPv6 relay agent, assists DHCPv6 clients like host A to deliver DHCPv6 packets to the DHCPv6 server.

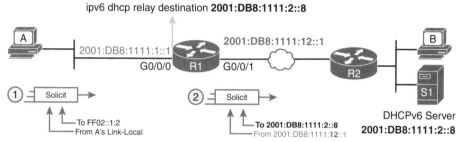

Figure 28-7 *DHCPv6 Relay Agent and DHCP IPv6 Addresses*

In the figure, Step 1 shows the DHCPv6 Solicit message, which would otherwise stay on the link due to the link-local scope of destination multicast address FF02::1:2. Step 2 then shows the action of the DHCP relay agent on Router R1. Router R1 changes the destination IPv6 address to the configured DHCP server's address (2001:DB8:1111:2::8). The DHCP relay agent also sets the source IPv6 address to the address of its outgoing interface (G0/0/1) as the source IPv6 address, which is slightly different from the DHCPv4 relay agent. R1 then forwards the Solicit message to the server.

Continuing the story beyond the figure, the server sends a reply, specifically a DHCPv6 Advertise message. That message reverses the IPv6 addresses used compared to the Solicit message, so the Advertise message uses a destination address of 2001:DB8:1111:12::1. The relay agent in Router R1 reacts by converting the destination address to host A's LLA and forwarding the packet out the interface toward the client.

Example 28-5 shows the DHCPv6 relay agent configuration for R1 in Figure 28-6. The top of the example shows the **ipv6 dhcp relay** interface subcommand, with reference to the IPv6 address of the DHCPv6 server. The bottom of the figure shows the output of the **show ipv6 interface** command, which confirms that R1 is now listening for multicasts sent to the all-DHCP-agents multicast address FF02::1:2.

Example 28-5 *Configuring Router R1 to Support Remote DHCPv6 Server*

```
interface GigabitEthernet0/0/0
 ipv6 dhcp relay destination 2001:DB8:1111:2::8

R1# show ipv6 interface g0/0/0
GigabitEthernet0/0/0 is up, line protocol is up
  IPv6 is enabled, link-local address is FE80::11FF:FE11:1111
```

```
No Virtual link-local address(es):
Global unicast address(es):
  2001:DB8:1111:1::1, subnet is 2001:DB8:1111:1::/64
Joined group address(es):
  FF02::1
  FF02::2
  FF02::5
  FF02::6
  FF02::1:2
  FF02::1:FF00:1
  FF02::1:FF11:1111
! Lines omitted for brevity
```

As an aside, note that of the multicast addresses listed under the heading "Joined group address(es)," the first five are well-known multicast addresses (FF02::1, FF02::2, FF02::5, FF02::6, and FF02::1:2), with two solicited-node multicast addresses that begin with FF02::1:FF.

Using Stateless Address Autoconfiguration

Most companies extensively use DHCPv4, and stateful DHCPv6 makes sense for those same reasons; however, using a stateful DHCP process does have some negatives. Someone has to configure, administer, and manage the DHCP server(s). The configuration includes ranges of IP addresses for every subnet. Then, when a host (client) leases the address, the server notes which client is using which address. All these functions work well, and knowing the information in the DHCP server can be pretty valuable; however, the reliance on a stateful DHCP server requires some thought and attention from the IT staff.

IPv6's **Stateless Address Autoconfiguration (SLAAC)** provides an alternative method for dynamic IPv6 address assignment—without needing a stateful server. In other words, SLAAC does not require a server to assign or lease the IPv6 address, does not require the IT staff to preconfigure a pool of addresses per subnet, and does not require the server to track state information about which device uses which IPv6 address.

The term *SLAAC* refers to both a specific part of how a host learns one IPv6 setting—its IPv6 address—plus the overall process of learning all four key host IPv6 settings (address, prefix length, default router, and the list of DNS server addresses). This next topic begins by looking at the tasks done by SLAAC related to the IPv6 address. Then the text looks at the overall SLAAC process to find all four host settings—a process that also uses NDP and stateless DHCP.

Building an IPv6 Address Using SLAAC

When using SLAAC, a host does not lease its IPv6 address. Instead, the host learns part of the address from the nearby router—the prefix—and then makes up the rest of its IPv6 address. Specifically, a host using SLAAC to choose its IPv6 address uses the following steps:

1. Learn the IPv6 prefix used on the link from any router, using NDP RS/RA messages.

2. Choose its IPv6 address by making up the interface ID (IID) value to follow the just-learned IPv6 prefix.

3. Before using the address, use DAD to ensure that no other host is already using the same address.

Figure 28-8 depicts the first two steps while noting the two most common ways a host completes the address. Hosts can use modified EUI-64 rules, as discussed in the section, "Generating a Unique Interface ID Using Modified EUI-64," in Chapter 27, "Implementing IPv6 Addressing on Routers," or a random number.

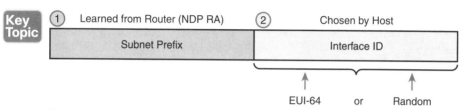

Figure 28-8 *Host IPv6 Address Formation Using SLAAC*

Combining SLAAC with Stateless DHCP

When using SLAAC, a host uses three tools to find its four IPv6 settings, as noted in Figure 28-9. SLAAC itself focuses on the IPv6 address only. The host then uses NDP messages to learn the prefix length and the IPv6 addresses of the default routers on the link. Finally, the host uses stateless DHCP to learn the IPv6 addresses of any DNS servers.

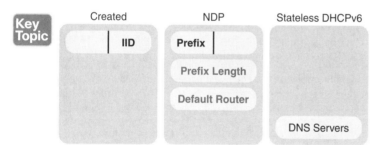

Figure 28-9 *Sources of Specific IPv6 Settings When Using SLAAC*

When SLAAC uses DHCP to supply the list of DNS servers, the server implements stateless DHCP. With stateless DHCPv6, the DHCPv6 server

- Needs simple configuration only, specifically the short list of DNS server addresses

- Needs no per-subnet configuration: no subnet list, no per-subnet address pools, no list of excluded addresses per subnet, and no per-subnet prefix lengths

- Has no need to track state information about DHCP leases—that is, which devices lease which IPv6 address—because the server does not lease addresses to any clients

Table 28-3 summarizes the key comparison points between stateful and stateless DHCP.

Table 28-3   Comparison of Stateless and Stateful DHCPv6 Services

Feature	Stateful DHCP	Stateless DHCP
Remembers IPv6 address (state information) of clients	Yes	No
Leases IPv6 address to client	Yes	No
Supplies list of DNS server addresses	Yes	Yes
Commonly used with SLAAC	No	Yes

Combining SLAAC with RA-Based DNS Server Configuration

SLAAC originally relied on a stateless DHCP server to supply the DNS server list. IPv6 now supports another option to deliver the DNS server list, called RA-based DNS configuration, which removes the need for a stateless DHCP server.

With RA-based DNS Server (RDNSS) configuration, you configure each router interface with the list of DNS servers. Then, when sending each NDP RA message, the router supplies the DNS list in its NDP RA (Router Advertisement) messages. As a result, RDNSS configuration provides a means for automatic assignment of all client IPv6 settings using router configuration only, with no DHCP server at all. However, note that it also requires configuration of the DNS server list on all routers that support IPv6 so that a centralized stateless DHCPv6 server may be more practical to manage.

Permanent and Temporary SLAAC Addresses

In practice, hosts use SLAAC to generate multiple unicast addresses, specifically a **permanent IPv6 address** plus a series of **temporary IPv6 addresses** over time. The permanent address remains unchanged over time. If that host runs as a server, the host will use the permanent address for all incoming connections. You would also typically add a DNS entry for that address in the DNS server so clients could easily connect.

Hosts use temporary addresses for client applications. For instance, when you open a web browser tab and connect to a website, your host connects using the temporary address rather than the permanent address.

Using temporary addresses makes hosts more secure, as detailed in a series of related RFCs that revolve around RFC 8981. Attackers may gather information and packets sent by a host through various attacks. If the captured packets over time have the same address, the attacker can more easily correlate the information to find a way to gain access to the host or deny services to it. By frequently changing the address, you can prevent the attacker's data analysis from giving them an edge in attacking your host.

When created, a host assigns all SLAAC-created addresses a **preferred lifetime** and **valid lifetime** setting. Each temporary address moves through stages called preferred, valid, and deprecated. During the preferred phase, the host uses the address for new connections. When the preferred lifetime expires, the address becomes valid. The host can continue using a valid address for existing connections but not for new ones. After the valid lifetime expires, the host considers the address deprecated and does not use the address again. Figure 28-10 shows the concepts.

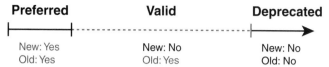

Figure 28-10   *SLAAC Preferred and Valid Lifetimes for One Temporary Address*

With temporary addresses, the preferred and valid lifetimes have short settings. A typical setting might be 24 hours for the preferred lifetime and one week for the valid lifetime. In that case, every 24 hours, the host would need a new temporary address because the last temporary address moves from a preferred to a valid state. Basically, at any one time, the host needs one temporary address in its preferred lifetime state. Figure 28-11 shows the idea, with the timelines for three consecutive temporary addresses appearing 24 hours after the previous one. At any point, the host has one temporary address with some preferred lifetime remaining, so the host can use the new preferred address for new application connections.

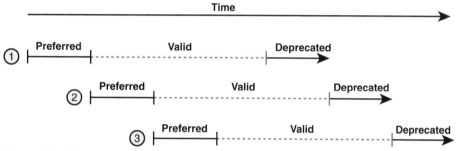

Figure 28-11   *Creating New Temporary Addresses to Ensure One Has Preferred Life Remaining*

You can see the permanent and temporary addresses in host commands like these:

macOS: **ifconfig en0 inet 6** or **ifconfig -aL inet6**

Linux: **ip -6 address**

Windows: **ipconfig /all** or **netsh interface ipv6 show address** (Windows netshell)

Windows: **Get-NetIPConfiguration -Detailed** (Windows PowerShell)

Example 28-6 shows output from the **netsh interface ipv6 show address** command on Windows. The example shows an excerpt of the output for the one working wireless LAN interface. The output shows its permanent (public) address used for incoming connections, with an infinite valid and preferred lifetime. It also shows the current temporary address, with a preferred lifetime of just under 24 hours and a valid lifetime of just under one week. Also, examine the IIDs of the addresses for ff:fe—again, their absence signals that this host did not use EUI-64 but instead generated a random IID.

Example 28-6 *Windows SLAAC Addresses with the* **netsh interface ipv6 show address** *Command*

```
C:\Users\Wendell> netsh
netsh> interface ipv6
netsh interface ipv6> show address


Interface 7: Wi-Fi


Addr Type  DAD State    Valid Life  Pref. Life Address
---------  -----------  ----------  ---------- -----------------------
Temporary  Preferred    6d23h57m58s  23h49m3s  2001:db8:1111:1:c1cd:7a44:45a5:58f1
Public     Preferred    infinite     infinite  2001:db8:1111:1:f1f5:5cbb:f395:6c51
Other      Preferred    infinite     infinite  fe80::f1f5:5cbb:f395:6c51%7
```

Note that upcoming Example 28-7 shows a sample of similar commands for macOS.

Troubleshooting Host IPv6 Addressing

This chapter's third and final major section examines a few commands to verify and trouble-shoot IPv6 addressing configuration on hosts. Specifically, this section examines the host's IPv6 settings and then looks at the usual commands to test whether a host can send packets: **ping** and **traceroute**.

Note that this section lists some commands on different host OSs; however, be aware that this and other chapters do not attempt to show each variation of every networking command on every OS. Instead, the host command examples reinforce the concepts seen earlier in the chapter.

Verifying IPv6 Connectivity from Hosts

Most end-user OSs support a convenient way to look at IPv6 settings from the graphical user interface. In some cases, all four of the key IPv6 host settings can be on the same window, whereas in other cases, seeing all the settings might require navigation to multiple windows or tabs in the same window. The following few pages first focus on how to find the IPv6 addresses used by hosts, followed by how to test connectivity using the **ping** and **traceroute** commands.

Host Commands to Find IPv6 Interface Addresses

For example, Figure 28-12 shows a macOS window that lists three IPv6 host settings. The one missing setting, the DNS server setting, is in another tab (as seen near the top of the image).

Take a moment to look at the details in Figure 28-12's image. The image shows the IPv4 settings at the top. The lower half of the window shows the IPv6 settings as having been learned "Automatically," which means that the host will use either stateful DHCP or SLAAC. In this case, the host used SLAAC to give itself two IPv6 addresses inside the same 2001:DB8:1111:1::/64 subnet. However, the graphical interface does not identify the permanent and temporary addresses or lifetimes.

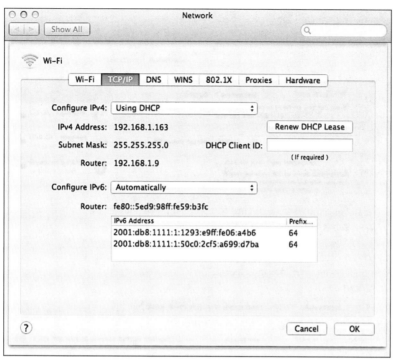

Figure 28-12 *Three IPv6 Settings for Dynamic Address Assignment on macOS*

Hosts support a range of commands to find more detail about the addresses, including lifetimes. Example 28-6 earlier showed the **netsh interface ipv6 show address** command for Windows, for example, with Linux using the **show -6 address** command. Example 28-7 shows these exact details on macOS with two commands. The first command, **ifconfig en8**, lists details about Ethernet, IPv4, and IPv6, on one specific interface (internally numbered as Ethernet number 8, or en8). The command also identifies the preferred address (using the keyword *secured*) and temporary address, as highlighted in the upper part of the example.

Example 28-7 *Sample* ifconfig *Commands from a Mac*

```
Mac% ifconfig en8
en8: flags=8863<UP,BROADCAST,SMART,RUNNING,SIMPLEX,MULTICAST> mtu 1500
       options=6467<RXCSUM,TXCSUM,VLAN_MTU,TSO4,TSO6,CHANNEL_IO,PARTIAL_
CSUM,ZEROINVERT_CSUM>
           ether 00:e0:4c:68:1f:26
           inet6 fe80::184c:56f9:fd3b:d6e7%en8 prefixlen 64 secured scopeid 0x14
           inet6 2001:db8:1111:1:106a:dd3e:8e22:a6fb prefixlen 64 autoconf secured
           inet6 2001:db8:1111:1:ec69:15f9:b4fc:fe2c prefixlen 64 autoconf temporary
           inet 192.168.1.120 netmask 0xffffffff broadcast 192.168.1.120
           nd6 options=201<PERFORMNUD,DAD>
           media: autoselect (1000baseT <full-duplex>)
           status: active
```

```
Mac% ifconfig -aL inet6
! Only interface en8 shown for brevity
en8: flags=8863<UP,BROADCAST,SMART,RUNNING,SIMPLEX,MULTICAST> mtu 1500
     options=6467<RXCSUM,TXCSUM,VLAN_MTU,TSO4,TSO6,CHANNEL_IO,PARTIAL_
CSUM,ZEROINVERT_CSUM>
     inet6 fe80::8ad:f140:a952:9a46%en8 prefixlen 64 secured scopeid 0xc
     inet6 2001:db8:1111:1:106a:dd3e:8e22:a6fb prefixlen 64 autoconf secured
pltime 604654 vltime 2591854
     inet6 2001:db8:1111:1:a968:a6d9:7fbf:38a6 prefixlen 64 autoconf temporary
pltime 85782 vltime 604654
     nd6 options=201<PERFORMNUD,DAD>
```

The lower part of the output shows how to find the preferred (pltime) and valid (vltime) life-times for each address using the **ifconfig -aL inet6** command. The output also lists the word *autoconf*, which implies the host used SLAAC. The output also identifies one permanent address (secured) and the other as the temporary address. Finally, note that the SLAAC-derived addresses appear to use random interface IDs, because the string ff:fe does not exist in the middle of the interface ID.

Testing IPv6 Connectivity with ping and traceroute

The **ping** and **traceroute** commands make for great connectivity testing tools for IPv4 as well as for IPv6. Some OSs (notably Microsoft Windows variants and Cisco routers and switches) let you use the same **ping** and **traceroute** commands used with IPv4. Some other OSs require a different command, like the **ping6** and **traceroute6** commands used with macOS and Linux. (The upcoming examples show both variations.)

As for the output of the **ping** and **traceroute** commands, most people who understand the commands as used with IPv4 need no coaching to use the commands with IPv6. The output is mostly unchanged compared to the IPv4 equivalents, other than the obvious differences with listing IPv6 addresses. For comparison, the upcoming examples use the internetwork displayed in Figure 28-13.

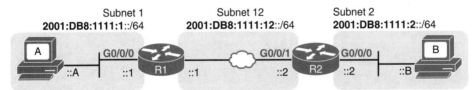

Figure 28-13 *IPv6 Internetwork for* **ping** *and* **traceroute** *Examples*

Example 28-8 shows three **ping6** commands, taken from PC1, a Linux host. (Linux uses **ping6** and **traceroute6** commands for IPv6.) The first two commands show IPv6 pings, the first to R1's LAN IPv6 address, followed by PC1 pinging PC B's IPv6 address. The final command shows an IPv4 ping for comparison.

Example 28-8 *The* ping6 *Command from PC1, for R1 and PC2*

```
! An IPv6 ping, PC A pings R1's address in the same subnet
Linux_A:$ ping6 2001:db8:1111:1::1
PING 2001:db8:1111:1::1 (2001:db8:1111:1::1) 56 data bytes
64 bytes from 2001:db8:1111:1::1: icmp_seq=1 ttl=64 time=1.26 ms
64 bytes from 2001:db8:1111:1::1: icmp_seq=2 ttl=64 time=1.15 ms
^C
--- 2001:db8:1111:1::1 ping statistics ---
2 packets transmitted, 2 received, 0% packet loss, time 1001 ms
rtt min/avg/max/mdev = 1.156/1.210/1.263/0.062 ms


! An IPv6 ping next, ping of PC B from PC A
Linux_A:$ ping6 2001:db8:1111:2::b
PING 2001:db8:1111:2::b (2001:db8:1111:2::b) 56 data bytes
64 bytes from 2001:db8:1111:2::b: icmp_seq=1 ttl=64 time=2.33 ms
64 bytes from 2001:db8:1111:2::b: icmp_seq=2 ttl=64 time=2.59 ms
64 bytes from 2001:db8:1111:2::b: icmp_seq=3 ttl=64 time=2.03 ms
^C
--- 2001:db8:1111:2::b ping statistics ---
3 packets transmitted, 3 received, 0% packet loss, time 2003 ms
rtt min/avg/max/mdev = 2.039/2.321/2.591/0.225 ms


! An IPv4 ping next, for comparison - ping of PC B from PC A
Linux_A:$ ping 10.1.2.22
PING 10.1.3.22 (10.1.2.22) 56 data bytes
64 bytes from 10.1.2.22: icmp_seq=1 ttl=64 time=2.45 ms
64 bytes from 10.1.2.22: icmp_seq=2 ttl=64 time=2.55 ms
64 bytes from 10.1.2.22: icmp_seq=3 ttl=64 time=2.14 ms
^C
--- 10.1.3.22 ping statistics ---
3 packets transmitted, 3 received, 0% packet loss, time 2014 ms
rtt min/avg/max/mdev = 2.04/2.318/2.604/0.224 ms
```

28

Example 28-9 shows a **traceroute6** command on PC A, finding the route to PC B. The output mirrors the style of output for most IPv4 **traceroute** commands, other than the obvious difference of listing IPv6 addresses. Note that the output lists R1's G0/0/0 IPv6 address, R2's G0/0/1 IPv6 address, and then PC B's address to end the output.

Example 28-9 *The* traceroute6 *Command from PC1, for PC2*

```
Linux_A:$ traceroute6 2001:db8:1111:2::b
traceroute to 2001:db8:1111:2::b (2001:db8:1111:2::b) from 2001:db8:1111:1::a,
   30 hops max, 24 byte packets
1   2001:db8:1111:1::1 (2001:db8:1111:1::1)  0.794 ms  0.648 ms  0.604 ms
2   2001:db8:1111:12::2 (2001:db8:1111:12::2)  1.606 ms  1.49 ms  1.497 ms
3   2001:db8:1111:2::b (2001:db8:1111:2::b)  2.038 ms  1.911 ms  1.899 ms
```

> **NOTE** The **traceroute/traceroute6** commands learn the addresses using the ICMPv6 time exceeded message. That mechanism results in the command output listing the GUA of the various routers and destination host.

Verifying Host Connectivity from Nearby Routers

For router verification commands for IPv6, some IPv6 features use the same command as with IPv4, but some substitute "ipv6" for "ip." And in some cases, particularly with functions that do not exist in IPv4 or have changed quite a bit, routers support brand-new commands. This section looks at a couple of router commands useful to verify IPv6 host connectivity, some old and some new for IPv6.

First, for connectivity testing, Cisco routers and switches support the **ping** and **traceroute** commands with the same basic features for IPv6 as with IPv4. The commands accept either an IPv4 or an IPv6 address as input for the standard version of the commands. For the extended versions of these commands, the first prompt question asks for the protocol. Just type **ipv6** instead of using the default of **ip**, and answer the rest of the questions.

Of course, an example helps, particularly for the extended commands. Example 28-10 begins with an extended IPv6 **ping** from R1 to PC B from Figure 28-13, using R1's G0/0/0 interface as the source of the packets. The second command shows a standard IPv6 **traceroute** from R1 to PC B.

Example 28-10 *Extended* **ping** *and Standard* **traceroute** *for IPv6 from Router R1*

```
R1# ping
Protocol [ip]: ipv6
Target IPv6 address: 2001:db8:1111:2::b
Repeat count [5]:
Datagram size [100]:
Timeout in seconds [2]:
Extended commands? [no]: yes
Source address or interface: GigabitEthernet0/0/0
UDP protocol? [no]:
Verbose? [no]:
Precedence [0]:
DSCP [0]:
Include hop by hop option? [no]:
Include destination option? [no]:
Sweep range of sizes? [no]:
Type escape sequence to abort.
Sending 5, 100-byte ICMP Echos to 2001:DB8:1111:2::b, timeout is 2 seconds:
Packet sent with a source address of 2001:DB8:1111:1::1
!!!!!
Success rate is 100 percent (5/5), round-trip min/avg/max = 0/1/4 ms
```

```
R1# traceroute 2001:db8:1111:2::b
Type escape sequence to abort.
Tracing the route to 2001:DB8:1111:2::b

  1 2001:DB8:1111:12::2 4 msec 0 msec 0 msec
  2 2001:DB8:1111:2::b 0 msec 4 msec 0 msec
```

Another way to verify host settings from a router is to look at the router's NDP neighbor table. All IPv6 hosts, routers included, keep an IPv6 neighbor table: a list of all neighboring IPv6 addresses and matching MAC addresses.

One way to verify whether a neighboring host is responsive is to determine whether it will send back an NDP NA when the router sends it an NDP NS (to discover the host's MAC address). To do so, the router could clear its neighbor table (**clear ipv6 neighbor**) and ping a host on some connected interface. The router will first need to send an NDP NS, and the host must send an NDP NA back. If the router shows that host's MAC address in the neighbor table, the host must have just replied with an NDP NA. Example 28-11 shows a sample of an IPv6 neighbor table from Router R2 in Figure 28-13, using the **show ipv6 neighbors** command.

Example 28-11   *The* show ipv6 neighbors *Command on Router R2*

```
R2# show ipv6 neighbors
IPv6 Address                     Age Link-layer Addr State Interface
2001:DB8:1111:2::B                 0 0200.bbbb.bbbb  STALE Gi0/0/0
FE80::BBFF:FEBB:BBBB               0 0200.bbbb.bbbb  STALE Gi0/0/0
FE80::FF:FE01:1                    0 2436.dadf.5681  REACH Gi0/0/1
```

Finally, routers can also list information about the available routers on a LAN subnet, which impacts the connectivity available to hosts. As a reminder, routers send NDP RA messages to announce their willingness to act as an IPv6 router on a particular LAN subnet. Cisco routers watch for RA messages from other routers, typically receiving unsolicited RA messages that routers send to the FF02::1 all IPv6 hosts multicast address. The **show ipv6 routers** command lists any other routers but not the local router. Refer to earlier Example 28-3 for a sample of the **show ipv6 routers** command output.

Chapter Review

One key to doing well on the exams is to perform repetitive spaced review sessions. Review this chapter's material using either the tools in the book or interactive tools for the same material found on the book's companion website. Refer to the "Your Study Plan" element for more details. Table 28-4 outlines the key review elements and where you can find them. To better track your study progress, record when you completed these activities in the second column.

Table 28-4   Chapter Review Tracking

Review Element	Review Date(s)	Resource Used
Review key topics		Book, website
Review key terms		Book, website
Answer DIKTA questions		Book, PTP
Review memory table		Book, website
Review command tables		Book

Review All the Key Topics

Table 28-5   Key Topics for Chapter 28

Key Topic Element	Description	Page Number
List	Four functions for which NDP plays a major role	699
List	Descriptions of the NDP NS and NA messages	699
Figure 28-1	Example use of NDP RS and RA	700
List	Descriptions of the NDP RS and RA messages	702
Figure 28-3	Example use of NDP NS and NA	703
List	Two important routes created by IPv6 hosts based on the RA message	704
Figure 28-4	Example use of NDP for Duplicate Address Detection (DAD)	705
Table 28-2	Summary of NDP functions discussed in this chapter	706
List	Similarities between DHCP for IPv4 and stateful DHCP for IPv6	707
Figure 28-5	Sources of host IPv6 configuration when using stateful DHCPv6	708
Figure 28-8	SLAAC address creation concepts	711
Figure 28-9	Sources of host IPv6 configuration when using SLAAC	711
Example 28-8	Examples of the **ping6** command	717
Example 28-10	Using extended **ping** and standard **traceroute** for IPv6	718

Key Terms You Should Know

Duplicate Address Detection (DAD), IPv6 neighbor table, Neighbor Advertisement (NA), Neighbor Discovery Protocol (NDP), Neighbor Solicitation (NS), on-link prefix, permanent IPv6 address, preferred lifetime, prefix discovery, Router Advertisement (RA), Router Solicitation (RS), stateful DHCPv6, Stateless Address Autoconfiguration (SLAAC), stateless DHCPv6, temporary IPv6 address, valid lifetime

Command References

Tables 28-6, 28-7, and 28-8 list configuration and verification commands used in this chapter, respectively. As an easy review exercise, cover the left column in a table, read the right column, and try to recall the command without looking. Then repeat the exercise, covering the right column, and try to recall what the command does.

Table 28-6 Chapter 28 Configuration Command Reference

Command	Description
ipv6 dhcp relay destination *server-address*	Interface subcommand that enables the IPv6 DHCP relay agent

Table 28-7 Chapter 28 EXEC Command Reference

Command	Description
ping {*host-name* | *ipv6-address*}	Tests IPv6 routes by sending an ICMP packet to the destination host
traceroute {*host-name* | *ipv6-address*}	Tests IPv6 routes by discovering the IP addresses of the routes between a router and the listed destination
show ipv6 neighbors	Lists the router's IPv6 neighbor table
show ipv6 routers	Lists any neighboring routers that advertised themselves through an NDP RA message

Table 28-8 Chapter 28 Host Command Reference

Command (Windows/macOS/Linux)	Description
ipconfig / ifconfig / ifconfig	(Windows/macOS/Linux) Lists interface settings, including IPv4 and IPv6 addresses
ping / ping6 / ping6	(Windows/macOS/Linux) Tests IP routes by sending an ICMPv6 packet to the destination host
tracert / traceroute6 / traceroute6	(Windows/macOS/Linux) Tests IP routes by discovering the IPv6 addresses of the routes between a router and the listed destination
netsh interface ipv6 show neighbors / get-Neighbor -AddressFamily IPv6	(Windows only) Lists IPv6 neighbors with network shell and PowerShell
ndp -an / ip -6 neighbor show	(macOS/Linux) Lists IPv6 neighbors
netsh interface ipv6 show route / netstat -rnf inet6 / ip -6 route	(Windows/macOS/Linux) Lists a host's IPv6 routing table
netsh interface ipv6 show address / ifconfig -aL inet6 / ip -6 address	(Windows/macOS/Linux) Lists a host's interface IPv6 addresses

28

CHAPTER 29

Implementing IPv6 Routing

This chapter covers the following exam topics:

3.0 IP Connectivity

    3.1 Interpret the components of routing table

        3.1.a Routing protocol code

        3.1.b Prefix

        3.1.c Network mask

        3.1.d Next hop

        3.1.e Administrative distance

    3.3 Configure and verify IPv4 and IPv6 static routing

        3.3.a Default route

        3.3.b Network route

        3.3.c Host route

        3.3.d Floating static

This last chapter in Part VII of the book completes the materials about IPv6 by examining four major topics. The first section examines IPv6 connected and **local routes**—the routes a router adds to its routing table in reaction to IPv6 address configuration. The second major section discusses static network routes, that is, routes configured by the **ipv6 route** command with a destination of an IPv6 prefix (subnet). The third major section examines other IPv6 static route topics, including default routes, host routes, and floating static routes, with some notes about troubleshooting all static IPv6 routes. The final short section discusses a few tools and tips to troubleshoot IPv6 static routes.

"Do I Know This Already?" Quiz

Take the quiz (either here or use the PTP software) if you want to use the score to help you decide how much time to spend on this chapter. The letter answers are listed at the bottom of the page following the quiz. Appendix C, found both at the end of the book as well as on the companion website, includes both the answers and explanations. You can also find both answers and explanations in the PTP testing software.

Table 29-1 "Do I Know This Already?" Foundation Topics Section-to-Question Mapping

Foundation Topics Section	Questions
Connected and Local IPv6 Routes	1, 2
Static IPv6 Network Routes	3, 4
Static Default, Host, and Floating Static IPv6 Routes	5, 6
Troubleshooting Static IPv6 Routes	7

Refer to the following figure for questions 1, 3, and 4.

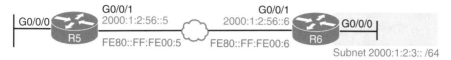

1. Router R6 in the figure has been configured with the **ipv6 address 2000:1:2:3::1/64** command on its G0/0/0 interface. The router also creates a link-local address of FE80::FF:FE00:1. All router interfaces have an up/up status. Which of the following routes will R6 add to its IPv6 routing table? (Choose two answers.)

   a. A route for 2000:1:2:3::/64

   b. A route for FE80::FF:FE00:1/64

   c. A route for 2000:1:2:3::1/128

   d. A route for FE80::FF:FE00:1/128

2. A router has been configured with the **ipv6 address 3111:1:1:1::1/64** command on its G0/0/0 interface and **ipv6 address 3222:2:2:2::1/64** on its G0/0/1 interface. Both interfaces have an up/up state. Which of the following routes would you expect to see in the output of the **show ipv6 route connected** command? (Choose two answers.)

   a. A route for 3111:1:1:1::/64

   b. A route for 3111:1:1:1::1/64

   c. A route for 3222:2:2:2::/64

   d. A route for 3222:2:2:2::2/128

3. An engineer needs to add a static IPv6 route for prefix 2000:1:2:3::/64 to Router R5 in the figure. Which of the following **ipv6 route** commands would result in a working IPv6 route for this subnet prefix? (Choose two answers.)

   a. ipv6 route 2000:1:2:3::/64 G0/0/1 2000:1:2:56::6

   b. ipv6 route 2000:1:2:3::/64 2000:1:2:56::6

   c. ipv6 route 2000:1:2:3::/64 G0/0/1 2001:1:2:56::5

   d. ipv6 route 2000:1:2:3::/64 G0/0/1

4. An engineer needs to add a static IPv6 route for prefix 2000:1:2:3::/64 to Router R5 in the figure. Which of the following answers shows a valid static IPv6 route for that subnet on Router R5?

   a. ipv6 route 2000:1:2:3::/64 2000:1:2:56::5

   b. ipv6 route 2000:1:2:3::/64 2000:1:2:56::6

   c. ipv6 route 2000:1:2:3::/64 FE80::FF:FE00:5

   d. ipv6 route 2000:1:2:3::/64 FE80::FF:FE00:6

5. When displaying an IPv6 static default route, how does the **show ipv6 route** command represent the concept of the default destination?

   a. With the phrase "Gateway of Last Resort" just above the list of routes

   b. With a prefix value ::/0 in the line for the route

   c. With a prefix value ::/128 in the line for the route

    d. With a prefix value 2000::/3 in the line for the route

    e. With the keyword "default" in the line for the route

6. Router R1 has a useful IPv6 configuration so that Router R1 learns a route for subnet 2001:db8:1:2::/64 with OSPF. The route lists an outgoing interface that is an Ethernet WAN link. The engineer then installs cellular interfaces on both routers for WAN backup. As part of the configuration, the engineer configures the **ipv6 route 2001:db8:1:2::/64 cellular0/2/0 200** command. What does the router do in response?

    a. It rejects the **ipv6 route** command because of the existing OSPF route for the same prefix.

    b. It accepts the **ipv6 route** command into the configuration but does not add a route to the routing table.

    c. It accepts the **ipv6 route** command into the configuration and adds the route to the routing table, but it leaves the OSPF-learned route in the routing table.

    d. It accepts the **ipv6 route** command into the configuration, adds the route to the routing table, and removes the OSPF-learned route in the routing table.

7. An engineer types the command **ipv6 route 2001:DB8:8:8::/64 2001:DB8:9:9::9 129** in configuration mode of Router R1 and presses Enter. Later, a **show ipv6 route** command lists no routes for subnet 2001:DB8:8:8::/64. Which of the following could have caused the route to not be in the IPv6 routing table?

    a. The command uses a next-hop global unicast address, which is not allowed, preventing the router from adding a route.

    b. The command must include an outgoing interface parameter, so IOS rejected the **ipv6 route** command.

    c. The router has no routes that match the next-hop address 2001:DB8:9:9::9.

    d. A route for 2001:DB8:8:8::/64 with administrative distance 110 already exists.

Foundation Topics

Connected and Local IPv6 Routes

A Cisco router adds IPv6 routes to its IPv6 routing table for several reasons. Many of you could predict those reasons at this point in your reading, in part because the logic mirrors the logic routers use for IPv4. Specifically, a router adds IPv6 routes based on the following:

- The configuration of IPv6 addresses on working interfaces (connected and local routes)

- The direct configuration of a static route (static routes)

- The configuration of a routing protocol, like OSPFv3, on routers that share the same data link (dynamic routes)

The first two sections of this chapter examine the first of these two topics, with discussions of IPv6 routing protocols residing in the CCNP Enterprise exams.

Also, as an early reminder of a few essential acronyms from earlier chapters, remember that GUA refers to global unicast addresses, the most common routable unicast address configured on Enterprise router interfaces. Unique local addresses (ULA) serve as private addresses. Finally, routes frequently use a neighboring router's link-local address (LLA), a unicast address that exists on every router and host interface, useful for sending packets over the local link.

Rules for Connected and Local Routes

Routers add and remove IPv6 connected and **IPv6 local routes** based on the interface configuration and state. First, the router looks for configured unicast addresses on any interfaces by looking for the **ipv6 address** command. Then, if the interface is working—if the interface has a "line status is up, protocol status is up" notice in the output of the **show interfaces** command—the router adds both a connected and local route.

> **NOTE**   Routers do not create connected or local IPv6 routes for link-local addresses.

The connected and local routes follow the same general logic as with IPv4. The connected route represents the subnet connected to the interface, whereas the local route is a host route for only the specific IPv6 address configured on the interface.

For example, consider a router configured with a working interface with the **ipv6 address 2000:1:1:1::1/64** command. The router will calculate the subnet ID based on this address and prefix length and place a connected route for that subnet (2000:1:1:1::/64) into the routing table. The router also takes the listed IPv6 address and creates a local route for that address, with a /128 prefix length. (With IPv4, local routes have a /32 prefix length, while IPv6 uses a /128 prefix length, meaning "exactly this one address.")

The following list summarizes the rules about how routers create routes based on the configuration of an interface IPv6 unicast address, for easier review and study:

1. Routers create IPv6 routes based on each unicast IPv6 address on an interface, as configured with the **ipv6 address** command, as follows:

    a. The router creates a route for the subnet (a connected route).

    b. The router creates a local route (/128 prefix length) for the router IPv6 address (a local route).

2. Routers do not create routes based on the link-local addresses associated with the interface.

3. Routers remove the connected and local routes for an interface if the interface fails, and they re-add these routes when the interface is again in a working (up/up) state.

Example of Connected IPv6 Routes

While the concept of connected and local IPv6 routes works much like IPv4 routes, seeing a few examples can certainly help. To show some sample routes, Figure 29-1 details one sample internetwork used in this chapter. The figure shows the IPv6 subnet IDs. The upcoming examples focus on the connected and local routes on Router R1.

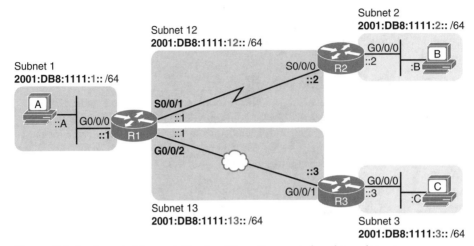

Figure 29-1 *Sample Network Used to Show Connected and Local Routes*

To clarify the notes in Figure 29-1, note that the figure shows IPv6 prefixes (subnets), with a shorthand notation for the interface IPv6 addresses. The figure shows only the abbreviated interface ID portion of each interface address near each interface. For example, R1's G0/0/0 interface address would begin with subnet ID value 2001:DB8:1111:1, added to ::1, for 2001:DB8:1111:1::1.

Now on to the example of connected routes. To begin, consider the configuration of Router R1 from Figure 29-1, as shown in Example 29-1. The excerpt from the **show running-config** command on R1 shows three working interfaces. Also note that no static route or routing protocol configuration exists.

Example 29-1 *IPv6 Addressing Configuration on Router R1*

```
ipv6 unicast-routing
!
! Unused interfaces omitted
!
interface GigabitEthernet0/0/0
 ipv6 address 2001:DB8:1111:1::1/64
!
interface Serial0/0/1
 ipv6 address 2001:db8:1111:12::1/64
!
interface GigabitEthernet0/0/2
 ipv6 address 2001:db8:1111:13::1/64
```

Based on Figure 29-1 and Example 29-1, R1 should have three connected IPv6 routes, as highlighted in Example 29-2.

Answers to the "Do I Know This Already?" quiz:

1 A, C **2** A, C **3** A, B **4** B **5** B **6** B **7** C

Example 29-2   *Routes on Router R1 Before Adding Static Routes or Routing Protocols*

```
R1# show ipv6 route
IPv6 Routing Table - default - 7 entries
Codes: C - Connected, L - Local, S - Static, U - Per-user Static route
       B - BGP, HA - Home Agent, MR - Mobile Router, R - RIP
       H - NHRP, I1 - ISIS L1, I2 - ISIS L2, IA - ISIS interarea
       IS - ISIS summary, D - EIGRP, EX - EIGRP external, NM - NEMO
       ND - ND Default, NDp - ND Prefix, DCE - Destination, NDr - Redirect
       RL - RPL, O - OSPF Intra, OI - OSPF Inter, OE1 - OSPF ext 1
       OE2 - OSPF ext 2, ON1 - OSPF NSSA ext 1, ON2 - OSPF NSSA ext 2
       la - LISP alt, lr - LISP site-registrations, ld - LISP dyn-eid
       lA - LISP away, a - Application
C   2001:DB8:1111:1::/64 [0/0]
     via GigabitEthernet0/0/0, directly connected
L   2001:DB8:1111:1::1/128 [0/0]
     via GigabitEthernet0/0/0, receive
C   2001:DB8:1111:12::/64 [0/0]
     via Serial0/0/1, directly connected
L   2001:DB8:1111:12::1/128 [0/0]
     via Serial0/0/1, receive
C   2001:DB8:1111:13::/64 [0/0]
     via GigabitEthernet0/0/2, directly connected
L   2001:DB8:1111:13::1/128 [0/0]
     via GigabitEthernet0/0/2, receive
L   FF00::/8 [0/0]
     via Null0, receive
```

All three highlighted routes show the same basic kinds of information, so for discussion, focus on the first pair of highlighted lines, which details the connected route for subnet 2001:DB8:1111:1::/64. The first pair of highlighted lines states: The route is a "directly connected" route; the interface ID is GigabitEthernet0/0/0; and the prefix/length is 2001:DB8:1111:1::/64. At the far left, the code letter "C" identifies the route as a connected route (per the legend above). Also note that the numbers in brackets mirror the same ideas as IPv4's **show ip route** command: The first number represents the administrative distance, and the second is the metric.

Examples of Local IPv6 Routes

Continuing this same example, three local routes should exist on R1 for the same three interfaces as the connected routes. Indeed, that is the case, with one extra local route for other purposes. Example 29-3 shows only the local routes, as listed by the **show ipv6 route local** command, with highlights of one particular local route for discussion.

29

Example 29-3 *Local IPv6 Routes on Router R1*

```
R1# show ipv6 route local
! Legend omitted for brevity


L   2001:DB8:1111:1::1/128 [0/0]
      via GigabitEthernet0/0/0, receive
L   2001:DB8:1111:4::1/128 [0/0]
      via Serial0/0/1, receive
L   2001:DB8:1111:5::1/128 [0/0]
      via GigabitEthernet0/0/2, receive
L   FF00::/8 [0/0]
      via Null0, receive
```

For the highlighted local route, look for a couple of quick facts. First, look back to R1's configuration in Example 29-1, and note R1's IPv6 address on its G0/0/0 interface. This local route lists the exact same address. Also note the /128 prefix length, meaning this route matches packets sent to that address (2001:DB8:1111:1::1), and only that address.

> **NOTE** While the **show ipv6 route local** command shows all local IPv6 routes, the **show ipv6 route connected** command shows all connected routes.

Static IPv6 Network Routes

IPv6 static routes require direct configuration with the **ipv6 route** command. Simply put, someone configures the command, and the router places the details from the command into a route in the IPv6 routing table.

The IPv6 network route is the most common type of static route among the types mentioned in the CCNA exam topics (network, host, default, and floating static). A network route, by definition, defines a route to the addresses in a subnet based on the listed prefix and prefix length. The **ipv6 route** global command also lists the forwarding instructions of how this router should forward packets toward that destination prefix by listing the outgoing interface or the address of the next-hop router.

Figure 29-2 shows the general concepts behind a single **ipv6 route** command for a network route. The figure shows the ideas behind a static route on Router R1 for the subnet on the right (subnet 2, or 2001:DB8:1111:2::/64). The command begins with **ipv6 route 2001:DB8:1111:2::/64**, defining the destination subnet. The rest of the command defines the forwarding instructions—either the outgoing interface (S0/0/1), the next-hop IPv6 address, or both.

Now that you understand the big ideas with IPv6 static network routes, the next few pages walk you through a series of examples. In particular, the examples look at configuring static routes with an outgoing interface, then with a next-hop GUA, and then with a next-hop LLA.

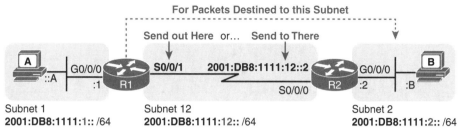

Figure 29-2 *Logic Behind IPv6 Static Route Commands (IPv6 Route)*

Static Network Routes Using an Outgoing Interface

This first IPv6 static route example uses the outgoing interface option. As a reminder, for both IPv4 and IPv6 static routes, when the command references an interface, the interface is a local interface; that is, it is an interface on the router where the command is added. In this case, as shown in Figure 29-2, R1's **ipv6 route** command would use interface S0/0/1, as shown in Example 29-4.

Example 29-4 *Static IPv6 Routes on Router R1*

```
! Static route on router R1
R1(config)# ipv6 route 2001:db8:1111:2::/64 S0/0/1
```

If you were attempting to support packet flow between all hosts, like PCs A and B in the figure, you need static routes on each router for each remote subnet. For example, to support traffic between hosts A and B, R1 is now prepared. Host A will forward all its IPv6 packets to its default router (R1), and R1 can now route those packets destined for host B's subnet out R1's S0/0/1 interface to R2 next. However, Router R2 does not yet have a route that matches addresses in host A's subnet (2001:DB8:1111:1::/64), so a complete static routing solution requires more routes.

Example 29-5 solves this problem by giving Router R2 a static route for subnet 1 (2001:DB8:1111:1::/64). After this route is added, hosts A and B should be able to ping each other.

Example 29-5 *Static IPv6 Routes on Router R2*

```
! Static route on router R2
R2(config)# ipv6 route 2001:db8:1111:1::/64 s0/0/0
```

Many options exist for verifying the existence of the static route and testing whether hosts can use the route. **ping** and **traceroute** can test connectivity. From the router command line, the **show ipv6 route** command will list all the IPv6 routes. The shorter output of the **show ipv6 route static** command, which lists only static routes, could also be used; Example 29-6 shows that output, with the legend omitted.

29

Example 29-6 *Verification of Static Routes Only on R1*

```
R1# show ipv6 route static
! Legend omitted for brevity
S   2001:DB8:1111:2::/64 [1/0]
     via Serial0/0/1, directly connected
```

This command lists many facts about the one static route on R1. First, the code "S" in the left column does identify the route as a static route. (However, the later phrase "directly connected" might mislead you to think this is a connected route; trust the "S" code.) Note that the prefix (2001:DB8:1111:2::/64) matches the configuration (in Example 29-4), as does the outgoing interface (S0/0/1).

When working with IPv6 routes, you will often wonder which route the router will match for a given destination address. You should be ready to think through that question while examining a full IPv6 routing table, but if answering a lab question on the exam, you can use a command that tells you the specific route, as seen in Example 29-7. For example, if host A sent an IPv6 packet to host B (2001:DB8:1111:2::B), would R1 use this static route? As it turns out, R1 would use that route, as confirmed by the **show ipv6 route 2001:DB8:1111:2::B** command. This command asks the router to list the route that the router would use when forwarding packets to that particular address.

Example 29-7 *Displaying the Route R1 Uses to Forward to Host B*

```
R1# show ipv6 route 2001:db8:1111:2::b
Routing entry for 2001:DB8:1111:2::/64
  Known via "static", distance 1, metric 0
  Route count is 1/1, share count 0
  Routing paths:
    directly connected via Serial0/0/1
      Last updated 00:01:29 ago
```

NOTE   Only serial interfaces, and not Ethernet interfaces, support using an **ipv6 route** command with only an outgoing interface as the forwarding instructions. With Ethernet interfaces, the router will accept the command, but the router cannot forward packets using the route. See the later section, "Troubleshooting Static IPv6 Routes," for more details on this case and other challenges with static IPv6 routes.

Static Network Routes Using Next-Hop IPv6 Address

IPv6 static route commands can use only the next-hop router address or a combination of the next-hop router address plus the outgoing interface. Note that these options work when the route forwards packets out any kind of interface, including Ethernet and serial links, but the upcoming examples show an Ethernet WAN link.

Interestingly, IPv6 supports using the neighbor's GUA, ULA, or LLA as the next-hop IPv6 address. The following list provides the working combinations, with Figure 29-3 depicting the logic from R1's perspective for a route with R3 as the next-hop router:

- Next-hop GUA or ULA only

- Next-hop GUA or ULA and outgoing interface

- Next-hop LLA and outgoing interface

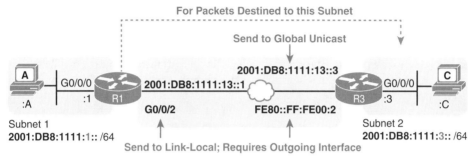

Figure 29-3 *Using GUA or LLA as the Next-Hop Address for Static IPv6 Routes*

The next few pages walk you through examples, first with a GUA and then with an LLA as a next-hop router.

Example Static Network Route with a Next-Hop GUA

In Example 29-8, R1 adds a static route that refers to neighbor R3's GUA per Figure 29-3. The command lists subnet 3 (2001:DB8:1111:3::/64), which exists on the far side of Router R3. The route then lists R3's GUA (ending in 13::3), the GUA on the shared subnet between R1 and R3, as the next-hop address.

Example 29-8 *Static IPv6 Routes Using Global Unicast Addresses*

```
!
R1(config)# ipv6 route 2001:db8:1111:3::/64 2001:DB8:1111:13::3
```

The first two commands in Example 29-9 list detail about the static route config-ured in Example 29-8. The first command lists all static routes on Router R1, currently just the one static route per Example 29-8. The second command, **show ipv6 route 2001:DB8:1111:3::33**, asks R1 to identify the route it would use to forward packets to the address listed in the command (Host C in the figure uses address **2001:DB8:1111:3::33**). The output details the just-configured static route, proving that R1 uses this new static route when forwarding packets to that host.

Example 29-9 *Verification of Static Routes to a Next-Hop Global Unicast Address*

```
R1# show ipv6 route static
! Legend omitted for brevity
S    2001:DB8:1111:3::/64 [1/0]
      via 2001:DB8:1111:13::3
```

```
R1# show ipv6 route 2001:db8:1111:3::33
Routing entry for 2001:DB8:1111:3::/64
  Known via "static", distance 1, metric 0
  Route count is 1/1, share count 0
  Routing paths:
    2001:DB8:1111:13::3
      Route metric is 0, traffic share count is 1
      Last updated 00:07:43 ago
```

Interestingly, the **ipv6 route 2001:db8:1111:3::/64 2001:db8:1111:13::3** command in
Example 29-8 works, but you might wonder how the router knows what outgoing interface
to use because the command does not list it. The router does need to identify the outgoing
interface, so it uses an iterative process by finding the route to reach the next-hop GUA. The
first iteration happens when the router matches the packet's destination address to the static
route. The second iteration occurs when the router finds the route to use when forwarding
packets to the next-hop address in the first route. That second iteration matches the route
for the subnet to which both the local router and the next-hop router connect—in this case,
subnet prefix 2001.db8:1111:13::/64 connected to R1's G0/0/2.

Example 29-10 shows some notes about the iterative lookup to find the outgoing interface.
The first command lists the connected route that Router R1 uses that matches next-hop GUA
2002:db8:1111:13::3, namely the route for prefix 2001:db8:1111:13::/64. But the **show ipv6
static detail** command shows the results of the router's iterative route lookup, listing interface G0/0/2 as the outgoing interface. It also lists a code of *, informing us that the router
added the route to the Routing Information Base (RIB), referring to the IPv6 routing table.

Example 29-10 *Understanding the Iterative Lookup to Find the Outgoing Interface*

```
R1# show ipv6 route connected
! Lines omitted to reveal route to the subnet between R1 and R3
C   2001:DB8:1111:13::/64 [0/0]
      via GigabitEthernet0/0/2, directly connected

R1# show ipv6 static detail
IPv6 Static routes Table - default
Codes: * - installed in RIB, u/m - Unicast/Multicast only
Codes for []: P - permanent I - Inactive permanent
        U - Per-user Static route
        N - ND Static route
        M - MIP Static route
        P - DHCP-PD Static route
        R - RHI Static route
        V - VxLan Static route
*   2001:DB8:1111:3::/64 via 2001:DB8:1111:13::3, distance 1
      Resolves to 1 paths (max depth 1)
      via GigabitEthernet0/0/2
```

You can also configure a static IPv6 route with the next-hop GUA plus the outgoing interface (sometimes called a fully specified route). Doing so means that the router does not need to perform the iterative route lookup. Example 29-11 shows just such a case, replacing the static route in Example 29-8 with one that also lists both the next-hop GUA plus G0/0/2 as the outgoing interface. The end of the example confirms that the route listed in the IPv6 routing table lists the next-hop GUA and outgoing interface.

Example 29-11 *Alternate IPv6 Static Route with Outgoing Interface and GUA*

```
R1# show running-config | include ipv6 route
ipv6 route 2001:DB8:1111:3::/64 GigabitEthernet0/0/2 2001:DB8:1111:13::3


R1# show ipv6 route | section 2001:DB8:1111:3::/64
S    2001:DB8:1111:3::/64 [1/0]
      via 2001:DB8:1111:13::3, GigabitEthernet0/0/2


R1# show ipv6 static detail
! Legend omitted
*    2001:DB8:1111:3::/64 via 2001:DB8:1111:13::3, GigabitEthernet0/0/2, distance 1
```

Example Static Network Route with a Next-Hop LLA

Static routes that refer to a neighbor's LLA work a little like the preceding two styles of static routes. First, the **ipv6 route** command refers to a next-hop address, namely an LLA; however, the command must also refer to the router's local outgoing interface. Why both? The **ipv6 route** command cannot simply refer to an LLA next-hop address by itself because the iterative route lookup used with GUAs will not work with LLAs. There are no routes for LLAs, so there is no way for a router to use only the LLA as a static route's forwarding instructions. In short, if using the LLA, you also need to configure the outgoing interface.

Figure 29-4 depicts the logic for using both the LLA and outgoing interface to replace the example static route configured in Example 29-8 and explained with Examples 29-9 and 29-10. In this case, the R1 configuration refers to R1's outgoing interface and to Router R2's LLA. The figure also shows the global configuration command required on Router R1.

```
ipv6 route 2001:db8:1111:3::/64 G0/0/2 fe80::ff:fe01:3
```

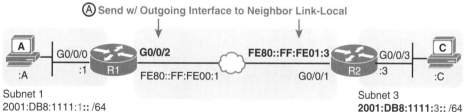

Figure 29-4 *Example Using LLAs and Outgoing Interface for IPv6 Static Routes*

Example 29-12 shows the configuration of the LLA-based static route on Router R1, with some purposeful mistakes along the way. The first attempt with the **ipv6 route** command omits the outgoing interface, so IOS rejects the command. The second attempt shows the command after using the up-arrow to retrieve the command and then adding the outgoing interface (G0/0/2) to the end of the command, but that command uses incorrect syntax. The interface ID should *precede* the address. The final **ipv6 route** command shows the correct syntax with IOS accepting the command.

Example 29-12 *Static IPv6 Network Route Using LLA*

```
R1# configure terminal
Enter configuration commands, one per line.  End with CNTL/Z.
R1(config)# ipv6 route 2001:db8:1111:3::/64 fe80::ff:fe01:3
% Interface has to be specified for a link-local nexthop
R1(config)# ipv6 route 2001:db8:1111:3::/64 fe80::ff:fe00:2 g0/0/2
                                                              ^

% Invalid input detected at '^' marker.

R1(config)# ipv6 route 2001:db8:1111:3::/64 g0/0/2 fe80::ff:fe01:3
R1(config)#^Z
```

Example 29-13 verifies the configuration in Example 29-12 by repeating the **show ipv6 route static** and **show ipv6 route 2001:DB8:1111:3::33** commands used in Example 29-9. Note that the output from both commands differs slightly versus the earlier example. Because the new configuration commands list both the next-hop address and outgoing interface, the **show** commands in Example 29-13 also list both the next-hop (LLA) and the outgoing interface. If you refer back to Example 29-9, you will see only a next-hop address listed.

Example 29-13 *Verification of Static Routes to a Next-Hop Link-Local Address*

```
R1# show ipv6 route static
! Legend omitted for brevity

S   2001:DB8:1111:3::/64 [1/0]
       via FE80::FF:FE00:2, GigabitEthernet0/0/2

R1# show ipv6 route 2001:db8:1111:3::33
Routing entry for 2001:DB8:1111:3::/64
  Known via "static", distance 1, metric 0
  Route count is 1/1, share count 0
  Routing paths:
    FE80::FF:FE00:2, GigabitEthernet0/0/2
      Route metric is 0, traffic share count is 1
      Last updated 00:01:01 ago
```

In summary, IPv6 static network routes list a prefix/prefix-length along with forwarding instructions. The forwarding instructions allow for unicast address types—GUA, ULA, or even LLAs. However, there are some restrictions about which options you can use with forwarding instructions. Table 29-2 summarizes the options.

Table 29-2   Summary Table for IPv6 Network Route Configuration

Forwarding Instructions	Serial	Ethernet
Interface only	Yes	No*
GUA/ULA only	Yes	Yes
Interface plus GUA/ULA	Yes	Yes
Interface plus LLA	Yes	Yes
LLA only	No	No

* The **ipv6 route** command can be configured with an outgoing Ethernet interface but no next-hop address, but the route does not forward packets.

Static Default, Host, and Floating Static IPv6 Routes

If you have been reading this book sequentially, the following topics should be relatively easy. Engineers use IPv6 default, host, and floating static routes for the same purposes as their IPv4 cousins. The only difference comes in the combinations of how to configure the next-hop addresses and outgoing interfaces for IPv6, a topic you just finished learning about in this chapter. Hopefully, most of the following few pages will be both a review of IPv4 default, host, and floating static concepts, along with helpful examples for IPv6 routes.

Static IPv6 Default Routes

IPv6 supports a default route concept, similar to IPv4. The default route tells the router what to do with an IPv6 packet when the packet matches no other IPv6 route. The straightforward router forwarding logic when no routes match a packet's destination is

- With no default route, the router discards the IPv6 packet.

- With a default route, the router forwards the IPv6 packet based on the default route.

Default routes can be beneficial in a couple of network design cases. For example, with an enterprise network design that uses a single router at each branch office, with one WAN link to each branch, the branch routers have only one possible path over which to forward packets. When using a routing protocol in a large network, the branch router could learn thousands of routes, all of which forward packets over that one WAN link.

Branch routers could use default routes instead of a routing protocol. The branch router would forward all traffic to the core of the network. Figure 29-5 shows just such an example, with two sample branch routers on the right and a core site router on the left, with the default route shown as the dashed line.

To configure a static default route, use a specific value to note the route as a default route: ::/0. An entire prefix of a double colon (::) with no other digits represents an all 0s prefix, and the /0 prefix length signifies that zero of the initial bits must match to be part of the same group. So, ::/0 serves as the abbreviation of "all IPv6 addresses." This idea mirrors the IPv4 convention to refer to the default route as 0.0.0.0/0 in **show** command output or 0.0.0.0 0.0.0.0 in the **ip route** command.

29

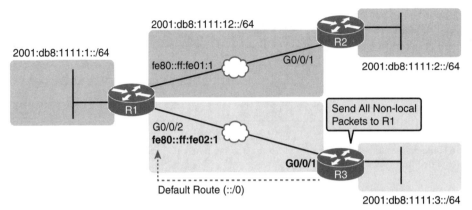

Figure 29-5 *Using Static Default Routes at Branch Routers*

To configure a static default route, use ::/0 as the destination, and otherwise, just configure the **ipv6 route** command as normal, with the same conventions about forwarding instructions as discussed earlier in this chapter. Example 29-14 shows one such sample static default route on Router R3 from Figure 29-5. The configuration uses next-hop LLA and, therefore, also requires the outgoing interface.

Example 29-14 *Static Default Route for Branch Router R3*

```
! Forward out R3's G0/0/1 local interface to R1's G0/0/2 LLA FE80::FF:FE02:1.
R3(config)# ipv6 route ::/0 g0/0/1 fe80::ff:fe02:1
```

Cisco IOS provides a simpler representation of IPv6 default routes compared to IPv4 default routes. For instance, the **show ipv6 route** command output does not list a "Gateway of Last Resort" as with IPv4. Instead, it lists the default route destination as ::/0, just as in the **ipv6 route** configuration command. Example 29-15 shows Router R3's routing table, with only the default route, plus the expected connected and local routes for its two working interfaces. The **show ipv6 route ::/0** command output, at the bottom of the example, shows more detail about the default route, including confirmation of the configured prefix of ::/0 and the next-hop LLA and outgoing interface.

Example 29-15 *Router R3's Static Default Route (Using Outgoing Interface)*

```
R3# show ipv6 route
IPv6 Routing Table - default - 6 entries
Codes: C - Connected, L - Local, S - Static, U - Per-user Static route
       B - BGP, R - RIP, H - NHRP, I1 - ISIS L1
       I2 - ISIS L2, IA - ISIS interarea, IS - ISIS summary, D - EIGRP
       EX - EIGRP external, ND - ND Default, NDp - ND Prefix, DCE - Destination
       NDr - Redirect, O - OSPF Intra, OI - OSPF Inter, OE1 - OSPF ext 1
       OE2 - OSPF ext 2, ON1 - OSPF NSSA ext 1, ON2 - OSPF NSSA ext 2
       a - Application, m - OMP
S    ::/0 [1/0]
     via FE80::FF:FE02:1, GigabitEthernet0/0/1
```

```
C    2001:DB8:1111:3::/64 [0/0]
       via GigabitEthernet0/0/0, directly connected
L    2001:DB8:1111:3::3/128 [0/0]
       via GigabitEthernet0/0/0, receive
C    2001:DB8:1111:13::/64 [0/0]
       via GigabitEthernet0/0/1, directly connected
L    2001:DB8:1111:13::3/128 [0/0]
       via GigabitEthernet0/0/1, receive
L    FF00::/8 [0/0]
       via Null0, receive


R3# show ipv6 route ::/0
Routing entry for ::/0
  Known via "static", distance 1, metric 0
  Route count is 1/1, share count 0
  Routing paths:
    FE80::FF:FE02:1, GigabitEthernet0/0/1
        Route metric is 0, traffic share count is 1
        Last updated 00:04:04 ago
```

Static IPv6 Host Routes

Both IPv4 and IPv6 allow the definition of static host routes—that is, a route to a single host IP address. With IPv4, those routes use a /32 mask, which identifies a single IPv4 address in the **ip route** command; with IPv6, a /128 mask identifies that single host in the **ipv6 route** command.

As for the syntax, an **IPv6 host route** follows the same rules as an IPv6 network route regarding the forwarding instructions. The only difference comes in the configuration of a full 128-bit address along with a prefix length of /128 so that the route matches a single IPv6 address.

You might never need to use a host route in a real network, but the motivation usually comes from some business reason to forward packets to one host over a different route that the routing protocol would choose. Figure 29-6 shows just such an example. The route for all hosts in the subnet flows over the lower part of the topology; however, you might have business reasons to forward traffic sent to host D over the upper path through Router R2, requiring a host route.

Example 29-16 shows the configuration based on Figure 29-6, with the host route for host D using R2 as the next-hop router, and a static network route for host D's subnet using Router R3 as the next-hop router.

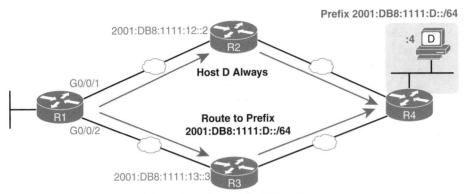

Figure 29-6   *An Example Topology for an IPv6 Host Route*

Example 29-16   *Static Host IPv6 Routes on R1, for Host D*

```
! The first command shows the host route, and the second shows the network route.
! Both use next-hop GUA and outgoing interface for clarity.
R1# configure terminal
Enter configuration commands, one per line.  End with CNTL/Z.
R1(config)# ipv6 route 2001:db8:1111:d::4/128 g0/0/1 2001:db8:1111:12::2
R1(config)# ipv6 route 2001:db8:1111:d::/64 g0/0/2 2001:db8:1111:13::3
R1(config)#^Z
R1#
```

Adding IPv6 host routes typically causes overlapping routes, as seen in this case. When choosing to place routes into the IPv6 routing table, a router always attempts to place the best route for each prefix (subnet) into the IP routing table. That rule applies to each subnet prefix, defined by each combination of prefix and prefix length. In this case, the two static routes have different prefix lengths, so it places both routes into the routing table, as seen in the output from the first command in Example 29-17.

Example 29-17   *IPv6 Host Route for Host D with Overlapping Network Route*

```
R1# show ipv6 route static
! Legend omitted
S    2001:DB8:1111:D::/64 [1/0]
     via 2001:DB8:1111:13::3, GigabitEthernet0/0/2
S    2001:DB8:1111:D::4/128 [1/0]
     via 2001:DB8:1111:12::2, GigabitEthernet0/0/1

R1# show ipv6 route 2001:db8:1111:d::4
Routing entry for 2001:DB8:1111:D::4/128
  Known via "static", distance 1, metric 0
  Route count is 1/1, share count 0
  Routing paths:
    2001:DB8:1111:12::2, GigabitEthernet0/0/1
      Route metric is 0, traffic share count is 1
```

```
      Last updated 00:02:28 ago

R1# show ipv6 route 2001:db8:1111:d::3
Routing entry for 2001:DB8:1111:D::/64
  Known via "static", distance 1, metric 0
  Route count is 1/1, share count 0
  Routing paths:
    2001:DB8:1111:13::3, GigabitEthernet0/0/2
      Route metric is 0, traffic share count is 1
      Last updated 00:00:43 ago
```

As with IPv4 routes, IPv6 matches a packet to the IPv6 routing table using longest-match logic. Packets sent to host D's address match both routes configured in Example 29-16, but the router chooses the longer prefix (more binary 1s in the prefix length) /128 host route. Stated differently, when matching more than one route, the router uses the route that defines the most specific set of addresses.

The final two **show** commands in Example 29-17 demonstrate Router R1's matching logic. The **show ipv6 route 2001:db8:1111:d::4** command asks the router what route it would use to match packets sent to host D's address, and the output describes the /128 host route, with R2's GUA as the next-hop address. Conversely, the final command lists a different IPv6 address in the same subnet as host D, so R1 will not match the host route. Instead, it matches the network route, listing outgoing interface G0/0/2 with R3's GUA as next-hop address.

Floating Static IPv6 Routes

Floating static routes are the last of the four specific static route types mentioned in the CCNA exam topics. The general concept works the same for both IPv4 and IPv6 floating static routes, so this section will provide a brief introduction. For more detail on the concepts, please refer to the section "Floating Static Routes" in Chapter 17, "Configuring IPv4 Addresses and Static Routes."

Floating static routes let a router direct traffic over a switched WAN connection, for instance, over a cellular interface—but only when the normally working WAN link fails. For instance, in Figure 29-7, the Ethernet WAN link typically works for months. OSPF learns IPv6 routes using that link. During those same times, the cellular interfaces remain unused, with no cellular call/link between the routers, and no IPv6 routes that use the cellular interfaces.

Floating static routes provide a method to direct packets over the cellular link, which triggers a phone call to create a link between the two routers—but only when the routes that use the primary link fail. To do so, you configure a static route that uses the cellular interface, and the router stores that route in its configuration. However, the router does not add the route to the routing table because of the existing OSPF-learned route for the exact same prefix/length. Once the primary routes fail, the routers add the floating static routes to their routing tables, directing traffic over the cellular link. In this scenario, the cellular link and the floating static route get used only during outages to the primary link.

29

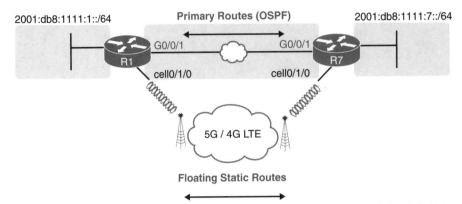

Figure 29-7 *Using a Floating Static Route to Key Subnet 2001:DB8:1111:7::/64*

Routers rely on each route's **IPv6 administrative distance** (AD) parameter to judge between different sources of routing information (for example, OSPF, EIGRP, or static routes) for routes for the same prefix/length. For instance, in Figure 29-7, an OSPF-learned route on R1, for prefix 2001:db8:1111:7::/64, would have a default AD of 110. Static routes default to an AD of 1, so Router R1 would normally prefer the static route configured with the **ipv6 route 2001:db8:1111:7::/64 cell0/1/0** command versus the OSPF-learned AD 110 route to that same subnet, and replace the OSPF-learned route with the static route.

Floating static routes remain out of the routing table by using a higher (worse) AD setting than the normally used routes. In the recent example, by setting the static route's AD to something higher than OSPF's 110—for instance, with the **ipv6 route 2001:db8:1111:7::/64 cell0/1/0 130** command—Router R1 will instead prefer the AD 110 OSPF-learned route instead of the AD 130 static route.

You can find the AD of a route in the routing table with the usual **show** commands. For instance, the **show ipv6 route** command lists each route's administrative distance as the first of the two numbers inside the brackets. The second number in brackets is the metric. Also, commands like **show ipv6 route** *prefix/length* give detail about one specific route; this command lists the AD simply as "distance."

Table 29-3 lists the various default IPv6 AD values. These defaults mirror the same default AD settings for IPv4 as seen in Table 24-4 in this book. Compared to Table 24-4, this table adds the entry for NDP (which does not apply to IPv4) and removes the mention of the IPv4 DHCP-based default route (AD 254) because IPv6 does not advertise default routes with DHCP.

Table 29-3   Default IPv6 Administrative Distances

Route Type	Administrative Distance
Connected	0
Static	1
NDP default route	2
BGP (external routes [eBGP])	20
EIGRP (internal routes)	90
IGRP	100

Route Type	Administrative Distance
OSPF	110
IS-IS	115
RIP	120
EIGRP (external routes)	170
BGP (internal routes [iBGP])	200
Unusable	255

Troubleshooting Static IPv6 Routes

IPv6 static routes have the same potential issues and mistakes as do static IPv4 routes, as discussed in Chapter 17. However, IPv6 static routes do have a few small differences. This last part of the static route content in the chapter looks at troubleshooting IPv6 static routes, reviewing many of the same troubleshooting rules applied to IPv4 static routes, while focusing on the details specific to IPv6.

This topic breaks static route troubleshooting into two perspectives: cases in which the router adds the route to the routing table but the route does not work, and cases in which the router does not add the route to the routing table.

Troubleshooting Incorrect Static Routes That Appear in the IPv6 Routing Table

A static route is only as good as the input typed into the **ipv6 route** command. IOS checks the syntax of the command, of course. However, IOS cannot tell if you choose the incorrect outgoing interface, next-hop address, or prefix/prefix-length in a static route. If the parameters pass the syntax checks, IOS places the **ipv6 route** command into the running-config file. Then, if no other problem exists (as discussed at the next heading), IOS puts the route into the IP routing table—even though the route may not work because of the poorly chosen parameters.

For instance, a static route that references a next-hop address should list the address of some other router on a subnet that connects the two routers. Imagine Router R1 uses an address 2001:1:1:1::1 on that subnet, with Router R2 using 2001:1:1:1::2. R1's **ipv6 route** command ought to refer to Router R2' 2001:1:1:1::2 address, but nothing prevents the mistake of configuring Router R1's 2001:1:1:1::1 address or any other address in that subnet other than 2001:1:1:1::/64. Router R1 allows the command and adds the route to the IPv6 routing table, but the route cannot possibly forward packets correctly.

When you see an exam question that has static routes, and you see them in the output of **show ipv6 route**, remember that the routes may have incorrect parameters. Mentally review this list of questions that confirm correct configuration and reveal common mistakes, ensuring an answer of yes to each relevant question.

Step 1. **Prefix/Length:** Does the **ipv6 route** command reference the correct subnet ID (prefix) and mask (prefix length)?

Step 2. **Next-hop LLA:** If configuring a next-hop LLA:

    a. Does the command also include an outgoing interface?

29

> **b**   Is the outgoing interface the correct interface (on the router on which the command is configured) based on the topology?
>
> **c.**   Is the configured LLA the LLA of the neighboring router on the same link as the listed outgoing interface?

Step 3.   **Next-hop GUA/ULA only:** If configuring a next-hop GUA or ULA but no outgoing interface:

> **a.**   Does the configured GUA/ULA refer to the neighbor's address, specifically on the neighbor's interface that connects to the local router?
>
> **b.**   Does the local router have a working route that matches the next-hop GUA/ULA? (Usually a connected route.)

Step 4.   **Outgoing Interface only:** If configuring an outgoing interface but no next-hop address:

> **a.**   Is the outgoing interface a serial interface—the only interface type that works in the **ipv6 route** command without also configuring a next-hop address?
>
> **b.**   Is the outgoing interface the correct interface (on the router on which the command is configured) based on the topology?

The preceding troubleshooting checklist works through the various cases in which IOS would accept the configuration of the static IPv6 route, but the route would not work because of the incorrect parameters in context. It helps to see a few examples. Figure 29-8 shows a sample network to use for the examples; all the examples focus on routes added to Router R1, for the subnet on the far right (note that this network uses different IPv6 addresses than the earlier figures).

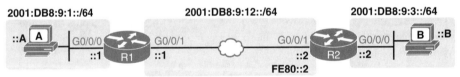

Figure 29-8   *Sample Topology for Incorrect IPv6 Route Examples*

Example 29-18 shows several **ipv6 route** commands. Of the commands shown, IOS rejects the second command in the example (step 2A), but it accepts and adds routes to the routing table for the others. However, the routes in the accepted commands all have some issue that prevents the route from working as designed. Look for the short comment at the end of each configuration command to see why each is incorrect, and the list following the example for more detail.

Example 29-18   ipv6 route *Commands with Correct Syntax but Incorrect Ideas*

```
ipv6 route 2001:DB8:9:33::/64 2001:DB8:9:12::2 ! Step 1: Wrong prefix
ipv6 route 2001:DB8:9:3::/64 FE80::2              ! Step 2A: Missing outgoing interface
ipv6 route 2001:DB8:9:3::/64 G0/0/0 FE80::2       ! Step 2B: Wrong interface on R1
ipv6 route 2001:DB8:9:3::/64 G0/0/1 FE80::1       ! Step 2C: Wrong neighbor link local
ipv6 route 2001:DB8:9:3::/64 2001:DD8:9:13::3     ! Step 3A: Wrong neighbor address
ipv6 route 2001:DB8:9:3::/64 G0/0/1               ! Step 4A: Also needs next-hop
```

Step 1. The prefix (2001:DB8:9:33::) has a typo in the fourth quartet (33 instead of 3). IOS accepts the command and now has a route for a nonexistent subnet.

Step 2A. The command uses the correct LLA as the next-hop address but fails to include any outgoing interface. IOS rejects the command.

Step 2B. The command uses the correct R2 LLA on the R1-R2 link (FE80::2 per the figure) but uses the incorrect R1 local interface of G0/0/0. (See the next example for more detail.)

Step 2C. The figure shows R2's G0/0/1 as using link-local address FE80::2, but the command uses FE80::1, R1's LLA.

Step 3A. The figure shows the subnet in the center as 2001:DB8:9:12::/64, with R1 using the ::1 address and R2 using ::2. This command uses a next-hop address ending in ::3 in that subnet that neither router uses.

Step 4A. The command lists only an outgoing interface of G0/0/1 (the correct interface), but no next-hop address. Only serial interfaces can be used with this syntax and have the route function correctly. Because it uses an Ethernet outgoing interface, the router needs the next-hop address in the command.

The key takeaway for this section is to know that a route in the IPv6 routing table might be incorrect due to poor choices for the parameters. The fact that a route is in the IPv6 routing table, particularly a static route, does not mean that it is correct.

The Static Route Does Not Appear in the IPv6 Routing Table

The preceding few pages focused on IPv6 static routes that show up in the IPv6 routing table but unfortunately have incorrect parameters. The next page looks at IPv6 routes that have correct parameters, but IOS does not place them into the IPv6 routing table.

When you add an **ipv6 route** command to the configuration, and the syntax is correct, IOS has a second step in which it considers whether to add that route to the IPv6 routing table. IOS makes the following checks before adding the route; note that IOS uses this same kind of logic for IPv4 static routes:

- For **ipv6 route** commands that list an outgoing interface, that interface must be in an up/up state.

- For **ipv6 route** commands that list a GUA or ULA (that is, not an LLA), the local router must have a route to reach that next-hop address.

- If another IPv6 route exists for that exact same prefix/prefix-length, the static route must have a better (lower) administrative distance than the competing route.

Note that the first two bullet items can change even without any configuration. For instance, as interfaces fail and recover, the interface state will change and the connected IPv6 routes will be removed and reappear in the IPv6 routing table. Depending on the current status, the static routes that rely on those interfaces and routes will be added and removed from the IPv6 routing table.

29

Chapter Review

One key to doing well on the exams is to perform repetitive spaced review sessions. Review this chapter's material using either the tools in the book or interactive tools for the same material found on the book's companion website. Refer to the "Your Study Plan" element for more details. Table 29-4 outlines the key review elements and where you can find them. To better track your study progress, record when you completed these activities in the second column.

Table 29-4 Chapter Review Tracking

Review Element	Review Date(s)	Resource Used
Review key topics		Book, website
Answer DIKTA questions		Book, PTP
Review command tables		Book
Review memory tables		Book, website
Do labs		Blog
Watch video		Website

Review All the Key Topics

Table 29-5 Key Topics for Chapter 29

Key Topic Element	Description	Page Number
List	Methods by which a router can build IPv6 routes	724
List	Rules for IPv6 connected and local routes	725
Figure 29-2	IPv6 static route concepts	729
Table 29-2	Summary of IPv6 network route configuration	735
Table 29-3	IPv6 default administrative distance values	740
Checklist	List of reasons for IPv6 static route problems that result in a route in the routing table but the route does not work correctly	741
Checklist	List of reasons for IPv6 static route problems that result in the route not appearing in the routing table	743

Key Terms You Should Know

IPv6 administrative distance, IPv6 host route, IPv6 local route, local route

Command References

Tables 29-6 and 29-7 list configuration and verification commands used in this chapter. As an easy review exercise, cover the left column in a table, read the right column, and try to recall the command without looking. Then repeat the exercise, covering the right column, and try to recall what the command does.

Table 29-6   Chapter 29 Configuration Command Reference

Command	Description
ipv6 route *prefix/length outgoing-interface*	Global command to define an IPv6 static route, with packets forwarded out the local router interface listed in the command
ipv6 route *prefix/length outgoing-interface next-hop-lla*	Global command to define an IPv6 static route, with a next-hop link-local address and the required local router outgoing interface
ipv6 route *prefix/length [outgoing-interface] next-hop-gua*	Global command to define an IPv6 static route, with the next-hop global unicast address and the optional local router outgoing interface
ipv6 route ::/0 *{[next-hop-address] [outgoing-interface]}*	Global command to define a default IPv6 static route

Table 29-7   Chapter 29 EXEC Command Reference

Command	Description
show ipv6 route [connected | local | static]	Lists routes in the routing table.
show ipv6 route *address*	Displays detailed information about the router's route to forward packets to the IPv6 address listed in the command. If no route matches, it displays "No route found."
show ipv6 route *prefix/length*	If a route that matches the listed prefix/length exists, the router displays detailed information about the route.
show ipv6 route | **section** *prefix/length*	Displays an excerpt of the output from the **show ipv6 route** command of only the lines related to routes for the listed prefix/length.
show ipv6 static detail	Displays a static route legend with multiple output lines about each static route, noting whether it is installed in the routing table (RIB) and the administrative distance.

29

Part VII Review

Keep track of your part review progress with the checklist in Table P7-1. Details on each task follow the table.

Table P7-1   Part VII Part Review Checklist

Activity	1st Date Completed	2nd Date Completed
Repeat All DIKTA Questions		
Answer Part Review Questions		
Review Key Topics		
Do Labs		
Watch Videos		
Use Per-Chapter Interactive Review		

Repeat All DIKTA Questions

For this task, use the PTP software to answer the "Do I Know This Already?" questions again for the chapters in this part of the book.

Answer Part Review Questions

For this task, use PTP to answer the Part Review questions for this part of the book.

Review Key Topics

Review all key topics in all chapters in this part, either by browsing the chapters or using the Key Topics application on the companion website.

Do Labs

Depending on your chosen lab tool, here are some suggestions for what to do in lab:

Pearson Network Simulator: If you use the full Pearson simulator, focus more on the configuration scenario and troubleshooting scenario labs associated with the topics in this part of the book. These types of labs include a larger set of topics and work well as Part Review activities. (See the Introduction for some details about how to find which labs are about topics in this part of the book.)

Blog: Config Labs: The author's blog includes a series of configuration-focused labs that you can do on paper or with Cisco Packet Tracer in about 15 minutes. To find them, open https://www.certskills.com and look under the Labs menu item.

Other: If using other lab tools, here are a few suggestions: configure IPv6 addresses on interfaces, and before using any **show** commands, predict the connected and local routes that should be added to the IPv6 routing table, and predict the link-local (unicast) address and various multicast addresses you expect to see in the output of the **show ipv6 interfaces** command.

Watch Video

The companion website includes a variety of common mistake and Q&A videos organized by part and chapter. Use these videos to challenge your thinking, dig deeper, review topics, and better prepare for the exam. Make sure to bookmark a link to the companion website and use the videos for review whenever you have a few extra minutes.

Part VIII

Exam Updates

Chapter 30: *CCNA 200-301 Official Cert Guide, Volume 1*, Second Edition Exam Updates

CHAPTER 30

CCNA 200-301 Official Cert Guide, Volume 1, Second Edition Exam Updates

The Purpose of This Chapter

For all the other chapters, the content should remain unchanged throughout this edition of the book. Instead, this chapter will change over time, with an updated online PDF posted so you can see the latest version of the chapter even after you purchase this book.

Why do we need a chapter that updates over time? For two reasons:

1. To add more technical content to the book before it is time to replace the current book edition with the next edition. This chapter will include additional technology content and possibly additional PDFs containing more content.

2. To communicate detail about the next version of the CCNA exam, to tell you about our publishing plans for that edition, and what that means to you.

To find the latest version of this chapter, follow the process below. Bookmark the link so that any time you refer to this chapter, begin by downloading a new copy. Use these steps:

Step 1. Browse to www.ciscopress.com/register.

Step 2. Enter the print book ISBN (even if you are using an eBook): 9780138229634.

Step 3. After registering the book, go to your account page and select the Registered Products tab.

Step 4. Click on the Access Bonus Content link to access the companion website. Select the **Exam Updates Chapter** link or scroll down to that section to check for updates.

Table 30-1 summarizes the information that this version of the chapter includes. Use the table as a quick reference for the detail to expect in the rest of the chapter.

Table 30-1 Status for Available New Technical Content for This Edition

Chapter Version	1
Most recent CCNA 200-301 blueprint version when this chapter was most recently released	1.1
Is there technology content in the latter part of this chapter?	No
Is there technology content in other downloadable files?	No
Links to other file downloads:	N/A
Is there information about the specifics of the new exam?	No

Any additional file downloads, or further instructions for file downloads, will be posted at this book's companion website. See the heading "How to Access the Companion Website" in the Introduction to this book for details on finding this book's companion website.

The following two sections give more detail about the primary purposes of the chapter. Any technical content or exam update detail follows later in the chapter.

Additional Technical Content

On rare occasions, the need exists for additional book content outside the normal process of creating a new book edition. Several factors might make an author want to add content. However, once an author decides to add content, the question becomes how to deliver the content and reach as many existing readers as possible. This chapter and its electronic update process give us the means to get the content to you.

Looking back at prior *CCNA Official Cert Guide* editions, the need to add content has happened only a few times over more than ten years of using chapters like this one. However, when needed, it has worked well. Using other means, like book registration, social media, and so on, reaches fewer of you, the readers.

You do not need to check frequently for a new PDF. You may want to check more regularly about exam updates, as discussed in the next section. But to check for new technical content, I suggest downloading the PDF again on this cadence:

- After your first reading of this book
- After your first reading of the Volume 2 book

NOTE An equivalent chapter exists in the *CCNA 200-301 Official Cert Guide, Volume 2*, Second Edition. I would also suggest downloading that chapter when you download this chapter.

Of course, if this chapter adds new technical content, treat it like any of the other chapters in the book, and study the content!

About Possible Exam Updates

Cisco introduced CCNA and CCNP in 1998. For the first 25 years of those certification tracks, Cisco updated the exams on average every 3–4 years. However, Cisco did not pre-announce the exam changes, so exam changes felt very sudden. Usually, a new exam would be announced, with new exam topics, giving you 3–6 months before your only option was to take the new exam. As a result, you could be studying with no idea about Cisco's plans, and the next day, you had a 3–6-month timeline to either pass the old exam or pivot to prepare for the new exam.

Thankfully, Cisco changed their exam release approach in 2023. Called the Cisco Certification Roadmap (https://cisco.com/go/certroadmap), the new plan includes these features:

1. Cisco considers changes to all exam tracks (CCNA, CCNP Enterprise, CCNP Security, and so on) annually.

2. Cisco uses a predefined annual schedule for each track, so you know the timing of possible changes to the exam you are studying for, even before any announcements.

3. The schedule moves in a quarterly sequence:

    a. Privately review the exam to consider what to change.

    b. Publicly announce if an exam is changing, and if so, announce details like exam topics and release date.

    c. Release the new exam.

4. Exam changes might not occur each year. If changes occur, Cisco characterizes them as minor (less than 20 percent change) or major (more than 20 percent change).

The specific dates for a given certification track can be confusing because Cisco organizes the work by fiscal year quarters. As an example, Figure 30-1 shows the 2024 fiscal year. Their fiscal year begins in August, so, for example, the first quarter (Q1) of fiscal year (FY) 2024 began in August 2023.

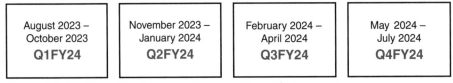

Figure 30-1 *Cisco Fiscal Year and Months Example (FY2024)*

Focus more on the sequence of the quarters to understand the plan. Figure 30-2 shows an example sequence in which Cisco updates the CCNA 200-301 exam, assuming a minor release (less than 20 percent change).

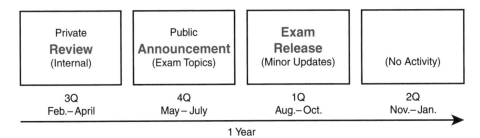

Figure 30-2 *Cisco CCNA Annual Roadmap with a Minor Release*

Over time, Cisco might make no changes in some years and minor changes in others. For example, Cisco announced CCNA 200-301 version 1.1 in the FY24-FY25 cycle (February 2024–January 2025). Figure 30-3 shows what could happen in the next four years. It first shows a year with no changes, then a year with minor changes, another year with no changes, and a year with major changes.

Figure 30-3 shows an example and does not reveal any secret knowledge about Cisco's plans; however, it shows a volume of change that matches the rate of change to the exam over its long history.

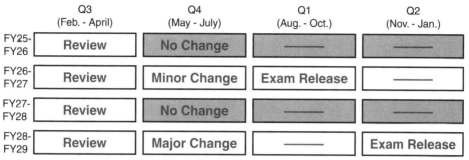

Figure 30-3 *An Example of What Could Happen with CCNA over Four Years*

Impact on You and Your Study Plan

Cisco's new policy helps you plan, but it also means that the CCNA exam might change before you pass the current exam. That impacts you, affecting how we deliver this book to you. This chapter gives us a way to communicate in detail about those changes as they occur. But you should watch other spaces as well.

Your study plan ongoing should follow this general process:

Step 1. Continue to use the *CCNA 200-301 Official Cert Guides, Volumes 1 and 2*, Second Edition, as is.

Step 2. Monitor for updates to this Exam Updates chapter, plus the equivalent chapter in Volume 2, to find additional content for topics Cisco may add to the exam.

Step 3. To be aware of changes to the CCNA exam, monitor the information sources listed below.

For those other information sources to watch, bookmark and check these sites for news. In particular:

Cisco: Check their Certification Roadmap page: https://cisco.com/go/certroadmap. Make sure to sign up for automatic notifications from Cisco on that page.

Publisher: Check this page about new certification products, offers, discounts, and free downloads related to the more frequent exam updates: www.ciscopress.com/newcert.

Cisco Learning Network: Subscribe to the CCNA Community at learningnetwork.cisco. com, where I expect ongoing discussions about exam changes over time. If you have questions, search for "roadmap" in the CCNA community, and if you do not find an answer, ask a new one!

Author: Look for blog posts labeled as News at www.certskills.com. For every new edition, I post about the new exam, new topics, and how to manage the transition. I will continue to do so now with more detail about the new annual cycle.

As changes arise, I will update this chapter with more detail about exam and book content. Given Cisco's certification roadmap, that means somewhere in each year's fiscal fourth quarter (May–July). At that point, I will publish an updated version of this chapter, listing our content plans. That detail will likely include the following:

■ Content removed, so if you plan to take the new exam version, you can ignore those when studying

■ New content planned per new exam topics, so you know what's coming

While I do not think Cisco will change CCNA every year—I predict Cisco will change it less than half the years—everyone needs to be aware of the possibility and timing of exam changes and new exam releases. I will use this chapter to communicate the exam and book content details. Look to the other sites for brief news about plans, but look here for the detail.

The remainder of the chapter shows the new content that may change over time.

News about the Next CCNA Exam Release

This statement was last updated in March 2024, before the publication of the *CCNA 200-301 Official Certification Guide, Volume 1*, Second Edition.

This version of this chapter has no news to share about the next CCNA exam release.

At the most recent version this chapter, the CCNA 200-301 exam version number was Version 1.1.

Updated Technical Content

The current version of this chapter has no additional technical content.

Part IX

Appendixes

Appendix A: Numeric Reference Tables

Appendix B: Exam Topics Cross-Reference

Appendix C: Answers to the "Do I Know This Already?" Quizzes

Glossary

Numeric Reference Tables

This appendix provides several useful reference tables that list numbers used throughout this book. Specifically:

Table A-1: A decimal-binary cross reference, useful when converting from decimal to binary and vice versa.

Table A-1   Decimal-Binary Cross Reference, Decimal Values 0–255

Decimal Value	Binary Value	Decimal Value	Binary Value	Decimal Value	Binary Value	Decimal Value	Binary Value
0	00000000	32	00100000	64	01000000	96	01100000
1	00000001	33	00100001	65	01000001	97	01100001
2	00000010	34	00100010	66	01000010	98	01100010
3	00000011	35	00100011	67	01000011	99	01100011
4	00000100	36	00100100	68	01000100	100	01100100
5	00000101	37	00100101	69	01000101	101	01100101
6	00000110	38	00100110	70	01000110	102	01100110
7	00000111	39	00100111	71	01000111	103	01100111
8	00001000	40	00101000	72	01001000	104	01101000
9	00001001	41	00101001	73	01001001	105	01101001
10	00001010	42	00101010	74	01001010	106	01101010
11	00001011	43	00101011	75	01001011	107	01101011
12	00001100	44	00101100	76	01001100	108	01101100
13	00001101	45	00101101	77	01001101	109	01101101
14	00001110	46	00101110	78	01001110	110	01101110
15	00001111	47	00101111	79	01001111	111	01101111
16	00010000	48	00110000	80	01010000	112	01110000
17	00010001	49	00110001	81	01010001	113	01110001
18	00010010	50	00110010	82	01010010	114	01110010
19	00010011	51	00110011	83	01010011	115	01110011
20	00010100	52	00110100	84	01010100	116	01110100
21	00010101	53	00110101	85	01010101	117	01110101
22	00010110	54	00110110	86	01010110	118	01110110
23	00010111	55	00110111	87	01010111	119	01110111
24	00011000	56	00111000	88	01011000	120	01111000
25	00011001	57	00111001	89	01011001	121	01111001
26	00011010	58	00111010	90	01011010	122	01111010
27	00011011	59	00111011	91	01011011	123	01111011
28	00011100	60	00111100	92	01011100	124	01111100
29	00011101	61	00111101	93	01011101	125	01111101
30	00011110	62	00111110	94	01011110	126	01111110
31	00011111	63	00111111	95	01011111	127	01111111

Decimal Value	Binary Value	Decimal Value	Binary Value	Decimal Value	Binary Value	Decimal Value	Binary Value
128	10000000	160	10100000	192	11000000	224	11100000
129	10000001	161	10100001	193	11000001	225	11100001
130	10000010	162	10100010	194	11000010	226	11100010
131	10000011	163	10100011	195	11000011	227	11100011
132	10000100	164	10100100	196	11000100	228	11100100
133	10000101	165	10100101	197	11000101	229	11100101
134	10000110	166	10100110	198	11000110	230	11100110
135	10000111	167	10100111	199	11000111	231	11100111
136	10001000	168	10101000	200	11001000	232	11101000
137	10001001	169	10101001	201	11001001	233	11101001
138	10001010	170	10101010	202	11001010	234	11101010
139	10001011	171	10101011	203	11001011	235	11101011
140	10001100	172	10101100	204	11001100	236	11101100
141	10001101	173	10101101	205	11001101	237	11101101
142	10001110	174	10101110	206	11001110	238	11101110
143	10001111	175	10101111	207	11001111	239	11101111
144	10010000	176	10110000	208	11010000	240	11110000
145	10010001	177	10110001	209	11010001	241	11110001
146	10010010	178	10110010	210	11010010	242	11110010
147	10010011	179	10110011	211	11010011	243	11110011
148	10010100	180	10110100	212	11010100	244	11110100
149	10010101	181	10110101	213	11010101	245	11110101
150	10010110	182	10110110	214	11010110	246	11110110
151	10010111	183	10110111	215	11010111	247	11110111
152	10011000	184	10111000	216	11011000	248	11111000
153	10011001	185	10111001	217	11011001	249	11111001
154	10011010	186	10111010	218	11011010	250	11111010
155	10011011	187	10111011	219	11011011	251	11111011
156	10011100	188	10111100	220	11011100	252	11111100
157	10011101	189	10111101	221	11011101	253	11111101
158	10011110	190	10111110	222	11011110	254	11111110
159	10011111	191	10111111	223	11011111	255	11111111

Table A-2: A hexadecimal-binary cross reference, useful when converting from hex to binary and vice versa.

Table A-2   Hex-Binary Cross Reference

Hex	4-Bit Binary
0	0000
1	0001
2	0010
3	0011
4	0100
5	0101
6	0110
7	0111
8	1000
9	1001
A	1010
B	1011
C	1100
D	1101
E	1110
F	1111

Table A-3: Powers of 2, from 2^1 through 2^{32}.

Table A-3 Powers of 2

X	2^X	X	2^X
1	2	17	131,072
2	4	18	262,144
3	8	19	524,288
4	16	20	1,048,576
5	32	21	2,097,152
6	64	22	4,194,304
7	128	23	8,388,608
8	256	24	16,777,216
9	512	25	33,554,432
10	1024	26	67,108,864
11	2048	27	134,217,728
12	4096	28	268,435,456
13	8192	29	536,870,912
14	16,384	30	1,073,741,824
15	32,768	31	2,147,483,648
16	65,536	32	4,294,967,296

Table A-4: Table of all 33 possible subnet masks, in all three formats.

Table A-4 All Subnet Masks

Decimal	Prefix	Binary
0.0.0.0	/0	00000000 00000000 00000000 00000000
128.0.0.0	/1	10000000 00000000 00000000 00000000
192.0.0.0	/2	11000000 00000000 00000000 00000000
224.0.0.0	/3	11100000 00000000 00000000 00000000
240.0.0.0	/4	11110000 00000000 00000000 00000000
248.0.0.0	/5	11111000 00000000 00000000 00000000
252.0.0.0	/6	11111100 00000000 00000000 00000000
254.0.0.0	/7	11111110 00000000 00000000 00000000
255.0.0.0	/8	11111111 00000000 00000000 00000000
255.128.0.0	/9	11111111 10000000 00000000 00000000
255.192.0.0	/10	11111111 11000000 00000000 00000000
255.224.0.0	/11	11111111 11100000 00000000 00000000
255.240.0.0	/12	11111111 11110000 00000000 00000000
255.248.0.0	/13	11111111 11111000 00000000 00000000
255.252.0.0	/14	11111111 11111100 00000000 00000000
255.254.0.0	/15	11111111 11111110 00000000 00000000
255.255.0.0	/16	11111111 11111111 00000000 00000000
255.255.128.0	/17	11111111 11111111 10000000 00000000
255.255.192.0	/18	11111111 11111111 11000000 00000000
255.255.224.0	/19	11111111 11111111 11100000 00000000
255.255.240.0	/20	11111111 11111111 11110000 00000000
255.255.248.0	/21	11111111 11111111 11111000 00000000
255.255.252.0	/22	11111111 11111111 11111100 00000000
255.255.254.0	/23	11111111 11111111 11111110 00000000
255.255.255.0	/24	11111111 11111111 11111111 00000000
255.255.255.128	/25	11111111 11111111 11111111 10000000
255.255.255.192	/26	11111111 11111111 11111111 11000000
255.255.255.224	/27	11111111 11111111 11111111 11100000
255.255.255.240	/28	11111111 11111111 11111111 11110000
255.255.255.248	/29	11111111 11111111 11111111 11111000
255.255.255.252	/30	11111111 11111111 11111111 11111100
255.255.255.254	/31	11111111 11111111 11111111 11111110
255.255.255.255	/32	11111111 11111111 11111111 11111111

Exam Topics Cross-Reference

This appendix lists the exam topics associated with the CCNA 200-301 exam blueprint Version 1.1. Cisco lists the exam topics on its website. Even though changes to the exam topics are rare, you should always review those exam topics for any updates; check www.cisco.com/go/certifications and navigate to the correct exam.

Cisco organizes each list of exam topics by domains, which are major topic areas. Cisco states the percentage of the exam that should come from each domain, so you get some idea of the areas of importance. Traditionally, the score report you receive after taking the exam shows your percentage score in each domain.

This appendix includes two separate types of indices for exam topics:

- **CCNA 200-301 Exam Topic Order:** This section lists the CCNA 200-301 V1.1 exam topics in the same order Cisco lists them on its website, with a list of associated book chapters. This first list shows a cross-reference from each exam topic to the chapters that include at least some material about each topic.

- **Book Chapter Order Versus CCNA 200-301 Exam Topics:** This lists the same CCNA 200-301 V1.1 exam topics but indexed by chapter instead of exam topic. This section lists the chapters in this book, along with the exam topics that the chapter includes. This section basically relists the kind of information found on the first page of each chapter, just in condensed form in one place.

CCNA 200-301 Exam Topic Order

The CCNA 200-301 exam includes six major topic areas (domains), each with a percentage listed. Table B-1 lists the domains and their percentages.

Table B-1   CCNA 200-301 V1.1 Exam Topic Domains

Domain	Percentage
Domain 1: Network Fundamentals	20%
Domain 2: Network Access	20%
Domain 3: IP Connectivity	25%
Domain 4: IP Services	10%
Domain 5: Security Fundamentals	15%
Domain 6: Automation and Programmability	10%

Tables B-2 through B-7 list the exam topics within each of the six domains. Note that the *CCNA 200-301 Official Cert Guide, Volume 2*, Second Edition, covers some of the exam topics, while this book covers the rest.

Table B-2   CCNA 200-301 V1.1 Domain 1 Exam Topics (Network Fundamentals)

Exam Topic	Vol 1 Chapter(s)	Vol 2 Chapter(s)
1.1 Explain the role and function of network components	2, 3, 5, 7	1, 10, 18, 21, 22
1.1.a Routers	3, 16, 18	
1.1.b Layer 2 and Layer 3 Switches	2, 5, 7, 18	
1.1.c Next-generation firewalls and IPS		10
1.1.d Access points		1
1.1.e Controllers		4, 22
1.1.f Endpoints		21
1.1.g Servers		21
1.1.h PoE		18
1.2 Describe characteristics of network topology architectures	2, 3	18–21
1.2.a Two-tier		18
1.2.b Three-tier		18
1.2.c Spine-leaf		21
1.2.d WAN	3	19
1.2.e Small office/home office (SOHO)	2, 16	18
1.2.f On-premises and cloud		20
1.3 Compare physical interface and cabling types	1, 2, 7	18
1.3.a Single-mode fiber, multimode fiber, copper	1, 2	18
1.3.b Connections (Ethernet shared media and point-to-point)	1, 2, 7	18
1.4 Identify interface and cable issues (collisions, errors, mismatch duplex, and/or speed)	7	
1.5 Compare TCP to UDP		5
1.6 Configure and verify IPv4 addressing and subnetting	6, 11–16, 18	
1.7 Describe private IPv4 addressing	11, 12, 17	14
1.8 Configure and verify IPv6 addressing and prefix	25–28	
1.9 Describe IPv6 address types	25–28	
1.9.a Unicast (global, unique local, and link local)	26–28	
1.9.b Anycast	26, 27	
1.9.c Multicast	27	
1.9.d Modified EUI 64	27, 28	
1.10 Verify IP parameters for Client OS (Windows, Mac OS, Linux)	19	
1.11 Describe wireless principles		1, 3
1.11.a Nonoverlapping Wi-Fi channels		1
1.11.b SSID		1

Exam Topic	Vol 1 Chapter(s)	Vol 2 Chapter(s)
1.11.c RF		1
1.11.d Encryption		3
1.12 Explain virtualization fundamentals (server virtualization, containers, and VRFs)		20
1.13 Describe switching concepts	5, 8	
1.13.a MAC learning and aging	5, 8	
1.13.b Frame switching	5, 8	
1.13.c Frame flooding	5, 8	
1.13.d MAC address table	5, 8	

Table B-3 CCNA 200-301 V1.1 Domain 2 Exam Topics (Network Access)

Exam Topic	Vol 1 Chapter(s)	Vol 2 Chapter(s)
2.1 Configure and verify VLANs (normal range) spanning multiple switches	8, 18	
2.1.a Access ports (data and voice)	8	
2.1.b Default VLAN	8	
2.1.c InterVLAN Connectivity	8, 18	
2.2 Configure and verify interswitch connectivity	8	
2.2.a Trunk ports	8	
2.2.b 802.1Q	8	
2.2.c Native VLAN	8	
2.3 Configure and verify Layer 2 discovery protocols (Cisco Discovery Protocol and LLDP)		13
2.4 Configure and verify (Layer 2/Layer 3) EtherChannel (LACP)	8–10, 18	
2.5 Interpret basic operations of Rapid PVST+ Spanning Tree Protocol	5, 9, 10	
2.5.a Root port, root bridge (primary/secondary), and other port names	9, 10	
2.5.b Port states and roles	9, 10	
2.5.c PortFast	9, 10	
2.5.d Root Guard, loop guard, BPDU filter, BPDU guard	9, 10	
2.6 Compare Cisco Wireless Architectures and AP modes		2
2.7 Describe physical infrastructure connections of WLAN components (AP, WLC, access/trunk ports, and LAG)		4

B

Exam Topic	Vol 1 Chapter(s)	Vol 2 Chapter(s)
2.8 Describe network device management access (Telnet, SSH, HTTP, HTTPS, console, and TACACS+/RADIUS, and cloud managed)	4, 6, 20	4
2.9 Interpret the wireless LAN GUI configuration for client connectivity, such as WLAN creation, security settings, QoS profiles, and advanced settings		4

Table B-4   CCNA 200-301 Domain 3 Exam Topics (IP Connectivity)

Exam Topic	Vol 1 Chapter(s)	Vol 2 Chapter(s)
3.1 Interpret the components of routing table	17, 29	
3.1.a Routing protocol code	17, 29	
3.1.b Prefix	17, 29	
3.1.c Network mask	17, 29	
3.1.d Next hop	17, 29	
3.1.e Administrative distance	17, 24, 29	
3.1.f Metric	17	
3.1.g Gateway of last resort	17	
3.2 Determine how a router makes a forwarding decision by default	17, 21–24	
3.2.a Longest prefix match	17, 24	
3.2.b Administrative distance	17, 21–24	
3.2.c Routing protocol metric	21, 21–24	
3.3 Configure and verify IPv4 and IPv6 static routing	17, 20, 29	
3.3.a Default route	17, 20, 29	
3.3.b Network route	17, 20, 29	
3.3.c Host route	17, 20, 29	
3.3.d Floating static	17, 20, 29	
3.4 Configure and verify single area OSPFv2	21–24	
3.4.a Neighbor adjacencies	21–24	
3.4.b Point-to-point	21–24	
3.4.c Broadcast (DR/BDR selection)	21–24	
3.4.d Router ID	21–24	
3.5 Describe the purpose, functions, and concepts of first hop redundancy protocols		16

Table B-5   CCNA 200-301 V1.1 Domain 4 Exam Topics (IP Services)

Exam Topics	Vol 1 Chapter(s)	Vol 2 Chapter(s)
4.1 Configure and verify inside source NAT using static and pools		14
4.2 Configure and verify NTP operating in a client and server mode		13
4.3 Explain the role of DHCP and DNS within the network	19	5
4.4 Explain the function of SNMP in network operations		17
4.5 Describe the use of syslog features including facilities and severity levels		13
4.6 Configure and verify DHCP client and relay	6, 19	
4.7 Explain the forwarding per-hop behavior (PHB) for QoS such as classification, marking, queuing, congestion, policing, and shaping		15
4.8 Configure network devices for remote access using SSH	6	10
4.9 Describe the capabilities and functions of TFTP/FTP in the network		17

Table B-6   CCNA 200-301 Domain 5 Exam Topics (Security Fundamentals)

Exam Topics	Vol 1 Chapter(s)	Vol 2 Chapter(s)
5.1 Define key security concepts (threats, vulnerabilities, exploits, and mitigation techniques)		9
5.2 Describe security program elements (user awareness, training, and physical access control)		9
5.3 Configure device access control using local passwords	6	10
5.4 Describe security password policies elements, such as management, complexity, and password alternatives (multifactor authentication, certificates, and biometrics)		9
5.5 Describe IPsec remote access and site-to-site VPNs		19
5.6 Configure and verify access control lists		6, 7, 8
5.7 Configure Layer 2 security features (DHCP snooping, dynamic ARP inspection, and port security)		11, 12
5.8 Compare authentication, authorization, and accounting concepts		9

B

Exam Topics	Vol 1 Chapter(s)	Vol 2 Chapter(s)
5.9 Describe wireless security protocols (WPA, WPA2, and WPA3)		3
5.10 Configure and verify WLAN within the GUI using WPA2 PSK		4

Table B-7   CCNA 200-301 V1.1 Domain 6 Exam Topics (Programmability and Automation)

Exam Topics	Vol 1 Chapter(s)	Vol 2 Chapter(s)
6.1 Explain how automation impacts network management		21
6.2 Compare traditional networks with controller-based networking		
6.3 Describe controller-based, software-defined architecture (overlay, underlay, and fabric)		21
6.3.a Separation of control plane and data plane		21, 22
6.3.b Northbound and Southbound APIs		21, 22
6.4 Explain AI (generative and predictive) and machine learning in network operations		22
6.5 Describe characteristics of REST-based APIs (authentication types, CRUD, HTTP verbs, and data encoding)		23
6.6 Recognize the capabilities of configuration management mechanisms such as Ansible and Terraform		24
6.7 Recognize components of JSON-encoded data		23

Book Chapter Order Versus CCNA 200-301 Exam Topics

Cisco organizes its exam topics based on the outcome of your learning experience, which is typically not a reasonable order for building the content of a book or course. This section lists the book chapters in sequence, with the exam topics covered in each chapter.

Table B-8   CCNA 200-301 V1.1: Chapter-to-Exam Topic Mapping

Book Chapter	Exam Topics Covered
Part I: Introduction to Networking	
Chapter 1: Introduction to TCP/IP Networking	1.0 Network Fundamentals 1.3 Compare physical interface and cabling types 1.3.a Single-mode fiber, multimode fiber, copper 1.3.b Connections (Ethernet shared media and point-to-point)

B

Book Chapter	Exam Topics Covered
Chapter 2: Fundamentals of Ethernet LANs	**1.0 Network Fundamentals** 1.1 Explain the role and function of network components *1.1.b Layer 2 and Layer 3 switches* 1.2 Describe characteristics of network topology architectures *1.2.e Small office/home office (SOHO)* 1.3 Compare physical interface and cabling types *1.3.a Single-mode fiber, multimode fiber, copper* *1.3.b Connections (Ethernet shared media and point-to-point)*
Chapter 3: Fundamentals of WANs and IP Routing	**1.0 Network Fundamentals** 1.1 Explain the role and function of network components *1.1.a Routers* 1.2 Describe characteristics of network topology architectures *1.2.d WAN*
Part II: Implementing Ethernet LANs	
Chapter 4: Using the Command-Line Interface	**2.0 Network Access** 2.8 Describe network device management access (Telnet, SSH, HTTP, HTTPs, console, TACACS+/RADIUS, and cloud managed)
Chapter 5: Analyzing Ethernet LAN Switching	**1.0 Network Fundamentals** 1.1 Explain the role and function of network components *1.1.b Layer 2 and Layer 3 switches* 1.13 Describe switching concepts *1.13.a MAC learning and aging* *1.13.b Frame switching* *1.13.c Frame flooding* *1.13.d MAC address table* **2.0 Network Access** 2.5 Interpret basic operations of Rapid PVST+ Spanning Tree Protocol

Book Chapter	Exam Topics Covered
Chapter 6: Configuring Basic Switch Management	**1.0 Network Fundamentals** 1.6 Configure and calculate IPv4 addressing and subnetting **2.0 Network Access** 2.8 Describe network device management access (Telnet, SSH, HTTP, HTTPs, console, TACACS+/RADIUS, and cloud managed) **4.0 IP Services** 4.6 Configure and verify DHCP client and relay 4.8 Configure network devices for remote access using SSH **5.0 Security Fundamentals** 5.3 Configure device access control using local passwords
Chapter 7: Configuring and Verifying Switch Interfaces	**1.0 Network Fundamentals** 1.1 Explain the role and function of network components *1.1.b Layer 2 and Layer 3 Switches* 1.3 Compare physical interface and cabling types *1.3.b Connections (Ethernet shared media and point-to-point)* 1.4 Identify interface and cable issues (collisions, errors, mismatch duplex, and/or speed)
Part III: Implementing VLANs and STP	
Chapter 8: Implementing Ethernet Virtual LANs	**1.0 Network Fundamentals** 1.13 Describe switching concepts *1.13.a MAC learning and aging* *1.13.b Frame switching* *1.13.c Frame flooding* *1.13.d MAC address table* **2.0 Network Access** 2.1 Configure and verify VLANs (normal range) spanning multiple switches *2.1.a Access ports (data and voice)* *2.1.b Default VLAN* *2.1.c InterVLAN Connectivity*

Book Chapter	Exam Topics Covered
	2.2 Configure and verify interswitch connectivity
	2.2.a Trunk ports
	2.2.b 802.1Q
	2.2.c Native VLAN
Chapter 9: Spanning Tree Protocol Concepts	**2.0 Network Access**
	2.4 Configure and verify (Layer 2/Layer 3) EtherChannel (LACP)
	2.5 Interpret basic operations of Rapid PVST+ Spanning Tree Protocol
	2.5.a Root port, root bridge (primary/secondary), and other port names
	2.5.b Port states and roles
	2.5.c PortFast
	2.5.d Root Guard, loop guard, BPDU filter, BPDU guard
Chapter 10: RSTP and EtherChannel Configuration	**2.0 Network Access**
	2.4 Configure and verify (Layer 2/Layer 3) EtherChannel (LACP)
	2.5 Interpret basic operations of Rapid PVST+ Spanning Tree Protocol
	2.5.a Root port, root bridge (primary/secondary), and other port names
	2.5.b Port states and roles
	2.5.c PortFast
	2.5.d Root Guard, loop guard, BPDU filter, BPDU guard
Part IV: IPv4 Addressing	
Chapter 11: Perspectives on IPv4 Subnetting	**1.0 Network Fundamentals**
	1.6 Configure and verify IPv4 addressing and subnetting
	1.7 Describe the need for private IPv4 addressing
Chapter 12: Analyzing Classful IPv4 Networks	**1.0 Network Fundamentals**
	1.6 Configure and verify IPv4 addressing and subnetting
	1.7 Describe the need for private IPv4 addressing

B

Book Chapter	Exam Topics Covered
Chapter 13: Analyzing Subnet Masks	**1.0 Network Fundamentals** 1.6 Configure and verify IPv4 addressing and subnetting
Chapter 14: Analyzing Existing Subnets	**1.0 Network Fundamentals** 1.6 Configure and verify IPv4 addressing and subnetting
Chapter 15: Subnet Design	**1.0 Network Fundamentals** 1.6 Configure and verify IPv4 addressing and subnetting
Part V: IPv4 Routing	
Chapter 16: Operating Cisco Routers	**1.0 Network Fundamentals** 1.1 Explain the role and function of network components *1.1.a Routers* 1.2 Describe characteristics of network topology architectures *1.2.e Small office/home office (SOHO)* 1.6 Configure and verify IPv4 addressing and subnetting
Chapter 17: Configuring IPv4 Addresses and Static Routes	**1.0 Network Fundamentals** 1.6 Configure and verify IPv4 addressing and subnetting **3.0 IP Connectivity** 3.1 Interpret the components of routing table *3.1.a Routing protocol code* *3.1.b Prefix* *3.1.c Network mask* *3.1.d Next hop* *3.1.e Administrative distance* *3.1.f Metric* *3.1.g Gateway of last resort* 3.2 Determine how a router makes a forwarding decision by default *3.2.a Longest prefix match* *3.2.b Administrative distance* 3.3 Configure and verify IPv4 and IPv6 static routing *3.3.a Default route* *3.3.b Network route* *3.3.c Host route* *3.3.d Floating static*

Book Chapter	Exam Topics Covered
Chapter 18: IP Routing in the LAN	**1.0 Network Fundamentals** 1.1 Explain the role and function of network components *1.1.a Routers* *1.1.b Layer 2 and Layer 3 Switches* 1.6 Configure and verify IPv4 addressing and subnetting **2.0 Network Access** 2.1 Configure and verify VLANs (normal range) spanning multiple switches *2.1.c InterVLAN connectivity* 2.4 Configure and verify (Layer 2/Layer 3) EtherChannel (LACP)
Chapter 19: IP Addressing on Hosts	**1.0 Network Fundamentals** 1.10 Verify IP parameters for Client OS (Windows, Mac OS, Linux) **4.0 IP Services** 4.3 Explain the role of DHCP and DNS within the network 4.6 Configure and verify DHCP client and relay
Chapter 20: Troubleshooting IPv4 Routing	**2.0 Network Access** 2.8 Describe network device management access (Telnet, SSH, HTTP, HTTPS, console, TACACS+/RADIUS, and cloud managed) **3.0 IP Connectivity** 3.3 Configure and verify IPv4 and IPv6 static routing *3.3.a Default route* *3.3.b Network route* *3.3.c Host route* *3.3.d Floating static*

B

Book Chapter	Exam Topics Covered
Part VI: OSPF	
Chapter 21: Understanding OSPF Concepts	**3.0 IP Connectivity** 3.2 Determine how a router makes a forwarding decision by default *3.2.b Administrative distance* *3.2.c Routing protocol metric* 3.4 Configure and verify single area OSPFv2 *3.4.a Neighbor adjacencies* *3.4.b Point-to-point* *3.4.c Broadcast (DR/BR selection)* *3.4.d Router ID*
Chapter 22: Implementing Basic OSPF Features	**3.0 IP Connectivity** 3.2 Determine how a router makes a forwarding decision by default *3.2.b Administrative distance* *3.2.c Routing protocol metric* 3.4 Configure and verify single area OSPFv2 *3.4.a Neighbor adjacencies* *3.4.c Broadcast (DR/BR selection)* *3.4.d (Router ID)*
Chapter 23: Implementing Optional OSPF Features	**3.0 IP Connectivity** 3.2 Determine how a router makes a forwarding decision by default *3.2.b Administrative distance* *3.2.c Routing protocol metric* 3.4 Configure and verify single area OSPFv2 *3.4.a Neighbor adjacencies* *3.4.b Point-to-point* *3.4.c Broadcast (DR/BR selection)* *3.4.d Router ID*

Book Chapter	Exam Topics Covered

Chapter 24: OSPF Neighbors and Route Selection	**3.0 IP Connectivity**
	
	3.1 Interpret components of the routing table
	
	   3.1.e Administrative distance
	
	3.2 Determine how a router makes a forwarding decision by default
	
	   3.2.a Longest prefix match
	
	   3.2.b Administrative distance
	
	   3.2.c Routing protocol metric
	
	3.4 Configure and verify single area OSPFv2
	
	   3.4.a Neighbor adjacencies
	
	   3.4.b Point-to-point
	
	   3.4.c Broadcast (DR/BR selection)
	
	   3.4.d Router ID

Part VII: IP Version 6	
Chapter 25: Fundamentals of IP Version 6	**1.0 Network Fundamentals** 1.8 Configure and verify IPv6 addressing and prefix
Chapter 26: IPv6 Addressing and Subnetting	**1.0 Network Fundamentals** 1.8 Configure and verify IPv6 addressing and prefix 1.9 Describe IPv6 address types

Chapter 27: Implementing IPv6 Addressing on Routers	**1.0 Network Fundamentals**
	
	1.8 Configure and verify IPv6 addressing and prefix
	
	1.9 Compare and contrast IPv6 address types
	
	   1.9.a Unicast (global, unique local, and link local)
	
	   1.9.b Anycast
	
	   1.9.c Multicast
	
	   1.9.d Modified EUI 64

Chapter 28: Implementing IPv6 Addressing on Hosts	**1.0 Network Fundamentals**
	
	1.8 Configure and verify IPv6 addressing and prefix
	
	1.9 Describe IPv6 address types
	
	   1.9.a Unicast (global, unique local, and link local)
	
	   1.9.d Modified EUI 64

B

Book Chapter	Exam Topics Covered
Chapter 29: Implementing IPv6 Routing	**3.0 IP Connectivity** 3.1 Interpret components of the routing table *3.1.a Routing protocol code* *3.1.b Prefix* *3.1.c Network mask* *3.1.d Next hop* *3.1.e Administrative distance* 3.3 Configure and verify IPv4 and IPv6 static routing *3.3.a Default route* *3.3.b Network route* *3.3.c Host route* *3.3.d Floating static*

Answers to the "Do I Know This Already?" Quizzes

Chapter 1

1. D and F. Of the remaining answers, Ethernet defines both physical and data-link protocols, PPP is a data-link protocol, IP is a network layer protocol, and SMTP and HTTP are application layer protocols.

2. A and G. Of the remaining answers, IP is a network layer protocol, TCP and UDP are transport layer protocols, and SMTP and HTTP are application layer protocols.

3. B. Adjacent-layer interaction occurs on one computer, with two adjacent layers in the model. The higher layer requests services from the next lower layer, and the lower layer provides the services to the next higher layer.

4. B. Same-layer interaction occurs on multiple computers. The functions defined by that layer typically need to be accomplished by multiple computers—for example, the sender setting a sequence number for a segment and the receiver acknowledging receipt of that segment. A single layer defines that process, but the implementation of that layer on multiple devices is required to accomplish the function.

5. A. Encapsulation is defined as the process of adding a header in front of data supplied by a higher layer (and possibly adding a trailer as well).

6. D. By convention, the term *frame* refers to the part of a network message that includes the data-link header and trailer, with encapsulated data. The term *packet* omits the data-link header and trailer, leaving the network layer header with its encapsulated data. The term *segment* omits the network layer header, leaving the transport layer header and its encapsulated data.

Chapter 2

1. A. The IEEE defines Ethernet LAN standards, with standard names that begin with 802.3, all of which happen to use cabling. The IEEE also defines wireless LAN standards, with standard names that begin with 802.11, which are separate standards from Ethernet.

2. C. The number before the word *BASE* defines the speed, in megabits per second (Mbps): 1000 Mbps equals 1 gigabit per second (1 Gbps). The *T* in the suffix implies twisted-pair or UTP cabling, so 1000BASE-T is the UTP-based Gigabit Ethernet standard name.

3. B. Crossover cables cross the wire at one node's transmit pin pair to the different pins used as the receive pins on the other device. For 10- and 100-Mbps Ethernet, the specific crossover cable wiring connects the pair at pins 1 and 2 on each end of the cable to pins 3 and 6 on the other end of the cable, respectively.

4.   B, D, and E. Routers, wireless access point Ethernet ports, and PC NICs all send using pins 1 and 2, whereas hubs and LAN switches transmit on pins 3 and 6. Straight-through cables connect devices that use opposite pin pairs for sending, because the cable does not need to cross the pairs.

5.   B and D. Multimode fiber works with LED-based transmitters rather than laser-based transmitters. Two answers mention the type of transmitters, making one of those answers correct and one incorrect.

Two answers mention distance. The answer that mentions the longest distance possible is incorrect because single-mode cables, not multimode cables, provide the longest distances. The other (correct) answer mentions the tradeoff of multimode being used for distances just longer than UTP's 100-meter limit, while happening to use less expensive hardware than single mode.

6.   B. NICs (and switch ports) use the carrier sense multiple access with collision detection (CSMA/CD) algorithm to implement half-duplex logic. CSMA/CD attempts to avoid collisions, but it also notices when collisions do occur, with rules about how the Ethernet nodes should stop sending, wait, and try again later.

7.   C. The 4-byte Ethernet FCS field, found in the Ethernet trailer, allows the receiving node to see what the sending node computed with a math formula that is a key part of the error-detection process. Note that Ethernet defines the process of detecting errors (error detection), but not error recovery.

8.   B, C, and E. The pre-assigned universal MAC address, given to each Ethernet port when manufactured, breaks the address into two 3-byte halves. The first half is called the organizationally unique identifier (OUI), which the IEEE assigns to the company that builds the product as a unique hex number to be used only by that company.

9.   C and D. Ethernet supports unicast addresses, which identify a single Ethernet node, and group addresses, which can be used to send one frame to multiple Ethernet nodes. The two types of group addresses are the *broadcast address* and *multicast address*.

Chapter 3

1.   D. The correct answer lists one term for an Ethernet WAN link between two sites: E-line, short for Ethernet line. The other answers list common synonyms for a serial link.

2.   B and D. The physical installation uses a model in which each router uses a physical Ethernet link to connect to some SP device in an SP facility called a point of presence (PoP). The Ethernet link does not span from each customer device to the other. From a data-link perspective, both routers use the same Ethernet standard header and trailer used on LANs; HDLC does not matter on these Ethernet WAN links.

3.   A. PC1 will send an Ethernet frame to Router1, with PC1's MAC address as the source address and Router1's MAC address as the destination address. Router1 will remove the encapsulated IP packet from that Ethernet frame, discarding the frame header and trailer, not using it again. Router1 will forward the IP packet by first encapsulating it inside a PPP frame. Router1 will not encapsulate the original

Ethernet frame in the PPP frame but rather the IP packet. The PPP header uses different addresses than Ethernet, so the original frame's Ethernet addresses are not used.

4. C. Routers compare the packet's destination IP address to the router's IP routing table, making a match and using the forwarding instructions in the matched route to forward the IP packet.

5. C. IPv4 hosts generally use basic two-branch logic. To send an IP packet to another host on the same IP network or subnet that is on the same LAN, the sender sends the IP packet directly to that host. Otherwise, the sender sends the packet to its default router (also called the default gateway).

6. A and C. Routers perform all the actions listed in the answers. However, the routing protocol does the functions in the two correct answers. Independent of the routing protocol, a router learns routes for IP subnets and IP networks directly connected to its interfaces. Routers also forward (route) IP packets, but that process is called IP routing, or IP forwarding, and is an independent process compared to the work of a routing protocol.

7. C. Address Resolution Protocol (ARP) does allow PC1 to learn information, but the information is not stored on a server. The **ping** command does let the user at PC1 learn whether packets can flow in the network, but it again does not use a server. With the Domain Name System (DNS), PC1 acts as a DNS client, relying on a DNS server to respond with information about the IP addresses that match a given hostname.

Chapter 4

1. A and B. The command in the question is an EXEC command that happens to require only user mode access. As such, you can use this command in both user mode and enable mode. Because it is an EXEC command, you cannot use the command (as shown in the question) in configuration mode. Note that you can put the word **do** in front of the EXEC command while in configuration mode (for example, **do show mac address-table**) to issue the command from inside any configuration mode.

2. B. The command referenced in the question, the **reload** command, is an EXEC command that happens to require privileged mode, also known as enable mode. This command is not available in user mode. Note that you can put the word **do** in front of the EXEC command while in configuration mode (for example, **do reload**) to issue the command from inside any configuration mode.

3. B. SSH provides a secure remote login option, encrypting all data flows, including password exchanges. Telnet sends all data (including passwords) as clear text.

4. A. Switches (and routers) keep the currently used configuration in RAM, using NVRAM to store the configuration file that is loaded when the switch (or router) next loads the IOS.

5. F. The startup-config file is in NVRAM, and the running-config file is in RAM.

6. B and C. The **exit** command moves the user one config mode backward, toward global configuration mode, or if already in global configuration mode, it moves the user back to enable mode. From console mode, it moves the user back to global configuration mode. The **end** command and the Ctrl+Z key sequence both move the user back to enable mode regardless of the current configuration submode.

Chapter 5

1. A. A switch compares the destination MAC address to the MAC address table. If a matching entry is found, the switch forwards the frame out the appropriate interface. If no matching entry is found, the switch floods the frame.

2. B. A switch floods broadcast frames, multicast frames (if no multicast optimizations are enabled), and unknown unicast destination frames (frames whose destination MAC address is not in the MAC address table). FFFF.FFFF.FFFF is the Ethernet broadcast address, so the switch floods the frame, which means that the switch forwards copies of the frame out all other ports except the arrival port.

3. A. A switch floods broadcast frames, multicast frames (if no multicast optimizations are enabled), and unknown unicast destination frames (frames whose destination MAC address is not in the MAC address table). Of the available answers, the correct answer defines how a switch floods a frame.

    Of the incorrect answers, one incorrect answer describes how a switch forwards known unicast frames by finding the matching entry in the MAC address table. Another describes MAC learning, in which the switch learns the source MAC address of incoming frames. Yet another incorrect answer mentions comparing the destination IP address to the destination MAC address, which the switch does not do.

4. B. Switches need to learn the location of each MAC address used in the LAN relative to that local switch. When a switch receives a frame, the source MAC identifies the sender. The interface in which the frame arrives identifies the local switch interface closest to that node in the LAN topology.

5. C. The **show interfaces status** command lists one line of output per interface. Cisco Catalyst switches name the type of interface based on the fastest speed of the interface, so 10/100 interfaces would be Fast Ethernet. With a working connection, ports from FastEthernet 0/1 through 0/10 would be listed in a connected state, while the rest would be listed in a notconnected state.

6. D. For the correct answer, each entry lists the learned MAC address. By definition, dynamically learned MAC addresses are learned by looking at the source MAC address of received frames. (That fact rules out one of the incorrect answers as well.)

    The **show mac address-table dynamic** command lists the current list of MAC table entries, with three known entries at the point at which the command output was gathered. The counter in the last line of output lists the number of current entries, not the total number of learned MAC addresses since the last reboot. For instance, the switch could have learned other MAC addresses whose entries timed out from the MAC address table.

    Finally, the answer that claims that port Gi0/2 connects directly to a device with a particular MAC address may or may not be true. That port could connect to another switch, and another, and so on, with one of those switches connecting to the device that uses the listed MAC address.

Chapter 6

1.   B. If both commands are configured, IOS accepts only the password as configured in the **enable secret** command.

2.   A. To answer this question, it might be best to first think of the complete configuration and then find any answers that match the configuration. The commands, in vty line configuration mode, would be **password** *password* and **login**. Only one answer lists a vty subcommand that is one of these two commands.

     Of note in the incorrect answers:

     One answer mentions console subcommands. The console does not define what happens when remote users log in; those details sit in the vty line configuration.

     One answer mentions the **login local** command; this command means that the switch should use the local list of configured usernames/passwords. The question stated that the engineer wanted to use passwords only, with no usernames.

     One answer mentions the **transport input ssh** command, which, by omitting the **telnet** keyword, disables Telnet. While that command can be useful, SSH does not work when using passwords only; SSH requires both a username and a password. So, by disabling Telnet (and allowing SSH only), the configuration would allow no one to remotely log in to the switch.

3.   B and C. SSH requires the use of usernames in addition to a password. Using the **username** global command would be one way to define usernames (and matching passwords) to support SSH. The vty lines would also need to be configured to require the use of usernames, with the **login local** vty subcommand being one such option.

     The **transport input ssh** command could be part of a meaningful configuration, but it is not a global configuration command (as claimed in one wrong answer). Likewise, one answer refers to the **username** command as a command in vty config mode, which is also the wrong mode.

4.   A, D, and F. To allow access through Telnet, the switch must have password security enabled, at a minimum using the **password** vty line configuration subcommand. In addition, the switch needs an IP address (configured under one VLAN interface) and a default gateway when the switch needs to communicate with hosts in a different subnet.

5.   B and C. To allow SSH or Telnet access, a switch must have a correct IP configuration. That includes the configuration of a correct IP address and mask on a VLAN interface. That VLAN interface then must have a path out of the switch via ports assigned to that VLAN. In this case, with all ports assigned to VLAN 2, the switch must use interface VLAN 2 (using the **interface vlan 2** configuration command).

     To meet the requirement to support login from hosts outside the local subnet, the switch must configure a correct default gateway setting with the **ip default-gateway 172.16.2.254** global command in this case.

6.   A. The **logging synchronous** line subcommand synchronizes the log message display with other command output so the log message does not interrupt a **show**

command's output. The **no ip domain-lookup** command is not a line subcommand. The other two incorrect answers are line subcommands but do not configure the function listed in the question.

Chapter 7

1. A and C. Because both devices use IEEE autonegotiation, they declare their speed and duplex capabilities to the other via messages sent out-of-band using Fast Link Pulses (FLPs). Then both devices choose the fastest speed that both support. They also use the best duplex setting that both support, with full duplex being better than half.

2. E. Cisco switches support per-interface settings for speed (with the **speed** command) and duplex (with the **duplex** command) in interface configuration mode.

3. B and E. Because the PC disables autonegotiation, it does not send autonegotiation FLP messages. However, it does start sending Ethernet frames based on the physical layer standard configured on the PC. After not receiving any autonegotiation FLP messages, the switch port analyzes the incoming signal to determine the standard used by the PC to send Ethernet frames. That analysis identifies the speed used by the PC, so the switch chooses to also use that speed. The switch then chooses the duplex based on a table of defaults: full duplex for speeds of 1 Gbps and faster or half duplex for speeds slower than 1 Gbps.

4. C. The **shutdown** interface subcommand administratively disables the interface, while the engineer can log in remotely on the weekend and configure the **no shutdown** interface subcommand to re-enable the interface. Note that unplugging the cable would prevent the interface from being used but would not allow the engineer to enable the interface remotely during the weekend change window. The **disable** and **enable** commands shown in a few answers do not exist.

5. B and D. The **interface range** global configuration command identifies a set of interfaces and moves the user into interface configuration mode. At that point, the switch applies any interface subcommands to all the interfaces in that range. However, the switch does not keep the **interface range** command in the configuration. For instance, in this case, the switch would list the **description** command under all the interfaces in the range: interfaces GigabitEthernet1/0/10 through GigabitEthernet 1/0/20 (11 interfaces in total).

6. A, B, and D. The disabled state in the **show interfaces status** command is the same as an "administratively down and down" state shown in the **show interfaces** command. The interface must be in a connected state (per the **show interfaces status** command) before the switch can send frames out of the interface.

7. A and C. First, note that some Cisco switch ports disable autonegotiation when configured with both **speed** and **duplex** on a port, as described in this question. A problem occurs when the combination of configured speed and duplex leads the autonegotiating device on the other end of the link to choose a different duplex setting—an effect called a duplex mismatch.

To summarize the scenario in this case, SW1 uses autonegotiation but receives no autonegotiation messages from SW2. As a result, SW1 then begins using alternate logic (called parallel detection) that does not rely on autonegotiation messages. SW2 does not use autonegotiation but has a speed set, so SW2 begins sending Ethernet frames per that speed on the link. SW1 senses the speed of those signals and uses the same speed, so a speed mismatch will not exist. However, SW1 then has to choose the duplex based on a default table, choosing half duplex if the speed is 10 or 100 Mbps, and full duplex if the speed is 1 Gbps or faster.

In the case of SW2 using **speed 100** and **duplex full** settings, SW1 senses the 100-Mbps speed and defaults to use half duplex, resulting in a duplex mismatch. Similar logic applies to the **speed 10** and **duplex full** case.

8. D. For the two answers about a duplex mismatch, that condition does cause collisions, particularly late collisions. However, only the side using CSMA/CD logic (the half-duplex side) has any concept of collisions. So, if switch SW1 were using half duplex and SW2 using full duplex, SW1 would likely see late collisions and show the counter incrementing over time.

   If switch SW2 had shut down its interface, switch SW1's interface would be in a down/down state, and none of the counters would increment. Also, if both switch ports use different speed settings, the ports would be in a down/down state, and none of the interface counters would increment.

Chapter 8

1. B. A VLAN is a set of devices in the same Layer 2 broadcast domain. A subnet often includes the exact same set of devices, but it is a Layer 3 concept. A collision domain refers to a set of Ethernet devices, but with different rules than VLAN rules for determining which devices are in the same collision domain.

2. D. Although a subnet and a VLAN are not equivalent concepts, the devices in one VLAN are typically in the same IP subnet and vice versa.

3. B. The 802.1Q trunking defines a 4-byte header, inserted after the original frame's destination and source MAC address fields. The insertion of this header does not change the original frame's source or destination address. The header itself holds a 12-bit VLAN ID field, which identifies the VLAN associated with the frame.

4. A and C. The **dynamic auto** setting means that the switch can negotiate trunking, but it can only respond to negotiation messages, and it cannot initiate the negotiation process. So, the other switch must be configured to trunk (**switchport mode trunk**) or to initiate the dynamic negotiation process (**switchport mode dynamic desirable**).

5. A and B. The configured VTP setting of VTP transparent mode means that the switch can configure VLANs, so the VLAN is configured. In addition, the VLAN configuration details, including the VLAN name, show up as part of the running-config file.

6. B and C. The **show interfaces switchport** command lists both the administrative and operational status of each port. When a switch considers a port to be trunking, this command lists an operational trunking state of "trunk." The **show interfaces trunk** command lists a set of interfaces—the interfaces that are currently operating as trunks. So, both of these commands identify interfaces that are operational trunks.

7. A and B. On switches that do not use VTP (by using VTP modes off or transparent), the switch lists all VLAN configuration in the configuration file (making one answer correct). Also, the **show vlan brief** command lists all defined VLANs, regardless of VTP mode and regardless of shutdown state. As a result, the two answers that mention commands are correct.

The other two answers are incorrect because VLAN 30 has been shut down, which means the switch will not forward frames in that VLAN, regardless of whether they arrive on access or trunk ports.

8. B. The first list of VLAN IDs includes all VLANs (1–4094) except those overtly removed per the details in any **switchport trunk allowed vlan** interface subcommands on the trunk interface. If no such commands are configured, the first list in the output will include 1–4094. The two incorrect answers that mention VLAN 30 list conditions that change the second of two lists of VLANs in the command output, while STP's choice to block an interface would impact the third list.

Chapter 9

1. A and B. Listening and learning are transitory port states, used only when moving from the blocking to the forwarding state. Discarding is not an STP port state.

2. C. The smallest numeric bridge ID wins the election. The bridge IDs in the answers break into a decimal priority on the left, a colon, and then the 12-digit hexadecimal MAC address of the switch. Of all the answers, two tie with the lowest priority (4097). Of those, the correct answer lists a lower MAC address.

3. C and D. Listening and learning are transitory port states used only when moving from the blocking to the forwarding state. Discarding is not an STP port state. Forwarding and blocking are stable states.

4. B. Nonroot switches forward Hellos received from the root; the root sends these Hellos based on the root's configured Hello timer.

5. B and D. RSTP uses port states forwarding, learning, and discarding. Forwarding and learning perform the same functions as the port states used by traditional STP.

6. A and D. With RSTP, an alternate port is an alternate to the root port when a switch's root port fails. A backup port takes over for a designated port if the designated port fails.

7. D. The PortFast feature allows STP/RSTP to move a port from blocking to forwarding without going through the interim listening and learning states. STP allows this exception when the link is known to have no switch on the other end of the link, removing the risk of a switching loop. Cisco created PortFast before the IEEE released RSTP, but RSTP included the equivalent feature as well, so it is a feature of both STP and RSTP.

BPDU Guard is a common feature to use at the same time as PortFast because it watches for incoming bridge protocol data units (BPDUs), which should not happen on an access port, and prevents the loops from a rogue switch by disabling the port.

8. C. Root Guard on a switch interface monitors incoming STP BPDUs, processing them as normal with STP, with one exception: superior BPDUs. Superior BPDUs identify a new root switch with a better (lower) Bridge ID. Root Guard reacts to receiving such a BPDU and disables the port.

For the other answers, BPDU Guard monitors for incoming BPDUs but disables the port for any received BPDU on the port. Neither PortFast nor Loop Guard monitor incoming BPDUs or react to them.

Chapter 10

1. A. Of the four answers, only **pvst** and **rapid-pvst** are valid options on the command. Of those, the **rapid-pvst** option enables Rapid Per VLAN Spanning Tree (RPVST+), which uses RSTP. The **pvst** option enables Per VLAN Spanning Tree (PVST), which uses STP, not RSTP. The other two options, if attempted, would cause the command to be rejected because these option do not exist.

2. A and C. The system ID extension (or extended system ID) part of a bridge ID contains 12 bits and sits after the 4-bit priority field and before the 48-bit system ID. Switches use this field to store the VLAN ID when using STP or RSTP to build spanning trees per VLAN. So, of the two answers that mention the system ID extension, the one that lists the VLAN ID, in this case 5, is correct.

    The output also lists a priority of 32773. However, that output lists the decimal equivalent of the 16-bit priority value. In reality, this decimal value is the sum of the configured decimal priority plus the VLAN ID: 32768 + 5 = 32773. So in this case, the root's configured priority is 32,768.

3. A, B, and D. Cisco's Rapid Per VLAN Spanning Tree (RPVST+) creates one spanning tree instance per VLAN. To do so, it sends BPDUs per VLAN. Each switch identifies itself with a unique Bridge ID (BID) per VLAN, made unique per VLAN by adding the VLAN ID to the system ID extension 12-bit field of the BID. RVPST also adds a new Type-Length Value (TLV) to the BPDU itself, which includes a place to list the VLAN ID. Finally, when transmitting the BPDUs over VLAN trunks, the switch uses a trunking header that lists the VLAN ID (a practice sometimes called tunneling in 802.1Q). The receiving switch can check all three locations that list the VLAN ID to ensure that they all agree about what VLAN the BPDU is describing. Of the four answers, the three correct answers describe the three actual locations in which RPVST+ lists the VLAN ID.

4. B and C. BPDU Guard disables a port by placing it into an error disabled (errdisabled) interface state. BPDU Guard does so when it is enabled on the interface, regardless of whether PortFast is also enabled. The two correct answers both state that BPDU Guard is enabled, while the two incorrect answers list it as disabled.

5. A and E. Root Guard reacts to the receipt of a superior BPDU by disabling the port. To do so, it leaves the interface state as is in a connected state. Instead, it manipulates the STP port state, changing it to a special state called broken. The commands display the broken state with letters BRK. So, the **show interfaces status** command lists a connected interface state, while the **show spanning-tree** command lists a port state of BRK, or broken, which stops all traffic on the interface.

6. D. IOS uses the **channel-group** configuration command to create an EtherChannel. Then the term *etherchannel* is used in the **show etherchannel** command, which displays the status of the channel. The output of this **show** command then names the channel a *PortChannel*. The only answer that is not used somewhere in IOS to describe this multilink channel is *Ethernet-Channel*.

7. B and D. The **channel-group** command will direct the switch to use LACP to dynamically negotiate to add a link to an EtherChannel when the command uses the **active** and **passive** keywords, respectively. The **desirable** and **passive** keywords direct the switch to use PAgP instead of LACP. Of the four answers, the two correct answers use two LACP values, while the two incorrect answers use at least one value that would cause the switch to use PAgP, making the answers incorrect.

    Of the two correct answers, both combinations result in the switches attempting to add the link to an EtherChannel using LACP as the negotiation protocol. If both switches used the **passive** keyword, they would both sit and wait for the other switch to begin sending LACP messages and therefore never attempt to add the link to the channel.

8. C. EtherChannel load distribution, or load balancing, on Cisco Catalyst switches uses an algorithm. The algorithm examines some fields in the various headers, so messages that have the same values in those fields always flow over the same link in a particular EtherChannel. Note that it does not break the frames into smaller fragments or use a round-robin approach that ignores the header values, and it does not examine link utilization when making the choice.

Chapter 11

1. B and D. The general rule to determine whether two devices' interfaces should be in the same subnet is whether the two interfaces are separated from each other by a router. To provide a way for hosts in one VLAN to send data to hosts outside that VLAN, a local router must connect its LAN interface to the same VLAN as the hosts and have an address in the same subnet as the hosts. All the hosts in that same VLAN on the same switch would not be separated from each other by a router, so these hosts would also be in the same subnet. However, another PC, connected to the same switch but in a different VLAN, will require its packets to flow through a router to reach Host A, so Host A's IP address would need to be in a different subnet compared to this new host.

2. D. By definition, two address values in every IPv4 subnet cannot be used as host IPv4 addresses: the first (lowest) numeric value in the subnet for the subnet ID and the last (highest) numeric value in the subnet for the subnet broadcast address.

3. B and C. At least 7 subnet bits are needed because $2^6 = 64$, so 6 subnet bits could not number 100 different subnets. Seven subnet bits could because $2^7 = 128 => 100$. Similarly, 6 host bits is not enough because $2^6 - 2 = 62$, but 7 host bits is enough because $2^7 - 2 = 126 => 100$.

    The number of network, subnet, and host bits must total 32 bits, making one of the answers incorrect. The answer with 8 network bits cannot be correct because the question states that a Class B network is used, so the number of network bits must always be 16. The two correct answers have 16 network bits (required because the question states the use of a Class B network) and at least 7 subnet and host bits each.

4. A and C. The private IPv4 networks, defined by RFC 1918, are Class A network 10.0.0.0, the 16 Class B networks from 172.16.0.0 to 172.31.0.0, and the 256 Class C networks that begin with 192.168.

5. A, D, and E. The private IPv4 networks, defined by RFC 1918, are Class A network 10.0.0.0, the 16 Class B networks from 172.16.0.0 to 172.31.0.0, and the 256 Class C networks that begin with 192.168. The three correct answers are from the public IP network range, and none are reserved values.

6. A and C. An unsubnetted Class A, B, or C network has two parts: the network and host parts.

7. B. An unsubnetted Class A, B, or C network has two parts: the network and host parts. The subnet part does not exist in that case. To perform subnetting, the engineer creates a new subnet part by choosing to use a subnet mask, defining a smaller number of host bits, which makes space for some bits to be used to number different subnets. So, the host part of the address structure gets smaller in the after-subnetting case. The subnet part of the address structure moves from size 0 (nonexistent) to some number of subnet bits after the engineer chooses a subnet (nondefault) mask. The network part remains a constant size throughout, whether subnetting or not.

Chapter 12

1. B and C. Class A networks have a first octet in the range of 1–126, inclusive, and their network IDs have a 0 in the last three octets. A network ID of 130.0.0.0 is actually a Class B network (first octet range 128–191, inclusive). All addresses that begin with 127 are reserved, so 127.0.0.0 is not a Class A network.

2. E. All Class B networks begin with values between 128 and 191, inclusive, in their first octets. The network ID has any value in the 128–191 range in the first octet, and any value from 0 to 255 inclusive in the second octet, with decimal 0s in the final two octets. Two of the answers show a 255 in the second octet, which is acceptable. Two of the answers show a 0 in the second octet, which is also acceptable.

3. B and D. The first octet (172) is in the range of values for Class B addresses (128–191). As a result, the network ID can be formed by copying the first two octets (172.16) and writing 0s for the last two octets (172.16.0.0). The default mask for all Class B networks is 255.255.0.0, and the number of host bits in all unsubnetted Class B networks is 16.

4. A and C. The first octet (192) is in the range of values for Class C addresses (192–223). As a result, the network ID can be formed by copying the first three octets (192.168.6) and writing 0 for the last octet (192.168.6.0). The default mask for all Class C networks is 255.255.255.0, and the number of host bits in all unsubnetted Class C networks is 8.

5. D. To find the network broadcast address, first determine the class, and then determine the number of host octets. At that point, convert the host octets to 255 to create the network broadcast address. In this case, 10.1.255.255 is in a Class A network, with the last three octets as host octets, for a network broadcast address of

10.255.255.255. For 192.168.255.1, it is a Class C address, with the last octet as the host part, for a network broadcast address of 192.168.255.255. Address 224.1.1.255 is a Class D address, so it is not in any unicast IP network and the question does not apply. For 172.30.255.255, it is a Class B address, with the last two octets as host octets, so the network broadcast address is 172.30.255.255.

Chapter 13

1. C. If you think about the conversion one octet at a time, the first two octets each convert to 8 binary 1s. The 254 converts to 8-bit binary 11111110, and the decimal 0 converts to 8-bit binary 00000000. So, the total number of binary 1s (which defines the prefix length) is 8 + 8 + 7 + 0 = /23.

2. B. If you think about the conversion one octet at a time, the first three octets each convert to 8 binary 1s. The 240 converts to 8-bit binary 11110000, so the total number of binary 1s (which defines the prefix length) is 8 + 8 + 8 + 4 = /28.

3. B. Remember that /30 is the equivalent of the mask that in binary has 30 binary 1s. To convert that to DDN format, write down all the binary 1s (30 in this case), followed by binary 0s for the remainder of the 32-bit mask. Then take 8 bits at a time and convert from binary to decimal (or memorize the nine possible DDN mask octet values and their binary equivalents). Using the /30 mask in this question, the binary mask is 11111111 11111111 11111111 11111100. Each of the first three octets is all binary 1s, so each converts to 255. The last octet, 11111100, converts to 252, for a DDN mask of 255.255.255.252. See Appendix A, "Numeric Reference Tables," for a decimal/binary conversion table.

4. C. The size of the network part is always either 8, 16, or 24 bits, based on whether it is Class A, B, or C, respectively. As a Class A address, N=8. The mask 255.255.255.0, converted to prefix format, is /24. The number of subnet bits is the difference between the prefix length (24) and N, so S=16 in this case. The size of the host part is a number that, when added to the prefix length (24), gives you 32, so H=8 in this case.

5. A. The size of the network part is always either 8, 16, or 24 bits, based on whether it is Class A, B, or C, respectively. As a Class C address, N=24. The number of subnet bits is the difference between the prefix length (27) and N, so S=3 in this case. The size of the host part is a number that, when added to the prefix length (27), gives you 32, so H=5 in this case.

6. D. Classless addressing rules define a two-part IP address structure: the prefix and the host part. This logic ignores Class A, B, and C rules and can be applied to the 32-bit IPv4 addresses from any address class. By ignoring Class A, B, and C rules, classless addressing ignores any distinction as to the network part of an IPv4 address.

7. A and B. The masks in binary define a number of binary 1s, and the number of binary 1s defines the length of the prefix (network + subnet) part. With a Class B network, the network part is 16 bits. To support 100 subnets, the subnet part must be at least 7 bits long. Six subnet bits would supply only 2^6 = 64 subnets, while 7 subnet bits supply 2^7 = 128 subnets. The /24 answer supplies 8 subnet bits, and the 255.255.255.252 answer supplies 14 subnet bits.

Chapter 14

1.   D. When using classful IP addressing concepts as described in Chapter 13, "Analyzing Subnet Masks," addresses have three parts: network, subnet, and host. For addresses in a single classful network, the network parts must be identical for the numbers to be in the same network. For addresses in the same subnet, both the network and subnet parts must have identical values. The host part differs when comparing different addresses in the same subnet.

2.   B and D. In any subnet, the subnet ID is the smallest number in the range, the subnet broadcast address is the largest number, and the usable IP addresses sit between them. All numbers in a subnet have identical binary values in the prefix part (classless view) and network + subnet part (classful view). To be the lowest number, the subnet ID must have the lowest possible binary value (all 0s) in the host part. To be the largest number, the broadcast address must have the highest possible binary value (all binary 1s) in the host part. The usable addresses do not include the subnet ID and subnet broadcast address, so the addresses in the range of usable IP addresses never have a value of all 0s or 1s in their host parts.

3.   C. The mask converts to 255.255.255.0. To find the subnet ID, for each octet of the mask that is 255, you can copy the IP address's corresponding values. For mask octets of decimal 0, you can record a 0 in that octet of the subnet ID. As such, copy the 10.7.99 and write a 0 for the fourth octet, for a subnet ID of 10.7.99.0.

4.   C. First, the resident subnet (the subnet ID of the subnet in which the address resides) must be numerically smaller than the IP address, which rules out one of the answers. The mask converts to 255.255.255.252. As such, you can copy the first three octets of the IP address because of their value of 255. For the fourth octet, the subnet ID value must be a multiple of 4, because 256 – 252 (mask) = 4. Those multiples include 96 and 100, and the right choice is the multiple closest to the IP address value in that octet (97) without going over. So, the correct subnet ID is 192.168.44.96.

5.   C. The resident subnet ID in this case is 172.31.77.192. You can find the subnet broadcast address based on the subnet ID and mask using several methods. Following the decimal process in the book, the mask converts to 255.255.255.224, making the interesting octet be octet 4, with magic number 256 – 224 = 32. For the three octets where the mask = 255, copy the subnet ID (172.31.77). For the interesting octet, take the subnet ID value (192), add magic (32), and subtract 1, for 223. That makes the subnet broadcast address 172.31.77.223.

6.   C. To answer this question, you need to find the range of addresses in the subnet, which typically then means you need to calculate the subnet ID and subnet broadcast address. With a subnet ID/mask of 10.1.4.0/23, the mask converts to 255.255.254.0. To find the subnet broadcast address, following the decimal process described in this chapter, you can copy the subnet ID's first two octets because the mask's value is 255 in each octet. You write a 255 in the fourth octet because the mask has a 0 on the fourth octet. In octet 3, the interesting octet, add the magic number (2) to the subnet ID's value (4), minus 1, for a value of 2 + 4 – 1 = 5. (The magic number in this case is calculated as 256 – 254 = 2.) That makes the broadcast address 10.1.5.255. The last usable address is 1 less: 10.1.5.254. The range that includes the last 100 addresses is 10.1.5.155 – 10.1.5.254.

Chapter 15

1. A. With 50 percent growth, the mask needs to define enough subnet bits to create 150 subnets. As a result, the mask needs at least 8 subnet bits (7 subnet bits supply 2^7, or 128, subnets, and 8 subnet bits supply 2^8, or 256, subnets). Similarly, the need for 50 percent growth in the size for the largest subnet means that the host part needs enough bits to number 750 hosts/subnet. Nine host bits are not enough ($2^9 - 2 = 510$), but 10 host bits supply 1022 hosts/subnet ($2^{10} - 2 = 1022$). With 16 network bits existing because of the choice to use a Class B network, the design needs a total of 34 bits (at least) in the mask (16 network, 8 subnet, 10 host), but only 32 bits exist—so no single mask meets the requirements.

2. B. With a growth of 20 percent, the design needs to support 240 subnets. Seven subnet bits do not meet the need ($2^7 = 128$), but 8 subnet bits do meet the need ($2^8 = 256$). To support 120 hosts/subnet, with 20% growth, the mask should support 144 hosts/subnet. That number requires 8 host bits ($2^8 - 2 = 254$). As a result, you need a minimum 8 subnet bits and 8 host bits.

   The right answer, 10.0.0.0/22, has 8 network bits because the network class is Class A, 14 subnet bits (/22 − 8 = 14), and 10 host bits (32 − 22 = 10). This mask supplies at least 8 subnet bits and at least 8 host bits.

   The answer with the /25 mask supplies only 7 host bits, making it incorrect. The answer showing 172.16.0.0/23 supplies 9 host bits, which is enough; however, it uses 16 network bits with the Class B network, leaving too few subnet bits (7). The answer that shows Class C network 192.168.7.0 with mask /24 supplies 8 host bits but 0 subnet bits.

3. B. To support 1000 subnets, 10 subnet bits ($2^{10} = 1024$) are needed. The design uses a Class B network, which means that 16 network bits exist as well. So, the shortest mask that meets the requirements is 255.255.255.192, or /26, composed of 16 network plus 10 subnet bits. The /28 answer also supplies enough subnets to meet the need, but compared to /26, /28 supplies fewer host bits and so fewer hosts/subnet.

4. C and D. The mask converts to 255.255.252.0, so the difference from subnet ID to subnet ID (called the magic number in this chapter) is 256 − 252 = 4. So, the subnet IDs start with 172.30.0.0, then 172.30.4.0, then 172.30.8.0, and so on, adding 4 to the third octet. The mask, used with a Class B network, implies 6 subnet bits, for 64 total subnet IDs. The last of these, 172.30.252.0, can be recognized in part because the third octet, where the subnet bits sit, has the same value as the mask in that third octet.

5. A. The first (numerically lowest) subnet ID is the same number as the classful network number, or 192.168.9.0. The remaining subnet IDs are each 8 larger than the previous subnet ID, in sequence, or 192.168.9.8, 192.168.9.16, 192.168.9.24, 192.168.9.32, and so on, through 192.168.9.248.

6. D. Using mask /24 (255.255.255.0), the subnet IDs increment by 1 in the third octet. The reasoning is that with a Class B network, 16 network bits exist, and with mask /24, the next 8 bits are subnet bits, so the entire third octet contains subnet bits. All the subnet IDs will have a 0 as the last octet, because the entire fourth octet consists of host bits. Note that 172.19.0.0 (the zero subnet) and 172.19.255.0 (the broadcast subnet) might look odd but are valid subnet IDs.

Chapter 16

1. B and D. Cisco routers originally used IOS, with some models today still using IOS. Most of the enterprise router product line uses the newer IOS XE operating system. CatOS, short for Catalyst OS, refers to the original Cisco switch operating system.

2. B. The switch and router CLI follows the same basic flow with many commands in common. The three incorrect answers are incorrect because they describe actions that can occur on both routers and switches. However, the user must configure router interfaces with IP addresses. Switches, when used as Layer 2 switches only, do not need any IP addresses on their Layer 2 physical interfaces.

3. A and C. To route packets on an interface, the router interface configuration must include an IP address and mask. One correct command shows the correct single command used to configure both values, while one incorrect command shows those settings as two separate (nonexistent) commands. Also, to route packets, the interface much reach an "up/up" state; that is, the **show interfaces** and other commands list two status values, and both must be "up." The **no shutdown** command enables the interface so that it can reach an up/up state, assuming the interface has correct cabling and is connected to an appropriate device. One incorrect answer mentions the **description** command, which is useful but has nothing to do with making the interface work properly.

4. B. If the first of the two status codes is "down," it typically means that a Layer 1 problem exists. In this case, the question states that the router connects to a switch with a UTP straight-through cable, which is the correct cable pinout. Of the two answers that mention the **shutdown** command, if the router interface were shut down, the first router status code would be "administratively down," so that answer is incorrect. However, if the neighboring device interface sits in a shutdown state, the router will sense no electrical signals over the cable, seeing that as a physical problem, and place the interface into a "down/down" state, making that answer correct.

   Second, the two answers that mention interface IP addresses have no impact on the status codes of the **show interfaces brief** command. Both answers imply that the interface does not have an IP address configured; however, the IP address configuration has no effect on the interface status codes, making both answers incorrect.

5. C. The **show ip interface brief** command lists all the interface IPv4 addresses but none of the masks. The other three commands list both the address and mask.

6. B. A router has one IPv4 address for each interface in use, whereas a LAN switch has a single IPv4 address that is just used for accessing the switch. The rest of the answers list configuration settings that use the same conventions on both routers and switches.

Chapter 17

1. A and C. The route defines the group of addresses represented by the route using the subnet ID and mask. The router can use those numbers to find the range of addresses that should be matched by this route. The other two answers list facts useful when forwarding packets that happen to match the route.

2. D. Each time a router routes an IP packet, it de-encapsulates (removes) the IP packet from the incoming data-link frame. Once it decides where to forward the packet next, it re-encapsulates the packet in a new data-link frame. That occurs even if the incoming and outgoing data links happen to be the same type, as is the case in this scenario. So, all three routers de-encapsulate the IP packet. Since all links are Ethernet links, all three de-encapsulation actions removed the packet from an Ethernet frame.

3. A and D. First, for the subnetting math, address 10.1.1.100, with mask /26, implies a subnet ID of 10.1.1.64. Also, mask /26 converts to a DDN mask of 255.255.255.192. For any working router interface, after adding the **ip address** command to configure an address and mask, the router adds a connected route for the subnet. In this case, that means the router adds a connected route for subnet 10.1.1.64 255.255.255.192. The router also adds a route called a local route, which is a route for the interface IP address with a 255.255.255.255 mask. In this case, that means the router adds a local route for address 10.1.1.100 with mask 255.255.255.255.

4. B and C. The **ip route** command can refer to the IP address of the next-hop router on the link between the two routers, or to the local router's outgoing interface ID. The incorrect answers reverse those items, mentioning the local router's IP address and the next-hop router's interface ID.

5. A. The correct syntax lists a subnet number, then a subnet mask in dotted-decimal form, and then either an outgoing interface or a next-hop IP address. Of the incorrect answers, one omits the subnet mask, while two use a prefix-style mask instead of a DDN mask.

6. B. The network engineer issued the command, but the router did not add an IP route. So, either the command had a syntax error, or the router accepted the command but has some reason to believe that it should not add a route to the table.

Two (incorrect) answers suggest the command has a syntax error: one answer with a general claim of a syntax error, and another explicitly stating that the next-hop IP address is missing. However, the **ip route 10.1.1.0 255.255.255.0 s0/0/0** command is syntactically correct. Note that with outgoing interface S0/0/0 listed, the command does not need a next-hop IP address.

As for reasons why IOS would not add a route once it accepts the command into the configuration, IOS performs several checks of the contents of a valid **ip route** command before adding the route to the routing table. It checks whether the outgoing interface is up/up (as noted in this question's correct answer) and whether it has a route to reach the next-hop address. Also, if the router already has a route to the same subnet learned from another source, the router checks whether the other route has a better administrative distance.

Chapter 18

1. A and F. Of all the commands listed, only the two correct answers are syntactically correct router configuration commands. The command to enable 802.1Q trunking is **encapsulation dot1q** *vlan_id*.

2. B and C. Subinterface G0/1.1 must be in an administratively down state due to the **shutdown** command being issued on that subinterface. For subinterface G0/1.2, its status cannot be administratively down because of the **no shutdown** command. G0/1.2's state will then track to the state of the underlying physical interface. With a physical interface state of down/down, subinterface G0/1.2 will be in a down/down state in this case.

3. C. The configuration of the Layer 3 switch's routing feature uses VLAN interfaces. The VLAN interface numbers must match the associated VLAN ID, so with VLANs 1, 2, and 3 in use, the switch will configure **interface vlan 1**, **interface vlan 2** (which is the correct answer), and **interface vlan 3**. The matching connected routes, like all connected IP routes, will list the VLAN interfaces.

   As for the incorrect answers, a list of connected routes will not list any next-hop IP addresses. Each route will list an outgoing interface; the outgoing interface will not be a physical interface, but rather a VLAN interface, because the question states that the configuration uses SVIs. Finally, all the listed subnets have a /25 mask, which is 255.255.255.128, so none of the routes will list a 255.255.255.0 mask.

4. C and D. First, for the correct answers, a Layer 3 switch will not route packets on a VLAN interface unless it is in an up/up state. When using autostate, a VLAN interface will only be up/up if the matching VLAN (with the same VLAN number) exists on the switch, is not shut down, and at least one port is up and active in that VLAN. For one correct answer, if the **no vlan 2** command were issued, deleting VLAN 2, the switch would move interface VLAN 2 to a up/down state so it could no longer route packets. For the other correct answer, disabling VLAN 2 with the **shutdown** command in VLAN configuration mode has the same result.

   As for the incorrect answers, when using autostate, a Layer 3 switch needs only one access port or trunk port forwarding for a VLAN to enable routing for that VLAN, so nine of the ten access ports in VLAN 2 could fail, leaving one working port, and the switch would keep routing for VLAN 2.

   A **shutdown** of VLAN 4 does not affect routing for VLAN interfaces 2 and 3. Had that answer listed VLAN 2 or 3, it would be a reason to make routing fail for that VLAN interface.

5. A and C. With a Layer 3 EtherChannel, the physical ports and the port-channel interface must disable the behavior of acting like a switch port and therefore act like a routed port, through the configuration of the **no switchport** interface subcommand. (The **routedport** command is not an IOS command.) Once created, the physical interfaces should not have an IP address configured. The port-channel interface (the interface representing the EtherChannel) should be configured with the IP address.

6. B and C. With a Layer 3 EtherChannel, two configuration settings must be the same on all the physical ports, specifically the speed and duplex as set with the **speed** and **duplex** commands. Additionally, the physical ports and port-channel port must all have the **no switchport** command configured to make each act as a routed port. So, having a different speed setting, or being configured with **switchport** rather than **no switchport**, would prevent IOS from adding interface G0/2 to the Layer 3 EtherChannel.

   As for the wrong answers, both would cause an issue adding the port to a Layer 2 EtherChannel but do not cause a problem with a Layer 3 EtherChannel. Once Layer 2 operations have been disabled because of the **no switchport** command, those settings do not then cause problems for the Layer 3 EtherChannel. So, Layer 2 settings about access VLANs, trunking allowed lists, and STP settings, which must match before an interface can be added to a Layer 2 EtherChannel, do not matter for a Layer 3 EtherChannel.

7. A. On a router that has some routed ports, plus some switched ports, IOS supports LAN switching subcommands on the switched ports only. So, when in interface configuration mode for one of a router's switched interfaces, IOS accepts the **switchport access** command but not the **ip address** command. The router supports the **description** subcommand on both switched and routed ports, making that answer incorrect. Finally, one answer lists a global command (**hostname**), making that answer incorrect because the question asks for interface subcommands.

Chapter 19

1. B and D. The client sends a Discover message, with the server returning an Offer message. The client then sends a Request, with the server sending back the IP address in the Acknowledgment message.

2. A and B. The two correct answers list the two primary facts that impact which IP addresses the server will lease to clients. For the incorrect answer about DNS servers, the DHCP server does supply the IP address of the DNS servers, but not the hostnames of the DNS servers. Also, the DHCP server supplies the IP address (but not the MAC address) of the default gateway in each subnet.

3. A and C. A router needs to act as a DHCP relay agent if DHCP clients exist on the connected subnet and there is no DHCP server in that subnet. If a DHCP server exists in the subnet, the router does not need to forward DHCP messages to a remote DHCP server (which is the function of a DHCP relay agent). The answer that mentions the **ip address dhcp** command makes the router interface act as a DHCP client and has nothing to do with DHCP relay agent.

4. D. The **ip address dhcp** command tells the router to obtain its address using DHCP. The router learns all the same information that a normal DHCP client would learn. The router uses the address listed as the default gateway to build a default route, using the default gateway IP address as the next-hop address. The router continues to work like a router always does, forwarding packets based on its IP routing table.

5. B and C. The output shows the MAC address, IP address, subnet mask (in hex format), and the subnet broadcast address. Of those, the DHCP server supplies the information in the two correct answers. The two incorrect answers mention the MAC address (not supplied by DHCP, but known to the device's NIC) and the subnet broadcast address (calculated by the host).

6. D. Windows supports both **ipconfig** and **ipconfig /all** commands, but the **ipconfig** command does not mention the DNS servers. Note that the **ifconfig** command works on Linux and macOS but not Windows, and the **ifconfig /all** command is an invalid command on all three.

Chapter 20

There are no questions for this chapter.

Chapter 21

1. D. Both versions of RIP use distance vector logic, and EIGRP uses a different kind of logic, characterized either as advanced distance vector or a balanced hybrid.

2. C and D. Both versions of RIP use the same hop-count metric, neither of which is affected by link bandwidth. EIGRP's metric, by default, is calculated based on bandwidth and delay. OSPF's metric is a sum of outgoing interfaces costs, with those costs (by default) based on interface bandwidth.

3. B, C, and D. Of the listed routing protocols, only the old RIP Version 1 (RIP-1) protocol does not support variable-length subnet masks (VLSM).

4. C. LSAs contain topology information that is useful in calculating routes, but the LSAs do not directly list the route that a router should add to its routing table. In this case, R1 would run a calculation called the Shortest Path First (SPF) algorithm, against the LSAs, to determine what IP routes to add to the IP routing table.

5. B. Neighboring OSPF routers that complete the database exchange are considered fully adjacent and rest in a full neighbor state. The up/up and final states are not OSPF states at all. The 2-way state is either an interim state or a stable state between some routers on the same VLAN.

6. C. The correct answer is the one advantage of using a single-area design. The three wrong answers are advantages of using a multiarea design, with all reasons being much more important with a larger internetwork.

Chapter 22

1. B. The **network 10.0.0.0 0.255.255.255 area 0** command matches all three interface IP addresses because it compares the first octet only (10) and matches in each case.

   The three incorrect answers do not match all three interface IP addresses because they each compare at least one octet that does not match the address in the **network** command:

   > **network 10.0.0.0 0.0.0.0** requires an exact match of all four octets (10.0.0.0), which matches no interfaces.

   > **network 10.0.0.0 0.0.0.255** requires an exact match of the first three octets (10.0.0), which matches none of the interface IP addresses.

   > **network 10.0.0.0 0.0.255.255** requires an exact match of the first two octets (10.0), which matches none of the interface IP addresses.

2. A. The **network 10.1.0.0 0.0.255.255 area 0** command matches all IP addresses that begin with 10.1, enabling OSPF in area 0 on all interfaces. The three incorrect answers do not match all three interface IP addresses because they each compare at least one octet that does not match the address in the **network** command:

   > **network 10.0.0.0 0.255.255.0** ignores the middle two octets but compares the first (10) and last (0) octets to the interface addresses. The first octet matches, but the fourth octet matches none of the addresses.

network **10.1.1.0 0.x.1x.0** does not meet syntax requirements because of the letters (x) in the wildcard mask. It would be rejected when attempted in configuration mode.

network **10.1.1.0 255.0.0.0** ignores the first octet but compares the last three octets (1.1.0) to the addresses. None of the addresses end in 1.1.0, so no addresses match this command.

3. A and E. Of the three wrong answers, two are real commands that simply do not list the OSPF neighbors. **show ip ospf interface brief** lists interfaces on which OSPF is enabled but does not list neighbors. **show ip interface** lists IPv4 details about interfaces, but none related to OSPF. One incorrect answer, **show ip neighbor**, is not a valid IOS command.

4. B. The rule for choosing the OSPF RID begins with the **router-id** command in the OSPF process configuration, but the router had no such command. The next rule considers all working (up/up) loopback interfaces, and among those, OSPF chooses the numerically highest IP address. In this case, two such loopback interfaces exist, with loopback 1, with address 10.8.8.8, having the numerically highest IP address.

5. B. With OSPFv2 interface configuration mode, the configuration looks just like the traditional configuration, with a couple of exceptions. The **network** router subcommand is no longer required. Instead, each interface on which OSPF should be enabled is configured with an **ip ospf** *process-id* **area** *area-id* interface subcommand. This command refers to the OSPF routing process that should be enabled on the interface and specifies the OSPFv2 area.

6. A and D. Many of the **show** commands for OSPF do not happen to note whether OSPF happens to be enabled due to an interface subcommand the (**ip ospf** interface subcommand) or a router subcommand (the **network** command). The **show ip protocols** command lists all interfaces on which OSPF has been enabled using the **ip ospf interface** subcommand under the heading "Routing on Interfaces Configured Explicitly." Additionally, the **show ip ospf interface** command, which lists many lines of output per interface, lists the phrase "Attached via Interface Enable." Also, although not in the answers, you can also look at the configuration with the **show running-config** or **show startup-config** command.

Chapter 23

1. B and D. By default, IOS assigns Ethernet interfaces an OSPF network type of broadcast, with an OSPF interface priority of 1. As a result, both routers attempt to discover the other routers on the link (which identifies one correct answer).

The broadcast network type means that the routers also attempt to elect a DR and BDR. With a priority tied, the routers choose the DR based on the highest router ID (RID) values, meaning that R2 will become the DR and R1 will become the BDR. These facts show why the two incorrect answers are incorrect. The other correct answer is correct because the **show ip ospf neighbor** command lists the local router's neighbor relationship state (FULL) and the role filled by that neighbor (DR), which would be the output shown on R1 when R2 is acting as DR.

2. B and C. First, the OSPF point-to-point network type causes the two routers to dynamically discover neighbors, making one answer correct.

    Next, IOS assigns a default OSPF interface priority of 1, so R1's configured priority of 11 would be better in a DR/BDR election. However, the point-to-point network type causes the router to not use a DR/BDR on the interface. As a result, the answer about R1 becoming the DR is incorrect (because no DR exists at all), and the answer listing a state of "FULL/DR" is incorrect for the same reason. However, the answer that claims that R2 will be neither DR nor BDR is true because no DR or BDR is elected.

3. D. The **show ip ospf interface brief** command lists a pair of counters under the heading "Nbrs F/C" on the far right of the output. The first of the two numbers represents the number of fully adjacent neighbors (2 in this case), and the second number represents the total number of neighbors.

4. B. The default OSPF priority setting is 1. Once configured with 100, R2 has a higher priority. However, the routers only use the priority values when electing a new DR, so as long as the neighbor relationship is stable, no new DR election will occur. So, any change to make R2 (with higher priority) the DR occurs only after a failure that breaks the current neighbor relationship. Two of the answers refer to other timing as to when R2 becomes the DR. Another distractor states that R2 will cease to serve as BDR, which is not the case.

5. B. SPF calculates the cost of a route as the sum of the OSPF interface costs for all outgoing interfaces in the route. The interface cost can be set directly (**ip ospf cost**), or IOS uses a default based on the reference bandwidth and the interface bandwidth. Of the listed answers, **delay** is the only setting that does not influence OSPFv2 metric calculations.

6. D. The configuration of the interface subcommand **ip ospf hello-interval 15** sets the Hello interval to 15. Also, without any explicit configuration of a Dead interval, IOS also sets the Dead interval to 4X the Hello interval or 60 in this case. The question stem describes the timing and purpose of the Dead interval: how long to wait after not receiving any more Hellos before believing the neighbor has failed.

Chapter 24

1. A and D. As worded, the correct answers list a scenario that would prevent the neighbor relationship. One correct answer mentions the use of two different OSPF areas on the potential OSPF neighbors; to become neighbors, the two routers must use the same area number. The other correct answer mentions the use of two different Hello timers, a mismatch that causes two routers to reject each other and to not become neighbors.

    The two incorrect answers list scenarios that do not cause issues, making them incorrect answers. One mentions mismatched OSPF process IDs; OSPF process IDs do not need to match for two routers to become neighbors. The other incorrect answer (that is, a scenario that does not cause a problem) mentions the use of two different priority values. The priority values give OSPF a means to prefer one router over the other when electing a DR/BDR, so the setting is intended to be set to different values on different routers and does not cause a problem.

2. C. As worded, the correct answers should be a scenario that would prevent the neighbor relationship. The answers all list values that are identical or similar on the two routers. Of those, the use of an identical OSPF Router ID (RID) on the two routers prevents them from becoming neighbors, making that one answer correct.

Of the incorrect answers, both routers must have the same Dead interval, so both using a Dead interval of 40 causes no issues. The two routers can use any OSPF process ID (the same or different value, it does not matter), making that answer incorrect. Finally, the two routers' IP addresses must be in the same subnet, so again that scenario does not prevent R13 and R14 from becoming neighbors.

3. D. The OSPF **shutdown** command tells the OSPF process to stop operating. That process includes removing any OSPF-learned routes from the IP routing table, clearing the router's LSDB, and closing existing OSPF neighbor relationships. In effect, it causes OSPF to stop working on the router, but it does retain the configuration so that a **no shutdown** command in OSPF configuration mode will cause the router to start using OSPF again with no changes to the configuration.

4. B. OSPF uses an equal-cost multipath feature, in which when it calculates multiple routes for the same subnet that tie with the lowest metric, the router places multiple routes into the routing table. IOS limits the number of such routes for one destination subnet per the **maximum-paths** setting on the router, which typically defaults to 6. The router would not use the route with metric 15001, as it is worse than the other two routes' metric of 15000.

5. D. Within a routing protocol, the routing protocol will choose the best route based on the metric. As a result, OSPF picks the metric 1000 route while EIGRP chooses its metric 1,000,000 route. Then the router must choose between the two routing protocol sources using the administrative distance. With default settings, EIGRP has a better administrative distance of 90 versus OSPF's 110. As a result, the router places the best EIGRP route into its routing table, the route learned by EIGRP with metric 1,000,000.

6. D. Each route defines a range of IP addresses as follows:

- 172.20.90.9/32: 172.20.90.9 only
- 172.20.88.0/23: 172.20.88.0–172.20.89.255
- 172.20.80.0/20: 172.20.80.0–172.20.95.255
- 172.20.0.0/16: 172.20.0.0–172.20.255.255
- 0.0.0.0/0: 0.0.0.0–255.255.255.255

Given those ranges, a packet destined for address 172.20.89.100 matches all but the first route in the list.

7. C. Each route defines a range of IP addresses, as follows:

- 172.20.90.9/32: 172.20.90.9 only
- 172.20.88.0/23: 172.20.88.0–172.20.89.255
- 172.20.80.0/20: 172.20.80.0–172.20.95.255

- 172.20.0.0/16: 172.20.0.0–172.20.255.255

- 0.0.0.0/0: 0.0.0.0–255.255.255.255

Given those ranges, a packet destined for address 172.20.90.1 matches the last three routes in the list. Among those, the router will use the most specific route, the route with the largest number of prefix bits. As a result, the router uses the route with prefix length /20, which has a next-hop address of 172.20.13.3.

Chapter 25

1. C. NAT, specifically the PAT feature that allows many hosts to use private IPv4 addresses while being supported by a single public IPv4 address, was one short-term solution to the IPv4 address exhaustion problem. IP version 5 existed briefly as an experimental protocol and had nothing to do with IPv4 address exhaustion. IPv6 directly addresses the IPv4 address exhaustion problem, but it is a long-term solution. ARP has no impact on the number of IPv4 addresses used.

2. A. Routers use the same process steps when routing IPv6 packets as they do when routing IPv4 packets. Routers route IPv6 packets based on the IPv6 addresses listed inside the IPv6 header by comparing the destination IPv6 address to the router's IPv6 routing table. As a result, the router discards the incoming frame's data-link header and trailer, leaving an IPv6 packet. The router compares the destination (not source) IPv6 address in the header to the router's IPv6 (not IPv4) routing table and then forwards the packet based on the matched route.

3. D. If you are following the steps in the book, the first step removes up to three leading 0s in each quartet, leaving FE80:0:0:0:100:0:0:123. This value leaves two strings of consecutive all-0 quartets; when you change the longest string of all 0s to ::, the address is FE80::100:0:0:123.

4. B. This question has many quartets that make it easy to make a common mistake: removing trailing 0s in a quartet of hex digits. Only leading 0s in a quartet and not trailing 0s should be removed. Many of the quartets have trailing 0s (0s on the right side of the quartet), so make sure not to remove those 0s.

5. A. The unabbreviated version of an IPv6 address must have 32 digits, and only one answer has 32 hex digits. In this case, the original number shows four quartets and a ::. So, the :: was replaced with four quartets of 0000, making the number eight. Then, for each quartet with fewer than four digits, leading 0s were added, so each quartet has four hex digits.

6. C. The /64 prefix length means that the last 64 bits, or last 16 digits, of the address should be changed to all 0s. That process leaves the unabbreviated subnet prefix as 2000:0000:0000:0005:0000:0000:0000:0000. The last four quartets are all 0s, making that string of all 0s be the longest and best string of 0s to replace with ::. After removing the leading 0s in other quartets, the answer is 2000:0:0:5::/64.

Chapter 26

1. C. Unique local addresses begin with FD in the first two digits.

2. A. Global unicast addresses begin with a hex 2 or 3.

3. D. The global routing prefix defines the address block, represented as a prefix value and prefix length, assigned to an organization by some numbering authority. The global routing prefix acts as the initial part of IPv6 addresses within the company for the number of bits defined by the prefix length. Similarly, when a company uses a public IPv4 address block, all the addresses have the same value in the network part, which also acts as the initial part of IPv4 addresses.

4. B. Subnetting a global unicast address block, using a single prefix length for all subnets, breaks the addresses into three parts. The parts are the global routing prefix, subnet ID, and interface ID.

5. D. Unique local addresses begin with a 2-hex-digit prefix of FD, followed by the 10-hex-digit global ID.

Chapter 27

1. A. The one correct answer lists the exact same IPv6 address listed in the question, with a /64 prefix length and no spaces in the syntax of the answer. Another (incorrect) answer is identical, except that it leaves a space between the address and prefix length, which is incorrect syntax. The two answers that list the **eui-64** parameter list an address and not a prefix; they should list a prefix to be correct. However, even if these two incorrect answers had listed the prefix of the address shown (2001:1:1:1::), the EUI-64 process would not have resulted in the IPv6 address listed in the question.

2. B. With the **eui-64** parameter, the router will calculate the interface ID portion of the IPv6 address based on its MAC address. Beginning with 5055.4444.3333, the router injects FF FE in the middle (5055.44FF.FE44.3333). Then the router inverts the seventh bit in the first byte. To see the change, hex 50 to binary 0101 0000. Then change bit 7, so the string becomes 0101 0010, which converts back to hex 52. The final interface ID value is 5255:44FF:FE44:3333. The wrong answers simply list a different value.

3. A and C. Of the four answers, the two correct answers show the minimal required configuration to support IPv6 on a Cisco router: enabling IPv6 routing (**ipv6 unicast-routing**) and enabling IPv6 on each interface, typically by adding a unicast address to each interface (**ipv6 address...**). The two incorrect answers list nonexistent commands.

4. B and D. The **show ipv6 route connected** command lists all known connected routes, with each route listing the prefix/length of the route. The **show ipv6 interface g0/0/0** command lists the interface address and the prefix/length calculated from the configured address/length.

Of the incorrect answers, the **show ipv6 interface brief** command lists the interface address but not the prefix/length of the connected subnet. The **show ipv6 address** command does not exist, but is simply rejected as an invalid command if attempted.

5. A. With an **ipv6 address** command configured for a global unicast address but without a link-local address configured with an **ipv6 address** command, the router calculates its link-local address on the interface based on its MAC address and EUI-64 rules. The router does not use the global unicast IPv6 address to calculate the link-local address.

The first half of the link-local address begins FE80:0000:0000:0000. The router then calculates the second half of the link-local address value by taking the MAC address (0200.0001.000A), injecting FF FE in the middle (0200.00FF.FE01.000A), and flipping the seventh bit (0000.00FF.FE01.000A).

6. B. FF02::1 is used by all IPv6 hosts on the link, FF02::5 is used by all OSPFv3 routers, and FF02::A is used by all EIGRPv6 routers. FF02::2 is used to send packets to all IPv6 routers on a link.

7. A. The router sends the NDP NS message to the solicited-node multicast address based on the unicast address of 2001:db8:1:1::1234:5678. To create the correct solicited-node address, take the last six hex digits (34:5678 in this case), and prepend FF02::1:FF. The correct answer is FF02::1:FF34:5678. The other answers are similar values that do not follow the correct solicited-node rules.

8. B and C. First, for G0/0/1, with the **ipv6 enable** command, the router enables IPv6, creating an LLA using EUI-64 rules for the interface ID. Those facts identify one correct and one incorrect answer.

Then, for the answer interface G0/0/2 and the **ipv6 autoconfig** command, the command enables IPv6 with SLAAC. As a result, it generates an LLA, using EUI-64 rules, and generates a routable unicast address using SLAAC, again using EUI-64 rules for the interface ID. As a result, G0/0/2's LLA and global unicast address use the same interface ID values.

Finally, for the answer about interface G0/0/3 and the **ipv6 address** subcommand, every interface that supports IPv6 must have an LLA. The router will again use EUI-64 to self-assign the interface ID portion of the interface's LLA.

Chapter 28

1. B. PC1 needs to discover PC2's MAC address. Unlike IPv4, IPv6 does not use ARP, instead using NDP. Specifically, PC1 uses the NDP Neighbor Solicitation (NS) message to request that PC2 send back an NDP Neighbor Advertisement (NA). SLAAC relates to address assignment and not to discovering a neighbor's MAC address.

2. A and C. The NDP RA lists the router IPv6 address, the IPv6 prefixes known on the link, and the matching prefix lengths. The incorrect answers happen to list facts not included in the NDP RA message.

3. A. The **show ipv6 neighbors** command lists all IPv6 addresses of neighbors (both routers and hosts), plus their matching MAC addresses. It does not note which are routers, leaving that information for the **show ipv6 routers** command.

4. D. For the one correct answer, hosts can ask for (solicit) all routers to identify themselves by sending an NDP Router Solicitation (RS) message, with the routers sending back an NDP Router Advertisement (RA) message. For the incorrect answers, PC1 uses NDP Neighbor Solicitation (NS) but not for learning its default router IPv6 address. DAD is a function that uses NDP NS and NA messages, but its function does not include the discovery of the default router address. Finally, EUI-64 does not define a protocol or message, but is rather a convention to define 64-bit values to use as an IPv6 IID.

5. D. SLAAC gives the host a means to choose its unicast address. The host also uses NDP to learn its prefix length, plus the address(es) of any default routers. It then uses stateless DHCP to learn the addresses of the DNS server(s).

6. B and D. With SLAAC, the host learns the subnet prefix from a router using NDP RS/RA messages, and then the host builds the rest of the address (the interface ID). The host can randomly generate the interface ID or use modified EUI-64 rules. The host does not learn the interface ID from any other device, which helps make the process stateless because no other device needs to assign the host its full address.

7. A. The DHCPv6 protocol uses well-known multicast addresses, specifically FF02::1:2, for messages directed to DHCPv6 servers. However, because this multicast address has a link-local scope, those messages remain on the local LAN. A router connected to the LAN must implement a DHCPv6 relay agent function so that the router will replace the packet's FF02::1:2 multicast destination address with the unicast address of the DHCPv6 server. The routers then use normal unicast routing to forward the packet.

For the two other incorrect answers, note that IPv6 does not use broadcast addresses at all. For instance, the all F's address in the answer is not an IPv6 broadcast address because there is no such thing in IPv6. Also, there is no mechanism to learn a DHCPv6 server's unicast address using NDP.

8. C. IPv6 routes on hosts and routers typically use the LLA of the next-hop device. For instance, PC1's default route would reference a router's LLA, not GUA. The **traceroute** command relies on those routes. However, the NDP messages that help the **traceroute** command identify how each router identifies the routable unicast address like the global unicast address. So, the **traceroute** command lists only GUAs in its output. Those facts determine the correct answer and rule out two answers as incorrect. One answer mentions the last line of **traceroute** output; because the command succeeded, that line lists the IPv6 address of the destination host rather than the address of the last router.

Chapter 29

1. A and C. With an IPv6 address on a working interface, the router adds a connected route for the prefix (subnet) implied by the **ipv6 address** command. It also adds a local route (with a /128 prefix length) based on the unicast address. The router does not add a route based on the link-local address.

2. A and C. The two correct answers show the correct subnet ID (subnet prefix) and prefix length for the two connected subnets: 3111:1:1:1::/64 and 3222:2:2:2::/64. The answer with the /128 prefix length exists in a local route, but the **show ipv6 route connected** command does not list local routes. The other incorrect answer lists the entire IPv6 address with a /64 prefix length rather than the prefix ID.

3. A and B. All the answers list the same destination subnet prefix (2000:1:2:3::/64), which is the subnet prefix on the LAN to the right of Router R1. The differences exist in the forwarding instructions in each route.

For the two commands that list both the outgoing interface (G0/0/1) and the next-hop address, both refer to the correct outgoing interface on Router R5. One refers to the incorrect next-hop address—R1's own global unicast address (GUA), whereas the correct command lists neighboring Router R6's GUA (which ends in :6).

For the incorrect answer that lists only an outgoing interface, it lists the correct interface, and the router adds it to its routing table, but the route does not work. IPv6 static routes that refer to an outgoing Ethernet interface must also list a next-hop address for the router to know enough information to forward packets.

For the correct answer that lists only a next-hop GUA, it lists the correct GUA: R6's GUA on the link between R5 and R6 (which ends in :6).

4. B. All four answers show examples of commands that use a next-hop router IPv6 address.

Two incorrect answers list a next-hop address for R5's WAN interface (one global unicast, one link-local). A correct next-hop address reference on Router R1 should refer to an address on Router R6 instead.

For the two answers that list addresses on Router R6, the one that lists R6's global unicast address (2001:1:2:56::6) is correct. The command that lists R6's link-local address also requires R5's outgoing interface, so the router would reject the command in the answer that lists FE80::FF:FE00:6.

5. B. The **show ipv6 route** command, unlike the **show ip route** command, does not designate a gateway of last resort. Instead, it lists the default route like the other IPv6 routes, but with the special prefix/length of ::/0, which matches all possible IPv6 addresses.

For the other incorrect answers, the prefix of ::/128 would match the host address of all 0s, rather than matching all addresses. A route that matches prefix 2000::/3 will match all global unicast addresses, but it does not match all IPv6 addresses, so it would not be a default route.

6. B. The **ipv6 route** command in the question uses correct syntax, so the router will at least accept the command into the configuration. Of note, the command uses the administrative distance (AD) setting at the end, with a value of 200. As a result, Router R1 treats this route as a floating static route because its AD value (200) is greater than the default OSPF AD (110). As such, R1 continues to use the better OSPF-learned route based on the better (lower) AD and does not add the static route to the routing table.

7. C. The question asks what could have caused the conditions in the question. The user typed the command and pressed Enter, but the question did not say whether the router accepted the command. The question also tells us that the IPv6 routing table lists no routes for prefix/length (2001:DB8:8:8::/64). The goal then is to consider the answers to determine if any of those answers could result in no routes appearing for this prefix.

IOS will add a new static route to the IPv6 routing table if, when using a next-hop global unicast address, the router has a working route to reach that next-hop address and there is no better (lower administrative distance) route for the exact same subnet. So, the correct answer identifies one reason why the route would not appear.

The answer that mentions a better route with administrative distance of 110 is a valid reason for the static route not to appear. Still, the question states that no route for the subnet appears in the routing table, so clearly that competing route does not exist.

The other two incorrect answers mention the **ipv6 route** command. This command can use a link-local next-hop address but does not have to do so, showing the incorrect claim on one of those answers. For the other answer, when using a global unicast address as next-hop, the command does not also require an outgoing interface parameter, showing that answer as incorrect.

NUMERIC

10/100   A short reference to an Ethernet NIC or switch port that supports speed of 10 Mbps and 100 Mbps.

10/100/1000   A short reference to an Ethernet NIC or switch port that supports speeds of 10 Mbps, 100 Mbps, and 1000 Mbps (that is, 1 Gbps).

10BASE-T   The 10-Mbps baseband Ethernet specification using two pairs of twisted-pair cabling (Categories 3, 4, or 5): one pair transmits data and the other receives data. 10BASE-T, which is part of the IEEE 802.3 specification, has a distance limit of approximately 100 m (328 feet) per segment.

100BASE-T   A name for the IEEE Fast Ethernet standard that uses two-pair copper cabling, a speed of 100 Mbps, and a maximum cable length of 100 meters.

1000BASE-T   A name for the IEEE Gigabit Ethernet standard that uses four-pair copper cabling, a speed of 1000 Mbps (1 Gbps), and a maximum cable length of 100 meters.

2-way state   In OSPF, a neighbor state that implies that the router has exchanged Hellos with the neighbor and that all required parameters match.

802.1Q   802.1Q is the standard protocol for this tag. The most critical piece of information (for this discussion) in this tag is the VLAN ID.

A

AAA   Authentication, authorization, and accounting. Authentication confirms the identity of the user or device. Authorization determines what the user or device is allowed to do. Accounting records information about access attempts, including inappropriate requests.

AAA server   A server that holds security information and provides services related to user login, particularly authentication (is the user who he says he is?), authorization (once authenticated, what do we allow the user to do?), and accounting (tracking the user).

ABR   *See* Area Border Router.

access interface   A LAN network design term that refers to a switch interface connected to end-user devices, configured so that it does not use VLAN trunking.

access layer   In a campus LAN design, the switches that connect directly to endpoint devices (servers, user devices), and also connect into the distribution layer switches.

access link   In Frame Relay, the physical serial link that connects a Frame Relay DTE device, usually a router, to a Frame Relay switch. The access link uses the same physical layer standards as do point-to-point leased lines.

access point (AP)   A device that provides wireless service for clients within its coverage area or cell, with the AP connecting to both the wireless LAN and the wired Ethernet LAN.

accounting   In security, the recording of access attempts. *See also* AAA.

address block   A set of consecutive IPv4 addresses. The term is most often used for a class-less prefix as defined by CIDR but can also refer to any subnet or IPv4 network.

adjacent-layer interaction   The general topic of how, on one computer, two adjacent layers in a networking architectural model work together, with the lower layer providing services to the higher layer.

administrative distance   In Cisco routers, a means for one router to choose between multiple routes to reach the same subnet when those routes were learned by different routing protocols. The lower the administrative distance, the better the source of the routing information.

all-nodes multicast address   A specific IPv6 multicast address, FF02::1, with link-local scope, used to send packets to all devices on the link that support IPv6.

all-routers multicast address   A specific IPv6 multicast address, FF02::2, with link-local scope, used to send packets to all devices that act as IPv6 routers on the local link.

alternate port role   With RSTP, a port role in which the port acts as an alternative to a switch's root port, so that when the switch's root port fails, the alternate port can immediately take over as the root port.

anycast address   An address shared by two or more hosts that exist in different parts of the network, so that by design, the routers will forward packets to the nearest of the two servers, allowing clients to communicate with the nearest such server, not caring which particular server with which the client communicates.

APIPA   Automatic Private IP Addressing. A convention per RFC 3927 for a process and reserved set of IPv4 addresses (169.254.0.0/16) that hosts use when they need to use an IPv4 address but they fail to lease an IPv4 address using dynamic processes like DHCP.

Area Border Router (ABR)   A router using OSPF in which the router has interfaces in multiple OSPF areas.

ARP   Address Resolution Protocol. An Internet protocol used to map an IP address to a MAC address. Defined in RFC 826.

ARP table   A list of IP addresses of neighbors on the same VLAN, along with their MAC addresses, as kept in memory by hosts and routers.

ARPANET   The first packet-switched network, first created around 1970, which served as the predecessor to the Internet.

ASBR   Autonomous System Border Router. A router using OSPF in which the router learns routes via another source, usually another routing protocol, exchanging routes that are external to OSPF with the OSPF domain.

authentication   In security, the verification of the identity of a person or a process. *See also* AAA.

authentication server (AS)   An 802.1x entity that authenticates users or clients based on their credentials, as matched against a user database. In a wireless network, a RADIUS server is an AS.

authenticator   An 802.1x entity that exists as a network device that provides access to the network. In a wireless network, a WLC acts as an authenticator.

authorization   In security, the determination of the rights allowed for a particular user or device. *See also* AAA.

auto-MDIX   An Ethernet standard feature, introduced at the same time as Gigabit Ethernet in 1998, that senses whether the link uses the correct UTP cable pinout (straight-through or cross-over), and automatically swaps the signals internally to make the link work if the wrong UTP cable pinout is used.

autonegotiation   An IEEE standard mechanism (802.3u) with which two nodes can exchange messages for the purpose of choosing to use the same Ethernet standards on both ends of the link, ensuring that the link functions and functions well.

autonomous system   An internetwork in the administrative control of one organization, company, or governmental agency, inside which that organization typically runs an interior gateway protocol (IGP).

auxiliary port   A physical connector on a router that is designed to be used to allow a remote terminal, or PC with a terminal emulator, to access a router using an analog modem.

B

backbone area   In OSPFv2 and OSPFv3, the special area in a multiarea design, with all non-backbone areas needing to connect to the backbone area, area 0.

back-to-back link   A serial link between two routers, created without CSU/DSUs, by connecting a DTE cable to one router and a DCE cable to the other. Typically used in labs to build serial links without the expense of an actual leased line from the telco.

backup designated router   An OSPF router connected to a multiaccess network that monitors the work of the designated router (DR) and takes over the work of the DR if the DR fails.

backup port role   With RSTP, a port role in which the port acts as a backup to one of the switch's ports acting as a designated port. If the switch's designated port fails, the switch will use the backup port to immediately take over as the designated port.

bandwidth   A reference to the speed of a networking link. Its origins come from earlier communications technology in which the range, or width, of the frequency band dictated how fast communications could occur.

binary mask   An IPv4 subnet mask written as a 32-bit binary number.

bitwise Boolean AND   A Boolean AND between two numbers of the same length in which the first bit in each number is ANDed, and then the second bit in each number, and then the third, and so on.

blocking state   In STP, a port state in which no received frames are processed and the switch forwards no frames out the interface, with the exception of STP messages.

Boolean AND   A math operation performed on a pair of one-digit binary numbers. The result is another one-digit binary number. 1 AND 1 yields 1; all other combinations yield a 0.

BPDU   Bridge protocol data unit. The generic name for Spanning Tree Protocol messages.

BPDU Guard   A Cisco switch feature that listens for incoming STP BPDU messages, disabling the interface if any are received. The goal is to prevent loops when a switch connects to a port expected to only have a host connected to it.

BPDU Filter   A Cisco switch feature that uses the monitoring and filtering (discarding) of STP BPDUs to achieve goals, such as protecting against forwarding loops on PortFast ports and disabling STP by filtering all BPDU messages.

bridge ID (BID)   An 8-byte identifier for bridges and switches used by STP and RSTP. It is composed of a 2-byte priority field followed by a 6-byte System ID field that is usually filled with a MAC address.

bridge protocol data unit   *See* BPDU.

broadcast address   Generally, any address that represents all devices, and can be used to send one message to all devices. In Ethernet, the MAC address of all binary 1s, or FFFF.FFFF.FFFF in hex. For IPv4, *see* subnet broadcast address.

broadcast domain   A set of all devices that receive broadcast frames originating from any device within the set. Devices in the same VLAN are in the same broadcast domain.

broadcast frame   An Ethernet frame sent to destination address FFFF.FFFF.FFFF, meaning that the frame should be delivered to all hosts on that LAN.

broadcast network type   An OSPF interface setting, useful on links with more than two routers, resulting in an LSA flooding process managed by an elected designated router (DR).

broadcast subnet   When subnetting a Class A, B, or C network, the one subnet in each classful network for which all subnet bits have a value of binary 1. The subnet broadcast address in this subnet has the same numeric value as the classful network's networkwide broadcast address.

broken (state)   An STP port state on Cisco switches, used by Root Guard and Loop Guard as a method for STP to disable the use of the port. A port in the broken state does not forward or process received frames.

C

Channel-group   One term Cisco switches use to reference a bundle of links that are, in some respects, treated like a single link. Other similar terms include *EtherChannel* and *PortChannel*.

CIDR   Classless interdomain routing. An RFC-standard tool for global IP address range assignment. CIDR reduces the size of Internet routers' IP routing tables, helping deal with the rapid growth of the Internet. The term *classless* refers to the fact that the summarized groups of networks represent a group of addresses that do not conform to IPv4 classful (Class A, B, and C) grouping rules.

CIDR Block   A set of consecutive public IPv4 addresses whose size can be any power of 2. Used as an alternative to the original process with public IP networks of three set sizes.

CIDR mask   Another term for a prefix mask, one that uses prefix or CIDR notation, in which the mask is represented by a slash (/) followed by a decimal number.

CIDR notation   *See* prefix notation.

Cisco Catalyst Edge Platform   The brand name created by Cisco for a product family. The products primarily act as routers, but they also create a platform to run many other networking services, including SD-WAN, SASE, and cloud features.

cladding   In fiber-optic cabling, the second layer of the cable, surrounding the core of the cable, with the property of reflecting light back into the core.

classful addressing   A concept in IPv4 addressing that defines a subnetted IP address as having three parts: network, subnet, and host.

classful IP network   An IPv4 Class A, B, or C network; called a classful network because these networks are defined by the class rules for IPv4 addressing.

classful routing protocol   Does not transmit the mask information along with the subnet number and therefore must consider Class A, B, and C network boundaries and perform auto-summarization at those boundaries. Does not support VLSM.

classless addressing   A concept in IPv4 addressing that defines a subnetted IP address as having two parts: a prefix (or subnet) and a host.

classless interdomain routing   The name of an RFC that defines several important features related to public IPv4 addressing: a global address assignment strategy to keep the size of IPv4 routing tables smaller, and the ability to assign public IPv4 addresses in sizes based on any prefix length.

classless prefix   A range of public IPv4 addresses as defined by CIDR.

classless prefix length   The mask (prefix length) used when defining a classless prefix.

classless routing protocol   An inherent characteristic of a routing protocol, specifically that the routing protocol does send subnet masks in its routing updates, thereby removing any need to make assumptions about the addresses in a particular subnet or network, making it able to support VLSM and manual route summarization.

CLI   Command-line interface. An interface that enables the user to interact with the operating system by entering commands and optional arguments.

collision domain   A set of network interface cards (NIC) for which a frame sent by one NIC could result in a collision with a frame sent by any other NIC in the same collision domain.

command-line interface   *See* CLI.

configuration mode   A part of the Cisco IOS Software CLI in which the user can type configuration commands that are then added to the device's currently used configuration file (running-config).

connected   The single-item status code listed by a **switch show interfaces status** command, with this status referring to a working interface.

connected route   On a router, an IP route added to the routing table when the router interface is both up and has an IP address configured. The route is for the subnet that can be calculated based on the configured IP address and mask.

console port   A physical socket on a router or switch to which a cable can be connected between a computer and the router/switch, for the purpose of allowing the computer to use a terminal emulator and use the CLI to configure, verify, and troubleshoot the router/switch.

contiguous network   A network topology in which subnets of network X are not separated by subnets of any other classful network.

convergence   The time required for routing protocols to react to changes in the network, removing bad routes and adding new, better routes so that the current best routes are in all the routers' routing tables.

core   In fiber-optic cabling, the center cylinder of the cable, made of fiberglass, through which light passes.

crossover cable   An Ethernet cable that swaps the pair used for transmission on one device to a pair used for receiving on the device on the opposite end of the cable. In 10BASE-T and 100BASE-TX networks, this cable swaps the pair at pins 1,2 to pins 3,6 on the other end of the cable, and the pair at pins 3,6 to pins 1,2 as well.

CSMA/CD   Carrier sense multiple access with collision detection. A media-access mechanism in which devices ready to transmit data first check the channel for a carrier. If no carrier is sensed for a specific period of time, a device can transmit. If two devices transmit at once, a collision occurs and is detected by all colliding devices. This collision subsequently delays retransmissions from those devices for some random length of time.

D

data VLAN   A VLAN used by typical data devices connected to an Ethernet, like PCs and servers. Used in comparison to a voice VLAN.

Database Description   An OSPF packet type that lists brief descriptions of the LSAs in the OSPF LSDB.

DDN   *See* dotted-decimal notation.

Dead Interval   In OSPF, a timer used for each neighbor. A router considers the neighbor to have failed if no Hellos are received from that neighbor in the time defined by the timer.

decimal mask   An IPv4 subnet mask written in dotted-decimal notation; for example, 255.255.255.0.

de-encapsulation   On a computer that receives data over a network, the process in which the device interprets the lower-layer headers and, when finished with each header, removes the header, revealing the next-higher-layer PDU.

default gateway/default router   On an IP host, the IP address of some router to which the host sends packets when the packet's destination address is on a subnet other than the local subnet.

default mask   The mask used in a Class A, B, or C network that does not create any subnets; specifically, mask 255.0.0.0 for Class A networks, 255.255.0.0 for Class B networks, and 255.255.255.0 for Class C networks.

default route   On a router, the route that is considered to match all packets that are not otherwise matched by some more specific route.

default VLAN   A reference to the default setting of 1 (meaning VLAN ID 1) on the **switchport access vlan** *vlan-id* **interface** subcommand on Cisco switches, meaning that by default, a port will be assigned to VLAN 1 if acting as an access port.

designated port   In both STP and RSTP, a port role used to determine which of multiple interfaces on multiple switches, each connected to the same segment or collision domain, should forward frames to the segment. The switch advertising the lowest-cost Hello BPDU onto the segment becomes the DP.

designated router   In OSPF, on a multiaccess network, the router that wins an election and is therefore responsible for managing a streamlined process for exchanging OSPF topology information between all routers attached to that network.

DHCP   Dynamic Host Configuration Protocol. A protocol used by hosts to dynamically discover and lease an IP address, and learn the correct subnet mask, default gateway, and DNS server IP addresses.

DHCP client   Any device that uses DHCP protocols to ask to lease an IP address from a DHCP server, or to learn any IP settings from that server.

DHCP relay agent   The name of the router IOS feature that forwards DHCP messages from client to servers by changing the destination IP address from 255.255.255.255 to the IP address of the DHCP server.

DHCP server   Software that waits for DHCP clients to request to lease IP addresses, with the server assigning a lease of an IP address as well as listing other important IP settings for the client.

Dijkstra Shortest Path First (SPF) algorithm   The name of the algorithm used by link-state routing protocols to analyze the LSDB and find the least-cost routes from that router to each subnet.

directed broadcast address   *See* subnet broadcast address.

disabled port role   In STP, a port role for nonworking interfaces—in other words, interfaces that are not in a connect or up/up interface state. The reason can be due to administrative setting (shutdown) or interface failure.

disabled state   In STP but not RSTP, the state to be used for interfaces in the disabled port role.

discarding state   An RSTP interface state, which primarily replaces the STP blocking state, as used for interfaces with port roles other than designated or root ports. In this state, the switch does not forward data frames out the interface, nor does it process received frames other than RSTP messages.

discontiguous network   A network topology in which subnets of network X are separated by subnets of some other classful network.

distance vector   The logic behind the behavior of some interior routing protocols, such as RIP. Distance vector routing algorithms call for each router to send its entire routing table in each update, but only to its neighbors. Distance vector routing algorithms can be prone to routing loops but are computationally simpler than link-state routing algorithms.

distribution layer   In a campus LAN design, the switches that connect to access layer switches as the most efficient means to provide connectivity from the access layer into the other parts of the LAN.

DNS   Domain Name System. An application layer protocol used throughout the Internet for translating hostnames into their associated IP addresses.

DNS Reply   In the Domain Name System (DNS), a message sent by a DNS server to a DNS client in response to a DNS Request, identifying the IP address assigned to a particular hostname or fully qualified domain name (FQDN).

DNS Request   In the Domain Name System (DNS), a message sent by a DNS client to a DNS server, listing a hostname or fully qualified domain name (FQDN), asking the server to discover and reply with the IP address associated with that hostname or FQDN.

DNS server   An application acting as a server for the purpose of providing name resolution services per the Domain Name System (DNS) protocol and worldwide system.

DNS server list   A list of IP addresses of DNS servers, known to an IP host, used by a host when sending DNS name resolution requests.

dotted-decimal notation (DDN)   The format used for IP version 4 addresses, in which four decimal values are used, separated by periods (dots).

dual stack   A mode of operation in which a host or router runs both IPv4 and IPv6.

duplex mismatch   On opposite ends of any Ethernet link, the condition in which one of the two devices uses full-duplex logic and the other uses half-duplex logic, resulting in unnecessary frame discards and retransmissions on the link.

duplicate address detection (DAD)   A term used in IPv6 to refer to how hosts first check whether another host is using a unicast address before the first host uses that address.

E

EIGRP   Enhanced Interior Gateway Routing Protocol. An advanced version of IGRP developed by Cisco. Provides superior convergence properties and operating efficiency and combines the advantages of link-state protocols with those of distance vector protocols.

EIGRP version 6   The version of the EIGRP routing protocol that supports IPv6, and not IPv4.

electromagnetic interference (EMI)   The name of the effect in which electricity passes through one cable as normal, inducing a magnetic field outside the conductor. That magnetic field, if it passes through another conductor, like a nearby cable, induces new electrical current in the second cable, interfering with the use of electricity to transmit data on the second cable.

enable mode   A part of the Cisco IOS CLI in which the user can use the most powerful and potentially disruptive commands on a router or switch, including the ability to then reach configuration mode and reconfigure the router.

encapsulation   The placement of data from a higher-layer protocol behind the header (and in some cases, between a header and trailer) of the next-lower-layer protocol. For example, an IP packet could be encapsulated in an Ethernet header and trailer before being sent over an Ethernet.

encryption   Applying a specific algorithm to data to alter the appearance of the data, making it incomprehensible to those who are not authorized to see the information.

enterprise router   A term to describe the general role of a router as a router at a permanent site owned or leased by the enterprise, like an office building, manufacturing facility, branch office, or retail location. These sites typically have enough users to justify separate routers, switches, and wireless access points, and are more likely to justify private WAN services, in comparison to SOHO routers.

equal-cost multipath (ECMP)   A term for a router's forwarding logic when it has more than one route for the same subnet with the same metric (cost).

equal-cost route   When a routing protocol computes all possible routes to one subnet, the case for which multiple of those routes have the same metric (cost).

error detection   The process of discovering whether a data-link level frame was changed during transmission. This process typically uses a Frame Check Sequence (FCS) field in the data-link trailer.

error disabled   An interface state on LAN switches that can be the result of one of many security violations.

error recovery   The process of noticing when some transmitted data was not successfully received and resending the data until it is successfully received.

EtherChannel   A feature in which up to eight parallel Ethernet segments exist between the same two devices, each using the same speed. May be a Layer 2 EtherChannel, which acts like a single link for forwarding and Spanning Tree Protocol logic, or a Layer 3 EtherChannel, which acts like a single link for the switch's Layer 3 routing logic.

EtherChannel Load Distribution   The logic used by switches when forwarding messages over EtherChannels by which the switch chooses the specific physical link out which the switch will forward the frame.

Ethernet   A series of LAN standards defined by the IEEE, originally invented by Xerox Corporation and developed jointly by Xerox, Intel, and Digital Equipment Corporation.

Ethernet address   A 48-bit (6-byte) binary number, usually written as a 12-digit hexadecimal number, used to identify Ethernet nodes in an Ethernet network. Ethernet frame headers list a destination and source address field, used by the Ethernet devices to deliver Ethernet frames to the correct destination.

Ethernet frame   A term referring to an Ethernet data-link header and trailer, plus the data encapsulated between the header and trailer.

Ethernet Line Service (E-Line)   A specific carrier/metro Ethernet service defined by MEF (MEF.net) that provides a point-to-point topology between two customer devices, much as if the two devices were connected using an Ethernet crossover cable.

Ethernet link   A generic term for any physical link between two Ethernet nodes, no matter what type of cabling is used.

Ethernet over MPLS (EoMPLS)   A term referring specifically to how a service provider can create an Ethernet WAN service using an MPLS network. More generally, a term referring to Ethernet WAN services.

Ethernet port   A generic term for the opening on the side of any Ethernet node, typically in an Ethernet NIC or LAN switch, into which an Ethernet cable can be connected.

EtherType   Jargon that shortens the term *Ethernet Type*, which refers to the Type field in the Ethernet header. The Type field identifies the type of packet encapsulated inside an Ethernet frame.

EUI-64   Literally, a standard for an extended unique identifier that is 64 bits long. Specifically for IPv6, a set of rules for forming a 64-bit identifier, used as the interface ID in IPv6 addresses, by starting with a 48-bit MAC address, inserting FFFE (hex) in the middle, and inverting the seventh bit.

extended ping   An IOS command in which the **ping** command accepts many other options besides just the destination IP address.

F

Fast Ethernet   The common name for all the IEEE standards that send data at 100 megabits per second.

fiber-optic cable   A type of cabling that uses glass fiber as a medium through which to transmit light.

filter   Generally, a process or a device that screens network traffic for certain characteristics, such as source address, destination address, or protocol, and determines whether to forward or discard that traffic based on the established criteria.

firewall   A device that forwards packets between the less secure and more secure parts of the network, applying rules that determine which packets are allowed to pass and which are not.

flash memory   A type of read/write permanent memory that retains its contents even with no power applied to the memory, and uses no moving parts, making the memory less likely to fail over time.

floating static route   A static IP route that uses a higher administrative distance than other routes, typically routes learned by a routing protocol. As a result, the router will not use the static route if the routing protocol route has been learned, but then use the static route if the routing protocol fails to learn the route.

flood/flooding   The result of the LAN switch forwarding process for broadcasts and unknown unicast frames. Switches forward these frames out all interfaces, except the interface in which the frame arrived. Switches also flood multicasts by default, although this behavior can be changed.

forward   To send a frame received in one interface out another interface, toward its ultimate destination.

forward delay   An STP timer, defaulting to 15 seconds, used to dictate how long an interface stays in the listening state and the time spent in learning state. Also called the forward delay timer.

forward route   From one host's perspective, the route over which a packet travels from that host to some other host.

forwarding state   An STP and RSTP port state in which an interface operates unrestricted by STP.

frame   A term referring to a data-link header and trailer, plus the data encapsulated between the header and trailer.

Frame Check Sequence   A field in many data-link trailers used as part of the error-detection process.

full duplex   Generically, any communication in which two communicating devices can concurrently send and receive data. In Ethernet LANs, the allowance for both devices to send and receive at the same time, allowed when both devices disable their CSMA/CD logic.

full state   In OSPF, a neighbor state that implies that the two routers have exchanged the complete (full) contents of their respective LSDBs.

full update   With IP routing protocols, the general concept that a routing protocol update lists all known routes.

fully adjacent   In OSPF, a characterization of the state of a neighbor in which the two neighbors have reached the full state.

fully adjacent neighbor   In OSPF, a neighbor with which the local router has also reached the OSPF full state, meaning that the two routers have exchanged their LSDBs directly with each other.

G

Gigabit Ethernet   The common name for all the IEEE standards that send data at 1 gigabit per second.

global routing prefix   An IPv6 prefix that defines an IPv6 address block made up of global unicast addresses, assigned to one organization, so that the organization has a block of globally unique IPv6 addresses to use in its network.

global unicast address   A type of unicast IPv6 address that has been allocated from a range of public globally unique IP addresses, as registered through IANA/ICANN, its member agencies, and other registries or ISPs.

H

half duplex   Generically, any communication in which only one device at a time can send data. In Ethernet LANs, the normal result of the CSMA/CD algorithm that enforces the rule that only one device should send at any point in time.

HDLC   High-Level Data Link Control. A bit-oriented synchronous data-link layer protocol developed by the International Organization for Standardization (ISO).

header   In computer networking, a set of bytes placed in front of some other data, encapsulating that data, as defined by a particular protocol.

Hello (Multiple definitions)   1) A protocol used by OSPF routers to discover, establish, and maintain neighbor relationships. 2) A protocol used by EIGRP routers to discover, establish, and maintain neighbor relationships. 3) In STP, refers to the name of the periodic message sourced by the root bridge in a spanning tree.

Hello BPDU   The STP and RSTP message used for the majority of STP communications, listing the root's bridge ID, the sending device's bridge ID, and the sending device's cost with which to reach the root.

Hello Interval   With OSPF and EIGRP, an interface timer that dictates how often the router should send Hello messages.

Hello timer   In STP, the time interval at which the root switch should send Hello BPDUs.

history buffer   In a Cisco router or switch, the function by which IOS keeps a list of commands that the user has used in this login session, both in EXEC mode and configuration mode. The user can then recall these commands for easier repeating or making small edits and issuing similar commands.

hop count   The metric used by the RIP routing protocol. Each router in an IP route is considered a hop, so for example, if two other routers sit between a router and some subnet, that router would have a hop count of two for that route.

host   Any device that uses an IP address.

host address   The IP address assigned to a network card on a computer.

host part   A term used to describe a part of an IPv4 address that is used to uniquely identify a host inside a subnet. The host part is identified by the bits of value 0 in the subnet mask.

host route   A route with a /32 mask, which by virtue of this mask represents a route to a single host IP address.

hostname   The alphanumeric name of an IP host.

hub   A LAN device that provides a centralized connection point for LAN cabling, repeating any received electrical signal out all other ports, thereby creating a logical bus. Hubs do not interpret the electrical signals as a frame of bits, so hubs are considered to be Layer 1 devices.

I

IANA   The Internet Assigned Numbers Authority (IANA). An organization that owns the rights to assign many operating numbers and facts about how the global Internet works, including public IPv4 and IPv6 addresses. *See also* ICANN.

ICANN The Internet Corporation for Assigned Names and Numbers. An organization appointed by IANA to oversee the distributed process of assigning public IPv4 and IPv6 addresses across the globe.

ICMP Internet Control Message Protocol. A TCP/IP network layer protocol that reports errors and provides other information relevant to IP packet processing.

ICMP echo reply One type of ICMP message, created specifically to be used as the message sent by the ping command to test connectivity in a network. The ping command expects to receive these messages from other hosts, after the ping command first sends an ICMP echo request message to the host.

ICMP echo request One type of ICMP message, created specifically to be used as the message sent by the ping command to test connectivity in a network. The ping command sends these messages to other hosts, expecting the other host to reply with an ICMP echo reply message.

IEEE Institute of Electrical and Electronics Engineers. A professional organization that develops communications and network standards, among other activities.

IEEE 802.11 The IEEE base standard for wireless LANs.

IEEE 802.1Q The IEEE standard VLAN trunking protocol. 802.1Q includes the concept of a native VLAN, for which no VLAN header is added, and a 4-byte VLAN header is inserted after the original frame's Type/Length field.

IEEE 802.2 An IEEE LAN protocol that specifies an implementation of the LLC sublayer of the data-link layer.

IEEE 802.3 A set of IEEE LAN protocols that specifies the many variations of what is known today as an Ethernet LAN.

IEEE 802.3 AD The IEEE standard for the functional equivalent of the Cisco-proprietary EtherChannel.

IETF The Internet Engineering Task Force. The IETF serves as the primary organization that works directly to create new TCP/IP standards.

IGP *See* interior gateway protocol.

inactivity timer For switch MAC address tables, a timer associated with each entry that counts time upward from 0 and is reset to 0 each time a switch receives a frame with the same MAC address. The entries with the largest timers can be removed to make space for additional MAC address table entries.

infrastructure mode The operating mode of an AP that is providing a BSS for wireless clients.

Integrated Services Router (ISR) Cisco's long-running term for several different model series of Enterprise-class routers, intended mostly for use as enterprise routers and some use as SOHO routers. ISR routers first serve as routers but, depending on the family or specific model, support all current types of WAN connections (private and Internet), LAN switching ports, Wireless APs, VPNs, and other integrated functions supported in a single device.

interface bandwidth   In OSPF, the numerator in the calculation of an interface's default OSPF cost metric, calculated as the interface bandwidth divided by the reference bandwidth.

Interface ID   The ending (rightmost) portion of the structure of an IPv6 address, usually 64 bits long.

interface-local scope   A concept in IPv6 for which packets sent to an address using this scope should not physically exit the interface, keeping the packet inside the sending host.

interior gateway protocol (IGP)   A routing protocol designed to be used to exchange routing information inside a single autonomous system.

interior routing protocol   A synonym of interior gateway protocol. *See* interior gateway protocol.

Internal Border Gateway Protocol (iBGP)   The use of BGP between two routers in the same ASN, with different rules compared to External BGP (eBGP).

internal router   In OSPF, a router with all interfaces in the same nonbackbone area.

Internetwork Operating System   The operating system (OS) of Cisco routers and switches, which provides the majority of a router's or switch's features, with the hardware providing the remaining features.

IOS   *See* Internetwork Operating System.

IOS XE   A Cisco operating system (OS) with a modern Linux-based multitasking software architecture used as the OS for many enterprise-class LAN switch and router products.

IP   Internet Protocol. The network layer protocol in the TCP/IP stack, providing routing and logical addressing standards and services.

IP address (IP version 4)   In IP version 4 (IPv4), a 32-bit address assigned to hosts using TCP/IP. Each address consists of a network number, an optional subnetwork number, and a host number. The network and subnetwork numbers together are used for routing, and the host number is used to address an individual host within the network or subnetwork.

IP address (IP version 6)   In IP version 6 (IPv6), a 128-bit address assigned to hosts using TCP/IP. Addresses use different formats, commonly using a routing prefix, subnet, and interface ID, corresponding to the IPv4 network, subnet, and host parts of an address.

IP network   *See* classful IP network.

IP packet   An IP header, followed by the data encapsulated after the IP header, but specifically not including any headers and trailers for layers below the network layer.

IP routing table   *See* routing table.

IP subnet   Subdivisions of a Class A, B, or C network, as configured by a network administrator. Subnets allow a single Class A, B, or C network to be used instead of multiple networks, and still allow for a large number of groups of IP addresses, as is required for efficient IP routing.

IP version 4   Literally, the version of the Internet Protocol defined in an old RFC 791, standardized in 1980, and used as the basis of TCP/IP networks and the Internet for over 30 years.

IP version 6   A newer version of the Internet Protocol defined in RFC 2460, as well as many other RFCs, whose creation was motivated by the need to avoid the IPv4 address exhaustion problem.

IPv4   *See* IP version 4.

IPv4 address exhaustion   The process by which the public IPv4 addresses, available to create the Internet, were consumed through the 1980s until today, with the expectation that eventually the world would run out of available IPv4 addresses.

IPv6   *See* IP version 6.

IPv6 address scope   The concept of how far an IPv6 packet should be forwarded by hosts and routers in an IPv6 network. Includes interface-local, link-local, site-local, and organization-local scopes.

IPv6 administrative distance   In Cisco routers, a means for one router to choose between multiple IPv6 routes to reach the same subnet when those routes were learned by different routing protocols. The lower the administrative distance, the better the source of the routing information.

IPv6 host route   A route with a /128 mask, which by virtue of this mask represents a route to a single host IPv6 address.

IPv6 local route   A route added to an IPv6 router's routing table for the router's interface IP address, with a /128 mask, which by virtue of this mask represents a route to only that router's IPv4 address.

IPv6 neighbor table   The IPv6 equivalent of the ARP table. A table that lists IPv6 addresses of other hosts on the same link, along with their matching MAC addresses, as typically learned using Neighbor Discovery Protocol (NDP).

ISO   International Organization for Standardization. An international organization that is responsible for a wide range of standards, including many standards relevant to networking. The ISO developed the OSI reference model, a popular networking reference model.

K–L

keepalive   A proprietary feature of Cisco routers in which the router sends messages on a periodic basis as a means of letting the neighboring router know that the first router is still alive and well.

known unicast frame   An Ethernet frame whose destination MAC address is listed in a switch's MAC address table, so the switch will forward the frame out the one port associated with that entry in the MAC address table.

LACP   Link Aggregation Control Protocol is a messaging protocol defined by the IEEE 802.3ad standard that enables two neighboring devices to realize that they have multiple parallel links connecting to each other and then to decide which links can be combined into an EtherChannel.

Layer 2 EtherChannel (L2 EtherChannel)   An EtherChannel that acts as a switched port (that is, not a routed port), and as such, is used by a switch's Layer 2 forwarding logic. As a result, the Layer 2 switch lists the Layer 2 EtherChannel in switch MAC address tables, and when forwarding a frame based on one of these MAC table entries, the switch balances traffic across the various ports in the Layer 2 EtherChannel.

Layer 3 EtherChannel (L3 EtherChannel)   An EtherChannel that acts as a routed port (that is, not a switched port), and as such, is used by a switch's Layer 3 forwarding logic. As a result, the Layer 3 switch lists the Layer 3 EtherChannel in various routes in the switch's IP routing table, with the switch balancing traffic across the various ports in the Layer 3 EtherChannel.

Layer 3 protocol   A protocol that has characteristics like OSI Layer 3, which defines logical addressing and routing. IPv4 and IPv6 are Layer 3 protocols.

Layer 3 switch   *See* multilayer switch.

learning   The process used by switches for discovering MAC addresses, and their relative location, by looking at the source MAC address of all frames received by a bridge or switch.

learning state   In STP, a temporary port state in which the interface does not forward frames, but it can begin to learn MAC addresses from frames received on the interface.

leased line   A serial communications circuit between two points, provided by some service provider, typically a telephone company (telco). Because the telco does not sell a physical cable between the two endpoints, instead charging a monthly fee for the ability to send bits between the two sites, the service is considered to be a leased service.

link state   A classification of the underlying algorithm used in some routing protocols. Link-state protocols build a detailed database that lists links (subnets) and their state (up, down), from which the best routes can then be calculated.

link-local address (LLA)   A unicast IPv6 address that begins FE80, used on each IPv6-enabled interface, used for sending packets within the attached link by applying a link-local scope.

link-local multicast address   A multicast IPv6 address that begins with FF02, with the fourth digit of 2 identifying the scope as link-local, to which devices apply a link-local scope.

link-local scope   With IPv6 multicasts, a term that refers to the parts (scope) of the network to which a multicast packet can flow, with link-local referring to the fact that the packet stays on the subnet in which it originated.

link-state advertisement (LSA)   In OSPF, the name of the data structure that resides inside the LSDB and describes in detail the various components in a network, including routers and links (subnets).

link-state database (LSDB)   In OSPF, the data structure in RAM of a router that holds the various LSAs, with the collective LSAs representing the entire topology of the network.

Link-State Request   An OSPF packet used to ask a neighboring router to send a particular LSA.

Link-State Update An OSPF packet used to send an LSA to a neighboring router.

listening state A temporary STP port state that occurs immediately when a blocking interface must be moved to a forwarding state. The switch times out MAC table entries during this state. It also ignores frames received on the interface and doesn't forward any frames out the interface.

LLC Logical Link Control. The higher of the two sublayers of the data-link layer defined by the IEEE. Synonymous with IEEE 802.2.

local broadcast IP address IPv4 address 255.255.255.255. A packet sent to this address is sent as a data-link broadcast, but only flows to hosts in the subnet into which it was originally sent. Routers do not forward these packets.

local mode The default mode of a Cisco lightweight AP that offers one or more functioning BSSs on a specific channel.

local route A route added to an IPv4 router's routing table for the router's interface IP address, with a /32 mask, which by virtue of this mask represents a route to only that router's IPv4 address.

local username A username (with matching password), configured on a router or switch. It is considered local because it exists on the router or switch, and not on a remote server.

logical address A generic reference to addresses as defined by Layer 3 protocols that do not have to be concerned with the physical details of the underlying physical media. Used mainly to contrast these addresses with data-link addresses, which are generically considered to be physical addresses because they differ based on the type of physical medium.

longest prefix match When a router's IP routing table has more than one route that matches a packet's destination address, the choice to use the matching route with the longest mask (the mask with the largest number of binary 1s in the mask).

Loop Guard A complex Cisco switch mechanism that protects against STP loops in a specific common case. For switches whose switch-to-switch links settle into either a root port or an alternate port role, as expected per the STP design, Loop Guard disables use of those ports if normal STP operation attempts to assign them the designated port role.

LSA *See* link-state advertisement.

LSDB *See* link-state database.

M

MAC Media Access Control. The lower of the two sublayers of the data-link layer defined by the IEEE. Synonymous with IEEE 802.3 for Ethernet LANs.

MAC address A standardized data-link layer address that is required for every device that connects to a LAN. Ethernet MAC addresses are 6 bytes long and are controlled by the IEEE. Also known as a hardware address, a MAC layer address, and a physical address.

MAC address table   A table of forwarding information held by a Layer 2 switch, built dynamically by listening to incoming frames and used by the switch to match frames to make decisions about where to forward the frame.

MaxAge   In STP, a timer that states how long a switch should wait when it no longer receives Hellos from the root switch before acting to reconverge the STP topology. Also called the MaxAge timer.

media access control (MAC) layer   A low-level function performed as part of Layer 2; in wireless networks, this function can be divided between a wireless LAN controller and a light-weight AP to form a split-MAC architecture.

message of the day   One type of login banner that can be defined on a Cisco router or switch.

metric   A unit of measure used by routing protocol algorithms to determine the best route for traffic to use to reach a particular destination.

Modified EUI-64   *See* EUI-64.

multiarea   In OSPFv2 and OSPFv3, a design that uses multiple areas.

multiarea OSPF   In OSPFv2 and OSPFv3, a design that uses more than one area within one OSPF domain (typically a single company).

multicast IP address   A class D IPv4 address. When used as a destination address in a packet, the routers collectively work to deliver copies of the one original packet to all hosts who have previously registered to receive packets sent to that particular multicast address.

multilayer switch   A LAN switch that can also perform Layer 3 routing functions. The name comes from the fact that this device makes forwarding decisions based on logic from multiple OSI layers (Layers 2 and 3).

multimode fiber   A type of fiber cable that works well with transmitters like LEDs that emit multiple angles of light into the core of the cable; to accommodate the multiple angles of inci-dent, the cable has a larger core in comparison to single-mode fiber cables.

N

name resolution   The process by which an IP host discovers the IP address associated with a hostname, often involving sending a DNS request to a DNS server, with the server supplying the IP address used by a host with the listed hostname.

name server   A server connected to a network that resolves network names into network addresses.

NAT   Network Address Translation. A mechanism for reducing the need for globally unique IP addresses. NAT allows an organization with addresses that are not globally unique to connect to the Internet, by translating those addresses into public addresses in the globally routable address space.

native VLAN   The one VLAN ID on any 802.1Q VLAN trunk for which the trunk forwards frames without an 802.1Q header.

neighbor   In routing protocols, another router with which a router decides to exchange routing information.

Neighbor Advertisement (NA)   A message defined by the IPv6 Neighbor Discovery Protocol (NDP), used to declare to other neighbors a host's MAC address. Sometimes sent in response to a previously received NDP Neighbor Solicitation (NS) message.

Neighbor Discovery Protocol (NDP)   A protocol that is part of the IPv6 protocol suite, used to discover and exchange information about devices on the same subnet (neighbors). In particular, it replaces the IPv4 ARP protocol.

Neighbor Solicitation (NS)   A message defined by the IPv6 Neighbor Discovery Protocol (NDP), used to ask a neighbor to reply with a Neighbor Advertisement, which lists the neighbor's MAC address.

neighbor table   For OSPF and EIGRP, a list of routers that have reached neighbor status.

network   A collection of computers, printers, routers, switches, and other devices that can communicate with each other over some transmission medium.

network address   *See* network number.

network broadcast address   In IPv4, a special address in each classful network that can be used to broadcast a packet to all hosts in that same classful network. Numerically, the address has the same value as the network number in the network part of the address and all 255s in the host octets; for example, 10.255.255.255 is the network broadcast address for classful network 10.0.0.0.

network ID   A number that identifies an IPv4 network, using a number in dotted-decimal notation (like IP addresses); a number that represents any single Class A, B, or C IP network.

network interface card (NIC)   A computer card, sometimes an expansion card and sometimes integrated into the motherboard of the computer, that provides the electronics and other functions to connect to a computer network. Today, most NICs are specifically Ethernet NICs, and most have an RJ-45 port, the most common type of Ethernet port.

Network LSA   In OSPF, a type of LSA that a designated router (DR) creates for the network (subnet) for which the DR is helping to distribute LSAs.

network number   A number that uses dotted-decimal notation like IP addresses, but the number itself represents all hosts in a single Class A, B, or C IP network.

network part   The portion of an IPv4 address that is either 1, 2, or 3 octets/bytes long, based on whether the address is in a Class A, B, or C network.

network route   A route for a classful network.

networking model   A generic term referring to any set of protocols and standards collected into a comprehensive grouping that, when followed by the devices in a network, allows all the devices to communicate. Examples include TCP/IP and OSI.

next-hop router In an IP route in a routing table, part of a routing table entry that refers to the next IP router (by IP address) that should receive packets that match the route.

NIC *See* network interface card.

NVRAM Nonvolatile RAM. A type of random-access memory (RAM) that retains its contents when a unit is powered off.

O

on-link prefix An IPv6 subnet prefix, advertised by a router in an NDP Router Advertisement (RA) message, that identifies to on-link hosts a subnet considered to exist on the local link.

Organization-local scope A concept in IPv6 for which packets sent to an address using this scope should be forwarded by routers inside the organization but not over any links connected to other organizations or over links connected to the Internet.

OSI Open System Interconnection reference model. A network architectural model developed by the ISO. The model consists of seven layers, each of which specifies particular network functions, such as addressing, flow control, error control, encapsulation, and reliable message transfer.

OSPF Open Shortest Path First. A popular link-state IGP that uses a link-state database and the Shortest Path First (SPF) algorithm to calculate the best routes to reach each known subnet.

OSPF neighbor A local router's attitude toward a second router that resides on a common subnet, when both use OSPF and use appropriate OSPF settings so that the routers will choose to exchange routing information with each other.

OSPF priority An OSPF interface setting that serves as the first comparison point in the designated router (DR) election process, with the router interface with the highest priority winning the election.

OSPF router-id In OSPF, the 32-bit number, normally shown in dotted-decimal notation but also allowed to be listed as an integer, intended as a unique identifier for each OSPF router in an OSPF domain.

OSPF version 2 The version of the OSPF routing protocol that supports IPv4, and not IPv6, and has been commonly used for over 20 years.

OSPF version 3 The version of the OSPF routing protocol that originally supported only IPv6, and not IPv4, but now supports IPv4 through the use of address family configuration.

outgoing interface In an IP route in a routing table, part of a routing table entry that refers to the local interface out which the local router should forward packets that match the route.

overlapping subnets An (incorrect) IP subnet design condition in which one subnet's range of addresses includes addresses in the range of another subnet.

P

packet   A logical grouping of bytes that includes the network layer header and encapsulated data, but specifically does not include any headers and trailers below the network layer.

PAgP   Port Aggregation Protocol (PAgP) is a messaging protocol defined by Cisco that enables two neighboring devices to realize that they have multiple parallel links connecting to each other and then to decide which links can be combined into an EtherChannel.

parallel detection   The term for the branch of IEEE autonegotiation steps that applies to a device that uses autonegotiation but the device on the other end of the link does not.

partial mesh   A network topology in which more than two devices could physically communicate but, by choice, only a subset of the pairs of devices connected to the network is allowed to communicate directly.

passive interface   With a routing protocol, a router interface for which the routing protocol is enabled on the interface, but for which the routing protocol does not send routing protocol messages out that interface.

patch cable   An Ethernet cable, usually short, that connects from a device's Ethernet port to a wall plate or switch. With wiring inside a building, electricians prewire from the wiring closet to each cubicle or other location, with a patch cable connecting the short distance from the wall plate to the user device.

periodic update   With routing protocols, the concept that the routing protocol advertises routes in a routing update on a regular periodic basis. This is typical of distance vector routing protocols.

permanent IPv6 address   When using IPv6 SLAAC, a host creates an address with an infinite preferred and valid lifetime, making the address permanent, using the address when listening for incoming connections to any services running on that host.

ping   An Internet Control Message Protocol (ICMP) echo message and its reply; ping often is used in IP networks to test the reachability of a network device.

pinout   The documentation and implementation of which wires inside a cable connect to each pin position in any connector.

point-to-point network type   An OSPF interface setting, useful on links in a point-to-point topology with only two routers, resulting in flooding directly between the routers without the use of a designated router (DR).

port   In TCP and UDP, a number that is used to uniquely identify the application process that either sent (source port) or should receive (destination port) data. In LAN switching, another term for *switch interface*.

PortChannel   One term Cisco switches use to reference a bundle of links that are, in some respects, treated like a single link. Other similar terms include *EtherChannel* and *Channel-group*.

PortFast   A switch STP feature in which a port is placed in an STP forwarding state as soon as the interface comes up, bypassing the listening and learning states. This feature is meant for ports connected to end-user devices.

preferred lifetime   In the context of IPv6 addresses, a timer applied to a SLAAC-created address defining how long the address is preferred, meaning the host uses the address for new and existing application flows.

Prefix (prefix ID)   In both IPv4 and IPv6, this term refers to the number that identifies a group of IPv4 or IPv6 addresses, respectively. Another term for *subnet identifier*.

prefix discovery   IPv6 neighbor discovery protocol (NDP) function, specifically part of the Router Advertisement (RA) message, in which the router supplies a list of IPv6 subnet prefixes and prefix lengths that exist on the local link.

prefix length   In IPv6, the number of bits in an IPv6 prefix.

prefix mask   A term to describe an IPv4 subnet mask when represented as a slash (/) followed by a decimal number. The decimal number is the number of binary 1s in the mask.

prefix notation (IP version 4)   A shorter way to write a subnet mask in which the number of binary 1s in the mask is simply written in decimal. For example, /24 denotes the subnet mask with 24 binary 1 bits in the subnet mask. The number of bits of value binary 1 in the mask is considered to be the prefix length.

primary root   This term refers to the switch configured with the primary keyword on the **spanning-tree vlan x root {primary | secondary}** command. At time of configuration, this command causes the switch to choose a new priority setting that makes the switch become the root switch in the network.

private addresses   IP addresses in several Class A, B, and C networks that are set aside for use inside private organizations. These addresses, as defined in RFC 1918, are not routable through the Internet.

private IP network   Any of the IPv4 Class A, B, or C networks as defined by RFC 1918, intended for use inside a company but not used as public IP networks.

Protocol Type field   A field in a LAN header that identifies the type of header that follows the LAN header. Includes the DIX Ethernet Type field, the IEEE 802.2 DSAP field, and the SNAP protocol Type field.

public IP address   An IP address that is part of a registered network number, as assigned by an Internet Assigned Numbers Authority (IANA) member agency, so that only the organization to which the address is registered is allowed to use the address. Routers in the Internet should have routes allowing them to forward packets to all the publicly registered IP addresses.

public IP network   Any IPv4 Class A, B, or C network assigned for use by one organization only, so that the addresses in the network are unique across the Internet, allowing packets to be sent through the public Internet using the addresses.

PVST+   An STP option in Cisco switches that creates an STP instance per VLAN. Cisco proprietary.

Q–R

quartet   A term used in this book, but not in other references, to refer to a set of four hex digits in an IPv6 address.

RADIUS server   An authentication server used with 802.1x to authenticate wireless clients.

RAM   Random-access memory. A type of volatile memory that can be read and written by a microprocessor.

Rapid PVST+   An STP option in Cisco switches that creates an RSTP instance per VLAN. Cisco proprietary.

Rapid Spanning Tree Protocol (RSTP)   Defined in IEEE 802.lw. Defines an improved version of STP that converges much more quickly and consistently than STP (802.Id).

reference bandwidth   In OSPF, a configurable value for the OSPF routing process, used by OSPF when calculating an interface's default OSPF cost metric, calculated as the interface's bandwidth divided by the reference bandwidth.

Regional Internet Registry   An organization (five globally) that receives allocations of public IPv4 addresses from IANA and then manages that address space in their major geographic region, performing public address allocations to ISPs and assignments directly to companies that use the addresses.

repeater   A device that repeats or retransmits signals it receives, effectively expanding the wireless coverage area.

resident subnet   Each IP subnet contains a number of unicast IP addresses; that subnet is the resident subnet for each of those addresses—that is, the subnet in which those addresses reside.

reverse route   From one host's perspective, for packets sent back to the host from another host, the route over which the packet travels.

RFC   Request For Comments. A document used as the primary means for communicating information about the TCP/IP protocols. Some RFCs are designated by the Internet Architecture Board (IAB) as Internet standards, and others are informational. RFCs are available online from numerous sources, including http://www.rfc-editor.org.

RIP   Routing Information Protocol. An interior gateway protocol (IGP) that uses distance vector logic and router hop count as the metric. RIP version 2 (RIPv2) replaced the older RIP version 1 (RIPv1), with RIPv2 providing more features, including support for VLSM.

RIR   *See* Regional Internet Registry.

RJ-45   A popular type of cabling connector used for Ethernet cabling. It is similar to the RJ-11 connector used for telephone wiring in homes in the United States. RJ-45 allows the connection of eight wires.

ROAS   *See* Router-on-a-Stick.

rollover cable   For connections to the RJ-45 console port rather than USB console port of a Cisco device, the type of cable used between the user PC and the console port. The UTP rollover cable uses a rollover pinout with eight pins, connecting pin 1 to pin 8, pin 2 to pin 7, and so on.

ROM   Read-only memory. A type of nonvolatile memory that can be read but not written to by the microprocessor.

ROMMON   A shorter name for ROM Monitor, which is a low-level operating system that can be loaded into Cisco routers for several seldom-needed maintenance tasks, including password recovery and loading a new IOS when flash memory has been corrupted.

root bridge   *See* root switch.

root cost   The STP cost from a nonroot switch to reach the root switch, as the sum of all STP costs for all ports out which a frame would exit to reach the root.

Root Guard   A Cisco switch feature that protects against unexpected new root switches. When enabled on an interface, IOS uses normal STP rules except to disable the use of the port after receiving a superior BPDU.

root port role   In STP and RSTP, the one port on a nonroot switch in which the least-cost Hello is received. Switches put root ports in a forwarding state.

root switch   In STP and RSTP, the switch that wins the election by virtue of having the lowest bridge ID and, as a result, sends periodic Hello BPDUs (default, 2 seconds).

routed port   A reference to the default logic on an interface on a router, such as de-encapsulating the Layer 3 packet from incoming Layer 2 frames and passing the packet to the Layer 3 forwarding logic of the device.

routed protocol   A protocol that defines packets that can be routed by a router. Examples of routed protocols include IPv4 and IPv6.

Router Advertisement (RA)   A message defined by the IPv6 Neighbor Discovery Protocol (NDP), used by routers to announce their willingness to act as an IPv6 router on a link. These can be sent in response to a previously received NDP Router Solicitation (RS) message.

router ID (RID)   In EIGRP and OSPF, a 32-bit number, written in dotted-decimal notation, that uniquely identifies each router.

router LSA   In OSPF, a type of LSA that a router creates to describe itself and the networks connected to it.

Router-on-a-Stick (ROAS)   Jargon to refer to the Cisco router feature of using VLAN trunking on an Ethernet interface, which then allows the router to route packets that happen to enter the router on that trunk and then exit the router on that same trunk, just on a different VLAN.

Router Solicitation (RS)   A message defined by the IPv6 Neighbor Discovery Protocol (NDP), used to ask any routers on the link to reply, identifying the router, plus other configuration settings (prefixes and prefix lengths).

routing protocol   A set of messages and processes with which routers can exchange information about routes to reach subnets in a particular network. Examples of routing protocols include Enhanced Interior Gateway Routing Protocol (EIGRP), Open Shortest Path First (OSPF), and Routing Information Protocol (RIP).

routing table   A list of routes in a router, with each route listing the destination subnet and mask, the router interface out which to forward packets destined to that subnet, and as needed, the next-hop router's IP address.

routing update   A generic reference to any routing protocol's messages in which it sends routing information to a neighbor.

RSTP   *See* Rapid Spanning Tree Protocol.

running-config file   In Cisco IOS switches and routers, the name of the file that resides in RAM, holding the device's currently used configuration.

S

same-layer interaction   The communication between two networking devices for the purposes of the functions defined at a particular layer of a networking model, with that communication happening by using a header defined by that layer of the model. The two devices set values in the header, send the header and encapsulated data, with the receiving devices interpreting the header to decide what action to take.

secondary root   This term refers to the switch configured with the secondary keyword on the **spanning-tree vlan x root {primary | secondary}** command. At time of configuration, this command causes the switch to set its base priority to 28,762.

Secure Shell (SSH)   A TCP/IP application layer protocol that supports terminal emulation between a client and server, using dynamic key exchange and encryption to keep the communications private.

segment   In TCP, a term used to describe a TCP header and its encapsulated data (also called an L4PDU). Also in TCP, the process of accepting a large chunk of data from the application layer and breaking it into smaller pieces that fit into TCP segments. In Ethernet, a segment is either a single Ethernet cable or a single collision domain (no matter how many cables are used).

shared Ethernet   An Ethernet that uses a hub, or even the original coaxial cabling, that results in the devices having to take turns sending data, sharing the available bandwidth.

shortest path first (SPF) algorithm   The name of the algorithm used by link-state routing protocols to analyze the LSDB and find the least-cost routes from that router to each subnet.

single-area OSPF   In OSPFv2 and OSPFv3, a design that uses a single area within one OSPF domain (typically a single company).

single-mode fiber   A type of fiber cable that works well with transmitters like lasers that emit a single angle of light into the core of the cable, allowing for a smaller core in comparison to multimode fiber cables.

site-local scope   A concept in IPv6 for which packets sent to an address using this scope should be forwarded by routers, but not forwarded over WAN links to other sites.

SOHO router   A term to describe the general role of a router that exists as part of the enterprise network but resides at an employee's home or at a smaller business site, possibly with a short-term lease compared to larger enterprise sites. These sites typically have few devices, so it makes sense to use one device that integrates routing, switches, wireless, and other features into a single device (the SOHO router) and are more likely to justify Internet access as the primary WAN access method.

solicited-node multicast address   A type of IPv6 multicast address, with link-local scope, used to send packets to all hosts in the subnet that share the same value in the last six hex digits of their unicast IPv6 addresses. Begins with FF02::1:FF00:0/104.

Spanning Tree Protocol (STP)   A protocol defined by IEEE standard 802.ID. Allows switches and bridges to create a redundant LAN, with the protocol dynamically causing some ports to block traffic, so that the bridge/switch forwarding logic will not cause frames to loop indefinitely around the LAN.

SSH   *See* Secure Shell.

standard access list   A list of IOS global configuration commands that can match only a packet's source IP address, for the purpose of deciding which packets to discard and which to allow through the router.

star topology   A network topology in which endpoints on a network are connected to a common central device by point-to-point links.

startup-config file   In Cisco IOS switches and routers, the name of the file that resides in NVRAM memory, holding the device's configuration that will be loaded into RAM as the running-config file when the device is next reloaded or powered on.

stateful DHCPv6   A term used in IPv6 to contrast with stateless DHCP. Stateful DHCP keeps track of which clients have been assigned which IPv6 addresses (state information).

stateless address autoconfiguration (SLAAC)   A feature of IPv6 in which a host or router can be assigned an IPv6 unicast address without the need for a stateful DHCP server.

stateless DHCPv6   A term used in IPv6 to contrast with stateful DHCP. Stateless DHCP servers don't lease IPv6 addresses to clients. Instead, they supply other useful information, such as DNS server IP addresses, but with no need to track information about the clients (state information).

static access interface   A LAN network design term, synonymous with the term *access interface*, but emphasizing that the port is assigned to one VLAN as a result of static configuration rather than through some dynamic process.

static route   An IP route on a router created by the user configuring the details of the route on the local router.

STP   Shielded twisted-pair. This type of cabling has a layer of shielded insulation to reduce electromagnetic interference (EMI).

straight-through cable   In Ethernet, a cable that connects the wire on pin 1 on one end of the cable to pin 1 on the other end of the cable, pin 2 on one end to pin 2 on the other end, and so on.

subinterface   One of the virtual interfaces on a single physical interface.

subnet   Subdivisions of a Class A, B, or C network, as configured by a network administrator. Subnets allow a single Class A, B, or C network to be used instead of multiple networks, and still allow for a large number of groups of IP addresses, as is required for efficient IP routing.

subnet address   *See* subnet number.

subnet broadcast address   A special address in each IPv4 subnet, specifically the largest numeric address in the subnet, designed so that packets sent to this address should be delivered to all hosts in that subnet.

subnet ID (IPv4)   *See* subnet number.

subnet ID (IPv6)   The number that represents the IPv6 subnet. Also known as the IPv6 prefix, or more formally as the subnet-router anycast address.

subnet ID (prefix ID)   *See* subnet number.

subnet mask   A 32-bit number that numerically describes the format of an IP address, by representing the combined network and subnet bits in the address with mask bit values of 1, and representing the host bits in the address with mask bit values of 0.

subnet number   In IPv4, a dotted-decimal number that represents all addresses in a single subnet. Numerically, the smallest value in the range of numbers in a subnet, reserved so that it cannot be used as a unicast IP address by a host.

subnet part   In a subnetted IPv4 address, interpreted with classful addressing rules, one of three parts of the structure of an IP address, with the subnet part uniquely identifying different subnets of a classful IP network.

subnet prefix   The term for a number that represents an IPv6 subnet.

subnet router anycast address   A special anycast address in each IPv6 subnet, reserved for use by routers as a way to send a packet to any router on the subnet. The address's value in each subnet is the same number as the subnet ID.

subnet zero   An alternative term for *zero subnet*. *See* zero subnet.

subnetting   The process of subdividing a Class A, B, or C network into smaller groups called subnets.

summary LSA   In OSPFv2, a type of LSA, created by an Area Border Router (ABR), to describe a subnet in one area in the database of another area.

superior BPDU   An STP bridge protocol data unit (BPDU) that lists a better (lower) root bridge ID (BID) as compared to the current bridge. A switch that receives a superior BPDU under normal conditions would begin using the new switch with the lower BID as the root switch.

switch   A network device that filters, forwards, and floods Ethernet frames based on the destination address of each frame.

switched Ethernet   An Ethernet that uses a switch, and particularly not a hub, so that the devices connected to one switch port do not have to contend to use the bandwidth available on another port. This term contrasts with *shared Ethernet*, in which the devices must share bandwidth, whereas switched Ethernet provides much more capacity, as the devices do not have to share the available bandwidth.

switched port   A reference to the default logic on a Layer 2 switch port, such as learning the source MAC address of received frames and passing incoming frames to the Layer 2 forwarding logic of the device.

switched virtual interface (SVI)   Another term for any VLAN interface in a Cisco switch. *See also* VLAN interface.

system ID extension   The term for the formatting applied to the original 16-bit STP priority field to break it into a 4-bit priority field and a 12-bit VLAN ID field.

T

TCP   Transmission Control Protocol. A connection-oriented transport layer TCP/IP protocol that provides reliable data transmission.

TCP/IP   Transmission Control Protocol/Internet Protocol. A common name for the suite of protocols developed by the U.S. Department of Defense in the 1970s to support the construction of worldwide internetworks. TCP and IP are the two best-known protocols in the suite.

telco   A common abbreviation for *telephone company*.

Telnet   The standard terminal-emulation application layer protocol in the TCP/IP protocol stack. Telnet is used for remote terminal connection, enabling users to log in to remote systems and use resources as if they were connected to a local system. Telnet is defined in RFC 854.

temporary IPv6 address   When using IPv6 SLAAC, a host creates an address with a relatively short preferred and valid lifetime, usually days long for each, making the address temporary. The host uses the temporary address for outgoing application connections.

topology database   The structured data that describes the network topology to a routing protocol. Link-state and balanced hybrid routing protocols use topology tables, from which they build the entries in the routing table.

trace   Short for traceroute. A program available on many systems that traces the path that a packet takes to a destination. It is used mostly to troubleshoot routing problems between hosts.

traceroute   A program available on many systems that traces the path that a packet takes to a destination. It is used mostly to debug routing problems between hosts.

trailer   In computer networking, a set of bytes placed behind some other data, encapsulating that data, as defined by a particular protocol. Typically, only data-link layer protocols define trailers.

transceiver   A term formed from the words *transmitter* and *receiver*. The hardware used to both send (transmit) energy over some communications medium (e.g., wires in a cable), as well as to process received energy signals to interpret as a series of 1s and 0s.

trunk   In campus LANs, an Ethernet segment over which the devices add a VLAN header that identifies the VLAN in which the frame exists.

trunk interface   A switch interface configured so that it operates using VLAN trunking (either 802.1Q or ISL).

trunking   Also called *VLAN trunking*. A method (using either the Cisco ISL protocol or the IEEE 802.1Q protocol) to support multiple VLANs, allowing traffic from those VLANs to cross a single link.

trunking administrative mode   The configured trunking setting on a Cisco switch interface, as configured with the switchport mode command.

trunking operational mode   The current behavior of a Cisco switch interface for VLAN trunking.

twisted-pair   Transmission medium consisting of two insulated wires, with the wires twisted around each other in a spiral. An electrical circuit flows over the wire pair, with the current in opposite directions on each wire, which significantly reduces the interference between the two wires.

U

UDP   User Datagram Protocol. Connectionless transport layer protocol in the TCP/IP protocol stack. UDP is a simple protocol that exchanges datagrams without acknowledgments or guaranteed delivery.

ULA global ID   The unique local address (ULA) for one organization uses a /48 prefix, composed of a set hex FD in the first 8 bits, with a 10-hex digit (40 bit) global ID, which should be generated by a pseudo-random algorithm.

unicast address   Generally, any address in networking that represents a single device or interface, instead of a group of addresses (as would be represented by a multicast or broadcast address).

unicast IP address   An IP address that represents a single interface. In IPv4, these addresses come from the Class A, B, and C ranges.

unidirectional link   A condition on fiber optic links in which one of the two required fibers fails in a way that also results in both attached switches leaving their interfaces in a working (connected) state—when, in reality, the link can pass frames only in a single direction.

unique local address   A type of IPv6 unicast address meant as a replacement for IPv4 private addresses.

unknown unicast frame   An Ethernet frame whose destination MAC address is not listed in a switch's MAC address table, so the switch must flood the frame.

up and up   Jargon referring to the two interface states on a Cisco IOS router or switch (line status and protocol status), with the first "up" referring to the line status and the second "up" referring to the protocol status. An interface in this state should be able to pass data-link frames.

update timer   The time interval that regulates how often a routing protocol sends its next periodic routing updates. Distance vector routing protocols send full routing updates every update interval.

user mode   A mode of the user interface to a router or switch in which the user can type only nondisruptive EXEC commands, generally just to look at the current status, but not to change any operational settings.

UTP   Unshielded twisted-pair. A type of cabling, standardized by the Telecommunications Industry Association (TIA), that holds twisted pairs of copper wires (typically four pair) and does not contain any shielding from outside interference.

V

valid lifetime   In the context of IPv6 addresses, a timer applied to a SLAAC-created address defining how long the address is valid, meaning the host can continue to support existing application flows using the address.

variable-length subnet mask (VLSM)   The capability to specify a different subnet mask for the same Class A, B, or C network number on different subnets. VLSM can help optimize available address space.

virtual LAN (VLAN)   A group of devices, connected to one or more switches, with the devices grouped into a single broadcast domain through switch configuration. VLANs allow switch administrators to separate the devices connected to the switches into separate VLANs without requiring separate physical switches, gaining design advantages of separating the traffic without the expense of buying additional hardware.

virtual private network (VPN)   The process of securing communication between two devices whose packets pass over some public and unsecured network, typically the Internet. VPNs encrypt packets so that the communication is private, and authenticate the identity of the endpoints.

VLAN   *See* virtual LAN.

VLAN interface   A configuration concept inside Cisco switches, used as an interface between IOS running on the switch and a VLAN supported inside the switch, so that the switch can assign an IP address and send IP packets into that VLAN.

VLAN Trunking Protocol (VTP)   A Cisco-proprietary messaging protocol used between Cisco switches to communicate configuration information about the existence of VLANs, including the VLAN ID and VLAN name.

voice VLAN   A VLAN defined for use by IP Phones, with the Cisco switch notifying the phone about the voice VLAN ID so that the phone can use 802.1Q frames to support traffic for the phone and the attached PC (which uses a data VLAN).

VoIP   Voice over IP. The transport of voice traffic inside IP packets over an IP network.

VTP   *See* VLAN Trunking Protocol.

VTP transparent mode   One of three VTP operational modes. Switches in transparent mode can configure VLANs, but they do not tell other switches about the changes, and they do not learn about VLAN changes from other switches.

W

WAN   *See* wide-area network.

web server   Software, running on a computer, that stores web pages and sends those web pages to web clients (web browsers) that request the web pages.

wide-area network (WAN)   A part of a larger network that implements mostly OSI Layer 1 and 2 technology, connects sites that typically sit far apart, and uses a business model in which a consumer (individual or business) must lease the WAN from a service provider (often a telco).

Wi-Fi Alliance   An organization formed by many companies in the wireless industry (an industry association) for the purpose of getting multivendor certified-compatible wireless products to market in a more timely fashion than would be possible by simply relying on standardization processes.

wildcard mask   The mask used in Cisco IOS ACL commands and OSPF and EIGRP network commands.

wired LAN   A local-area network (LAN) that physically transmits bits using cables, often the wires inside cables. A term for local-area networks that use cables, emphasizing the fact that the LAN transmits data using wires (in cables) instead of wireless radio waves. *See also* wireless LAN.

wireless LAN   A local-area network (LAN) that physically transmits bits using radio waves. The name "wireless" compares these LANs to more traditional "wired" LANs, which are LANs that use cables (which often have copper wires inside).

Z

zero subnet   For every classful IPv4 network that is subnetted, the one subnet whose subnet number has all binary 0s in the subnet part of the number. In decimal, the zero subnet can be easily identified because it is the same number as the classful network number.

Index

Symbols

Numbers

A

B

E

G

H

O

Q

R

T

UTP (Unshielded Twisted-Pair) cabling

10BASE-T pinouts, 46–47

100BASE-T pinouts, 46–47

1000BASE-T pinouts, 49

cabling comparisons, 52–53

data transmission, 43–44

Ethernet LAN builds, 43–49

Ethernet links, 44–46

V

valid lifetimes, SLAAC, 712–713

verifying

broadcast network operations, 588–590

data VLAN, 209–212

embedded switch port routing, 480–481

Ethernet LAN switching, 121–123

host connectivity, IPv6 addressing, 718–719

IPv4 configurations, switches, 150–151

Layer 3 Switch SVI configurations, 466

OSPFv2 verification commands, 568–573

ROAS configurations, 461–463

static network routes, 442

VLAN

data VLAN, 209–212

voice VLAN, 209–212

voice VLAN, 209–212

VLAN (Virtual LAN), 188. *See also* **LAN; WLAN**

access interfaces, 197–198

assigning to interfaces, 197–201, 213

broadcast domains, 191–192

configuring, 197–201

creating, 197–201

data VLAN

configuring, 209–212

verifying, 209–212

disabled/undefined VLAN, 212–218

forwarding data between VLAN, 195–197

interfaces, 464–466

load balancing with STP, 260

native VLAN, 195

phone connections, 207–212

PVST+260, 261

routing

Layer 3 Switch Routed Ports, 455, 469–477

Layer 3 Switch SVI, 455, 464–469

ROAS, 454

ROAS, configuring, 458–461

ROAS, troubleshooting, 463–464

ROAS, verifying configurations, 461–463

Router 802.1Q Trunks, 454, 457–464

Router LAN Switch Ports, 455, 477–482

routing between VLAN, 195–197

RPVST+260, 261

static access interfaces, 197–198

switches, IP settings, 147–149

troubleshooting, 212–218

trunking, 192–195, 201–207, 215–218

undefined/disabled VLAN, 213–215

voice VLAN

configuring, 209–212

verifying, 209–212

VTP, 194, 201–202

Register your product at **ciscopress.com/register**
to unlock additional benefits:

- Save 35%* on your next purchase with an exclusive discount code

- Find companion files, errata, and product updates if available

- Sign up to receive special offers on new editions and related titles

Get more when you shop at **ciscopress.com**:

- Everyday discounts on books, eBooks, video courses, and more

- Free U.S. shipping on all orders

- Multi-format eBooks to read on your preferred device

- Print and eBook Best Value Packs

Cisco Press